A Variorum Edition of the Works of Geoffrey Chaucer

VOLUME I

Paul G. Ruggiers
General Editor

Donald C. Baker
Associate Editor

Helen Storm Corsa
Charles Moorman
Roy J. Pearcy
Roy Vance Ramsey
Thomas Ross

Consultants

The Canterbury Tales

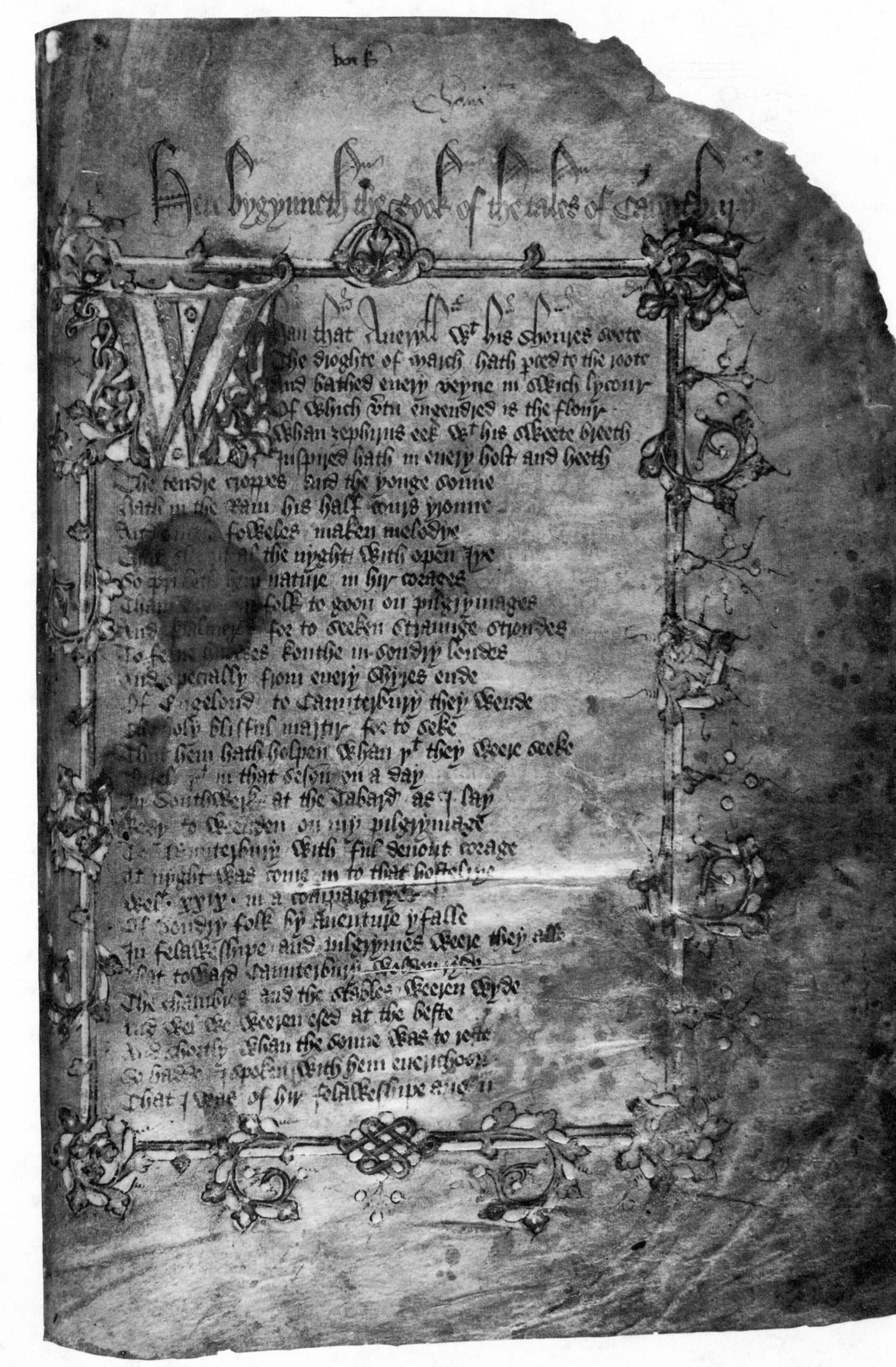

Here bygynneth the book of the tales of Caunterbury

Whan that Aueryll wt his shoures soote
The droghte of march hath perced to the roote
And bathed euery veyne in swich lycour
Of which vertu engendred is the flour
Whan zephirus eek wt his swete breeth
Inspired hath in euery holt and heeth
The tendre croppes and the yonge sonne
Hath in the Ram his half cours yronne
And smale fowles maken melodye
That slepen al the nyght with open eye
So priketh hem nature in hir corages
Thanne longen folk to goon on pilgrymages
And Palmeres for to seken straunge strondes
To ferne halwes kouthe in sondry londes
And specially from euery shyres ende
Of Engelond to Caunterbury they wende
The holy blisful martir for to seke
That hem hath holpen whan þt they were seeke
Bifel þt in that seson on a day
In Southwerk at the Tabard as I lay
Redy to wenden on my pilgrymage
To Caunterbury with ful deuout corage
At nyght was come in to that hostelrye
Wel .xxix. in a compaignye
Of sondry folk by auenture yfalle
In felaweshipe and pilgrymes were they alle
That toward Caunterbury wolden ryde
The chambres and the stables weren wyde
And wel we weren esed at the beste
And shortly whan the sonne was to reste
So hadde I spoken with hem euerichon
That I was of hir felaweshipe anon

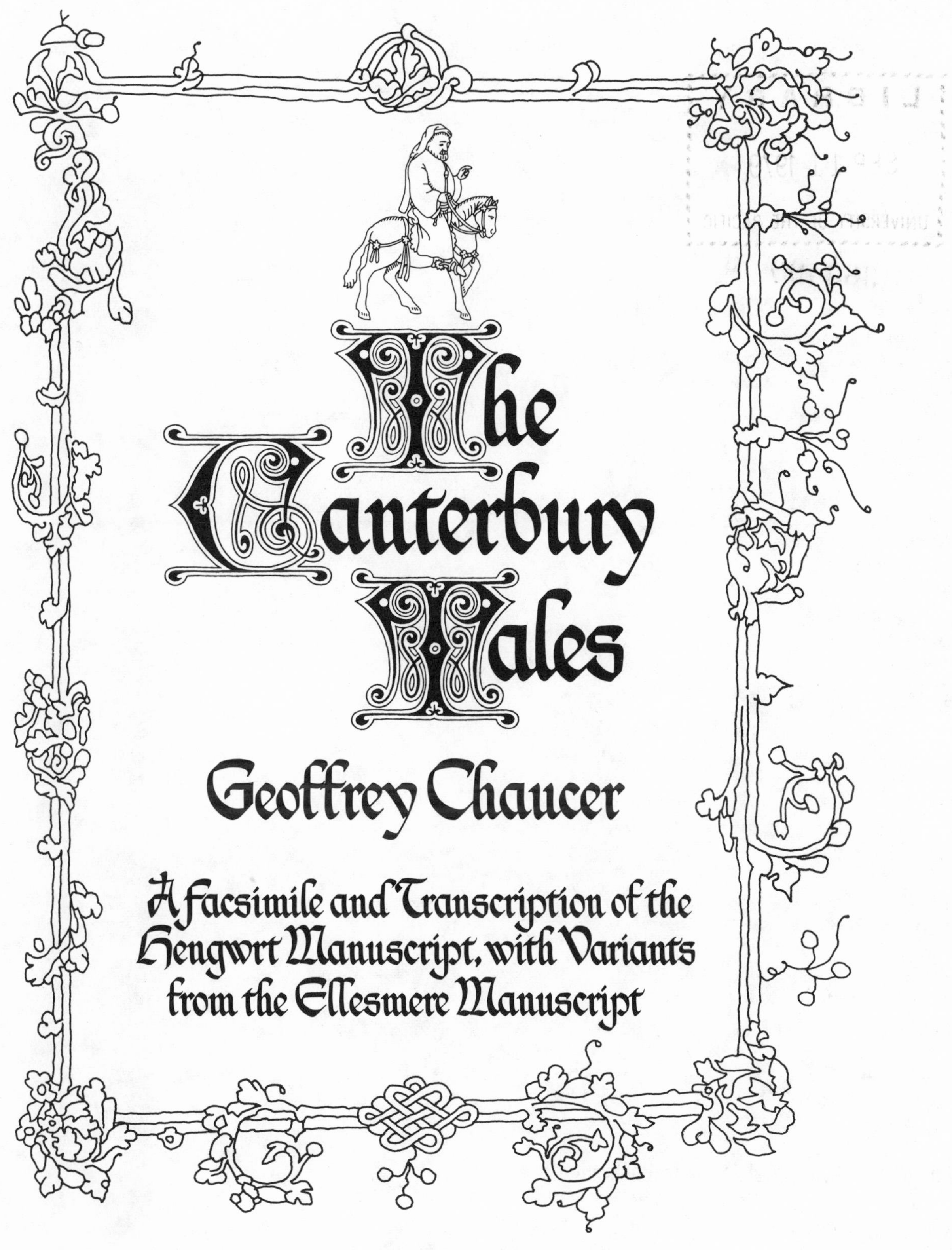
The Canterbury Tales
Geoffrey Chaucer
A Facsimile and Transcription of the
Hengwrt Manuscript, with Variants
from the Ellesmere Manuscript

Edited by Paul G. Ruggiers

Introductions by Donald C. Baker and by
A. I. Doyle and M. B. Parkes

University of Oklahoma Press, Norman, and Wm. Dawson & Sons, Ltd., Folkestone

Library of Congress Cataloging in Publication Data

Chaucer, Geoffrey, d. 1400.
The Canterbury tales.

1. Manuscripts, English—Facsimiles. I. Hengwrt manuscript. II. Ruggiers, Paul G. III. Title.
PR1866.R8 1978 821′.1 77-18611

 Manufactured in the U.S.A. First edition. ISBN: 0-8061-1416-9.

Published in Great Britain by Wm. Dawson & Sons, Ltd., Cannon House, Folkestone, Kent, England. ISBN: 0-7129-0903-6.

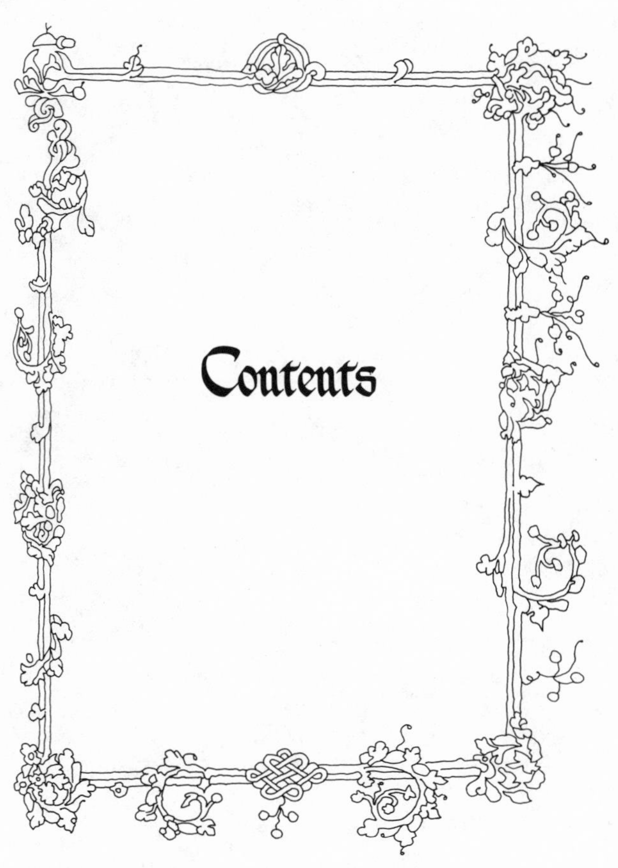

Contents

Illustrations

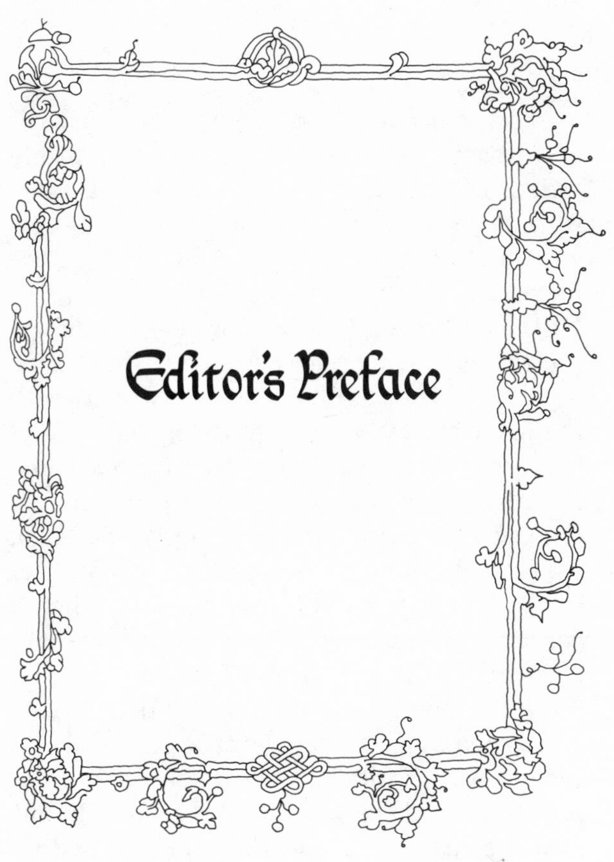

Editor's Preface

It is a singular pleasure to present the facsimile of the Hengwrt (Aberystwyth, National Library of Wales, Peniarth 392) manuscript of the *Canterbury Tales* with transcription of the Hengwrt and comparative readings from the Ellesmere text. This presentation provides an opportunity to explain the principles that have come to inform the *Variorum Chaucer* over the past decade and now give good warrant of continuing to inform the project in its future phases. And since there will be no other place to recount the stages by which cooperatively we have come to offer the Hengwrt text as the basis of our edition, I take this occasion to recount first decisions leading to the publication of this volume.

In 1967, Donald Baker and I, after several years of discussion of the need for an instrument to assess the vicissitudes of almost six hundred years of Chaucer scholarship, decided to ask various scholars in the field whether they would consider such a research tool useful and feasible. Encouraged by their replies, we convened a small group of advisers, Marie Padgett Hamilton, Charles Muscatine, Thomas Kirby, and Robert Jordan, to discuss the implications of the decision to create a Chaucer commentary. The discussion was rich and fruitful: there seemed no doubt about the need for a reference work aimed at making sense of an enormous diversity of scholarship. Even taking into account the availability of the various editions of Chaucer utilizing the scholarship of their time—sometimes unfortunately blocking our view of the scholarship from which their notes were composed—we felt that the time was right for launching the present project. Out of this first meeting came the conviction, most ably advanced and defended by Hamilton, that any commentary made should be securely anchored in its own text; and that suggestion, received at the time without full regard to its implications, was the germ from which this present volume grew.

Thereafter, at two-year intervals beginning in 1968, five plenary conferences were held at the University of Oklahoma for those scholars who had accepted our invitation to participate in the project. The conferences have proved extremely valuable, allowing the editors to become fully involved in the problems of a commentary and giving all of us the responsibility, both exhilarating and sobering, of creating a reference work for which no precise model exists. And more specifically, each conference has given us an increased sense of what can be done.

I recount here only the larger events which have preceded this publication, reminding the reader that many of the developments occurred more or less simultaneously, as the settling of earlier problems made possible the approach to problems just emerging. Thus what follows here must not be taken to be a chronological account.

1. Over a period of three years a set of guidelines was written, part of which, a section dealing with printed editions, was generously prepared by Roy Pearcy. Though the guidelines have undergone steady revision since their first appearance, they have continued to provide a focus for our collective efforts and have remained the basis for continued debate.

2. Donald Baker produced a sample fascicle of the *Manciple's Tale,* which made it abundantly clear that a form of presentation was emerging. Polished and expanded for reexamination at the conference of 1976, the fascicle in its later form demonstrated finally that a coherent presentation of the accumulated Chaucer scholarship could be made.

3. Five editors, Charles A. Owen, Jr., Richard Hoffman, Thomas Garbàty, Charles Moorman, and Charles Dahlberg, addressed themselves to particular problems of the fascicle format, helping to decide on the range and limits of the introduction, the survey of criticism, and the explanatory and textual notes; the possibility of including a compendium of commentary was given long consideration before the idea was rejected.

4. The editors as a group made the important decision to adopt the Hengwrt manuscript (explained and defended below by Professor Baker) as base text for the *Variorum Chaucer.* They further decided that the Hengwrt text would be utilized as a "best" text and that in the individual fascicles the editors would emend it cautiously and conservatively, "correcting" the scribe where such correction is deemed necessary and explaining such departures from the manuscript reading in their textual notes. In these instances pragmatic dependence upon their own collation of principal manuscripts and upon the further collations provided by Joseph Manly and Edith Rickert's *Corpus of Variants* in their *Text of the Canterbury Tales* has been urged.

I remind all future users of the *Variorum Chaucer* that our goal here has been to present in the forthcoming fascicles not a new critical text but a modestly emended or corrected Hengwrt text. This text, we believe—and the labors of Manly and Rickert bear us out—is as close as we will come to Chaucer's own intentions for large parts of the *Canterbury Tales.* And, as Baker states below, the best-text method, modified for our purposes, provides a neutral text of the *Canterbury Tales* to which the commentary may be appended and referred.

5. Additionally, we wished to provide a textual apparatus in which two demonstrations might be made: *(a)* We wanted to present the Hengwrt manuscript against the background principally of those other landmark manuscripts, or their descendants, of the earliest period of the manuscripts of the *Canterbury Tales.* This core group is made up of Ad[3] (Additional 35286), Cp (Corpus Christi 198), Cambridge Dd 4.24, El (Ellesmere), Cambridge Gg 4.27, Ha[4] (Harley 7334), He (Helmingham), La (Lansdowne 851), and Pw (Petworth). Caxton's 1478 edition of the *Canterbury Tales,* collated by Manly and Rickert with the manuscripts, we have placed at the head of our list of printed editions. It is expected that the core group will be amplified from time to time by other representative manuscripts, when, for example, one of the core is *Out* and another manuscript in a family replaces it, or when a particular manuscript may be shown to have been influential in the establishment of some readings, for example, En[1] (Egerton 2776), or Se (Selden). Accordingly, over a period of two years, a set of collations based upon the manuscripts given above was prepared by me and my staff and subsequently distributed as a first-draft effort, with microfilms and printouts, to the individual authors. For several of the tales I had the additional assistance of Thomas Ross and Vance Ramsey, to whom I now express my formal thanks. *(b)* We wanted the collational apparatus to be crowned by a survey of the texts prepared by the various editors of the *Canterbury Tales* from Caxton on, so that it would be possible to see historically the evolution of the several traditions of the printed editions. More specifically, the apparatus should demonstrate the various relationships between the individual lemmata of the printed editions and those of the manuscripts and should show clearly those instances in which the reading of the printed edition has no source in any known manuscript. Here our dependence upon Manly's *Corpus of Variants* for evidence outside the scope of our collational apparatus will be explained at length in the first fascicle of the *Canterbury Tales* to be published.

6. Almost simultaneously with the previous decisions we came to the decision—logical and inevitable, it seemed to us—to present the Hengwrt manuscript in facsimile as our inaugural publication, and to accompany it with a semidiplomatic transcription and running comparison with the Ellesmere readings. I have worked with my

diligent staff for five years to implement that decision and to produce the present volume. Our labors were considerably lightened by the kind support of Richard Hoffman, who prepared the text and variants of the *Tale of Melibee,* and of Joseph Mogan, who performed the same services for the *Parson's Tale.* Thus with great satisfaction we present in facsimile a text which occupies so important a place in the tradition of the *Canterbury Tales.*

Acknowledgments

The text and transcription here offered could not have been brought to this final stage without the assistance of many. It is my pleasure to thank them now. My profoundest gratitude must go first to Richard Hoffman and to Joseph Mogan, who set aside much of their own work to prepare the transcription and variants, respectively, of the *Tale of Melibee* and the *Parson's Tale;* to Helen Corsa, Roy Pearcy, Charles Moorman, Vance Ramsey, and Thomas Ross for acting as consulting editors and offering sane and prompt attention to problems as they arose; to Professor Ramsey and to Professor Ross I am further indebted for assistance in the second of our five corrections of the text transcription, during which each read five tales.

I am indebted to Ian Doyle and to Daniel Huws for their meticulous transcriptions of the memoranda on 128v, 152v, and 165r, and of the mock-writ on 169v.

My labors have been lightened greatly by the cheerful assistance of my former students Mende Snodgress, Kenneth Rogers, Peggy Epperson, Lynne Hunt Levy, Nan Arbuckle, and Anne Marie Candido; their scrupulous attention to the details of transcription and variations has saved me from innumerable errors and oversights. And Sally Mussetter has always given sound paleographical advice and has applied her bracing wit to many a difficult case.

A very special debt must be acknowledged for the unstinting loyalty to me and to the project of Lane Goodall, whose sharp eye and clear intelligence have been ever at my disposal; and that of Donald Rose, who, as managing editor, has assumed the responsibility for systematizing and coordinating the procedures by which the text has been brought to completion; his patient good humor has sustained us all.

I wish also to express my gratitude to Mildred Logan, Julie Blissert, and Howard McElhany, of the University of Oklahoma Press, who have borne with us with kindness and understanding. Mr. McElhany's ingenuity has more than once saved us both money and time.

And special thanks must be offered to the National Library of Wales for permission to reproduce the Hengwrt manuscript, and in particular to Daniel Huws, Assistant Keeper of Manuscripts, and to Colin Venus, who photographed our text, for their kindness on our visits to their country; to the Huntington Library at San Marino, California, for kind services relating to the Ellesmere manuscript.

And to the National Endowment for the Humanities, for providing us with support to discharge many of the obligations incurred in the course of this project, and to my friend, the anonymous donor who has made the publication of this edition possible, my profoundest gratitude.

PAUL G. RUGGIERS

Norman, Oklahoma

Introduction

THE RELATION OF THE HENGWRT MANUSCRIPT TO THE VARIORUM CHAUCER TEXT

Donald C. Baker

The publication of the Hengwrt manuscript of the *Canterbury Tales* at the outset of the *Variorum Chaucer* project presents, for the first time in facsimile, this exceedingly important manuscript, which will serve as the base text for the *Canterbury Tales* in the *Variorum.* Its importance has been increasingly recognized since publication of the Manly-Rickert text of the *Canterbury Tales;* the evidence of its singularity was presented there by the editors and in subsequent important articles by Mrs. Germaine Dempster, next to Manly the greatest of the textual scholars of the *Canterbury Tales.* Hengwrt's age (1400–10), its unedited state, and its accuracy (Manly-Rickert's textual reconstruction is very, very close to Hengwrt[1]), have now placed it in the forefront of the *Canterbury Tales* manuscripts, ahead even of the magnificent and more nearly complete, but heavily edited, Ellesmere. Our text will be a very conservatively edited Hengwrt with apparatus drawn from firsthand collation of ten or more manuscripts representing Manly's chief groups (with Ellesmere serving as the base when Hengwrt is incomplete) and a collation of the chief printed texts, which, of course, Manly-Rickert did not provide.

It must be admitted, however, that there is no overwhelming case on the face of it for still another text of the *Canterbury Tales.* There are many in the field. A variorum text, as the term is generally understood, is primarily a text which will bear the weight of the notes *variorum.* It should, of course, be as good and as useful a text as it is possible to achieve, but it must always be borne in mind that its purpose is not chiefly to be a text but to serve as a means of sorting and organizing the mass of commentary. While important, it is, therefore, in a sense, secondary. Thus, the *Variorum Milton* has provided no text at all but keyed its commentary to the Columbia edition of Milton, an admirable text which, though it may not at all points meet with the approval of Milton scholars, is universally known, is normally quoted from, has been standard for many years, and certainly represents the basic tradition of Milton's text.

Why, therefore, have we not in the case of the *Canterbury Tales* simply borrowed the most popular edition since the now-obsolete Skeat, that of F. N. Robinson? One principal reason is that Robinson, even in his second edition, is too committed to the Ellesmere manuscript, which we believe to be only the second-best manuscript of the *Canterbury Tales.* Then why have we not used the great Manly-Rickert text, which does give much greater weight to what is clearly the best over-all text, the Hengwrt? One reason is that the Manly-Rickert text, not being punctuated, is almost never cited for purpose of quotation. In view of this, why create

[1] Germaine Dempster remarked, in "The First Canterbury Tales MSS after the Death of Chaucer," a paper read to the Rocky Mountain Modern Language Association in October, 1951, that many scholars had assumed that Manly-Rickert had adopted the Hengwrt as their base, though this had been far from their intention, but that their text was much closer to Hengwrt than to any other manuscript.

a text which has never been cited at all? The real answer is twofold: one, that Chaucer's text has never had the stable tradition that Milton's has had, and as a result each century has had its own Chaucer; and two, that a reasonably uniform practice seems desirable for so extensive a project as a variorum, and since several of Chaucer's poems have never had a really adequate edition, the base-text method which will be required by several seems best to adopt over all.

What we are attempting is the difficult task of providing at one time the text which is as near as it is possible to get to what Chaucer must have written (and we believe that for most of the *Canterbury Tales* it is that of the Hengwrt manuscript—as slightly emended—to a greater extent even than that of the Manly-Rickert text) and, easily accessible on the same page, the collated readings from both the chief manuscript families and the principal printed editions, which will, taken together, provide the text of Chaucer that every writer upon the poet has used. The manuscript readings will be drawn both from those manuscripts representing the most accurate versions and from those manuscripts representing the most important traditions that went into the formation of Chaucer's text over the centuries and upon which all writers drew; likewise, from the printed editions, those that played a role in the transmission of Chaucer's text. Clearly, the chief reason for not selecting an existing printed text is that it would present a single reading, or a single statistic in the larger body of evidence, and the very fact that our new text had not been cited would free the new text from too close an association with other texts and it would therefore provide a structure around which all other readings and the commentary bearing upon those readings could be grouped without the danger of bias arising. The very considerable variation in the tradition of Chaucer's text may in itself be seen as cause of some commentary (for example, the consistently "cruder" text of Caxton's edition and his sixteenth-century followers, which may have contributed to the notion of Chaucer's "coarseness").

In short, we hope to provide both what Chaucer wrote and what, for centuries, it was assumed that he wrote. In following our text, the collations, and the commentary, the scholar may get a clearer idea of the way in which Chaucer's text slowly came into being and the commentary upon it developed. For this purpose it has seemed best to adopt the Hengwrt manuscript as our base text.

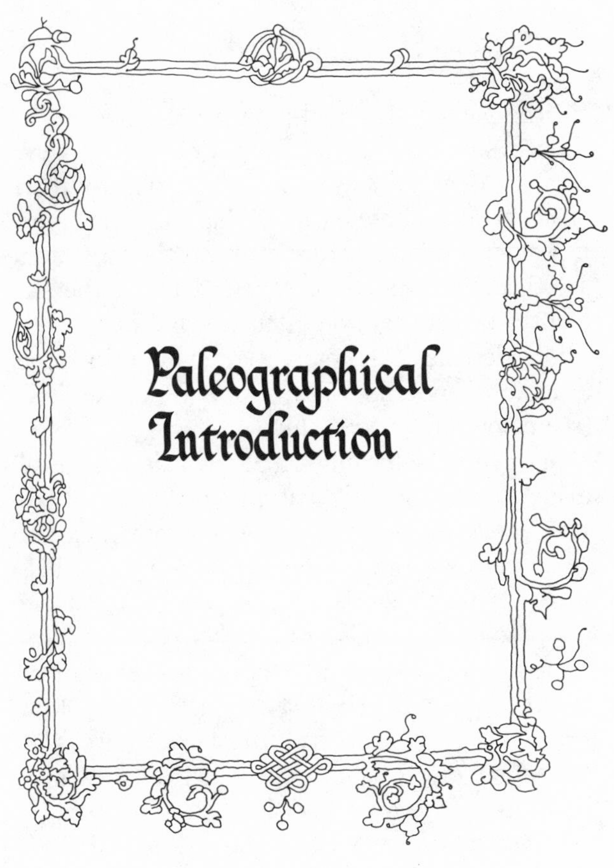

Paleographical Introduction

A. I. Doyle and M. B. Parkes

The importance of the Hengwrt manuscript of the *Canterbury Tales* is that it is probably the earliest surviving copy of that unfinished work, that it shows, through its makeup and various deficiencies, the lack of an established sequence of the whole collection, alterations in the relative arrangement and personal assignment of particular tales and their links, and delays in receiving them, yet that it reproduces with remarkable fidelity sources better than those used by most other known copies and subjected to less adaptation and amendment (cf. Tatlock 1935:128–29, 133–39; Manly and Rickert 1940: 1.175–76; Dempster 1946:392–95; 1949:1131–32, 1139–40).

CODICOLOGICAL AND PALEOGRAPHICAL OBSERVATIONS[1]

The closest relationships of the Hg manuscript, paleographically and in some portions textually, are with the Ellesmere manuscript (San Marino, Huntington Library, MS.El.26.C.9), which we follow others (Tatlock 1935:128; Manly and Rickert 1940:1.149) in believing to be by the same copyist as most of Hg (pp. xx, xxxiv, xliii). There are, however, conspicuous contrasts between the two manuscripts, which force us to suppose great differences in the circumstances and manner of their preparation. Hg, although by no means a cheap product, is inferior in page size and design, in textual and structural coherence, and in extent of decoration, to El. The exceptionally lavish and smoothly executed character of the latter implies superior planning and provision of resources, and closer collaboration of those concerned, than do the irregularities and improvisations in Hg. Whereas El must always have been a most acceptable presentation of *CT,* the more rough-and-ready Hg may have been accepted as the best that could be achieved in less favorable conditions.

ORIGINAL CONTENT AND AUTHORSHIP

The volume's prime and, so far as we know, sole scope is stated by the heading in the display script of the main scribe at the head of the first page (now folio 2r). In fact it contains the whole of the *Canterbury Tales* with the exception of the *Canon's Yeoman's Tale,* some links and a few shorter passages, and it is defective at the end, having lost part of the *Parson's Tale* (Block/Group I, line 550–end) and possibly the *Retraccioun*s. Because of this there is no final colophon, but the work is attributed by the original scribe in an added note on fol. 57v, "Of this Cokes Tale maked Chaucer na moore" is implied by "Lenvoy de Chaucer," 190v, and by an interlinear gloss on the word "me," 213r, while the author's name also occurs in the headings and explicits to *Thopas* and *Melibeus,* and in the

[1] The description which follows is greatly indebted to that by Manly and Rickert (1940:1.266–83; 2.477–79) but their observations and arguments have been amplified or corrected after fresh examinations of the manuscript by both authors of this introduction and by Daniel Huws, of the National Library of Wales, to whom particular thanks are owed.

running titles added by a second contemporaneous hand.

DATE AND PLACE OF MAKING

The principal criterion for dating the manuscript is the handwriting of its copyists (see below, pp. xxxiv–xxxvii). The main scribe is known in two[2] other volumes, El and, we believe, Trinity College, Cambridge (England), MS.R.3.2, where he is one of five working contemporaneously, one of whom, Thomas Hoccleve, died in 1426, while the text, John Gower's *Confessio Amantis,* has appended to it a Latin poem which must have been composed shortly before or after Gower's death in 1408 (Doyle and Parkes 1978:163–85). The main scribe of Hg was therefore active at some time in the first quarter of the fifteenth century, although the style of his writing suggests that he had learned it in the second half of the fourteenth century. Of the other hands which supply his omissions, some can be confidently assigned to the later period: one of the closest parallels is firmly dated 1412–13.

The style of the illumination of the first page is, like that of El, of the end of the fourteenth century, without the features which developed in the first decade or so of the fifteenth, although the executants may have been old-fashioned. Margaret Rickert (Manly and Rickert 1940:1. 565, 567–69) discerned successive stages of that development in two other early copies of the *Canterbury Tales,* the eclectic B. L. Harley 7334 and Corpus Christi College, Oxford, 198, the best representative of the related *c* tradition of the text. Both were, except for corrections, copied by the same prolific scribe whose other work, including a share of the Trinity Gower (Doyle and Parkes 1978:174–82), is datable at the least from after 1398 to after 1408. If we also accept Dempster's argument (1949:1124–25, 1139–42) that the arrangement of the tales in Hg influenced that in Harley and the *c* tradition, then Hg is likely to have been completed before the creation of those other arrangements. Since it is generally thought that the sources of Hg were near enough to Chaucer to provide exemplars of unrivaled quality, yet without the ability to fill the gaps within and between the pieces authentically, or to arrange them authoritatively, it is reasonable to suppose that he was by then dead or incapacitated; that is, that the work, even if perhaps initiated before, was mostly done after 1400, perhaps in the first few years of the fifteenth century, although there may have been a considerable delay before the supplying of some omissions and the binding up of the sections (see below, pp. xxxix, xliii).

We cannot determine on purely paleographical evidence whether Hg was written before El or vice versa, or how long may separate them; it is conceivable that to some extent the scribe's work on them overlapped, as the variations in his practices do. The time taken cannot have been less than several months on each,[3] more if the copying was not a full-time occupation and if, as appears to have happened with Hg, the supply of exemplars was interrupted; it may have run into years, especially if we add planning and decoration, at least in the case of El. It is easier to believe that Hg was copied before El than the contrary; it would be surprising that a scribe who had already copied the more straightforward sequence of El, however subordinate his role, should not have helped to improve that of Hg more than he seems to have done.[4] And other early arrangements superior to that of Hg, although differing from that in El, were copied by another scribe whose hand appears in the Trinity Gower together with that of Hg and El and who may therefore have been known to him: i.e., those of Corpus Christi College, Oxford, 198 and B. L. Harley 7334. So Hg may well antedate these too. However, Hg cannot be regarded simply as a trial run for El, since their texts exhibit substantial differences. The resemblances and contrasts between Hg and El are most comprehensible if the two were produced for different employers with some interval between, or possibly for the same employer with two different clients.

The employer for Hg could have been an admirer of the author dealing directly with the

[2] Since this introduction was written, we have identified a fragment of a third, at Hatfield House: see Jackson J. Campbell, "A New *Troilus* Fragment," *PMLA,* Vol. 73 (1958), pp. 305–308, with reduced facsimile.

[3] Cf. H. E. Bell, "The Price of Books in Medieval England," *The Library,* 4th ser., Vol. 17 (1936–37), pp. 312–32, esp. 314–16.

[4] The arguments over whether Hengwrt or Ellesmere was copied first are so complex that the present writers are not in complete agreement on this particular issue.

holders of exemplars on the one hand and the scribe on the other, in order to obtain as fully and as soon as possible a collection of the *CT* for his own and his friends' pleasure, with perhaps a concern for posterity too. It could, alternatively, have been a stationer as agent for such a client, either merely arranging the copying and decoration, or also procuring the exemplars. Or it could have been a stationer performing the same functions with a view to selling the product to an as yet uncertain customer, or else to retain it for use as an exemplar for further (better-ordered) copies. If the last were the case, we would expect to find rather more textual derivation from Hg than seems to survive in other manuscripts (see Manly and Rickert 1940:1.252–53, 275–76, 441; 2.479); the early influence mentioned above is restricted to the arrangement and some wording of links, in a way which (to take up a suggestion of Dempster) could have been copied or carried in his head by the scribe or a compiler of another collection, from a book in private ownership. According to Dempster (1948b:465; 1949:1124, 1136–38, 1140–42) Manly and Rickert seem to have thought of Hg and El as produced by privately employed scribes, and of Harley 7334, Corpus 198, and others as commercial in the sense that the initiative for copying (and perhaps compilation) came from the London book trade. We think that this may suggest a sharper division in the modes of production of new vernacular literature than had developed by that time. At the earliest stage the stationers were more likely to be intermediaries than speculators, and the same scribes and decorators might be hired for similar copies of the same books from diverse exemplars, following rather than anticipating individual commissions (cf. Tatlock 1935:107–109; Pollard 1937:14–16; Dempster 1946:403–404; Doyle and Parkes 1978:196–98).

The work so far identified as by the main scribe of Hg and El, one of five sharing the Trinity Gower, shows that he was a very proficient copyist of recent English poetry and was also familiar with Latin texts. He may also have been a professional in the sense that he earned his living at least in part by his pen, but possibly in an ecclesiastical, administrative, or legal capacity, not necessarily as a full-time literary copyist. His repeated copying of *CT,* in one instance without and the other with extensive editorial changes (for which he is unlikely to have been personally responsible), argues that he was not an enthusiastic amateur so much as a reliable amanuensis. His spelling reveals no fundamental incompatibility with what can be recovered of Chaucer's and Gower's original orthographies (differing as they do), which suggests that he did not habitually write in a distant dialect.[5] Variations in his practice among the three manuscripts and within each (reflecting no doubt various exemplars and even changes of fashion) indicate that it was fairly flexible.[6] These characteristics, besides his particular usages, would suit the situation in a metropolitan milieu about the turn of the fourteenth into the fifteenth century.

When, where, by whom, and for whom was Hg made? We cannot give a conclusive answer to any of these questions. If other manuscripts containing any of the hands found in Hg (or, of course, related texts) should fortunately be discovered in future, its connections may be enlarged and defined better than we can venture now.[7]

MATERIAL AND PREPARATION

The membrane employed, more probably sheep than calf, is fairly uniform, of middling thickness and quality, with a good mat (velvety) finish, but with small original holes in a number of sheets, some of them formerly stitched up and avoided by the scribe (e.g., on fol. 7, 14, 39, 102). Where the hair and flesh sides can be distinguished, they appear to have been gathered conventionally with like facing like, normally in quaternions (quires of eight leaves—for exceptions see pp. xxiv–xxv). The approximate size of each leaf is now 11 1/2 × 8 1/4 inches (292 × 210 mm.), but originally the unfolded cut sheet must have measured at least 12 × 17 inches (305 × 408 mm.), estimated from the extent of later

[5] Cf. M. L. Samuels, "Some Applications of Middle English Dialectology," *English Studies,* Vol. 44 (1963), pp. 81–94, esp. 87–89.

[6] Cf. Manly and Rickert 1940:1.151, 276, 557–60; Price 1955: 137–48; F. Wild, *Die sprachlichen Eigentümlichkeiten der wichtigeren Chaucer-Handschriften und die Sprache Chaucers* (Wiener Beiträge zur Englischen Philologie 44, 1915), esp. pp. 8–12. R. Vance Ramsey has shown us some statistics of the variations, which need further discussion.

[7] The *Troilus* fragment mentioned in n. 2 is too short to reveal much, except to strengthen the association of the scribe with recent English poetry.

cropping of running titles (fol. 42r, 120r, 136r), catchwords (41v, 65v, 95v), and side notes (109r, 162r, 190r, 236v, 242r, 249v).

Subsequent use and maltreatment have obscured much of the original surface (stains on fol. 2r, 52, ingrained dirt elsewhere), and the top outside corners throughout the volume have been eroded, as well as the lower fore edge from about fol. 90 to 200, and the bottom margin from fol. 210 to 212 with portions of the last line or two of the text, probably by the teeth of mice or rats. There are some offsets of initials by damp. The lost corners were replaced with blank parchment in 1956, but, unfortunately, in the process a little of the writing has been scarfed over (cf. Manly and Rickert 1939: pl. opp. p. 64 with fol. 153r in the present facsimile).

Pricks to guide the ruling survive on many leaves, near the fore edge only, repeated irregularities in the pattern indicating that the sheets were pricked in batches, perhaps already folded into quires, then unfolded for ruling. The pricking takes the form of a horizontal knife point on fol. 2–4, at an angle and less penetrating in the second half of the quire, elsewhere varying between a point and a deeper cut. Ruling where discernible is chiefly blind, imposed by dry point on both sides of each sheet, but a number of sides, pages, or parts of pages are ruled or reruled in gray lead (e.g., fol. 9v, 18r, 88r, 93v, 94r–v, 95v, 99v–100r, top two lines of 108r, 153r–v, 165r top half, 226–33). It is possible that the lead has been erased or rubbed off in other places. On some pages and leaves there is no sign now of horizontal ruling. The blind ruling was sometimes done by sides of sheets (e.g., fol. 76r–79v), in advance of writing, though with regard to the expected contents, and supplemented by the lead where insufficient or unprovided (e.g., the supernumerary leaf 153 and within the augmented quire 29).

The employment of dry point on membrane of this velvety finish seems to us somewhat unusual at this period. The furrows are not easy to see and may have been intended as an inconspicuous guide to the alignment of the text, headings, and explicits.[8] There is no ruling for the writing of marginalia and other apparatus, difficult to predict at the outset if, as it appears, a complete exemplar of the whole work was not then to hand. In the ampler space of El a separate frame was ruled in ink for the marginalia, but no lines were provided for them. And in Hg, unlike El, there is no pricking or ruling for running titles or catchwords.

The ruling comprises a roughly rectangular frame of intersecting lines, within which the single column is ruled for 40, 39, or 44 written or blank lines below the top ruled line, according to the several forms of the text, the top and bottom two lines being generally carried across both margins. The other line ruling extends irregularly into both margins. The size of the frame varies in relation to the forms of the text and number of lines, with a range of 216–27 × 115–20 mm. for 40 lines of decasyllabic couplets, about 215 × 115–20 mm. for 39 lines of seven-line stanzas, and 225 × 115–20 mm. for 44 lines of eight-line stanzas (five stanzas per page with intervening blank lines for each type), 210 × 160 mm. for tail rhyme, and 220–30 × 120–30 mm. for prose. There are also substantial variations from quire to quire (e.g., qq. 27, 28, 29) and page to page within the same tale (e.g., fol. 112–26 and 220–27) of the actual space occupied by writing, where there is no correspondence on the same sides of bifolia because of independent or indistinct ruling. The results are not always straight, parallel, or rectangular (e.g., fol. 51r, 72v, 113r, 135r). While some of these things are not obtrusive it is evident that the demands of uniformity and neatness were not as high for Hg as for El, and haste often made the scribe manage without careful preparation for his writing.

CONSTRUCTION OF THE VOLUME

The manuscript now consists of 249 leaves (numbered 2–250 by modern hands) in 31 quires, chiefly of eight leaves each; one more of ten would have accommodated the remainder of the *Parson's Tale* and the *Retraccciouns.*[9] There are early gathering signatures in the form of small letters (apart from *N*) and Roman numerals lightly and informally written in ink in the bot-

[8] We have used "headings" because "incipits" often mean the opening words of the text itself; although "explicits" can be used correspondingly for the actual closing words, "endings" would be still more misleading, and they are not colophons. Our practice here thus accords with Petti, 1977, not Doyle and Parkes, 1978.

[9] Manly and Rickert 1940:1.268 suggest two more quires of eight, but that would be far too much.

tom right-hand corners of the first halves of quires in section IV only, with an extra set on the left in quire 29 (see p. xxix). That such signatures are found only in section IV and not throughout the volume may mean that they are not a binder's but the scribe's or his director's doing, to assist maintenance of correct gathering where the contents are most disjointed and the requisite ruling most changeable. The start halfway through the alphabet presumes the assignment of the previous letters to other quires expected to precede, but none are visible there, and all are very difficult to decipher. They are mostly faint or cropped. Manly and Rickert (1940:1.266–67) offer readings confirmed from ultraviolet photographs, but Daniel Huws, of the National Library of Wales, has produced for us partly divergent results, not supporting as straightforward a pattern as theirs and perhaps reflecting the disordered origins of that portion of the volume.[10] On their evidence, taken with the physical structure of the manuscript and the internal relationships of the tales, Manly and Rickert conjectured one intended sequence of quires running from section I into section IV, interrupted by the insertion of sections II and III. In the following table their readings of quire signatures are in Roman letters, queried if doubtful, in square brackets if conjectural; Huws's readings in italics, queried if doubtful, with our conjectures also italicized in square brackets.

[10] Huws confirms the presence of all the signatures recorded by Manly and Rickert, except on fol. 145, where it is probably concealed by a repair, but he has found others and questions some of their readings: on fol. 113–15 "a horizontal line and below it on 115 what looks more like *b* than *k*"; 154–55 "cannot make a *p* of it; looks like *k* on each"; 163–64 "something, hardly *q*"; "on 167 a horizontal line above it, a similar line on 168"; 178–80 "*p* on all three under ultra-violet lamp"; 186 "upper part of a quire signature"; 193–96 "on each a small circle, below it on 194 a – and on 196 a +"; 202–203 "looks like *q*"; 209 "indistinct mark"; 217–20 "what I take to be a long *r* on each, not *y*"; "*s iiii* clear on 228, the *s* less clear on 226–27 and I think just visible on 225." The results would be more intelligible if the tales were in self-contained interchangeable booklets. Some may be arbitrary identifications of the sheets belonging to a particular quire, not relating quire to quire, which was done by the catchwords, as often at an earlier period than this.

Quire 29, fol. 225–29, has additional leaf numbering with Roman digits clearly in ink in the left-hand corner of the lower margin, aligned with the vertical ruling, on the first five rectos, the last number boxed and repeated on the verso, with a cross for the middle fold of the quire (as is common). It seems possible that this was done before writing, along with the distinct lead ruling of both sides of each sheet, to ensure that the scribe would not make mistakes in the order of the extended quire. Cf. Manly and Rickert 1940:1.18, 278–79.

The horizontal rules represent the points of coincidence of physical and content division, that is, the separable sections of the codex, denoted also by Roman numerals in the extreme left-hand column (the beginning of each section and of each quire is recorded also in the top left-hand corner of the corresponding page of the transcription, facing the facsimile). In the extreme right-hand column of the table the sigla for the blocks, groups, or fragments of the text are bracketed with the folios occupied by each element.

There is no doubt that section III is simply misplaced and should and could come logically between sections IV and V (Manly and Rickert 1940:1.270), although it was decided before the rebinding of the volume in 1956 by the National Library not to correct the situation (see below, p. xlii). Section II is also obviously out of place in the narrative order but there is no point in the structure of the volume where it could be inserted more satisfactorily (Manly and Rickert 1940:1.273). From these facts it may be inferred that the sections were not copied in the most logical order, but there is no reason to suppose that the order in which they are found now is chronologically that in which they were made. The very divisions of the volume, the abnormal makeup of some quires, the occurrence of blank pages or parts of pages, changes in the character of the writing and shades of ink, and the disorder of the contents, particularly in section IV, afford clues to how the copying may have proceeded in relation to the supply of exemplars.

The structural sections, within which linked and unlinked matter is copied across quire divisions, are contrived to finish a unit of the text on the last leaf of a quire of normal length or one shortened or lengthened for the purpose (q. 12 of six, q. 29 of ten leaves). They suggest that the copyist was provided either with a single corresponding exemplar (as perhaps for sections I and V) or else with a succession of exemplars (as for sections IV, III, and possibly II) and instructed, or allowed to decide, how far he should copy each consecutively after the last and where it was advisable to leave a limited space within a quire or an indefinite one at the end of a section to accommodate, respectively, a short piece of text known or thought to be wanting at that point, or a longer portion not yet available or

STRUCTURAL SECTIONS	PRESENT QUIRING	QUIRE LETTERS	PRESENT FOLIOS	SPREAD OF CONTENTS	BLOCK/ GROUP
I	1^8	[a]	2–9	2r–12v *GP*	A
	2^8	[b]	10–17		
	3^8	[c]	18–25	12v–41r *KnT*	
	4^8	[d]	26–33		
	5^8	[e]	34–41		
	6^2	[f]	42–43	41r–50v *MilPT*	
	7^6	[g]	44–49		
	8^8	[h]	50–57	50v–56v *RvPT* 56v–57v *CkPT*	
		[j] (reserved for conclusion of *CkT*?)			
II	9^8		58–65	58r–73v *WBPT*	D
	10^8		66–73	73v–78v *FrPT*	
	11^8		74–81	78v–86v *SumPT*	
	12^6		82–87	87v blank	
III	13^8		88–95	88r–98v *MkPT*	B^{2b}
	14^8		96–103	99r–107r *NPPT*	
	15^8		104–11	107r–111v *ManPT*	= H

STRUCTURAL SECTIONS	PRESENT QUIRING	QUIRE LETTERS	PRESENT FOLIOS	SPREAD OF CONTENTS	BLOCK/ GROUP
	16^{8}	k? *h?*	112–19		
	17^{8}	l	120–27	112r–128r *MLHPT* 128v blank	= B^{1}
	18^{8}	m	128–35		
				129r–137v *SqT*	= F^{a}
	19^{8}	N	136–43	137v *Sq-FranL* as *MerP*	(F673–708)
	20^{8}	o	144–51	138r–152v *MerT*	E^{b}
	$21^{8 + \text{one}}$	p *k*	152–60	153r–v *MerE-SqP* as *FranH*	(E2419–40 & F1-8)
				153v–165r *FranPT*	= F^{b}
	22^{16}	q? *-?*	161–76	165v–173r *SNPT*	= G^{a}
	23^{8}	[r] *p*	177–84	173v–191r *ClPTE*	= E^{a}
IV	24^{8}	[s] *?*	185–92		
				191v–195r *PhyT*	
	25^{8}	[t] *o?*	193–200	195r–v *Phy-PardL*	C
				195v–203v *PardPT*	
	26^{8}	v? *q?*	201–208		
				204r–209r *ShT*	
				209v *Sh-PrL* 209v–213r *PrPT*	
	27^{8}	[x] *?*	209–16	213r–v *Pr-ThL*	B^{2a}
				213v–215r *Th* 215r–216r *Th-MelL* 216r–234v *Mel*	
	28^{8}	y *r*	217–24		
	29^{10}	[z] *s*	225–34		
	30^{8}		235–42		
	31^{8}		243–50	235r–250v *ParsPT* (defective)	
V					I
	$[32^{10?}]$			[end of *ParsT*; & *Ret?*]	

of uncertain existence. It could also be that when (by the time he began its final quire) he terminated a section it was because he, or his director, was not sure what should immediately follow for the best eventual order, although he may have already copied it in another section.

THE PROGRESS OF COPYING

The continuity of copying through tales and quires was not uninterrupted. There were naturally breaks between one day's and the next's work, and within each day for meals and other necessities, such as ruling, cutting fresh nibs, and mixing or stirring ink, which may or may not be noticeable on the pages today; some are, even in photographic reproduction (e.g., fol. 42r, new quire; 50r, new quire; 123v, near end of second stanza; 144r, new quire; 151r, near foot of page; 165v, new tale; 218r, second paragraph; 236v, second paragraph; 249r, second paragraph). But besides these routine halts, and more gradual changes in the size, slant, and currency of the script in the course of stretches of continuous writing, which reflect the copyist's state of mind and body or the condition of his implements and materials, there are disconformities which can be explained most intelligibly by interruptions in the availability of exemplars of consecutive portions of the series of tales and links and by attempts to take advantage of what was available while it was so, with a minimum of adaptation, if unavoidable, and some anticipation of the possibility of future insertions. There are obvious signs of haste in the writing (growing size, unevenness, and current features) in the course of some pieces (e.g., *MilT, RvT, CkT,* concluding section I), after careful opening stretches, which suggest that, while eager to maintain a high standard where it would be most noticeable (and he would have to pause to space and engross explicits and headings, as he apparently did as he came to them), he was not at indefinite leisure to do all the copying as deliberately.

Catchwords he also seems to have written as he came to them. The absence of catchwords at the section ends may therefore indicate either ignorance or caution at the time of copying, since within the sections each quire has them usually in the same ink as well as the same hand as the page above, with a penwork underline, apart from fol. 95v, where only the tops of the letters survive as a result of cropping.[11] The fact that no catchwords were added at a later stage at the ends of sections I, IV, and III to connect them straightforwardly with V may reflect the state of uncertainty about the completeness and correct order of the manuscript which its collectors may have remained in and their acceptance of its irremediably jumbled and interim character.

The sectionalization and the absence of final catchwords could be owing in part to the copyist pursuing his work from exemplars in different places, having left what he had already done with his director or customer or at home and having no note of its scope or start. We must also allow for the possibility that more than one section may have been in progress, or suspense, at the same time and that some of the present sections might be survivors of parallel copies made by the same scribe, while there may once have been still another section for the missing *Canon's Yeoman's Prologue* and *Tale.*

Subject to such provisos, examination of the separate sections and their contents affords arguments for a possible progress of the main scribe through sections V, IV (except fol. 137v, 153), I, III (fol. 88r–98v), II, III (fol. 98v–111v), fol. 137v and 153, a second hand intervening to supply one explicit in IV and all the running titles except some in V and those in the second half of III, the latter being added by the main hand later. But several alternatives are conceivable with I, V, and II in other orders, as will appear below.

Section I (fol. 2–57) commences with the heading for the whole work, distinctly paler in ink than the rest of the page and so possibly a later insertion by the scribe (cf. fol. 98v–111, 137v, 153), but this may be partly an effect of the enlarged pen strokes or the damp and attrition to which it has obviously been exposed. The first line of text is dropped well below the top of the normal page, or of those that begin other units of the work, and the space left for the decorated initial was larger. The scribe probably envisaged the top bar of the vinet going above his heading and left sufficient space, but in fact

[11] They are mostly written somewhat aslant, although this is accentuated in the facsimile by the curvature of the gutter.

it is cramped between heading and text, the gold and blue of the central feature superimposed on downstrokes of the heading, thus confirming the latter's priority in execution, which might be in doubt.

The text runs straight through block A with no spare space save a line or two before and after explicits and headings. The only structural anomaly concerns quire 6, of two leaves only, and quire 7, of six, both within the extent of the *Miller's Tale.* Manly and Rickert (1940:1. 167) explain this as a simple error of the scribe, after writing the first leaf in what was meant to be a normal quire of eight, continuing directly on to the conjoint leaf, instead of the first of another loose bifolium and then two more before commencing the second half of the full gathering. In their view, when he discovered his mistake, he decided to retain the bifolia as he had written them, in the present state. For that to be economical he must have filled more than half of the eight leaves before he realized the situation. If he had noticed before he got far down the third page, he could have erased it, and if he had finished or nearly finished no more than the second, third, or fourth leaf, he could still have cut the first bifolium in two and attached the singletons by stubs to counterparts concluding the quaternion, though that might have been thought somewhat insecure before the book was bound. That there is no visible catchword to quire 6, whereas there is one to quire 7, tends to confirm that the mistake was not noticed till a late stage in assembling the sheets of the quire or section. Manly and Rickert did not notice that there is some difference of membrane, frame, and ink between quires 6 and 7 and those on either side. These could be simply signs of a separate stint, but possibly also of a substitution, involving the end of the *Miller's Prologue* and most of his *Tale.* There are parallels in other manuscripts for textual change at that point, but not reflected in Hg (Manly and Rickert 1940:2.153–54).

The *Cook's Tale* expires (as normal) on fol. 57v, with room for ten more lines on the page, the last of the quire and section. That the scribe had no more of the tale to hand, and already thought none was likely, is indicated by his writing the minims of the last line (exceptionally for the English of the text) with angular heads and feet, in the bastard style of his headings, explicits, Latin quotations, and some sidenotes.[12] Nonetheless he, or his director, did not give up all hope or obstruct continuation at a later date, since they did not fill the space with an explicit as done elsewhere in the manuscript. If Manly's and Rickert's conjecture is correct concerning the assignment of quire signatures, allowance was made, whenever that was done, for another quire (to be signed *j*) to follow section I if necessary. Sometime after writing the *CkT,* on the evidence of a paler shade of ink, like that of section II (which was not necessarily the next written after I), the same scribe, relying on reputable information or reasonable probability, added, "Of this Cokes tale maked Chaucer na moore," yet even then only in the margin, so as to leave open the possibilities of supplying a spurious continuation or a link like that which follows the truncated *Squire's Tale,* if either should be found.

If those were the thoughts at the finishing of the *CkT,* it is not impossible that there were other portions of the collection then ready for copying, or already copied, by this scribe, and equally so when the marginal note was added. Section I need not have been the very first to be copied, in any case, although there is a natural likelihood that block A was in better order and would be first obtained for the purpose. If the quire-letter conjectures of Manly and Rickert are accepted, section I was finished by the time the quires of IV came to be signed, though that may not have been at the time of their writing.

Section II (fol. 58–87) is all written in a lighter shade of brown ink than most of the rest of the manuscript, and therefore presumably at a somewhat different time and in one closely consecutive series of sessions. If its exemplar or exemplars, making up the whole of block D, had been available in the course of the copying of section III or IV, the material could have been as well fitted in either before block H or before B^{2a}, as what is accommodated there; or if it had already been copied separately, one

[12] On fol. 7r lines 13–15 are similarly written (*GP* 402–405), as if he was slowing down for some reason, perhaps writing more mechanically with his mind half-distracted since he omitted the word *herberwe* and had to insert it later with a thinner nib and ink. The very first catchword of section I, on fol. 9v, is also bastard in tendency, and other catchwords show it with related symptoms.

of those sections could have been divided to allow for its insertion. If the original name of the previous narrator in the first line of the *Parson's Tale,* at the beginning of section V, subsequently erased and rewritten as "Maunciple," were "Somnour" (rather than "Frankeleyn," as surmised by Manly and Rickert 1940: 1.276–77), section II, where the *Summoner's Tale* comes last,[13] might have been completed later than V and at first intended to precede it; but after the alteration, whereby sections IV, III, and V are linked in that order, II could be placed only as it is today. That the note about the *Cook's Tale* on the last page of section I is in the same shade of ink as section II, however, suggests that it was being completed for that position. Section II could have been the very last done, apart from the addition of running titles.

Manly and Rickert offer two different (unnecessary) accounts of the structure of quire 12, the last of section II (1940:1.14, wrongly called q. 11; 267: both say the text ends on fol. 86r instead of 86v), alleging that fol. 87 is thinner, which is not true, and ignoring the fact of its ruling. The first and last leaves (fol. 82 and 87) had undoubtedly become separated and before the latest rebinding were stitched to their neighbors, though now joined by a new strip of parchment.

The blank ruled fol. 87 was an inevitable surplus; the quire had already been reduced to six leaves in anticipation of the end of the tale, with no certain or convenient sequel waiting to be copied. The ruling may have been automatic (across a bifolium), but it would have facilitated the addition of more matter later. That it was not utilized to commence appropriate matter from sections III, IV, or V tends to confirm the probability that they were already completed, and that the *Canon's Yeoman's Prologue* and *Tale* were not attached here (or at the end of section I) suggests that they were never obtained for Hg, unless they occupied a short separate section (a single quire of twelve?) that has been lost.

Section III (fol. 88–111) is in the darker brown ink up to and including the last line of the *Monk's Tale* on fol. 98v, but the explicit on the same page is in a paler yellowish ink employed for the remainder of the section (fol. 99–111), suggestive of an interval before copying was resumed. It may mean that the *Nun's Priest's Prologue* and *Tale,* though linked with the *Monk's,* was not immediately available, and that the exemplar of the *Manciple's,* not so linked to the *NPPT,* nevertheless came to the scribe with it and that he was encouraged or permitted to copy *ManPT* consecutively to fill up the quire of eight already begun, with noticeably less than the usual space between the explicit of the one and the heading of the other on fol. 107r.

The absence of a catchword at the end of the section may mean that what should follow was still uncertain, that, although section V may have been written before the second part of III, the name in V's first line had not yet been changed to *Mauncíple* and was not immediately since it is not in the yellowish ink. A similar shade is, however, used for two additions to section IV, on fol. 137v and the inserted fol. 153, which may therefore have been made about the same time as the second part of section III. The unsupplemented state of IV is thus earlier, but not necessarily before the *first* part of III, and the remainder of IV was possibly completed after III had been begun; the *Monk's Prologue* makes it clear that the *Tale of Melibeus* should precede; so, if the former had been copied before the latter, a catchword on fol. 235v could have connected them; but, ambiguously, IV may have been completed with an enlarged quire either because its sequel was already copied or because it was unknown.

The running titles to the second part of section III, where the text is in the yellowish ink, are (unlike all others except the names of the sins with the *Parson's Tale*) by the main hand, but in a darker ink than the text, and it seems that they were an afterthought, imitating the initiative of the second hand, which provided

[13] This hypothesis about *SumT* (cf. Tatlock 1935:139), pursued from an article by Norman Blake on "The Relationship Between the Hengwrt and Ellesmere Manuscripts of the *Canterbury Tales,*" which he has been kind enough to communicate before publication, has in its favor, apart from its placing at the end of section II, the last line (D 2294): *My tale is doon, we been almoost at towne* (Hg). On the other hand, no extant copy puts it in the penultimate place of the series, and, as Manly and Rickert say, there are remains of a straight descender from the initial letter of the erased name, as well as the outline of a nearby ascender; Huws thinks there can hardly have been any other descenders in the erased area. *Plowman* would fit it better than any other available pilgrim.

the rest, including those in the first part of section III. If the second scribe had not already done so, it would be strange if the main scribe had not supplied them there, instead of commencing as he does in the middle of quire 14. It appears, therefore, that the second hand was engaged on the manuscript at least a little time before the first ceased to be.

Section IV (fol. 112–234) is the longest and, as may be seen from the table (pp. xxiv–xxv), the most disturbed and fragmented in content sequence. That the scribe was aware of its disjointed character is shown by his leaving blank pages or parts of pages at several points between tales and prologues. That there were delays in copying is suggested by changes of ink, and that there were changes of content in the course of copying is indicated by the structural abnormalities of quires 21 and 22. Even if the latter is disregarded, it is extremely unlikely that the scribe had a single exemplar in the same order for the whole length of the section, and it seems that he must have obtained a number of shorter ones, not fewer than six and perhaps considerably more, and not all at one time. He or his director could hardly have created the present effect if they had had all the material of the section simultaneously in its separate or linked pieces, to arrange for themselves without authoritative guidance or previous pattern, on principles of internal evidence or of superficial smoothness. It seems that, for at least the first two-thirds of the section (fol. 112–91) the scribe copied what he was given or told to copy, consecutively except where he, for whatever reason, left a gap for possible later insertions, that his director did his best with the minimum of alteration to the most glaring loose ends as he got them, but that neither had time or patience to wait for the several tales and links involved to be sorted out more satisfactorily when they were all in hand together; indeed, that they were for much of the time uncertain what pieces might come to hand and in what order, yet felt that they must be transcribed very nearly *tel quel,* piecemeal, and perhaps pell-mell. If so, it is likely that the exemplars were available only by installments for limited periods because they were in demand elsewhere or had to be got at in different places. It may be that such or other reasons or urgency pushed the scribe harder and more unthinkingly than his director or customer envisaged, who may not have been constantly with him during the operation and who had thereafter to accept the results, subject to minor modifications which might be practicable, as inevitable in the circumstances, a first and interim attempt. What is most revealing is that the well-established device of smaller sections, self-contained booklets, was not adopted for the separate fragments of the text, enabling them to be reshuffled freely, with additions later. This points to section IV having been started and pursued at a very early stage in the formation of a collection of the *Canterbury Tales,* when the advantages of flexibility were not as plain to the initiator or the copyist as they are to us now, or as they became perforce to them when sections III and II were probably, and even I and V possibly, written later. An alternative hypothesis, that section IV in particular, and also the rest of the manuscript, represents a surrender or indifference of the collectors to the difficulty of the problems of authentic arrangement, does not seem to us to square with the scruples shown by those responsible for Hg, against supplying spurious material to fill gaps (see p. xliii) and the very restricted amount of belated patching done by it on fol. 137v and 153 (see below, pp. xxx–xxxi).[14]

The quire signatures of section IV as interpreted by Manly and Rickert (1940:1.266–67, 274) imply that section I was complete and expected to precede it, without the interposition of section III (which is accidental) or II (which is unavoidable and is therefore presumably subsequent). The signatures, however, need not have been inscribed immediately before or after the writing of the respective quires but some time subsequently, after the augmentation of quire 22 if their reading is accepted (p. xxxi). It may not have been thought necessary to sign sections I and V, if they already existed, since their placing at the beginning and end was self-evident.

Section IV begins with a similar dark brown ink to that found in I and the first half of III, though it goes suddenly grayer near the end of the second stanza on fol. 123v (just possibly only one day's but more likely two days' work from

[14] This is further in response to questions raised by Blake.

112r) and so continues, gradually darkening, as if it were a result of stirring the pot after it had settled for a while, possibly only overnight. The *Man of Law's Tale* ends at the foot of fol. 128r, the first page of quire 18, and the verso is left not only without writing but also unruled. Since the scribe did not refuse elsewhere in this and other sections to start a new prologue or tale on the back of a leaf or even partway down a page—unless this was his very first encounter with the question—his behavior suggests he had some hope of getting later a link with the *Squire's Tale* that he proceeded to copy from the top of fol. 129r. As *MLT* is in seven-line stanzas, ruled for 39 writing-lines per page, whereas *SqT* is in decasyllabic couplets, at 40 per page, he may have been uncertain what ruling would be required for a link on fol. 128v. The *Epilogue* to *MLT* (B 1163–90) would have fitted into the space, but it may have been rejected (Manly and Rickert 1940:1.271–72) because it announced a tale by the Shipman (or, as in other copies, the Summoner) and could not easily be tailored to the Squire whose tale was the next to hand and may have been begun before *MLE* was seen, or while a decision by the director was pending. The *Squire's Prologue* (F 1–8) could have been used in addition, or by itself, but in other copies it is almost invariably attached to the *Merchant's End Link* (E 2419–40), so it was probably not yet available, like *MerT* itself which would properly and easily have preceded *SqT.*

When the scribe came to the enforced end of *SqT* at the top of fol. 137v, he appears at first to have left the remainder of the page (the second of quire 19) blank, either not knowing if there might be a continuation or else to accommodate a possible link, and went on to begin *MerT* at the top of fol. 138r, since it is in the same shade of ink whereas the remainder of fol. 137v is in the yellow shade and larger writing of the second part of section III (see p. xxviii). It would seem that the genuine *MerP* (E 1213–44), which would have fitted in the space, either was not available or was rejected because of unalterable inappropriateness to the preceding *SqT.* What was in fact subsequently inserted is the *Franklin's Head Link,* which rightly follows and refers to *SqT* but with the name of the next narrator, and the heading, changed to the Merchant. The delay in making this neat adaptation may have been owing again to the director, but if *FranPT* had been available earlier, there would have been no need since *MerPT* could have been postponed for a potentially better placing, after *ClPTE* indeed, to which it refers—unless urgency in transcribing whatever tale was at the moment to hand and ignorance of what might come were overriding factors.

The first two lines on fol. 144r, which is the first page of quire 20, are noticeably darker and larger in scale than the remainder, suggestive of a pause before the work proceeded. In quire 21, toward the end of *MerT,* with the second line from the foot of fol. 151r (E 2319), there is a probably more significant change of ink from the darkish brown to a grayer shade, which then persists up to the end of *FranT* on fol. 165r, with the exception of fol. 153. Dempster (1948a: 325–30) has discussed the coincidence of this change with the point at which the text breaks off in the three copies of tradition *c* and where there is a shift of affiliation and an irregular quire in the related Harley 7334. She argued that there must have been a physical break in the exemplar for Hg at that point, which corresponded with one in the independent derivation, and must therefore have originated very early and been duplicated in divided exemplars; and, while the other manuscripts could not obtain the continuation of the same exemplar they started with, Hg did get its own returned after an interval.

On the evidence of the uniformity of the grayish ink, the scribe must have obtained an exemplar of the *Franklin's Tale* about the same time and attempted to allow for the later insertion of a link before going on. He left the lower half of fol. 152v, after the end of *MerT,* blank, and appears to have recommenced writing at the top of fol. 154r (the next page of the original quaternion) with the thirteenth line of *FranPT* (F 721). Manly and Rickert argued (1940:1.271–72; 2.478) that the scribe must have reckoned that he would not be able to fit both a link and the first dozen lines into the blank space on fol. 152v but that, if no link materialized, he could then fill in the latter. When he was provided with a link some time later, about the same time as he inserted the adapted *Sq-FranL* as the *Merchant's Prologue* on fol. 137v, it was in fact *MerE* together with *SqP* adapted, again by a change of name and a few other words, to the

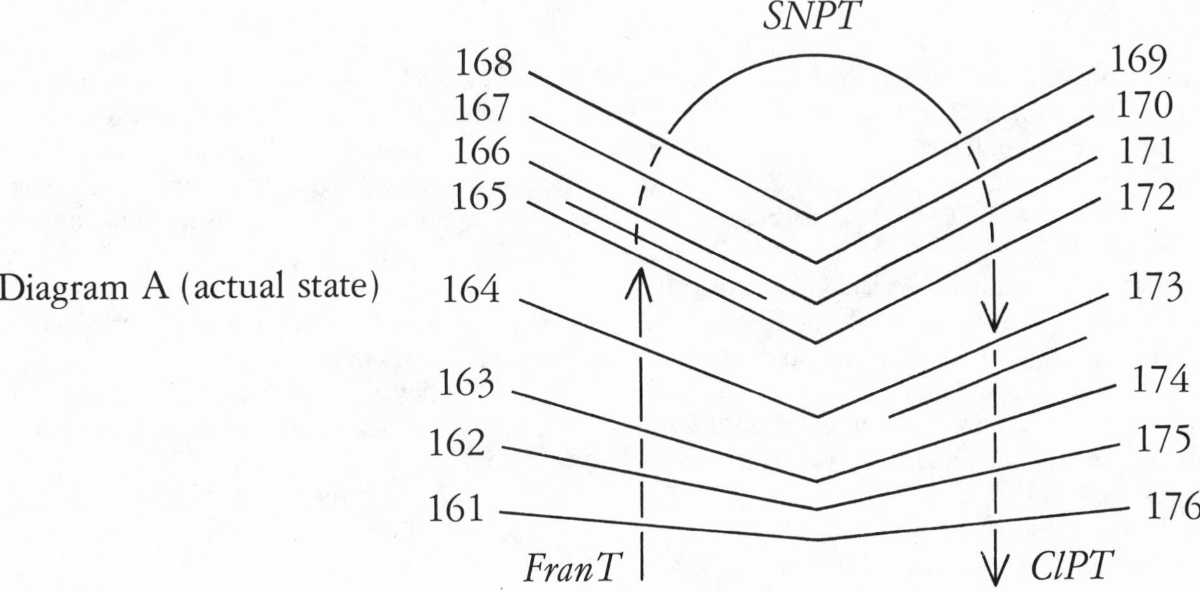

Franklin, which he copied, followed by the first dozen lines of *FranP* in the yellowish ink, on an extra single leaf ruled in gray lead and inserted (as fol. 153) at the appropriate place in the quire. Since the number of lines of verse was insufficient to fill the leaf, he disposed them on the two sides with unusually generous space after the headings and explicit and enlarged decorative ascenders. The only addition we can make to this hypothesis is the possibility that at first the exemplar of *FranPT* lacked the very opening lines (on a leaf removed with *Sq-FranL* in the course of adaptation for fol. 137v), and the scribe might not know how many. But in either case it is clear that he knew he had to make good at least one defect here, unlike the other points where he left gaps which might be merely guesses, filled eventually in one place (fol. 137v), not in another (fol. 128v).

Quire 22 is also abnormal, being double the normal length, and presumably reflects another and larger interpolation or rearrangement in the course of production of section IV, for which no or not enough allowance had been made in advance. Manly and Rickert suggested (1940: 1.274–75) that an original quire of eight containing the end of the *Franklin's Tale* followed by the *Clerk's Prologue* and *Tale* had the *Second Nun's Prologue* and *Tale* subsequently interposed, the central bifolium (including the junction of *FranT* and *ClP)* being replaced by five new bifolia bearing the last three pages of *FranT,* then the whole of *SNPT,* and finally the first page of *ClP* (diagram).

Manly and Rickert did not notice one objection to their reconstruction. As they themselves observed (1940:1.268), the grayer shade of ink runs, excepting fol. 153, from fol. 151r to the end of *FranT* on 165r. If the final pages had been recopied after an interval, as they suggest, one would expect to see the change of ink at an earlier point (between 163v and 164r) and perhaps another after the beginning of *ClP* (between 173v and 174r). In fact the distinct changes occur simply at the beginning and end of *SNPT* (fol. 165v–173r), which is all darker; *ClPT* reverts to a grayer shade, which continues to the end of the quire at least. It looks (diagram) as if, after commencing quire 22, very near finishing *FranT,* the scribe learned that he would have to place *SNPT,* the exemplar of which was not yet to hand, before *ClPT,* which he already had. Instead of ending *FranT* on the fifth leaf of a quaternion, leaving the remainder (7 pages) blank and starting *ClP* after a further 9 blank pages in the next quire, he decided to double the size of quire 22 by finishing *FranT* on the first page (fol. 165r) of a fifth bifolium, inserting three more bifolia and leaving 16 pages blank before going on to copy *ClPTE* from fol. 173v in similar ink. He must have known the right length if not necessarily the content of the missing piece. That it was added after the completion of section IV is suggested by the absence of the flourished underlining of the explicit which occurs everywhere else in IV (and V) but not in the other sections. The running title (by the second scribe) is accompanied by punctuation-like motifs which otherwise occur only with the *Parson's Tale* in section V in that form.[15]

A related fact of interest not noticed by Manly and Rickert is that the main scribe did not write the explicit to *FranT,* perhaps because of uncertainty about what was to follow or because he was distracted by his calculations; since the lower half of the page was left blank when *SNPT* came to be copied eventually, he may have been allowing for a link. The explicit is by a distinct contemporary hand writing an enlarged Bastard Anglicana resembling that of the main scribe, underlined and terminated with a pen flourish or knot different from his. It appears to be the same hand as most of the running titles, and probably of many of the sidenotes of the *Parson's Tale* (see p. xliii). This second scribe seems to have been working before the first finished with the manuscript (p. xxviii) and the blue paragraph mark prefixed to his explicit on fol. 165r is uniform in style and color with those throughout the text and ancillary matter.

One may wonder if there is any connection between the temporary hiatus after *FranT* and the erased name of the preceding narrator in the first line of the *Parson's Prologue* (fol. 235r), at the beginning of section V, surmised to be *Frankeleyn* by Manly and Rickert (1940:1.276–77). If the scribe had already written that name in section V, he might well have halted at the end of *FranT* for guidance, although in midquire as he was then he could not have made a neat junction without more ado.[16]

In other manuscripts *SNPT* is followed and linked to the *Canon's Yeoman's Tale* by the latter's *Prologue.* That they do not occur at this point in Hg may be another instance of the dislocation of exemplars of connected portions of the *CT,* but it could be due to the constriction of space between *FranT* and *ClPT* in quire 22 or deliberate choice (cf. Tatlock 1935:128n.77). We do not feel that editorial liberty is lightly to be invoked to explain the specific contents and shape of Hg, unlike some other copies of the *CT,* for, if that had been a major factor, we cannot see why a more coherent sequence was not maintained or contrived. There are signs of forethought on the part of the scribe in leaving space between tales where he had some information or suspicion that short links might have to be fitted in later, but only as he came to those points, and not all were filled (cf. Tatlock 1935: 135). The only verbal adaptations were extremely restrained and very conspicuously occasioned by the reversed order and delay in the supply of exemplars, the chief factor to which most of the peculiarities of section IV, and of other portions of the manuscript, may be attributed.

In contrast with the first two-thirds of section IV, the last third (fol. 191v–234v) is less fragmented in contents and without structural abnormalities. As, according to Manly and Rickert (1940:1.275–76), Hg is independent of all other manuscripts for the text of block C and the *Shipman's Tale* (but cf. Dempster 1946:394n.83, on the latter), the scribe may have got his exemplars from the same source and together with the other linked (and also genetically related) pieces of B^{2a}. It would appear, however, that the exemplar ended with the *Tale of Melibeus,* or B^{2b} had already been copied in the first part of section III, for it was decided to terminate section IV with a quire of ten, and the absence of a catchword may mean that the sequel was not known.

Section V (fol. 235–50), in a dark brown ink, has in its first line, as already mentioned, *Maunciple* as the name of the preceding narrator in the main scribe's hand and similar ink, over an erasure. The previous name may have been in the exemplar or else supplied by the director or scribe to suit a different arrangement of the tales from that finally thought right or best. Manly and Rickert (1940:1.276–77) came to the conclusion that only *Frankeleyn,* possibly with abbreviation of the *n*s, would fit the space and traces of the original writing. That abbreviation of the name is unparalleled in the manuscript; the *ra* is, however, abbreviated on fol. 6r, inner margin, but there was originally no such constraint on fol. 235r. Whatever the name first written there, it was probably altered after a decision by the director or scribe, when they got an exemplar of *ManP* (or advice) that its reference to Bobbeupanddown as near Canterbury justified its placing, with its tale, immediately before *ParsPT.* The copying of *ManPT* at the

[15] These variations suggest that the running titles may not have been added to the sections or parts thereof in precisely the same order as the latter were written.

[16] Only two later manuscripts actually place *FranT* next to last: Manly and Rickert 1940:2 chart II.

end of the second part of section III, whereby it could be thus placed, may have preceded that decision (if the absence of a catchword is significant) or followed it.

If section V was written before IV was half-finished, it could in fact have been the first or second to be done, even before I. The main scribe provided running titles of the Latin names of the deadly sins on both rectos and versos of the relevant portions of *ParsT,* evidently before the second hand wrote the name of the narrator on the rectos, since it is displaced to the right on those pages.[17] The desirability of the name of the narrator or tale had not become obvious to the first scribe at that stage, but it had by the second part of section III (see p. xxviii) after the other's intervention.

LAYOUT AND ARTICULATION OF THE TEXT

It is simplest to suppose that the main scribe himself gathered, pricked, ruled, and reruled the sheets according to a size agreed with his employer in relation to their initial knowledge of the matter to be copied and the modes of writing and decoration preferred. We do not know if the number of lines per page was that of the exemplars, or that they were uniform in that respect, since the choices were probably made before all were seen. His module varied from 5 to 6 mm. between the ruled lines, with a full page of 40 written below the top line of the frame for most of the verse and all the prose, or five stanzas per page with blank lines between, making 44 lines below the top for eight-line units and 39 for seven.

The treatment of the headings, subheadings, and explicits and their wording and indentations for major and minor painted capitals must have been present in the exemplars, introduced therein by the director of the copying, or devised by the scribe in the course of the work in accordance with general instructions. Although the pattern of wording of headings and explicits is repetitive enough to reflect precedents in the original manuscripts, the variations in the earlier copies are sufficiently substantial to mean that it was not found or respected as fully as the actual text and may be in part the invention of the particular director or copyist (Tatlock 1935: 111; Manly and Rickert 1940:3.528–29). The mention of the Wife of Bath is squeezed below the heading on fol. 58r as if it were an afterthought. It appears that the scribe forgot to drop the head of the text (despite remembering the space for a decorated initial) on fol. 197v and had to write the heading for the *Pardoner's Tale* subsequently in the top margin, his exemplar presumably having none at that point but only the one copied on fol. 195v, to which he had to add, by a caret mark and interlineation, "Prologe of the." Part subheadings in the upper margins of fol. 180r and 185r, however, seem to have been intended as an economy, not to displace a whole stanza from the page, and on 137v it may be so too, since previous subheadings in *SNT* and *SqT* occur within the text.

The manner of display of the headings, subheadings, and explicits, in enlarged Bastard Anglicana or Anglicana Formata, with exaggerated ascenders and penwork decoration, prefixed and terminated with a tremolo or knot, with the addition in section IV and V of a connecting underline chiefly for explicits (excepting *SNT),* sometimes increased to a complete cartouche (in *PrT* and *Mel),* is paralleled in some manuscripts of *Piers Plowman,* such as Trinity College, Cambridge, B.15.17 of the B text, close in date and spelling to Hg.[18] The same form of underline is used for all the visible catchwords except the last surviving in section V, on fol. 250v, which is a parallelogram (rhomboid). The inner sidenotes to *MkT* have the same underlining—that is, the first part of section III. It could be that the amount of underlining diminished as the work proceeded; it does not appear to have been added afterward.

ANCILLARY APPARATUS

The size and design of the pages were not really adequate for all the content they were to take,

[17] The second hand's title is displaced on fol. 245r, although there is no trace of any there by the main hand; did the second perhaps work forward from the back of section V? On 244r it is still not quite central, but on 243r it is. Having got into the habit of placing the titles to the right he could have been slow to realize it was no longer necessary.

[18] Cf. W. W. Greg, *Facsimiles of Twelve Early English Manuscripts in the Library of Trinity College, Cambridge* (Oxford, 1913), pl. VII, the treatment of the ascenders with Hg fol. 88r and the cartouche with 234v; Samuels, *English Studies,* Vol. 44, p. 88, for spelling.

for apparently the extent of the Latin marginal annotations to some tales was not anticipated at the outset of the enterprise, either because the exemplars for them had not been seen or else because they had not yet been fully annotated. The ruling provided for a narrow inner and a wider outer margin, the shorter sidenotes being placed in the one and the longer in the other, but the result is that the former are cramped on recto pages and the latter on versos (e.g., fol. 139v). With the prose tales occupying a wider column, the inner margin is avoided. In El both types of notes are placed in a column ruled for them in the much broader outer margin, which could well be one benefit of the experience of the scribe or his director in Hg (cf. Doyle and Parkes 1978:pl. 56).

The sidenotes in the left-hand margins, which are mostly names, were probably written before the adjacent lines of the text, which occasionally they displace—conspicuously on fol. 107r and less so on 98r, fourth stanza, second line. Although the scribe may have used the projection of the ruled writing lines as a rough guide for these notes, he did not follow it closely (e.g., fol. 6v). Most of the sidenotes in *ParsT,* which are analytical in function, were written by the second scribe, it seems.

The sidenotes in the right-hand margins are mostly longer citations and quotations from Latin sources and were probably copied in small batches shortly after the related text, since they are generally in the same ink and sometimes cramped or displaced (e.g., fol. 212v). Where the text on the same page has blue paragraph marks but accompanying notes do not, despite scribal indicators for such marks (e.g., fol. 174v longer note, 179r, 180v, 182v, 198r), that annotation must be subsequent, except for occasional oversights by the decorator. Others, in different shades of ink and unparagraphed, are certainly later (e.g., fol. 16v, 37v, 49r, 174v shorter note, 210r near foot). Some marginal notes, also not paragraphed, are by other early hands (e.g., fol. 139r, 144v, 145v, 237v).

There are a number of interlinear and a few marginal Latin glosses explaining single words or phrases, apparently inserted by the main scribe more or less at once, most but not all of which are found in El and not elsewhere, which is also true of some of the longer marginal quotations and citations (Manly and Rickert 1940:3.525–27). The incidence of the longer sidenotes in Hg is uneven: there are few in section I, none in II or V (by the main scribe); in III, *MkT* and *ManT* have some, but most occur in IV. If IV could be, as already argued, one of the earliest sections written, and as *MLT,* which opens it, has a substantial number of such notes, they cannot have sufficiently affected the page size, and perhaps, after the difficulties they occasioned, or for the sake of speed, they were not so fully copied in subsequent sections. There are, however, discrepancies between the annotation in Hg and El which suggest that a high proportion of it may have been added to their exemplars independently, since some occurs in Hg but not in El, where space and time do not seem to have been pressing. The fact that the longer notes are placed in Hg in a different column from most of the shorter notes may be not merely for convenience but also a recognition of their different purpose and perhaps origin.

Running titles were not envisaged in ruling, nor by the main scribe when he put subheadings in the top margins (fol. 137v, 180r, 185r); he did, however, provide them on each page for the deadly sins in *ParsT* (fol. 247v–50v) and added them for the rectos for *NPT* and *ManPT* following the example, in the earlier part of section III, of the second scribe, who supplied them for the rest of the volume except the *General Prologue.* The style of script adopted by the second scribe for these running titles and one explicit (fol. 165r) is sufficiently like the Bastard Anglicana of the first scribe and so conventional as easily to escape differentiation (cf. Manly and Rickert 1940:1.276). Where the first scribe had already occupied the center of the top margin, the second scribe's titles are pushed to the right. There are some additional running titles by sixteenth-century hands (see p. xlviii).

HANDWRITING: *A,* THE MAIN COPYIST

All the text and accompanying apparatus of *CT* in Hg (with the exception of some early supplies of a few original omissions, one explicit, most of the running titles, and a number of sidenotes) appear to have been written by one hand, in two grades or varieties of script utilized for different functions: (1) Anglicana Formata for the main body of English verse and prose and the longer Latin sidenotes; (2) a larger size of Anglicana Formata or else Bastard Anglicana for headings, colophons, Latin and French quotations within the text, and some shorter sidenotes (cf. Parkes 1969:xvii–xviii).

The styles of both varieties of Anglicana were developed in the middle of the fourteenth century, during the reign of Edward III (1327–77), from earlier models with a more rounded duct, and used for both documents and books. In the last quarter of the fourteenth century the introduction of the new Secretary script (Parkes 1969: xix–xx) began to influence the duct and letter forms of hands which were otherwise still traditionally Anglicana. The Hg main hand shows only a few of those forms, chiefly in the interlinear glosses and Latin sidenotes, such as the single-compartment Secretary *a* (e.g., 26v, 31r, 116r, 162r, 167r, 172r, 174r–v, 177v–78v, 199r, 206v, but occasionally also in the text, e.g., fol. 26r, 33r, 65v, 102v, 119v, 191v, 192v catchword) or the down curve of the tail of a final *m* (e.g., fol. 20v, 37v, 107r, sidenotes). The restriction of these features of the new script suggests that the scribe's repertoire had been only slightly affected by it or else that he, or his director, felt the traditional style more appropriate for the copying of vernacular texts.

The scribe's performance is expert, but not mechanical. The height, spread, and slant of his graphs and the straightness of his written lines (e.g., 51r–v, 113r) vary from section to section, tale to tale, passage to passage, and even within pages (where there is a tendency to increase in size, e.g., 5v, 6r, 53v), yet not to the detriment of a general uniformity. His work was probably rapid despite the complexities of the script and his duct, and the most conspicuous variations in Hengwrt may perhaps be due to the interrupted and possibly protracted circumstances of its copying.

Although well schooled in highly conventional models of writing, his hand is recognizably individual. Other manuscripts from the same period (though not many in English) have the same general characteristics and even similarities of detail, but they are not identical in that they do not manifest the specific assortment of forms and usages combined in the work of this scribe. The nearest we know is one leaf of a copy of *CT,* Cambridge University Library MS Kk. 1.3 (20) which, as Manly and Rickert (1940:1.303) say, is also close in spelling and punctuation. It differs more at first sight than after further inspection. It may be his work, but we hesitate to assert it, whereas we have no doubt about the Hatfield fragment of *Troilus* (see footnote 2). The general aspect of a hand is not easily definable in that, like a personal physiognomy, it is a unique ensemble of common elements which is only recognized after some (though not necessarily a long) extent of acquaintance, in comparison with others of the same genetic group. It is also affected by the circumstances in which it was written and the context in which it appears, which determine more or less favorable conditions of display. To satisfy oneself of the identities and differences, there is no substitute for going through lengthy stretches of the handwriting in question, analyzing and imitating its practices.[19] To persuade other observers to agree, one can only point out instances and invite them to perform the same exercise. There can be no absolute certainty that one scribe did not imitate another indistinguishably, and, in some circumstances, with simple conventions and strict discipline, it may be very difficult or impossible to isolate one's work from another's, but that was more common for other periods, places, and styles than for those with which we are concerned here. There are hands of clerks of the English Chancery at this time, on whom such regularity must have been imposed, which defy one to distinguish easily individuals, but no one has hitherto remarked on any very close resemblance to the Hengwrt hand except that of the Ellesmere Chaucer, to which we can now add the Trinity Cambridge Gower (Doyle and Parkes 1978:170–74) and the Hatfield fragment of *Troilus.*

The following variants and details may be pointed out: three forms of *A,* the most usual of two compartments, the top often leaning well to the left and the lower sometimes angular; the second form, preferred in some stretches and at page or line beginnings, is made as an elegant clockwise curve open at the bottom, crossed by an oblique straight stroke with two short cross-

[19] Cf. T. A. M. Bishop, *Scriptores Regis* (Oxford, 1961), pp. 7, 9.

bars (e.g., fol. 8r lines 1–3, 138r passim, 144v sidenote, 187r last line); the third form, rare in Hg, has a wide, open curve for its head and an open, angular lower compartment (e.g., fol. 6v lines 24–25, 27–29, 243r last line). The single-compartment Secretary *a,* as already noticed, is found so rarely in the English text that its presence there may be due to inadvertence, whereas it occurs frequently though sporadically in the Latin sidenotes (see p. xxxiv).

The small *b, h,* and *l* have versions with angular heels and heads, as well as more rounded ones, and closed loops, as well as (more frequently) open hooks, depending on the position within words and the comparative currency of writing in the passage.

D is normally an enlargement of the small looped letter, but occasionally the scribe used an older, broader form with an open head stroke, which is found also in the display script of headings (in the text, fol. 6v penultimate line, 63r line 5, 68r line 31 variant, 76v line 22, 90r line 17, 172r line 4, 204v line 1).

The round (reverse) form of *e* is used only in final positions and apparently according to the whim of the moment, although probably influenced by its greater ease of construction, especially following certain other letters (e.g., long *r*). Sometimes it is finished with a tongue, particularly in the headings (e.g., 56v and 190v–91r, where the text is graduating into the display script).

The duct of the *g* is very distinctive. It is apparently made most often of three strokes: the second, which closes the upper lobe on the left, commonly extends down to the right, projecting just beyond the point of contact with the lower lobe, and the anticlockwise stroke of the lower lobe does not always quite meet that point. (See fol. 3v line 29, 33r line 19, 71v line 4, 133r line 12, for clear examples of the gap.)

There is a varied and sometimes awkward handling of the tail of both *H* and *h,* to avoid cramping the line below, and sometimes it is carried round into a complete loop suggestive of haste (e.g., fol. 41r last line).

I, mostly with a long sloping head stroke, sometimes tied back to the stem, has one or two budding crossbars on the left of the stem (e.g., fol. 140v, lines 8–9, 10–11); it is often more upright than the slant of surrounding letters. The *i* has a curved tick only in a few instances, especially when in a group of minims, usually falling over the next letter of the word (most frequently *in*).

The minims of *m, n,* and *u* are quite well differentiated, sometimes linked, usually with distinct heads or feet.

The round (or *2*-shaped) *r* is used after *o* and sometimes after *p* (e.g., 99r passim, *preest,* perhaps influenced by the bastard heading on the same page). It generally but not always has an added lower hook. Short *r* almost never occurs except in bastard headings and marginalia. Long *r* is always joined to the following letter (or abbreviation) and stands out in final positions by the wide sweep of its upstroke and right arm.

Small *s* of the sigma shape is predominant at the beginnings of words, very rarely at the ends (179r sidenote, 225r line 15), but long *s* (invariable medially) alternates sometimes initially on no discernible rule (e.g., fol. 183r–84v). Final (8-shaped) *s* is a complex form: as with *g* the three or four strokes do not always join up completely or neatly (e.g., 77r lines 23–24, 118r line 29, 122r first and last stanzas).

T has a considerable range of variations of the same basic form: the head stroke is flat or arched, left free or looped closely or widely back into the bowl, or underneath; the straight vertical stroke is sometimes taken right through the bowl and sometimes not. For variation on a single page see fol. 4r.

There are two forms of *v,* in which the first stroke is made from opposite directions, used indifferently, it seems.

W and *w* are distinguished solely by size and placing; in the treatment of the base and upper strokes there is a good deal of elegant variation on the same basic form, depending on the space available above or on either side (see fol. 21v first two and last two lines).

Small *y* is generally dotted, to distinguish it from þ (thorn), though in this hand unnecessarily, and it sits somewhat awkwardly with the fork below the general level of other letters; the vertical right limb is not parallel to the general slant. The þ itself is employed only with following raised *t* for þ*at* and as an insertion in the last line of fol. 203v. *That* is preferred for line beginnings.

ȝ is used by the scribe for the function of

yogh only in *veʒe* (fol. 27r line 12) but is also found as a painted capital over his guide letter *y* on fol. 214v. The same scribal form is used for *z* in English and Latin.

The *and/et* sign is not very common in the English (e.g., fol. 91v line 16, 154r line 22), except in *Thopas, Melibeus,* and the *Parson's Tale,* which occupy a tight page width. It is comparatively frequent in a simpler form in the Latin sidenotes (e.g., 125r, 139r, 188v). Other abbreviations are surprisingly little used, except in the longer Latin marginalia, where they may be taken over from the exemplar but probably also encouraged by shortage of space, which did not usually affect the English verse since it came first and did not take up as much page width. The forms of abbreviation confirm the scribe's familiarity with Latin texts.[20]

Although the scribe employs a "set" style of writing with a large proportion of pen lifts, many pairs and groups of letters are joined, some habitually, others occasionally. The *st* ligature with two peaks is constant and conspicuous. Small *c* is always linked with the following letter; *de, do,* are often and *pp* always fused. The final tags on certain letters or groups of letters are mostly mere mannerisms, possibly fossilized abbreviations, imitated in the diplomatic transcript. (Cf. Parkes 1969:xxix.) Final *d, f, g, k, t* may have a down stroke, especially at line ends; *gh, sh, th,* and *ll* occasionally have a crossbar which could imply a final *e;* final *on* and *p* often have a curved stroke over them, the first of which may be expanded as *oun,* but the other not found extended (cf. Price 1955:139).

There is not room here to compare the writing in El and the same scribe's share of the Trinity Gower (cf. Petti 1977:pl. 3, p. 47). All the same forms and features can be found in El, and nearly all in the shorter stretch of Trinity, with varying preponderance of alternatives, and an increase in El of symptoms of more liberal space and time, such as otiose strokes and fuller punctuation.

PUNCTUATION[21]

In verse texts (apart from *Sir Thopas,* requiring separate description below) each rhyming line is written separately and begins with a *littera notabilior.* Since the principal purpose of punctuation of verse is to indicate metrical form, this layout was often sufficient (Parkes 1978: 130), but here the *caesura* is regularly marked by a *virgula suspensiva* (/), sometimes more than one to a line, as done by the same scribe (but not always in identical positions) in El. There is only very occasionally other pointing: e.g., on fol. 9v lines 2, 10, 13, 22, fol. 20v lines 1, 11, fol. 33r line 26; where the tag attached to certain letters serves also as a *virgula,* it is followed by a plain *punctus.* In contrast with El, the *punctus interrogativus* is rare: on fol. 49v line 22, 59v line 7, and in a somewhat different form on 75r line 32. Its shapes are not really distinguished from those of the *punctus elevatus,*[22] which is found with and without the lower point: e.g., on fol. 84v line 21 (after a virgule), 185r last line, 188v line 25 (with a point preceding the previous word), and 195v line 17.

The scribe provided a sign resembling *cc* in front of the first line of passages of varying length, both narrative and speech, in the decasyllabic couplets, and of certain stanzas, not all, though his discriminations among the latter have been disguised by the subsequent painting of blue ¶ marks on or by them and automatically at the beginning of all other stanzas. The scribe separated stanzas by a blank line, for which paragraph marks might be thought strictly an alternative, if they were not also applied as decoration. Colored capitals had the same dual function, and the scribe provided a few spaces for one-line versal initials at the beginning of fresh episodes, speeches, and so on, in each kind of verse, as well as the larger indentations and guide letters at more important divisions of the text (e.g., fol. 165r, 166v, 167r), for both of which he presumably had indications in his exemplars, since they are uneven in incidence and sometimes unexpected.

In *Thopas* the couplet rhymes of each stanza are linked by braces and with the tail line set midway between them to the right, the rhyming tail lines being similarly connected and with a final pen flourish. For the extended stanzas the

[20] Not merely in the Latin sidenotes: on fol. 60v line 22 he writes *Essex* with a tail carried above the last letter as its termination would be suspended in a legal document in Latin.

[21] Cf. Manly and Rickert 1940:1.278; Petti 1977:47.

[22] The curve of the one should be the reverse of the other. The Hatfield fragment has the same form twice as an interrogative.

"bob" is written after the second tail rhyme, preceded by a double virgule (as indicator for a painted paragraph mark) and followed by a *punctus elevatus,* besides being braced with the next tail rhyme (by contrast, in El the *punctus elevatus* follows the second tail rhyme, indicating more appropriately that the *sensus* is incomplete). There is a *punctus elevatus* (without lower point) appropriately after the second line of the defective stanza (B 1996) at the top of fol. 214v in Hg. Indentation and guide letters were provided for painted versals at the beginning of the second and third fits,[23] though the last, like some of the bob marks, escaped the decorator.

In the English prose the *virgula suspensiva* was used for minor medial pauses in the *sensus* and the *punctus elevatus* (with and without point) for major medial pauses. The *virgula* is sometimes followed by a *punctus* in lists (fol. 239v line 25, 245v lines 25–26) or the *elevatus* (245v line 12). The beginning of a new *sententia,* especially before a quotation, is indicated by a form of the *paragraphus* proper, here and in El like an inverted triangle, exactly as it is found in Peterhouse MS.75, the *Equatorie of the Planetis,* very arguably Chaucer's autograph (cf. Equatorie 1955:135–36; Petti 1977:45–46). This is in addition to the double virgules (and perhaps occasionally other points before *litterae notabiliores*) painted over with paragraph signs. The scribe also employs a single oblique hyphen and wavy line fillers.

The longer Latin sidenotes generally begin with a double virgule or tremolo, painted over with a paragraph sign, and a *littera notabilior,* and employ the plain *punctus, virgula,* and *punctus elevatus,* a single hyphen, and wavy line fillers.

The tremolo stroke with knot above at the end of many of the main scribe's headings, subheadings, explicits, and underlining of the last, most catchwords and some sidenotes, may incorporate an "end-of-section" mark *(positura),* as after the last complete stanza of *Sir Thopas,* but it is used interchangeably with the tremolo alone in the same positions and also in purely decorative ones, such as with the ascenders of the first text line on fol. 2r. The knot after the explicit on fol. 165r is the second scribe's version of the same formula.[24] The dot and wavy line after most of the running titles, rendered in the transcription as a *punctus interrogativus* or *elevatus,* may have been felt to have some of the latter's significance there, but when (as on fol. 113r and 116r or 145r or 155r etc.) it also is placed in front, or when *SNPT* has two or three dots and a descending flourish, it is clearly conventional framing.[25] Similar forms will be seen in front of the last lines of sidenotes on fol. 179v.

We must ask how far the significant punctuation was derived from the exemplars or is owing to the scribe's own system and judgment. Copyists of Middle English works (and perhaps their authors) tend to fall into one of two classes in respect of punctuation: those seemingly indifferent to it and those for whom it was meaningful; and though the latter did not necessarily repeat precisely what was in their originals, if any, they were more likely to grasp and carry out its principles. The Hg-El scribe was one of this class. The placing of his virgules in Hg and El is not always identical (as may be seen from the transcription), even in tales where their exemplars were closely related or identical. In Trinity College, Cambridge, R.3.2 he provides them, attached and unattached, in the same fashion, although most of the other copyists there, working probably from the same source, close to Gower, do not do so. It looks as if they were habitual to him, or else he was exceptionally meticulous, possibly both. For the more selective paragraph marks of each kind, the case for the author's or an editor's indications being followed in most instances is stronger, as for the painted initial spaces. It would have been much more difficult to improvise them neatly and convincingly in the course of writing, except for automatic stanza treatment, and it is there that the decorator's routine obscures most the deliberate choice of the scribe (e.g., fol. 96v, 97r, 113v, 114r, 166v, 167v, 174v, 177r). The *cc* signs could have been added retrospectively in the left-hand margin, of course, page by page, but we can see no positive evidence of that, and if they were

[23] Cf. J. A. Burrow, *"Sir Thopas,* an Agony in Three Fits," *Review of English Studies,* n.s., Vol. 22 (1971), pp. 54–58.

[24] Cf. the frame of Richard II's sign manual, 1389; P. Chaplais, *English Royal Documents 1199–1461* (Oxford, 1971), pl. 18a, and the first and last entries on pl. IV, H. Jenkinson, *The Later Court Hands in England* (Cambridge, 1927), 1437, 1440.

[25] Cf. Jenkinson, pl. II(i), c. 1400, and also the flourishes on ascenders there with headings in Hg.

mainly at the scribe's own judgment, one might expect fewer in some places and more in others. Moreover, he may not have expected the *cc* to attract painting as the // normally did.

DECORATION

The main scribe employs a number of penwork decorative conventions already well established in documents and books, especially in the enlarged script of headings, subheadings, explicits, and some sidenotes: exaggerated initials and ascenders with crossbars and flourishes, preceded or followed by knots or tremolo lines, often connected by underlining. The ascenders of the first line of every page, tale, prologue, or link are also somewhat enhanced, as had long been customary.

At the beginning of a prologue, tale, or link the scribe indents his text to the extent of half a dozen graphs or so and two, three, or four lines down, writing the first letter (still visible on 204r and 213v) minutely in the space to guide the flourisher, with the next letter as a small capital. The initials subsequently painted in these spaces are of blue with red serrated penwork flourishing of the style standardized in England with few variations from the latter part of the fourteenth century until the early sixteenth. There is no reason to doubt that they were provided here soon after the completion of the several sections of the text, including an explicit and a running title by the second hand, probably all by a single flourisher or team at one time. In some places the scribe indented a two-graph space at the beginning of certain lines or stanzas, with or without a guide letter, for a plain blue Lombardic capital, which was probably executed at the same time as the larger flourished initials and the blue (¶) paragraph marks throughout the manuscript. The latter were applied (except for occasional oversights) on or alongside the scribe's own *cc* paragraph signs as well as on the conventional indicator of a double virgule // in prose and in front of sidenotes, and automatically before headings, subheadings, explicits, and distinct stanzas.

The indented space for the very first initial on fol. 2r was conventionally larger, about sixteen graphs wide by six lines deep, and the number of text lines on the page was substantially reduced (to 32, instead of 40) in order to accommodate a dropped heading in enlarged Bastard Anglicana. From the placing it seems likely that the illuminated border, a full vinet extending from the initial, was expected to enclose the heading as well as the text, but in fact its top bar goes rather awkwardly between, leaving a disproportionately large space above.

It is probable that, as in other copies of *CT* of second-class quality (Manly and Rickert 1940: 563–64), no other full illumination, even of demivinets or champs for subsidiary divisions of the text, was planned. The one page, which has suffered badly from subsequent ill-treatment, is in the same later fourteenth-century style much more lavishly displayed in the Ellesmere manuscript, which Margaret Rickert thought attributable to a group of old-fashioned illuminators in London at the beginning of the fifteenth century (Manly and Rickert 1940:1.269, 566). In Hengwrt it is not better or more distinctive than in a number of middle-quality contemporaneous English manuscripts and, if it were not for the relationships of script and text with those of Ellesmere, the similarity would hardly have attracted attention. All other illuminated copies of the *Canterbury Tales,* however, according to Rickert (*ibid.* 565), are in more developed styles than that of El and Hg, and probably later in date. The illumination, like the flourishing, is of professional competence; it is likely that the one followed on the other, whether in the same workshop or not.

BINDING

Illumination was not advisable long before binding, to avoid the risks of rubbing or cracking while in loose gatherings (Pollard 1937:14). Some of the deterioration in Hengwrt, and the rubbing of some of the flourished initials, may be owing to its remaining unbound for a considerable time after the decoration. Manly and Rickert (1940:269–70) argued that the gnawing of the leaves by rats must have taken place while the volume was unbound, since the extant boards of the old binding are uneroded.[26] The unifor-

[26] Many Hengwrt manuscripts were gnawed by rats: cf. *Handlist of Manuscripts in the National Library of Wales,* 1–3 (Aberystwyth, 1940–59), pp. 1, ix–xi.

Original board bindings of the Hengwrt MS, front (left)

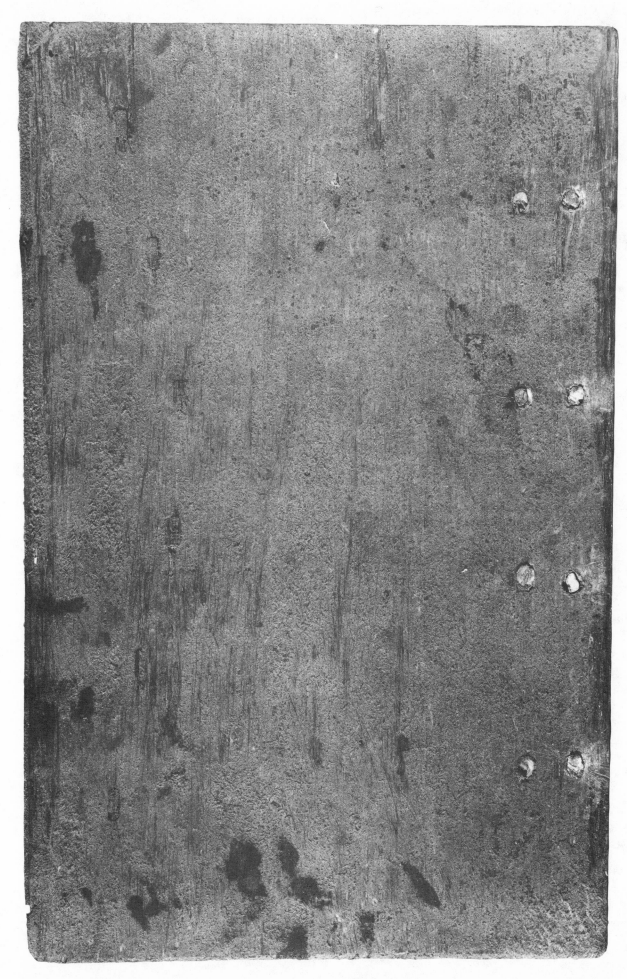

and back, slightly reduced. Original size 20.5 × 31.2 cm.

mity of the erosion, however, is such that the quires must have been firmly connected, at least within a limp membrane wrapper, when that happened. The old oak boards were taken off in 1930 and are now kept separately. They appear to have been made for a binding of the later Middle Ages, beveled as then customary, probably of the fourteenth century, with six trenches in each board for thongs, pieces of which survive.[27] The boards were turned before re-covering with the present dark tanned skin (thought to be the goat), decorated with a single large lozenge within a rectangular panel, both formed by quadruple blind fillets, when bound probably in the late sixteenth or early seventeenth century (see p. xlviii). It is therefore uncertain if they were the earlier Hg covers or came from another book. The sewing on four cords pre-1930 did not relate to the thong positions of the covers, and must have dated from that postmedieval rebinding, and only refixing of the covers by glue had taken place subsequently.

The misplacing of fol. 88–111 must have taken place before the erosion of the edges, and the erosion affected a number of later sixteenth-century additions (e.g., fol. 78r, 110v, 125r, 126r, 128v, 165r, 169v). The authorities of the National Library, after careful consideration in 1930, decided not to rectify the misbinding (rightly, in view of the confusion it could have caused with previous references), but the book was not in fact rebound in new covers (bearing an imitation of the old pattern on red morocco) until 1956. Unfortunately no record appears to have been kept then of what was found concerning the number of sewing holes or the ways in which certain leaves were secured before and after, the present state of which does not agree with Manly's and Rickert's observations (1940: 1.266–68). The blank fol. 87, which they thought a thinner singleton added, oddly, to an already anomalous quire of five, but in fact uniform in weight and ruled like the rest, must have been detached by accident from its counterpart, fol. 82, to which it is now secured on the outside by a modern strip, each leaf having been secured by stitching previously to its neighbor in the quire. Fol. 153, an indubitable singleton, now has a stub immediately following it (secured somehow by adhesive), not, as they saw it, after 159.

Folio 1 (in the operative modern numeration —that in the top right-hand corner, not that in the bottom left corner) now kept with the old boards, is a single leaf from an early-fourteenth-century Sarum breviary with musical notation.[28] A cursive textual correction of late fourteenth- or early fifteenth-century date (1r col. 2 line 11 from bottom) shows that it was still in use then. Reuse of leaves from discarded manuscripts, especially liturgical ones, for pastedowns, flyleaves, and strengthening pieces was quite common both before and after the advent of printing and the Reformation,[29] and this instance tells us nothing more about the origin of Hg, since the Sarum use prevailed in Wales as well as the Diocese of Coventry and Lichfield, which included Cheshire, where Hg seems to have been in the sixteenth and seventeenth centuries (p. xlvii). The waste leaf was attached to Hg before the erosion of the upper corners, it seems (although that edge is unusually smooth, perhaps prepared for repair), and shares stains with fol. 2r. It was not apparently a pastedown nor, even with its lost conjoint, substantial or worn enough to have been an outside wrapper for the whole volume, so it was presumably always a flyleaf. There are marks of later oversewing on the inner margins (see plates, pp. xliv–xlv).

OMISSIONS, ERRORS, AND CORRECTIONS

The manuscript is credited by Manly and Rickert with "great freedom from accidental errors" (1940:1.276), and the copyist was obviously careful in catching and neatly correcting his mistakes, usually (to judge from the ink) soon after they occurred, perhaps because he checked his own work page by page or leaf by leaf. Where couplets are skipped and not subsequently sup-

[27] Cf. G. Pollard, "Describing Medieval Bookbindings," in *Medieval Learning and Literature: Essays Presented to R. W. Hunt,* ed. J. J. G. Alexander and M. T. Gibson (Oxford, 1976), pp. 50–65, esp. p. 57, fig. 4; the boards from Hg had staggered thongs in a different pattern and short grooves at each end and on the fore edge, no doubt for clasps.

[28] Dr. J. A. Caldwell kindly confirms from the form of the notes our judgment of the date from the writing. The text is from the office of Matins for Holy Saturday: *Breviarium ad usum Sarum,* ed. F. Procter and C. Wordsworth (Cambridge, 1882), Vol. 1, pp. dccxcvi–ix.

[29] See N. R. Ker, *Pastedowns in Oxford Bindings* (Oxford Bibliographical Society Publications, n.s., 5, 1954), esp. p. vii.

plied, it may have been owing to haste (e.g., fol. 41v, A 3155–56, very noticeable in the writing of that and the following pages), or homoioteleuton (fol. 99r, B 3979 *Youre tale,* B 3981 *Youre Tales*), if it had not already happened in his exemplars. To indicate the place to insert a full line or more, he uses an embellished cross (40r, 64r) and *a* and *b* in the margin to reverse line order (45r). Most of his corrections are interlinear or marginal insertions of single words, with a caret sign (e.g., fol. 3v line 32, 7r line 13, 59v line 5, 64v line 37, 216r line 27). Substitutions are by rewriting on erasures (fol. 159v line 21 *dede were,* 235r line 2 *Maunciple*) and are often difficult to discern in photographic reproduction. A simple erasure in a completed line he covers with a dash (16v line 14, 83v line 28). There are rarely any visible indicators for the corrections in the margins: *forbedeth* in plummet on fol. 199v relates to a neat rewriting of the *d* of the word in the adjacent line, and there is a cross, saltirewise, on fol. 224v line 7, for a substitution. Other upright crosses in *Mel* and *ParsT,* some between lines and not obviously related to alterations, may relate to checking or even subsequent copying (fol. 230v line 10, 241v line 26, 242v line 8, 244v line 35, 246v line 33), like the word *huc* by an early hand (probably not the main scribe's) in the outer margin of fol. 231r. From the end of *WBP* (D 829 fol. 68r line 7) through *WBT* (to fol. 73r last line) three bold dots in the left-hand margin at 72-line intervals (with space for rubrics) look like marking-off for a copy, possibly of 36-line pages, but that is not the norm of the Hatton manuscript, which Manly and Rickert (1940:1.275, 2.210, 216) thought probably copied from Hg there. There are a few small amendments by other early hands (79v line 2 *ra* over erasure, 107v line 18 *Ye* in margin) but nothing systematic.

SUPPLEMENTARY HANDS: *B–F*

Other early hands did, however, supply deficiencies in the ancillary apparatus and lacunae within the text left by the main scribe *(A),* presumably because he had nothing in his exemplars and no instructions to fill them. The first of these supplementary hands, *(B),* may be that of someone who worked as a partner or supervisor to some extent, since its provision of running titles through the rest of the volume appears to be followed by the main hand *(A)* in the second part of section III; the explicit to *FranT* on fol. 165r is also by *B* (cf. running title on 164r and previous leaves) and has been given a painted paragraph mark uniform with those of the text, annotations, headings, and explicits by *A.*

We believe that most of the sidenotes to *ParsT* are also by *B.* They are in the same grayish ink as his running titles there (i.e., the narrator's name, not those of the deadly sins done by *A,* who also wrote the sidenote *Superbia* on fol. 245v, on the evidence of ink and decorative features—cf. the *S* of the sidenote on fol. 89v) and show various details in common with those elsewhere, although they are mostly in two smaller sizes and a rather different style. The second and third lines of the notes on fol. 245v are in a large Bastard Anglicana imitating the first by *A* and his subheading, particularly in the ascenders. Those on 240r (cf. *The* in running titles, especially the tongue of the *e*), 241r, 242r, the last two on 245v, all on 246r–47r (cf. the *S* and *g* in running titles on 13r, 19r, 84r, 205r, etc.), four on 247v, and three on 249v are all in a compatible small Bastard Anglicana but with Secretary forms of final *s* which recur in the somewhat smaller notes on 236v, 237v, one on 247v, 248v, and 249r–v (cf. *The* again). There are other shared details which make it difficult to separate them consistently. The open neck left in the formation of the two-compartment *a* ties them to each other and the running titles, despite the appearance of the unitary form in some of the notes as part of a more Secretary aspect (e.g., 249r). Their wording, like the titles, may have been improvised.[30]

The chronological relationship of the other supplementary hands to *A* and *B* and to each other is uncertain, but they can be listed according to the importance and authenticity of their contributions.

Hand *C* is a (necessarily) minute calligraphic Secretary which supplies the Adam stanza of *MkT* (*B* 3197–204) on the inner margin of fol.

[30] This annotator did not give any indications for paragraph marks, but one may wonder if he did not do this work after the blue marks had been added to the accompanying text. Most of the running titles *could* also be later than the decoration, although at least one, and one explicit, by hand *B* are earlier.

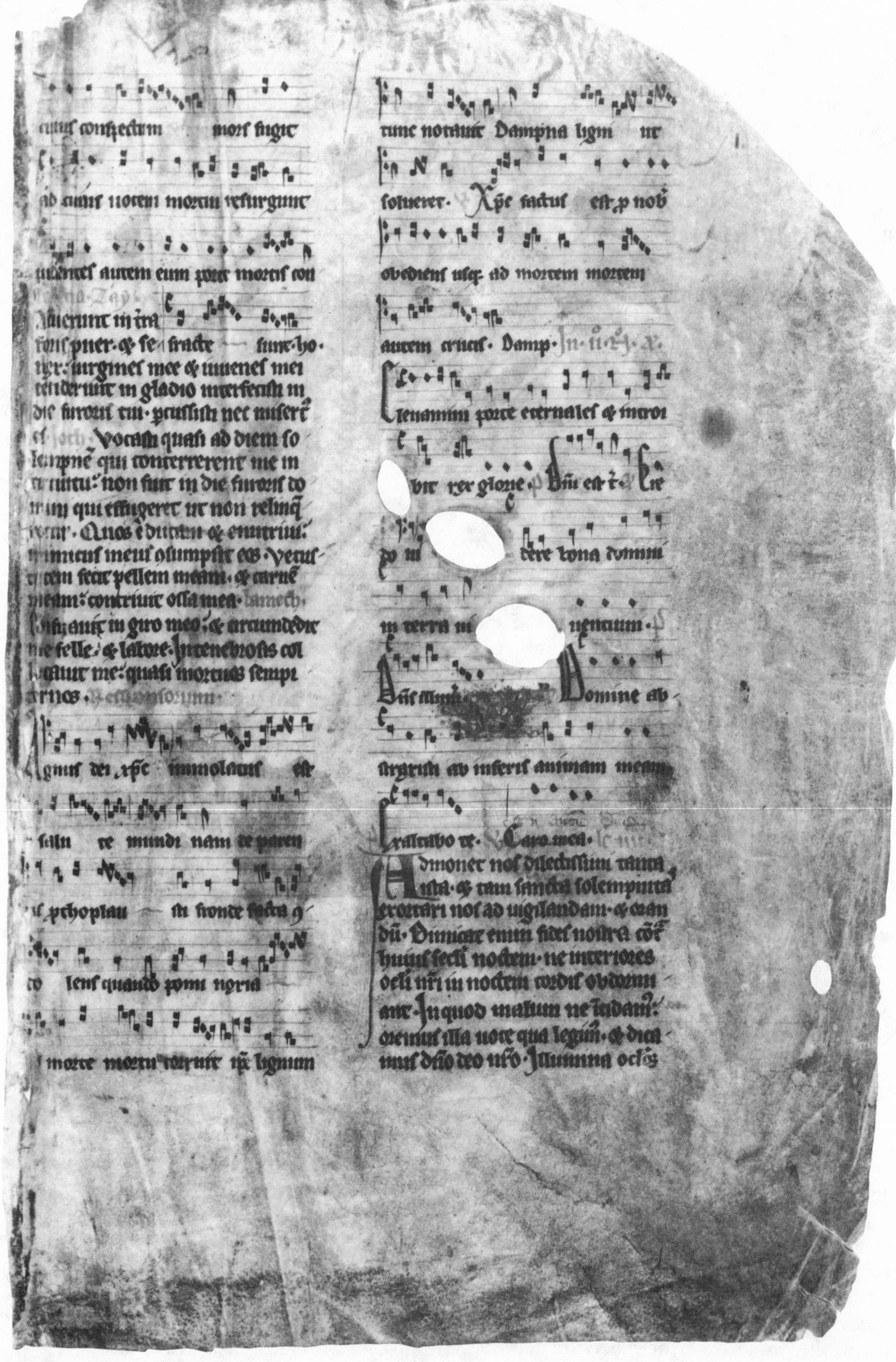

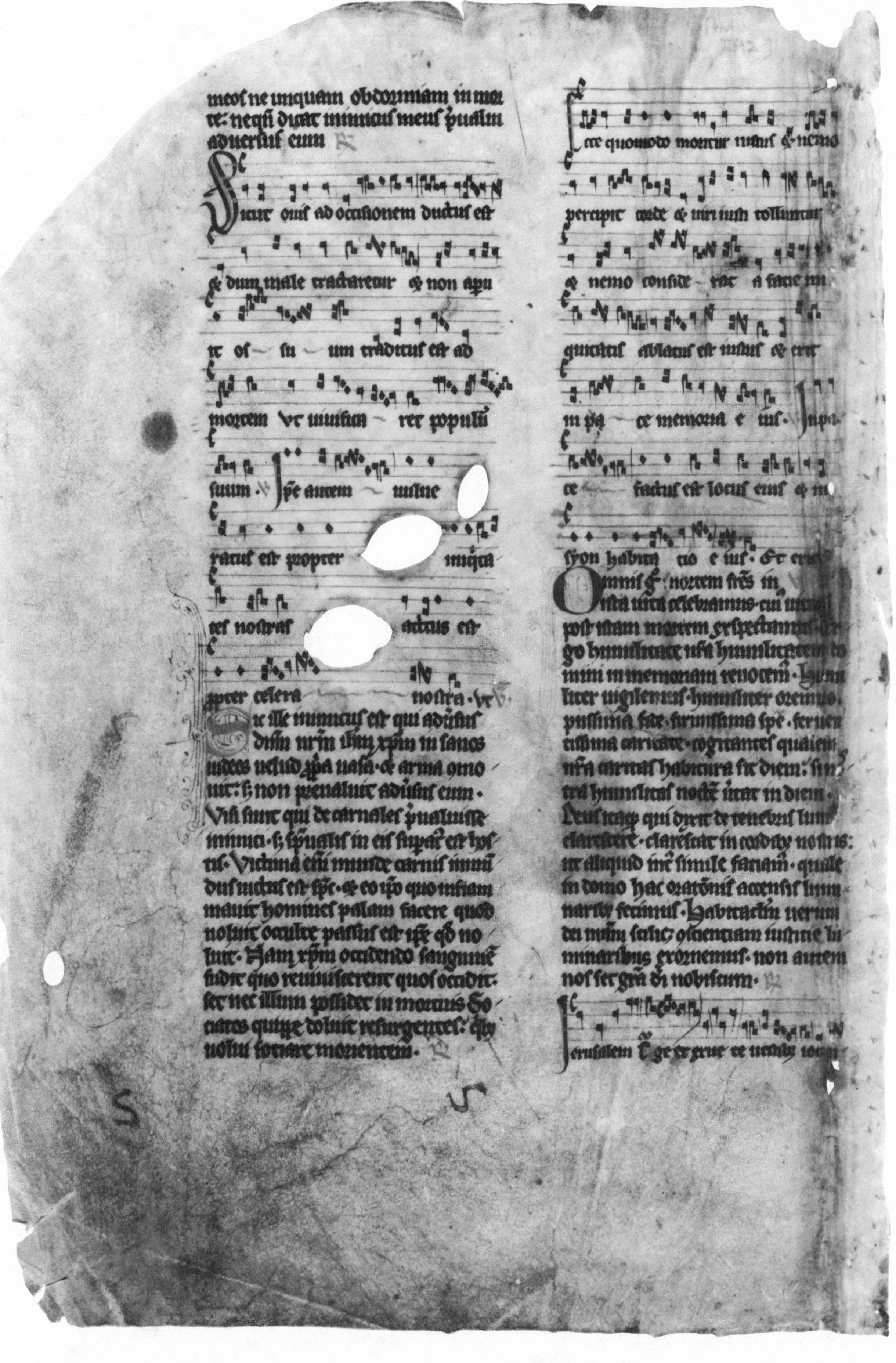

Leaf from Sarum Missal (folio 1).

89v, with pen lines to indicate its right placing, for which *A* had made no allowance. It is divided by *punctus* and *litterae notabiliores,* not line by line. It goes so far into the gutter that it can hardly have been added after the volume was bound, even in limp wrappers, in so neat a manner. The style of script is very like that of B.L. MS.Arundel 38, the presentation copy to Prince Henry of Thomas Hoccleve's *Regiment of Princes,* which must have been completed in 1412–13, and is the work of an equally practiced scribe.[31] The last five letters of line 38 on fol. 135v (in a word omitted by *A*?) look most like *C* (cf. *e* and *h*).

Hand *D* is a less fine yet neat Secretary of the same period (i.e., the first quarter of the fifteenth century approximately), in more difficult conditions. It supplies more than the second half of each of the last ten lines (D 1311–20) on fol. 74r, where either hand *A* failed to copy them because of obliteration in his exemplar or his own writing was obscured, possibly by a spillage of ink, which had to be erased (it is the first page of a quire, more exposed to accidents). No more writing by *A* can be seen under ultraviolet light, but the surface has been very badly damaged by erasure and dirt here, and there are some traces of other writing in the outer margin, perhaps in preparation for the present patching. Hand *D* found it hard to hold straight lines and an upright formal duct (with bastard minims) and after half a dozen relaxed to a more slanting current style (with simpler *w* and long *r*). Manly and Rickert (1940:1.277–78) refer the lacuna to damage in the exemplar, but that would not account for all the phenomena here. The text is authentic.

Hand *E* is a large slanting Secretary, probably of the second quarter of the fifteenth century, which supplies the words *at messe* needed to complete the rhyme, left blank by *A,* on fol. 80v line 4 (D 1788). The phrase is authentic.

Hand *F* is a large set Secretary, of the first or second quarter of the fifteenth century, which supplies the last five words of line 24 on fol. 83v (D 2048), the last three words of line 25, and the whole of line 26 on fol. 138v (E 1305–1306) and line 30 on fol. 150r (E 2230), all in blanks left by *A;* probably also the word *the* inserted above line 27 on 150r, and the *b* before and *a* below the last line of 83v directing a shift of the word *leet,* it seems. These contributions are all spurious.

There is still one conspicuous short gap of two consecutive half lines, for a French or Latin dictum (*Mel* 1777, B 2965), which no one was able or remembered to fill (supplied in modern pencil).

If fol. 74r had been left incomplete by *A,* one would expect such a large lacuna to have been filled as soon as possible, and not later than the smaller ones supplied by *E* and *F.* But if it was the result of damage to Hg, repair may have come later. Unlike hands *C, D,* and *E,* hand *F* was trying to deal with lacunae for which sufficient manuscript authority was not readily available (Manly and Rickert 1940:1.278–79; Brusendorff 1925:65–67, 98–99). He may have relied on his own invention, or his director's. *F* is very like Thomas Hoccleve's hand in his own poetical anthologies, Huntington Library HM 144 and 744 and Durham University Library (England), Cosin V.III.9, which can be dated respectively not before 1422 (both HM), not before 1419 and not after 1426, the year of his death. He had, however, been writing since at least 1388, as a Privy Seal clerk, and English poetry from at least 1402. Unfortunately some of his most characteristic letter forms are absent from the words in Hg (a *g* and a *w* in particular), but there are enough close similarities to leave the question open, alerted as we have been to the possibility by his presence in the Trinity Gower (as scribe *E* there) along with *A* (there *B*) and the copyist of Harley 7334 (*D* there) (Doyle and Parkes 1978:182–85).[32] Conjecture about the circumstances in which four skilled Secretary hands (*C–F* here) came to make the

[31] Cf. Doyle and Parkes 1978:pl. 57; British Museum, *Schools of Illumination* (London, 1922), Vol. 4, pl. 11.

[32] Cf. Doyle and Parkes pl. 53–54; Petti 1977:pl. 7; P. J. Croft, *Autograph Poetry in the English Language* (London, 1973), Vol. 1, pl. 3; H. C. Schulz, "Thomas Hoccleve, Scribe," *Speculum,* Vol. 12 (1937), pp. 71–81, pl. I, II. *H* and *h* are very like, on fol. 138v and 150r low in relation to the following letters, on 83v however level. The *y* with its tail carried up to produce a dot or curl above is on 138v and 150r. Both details occur in B.L. MS. Cotton Vespasian B.XXII, Admiralty ordinances, not before 1413, first portion, in a hand of the same school as Hoccleve's and other Privy Seal clerks: see British Museum, *Schools of Illumination,* Part 4, pl. 10; and *Illuminated Manuscripts in the British Museum,* described by G. F. Warner (London, 1900), Part 2 [pl. 12]; P. Chaplais, *English Royal Documents, 1199–1461* (Oxford, 1971), pl. 22(a) [Hoccleve], 1415.

additions to Hg, independently or in concert, would be out of place.

MARGINALIA BY OTHER FIFTEENTH-CENTURY HANDS: *H–O*

There are some additional annotations in several hands of early rather than late fifteenth-century appearance which may be those of scholarly users rather than supplementary copyists (classes which are of course not mutually exclusive):

G: an expert Anglicana Formata adds the Latin equivalent of lines 15–16 (E 1335–36) on fol. 139r.

H: a small Anglicana adds a Latin note on the words *arke diurne* at line 35 of fol. 144v (E 1795) and a shorter English one on *Venus* at line 35 of fol. 145v (E 1875), both badly faded and the first also eroded at the fore edge.

I: a small elaborate Bastard Anglicana gives in the bottom margin of fol. 219v the Latin distich translated in *Mel* (2298) above (Walther 1963:1810).

There are shorter notes and jottings which, from their content and manner, are probably by fifteenth-century readers:

J: *caue* in ink opposite line 7 or 8 on fol. 69r in *WBT* (D 898), early.

K: *Amen dicat* in faded ink opposite line 30 on fol. 81r in *SumT* (D 1854).

L: *Jesus,* irrelevantly, opposite line 27 on fol. 159v (E 1187), late.

M: *Melibeus* in red ink with an elongated red-stroked mark on fol. 222v (cf. the same form at the top of 22v), leading to his name in the text (B 2422), by an Anglicana Formata having resemblances to *B* (cf. running title on 222r etc.).

N: *Nota de pulcritudine mulierum malarum* against line 21 of fol. 238r, *ParsT* (I 154) by an early leftward-leaning Anglicana, which may also be that of *nota bene* on 239v, line 37 (the larger *nota* on 242v and 248r is probably by hand *A*).

O: *vomite* as a gloss to *spewyng,* fol. 237v line 25, by an early hand.

There is a sketch of a hand with pointing index finger at the third line from the bottom of fol. 237r, and on 244v line 6, probably medieval.

Other early inscriptions have no obvious relation to the text but may bear on the provenance of the volume. The word written by dry point on fol. 13v and read by Manly and Rickert (1940: 1.282) as the Welsh place name *builth* should in fact be seen the other way up as *smug* or *snug,* and there is another unintelligible dry-point inscription upside down on fol. 14r. On fol. 85v there is a large red plummet inscription read by Manly and Rickert and Huws as *Stokes* but perhaps *Stoker,* conceivably a user's or a maker's name. There are also various traces of erased inscriptions in the margins, notably one of two or three lines, perhaps in *textura,* at the foot of fol. 159r–v, which neither Huws nor we can make anything of.

SIXTEENTH- AND SEVENTEENTH-CENTURY ADDITIONS

There is not much doubt about the assignment of additions between the fifteenth and the sixteenth centuries, except on fol. 43v, where below line 32 the last three words are imitated by a hand apparently of the former (cf. hand *J* on fol. 69r) and higher up on the page a repetition of the last word of line 21 in a current hand of much more sixteenth-century character.

At the top of fol. 110v *Ryght wurshypeffull* (the opening formula of a letter) is written in a current hand of probably the first half of the sixteenth century, employing a long *r,* as do two English marginalia on 247v, which could be from the same hand and date, with the additions of the words *In* and *ye* to the beginnings of lines 26 and 28 on the same page. Neither note seems particularly relevant to the adjoining text: the first is defective and corrected, and the second sounds rather like a line of alliterative verse. On 248r *Jhesu send Jhūs* (?) *send* in the outer margin is of the same period.

Manly and Rickert (1940:1.279–82) picked out the partly erased and eroded inscription on fol. 87v *Fouke Dutton Huius ly(bri) est possesoer (sic)* as the earliest certain ownership evidence and identified him as a draper of Chester who died in 1558, which the writing would fit. The penwork knots and underline would not be inappropriate for someone who became mayor of the city. To the same milieu they ascribe the name *R Wryne* with a more professional-looking notary's knot *(paraff); Maria mater omnium virtutum* in the same set Secretary hand on fol. 125v, would suit the man who was recorder of Chester in the reign of Henry VIII. From the style of writing it is quite likely that the added running title on the inner margin of the previous page, 125r, is also by him, and perhaps that eroded from the outer corner there and on 126r; not so certainly those on 78r and 218v, which are of the same period and *H* on fol. 195r.

There are a number of additions by one neat Anglicana of the type still used by practitioners of the common law in the sixteenth and seventeenth centuries:[33] on fol. 44r *Gilbart Nelsoun;* 145v *Johannes Barcomsted generosus huius libri magister et verus et solus possessor teste G N;* 169v, a defective and possibly fictional writ of gaol delivery from Queen Elizabeth concerning Ralph Hot . . . gentleman of Chester; 171v *James pratri* (?), *William Dymmocke;* 187v *Henricus octavus Rex An(g)lie;* 234r *Radix omnium malorum est Cupiditas,* against the English equivalent in *Mel* (B 3029). Manly and Rickert were not able to make any firm identifications of these names, though offering ones in the Chester area.

Of the same period, and certainly well after 1534 when it was initiated by law, are the cancellations of the word *Pope* and the insertion of *bishop* or *byshop* on fol. 115r, 169v, 170r, 173r by a current hand somewhat resembling that on fol. 43v.

On fol. 165r are details of the births of five children named Banestar and Bannester: from the writing the first two, of 1571–73, were probably recorded together; the third, by the same painstaking italic hand, 1575; the fourth by a mixed hand, 1576; the last by the previous or a similar italic, 1578, sideways at the top of the page. Some details such as *having one tothe at his byrth* added to the first by the italic hand, agree with the evidence on fol. 128v, where the first five lines (eroded) of moral verses in that script are ascribed by a later hand or hands *per Ellenour Banester the graundmother of this under-named (Children* added), followed by five births of the Brereton family, 1605–12, the first at Newington, the second at Chester, and three at Llanvair (Caernarvon). Manly and Rickert traced the alliances by which Hg may have passed from Fulke Dutton (but not via Barcomsted?) to Eleanor Starkey, who married John Banester of Chester (d. 1581) and their daughter Martha, who married Andrew Brereton. On fol. 152v there is a memorandum of a debt of the last named as of Llanvair iscaire, 1625.

The added running title on fol. 16v could be by the hand of the fourth Banester birth note or another of similar date. The marginal notes on fol. 206r and 227v, by a single current hand, it seems, paraphrasing the adjacent texts *(ShT* and *Mel),* are probably from the period of Banester or Brereton ownership. That on 221v appears to be in Eleanor Banester's italic. *R s* in Roman capitals on fol. 79r is of uncertain date and significance, as is the drawing on 44r. The sketch of a queen's head on fol. 123r (outer margin), no doubt illustrating *MLT* (B 786), and of a man with a feathered cap on fol. 153v (inner margin), could be of the sixteenth century.

LATER PROVENANCE

Preserved with the remains of the old binding is a quarter sheet of paper bearing the numbers 152 and 72a in modern hands (indicating different points in the volume where it had lain loose?) and two Latin poems in an elegant scholarly current italic of late sixteenth- or early seventeenth-century appearance: one on Gellia throwing a snowball, the other on a Thracian boy killed by breaking ice, both neoclassical compositions of considerable accomplishment (the latter derived in part from Ovid *Tristia* 3.10. 38)[34] but having no relevance to the text of Hg and presumably placed in it merely as a bookmark by a reader, perhaps when, before or after Andrew Brereton's death in 1649, the manuscript entered the collection of Robert Vaughan of Hengwrt (Merioneth), d. 1667. It occurs as 154 of the Membrana in a catalogue of 1658, N. L. W. Wynnstay MS 10.

The Hengwrt library was bequeathed to W. W. E. Wynne, of Peniarth, in 1859. It was while it was in his possession that Hg was transcribed and fol. 204r reproduced for the Chaucer Society.[35] The manuscripts were purchased by Sir John Williams in 1904 and given to the National Library of Wales in 1909.[36]

[33] Cf. Jenkinson, *The Later Court Hands in England,* Vol. 2, alphabet 18.

[34] We owe this reference and other comments to G. B. Townend.

[35] *Six-Text Edition* (1868); *Autotype Specimens* (1877), Part 1.

[36] Manly and Rickert 1940:282–83; *Handlist of Manuscripts in the National Library of Wales,* pp. iii–xxiv.

REFERENCES

Brusendorff, A. A. 1925. The Chaucer Tradition. London and Copenhagen.

Dempster, Germaine 1946. Manly's Conception of the Early History of the Canterbury Tales. PMLA 61:379–415.

——— 1948*a*. On the Significance of Hengwrt's Change of Ink in the Merchant's Tale. MLN 63:325–30.

——— 1948*b*. A Chapter of the Manuscript History of the Canterbury Tales. PMLA 63:456–84.

——— 1949. The Fifteenth-Century Editors of the Canterbury Tales and the Problem of Tale Order. PMLA 64:1123–42.

Doyle, A. I., and M. B. Parkes 1978. The Production of Copies of the Canterbury Tales and the Confessio Amantis in the Early Fifteenth Century. In Medieval Scribes, Manuscripts and Libraries: Essays presented to N. R. Ker. Ed. M. B. Parkes and Andrew G.Watson. London: Scolar Press. 163–210.

Manly, J. M., and Edith Rickert 1939. The 'Hengwrt' Manuscript of Chaucer's Canterbury Tales. National Library of Wales Journal 1:59–75.

——— and ——— 1940. The Text of the Canterbury Tales. Chicago: University of Chicago Press. 1.266–83; 2.477–79.

Parkes, M. B. 1969. English Cursive Book Hands 1250–1500. Oxford: Clarendon Press.

——— 1978. Punctuation or Pause and Effect. In: Medieval Eloquence. Ed. J. J. Murphy. Berkeley: University of California Press.

Petti, A. G. 1977. English Literary Hands from Chaucer to Dryden. London: E. Arnold.

Pollard, Graham 1937. The Company of Stationers Before 1557. Library. 4th ser., 18: 1–38.

Price, Derek J., ed. 1955. The Equatorie of the Planetis, Edited from Peterhouse MS. 75.1. Linguistic analysis by R. M. Wilson. Cambridge: Cambridge University Press.

Tatlock, J. S. P. 1935. The Canterbury Tales in 1400. PMLA 50:100–39.

Walther, Hans 1963. Carmina Medii Aevi Posterioris Latina: II/1, Proverbia sententiaeque . . . Teil 1. Gottingen: Vandenhoeck and Ruprecht.

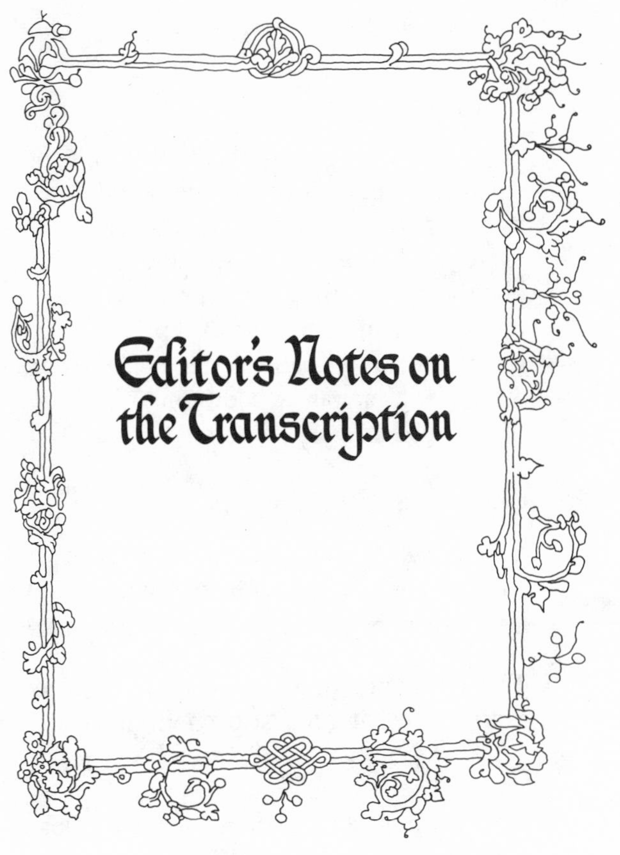

Editor's Notes on the Transcription

Paul G. Ruggiers

1. *Presentation of the Text:* The following clarifications should facilitate the use of this volume:

   a. The transcription matches the text of the manuscript page line for line, in both the verse and the prose tales. It is accompanied by a matching column of comparisons with Ellesmere readings, except for the prose tales, where we have been forced to place the Ellesmere readings after the tales.

   b. All page headings have been retained, as have catchwords and quire signatures. Page headings are given in slightly larger typeface than that of the body of the text.

   c. All marginal glosses longer than three words are printed at the bottom of the page, on the left side, with manuscript identification. Paragraph signs have been omitted, and all abbreviations have been expanded silently. Shorter glosses are retained where they occur in the transcription.

   d. All *Outs,* footnotes, and Ellesmere foliation numbers are given at the bottom of the page, on the right side.

   Each transcription page thus presents four blocks of materials: on the left side, 1) the transcription; 2) the longer marginal glosses. And on the right side, 3) the Ellesmere variant column; and 4) all footnotes, *Outs,* and Ellesmere foliation.

   e. The foliation of the Hengwrt manuscript is given in the top left-hand side of the transcription page.

   f. A continuous numbering system for the entire volume is carried in the outside bottom corner of each transcription page.

   g. Latin within the text is given in boldface and in slightly larger type in the rubrics.

   h. Owing to the length of line in the prose tales, the Ellesmere comparisons have had to be placed at the end of the volume. Further it should be noted that the prose tales have been given a double numbering system: the traditional numbering and a simpler marginal numbering by 5's for easy correlation of text and glosses. Both numbers are given with the glosses at the bottom of the transcription page.

   i. All illuminated and large letters occurring in the Hengwrt manuscript have been approximated in our type faces. Such letters in the Ellesmere column are given in boldface.

2. *Symbols:* We employ the following symbols:

   a. []: Square brackets are used to indicate damaged places in the manuscript.

   b. ⟨⟩: Diamond brackets are used to indicate additions to the manuscript by any scribe. These are usually insertions by a later hand into a line to restore an omitted word.

   c. ( ): Parentheses are used to indicate all modern editorial comment.

d. [ ]: Modified brackets are used to indicate marginalia of fewer than three words occuring on the right margin of a leaf. These are always recorded last in the variant line.

A knyght [Knyght]

e.]: A single modified bracket pointing left is used to indicate that the marginal gloss occurs on the left margin of the leaf. It is always printed first in any series.

f. |: A straight bar is used to indicate that an Ellesmere line of verse closes with a different word from that in the corresponding line in Hengwrt.

RvT 4322: in magestee in Trinitee |

3. *Punctuation:* We have observed the following:

a. /: Virgule, occasionally with a *punctus* after it.

b. ⁊: Attached virgule, usually with *d, f, g, k, t,* and occasionally even with *c* and *r.* When the *d* is flourished, the virgule is often attached to the flourish.

c. //: Double virgules.

d. ·: *Punctus,* usually on either side of numbers and occasional capital letters. Sometimes it sits on the line; other times it is raised off the line.

e. ⸮: *Punctus elevatus.* We have attempted to imitate the form in designed type face. Sometimes the elevatus appears without the *punctus.* It is virtually impossible, in the hands of the Hengwrt and Ellesmere scribes, to distinguish an *interrogativus,* even when one is intended, from the *elevatus.*

f. ⁊: A wedge most often found in our two manuscripts in the prose tales, used to divide quoted matter from the rest of the sentence; generally interchangeable with the *paragraphus.*

g. ¶: The paragraph sign is always given in the form shown here, though in the manuscript, sometimes only the signal for a painted letter appears. They may be seen together at *KnT* 905, 915, 931.

4. *Capitalization:*

a. All capitals have been recorded as they occur in the manuscripts. It should be noted, however, that, for the letters *a, d, h, l, s, v, w, y,* when a clear majuscule is not explicitly given, the tests used have been mainly size of letter and comparison with instances in which the letter is clearly intended as a capital. In addition, *ff* is always transcribed as a capital letter.

5. *Abbreviations and Brevigraphs:*

a. In general, all abbreviations have been expanded, the expansions being given in italics, except for *.i. (id est)* and *.s. (scilicet).*

b. The Tironian sign for *et* has been expanded as *and* when it occurs in an English line.

c. *Xpofere* has been expanded as *Cristofere.*

d. The various abbreviations for the Deity have been expanded as follows:

Ihs: Ie*sus*
Ihc: Ie*sus*
Ihus: Ie*s*us
Ihu: Ie*s*u

e. Expansion of the brevigraphs has been made as routinely as possible in keeping with the practices of Latin manuscripts. The practices of vernacular manuscripts in English in the fifteenth century are somewhat less stable. The scribe(s) of the Hengwrt and Ellesmere manuscripts maintains a high degree of consistency.

It has not always been possible to observe a rule of total consistency. For example, the scribe occasionally places a brevigraph signal on the last syllable of a line but omits it in the rhyming word of the succeeding line. Or he may indicate the possibility of expansion of a word for which no reasonable expansion can be made. In such cases we have allowed the word to stand with the brevigraph sign.

f. The barred double *l* (ɫɫ) has been allowed to stand without expansion. For these manuscripts the argument for expansion would depend largely on metrics; and it is possible to argue both for and against expansion.

g. We have expanded p̄ to p*e*, though the decision to do so, as with ħ, is somewhat arbitrary.

h. The sign used to indicate a terminal *s* sound *(ꝭ)* has been expanded to make the word bearing the sign into a plural or possessive form.

6. *Recording the Ellesmere Variants:* The following notes will help to clarify the system used to record all of the differences between the Hengwrt and Ellesmere manuscripts. In the examples that follow, the lemma in the left column is drawn from Hengwrt, the lemma in the right column from Ellesmere.

a. All differences in punctuation are recorded:

GP 20:	Southwerk⁊ Tabardꝉ /	Southwerk / Tabardꝉ

b. All differences in spelling are recorded:

GP 26:	felaweshipe / pilgrymes weere	felaweship*e* pilg*ri*mes were

c. All uses of the barred *h* (ħ) and flourished *d* (dꝉ) are observed:

GP 23:	nyght⁊ was	nygħt / were
GP 408:	Gootlond /	Gootlandꝉ /

d. Presence or absence of the paragraph sign is noted:

GP 425:	¶Ful	Ful
GP 784:	Hoold	¶Hoold

e. All differences in the use of brevigraphs are noted:

GP 72:	p*ar*fit	parfit
GP 183:	opynyon	opiniou*n*
GP 191:	prikyng /	p*ri*kyng

f. All omissions in one manuscript are indicated by the use of the word on either side of the omitted word in the other manuscript:

GP 205:	as is a	as a

g. All inversions are recorded without giving bracketing words on either side:

GP 375:	they weere	were they

h. All substitutions within the line are bracketed by the word on either side of it:

GP 70:	vileynye he sayde	vileynye ne sayde
GP 252:	beggere / of his	begger*e* in his

Where necessary, a whole line, or almost all of a line, has been given in the variant column to prevent misunderstanding:

GP 82:	Of .xx. yeer / he was of age I gesse	twenty yeer of Age / he was I
GP 95:	He koude songes wel make / and endite	songes make / and wel endite
GP 110:	Of wodecraft / koude he wel al the vsage	wodecraft / wel koude he al

i. All additions are bracketed by the word on either side of it:

GP 258:	louedayes / koude	louedayes / ther koude

The Canterbury Tales

Here bygynneth the Book of the tales of Cant*er*bury [1]

When that Aueryłł w*ith* his shoures soote	WHan Apriłł with hise
The droghte of March / hath p*er*ced to the roote	perced
And bathed euery veyne in swich lycour	veyne / licour
Of which v*er*tu engendred is the flour	v*er*tu /
Whan zephirus eek / w*ith* his sweete breeth	Zephirus breeth
Inspired hath in euery holt and heeth	hath / heeth
The tendre croppes / and the yonge sonne	
Hath in the Ram / his half cours yronne	
And sm[a]le foweles / maken melodye	smale
That sl[epen] al the nyght with open Iye	slepen nyght / eye
So priketh hem nature / in hir corages	nature
Than[ne longen] folk to goon on pilgrymages	Thanne longen folk / pilg*ri*mages
And Palmere[s] for to seeken straunge strondes	Palm*er*es / seken
To ferne halwes / kouthe in sondry londes	kowthe
And specially / from euery shyres ende	fram shires
Of Engelond / to Caunterbury they wende	
The holy blisful martir / for to seke	hooly martir
That hem hath holpen whan *þat* they weere seeke	holpen / were
Bifel *þat* in that sesou*n* on a day	Bifil that / seson
In Southwerk at the Tabard / as .I. lay	Southwerk / Tabard I
Redy to weenden / on my pilgrymage	Redy / wenden
To [Ca]unterbury / with ful deuout corage	Caunt*er*bury /
At nyght was come / in to that hostelrye	nyght / were
Wel .xxix. in a compaignye	nyne and twenty
Of sondry folk / by auenture yfalle	
In felaweshipe / and pilgrymes weere they alle	felaweship*e* / pilg*ri*mes were
That toward Caunterbury wolden ryde	Caunt*er*bury
The chambres and the stables / weeren wyde	stables weren
And wel we weeren esed / at the beste	weren esed atte
And shortly whan the sonne was to reste	shortly / Sonne
So hadde I spoken with hem euerichoon	spoken / w*ith* euerichon
That I was of hir felaweshipe ano n	was / felaweship*e* anon

8 .i. sol in Ariete El

[1] *1r* Rubric *Out* El.

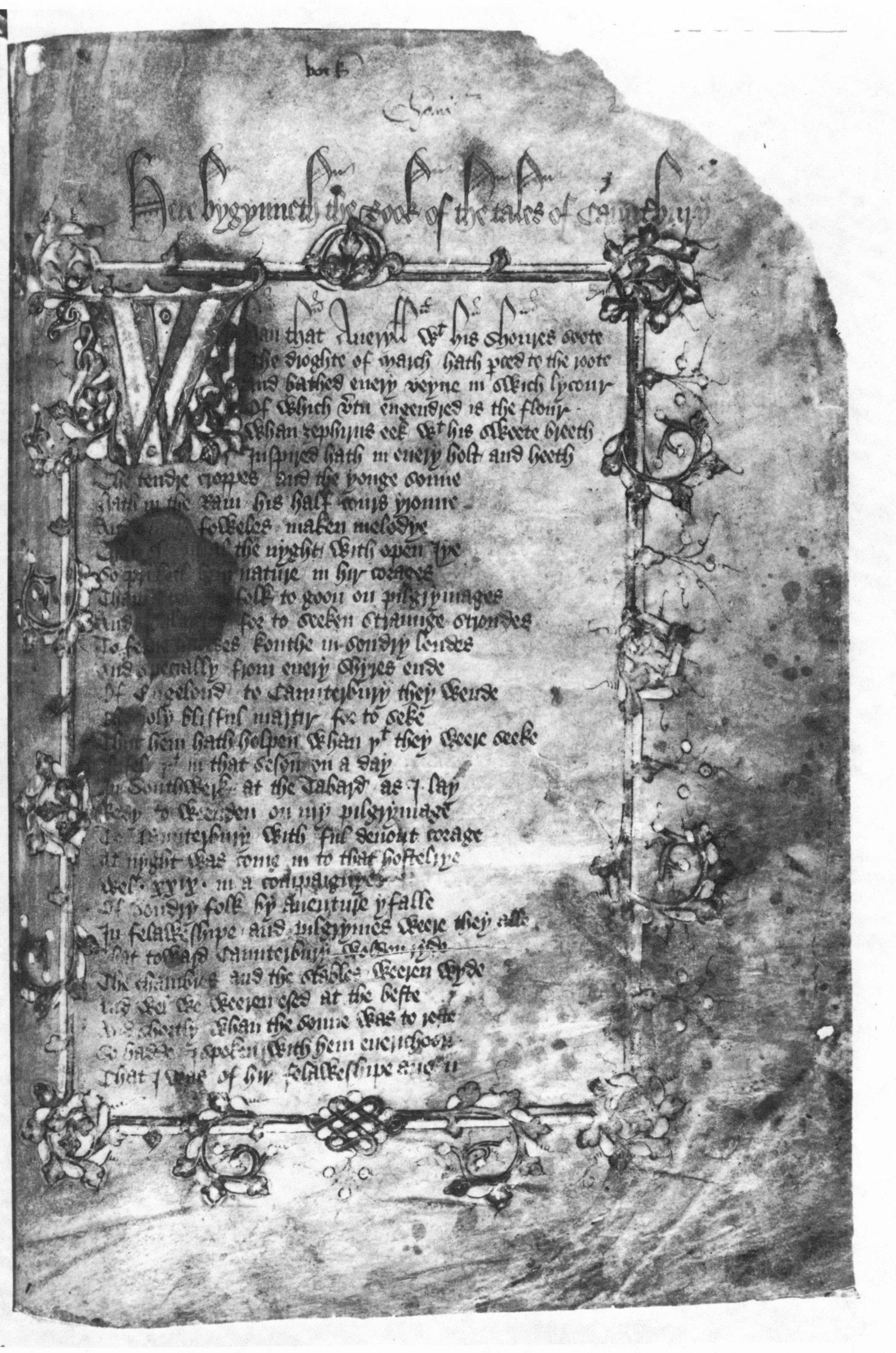

Here bygynneth the book of the tales of Caunterbury

Whan that Aueryll wt his shoures soote
The droghte of March hath perced to the roote
And bathed euery veyne in swich lycour
Of which vertu engendred is the flour
Whan zephirus eek wt his swete breeth
Inspired hath in euery holt and heeth
The tendre croppes and the yonge sonne
Hath in the Ram his half cours yronne
And [illegible] foweles maken melodye
[illegible] the nyght with open Iye
So priketh [illegible] nature in hir corages
Thanne [illegible] folk to goon on pilgrymages
And [illegible] for to seken straunge strondes
To ferne halwes kouthe in sondry londes
And specially from euery shires ende
Of Engelond to Caunterbury they wende
The holy blisful martir for to seke
That hem hath holpen whan yt they were seeke
[illegible] yt in that seson on a day
In Southwerk at the Tabard as I lay
Redy to wenden on my pilgrymage
To Caunterbury with ful deuout corage
At nyght was come in to that hostelrye
Wel .xxix. in a compaignye
Of sondry folk by auenture yfalle
In felaweshipe and pilgrymes were they alle
That toward Caunterbury wolden ryde
The chambres and the stables weren wyde
And wel we weren esed at the beste
And shortly whan the sonne was to reste
So hadde I spoken with hem euerichoon
That I was of hir felaweshipe anon

And made forward erly for to ryse
To take oure wey ther as I yow deuyse
But nathelees / whil I haue tyme and space
Er that I ferther / in this tale pace
Me thynketh it / acordant to resoun
To telle yow / al the condicioun
Of ech of hem / so as it semed me
And whiche they weere / and of what degree
And eek in what array þt they weere inne
And at a knyght / thanne wol I first bigynne
Knyght / A knyght ther was / and that a worthy man
That fro the tyme / þt he first bigan
To ryden out / he loued chiualrye
Trouthe and honour / fredom and curteisye
Ful worthy was he / in his lordes werre
And ther to hadde he riden / no man ferre
As wel in cristendom / as hethenesse
And euere honured / for his worthynesse
At Alisaundre he was / whan it was wonne
Ful ofte tyme / he hadde the bord bigonne
Abouen alle nacions / in Pruce
In lettow hadde he reysed and in Ruce
No cristen man so ofte / of his degree
In Gernade at the seege eek hadde he be
At Algezir / and ryden in Belmarye
At lyeys was he / and at Satalye
Whan they were wonne / and in the grete see
At many a noble armee / hadde he be
At mortal batailles / hadde he been fiftene
And foghten for oure feyth / at Tramyssene
In lystes thryes and ay slayn his foo
This ilke worthy knyght / hadde been also
Somtyme / with the lord of Palatye
Agayn another ~~hethen in Turkye~~
And eueremoore / he hadde a souereyn prys
And though þt he were worthy / he was wys
And of his poort / as meke as is a mayde
He neuere yet / no vileynye he sayde
In al his lyf / vn to no maner wight
He was a verray parfit / gentil knyght /

And maade forward / erly for to ryse	made
To take oure wey / ther as .I. yow deuyse	I
¶But nathelees / while .I. haue tyme and space	But whil I *and*
Er that I ferther / in this tale pace	that
Me thynketh it acordant to resou*n*	thynketh / it acordaunt
To telle yow / al the condiciou*n*	
Of eech of hem / so as it seemed me	ech semed
And whiche they weere / and of what degree	were /
And eek in what array / þat they weere Inne	that were
And at a knyght thanne wol I first bigynne	knyght than
Knyght ¶A knyght ther was / and that a worthy man	A knyght ⌈¶Knyght⌉
That fro the tyme / þat he first bigan	tyme / that
To ryden out he loued chiualrye	riden out / chiualrie
Trouthe and hono*ur* / fredom and curteisye	honour / curteisie
Ful worthy was he / in his lordes werre	
And ther to hadde he ryden / no man ferre	to / riden /
As wel in cristendom / as hethenesse	2 as in Hethenesse
And euere honured / for his worthynesse	euere / honoured
¶At Alisaundre he was / whan it was wonne	
Ful ofte tyme / he hadde the bord bigonne	
Abouen alle nacions / in Pruce	nacions
In lectow / hadde he reysed / and in Ruce	Lettow / reysed
No cristen man so ofte / of his degree	ofte
In Gernade at the seege eek hadde he be	Gernade /
At Algizir / and ryden in Belmarye	Of Algezir /. riden
At lyeys was he / and at Satalye	Lyeys
Whan they weere wonne / and in the grete See	were *and*
At many a noble armee / hadde he bee	Armee / be
¶At mortal batailles / hadde he been fiftene	At
And foghten for oure feyth / at Tramyssene	foughten feith
In lystes thryes / and ay slayn his foo	Lystes thries /
¶This ilke worthy knyght hadde been also	This knight
Som tyme / with the lord of Palatye	
Agayn another hethen in Turkye	Agayn /
And euere moore / he hadde a souereyn prys	eueremoore /
And thogh þat he weere worthy / he was wys	though were worthy
And of his poort. as meke / as is a mayde	port meeke
Ne neuere yet no vileynye he sayde	He neuere yet / vileynye ne sayde
In al his lyf vn to no manere wight	lyf / maner wight
He was a verray p*ar*fit gentil knyght	parfit knyght

21v

But for to tellen yow / of his array
Hise hors weere goode / but he ne was nat gay
Of Fustian / he wered a gypou*n*
Al bismotered / with his haubergeou*n*
For he was laate / comen from his viage
And wente / for to doon his pilgrymage
Squyer ¶With hym / ther was his sone a yong' Squyer
A louere / and a lusty Bachiler
With lokkes crulle / as they weere leyd in p*re*sse
Of .xx. yeer / he was of age I gesse
Of his stature / he was of euene lengthe
And wonderly delyuere / and of greet strengthe
And he hadde been som tyme / in chiu[ac]hye
In Flaundres / in Artoys / and Picardye
And born hym wel / as in so litel space
In hope / to stonden / in his lady grace
¶Embrouded was he / as it weere a meede
Al ful of fresshe floures / white and reede
Syngynge he was / or floytynge al the day
He was as fressħ / as is the Monthe of May
Short was his gowne / with sleues / longe *and* wyde
Wel koude he sitte on hors / and faire ryde
He koude songes wel make / and endite
Iuste and eek daunce / and wel portreye and write
So hoote he loued / that by nyghtertale
He slepte namoore / than dooth a nyghtyngale
Curteys he was / lowely / and seruysable
And carf biforn his fader / at the table
Yeman ¶A yeman he hadde / and seruantz namo
At that tyme / for hym liste ryde so
And he was clad / in coote and hood of greene
A sheef of Pecok arwes / bright' and keene
Vnder his belt' he bar ful thriftily
Wel koude he dresse his takel yemanly
His arwes drowped noght' with fetheres lowe
And in his hand / he bar a myghty bowe
A not heed hadde he / with a broun visage
Of wodecraft / koude he wel al the vsage
Vp on his arm / he bar a gay bracer
And by his syde / a swerd and a Bokeler

ELLESMERE

¶But
His weren he was

bismotered habergeou*n*
late / ycome

¶Squier] **W**ith hym Squier
louyer*e* / Bacheler
W*ith* were presse
twenty yeer of Age / he was I

somtyme chyuachie
Artoys Pycardie
weel / as of so
stonden
Embrouded were
fressħe whyte

w*ith* sleues
hors
songes make / and wel endite
and and weel purtreye *and*
3 louede /
namoore nygħtyngale
Curteis
carf / fader
A hadde he / [¶Yeman]
ride
cote *and* grene
pecok brigħt kene

he /
Hise drouped
baar mygħty

wodecraft / wel koude he al
baar
swerd / bokeler

32r

But for to tellen yow of his array
His hors weere goode but he ne was nat gay
Of ffustian he wered a gypon
Al bismotered with his habergeon
ffor he was laate comen from his viage
And wente for to doon his pilgrymage
Squyer. With hym ther was his sone a yong Squyer
A louere and a lusty bacheler
With lokkes crulle as they were leyd in presse
Of .xx. yeer he was of age I gesse
Of his stature he was of euene lengthe
And wonderly delyuere and of greet strengthe
And he hadde been som tyme in chyuachye
In fflaundres in Artoys and Picardye
And born hym wel as in so litel space
In hope to stonden in his lady grace
Embrouded was he as it were a meede
Al ful of fresshe floures white and reede
Syngynge he was or floytynge al the day
He was as fressh as is the monthe of may
Short was his gowne with sleues longe and wyde
Wel koude he sitte on hors and faire ryde
He koude songes wel make and endite
Iuste and eek daunce and wel portreye and write
So hoote he louede that by nyghtertale
He sleep namoore than dooth a nyghtyngale
Curteys he was lowely and seruysable
And carf biforn his fader at the table
Yeman. A yeman hadde he and seruantz namo
At that tyme for hym liste ryde so
And he was clad in cote and hood of greene
A sheef of Pecok arwes bright and keene
Vnder his belt he bar ful thriftily
Wel koude he dresse his takel yemanly
His arwes drouped noght with fetheres lowe
And in his hand he bar a myghty bowe
A not heed hadde he with a broun visage
Of wodecraft koude he wel al the vsage
Vp on his arm he bar a gay bracer
And by his syde a swerd and a bokeler

And on that oother syde a gay daggere
Harneysed wel and sharp as poynt of spere
A Cristofre on his brest of siluer sheene
An horn he bar the bawdryk was of greene
A fforster was he soothly as I gesse

Prioresse.

Ther was also a Nonne a Prioresse
That of hir smylyng was ful symple and coy
Hir gretteste ooth was but by seint Loy
And she was cleped madame Eglentyne
fful wel she soong the seruyce dyuyne
Entuned in hir nose ful semely
And frenssh she spak ful faire and fetisly
After the scole of Stratford at the Bowe
ffor frenssh of Parys was to hire vnknowe
At mete wel ytaught was she with alle
She leet no morsel from hir lyppes falle
Ne wette hir fyngres in hir sauce depe
Wel koude she carye a morsel and wel kepe
That no drope fille vp on hir brest
In curteisye was set muchel hir lest
Hir ouer lyppe wyped she so clene
That in hir coppe ther was no ferthyng sene
Of grece whan she dronken hadde hir draghte
fful semely after hir mete she raghte
And sikerly she was of greet desport
And ful plesaunt and amyable of port
And peyned hire to countrefete cheere
Of Court and been estatlich of manere
And to been holden digne of reuerence
But for to speken of hir conscience
She was so charitable and so pitous
She wolde wepe if þt she sawe a mous
Caught in a trappe if it were deed or bledde
Of smale houndes hadde she þt she fedde
With rosted flessh or mylk and wastel breed
But soore wepte she if oon of hem were deed
Or if men smoot it with a yerde smerte
And al was conscience and tendre herte
fful semely hir wympel pynched was
Hir nose tretys hir eyen greye as glas

	ELLESMERE
And on that oother syde / a gay daggere	
Harneysed wel / and sharp*e* / as poynt of spere	Harneised sharp*e* point
A *Crist*ofre on his brest of siluer sheene	Cristophere
An horn he bar / the bawdryk was of greene	bawdryk grene
A Forster was he / soothly as I gesse	
Prioresse ¶Ther was also / a Nonne a Prioresse	Ther ⌈¶Prioresse⌉
That of hir smylyng was ful symple and coy	smylyng / *and*
Hir gretteste ooth / was but by Seint Loy	Hir*e* seint
And she was clepyd / madame Eglentyne	cleped /
Ful wel she soong the seruyce dyuyne	weel seruice
Entuned in hir nose / ful semely	semeely
And frenssħ she spak / ful faire and fetisly	frenssħ /
After the scole / of Stratford at the Bowe	Stratford atte Bowe
For frenssħ of Parys / was to hire vnknowe	hir*e*
At mete / wel ytaught was she with alle	ytaught
She leet no morsel / from hir lyppes falle	leet lippes
Ne wette hir fyngres / in hir sauce deepe	depe
Wel koude she carye a morsel / and wel keepe	carie kepe
That no drope / fille vp on hir brist	drope / ne fille hir*e* brist
In curteisye / was set muchel hir list	curteisie set ful muchel list /
Hir ouer lyppe / wyped she so cleene	lippe / clene
That in hir coppe / ther was no ferthyng seene	ferthyng sene
Of grece / whan she dronken hadde hir draghte	draughte
Ful semely / after hir mete she raghte	raughte
And sikerly / she was of greet desport	greet
And ful plesaunt and amyable of port	plesaunt /
And peyned hire / to countrefete chiere	hir*e* cheere
Of Court and been estatlich of manere	and to been
And to been holden / digne of reu*er*ence	ben holden reuerence
But for to speken / of hir conscience	speken hir*e*
She was so charitable / and so pitous	charitable
She wolde ⟨wepe⟩ / if *þat* she sawe a Mous	wepe / that saugh
Caught in a trappe / if it weere deed / or bledde	4 Kaught were deed
Of smale houndes / hadde she / *þat* she fedde	she
With rosted flessħ / or mylk and wastel breed	Milk /
But soore wepte she / if oon of hem weere deed	if any of were
Or if men smoot it / with a yerde smerte	smoot it
And al was conscience / and tendre herte	conscience
Ful semely / hir wympel pynched was	semyly / wympul
Hir nose tretez / hir eyen / greye as glas	tretys / eyen

[4] 2v

	ELLESMERE
Hir mouth ful smal / and ther to / softe and reed	to *and*
But sikerly / she hadde a fair forheed	forheed
It was almoost a spanne brood I trowe	almoost .
For hardily / she was nat vndergrowe	
Ful fetys was hir cloke / as I was war	
Of smal Coral / aboute hir arm she bar	coral / hir*e* Arm
A peyre of bedes / gauded al with greene	peire grene
And ther on heeng a brooch of gold ful sheene	on / heng
On which / was first writen / a crowned .A.	which / ther was write
And after / **Amor vincit omnia**	vincit
¶Another Nonne / with hire hadde she	¶Nonne *and* .iij. preestes] Another *with* hire
That was hire Chapeleyne / and preestes thre	hir Chapeleyne
Monk ¶A Monk ther was / a fair for the maystrye	¶Monk /] A maistrie
An outrydere / that louede venerye	outrider*e* / that venerie
A manly man / to been an Abbot able	
Ful many a deyntee hors / hadde he in stable	
And whanne he rood / men myghte his brydel heere	whan
Gyngle in a whistlynge wynd / as cleere	Gynglen / wynd als
And eek as loude / as dooth the Chapel belle	eek ⟨þe⟩
There as this lord / is kepere of the Selle	Ther was keper*e* Celle
The rule of Seint Maure / or of Seint Beneyt	reule Beneit /
By cause þat it was oold / and som deel streyt	that old / del streit /
This ilke Monk / leet oolde thynges pace	olde
And heeld / after the newe world the space	
He yaf noght of that text a pulled hen	nat text
That seith / þat hunterys been none holy men	that hunters beth nat hooly
Ne þat a Monk. whan he is recchelees	that Monk /
Is likned / til a fissħ / þat is waterlees	
This is to seyn / a Monk / out of his Cloystre	Monk
But thilke text heeld he nat worth an Oystre	text /
And I seyde / his opynyon was good	opiniou*n*
What sholde he studie / and make hym seluen wood	*and*
Vp on a book in Cloystre alwey to poure	book /
Or swynke with his handes / and laboure	swynken *with* handes
As Austyn bit. how shal the world be serued	bit /
Lat Austyn haue his swynk. to hym reserued	Austyn / his owene swynk / res*er*ued
Ther fore / he was a prykasour aryght	Therfore / prikasour aright
Grehoundes he hadde / as swift as fowel in flyght	flight /
Of prikyng and of huntyng for the haare	p*ri*kyng / hare
Was al his lust. for no cost wolde he spaare	spare

Nonne Chapeleyne / and thre prestes

Hir mouth ful smal / and ther to softe and reed
But sikerly / she hadde a fair forheed
It was almoost a spanne brood I trowe
ffor hardily / she was nat vndergrowe
fful fetys was hir cloke / as I was war
Of smal coral / aboute hir arm she bar
A peire of bedes / gauded al with greene
And ther on heng / a brooch of gold ful sheene
On which / was first writen / a crowned . A .
And after / Amor vincit omnia .
Another Nonne / with hire hadde she
That was hire Chapeleyne / and preestes thre
Monk. A Monk ther was / a fair for the maistrie
An outridere / that louede venerie
A manly man / to been an Abbot able
fful many a deyntee hors / hadde he in stable
And whanne he rood / men myghte his brydel heere
Gyngle in a whistlynge wynd / as cleere
And eek as loude / as dooth the Chapel belle
Ther as this lord / is kepere of the Celle
The rule of Seint Maure / or of Seint Beneyt
By cause þt it was old / and som deel streyt
This ilke Monk / leet olde thynges pace
And heeld / after the newe world the space
He yaf noght of that text / a pulled hen
That seith / þt hunterys been none holy men
Ne þt a Monk . whan he is recchelees
Is likned / til a fissh / þt is waterlees
This is to seyn / a Monk out of his Cloystre
But thilke text / heeld he nat worth an Oystre
And I seyde / his opynyon was good
What sholde he studie / and make hym seluen wood
Vp on a book / in Cloystre alwey to poure
Or swynke with his handes / and laboure
As Austyn bit . how shal the world be serued
lat Austyn haue his swynk . to hym reserued
Ther fore / he was a prikasour aryght
Grehoundes he hadde / as swift as fowel in flyght
Of prikyng / and of huntyng for the haare
Was al his lust / for no cost wolde he spaare

Nonne Chapeleyne
and thre prestes ...

I saugh his sleues/ p[ur]filed at the hond
With grys/ and that the fyneste of a lond
And for to festne his hood/ vnder his chyn
He hadde of gold/ wroght a ful curious pyn
A loue knotte/ in the gretter ende ther was
His heed was balled/ that shoon as any glas
And eek his face/ as he hadde been enoynt/
He was a lord ful fat/ and in good poynt/
Hise eyen steepe/ and rollynge in his heed
That stemed/ as a fourneys of a leed
Hise bootes souple/ his hors/ in greet estaat/
Now certeynly/ he was a fair p[re]lat/
He was nat paale/ as is a forpyned goost/
A fat swan/ loued he/ best of any roost/
His palfrey/ was as broun as any berye

Ffrere – A frere ther was/ a wantowne and a merye
A lymytour/ a ful solempne man
In alle the ordres foure/ is noon þt kan
So muche of daliaunce/ and fair langage
He hadde maked/ ful many a mariage
Of yonge wommen/ at his owene cost/
Vn to his ordre/ he was a noble post/
fful wel biloued/ and famylier was hee
With ffrankeleyns/ ouer al in his contree
And eek with worthy wommen/ of the toun
ffor he hadde/ power of confessioun
As seyde hym self/ moore than a curaat/
ffor of his ordre/ he was licenciaat/
fful swetely/ herde he confessioun
And plesaunt/ was his absolucioun
He was an esy man/ to yeue penaunce
Ther as he wiste/ to haue a good pitaunce
ffor vn to a poure ordre/ for to yeue
Is signe/ that a man/ is wel yshryue
ffor if he yaf/ he dorste make auaunt/
He wiste/ þt a man was repentaunt/
ffor many a man/ so hard is of his herte
He may nat wepe/ though þt he sore smerte
Ther fore/ in stede of wepynge/ and preyeres
Men moote yeue siluer/ to the poure freres

	ELLESMERE
I saugh his sleues / p*ur*filed at the hond	5 seigh ypurfiled hond
With grys / and that the fyneste of a lond	lond
And for to festne his hood / vnder his chyn	hood
He hadde / of gold / wroght a ful curious pyn	hadde ywroght
A loue knotte / in the gretter ende ther was	
His heed was balled / that shoon as any glas	þ*a*t
And eek his face / as he hadde been enoynt	as it hadde enoynt /
He was a lord ful fat and in good poynt	fat /
Hise eyen steepe / and rollynge in his heed	stepe /
That stemed / as a fourneys of a leed	forneys
Hise bootes souple / his hors / in greet estaat	His hors
Now certeynly / he was a fair p*re*lat	ce*r*teinly / prelaat
He was nat paale / as is a forpyned goost	He nas nat pale / as a
A fat swan / loued he / best of any roost	swan he
His palfrey / was as broun as any berye	as is a berye
¶Frere ¶A frere ther was / a wantowne and a merye	A Frere *and* [¶Frere]
A lymytour / a ful solempne man	
In alle the ordres foure / is noon þ*a*t kan	
So muche of daliaunce / and fair langage	muchel
He hadde maked / ful many a mariage	maad /
Of yonge wommen / at his owene cost	wo*mm*en /
Vn to his ordre / he was a noble post	
Ful wel biloued / and familier was hee	And wel famulier he
With Frankeleyns / ouer al in his contree	frankeleyns /
And eek with worthy wommen / of the town	And with wo*mm*en toun
For he hadde / power of confessioun	hadde
As seyde hym self / moore than a curaat	Curat
For of his ordre / he was licenciaat	licenciat
Ful swetely / herde he confessiou*n*	
And plesant. was his absoluciou*n*	plesaunt Absoluciou*n*
He was an esy man / to yeue penaunce	
Ther as he wiste / to haue a good pitaunce	
For vn to a poure ordre / for to yeue	vnto yiue
Is signe / that a man / is wel yshryue	þ*a*t man
For if he yaf he dorste make auaunt	yaf /
He wiste / þ*a*t a man was repentaunt	that
For many a man / so hard is of his herte	
He may nat weepe / thogh þ*a*t he soore smerte	wepe / al thogh hym soore
Ther fore / in stede of wepynge / and preyeres	Therfore wepynge
Men moote yeue siluer / to the poure freres	

53r

		ELLESMERE
	¶His typet was ay farsed ful of knyues	His
	And pynnes / for to yeuen faire wyues	yeuen yonge wyues
	And certeynly / he hadde a murye noote	certeinly / note
	Wel koude he synge / and pleyen on a roote	rote
	Of yeddynges / he bar outrely the prys	baar pris
	His nekke whit was / as the flour delys	nekke / whit
	Ther to he stroong was / as a Champioun	to / strong was Champiou*n*
	He knew the tauernes wel in euery town	Tauernes in al the toun
	And euery hostiler / and Tappestere	[6] euerich Hostiler /
	Bet / than a lazer / or a beggestere	Bet lazar
	For vn to swich a worthy man / as he	man
	Acorded nat / as by his facultee	nat
	To haue / with syke lazers aqueyntaunce	haue sike lazars Aqueyntau*n*ce
	It is nat honeste / it may noght auaunce	nat auau*n*ce
	For to deelen / with no swich poraille	
	But al with riche / and sellerys of vitaille	wit*h* selleres
	And ouer al / ther as p*ro*fit sholde aryse	arise
	Curteys he was / and lowely of seruyse	Curteis
	Ther was no man / nowheer / so v*er*tuous	Ther nas no nowher
	He was the beste beggere / of his hous	was / beggere in his
252b	And yaf a c*er*teyn ferme / for the graunt	[7]
252c	Noon of his bretheren / cam ther in his haunt	[8]
	For thogh a wydwe / hadde noght a sho	thogh noght
	So plesant was his **In principio**	plesaunt p*ri*ncipio
	Yet wolde he haue a ferthyng er he wente	haue /
	His purchaas / was wel bettre than his rente	purchas /
	And rage he koude / as it weere right a whelp*e*	were right
	In louedayes / koude he muchel help*e*	louedayes / ther koude
	For there / he was nat lyk a Cloystrer	ther lyk
	With a threedbare cope / as is a poure scoler	thredbare
	But he was lyk a maister / or a Pope	lyk / pope
	Of double worstede / was his semycope	
	And rounded as a belle / out of the presse	That rounded
	Somwhat he lypsed / for his wantownesse	lipsed /
	To make his englyssh / sweete vp on his tonge	englissh /
	And in his harpyng whan þat he hadde songe	harpyng.
	Hise eyen twynkled / in his heed aryght	twynkled aryght
	As doon the sterres / in the frosty nyght	nyght
	This worthy lymytour / was cleped huberd	
Marchant	¶A Marchant was ther / with a forked berd	¶Marchau*n*t] A wit*h*

[6] *3v*

[7] *Out* El.

[8] *Out* El.

5

His typet was ay farsed ful of knyues
And pynnes for to yeuen faire wyues
And certeynly he hadde a murye noote
Wel koude he synge and pleyen on a rote
Of yeddynges he bar outrely the prys
His nekke whit was as the flour delys
Ther to he strong was as a champioun
He knew the tauernes wel in euery toun
And euery hostiler and Tappestere
Bet than a lazer or a beggestere
For vn to swich a worthy man as he
Acorded nat as by his facultee
To haue with syke lazers aqueyntaunce
It is nat honeste it may noght auaunce
For to deelen with no swich poraille
But al with riche and selleres of vitaille
And ouer al ther as profit sholde aryse
Curteys he was and lowely of seruyse
Ther was no man nowher so vertuous
He was the beste beggere of his hous
And yaf a certeyn ferme for the graunt
Noon of his bretheren cam ther in his haunt
For thogh a wydwe hadde noght a sho
So plesant was his In principio
Yet wolde he haue a ferthyng er he wente
His purchaas was wel bettre than his rente
And rage he koude as it were right a whelp
In louedayes koude he muchel help
For there he was nat lyk a Cloysterer
With a thredbare cope as is a poure scoler
But he was lyk a maister or a pope
Of double worstede was his semycope
And rounded as a belle out of the presse
Somwhat he lipsed for his wantownesse
To make his englyssh sweete vp on his tonge
And in his harpyng whan þt he hadde songe
Hise eyen twynkled in his heed aryght
As doon the sterres in the frosty nyght
This worthy lymytour was cleped Huberd
marchaunt A Marchant was ther with a forked berd

In motlee / and hye on hors he sat /
Vp on his heed / a fflaundryssh beuere hat /
His bootes clasped / faire and fetisly
Hise resons he spak ful solempnely
Sownynge / alwey / thencrees of his wynnyng /
He wolde / the see were kept / for any thyng /
Bitwixen Middelburgh / and Orewelle
Wel koude he in eschaunge / sheeldes selle
This worthy man / ful wel his wit bisette
Ther wiste no wight · that he was in dette
So estatly was he / of his gouernaunce
With his bargaynes / and with his cheuyssaunce
ffor sothe / he was a worthy man with alle
But sooth to seyn / I noot how men hym calle

Clerk of Oxenford · A clerk ther was / of Oxenford also
That vn to logyk · hadde longe ygo
As leene was his hors / as is a rake
And he was noght right fat / I vndertake
But looked holwe / and ther to sobrely
fful thredbare / was his ouereste Courtepy
ffor he hadde geten hym yet no benefice
Ne was so worldly / for to haue office
ffor hym was leuere / haue at his beddes heed
Twenty bookes / clad in blak / or reed
Of Aristotle / and his Philosophye
Than robes riche / or ffithele / or gay Sautrye
But al be / that he was a Philosophre
yet hadde he but litel gold in Cofre
But al that he myghte / of his frendes hente
On bookes and on lernynge / he it spente
And bisily gan for the soules preye
Of hem / that yaf hym / wher with to scoleye
Of studye / took he moost cure and moost heede
Noght o word spak he moore than was neede
And that was spoke in forme / and reuerence
And short / and quyk / and ful of heigh sentence
Sownynge in moral vertu / was his speche
And gladly / wolde he lerne / and gladly teche

Sergeaunt of lawe A sergeaunt of lawe / waar / and wys
That often / hadde been at the Paruys

	ELLESMERE
In Motlee / and hye on hors he sat	horse
Vp on his heed / a Flaundryssh Beu*er*e hat	heed
His bootes clasped / faire and fetisly	
Hise resons / he spak ful solempnely	resons spak /
Sownyng alwey / thencrees of his wynnyng	Sownynge alwey
He woolde / the see weere kept for any thyng	wolde were
Bitwixen Myddelburgh / and Orewelle	Bitwixe Middelburgh
Wel koude he / in eschaunge / sheeldes selle	he eschaunge
This worthy man / ful wel his wit bisette	
Ther wiste no wight. that he was in dette	wight / þ*at*
So estaatly was he / of his gou*er*naunce	estatly / he gouernaunce
With his bargaynes / and w*ith* his cheuysaunce	cheuyssaunce
For soothe / he was a worthy man with alle	sothe /
But sooth to seyn / I noot how men hym calle	
¶Clerc of Oxenford ¶A Clerc ther was / of Oxenford also	¶Clerk of Oxenford] A Clerk Oxenford
That vn to logyk. hadde longe ygo	logyk /
As leene was his hors / as is a rake	And leene hors
And he was noght right fat I vndertake	he nas nat right fat
But looked holwe / and ther to sobrely	9
Ful threedbaare / was his ou*er*este Courtepy	thredbare / ouereste courtepy
For he hadde / geten hym yet no benefice	hadde yet
Ne was so worldly / for to haue office	
For hym was leuere / haue at his beddes heed	
Twenty bookes / clad / in blak / or reed	clad blak
Of Aristotle / and his Philosophye	Philophie
Than robes riche / or Fithele / or gay Sautrye	fithele / Sautrie
But al be / that he was a Philosophre	
Yet hadde he / but litel gold in Cofre	cofre
But al that he myghte / of his frendes hente	þ*at* myghte / freendes
On bookes / and on lernynge / he it spente	lernynge
And bisily / gan for the soules preye	
Of hem / that yaf hym / wher with to scoleye	þ*at* hym w*ith*
Of studye / took he moost cure and moost heede	studie *and*
Noght oo word spak he / moore than was neede	Noght o word / spak he
And that was spoke / in forme / and reuerence	was seyd / in forme
And short and quyk and ful of heigh sentence	hy
Sownynge in moral v*er*tu / was his speche	
And gladly wolde he lerne / and gladly teche	lerne
¶Sergeaunt of Lawe ¶A Sergeaunt of lawe / waar / and wys	A Sergeant of the lawe / war [¶Sergeant of lawe]
That often / hadde been at the Parvys	often

94r

		ELLESMERE
	Ther was also / ful ryche of excellence	riche
	Discreet he was / and of greet reue*r*ence	reuerence
	He seemed swich / hise wordes weeren so wyse	semed weren wise
	Iustice he was / ful often in Assise	
	By patente / and by pleyn co*m*missiou*n*	
	For his science / and for his heigh renou*n*	heigh
	Of fees and robes / hadde he many oon	
	So greet a purchasour / was nowher noon	greet
	Al was fee symple / to hym / in effect	symple hym
	His purchasyng myghte nat been infect	
	Nowher so bisy a man as he / ther nas	Nowher he
	And yet he seemed / bisyer than he was	semed / bisier
	In te*r*mes / hadde he caas / and doomes alle	te*r*mes caas
	That from tyme of kyng william / weere falle	from the tyme / william were yfalle
	Ther to / he koude endite / and make a thyng	endite
	Ther koude no wight pynchen at his writyng	wight /
	And euery statut. koude he pleyn by roote	statut / rote
	He rood but hoomly / in a medlee coote	cote
	Girt with a ceynt of sylk. with barres smale	wi*th* ceint silk / wi*th*
	Of his array / telle I no lenger tale	array
[¶]Fr*a*nke-leyn	¶A Frankeleyn / was in his compaignye	A [¶Frankeleyn]
	Whit was his berd / as is the dayesye	his heed / as is a dayeseye
	Of his complexcion / he was sangwyn	complexiou*n* /
	Wel loued he by the morwe / a sop*e* in wyn	morwe
	To lyuen in delyt was euere his wone	delit
	For he was / Epicurus owene sone	
	That heeld opynyou*n* / þ*a*t pleyn delit	10 opiniou*n* / that
	Was verray / felicitee parfit	verray
	An housholdere / and that a greet was hee	housholder*e* / he
	Seint Iulyan he was / in his contree	Seint Iulian was he
	His breed / his ale / was alweys after oon	Ale /
	A bettre envyned man / was neuere noon	nu*er*e
	With outen bake mete / was neuere his hous	oute neu*er*e
	Of fressh fissh / and flessh / and that so plentevous	Of fissh plenteuous
	It snewed in his hous / of mete and drynke	
	Of alle deyntees / þ*a*t men koude bithynke	that thynke
	After / the sondry sesons / of the yeer	After
	So chaunged he / his mete / and his soper	mete
	Ful many a fat partrych / hadde he in Muwe	partrich /
	And many a breem / and many a luce in Stuwe	Breem / Luce

10*4v*

Ther was also / ful ryche of excellence
Discreet he was / and of greet reuerence
He semed swich / hise wordes weren so wyse
Iustice he was / ful often in Assise
By patente / and by pleyn commissioun
ffor his science / and for his heigh renoun
Of fees and robes / hadde he many oon
So greet a purchasour / was nowher noon
Al was fee symple / to hym / in effect
His purchasyng / myghte nat been infect
Nowher so bisy a man as he / ther nas
And yet he semed / bisier than he was
In termes / hadde he caas / and domes alle
That from tyme of kyng William / weere falle
Ther to / he koude endite / and make a thyng
Ther koude no wight / pynchen at his writyng
And euery statut · koude he pleyn by roote
He rood but hoomly / in a medlee coote
Gyrt with a ceynt of sylk / · with barres smale
Of his array / telle I no lenger tale
[Fra]nkeleyn A ffrankeleyn / was in his compaignye
Whit was his berd / as is the dayesye
Of his complexion / he was sangwyn
Wel loued he by the morwe / a sop in wyn
To lyuen in delyt / was euere his wone
ffor he was / Epicurus owene sone
That heeld opynyon / þt pleyn delit
Was verray / felicitee parfit
An housholdere / and that a greet was hee
Seint Iulyan he was / in his contree
His breed / his ale / was alweys after oon
A bettre envyned man / was neuere noon
With outen bake mete / was neuere his hous
Of fiessh fissh and flessh / and that so plentevous
It snewed in his hous / of mete and drynke
Of alle deyntees / þt men koude bithynke
After / the sondry sesons / of the yeer
So chaunged he / his mete / and his soper
ffful many a fat partrych / hadde he in muwe
And many a breem / and many a luce in stuwe

Wo was his cook / but if his Sauce weere
Poynaunt and sharp / and redy al his geere
His table dormant in his halle alway
Stood redy couered / al the longe day
At Sessions ther was he lord and Sire
fful ofte tyme he was knyght of the Shire
An Anlaas and a gipser al of Sylk
Heeng at his girdel / whit as morne milk
A Shirreue hadde he been / and Countour
Was nowher swich a worthy vauasour

Haberdasshere · Carpenter · Webbe · Dyere · Tapycer

An haberdasshere and a Carpenter
A webbe a Dyere and a Tapycer
And they weere clothed alle in oo lyuree
Of a solempne and a greet fraternytee
fful fressh and newe hir geere apyked was
Hir knyues weere chaped noght with bras
But al with siluer / wroght ful cleene and wel
Hir girdles and hir pouches euerydel
Wel semed ech of hem a fair burgeys
To sitten in a yeldehalle on a deys
Eueryich for the wisdom þt he kan
Was shaply for to been an Alderman
ffor catel hadde they ynogh / and rente
And eek hir wyues wolde it wel assente
And ellis certeyn they weere to blame
It is ful fair to been ycleped madame
And goon to vigilies / al bifore
And haue a mantel / roialliche ybore

Cook

A Cook they hadde with hem / for the nones
To boille the chiknes / with the marybones
And poudre marchaunt tart and Galyngale
Wel koude he knowe a draghte of london ale
He koude rooste and seethe and broille and frye
Maken mortreux / and wel bake a pye
But greet harm was it as it thoughte me
That on his Shyne a mormal hadde he
ffor blankmanger that made he with the beste

Shipman

A Shipman was ther wonyng fer by weste
ffor aught I woot he was of Dertemouthe
He rood vp on a Rouncy / as he kouthe

Wo was his Cook' / but if his sauce weere
Poynaunt' and sharp*e* / and redy al his geere
Hys table dormaunt' in his halle alway
Stood redy couered / al the longe day
At sessions / ther was he / lord and sire
Ful ofte tyme / he was knyght of the Shire
An Anlaas / and a Gipser / al of sylk'
Heeng' at his girdel / whit as morne mylk'
A shirreue hadde he been / and Countour
Was nowheer / swich a worthy vauasour
[Haber-dassher*e* Carpenter Webbe Dyere Tapycer] ¶An haberdasshere / and a Carpenter
A Webbe / a Dyere / and a Tapycer
And they weere clothed alle / in oo lyu*er*ee
Of a solempne / and a greet frat*er*nytee
Ful fressħ and newe / hir geere apyked was
Hir knyues weere chaped / noght with bras
But al with siluer / wroght ful cleene and wel
Hir girdles / and hir pouches / euerydel
Wel seemed eech of hem / a fair Burgeys
To sitten in a yeldehalle / on a deys
Euerych / for the wisdom / *þa*t he kan
Was shaply / for to been an Alderman
For catel / hadde they ynogh / and rente
And eek hir wyues / wolde it wel assente
And ellis certeyn / they weere to ƀlame
It is ful fair / to been yclepyd madame
And goon to vigilies / al bifore
And haue a Mantel / realliche ybore
Cook / ¶A Cook they hadde with hem / for the nones
To boille the chiknes / with the Marybones
And poudre marchaunt'. tart' and / Galyngale
Wel koude he knowe / a draghte of london ale
He koude rooste / and seethe / and broille / *and* frye
Maken Mortreux / and wel bake a pye
But greet harm was it / as it thoughte me
That on his Shyne / a Mormal hadde he
For Blankmanger / that maade he with the beste
Shipman ¶A Shipman was ther / wonyng fer by weste
For aught I woot' he was of Dertemouthe
He rood vp on a Rouncy / as he kouthe

ELLESMERE

Cook' were
Poynaunt /
His dormant'
sessiou*ns* / he
knyght shire
gipser silk'
Heeng Milk /
been
nowher /
¶Haberdassħer*e*] AN haberdassħer*e*
¶Carpenter]
¶Webbe] were alle o
¶Dyere] fraternitee
¶Tapicer] apiked
knyues / were chaped
w*ith* wroght clene weel
Hir*e* girdles / pouches euerydeel
semed ech burgeys
Euerich / wisdom
catel ynogh
wyues
elles were they
ycleped
Mantel roialliche
¶Cook] A w*ith* hem
chiknes w*ith*
Marchant' and galyngale
draughte Londou*n* Ale
rooste sethe / and boille and
11 it'
shyne / mormal
blankmanger' made
A wonynge [¶Shipman]
aught woot /

11 5*r*

	ELLESMERE
In a gowne of faldyngꝫ to the knee	
A daggere hangynge on a laas / hadde he	dagger*e* / laas
Aboute his nekke / vnder his arm adown	Arm adoun
The hoote Somer / hadde maad his hewe al brown	somer / broun
And certeynly / he was a good felawe	certeinly /
Ful many a draghte of wyn / hadde he drawe	draughte had
Fro Burdeuxwardꝭ whil þ*at* the Chapman sleep*e*	that
Of nyce conscience / took he no keep*e*	
If þ*at* he faughtꝫ and hadde the hyer hondꝭ	faughtꝫ
By watre he sente hem hoom / to euery londꝭ	water / hoom
But of his craftꝫ to rekene wel his tydes	
His stremys / and his daungers hym bisydes	stremes / bisides
His ⟨herberwe⟩ and his moone / his lodmenage	herberwe / Lodemenage
Ther was noon swich / from huƚƚ to Cartage	Ther nas noon Huƚƚ
Hardy he was / and wys to vndertake	was wys /
With many a tempestꝫ hadde his beerd been shake	tempest / berd
He knew alle the hauenes / as they weere	Hauenes / were
Fro Gootlond / to the cape of Fynysteere	Gootlandꝭ Cape of Fynystere
And euery cryke / in Britaigne / and in Spaigne	Britaigne Spayne
His barge / yclepyd was the Mawdelayne	Barge / ycleped Maudelayne
Docto*ur* of Phisykꝫ ¶With vs / ther was / a Doctour of Phisykꝫ	With vs Phisik [¶Doctour of Phisik/]
In al this world / ne was ther noon hym lykꝫ	lik /
To speken of Phisykꝫ and of Surgerye	speke phisik /
For he was grounded / in Astronomye	grounded
He kepte his pacientꝫ a ful greet deel	
In houres / by his magyk natureel	
Wel koude he fortunen / the ascendentꝫ	fortunen Ascendentꝫ
Of hise ymages / for his pacientꝫ	
He knew the cause / of euery maladye	euerich
Weere itꝫ of hootꝫ or coold / or moyste / or drye	Were it
And where it engendred / and of what humour	where they engendred / humo*ur*
He was a verray / p*ar*fit practisour	verray parfit praktisour
The cause yknowe / and of his harm the roote	
Anoon he yaf / the sike man his boote	Anon
¶Ful redy hadde he / hise Apothecaryes	Ful Apothecaries
To senden hym / his drogges / and his letuaryes	sende hym drogges Letuaries
For eech of hem / maade oother for to wynne	ech made
Hir frendshipe / was noght newe to bigynne	frendshipe / nas nat newe
Wel knew he / the oolde Esculapyus	olde Esculapius
And Discorides / and eekꝫ Rusus	Deyscorides / eek Risus

In a gowne of faldyng to the knee
A daggere hangynge on a laas hadde he
Aboute his nekke vnder his arm adoun
The hoote somer hadde maad his hewe al broun
And certeynly he was a good felawe
fful many a draghte of wyn hadde he drawe
ffro Burdeux ward whil þt the Chapman sleep
Of nyce conscience took he no keep
If þt he faught and hadde the hyer hond
By water he sente hem hoom to euery lond
But of his craft to rekene wel his tydes
His stremys and his daungers hym bisydes
His herberwe and his moone his lodmenage
Ther was noon swich from Hulle to Cartage
Hardy he was and wys to vndertake
With many a tempest hadde his berd been shake
He knew alle the hauenes as they were
ffro Gootlond to the cape of ffynystere
And euery cryke in Britaigne and in Spaigne
His barge ycleped was the Maudelayne
Doctour of Phisyk
With vs ther was a doctour of Phisyk
In al this world ne was ther noon hym lyk
To speken of Phisyk and of Surgerye
ffor he was grounded in Astronomye
He kepte his pacient a ful greet deel
In houres by his magyk natureel
Wel koude he fortunen the ascendent
Of hise ymages for his pacient
He knew the cause of euery maladye
Were it of hoot or cold or moyste or drye
And where it engendred and of what humour
He was a verray parfit praktisour
The cause yknowe and of his harm the roote
Anoon he yaf the sike man his boote
fful redy hadde he hise Apothecaryes
To senden hym his drogges and his letuaryes
ffor ech of hem made oother for to wynne
Hir frendshipe was noght newe to bigynne
Wel knew he the olde Esculapyus
And Discorides and eek Rufus

Olde ypocras / haly / and Galyen
Serapion / Razis and Avycen
Auerroys / Damascien / and Constantyn
Bernard / and Gatesden / and Gilbertyn
Of his diete / me[illegible]surable was he
For it was / of no superfluytee
But of greet norissynge and digestible
His studye / was but litel on the Bible
In Sangwyn and in Pers / he clad was al
Lyned with Taffata / and with Sendal
And yet he was / but esy of dispence
He kepte / þt he wan in pestilence
For gold in Phisyk / is a cordial
Ther fore he loued gold in special

.. The goode wyf .. of bisyde Bathe ..

A good wyf was ther / of bisyde Bathe
But she was som del deef / and that was scathe
Of clooth makynge / she hadde swich an haunt
She passed hem / of ypres / and of Gaunt
In al the parisshe / wyf ne was ther noon
That to the offrynge / bifore hire sholde goon
And if ther dide / certeyn / so wrooth was she
That she was / out of alle charitee
Hir couerchiefs / ful fyne weere of grownd
I dorste swere / they weyeden ten pownd
That on a Sonday / weeren vp on hir heed
Hir hosen weeren / of fyn Scarlet reed
Ful streyte yteyd / and shoes ful moyste & newe
Boold was hir face / and fair and reed of hewe
She was a worthy womman / al hir lyue
Housbondes at chirche dore / she hadde fyue
With outen oother compaignye / in youthe
But ther of nedeth nought to speke as nowthe
And thryes / hadde she been at Ierusalem
She hadde passed many a straunge strem
At Rome she hadde been / and at Boloyne
In Galyce at Seint Iame / and at Coloyne
She koude muchel / of wandrynge by the weye
Gattothed was she / soothly for to seye
Vp on an Amblere / esily she sat
Ywympled wel / and on hir heed an hat

	Olde ypocras / Haly / and Galyen	haly /
	Serapion / Razis / and Avycen	Serapiou*n* Auycen
	Auerroys / Damascien / and Constantyn	12 Auerrois /
	Bernard / and Gatesden / and Gilbertyn	Bernard /
	Of his diete / mesurable was hee	he
	For it was / of no sup*er*fluytee	sup*er*fluitee
	But of greet norissynge / and digestible	norissyng
	His studye / was but litel on the Bible	studie /
	In sangwyn and in Pers / he clad was al	pers /
	Lyned with Taffata / and with Sendal	
	And yet he was / but esy of dispence	
	He kepte / þat he wan in pestilence	that
	For gold in Phisyk. is a Cordial	Phisik cordial
	Ther fore / he loued gold in special	Therfore louede
The goode Wyf of bisyde Bathe	¶A good wyf was ther / of bisyde Bathe	¶The goode Wif of] A wif ther biside
	But she was somdel deef and that was scathe	¶Bathe] deef *and* þat
	Of clooth makynge / she hadde swich an haunt	makyng
	She passed hem / of Ipres / and of Gaunt	hem of ypres
	In al the parysshe / wyf ne was ther noon	parisshe / wif
	That to the offrynge / bifore hire sholde goon	hir*e*
	And if ther dide / certeyn / so wrooth was shee	certeyn she
	That she was / out of alle charitee	
	Hir Cou*er*chiefes / ful fyne weere of grownd	cou*er*chiefs / were of ground
	I dorste swere / they weyeden . ten pownd	weyeden ten pound
	That on a Sonday / weeren vp on hir heed	sonday / weren vpon heed
	Hir hosen weeren / of fyn scarlet reed	weren / reed
	Ful streyte yteyd / and shoes / ful moyste *and* newe	streite shoes
	Boold was hir face / and fair and reed of hewe	
	She was a worthy wo*m*man / al hir lyue	wo*m*man
	Housbondes at chirche dore / she hadde fyue	
	With outen oother compaignye / in yowthe	Withouten compaignye youthe
	But ther of / nedeth noght to speke as nowthe	nat
	And thries / hadde she been at Ierusalem	
	She hadde passed / many a straunge strem	
	At Rome she hadde been / and at Boloyne	been Boloigne
	In Galyce at Seint Iame / and at Coloyne	Galice Cologne
	She koude muchel / of wandrynge by the weye	
	Gattothed was she / soothly for to seye	Gat tothed
	Vp on an Amblere / esily she sat	Amblere / sat
	Ywympled wel / and on hir heed an hat	

125*v*

ELLESMERE

As brood as is / a Bokeler / or a Targe
A foot mantel / aboute hir hypes large
And on hir feet’ a peyre of spores sharpe
In felaweshipe / wel koude she laughe. and carpe
Of remedies of loue / she knew p*ar* chaunce
For she koude of that art’ the olde daunce
[P*er*so]u*n* of a town ¶A good man / was ther / of Religioun
And was a poure p*er*son / of a toun
But riche he was / of holy thoght and werk’
He was also / a lerned man a Clerk’
That Cristes gospel / trewely wolde p*re*che
His parisshens / deuoutly wolde he teche
Benygne he was / and wonder diligent
And in aduersitee / ful pacient’
And swich he was proeued / ofte sythes
Ful looth weere hym / to cursen for his tythes
But rather wolde he yeuen / out of doute
Vn to his poure parisshens aboute
Of his offrynge / and eek’ of his substaunce
He koude / in litel thyng’ haue suffisaunce
Wyd was his parisshe / and houses fer a sonder
But he ne lafte noght’ for reyn ne thonder
In siknesse / nor in meschief’ to visite
The ferreste in his parisshe / muche and lyte
Vp on his feet’ and in his hond a staf’
This noble ensample / to his sheep he yaf’
That first he wroghte / and afterward he taughte
Out of the gospel / he tho wordes caughte
And this figure / he added eek ther to
That if gold ruste / what sholde Iren do
For if a preest be foul / in whom we truste
No wonder is / a lewed man to ruste
And shame it is / if a preest take keep*e*
A shiten shepherde / and a clene sheep*e*
Wel oghte a preest’ ensample for to yiue
By his clennesse / how ꝥat his sheep sholde lyue
He sette noght’. his benefice to hyre
And leet his sheep / encombred in the Myre
And ran to Londou*n* / vn to Seint Poules
To seeken hym / a Chauntrye for soules

brood / is bokeler / targe
hipes
paire
felaweshipe / *and*

Art’
¶P*er*sou*n* of a toun] A man ther
was / p*er*sou*n*
hooly thogħt *and* werk /
clerk’
13 cristes preche
Hise parissħens /

Adu*er*sitee
swich / preued sithes
were hise tithes
yeuen
parissħens
offryng’ eek

parissħe /
lefte nat’
siknesse meschief /
parisshe lite
hand staf
sheep*e* yaf
firste afterward that he

what shal Iren
foul / on whom

preest / yeue
sheep*e*
sette nat his
sheep*e* /
londou*n* / seint
seken hym chauntrie

136r

As brood as is / a Bokeler / or a Targe
A foot mantel / aboute hir hypes large
And on hir feet / a peyre of spores sharpe
In felaweshipe / wel koude she laughe and carpe
Of remedies of loue / she knew perchaunce
For she koude of that art / the olde daunce
[illegible] A good man / was ther / of Religioun
And was a poure persoun / of a toun
But riche he was / of holy thoght and werk
He was also / a lerned man a clerk
That Cristes gospel / trewely wolde preche
His parisshens / deuoutly wolde he teche
Benygne he was / and wonder diligent
And in aduersitee / ful pacient
And swich he was preued / ofte sythes
Ful looth were hym / to cursen for his tythes
But rather wolde he yeuen / out of doute
Vn to his poure parisshens aboute
Of his offrynge / and eek / of his substaunce
He koude in litel thyng / haue suffisaunce
Wyd was his parisshe / and houses fer a sonder
But he ne lafte noght / for reyn ne thonder
In siknesse / nor in meschief / to visite
The ferreste in his parisshe / muche and lyte
Vp on his feet / and in his hond a staf
This noble ensample / to his sheep he yaf
That first he wroghte / and afterward he taughte
Out of the gospel / he tho wordes caughte
And this figure / he added eek ther to
That if gold ruste / what sholde iren do
For if a preest be foul / in whom we truste
No wonder is / a lewed man to ruste
And shame it is / if a preest take keep
A shiten shepherde / and a clene sheep
Wel oghte a preest / ensample for to yiue
By his clennesse / how that his sheep sholde lyue
He sette noght / his benefice to hyre
And leet his sheep / encombred in the myre
And ran to londoun / vn to Seint Poules
To seken hym / a Chauntrye for soules

Or with a bretherede / to been withholde
But dwelte at hoom / and kepte wel his folde
So þt the wolf / ne made it noght myscarye
He was a shepherde / and noght a mercenarye
And though he hooly were / and vertuous
He was noght / to synful men despitous
Ne of his speche / daungerous ne digne
But in his techyng / discreet and benygne
To drawen folk to heuene / wt fairnesse
By good ensample / this was his bisynesse
But it were / any persone obstinaat
What so he were / of heigh / or lowe estaat
Hym wolde he snybben / sharply for the nonys
A bettre preest / I trowe ther nowher noon ys
He wayted after no pomp / and reuerence
Ne maked hym / a spiced conscience
But Cristes loore / and hise Apostles twelue
He taughte / but first / he folwed it hym selue
Plowman ¶ With hym ther was a Plowman / was his brother
That hadde ylad of donge / ful many a fother
A trewe swynkere / and a good was he
Lyuynge in pees / and parfit charitee
God loued he best / with al his hoole herte
At alle tymes / though hym gamed or smerte
And thanne his neighebore / right as hym selue
He wolde thresshe / and ther to dyke and delue
For Cristes sake / for euery poure wight
With outen hyre / if it laye in his myght
His tythes payde he / ful faire and wel
Bothe of his propre swynk / and his catel
In a Tabard he rood / vp on a mere
Ther was also / a Reue / and a Millere
A Somonour / and a Pardoner also
A Maunciple / and my self / ther were namo
Millere ¶ The Millere / was a stout carl / for the nones
Ful byg he was of brawen / and eek of bones
That proued wel / for ouer al ther he cam
At wrastlynge / he wolde haue alwey the Ram
He was short shuldred / brood a thikke knarre
Ther was no dore / that he nolde heue of harre

Or with a breetherede / to been withhoolde
But dwelte at hoom / and kepte wel his fooldе
So þ*at* the wolf ne maade it noght myscarye
He was a sheepherde / and noght a Mercenarye
And thogh he hooly weere / and vertuous
He was noght to synful men despitous
Ne of his speche / daungerous / ne digne
But in his techyng discreet and benygne
To drawen folk to heuene / w*ith* fairnesse
By good ensample / this was his bisynesse
But it weere / any p*er*sone obstynaat
What so he weere / of heigh / or lowe estaat
Hym wolde he snybben / sharply for the nonys
A bettre preest I trowe ther nowher noon ys
He wayted / after no pomp*e* / and reuerence
Ne maked hym / a spyced conscience
But Cristes loore / and hise Apostles twelue
He taughte / but first he folwed it hym selue
Plowman ¶With hym ther was a Plowman / was his broother
That hadde ylad of donge / ful many a Foother
A trewe swynkere / and a good was he
Lyuynge in pees / and p*ar*fit charitee
God loued he best with al his hoole herte
At alle tymes / thogh hym gamed / or smerte
And thanne his Neighebore / right as hym selue
He wolde thresshe / and ther to / dyke and delue
For Cristes sake / for euery poure wight
With outen hyre / if it laye in his myght
His tythes payde he / ful faire and wel
Bothe of his p*ro*pre swynk and his catel
In a Tabard he rood / vp on a Mere
Ther was also / a Reue / and a Millere
A Somonour / and a Pardoner also
A Maunciple / and my self ther weere namo
Millere ¶The Millere / was a stout carl / for the nones
Ful byg he was / of brawen / and eek of bones
That proeued wel / for ouer al ther he cam
At wrastlynge / he wolde haue alwey the Ram
He was short shuldred / brood / a thikke knarre
Ther was no dore / that he noolde heue of harre

ELLESMERE

bretherhed / withholde
dwelleth hoom kepeth folde
that wolf / made nat myscarie
shepherde / Mercenarie
though were / v*er*tuous
nat
daungerous
discreet
folk heuene by fairnesse

were / persone obstinat
were / heigh lough estat
snybben
trowe / þ*a*t nowher
waiteth / pompe
hym spiced
cristes

14 ¶Plowman] With Plowman brother
dong fother
swynker*e* /
parfit
best /
thogh he gamed
neighebore / right
thresshe / therto
cristes wight
W*ith* hire / lay myght
Hise tithes / he

Tabard vpon
¶Miller*e*] Ther Reue
Somnour /
self were
The Miller*e* carl
byg brawn /
proued oue*r*al

sholdred /
þ*a*t he ne wolde heue

146*v*

		ELLESMERE
	Or breke it at a rennynge / with his heed	itꝭ rennyngꝭ
	His beerd / as any sowe / or fox / was reed	berd / fox
	And ther to brood / as thogh it weere a spaade	though were spade
	Vp on the cop*e* right of his nose he haade	cop*e* / right hade
	A werte / and ther on stood / a tuftꝭ of heerys	stood toft herys
	Reede / as the bristles / of a sowes eerys	Reed / brustles / erys
	Hise nosethirles / blake weere and wyde	were
	A swerd and a bokeler / baar he by his syde	bar
	His mouth as greet was / as a greet fourneys	forneys
	He was a Ianglere / a Golyardeys	Iangler*e* / and a goliardeys
	And that was moostꝭ of synne and harlotryes	harlotries
	Wel koude he stelen corn / and tollen thryes	thries
	And yet he hadde / a thombe of gold p*ar*dee	
	A whit coote / and a blew hood wered hee	cote / he
	A Baggepipe / wel koude he / blowe and sowne	baggepipe / he
	And ther with al / he broghte vs out of towne	
[M]aunciple	¶A gentil Maunciple / was ther / of a Temple	¶Maunciple] A ther temple
	Of which / Achatours myghte take exemple	which Achatours /
	For to been wyse / in byynge of vitaille	be wise /
	For wheither *þat* he payde / or took by taille	that
	Algate / he wayted so / in his achaatꝭ	Achaatꝭ
	That he was ay biforn / and in good staatꝭ	
	¶Now is nat that of god / a ful greet grace	Now god ful fair grace
	That swich a lewed mannes witꝭ shal pace	wit
	The wysdom / of an heep*e* / of lerned men	wisdom / heep*e*
	Of Maistres hadde he mo / than thryes ten	maistres he / mo thries
	That weeren / of lawe / expertꝭ and curious	15 weren
	Of whiche / ther weere a dozeyne / in that hous	þer weren duszeyne
	Worthy / to been Stywardes / of rente / and lond'	Worthy rente
	Of any lord / that is in Engelond'	
	To make hym lyue / by his p*ro*pre good	maken
	In honour dettelees / but if he weere wood	honou*r* were
	Or lyue as scarsly / as hym lyst desire	listꝭ
	And able / for to helpen / al a Shire	helpen shire
	In any caas / that myghte falle / or happe	*þat* falle
	And yet this Maunciple / sette hir aller cappe	manciple /
Reue	¶The Reue / was a sclendre coleryk man	The Reue was / colerikꝭ [¶Reue]
	His beerd was shaue / as neigh as euer he kan	berd ny eue*r*
	His heer was by his eerys / ful rownd yshorn	erys / round
	His top*e* was dokked / lykꝭ a preest byforn	lyk biforn

157*r*

Or breke it at a rennynge with his heed
His berd as any sowe or fox was reed
And ther to brood as thogh it were a spaade
Vp on the cop right of his nose he haade
A werte and ther on stood a tuft of herys
Reede as the brustles of a sowes erys
His nosethirles blake were and wyde
A swerd and a bokeler bar he by his syde
His mouth as greet was as a greet forneys
He was a Ianglere and a Golyardeys
And that was moost of synne and harlotryes
Wel koude he stelen corn and tollen thryes
And yet he hadde a thombe of gold pardee
A whit cote and a blew hood wered hee
A baggepipe wel koude he blowe and sowne
And ther with al he broghte vs out of towne
Manciple A gentil Maunciple was ther of a temple
Of which achatours myghte take exemple
ffor to been wyse in byynge of vitaille
ffor wheither þt he payde or took by taille
Algate he wayted so in his achaat
That he was ay biforn and in good staat
Now is nat that of god a ful greet grace
That swich a lewed mannes wit shal pace
The wysdom of an heep of lerned men
Of maistres hadde he mo than thryes ten
That weren of lawe expert and curious
Of whiche ther were a dozeyne in that hous
Worthy to been Stywardes of rente and lond
Of any lord that is in Engelond
To make hym lyue by his propre good
In honour dettelees but if he were wood
Or lyue as scarsly as hym lyst desire
And able for to helpen al a Shire
In any caas that myghte falle or happe
And yet this Maunciple sette hir aller cappe
Reue The Reue was a sclendre colerik man
His berd was shaue as neigh as euere he kan
His heer was by his erys ful rownd yshorn
His top was dokked lyk a preest biforn

Ful longe were his legges / and ful lene
Ylik a staf / ther was no calf ysene
Wel koude he kepe / a Gerner and a Bynne
Ther was noon Auditour / koude on hym wynne
Wel wiste he / by the droghte and by the reyn
The yeldynge of his seed / and of his greyn
His lordes sheep / his neet / his dayerye
His swyn / his hors / his stoor / and his pultrye
Was hoolly / in this Reues gouernynge
And by his couenant / yaf the rekenynge
Syn that his lord / was twenty yeer of age
Ther koude no man / brynge hym in Arrerage
Ther nas Baillyf / hierde / nor oother hyne
That he ne knew / his sleighte / and his couyne
They were adrad of hym / as of the deeth
His wonyng was ful faire vp on an heeth
With greene trees / shadwed was his place
He koude bettre than his lord / purchace
Ful riche he was astored pryuely
His lord wel koude he plesen subtilly
To yeue and lene hym / of his owene good
And haue a thank / and yet a cote and hood
In youthe he lerned hadde a good myster
He was a wel good wrighte a Carpenter
This Reue sat / vp on a wel good stot
That was a pomely gray / and highte Scot
A long Surcote of pers / vp on he hadde
And by his syde / he baar a rusty blade
Of Northfolk was this Reue / of which I telle
Bisyde a toun / men clepyn Baldeswelle
Tukked he was / as is a ffrere aboute
And euere he rood / the hyndreste of oure route

~ Somonour ~ A Somonour was ther with vs in that place
That hadde a fyr reed Cherubynnes face
For Sawcefleem he was / with eyen narwe
And hoot he was / and lecherous as a Sparwe
With scaled browes blake / and pyled berd
Of his visage / children were aferd
Ther nas quyk siluer / lytarge / ne Brymstoon
Boras / Ceruce / ne Oille of Tartre noon

Ne oynement

	ELLESMERE
Ful longe weere hise legges / and ful leene	were his lene
Ylik a staf /. ther / was no calf yseene	Ylyk staf / ther ysene
Wel koude he keepe / a Gerner and a Bynne	kepe gerner / bynne
Ther was noon Auditour / koude on hym wynne	koude of hym
Wel wiste he / by the droghte and by the reyn	droghte /
The yeldynge / of his seed / and of his greyn	
His lordes sheep*e* / his neet / his dayerye	neet'
His swyn / his hors / his stoor / and his pultrye	
Was hoolly / in this Reues gou*er*nynge	gouernyng /
And by his couenant'. yaf the rekenynge	couenant' rekenyng'
Syn that his loord / was twenty yeer of age	lord /
Ther koude no man / brynge hym in arrerage	Arrerage
Ther nas Baillyf'. hierde / nor oother hyne	baillif ne hierde /
That he ne knew / his sleyghte / and his couyne	he knew sleighte
They weere adrad of hym / as of the deeth	were
His wonyng' was ful faire vp on an heeth	
With greene trees / shadwed was his place	grene
He koude bettre / than his lord purchace	bettre
Ful riche / he was astoored pryuely	riche astored
His lord / wel koude he plesen subtilly	
To yeue / and leene hym / of his owene good	yeue lene
And haue a thank'. and yet a coote and hood	thank / a gowne and
In youthe / he lerned hadde / a good Mister	youthe he hadde lerned myster
He was a wel good wrighte / a Carpenter	wrigħte
This Reue sat' vp on a wel good Stot'	a ful good
That was a Pomely gray / and highte Scot'	was al pomely grey / higħte
A long Surcote of Pers / vp on he haade	surcote pers / hade
And by his syde / he baar a rusty blaade	blade
Of Northfolk was this Reue / of which I telle	Northfolk'
Bisyde a town / men clepyn Baldeswelle	Biside toun / clepen
Tukked he was / as is a Frere aboute	frere
And euere he rood / the hyndreste of oure route	eu*er*e
Somonour ¶A Somonour' was ther was with vs / in that place	A Somonour *with* vs ⌈¶Somonour⌉
That hadde / a fyr reed Cherubynnes face	
For Sawceflewm he was / with' eyen narwe	16 saucefleem was with eyen
And hoot he was / and lecherous as a Sparwe	As hoot sparwe
With scaled browes blake / and pyled berdˡ	blake piled
Of his visage / children weere aferdˡ	were
Ther nas quyk' siluer / lytarge / ne Brymstoon	siluer' lytarge brymstoon
Borace / Ceruce / ne Oille of Tartre noon	Boras / oille

167*v*

Ne oynement'

	ELLESMERE
Ne oynementꝭ. that wolde clense and byte	oynementꝭ
That hym myghte helpen / of his whelkes whyte	myghte of the whelkes white
Nor of the knobbes / sittynge on his chekes	
Wel loued he garlekꝭ oynons and eek lekes	garleekꝭ oynons /
And for to drynke strong wyn / reed as blood	drynken
Thanne wolde he speke / and crye as he were wood[17]	crie
A fewe t*er*mes hadde he / two / or thre	two
That he hadde lerned / out of som decree	had
No wonder is / he herde it al the day	
And eek ye knowe wel / how þ*at* a Iay	knowen
Kan clepen watte / as wel as kan the Pope	pope
But who so koude / in oother thyng hym grope	thyngꝭ
Thanne hadde he spentꝭ al his philosophie	Philosophie
Ay / **Questio quid iuris** / wolde he crye	questio crie
¶He was a gentil harlotꝭ and a kynde	He was /
A bettre felawe / sholde men noght fynde	
He wolde suffre / for a quartꝭ of wyn	quart
A good felawe / to haue his concubyn	
A twelf monthe / and excusen hym at the fulle	excuse atte fulle
Ful pryuely / a fynch eek koude he pulle	pr*i*uely /
And if he foond owher / a good felawe	
He wolde techen hym / to haue noon awe	Awe
In swich caas / of the Ercedeknes curs	Ercedekenes
But if a mannes soule / were in his purs	Butꝭ
For in his purs / he sholde ypunysshed be	
Purs is the Ercedeknes helle / seyde he	Purs / Ercedekenes helle
¶But wel I woot / he lyed right in dede	But right
Of cursyngꝭ oghte ech gilty man drede	
For curs wol sle / right as assoillyngꝭ sauyth	slee / right sauith
And also / war hym of a **Significauitꝭ**	
¶In daunger hadde he / at his owene gyse	In gise
The yonge gerles / of the diocise	girles /
And knew hir conseil / and was al hir reed	
A gerland / hadde he setꝭ vp on his heed	gerlandꝭ / set
As greetꝭ. as it were / for an Ale stake	greet /
A bokeler / hadde he maad hym of a cake	bokeleer / Cake
Pardoner ¶With hym ther rood / a gentil Pardoner	¶Pardoner] **W**ith ther was / a
Of Rouncyual / his freend / and his comper	Rounciuale / freend compeer
That streight was comen / fro the Court of Rome	co*ur*t
Ful loude he soongꝭ com hyder loue to me	hider

17 *Out* Hg 637-38. El reads:

And whan þ*at* he / wel dronken hadde the wyn
Thanne wolde he speke no word but latyn

Ne oynement · that wolde clense and byte
That hym myghte helpen of his whelkes whyte
Nor of the knobbes sittynge on his chekes
Wel loued he garlek oynons and eek lekes
And for to drynke strong wyn reed as blood
Thanne wolde he speke and crye as he were wood
A fewe termes hadde he two or thre
That he hadde lerned out of som decree
No wonder is he herde it al the day
And eek ye knowe wel how þt a Iay
Kan clepen watte as wel as kan the Pope
But who so koude in oother thyng hym grope
Thanne hadde he spent al his philosophie
Ay Questio quid iuris wolde he crye
He was a gentil harlot and a kynde
A bettre felawe sholde men noght fynde
He wolde suffre for a quart of wyn
A good felawe to haue his concubyn
A twelf monthe and excusen hym at the fulle
Ful pryuely a fynch eek koude he pulle
And if he foond owher a good felawe
He wolde techen hym to haue noon awe
In swich cas of the Erchedekenes curs
But if a mannes soule were in his purs
For in his purs he sholde ypunysshed be
Purs is the Erchedekenes helle seyde he
But wel I woot he lyed right in dede
Of cursyng oghte ech gilty man drede
For curs wol slee right as assoillyng sauyth
And also war hym of a Significauit
In daunger hadde he at his owene gyse
The yonge gerles of the diocise
And knew hir conseil and was al hir reed
A gerland hadde he set vp on his heed
As greet as it were for an Ale stake
A bokeler hadde he maad hym of a cake
Pardoner With hym ther rood a gentil Pardoner
Of Rouncyuale his freend and his compeer
That streight was comen fro the Court of Rome
Ful loude he soong com hyder loue to me

This Somonour baar to hym a styf burdoun
Was neuere trompe of half so greet a soun
This Pardoner hadde heer as yelow as wex
But smothe it heeng as dooth a stryke of flex
By ounces henge his lokkes þt he hadde
And ther with he his shuldres ouerspradde
But thynne it lay by colpons oon and oon
But hood for Iolitee wered he noon
ffor it was trussed vp in his walet
Hym thoughte he rood al of the newe iet
Dischenelee saue his cappe he rood al bare
Swiche glarynge eyen hadde he as an hare
A vernycle hadde he sowed vp on his cappe
His walet biforn hym in his lappe
Bretful of pardon comen from Rome al hoot
A voys he hadde as smal as hath a goot
No berd hadde he ne neuere sholde haue
As smothe it was as it were late yshaue
I trowe he were a geldyng or a mare
But of his craft fro Berwyk in to Ware
Ne was ther swich another Pardoner
ffor in his male he hadde a pilwe beer
Which þt he seyde was oure lady veyl
He seyde he hadde a gobet of the seyl
That Seint Peter hadde whan þt he wente
Vp on the see til Ihu Cryst hym hente
He hadde a croys of latoun ful of stones
And in a glas he hadde pigges bones
But with thise relykes whan þt he foond
A poure persoun dwellyng vp on lond
Vp on a day he gat hym moore moneye
Than þt the persoun gat in monthes tweye
And thus with feyned flaterye and Iapes
He made the persoun and the peple his apes
But trewely to tellen at the laste
He was in chirche a noble Ecclesiaste
Wel koude he rede a lesson and a storie
But alderbest he song an Offertorie
ffor wel he wiste whan þt song was songe
He moste preche and wel affyle his tonge

	ELLESMERE
This Somono*ur* baar to hym / a styf burdoun	18 Somono*ur* / bar hym stif
Was neu*ere* trompe / of half so greet a soun	neuere
¶This P*ar*doner / hadde heer / as yelow as wex	This Pardoner
But smothe it heeng as dooth a stryke of flex	strike
By ounces / henge his lokkes þ*at* he hadde	hise
And ther with / he his shuldres ouerspradde	hise ou*er*spradde
But thynne it lay / by colpons oon and oon	
But hood for Iolitee / wered he noon	
For it was trussed vp / in his walet	trussed / vp
Hym thoughte / he rood al of the newe Iet	rood /
Discheuelee saue his cappe / he rood al bare	
Swiche glarynge eyen / hadde he as an hare	eyen
A vernycle / hadde he sowed / vp on his cappe	vernycle
His walet biforn hym / in his lappe	
Bretful of pardou*n* / comen from Rome al hoot	Bret ful hoot /
A voys he hadde / as smal / as hath a Goot	smal goot /
No berd hadde he / ne neuere sholde haue	neu*ere*
As smothe it was / as it were late yshaue	shaue
I trowe he were a geldyng or a Mare	trowe / geldyng mare
But of his craft. fro Berwyk in to Ware	craft Berwyk /
Ne was ther / swich another Pardoner	
For in his Male / he hadde a pilwe beer	male /
Which þ*at* he seyde / was oure lady veyl	
He seyde he hadde / a gobet of the seyl	gobet
That Seint Peter hadde / whan þ*at* he wente	seint
Vp on the See / til I*es*u Crist hym hente	crist
He hadde a cros of latou*n* / ful of stones	croys
And in a glas / he hadde pigges bones	
But with thise relykes / whan þ*at* he foond	*with* relikes / fond
A poure p*er*son / dwellyng vp on lond	p*er*sou*n* / dwellynge lond
Vp on a day / he gat hym moore moneye	
Than þ*at* the p*er*sou*n* gat in Monthes tweye	p*er*son gat /
And thus / with feyned flaterye and Iapes	
He made the p*er*son / and the peple his apes	p*er*sou*n* Apes
But trewely / to tellen at the laste	atte laste
He was in chirche / a noble Ecclesiaste	chirche ecclesiaste
Wel koude he / rede a lesson / and a Storie	he rede / lesso*un* or a storie
But alderbest he soong an Offertorie	alderbest / song
For wel he wiste / whan þ*at* soong was songe	þ*at* song
He moste p*re*che / and wel affyle his tonge	affile
	188r

	ELLESMERE
To wynne siluer / as he ful wel koude	
Ther fore he soong the muryerly and loude	Therfore song murierly
¶Now haue I toold yow / soothly in a clause	NOw yow shortly
Thestaat / tharray / the nombre / and eek the cause	Thestaat nombre *and*
Why þ*at* assembled was this compaignye	
In Southwerk. at this gentil hostelrye	Southwerk / as this
That highte the tabard / faste by the belle	Tabard /
But now is tyme / to yow for to telle	
How þ*at* we baren vs / that ilke nyght	19 that vs nyght
Whan we weere / in that hostelrye alyght	were / hostelrie alyght
And after wol I telle / of oure viage	
And al the remenant of oure pilgrymage	remenaunt pilg*ri*mage
¶But first I pray yow / of youre curteisye	But first
That ye narette it / noght my vileynye	it nat
Though þ*at* I pleynly speke / in this matere	Thogh þ*at* / speke mateere
To telle yow / hir wordes / and hir cheere	wordes
Ne thogh I speke / hir wordes p*ro*prely	speke
For this ye knowen / also wel as I	
Who so shal telle a tale / after a man	
He moot reherce / as neigh as eu*er*e he kan	ny
Euerich a word / if it be in his charge	
Al speke he / neuer so rudeliche and large	rudeliche or large
Or ellis / he moot telle his tale vntrewe	
Or feyne thyng or fynde wordes newe	thyng.
He may noght spare / al thogh he weere his brother	nat were
He moot as wel / seye o word / as another	word
Crist spak hym self ful brode in holy writ /	Crist self / hooly
And wel ye woot no vileynye is it	
Ek Plato seith / who so kan hym rede	Eek
The wordes / mote be cosyn / to the dede	moote cosyn
¶Also I pray yow / to foryeue it me	Also prey
Al haue I nat set folk / in hir degree	folk
Here in this tale / as þ*at* they sholde stonde	Heere
My wit is short ye may wel vnderstonde	
¶Greet cheere / made oure hoost vs euerichon	chiere
And to the souper / sette he vs anon	soper /
He serued vs / with vitaille / at the beste	vitaille
Strong was the wyn / and wel to drynke vs leste	
A semely man / oure hoost was with alle	
For to been / a Marchal in an halle	

198*v*

To wynne silver / as he ful wel koude
Ther fore he song / the murierly / and loude
Now haue I told yow / soothly in a clause
Thestaat / tharray / the nombre / and eek the cause
Why þt assembled was this compaignye
In Southwerk / at this gentil hostelrye
That highte the tabard / faste by the belle
But now is tyme / to yow for to telle
How þt we baren vs / that ilke nyght
Whan we were / in that hostelrye alyght
And after wol I telle / of oure viage
And al the remenant / of oure pilgrymage
But first I pray yow / of youre curteisye
That ye narette it noght my vileynye
Though þt I pleynly speke / in this matere
To telle yow hir wordes / and hir cheere
Ne though I speke hir wordes proprely
ffor this ye knowen / also wel as I
Who so shal telle a tale / after a man
He moot reherce / as neigh as euere he kan
Euerich a word / if it be in his charge
Al speke he neuer so rudeliche and large
Or ellis / he moot telle his tale vntrewe
Or feyne thyng / or fynde wordes newe
He may noght spare / al though he were his brother
He moot as wel / seye o word / as another
Crist spak hym self / ful brode in holy writ
And wel ye woot / no vileynye is it
Ek Plato seith / who so kan hym rede
The wordes / mote be cosyn / to the dede
Also I pray yow / to foryeue it me
Al haue I nat set folk / in hir degree
Here in this tale / as þt they sholde stonde
My wit is short / ye may wel vnderstonde
Greet cheere made oure hoost vs euerichon
And to the souper / sette he vs anon
He serued vs / with vitaille at the beste
Strong was the wyn / and wel to drynke vs leste
A semely man / oure hoost was with alle
ffor to been / a marchal in an halle

A large man he was / with eyen stepe
A fairer burgeys / was ther noon in Chepe
Boold of his speche / and wys / and wel ytaught /
And of manhode / hym lakked right naught /
Eke ther to / he was right a myrie man
And after souper / pleyen he bigan
And spak of myrthe / amonges othere thynges
Whan þt we hadde maad oure rekenynges
And seyde thus / now lordes trewely
Ye been to me / right welcome hertely
For by my trouthe / if þt I shal nat lye
I saugh noght this yeer / so myrie a compaignye
Atones in this herberwe / as is now
Fayn wolde I doon yow myrthe / wiste I how
And of a myrthe / I am right now bythoght /
To doon yow ese / and it shal coste noght /
Ye goon to Caunterbury / god yow spede
The blisful martir / quyte yow youre mede
And wel I woot / as ye goon by the weye
Ye shapen yow / to talen and to pleye
For trewely / confort / ne myrthe is noon
To ryde by the weye / doumb as stoon
And therfore wol I maken yow desport /
As I seyde erst / and doon yow som confort /
And if yow liketh alle / by oon assent /
For to stonden / at my juggement /
And for to werken / as I shal yow seye
Tomorwe / whan ye riden by the weye
Now by my fader soule / þt is deed
But ye be myrie / I wol yeue yow myn heed
Hoold vp youre hondes / withouten moore speche
Oure conseil / was nat longe for to seche
Vs thoughte / it was nat worth to make it wys
And graunted hym / withouten moore avys
And bad hym seye / his voirdit as hym leste
Lordynges quod he / now herkneth for the beste
But taketh it noght / I prey yow in desdeyn
This is the poynt / to speken short and pleyn
That ech of yow / to shorte with oure weye
In this viage / shal tellen tales tweye

	ELLESMERE
A large man he was / with eyen stepe	
A fairer burgeys / was ther noon in Chepe	Burgeys /
Boold of his speche / and wys / and wel ytaught	wys ytaught
And of manhode / hym lakked right naught	manhod / right naught
Eke ther to / he was right a murye man	Eek therto / myrie
And after souper / pleyen he bigan	soper /
And spak of murthe / amonges othere thynges	myrthe /
Whan þat we hadde maad oure rekenynges	that we /
And seyde thus / now lordes trewely	lordynges
Ye been to me / right wel come hertely	right welcome
For by my trouthe / if þat I shal nat lye	that
I seigh noght this yeer / so murye a compaignye	saugh nat myrie co*m*paignye
Atones in this herberwe / as is now	herberwe
Fayn wolde I doon yow myrthe / wiste I how	
And of a myrthe / I am right now bithoght	right bythoght
To doon yow ese / and it shal coste noght	noght
¶Ye goon to Caunt*er*bury / god yow spede	20 Caunterbury / speede
The blisful Martir / quyte yow youre mede	martir / quite meede
And wel I woot as ye goon by the weye	
Ye shapen yow / to talen and to pleye	
For trewely / confort / ne murthe is noon	confort myrthe
To ryde by the weye / domb as stoon	ride weye doumb as the stoon
And ther fore / wol I maken yow desport	therfore / disport
As I seyde erst and doon yow som confort	
And if yow liketh alle / by oon assent	
For to stonden / at my Iuggement	
And for to werken / as I shal yow seye	
Tomorwe / whan ye ryden by the weye	riden
Now by my fader soule / þat is deed	soule that deed
But ye be murye / I wol yeue yow myn heed	But if ye myrie / heed
Hoold vp youre hondes / with outen moore speche	¶Hoold hond w*ith*outen
¶Oure conseil / was nat longe for to seche	Oure
Vs thoughte / it was nat worth / to make it wys	noght
And graunted hym / with outen moore avys	wit outen auys
And bade hym seye / his voirdit as hym leste	bad seye
¶Lordynges quod he / now herkneth for the beste	
But taketh it noght I pray yow in desdeyn	taak nought / prey
This is the poynt to speken short and pleyn	
That ech of yow / to shorte with oure weye	
In this viage / shal tellen tales tweye	telle
	209*r*

	ELLESMERE
To Caunterburyward / I mene it so	Caunterburyward /
And homward / he shal tellen othere two	
Of auentures / þat whilom haue bifalle	that han
And which of yow / þat bereth hym best of alle	that
That is to seyn / that telleth in this cas	caas
Tales of best sentence / and moost solas	solaas
Shal haue a Souper / at oure aller cost /	soper cost
Here in this place / sittynge by this post	Heere
Whan that we come agayn / fro Caunterbury	agayn Caunterbury
And for to make yow / the moore mury	
I wol my self goodly wit yow ryde	self / with
Right at myn owene cost and be youre gyde	Right youre
And who so wole / my Iuggement with seye	withseye
Shal paye / al that we spende by the weye	spenden
And if ye vouche sauf / þat it be so	sauf that
Tel me anoon / with outen wordes mo	anon /
And I wol erly / shape me ther fore	therfore
¶This thyng was graunted / and oure othes swore	graunted
With ful glad herte / and preyden hym also	
That he wolde vouche sauf / for to do so	
And that he wolde been / oure gouernour	he / been gouernour
And of oure tales / Iuge and reportour	Reportour
And sette a Souper / at a certeyn prys	soper pris
And we wol ruled been / at his deuys	we / reuled been
In heigh and logh / and thus by oon assent	21 ¶In heigh and lough /
We been acorded / to his Iuggement	
And ther vp on / the wyn was fet anoon	anon
We dronken / and to reste wente echon	echon
With outen / any lenger taryynge	
¶A morwe / whan þat day bigan to sprynge	A day / gan for to
Vp roos oure hoost and was oure aller cok	
And gadred vs / togydres in a flok /	gadrede vs togidre / alle in a flok
And forth we ryden / a litel moore than pas	riden / paas
Vn to the wateryng of Seint Thomas	
And there oure hoost / bigan his hors areste	hoost
And seyde / lordes / herkneth if yow leste	seyde lordynges /
¶Ye woot youre forward / and it yow recorde	foreward /
If euensong / and morwesong acorde	morwesong accorde
Lat se now / who shal telle the firste tale	
As euere mote I drynke wyn / or Ale	drynke / wyn
	219v

To Caunterbury ward I mene it so
And homward he shal tellen othere two
Of auentures pt whilom haue bifalle
And which of yow pt bereth hym best of alle
That is to seyn that telleth in this cas
Tales of best sentence and moost solas
Shal haue a souper at oure aller cost
Heere in this place sittynge by this post
Whan that we come agayn fro Caunterbury
And for to make yow the moore mury
I wol my self goodly with yow ryde
Right at myn owene cost and be youre gyde
And who so wole my juggement withseye
Shal paye al that we spende by the weye
And if ye vouche sauf pt it be so
Tel me anoon with outen wordes mo
And I wol erly shape me ther fore
This thyng was graunted and oure othes swore
With ful glad herte and preyden hym also
That he wolde vouche sauf for to do so
And that he wolde been oure gouernour
And of oure tales juge and reportour
And sette a souper at a certeyn prys
And we wol reuled been at his deuys
In heigh and lough and thus by oon assent
We been acorded to his juggement
And ther vp on the wyn was fet anoon
We dronken and to reste wente echon
With outen any lenger taryynge
A morwe whan pt day bigan to sprynge
Vp roos oure hoost and was oure aller cok
And gadred vs togydres in a flok
And forth we ryden a litel moore than pas
Vn to the wateryng of Seint Thomas
And there oure hoost bigan his hors areste
And seyde lordes herkneth if yow leste
Ye woot youre forward and it yow recorde
If euensong and morwesong acorde
Lat se now who shal telle the firste tale
As euere mote I drynke wyn or ale

Who so be rebel to my juggement
Shal paye for al that by the wey is spent
Now draweth cut er þt we ferrer twynne
He which þt hath the shorteste shal bigynne
Sire knyght quod he my mayster and my lord
Now draweth cut for that is myn acord
Cometh neer quod he my lady Prioresse
And ye sire Clerk lat be youre shamefastnesse
Ne studieth noght ley hond to euery man
Anoon to drawen euery wight bigan
And shortly for to tellen as it was
Were it by auenture or sort or cas
The sothe is this the cut fil to the knyght
Of which ful blithe and glad was euery wight
And telle he moste his tale as was resoun
By forward and by composicioun
As ye han herd what nedeth wordes mo
And whan this goode man saugh þt it was so
As he þt wys was and obedient
To kepe his forward by his free assent
He seyde syn I shal bigynne the game
What wel come be the cut in goddes name
Now lat vs ryde and herkneth what I seye
And with that word we ryden forth oure weye
And he bigan with right a murye cheere
His tale anoon and seyde as ye may heere

Iamque domos patrias Scithice post aspera gentis
Prelia laurigero &c

Here bigynneth the knyghtes tale

Whilom as olde stories tellen vs
Ther was a duc þt highte Theseus
Of Athenes he was lord and gouernour
And in his tyme swich a conquerour
That gretter was ther noon vnder the sonne
Ful many a riche contree hadde he wonne
What with his wysdom and his chiualrye
He conquered al the regne of Femenye

Who so be rebel / to my Iuggement
Shal paye / for al / that by the wey is spent
Now draweth cut er *þat* we ferrer twynne
He which *þat* hath the shorteste / shal bigynne
¶Sire knyght quod he / my mayster and my lord
Now draweth cut for that is myn acord
Cometh neer quod he / my lady Prioresse
And ye sire Clerc. lat be youre shamefastnesse
Ne studieth noght ley hond to / euery man
¶Anoon to drawen / euery wight bigan
And shortly / for to tellen / as it was
Were it by auenture / or sort or cas
The sothe is this / the Cut fil to the knyght
Of which ful blithe and glad was euery wight
And telle he moste his tale / as was resoun
By forward / and by composiciou*n*
As ye han herd / what nedeth wordes mo
And whan this goode man / saugh *þat* it was so
As he / *þat* wys was / and obedient
To kepe his forward / by his free assent
He seyde / syn I shal bigynne the game
What wel come be the Cut in goddes name
Now lat vs ryde / and herkneth what I seye
And with that word / we ryden forth oure weye
And he bigan / with right a murye cheere
His tale anoon / and seyde as ye may heere

¶Iamq*ue* domos patria Scithice post asp*er*a
gentis prelia laurigero

W Here bigynneth / the Knyghtes tale

Whilom / as olde stories tellen vs
Ther was a duc *þat* highte Theseus
Of Atthenes / he was lord and gouernour
And in his tyme / swich a conquerour
That gretter was ther noon vnder the sonne
Ful many a riche contree / hadde he wonne
What with his wysdom / and his chiualrye
He conquered / al the regne of femenye

ELLESMERE

be / rebel
al *þat* spent
draweth
He / shorteste
Sire knyght lord
cut / accord
sire clerk /
noght / to
Anon wight
tellen
cut knyght
which / wyght
A telle resou*n*
foreward /
An whan
that was
foreward /
What cut / a goddes
with
right myrie
anon / seyde in this manere

Iam*que* domos patrias Scithice post aspera
gentis prelia laurigero *et cetera.*[1]

¶Heere bigynneth the Knyghtes tale

WHilom / stories /
gou*er*nour
tyme Conquerour
gretter / Sonne
contree
chiualrie
Femenye

1 ¶Knyght *10r.* Miniature of Knight in right margin.

	ELLESMERE
That whilom / was ycleped Scithia	
And wedded / the queene ypolita	wedded
And broghte hire hom with hym / in his contree	hir*e* hoom w*ith* hym
With muchel glorie / and greet solempnitee	solempnytee
And eek / hir yonge suṣter Emelye	eekꝰ hir faire suster
And thus with victorie / and with melodye	thus / victorie
Lete I this noble ducꝰ to Atthenes ryde	duc /
And al his hoostꝰ. in armes hym bisyde	hoostꝰ Armes
¶And c*er*tes / if it nere to longꝰ to heere	nere / long
I wolde haue toold / fully the manere	wolde yow haue
How / wonnen was the regne of Femenye	
By Theseus / and by his Chiualrye	chiualrye
And of the grete bataille / for the nones	bataille
Bitwixen Atthenes / and Amazones	Atthenes
And how assegeged was ypolita	asseged
The faire hardy queene of Scithia	
And of the feste / þ*at* was at hir weddynge	
And of the tempestꝰ at hir hom comynge	tempest / hoom
But al that thyngꝰ I moot as now forbere	
I haue god woot / a large feeld to ere	
And wayke / been the oxen in my plogh	wayke been / Oxen Plougħ
The remenant of the tale / is long ynogh	ynougħ
I wol nat letten eek / noon of this route	eekꝰ
Lat euery felawe / telle his tale aboute	
And lat se now / who shal the souper Wynne	soper wynne
And ther I lefte / I wol ayein bigynne	.I ayeyn[2]
Incipitꝰ narracio	
This ducꝰ of whom I make menciou*n*	mencioun [¶Narratꝰ]
Whanne he was come / almoost to the town	Whan almoost vn to toun
In al his wele / and in his mooste pryde	pride
He was war / as he caste his eye asyde	warꝰ aside
Wher þ*at* ther kneled / in the heighe weye	Where that kneled the weye
A compaignye of ladyes / tweye and tweye	
Ech after oother / clad in clothes blake	3
But swich a cry / and swich a wo they make	
That in this world / nys creature lyuynge	
That herde / swich another waymentynge	

[2] No break in El.

[3]¶Knygħtꝰ *10v*

That whilom was ycleped Scithia
And wedded the queene ypolita
And broghte hire hom with hym in his contree
With muchel glorie and greet solempnytee
And eek hir yonge suster Emelye
And thus with victorie and with melodye
Lete I this noble duc to Atthenes ryde
And al his hoost in armes hym bisyde
And certes if it nere to long to heere
I wolde haue toold fully the manere
How wonnen was the regne of ffemenye
By Theseus and by his chiualrye
And of the grete bataille for the nones
Bitwixen Atthenes and Amazones
And how asseged was ypolita
The faire hardy queene of Scithia
And of the feste þt was at hir weddynge
And of the tempest at hir hom comynge
But al that thyng I moot as now forbere
I haue god woot a large feeld to ere
And wayke been the oxen in my plogh
The remenant of the tale is long ynogh
I wol nat letten eek noon of this route
Lat euery felawe telle his tale aboute
And lat se now who shal the soper wynne
And ther I lefte I wol ayein bigynne

Incipit narracio

This duc of whom I make mencion
Whanne he was come almoost to the toun
In al his wele and in his mooste pryde
He was war as he caste his eye asyde
Wher þt ther kneled in the heighe weye
A compaignye of ladyes tweye and tweye
Ech after oother clad in clothes blake
But swich a cry and swich a wo they make
That in this world nys creature lyuynge
That herde swich another waymentynge

And of this cry they nolde neuere stenten
Til they the reynes of his brydel henten
What folk been ye þt at myn hom comynge
Perturben so my feste with cryynge
Quod Theseus haue ye so greet envie
Of myn honour that thus compleyne & crye
Or who hath yow mysboden or offended
And telleth me if it may been amended
And why þt ye been clothed thus in blak
The eldeste lady of hem alle spak
Whan she hadde swowned wt a deedly cheere
That it was routhe for to seen and heere
She seyde lord to whom ffortune hath yiuen
Victorie and as a Conquerour to lyuen
Noght greueth vs youre glorie and youre honour
But we biseken mercy and socour
Haue mercy on oure wo and oure distresse
Som drope of pitee thurgh thy gentillesse
Vp on vs wrecched wommen lat thow falle
ffor certes lord ther is noon of vs alle
That she ne hath been a duchesse or a queene
Now be we caytyues as it is wel seene
Thanked be ffortune and hir false wheel
That noon estaat assureth to been weel
Now certes lord to abiden youre presence
Heere in this temple of the goddesse Clemence
We haue been waytynge al this fourtenyght
Now help vs lord sith it is in thy myght
I wrecche which þt wepe and waille thus
Was whilom wyf to kyng Cappaneus
That starf at Thebes cursed be the day
And alle we þt been in this array
And maken al this lamentacioun
We losten alle oure housbondes at that town
Whil þt the seege ther aboute lay
And yet now the olde Creon weylaway
That lord is now of Thebes the Citee
ffulfild of Ire and of Iniquitee
He for despit and for his tyrannye
To doon the dede bodyes vileynye

	ELLESMERE
And of this cry / they nolde neu*er*e stenten	neuere
Til they / the reynes of his brydel henten	
¶What folk been ye / *þat* at myn hom comynge	that
P*er*turben so my feste / with cryynge	criynge
Quod Theseus / haue ye so greet envie	enuye
Of myn honour / that thus compleyne *and* crye	*þat* and
Or who hath yow mysboden / or offended	yow / mysboden
And telleth me / if it may been amended	
And why *þat* ye / been clothed thus in blak /	why / ye been / blak
The eldeste lady / of hem alle spak	¶The lady spak
Whan she hadde swowned / *with* a deedly cheere	
That it was routhe / for to seen and heere	
¶She seyde / lord / to whom Fortune hath yiuen	And seyde yeuen
Victorie / and as a Conquerour to lyuen	
Noght greueth vs youre glorie / and youre hono*ur*	Nat vs / glorie honour
But we biseken / mercy and socour	we / biseken
Haue mercy on oure wo / and oure distresse	
Som drope of pitee / thurgh thy gentillesse	
Vp on vs wrecched wommen / lat thow falle	wo*m*men / thou
For c*er*tes lord / ther is noon of vs alle	certes
That she ne hath been / a duchesse / or a queene	
Now be we caytyues / as it is wel seene	
Thanked be Fortune / and hir false wheel	hir*e*
That noon estaat assureth to been weel	be
Now certes lord / to abiden your*e* p*re*sence	And c*er*tes abyden youre
Heere in this temple / of the goddesse clemence	in the temple /
We haue been waytynge / al this fourtenyght	han waitynge / fourtenyght
Now help vs lord / syth it is in thy myght	sith myght
¶I wrecche / which *þat* wepe / and waille thus	wepe and crie thus
Was whilom wyf / to kyng Cappaneus	kyng
That starf at Thebes / cursed be the day	be that day
And alle we / *þat* been in this array	that
And maken / al this lamentacioun	lamentaciou*n*
We losten alle oure housbondes / at that town	losten / housbondes toun
Whil *þat* the sege / ther aboute lay	that seege /
And yet now / the olde Creon weylaway	now Creon
That lord is now / of Thebes the Citee	
Fulfild of Ire / and of Iniquitee	
He for despit and for his tyrannye	tirannye
To doon / the dede bodyes vileynye	do /

¶The Knyght ¶	ELLESMERE
Of alle oure lordes / whiche þat been slawe	that
Hath alle the bodyes / on an heepe ydrawe	He hath
And wol nat suffren hem / by noon assent	
Neyther to been yburyed / nor ybrent	Neither yburyed
But maketh houndes / ete hem in despit	4
And with that word / with outen moore respit	*with*
They fillen gruf and cryden pitously	criden
Haue / on vs wrecched wommen / som mercy	Haue wommen /
And lat oure sorwe / synken in thyn herte	
¶This gentil duc doun from his courser sterte	
With herte pitous / whan he herde hem speke	
Hym thoughte / þat his herte wolde breke	thoughte /
Whan he saugh hem / so pitous / and so maat	saugh pitous
That whilom weren / of so greet estaat	
And in hise armes / he hem alle vp hente	his Armes /
And hem conforteth / in ful good entente	
And swoor his ooth / as he was trewe knyght	
He wolde doon / so ferforthly his myght	
Vp on the tiraunt Creon / hem to wreke	
That al the peple of Grece / sholde speke	
How Creon was / of Theseus yserued	Creon / was
As he þat hadde his deeth / ful wel disserued	hadde / deeth deserued
And right anoon / with outen moore abood	right *with*
His baner he desplayeth / and forth rood	Baner deplayeth
To Thebesward / and al his oost bisyde	Thebesward / hoost biside
No neer Atthenes / wolde he go ne ryde	ride
Ne take his ese / fully half a day	
But onward in his wey / that nyght he lay	onward on his nyght
And sente anoon / ypolita the queene	anon /
And Emelye / hir yonge suster sheene	
Vn to the town of Atthenes / to dwelle	toun Atthenes
And forth he ryt ther nys namoore to telle	rit ther is namoore
¶The rede statue of Mars / with spere and targe	The Statue *with*
So shyneth / in his white Baner large	baner
That alle the feeldes / glitren vp and doun	glyteren
And by his Baner / born was his penoun	born is his
Of gold ful ryche / in which ther was ybete	riche /
The Mynotaur / which þat he wan in Crete	he slough in
¶Thus ryt this duc. thus ryt this conquerour	rit duc rit Conquerour
And in his oost / of Chiualrye the flour	hoost Chiualrie

4¶Knyght *11r*

Of alle oure lordes / whiche yt been yslawe
Hath alle the bodyes / on an heep ydrawe
And wol nat suffren hem / by noon assent
Neyther to been yburyed / nor ybrent
But maketh houndes / ete hem in despit
And with that word / with outen moore respit
They fillen gruf / and cryden pitously
Haue on vs wrecched wommen / som mercy
And lat oure sorwe / synken in thyn herte
¶ This gentil duc / doun from his courser sterte
With herte pitous / whan he herde hem speke
Hym thoughte / yt his herte wolde breke
Whan he saugh hem / so pitous and so maat
That whilom weren / of so greet estaat
And in hise armes / he hem alle vp hente
And hem conforteth / in ful good entente
And swoor his ooth / as he was trewe knyght
He wolde doon / so ferforthly his myght
Vp on the tiraunt Creon / hem to wreke
That al the peple of Grece / sholde speke
How Creon was of Theseus / yserued
As he yt hadde his deeth / ful wel disserued
And right anoon / with outen moore abood
His baner he desplayeth / and forth rood
To Thebes ward / and al his oost bisyde
No neer Atthenes / wolde he go ne ryde
Ne take his ese / fully half a day
But onward in his wey / that nyght he lay
And sente anoon / Ypolita the queene
And Emelye hir yonge suster sheene
Vn to the town of Atthenes / to dwelle
And forth he ryt / ther nys namoore to telle
¶ The rede statue of Mars / with spere and targe
So shyneth in his white baner large
That alle the feeldes / glyteren vp and doun
And by his baner / born was his penoun
Of gold ful ryche / in which ther was ybete
The Mynotaur / which yt he wan in Crete
¶ Thus ryt this duc / thus ryt this conquerour
And in his oost / of chiualrye the flour

Til yt he cam to Thebes / and alighte
ffaire in a feeld / ther as he thoghte fighte
But shortly / for to speken of this thyng
With Creon / which yt was of Thebes kyng
He faught / and slough hym manly / as a knyght
In pleyn bataille / and putte the folk to flyght
And by assaut / he wan the Citee after
And rente adoun / bothe wal / and sparre and rafter
And to the ladyes / he restored agayn
The bones of hir freendes / yt weere slayn
To doon obsequies / as was tho the gyse
But it weere al to long / for to deuyse
The grete clamour / and the waymentynge
That the ladyes made / at the brennynge
Of the bodies / and the grete honour
That Theseus / the noble conquerour
Dooth to the ladys / whan they from hym wente
But shortly / for to telle is myn entente
Whan yt this worthy duc / this Theseus
hath Creon slayn / and wonne Thebes thus
Stille in that feeld / he took al nyght his reste
And dide with al the [illegible] contree / as hym leste
To ransake in the taas [illegible] of bodies dede
hem for to strepe / of harneys / and of wede
The pilours / diden bisynesse and cure
After the bataille / and disconfiture
And so bifel / in the taas they founde
Thurgh girt / with many a greuous blody wounde
Two yonge knyghtes / liggynge by and by
Bothe in oon armes / wroght ful richely
Of whiche two / Arcita highte that oon
And that oother knyght / highte Palamon
Nat fully quyk / ne fully deed / they weere
But by hir cote armures / and by hir geere
The heraudes / knewe hem best in special
As they yt weren / of the blood roial
Of Thebes / and of sustren two yborn
Out of the taas / the pilours han hem torn
And han hem caryed / softe vn to the tente
Of Theseus / and he ful soone hem sente

	ELLESMERE
Til *þat* he cam to Thebes / and alighte	Thebes alighte
Faire in a feeld / ther as he thoghte fighte	thoughte fighte
¶But shortly / for to speken of this thyng	But
With Creon / which *þat* was of Thebes kyng	Creon /
He faught and slow him manly / as a knyght	faught slough manly
In pleyn bataille / and putte the folk to flyght	folk flyght
And by assaut he wan the Citee after	
And rente adoun / bothe wal / and sparre / and rafter	wall*e* sparre *and*
And to the ladyes / he restored agayn	
The bones / of hir freendes / *þat* were slayn	hir housbondes that weren
To doon obsequies / as was tho the gyse	
But it weere al to long for to deuyse	were longe /
The grete clamour / and the waymentynge	5
That the ladyes made / at the brennynge	
Of the bodies / and the grete honour	
That Theseus / the noble Conquerour	
Dooth to the ladys / whan they from hym wente	ladyes /
But shortly / for to telle is myn entente	shortly telle /
¶Whan *þat* this worthy duc this Theseus	
Hath Creon slayn / and wonne Thebes thus	Creon
Stille in that feeld / he took al nyght his reste	nyght
And dide with al the contree / as hym leste	wi*th*
¶To ransake in the taas / of bodies dede	of the bodyes
Hem for to strepe / of harneys / and of wede	harneys
The pilours / diden bisynesse / and cure	bisynesse
After the bataille / and disconfiture	bataille
And so bifel / in the taas they founde	bifel / *þat* in
Thurgh girt with many a greuous blody wownde	Thurgh wounde
Two yonge knyghtes / liggynge by and by	knyghtes /
Bothe in oon armes / wroght ful richely	Armes / wroght
Of whiche two / Arcita highte that oon	highte
And that oother knyght highte Palamon	knyght /
Nat fully quyk / ne fully deed they weere	quyke / dede were
But by hir Cote armures / and by hir geere	CoteArmures / gere
The heraudes / knewe hem best in special	
As they *þat* weren / of the blood roial	
Of Thebes / and of sustren two yborn	
Out of the taas / the pilours han hem torn	
And han hem caryed / softe vn to the tente	caried /
Of Theseus / and he ful soone hem sente	and ful soone he hem

5 ¶Knyght *11v*

Hengwrt	ELLESMERE
To Atthenes / to dwellen in prisou*n*	
P*er*petuelly / he nolde no raunsou*n*	Perpetuelly /
¶And whan this worthy duc / hath thus ydoon	And duc ydon
He took his oost / and hom he ryt anoon	hoost hoom he rood anon
With laurer corouned / as a conquerour	crowned / Conquerour
And there he lyueth / in ioye / and in honour	ther ioye
Terme of his lyf / what nedeth wordes mo	of lyue /
And in a tour / in angwissh and in wo	tour angwissh
Dwellen this Palamon / and eek Arcite	This Palamon / and his felawe Arcite
For eu*er*e moore / ther may no gold hem quyte	eu*er*emoore / quite
¶This passeth yeer by yeer / and day by day	passeth /
Til it fil ones / in a morwe of May	
That Emelye / þat fairer was to seene	sene
Than is the lilie / vp on his stalke greene	lylie / vpon grene
And fressher than the May / with floures newe	fressher *with*
For with the Rose colour stroof hir hewe	*with* hir*e*
I noot which was / the fairer of hem two	noot was the fyner of
Er it were day / as was hir wone to do	
She was arysen / and al redy dight	arisen / dight
For May wol haue / no slogardye a nyght	slogardrie nyght
The sesou*n* pryketh / euery gentil herte	6 sesou*n* / priketh /
And maketh it out of his sleep to sterte	maketh hym / out slep*e*
And seith arys / and do thyn obseruance	obseruau*n*ce
This maketh Emelye / haue remembrance	maked remembrau*n*ce
To doon honour to May / and for to ryse	
Yclothed was she fressh / for to deuyse	she / fressh
Hir yelow heer / was broyded in a tresse	
Bihynde hir bak a yerde long I gesse	bak /
And in the gardyn / at the sonne vp riste	
She walketh vp and doun / and as hir liste	hir*e*
She gadreth floures / party white and rede	gadereth floures party /
To make a subtil gerland for hir hede	gerland hir*e*
And as an Aungel / heuenysshly she soong	heuenysshly
¶The grete tour / þat was so thikke and strong	The stroong
Which of the Castel / was the chief dongeou*n*	
Ther as the knyghtes / weren in prisou*n*	knyghtes /
Of whiche I tolde yow / and tellen shal	
Was euene ioynant / to the gardyn wal	ioynant
Ther as this Emelye / hadde hir pleyyng	pleyynge
Bright was the sonne / and cleer / in that mornyng	Bright so*n*ne / *and* cleer that morwenynge

6¶Knyght *12r*

To Atthenes / to dwellen in prison
Perpetuelly / he nolde no raunson
And whan this worthy duc / hath thus ydoon
He took his oost / and hom he rit anoon
With laurer corouned / as a conquerour
And there he lyueth in ioye / and in honour
Terme of his lyf / what nedeth wordes mo
And in a tour / in angwyssh and in wo
Dwellen this Palamon / and eek Arcite
For eue moore / ther may no gold hem quyte
This passeth yeer by yeer / and day by day
Til it fil ones / in a morwe of May
That Emelye / þt fairer was to seene
Than is the lilie / vp on his stalke greene
And fressher than the May / with floures newe
For with the rose colour / stroof hir hewe
I noot which was / the fairer of hem two
Er it were day / as was hir wone to do
She was arisen / and al redy dight
For May wol haue / no slogardye a nyght
The sesoun priketh euery gentil herte
And maketh it / out of his sleep to sterte
And seith arys / and do thyn obseruaunce
This maketh Emelye haue remembraunce
To doon honour to May / and for to ryse
yclothed was she fressh / for to deuyse
Hir yelow heer / was broyded in a tresse
Bihynde hir bak / a yerde long I gesse
And in the gardyn / at the sonne vp riste
She walketh vp and doun / and as hir liste
She gadreth floures / party white and rede
To make a subtil gerland for hir hede
And as an Aungel / heuenysshly she soong
The grete tour / þt was so thikke and strong
Which of the Castel / was the chief dongeoun
Ther as the knyghtes / weren in prisoun
Of whiche I tolde yow / and tellen shal
Was euene ioynant / to the gardyn wal
Ther as this Emelye / hadde hir pleyyng
Bright was the sonne / and cleer in that morwenyng

And Palamon the woful prisoner
As was his wone by leue of his gayler
Was risen and romed in a chambre an heigh
In which he al the noble Citee seigh
And eek the gardyn ful of braunches grene
Ther as the fresshe Emelye the sheene
Was in hir walk and romed vp and down
This sorweful prisoner this Palamon
Gooth in the chambre romyng to and fro
And to hym self compleynyng of his wo
That he was born ful ofte he seyde allas
And so bifel by auenture or cas
That thurgh a wyndow thikke of many a barre
Of Iren greet and square as any sparre
He caste his eye vp on Emelya
And ther with al he bleynte and cryde a
As though he stongen were vn to the herte
And with that cry Arcite anon vp sterte
And seyde Cosyn myn what eyleth thee
That art so pale and deedly on to see
Why cridestow who hath thee doon offence
ffor goddes loue tak al in pacience
Oure prison for it may noon oother be
ffortune hath yeuen vs this aduersitee
Som wikked aspect or disposicion
Of Saturne by som constellacion
Hath yeuen vs this al though we hadde it sworn
So stood the heuene whan þt we were born
We moste endure it this is the short and playn
This Palamon answerde and seyde agayn
Cosyn for sothe of this opinion
Thow hast a vayn ymaginacion
This prison caused me noght to crye
But I was hurt right now thurgh out myn ye
In to myn herte that wol my bane be
The fairnesse of that lady þt I se
Yond in the gardyn romen to and fro
Is cause of al my cryyng and my wo
I noot wher she be womman or goddesse
But Venus is it soothly as I gesse

	ELLESMERE
And Palamon / this woful prisoner	And this Palamou*n* /
As was his wone / by leue of his Gailler	gayler
Was risen / and romed in a chambre anheigh	romed / an heigħ
In which / he al the noble Citee seigh	seigħ
And eek the gardyn / ful of braunches greene	grene
Ther as / the fresshe Emelye the sheene	as this fressħe shene
Was in hir walk / and romed vp and down	walk⁊ doun
This sorweful prisoner / this Palamou*n*	
Gooth in the chambre / romyng to and fro	Goth romynge
And to hym self / compleynyng⁊ of his wo	compleynynge
That he was born / ful ofte he seyde allas	
And so bifel / by auenture / or cas	auenture
That thurgh a wyndow / thikke of many a barre	
Of Iren greet⁊ and square as any sparre	Iren / greet
He caste his eye / vp on Emelya	EmelyA
And ther with al he bleynte / and cryde .A.	bleynte cride
As thogh / he stongen weere / vn to the herte	though were
¶And with that cry / Arcite anoon vp sterte	And anon
And seyde cosyn myn / what eyleth thee	
That art so pale / and deedly on to see	
Why cridestow / who hath thee doon offence	
For goddes loue / tak al in pacience	taak
Oure p*ri*son / for it may noon oother be	prisou*n* /
Fortune / hath yeuen vs this aduersitee	Adu*er*sitee
Som wikked aspect⁊ or disposiciou*n*	wikke aspect /
Of Saturne / by som constellaciou*n*	
Hath yeuen vs this / al thogh we hadde it sworn	though
So stood the heuene / whan *þat* we were born	
We mote endure it⁊ this is the short and playn	7 moste endure / this
This Palamou*n* answerde / and seyde agayn	¶This Palamon
¶Cosyn for sothe / of this opiniou*n*	Cosyn
Thow hast⁊ a vayn ymaginaciou*n*	hast veyn
This prisou*n* / caused me noght to crye	prison nat for to
But I was hurt right now / thurgh out myn Iye	hurt⁊ rigħt now eye
In to myn herte / that wol my bane be	
The fairnesse / of that lady *þat* I se	see
Yond in the gardyn / romen to and fro	
Is cause / of al my cryyng⁊ and my wo	criyng⁊
I noot⁊ wher she be womman / or goddesse	be / wo*m*man
But Venus / is it soothly / as I gesse	Venus it / soothly

7¶Knygħt *12v*

	ELLESMERE
And ther with al / on knees down he fil	doun
And seyde / Venus if it be thy wil	seyde Venus /
Yow in this gardyn / thus to t*ra*nsfigure	
Bifore me / sorweful wrecched creature	wrecche
Out of this prisou*n* / help þ*at* we may scape	helpe scapen
And if so be / my destynee be shape	shapen
By eterne word / to dyen in prisou*n*	
Of oure lynage / haue som compassiou*n*	
That is so lowe ybroght' by tirannye	ybroght'
¶And with that word / Arcite gan espye	And
Wher*e* as this lady / romed to and fro	Wher
And with that sighte / hir beautee hurte hym so	wit*h* sigħte /
That if þ*at* Palamon / was wounded soore	that Palamon / wounded
Arcite is hurt'. as muche as he / or moore	hurt'
And with a syk /. he seyde pitously	wit*h* sigħ /
The fresshe beautee / sleeth me sodeynly	
Of hir*e* / þ*at* rometh in the yonder place	that rometh /
And but' I haue / hir mercy / *and* hir grace	but mercy and
That I may seen hir*e* / at the leeste weye	atte leeste
I nam but deed / ther nys namoore to seye	ther is namoore
¶This Palamon / whan he tho wordes herde	
Despitously / he loked / and answerde	Dispitously / looked
Wheither seistow this / in ernest' or in pley	pley /
¶Nay quod Arcite / in ernest by my fey	
God help me so / me list ful yuele pleye	help*e*
This Palamon / gan knytte his browes tweye	¶This
¶It were to thee quod he / no greet honour	It nere quod he to thee /
For to be fals / ne for to be traytour	traitour
To me / that am thy cosyn *and* thy brother	þ*at* and
Ysworn ful depe / and ech of vs til oother	
That neuere / for to dyen in the peyne	neu*ere* /
Til þ*at* the deeth / departe shal vs tweyne	þ*at* deeth /
Neither of vs / in loue to hyndre oother	
Ne in noon oother caas / my leeue brother	cas /
But þ*at* thow sholdest' trewely forthre me	thou forthren
In euery caas / as I shal forthren thee	cas /
This was thyn ooth / and myn also certeyn	8
I woot right wel / thow darst it nat withseyn	rigħt thou
Thus artow of my conseil / out of doute	conseil
And now / thow woldest falsly been aboute	woldest'
	[8]¶Knygħt' | *13r*

And ther with al on knees adoun he fil
And seyde Venus if it be thy wil
Yow in this gardyn thus to transfigure
Bifore me sorweful wrecched creature
Out of this prisoun help þt we may scape
And if so be my destynee be shape
By eterne word to dyen in prisoun
Of oure lynage haue som compassioun
That is so lowe ybroght by tirannye
And with that word Arcite gan espye
Wher as this lady romed to and fro
And with that sighte hir beautee hurte hym so
That if þt Palamon was wounded sore
Arcite is hurt as muche as he or moore
And with a sik he seyde pitously
The fresshe beautee sleeth me sodeynly
Of hire þt rometh in the yonder place
And but I haue hir mercy & hir grace
That I may seen hire at the leeste weye
I nam but deed ther nys namoore to seye
This Palamon whan he tho wordes herde
Despitously he looked and answerde
Wheither seistow this in ernest or in pley
Nay quod Arcite in ernest by my fey
God help me so me list ful yuele pleye
This Palamon gan knytte his browes tweye
It were to thee quod he no greet honour
For to be fals ne for to be traytour
To me that am thy cosyn & thy brother
Ysworn ful depe and ech of vs til oother
That neuere for to dyen in the peyne
Til þt the deeth departe shal vs tweyne
Neither of vs in loue to hyndre oother
Ne in noon oother cas my leeue brother
But þt thow sholdest trewely forthren me
In euery cas as I shal forthren thee
This was thyn ooth and myn also certeyn
I woot right wel thow darst it nat withseyn
Thus artow of my conseil out of doute
And now thow woldest falsly been aboute

To loue my lady / whom I loue and serue
And euere shal / til þt myn herte sterue
Now certes false Arcite thow shalt nat so
I loued hire first / and tolde thee my wo
As to my conseil / and my brother sworn
To forthre me / as I haue told biforn
For which thow art ybounden as a knyght
To helpe me / if it laye in thy myght
Or ellis artow fals / I dar wel sayn
This Arcite ful proudly spak agayn
¶ Thow shalt quod he be rather fals than I
And thow art fals / I telle thee outrely
For paramour / I loued hire first er thow
What wiltow seyn / thow woost nat yet now
Wheither she be a womman or goddesse
Thyn is affeccion of holynesse
And myn is loue / as to a creature
For which I tolde thee myn auenture
As to my cosyn / and my brother sworn
I pose that thow louedest hire biforn
Wostow nat wel / the olde clerkes sawe
That who shal yeue a louere any lawe — Quis legem det amant
Loue is a gretter lawe by my pan
Than may be yeue to any erthely man
And therfore positif lawe / and swich decree
Is broke al day for loue in ech degree
A man moot nedes loue / maugree his heed
He may nat fleen it / thogh he sholde be deed
Al be she mayde / wydwe / or ellis wyf
And eek it is nat likly al thy lyf
To stonden in hir grace / namoore shal I
For wel thow woost thy self verraily
That thow and I been dampned to prisoun
Perpetuelly / vs gayneth no raunsoun
We stryue as dide the houndes for the boon
They foghte al day / and yet hir part was noon
Ther cam a kyte / whil þt they were so wrothe
That bar awey the boon bitwix hem bothe
And therfore at the kynges court my brother
Ech man for hym self / ther is noon oother

	ELLESMERE
To loue my lady / whom I loue and serue	
And euere shal / til þ*at* myn herte sterue	eu*er*e
Now certes false Arcite / thow shalt nat so	Nay c*er*tes
I loued hir*e* first and tolde thee my wo	
As to my conseil / and my brother sworn	and to my
To forthre me / as I haue told biforn	toold
For which / thow art ybounden / as a knyght	thou ybounden knyght
To helpe me / if it laye in thy myght	helpen lay myght
Or ellis artow fals / I dar wel sayn	elles seyn
This Arcite / ful proudly spak agayn	¶This ageyn
¶Thow shalt quod he / be rather fals than I.	Thow I
And thow art fals / I telle thee outrely	thou
For p*ar*amour / I loued hire first er thow	p*ar*amour hir*e*
What wiltow seyn / thow woost nat yet now	thou wistest nat
Wheither she be a womman / or goddesse	be / wo*m*man
Thyn is / affecciou*n* of holynesse	hoolynesse
And myn is loue / as to a creature	as to
For which / I tolde thee myn auenture	
As to my cosyn / and my brother sworn	
I pose / that thow louedest hir*e* biforn	
Wostow nat wel / the olde clerkes sawe	
That who shal / yeue a louere any lawe	That / shal lou*er*e
Loue is a gretter lawe / by my pan	
Than may be yeue / to any erthely man	yeue / of any
And therfore / posityf lawe / and swich decree	positif lawe
Is broke alday for loue / in ech degree	broken loue
A man moot nedes loue / maugree his heed	
He may nat fleen it / thogh he sholde be deed	flee it
Al be she mayde / wydwe / or ellis wyf	mayde / or wydwe / elles
And eek it is nat likly / al thy lyf	likly lyf
To stonden in hir g*ra*ce / namoore shal .I.	grace / I
For wel thow woost thy self v*er*raily	thou seluen verraily
That thow and I / been dampned to prisou*n*	thou be
P*er*petuelly / vs gayneth no raunsou*n*	
We stryue / as dide the houndes for the boon	stryuen / dide / boon
They foghte alday / and yet hir part was noon	foughte al day /
Ther cam a kyte / whil þ*at* they were so wrothe	whil they weren
That bar awey the boon / bitwix hem bothe	And baar bitwixe
And therfore / at the kynges court my brother	
Ech man for hym self / ther is noon oother	

1164 Quis legem det amantibus Hg El

	ELLESMERE
Loue if thee lest'. for I loue / and ay shal	list' loue
And soothly / leue brother this is al	leeue
Heere in this prisou*n* / moote we endure	
And euerich of vs / take his auenture	
¶Greet was the stryf / and long bitwix hem tweye	9 GReet strif / long'
If þat' I hadde leyser for to seye	that hadde /
But to theffect / it happed on a day	theffect'
To telle it yow / as shortly as I may	
A worthy duc'. þat highte Parotheus	duc' that highte P*er*otheus
That felawe was / vn to duc Theseus	was / to
Syn thilke day / þat they were children lyte	that lite
Was come to Atthenes / his felawe to visite	
And for to pleye / as he was wont to do	won
For in this world / he loued no man so	
And he loued hym / as tendrely agayn	als
So wel they loued / as olde bookes sayn	louede /
That whan þat oon was deed / soothly to telle	That'
His felawe wente / and soghte hym down in helle	felawe / soughte doun
But of that storie / list me noght to write	nat
Duc P*ar*otheus / loued wel Arcite	
And hadde hym knowe at Thebes / yeer by yere	Thebes
And finally / at requeste and prayere	preyere
Of P*ar*otheus / with outen any raunsou*n*	
Duc Theseus / hym leet' out of prisou*n*	leet
Frely to goon / wher þat hym liste ouer al	ou*er*
In swich a gyse / as I yow tellen shal	you
This was the forward / pleynly for tendite	¶This
Bitwixe Theseus / and hym Arcite	Bitwixen
That if so weere þat Arcite weere yfounde	were / were
Euere in his lyf' by day / or nyght' or stounde	lif / nyght
In any contree / of this Theseus	
And he weere caught'. it was acorded thus	were caught'
That with a swerd / he sholde lese his heed	
Ther nas noon oother / remedye ne reed	nas / oother remedie
But taketh his leue / and homward he hym spedde	hi*m*
Lat hym be war / his nekke lyth to wedde	war' lith
¶How greet a sorwe / suffreth now Arcite	
The deeth he feeleth / thurgh his herte smyte	
He wepeth / wayleth / cryeth pitously	crieth
To sleen hym self' he wayteth pryuely	self / waiteth p*ri*uely
	9¶Knyght' *13v*

Loue if thee lest . for I loue and ay shal
And soothly leue brother this is al
Heere in this prisoun moote we endure
And euerich of vs take his auenture
Greet was the stryf and long bitwix hem tweye
If þt I hadde leyser for to seye
But to theffect it happed on a day
To telle it yow as shortly as I may
A worthy duc . þt highte Perotheus
That felawe was vn to duc Theseus
Syn thilke day þt they were children lyte
Was come to Athenes his felawe to visite
And for to pleye as he was wont to do
ffor in this world he loued no man so
And he loued hym as tendrely agayn
So wel they loued as olde bookes sayn
That whan þt oon was deed soothly to telle
His felawe wente and soghte hym doun in helle
But of that storie list me noght to write
Duc Potheus loued wel Arcite
And hadde hym knowe at Thebes yeer by yere
And finally at requeste and prayere
Of Potheus with outen any raunsoun
Duc Theseus hym leet out of prisoun
ffrely to goon wher þt hym liste ouer al
In swich a gyse as I yow tellen shal
This was the forward pleynly for tendite
Bitwixe Theseus and hym Arcite
That if so were þt Arcite were yfounde
Euere in his lyf by day or nyght oo stounde
In any contree of this Theseus
And he were caught it was acorded thus
That with a swerd he sholde lese his heed
Ther nas noon oother remedye ne reed
But taketh his leue and homward he hym spedde
Lat hym be war his nekke lyth to wedde
How greet a sorwe suffreth now Arcite
The deeth he feeleth thurgh his herte smyte
He wepeth wayleth cryeth pitously
To sleen hym self he wayteth pryuely

He cryde allas the day þt I was born
Now is my prisoun worse than biforn
Now is me shape eternally to dwelle
Noght in purgatorie but in helle
Allas þt euere knew I Perotheus
For ellis hadde I dwelled with Theseus
Yfetered in his prisoun euermo
Thanne hadde I been in blisse and nat in wo
Oonly the sighte of hire whom þt I serue
Though þt I neuere hir grace may disserue
Wolde haue suffised right ynogh for me
O deere cosyn Palamon quod he
Thyn is the victorie of this auenture
Ful blisfully in prison maystow dure
In prison? nay certes but in paradys
Wel hath Fortune yturned thee the dys
That hast the sighte of hire and I thabsence
For possible is syn thow hast hire presence
And art a knyght a worthy and an able
That by som cas syn Fortune is chaungeable
Thow mayst to thy desir som tyme atteyne
But I that am exiled and bareyne
Of alle grace and in so greet despeir
That ther nys erthe water fyr ne eyr
Ne creature that of hem maked is
That may me helpe or do confort in this
Wel oghte I sterue in wanhope and distresse
Fare wel my lyf my lust and my gladnesse
Allas why pleynen folk so in commune
On purueiance of god or of Fortune
That yeueth hem ful ofte in many a gyse
Wel bettre than they kan hem self deuyse
Som man desireth for to haue richesse
That cause is of his moerdre or greet siknesse
And som man wolde out of his prisoun fayn
That in his hous is of his meynee slayn
Infinite harmes been in this matere
We woot nat what thyng þt we prayen heere
We fare as he þt dronke is as a mous
A dronke man woot wel he hath an hous

But he noot &c

	ELLESMERE
He seyde allas / the day þat I was born	allas / that day þat he was
Now is my prisoun / worse than biforn	
Now is me shape / eternally to dwelle	
Noght in purgatorie / but in helle	Nat in my purgatorie /
Allas / þat euere knew I Parotheus	Perotheus
For ellis / hadde I dwelled with Theseus	elles / hadde I.
Yfettred in his prisoun eueremo	Yfetered
Thanne hadde I been in blisse / and nat in wo	blisse *and*
Oonly the sighte of hire / whom þat I serue	Oonly / sighte
Thogh þat I neuere / hir grace may disserue	Though deserue
Wolde haue suffised / right ynogh for me	han ynough
¶O deere cosyn / Palamon / quod he	O Palamon
Thyn is the victorie / of this auenture	10
Ful blisfully / in prisoun maystow dure	blisfully prisoun maistow
In prison.// / nay certes / but in paradys	prisoun// certes nay / Paradys
Wel hath Fortune / yturned thee / the dys	thee
That hast the sighte of hire / and I thabsence	sighte
For possible is / syn thow hast hire presence	thou hire
And art a knyght a worthy and an able	knyght
That by som caas / syn Fortune is chaungeable	That som cas / syn /
Thow mayst to thy desir / som tyme atteyne	maist
But I / that am exiled and bareyne	þat
Of alle grace / and in so greet despeyr	dispeir
That ther nys Erthe / water / fyr / ne Eyr	erthe / fir eir
Ne creature / that of hem maked is	þat
That may me helpe / or do confort in this	me heele / or doon
Wel oghte I sterue / in wanhope / and distresse	oughte wanhope
Farwel my lyf / my lust and my gladnesse	Farwel / my lif /
¶Allas / why pleynen folk so / in commune	folk so
On purueiance of god / or of Fortune	purueiaunce
That yeueth hem ful ofte / in many a gyse	
Wel bettre / than they kan hem self deuyse	
¶Som man desireth / for to haue richesse	Som han
That cause is ofte / of his moerdre / or gret siknesse	is of greet
And som man wolde / out of his prison fayn	prisoun
That in his hous / is of his meynee slayn	
Infinite harmes / been in this matere	mateere
We woot nat what thyng þat we prayen heere	witen nat what we preyen
We fare as he / þat dronke is as a Mous	faren / he that
A dronke man woot wel / he hath an hous	wel / þat he

But he noot

[10]¶Knyght *14r*

.The Knyght.	ELLESMERE
But he noot' / which the righte wey is thider	noot' rigħte
And to a dronke man / . the wey ⟨is⟩ slider	man / is
And certes / in this world / so faren we	world
We seken faste / after felicitee	
But we goon wrong' ful ofte trewely	often
Thus may we seyn alle / and nameliche .I.	namely I
That wende / and hadde a greet opiniou*n*	
That if I myghte / scapen fro prisou*n*	myghte / escapen / from
Thanne hadde I been in ioye / and p*ar*fit heele	
Ther now / I am exiled fro my wele	That now / exiled /
Syn þ*at* / I may nat seen yow Emelie	þ*at* nat' you Emelye
I nam but deed / ther nys no remedie	remedye
¶Vp on that oother syde Palamon	syde /
Whan þ*at* he wiste / Arcite was agon	
Swich sorwe he maketh / þ*at* the grete tour	
Resowneth / of his yowlyng' and clamour	Resouned / youlyng'
The pure fettres / of his shynes grete	fettres / on his
Were / of his bittre salte teeris wete	Weren / teeres
Allas quod he / Arcita cosyn myn	
Of al oure stryf / god woot' the fruyt is thyn	strif / woot
Thow walkest now / in Thebes at thy large	11 now
And of my wo / thow yeuest litel charge	
Thow mayst' syn thou hast wisdom / and manhede	Thou mayst / wisdom *and*
Assemblen / al the folk' of oure kynrede	alle folk /
And make a werre / so sharp / on this Citee	sharp*e*
That by som auenture / or som tretee	
Thow mayst haue hire / to lady and to wyf	hir*e* wyf'
For whom / þ*at* I moste nedes lese my lyf	lyf'
For as by wey / of possibilitee	For / wey
Sith thow art' at thy large / of prisou*n* free	thou art
And art a lord / greet is thyn auantage	auauntage
Moore than is myn / that sterue her*e* in a cage	þ*at* here
For I moot wepe / and waille whil I lyue	wayle
With al the wo / þ*at* prison may me yeue	W*ith*
And eek w*ith* peyne / þ*at* loue me yeueth also	
That doubleth / al my torment' and my wo	torment /
Ther with / the fyr of Ialousie vp sterte	
With Inne his brest' and hente hym by the herte	hi*m*
So woodly / þ*at* he lyk was to byholde	that biholde
The Boxtree / or the Asshen dede / and colde	dede

[11]¶Knyghtʼ *14v*

But he noot which the righte wey is thider
And to a dronke man the wey slider
And certes in this world so faren we
We seken faste after felicitee
But we goon wrong ful ofte trewely
Thus may we seyn alle and namelich I
That wende and hadde a greet opinion
That if I myghte escapen fro prison
Thanne hadde I been in ioye and pfit heele
Ther now I am exiled fro my wele
Syn þt I may nat seen yow Emelye
I nam but deed ther nys no remedie
Vp on that oother syde Palamon
Whan þt he wiste Arcite was agon
Swich sorwe he maketh þt the grete tour
Resouneth of his youlyng and clamour
The pure fettres of his shynes grete
Were of his bittre salte teerys wete
Allas quod he Arcita cosyn myn
Of al oure stryf god woot the fruyt is thyn
Thow walkest now in Thebes at thy large
And of my wo thow yeuest litel charge
Thow mayst syn thou hast wisdom and manhede
Assemblen al the folk of oure kynrede
And make a werre so sharp on this Citee
That by som auenture or som tretee
Thow mayst haue hire to lady and to wyf
ffor whom þt I moste nedes lese my lyf
ffor as by wey of possibilitee
Sith thow art at thy large of prison free
And art a lord greet is thyn auantage
Moore than is myn that sterue heer in a cage
ffor I moot wepe and waille whil I lyue
With al the wo þt prison may me yeue
And eek with peyne þt loue me yeueth also
That doubleth al my torment and my wo
Ther with the fyr of Ialousie vp sterte
With inne his brest and hente hym by the herte
So woodly þt he lyk was to biholde
The Boxtree or the asshen deede and colde

Thanne seyde he / o cruel goddes þt gouerne
This world / with byndyng of youre word eterne
And writen in the table of atthamaunt
Youre parlement / and youre eterne graunt /
What is mankynde moore vn to yow holde
Than is the sheep / þt rouketh in the folde
For slayn is man / right as another beest /
And dwelleth eek in prison and arrest /
And hath siknesse / and greet aduersitee
And ofte tymes / giltelees pardee
What gouernance is in this prescience
That giltelees / tormenteth innocence
And yet encreeceth this al my penance
That man is bounden to his obseruance
For goddes sake to letten of his wille
Ther as a beest / may al his lust fulfille
And whan a beest is deed / it hath no peyne
But man after his deeth / moot wepe and pleyne
Though in this world / he haue care and wo
With outen doute / it moot stonden so
The answere of this / lete I to dyuynys
But wel I woot / þt in this world greet pyne is
Allas I se a serpent / or a theef
That many a trewe man / hath doon mescheef
Goon at his large / and wher hym list may turne
But I moot been in prison / thurgh Saturne
And eek thurgh Juno / Jalous / and eek wood
That hath destroyed / wel neigh al the blood
Of Thebes / with his waste walles wyde
And Venus sleeth me / on that oother syde
For Jalousie / and fere of hym Arcite
Now wol I stynte / of Palamon a lite
And lete hym in his prison stille dwelle
And of Arcita forth I wol yow telle
The somer / and the nyghtes longe
Encreessen double wise the peynes stronge
Bothe of the louere / and the prisoner
I noot / which hath the wofuller myster
For soothly for to seyn this Palamon
Perpetuelly is dampned to prison

	ELLESMERE
¶Thanne seyde he / o crewel goddes / þat gou*er*ne	crueel goddes
This world / with byndyngꝭ of youre word et*er*ne	wi*th*
And writen / in the table of Atthamau*n*t	writen Atthamauntꝭ
Youre p*ar*lementꝭ. and youre eterne grau*n*tꝭ	p*ar*lementꝭ graunt
What is man kynde / moore vn to yow holde	you
Than is the sheep*e* / þat rowketh in the folde	rouketh
For slayn is man / right as another beestꝭ	
And dwelleth eekꝭ in prison and arrestꝭ	eek / arreestꝭ
And hath siknesse / and greet adu*er*sitee	Adu*er*sitee
And ofte tymes / giltlees pardee	
¶What gouernance / is in this p*re*science	
That giltlees / tormenteth Innocence	
And yetꝭ encreeceth this / al my penance	yet encresseth penaunce
That man is bounden / to his obseruance	obseruau*n*ce
For goddes sake / to letten of his wille	
Ther as a beestꝭ may al his lust fulfille	beest /
And whan a beest is deed / it hath no peyne	deed / he hath
But man after his deeth / moot wepe and pleyne	But after his deeth / man
Thogh in this world / he haue care and wo	Though
With outen doute / it moot stonden so	it may stonden
The answere of this / lete I to diuynys	dyuynys
But wel I wootꝭ þat in this world / greet pyne is	world ys
¶Allas / I se a serpentꝭ or a theef /	Allas /
That many a trewe man / hath doon mescheefꝭ	
Goon at his large / and wher*e* hym lust may turne	where listꝭ
But I moot been in prison / thurgh Saturne	prisou*n* / thurgħ
And eek thurgh Iuno / Ialous / and eek wood	thurgħ Ialous
That hath destroyed / wel neigh al the blood	ny
Of Thebes / with his waste walles wyde	12 hise
And Venus / sleeth me / on that oother syde	me
For Ialousie / and feere / of hym Arcite	fere
¶Now wol I stynte / of Palamon alite	stynte
And lete hym / in his prisou*n* stille dwelle	
And of Arcita / forth I wol yow telle	
¶The Somer / and the nyghtes longe	¶The sonne passeth / and
Encreecen / double wise / the peynes stronge	Encressen
Bothe of the louere / and the prisoner	Bothe /
I nootꝭ which hath / the sorwefuller myster	hath the wofuller mester
For soothly for to seyn / this Palamon	For shortly for Palamou*n*
P*er*petuelly / is dampned to prisou*n*	

12 ¶Knyghtꝭ *15r*

		ELLESMERE
In cheynes / and in fettres / to been deed		cheynes
And Arcite / is exiled / vp on his heed		exiled vpon
For euere mo / as out of that contree		eu*er*e
Ne neueremo / ne shal his lady see		neu*er*e mo / he shal
¶Yow loueris / axe I now / this questiou*n*		YOw loueres / now
Who hath the worse / Arcite / or Palamou*n*		Palamou*n*
That oon may seen his lady / day by day		
But in p*ri*sou*n* / moot he dwelle alway		prison / he moot dwelle
That oother / where hym list⁊ may ride or go		wher
But seen his lady / shal he neuere mo		neueremo
Now demeth as yow list⁊ ye þ*at* kan		that
For I wol telle forth / as .I. bigan[13]		forħ / I[14]
¶Whan þ*at* Arcite / to Thebes comen was		Whan that
Ful ofte a day / he swelte / and seyde allas		swelte
For seen his lady / shal he neu*er*e mo		neueremo
And shortly / to concluden al his wo		
So muchel sorwe / hadde neuere creature		muche
That is ⟨or⟩ shal / whil þ*at* the world may dure		is / or
¶His sleep*e* / his mete / his drynke / is hym biraft⁊		His slep*e* /
That leene he weex / and drye as is a shaft⁊		lene wexeth /
Hise eyen holwe / and grisly to biholde		
His hewe falow / and pale as asshen colde		Assħen
And solitarie he was / and euere alloone		allone
And waillynge al the nyght⁊. makynge his moone		nyght⁊ mone
And if he herde / soong⁊ or Instrument⁊		song⁊
Thanne wolde he wepe / he myghte nat be stent⁊		mygħte
So feble eek were his spiritz / and so lowe		hise spiritz
And chaunged so / þ*at* no man koude knowe		that
His speche / nor his voys / thogh men it herde		speche though
And in his gere / for al the world he ferde		geere /
Nat oonly / lyk the loueris maladye		15 lik
Of Hereos / but rather lyk Manye	Mania	¶Mania]
Engendred / of humour malencolyk⁊		malencolik⁊
Biforn his Celle fantastyk⁊		his owene Celle fantastik⁊
And shortly / turned was / al vp so down		was doun
Bothe habit⁊ and eek disposicioun		habit /
Of hym / this woful louere daun Arcite		hym
¶What sholde I al day / of his wo endite		I / day
Whanne he endured hadde / a yeer / or two		Whan yeer
This cruel torment⁊ and this peyne and wo		crueel *and* wo

[13] No break in Hg.

[14] Break in El followed by:
¶Explicit prima pars
¶Sequitur pars secunda

[15] ¶Knygħt⁊ *15v*

In cheynes and in fettres to been deed
And Arcite is exiled / vp on his heed
ffor euere mo / as out of that contree
Ne neuere mo ne shal his lady see
Yow loueres axe I now / this questioun
Who hath the worse / Arcite / or Palamoun
That oon may seen his lady / day by day
But in prison / moot he dwelle alway
That oother / where hym list / may ryde or go
But seen his lady / shal he neuere mo
Now demeth as yow list / ye þt kan
ffor I wol telle forth / as . I . bigan
Whan þt Arcite / to Thebes comen was
fful ofte a day / he swelte / and seyde allas
ffor seen his lady / shal he neue mo
And shortly / to concluden al his wo
So muchel sorwe / hadde neuere creature
That is or shal / whil þt the world may dure
His sleep / his mete / his drynke / is hym biraft
That lene he wex / and drye as is a shaft
Hise eyen holwe / and grisly to biholde
His hewe falow / and pale as asshen colde
And solitarie he was / and euere allone
And waillynge al the nyght / . makynge his moone
And if he herde / soong / or instrument
Thanne wolde he wepe / he myghte nat be stent
So feble eek were his spiritz / and so lowe
And chaunged so / þt no man koude knowe
His speche / nor his voys / though men it herde
And in his gere / for al the world he ferde
Nat oonly / lyk the loueris maladye
Of Hereos / but rather lyk manye   ymania
Engendred of humour malencolyk
Biforn his celle fantastyk
And shortly / turned was al vp so doun
Bothe habit / and eek disposicioun
Of hym / this woful louere daun Arcite
What sholde I al day / of his wo endite
Whanne he endured hadde / a yeer or two
This cruel torment / and this peyne and wo

At Thebes in his contree as I seyde
Up on a nyght in sleep / as he hym leyde
Hym thoughte / how þt the wynged god Mercurie
Biforn hym stood and bad hym to be murye
His slepy yerde in honde he bar upryghte
An hat he werede / up on his heris brighte
Arrayed was this god / as he took keep
As he was whan þt Argus took his sleep
And seyde hym thus to Atthenes shaltow wende
Ther is thee shapen / of thy wo an ende
And with that word Arcite wook and sterte
Now trewely / how sore þt me smerte
Quod he to Atthenes right now wol I fare
Ne for the drede of deeth / shal I nat spare
To se my lady / þt I love and serve
In hir presence I recche nat to sterve
And with that word / he caughte a greet myrour
And saugh þt chaunged was al his colour
And saugh his visage / al in another kynde
And right anoon / it ran hym in his mynde
That sith his face / was so disfigured
Of maladie / the which he hadde endured
He myghte wel / if þt he bar hym lowe
Lyve in Atthenes / evermoore unknowe
And seen his lady / wel ny day by day
And right anoon he chaunged his array
And cladde hym / as a povre laborer
And al allone / save oonly a squier
That knew his pryvetee / and al his cas
Which was disgised / povrely as he was
To Atthenes is he goon the nexte way
And to the court / he wente up on a day
And at the gate / he profreth his servyse
To drugge and drawe / what so men wol devyse
And shortly of this matere for to seyn
He fil in office / with a chamberleyn
The which þt dwellyng was with Emelye
ffor he was wys / and koude soone espye
Of every servant / which þt serveth here
Wel koude he hewen wode / and water bere

	ELLESMERE
At Thebes in his contree / as I seyde	
Vp on a nyght' in sleep / as he hym leyde	nyħt' sleep*e*
Hym thoughte / how *pat* the wynged god M*er*curye	that' M*er*curie
Biforn hym stood / and bad hym to be murye	murie
His slepy yerde / in honde he bar vp righte	hond riħte
An hat he wered / vp on his herys brighte	werede / vp hise heris briħte
Arrayed was this god / as he took keep*e*	as I took
As he was / whan *pat* Argus took his sleep*e*	
And seyde hym thus / to Atthenes shaltow wende	shaltou
Ther is thee shapen / of thy wo an ende	
¶And with that word / Arcite wook and sterte	And wook'
Now trewely / how sore *pat* me smerte	hou soore
Quod he / to Atthenes right now wol I fare	Atthenes / riħt
Ne for the drede of deeth / shal I nat spare	
To se my lady / *pat* I loue and serue	that
In hir presence / I recche nat to sterue	hir*e*
¶And with that word / he caughte a greet Miro*ur*	w*ith* Mirour
And saugh / *pat* chaunged was al his colour	sauħ /
And saugh his visage / al in another kynde	sauħ
And right anoon / it ran hym in his mynde	riħt anon /
That sith his face / was so disfigured	
Of maladie / the which he hadde endured	maladye /
He myghte wel / if *pat* he bar hym lowe	
Lyue in Atthenes / eu*er*emoore vnknowe	
And seen his lady / wel ny / day by day	ny
And right anoon / he chaunged his array	riħt anon /
And cladde hym / as a poure laborer	
And al allone / saue oonly a Squyer	Squier
That knew his pryuetee / and al his cas	p*ri*uetee /
Which was disgised / pourely as he was	
To Atthenes / is he goon / the nexte way	goon
And to the Court' he wente vp on a day	court'
And at the gate / he p*ro*freth his seruyse	profreth
To drugge and drawe / what so men wol deuyse	
¶And shortly / of this matere / for to seyn	And matere
He fil in office / with a Chambreleyn	Chamberleyn
The which / *pat* dwellyng was w*ith* Emelye	which dwellynge with
For he was wys / and koude soone espye	
Of euery seruant' which *pat* serueth here	16 seruau*n*t that
Wel koude he / hewen wode / and water bere	

16 ¶Knyħt' *16r*

The Knyght	ELLESMERE
For he was yong. and myghty for the nones	yong /
And ther to / he was strong and byg of bones	was long / and big
To doon / what any wight kan hym deuyse	doon / that any wigħt /
A yeer / or two / he was in this seruyse	yeer
Page of the chambre / of Emelie the brighte	Emelye brigħte
And Philostrate / he seyde þ*at* he highte	higħte
¶But half so wel biloued a man / as he	But half / wel / man
Ne was ther neuere in Court of his degree	neu*er*e
He was so gentil / of condiciou*n*	gentil
That thurgh out al the Court was his renou*n*	thurghout
They seiden / þ*at* it were a charitee	seyden / that
That Theseus / wolde enhauncen his degree	
And putten hym / in worshipful seruyse	
Ther as he myghte / his v*er*tu excercise	vertu
And thus with Inne a while / his name is spronge	thus /
Bothe of his dedes / and his goode tonge	hise dedes /
That Theseus / hath taken hym so ner	neer
That of his chambre / he made hym a Squier	
And gaf hym gold / to mayntene his degree	
And eek men broghte hym / out of his contree	eek
Fro yeer to yeer / ful pryuely his rente	From
But honestly / and sleighly / he it spente	But slyly
That no man wondred / how þ*at* he it hadde	
And thre yeer in this wise / his lyf he ladde	lif
And bar hym so / in pees / and ek in werre	eek
Ther was no man / that Theseus hath derre	þ*at*
And in this blisse / lete I now Arcite	
And speke I wole / of Palamon alite	
¶In derknesse / and horrible / and strong p*ri*sou*n*	IN derknesse strong prisou*n*
This seuen yeer / hath seten Palamou*n*	Thise Palamon
Forpyned / what for wo / and for distresse	
Who feeleth / double soor / and heuynesse	soor
But Palamon / that loue destreyneth so	
That wood out of his wit he gooth for wo	goth
And eek ther to / he is a prisoner	
P*er*petuelly / nat oonly for a yer	Perpetuelly / noght oonly /
Who koude ryme / in englissh p*ro*prely	¶Who englyssħ
His martirdom / for sothe it am noght I	nat I.
Ther fore I passe / as lightly / as I may	Therfore lightly
¶It fil / þ*at* / in that seuenthe yeer of May	fel / that in the Seuenthe yer in May

ffor he was yong/ and myghty for the nones
And ther to/ he was strong/ and byg/ of bones
To doon/ what any wight/ kan hym devyse
A yeer/ or two/ he was in this servyse
Page of the chambre/ of Emelie the brighte
And Philostrate/ he seyde þt he highte
But half so wel biloved a man/ as he
Ne was ther nevere in Court/ of his degree
He was so gentil/ of condicion
That thurgh out al the Court/ was his renon
They seiden/ þt it were a charitee
That Theseus/ wolde enhaunceu his degree
And putten hym/ in worshipful servyse
Ther as he myghte/ his vertu excercise
And thus with inne a while/ his name is spronge
Bothe of his dedes/ and his goode tonge
That Theseus/ hath taken hym so neer
That of his chambre/ he made hym a Squier
And gaf hym gold/ to mayntene his degree
And eek men broghte hym/ out of his contree
ffro yeer to yeer/ ful pryvely his rente
But honestly/ and sleighly/ he it spente
That no man wondred/ how þt he it hadde
And thre yeer in this wise/ his lyf he ladde
And bar hym so/ in pees/ and ek in werre
Ther was no man/ that Theseus hath derre
And in this blisse/ lete I now Arcite
And speke I wole/ of Palamon alite
In derknesse/ and horrible/ and strong prisoun
This seven yeer/ hath seten Palamoun
fforpyned what for wo/ and for distresse
Who feeleth double soor/ and hevynesse
But Palamon/ that love destreyneth so
That wood out of his wit/ he gooth for wo
And eek ther to/ he is a prisoner
Perpetuelly/ nat oonly for a yer
Who koude ryme/ in englissh proprely
His martirdom/ for sothe it am noght I
Ther fore I passe/ as lightly/ as I may
It fil/ þt in that seventhe yeer of May

The thridde nyght · as olde bokes seyn
That al this storie / tellen moore pleyn
Were it by auenture / or destynee
As whan a thyng is shapen / it shal be
That soone after the mydnyght / Palamon
By helpyng of a freend / brak his prisoun
And fleeth the Citee / faste as he may go
ffor he hadde yeue his Gailler drynke so
Of a clarree / maad of certeyn wyn
With Narcotikes and opye / of Thebes fyn // Opiu Thebaicum
That al that nyght / thogh þt men wolde hym shake
The Gailler sleep / he myghte noght awake
¶ And thus he fleeth / as faste as euere he may
The nyght was short / and faste by the day
That nedes cost / he moste hym seluen hyde
And til a groue / faste ther byside
With dredeful foot / thanne stalketh Palamon
ffor shortly / this was his opynyon
That in that groue / he wolde hym hyde al day
And in the nyght / thanne wolde he take his way
To Thebes ward / his freendes for to preye
On Theseus / to helpe hym to werreye
And shortly / outher he wolde lese his lyf
Or wynnen Emelie / vn to his wyf
This is theffect / and his entente pleyn
¶ Now wol I turne / to Arcite ageyn
That litel wiste / how neigh þt was his care
Til þt ffortune / hadde broght hym in the snare
¶ The bisy larke / messager of day
Salueth in hir song / the morwe gray
And firy Phebus / riseth vp so brighte
That al the Orient · laugheth of the lighte
And with his stremes / dryeth in the greues
The siluer dropes / hangynge on the leues
And Arcita / that in the court roial
With Theseus / is Squyer principal
Is risen / and looketh on the murye day
And for to doon his obseruance to May
Remembrynge / on the poynt of his desir
He on a Courser / stertlynge as the fir

	ELLESMERE
The thridde nyght'. as olde bokes seyn	nygħt' bookes
That al this storie / tellen moore pleyn	
Were it by auenture / or destynee	it'
As whan a thyng is shapen / it shal be	
That soone after the mydnyght' Palamou*n*	mydnygħt'
By helpyng of a freend / brak his prisou*n*	helpyng'
And fleeth the Citee / faste as he may go	17 ¶And
For he hadde yeue / his Gailler drynke so	gayler
Of a Clarree / maad of certeyn wyn	Clarree maad / of a certeyn
With Nercotikes / and opye / of Thebes fyn // Opiu*m* Thebaicum	¶Opium Thebaicum] Of Nercotikes / Opie
That al that nyght'. thogh *þ*at men wolde hym shake	nygħt' thogħ hi*m*
The Gailler sleep*e* / he myghte noght awake	This gayler nat
¶And thus he fleeth / as faste as euere he may	eu*ere*
The nyght was short' and faste by the day	nygħt
That nedes cost' he moste hym seluen hyde	moot
And til a groue / faste ther bisyde	
With dreedful foot' thanne stalketh Palamou*n*	W*ith* dredeful Palamon
For shortly / this was his opynyou*n*	opiniou*n*
That in that groue / he wolde hym hyde alday	al day
And in the nyght' thanne wolde he take his way	nyght /
To Thebesward / his freendes for to preye	Thebes ward /
On Theseus / to helpe hym to werreye	
And shortly / outher he wolde lese his lyf /	lif
Or wynnen Emelie / vn to his wyf	Emelye /
This is theffect / and his entente pleyn	theffect'
¶Now wol I turne / to Arcite ageyn	
That litel wiste / how neigh *þ*at was his care	ny
Til *þ*at Fortune / hadde broght hym / in the snare	had brogħt hi*m*
¶The bisy larke / messager of day	The
Salueth in hir song' the morwe gray	song /
And firy Phebus / riseth vp so brighte	brigħte
That al the Orient'. laugheth of the lighte	Orient' ligħte
And w*ith* his stremes / dryeth in the greues	hise
The siluer dropes / hangynge on the leues	
And Arcita / that in the Court roial	that is in court Roial
With Theseus / [h]is Squyer principal	Theseus / his Squier
Is risen / and looketh on the murye day	myrie
And for to doon / his obseruance to May	obseruaunce
Remembrynge / on the point of his desir	poynt
He on a Courser / startlynge as the fir	

17 ¶Knygħt' *16v*

The Knyght /	ELLESMERE
Is riden in to the feldes / hym to pleye	feeldes /
Out of the Courtꝰ. were it a myle / or tweye	Courtꝰ myle
And to the groue / of which þ*at* I yow tolde	
By auenture / his wey he gan to holde	wey /
To maken hym / a gerland of the greues	gerland /
Were it of wodebynde / or hawethorn leues	
And loude he soongꝰ. ayein the sonne shene	songꝰ ayeyn
May / with alle thy floures / and thy grene	wi*th* floures
Wel come be thow / faire fresshe May	thou /
In hope / þ*at* I som grene gete may	
And from his courser / with a lusty herte	
In to the groue / ful hastily he sterte	to a groue /
And in a path / he rometh vp and doun	
Ther as by auenture / this Palamou*n*	
Was in a bussħ / þ*at* no man myghte hym se	18 that mygħte
For soore afered / of his deeth was he	aferd deeth / thanne was
No thyng knew he / þ*at* it was Arcite	thyngꝰ ne knew that
God wootꝰ he wolde haue trowed it ful lite	
But sooth is seyd / go sithen many yeris	yeres
That feeld hath eyen / and the wode hath erys	eres
It is ful fair / a man to bere hym euene	
For alday meeten men / at vnset steuene	al day / meeteth
Ful litel woot Arcite / of his felawe	Arcite
That was so neigh / to herknen al his sawe	ny /
For in the bussh / he sitteth now ful stille	
¶Whan þ*at* Arcite / hadde romed al his fille	
And songen al the roundel lustily	
In to a studie / he fil sodeynly	fil al sodeynly
As doon thise louerys / in hir queynte gerys	loueres / geres
Now in the crop*e* / now down in the brerys	doun breres
Now vp / now down / as boket in a welle	doun / boketꝰ
Right as the friday / soothly for to telle	Rigħt
Now it shyneth / now it reyneth faste	
Rightꝰ so / kan gery Venus ouercaste	Rigħt geery ouer caste
The hertes of hir folkꝰ. right as hir day	folkꝰ rigħt
Is gerful / right so chaungeth she array	gereful / rigħt
Selde is the friday / al the wike ylike	wowke
¶Whan þ*at* Arcite hadde songe / he gan to syke	had sike
And sette hym down / with outen any moore	doun / wi*th*
Allas quod he / that day / þ*at* I was bore	day

18 ¶Knygħtꝰ *17r*

Is riden in to the feldes / hym to pleye
Out of the Court / were it a myle / or tweye
And to the groue / of which þt I yow tolde
By auenture / his wey he gan to holde
To maken hym a gerland of the greues
Were it of wodebynde / or hawethorn leues
And loude he song / ayein the sonne shene
May / with alle thy floures and thy grene
Wel come be thow faire fresshe may
In hope / þt I som grene gete may
And from his courser / with a lusty herte
In to the groue / ful hastily he sterte
And in a path / he rometh vp and doun
Ther as by auenture / this Palamon
Was in a bussh / þt no man myghte hym se
ffor soore afered / of his deeth was he
No thyng knew he / þt it was Arcite
God woot he wolde haue trowed it ful lite
But sooth is seyd / go sithen many yeres
That feeld hath eyen / and the wode hath erys
It is ful fair / a man to bere hym euene
ffor al day meeten men / at vnset steuene
fful litel woot Arcite / of his felawe
That was so neigh / to herknen al his sawe
ffor in the bussh / he sitteth now ful stille
Whan þt Arcite / hadde romed al his fille
And songen al the roundel lustily
In to a studie / he fil sodeynly
As doon thise loueres / in hir queynte geres
Now in the crop / now down in the breres
Now vp / now down / as boket in a welle
Right as the friday / soothly for to telle
Now it shyneth / now it reyneth faste
Right / so kan gery Venus ouercaste
The hertes of hir folk / right as hir day
Is gerful / right so chaungeth she array
Selde is the friday / al the wike ylike
Whan þt Arcite hadde songe / he gan to syke
And sette hym down / with outen any moore
Allas quod he / that day / þt I was bore

How longe Juno thurgh thy crueltee
Woltow werreyen Thebes the Citee
Allas ybroght is to confusioun
The blood roial of Cadmus and Amphioun
¶ Cadmus which þt was the firste man
That Thebes bulte and first bigan
And of the Citee first was crowned kyng
Of his lynage am I and his ofspryng
By verray ligne as of the stok roial
And now I am so caytyf and so thral
That he þt is my mortal enemy
I serue hym as his squyer pourely
And yet doth Juno me wel moore shame
ffor I dar noght biknowe myn owen name
But ther as I was wont to highte Arcite
Now highte I Philostrate noght worth a myte
¶ Allas thow felle Mars allas Juno
Thus hath youre ire oure lynage al fordo
Saue oonly me and wrecched Palamoun
That Theseus martyreth in prisoun
¶ And ouer al this to sleen me outrely
Loue hath his firy dart so brennyngly
ystiked thurgh my trewe careful herte
That shapen was my deeth erst than my sherte
ye sleen me wt youre eyen Emelye
ye been the cause wherfore þt I dye
Of al the remenant of myn oother care
Ne sette I noght the mountaunce of a tare
So þt I koude doon aught to youre plesaunce
And with that word he fil doun in a traunce
A longe tyme and afterward he vp sterte
¶ This Palamoun that thoughte þt thurgh his herte
He felte a cold swerd sodeynly glyde
ffor ire he quook no lenger wolde he byde
And whan þt he had herd Arcites tale
As he were wood wt face deed and pale
He stirte hym vp out of the buskes thikke
And seyde Arcite false traytour wikke
Now artow hent that louest my lady so
ffor whom þt I haue al this peyne and wo

	ELLESMERE
How longe Iuno / thurgh thy crueltee	
Woltow werreyen / Thebes the Citee	werreyen
Allas / ybroght is to confusiou*n*	
The blood roial / of Cadme and Amphiou*n*	⌈¶Cadmus⌉
¶Cadm*us* / which *þat* was the firste man	Of Cadmus /
That Thebes bulte / and first bigan	bulte / or first the toun bigan
And of the Citee / first was crowned kyng7	crouned
Of his lynage am I / and his of spryng7	spryng /
By verray ligne / as of the stok roial	
And now I am / so caytyf and so thral	caytyf /
That he *þat* is / my mortal enemy	he / that is
I serue hym / as his Squyer pourely	squier
And y[et] dooth Iuno / me wel moore shame	yet / Iuno me /
For I dar noght7 biknowe myn owen name	owene
But ther as I was wont7 to highte Arcite	I /
Now highte I Philostrate / noght worth a myte	
¶Allas thow felle Mars / allas Iuno	Allas thou
Thus hath youre Ire / oure lynage al fordo	oure kynrede al
Saue oonly me / and wrecched Palamou*n*	
That Theseus / martireth in prisou*n*	
¶And ouer al this / to sleen me outrely	And
Loue hath his firy dart7 so brennyngly	hath /
Ystiked / thurgh my trewe careful herte	19 thurgħ
That shapen was my deeth / erst than my sherte	
Ye sleen me wi*th* youre eyen / Emelye	me / with eyen
Ye been the cause / wherfore *þat* .I. dye	I
Of al the remenant7 of myn oother care	
Ne sette I noght7. the mountaunce of a tare	nat7 montance
So *þat* I koude doon aught7. to your*e* plesaunce	koude / aught7 youre plesau*n*ce
And with that word / he fil down in a traunce	doun
A longe tyme / and afterward he vp sterte	and after he
¶This Palamou*n* / that thoughte / *þat* thurgh his herte	*þat* thoughte
He felte a coold swerd / sodeynly glyde	sodeynliche
For Ire he quook7. no lenger wolde he byde	quook /
And whan *þat* he had herd / Arcites tale	he / herd
As he were wood / wi*th* face deed and pale	face /
He stirte hym vp / out of the buskes thikke	
And seyde Arcite / false traytour wikke	seide
Now artow hent7 that louest my lady so	
For whom *þat* I haue / al this peyne and wo	

[19]¶Knyghŧ7 *17v*

And art my blood / and to my conseil sworn	
As I ful ofte / haue toold thee her biforn	haue seyd thee heer
And hast byiaped here / duc Theseus	heere / duc'
And falsly / chaunged hast thy name thus	hast'
I wol be deed / or ellis thow shalt dye	elles thou
Thow shalt' noght / loue my lady Emelye	Thou shalt nat /
But I wol loue hir*e* oonly / and namo	hire
For I am Palamon / thy mortal foo	
And thogh *þat* I / no wepne haue in this place	though I wepene
But out of prisou*n* / am astert by grace	prison /
I drede noght' *þat* outher thow shalt dye	nogħt /
Or thow ne shalt' noght louen Emelye	shalt nat'
Chees which thow wolt' or thow shalt' noght asterte	thou thou shalt nat
¶This Arcite / with ful despitous herte	
Whan he hym knew / and hadde his tale herd	herd'
As fiers as leou*n* / pulled out his swerd	Leou*n* / swerd'
And seyde thus / by god *þat* sitteth aboue	sit
Nere it *þat* thow art syk' and wood for loue	it / thou art' sik'
And eek' *þat* thow / no wepne hast in this place	thow hast /
Thow sholdest neu*ere* / out of this groue pace	Thou
That thow ne sholdest' dyen of myn hond	thou hond'
For I diffye / the seuretee and the bond	defye / seurete bond'
Which *þat* thow seist' *þat* I haue maad to thee	that thou
What verray fool / thynk wel *þat* loue is free	thynk' wel /
And I wol loue hire / maugree al thy myght'	hir*e* / mygħt
¶But for as muche / ⟨as⟩ thow art a worthy knyght'	But muche / thou knygħt'
And wilnest' to darreyne hire by bataille	
Haue here my trouthe / tomorwe I nyl nat faille	heer I wol nat
With outen wityng' of any oother wight'	oute wigħt
That here / I wol be founden / as a knyght'	heere / founden knygħt'
And bryngen harneys / right ynogh for thee	[20] rigħt ynougħ
And chees the beste / and leef the worste to me	chese leue worste for me
And mete and drynke / this nyght wol I brynge	nygħt
Ynogh for thee / and clothes for thy beddynge	Ynougħ
And if so be / *þat* thow my lady wynne	that thou
And sle me in this wode / ther I am Inne	
Thow mayst wel haue thy lady / as for me	
¶This Palamon answerde / I graunte it thee	
And thus they been departed / til amorwe	
Whan ech of hem / hadde leyd his feith to borwe	had

[20] ¶Knygħt' *18r*

And art my blood / and to my conseil sworn
As I ful ofte haue told thee her-biforn
And hast byiaped here / duc Theseus
And falsly / chaunged hast thy name thus
I wol be deed / or ellis thow shalt dye
Thow shalt noght / loue my lady Emelye
But I wol loue hire oonly / and namo
ffor I am Palamon / thy mortal foo
And though þt I / no wepne haue in this place
But out of prisoun / am astert by grace
I drede noght / þt outher thow shalt dye
Or thow ne shalt noght louen Emelye
Chees which thow wolt / or thow shalt noght asterte
This Arcite / with ful despitous herte
Whan he hym knew / and hadde his tale herd
As fiers as leoun / pulled out his swerd
And seyde thus / by god þt sitteth aboue
Nere it þt thow art syk / and wood for loue
And eek þt thow / no wepne hast in this place
Thow sholdest neue / out of this groue pace
That thow ne sholdest / dyen of myn hond
ffor I diffye / the seuretee and the bond
Which þt thow seist þt I haue maad to thee
What verray fool / thynk wel þt loue is free
And I wol loue hire / maugree al thy myght
But for as muche / thow art a worthy knyght
And wilnest / to darreyne hire by bataille
Haue here my trouthe / tomorwe I nyl nat faille
With outen wityng / of any oother wight
That here I wol be founden / as a knyght
And bryngen harneys / right ynogh for thee
And chees the beste / and leef the worste to me
And mete and drynke / this nyght wol I brynge
ynogh for thee / and clothes for thy beddynge
And if so be / þt thow my lady wynne
And sle me in this wode / ther I am inne
Thow mayst wel haue thy lady / as for me
This Palamon answerde / I graunte it thee
And thus they been departed / til amorwe
Whan ech of hem / hadde leyd his feith to borwe

O Cupide out of alle charitee
O regne that wolde no felawe haue to thee
fful sooth is seyd þt loue ne lordshipe
Wol noght his thankes haue no felaweshipe
Wel fynden that Arcite and Palamon
Arcite is riden anoon vn to the toun
And on the morwe er it were dayes lyght
fful priuely two harneys hath he dyght
Bothe suffisaunt and mete to darreyne
The bataille in the feeld bitwixe hem tweyne
And on his hors allone as he was born
He carieth al this harneys hym biforn
And in the groue at tyme and place yset
This Arcite and this Palamon been met
To chaungen gan the colour in hir face
Right as the hunterys in the regne of Trace
That stonden at the gappe with a spere
Whanne hunted is the leon or the bere
And hereth hym come russhynge in the greues
And breketh bothe bowes and the leues
And thynketh here cometh my mortal enemy
With oute faille he moot be deed or I
ffor outher I moot sleen hym at the gappe
Or he moot sle me if þt me mysshappe
So ferden they in chaungyng of hir hewe
As fer as euerich oother of hem knewe
Ther nas no good day ne no saluynge
But streight with outen word or rehersynge
Euerich of hem heelp for to armen oother
As frendly as he were his owene brother
And after that with sharpe speres stronge
They foynen ech at oother wonder longe
Thou myghtest wene þt this Palamon
In his fightyng were a wood leon
And as a cruel tygre was Arcite
As wilde boores gonnen they to smyte
That frothen whit as foom for ire wood
Vp to the ancles foghte they in hir blood
And in this wyse I lete hem fightyng dwelle
And forth I wol of Theseus yow telle

	ELLESMERE
¶O Cupide / out of alle charitee	O
O regne / that wolde no felawe haue to thee	regne þ*at* wolt haue w*ith* thee
Ful sooth is seyd / þ*at* loue ne lordshipe	
Wol noght his thankes / haue no felaweshipe	noght hir thankes /
Wel fynden that Arcite and Palamou*n*	
¶Arcite / is riden anoon / vn to the town	Arcite anon / toun
And on the morwe / er it were dayes lyght	light
Ful p*ri*uely / two harneys hath he dyght	dight
Bothe suffisaunt and mete to darreyne	
The bataille in the feeld / bitwix hem tweyne	feeld /
And on his hors / allone / as he was born	allone
He carieth al this harneys / hym biforn	carieth / al the harneys /
And in the groue / at tyme and place yset	yset
This Arcite / and this Palamon been met	ben
¶To chaungen / gan the colour in hir face	To colour
Right as the hunterys / in the regne of Trace	Right hunters /
That stonden at the gappe / with a spere	stondeth gappe
Whanne hunted is / the leou*n* or the Bere	Whan leou*n* and the bere
And hereth hym / come russhynge in the greues	russhyng
And breketh / bothe bowes / and the leues	
And thynketh / here cometh my mortal enemy	heere
With oute faille / he moot be deed / or .I.	I
For outher / I moot sleen hym / at the gappe	hym
Or he moot sle me / if þ*at* me myshappe	sleen
So ferden they / in chaungyng of hir hewe	
As fer / as euerich / oother of hem knewe	euerich of hem oother knewe
¶Ther nas no good day / ne no saluynge	day saluyng
But streight with outen word / or rehersynge	w*ith* rehersyng
Euerich of hem / heelp for to armen oother	heelp*e*
As frendly / as he weere / his owene brother	freenly / were
And after that with sharpe speres stronge	
They foynen / ech at oother / wonder longe	foynen oother
Thou myghtest wene / þ*at* this Palamou*n*	myghtest that
In his fightyng were a wood leou*n*	
And as a crewel Tygre / was Arcite	crueel Tigre
As wilde boores / gonnen they to smyte	bores / gonne
That frothen / whit as foom / for Ire wood	frothen
Vp to the Anclees / foghte they in hir blood	Anclee /
And in this wise / I lete hem fightyng dwelle	[21] ¶And fightyng
And forth I wole / of Theseus yow telle	

[21] ¶Knyght *18v*

	ELLESMERE
¶The destynee / Ministre general	The destinee /
That executeth / in the world ou*er* al	
The purueiance / that god hath seyn biforn	purueiaunce /
So stroong it is / þ*at* thogh the world hadde sworn	strong though had
The contrarie of a thyng by ye / or nay	ye
Yet som tyme / it shal fallen on a day	somtyme /
That falleth nat eft / with Inne a thousand yeer	eft w*ith* yeere
For *cer*teinly / oure appetites heer	Appetites heere
Be it of werre / or pees / or hate / or loue	it
Al is this ruled / by the sighte aboue	reuled / sighte
¶This mene I now / by myghty Theseus	myghty
That for to hunten / is so desirus	
And namely / at the grete hert in May	
That in his bed / ther daweth hym no day	
That he nys clad / and redy for to ryde	
With hunte and horn / and houndes hym bisyde	
For in his huntyng hath he swich delit	huntyng. delit
That it is / al his ioye and appetit	Appetit
To been hym self / the grete hertes bane	
For after Mars / he serueth now Diane	Dyane
¶Cleer was the day / as I haue told er this	toold
And Theseus / with alle ioye and blys	blis
With his ypolita / the faire queene	
And Emelie / clothed al in greene	Emelye / grene
On huntyng be they riden roially	huntyng
And to the groue / that stood ful faste by	
In which ther was an hert as men hym tolde	
Duc Theseus / the streighte wey hath holde	Duc
And to the launde / he rideth hym ful right	right /
For thider was the hert wont haue his flight	flight
And ouer a brook / and so forth on his weye	forth in his
This duc / wol han a cours at hym / or tweye	duc. hym
With houndes swiche / as þ*at* hym list comaunde	houndes / swiche as hym
And whan this duc. was come vn to the launde	¶And Duc
Vnder the sonne he looketh / and anon	
He was war / of Arcite and Palamou*n*	
That foghten breme / as it were boles two	foughten were bores two
The brighte swerdes / wenten to and fro	
So hidously / that with the leeste strook	w*ith*
It semed / as it wolde felle an ook	fille

The knyght.

The destynee / mynistre general
That executeth / in the world ouer al
The purueiance / that god hath seyn biforn
So strong it is / þt though the world hadde sworn
The contrarie of a thyng / by ye or nay
Yet som tyme / it shal fallen on a day
That falleth nat eft / with Inne a thousand yeer
ffor certeinly / oure appetites heer
Be it of werre / or pees / or hate / or loue
Al is this ruled / by the sighte aboue
This mene I now / by myghty Theseus
That for to hunten / is so desirus
And namely / at the grete hert in May
That in his bed / ther daweth hym no day
That he nys clad / and redy for to ryde
With hunte and horn / and houndes hym bisyde
ffor in his huntyng / hath he swich delit
That it is / al his ioye and appetit
To been hym self / the grete hertes bane
ffor after Mars / he serueth now Diane
Cleer was the day / as I haue told er this
And Theseus / with alle ioye and blys
With his ypolita / the faire queene
And Emelye / clothed al in greene
On huntyng be they riden roially
And to the groue / that stood ful faste by
In which ther was an hert / as men hym tolde
Duc Theseus / the streighte wey hath holde
And to the launde / he rideth hym ful right
ffor thider was the hert / wont haue his flight
And ouer a brook / and so forth on his weye
This duc / wol han a cours at hym / or tweye
With houndes swiche / as þt hym list comaunde
And whan this duc / was come vn to the launde
Vnder the sonne / he looketh and anon
He was war / of Arcite and Palamon
That foghten breme / as it were bores two
The brighte swerdes / wenten to and fro
So hidously / that with the leeste strook
It semed / as it wolde felle an ook

But what they were / no thyng he ne woot /
This duc his courser / with the spores smoot /
And at a stert / he was bitwix hem two
And pulled out a swerd / and cryed hoo
Namoore / vp on peyne / of lesyng of your heed
By myghty mars / he shal anon be deed
That smyteth any strook / þt I may seen
But telleth me / what myster men ye been
That been so hardy / for to fighten heer
With outen Iuge / or oother officer
As it were in a lystes roially
This Palamon / answerde hastily
And seyde / Sire / what nedeth wordes mo
We haue the deeth disserued / bothe two
Two woful wrecches been we / two caytyues
That been encombred / of oure owene lyues
And as thow art / a rightful lord and Iuge
Ne yif vs / neither mercy ne refuge
But slee me first / for seinte charitee
But slee my felawe eek / as wel as me
Or slee hym first / for though thow knowe it lite
This is thy mortal foo / this is Arcite
That fro thy lond / is banysshed on his heed
For which / he hath deserued to be deed
For this is he þt cam vn to thy yate
And seyde / þt he highte Philostrate
Thus hath he iaped thee / ful many a yeer
And thow hast maked hym / thy chief Squyer
And this is he / þt loueth Emelye
For sith the day is come / þt I shal dye
I make pleynly / my confessioun
That I am thilke woful Palamon
That hath thy prisoun / broken wikkedly
I am thy mortal foo / and it am I
That loueth so hoote / Emelye the brighte
That I wol dyen / present in hir sighte
Wherfore I axe deeth / and my Iuwise
But slee my felawe / in the same wise
For bothe haue we / deserued to be slayn
This worthy duc / answerde anon agayn

But what they weere / no thyng he ne woot	were / thyng
This duc his courser / with the spores smoot	wi*th* his spores
And at a stert he was bitwix hem two	stert /
And pulled out a swerd / and cryed hoo	cride
Namoore / vp on peyne / of lesyng of your*e* heed	peyne lesynge youre
By myghty Mars / he shal anon be deed	myghty
That smyteth any strook / þ*at* I may seen	22 strook*es*. that
But telleth me / what myster men ye been	mystiers
That been so hardy / for to fighten heer	heere
With outen Iuge / or oother officer	Officere
As it weere in a lystes roially	were /
¶This Palamon / answerde hastily	
And seyde / sire / what nedeth wordes mo	sire /
We haue the deeth disserued / bothe two	haue / deeth / disserued
Two woful wrecches been we / two caytyues	
That been encombred / of oure owene lyues	
And as thow art a rightful lord and Iuge	thou rightful
Ne yif vs / neither mercy ne refuge	yeue
But slee me first. for seinte charitee	sle first
But slee my felawe eek as wel as me	sle
Or slee hym first. for thogh thow knowe it lite	sle though knowest
This is thy mortal foo / this is Arcite	
That fro thy lond / is banysshed on his heed	banysshed
For which / he hath deserued to be deed	
For this is he / þ*at* cam vn to thy yate	gate
And seyde / þ*at* he highte Philostrate	highte
Thus hath he iaped thee / ful many a yeer	yer
And thow hast maked hym / thy chief Squyer	thou hast hym Squier
And this is he / þ*at* loueth Emelye	that
For sith the day is come / þ*at* I shal dye	
I make pleynly / my confessiou*n*	
That I am / thilke woful Palamou*n*	
That hath thy prisou*n* / broken wikkedly	hath / prisou*n*
I am thy mortal foo / and it am I	
That loueth so hoote / Emelye the brighte	brighte
That I wol dyen / p*re*sent in hir sighte	dye / sighte
Wherfore I axe deeth / and my Iuwise	
But slee my felawe / in the same wise	sle
For bothe haue we / deserued to be slayn	bothe / han we
¶This worthy duc answerde anoon agayn	Duc anon

22 ¶Knyght *19r*

	ELLESMERE
And seyde / this is a short conclusiou*n*	
Youre owene mouth / by your*e* confessiou*n*	
Hath dampned yow / and I wol it recorde	
It nedeth noght to pyne yow w*ith* the corde	noght /
Ye shul be deed / by myghty Mars the rede	shal
¶The queene anoon / for verray wommanhede	anon / wo*m*manhède
Gan for to wepe / and so dide Emelye	
And alle the ladies / in the compaignye	ladyes /
Greet pitee was it / as it thoughte hem alle	was it
That euere swich a chaunce / sholde falle	eu*er*e / chaunce
For gentil men they weere / of greet estaat	were / estaat
And no thyng but for loue / was this debaat	thyng loue
And sawe / hir blody wowndes / wide and soore	saugh woundes / wyde
And alle cryden / bothe lasse and moore	crieden /
Haue mercy lord / vp on vs wommen alle	23 m*er*cy Lord / wo*m*men
And on hir bare knees / adown they falle	adoun
And wolde haue kist his feet ther as he stood	
Til at the laste / aslaked was his mood	
For pitee / renneth soone in gentil herte	
And thogh he first. for Ire quook and sterte	though / he first
He hath considred / shorthly in a clause	considered / shortly
The trespas of hem bothe / and eek the cause	
And al thogh þ*a*t his Ire / hir gilt accused	though
Yet in his resou*n* / he hem bothe excused	
¶As thus / he thoghte wel þ*a*t euery man	As
Wol helpe hym self in loue / if þ*a*t he kan	that
And eek / deliuere hym self / out of prisou*n*	eek deliu*er*e self
And eek / his herte hadde compassiou*n*	eek
Of wommen / for they wepten eu*er*e in oon	wo*m*men / wepen euere
And in his gentil herte / he thoghte anoon	And / thoughte anon
And softe vn to hym self / he seyde fy	fy /
Vp on a lord / that wol haue no mercy ¶no*ta*	[¶No*ta*te d*omi*ni]
But be a leou*n* / bothe in word / and dede	been word
To hem / that been in repentaunce and drede	þ*a*t repentau*n*ce
As wel / as to a proud despitous man	
That wol mayntene / that he first bigan	
That lord / hath litel of discreciou*n*	
That in swich caas / kan no dyuysiou*n*	cas / diuisiou*n*
But weyeth pryde / and humblesse / after oon	weyeth / pride humblesse
And shortly / whan his Ire is thus agoon	Ire /

23 ¶Knyght *19v*

And seyde / this is a short conclusion
Youre owene mouth / by youre confession
Hath dampned yow / and I wol it recorde
It nedeth noght / to pyne yow with the corde
Ye shul be deed / by myghty Mars the rede
¶ The queene anoon / for verray wommanhede
Gan for to wepe / and so dide Emelye
And alle the ladies / in the compaignye
Greet pitee was it / as it thoughte hem alle
That euere swich a chaunce / sholde falle
ffor gentil men they were / of greet estaat
And no thyng but for loue / was this debaat
And saugh hir blody woundes / wyde and soore
And alle cryden / bothe lasse and moore
Haue mercy lord / vp on vs wommen alle
And on hir bare knees / adoun they falle
And wolde haue kist his feet / ther as he stood
Til at the laste / aslaked was his mood
ffor pitee renneth soone / in gentil herte
And thogh he first / for ire quook and sterte
He hath considered / shortly in a clause
The trespas of hem bothe / and eek the cause
And al thogh þt his ire / hir gilt accused
Yet in his resoun / he hem bothe excused
¶ As thus / he thoghte wel þt euery man
Wol helpe hym self in loue / if þt he kan
And eek deliuere hym self / out of prisoun
And eek his herte hadde compassioun
Of wommen / for they wepten euere in oon
And in his gentil herte / he thoghte anoon
And softe vn to hym self / he seyde fy Cuo
Vp on a lord / that wol haue no mercy
But be a leoun / bothe in word and dede
To hem / that been in repentaunce and drede
As wel as to a proud despitous man
That wol mayntene / that he first bigan
That lord hath litel of discrecioun
That in swich cas / kan no diuysioun
But weyeth pride and humblesse after oon
And shortly whan his ire is thus agoon

He gan to looken vp / with eyen lighte
And spak thise same wordes / al on highte
¶ The god of loue / a benedicitee
How myghty / and how greet a lord is he
Agayns his myght / ther gayneth none obstacles
He may be cleped a god / for his myracles
ffor he kan maken / at his owene gyse
Of euerich herte / as þt hym list deuyse
¶ Lo heere / this Arcite / and this Palamoun
That quitly were / out of my prisoun
And myghte haue lyued in Thebes roially
And witen / I am hir mortal enemy
And þt hir deeth / lyth in my myght also
And yet hath loue / maugree hir eyen two
Broght hem hyder / bothe for to dye
Now looketh / is nat that an heigh folye
¶ Who may been a fool / but if he loue
Bihoold for goddes sake / þt sit aboue
Se how they blede / be they noght wel arrayed
Thus hath hir lord / the god of loue ypayed
Hir wages and hir fees / for hir seruyse
And yet they wenen / for to be ful wyse
That seruen loue / for aught þt may bifalle
But this is yet / the beste game of alle
That she for whom / they haue this jolitee
Kan hem therfore / as muche thank as me
She woot namoore / of al this hoote fare
By god / than woot a cokkow of an hare
But al moot been assayed / hoot and coold
A man moot been a fool / or yong or oold
I woot it by my self / ful yoore agoon
ffor in my tyme / a seruant was I oon
And therfore / syn I knowe of loues peyne
And woot how soore / it kan a man distreyne
As he þt hath been caught / ofte in his laas
I yow foryeue / al hoolly this trespaas
At requeste of the queene / þt kneleth heere
And eek of Emelye / my suster deere
And ye shal bothe anoon / vn to me swere
That neuere mo / ye shal my contree dere

He gan to loken vp / with eyen lighte
And spak thise same wordes / al on highte
¶The god of loue / a benedicitee
How myghty / and how greet a lord is he
Agayns his myghtꝰ. ther gayneth none obstacles
He may be clepid a god / for his miracles
For he kan maken / at his owene gyse
Of euerich herte / as *þat* hym list deuyse
¶Lo here / this Arcite / and this Palamou*n*
That quitly were / out of my prisou*n*
And myghte haue lyued in Thebes roially
And witen / I am hir mortal enemy
And *þat* hir deeth / lyth in my myght also
And yet hath loue / maugree hir eyen two
Broght hem hyder / bothe for to dye
Now looketh / is nat thatꝰ an heigh folye
¶Who may been a fool / but if he loue
Bihoold for goddes sake / *þat* sit aboue
Se how they blede / be they noght wel arrayed
Thus hath hir lord / the god of loue ypayed
Hir wages / and hir fees / for hir seruyse
And yet they wenen / for to be ful wyse
That seruen loue / for aught *þat* may bifalle
But this is yetꝰ the beste game of alle
That she / for whom / they haue this Iolitee
Kan hem therfore / as muche thank as me
She woot namoore / of al this hoote fare
By god / than wootꝰ a cokkow of an hare
But al moot been assayed / hoot and coold
A man moot been a fool / or yongꝰ or oold
I woot it by my self / ful yoore agoon
For in my tyme / a seruant was I oon
And ther fore / syn I knowe of loues peyne
And woot how soore / it kan a man distreyne
As he *þat* hath been caughtꝰ ofte in his laas
I yow foryeue / al hoolly this trespas
At requeste of the queene / *þat* kneeleth heere
And eek of Emelye / my suster deere
And ye shal bothe anoon / vn to me swere
That neuere mo / ye shal my contree dere

ELLESMERE

looken lighte
highte
benedicite

Ayeyns myghtꝰ
cleped hise myracles

diuyse
Lo heere
weren /
myghte / han

deth / lith myght

Broght
heigh

Bihoold / sake
noght

been
24 aughtꝰ that

whom han
ther fore / thank /
wootꝰ
woot Cokkow
coold
oold
yore agon

therfore /
hou
he / hath / caught
trespaas
kneleth

shul bothe / anon
neu*ere*

24 ¶Knyghtꝰ *20r*

	ELLESMERE
Ne make werre vp on me / nyght nor day	nyght ne
But been my freendes / in al that ye may	
I yow foryeue / this trespas eu*er*ydel	euery deel
And they hym sworen / his axing faire and wel	axyng *and* weel
And hym of lordshipe / and of mercy preyde	lordshipe /
And he hem graunteth g*ra*ce / and thanne he seyde	and thus he
¶To speke of roial lynage / and richesse	To speke / lynage
Thogh þ*at* she weere a queene / or a princesse	Though were queene p*r*incesse
Ech of yow bothe / is worthy doutelees	you
To wedden whan tyme is / but nathelees	is doutelees |
I speke / as for my suster Emelye	
For whom / ye haue this stryf and Ialousye	whom haue / strif *and*
Ye woot your self. she may nat wedden two	self
Atones / thogh ye fighten eueremo	though eu*er*emo
That oon of yow / al be hym looth / or lief	you / looth lief /
He moot go pipen / in an yuy leef	moot pipen / leef
This is to seyn / she may nat now haue bothe	han
Al be ye neu*er*e so Ialous / ne so wrothe	neuer Ialouse /
And for thy / I yow putte in this degree	.I
That ech of yow / shal haue his destynee	
As hym is shape / and herkneth in what wyse	
Lo here your*e* ende / of that I shal deuyse	heere youre
¶My wyl is this / for plat conclusiou*n*	My
With outen any replicaciou*n*	outen / repplicaciou*n*
If that yow liketh / take it for the beste	you it
That euerich of yow / shal goon wher*e* hym leste	you /
Frely / with outen raunsou*n* / or daunger	raunson /
And this day fifty wykes / fer ne neer	ner
Euerich of yow / shal brynge an hundred knyghtes	you / knyghtes
Armed for listes / vp at alle rightes	lystes / rightes
Al redy / to darreyne hire by bataille	25 ¶Al
And this bihoote I yow / with outen faille	bihote
Vp on my trouthe / and as I am a knyght	knyght /
That wheither of yow bothe / þ*at* hath myght	bothe myght
This is to seyn / þ*at* wheither he or thou	that thow
May with his hundred / as I spak of now	wit*h*
Sleen his contr*ar*ie / or out of lystes dryue	contrarie /
Thanne shal I yeue / Emelye to wyue	EmelyA
To whom þ*at* Fortune / yeueth so fair a g*ra*ce	grace
The lystes / shal I maken in this place	Tho lystes /

25 ¶Knyght *20v*

Ne make werre vp on me nyght ne day
But been my freendes in al that ye may
I yow foryeue this trespas euerydel
And they hym sworen his axyng faire and wel
And hym of lordshipe and of mercy preyde
And he hem graunteth grace and thanne he seyde
To speke of roial lynage and richesse
Though þt she were a queene or a princesse
Ech of yow bothe is worthy doutelees
To wedden whan tyme is but nathelees
I speke as for my suster Emelye
ffor whom ye haue this stryf and Ialousye
ye woot youre self she may nat wedden two
Atones though ye fighten eueremo
That oon of yow al be hym looth or lief
he moot go pipen in an yuy leef
This is to seyn she may nat now haue bothe
Al be ye neuere so Ialous ne so wrothe
And for thy I yow putte in this degree
That ech of yow shal haue his destynee
As hym is shape and herkneth in what wyse
lo heere youre ende of that I shal deuyse
My wyl is this for plat conclusion
With outen any replicacion
If that yow liketh take it for the beste
That euerich of yow shal goon where hym leste
ffrely with outen raunson or daunger
And this day fifty wykes fer ne neer
Euerich of yow shal brynge an hundred knyghtes
Armed for lystes vp at alle rightes
Al redy to darreyne hire by bataille
And this bihoote I yow with outen faille
Vp on my trouthe and as I am a knyght
That wheither of yow bothe þt hath myght
This is to seyn þt wheither he or thou
May with his hundred as I spak of now
Sleen his contrarie or out of lystes dryue
Thanne shal I yeue Emelye to wyue
To whom þt fortune yeueth so fair a grace
The lystes shal I maken in this place

And god so wisly on my soule rewe
As I shal euene Iuge been and trewe
Ye shul noon oother ende with me maken
That oon of yow ne shal be deed or taken
And if yow thynketh this is wel ysayd
Sey youre auys and holdeth yow apayd
This is youre ende and youre conclusioun
Who looketh lightly now but Palamoun
Who spryngeth vp for ioye but Arcite
Who koude telle or who koude it endite
The ioye that is maked in the place
Whan Theseus hath doon so fair a grace
But doun on knees wente euery maner wight
And thonken hym with al hir herte and myght
And namely the Thebans ofte sythe
And thus with good hope and herte blythe
They take hir leue and homward gonne they ryde
To Thebes with olde walles wyde

Explicit prima pars

Incipit pars secunda

I trowe men wolde deme it necligence
If I foryete to tellen the dispence
Of Theseus that gooth so bisily
To maken vp the lystes roially
That swich a noble theatre as it was
I dar wel seyn in this world ther nas
The circuit a myle was aboute
Walled of stoon and dyched al withoute
Round was the shap in manere of compas
Ful of degrees the heighte of sixty paas
That whan a man was set on o degree
He letted noght his felawe for to see
Estward ther stood a gate of marbul whit
Westward right swich another in the opposit
And shortly to concluden swich a place
Was noon in erthe as in so lite a space

	ELLESMERE
And god so wisly / on my soule rewe	
As I shal / euene Iuge been and trewe	shal
Ye shul noon oother ende / with me maken	*with*
That oon of yow / ne shal be deed / or taken	deed
And if yow thynketh / this is wel ysayd	weel
Sey youre auys / and holdeth yow apayd	Seyeth you
This is youre ende / and you*re* conclusiou*n*	youre
¶Who looketh lightly now / but Palamou*n*	
Who spryngeth vp for ioye / but Arcite	
Who koude telle / or who koude it endite	kouthe kouthe endite
The ioye / that is maked in the place	þ*a*t
Whan Theseus / hath doon so fair a *gra*ce	grace
But doun on knees / wente euery maner wightꝰ	man*er* wighħtꝰ
And thonken hym / with al hir herte and myghtꝰ	*with* myghħtꝰ
And namely the Thebans ofte sythe	often sithe
And thus with good hope / and herte blythe	and *with* herte blithe
They take hir leeue / and homward gonne they ryde	taken leue / ride
To Thebes / with olde walles wyde	with hise olde
¶Explicitꝰ prima pars	¶Explicitꝰ secunda pars
¶Incipitꝰ pars secunda	¶Sequit*ur* pars tercia
I trowe / men wolde deme it necligence	I Trowe /
If I foryete / to tellen the despence	dispence
Of Theseus / that gooth so bisily	
To maken vp the lystes / roially	vp / lystes
That swich a noble Theatre / as it was	
I dar wel seyn / in this world ther nas	
The circuitꝰ a myle was aboute	circuit /
Walled of stoon / and dyched al with oute	
Round was the shap*e* / in manere of compas	
Ful of degrees / the heighte of sixty paas	Sixty pas
That whan a man / was setꝰ on o degree	set /
He letted noghtꝰ his felawe for to see	lette natꝰ
¶Estward ther stood a gate / of Marbul whit	¶Estward / whit /
Westward / right swich another / in the opositꝰ	Westward righħt another opositꝰ
And shortly to concluden / swich a place	26 ¶And concluden / ⸍ swich
Was noon in erthe / as in so lite a space	so litel space

For in the lond

26 ¶Knyghħtꝰ *21r*

	ELLESMERE
For in the lond / ther was no crafty man	
That Geometrye / or Ars metrik kan	geometrie / Metrik
Ne purtreyour / ne keruere of ymages	portreit*our* / kerue*re*
That Theseus / ne yaf mete and wages	
The Theatre / for to maken and deuyse	
And for to doon / his ryte and sacrifise	
He Estward hath / vp on the gate aboue	Estward / hath
In worship of Venus / goddesse of loue	worship*e* Venus
Doon maad an Auter / and an oratorie	make Oratorie
And on the westward / in memorie	
Of Mars / he maked hath right swich another	right
That coste largely / of gold a fother	
And Northward / in a touret on the wal	Northward Touret /
Of Alabastre whit and reed Coral	coral
An oratorie / riche for to see	Oratorie /
In worship*e* / of Diane of chastitee	worship*e* Dyane Chastitee
Hath Theseus / doon wroght in noble wise	Theseus wroght wyse
¶But yet hadde I forgeten / to deuyse	yet foryeten
The noble keruyng / and the purtreit*ur*es	keruyng portreitures
The shap*e* / the contenance / and the figures	contenaunce
That weren / in thise oratories thre	Oratories
¶First / in the temple of Venus / maystow se	
Wroght on the wal / ful pitous to biholde	Wroght
The broken slepes / and the sykes colde	sikes
The sacred teerys / and the waymentynge	teeris /
The firy strokes / of the desirynge	strokes / and the
That loues seruantz / in this lyf enduren	
The othes / that hir couenantz assuren	
Plesance / and hope / desir / foolhardynesse	Plesaunce desir
Beautee and youthe / baudrye / richesse	bauderie
Charmes and force / lesynges / flaterye	lesynges
Despense / bisynesse / and Ialousye	bisynesse
That wered / of yelowe gooldes a gerland	wered yelewe
And a Cokkow / sittyng on hir hand	sittynge hand
Festes / Instrumentz / caroles / daunces	caroles
Lust and array / and alle the circumstaunces	circumstau*n*ces
Of loue / whiche þ*at* I rekned / and rekne shal	rekned haue / *and*
By ordre / weren peynted on the wal	
And mo / than I kan make of menciou*n*	
For soothly / al the Mount of Citherou*n*	mount

For in the lond / ther was no crafty man
That Geometrie / or ars metryk kan
Ne purtreyour / ne keruere of ymages
That Theseus / ne yaf mete and wages
The Theatre / for to maken and deuyse
And for to doon / his ryte and sacrifise
He Estward hath / vp on the gate aboue
In worship of Venus / goddesse of loue
Doon maad an Auter / and an oratorie
And on the westward / in memorie
Of Mars / he maked hath right swich another
That coste largely / of gold a fother
And northward / in a touret / on the wal
Of alabastre whit / and reed coral
An oratorie / riche for to see
In worship / of Diane of chastitee
Hath Theseus / doon wroght / in noble wise
But yet hadde I forgeten / to deuyse
The noble keruyng / and the purtreitures
The shap / the contenance / and the figures
That weren / in thise oratories thre
First / in the temple of Venus / maystow se
Wroght on the wal / ful pitous to biholde
The broken slepes / and the sykes colde
The sacred teerys / and the waymentynge
The firy strokes / of the desirynge
That loues seruantz / in this lyf enduren
The othes / that hir couenantz assuren
Plesance / and hope / desir / foolhardynesse
Beautee and youthe / baudrye / richesse
Charmes and force / lesynges / flaterye
Despense / bisynesse / and Jalousye
That wered / of yelowe gooldes a gerland
And a cokkow / sittyng on hir hand
Festes / Instrumentz / caroles / daunces
Lust and array / and alle the circumstaunces
Of loue / whiche þ^t I rekned / and rekne shal
By ordre / weren peynted on the wal
And mo / than I kan make of mencioun
For soothly / al the mount of Citheroun

Ther Venus hath hir principal dwellynge
Was shewed on the wal in portreyynge
With al the gardyn and the lustynesse
Nat was foryeten the porter ydelnesse
Ne Narcisus the faire of yoore agon
Ne yet the folie of kyng Salomon
Ne yet the grete strengthe of Ercules
Thenchantementz of Medea and Circes
Ne of Turnus with the hardy fiers corage
The ryche Cresus caytif in seruage
Thus may ye seen that wisdom ne richesse
Beautee ne sleighte strengthe hardynesse
Ne may with Venus maken champartie
For as hir list the world than may she gye
Lo al this folk so caught were in hir laas
Til they for wo ful ofte seyde allas
Suffiseth heere ensamples oon or two
And though I koude rekne a thousand mo
The statue of Venus glorious for to see
Was naked fletyng in the large See
And fro the nauele doun al couered was
With wawes grene and brighte as any glas
A Citole in hir right hand hadde she
And on hir heed ful semely for to se
A rose gerland fressh and wel smellynge
Aboue hir heed hir dowues flikerynge
Biforn hir stood hir sone Cupido
Up on his shuldres wynges hadde he two
And blynd he was as it is ofte seene
A bowe he bar and arwes brighte and keene
Why sholde I nat as wel eek telle yow al
The purtreyture that was vp on the wal
Withinne the temple of myghty Mars the rede
Al peynted was the wal in lengthe and brede
Lyk to the estres of the grisly place
That highte the grete temple of Mars in Trace
In thilke colde frosty Region
Ther as Mars hath his souereyn mansion
First on the wal was peynted a forest
In which ther dwelleth neither man ne best

	ELLESMERE		
Ther Venus / hath hir p*ri*ncipal dwellynge			
Was shewed on the wal / in purtreyynge	portreyynge		
With al the gardyn / and the lustynesse			
Nat was foryeten / the porter ydelnesse	Porter		
Ne Narcisus the faire / of yoore agon	yore		
Ne yet the folie / of kyng Salomon	And yet	folye /	kyng Salomon
Ne yet the grete streħgthe of Ercules	27	¶And eek the	
Thenchantementz / of Medea and Circes	Thenchauntementz		
Ne of Turnus / with the hardy fiers corage	*with*		
The ryche Cresus / caytif in seruage	riche	kaytyf /	
¶Thus may ye seen / þat wisdom ne richesse	Thus	wysdom	
Beautee / ne sleighte / strengthe hardynesse	Beautee	sleighte /	
Ne may with Venus / maken champ*ar*tie	Venus / holde champ*ar*tie		
For as hir lust the world than may she gye	list		
Lo al this folk / so caught were in hir laas	alle thise folk*es*	las	
Til they for wo / ful ofte seyde allas			
Suffiseth heere ensamples / oon or two	heere / ensamples		
And though / I koude rekne a thousand mo	rekene		
¶The statue of Venus / glorious for to see [ad vid]	The Statue	se	
Was naked / fletyng in the large See [.i. mare]	fletynge	See	
And fro the nauele down / al couered was	doun /	cou*er*ed	
With wawes grene / and brighte as any glas	*With*	brighte	
A Citole in hir right hand / hadde she	Citole /	right	
And on hir heed / ful semely for to se			
A rose gerland / fressh / and wel smellynge	A Rose gerland fressh /		
Aboue hir heed / hir dowues flikerynge			
Biforn hir*e* stood / hir sone Cupido	hir*e* / stood		
Vp on his shuldres / wynges hadde he two			
And blynd he was / as it is ofte seene	it was often		
A bowe he bar / and Arwes brighte and keene	brighte	kene	
¶Why sholde I nat as wel / eek telle yow al	noght /	wel	
The purtreyture / þat was vp on the wal	portreiture / that		
With Inne the temple / of myghty Mars the rede	*With*		
Al peynted was the wal / in lengthe and brede			
Lyk to the eestres / of the grisly place	estres /		
That highte the grete temple / of Mars in Trace	highte	temple	
In thilke colde / frosty Regiou*n*			
Ther as Mars / hath his souereyn mansiou*n*			
¶First on the wal / was peynted a Forest	forest		
In which ther dwelleth / neither man ne best			

27 ¶Knyght *21v*

The Knyght ./	ELLESMERE
With knotty / knarry / bareyne trees olde	knotty
Of stubbes sharpe / and hidouse to biholde	
In which / ther ran a rombul / in a swougħ	which ran / a rumbel and a
As thogh a storm / sholde bresten euery bougħ	though
And downward on an hil / vnder a bente	dounward from an hille /
Ther stood the temple / of Mars Armypotente	temple
Wroght al of burned steel / of which the entree	Wroghħt
Was long and streyt and gastly for to see	long streit
And ther out cam a rage / and swich a veze (.i. impet*us*)	
That it made / al the gate for to rese	
The Northren light in at the dores shoon	lyghħt
For wyndow on the wal / ne was ther noon	wyndowe / wal
Thurgh which men myghten / any light discerne	lighħt
The dore was al / of Athamant eterne	Adamant
Yclenched / oue*r*thwart and endelong /	28 ouerthwart endelong
With Iren togh / and for to make it strong	tougħ /
Euery piler / the temple to sustene	pyler
Was tonne greet of Iren bright and shene	brighħt
¶Ther say I first. the dirke ymagynynge	saughħ first ymaginyng
Of felonye / and al the compassynge	and the compassyng
The cruel Ire / reed as any gleede	crueel
The pike purs / and eek the pale drede	pykepurs / and the
The smyler*e* / with the knyf vnder the cloke	knyf*es*
The shipne brennyng with the blake smoke	shepne / brennynge / *with*
The tresou*n* / of the mordryng in the bed	mordrynge bedde
The open werre / with woundes al bibled	*with* bibledde
Contek / with blody knyf and sharp*e* manace	Contek knyf /
Al ful of chirkyng was that sory place	chirkyng
¶The sleer*e* of hym self / yet saugh I ther	
His herte blood / hath bathed al his heer	
The nayl ydryuen / in the shode a nyght	nyghħt
The colde deeth / with mouth gapyng vp right	gapyng righħt
Amyddes of the temple / sat meschaunce	
With disconfort / and sory contenaunce	disconfort
¶Yet saugh I woodnesse / laughyng in his rage	laughynge
Armed compleynt out hees / and fiers outrage	compleint
The caroyne in the bussħ / with throte ycorue	careyne busk *with*
A thousand slayn / and noght of qualm ystorue	nat oon of
The tiraunt with the praye / by force yraft	pray
The town destroyed / ther was no thyng laft	toun thy⟨ng laft⟩

[28]¶Knyghħt *22r*

With knotty / knarry / bareyne trees olde
Of stubbes sharpe / and hidouse to biholde
In which / ther ran a rumbul / in a swough
As though a storm / sholde bresten euery bough
And downward on an hil / vnder a bente
Ther stood the temple / of Mars armypotente
Wroght al of burned steel / of which the entree
Was long and streyt / and gastly for to see .i. impetus
And ther out cam a rage / and swich a veze
That it made al the gate for to rese
The northren light in at the dores shoon
For wyndowe on the wal / ne was ther noon
Thurgh which men myghten any light discerne
The dore was al / of Adamant eterne
yclenched / outhwart / and endelong
With iren tough / and for to make it strong
Euery piler / the temple to sustene
Was tonne greet / of iren bright and shene
Ther saugh I first / the derke ymaginynge
Of felonye / and al the compassynge
The cruel Ire / reed as any gleede
The pikepurs / and eek the pale drede
The smylere / with the knyf vnder the cloke
The shipne brennyng with the blake smoke
The tresoun / of the mordryng in the bed
The open werre / with woundes al bibled
Contek with blody knyf and sharp manace
Al ful of chirkyng was that sory place
The sleere of hym self / yet saugh I ther
His herte blood / hath bathed al his heer
The nayl ydryuen / in the shode anyght
The colde deeth / with mouth gapyng vp right
Amyddes of the temple / sat meschaunce
With disconfort / and sory contenaunce
Yet saugh I woodnesse / laughynge in his rage
Armed compleynt / out hees / and fiers outrage
The caroyne in the bussh / with throte ycorue
A thousand slayn / and noght of qualm ystorue
The tiraunt / with the praye / by force yraft
The town destroyed / ther was no thyng laft

¶ Yet saugh I brent / the shippes hoppesteres
The hunte strangled / with the wilde beres
The sowe freten the child / right in the cradel
The cook yscalded / for al his longe ladel
¶ Naught was forgeten / by the infortune of Marte
The carter / over ryden / with his carte
Under the wheel / ful lowe he lay adoun
Ther were also / of Martes divisioun
The barbour / and the bocher / and the smyth
That forgeth sharpe swerdes / on his styth
¶ And al above / depeynted in a tour
Saugh I Conquest / sittyng / in greet honour
With the sharpe swerd / over his heed
Hangynge by a subtil twynes threed
¶ Depeynted was the slaughtre of Julius
Of grete Nero / and of Anthonius
Al be that thilke tyme / they were unborn
Yet was hir deeth / depeynted ther biforn
By manasynge of Mars / right by figure
So was it shewed / in that portreiture
As is depeynted in the sertres above
Who shal be slayn / or ellis deed for love
Suffiseth oon ensample / in stories olde
I may nat rekne hem alle / though I wolde
¶ The Statue of Mars / up on a carte stood
Armed / and loked grym / as he were wood
And over his heed / ther shynen two figures
Of sterres / that been cleped in Scriptures
That oon Puella / that other Rubeus
This god of armes / was arrayed thus
A wolf ther stood / biforn hym at his feet /
With eyen rede / and of a man he eet
With subtil pencel / was depeynted this storie
In redoutynge of Mars / and of his glorie
¶ Now to the temple / of Diane the chaste
As shortly as I kan / I wol me haste
To telle yow / al the descripsioun
Depeynted been the walles / up and doun
Of huntyng / and of shamefast chastitee
Ther saugh I · how woful Calistopee

	ELLESMERE
¶Yet saugh I brentꝭ. the shippes hoppesteres	brentꝭ
The hunte strangled / with the wilde beres	
The sowe freten the child / right in the Cradel	sowe / child rigħt
The Cook yscalded / for al his longe ladel	
¶Naught was forgeten / by the Infortune of Marte	¶Nogħt foryeten /
The Carter*e* / ouer ryden / with his Carte	Cartere / ryden
Vnder the wheel / ful lowe he lay adown	lowe / adoun
Ther were also / of Martes deuysioun	¶Ther diuisioun
The Barbo*ur* / and the Bochier and the Smyth	The laborer / and Bocher Smytħ
That forgeth sharpe swerdes / on his styth	swerdes Styth
¶And al aboue / depeynted in a tour	
Saugh I Conquestꝭ sittyngꝭ in greet hono*ur*	Saugħ sittynge honour
With the sharpe swerd / ouer his heed	
Hangynge / by a subtil twynes threed	soutil
¶Depeynted was / the slaghtre of Iulius	slaughtre
Of grete Nero / and of Anthonius	Antonius
Al be / *þat* thilke tyme / they were vnborn	be
Yet was hir deeth / depeynted ther biforn	deth /
By manacynge of Mars / right by figure	manasynge rigħt
So was it shewed / in that purtreyture	shewed portreiture
As is depeynted / in the Sertres aboue	Certres
Who shal be slayn / or ellis deed for loue	elles
Suffiseth oon ensample / in stories olde	29
I may nat rekne hem alle / thogh I wolde	rekene alle though
¶The Statue of Mars / vp on a Carte stood	The vp vn
Armed / and loked grym / as he were wood	looked grym
And ouer his heed / ther shynen two figures	
Of sterres / *þat* been clepyd in Scriptures	that cleped scriptures
That oon Puella / that oother Rubeus	
This god of armes / was arrayed thus	Armes /
A wolf ther stood / bifore hym at his feetꝭ	biforn feet
With eyen rede / and of a man he eet	
With subtil pencel / was depeynted this storie	soutil
In redoutynge of Mars / and of his glorie	redoutynge / Mars
¶Now to the temple / of Diane the chaste	NOw / Dyane
As shortly as I kan / I wol me haste	kan
To telle yow / al the discripsioun	descripsioun
Depeynted been the walles / vp and doun	walles
Of huntyngꝭ and of shamefast chastitee	
Ther saw I. / how woful Calistopee	¶Ther saugh I /

29 ¶Knyghtꝭ *22v*

	Ellesmere
When þat Diane / agreued was with here	
Was turned / fro a womman / til a Bere	from wom*m*an
And after was she maad / the lode sterre // Vrsa maior	maad loode [¶Vrsa maior]
Thus was it peynted / I kan seye yow no ferre	sey
Hir sone is eek a sterre / as men may see	sterre
Ther saw I Dane / yturned to a tree	¶Ther saugh yturned til a
I mene nat / the goddesse Diane	nat
But Penneus doghter / which þat highte Dane	highte
¶Ther saw I Attheon / an hert ymaked	saugh
For vengeaunce / þat he saw Diane al naked	vengeau*n*ce / saugh
I seigh / how þat hise houndes haue hym caught	saugh / houndes / caught
And freten hym / for þat they knewe hym naught	freeten naught
¶Yet peynted was / a litel ferther moor	peynted / a forther
How Atthalante / hunted the wilde boor	
And Meleagree / and many another mo	
For which Diane / wroghte hym care and wo	Dyane /
Ther saw I. many another wonder storie	¶Ther saugh I /
The whiche / me list nat drawen to memorie	nat
¶This goddesse on hert ful hye seet	on an hert ful wel hye
With smale houndes / al aboute hir feet	
And vnder nethe hir feet. she hadde a moone	feet
Wexinge it was / and sholde wanye soone	Wexynge
In gaude grene / hir statue yclothed was	clothed
With bowe in honde / and arwes in a cas	Arwes
Hir eyen caste she / ful lowe adown	adoun
Ther Pluto / hath his dirke Regioun	derke regioun
A womman trauailyng was hir biforn	¶A wom*m*an trauaillynge / hir*e*
But for hir child / so longe was vnborn	
Ful pitously / lucina gan she calle	Lucyna /
And seyde help / for thow mayst best of alle	help*e* / mayst
Wel koude he peynte lyfly / that it wroghte	30 peynten lifly / wroghte
With many a floryn / he the hewes boghte	boghte
¶Now been thise listes maad / and Theseus	NOw the lystes
That at his grete cost arrayed thus	cost /
The temples / and the Theatre euery del	deel
Whan it was doon / hym liked wonder wel	lyked weel
But stynte I wole / of Theseus alite	
And speke of Palamon / and of Arcite	
¶The day approcheth / of hir retournynge	reto*ur*nynge
That euerich / sholde an hundred knyghtes brynge	knyghtes

30 ¶Knyght *23r*

Whan yt Diane / agreued was with here
Was turned fro a womman / til a bere
And after was she maad / the lode sterre — Vrsa maior
Thus was it peynted / I kan seye yow no ferre
Hir sone is eek a sterre / as men may see
Ther saugh I Dane / yturned to a tree
I mene nat / the goddesse Diane
But Penneus doghter / which yt highte Dane
¶ Ther saugh I Attheon / an hert ymaked
ffor vengeaunce / yt he saugh Diane al naked
I saugh / how yt hise houndes haue hym caught
And freten hym / for yt they knewe hym naught
¶ Yet peynted was / a litel ferther moor
How Atthalante / hunted the wilde boor
And Meleagree / and many another mo
ffor which Diane / wroghte hym care and wo
Ther saugh I . many another wonder storie
The whiche me list nat drawen to memorie
¶ This goddesse on hert / ful hye seet
With smale houndes / al aboute hir feet
And vnder nethe hir feet / she hadde a moone
Wexynge it was / and sholde wanye soone
In gaude grene / hir statue yclothed was
With bowe in honde / and arwes in a cas
Hir eyen caste she / ful lowe adoun
¶ Ther Pluto hath his derke regioun
A womman trauaillyng / was hir biforn
But for hir child / so longe was vnborn
ffvl pitously / Lucina gan she calle
And seyde help / for thow mayst best of alle
Wel koude he peynte lyfly / that it wroghte
With many a floryn / he the hewes boghte
¶ Now been thise listes maad / and Theseus
That at his grete cost / arrayed thus
The temples / and the theatre euerydel
Whan it was doon / hym liked wonder wel
But stynte I wole / of Theseus alite
And speke of Palamon / and of Arcite
¶ The day approcheth / of hir retournynge
That euerich sholde an hundred knyghtes brynge

The bataille to darreyne / as I yow tolde
And til Athenes / hir couenant for to holde
Hath euerich of hem / broght a hundred knyghtes
Wel armed for the werre / at alle rightes
And sikerly / ther trowed many a man
That neuere sithen / þt the world bigan
As for to speke / of knyghthod of hir hond
As fer / as god hath maked see and lond
Nas of so fewe / so noble a compaignye
ffor euery wight / þt loued chiualrye
And wolde his thankes / han a passant name
Hath prayd / that he myghte been of that game
And wel was hym / þt ther to chosen was
ffor if ther fille tomorwe swich a cas
Ye knowen wel / þt euery lusty knyght
That loueth paramours / and hath his myght
Were it in Engelond / or elles where
They wolde hir thankes / wilnen to be there
To fighten for a lady / benedicitee
It were a lusty sighte / for to see
And right so ferden they with Palamon
With hym ther wenten / knyghtes many oon
Som wol ben armed / in an haubergeon
And in a brestplate / and in a light gipoun
And som wol haue / a peyre plates large
And som wol haue / a Pruce sheeld / or a targe
Som wol been armed / on his legges weel
And haue an ax / and som a maas of steel
Ther nys no newe gyse / þt it nas old
Armed were they / as I haue yow told
Euerich / after his opinyon
Ther maystow seen / comynge with Palamon
Lygurge hym self / the grete kyng of Trace
Blak was his berd / and manly was his face
The cercles of his eyen / in his heed
They gloweden / bitwixen yelow and reed
And lyk a griffon / loked he aboute
With kempe heris / on his browes stoute
His lymes grete / his brawnes harde and stronge
His shuldres brode / hise armes rounde and longe

	ELLESMERE
The bataille to darreyne / as I yow tolde	
And til Atthenes / hir couenant for to holde	couenantz
Hath euerich of hem / broght a hundred knyghtes	eu*er*ich broght an hundred knyghtes
Wel armed for the werre / at alle rightes	rightes
And sikerly / ther trowed many a man	many a man[y]
That neuere sithen / þ*at* the world bigan	neu*er*e that
As for to speke / of knyghthod of hir hond	knyghthod hond
As fer / as god hath maked see and lond	see or lond
Nas of so fewe / so noble a compaignye	
For euery wight þ*at* loued chiualrye	wight that louede
And wolde his thankes / han a passant name	
Hath prayd / that he myghte been of that game	preyd / þ*at*
And wel was hym / þ*at* ther to chosen was	that
For if ther fille / tomorwe swich a cas	fille
Ye knowen wel / þ*at* euery lusty knyght /	knyght
That loueth p*ar*amours / and hath his myght	myght
Were it in Engelond / or ellis where	elles
They wolde hir thankes / wilnen to be there	
To fighten for a lady / benedicitee	fighte
It were a lusty sighte / for to see	sighte /
¶And right so / ferden they with Palamon	right wi*th* Palamou*n*
With hym ther wenten / knyghtes many oon	Wi*th* hym / wenten on
Som wol ben armed / in an haubergeou*n*	
And in a Brestplate / and in a light gypou*n*	in bristplate / light
And som wol haue / a peire plates large	so*m*me woln paire
And som wol haue / a Pruce sheeld / or a targe	so*m*me woln
Som wol been armed / on his legges weel	So*m*me woln ben on hir legges
And haue an Ax / and som a Maas of steel	so*m*me Mace
Ther nys no newe gyse / þ*at* it nas oold	Ther is no that old
Armed were they / as I haue yow toold	told
Euerich / after his opinyou*n*	Euerych / opiniou*n*
¶Ther maystow seen / comynge with Palamou*n*	Ther maistow wi*th* Palamon
Lygurge hym self the grete kyng of Trace	
Blak was his beerd / and manly was his face	berd /
The cercles of his eyen / in his heed	cercles / hise eyen
They gloweden / bitwixen yelow and reed	
And lyk a griffou*n* / loked he aboute	lik grifphon / looked
With keempe herys / on his browes stoute	kempe heeris / hise
His lymes grete / his brawnes / harde and stronge	31 Hise hise brawnes
Hys shuldres brode / hise armes rounde and longe	Hise shuldres

31 ¶Knyght *23v*

	ELLESMERE
And as the gyse was / in his contree	was
Ful hye / vp on a Chaar of gold stood he	vpon gold / ⟨he⟩
With foure white Boles / in the trays	boles
In stide of Cotearmure / ouer his harnays	stede Cote Armure / ou*er*
With nayles yelwe / and brighte as any gold	yelewe / brigħte goldꝭ
He hadde a Berys Skyn / colblak / for old	Beres skyn / oldꝭ
His longe heer / was kembed bihynde his bakꝭ	kembd / bak
As any Rauenes fethere / it shoon for blakꝭ	
A wrethe of gold / greet of huge wighte	gold Arm greetꝭ
Vp on his heed / and ful of stones brighte	Vpon heed / set ful brigħte
Of fyne Rubyes / and of Dyamau*n*tz	Dyamauntz
Aboute his Chaar / ther wente white Alauntz	Chaarꝭ wenten
Twenty and mo / as grete as any Steer	
To hunten at the leou*n* / and the deer	Leou*n* or / or the
And folwed hym / w*ith* mosel faste ybounde	
Colered of gold / and turrettes filed rounde	t*ur*rettes fyled
An hundred lordes / hadde he in his route	
Armed ful wel / with hertes stierne and stoute	w*ith*
¶With Arcita / in stories as men fynde	With Arcite /
The grete Emetrius / the kyng of Inde	Emetreus /
Vp on a Steede bay / trapped in steel	steede
Couered in a clooth of gold / dyapred weel	in clooth
Cam ridynge / lyk the god of Armes Mars	lykꝭ
His cote armure / was of clooth of Tars	Cote Armure /
Couched w*ith* perlys white / and rounde and grete	with p*er*les / white *and* grete
His sadel was / of brend gold newe ybete	Sadel / was
A Manteletꝭ vp on his shulder hangynge	Mantel /
Bretful of Rubies reede / as fyr sparklynge	Brat ful Rubyes rede /
His crispe heer / lyk rynges was yronne	
And that was yelow / and glitred as the sonne	glytered
His nose was heigh / hise eyen bright Citryn	heigħ / citryn
His lyppes rounde / his colour was sangwyn	Hise lippes
A fewe fraknes / in his face yspreynd	frakenes / yspreyndꝭ
Bitwixen yelow / and som del blak ymeynd	somdel ymeyndꝭ
And as a leou*n* / he his lookyng caste	Leou*n* / lookyngꝭ
Of .xxv. yeer / his age I caste	fyue and twenty
His beerd / was wel bigonne for to sprynge	berd /
His voys / was as a trompe thonderynge	thondrynge
Vp on his heed / he wered of laurer grene	
A gerland fresħ / and lusty for to seene	gerlandꝭ / sene

And as the gyse was / in his contree
Ful hye / vp on a Chaar of gold stood he
With foure white boles / in the trays
In stede of Cote armure / ouer his harnays
With nayles yelwe / and brighte as any gold
He hadde a Beres skyn / colblak for old
His longe heer / was kembd bihynde his bak
As any Rauenes fethere / it shoon for blak
A wrethe of gold / greet of huge wighte
Vp on his heed / and ful of stones brighte
Of fyne Rubyes / and of dyamauntz
Aboute his Chaar / ther wente white alauntz
Twenty and mo / as grete as any steer
To hunten at the leon / and the deer
And folwed hym / with mosel faste ybounde
Colered of gold / and turettes filed rounde
An hundred lordes hadde he in his route
Armed ful wel / with hertes sterne and stoute
With Arcita / in stories as men fynde
The grete Emetreus / the kyng of Inde
Vp on a steede bay / trapped in steel
Couered in a clooth of gold / dyapred weel
Cam ridynge lyk the god of Armes Mars
His cote armure / was of clooth of Tars
Couched with perlys white / and rounde and grete
His sadel was of brend gold newe ybete
A mantelet / vp on his shulder hangynge
Bret ful of Rubies rede / as fyr sparklynge
His crispe heer / lyk rynges was yronne
And that was yelow / and glitered as the sonne
His nose was heigh / hise eyen bright Citryn
His lippes rounde / his colour was sangwyn
A fewe frakenes / in his face yspreynd
Bitwixen yelow / and somdel blak ymeynd
And as a leon / he his lookyng caste
Of .xxv. yeer / his age I caste
His berd was wel bigonne for to sprynge
His voys was as a trompe thonderynge
Vp on his heed / he wered of laurer grene
A gerland fressh / and lusty for to seene

Vp on his hand / he bar for his deduyt /
An Egle tame / as any lilie whyt /
An hundred lordes / hadde he with hym there
Al armed saue hir heddes / in al hir gere
fful richely / in alle maner thynges
ffor trusteth wel / þt dukes / Erles / kynges
Were gadred / in this noble compaignye
ffor loue / and for encrees of chiualrye
Aboute this kyng / ther ran on euery part /
fful many a tame leon and leopart /
And in this wise / thise lordes alle and some
Been on the Sonday / to the Citee come
Aboute prime / and in the toun alight /
This Theseus / this duc / this worthy knyght /
Whan he hadde broght hem / in to his Citee
And Inned hem / euerich at his degree.
He festeth hem / and dooth so greet labour
To esen hem / and doon hem al honour
That yet men wenen / þt no mannes wit /
Of noon estaat / ne koude amenden it /
The mynstralcye / the seruyce / at the feeste
The grete yiftes / to the meeste and leeste
The riche array / of Theseus paleys
Ne who sat first or last / vp on the deys
What ladyes fairest been / and best daunsynge
Or which of hem / kan daunse best and synge
Ne who moost felyngly / speketh of loue
What haukes sitten / on the perche aboue
What houndes liggen / on the floor adoun
Of al this / make I now no mencioun
But al theffect / that thynketh me the beste
Now comth the point / and herkneth if yow leste
The Sonday nyght / er day bigan to sprynge
Whan Palamon / the larke herde synge
Al thogh it nere nat day / by houres two
Yet soong the larke / and Palamon right tho
With holy herte / and with an heigh corage
He roos / to wenden on his pilgrymage
Vn to the blisful / Citherea benygne
I mene Venus / honurable and digne

ELLESMERE

Vp on his hand / he bar for his deduyt
An Egle tame / as any lilie whyt
An hundred lordes / hadde he with hym there
Al armed saue hir heddes / in al hir gere
Ful richely / in alle manere thynges
For trusteth wel / *þ*at dukes / Erles / kynges
Were gadred / in this noble compaignye
For loue / and for encrees of chiualrye
Aboute this kyng ther ran on euery part
Ful many a tame leou*n* and leopart
¶And in this wise / thise lordes alle and some
Been on the Sonday / to the Citee come
Aboute pryme / and in the town alight
¶This Theseus / this duc this worthy knyght
Whan he hadde broght hem / in to his Citee
And Inned hem / euerich at his degree
He festeth hem / and dooth so gret labour
To esen hem / and doon hem al honour
That yet men wenen / *þ*at no mannes wit
Of noon estaat ne koude amenden it /
¶The Mynstralcye / the seruyce / at the feeste
The grete yiftes / to the meeste and leeste
The ryche array / of Theseus Paleys
Ne who sat first or last vp on the deys
What ladyes fairest been / and best daunsynge
Or which of hem / kan daunse best and synge
Ne who moost feelyngly / speketh of loue
What haukes sitten / on the p*er*che aboue
What houndes lyggen / on the floor adown
Of al this / make I now no mencioun
But al theffect that thynketh me the beste
Now comth the point and herkneth if yow leste
¶The Sonday nyght er day bigan to sprynge
Whan Palamon / the larke herde synge
Al thogh it nere nat day / by houres two
Yet soong the larke / and Palamon right tho
With holy herte / and with an heigh corage
He roos / to wenden on his pilgrymage
Vn to the blisful / Scitherea benygne
I mene Venus / honurable and digne

Vpon
lilye
Lordes / wit*h*
maner
Erles
32 gadered /
Leou*n* / leopard
And in
toun alight
knyght
had broght
euerich in his
greet
weneth / no maner wit
it
seruice /
riche paleys
sat first ne last
been / or best
dauncen
felyngly
haukes / sitten perche
houndes / liggen in the adoun
cometh
The nyght
though
song Palamon also |
hooly heigh
blisful Citherea benigne

32 ¶Knyght *24r*

	ELLESMERE
And in hir hour / he walketh forth a paas	houre / pas
Vn to the lystes / ther hir temple was	hire
And down he kneleth / and with hu*m*ble cheere	doun kneleth / with ful humble
And herte soor / he seyde as ye shal heere	soor / and seyde in this manere
¶Faireste of faire / o lady myn Venus	Faireste
Doghter of Ioue / and spouse to Vulcanus	Doughter to Ioue / spouse of Vulcanus
Thow gladere / of the mount of Cytheron	gladere / Mount Citheron
For thilke loue / thow haddest to Adoon	
Haue pitee / of my bittre teerys smerte	teeris
And taak myn humble prayere at thyn herte	preyere
¶Allas I ne haue no langage to telle	Allas / haue /
Theffect. ne the tormentz of myn helle	Theffectes /
Myn herte / may myne harmes nat biwreye	
I am so confus / þ*at* I kan noght seye	that
But mercy lady bright þ*at* knowest wele	33 m*er*cy bright that weele
My thoght and seest what harmes þ*at* I feele	thought seest
Considre al this / and rewe vp on my soore	Considere
As wisly / as I shal for euere moore	eueremoore
Emforth my myght thy trewe seruant be	myght
And holden werre / alwey with chastitee	
That make I myn avow / so ye me helpe	auow /
I kepe noght of armes for to yelpe	noght Armes
Ne I ne axe noght to morwe / to haue victorie	nat tomorwe
Ne renoun in this cas / ne veyne glorie	renou*n*
Of prys of armes / blowen vp and down	pris Armes / doun
But I wolde haue / fully possessioun	
Of Emelye / and dye in thy seruyse	
Fynd thow the manere / how / and in what wyse	hou *and*
I recche nat but it may bettre be	nat /
To haue victorie of hem / or they of me	
So þ*at* I haue / my lady in myn armes	that myne Armes
For thogh so be / þ*at* Mars is god of armes	though that Armes
Youre vertu is so greet in heuene aboue	
That if yow list I shal wel haue my loue	
¶Thy temple / wol I worshipe eu*er*emo	temple
And on thyn Auter / wher I ryde or go	where ride
I wol doon sacrifice / and fyres beete	fires
And if ye wol noght so / my lady sweete	nat
Thanne praye I thee / to morwe with a spere	preye tomorwe / *with*
That Arcita / me thurgh the herte bere	thurgh

2221 The preyere of Palamoun to Venus goddesse of loue El

33 ¶Knyght *24v*

And in hir hour / he walketh forth a paas
Vn to the lystes / ther hir temple was
And doun he kneleth / and with humble cheere
And herte soor / he seyde as ye shal heere
ffayreste of faire / o lady myn Venus
Doghter of Ioue / and spouse to Vulcanus
Thow gladere / of the mount of Citheron
ffor thilke loue / thow haddest to Adoon
Haue pitee / of my bittre teerys smerte
And taak myn humble prayere at thyn herte
Allas I ne haue no langage to telle
Theffect· ne the tormentz of myn helle
Myn herte / may myne harmes nat biwreye
I am so confus / þt I kan noght seye
But mercy lady bright / þt knowest weel
My thoght / and seest what harmes þt I feele
Considre al this / and rewe vp on my soore
As wisly / as I shal for euere moore
Emforth my myght / thy trewe seruant be
And holden werre / alwey with chastitee
That make I myn avow / so ye me helpe
I kepe noght of armes for to yelpe
Ne I ne axe noght tomorwe to haue victorie
Ne renoun in this cas / ne veyne glorie
Of prys of armes / blowen vp and doun
But I wolde haue fully possessioun
Of Emelye / and dye in thy seruyse
ffynd thow the manere how / and in what wyse
I recche nat / but it may bettre be
To haue victorie of hem / or they of me
So þt I haue / my lady in myn armes
ffor thogh so be / þt Mars is god of armes
Youre vertu is so greet / in heuene aboue
That if yow list / I shal wel haue my loue
Thy temple wol I worshipe eueremo
And on thyn auter / wher I ryde or go
I wol doon sacrifice / and fyres beete
And if ye wol noght so / my lady sweete
Thanne preye I thee / tomorwe with a spere
That Arcita / me thurgh the herte bere

Thanne rekke I noght/ whan I haue lost my lyf
Thogh þt Arcita/ wynne hire to his wyf
This is theffect/ and ende of my prayere
yif me my loue/ thow blisful lady deere
¶ Whan the orison was doon/ of Palamon
His sacrifice he dide/ and that anon
ffull pitously/ with alle circumstances
Al telle I nat as now/ his obseruances
But at the laste/ the Statue of Venus shook
And made a signe/ wher by þt he took
That his prayere/ accepted was that day
ffor thogh the signe/ shewed a delay
yet wiste he wel þt graunted was his boone
And with glad herte/ he wente hym hoom ful soone
¶ The thridde hour inequal/ þt Palamon
Bigan to Venus temple/ for to gon
Vp roos the sonne/ and vp roos Emelye
And to the temple of Diane gan hye
Hir maydens/ þt she thider wt hire ladde
ffull redily with hem the fyr they hadde
Thencens/ the clothes/ and the remenant al
That to the sacrifice longen shal
The hornes ful of mede/ as was the gyse
Ther lakked noght/ to doon hir sacrifise
¶ Smokynge the temple/ ful of clothes faire
This Emelye/ with herte debonaire
Hir body wessh/ with water of a welle
But hou she dide hir ryte/ I dar nat telle
But it be any thyng/ in general
And yet it were a game/ to heren al
To hym þt meneth wel/ it were no charge
But it is good/ a man be at his large
¶ Hir brighte heer was kembed/ vntressed al
A corone/ of a grene ook/ cerial
Vp on hir heed was set ful fair and meete
Two fyres on the Auter gan she beete
And dide hir thynges/ as men may biholde
In Stace of Thebes/ and othere bokes olde
Whan kyndled was the fyr/ with pitous cheere
Vn to Diane/ she spak as ye may heere

	ELLESMERE
Thanne rekke I noght⁊ whan I haue lost my lyf	Tha*n*ne nogħt⁊ lyf⁊
Thogh þ*at* Arcita / wynne hire to his wyf⁊	Thougħ that hir*e*
This is theffect⁊ and ende of my prayere	preyere
Yif me my loue / thow blisful lady deere	
¶When the orison was doon / of Palamon	orison / doon Palamou*n*
His sacrifice he dide / and that anon	
Ful pitously / with alle circumstances	circumstau*n*ce
Al telle I nat as now / his obseruances	nogħt obs*er*uau*n*ce
But at the laste / the Statue of Venus shook⁊	But atte laste / statue shook /
And made a signe / wher by þ*at* he took⁊	
That his prayere / accepted was that day	preyere /
For thogh the signe / shewed a delay	
Yet wiste he wel / þ*at* graunted was his boone	
And with glad herte / he wente hym hoom ful soone	w*ith*
¶The thridde hour in equal / þ*at* Palamon	The houre equal that
Bigan / to Venus temple / for to gon	temple
Vp roos the sonne / and vp roos Emelye	
And to the temple of Diane / gan hye	Dyane
Hir maydens / þ*at* she thider w*ith* hire ladde	hir*e*
Ful redily with hem / the fyr they hadde	redily / w*ith* hem they ladde
Thencens / the clothes / and the remenant al	
That to the sacrifice / longen shal	
The hor⟨n⟩es ful of Mede / as was the gyse	[34] hornes fulle Meeth /
Ther lakked noght⁊ to doon hir sacrifise	nogħt⁊
¶Smokynge the temple / ful of clothes faire	
This Emelye / with herte debonaire	
Hir body wessħ / with water of a welle	
But hou she dide hir ryte / I dar nat telle	
But it be / any thyng⁊ in general	thyng /
And yet⁊ it were a game / to heren al	heeren
To hym þ*at* meneth wel / it nere no charge	it were no
But it is good / a man be at his large	been
¶Hir brighte heer was kembed / vntressed al	kembd'
A corone / of a grene ook⁊ cerial	coroune / ook /
Vp on hir heed was set⁊ ful fair and meete	Vpon
Two fyres / on the Auter gan she beete	Auter /
And dide hir thynges / as men may biholde	
In Stace of Thebes / and othere bokes olde	and thise bookes
Whan kyndled was the fyr / with pitous cheere	w*ith*
Vn to Diane / she spak / as ye may heere	Dyane / spak⁊

[34]¶Knygħt⁊ *25r*

	ELLESMERE
¶O chaste goddesse / of the wodes grene	O
To whom / bothe heuene / and erthe / and .i. *mare* See is seene	whom heuene *and* erthe *and* see sene
Queene of the regne of Pluto / derk and lowe	Pluto derk /
Goddesse of maydens / þ*at* myn herte hast knowe	that
Ful many a yeer / and woost what I desire	
As keep*e* me / fro thy vengeance and thyn Ire	vengeau*n*ce
That Attheou*n* / aboghte crewelly	Attheon / aboughte cruelly
Chaste goddesse / wel wostow þ*at* I	.I.
Desire / to been a mayden / al my lyf	ben mayden lyf /
Ne neuere wol I be / no loue / ne wyf	neuer*e* be loue
I am thow woost yet of thy compaignye	
A mayde / and loue huntyng and venerye	huntynge
And for to walken / in the wodes wilde	
And noght to been a wyf / and be with childe	ben wit*h*
Noght wol I knowe / compaignye of man	knowe / the compaignye
Now help me lady / sith ye may and kan	help*e*
For tho thre formes / þ*at* thow hast in thee	thou
And Palamon / þ*at* hath swich loue to me	that
And eek Arcite / þ*at* loueth me so soore	that
This grace I praye thee / with oute moore	preye thee
As seend loue and pees / bitwix hem two	And sende bitwixe
And fro me / turn*e* awey / hir hertes so	turne awey
That al hir hote loue / and hir desir	hir*e* hoote
And al hir bisy torment and hir fyr	fir
Be queynt and turned in another place	queynt or turned /
And if so be / thow wolt noght do me grace	thou wolt do me no grace
Or if my destynee / be shape so	And if shapen
That I shal nedes / haue oon of hem two	nedes
As seend me hym / þ*at* moost desireth me	sende
Bihoold goddesse / of clene chastitee	
The bittre teerys / þ*at* on my chekes falle	35 teeris / that
Syn thow art mayde / and keper*e* of vs alle	thou kepere
My maydenhode thow kepe / and wel conserue	maydenhede thou kepe
And whil I lyue / a mayde I wol thee serue	
¶The fyres brenne / vp on the Auter cleere	fires
Whil Emelie / is thus in hir prayere	Emelye / was thus preyere
But sodeynly / she seigh a sighte queynte	saugh sigħte
For right anon / oon of the fyres queynte	
And quyked agayn / and after that anon	
That oother fyr was queynt and al agon	

2297 The preyere of Emelye to Dyane goddesse of Maydens El

35 ¶Knygħt *25v*

O chaste goddesse of the wodes grene
To whom bothe heuene and erthe and see is seene
Queene of the regne of Pluto derk and lowe
Goddesse of maydens þt myn herte hast knowe
ffful many a yeer and woost what I desire
As keep me fro thy vengeance and thyn ire
That Attheon aboghte cruelly
Chaste goddesse wel woostow þt I
Desire to been a mayden al my lyf
Ne neuere wol I be no loue ne wyf
I am thow woost yet of thy compaignye
A mayde and loue huntyng and venerye
And for to walken in the wodes wilde
And noght to been a wyf and be with childe
Noght wol I knowe compaignye of man
Now help me lady sith ye may and kan
ffor tho thre formes þt thow hast in thee
And Palamon þt hath swich loue to me
And eek Arcite þt loueth me so soore
This grace I praye thee with oute moore
As sende loue and pees bitwixe hem two
And fro me turn awey hir hertes so
That al hir hote loue and hir desir
And al hir bisy torment and hir fyr
Be queynt and turned in another place
And if so be thow wolt noght do me grace
Or if my destynee be shape so
That I shal nedes haue oon of hem two
As sende me hym þt moost desireth me
Bihoold goddesse of clene chastitee
The bittre teerys þt on my chekes falle
Syn thow art mayde and kepere of vs alle
My maydenhode thow kepe and wel conserue
And whil I lyue a mayde I wol thee serue
The fyres brenne vp on the Auter cleere
Whil Emelie is thus in hir preyere
But sodeynly she seigh a sighte queynte
ffor right anon oon of the fyres queynte
And quyked agayn and after that anon
That oother fyr was queynt and al agon

And as it queynte it made a whistlynge
As don thise weete brondes in hir brennynge
And at the brondes ende out ran anoon
As it were blody dropes many oon
Ffor which so soore agast was Emelye
That she was wel neigh mad and gan to crye
For she ne wiste what it signyfied
But oonly for the feere thus hath she cryed
And weep þt it was pitee for to heere
And ther with al Diane gan appeere
With bowe in honde right as an hunteresse
And seyde doghter stynt thyn heuynesse
Among the goddes hye it is affermed
And by eterne word writen and confermed
Thou shalt be wedded vn to oon of tho
That han for thee so muche care and wo
But vn to which of hem I may noght telle
Ffare wel for I ne may no lenger dwelle
The fires whiche þt on myn auter brenne
Shul thee declaren er þt thow go henne
Thyn auenture of loue as in this cas
And with that word the arwes in the caas
Of the goddesse clateren faste and rynge
And forth she wente and made a vanysshynge
Ffor which this Emelye astoned was
And seyde what amounteth this allas
I putte me in thy protection
Diane and in thy disposicion
And hoom she gooth anoon the nexte weye
This is theffect ther nys namoore to seye
The nexte houre of Mars folwynge this
Arcite vn to the temple walked is
Of fierse Mars to doon his sacrifise
With alle the rytes of his payen wyse
With pitous herte and heigh deuocion
Right thus to Mars he seyde his orison
O stronge god þt in the regnes colde
Of Trace honoured art and lord yholde
And hast in euery regne and euery lond
Of armes al the brydel in thyn hond

	ELLESMERE
And as it queynte / it made a whistlynge	
As doon thise weete brondes / in hir brennynge	wete brondes
And at the brondes ende / out ran anoon	anon
As it were / blody dropes many oon	
For which / so soore agast was Emelye	
That she was wel neigh mad / and gan to crye	ny mad
For she ne wiste / what it signyfied	
But oonly for the feere / thus hath she cryed	cried
And weep*e* / þ*a*t it was pitee for to heere	that
¶And ther with al / Diane gan appeere	And Dyane
With bowe in honde / right as an hunteresse	right
And seyde doghter / stynt thyn heuynesse	
Among the goddes hye / it is affermed	Among
And by eterne word / writen and confermed	
Thou shalt be wedded / vn to oon of tho	ben wedded
That han for thee / so muche care and wo	muchel
But vn to which of hem / I may noght telle	nat
Fare wel / for I ne may no lenger dwelle	Farwel /
The fires / whiche þ*a*t on myn Auter brenne	that
Shul thee declaren / er þ*a*t thow go henne	Shulle declare / that thou
Thyn auenture of loue / as in this cas	
And with that word / the Arwes in the Caas	wit*h*
Of the goddesse / clateren faste and rynge	
And forth she wente / and made a vanysshynge	vanysshynge
For which / this Emelye astoned was	Emelye /
And seyde / what amounteth this allas	
I putte me / in thy proteccioun*n*	p*ro*teccioun*n*
Diane / and in thy disposicioun*n*	Dyane /
And hoom she gooth anoon / the nexte weye	goth anon
This is theffect ther nys namoore to seye	ther is namoore
¶The nexte houre of Mars / folwynge this	The Mars
Arcite / vn to the temple walked is	
Of fierse Mars / to doon his sacrifise	
With alle the rytes / of his payen wise	wyse
With pitous herte / and heigh deuocioun*n*	
Right thus to Mars / he seyde his orisoun*n*	Right
¶O stronge god / þ*a*t in the regnes colde	O that
Of Trace / honoured art and lord yholde	
And hast in euery regne / and euery lond	36 ¶And lond
Of armes / al the brydel in thyn hond	Armes / hond

2349 The answere of Dyane to Emelye El

2373 The orisoun of Arcite to Mars god of Armes El

36 ¶Knyght *26r*

The Knyght.	ELLESMERE		
And hem fortunest as thee list deuyse	lyst		
Accepte of me / my pitous sacrifise			
If so be / þ*at* my youthe may disserue	be that	deserue	
And þ*at* my myght be worthy for to serue	myght		
Thy godhede / þ*at* I may be oon of thyne	been		
Thanne praye I thee / to rewe vp on my pyne	preye		
For thilke peyne / and thilke hote fyr	hoote fir		
In which / thow whilom brendest for desir			
Whan þ*at* thow vsedest the beautee			
Of faire yonge / fresshe Venus free	fresshe		
And haddest hire / in armes at thy wille	hir*e* /		
Al though thee ones / on a tyme mysfille			
Whan Vulcanus / hadde caught thee in his laas	las		
And foond thee lyggyng by his wyf allas	liggynge /		
For thilke sorwe / þ*at* was in thyn herte	that		
Haue routhe as wel / vp on my peynes sm*er*te	smerte		
I am yong / and vnkonnyng as thow woost /	yong	vnkonnynge	woost
And as I trowe / with loue offended moost			
That euere was / any lyues creature			
For she þ*at* dooth me / al this wo endure	she /		
Ne reccheth neuere / wher I synke or fleete			
And wel I woot er she me mercy heete			
I moot with strengthe / wynne hire in the place	wit*h*	hir*e*	
And wel I woot with outen help and grace	wit*h*	help*e* or grace	
Of thee / ne may my strengthe noght auaille			
Thanne help me lord / tomorwe in my bataille	help*e*		
For thilke fyr / þ*at* whilom brende thee	that	brente	
As wel as thilke fyr / now brenneth me	wel /		
And do þ*at* I tomorwe / may haue victorie	do / that	tomorwe haue	
Myn be the trauaille / and thyn be the glorie			
Thy souereyn temple / wol I moost honouren			
Of any place / and alwey moost labouren			
In thy plesaunce / and in thy craftes stronge	plesau*n*ce /		
And in thy temple / I wol my baner honge			
And alle the armes / of my compaignye	Armes /		
And euere mo / vn til þ*at* day I dye	vn to that		
Eterne fyr / I wol bifore thee fynde	fir /	biforn	
And eek to this auow / I wol me bynde	eek /		
My berd / myn heer / þ*at* hangeth long adown	beerd /	that hongeth	adoun
That neuere yet ne felte offensioun			

And hem fortunest as thee list deuyse
Accepte of me / my pitous sacrifise
If so be / þt my youthe may disserue
And þt my myght / be worthy for to serue
Thy godhede / þt I may be oon of thyne
Thanne praye I thee / to rewe vp on my pyne
ffor thilke peyne / and thilke hote fyr
In which thow whilom brendest for desyr
Whan þt thow vsedest the beautee
Of faire yonge / fresshe Venus free
And haddest hire in armes at thy wille
Al though thee ones / on a tyme mysfille
Whan Vulcanus / hadde caught thee in his laas
And foond thee liggyng / by his wyf allas
ffor thilke sorwe / þt was in thyn herte
Haue routhe as wel / vp on my peynes smerte
I am yong / and vnkonnyng / as thow woost /
And as I trowe / with loue offended moost /
That euere was / any lyues creature
ffor she þt dooth me / al this wo endure
Ne reccheth neuere / wher I synke or fleete
And wel I woot / er she me mercy heete
I moot with strengthe / wynne hire in the place
And wel I woot / with outen help and grace
Of thee / ne may my strengthe noght auaille
Thanne help me lord / tomorwe in my bataille
ffor thilke fyr / þt whilom brende thee
As wel as thilke fyr / now brenneth me
And do þt I tomorwe / may haue victorie
Myn be the trauaille / and thyn be the glorie
Thy souereyn temple / wol I moost honouren
Of any place / and alwey moost labouren
In thy plesaunce / and in thy craftes stronge
And in thy temple / I wol my baner honge
And alle the armes / of my compaignye
And eueremo / vn til þt day I dye
Eterne fyr / I wol bifore thee fynde
And eek to this auow / I wol me bynde
My berd / myn heer / þt hangeth long adoun
That neuere yet / ne felte offensioun

Of rasour / ne of shere / I wol thee yiue
And been thy trewe seruant / whil I lyue
Now lord haue routhe / vp on my sorwes soore
Yif me the victorie / I axe thee namoore
¶ The prayere stynt / of Arcita tho stronge
The rynges / on the temple dore þt honge
And eek the dores / clatereden ful faste
Of which Arcita / som what hym agaste
The fires brende / vp on the auter brighte
That it gan al the temple for to lighte
A swete smel / anoon the ground vp yaf
And Arcita / anoon his hand vp haf
And moore encens / in to the fyr he caste
With othere rytes mo / and at the laste
¶ The statue of Mars / bigan his hauberk rynge
And with that soun / he herde a murmurynge
Ful lowe and dym / and seyde thus / Victorie
For which he yaf to Mars / honour and glorie
¶ And thus with ioye / and hope / wel to fare
Arcite anoon / vn to his In is fare
As fayn as fowel / is of the brighte sonne
¶ And right anoon / swich stryf ther is bigonne
For thilke grauntyng / in the heuene aboue
Bitwixe Venus / the goddesse of loue
And Mars / the sterne god armypotente
That Iuppiter / was bisy it to stente
Til þt the pale / Saturnus the colde
That knew so manye / of auentures olde
Foond in his olde experience an art /
That he ful soone / hath plesed euery part /
As sooth is seyd / elde hath greet auantage
In elde / is bothe wisdom and vsage
Men may the olde atrenne / and nat atrede
Saturne anoon / to stynten stryf and drede
Al be it þt it is agayn his kynde
Of al this stryf he kan remedie fynde
¶ My deere doghter Venus / quod Saturne
My cours / that hath so wyde for to turne
Hath moore power / than woot any man
Myn is the drenchyng / in the see so wan

	ELLESMERE
Of Rasour / nor of Shere / I wol thee yiue	rasour / shere / yeue
And been thy trewe seruant’ whil I lyue	ben s*er*uant’
Now lord haue routhe / vp on my sorwes soore	routhe
Yif me the victorie / I axe thee namoore	aske
¶The prayere stynt’ of Arcita the stronge	The preyere
The rynges / on the temple dore þ*at* honge	that
And eek’ the dores / clatereden ful faste	37 ¶And
Of which Arcita / som what hym agaste	
The fires brende / vp on the Auter brighte	fyres brenden / brigħte
That it gan al the temple for to lighte	gan / ligħte
A swete smel / anoon the ground vp yaf’	And sweete smel / the ground anon vp yaf
And Arcita / anoon his hand vp haf’	anon
And moore encens / in to the fyr he caste	
With othere rytes mo / and at the laste	and atte laste
¶The Statue of Mars / bigan his hauberk’ rynge	The hauberk
And with that sown / he herde a m*ur*murynge	w*ith* soun /
Ful lowe and dym / and seyde thus / victorie	
For which / he yaf to Mars / honour and glorie	
¶And thus with ioye / and hope / wel to fare	And thus / hope
Arcite anoon / vn to his In is fare	anon /
As fayn as fowel / is of the brighte sonne	brigħte
¶And right anoon / swich stryf ther is bigonne	rigħt anon / strif /
For thilke grauntyng’ in the heuene aboue	
Bitwixe Venus / the goddesse of loue	
And Mars / the sterne god armipotente	stierne god Armypotente
That Iuppiter / was bisy it to stente	Iuppiter’
Til þ*at* the pale / Saturnus the colde	that
That knew so manye / of auentures olde	
Foond in his olde experience / an art’	Foond / exp*er*ience and Art’
That he ful soone / hath plesed euery part’	
As sooth is seyd / elde hath greet auantage	
In elde / is bothe wisdom and vsage	wysdom
Men may the olde atrenne / and nat atrede	at renne / noght at rede
Saturne anoon / to stynten stryf and drede	anon / strif
Al be it / þ*at* it is agayn his kynde	it’ that it is /
Of al this stryf’ he kan remedie fynde	strif / he gan remedie
¶My deere doghter Venus / quod Saturne	
My cours / that hath so wyde for to turne	
Hath moore power / than woot any man	
Myn is the drenchyng’ in the See so wan	see

[37] ¶Knyghħt’ *26v*

The Knyght	ELLESMERE
Myn is the prison / in the derke cote	
Myn is the stranglyng and hangyng by the throte	hangyng
The murmur / and the cherles rebellynge	m*ur*mure / rebellyng
The groynyng and the pryuee empoysonynge	groynynge / empoysonyng
I do vengeance / and pleyn correcciou*n*	
Whil I dwelle / in the signe of the leou*n*	in signe
Myn is the ruyne / of the heighe halles	hye
The fallyng of the toures / and of the walles	fallynge /
Vp on the Mynour / or the Carpenter	Mynour
I slow Sampson / shakyng the piler	Sampsou*n* / shakynge
And myne be / the maladies colde	maladyes
The derke tresons / and the castes olde	
My lookyng is the fader of pestilence	
Now weep namoore / I shal doon diligence	weep*e*
That Palamon / that is thyn owene knyght	38 knyght
Shal haue his lady / as thow hast hym hight	thou hight
Thogh Mars shal helpe his knyght yet nathelees	Though
Bitwixe yow / ther moot be som tyme pees	
Al be ye noght of o complexiou*n*	complecciou*n*
That causeth al day / swich diuisiou*n*	day
I am thyn Aiel / redy at thy wille	
Weep*e* now namoore / I wol thy lust fulfille	
¶Now wol I stynten / of the goddes aboue	
Of Mars / and of Venus / goddesse of loue	Venus
And telle yow / as pleynly as I kan	
The grete effect. for which þ*at* I bigan[39]	40 effect that bygan
¶Greet was the feeste / in Atthenes that day	GReet
And eek the lusty sesou*n* / of that May	eek / seson
Made euery wight to been in swich plesaunce	wight plesau*n*ce
That al that monday / Iusten they and daunce	Monday /
And spenden it in Venus heigh seruyse	spenten heigh
And by the cause / þ*at* they sholde ryse	that
Erly / for to seen the grete sight	Eerly / grete fight
Vn to hir reste / wente they at nyght	wenten nyght
And on the morwe / whan the day gan sprynge	what þ*at* day
Of hors and harneys / noyse and claterynge	
Ther was in hostelryes / al aboute	hostelryes
And to the paleys / rood ther many a route	
Of lordes / vp on steedes and palfreys	steedes /
Ther maistow seen / deuysynge of harneys	maystow seen diuisynge

38 ¶Knyght *27r*

39 No break in Hg.

40 Break in El after 2482 followed by:

¶Explicit tercia pars

¶Sequit*ur* pars quarta

Myn is the prison / in the derke cote
Myn is the stranglyng / and hangyng by the throte
The murmur / and the cherles rebellynge
The groynyng / and the pryuee enpoysonynge
I do vengeance / and pleyn correccion
Whil I dwelle / in the signe of the leon
Myn is the ruyne / of the heighe halles
The fallyng of the toures / and of the walles
Vp on the mynour / or the Carpenter
I slow Sampson / shakyng the piler
And myne be / the maladies colde
The derke tresons / and the castes olde
My lookyng / is the fader of pestilence
Now weep namoore / I shal doon diligence
That Palamon / that is thyn owene knyght /
Shal haue his lady / as thow hast hym hight /
Though Mars shal helpe his knyght / yet natheles
Bitwixe yow / ther moot be som tyme pees
Al be ye noght / of o complexion
That causeth al day / swich diuision
I am thyn aiel / redy at thy wille
Weep now namoore / I wol thy lust fulfille
Now wol I stynten / of the goddes aboue
Of Mars / and of Venus goddesse of loue
And telle yow / as pleynly as I kan
The grete effect . for which þt I bigan
Greet was the feeste / in Atthenes that day
And eek the lusty seson / of that May
Made euery wight to been in swich plesaunce
That al that Monday / justen they and daunce
And spenden it / in Venus heigh seruyse
And by the cause / þt they sholde ryse
Erly / for to seen the grete fight
Vn to hir reste / wente they at nyght /
And on the morwe / whan the day gan sprynge
Of hors and harneys / noyse and claterynge
Ther was in hostelryes / al aboute
And to the paleys / rood ther many a route
Of lordes / vp on steedes and palfreys
Ther maystow seen / deuysynge of harneys

So vnkouth / and so ryche / and wroght so weel
Of Goldsmythrye / of browdyng / and of steel
The sheldes brighte / testers / and trappures
Goldhewen helmes / hauberkes / cote armures
Lordes in parementz / on hir coursers
Knyghtes of retenue / and eek Squyers
Nailynge the speres / and the helmes bokelynge
Gyggynge of sheeldes / with layneres lasynge
Ther as nede is / they were no thyng ydel
The fomy steedes / on the golden brydel
Gnawynge / and faste the armurers also
With fyle and hamer / prykyng to and fro
Yemen on foote / and communes many oon
With shorte staues / thikke as they may goon
Pipes / trompes / nakers / clariounes
That in the bataille blowen blody sownes
The paleys ful of peples / vp and down
Heer thre / ther ten / holdynge hir questioun
Deuynynge / of thise Thebans knyghtes two
Somme seyde thus / somme seyden it shal be so
Somme helden with hym / with the blake berd
Somme wt the balled / somme wt the thikke herd
Somme seyde / he looked grym / and he wolde fighte
He hath a sparth of .xx. pound of wighte
Thus was the halle / ful of deuynynge
Longe after / þt the sonne gan to sprynge
¶ The grete Theseus / þt of his sleep awaked
With mynstralcye / and noyse þt was maked
Held yet the chambres / of his paleys ryche
Til þt tho Theban knyghtes / bothe yliche
Honoured / weren in to the paleys fet
¶ Duc Theseus / is at a wyndowe set
Arrayed / right as he were a god in Trone
The peple preesseth thiderward ful soone
Hym for to seen / and doon heygh reuerence
And eek to herkne his heste / and his sentence
¶ An heraud on a Scaffold / made an oo
Til al the noyse / of the peple was ydo
And whan he say the peple / of noyse al stille
Thus shewed he / the myghty dukes wille

The lord hath

	ELLESMERE
So vnkouth / and so ryche / and wroght so weel	vnkouth riche / wrogħt
Of Goldsmythrye / of Broudyngꝭ and of steel	goldsmythrye / browdynge /
The sheldes brighte / testers / and trappures	sheeldes testeres /
Goldhewen helmes / hauberkes / cote armures	Gold hewen hauberkes Cote Armures
Lordes in parementz / on hir coursers	courseres
Knyghtes of retenue / and eek Squyers	Squieres
Nailynge the speres / and the helmes bokelynge	and helmes
Gyggynge of sheeldes / with layners lasynge	Giggynge *with* layneres lacynge
Ther as nede is / they were no thyng ydel	There weren
The fomy steedes / on the golden brydel	
Gnawynge / and faste the Armurers also	
With fyle and hamer / prykyng to and fro	hamer prikynge
Yemen on foote / and co*m*munes many oon	
With shorte staues / thikke as they may goon	
Pipes / trompes / Nakers / Claryounes	Pypes / Nakerers / Clariounes
That in the bataille / blowen blody sownes	sounes
The paleys ful of peples / vp and down	41 paleys / peples doun
Heer thre / ther ten / holdynge hir questioun	Heere questiou*n*
Deuynynge / of thise Thebans knyghtes two	Dyuynynge / Thebane
So*m*me seyde thus / so*m*me seyden it shal be so	seyden thus / seyde it
So*m*me helden with hym / with the blake berd	*with* hym / *with* berd'
So*m*me w*ith* the balled / so*m*me w*ith* the thikke herd	So*m*me with the balled / herd'
So*m*me seyde / he looked grym / and he wolde fighte	grymme / figħte
He hath a Sparth / of .xx. pound of wighte	sparth / twenty wighte
Thus was the halle / ful of deuynynge	diuynynge
Longe after / *pat* the sonne gan to sprynge	that
¶The grete Theseus / *pat* of his sleep*e* awaked	The that
With mynstralcye / and noyse *pat* was maked	Mynstralcie /
Held yet the chambres / of his paleys ryche	Heeld chambre / Paleys riche
Til *pat* the Theban*e* knyghtes / bothe yliche	thatꝭ Thebane
Honoured /. weren in to the Paleys fet	Honured / were paleys fetꝭ
¶Duc Theseus / is at a wyndow setꝭ	Ducꝭ Theseus / was at
Arrayed / right as he weere a god in Trone	rigħt were
The peple preeseth / thiderward ful soone	peple / preesseth
Hym for to seen / and doon heigh reu*er*ence	reuerence
And eek / to herkne his heste / and his sentence	eekꝭ herkne / heste
¶An heraud on a Scaffold / made an .oo.	heraud' Scaffold Oo
Til al the noyse / of the peple was ydo	noyse of peple
And whan he say the peple / of noyse al stille	saugħ / the noyse of peple al
Thus shewed he / the myghty dukes wille	Tho shewed Dukes

The lord hath

41¶Knyghtꝭ *27v*

ELLESMERE

¶The lord hath / of his heighe discreciou*n*
Considred / þ*at* it were destrucciou*n*
To gentil blood / to fighten in the gyse
Of mortal bataille / now in this emprise
Wher fore / to shapen / þ*at* they shal noght dye
He wole / his firste purpos modifie
¶No man ther fore / vp on peyne / of los of lyf
No manere shot ne polax / ne short knyf
In to the lystes sende / or thider brynge
Ne short swerd for to stoke / with point bitynge
No man ne drawe / ne bere it by his syde
Ne no man / shal vn to his felawe ryde
But o cours / with a sharp ygrounde spere
Foyne if hym list on foote / hym self to were
And he þ*at* is at meschief / shal be take
And noght slayn / but be broght vn to the stake
That shal been ordeyned / on eyther syde
But thider he shal bi force / and ther abyde
And if so falle / the Chiefteyn be take
On outher syde / or ellis sleen his make
No lenger / shal the tourneying laste
God spede yow / go forth and ley on faste
With long swerd / and w*ith* mace / fighteth your fille
Go now youre wey / this is the lordes wille
¶The voys of peple / touched the heuene
So loude cryde they / with loude steuene
God saue swich a lord / that is so good
He wilneth / no destrucciou*n* of blood
¶Vp goon the trompes / and the melodye
And to the lystes / ryt the compaignye
By ordinance / thurgh out the Citee large
Hanged with clooth of gold / and noght w*ith* sarge
¶Ful lyk a lord / this noble duc gan ryde
Thise two Thebans / vp on eyther syde
And after rood the queene / and Emelye
And after that another compaignye
Of oon and oother / after hir degree
And thus they passen / thurgh out the Citee
And to the lystes / coome they bityme
It nas nat of the day / yet fully pryme

lord / hath heigh
Considered / that

Wherfore / nat
wolde / modifye
therfore / vp peyne
maner shot polax /
sende / ne thider
w*ith* poynt
bere by
man shal /
sharp*e*

he / that meschief
noght broght
ben either
by force / there
¶And if so be / the chieftayn
elles
lenger turneiynge
you / gooth forth /
W*ith* swerd / Maces / youre
Gooth
42 THe
cride with murie steuene

destruccion
Vp
rit

w*ith* gold nat
lik
either
rood / queene

thurgh
come by tyme

42 ¶Knyght *28r*

The lord hath / of his heighe discrecion
Considered / þt it were destruction
To gentil blood / to fighten in the gyse
Of mortal bataille / now in this emprise
Wher fore / to shapen / þt they shal noght dye
He wole / his firste purpos modifie
No man ther fore / up on peyne / of los of lyf
No manere shot / ne polax / ne short knyf
In to the lystes sende / or thider brynge
Ne short swerd for to stoke / with point bitynge
No man ne drawe / ne bere it by his syde
Ne no man / shal vn to his felawe ryde
But o cours / with a sharp ygrounde spere
ffoyne if hym list on foote / hym self to were
And he þt is at meschief / shal be take
And noght slayn / but be broght vn to the stake
That shal been ordeyned / on eyther syde
But thider he shal by force / and ther abyde
And if so falle / the chieftayn be take
On outher syde / or ellis sleen his make
No lenger / shal the tourneiyng laste
God spede yow / go forth and ley on faste
With long swerd / and wt mace / fighteth youre fille
Go now youre wey / this is the lordes wille
The voys of peple / touched the heuene
So loude cryde they / with loude steuene
God saue swich a lord / that is so good
He wilneth / no destruction of blood
Vp goon the trompes / and the melodye
And to the lystes / ryt the compaignye
By ordinance / thurgh out the Citee large
Hanged with clooth of gold / and noght wt sarge
Ful lyk a lord / this noble duc gan ryde
Thise two Thebans / up on eyther syde
And after rood the queene / and Emelye
And after that / another compaignye
Of oon and oother / after hir degree
And thus they passen / thurgh out the Citee
And to the lystes / coome they bytyme
It nas nat of the day / yet fully pryme

Whan set was Theseus ful ryche and hye
Ypolita the queene and Emelye
And othere ladyes in degrees aboute
Vn to the setes preesseth al the route
And westward thurgh the gates vnder marte · vnder marte
Arcite and eek the hundred of his parte
With baner reed is entred right anon
And in that selue moment Palamon
Is vnder Venus Estward in the place
With baner whit and hardy cheere and face
In al the world to seken vp and doun
So euene with outen variacioun
Ther nere swiche compaignyes tweye
ffor ther was noon so wys þt koude seye
That any hadde of oother auantage
Of worthynesse ne of estaat ne age
So euene were they chosen for to gesse
And in two renges faire they hem dresse
Whan þt hir names rad were euerichon
That in hir nombre gyle were ther noon
Tho were the gates shet and cryd was loude
Do now youre deuoir yonge knyghtes proude
The heraudes lefte hir prikyng vp and doun
Now ryngen trompes loude and clarioun
Ther is namoore to seyn but west and est
In goon the speres ful sadly in the arest
In gooth the sharpe spore in to the syde
Ther seen men who kan juste and who kan ryde
Ther shyueren shaftes vp on sheeldes thikke
He feeleth thurgh the herte spoon the prikke
Vp spryngeth speres twenty foot on highte
Out goon the swerdes as the siluer brighte
The helmes they tohewen and to shrede
Out brest the blood with sterne stremys rede
With myghty maces the bones they to breste
He thurgh the thikkest of the throng gan threste
Ther stomblen steedes stronge and doun gooth al
He rolleth vnder foot as dooth a bal
He foyneth on his feet with his tronchoun
And he hym hurteth with his hors adoun

	ELLESMERE
¶Whan set was Theseus / ful ryche and hye	Whan riche
Ypolita the queene / and Emelye	queene
And othere ladyes / in degrees aboute	ladys /
Vn to the setes / preeseth al the route	Seetes preesseth
.i. sub Marte	.i. s*u*b Marte
And westward / thurgh the gates vnder Marte	Marte
Arcite / and eek the hundred of his parte	hondred
With baner reed / is entred right anon	
¶And in that selue moment Palamou*n*	moment
Is vnder Venus / Estward in the place	
With baner whit / and hardy cheere and face	Baner whyt / chiere *and*
In al the world / to seken vp and down	doun
So euene / with outen variacioun	
Ther nere / swiche compaignyes tweye	
For ther was noon so wys / þ*at* koude seye	wys
That any hadde / of oother auantage	auauntage
Of worthynesse / ne of estaat ne age	
So euene / were they chosen for to gesse	euene were chosen /
And in two renges / faire they h⟨e⟩m dresse	hem
¶Whan þ*at* hir names / rad were euerichon	
That in hir nombre / gyle were ther noon	
Tho were the gates shet and cryd was loude	cried
Do now youre deuoir / yonge knyghtes proude	
¶The heraudes / lefte hir prikyng vp and down	prikyng doun
Now ryngen trompes loude / and Clarioun	loude clarioun
Ther is namoore to seyn / but west and Est	west
In goon the speres / ful sadly in the arest	in arrest
In gooth the sharpe spore / in to the syde	
Ther seen men / who kan Iuste / and who kan ryde	Iuste *and*
Ther shyueren shaftes / vp on sheeldes thikke	
He feeleth / thurgh the herte spoon the prykke	prikke
Vp spryngeth speres / twenty foot on highte	spryngen hiħte
Out goon the swerdes / as the siluer brighte	gooth briħte
The helmes they tohewen / and to shrede	43 toshrede
Out brest the blood / with sterne stremys rede	stierne stremes
With myghty maces / the bones they tobreste	to breste
He thurgh the thikkest of the throng gan threste	thikkeste /
Ther stomblen steedes stronge / and doun gooth al	Ther semblen steedes
He rolleth vnder foot as dooth a bal	
He foyneth on his feet with his tronchoun	tronchou*n*
And he hym hurteth / with his hors adoun	hurtleth /

43 ¶Knyghħt *28v*

ELLESMERE

He thurgh the body is hurt and sithen ytake
Maugree his heed / and broght vn to the stake
As forward was / right there he moste abyde
Another / lad is on that oother syde
¶And som tyme / dooth hem Theseus to reste
Hem to refresshe / and drynken if hem leste
Ful ofte a day / haue thise Thebans two
Togydre ymet and wroght his felawe wo
Vnhorsed hath ech oother / of hem tweye
Ther nas no tygre / in the vale of Galgopheye
Whan *þat* hir whelp is stole / whan it is lyte
So cruel on the hunte / as is Arcite
For Ialous herte / vp on this Palamou*n*
Ne in Belmarye / ther nys so fel leou*n*
That hunted is / or for his hunger wood
Ne of his praye / desireth so the blood
As Palamon / to sleen his foo Arcite
The Ialous strokes / on hir helmes byte
Out renneth blood / on bothe hir sydes rede
¶Som tyme an ende ther is / of euery dede
For er the sonne / vn to the reste wente
The stronge kyng Emetrius / gan hente
This Palamon / as he faught with Arcite
And made his swerd / depe in his flessh to byte
And by the force of twenty / is he take
Vnyolden / and ydrawen to the stake
And in the rescous / of this Palamou*n*
The stronge kyng lygurge / is born adoun
And kyng Emetrius / for al his strengthe
Is born out of his sadel / a swerdes lengthe
So hitte hym Palamon / er he were take
But al for noght he was broght to the stake
His hardy herte / myghte hym helpe naught
He moste abyde / whan *þat* he was caught
By force / and eek by composiciou*n*
¶Who sorweth now / but woful Palamou*n*
That moot namoore / goon agayn to fighte
And whan *þat* Theseus / hadde seen this sighte
Vn to the folk / that foghten thus echon
He cryde / hoo namoore / for it is doon

ELLESMERE

broght
was right
Another is /
to fresshen / and
han Thebanes
wroght
hath / oother
Tygre
whelp*e* lite
crueel
For Ielous
Palamou*n* /
The Ielous
ende / is
kyng Emetreus /
with
ydrawe vn to
rescus /
kyng
kyng Emetreus /
Palamou*n*
noght / broght
that caught
fighte
seyn sighte
folk / *þat*

He thurgh the body is hurt / and sithen ytake
Maugree his heed / and broght vn to the Stake
As forward was / right there he moste abyde
Another lad is on that oother syde
¶ And som tyme / dooth hem Theseus to reste
Hem to refresshe / and drynken if hem leste
ffful ofte a day / haue thise Thebans two
Togydre ymet / and wroght his felawe wo
Vnhorsed hath ech oother / of hem tweye
Ther nas no tygre / in the vale of Galgopheye
Whan þt hir whelp is stole / whan it is lyte
So cruel on the hunte / as is Arcite
ffor Ialous herte / vp on this Palamon
Ne in Belmarye / ther nys so fel leon
That hunted is / or for his hunger wood
Ne of his praye / desireth so the blood
As Palamon / to sleen his foo Arcite
The Ialous strokes / on hir helmes byte
Out renneth blood / on bothe hir sydes rede
¶ Som tyme an ende ther is / of euery dede
ffor er the sonne / vn to the reste wente
The stronge kyng Emetrius / gan hente
This Palamon / as he faught with Arcite
And made his swerd / depe in his flessh to byte
And by the force of twenty / is he take
Vnyolden / and ydrawen to the Stake
And in the rescous / of this Palamon
The stronge kyng lygurge / is born adoun
And kyng Emetreus / for al his strengthe
Is born out of his sadel / a swerdes lengthe
So hitte hym Palamon / er he were take
But al for noght / he was broght to the Stake
His hardy herte / myghte hym helpe naught /
He moste abyde / whan þt he was caught /
By force / and eek by composicion
¶ Who sorweth now / but woful Palamon
That moot namoore / goon agayn to fighte
And whan þt Theseus / hadde seen this sighte
Vn to the folk / that foghten thus echon
He cryde / hoo namoore / for it is doon

I wol be trewe Juge / and nat partye
Arcite of Thebes / shal haue Emelye
That by his fortune / hath hire faire ywonne
Anon ther is a noyse of peple bigonne
ffor ioye of this / so loude and heigh with alle
It semed / þt the lystes sholde falle
¶ What kan now faire Venus / doon aboue
What seith she now / what dooth this queene of loue
But wepeth so / for wantyng of hir wille
Til þt hir teeres / in the lystes fille
She seyde / I am ashamed doutelees
¶ Saturnus seyde / doghter hoold thy pees
Mars hath his wil / his knyght hath al his boone
And by myn heed / thow shalt been esed soone
¶ The trompours / wt the loude mynstralcye
The heraudes / þt ful loude yelle and crye
Been in hir wele / for ioye of daun Arcite
But herkneth me / and stynteth noyse a lite
Which a myracle / ther bifel anon
¶ This fierse Arcite / hath of his helm ydon
And on a courser / for to shewe his face
He priketh endelong / the large place
lookyng upward / vp on this Emelye
And she agayn / hym caste a freendly eye
And she was al his cheere / as in his herte
Out of the ground / a furye infernal sterte
ffrom Pluto sent / at requeste of Saturne
ffor which his hors / for feere gan to turne
And leep asyde / and foundred as he leep
And er þt Arcite / may taken keep
He pighte hym / on the pomel of his heed
That in the place / he lay as he were deed
His brest tobrosten / with his Sadel bowe
As blak he lay / as any col / or crowe
So was the blood / yronnen in his face
Anon he was yborn out of the place
With herte soor / to Theseus paleys
Tho was he coruen / out of his harneys
And in a bed ybroght / ful faire and blyue
ffor he was yet / in memorie and alyue

	ELLESMERE
I wol be trewe Iuge / and nat partye	44 ¶I and no partie
Arcite of Thebes / shal haue Emelye	Emelie
That by his fortune / hath hire faire ywonne	hir*e*
Anon ther is a noyse of peple bigonne	Anon /
For ioye of this / so loude and heigh with alle	Ioye heighe w*ith*
It semed / *þat* the lystes sholde falle	that
¶What kan now faire Venus / doon aboue	What Venus
What seith she now / what dooth this queene of loue	
But wepeth so / for wantyng of hir wille	wantynge
Til *þat* hir teerys / in the lystes fille	that teeres /
She seyde / I am ashamed doutelees	
¶Saturnus seyde / doghter hoold thy pees	
Mars hath his wyl / his knyght' hath al his boone	wille /
And by myn heed / thow shalt been esed soone	
¶The trompours / w*ith* the loude Mynstralcye	The trompes / with Mynstralcie
The heraudes / *þat* ful loude yelle and crye	that yolle crie
Been in hir wele / for ioye of daun Arcite	hir*e* Ioye
But herkneth me / and stynteth noyse alite	stynteth now alite
Which a myracle / ther bifel anon	
¶This fierse Arcite / hath of his helm ydon	
And on a Courser / for to shewe his face	
He priketh / endelong' the large place	priketh
Lookyng vpward / vp on this Emelye	Lokynge vpward vp on Emelye
And she agayn / hym caste a freendly eye[45]	freendlich
And she was al his cheere / as in his herte	And was chiere /
Out of the ground / a furye Infernal sterte	¶Out furie
From Pluto sent' at requeste of Saturne	
For which his hors / for feere gan to turne	fere
And leep asyde / and foundred as he leep*e*	leep*e* aside /
And er *þat* Arcite / may taken keep*e*	that
He pighte hym / on the pomel of his heed	pigħte [¶No*ta* peric*ulum*]
That in the place / he lay as he were deed	place lay /
His brest to brosten / with his Sadel bowe	brest' tobrosten / sadel
As blak he lay / as any col / or crowe	cole
So was the blood / yronnen in his face	
Anon he was yborn out of the place	was /
With herte soor / to Theseus Paleys	paleys
Tho was he coruen / out of his harneys	koruen /
And in a bed ybroght' ful faire and blyue	ybrouħt /
For he was yet' in memorie and alyue	memorie /

44 ¶Knygħt' *29r*

45 *Out* Hg El 2681-82. Cp reads:
For wo*m*men as to speken in comune
Thei folwen aƚƚ þe fauour of fortune

	ELLESMERE
And alwey cryinge / after Emelye	alwey / criynge
¶Duc Theseus / with al his compaignye	
Is comen hoom / to Atthenes his Citee	
With alle blisse / and greet solempnytee	solempnitee
Al be it *þat* this auenture was falle	that Auenture
He nolde noght disconforten hem alle	
¶Men seyde eek Arcite / shal nat dye	Men eek that Arcite
He shal been heelyd / of his maladye	heeled /
And of another thyng / they were as fayn	46 ¶And another thyng / weren
That of hem alle / was ther noon yslayn	
Al were they soore yhurt and namely oon	
That w*ith* a Spere / was thirled the brest boon	spere / thirled his brest
¶To oothere woundes / and to broken armes	To othere Armes
So*m*me hadden salues / and so*m*me hadden charmes	
Fermacyes of herbes / and eek saue	Fermacies
They dronken / for they wolde hir lymes haue	
For which this noble duc / as he wel kan	duc
Conforteth / and honoureth euery man	
And made reuel / al the longe nyght	nyght
Vn to the straunge lordes / as was right	right
¶Ne ther was holden / no disconfitynge	Ne
But as a Iustes / or a tourneyinge	tourneiynge
For soothly / ther was no disconfiture	
For fallyng. nys nat but an auenture	fallyng Auenture
Ne to been had by force / vn to the stake	to be lad by
Vnyolden / and with twenty knyghtes take	knyghtes
O p*er*sone allone / with outen mo	allone
And haryed forth / by arm / foot / and to	Arm / foot too
And eek his steede / dryuen forth w*ith* staues	
With footmen / bothe yemen and eek knaues	
It nas arretted hym / no vileynye	hym
Ther may no man / clepe it cowardye	clepen
¶For which anoon / duc Theseus leet crye	anon /
To stynten / al rancour and enuye	alle
The g[r]e / as wel of oo syde as of oother	gree / o
And eyther syde ylyk as otheres brother	ylik ootheres
And yaf hem yiftes / after hir degree	
And fully heeld a feeste / dayes three	fully /
And conueyed / the kynges worthily	conuoyed /
Out of his toun / a iournee largely	Iournee

46 ¶Knyght *29v*

And alwey cryinge after Emelye
Duc Theseus with al his compaignye
Is comen hoom to Atthenes his Citee
With alle blisse and greet Solempnytee
Al be it yt this auenture was falle
He nolde noght disconforten hem alle
Men seyde eek Arcite shal nat dye
He shal been heelyd of his maladye
And of another thyng they were as fayn
That of hem alle was ther noon yslayn
Al were they soore yhurt and namely oon
That wt a spere was thirled his brest boon
To othere woundes and to broken armes
Somme hadden salues and somme hadden charmes
Fermacyes of herbes and eek saue
They dronken for they wolde hir lymes haue
For which this noble Duc as he wel kan
Conforteth and honoureth euery man
And made reuel al the longe nyght
Vn to the straunge lordes as was right
Ne ther was holden no disconfitynge
But as a Iustes or a tourneyinge
For soothly ther was no disconfiture
For fallyng nys nat but an auenture
Ne to been lad by force vn to the stake
Vnyolden and with twenty knyghtes take
O persone allone with outen mo
And haryed forth by arm foot and to
And eek his steede dryuen forth wt staues
With footmen bothe yemen and eek knaues
It nas arretted hym no vileynye
Ther may no man clepe it cowardye
For which anoon Duc Theseus leet crye
To stynten al rancour and enuye
The gree as wel of o syde as of oother
And eyther syde ylyk as otheres brother
And yaf hem yiftes after hir degree
And fully heeld a feeste dayes three
And conueyed the kynges worthily
Out of his toun a iournee largely

And hoom wente every man the righte way
Ther was namoore but fare wel have good day
Of this bataille I wol namoore endite
But speke of Palamon and of Arcite

Explicit secunda pars

Incipit pars tercia et ultima

Swelleth the brest of Arcite and the soore
Encreesseth at his herte moore and moore
The clothered blood for any lechecraft
Corrupteth and is in his bouk ylaft
That neyther veyne blood ne ventusynge
Ne drynke of herbes may been his helpynge
The vertu expulsyf or animal
ffro thilke vertu cleped natural
Ne may the venym voyden ne expelle
The pipes of his longes gan to swelle
And every lacerte in his brest adoun
Is shent with venym and corrupcioun
Hym gayneth neither for to gete his lyf
Vomyt upward ne dounward laxatyf
Al is tobrosten thilke regioun
Nature hath no dominacioun
And certeinly ther nature wol nat wirche
ffare wel phisyk go ber the man to chirche
This al and som pt Arcita moot dye
ffor which he sendeth after Emelye
And Palamon pt was his cosyn deere
Thanne seyde he thus as ye shal after heere
Naught may the woful spirit in myn herte
Declare a point of alle my sorwes smerte
To yow my lady pt I love moost
But I biquethe the servyce of my goost
To yow aboven every creature
Syn pt my lyf may no lenger dure
Allas the wo allas the peynes stronge
That I for yow have suffred and so longe

And hoom wente eu*er*y man / the righte way
Ther was namoore / but fare wel haue good day
Of this bataille / I wol namoore endite
But speke of Palamon / and of Arcite

¶Explicit secunda pars

¶Incipit pars t*er*cia *et* vltim*a*

Swelleth the brest of Arcite / and the soore
Encreeseth at his herte / moore and moore
The clothered blood / for any lechecraft
Corrupteth / and is in his bouk / ylaft
That neyther veyne blood / ne ventusynge
Ne drynke of herbes / may been his helpynge
The v*er*tu expulsyf / or animal
Fro thilke v*er*tu / clepyd natural
Ne may the venym / voyden ne expelle
The pipes of his longes / gan to swelle
And euery lacerte / in his brest adown
Is shent with venym and corrupcioun
Hym gayneth neither / for to gete his lyf
Vomyt vpward / ne downward laxatyf
Al is to brosten / thilke regioun
Nature / hath no dominacioun
And c*er*teinly / ther nature wol nat werche
Fare wel Phisyk. go ber the man to cherche
This al and som / *pat* Arcita moot dye
For which / he sendeth after Emelye
And Palamon / *pat* was his cosyn deere
Thanne seyde he thus / as ye shal after heere
¶Nat may the woful spirit in myn herte
Declare a point of alle my sorwes smerte
To yow my lady / *pat* I loue moost
But I byquethe / the seruice of my goost
To yow / abouen euery creature
Syn *pat* my lyf / may no lenger dure
Allas the wo / allas the peynes stronge
That I for yow haue suffred / and so longe

ELLESMERE

euery man righte
wel /
47 Palamou*n*

Eucreesseth

bouk
neither
ben
vertu expulsif / Animal
vertu / cleped

gonne
adoun
corrupciou*n*
48 neither lif
dounward laxatif
tobrosten / Regioun
Nature hath now / no
certeinly / Nature wirche
Phisik chirche
that
sendeth /
that

¶Naught may /
Declare o point
that
biquethe / seruyce

suffred

[47] No break in El.

[48] ¶Knyght *30r*

The Knyght /	ELLESMERE
Allas the deeth / allas myn Emelye	
Allas / departyng of oure compaignye	departynge
Allas myn hertes queene / allas my wif	wyf
Myn hertes lady / ender*e* of my lyf	endere lyf
What is this world / what axeth men to haue	asketh
2778 Now with his loue / now in his colde graue[49]	
2783 ¶I haue heer / with my cosyn Palamon	I *with* Palamon
Had stryf and rancour / many a day gon	strif rancour agon
For loue of yow / and for my Ialousye	
And Iuppiter / so wys my soule gye	
To speken / of a seruaunt p*ro*prely	seruau*n*t proprely
With circumstaunces alle / trewely	With alle circumstances trewely
That is to seyn / trouthe / honour / knyghthede	hono*ur* / knyghthede
Wisdom / humblesse / estaat / and heigh kynrede	Wysdom / estaat
Fredom / and al / that longeth to that art	al Art
So Iuppiter / haue of my soule part	
As in this world / right now ne knowe I non	right
So worthy to been loued / as Palamon	ben
That serueth yow / and wol doon al his lyf	lyf
And if *þa*t euere / ye shal been a wyf	that shul ben wyf
Foryet nat Palamon / the gentil man	
And with that word / his speche faille gan	*with*
For from his feet vp to his brest was come	And from his herte / vp
The coold of deeth / *þa*t hadde hym ou*er*come	that
And yet moore ouer / for in his armes two	ouer hys*e* Armes
The vital strengthe / is lost and al ago	strengthe lost /
Oonly the Intellect with oute moore	50 Oonly / intellect outen
That dwelled in his herte / syk and soore	
Gan faillen / whan the herte felte deeth	
Dusked hise eyen two / and fayled breeth	failled
But on his lady / yet caste he his eye	lady yet
His laste word / was mercy Emelye	
His spirit chaunged hous / and wente ther	
As I cam neuere / I kan nat tellen wher	neu*er*e /
Therfore I stynte / I nam no dyuynystre	diuinistre
Of soules / fynde I nat in this Registre	
Ne me ne lyst / thilke opynyons to telle	list opinions
Of hem / thogh *þa*t they writen wher they dwelle	though
Arcite is coold / ther Mars his soule gye	
Now wol I speken / forth of Emelye	speken

[49] *Out* Hg 2779-82. El reads:

Allone / with outen any compaignye
Fare wel / my sweete foo / myn Emelye
And softe taak me / in youre Armes tweye
For loue of god / and herkneth what I seye

[50] ¶Knyght *30v*

Allas the deeth allas myn Emelye
Allas departyng of oure compaignye
Allas myn hertes queene allas my wyf
Myn hertes lady endere of my lyf
What is this world what axeth men to haue
Now with his loue now in his colde graue
I haue heer with my cosyn Palamon
Had stryf and rancour many a day gon
ffor loue of yow and for my Ialousye
And Iuppiter so wys my soule gye
To speken of a seruaunt proprely
With circumstaunces alle trewely
That is to seyn trouthe honour knyghthede
Wysdom humblesse estaat and heigh kynrede
ffredom and al that longeth to that art
So Iuppiter haue of my soule part
As in this world right now ne knowe I non
So worthy to been loued as Palamon
That serueth yow and wol doon al his lyf
And if þt euere ye shal been a wyf
fforyet nat Palamon the gentil man
And with that word his speche faille gan
ffor from his feet vp to his brest was come
The cold of deeth þt hadde hym ouercome
And yet moore ouer for in his armes two
The vital strengthe is lost and al ago
Oonly the Intellect with oute moore
That dwelled in his herte syk and soore
Gan faillen whan the herte felte deeth
Dusked hise eyen two and fayled breeth
But on his lady yet caste he his eye
His laste word was mercy Emelye
His spirit chaunged hous and wente ther
As I cam neuere I kan nat tellen wher
Ther fore I stynte I nam no dyuynystre
Of soules fynde I nat in this registre
Ne me ne lyst thilke opynyouns to telle
Of hem though þt they writen wher they dwelle
Arcite is coold ther Mars his soule gye
Now wol I speken forth of Emelye

Shrighte Emelye and howleth Palamon
And Theseus his suster took anon
Swownynge and baar hir fro the corps away
What helpeth it to tarien forth the day
To tellen how she weep bothe eue and morwe
For in swich cas wommen haue swich sorwe
Whan þt hir housbondes been from hem ago
That for the moore part they sorwen so
Or ellis fallen in swich a maladye
That at the laste certeinly they dye
Infinite been the sorwes and the teerys
Of olde folk and folk of tendre yeerys
In al the town for the deeth of this Theban
For hym ther wepeth bothe child a man
So greet wepyng was ther noon certayn
Whan Ector was broght al fressh yslayn
To Troye allas the pitee þt was ther
Cracchynge of chekes rentynge eek of heer
Why woldestow be deed thise wommen crye
And haddest gold ynow and Emelye
No man myghte gladen Theseus
Sauynge his olde fader Egeus
That knew this worldes transmutacioun
As he hadde seyn it chaungen bothe up and doun
Joye after wo and wo after gladnesse
And shewed hem ensample and lyknesse
Right as ther dyed neuere man quod he — Argumentum
That he ne lyued in erthe in som degree
Right so ther lyued neuere man he seyde
In al this world þt som tyme he ne deyde
This world nys but a thurghfare ful of wo
And we been pilgrymes passynge to and fro
Deeth is an ende of euery worldly soore
And ouer al this yet seyde he muchel moore
To this effect ful wysly to enhorte
The peple that they sholde hem reconforte
Duc Theseus with al his bisy cure
Caste now wher that the sepulture
Of goode Arcite may best ymaked be
And eek moost honurable in his degree

		ELLESMERE
¶Shrighte Emelye / and howleth Palamon		Shrighte
And Theseus / his suster took anon		
Swownynge / and baar hire fro the corps away		
What helpeth it to tarien forth the day		
To tellen how she weepe / bothe eue and morwe		tellen /
For in swich caas / wommen haue swich sorwe		cas / wommen
Whan þat hir housbondes / been from hem ago		housbond / is from
That for the moore part they sorwen so		
Or ellis fallen / in swich a maladye		ellis / fallen swich maladye
That at the laste / certeinly they dye		certeinly
¶Infinite / been the sorwes and the teerys		teeres
Of olde folk. and folk of tendre yeerys		folk / and eek of yeeres
In al the town / for the deeth of this Theban		toun / for deeth
For hym ther wepeth bothe child a man		wepeth / child and man
So greet wepyng was ther noon certayn		greet a wepyng
Whan Ector was broght al fressħ yslayn		ybroħt /
To Troye / allas the pitee þat was ther		
Cracchynge of chekes / rentyng eek of heer		rentynge
Why woldestow be deed / thise wommen crye		
And haddest gold ynow / and Emelye		ynougħ /
¶No man / myghte gladen Theseus		
Sauyng his olde fader Egeus		Sauynge /
That knew / this worldes transmutacioun		transmutacioun
As he hadde seyn it chaungen / bothe vp and down		hadde / it / vp doun
Ioye after wo / and wo after gladnesse		
And shewed hem / ensample and lyknesse		ensamples liknesse
¶Right as ther deyed neuere man / quod he	Argumentum	¶Argumentum] Rigħt ther dyed neuere man
That he ne lyued in erthe / in som degree		lyuede
Right so / ther lyued neuere man he seyde		lyuede neuer
In al this world / þat som tyme he ne deyde		
This world / nys but a thurghfare / ful of wo		thurghfare
And we been pilgrymes / passynge to and fro		
Deeth is an ende / of euery worldly soore		worldes
And ouer al this / yet seyde he muchel moore		
To this effect ful wysly / to enhorte		51 wisely /
The peple / that they sholde hem reconforte		
¶Duc Theseus / with al his bisy cure		Duc
Caste now / wher that the sepulture		Cast
Of goode Arcite / may best ymaked be		
And eek moost honurable / in his degree		eek honurable

51 ¶Knygħt *31r*

And at the laste / he took conclusiou*n*	
That ther / as firstꝛ Arcite and Palamou*n*	ther
Hadden for loue / the bataille hem bitwene	
That in the selue groue / swoote and grene	Thatꝛ in that selue
Ther as he hadde / hise amorouse desires	
His compleinte / and for loue his hote fyres	compleynte / hise hoote fires
He wolde make a fyr / in which the office	
Funeral / he myghte al acomplice	Fun*er*al / myghte accomplice
And leet anoon comaunde / to hakke and hewe	leet comande anon / to
The okes olde / and leyen hem on a rewe	leye
In colpons / wel arrayed for to brenne	
Hise officers / with swifte feetꝛ they renne	Officers / feet
And ryde anoon / at his comandementꝛ	ryden anon /
And after this / Theseus hath ysentꝛ	after /
After a Beere / and it al ouerspradde	beere / ouer spradde
With clooth of gold / the richeste / *þa*t he hadde	
And of the same suyte / he cladde Arcite	
Vp on his handes / his gloues white	hise hondes / hadde he gloues
Eek on his heed / a coroune of laurer greene	grene
And in his hand / a swerd ful bright and keene	hond / kene
He leyde hym bare the visage / on the beere	
Ther with he weep*e* / *þa*t pitee was to heere	that
And for the peple / sholde seen hym alle	
Whan it was day / he broghte hym to the halle	broghte
That roreth / of the cryyngꝛ and the sown	criyngꝛ soun
Tho cam / this woful Theban Palamou*n*	¶Tho cam
With flotry berd / and ruggy asshy heerys	flotery rugged Asshy heeres
In clothes blake / ydropped al with teerys	teeres
And passyngꝛ othere / of wepyng Emelye	passynge wepynge
The rufulleste / of al the compaignye	rewefulleste /
In as muche / as the seruyce sholde be	
The moore noble / and ryche in his degree	riche
Duc Theseus / leet forth thre steedes brynge	
That trapped weren in steel al gliterynge	were
And couered with the armes / of daun Arcite	Armes /
Vp on thise steedes / grete and whyte	white
Ther seten folk / of which oon baar his sheeld	sitten folkꝛ whiche sheeld
Another his spere / vp on his hondes heeld	spere / in his heeld
The thridde bar with hym / his bowe Turkeys	baar w*ith*
Of brend gold / was the caas / and eek the harneys	

And at the laste / he took conclusion
That ther / as first Arcite and Palamon
Hadden for loue / the bataille hem bitwene
That in the selue groue / swoote and grene
Ther as he hadde / hise amorouse desires
His compleynte / and for loue his hoote fires
He wolde make a fyr / in which the office
ffuneral / he myghte al accomplice
And leet anoon comaunde / to hakke and hewe
The okes olde / and leyen hem on a rewe
In colpons / wel arrayed for to brenne
Hise officers / with swifte feet they renne
And ryde anoon / at his comandement
And after this / Theseus hath ysent
After a beere / and it al ouerspradde
With clooth of gold / the richeste þt he hadde
And of the same suyte / he cladde Arcite
Vp on his handes / his gloues white
Eek on his heed / a coroune of laurer grene
And in his hand / a swerd ful bright and kene
He leyde hym bare the visage / on the beere
Ther with he weep / þt pitee was to heere
And for the peple / sholde seen hym alle
Whan it was day / he broghte hym to the halle
That roreth of the crying / and the sown
Tho cam this woful Theban Palamon
With flotery berd / and ruggy asshy heerys
In clothes blake / ydropped al with teerys
And passyng othere / of wepyng Emelye
The rewfulleste / of al the compaignye
In as muche / as the seruyce sholde be
The moore noble / and riche in his degree
Duc Theseus / leet forth thre steedes brynge
That trapped weren in steel al gliterynge
And couered with the armes / of daun Arcite
Vp on thise steedes / grete and white
Ther seten folk / of which oon bar his sheeld
Another his spere / vp on his hondes heeld
The thridde bar with hym / his bowe Turkeys
Of brend gold / was the cas / and eek the harneys

And ryden forth a paas with sorweful cheere
Toward the groue as ye shul after heere
The nobleste of the grekys þt ther weere
Vp on hir shuldres carieden the beere
With slak paas and eyen rede and weete
Thurgh out the Citee by the maister streete
That sprad was al with blak and wonder hye
Right of the same is the strete ywrye
Vp on the right hand wente olde Egeus
And on that oother syde duc Theseus
With vessels in hir hand of gold ful fyn
Al ful of hony melk and blood and wyn
Eek Palamon with ful greet compaignye
And after that cam woful Emelye
With fyr in hande as was that tyme the gyse
To do the office of funeral seruyse
Heigh labour and greet apparaillynge
Was at the seruyce and the fyr makynge
That wt his grene top the heuene raughte
And twenty fadme of brede the armes straughte
This is to seyn the bowes were so brode
Of stree first ther was leyd many a lode
But how the fyr was maked vp on highte
Ne eek the names how the trees highte
As ook firre birch asp alder holm popler
Wylow elm plane assh box chasteyn lynde laurer
Mapul thorn beech hasyl ew whippultree
How they were feld shal nat been told for me
Ne how the goddes ronnen vp and doun
Desherited of hir habitacioun
In which they woneden in reste and pees
Nymphes ffawnes and Amadrides
Ne how the beestes and the bryddes alle
ffledden for feere whan the wode was falle
Ne how the ground agast was of the light
That was nat wont to seen the sonne bright
Ne how the fyr was couched first with stree
And thanne with drye stikkes clouen a three
And thanne with grene wode and spicerye
And thanne with clooth of gold and with perrye

	ELLESMERE
And ryden forth a paas / with sorweful cheere	riden
Toward the groue / as ye shul after heere	
The nobleste of the Grekys / þat ther were	52 grekes / that
Vp on hir shuldres / carieden the beere	caryeden
With slak paas / and eyen rede and weete	wete
Thurgh out the Citee / by the maister streete	strete
That sprad was al with blak' and wonder hye	blak' /
Right of the same / is the strete ywrye	Rigħt Strete
Vp on the right hand / wente olde Egeus	rigħt hond /
And on that oother syde / duc' Theseus	
With vessels in hir hand / of gold ful fyn	vessel
Al ful of hony / melk / and blood and wyn	Milk'
Eek Palamon / with ful greet compaignye	
And after that / cam woful Emelye	
With fyr in hande / as was that tyme the gyse	*With* honde /
To do the office / of funeral seruyse	
¶Heigh labour / and greet apparaillynge	Heigh labour' and ful greet
Was at the seruyce / and the fyr makynge	seruice /
That *with* his grene top*e* / the heuene raughte	with heuene |
And twenty fadme of brede / the armes straughte	Armes
This is to seyn / the bowes / were so brode	bowes weren
Of stree first' ther was leyd many a lode	leyd ful many
But how the fyr was maked vp on highte	fyr / hiħte
Ne eek the names / how the trees highte	eek' names / that the hiħte
As ook / Fyrre / Birch / Asp / Alder / holm / popler	ook' firre / bircħ / Aspe / popeler
Wylow / Elm / Plane / Assh / Box / Chestayn / lynde / laurer	Wylugh / plane / Asħ / box / chasteyn /
Mapul / Thorn / Beech / hasyl / Ew / Whippultree	thorn / bech / hasel / Whippeltree
How they were feld / shal nat been told for me	weren fild' / be toold
Ne how the goddes / ronnen vp and doun	hou goddes
Desherited / of hir habitacioun	Disherited / hir*e*
In which they woneden / in reste and pees	whiche
Nymphes / Fawnes / and Amadrides	Nymphus /
Ne how the beestes / and the bryddes alle	hou briddes
Fledden / for fered / whan the wode was falle	Fledden fere /
Ne how the ground / agast was of the lyght'	ligħt'
That was nat wont' to seen the sonne bright'	brigħt'
Ne how the fyr / was couched first with stree	
And thanne with drye stikkes / clouen a three	stokkes / thre
And thanne with grene wode / and spicerye	wode
And thanne with clooth of gold / and with perrye	*with* *with*

52 ¶Knyght' *31v*

∫The Knyght / ∫

And gerlandes hangynge / ful of many a flour
The Mirre / thencens / with al so greet sauour
Ne how Arcite / lay among al this
Ne what richesse / aboute the body is
Ne how that Emelye / as was the gyse
Putte in the fyr / of funeral seruyse
Ne how she swowned / whan men made the fyr
Ne what she spak' ne what was hir desir
Ne what Iuels / men in the fyr caste
Whan *þat* the fyr was greet' and brente faste
Ne how so*m*me caste hir sheeld / and so*m*me hir spere
And of hir vestimentz / whiche *þat* they were
And coppes fulle of Milk / and wyn and blood
In to the fyr / *þat* brente as it were wood
Ne how the Grekys / with An huge route
Thries ryden / al the fyr aboute
Vp on the left hand / with a loud shoutynge
And thries / with hir speres claterynge
And thries / how the ladyes gonne crye
And how *þat* lad / was homward Emelye
Ne how Arcite / is brent to Asshen colde
Ne how that lychwake / was yholde
Al thilke nyght' ne how the grekys pleye
The wake pleyes / ne kepe I noght to seye
Who wrastleth best naked / with oille enoynt'
Ne who *þat* baar hym best' in no disioynt'
I wol nat tellen al / how they goon
Hoom til Atthenes / whan the pleye is doon
But shortly to the poynt' than wol I wende
And maken / of my longe tale an ende
¶By p*ro*ces / and by lengthe of certeyn yerys
Al stynt is / the moornynge and the terys
Of Grekys / by oon gene⟨r⟩al assent'
Thanne semed me / ther was a p*ar*lement'
At Atthenes / vp on a certeyn point' and caas
Among the whiche pointes / yspoken was
To haue / with certeyn contrees alliance
And haue fully / of Thebans obeisance
For which / this noble Theseus anon
Leet senden / after gentil Palamon

ELLESMERE

gerlandes / hangynge / with ful many
greet odour
aboute his body
fyr'
made fyr
Ieweles / fyr*e*
53 ¶Ne
hir*e*
of wyn / and Milk' and
that brente /
grekes / an
Tries riden / the place aboute
left' *with*
how / lad
Ne / lych wake /
nygħt / grekes
nat
that
¶I tellen eek' how that they
pley
point' thanne
By processe / yeres
stynted *and* teres
grekes / general assent
on certein pointz
Among' pointz /
certein alliau*n*ce
obeisau*n*ce

[53] ¶Knygħt' *32r*

And gerlandes hangynge / ful of many a flour
The myrre thencens / with al so greet sauour
Ne how Arcite lay among al this
Ne what richesse / aboute the body is
Ne how that Emelye / as was the gyse
Putte in the fyr / of funeral seruyse
Ne how she swowned / whan men made the fyr
Ne what she spak / ne what was hir desir
Ne what Iuels men in the fyr caste
Whan þt the fyr was greet / and brente faste
Ne how somme caste hir sheeld / and somme hir spere
And of hir vestimentz / whiche þt they were
And cuppes fulle of mylk and wyn and blood
In to the fyr / þt brente as it were wood
Ne how the Grekys / with an huge route
Thries ryden / al the fyr aboute
Vp on the left hand / with a loud shoutynge
And thries / with hir speres claterynge
And thries / how the ladyes gonne crye
And how þt lad was homward Emelye
Ne how Arcite / is brent to asshen colde
Ne how that lychewake / was yholde
Al thilke nyght / ne how the Grekys pleye
The wake pleyes / ne kepe I noght to seye
Who wrastleth best naked / with oille enoynt
Ne who þt baar hym best / in no disioynt
I wol nat tellen al / how they goon
Hoom til Atthenes / whan the pleye is doon
But shortly to the poynt / thanne wol I wende
And maken / of my longe tale an ende
By proces / and by lengthe of certeyn yeerys
Al stynt is the moornynge and the teerys
Of Grekys / by oon general assent
Thanne semed me / ther was a parlement
At Atthenes / vp on a certeyn poynt and caas
Among the whiche poyntes / yspoken was
To haue with certeyn contrees alliance
And haue fully of Thebans obeisance
For which this noble Theseus anon
Leet senden after gentil Palamon

vnwist of hym what was the cause and why
But in his blake clothes sorwefully
He cam at his comandement in hye
Tho sente Theseus for Emelye
Whan they were set and hust was al the place
And Theseus abiden hath a space
Er any word cam from his wise brest
His eyen sette he ther as was his lest
And with a sad visage he siked stille
And after that right thus he seyde his wille
Theseo. The firste moeuere of the cause aboue
Whan he first made the faire cheyne of loue
Greet was theffect and heigh was his entente
Wel wiste he why and what ther of he mente
For with that faire cheyne of loue he bond
The fyr the eyr the water and the lond
In certeyn boundes þt they may nat flee
That same Prince and that moeuere quod he
Hath stablissed in this wrecched world adoun
Certeyne dayes and duracioun
To al that is engendred in this place
Ouer the which day they may nat pace
Al mowe they yet tho dayes abregge
Ther nedeth noon auctoritee to allegge
For it is preued by experience
But þt me list declaren my sentence
Thanne may men wel by this ordre discerne
That thilke moeuere stable is and eterne
Wel may men knowe but it be a fool
That euery part is dirryued from his hool
For nature hath nat taken his bigynnyng
Of no partie or of cantel of a thyng
But of a thyng that parfit is and stable
Descendynge so til it be corrumpable
And therfore for his wise purueiaunce
He hath so wel biset his ordinaunce
That speces of thynges and progressions
Shullen enduren by successions
And noght eterne with outen any lye
This maystow vnderstonde and seen at eye

	ELLESMERE
Vnwist of hym / what was the cause and why	Vnwistʼ
But in his blake clothes / sorwefully	Butʼ hise
He cam at his comandement / in hye	cam / comandementʼ
Tho sente Theseus / for Emelye	sente / Theseus
¶Whan they were setʼ and hust was al the place	Whan
And Theseus / abiden hath a space	hadde
Er any word / cam from his wise brest /	fram brestʼ
His eyen sette he / ther as was his lestʼ	Hise eyen
And with a sad visage / he siked stille	
And after thatʼ right thus he seyde his wille	riħt
Nota ¶The firste moeuere / of the cause aboue	The
Whan he first made / the faire cheyne of loue	
Greet was theffectʼ and heigh was his entente	
Wel wiste he why / and what ther of he mente	
For with that faire cheyne of loue he boond	bondʼ
The fyr / the Eyr / the water / and the loond	fyrʼ the eyr / the water and the londʼ
In c*er*teyn boundes / þ*a*t they may nat flee	certeyn that
That same Prince / and that moeuere quod he	prince / that same moeuere
Hath stabliced / in this wrecched world adoun	54 stablissed /
Certeine dayes / and duracioun	Certeyne
To al / that is engendred / in this place	engendred
Ouer the which day / they may nat pace	
Al mowe they yet / tho dayes abregge	yetʼ dayes wel abregge
Ther nedeth / noon auctoritee to allegge	nedeth noħtʼ noon Auctoritee allegge
For it is proued / by experience	preeued /
But þ*a*t me listʼ declaren my sentence	that
Thanne may men wel / by this ordre discerne	men / by ordre wel discerne
That thilke moeuere / stable is and eterne	moeu*er*e /
Wel may men knowe / but it be a fool	
That euery partʼ. is diryued from his hool	partʼ dirryueth
For nature / hath nat taken his bigynnyngʼ	hath taken
Of no partie / or of cantel of a thyngʼ	
But of a thyngʼ. that p*ar*fit is and stable	thyngʼ
Descendynge so / til it be corrumpable	
And ther fore / for his wise purueiaunce	therfore / of his
He hath / so wel biset his ordinaunce	bisetʼ
That specis of thynges / and progressions	speces p*ro*gressiou*n*s
Shullen enduren / by successions	successiou*n*s
And noght eterne / with outen any lye	nat
This maistow vnderstonde / and seen at Iye	maystow seen it eye

[54] ¶Knyghtʼ *32v*

¶Loo the ook / that hath so long a norisshynge
Fro the tyme / that it first gynneth sprynge
And hath so long a lyf / as ye may see
Yet at the laste / wasted is the tree
¶Considreth eek / how þ*a*t the harde stoon
Vnder oure foot on which we ryde and goon
It wasteth / as it lyth by the weye
The brode Ryuer / som tyme wexeth dreye
The grete townes / se we wane and wende
Thanne se ye / þ*a*t al this thyng hath ende
⟨Of man and wo*m*man / se we wel also⟩
⟨That nedeth / in oon of thise te*r*mes two⟩
This is to seyn / in youthe / or ellis age
He moot be deed / the kyng as shal a page
Som in his bed / som in the depe see
Som in the large feeld / as ye may se
Ther helpeth noght al gooth that ilke weye
Thanne may I seyn / þ*a*t al this thyng moot deye
What maketh this ⸮ but Iuppiter the kyng
That is Prince / and cause of alle thyng
Conue*r*tyng al vn to his p*ro*pre welle
From which it is diryued sooth to telle
And heer agayns / no creature on lyue
Of no degree / auailleth for to stryue
¶Thanne is it wisdom / as it thynketh me
To maken v*er*tu / of necessitee
And take it wel / þ*a*t we may nat eschue
And nameliche / that to vs alle is due
And who so gruccheth oght he dooth folye
And rebel is / to hym þ*a*t al may gye
And certeinly / a man hath moost honour
To dyen / in his excellence and flour
Whan he is siker / of his goode name
Thanne hath he doon / his freend ne hym no shame
And gladder oghte / his freend been of his deeth
Whan with honour / yolden is vp his breeth
Than whan his name / apalled is for age
For al forgeten is his vasselage
Thanne is it best as for a worthy fame
To dyen / whan he is best of name
¶The contrarie of al this / is wilfulnesse
Why grucchen we / why haue we heuynesse

ELLESMERE

¶Exemplu*m*] Loo þ*a*t long
From tyme / þ*a*t first bigynneth
lif / as we may

¶Exemplu*m*] ¶Considereth eek that
feet we trede and
Yet wasteth it
somtyme
grete toures /
Thanne may ye se / þ*a*t thyng
¶Of seen
termes
elles

as men may see
noght goth
seyn / al thyng
¶What this /
prince /
Conue*r*tynge al / propre
dirryued /

wysdom /
vertu
55 ¶And weel / that
namely /
ought
that

gladder / oghte
honour / vp yolden is his

forgeten / vassellage

whan þ*a*t he

[55] ¶Knyght *33r*

Loo the ook / that hath so long a norisshynge
ffro the tyme / that it first gynneth sprynge
And hath so long a lyf / as ye may see
Yet at the laste / wasted is the tree
Considreth eek / how þt the harde stoon
Vnder oure foot / on which we ryde and goon
It wasteth / as it lyth by the weye
The brode ryuer / som tyme wexeth dreye
The grete townes / se we wane and wende
Thanne se ye / þt al this thyng hath ende
Of man and womman / se we wel also
That nedeth in oon of thise tmes two
This is to seyn / in youthe / or ellis age
He moot be deed / the kyng / as shal a page
Som in his bed / som in the depe see
Som in the large feeld / as ye may se
Ther helpeth noght / al gooth that ilke weye
Thanne may I seyn / þt al this thyng moot deye
What maketh this / but Iuppiter the kyng /
That is Prince / and cause of alle thyng /
Conuertyng al vn to his ppre welle
ffrom which it is diryued sooth to telle
And heer agayns / no creature on lyue
Of no degree / auailleth for to stryue
Thanne is it wysdom / as it thynketh me
To maken vtu / of necessitee
And take it wel / þt we may nat eschue
And namelich / that to vs alle is due
And who so grucceth oght / he dooth folye
And rebel is / to hym þt al may gye
And certeinly / a man hath moost honour
To dyen in his excellence and flour
Whan he is siker / of his goode name
Thanne hath he doon / his freend ne hym no shame
And gladder oghte / his freend been of his deeth
Whan with honour / yolden is vp his breeth
Than whan his name / apalled is for age
ffor al forgeten is his vasselage
Thanne is it best / as for a worthy fame
To dyen / whan he is best of name
The contrarie of al this / is wilfulnesse
Why grucchen we / why haue we heuynesse

That goode Arcite / of chiualrie flour
Departed is / with duetee and with honour
Out of this foule prison / of this lyf
Why grucchen heere / his cosyn and his wyf
Of his welfare / þt loueth hem so weel
Kan he hem thank / nay god woot neuer a deel
That bothe his soule / and eek hem self offende
And yet they mowe hir lustes nat amende
¶ What may I conclude of this longe serye
But after wo I rede vs to be merye
And thanken Iupiter / of al his grace
And er we departen from this place
I rede we make / of sorwes two
O parfit ioye / lastynge euere mo
And loketh now / wher moost sorwe is her inne
Ther wol I first / amenden and bigynne
¶ Suster quod he this is my ful assent
With al thauys / heer of my parlement
That gentil Palamon / youre owene knyght
That serueth yow / with wyl and herte myght
And euere hath doon / syn ye first hym knewe
That ye shal of youre grace vp on hym rewe
And taken hym / for housbond and for lord
Leen me youre hond / for this is oure acord
Lat se now / of youre wommanly pitee
He is a kynges brother sone pardee
And though he were / a poure Bacheler
Syn he hath serued yow / so many a yeer
And had for yow / so greet aduersitee
It moste been considred / leueth me
For gentil mercy / oghte to passen right
¶ Thanne seyde he thus / to Palamon the knyght
I trowe ther nedeth litel sermonyng
To make yow assente to this thyng
Com neer and taketh youre lady by the hond
Bitwixe hem was maad anon the bond
That highte matrymoigne / or mariage
By al the conseil / and the Baronage
And thus with alle blisse and melodye
Hath Palamon ywedded Emelye

	ELLESMERE
That goode Arcite / of chiualrie flour	Chiualrie
Departed is / with duetee / and with honour	duetee and honour
Out of this foule prison / of this lyf	prisou*n*
Why gruccheth heere / his cosyn and his wyf /	grucchen wyf
Of his welfare / þ*at* loueth hem so weel	that loued
Kan he hem thank⁊ ⸗ nay god woot neuer a deel	thank⸗ neu*er*
That bothe his soule / and eek hem self offende	
And yet they mowe / hir lustes nat amende	
¶What may I conclude / of this longe serye	What concluden /
But after wo / I rede vs to be merye	
And thanken Iuppiter / of al his grace	
And er we / departen from this place	er that we /
I rede we make / of sorwes two	
O p*ar*fit Ioye / lastynge euere mo	parfit ioye / eu*er*emo
And loketh now / wher moost sorwe is her Inne	looketh
Ther wol I first⁊ amenden and bigynne	wol we first⁊
¶Suster quod he / this is my ful assent⁊	Suster fulle
With al thauys / heer of my p*ar*lement	thavys / heere p*ar*lement⁊
That gentil Palamon / youre owene knyght⁊	Palamon / thyn owene knyght⁊
That serueth yow / with wyl and herte myght⁊	wit*h* wille / herte / and myght
And euere hath doon / syn ye first hym knewe	eu*er*e syn þ*at* ye
That ye shal of youre grace vp on hym rewe	shul grace /
And taken hym / for housbond and for lord	housbonde lord
Leen me youre hond / for this is oure acord	Lene accord
Lat se now / of youre wo*m*manly pitee	
He is / a kynges brother sone pardee	is
And thogh he were / a poure Bachiler	though bacheler
Syn he hath serued yow / so many a yeer	
And had for yow / so greet adu*er*sitee	Adu*er*sitee
It moste been considred / leueth me	considered / leeueth
For gentil mercy / oghte to passen right⁊	m*er*cy / right⁊
¶Thanne seyde he thus / to Palamon the knyght⁊	Palamon ful right⁊
I trowe / ther nedeth litel sermonyng⁊	56
To make yow / assente to this thyng⁊	
Com neer / and taketh youre lady by the hond	taak hond
Bitwixe hem / was maad anon the bond	Bitwixen bond
That highte matrymoigne / or mariage	matrimoigne /
By al the conseil / and the Baronage	
And thus / with alle blisse / and melodye	¶And blisse
Hath Palamon / ywedded Emelye	

56 ¶Knyght *33v*

	ELLESMERE
And god / that al this world hath wroght	þ*at* this wyde world wroghħt
Sende hym his loue / that hath it deere aboght	that it aboghħt
For now is Palamon / in alle wele	
Lyuynge in blisse / in richesse / and in heele	richesse
And Emelye / hym loueth so tendrely	
And he / hir serueth so gentilly	he hir*e* /
That was ther no word hem bitwene	That neu*ere* / was
Of Ialousie / or any oother teene	
Thus endeth Palamon / and Emelye	Palamon
And god saue / al this faire compaignye Amen	

¶Here is ended / the Knyghtes tale

¶Heere is ended the Knygħtes tale

¶The prologe of the Milleres tale

¶Heere folwen the wordes / bitwene the hoost and the Millere

WHan that the knyght hadde thus his tale ytoold	Whan knyghħt hath thus
In al the compaignie / nas ther yong ne oold	the route / ne was ther
That he ne seyde / it was a noble Storie	storie
And worthy / for to drawen to memorie	
And namely / the gentils euerichon	namely
¶Oure hoost lough / and swoor / so moot I gon	Oure lougħ / swoor
This gooth aright vnbokeled is the male	arigħt / Male
Lat se now / who shal telle another tale	
For trewely / the game is wel bigonne	
Now telleth ye sire Monk / if þ*at* ye konne	telleth on Sir*e* that
Som what / to quite with the knyghtes tale	Somwhat
¶The Millere / that for dronken was a pale	Miller*e* / was al pale
So that vnnethe / vp on his hors he sat	sat
He nolde aualen / neither hood ne hat	hat
Ne abiden no man / for his curteisye	abyde curteisie
But in Pilates voys / he gan to crye	crie
And swoor by armes / and by blood and bones	Armes / blood / *and*
I kan a noble tale / for the nones	tale
With which / I wol now quite the knyghtes tale	Wit*h* quite / knygħtes
¶Oure hoost saugh / þ*at* he was dronke of ale	Oure saugħ / that Ale

And god that al this world hath wroght
Sende hym his loue / that hath it deere aboght
For now is Palamon / in alle wele
Lyuynge in blisse / in richesse / and in heele
And Emelye hym loueth so tendrely
And he hir serueth so gentilly
That was ther no word hem bitwene
Of Ialousie / or any oother teene
Thus endeth Palamon / and Emelye
And god saue / al this faire compaignye Amen

Here is ended the knyghtes tale

¶ The prologe of the Milleres tale

Whan that the knyght hadde thus his tale ytoold
In al the compaignye / nas ther yong ne oold
That he ne seyde / it was a noble storie
And worthy for to drawen to memorie
And namely the gentils euerichon
¶ Oure hoost lough / and swoor so moot I gon
This gooth aright / vnbokeled is the male
Lat se now who shal telle another tale
For trewely / the game is wel bigonne
Now telleth ye sire monk / if þt ye konne
Som what / to quite with the knyghtes tale
¶ The Millere / that for dronken was al pale
So that vnnethe / vp on his hors he sat
He nolde aualen / neither hood ne hat
Ne abiden no man / for his curteisye
But in Pilates voys / he gan to crye
And swoor by armes / and by blood and bones
I kan a noble tale / for the nones
With which I wol now quite the knyghtes tale
¶ Oure hoost saugh / þt he was dronke of ale

And seyde abyde Robyn leeue brother
Som bettre man shal telle vs first another
Abyde and lat vs werken thriftily
By goddes soule quod he that wol nat I
ffor I wol speke or ellis go my wey
Oure hoost answerde tel on a deuele wey
Thow art a fool thy wit is ouercome
Now herkneth quod the millere alle and some
But first I make a protestacioun
That I am dronke I knowe it by my sown
And therfore if þt I mysspeke or seye
Wite it the ale of Southwerk I preye
ffor I wol telle a legende and a lyf
Bothe of a Carpenter and of his wyf
How þt a clerk hath set the wrightes cappe
The Reue answerde and seyde stynt thy clappe
Lat be thy lewed dronken harlotrye
It is a synne and eek a greet folye
To apeyren any man or hym diffame
And eek to bryngen wyues in swich fame
Thow mayst ynow of othere thynges seyn
This dronken millere spak ful soone ageyn
And seyde leeue brother Osewold
Who hath no wyf he is no cokewold
But I seye nat therfore þt thow art oon
Ther been ful goode wyues many oon
Why artow angry with my tale now
I haue a wyf pardee as wel as thow
Yet nolde I for the oxen in my plough
Take vp on me moore than ynough
As demen of my self þt I were oon
I wol bileeue wel þt I am noon
An housbonde shal noght been Inquisityf
Of goddes pryuetee nor of his wyf
So he may fynde goddes foyson there
Of the remenant nedeth noght enquere
What sholde I moore seyn but this Millere
He nolde his wordes for no man forbere
But tolde his cherles tale in his manere
Me athynketh that I shal reherce it heere

	ELLESMERE
¶And seyde / abyde / Robyn leeue brother	And abyd Robyn my leeue
Som bettre man / shal telle vs first another	
Abyde / and lat vs werken thriftily	[1]
¶By goddes soule quod he / that wol nat I	nat
For I wol speke / or ellis go my wey	elles
¶Oure hoost answerde / tel on a deuelewey	Oure deuele wey
Thow art a fool / thy wit is ouercome	Thou oue*r*come
¶Now herkneth quod the Millere / alle and some	Mille*r*e
But first I make a protestacioun	
That I am dronke / I knowe it by my sown	soun
And therfore / if þ*at* I mysspeke / or seye	that mysspeke
Wite it / the ale of Southwerk I preye	Wyte it Ale Southwerk
For I wol telle / a legende and a lyf	
Bothe of a Carpenter / and of his wyf	
How þ*at* a clerk hath set the wrightes cappe	that clerk /
¶The Reue answerde / and seyde stynt thy clappe	
Lat be / thy lewed dronken harlotrye	
It is a synne / and eek a greet folye	
To apeyren any man / or hym diffame	defame
And eek to bryngen wyues / in swich fame	eek wyues
Thow mayst ynow / of othere thynges seyn	Thou ynogh /
¶This dronken Mill*er*e / spak ful soone ageyn	dronke
And seyde / leeue brother Osewold	leue
Who hath no wyf / he is no Cokewold	
But I seye nat therfore / þ*at* thow art oon	sey that thou
Ther been ful goode wyues many oon[2]	
Why artow angry / wit my tale now	with
I haue a wyf p*ar*dee / as wel as thow	
Yet nolde I / for the oxen in my plough	plogh
Take vp on me / moore than ynough	ynogh
As demen of my self / þ*at* I were oon	that
I wol bileeue wel / þ*at* I am noon	bileue that
An housbonde / shal noght been Inquisityf /	nat Inquisityf
Of goddes pryuetee / nor of his wyf	wyf
So he may fynde / goddes foyson there	fynde foysou*n*
Of the remenant nedeth noght enquere	nat
¶What sholde I moore seyn / but this Millere	Mille*r*e
He nolde his wordes / for no man forbere	
But tolde his cherles tale / in his manere	tale
Me athynketh / that I shal reherce it heere	Mathynketh /

[And therfore]

[1] ¶Millere *34r*

[2] *Out* Hg 3155-56. El reads:
And eu*er*e / a thousand goode / ayeyns oon badde
That knowestow wel thy self but if thou madde

42r Quire 6² (begins)

.The Millere.

	ELLESMERE
And therfore / euery gentil wight I preye	
Demeth noght for goddes loue / þ*at* I seye	For goddes loue / demeth nat that
Of yuel entente / but for I moot reherse	but that I reherce
Hir tales alle / be they bet or werse	bettre or
Or ellis falsen / som of my matere	elles / falsen mateere
And therfore / who so list it noght yhere	nat yheere
Turne ouer the leef / and chese another tale	
For he shal fynde ynowe / grete and smale	
Of storial thyng that toucheth gentilesse	[3] gentillesse
And eek moralitee / and holynesse	hoolynesse
Blameth noght me / if þ*at* ye chese amys	nat that
The Millere is a cherl / ye knowe wel this	The Mill*er*e /
So was the Reue eek and othere mo	Reue / and othere manye mo
And harlotrye / they tolden bothe two	harlotrie /
Auyseth yow / and put me out of blame	yow / putteth me
And eek / men shal noght maken ernest of game	eek nat

¶Here bigynneth / the Millerys tale	¶Heere bigynneth the Mill*er*e his tale[4]
Whilom / ther was dwellyng in Oxenford	dwellynge at Oxenford
A riche gnof that gestes heeld to bord	gnof / bord
And of his craft he was a Carpenter	
With hym ther was dwellynge a poure Scoler	W*ith* hym /
Hadde lerned Art but al his fantasie	fantasye
Was turned / for to leere Astrologie	lerne Astrologye
And koude / a certeyn of conclusions	conclusiou*n*s
To demen / by interrogacions	Interrogaciou*n*s
If þ*at* men axed hym / in cer*tein* houres	asked certein
Whan þ*at* men sholde haue droghte / or ellis shoures	elles
Or if men axed hym / what shal bifalle	asked sholde
Of euery thyng / I may nat rekene hem alle	
¶This clerk / was clepyd Hende Nicholas	clerk cleped / hende
Of derne loue he koude / and of solas	deerne koude
And ther to he was sleigh / and ful pryuee	to / p*ri*uee
And lyk a mayde meke / for to see	mayden / meke
A chambre hadde he / in that hostelrie	he hostelrye
Allone / with outen any compaignye	
Ful fetisly dight / with herbes swoote	ydight
And he hym self as sweete as is the roote	self /

[3] ¶Mill*er*e *34v*

[4] Miniature of the Miller in right margin: ⟨Robin w*ith* hi*s* Bagpype⟩

And ther fore euery gentil wight I preye
Demeth noght for goddes loue þt I seye
Of yuel entente but for I moot reherse
Hir tales alle be they bet or werse
Or ellis falsen som of my matere
And ther fore who so list it noght yheere
Turne ouer the leef and chese another tale
ffor he shal fynde ynowe grete and smale
Of storial thyng that toucheth gentilesse
And eek moralitee and holynesse
Blameth noght me if þt ye chese amys
The Millere is a cherl ye knowe wel this
So was the Reue eek and othere mo
And harlotrye they tolden bothe two
Auyseth yow and put me out of blame
And eek men shal noght maken ernest of game

Heere bigynneth the Milleres tale

Whilom ther was dwellyng in Oxenford
A riche gnof that gestes heeld to bord
And of his craft he was a Carpenter
With hym ther was dwellynge a poure scoler
Hadde lerned art but al his fantasye
Was turned for to lere Astrologye
And koude a certeyn of conclusiouns
To demen by interrogaciouns
If þt men asked hym in certein houres
Whan þt men sholde haue droghte or ellis shoures
Or if men asked hym what shal bifalle
Of euery thyng I may nat rekene hem alle
This clerk was cleped hende Nicholas
Of deerne loue he koude and of solas
And ther to he was sleigh and ful pryuee
And lyk a mayde meke for to see
A chambre hadde he in that hostelrye
Allone with outen any compaignye
fful fetisly dight with herbes swoote
And he hym self as sweete as is the roote

Of lycreys or any Cetyale
His Almageste and bookes grete and smale
His Astrelabye longynge for his art
His augrym stones layen faire a part
On shelues couched at his beddes heed
His presse ycouered with a ffaldyng reed
And al aboue ther lay a gay sautrye
On which he made a nyghtes melodye
So swetely þt al the chambre rong
And Angelus ad virginem he song
And after that he song the kynges note
ffful often blessed was his myrie throte
And thus this swete clerk his tyme spente
After his freendes fyndyng and his rente
This Carpenter hadde wedded newe a wyf
Which þt he loued moore than his lyf
Of .xviij. yeer she was of age
Ialous he was and heeld hire narwe in cage
ffor she was wilde and yong and he was old
And demed hym self been lyk a Cokewold
He knew nat Caton for his wit was rude
That bad men sholde wedde his similitude
Men sholde wedden after hir estaat
ffor youthe and Elde is often at debaat
But sith þt he was fallen in the snare
He moste endure as oother folk his care
ffair was this yonge wyf and ther with al
As any wesele hir body gent and smal
A ceynt she werede barred al of sylk
A barmclooth as whit as morne mylk
Vp on hir lendes ful of many a goore
Whit was hir smok and broyden al bifoore
And eek bihynde on hir coler aboute
Of col blak silk with Inne and eek wt oute
The tapes of hir white voluper
Were of the same sute of hir coler
Hir filet brood of sylk and set ful hye
And sikerly she hadde a likerous ye
ffful smale ypulled were hir browes two
And tho were bent and blake as is a slo

	ELLESMERE
Of lycorys / or any Cetuale	Cetewale
His Almageste / and bookes grete and smale	
His Astrelabye / longynge for his Artꝭ	Astrelabie /
His Augrym stones / layen faire a partꝭ	Hise part /
On shelues couched / at his beddes heed	shelues / couched
His Presse / ycouered with a Faldyng reed	p*re*sse ycouered / faldyng
And al aboue / ther lay a gay Sautrye	Sautrie
On which / he made a nyghtes melodye	melodie
So swetely / þ*at* al the chambre roongꝭ	that rongꝭ
And **Angelus ad Virginem** / he soongꝭ	songꝭ
And after thatꝭ he soong the kynges note	song / noote
Ful often / blissed was / his murye throte	blessed was myrie
And thus this swete clerk / his tyme spente	thus / this sweete clerkꝭ
After his freendes fyndyngꝭ and his rente	
¶This Carpenter / hadde wedded newe a wyf	Carpenterꝭ
Which þ*at* he louede / moore than his lyf	that lyf /
Of .xviij. yeer / she was of age	5 xviij. Age
Ialous he was / and heeld hir*e* narwe in Cage	cage
For she was wilde and yong / and he was old	yong and wylde / oldꝛ
And demed hym self / been lyk a Cokewoldꝛ	selfꝭ lik /
He knew nat Catou*n* / for his wit was rude	
That bad / men sholde wedde his similitude	man simylitude
Men sholde wedden / after hir estaat	hir*e*
For youthe and Elde / is often at debaat	elde /
But sith þ*at* he / was fallen in the snare	that
He moste endure / as oother folkꝭ his care	folk
¶Fair was this yonge wyf / and ther with al	
As any wesele / hir body gent and smal	wezele / body /
A ceynt she werde / barred al of sylk /	werede / ybarred silk
A barmclooth / as whit as morne Mylkꝭ	Milk
Vp on hir lendes / ful of many a goore	
Whit was hir smokꝭ and broyden al bifoore	
And eek bihynde / on hir coler aboute	
Of col blak silk / with Inne and eek w*ith* oute	colblak silkꝭ w*ith* Inne
The tapes / of hir white voluper	
Were of the same sute / of hir coler	suyte
Hir filet brood of sylkꝭ and set ful hye	filetꝭ silkꝭ
And sikerly / she hadde a likerous Iye	eye
Ful smale ypulled / were hir browes two	hir*e*
And tho were bentꝭ and blake as is a slo	as any sloo

[5] ¶Miller*e* *35r*

The Millere

She was ful moore / blisful on to see
Than is the newe / Pereionette tree
And softer / than the wolle is of a wether
And by hir girdel / heeng a purs of lether
Tasseled with silk / and perled with latoun
In al this world / to seken vp and doun
Ther nys no man so wys / *þat* koude thenche
So gay a Popelote / or swich a wenche
Ful brighter was / the shynyng of hir hewe
Than in the Tour / the noble yforged newe
But of hir soong it was as loude and yerne
As any swalwe / sittyng on a Berne
Ther to / she koude skippe / and make game
As any kyde / or Calf / folwynge his dame
Hir mouth was sweete / as Bragot or the meeth
Or hoord of Apples / leyd in hey or heeth
Wynsynge she was / as is a ioly Colt
Loong as a Mast and vp righte as a bolt
A brooch she baar / vp on hir loue coler
As brood / as is the boos of a Bokeler
Hir shoes were laced / on hir legges hye
She was a Prymerole / a piggesnye
For any lord / to leggen in his bedde
Or yet for any good yeman to wedde
¶Now sire and eft sire / so bifel the cas
That on a day / this hende Nicholas
Fil with this yonge wyf / to rage *and* pleye
Whil *þat* hir housbonde / was at Osneye
As clerkes been / ful subtil and ful queynte
And pryuely / he caughte hir*e* by the queynte
And seyde ywys / but if ich haue my wille
For derne loue / of thee lemman I spille
And heeld hir*e* harde / by the haunche bones
And seyde lemman / loue me al atones
Or I wol dyen / al so god me saue
And she sproong as a Colt dooth in the Traue
And with hir heed / she wryed faste awey
She seyde I wol nat kisse thee by my fey
Wy lat be quod ich / lat be Nicholas
Or I wol crye / out harrow and allas

ELLESMERE

was / moore
is / pereionette
with grene / and p*er*led w*ith*
nas
popelote /
brighter was shynyng
tour /
¶But song / was /
sittynge berne
calf
bragot Meeth
colt
Long bolt
bokeler
prymerole /
6 NOw sire /
and
that housbonde Oseneye
clerkes / been subtile /
pr*i*uely /
ywis /
deerne loue thee /
seyde / lemman
also
colt traue
seyde / thee /
Why
crie / out harrow /

6 ¶Millere *35v*

She was ful moore / blisful on to see
Than is the newe perjonette tree
And softer / than the wolle is of a wether
And by hir girdel / heeng a purs of lether
Tasseled with silk / and perled with latoun
In al this world / to seken vp and doun
Ther nys no man so wys / þat koude thenche
So gay a popelote / or swich a wenche
Ful brighter was the shynyng of hir hewe
Than in the Tour / the noble yforged newe
But of hir song / it was as loude and yerne
As any swalwe sittyng on a berne
Ther to / she koude skippe and make game
As any kyde or calf / folwynge his dame
Hir mouth was sweete as bragot / or the meeth
Or hoord of apples / leyd in hey or heeth
Wynsynge she was / as is a ioly colt
Long as a mast / and vprighte as a bolt
A brooch she baar / vp on hir lowe coler
As brood as is the boos of a bokeler
Hir shoes were laced / on hir legges hye
She was a prymerole / a piggesnye
For any lord / to leggen in his bedde
Or yet for any good yeman to wedde
Now sire and eft sire / so bifel the cas
That on a day this hende Nicholas
Fil with this yonge wyf / to rage and pleye
Whil þat hir housbonde / was at Osneye
As clerkes been / ful subtil and ful queynte
And pryuely / he caughte hir by the queynte
And seyde ywys / but if ich haue my wille
For deerne loue / of thee lemman I spille
And heeld hir harde / by the haunche bones
And seyde lemman / loue me al atones
Or I wol dyen / also god me saue
And she sproong / as a colt dooth in the traue
And with hir heed / she wryed faste awey
She seyde I wol nat kisse thee by my fey
Why lat be quod ich / lat be Nicholas
Or I wol crye / out harrow and allas

Do wey youre handes for youre curteisye
¶ This Nicholas gan mercy for to crye
And spak so faire and profred hym so faste
That she hir loue hym graunted atte laste
And swoor hir ooth by Seint Thomas of Kent
That she wolde been at his comandement
Whan þt she may hir leyser wel espie
Myn housbonde is so ful of Ialousie
That but ye waite wel and been priuee
I woot right wel I nam but deed quod she
Ye moste been ful derne as in this cas
¶ Nay ther of care thee noght quod Nicholas
A clerk hadde litherly biset his whilo
But if he koude a Carpenter bigyle
And thus they been acorded and ysworn
To waite a tyme as I haue told biforn
Whan Nicholas hadde doon thus euerydel
And thakked hire vp on the lendes wel
He kiste hir sweete and taketh his sautrye
And pleyeth faste and maketh melodye
¶ Thanne fil it thus þt to the parissh chirche
Cristes owene werkes for to wirche
This goode wyf wente on an haliday
Hir forheed shoon as bright as any day
So was it wasshen whan she leet hir werk
¶ Now was ther of that chirche a parissh clerk
The which þt was ycleped Absolon
Crul was his heer and as the gold it shoon
And strouted as a ffanne large and brode
ffull streight and euene lay his ioly shode
His rode was reed his eyen greye as goos
With Poules wyndow coruen on his shoos
In hoses rede he wente fetisly
Yclad he was ful smal and proprely
Al in a kirtel of a light waget set
ffull faire and thikke been the pointes
And ther vp on he hadde a gay surplys
As whit as is the blosme vp on the rys
A myrie child he was so god me saue
Wel koude he laten blood and clippe and shaue

	ELLESMERE
Do wey youre handes / for youre curteisye	
¶This Nicholas / gan mercy for to crye	
And spak so faire / and profred hym so faste	profred hir*e* so
That she hir loue / hym graunted atte laste	
And swoor hir ooth / by Seint Thomas of Kent	
That she wolde been / at his comaundement	wol comandement
Whan *þa*t she may / hir leyser wel espie	
Myn housbonde / is so ful of Ialousie	
That but ye waite wel / and been pryuee	wayte p*ri*uee
I woot right wel / I nam but deed quod she	right
Ye moste been ful derne / as in this cas	deerne /
¶Nay ther of / care thee noght quod Nicholas	noght
A clerc hadde lutherly / biset his while	clerk whyle
But if he koude / a Carpenter bigyle	
And thus they been / acorded and ysworn	accorded
To waite a tyme / as I haue told biforn	wayte
Whan Nicholas / hadde doon thus euerydel	¶Whan had euerideel
And thakked hire / vp on the lendes wel	hire / aboute the weel
He kiste hir sweete / and taketh his sautrye	hir*e* sawtrie
And pleyeth faste / and maketh melodye	melodie
¶Thanne fil it thus / *þa*t to the parissh chirche	Thanne paryssh
Cristes owene werkes / for to wirche	Cristes /
This goode wyf / wente on an haliday	
Hir forheed shoon / as bright as any day	bright
So was it wasshen / whan she leet hir werk	wasshen / werk
¶Now was ther of that chirche a parissh clerk	parissh clerk
The which / *þa*t was yclepid Absolon	that ycleped
Crul was his heer / and as the gold it shoon	
And strouted as a Fanne / large and brode	
Ful streight and euene / lay his ioly shode	
His rode was reed / hise eyen greye as goos	
With Poules wyndow / coruen on his shoos	
In hoses rede / he wente fetisly	7
Yclad he was / ful smal and p*ro*prely	
Al in a kirtel / of a light waget ⟨set⟩	lyght waget
Ful faire and thikke / been the pointes	poyntes set
And ther vp on / he hadde a gay surplys	
As whit as is the blosme vp on the rys	whit is /
A murye child he was / so god me saue	myrie
Wel koude he laten blood / and clippe and shaue	

7 ¶Miller*e* *36r*

44r Quire 7^{6} (begins)

⸗The Millere⸗

	ELLESMERE
And maken a chartre of lond / or Aquitaunce	Acquitaunce
On twenty manere / koude he trippe and daunce	In twenty
After the scole / of Oxenford tho	Scole /
And with his legges / casten to and fro	
And pleyen songes / on a smal Rubible	
Ther to he soong som tyme / a loud quynyble	to / song
And as wel / koude he pleye on a gyterne	pleye / on his giterne
In al the town / nas Brewhous ne Tau*er*ne	toun / Tauerne
That he ne visited / with his solas	
Ther any / gaylard tappestere was	any Tappestere
But sooth to seyn / he was som del squaymous	somdeel
Of fartyng / and of speche daungerous	fartyng
¶This Absolon / *pa*t ioly was and gay	iolif
Gooth with a sencer / on the haliday	Sencer /
Sensynge the wyues / of the parisshe faste	parisshe
And many a louely look / on hem he caste	
And namely / on this Carpenters wyf	Carpenteris
To looke on hire / hym thoughte a murye lyf	hir*e* / myrie
She was so p*ro*pre and sweete and likerous	p*ro*pre /
I dar wel seyn / if she hadde been a Mous	
And he a cat he wolde hir hente anon	Cat hir*e*
This parisshe clerk this ioly Absolon	¶This parissh clerk /
Hath in his herte / swich a loue longynge	
That of no wyf / ne took he noon offrynge	wyf / took
For curteisye / he seyde he wolde noon	curteisie /
The Moone / whan it was nyght ful brighte shoon	nyght
And Absolon / his gyterne / hath ytake	gyterne
For p*ar*amours / he thoghte for to wake	paramours /
And forth he gooth / iolyf and amorous	iolif
Til he cam / to the Carpenters hous	Carpenteres
A litel / after cokkes hadde ycrowe	Alitel / Cokkes
And dressed hym vp / by a shot wyndowe	shotwyndowe
That was / vp on / the Carpenters wal	on Carpenteris
He syngeth / in his voys / gentil and smal	syngeth
Now deere lady / if thy wille be	
I prey yow / *pa*t ye wol rewe on me	pray that wole thynke on
Ful wel acordant to his giternynge	acordaunt gyternynge
This Carpenter awook and herde hym synge	awook / herde synge
And spak vn to his wyf / and seyde anon	spak
What Alison / herestow noght Absolon	nat

And maken a chartre of lond or Acquitaunce
In twenty manere / koude he trippe and daunce
After the scole of Oxenford tho
And with his legges casten to and fro
And pleyen songes on a smal Rubible
Ther to he song som tyme a loud quynyble
And as wel koude he pleye on a gyterne
In al the town nas brewhous ne Tauerne
That he ne visited with his solas
Ther any gaylard tappestere was
But sooth to seyn he was som del squaymous
Of fartyng and of speche daungerous
This Absolon yt ioly was and gay
Gooth with a sencer / on the haliday
Sensynge the wyues of the parisshe faste
And many a louely look on hem he caste
And namely on this Carpenteres wyf
To looke on hire / hym thoughte a murye lyf
She was so propre and sweete and likerous
I dar wel seyn if she hadde been a mous
And he a cat / he wolde hire hente anon
This parisshe clerk this ioly Absolon
Hath in his herte swich a loue longynge
That of no wyf / ne took he noon offrynge
For curteisye / he seyde he wolde noon
The moone whan it was nyght / ful brighte shoon
And Absolon his gyterne hath ytake
For paramours he thoghte for to wake
And forth he gooth iolyf and amorous
Til he cam to the Carpenteres hous
A litel after cokkes hadde ycrowe
And dressed hym vp by a shot wyndowe
That was vp on the Carpenteres wal
He syngeth in his voys / gentil and smal
Now deere lady / if thy wille be
I prey yow yt ye wol rewe on me
Ful wel acordaunt to his gyternynge
This Carpenter awook and herde hym synge
And spak vn to his wyf / and seyde anon
What Alison / herestow noght Absolon

That chaunteth thus vnder oure boures wal
And she answerde hir housbonde ther with al
Yis god woot John I here it euerydel
This passeth forth what wol ye bet than wel
ffro day to day this ioly Absolon
So woweth hir þt hym is wo bigon
He waketh al the nyght and al the day
He kembed his lokkes brode and made hym gay
He woweth hir by meenes and brocage
And swoor he wolde been hir owene page
He syngeth brokkyng as a nyghtyngale
He sente hir pyment meeth and spiced ale
And wafres pipyng hoot out of the gleede
And for she was of towne he profred meede
ffor som folk wol be wonnen for richesse
And som for strokes and som for gentilesse
Som tyme to shewe his lightnesse and maistrye
He pleyeth Herodes vp on a scaffold hye
But what auailleth hym as in this cas
She loueth so this hende Nicholas
That Absolon may blowe the bukkes horn
He ne hadde for his labour but a scorn
And thus she maketh Absolon hir ape
And al his ernest turneth til a Iape
fful sooth is this prouerbe it is no lye
Men seith right thus alwey the neighe slye
Maketh the ferre leeue to be looth
ffor though þt Absolon be wood or wrooth
By cause þt he fer was from hir sighte
This neighe Nicholas stood in his lighte
Now bere thee wel thow hende Nicholas
ffor Absolon may waille and synge allas
And so bifel it on a Saterday
This Carpenter was goon til Osenay
And hende Nicholas and Alison
Acorded been to this conclusion
That Nicholas shal shapen hem a wile
This sely Jalous housbonde to bigile
And if so be the game wente aright
She sholde slepen in his arm al nyght

	ELLESMERE
That chaunteth thus / vnder oure boures wal	8
¶And she / answerde hir housbonde / ther with al	And she
Yis god woot Iohn / I here it euerydel	heere euery deel
This passeth forth / what wol ye bet than wel	¶This weel
Fro day to day / this ioly Absolon	day to day / to day / this
So woweth hir*e* / þ*a*t hym is wo bigon	that
He waketh al the nyght and al the day	waketh / nyght /
He kembed his lokkes brode / and made hym gay	kembeth hise
He woweth hir*e* / by meenes / and brocage	
And swoor / he wolde been hir owene page	
He syngeth brokkyng as a nyghtyngale	brokkynge /
He sente hir pyment Meeth / and spiced Ale	hir*e* Meeth Spiced
And wafres pipyng hoot out of the gleede	wafres / pipyng / hoot /
And for she was of towne / he p*ro*fred meede	profreth
For som folk / wol be wonnen for richesse	folk ben
And som for strokes / and som for gentilesse	And so*m*me so*m*me gentillesse
Som tyme to shewe / his lightnesse and maistrye	¶Somtyme / shewe
He pleyeth Herodes / vp on a Scaffold hye	herodes
But what auailleth hym / as in this cas	
She loueth so / this hende Nicholas	
That Absolon / may blowe the Bukkes horn	bukkes
He ne hadde for his labour / but a scorn	hadde / labour
And thus she maketh / Absolon hir Ape	thus / maketh hir*e*
And al his ernest turneth til a Iape	
Ful sooth is this p*rouer*be / it is no lye	prou*er*be /
Men seith right thus / alwey the neighe slye	seyn right nye
Maketh / the ferre leeue to be looth	looth
For thogh þ*a*t Absolon / be wood or wrooth	though that wrooth
By cause / þ*a*t he fer was from hir sighte	that hir*e* sighte
This neighe Nicholas / stood in his lighte	nye lighte
¶Now bere thee wel / thow hende Nicholas	NOw thou
For Absolon / may waille / and synge allas	waille
¶And so bifel it on a Saterday	And it
This Carpenter / was goon til Osenay	Carpenter
And Hende Nicholas / and Alisou*n*	hende Nicholas
Acorded been / to this conclusiou*n*	
That Nicholas / shal shapen hem a wile	hym wyle
This sely Ialous housbonde / to bigile	housbonde bigyle
And if so be / the game wente aright	aright
She sholde slepen / in his arm al nyght	nyght

3382 Vnde Ouidius Ictibus Agrestis Hg El

8 ¶Millere *36v*

The Millere.

	ELLESMERE
For this was hir desir / and his also	was / his desir and hir*e*
And right anoon / with outen wordes mo	right anon /
This Nicholas / no lenger wolde tarie	
But dooth ful softe / vn to his chambre carie	
Bothe mete and drynke / for a day or tweye	
And to hir housbonde / bad hire for to seye	to hir*e* bad hir*e*
If þ*at* he axed / after Nicholas	that
She sholde seye / she nyste wher he was	where
Of al that day / she seigh hym noght w*ith* Iye	[9] saugh nat with eye
She trowed / þ*at* he was in maladye	that
For / for no cry / hir mayde koude hym calle	For /.
He nolde answere / for no thyng þ*at* myghte falle	for thyng that
¶This passeth forth / al thilke Saterday	
That Nicholas / stille in his chambre lay	
And eet and sleep*e* / or dide what hym leste	
Til Sonday / þ*at* sonne gooth to reste	that the sonne
¶This sely Carpenter / hath greet m*er*uaille	Carpenter m*er*ueyle
Of Nicholas / or what thyng myghte hym aille	eyle
And seyde / I am adrad / by Seint Thomas	adrad
It stondeth nat aright with Nicholas	aright
God shilde / þ*at* he deyde sodeynly	that
This world is now / ful tikel sikerly	world / now
I seigh to day a corps / born to chirche	saugh day / a cors yborn
That now a monday last I seigh hym wirche	now / on monday saugh
.b. Clepe at his dore / or knokke with a stoon	
.a. Go vp quod he / vn to his knaue anoon	[10] ¶Go
Looke how it is / and tel me boldely	
¶This knaue gooth hym vp / ful sturdily	knaue / vp
And at the chambre dore / whil þ*at* he stood	that
He cryde and knokked / as þ*at* he were wood	cride that
What how / what do ye maister Nicholay	
How may ye slepen / al the longe day	
But al for noght he herde nat a word	¶But
An hole he foond / ful lowe vp on a bord	
Ther as the Cat / was wont In for to crepe	Cat
And at that hole / he looked In ful depe	
And atte laste / he hadde of hym a sighte	Til at the laste /
¶This Nicholas / sat euere capyng vp righte	This sat capyng eu*er*e vp righte
As he hadde kiked / on the newe moone	had
Adown he gooth / and tolde his maister soone	Adoun

[9] ¶Miller*e* *37r*

[10] 3431-2 in proper sequence in El.

ffor this was his desir / and hire also
And right anoon / withouten wordes mo
This Nicholas / no lenger wolde tarie
But dooth ful softe / vn to his chambre carie
Bothe mete and drynke / for a day or tweye
And to hire housbonde / bad hire for to seye
If þt he axed / after Nicholas
She sholde seye / she nyste wher he was
Of al that day / she saugh hym noght wt iye
She trowed / þt he was in maladye
ffor for no cry / hir mayde koude hym calle
He nolde answere / for no thyng þt myghte falle
¶ This passeth forth / al thilke Saterday
That Nicholas / stille in his chambre lay
And eet and sleep / or dide what hym leste
Til Sonday / þt sonne gooth to reste
¶ This sely Carpenter / hath greet merueille
Of Nicholas / or what thyng myghte hym eille
And seyde I am adrad / by seint Thomas
It stondeth nat aright / with Nicholas
God shilde / þt he deyde sodeynly
This world is now / ful tikel sikerly
I saugh to day / a cors / born to chirche
That now a monday last / I saugh hym wirche
b Clepe at his dore / or knokke with a stoon
a Go vp quod he / vn to his knaue anoon
Looke how it is / and tel me boldely
¶ This knaue gooth hym vp / ful sturdily
And at the chambre dore / whil þt he stood
He cryde and knokked / as þt he were wood
What how / what do ye maister Nicholay
How may ye slepen / al the longe day
But al for noght / he herde nat a word
An hole he foond / ful lowe vp on a bord
Ther as the cat / was wont in for to crepe
And at that hole / he looked in ful depe
And atte laste / he hadde of hym a sighte
¶ This Nicholas / sat euere capyng vp righte
As he hadde kiked / on the newe moone
Adoun he gooth / and tolde his maister soone

In what array / he saugh this ilke man
This Carpenter / to blessen hym bigan
And seyde / help vs seinte ffrydeswyde
A man woot litel / what hym shal bitydе
This man is falle / with his Astromye
In som woodnesse / or in som Agonye
I thoghte ay wel / how þt it sholde be
Men sholde noght knowe / of goddes pryuetee
Ye blissed be alwey / a lewed man
That noght / but oonly his bileue kan
So ferde another clerk / with Astromye
He walked in the feeldes / for to prye
Vp on the sterres / what ther sholde bifalle
Til he was / in a marle pit yfalle
He saugh nat that / but yet by Seint Thomas
Me reweth sore / of hende Nicholas
He shal be rated / of his studiyng
If þt I may / by Ihesus heuene kyng
Get me a staf / þt I may vnderspore
Whil þt thow Robyn / heuest vp the dore
He shal out of his studiyng / as I gesse
And to the chambre dore / he gan hym dresse
His knaue was a strong carl / for the nones
And by the haspe / he haaf it vp atones
In to the floor / the dore fil anoon
This Nicholas / sat ay as stille as stoon
And euere caped vp / in to the Eyr
This Carpenter / wende he were in despeyr
And hente hym / by the sholdres myghtily
And shook hym harde / and cryde spitously
What Nicholay / what how looke adoun
Awake / and thenk on Cristes passioun
I crouche thee / from Elues and fro wightes
Ther with the nyght spel / seyde he anon rightes
On foure halues / of the hous aboute
And on the thresshfold / on the dore with oute
Ihesu crist / and Seint Benedight
Blesse this hous / from euery wikked wight
ffor the nyghtes verye / the white pater noster
Where wentestow / seinte Petres suster

	ELLESMERE
In what array / he saw this ilke man	saugh that ilke
¶This Carpenter / to blessen hym bigan	
And seyde / help vs seinte Frideswyde	Seinte Frydeswyde
A man woot litel / what hym shal bityde	
This man is falle / with his Astromye	
In som woodnesse / or in som Agonye	
I thoghte ay wel / how *pa*t it sholde be	that
Men sholde noght knowe / of goddes p*ri*uetee	nat pryuetee
Ye blissed be alwey / a lewed man	Ye / blessed alwey
That noght but oonly his bileue kan	
So ferde another clerk with Astromye	
He walked in the feeldes / for to prye	
Vp on the sterres / what ther sholde bifalle	
Til he was / in a Marlepit yfalle	Marleput
He saw nat that but yet by Seint Thomas	saugh that / ⟨Thomas⟩
Me reweth sore / of hende Nicholas	soore /
He shal be rated / of his studiyng	11
If *pa*t I may / by I*es*us heuene kyng	that
Get me a staf / *pa*t I may vnderspore	¶Get that
Whil *pa*t thow Robyn / heuest vp the dore	thou heuest of the
He shal out of his studyyng as I gesse	shal / studiyng
And to the chambre dore / he gan hym dresse	
His knaue / was a strong carl / for the nones	
And by the haspe / he haaf it vp atones	it of atones
In to the floor / the dore fil anoon	anon
This Nicholas / sat ay as stille as stoon	
And euere caped vp / in to the Eyr	eu*er*e vpward / in Eir
This Carpenter / wende he were in despeyr	despeir
And hente hym / by the sholdres myghtily	
And shook hym harde / and cryde spitously	cride
What Nicholay / what how looke adoun	what how / what looke
Awake / and thenk on Cristes passioun	
I crouche thee / from Elues / and fro wightes	
Ther with the nyght spel / seyde he anon rightes	*with* nyghtspel / anonrightes
On foure halues / of the hous aboute	
And on the thresshfold / on the dore with oute	thresshfold / of the
I*es*us crist and Seint Benedight	seint Benedight
Blesse this hous / from euery wikked wight	eu*er*y
For the nyghtesuerye / the white Pater noster	For nyghtes uerye / pater
Where wentestow / seinte Petres suster	seint soster

[11] ¶Miller*e* *37v*

The Millere	ELLESMERE
And at the laste / this hende Nicholas	¶And atte laste /
Gan for to sike soore / and seyde allas	
Shal al the world / be lost eft soones now	al this world / eftsoones now
¶This Carpenter answerde / what seistow	Carpenter / seystow
What thenk / on god / as we doon men *þat* swynke	thynk doon /
¶This Nicholas answerde / fecche me drynke	
And after / wol I speke in pryuetee	
Of *cer*tein thyng / *þat* toucheth me and thee	certeyn thyng that
I wol telle it / noon oother man *cer*tayn	it certeyn
¶This Carpenter gooth doun / and comth agayn	Carpenter / goth ageyn
And broghte of myghty ale / a large quart	broghte / Ale quart
And whan *þat* eech of hem / hadde dronke his part	ech had
This Nicholas / his dore faste shette	
And doun the Carpenter / by hym he sette	Carpenter
And seyde / Iohn / myn hoost lief and deere	¶He seyde / Iohn
Thou shalt vp on thy trouthe / swere me heere	shalt trouthe
That to no wight thou shalt this conseil wreye	wight
For it is cristes conseil / that I seye	is / conseil
And if thou telle it man thou art forlore	telle man /
For this vengeaunce / thow shalt haue therfore	vengeau*n*ce / thou han
That if thow wreye me / thow shalt be wood	if thou thou shalt
¶Nay Crist forbede it for his holy blood	crist hooly
Quod tho this sely man / I nam no labbe	
And thogh I seye / I nam nat lief to gabbe	Ne though I am nat
Sey what thow wolt I shal it neuere telle	12 thou wolt / neu*er*e
To child ne wyf by hym that harwed helle	wyf /
¶Now Iohn quod Nicholas / I wol noght lye	NOw nat
I haue yfounde / in myn Astrologye	
As I haue looked / in the moone bright	bright
That now a monday next at quarter nyght	nyght
Shal falle a reyn / and that so wilde and wood	
That half so greet was neu*er*e Nowels flood	neuere Noees
This world he seyde / in lasse than in an hour	than an hour
Shal al be dreynt so hidous is the shour	dreynt /
Thus shal man kynde drenche / and lese hir lyf	mankynde lyf
¶This Carpenter answerde / allas my wyf	wyf
And shal she drenche / allas myn Alisoun	
For sorwe of this / he fil almoost adoun	
And seyde / is ther no remedie in this cas	
¶Why yis for gode / quod Hende Nicholas	forgode / hende

[12] ¶Millere *38r*

And at the laste / this hende Nicholas
Gan for to sike soore / and seyde allas
Shal al this world / be lost eft sones now
¶ This Carpenter answerde / what seystow
What thenk on god / as we doon men þt swynke
¶ This Nicholas answerde / fecche me drynke
And after / wol I speke in pryuetee
Of certeyn thyng / þt toucheth me and thee
I wol telle it / noon oother man certayn
¶ This Carpenter gooth doun / and comth agayn
And broghte of myghty ale / a large quart
And whan þt ech of hem / hadde dronke his part
This Nicholas / his dore faste shette
And doun the Carpenter / by hym he sette
And seyde John / myn hoost / lief and deere
Thow shalt vp on thy trouthe / swere me heere
That to no wight / thou shalt this conseil wreye
For it is cristes conseil / that I seye
And if thou telle it / man thou art forlore
For this vengeaunce / thow shalt haue therfore
That if thow wreye me / thow shalt be wood
¶ Nay crist forbede it / for his holy blood
Quod tho this sely man / I nam no labbe
And though I seye / I nam nat lief to gabbe
Sey what thow wolt / I shal it neuere telle
To child ne wyf / by hym that harwed helle
¶ Now John quod Nicholas / I wol noght lye
I haue yfounde / in myn Astrologye
As I haue looked / in the moone bright /
That now a monday next / at quarter nyght /
Shal falle a reyn / and that so wilde and wood
That half so greet / was neuere Noes flood
This world he seyde / in lasse than in an hour
Shal al be dreynt / so hidous is the shour
Thus shal mankynde drenche / and lese hir lyf
¶ This Carpenter answerde / allas my wyf
And shal she drenche / allas myn Alisoun
For sorwe of this / he fil almoost adoun
And seyde / is ther no remedie in this cas
¶ Why yis for gode / quod hende Nicholas

If thow wolt werken after loore and reed
Thow mayst noght werken after thyn owene heed
ffor thus seith Salomon / þt was ful trewe
Werk al by conseil / and thow shalt noght rewe
And if thow werken wolt by good conseyl
I vndertake / with outen mast or sayl
yit shal I saue hire and thee and me
Hastow nat herd / how saued was Noe
Whan þt oure lord hadde warned hym biforn
That al the world / with water sholde be lorn
Yis quod this Carpenter / ful yore ago
Hastow nat herd / quod Nicholas also
The sorwe of Noe / with his felaweshipe
Er þt he myghte gete his wyf to shipe
Hym hadde leuere I dar wel vndertake
At thilke tyme than alle hise wetheres blake
That she hadde had a ship hir self allone
And therfore wostow what is best to done
This axeth haste / and of an hastyf thyng
Men may noght preche / or maken tariyng
Anoon go gete vs faste / in to this In
A knedyng trogh / or ellis a kymelyn
ffor eech of vs / but looke þt they be large
In whiche we mowen swymme as in a barge
And han ther inne vitaille suffisaunt
But for a day / fy on the remenaunt
The water shal aslake / and goon away
Aboute pryme / vp on the nexte day
But Robyn may nat wite of this thy knaue
Ne eek thy mayde Gille I may nat saue
Axe noght why / for though thou axe me
I wol noght tellen goddes pryuetee
Suffiseth thee but if thy wittes madde
To han as greet a grace as Noe hadde
Thy wif shal I wel sauen out of doute
Go now thy wey / and speed thee heer aboute
But whan thou hast for hire and thee and me
ygeten vs thise knedyng tubbes thre
Thanne shaltow hangen hem in the roof ful hye
That no man of oure purueiaunce espye

	ELLESMERE
If thow wolt werken / after loore and reed	thou
Thow mayst noght werken / after thyn owene heed	Thou nat
For thus seith Salomon / þat was ful trewe	Salomoun / that
Werk al by conseil / and thow shalt noght rewe	thou nat
And if thow werken wolt by good consayl	thou conseil
I vndertake / with outen mast or sayl	Mast and seyl
Yit shal I saue hire / and thee and me	Yet sauen / thee /
Hastow nat herd / how saued was Noe	Hastou hou Noe
Whan þat oure lord / hadde warned hym biforn	
That al the world / with water sholde be lorn	with
¶Yis quod this Carpenter ful yore ago	Carpenter / yoore
¶Hastow nat herd / quod Nicholas also	¶Hastou
The sorwe of Noe / with his felaweshipe	
Er þat he myghte / gete his wyf to shipe	myghte / brynge his
Hym hadde leuere / I dar wel vndertake	hadde be leuere /
At thilke tyme / than alle hise wetheres blake	
That she hadde had a shipe / hir self allone	
And therfore / wostow what is best to done	ther fore / woostou doone
This axeth haste / and of an hastyf thyng	asketh hastif
Men may noght preche / or maken tariyng	nat preche /
Anoon go gete vs faste / in to this In	¶Anon
A knedyng trogh / or ellis a kymelyn	knedyng
For eech of vs / but looke þat they be large	ech
In whiche we mowen swymme / as in a barge	whiche / mowe swymme
And han ther Inne / vitaille suffisaunt	suffissant
But for a day / fy on the remenaunt	remenant
The water shal aslake / and goon away	
Aboute pryme / vp on the nexte day	
But Robyn / may nat wite of this / thy knaue	
Ne eek thy mayde Gille / I may nat saue	Gille
Axe noght why / for thogh thou axe me	nat why / though aske
I wol noght tellen goddes pryuetee	nat
Suffiseth thee / but if thy wittes madde	13
To han as greet a grace / as Noe hadde	
Thy wif shal I wel sauen / out of doute	wyf
Go now thy wey / and speed thee heer aboute	
But whan thou hast / for hire and thee and me	¶But hast
Ygeten vs / thise knedyng tubbes thre	knedyng
Thanne shaltow hangen hem / in the roof ful hye	hange
That no man / of oure purueiance espye	purueiaunce spye
	13¶Millere 38v

The Millere	ELLESMERE
And whan thow thus hast doon / as I haue seyd	thou
And hast oure vitaille / faire in hem yleyd	
And eek an Ax / to smyte the corde atwo	
Whan þat the water cometh / þat we may go	comth / that
And breke an hole / an heigh vp on the gable	broke anheigh
Vn to the gardynward / ouer the stable	
That we may frely / passen forth oure wey	way
Whan þat the grete shour / is goon awey	away
Thanne shaltow swymme / as murye I vndertake	shal I swymme / myrie
As dooth the white doke / after his drake	after hire drake
Thanne woltow clepe / how Alison / how Iohn	wol I Alisoun /
Be murye / for the flood wol passe anon	myrie /
And thou wolt seyn / hail maister Nicholay	hayl
Good morwe / I see thee wel / for it is day	se
And thanne shal we be lordes al oure lyf	thanne / shul be / lyf /
Of al the world / as Noe and his wyf	wyf /
But of o thyng / I. warne thee ful right	¶But thyng I right
Be wel auysed / on that ilke nyght	nyght
That we been entred / in to shippes bord	ben
That noon of vs / ne speke noght a word	nat
Ne clepe ne crye / but been in his prayere	clepe / crie / preyere
For it is / goddes owene heste deere	heeste
Thy wyf and thow / mote hange fer atwynne	¶Thy thou / moote
For þat bitwix yow / shal be no synne	that bitwixe
Namoore in lookyng than ther shal in dede	lookyng / deede
This ordinaunce is seyd / go god thee spede	ordinance speede
Tomorwe at nyght whan men been alle aslepe	whan folk ben
In to oure knedyng tubbes / wol we crepe	knedyng
And sitten there / abidyng goddes grace	
Go now thy wey / I haue no lenger space	
To make of this / no lenger sermonyng	
Men seyn thus / seend the wise and sey no thyng	sende wise /
Thow art so wys / it nedeth thee nat teche	Thou wys nat to preche
Go saue oure lyf and that I thee biseche	lyf / the
¶This sely Carpenter / gooth forth his wey	goth
Ful ofte he seyde / allas and weylawey	ofte / seith
And to his wyf / he tolde his priuetee	pryuetee
And she was war / and knew it bet than he	
What al this queynte cast was for to seye	
But nathelees / she ferde as she wolde deye	

And whan thow thus hast doon as I haue seyd
And hast oure vitaille faire in hem yleyd
And eek an ax to smyte the corde atwo
Whan þt the water cometh þt we may go
And breke an hole an heigh vp on the gable
Vn to the gardyn ward ouer the stable
That we may frely passen forth oure wey
Whan þt the grete shour is goon awey
Thanne shaltow swymme as myrie I vndertake
As dooth the white doke after hir drake
Thanne wol I clepe how Alison how Iohn
Be myrie for the flood wol passe anon
And thow wolt seyn hail maister Nicholay
Good morwe I se thee wel for it is day
And thanne shal we be lordes al oure lyf
Of al the world as Noe and his wyf
But of o thyng I warne thee ful right
Be wel auysed on that ilke nyght
That we been entred in to shippes bord
That noon of vs ne speke noght a word
Ne clepe ne crye but been in his prayere
For it is goddes owene heste deere
Thy wyf and thow mote hange fer atwynne
For þt bitwix yow shal be no synne
Namoore in lookyng than ther shal in dede
This ordinance is seyd go god thee spede
Tomorwe at nyght whan men been alle aslepe
In to oure knedyng tubbes wol we crepe
And sitten there abidyng goddes grace
Go now thy wey I haue no lenger space
To make of this no lenger sermonyng
Men seyn thus send the wise and sey no thyng
Thow art so wys it nedeth thee nat teche
Go saue oure lyf and that I thee biseche
This sely carpenter gooth forth his wey
Ful ofte he seyde allas and weylawey
And to his wyf he tolde his pryuetee
And she was war and knew it bet than he
What al this queynte cast was for to seye
But nathelees she ferde as she wolde deye

And seyde allas go forth thy wey anon
Help vs to scape or we been dede echon
I am thy trewe verray wedded wyf
Go deere spouse and help to saue oure lyf
¶ Lo which a greet thyng is affeccion
Men may dyen of ymaginacion
So depe may impression be take
This sely Carpenter bigynneth quake
Hym thynketh verraily þt he may se
Noes flood come walwyng as the see
To drenchen Alison his hony deere
He wepeth wayleth maketh sory cheere
He siketh wt ful many a sory swogh
And gooth and geteth hym a knedyng trogh
And after a tubbe and a kymelyn
And pryuely he sente hem to his In
And heeng hem in the roof in pryuetee
His owene hand he made laddres thre
To clymben by the ronges and the stalkes
Vn to the tubbes hangyng in the balkes
And hem vitailled bothe trogh and tubbe
With breed and chese and good ale in a Iubbe
Suffisynge right ynogh as for a day
But er þt he hadde maad al this array
He sente his knaue and eek his wenche also
Vp on his nede to london for to go
And on the monday whan it drogh to nyght
He shette his dore with outen candel lyght
And dressed alle thyng as it sholde be
And shortly vp they clomben alle thre
They seten stille wel a furlong way
Now Pater noster clom seyde Nicholay
And clom quod Iohn and clom seyde Alison
This Carpenter seyde his deuocion
And stille he sit and biddeth his prayere
Awaitynge on the reyn if he it heere
¶ The dede sleep for wery bisynesse
Fil on this Carpenter right as I gesse
Aboute corfew tyme or litel moore
ffor trauaillyng of his goost he groneth soore

	ELLESMERE
And seyde allas / go forth thy wey anon	[14] ¶And
Help vs to scape / or we been dede echon	been lost echon
I am thy trewe / verray wedded wyf	wyf
Go deere spouse / and help to saue oure lyf	lyf
¶Lo which a greet thyng / is affecciou*n*	Lo / Affecciou*n* [¶Auctor]
Men may dyen / of ymaginaciou*n*	
So depe / may imp*re*ssiou*n* be take	impressiou*n*
This sely Carpenter / bigynneth quake	
Hym thynketh verrailiche / þ*at* he may se	verraily / that see
Noes flood / come walwyng as the see	Noees walwynge
To drenchen Alisou*n* / his hony deere	
He wepeth / waileth / maketh sory cheere	weyleth /
He siketh / w*ith* ful many a sory swogħ	
And gooth / and geteth hym a knedyng trogħ	He gooth / knedyng
And after / a tubbe and a kymelyn	after that a
And pryuely / he sente hem to his In	
And heeng hem / in the roof in p*ri*uetee	heng pryuetee
His owene hand / he made laddres thre	hand made
To clymben / by the ronges and the stalkes	
Vn to the tubbes / hangyng in the balkes	In to hangynge
And hem vitailed / bothe trogh and tubbe	vitailleth /
With breed and chese / and good ale in a Iubbe	W*ith* Ale
Suffisynge right ynogh / as for a day	
But er þ*at* he hadde maad / al this array	that he / maad
He sente his knaue / and eek his wenche also	
Vp on his nede / to londou*n* for to go	london
And on the monday / whan it drogh to nyght	Monday / drow nyght
He shette his dore / with outen candel lyght	oute lygħt
And dressed alle thyng as it sholde be	dresseth it shal be
And shortly / vp they clomben alle thre	
They seten stille / wel a furlong way	sitten
Now Pater noster / clom seyde Nicholay	¶Now
And clum quod Ioħn / and clum seyde Alisou*n*	And clom clom seyde
This Carpenter / seyde his deuociou*n*	
And stille he sit and biddeth his prayere	sit / preyere
Awaitynge on the reyn / if he it heere	
¶The dede sleep*e* / for wery bisynesse	
Fil on this Carpenter / right as I gesse	rigħt
Aboute corfew tyme / or litel moore	
For trauaillyng of his goost he groneth soore	trauaille

[14] ¶Miller*e* *39r*

The Millere.

	ELLESMERE
And eft he routeth / for his heed myslay	
¶Doun of the laddre / stalketh Nicholay	Doun
And Alisou*n* / ful softe adoun she spedde	
With outen wordes mo / they goon to bedde	
Ther as the Carpenter / is wont to lye	
Ther was the reuel / and the melodye	
And thus lyth Alisou*n* / and Nicholas	thus Alison /
In:busynesse of myrthe / and in solas	In bisynesse / myrthe and of solas
Til that the belle of laudees / gan to rynge	15 laudes
And freres in the chauncel / gonne synge	Chauncel
¶This parissh clerk this amorous Absolon	This clerk / Amorous Absolon
That is for loue / alwey so wo bigon	loue
Vp on the monday / was at Osneye	Monday / Oseneye
With compaignye / hym to disporte and pleye	With a compaignye /
And axed vp on caas / a Cloistrer	cas
Ful pryuely / after Iohn the Carpenter	p*ri*uely /
And he drogh hym a part out of the cherche	drough chirche
And seyde I noot I saugh hym here noght werche	heere nat wirche
Sith Saterday / I trowe þat he be went	Syn that went
For tymber / ther oure Abbot hath hym sent	
For he is wont for tymber for to go	
And dwellen atte graunge / a day or two	at the grange /
Or ellis / he is at his hous c*er*teyn	elles / certeyn
Where þat he be / I kan noght soothly seyn	Wher*e* that nat
¶This Absolon / ful iolyf was and lyght	ioly light
And thoghte / now is tyme to wake al nyght	tyme wake nyght
For sikerly / I saugh hym noght stirynge	sikirly nat
Aboute his dore / syn day bigan to sprynge	
So mote I thryue / I shal at Cokkes crowe	¶So moot cokkes
Ful p*ri*uely / knokken at his wyndowe	pryuely / knokke
That stant ful lowe / vp on his boures wal	
To Alison / now wol I tellen al	
My loue longyng . for yit I shal nat mysse	longynge / yet
That at the leeste wey / I shal hir kisse	hir*e*
Som manere confort / shal I haue parfay	maner confort p*ar*fay
My mouth hath icched / al this longe day	icched
That is a signe of kissyng at the leeste	atte leeste
Al nyght me mette eek / I was at a feeste	nyght
Ther fore I wol go slepe / an houre or tweye	Therfore goon
And al the nyght than wol I wake and pleye	thanne

[15] ¶Miller*e* *39v*

And eft he routeth for his heed myslay
Doun of the laddre / stalketh Nicholay
And Alisoun / ful softe adoun she spedde
With outen wordes mo / they goon to bedde
Ther as the Carpenter / is wont to lye
Ther was the reuel / and the melodye
And thus lyth Alisoun / and Nicholas
In bisynesse of myrthe / and in solas
Til that the belle of laudes gan to rynge
And freres in the chauncel gonne synge
This parissh clerk / this amorous Absolon
That is for loue / alwey so wo bigon
Vp on the monday / was at Oseneye
With compaignye / hym to disporte and pleye
And axed vp on cas / a Cloystrer
Ful pryuely / after Iohn the Carpenter
And he drogh hym apart / out of the chirche
And seyde I noot / I saugh hym heere noght werche
Sith Saterday / I trowe þt he be went
For tymber / ther oure Abbot hath hym sent
For he is wont / for tymber for to go
And dwellen atte grange / a day or two
Or ellis he is at his hous certeyn
Where þt he be / I kan noght soothly seyn
This Absolon / ful iolyf was and light
And thoghte now is tyme to wake al nyght /
For sikerly / I saugh hym noght stirynge
Aboute his dore syn day bigan to sprynge
So moot I thryue / I shal at cokkes crowe
Ful pryuely / knokken at his wyndowe
That stant ful lowe / vp on his boures wal
To Alisoun / now wol I tellen al
My loue longyng / for yet I shal nat mysse
That at the leeste wey / I shal hir kisse
Som maner confort / shal I haue parfay
My mouth hath icched / al this longe day
That is a signe of kissyng / at the leeste
Al nyght me mette eek / I was at a feeste
Ther fore I wol go slepe / an houre or tweye
And al the nyght / than wol I wake and pleye

Whan þt the firste cok hath crowe anon
Up rist this ioly louere Absolon
And hym arrayeth gay at point deuys
But first he cheweth grayn and likorys
To smellen swete er he hadde kembd his heer
Vnder his tonge a trewe loue he beer
ffor therby wende he to be gracious
He rometh to the Carpenteres hous
And stille he stant vnder the shot wyndowe
Vn to his brest it raughte it was so lowe
And softe he cogheth with a semy soun
What do ye hony comb swete Alisoun
My faire bryd my swete cynamome
Awaketh lemman myn and speketh to me
Wel litel thynken ye vp on my wo
That for youre loue I swete ther I go
No wonder is thogh þt I swelte and swete
I moorne as dooth a lamb after the tete
Ywis lemman I haue swich loue longyng
That lyk a turtle trewe is my moornyng
I may nat ete namoore than a mayde
Go fro the wyndowe Jakke fool she sayde
As help me god it wol nat be com pa me
I loue another and ellis I were to blame
Wel bet than thee by Jhu Absolon
Go forth thy wey or I wol caste a stoon
And lat me slepe a twenty deuelewey
Allas quod Absolon and weilawey
That trewe loue was euere so yuel biset
Thanne kys me syn þt it may be no bet
ffor Jhus loue and for the loue of me
Woltow thanne go thy wey ther with quod she
Ye certes lemman quod this Absolon
Thanne make thee redy quod she I come anon
This Absolon doun sette hym on his knees
And seyde I am a lord at alle degrees
ffor after this I hope ther cometh moore
Lemman thy grace and swete bryd thyn oore
The wyndowe she vndooth and that in haste
Haue do quod she com of and speed thee faste

	ELLESMERE
¶Whan *þat* the firste cok' hath crowe anon	Whan that
Vp rist / this ioly louere Absolon	rist' louer*e*
And hym arrayeth gay / at point deuys	arraieth / gay at poynt
But first / he cheweth grayn and likorys	first' greyn of lycorys
To smellen swete / er he hadde kembd his heer	sweete /
Vnder his tonge / a trewe loue he beer	
For ther by / wende he to be gracious	ben
He rometh / to the Carpenters hous	Carpenteres
And stille he stant' vnder the shot wyndowe	shotwyndowe
Vn to his brest' it raughte / it was so lowe	brist
And ofte he cogheth / with a semy sown	And softe he knokketh / soun
What do ye hony comb / swete Alisoun	sweete
My faire bryd / my swete cynamome	sweete
Awaketh lemman myn / and speketh to me	
Wel litel thynken ye / vp on my wo	Wel /
That for youre loue / I swete ther I go	
No wonder is / thogh *þat* I swelte and swete	[16] that
I moorne / as dooth a lamb / after the tete	lamb
Ywis lemman / I haue swich loue longyng'	longynge
That lyk a turtle trewe / is my moornyng'	lik turtel moornynge
I may nat ete / namoore than a mayde	
¶Go fro the wyndow / Iakke fool she sayde	
As help me god / it wol nat be com pa me	
I loue another / and ellis I were to blame	elles
Wel bet than thee / by I*es*u Absolon	
Go forth thy wey / or I wol caste a stoon	ston
And lat me slepe / a twenty deuelewey	deuelwey
¶Allas quod Absolon / and weilawey	weylawey
That trewe loue / was euere so yuel biset'	eu*er*e
Thanne kys me / syn *þat* it may be no bet'	syn it bet
For I*es*us loue / and for the loue of me	
¶Woltow thanne / go thy wey ther with quod she	¶Wiltow wey quod she ./
¶Ye certes lemman / quod this Absolon	
¶Thanne make thee redy quod she / I come anon[17]	she
¶This Absolon / doun sette hym on his knees	
And seyde / I am a lord / at alle degrees	am lord
For after this / I hope ther cometh moore	
Lemman thy grace / and swete bryd thyn oore	sweete
¶The wyndow she vndooth / and that in haste	wyndow / vndoth /
Haue do quod she / com of and speed thee faste	the

[16] ¶Mill*er*e *40r*

[17] *Out* Hg 3721-22. El reads:
And vn to Nicholas / she seyde stille
Now hust' and thou shalt laughen al thy fille

The Millere.ʃ	ELLESMERE
Lest *þa*t oure neghebores / thee espye	that Neighebores / espie
¶This Absolon / gan wipe his mouth ful drye	wype drie
Derk was the nyght' as pych / or as the cole	Dirk nygħt' pich /
And at the wyndow / out she putte hir hole	pitte
And Absolon / hym fil no bet ne wers	
But with his mouth / he kiste hir naked ers	*with*
Ful sauourly / er he were war of this	he was war
Abak he sterte / and thoghte it was amys	¶Abak stirte / thoughte
For wel he wiste / a womman hath no berd	
He felte a thyng al rogh / and longe yherd	rough /
And seyde / fy allas / what haue I do	allas
¶Te hee quod she / and clapte the wyndow to	¶Tehee
And Absolon / gooth forth a sory paas	pas
¶A berd / a berd / quod hende Nicholas	berd a berd /
By goddes corpus / this gooth faire and wel	goth weel
¶This sely : Absolon / herde euery del	seely deel
And on his lippe / he gan for anger byte	Anger
And to hym self' he seyde I shal thee quyte	self /
¶Who rubbeth now / who froteth now his lippes	
With dust' *with* sond / *with* straw / *with* clooth / *with* chippes	W*ith* dust'
But Absolon / *þa*t seith ful ofte allas	that
My soule / bitake vn to Sathanas	bitake I vn
But me were leuere / than al this town quod he	[18] toun
Of this despit' awreken for to be	awroken
Allas quod he / allas I ne hadde ybleynt'	ybleynt
His hote loue was coold / and al yqueynt	hoote loue / coold yqueynt'
For fro that tyme / *þa*t he hadde kist hir ers	that
Of p*ar*amours / he sette noght a kers	nat
For he was heelyd / of his maladye	was / heeled maladie
Ful ofte p*ar*amours / he gan defye	ofte / p*ar*amours deffie
And weep / as dooth a child *þa*t is ybete	weepe / that
A softe paas / he wente ouer the strete	
Vn til a smyth / men clepen daun Gerueys	cleped
That in his forge / smythed plogh harneys	plougħ
He sharpeth shaar / and cultour bisily	kultour
This Absolon / knokketh al esily	
And seyde / vndo Gerueys and that anon	Gerueys /
¶What who artowʃ / it' am I Absolon	artowʃ / I am heere Absolon
What Absolon / what Cristes swete tree	Absolon / for cristes sweete
Why rise ye so rathe / ey benedicitee	

3734 Nota malum quid Hg

[18] ¶Millere *40v*

Lest þt oure neghebores / thee espie
This Absolon / gan wype his mouth ful drye
Derk was the nyght / as pych / or as the cole
And at the wyndow / out she putte hir hole
And Absolon / hym fil no bet ne wers
But with his mouth / he kiste hir naked ers — No malu quid
Ful sauourly / er he were war of this
Abak he stirte / and thoghte it was amys
For wel he wiste / a womman hath no berd
He felte a thyng al rogh / and longe yherd
And seyde / fy allas / what haue I do
Tehee quod she / and clapte the wyndow to
And Absolon / gooth forth a sory paas
A berd / a berd / quod hende Nicholas
By goddes corpus / this gooth faire and wel
This sely Absolon / herde euery del
And on his lippe / he gan for anger byte
And to hym self / he seyde I shal thee quyte
Who rubbeth now / who froteth now his lippes
With dust / wt sond / wt straw / wt clooth / wt chippes
But Absolon / þt seith ful ofte allas
My soule / bitake I vn to Sathanas
But me were leuere / than al this toun quod he
Of this despit / awreken for to be
Allas quod he / allas I ne hadde yblejnt
His hote loue was coold / and al yqueynt
For fro that tyme / þt he hadde kist hir ers
Of paramours / he sette noght a kers
For he was heeled / of his maladye
Ful ofte paramours / he gan deffye
And weep / as dooth a child þt is ybete
A softe paas / he wente ouer the strete
Vn til a smyth / men clepen daun Gerueys
That in his forge / smythed plogh harneys
He sharpeth shaar / and cultour bisily
This Absolon / knokketh al esily
And seyde vndo Gerueys and that anon
What who artow / it am I Absolon
What Absolon / what Cristes swete tree
Why rise ye so rathe / ey benedicitee

What eyleth yow som gay gerl god it woot
Hath broght yow thus vp on the viritoot
By seinte note ye woot wel what I mene
This Absolon ne roghte nat a bene
Of al his pley no word agayn he yaf
He hadde moore tow on his distaf
Than Gerueys knew and seyde freend so deere
That hoote cultour in the chymenee heere
As lene it me I haue ther with to doone
I wol brynge it thee agayn ful soone
Gerueys answerde certes were it gold
Or in a poke nobles al vntold
Thow sholdest haue as I am trewe smyth
Ey Cristes foo what wol ye do ther with
Ther of quod Absolon be as be may
I shal wel telle it thee another day
And caughte the cultour by the colde stele
Ful softe out at the dore he gan to stele
And wente vn to the carpenteres wal
He cogheth first and knokketh ther with al
Vp on the wyndowe right as he dide er
This Alison answerde who is ther
That knokketh so I warante it a theef
Why nay quod he god woot my swete leef
I am thyn Absolon my derelyng
Of gold quod he I haue thee broght a ryng
My moder yaf it me so god me saue
Ful fyn it is and ther to wel ygraue
This wol I yeuen thee if thow me kisse
This Nicholas was risen for to pisse
And thoghte he wolde amenden al the iape
He sholde kisse his ers er þt he scape
And vp the wyndowe dide he hastily
And out his ers he putteth pryuely
Ouer the buttok to the haunche bon
And ther with spak this clerk this Absolon
Spek swete herte I noot noght wher thow art
This Nicholas anoon leet fle a fart
As greet as it hadde been a thonder dent
That with the strook he was almoost yblent

And he was redy

	ELLESMERE
What eyleth yow / som gay gerl / god it woot	gerl
Hath broght yow thus / vp on the viritoot	
By Seinte note / ye woot wel what I mene	seinte
¶This Absolon / ne roghte nat a bene	
Of al his pley / no word agayn he yaf	yaf
He hadde moore tow / on his dystaf	hadde / distaf
Than Gerueys knew / and seyde freend so deere	
That hoote cultour / in the chymenee heere	kultour /
As lene it me / I haue ther with to doone	
I wol brynge it thee / agayn ful soone	And I wol /
¶Gerueys answerde / certes were it gold	
Or in a poke / nobles al vntold	alle vntold
Thow sholdest haue / as I am trewe Smyth	Thou smyth
Ey Cristes foo / what wol ye do ther with	cristes with
¶Ther of quod Absolon / be as be may	
I shal wel telle it thee / another day	thee / tomorwe day
And caughte the cultour / by the colde stele	kultour /
Ful softe / out at the dore he gan to stele	
And wente / vn to the Carpenters wal	Carpenteris
He cogheth first and knokketh ther with al	first /
Vp on the wyndow / right as he dide er	wyndowe / right
¶This Alison answerde / who is ther	ther
That knokketh so / I warante it a theef	theef
¶Wy nay quod he god woot my swete lief	¶Why he / woot sweete leef
I am thyn Absolon / my derelyng	deerelyng
Of gold quod he / I haue thee broght a ryng	
My moder yaf it me / so god me saue	mooder
Ful fyn it is / and ther to wel ygraue	
This wol I yeuen thee / if thow me kisse	yeue thou
¶This Nicholas / was risen for to pisse	
And thoghte / he wolde amenden al the Iape	19 thoughte /
He sholde kisse his ers / er *þa*t he scape	his / er that
And vp the wyndow / dide he hastely	wyndowe / hastily
And out his ers / he putteth pryuely	
Ouer the buttok / to the haunche bon	Ou*er*
¶And ther with / spak this clerk this Absolon	And spak
Spek swete herte / I noot noght wher thow art	sweete bryd / I nat where thou
This Nicholas / anoon leet fle a fart	¶This anon
As greet as it hadde been a thonder dent	had dent
That with the strook he was almoost yblent	yblent

And he was redy

[19] ¶Millere *41r*

.The Millere.

	ELLESMERE
And he was redy / with his Iren hoot	
And Nicholas / in the ers he smoot	Nicholas / amydde ers
Of gooth the skyn / an handbrede aboute	¶Of hande brede
The hoote cultour / brende so his toute	kultour /
That for the smert he wende for to dye	And for
As he were wood / for wo he gan to crye	
Help water / water / help for goddes herte	Help / water /
¶This Carpenter / out of his slomber sterte	
And herde oon cryen water / as he were wood	crien
And thoghte allas / now cometh Nowelys flood	thoughte / Allas / comth Nowelis
He sette hym vp / with oute wordes mo	sit outen
And with his Ax / he smoot the corde atwo	
And down gooth al / he foond neither to selle	doun
Ne breed ne ale / til he cam to the Celle	Ale /
Vp on the floor / and ther*e* aswowne he lay	there
¶Vp stirte hir*e* / Alison and Nicholay	hire /
And cryden out and harrow / in the Strete	criden / out harrow
The neghebores / bothe smale and grete	neighebores /
In ronnen / for to gauren on this man	
That aswowne lay / bothe pale and wan	That yet aswowne he lay /
For with the fal / he brosten hadde his arm	Arm
But stonde he moste / vn to his owene harm	
For whan he spak / he was anon bore doun	
With hende Nicholas and Alisoun	Nicholas /
They tolden euery man / *þat* he was wood	that
He was agast so / of Nowelys flood	Nowelis
Thurgh fantasie / *þat* of his vanytee	that
He hadde yboght hym / knedyng tubbes thre	
And hadde hem hanged / in the roof aboue	the roue aboue
And *þat* he preyde hem / for goddes loue	
To sitten in the roof / p*ar* compaignye	
¶The folk gan laughen / at his fantasye	
In to the roof / they kiken and they cape	
And turned al his harm / vn to a Iape	
For what so / *þat* this Carpenter answerde	For /
It was for noght no man his reson herde	
With othes grete / he was so sworn adoun	
That he was holden wood / in al the toun	holde wood
For euery clerk / anon right heeld with oother	20 anonright /
They seyde / the man was wood / my leeue brother	broother

20 ¶Miller*e* *41v*

And he was redy / with his iren hoot /
And Nicholas / in the ers he smoot /
Of gooth the skyn / an handbrede aboute
The hoote cultour / brende so his toute
That for the smert / he wende for to dye
As he were wood / for wo he gan to crye
Help water / water / help for goddes herte
This carpenter / out of his slomber sterte
And herde oon cryen water / as he were wood
And thoghte allas / now cometh Nowelys flood
He sette hym vp / with oute wordes mo
And with his ax / he smoot the corde atwo
And down gooth al / he foond neither to selle
Ne breed ne ale / til he cam to the celle
Vp on the floor / and ther aswowne he lay
Vp sterte hire Alison / and Nicholay
And cryden out / and harrow in the strete
The neghebores / bothe smale and grete
In ronnen / for to gauren on this man
That aswowne lay / bothe pale and wan
ffor with the fal / he brosten hadde his arm
But stonde he moste / vn to his owene harm
ffor whan he spak / he was anon bore down
With hende Nicholas / and Alisoun
They tolden euery man / þt he was wood
He was agast so / of Nowelys flood
Thurgh fantasie / þt of his vanytee
He hadde yboght hym / knedyng tubbes thre
And hadde hem hanged / in the roof aboue
And þt he preyde hem / for goddes loue
To sitten in the roof / par compaignye
The folk gan laughen / at his fantasye
In to the roof / they kiken and they cape
And turned al his harm / vn to a Iape
ffor what so / þt this carpenter answerde
It was for noght / no man his reson herde
With othes grete / he was so sworn adoun
That he was holden wood / in al the toun
ffor euery clerk / anon right heeld with oother
They seyde the man was wood / my leeue brother

And euery wight gan laughen at this stryf
Thus swyued / was the Carpenteres wyf /
ffor al his kepyng / and his Ialousye
And Absolon / hath kist hir nether ye
And Nicholas / is scalded in the toute
This tale is doon / and god saue al the route

Here is ended / the Milleres tale

The prologe of the Reues tale

Whan folk hadde laughen / at this nyce cas
Of Absolon / and hende Nicholas
Diuerse folk / diuersely they seyde
But for the moore part / they lowe and pleyde
Ne at his tale / I seigh no man hym greue
But it were oonly / Osewold the Reue
By cause he was / of Carpenteres craft
A litel ire / is in his herte ylaft
He gan to grucche / and blamed it a lite
So the ik quod he / ful wel koude I thee quyte
With bleryng / of a proud Milleres eye
If yt me liste / speke of rybaudye
But ik am oold / me list no pleye for age
Gras tyme is doon / my fodder is now forage
This white top / writeth myne olde yeris
Myn herte / is also mowled / as myne heris
But if ik fare / as dooth an Openers
That ilke fruyt / is euer lenger the wers
Til it be roten / in mullok or in stree
We olde men / I drede so fare we
Til we be roten / kan we noght be rype
We hoppe alwey / whil yt the world wol pype
ffor in oure wil / ther stiketh euere a nayl
To haue an hoor heed / and a grene tayl
As hath a leek / for thogh oure myght be goon
Oure wil desireth folie / euere in oon
ffor whan we may noght / doon than wol we speke
Yet in oure asshen olde / is fyr yreke

	ELLESMERE
And eu*er*y wight gan laughen at this stryf	euery wight / … laughen of this stryf /
Thus swyued / was the Carpenters wyf	Thus / swyued was / this Carpenteris wyf /
For al his kepyng and his Ialousye	
And Absolon / hath kist hir nether Iye	kist … eye
And Nicholas / is scalded in the toute	towte
This tale is doon / and god saue al the route	rowte
¶Here is ended / the Millerys tale	¶Heere endeth the Millere his tale
¶The p*ro*loge / of the Reues tale	¶The Prologe / of the Reues tale
WHan folk hadde laughen / at this nyce cas	WHan … had
Of Absolon / and hende Nicholas	
Diu*er*se folk / diuersely they seyde	diu*er*sely
But for the moore part they lowe and pleyde	But … loughe
Ne at his tale / I seigh no man hym greue	at this tale / … saugh
But it were oonly / Osewold the Reue	Osewold
By cause he was / of Carpenters craft	cause / … Carpenteris
A litel Ire / is in his herte ylaft	
He gan to grucche / and blamed it alite	
So the ik quod he / ful wel koude I thee quyte	¶So theek quod … I yow quite
With bleryng of a proud Millerys Iye	bleryng / … Milleres eye
If *þat* me liste / speke of rybaudye	that … ribaudye
But ik am oold / me list no pleye for age	pley … Age
Gras tyme is doon / my fodder is now forage	
This white top*e* / writeth myne olde yerys	yeris
Myn herte / is also mowled / as myne herys	herte … is mowled also as … heris
But if ik fare / as dooth an Openers	if I fare /
That ilke fruyt is euer lenger the wers	¶That … fruyt / … euerleng
Til it be roten / in Mollok / or in stree	Mullok
We olde men / I drede so fare we	drede /
Til we be roten / kan we noght be rype	nat
We hoppe alwey / whil *þat* the world wol pipe	hoppen ay / whil that … pype
For in oure wil / ther stiketh euere a nayl	wyl / … eu*er*e
To haue an hoor heer / and a grene tayl	hoor heed / and
As hath a leek / for thogh oure myght be goon	leek
Oure wil desireth folie / euere in oon	wyl / … folie
For whan we may noght doon / than wol we speke	nat
Yet in oure asshen olde / is fyr yreke	Asshen

Foure gleedes haue we / whiche I shal deuyse
Auauntyng’ lyyng’ Anger Coueitise
Thise foure sparkles / longen vn to eelde
Oure lymes / mowe wel been vnweelde
But wil ne shal noght faillen / that is sooth
And yet I haue alwey / a coltes tooth
As many a yeer / as it is passed henne
Syn þ*at* my tappe of lyf / bigan to renne
For sikerlik’ whan ik was bore anon
Deeth drogh the tappe of lyf / and leet it goon
And euere sith / hath so the tappe yronne
Til þ*at* almoost / al empty is the tonne
The streem of lyf / now droppeth on the chymbe
The sely tonge / may wel rynge and chymbe
Of wrecchednesse / þ*at* passed is ful yoore
With olde folk / saue dotage is namoore
¶Whan þ*at* oure hoost’ hadde herd this sermonyng’
He gan to speke / as lordly as a kyng’
He seyde / what amounteth al this wit
What shal we speke alday / of holy writ
The deuel made / a Reue for to p*re*che
Or of a Souter*e* / a Shipman / or a leche
Sey forth thy tale / and tarie noght the tyme
Lo Depeford / and it is half wey pryme
Lo Grenewych / ther many a sherewe is Inne
It were al tyme / thy tale to bigynne
¶Now sires / quod this Osewold the Reue
I pray yow alle / þ*at* ye noght yow greue
Thogh I answere / and som del sette his howue
For leueful is / with force / force of showue
This dronken Miller*e* / hath ytoold vs heer
How þ*at* / bigiled was a Carpenter
P*ar*auenture in scorn / for I am oon
And by youre leue / I shal hym quyte anon
Right / in his cherles termes / wol I speke
I pray to god / his nekke mote to breke
He kan wel / in myn eye / seen a stalke
But in his owene / he kan noght seen a balke
Narrat’ AT Trompyngtou*n* / nat fer fro Cantebrygge
Ther gooth a brook / and ouer that a brygge

3912 vim vi repellere El

ELLESMERE

¶Foure han
liyng’ Anger /

Oure olde lemes /
1 wyl nat soothħ
yet’ ik alwey Coltes toothħ
yeer’
that lif /
sikerly / I bore /
droughħ leet’ gon
euer sithe /
that almoost’

that
folk’
Whan that hoost /

seide / wit’
What’ shul alday hooly writ’
deuel / made preche
And of Souter*e* / Shipman
nat
Depeford’ /
Grenewychħ / shrewe

NOw Osewold’
that nat
somdeel
force⸗force
¶This dronke Miller*e*
that’ bigyled Carpenteer

quite anoon
Righħt termes
mote breke
eye
2 nat
3 Trumpyngtou*n* / Cantebrigge
ou*er* brigge

1 ¶Reue *42r*

2 Break in El followed by:

¶Heere bigynneth / the Reues tale

3 Miniature of the Reeve in right margin.

The Reue.

ffoure gleedes haue we / whiche I shal deuyse
Auauntyng / lyyng / anger / Coueitise
Thise foure sparkles / longen vn to eelde
Oure lymes / mowe wel been vnweelde
But wil ne shal noght faillen / that is sooth
And yet I haue alwey / a coltes tooth
As many a yeer / as it is passed henne
Syn þt my tappe of lyf / bigan to renne
ffor sikerly / whan I was bore anon
Deeth drogh the tappe of lyf / and leet it goon.
And euere sith / hath so the tappe yronne
Til þt almoost / al empty is the tonne
The streem of lyf / now droppeth on the chymbe
The sely tonge / may wel rynge and chymbe
Of wrecchednesse / þt passed is ful yoore
With olde folk / saue dotage is namoore
¶ Whan þt oure hoost / hadde herd this sermonyng /
He gan to speke / as lordly as a kyng /
He seyde / what amounteth al this wit
What shal we speke alday / of holy writ
The deuel made a Reue for to preche
Or of a Souter / a Shipman / or a leche
Sey forth thy tale / and tarye noght the tyme
Lo Depeford / and it is half wey pryme
Lo Grenewych / ther many a shrewe is Inne
It were al tyme / thy tale to bigynne
¶ Now sires / quod this Osewold the Reue
I pray yow alle / þt ye noght yow greue
Thogh I answere / and som del sette his howue
ffor leueful is / with force force of showue
This dronken Millere / hath ytoold vs heer
How þt bigiled was a Carpenter
Parauenture in scorn / for I am oon
And by youre leue / I shal hym quyte anon
Right in his cherles termes / wol I speke
I pray to god / his nekke mote to breke
He kan wel in myn eye seen a stalke
But in his owene / he kan noght seen a balke

Narrat

At Trompyngton / nat fer fro Cantebrigge
Ther gooth a brook / and ouer that a brigge

Vp on the which brook ther stant a melle
And this is verray sooth / þt I yow telle
A millere was ther dwellyng many a day
As any Pecok he was proud and gay
Pipen he koude / and fisshe / and nettes beete
And turne coppes / and wel wrastle and sheete
And by his belt / he baar a long panade
And of a swerd / ful trenchaunt was the blade
A ioly poppere / baar he in his pouche
Ther was no man / for peril dorste hym touche
A Sheffeld thwitel / baar he in his hose
Round was his face / and camuse was his nose
As piled as an ape / was his skulle
He was a market betere / atte fulle
Ther dorste no wight / hand vp on hym legge
That he ne swoor / he sholde anon abegge
A theef he was for sothe / of corn and mele
And þt a sleigh / and vsaunt for to stele
His name was hoten / deynous Symkyn
A wyf he hadde / comen of noble kyn
The person of the toun / hir fader was
With hire he yaf / ful many a panne a bras
For þt Symkyn / sholde in his blood allye
She was yfostred / in a Nonnerye
For Symkyn / wolde no wyf as he sayde
But she were wel ynorissed and a mayde
To sauen his estaat of yomanrye
And she was proud / and pert as is a pye
A ful fair sighte / was it vp on hem two
On halydayes / biforn hire wolde he go
With his tipet / bounden aboute his heed
And she cam after / in a gyte of reed
And Symkyn / hadde hosen of the same
Ther dorste no wight / clepen hire but dame
Was noon so hardy / þt wente by the weye
That with hire dorste rage or ones pleye
But if he wolde be slayn of Symkyn
With panade / or with knyf / or boydekyn
For Ialous folk / been perilouse eueremo
Algate they wolde hir wyues wenden so

	ELLESMERE
Vp on the which brook ther stant a Melle	brook /
And this is verray sooth / þat I yow telle	
A Millere was ther dwellyng many a day	Millere / dwellynge
As any Pecok he was proud and gay	pecok
Pipen he koude / and fisshe / and nettes beete	koude fisshe /
And torne coppes / and wel wrastle and sheete	turne
And by his belt he baar a long Panade	panade
And of a swerd / ful trenchaunt was the blade	trenchant
A ioly poppere / baar he in his pouche	4
Ther was no man / for peril dorste hym touche	peril /
A sheffeld thwitel / baar he in his hose	Sheffeld
Round was his face / and camuse was his nose	
As piled as an Ape / was his skulle	
He was a Market betere / atte fulle	Market betere
Ther dorste no wight hand vp on hym legge	wight /
That he ne swoor / he sholde anon abegge	
A theef he was for sothe / of corn and mele	was / of corn and eek of Mele
And þat a sleigh / and vsant for to stele	that sly / vsaunt
His name was hoten / deynous Symkyn	hoote /
A wif he hadde / comen of noble kyn	wyf ycomen
The person of the toun / hir fader was	person
With hire he yaf / ful many a panne a bras	panne of bras
For þat Symkyn / sholde in his blood allye	that
She was yfostred / in a Nonnerye	yfostred
For Symkyn / wolde no wyf as he sayde	wyf /
But she were wel ynorissed and a mayde	But if she were /
To sauen / his estaat of yemanrye	sauen yomanrye
And she was proud / and peert as is a pye	peert
A ful fair sighte / was it vp on hem two	sighte /
On halidayes / biforn hire wolde he go	halydayes /
With his tipet wounden aboute his heed	typet bounde
And she cam after / in a gyte of reed	
And Symkyn / hadde hosen of the same	
Ther dorste no wight clepen hire but dame	wight / hire
Was noon so hardy / þat wente by the weye	that
That with hire / dorste rage / or ones pleye	hire /
But if he / wolde be slayn of Symkyn	if / he
With panade / or with knyf or boydekyn	knyf / boidekyn
For Ialous folk / been perilouse eueremo	perilous
Algate / they wolde hir wyues wenden so	hire

4 ¶Reue *42v*

·/·The Reue·/·	ELLESMERE
And eek / for she was som del smoterlich	somdel smoterlicħ
She was as digne / as water in a dich	dicħ
And ful of hoker / and of bismare	As ful
Hir thoghte / þ*a*t a lady sholde hir spare	thoughte / hir*e*
What for hir kynrede / and hir nortelrye	hir*e* hir nortelrie
That she hadde lerned / in the Nonnerye	lerned Nonnerie
A doghter hadde they / bitwix hem two	¶A they bitwixe
Of twenty yeer / with outen any mo	
Sauyng a child / þ*a*t was of hal yeer age	Sauynge half
In Cradel it lay / and was a p*ro*pre page	
This wenche / thikke and wel ygrowen was	wenche thikke /
With camuse nose / and eyen greye as glas	kamuse
With buttokes brode / and brestes rounde and hye	Buttokes
But right fair was hir heer' I wol nat lye	rigħt hir*e* heer /
¶The pe*r*son of the toun / for she was so feir	¶This was feir
In purpos was / to maken hir*e* his heir	
Bothe of his catel / and his Mesuage	5
And straunge he made it' of hir mariage	straunge / it
His purpos was / for to bistowe hir hye	hir*e*
In to som worthy blood of Auncetrye	
For holicherches good / moot been despended	hooly chirches
On holicherches blood / þ*a*t is descended	hooly chirches that
Ther fore / he wolde his holy blood honoure	Therfore / hooly
Thogh þ*a*t he / holy chirche sholde deuoure	Though / that' he hooly
¶Greet sokne / hath this Miller*e* out of doute	Greet sokene / Miller*e* /
With whete and malt' of al the land aboute	Malt'
And nameliche / ther was a greet Collegge	
Men clepeth / the soler halle at Cantebregge	clepen Soler
Ther was hir whete / and eek hir malt ygrounde	
And on a day / it happed in ⟨a⟩ stounde	a
Syk was this maunciple / on a maladie	Sik lay the Maunciple / maladye
Men wenden wisly / þ*a*t he sholde dye	that
For which this Millere / stal bothe mele and corn	which /
An hondred tyme / moore than biforn	hundred
For ther biforn / he stal but curteisly	
But now / he was a theef outrageously	
For which the wardeyn / chidde and made fare	which / wardeyn
But ther of / sette the Millere noght a tare	Miller*e* nat
He craked boost' and swoor it was noght so	And craketh boost / nat
Thanne were ther / yonge poure scolers two	¶Thanne poure clerkes two

5 ¶Reue *43r*

And eek for she was somdel smoterlich
She was as digne as water in a dich
And ful of hoker and of bismare
Hir thoghte þt a lady sholde hir spare
What for hir kynrede and hir nortelrye
That she hadde lerned in the nonnerye
A doghter hadde they bitwix hem two
Of twenty yeer with outen any mo
Savyng a child þt was of hal yeer age
In cradel it lay and was a ppre page
This wenche thikke and wel ygrowen was
With camuse nose and eyen greye as glas
With buttokes brode and brestes rounde and hye
But right fair was hir heer I wol nat lye
The pson of the toun for she was so feir
In purpos was to maken hire his heir
Bothe of his catel and his mesuage
And straunge he made it of hir mariage
His purpos was for to bistowe hir hye
In to som worthy blood of auncetrye
For holicherches good moot been despended
On holicherches blood þt is descended
Therfore he wolde his holy blood honoure
Though þt he holy chirche sholde devoure
Greet sokne hath this millere out of doute
With whete and malt of al the land aboute
And nameliche ther was a greet collegge
Men clepeth the Soler halle at Cantebregge
Ther was hir whete and eek hir malt ygrounde
And on a day it happed in a stounde
Syk was this manciple on a maladie
Men wenden wisly þt he sholde dye
For which this millere stal bothe mele and corn
An hundred tyme moore than biforn
For ther biforn he stal but curteisly
But now he was a theef outrageously
For which the wardeyn chidde and made fare
But ther of sette the millere noght a tare
He craked boost and swoor it was noght so
Thanne were ther yonge povre scolers two

That dwelten in the halle of which I seye
Testyf they were and lusty for to pleye
And oonly for hir myrthe and reuerye
Vp on the wardeyn bisily they crye
To yeue hem leue but a litel stounde
To go to mille and seen hir corn ygrounde
And hardily they dorste leye hir nekke
The millere sholde noght stelen hem half a pekke
Of corn by sleighte ne by force hem reue
And atte laste the wardeyn yaf hem leue
Iohn highte that oon and Aleyn highte that oother
Of oon town were they born þt highte Strother
Fer in the North I kan noght telle where
This Aleyn maketh redy al his gere
And on an hors the sak he caste anon
Forth gooth Aleyn the clerk and also Iohn
With good swerd and with bokeler by his syde
Iohn knew the wey hym neded no gyde
And at the mille the sak adoun he layth
Aleyn spak first al hayl Symkyn in faith
How fares thy faire doghter and thy wyf
Aleyn welcome quod Symkyn by my lyf
And Iohn also how now what do ye here
By god quod Iohn Symond nede has na peere
Hym bihoues serue hym self þt has na swayn
Or ellis he is a fool as clerkes sayn
Oure manciple I hope he wol be deed
Swa werkes ay the wanges in his heed
And therfore is I come and eek Alayn
To grynde oure corn and carie it heem agayn
I pray yow speed vs heythen that ye may
It shal be doon quod Symkyn by my fay
What wol ye doon whil þt it is in hande
By god right by the hoper wol I stande
Quod Iohn and se how the corn gas in
Yet saugh I neuere by my fader kyn
How þt the hoper wagges til and fra
Aleyn answerde Iohn wiltow swa
Thanne wol I be bynethe by my crown
And se how þt the mele falles down

	ELLESMERE
That⁊ dwelten in the halle / of which I seye	That in this halle /
Testyf they were / and lusty for to pleye	Testif
And oonly / for hir myrthe and reuerye	hire
Vp on the wardeyn / bisily they crye	
To yeue hem leue / but a litel stounde	
To go to Mille / and seen hir corn ygrounde	goon
And hardily / they dorste leye hir nekke	
The Millere / sholde noght stelen hem half a pekke	Millere nat stele hem /
Of corn by sleighte / ne by force hem reue	
And atte laste / the wardeyn yaf hem leue	at the laste /
Iohn̄ highte that oon / and Aleyn highte that oother	Aleyn heet
Of oon town were they born / þat highte Strother	Of o toun that
Fer in the North / I kan noght telle where	nat
This Aleyn / maketh redy al his gere	¶This
And on an hors / the sak he caste anon	sak⁊
Forth gooth Aleyn the clerk⁊. and also Iohn̄	goth clerk /
With good swerd / and with bokeler by his syde	swerd⁊ and bokeler by hir syde
Iohn̄ knew the wey / hym neded no gyde	wey / hem neded
And at the Mille / the sak adoun he layth	layth̄
¶Aleyn spak first⁊ alhayl Symkyn in fayth	Aleyn first / al hayl Symond⁊ yfayth
How fares / thy faire doghter / and thy wyf	Hou fares wyf /
¶Aleyn wel come / quod Symkyn by my lyf	welcome Symkyn / lyf /
And Iohn̄ also / how now / what do ye here	heer
¶By god quod Iohn̄ / Symond nede has na peere	¶Symond⁊ quod Iohn̄ / by god peer
Hym bihoues serue hym self / þat has na swayn	6 Hym boes serue selue / that
Or ellis / he is a fool / as clerkes sayn	elles /
Oure maunciple / I hope he wol be deed	Oure Manciple / hope / wil
Swa werkes ay / the wanges in his heed	
And ther fore is I come / and eek Alayn	And forthy / is
To grynde oure corn / and carie it heem agayn	it ham agayn
I pray yow / speed vs heythen / what ye may	spede heythen that ye
¶It shal be doon / quod Symkyn by my fay	
What wol ye doon / whil þat it is in hande	that
¶By god / right by the hoper / wol I stande	right hopur wil
Quod Iohn̄ / and se how the corn gas In	se / how that the
Yet saw I neuere / by my fader kyn	saugh̄ I neuere /
How þat the hoper / wagges til and fra	that hopur /
¶Aleyn answerde / Iohn̄ wiltow swa	
Thanne wol I be byneth / by my crown	wil byneth̄ / croun
And se / how þat the mele falles down	Mele doun

6¶Reue *43v*

In to the trogh / that sal be my desportꝛ	trougħ / disport /
For Ioħn in faith / I may been of youre sortꝛ	Ioħn yfaith / your*e*
I is as ille a Millere / as ar ye	I is / Miller*e* /
¶This Millere / smyled of hir nycetee	Miller*e* /
And thoghte / al this nys doon / but for a wyle	
They wene / þ*at* no man may hem bigile	bigyle
But by my thrift / yet shal I blere hir Iye	eye
For al the sleighte / in hir Phislophye	sleigħte / Philosophye
The moore queynte crekys / þ*at* they make	crekes / that
The moore wol I stele / whan I take	
In stede of flour / yet wol I yeue hem bren	stide
The grettest clerkes / been noght the wisest men	gretteste nogħt wisest
As whilom to the wolfꝛ thus spak the mare	wolf / Mare
Of al hir artꝛ counte I noght a tare	Artꝛ noghtꝛ
Out of the dore / he gooth ful pryuely	¶Out at the
Whan þ*at* he saugh his tyme / softely	saugħ / tyme
He looketh vp and doun / til he hath founde	
The clerkes hors / ther ⟨as⟩ it stood ybounde	as
Bihynde the Mille / vnder a leefsel	lefsel
And to the hors / he gooth hym faire and wel	goth
He strepeth of the bridel / right anon	brydel / rigħt
And whan the hors was laus / he gynneth gon	
Toward the fen / ther wilde mares renne	Mares
And forth with wehe / thurgh thikke and thenne	wehee / thikke *and* thurgh thenne
This Millere gooth ayein / no word he seyde	¶This Miller*e* agayn /
But dooth his note / and with the clerkes pleyde	
Til þ*at* hir corn / was faire and wel ygrounde	that weel
And whan the mele / was sakked and ybounde	Mele / is sakked
¶This Ioħn gooth outꝛ and fynt his hors away	This goth
And gan to crye / harrow and weilaway	crie / weylaway
Oure hors is lostꝛ. Alayn for goddes banes	lorn /
Step on thy feetꝛ com of man al atanes	Step*e* com out man
Allas oure wardeyn / has his palfrey lorn	7 Allas /
¶This Alayn al forgatꝛ bothe mele and corn	This Aleyn Mele
Al was out of his mynde / his housbondrye	housbondrie
What whilk wey is he gane / he gan to crye	whilkꝛ way geen / crie
¶The wyf cam lepyngꝛ Inward with a ren	lepynge
She seyde allas / youre hors gooth to the fen	goth
With wilde mares / as faste as he may go	
Vnthank come on his hand / þ*at* boond hym so	that

7 ¶Reue *44r*

In to the trogh / that shal be my desport
For Iohn in faith / I may been of youre sort
I is as ille a millere / as ar ye
This millere / smyled of hir nycetee
And thoghte / al this nys doon / but for a wyle
They wene / þt no man may hem bigile
But by my thrift / yet shal I blere hir ye
For al the sleighte / in hir philosophye
The moore queynte crekys / þt they make
The moore wol I stele / whan I take
In stede of flour / yet wol I yeue hem bren
The grettest clerkes / been noght the wisest men
As whilom to the wolf / thus spak the mare
Of al hir art / counte I noght a tare
Out of the dore / he gooth ful pryuely
Whan þt he saugh his tyme / softely
He looketh vp and doun / til he hath founde
The clerkes hors / ther as it stood ybounde
Bihynde the mille / vnder a leef sel
And to the hors / he gooth hym faire and wel
He strepeth of the brydel / right anon
And whan the hors was laus / he gynneth gon
Toward the fen / ther wilde mares renne
And forth with wehe / thurgh thikke and thenne
This millere gooth agayn / no word he seyde
But dooth his note / and with the clerkes pleyde
Til þt hir corn / was faire and wel ygrounde
And whan the mele / was sakked and ybounde
This Iohn gooth out / and fynt his hors away
And gan to crye / harrow and weilaway
Oure hors is lost / Alayn for goddes banes
Step on thy feet / com of man al atanes
Allas oure wardeyn / has his palfrey lorn
This Alayn al forgat / bothe mele and corn
Al was out of his mynde / his housbondrye
What whilk wey is he gane / he gan to crye
The wyf cam lepyng / inward with a ren
She seyde allas / youre hors gooth to the fen
With wilde mares / as faste as he may go
Vnthank come on his hand / þt boond hym so

And he þt bettre sholde haue knyt the reyne
¶ Allas quod John Aleyn for Cristes peyne
lay doun thy swerd and I wol myn alswa
I is ful wight god waat as is a ra
By god hert he sal nat scape vs bathe
Why ne hadstow pit the capil in the lathe
Ilhail by god Alayn thou is a fonne
¶ Thise sely clerkes haan ful faste yronne
Toward the fen bothe Alayn and eek John
And whan the millere saugh þt they were gon
He half a busshel of hir flour hath take
And bad his wyf go knede it in a cake
He seyde I trowe the clerkes were aferd
yet kan a millere maken a clerkes berd
ffor al his art ye lat hem goon hir weye
lo wher he gooth ye lat the children pleye
They gete hym noght so lightly by my croun
¶ Thise sely clerkes rennen vp and doun
With keep keep stand stand Jossa warderere
Ga whistle thou and I sal kepe hym heere
But shortly til þt it was verray nyght
They koude noght though they dide al hir myght
Hir capyl cacche he ran alwey so faste
Til in a dych they caughte hym at the laste
¶ Wery and weet as beest is in the reyn
Comth sely John and with hym comth Aleyn
Allas quod John the day þt I was born
Now ar we dryuen til hethyng and til scorn
Oure corn is stole men wil vs foolis calle.
Bothe the wardeyn and oure felawes alle
And namely the millere weilawey
¶ Thus pleyneth John as he gooth by the wey
Toward the mille and Bayard in his hond
The millere sittyng by the fyr he fond
ffor it was nyght and ferther myghte they noght
But for the loue of god they hym bisoght
Of herberwe and of ese as for hir peny
¶ The millere seide agayn if ther be eny
Swich as it is yet shal ye haue youre part
Myn hous is streit but ye han lerned art

	ELLESMERE
And he *þat* bettre / sholde haue knyt the reyne	han
¶Allas / quod Iohn̄ / Aleyn for Cristes peyne	¶Allas quod Aleyn / for cristes
Lay doun thy swerd / and I wol myn alswa	wil
I is ful wight / god waat as is a ra	wight raa
By god hert he sal nat scape vs bathe	herte /
Why ne had thow / pit the capil in the lathe	Why nadtow pit the Capul
Ilhail / by god Alayn / thow is a fonne	Ilhayl / thou
¶This sely clerkes / haan ful faste yronne	han
Toward the fen / bothe Alayn and eek Iohn̄	Aleyn
And whan the Millere seigh / *þat* they were gon	¶And Millere / saugh
He half a busshel / of hir flour hath take	busshel /
And bad his wyf / go knede it in a cake	in cake
He seyde / I trowe / the clerkes were aferd	trowe aferd
Yet kan a Millere / maken a clerkes berd	Millere / make berd
For al his art ye lat hem goon hir weye	Art now lat
Lo where he gooth / ye lat the children pleye	wher they goon /
They gete hym noght so lightly / by my croun	nat lightly /
¶Thise sely clerkes / rennen vp and doun	
With keep / keep / stand / stand / Iossa warderere	*With* keepe / keepe / stand / stand /
Ga whistle thow / and I sal kepe hym heere	thou / I shal
But shortly / til *þat* it was verray nyght	But that nyght
They koude noght thogh they dide al hir myght	nat / do myght
Hir capyl cacche / he ran alwey so faste	capul
Til in a dych / they caughte hym at the laste	atte laste
¶Wery and weet as beest is in the reyn	Wery
Comth sely Iohn̄ / and with hym comth Aleyn	*with*
Allas quod Iohn̄ / the day *þat* I was born	that
Now ar we dryuen / til hethyng *and* til scorn	are dryue / hethyng and
Oure corn is stole / men wil vs foolis calle	stoln / me / wil fooles
Bothe the wardeyn / and oure felawes alle	Bathe
And namely the Millere / weilawey	namely / Millere weylaway
¶Thus pleyneth Iohn̄ / as he gooth by the wey	way
Toward the Mille / and Bayard in his hond	bayard hond
The Millere / sittyng by the fyr he fond	Millere / sittynge / fond
For it was nyght and ferther myghte they noght	forther noght
But for the loue of god / they hym bisoght	bisoght
Of herberwe and of ese / as for hir peny	
¶The Millere seide agayn / if ther be eny	seyde
Swich as it is / yet shal ye haue youre part	
Myn hous is streyt but ye han lerned art	streit Art

Ye kan by argumentz / make a place	8 konne Argumentz /
A myle brood / of twenty foot of space	
Lat se now / if this place may suffise	
Or make it rowm with speche / as is your*e* gyse	youre gise
¶Now Symond seyde this Iohn / by Seint Cutberd	NOw Symond / seyde Iohn /
Ay is thou myrie / and that is faire answerd	and this is answerd
I haue herd seye / men sal tak of twa thynges	seyd / man sal taa /
Swilk as he fyndes / or tak swilk as he brynges	Slyk as or taa slyk as
But specialy / I pray thee hoost deere	specially /
Get vs som mete and drynke / and make vs cheere	
And we wol payen / trewely atte fulle	wil
With empty hand / men may none haukes tulle	
Lo heere oure siluer / redy for to spende	Loo
¶This Millere in to town / his doghter sende	Miller*e* / toun
For ale and breed / and rosted hem a goos	Ale
And boond hir hors / it sholde namoore go loos	hir*e* sholde nat goon loos
And in his owene chambre / hem made a bed	
With shetes and w*ith* chalons / faire yspred	sheetes and with
Noght from his owene bed / but ten foot or twelue	Noght bed / ten foot /
His doghter hadde a bed / al by hir selue	
Right in the same chambre by and by	Right chambre /
It myghte be no bet and cause why	why
Ther was no rowmer herberwe / in the place	ro*m*mer herberwe
They soupen / and they speken / hem to solace	speke
And drynken euere stroong ale / at the beste	drynke eu*er*e / strong Ale atte beste
Aboute mydnyght / wente they to reste	mydnyght
Wel hath this Millere / vernysshed his heed	¶Wel Miller*e* vernysshed
Ful pale he was for dronke / and noght reed	dronken / nat
He yexeth / and he speketh thurgh the nose	speketh /
As he were / on the quakke / or on the pose	
To bedde he goth / and w*ith* hym goth his wyf	with
As any Iay / she light was and iolyf	Iolyf
So was / hir ioly whistle / wel ywet	was whistle wel y wet
The Cradel / at hir beddes feet is set	set
To rokken / and to yeue the child to sowke	
And whan þ*at* dronken / al was in the Crowke	crowke
To bedde wente / the doghter right anon	bedde / wente right
To bedde gooth Aleyn / and also Iohn	bedde wente Aleyn /
Ther nas namoore / hem neded no dwale	
This Millere / hath so wisly bibbed ale	Miller*e* / wisely Ale

[8] ¶Reue *44v*

Ye kan by argumentz / make a place
A myle brood / of twenty foot of space
Lat se now / if this place may suffise
Or make it rowm with speche / as is youre gyse
Now Symond seyde this John / by Seint Cutberd
Ay is thou myrie / and that is faire answerd
I haue herd seye / men sal tak of twa thynges
Swilk as he fyndes / or tak swilk as he brynges
But specially / I pray thee hoost deere
Get vs som mete and drynke / and make vs cheere
And we wol payen / trewely atte fulle
With empty hand / men may none haukes tulle
Lo heere oure siluer / redy for to spende
This millere in to town / his doghter sende
For ale and breed / and rosted hem a goos
And boond hir hors / it sholde namoore go loos
And in his owene chambre / hem made a bed
With shetes and with chalons / faire yspred
Noght from his owene bed / but ten foot or twelue
His doghter hadde a bed / al by hir selue
Right in the same chambre by and by
It myghte be no bet / and cause why
Ther was no roumer herberwe in the place
They soupen / and they speken / hem to solace
And drynken euere strong ale / at the beste
Aboute mydnyght / wente they to reste
Wel hath this millere / vernysshed his heed
Ful pale he was for dronke / and noght reed
He yexeth / and he speketh thurgh the nose
As he were on the quakke / or on the pose
To bedde he goth / and with hym goth his wyf
As any Jay / she light was and iolyf
So was hir ioly whistle / wel ywet
The cradel / at hir beddes feet is set
To rokken / and to yeue the child to sokke
And whan þt dronken / al was in the crowke
To bedde wente / the doghter right anon
To bedde gooth Aleyn / and also John
Ther nas namoore / hem neded no dwale
This millere / hath so wisly bibbed ale

That as an hors he snorteth in his sleep
Ne of his tayl bihynde he took no keep
His wyf bar hym a burdon a ful strong
Men myghten hir rowtyng heren a furlong
The wenche rowteth eek par compaignye
Aleyn the clerk that herde this melodye
He poked John and seyde slepestow
Herd thow euere slyk a sang er now
Lo whilk a complyn is ymel hem alle
A wilde fyr on thair bodyes falle
Wha herkned euere swilk a ferly thyng
Ye they sal haue the flour of il endyng
This lang nyght ther tydes me na reste
But yet na force al sal be for the beste
For John seyde he als euere moot I thryue
If þt I may yon wenche wol I swyue
Som esement has lawe shapen vs
For John ther is a lawe þt says thus
That gif a man in a point be agreued
That in another he sal be releued
Oure corn is stoln sothly it is na nay
And we han had an ille fit to day
And syn I sal haue naan amendement
Agayn my los I wil haue esement
By goddes saule it sal naan other be
This John answerde Aleyn auyse thee
The millere is a perilous man he seyde
And if þt he out of his sleep abrayde
He myghte doon vs bathe a vileynye
Aleyn answerde I counte hym nought a flye
And vp he rist and by the wenche he crepte
This wenche lay vp righte and faste slepte
Til he so neigh was er she myghte espie
That it hadde been to late for to crie
And shortly for to seyn they were at oon
Now pley Aleyn for I wol speke of John
This John lith stille a furlang wey or two
And to hym self he maketh routhe and wo
Allas quod he this is a wikked jape
Now may I seyn þt I is but an ape

	ELLESMERE
That as an hors / he fnorteth in his sleep*e*	
Ne of his tayl bihynde / he took no keep*e*	
His wyf bar hym / a burdon / a ful strong	hym burdon
Men myghten hir routyng heren a furlong	myghte rowtyng heere two furlong
The wenche / routeth eek p*ar* compaignye	wenche rowteth eek /
¶Aleyn the clerc that herde this melodye	clerk /
He poked Ioħn / and seyde slepestow	
Herd thow euere / slyk a sang er now	Herdtow eu*er*e slyk /
Lo swilk a couplyng is ymel hem alle	9 whilk a cowplyng
A wilde fyr / on thair bodyes falle	fyr / vp on
Wha herkned euere / swilk a ferly thyng	euere / slyk a
Ye they sal haue / the flour of il endyng	
This lang nyght ther tydes me na reste	lange nyght /
But yet na force / al sal be for the beste	nafors /
For Ioħn seyde he / als eu*er*e moot I thryue	
If þ*at* I may / yon wenche wol I swyue	that wil
Som esement has lawe shapen vs	yshapen
For Ioħn / ther is a lawe / þ*at* says thus	that
That gif a man / in a point be agreued	point ygreued
That in another / he sal be releued	
Oure corn is stoln / soothly it is na nay	stoln / shortly is ne nay
And we han had / an ille fit to day	il fit al this day
And syn I sal / haue naan amendement	sal neen
Agayn my los / I wil haue esement	
By goddes saule / it sal naan other be	god sale / neen bee
¶This Ioħn answerde / Aleyn auyse thee	Alayn
The Millere / is a p*er*ilous man he sayde	Miller*e* / seyde
And if þ*at* he / out of his sleep abrayde	And gif that sleep*e* abreyde
He myghte doon vs bathe / a vileynye	myghte vs / bathe
¶Aleyn answerde / I counte hym noght a flye	nat
And vp he rist / and by the wenche he crepte	
This wenche lay vp righte / and faste slepte	righte /
Til he so neigh was / er she myghte espie	ny myghte
That it hadde been / to late for to crie	had
And shortly for to seyn / they were at oon	aton
Now pley Aleyn / for I wol speke of Ioħn	
¶This Ioħn lith stille / a furlang wey / or two	This furlong wey
And to hym self he maketh routhe and wo	self /
Allas quod he / this is a wikked Iape	
Now may I seyn / þ*at* I is but an ape	that Ape

9¶Reue | *45r*

	ELLESMERE
Yet has my felawe / som what for his harm	
He has the Milleris doghter / in his arm	has / Arm
He auntred hym / and has his nedes sped	
And I lye / as a draf sak / in my bed	sek /
And whan this iape / is told another day	Iape tald
I sal ben halden / a daf a Cokenay	been halde cokenay
I wil arise and auntre it⁊ by my fayth	arise / it faytħ
Vnhardy is vnsely / thus men sayth	vnseely / saytħ
¶And vp he roos / and softely he wente	And
Vn to the Cradel / and in his hand it hente	cradel /
And baar it softe / vn to his beddes feet⁊	to the beddes
Soone after this / the wyf hir routynt leet⁊	¶Soone rowtyng
And gan awake / and wente hir out to pisse	hir*e*
And cam agayn / and gan hir Cradel mysse	cradel
And groped heer and ther / but she foond noon	
Allas quod she / I hadde almoost mysgoon	
I hadde almoost⁊ goon to the clerkes bed	[10] almoost goon /
Ey benedicite / thanne had I foule ysped	hadde y sped
And forth she gooth / til she the Cradel fond	fond
She gropeth alwey / forther *with* hir hond	gropeth / alwey with hond
And foond the bed / and thoghte noght but good	
By cause / *þat* the Cradel by it stood	that
And nyste wher she was / for it was derk⁊	
But faire and wel / she creep in to the clerk⁊	creep*e* In
And lyth ful stille / and wolde haue caught a sleep*e*	lith han
With Inne a while / this Ioħn the clerk vp leep*e*	
And on this goode wyf / he leyth on soore	leith
So murie a fyt⁊ ne hadde she nat ful yoore	myrie a fit⁊ hadde
He priketh harde and depe / as he were mad	harde and soore / as
This ioly lyf / han thise two clerkes lad	
Til *þat* / the thridde cok⁊ bigan to synge	that⁊ cok /
¶Aleyn wax wery / in the dawenynge	
For he hadde swonken / al the longe nyght⁊	had nygħt⁊
And seyde / fare wel Malyn swete wight⁊	weel Malyne sweete wigħt⁊
The day is come / I may no lenger byde	
But euere mo / wher so I go or ryde	eueremo / go /
I is thyn awen clerk⁊ so haue I sel	clerk⁊ swa seel
¶Now deere lemman quod she / go fare wel	fareweel
But er thow go / o thyng⁊ I wol thee telle	
Whan that thow wendest / homward by the Melle	thou wendest⁊

[10] ¶Reue *45v*

yet has my felawe / som what for his harm
He has the milleris doghter / in his arm
He auntred hym / and has his nedes sped
And I lye / as a draf sak / in my bed
And whan this iape is told another day
I sal ben halden / a daf a cokenay
I wil arise and auntre it / by my fayth
Vnhardy is vnsely / thus men sayth
And vp he roos / and softely he wente
Vn to the cradel / and in his hand it hente
And bar it softe / vn to his beddes feet
Soone after this / the wyf hir routyng leet
And gan awake / and wente hir out to pisse
And cam agayn / and gan hir cradel mysse
And groped heer and ther / but she foond noon
Allas quod she / I hadde almoost mysgoon
I hadde almoost / goon to the clerkes bed
Ey benedicite / thanne had I foule yspeed
And forth she gooth / til she the cradel fond
She gropeth alwey forther / with hir hond
And foond the bed / and thoghte noght but good
By cause / þt the cradel by it stood
And nyste wher she was / for it was derk
But faire and wel / she creep in to the clerk
And lyth ful stille / and wolde haue caught a sleep
With inne a while / this Iohn the clerk vp leep
And on this goode wyf / he leyth on soore
So myrie a fyt / ne hadde she nat ful yoore
He priketh harde and depe / as he were mad
This ioly lyf / han thise two clerkes lad
Til þt / the thridde cok bigan to synge
Aleyn wax wery / in the dawenynge
For he hadde swonken / al the longe nyght
And seyde / fare wel Malyn swete wight
The day is come / I may no lenger byde
But eueremo / wher so I go or ryde
I is thyn awen clerk / so haue I sel
Now dere lemman quod she / go fare wel
But er thow go / o thyng I wol thee telle
Whan that thow wendest / homward by the melle

Right at the entree / of the dore bihynde
Thow shalt a cake / of half a busshel fynde
That was ymaked / of thyn owene mele
Which þt I heelp / my sire for to stele
And good lemman / god thee saue and kepe
And with that word / almoost she gan to wepe
Aleyn vp rist / and thoghte er þt it dawe
I wol go crepen in / by my felawe
And fond the cradel / with his hond anon
By god thoghte he / al wrang I haue mysgon
Myn heed is toty / of my swynk to nyght
That maketh me / þt I go noght aright
I woot wel by the cradel / I haue mysgo
Here lyth the millere / and his wyf also
And forth he gooth / on twenty deuelesway
Vn to the bed / ther as the millere lay
He wende haue cropen / by his felawe John
And by the millere / in he creep anoon
And caughte hym by the nekke / and softe he spak
He seyde thou John / thow swynesheed awak
ffor cristes saule / and here a noble game
ffor by that lord / þt called is seint Jame
As I haue thries / in this shorte nyght
Swyued the milleres doghter / bolt vp right
Whil thow hast / as a coward ben agast
Ye false harlot / quod the millere hast
A false traytour / false clerk quod he
Thou shalt be deed / by goddes dignytee
Who dorste be so bold / to disparage
My doghter / that is come of swich lynage
And by the throte bolle / he caughte Alayn
And he hente hym / despitously agayn
And on the nose / he smoot hym with his fest
Doun ran the blody streem / vp on his brest
And on the floor / with nose and mouth tobroke
They walwen / as doon two pigges in a poke
And vp they goon / and doun agayn anoon
Til þt the millere / sporned on a stoon
And doun he fil / bakward vp on his wyf
That wiste no thyng / of this nyce stryf

	ELLESMERE
Right at the entree / of the dore bihynde	Rigħt
Thow shalt a Cake / of half a busshel fynde	Thou busshel
That was ymaked / of thyn owene mele	
Which þat I heelp / my sire for to stele	that heelp*e* / my fader for
And good lemman / god thee saue and kepe	goode
And with that word / almoost he gan to wepe	almoost she gan
¶Aleyn vp rist and thoghte er þat it dawe	Aleyn rist / thoughte /
I wol go crepen In / by my felawe	
And fond the Cradel / with his hond anon	hand
By god thoghte he / al wrang I haue mysgon	thoughte wrang
Myn heed is toty / of my swynk to nyght	nygħt
That maketh me / þat I go noght aright	that nat arigħt
I woot wel by the Cradel / I haue mysgo	
Here lyth the Millere / and his wyf also	Heere lith
And forth he gooth / on twenty deueleway	goth / a twenty deuel way
Vn to the bed / ther as the Millere lay	Miller*e*
He wende haue cropen / by his felawe Ioħn	
And by the Millere / In he creep anoon	Miller*e* creep*e* anon
And caughte hym by the nekke / and softe he spak	caugħte
He seyde thou Ioħn / thow Swyneshed awak	seyde / thou swynesheed awak
For cristes saule / and here a noble game	heer
For by that lord / þat called is Seint Iame	that called seint
As I haue thries / in this shorte nyght	nygħt /
Swyued the Milleris doghter / bolt vp right	Milleres doghter right
Whil thow hast / as a coward been agast	11 hast Coward agast
¶Ye false harlot quod the Millere hast	Miller*e* hast
A false traytour / false clerk quod he	traitour / clerk
Thou shalt be deed / by goddes dignytee	Thow dignitee
Who dorste be so bold / to disparage	boold / disp*ar*age
My doghter / that is come of swich lynage	come /
And by the throte bolle / he caughte Alayn	
And he hente hym / despitously agayn	
And on the nose / he smoot hym with his fest	smoot
Doun ran the blody streem / vp on his brest	
And on the floor / with nose and mouth tobroke	And in the to broke
They walwen / as doon two pigges in a poke	walwe /
And vp they goon / and doun agayn anoon	anon
Til þat the Millere / sporned on a stoon	that Miller*e* / sporned at a
And doun he fil / bakward vp on his wyf	wyf /
That wiste no thyng of this nyce stryf	thyng / stryf /

11 ¶Reue *46r*

The Reue

For she was falle aslepe / alitel wight
With Iohn the clerk / that waked hadde al nyght
And with the fal / out of hir sleepe she brayde
Help holy cros of Bromholm / she sayde
In manus tuas / lord to thee I calle
Awake Symond / the feend is on me falle
Myn herte is broken / help I nam but ded
Ther lyth oon vp on my wombe / and vp myn hed
Help Symkyn / for the false clerkes fighte
¶This Iohn sterte vp / as faste as euere he myghte
And graspeth by the walles / to and fro
To fynde a staf / and she sterte vp also
And knew the estres / bet than dide this Iohn
And by the wal / a staf she foond anon
And saugh / a litel shymeryng of a light
For at an hole / in shoon the moone bright
And by that light she saugh hem bothe two
But sikerly / she nyste who was who
But as she saugh / a whit thyng in hir Iye
And whan she gan / this white thyng espye
She wende the clerk hadde wered a voluper
And with the staf / she drow ay ner and ner
And wende han hit this Aleyn atte fulle
And smoot the Millere / on the piled skulle
That doun he gooth / and cryde harrow I dye
Thise clerkes bette hym wel / and lete hym lye
And greithen hem / and toke hir hors anon
And eek hir mele / and on hir wey they gon
And at the Mille / yet they toke hir cake
Of half a busshel flour ful wel ybake
¶Thus is the proude Millere / wel ybete
And hath ylost the gryndyng of the whete
And payed for the souper / euerydel
Of Aleyn / and of Iohn / that bette hym wel
His wyf is swyued / and his doghter als
Lo which it is / a Millere to be fals
And ther fore this prouerbe / is seyd ful sooth
Hym thar nat wene wel / þat yuele dooth
A gilour shal hym self / bigiled be
And god / that sitteth heighe in magestee

ELLESMERE

aslepe alite wight
nyght
with breyde
hooly croys seyde

Awak Symond / on vs falle
deed
oon / and on myn heed
Helpe fighte
stirte as soone as euer myghte
walles
stirte
Estres /

light
In bright

nyste /
saugh / eye
gan / the white
volupeer
with neer and neer
at the fulle
Millere / pyled
And doun cride
beete weel /
greythen

tooke
busshel flour /
Thus Millere
ylost / gryndynge
12 soper euerideel
Aleyn þat weel

swich Millere
therfore / prouerbe /
that
gylour / self bigyled
þat in Trinitee

12 ¶Reue 46v

ffor she was falle aslepe/ a litel wight/
With Iohn the clerk/ that waked hadde al nyght/
And with the fal/ out of hir sleep she brayde
Help holy cros of Bromholm/ she sayde
In manus tuas/ lord to thee I calle
Awake Symond/ the feend is on me falle
Myn herte is broken/ help I nam but deed
Ther lyth oon vp on my wombe/ and vp myn heed
Help Symkyn/ for the false clerkes fighte
This Iohn stirte vp/ as faste as euere he myghte
And graspeth by the walles/ to and fro
To fynde a staf/ and she stirte vp also
And knewe the estres/ bet than dide this Iohn
And by the wal/ a staf she foond anon
And saugh/ a litel shymeryng of a light
ffor at an hole/ in shoon the moone bright/
And by that light/ she saugh hem bothe two
But sikerly/ she nyste who was who
But as she saugh/ a whit thyng in hir iye
And whan she gan/ this white thyng espye
She wende the clerk/ hadde wered a voluper
And with the staf/ she drow ay neer and neer
And wende han hit/ this Aleyn atte fulle
And smoot the millere/ on the pyled skulle
That doun he gooth/ and cryde harrow I dye
Thise clerkes bette hym wel/ and lete hym lye
And greythen hem/ and tooke hir hors anon
And eek hir mele/ and on hir wey they gon
And at the mille/ yet they toke hir cake
Of half a busshel flour/ ful wel ybake
Thus is the proude millere wel ybete
And hath ylost/ the gryndyng of the whete
And payed for the souper/ euerydel
Of Aleyn and of Iohn/ that bette hym wel
His wyf is swyued/ and his doghter als
Lo which it is/ a millere to be fals
And therfore this prouerbe/ is seyd ful sooth
Hym thar nat wene wel/ yt yuele dooth
A gilour shal hym self/ bigiled be
And god/ that sitteth heighe in magestee

Saue al this compaignye grete and smale
Thus haue I quyt the Millere in my tale

Here endeth the Reues tale

The prologe of the Cookes tale

The Cook of londoun whil the Reue spak
ffor ioye hym thoughte he clawed hym on the bak
haha quod he for Cristes passion
This Millere hadde a sharp conclusion
Vp on his argument of herbergage
Wel seyde Salomon in his langage
Ne bryng nat euery man in to thyn hous
ffor herberwyng by nyghte is perilous
Wel oghte a man auysed for to be
Whom þt he broghte in to his pryuetee
I pray to god so yeue me sorwe and care
If euere sith I highte hogge of Ware
Herde I a Millere bettre yset awerk
He hadde a iape of malice in the derk hic
But god forbede that we stynten heere
ffor if ye vouche sauf to heere
A tale of me that am a poure man
I wol yow telle as wel as euere I kan
A litel iape that fil in oure Citee
Oure hoost answerde and seyde I graunte it thee
Now tel on Roger looke that it be good
ffor many a pastee hastow laten blood
And many a Iakke of Douere hastow soold
That hath been twies hoot and twies coold
Of many a pilgrym hastow Cristes curs
ffor of thy persle yet they fare the wors
That they han eten with thy stubbul goos
ffor in thy shoppe is many a flye loos
Now tel on gentil Roger by thy name
But yet I praye thee be nat wrooth for game
A man may seye ful sooth in game and pley
Thow seist ful sooth quod Roger by my fey

	ELLESMERE
Saue al this compaignie / grete and smale	compaignye /
Thus haue I quyt the Millere / in my tale	quyt' Miller*e*
¶Here endeth the Reues tale	¶Heere is ended the Reues tale
¶The prologe of the Cookes tale	¶The prologe of the Cokes tale
The Cook / of Londou*n* / whil the Reue spak'	Cook whil that the spak
For ioye hym thoughte / he clawed hym on the bak'	hi*m* hi*m*
Haha quod he / for Cristes passiou*n*	Ha. ha. cristes
This Millere / hadde a sharp*e* conclusiou*n*	Miller*e* /
Vp on his argument' of herbergage	Argument /
Wel seyde Salomon / in his langage	Salomo*n* /
Ne bryng nat euery man / in to thyn hous	brynge man
For herberwyng' by nyghte is p*er*ilous	herberwynge
Wel oghte a man / auysed for to be	
Whom *þat* he broghte / in to his p*ri*uetee	that pryuetee
I pray to god / so yeue me sorwe and care	
If euer sith / I highte hogge of ware	eu*er*e sitthe / highte Hogge
Herde I a Millere / bettre yset awerk /	Miller*e* / awerk
He hadde a iape of malice / in the derk'	Iape malice derk
But god forbede / that we stynten heere [hic]	stynte
For if ye / vouche sauf to heere [audire]	And therfore / if ye
A tale of me / that am a poure man	
I wol yow telle / as wel as eu*er*e I kan	
A litel iape / that fil in oure Citee	
¶Oure hoost answerde / and seyde I graunte it thee	seide
Now tel on Roger / looke that it be good	telle
For many a pastee / hastow laten blood	
And many a Iakke of Douere / hastow soold	Douere
That hath been twies hoot' and twies coold	been /
Of many a pilgrym / hastow Cristes curs	cristes
For of thy p*er*sle / yet they fare the wors	p*er*cely /
That they han eten / with thy stubbul goos	stubbel
For in thy shoppe / is many a flye loos	
Now tel on / gentil Roger / by thy name	telle Roger
But yet I praye thee / be nat wrooth for game	yet' pray wroth
A man may seye ful sooth / in game and pley	[1]
¶Thow seist ful sooth / quod Roger by my fey	¶Thou

[1] ¶Cook *47r*

	ELLESMERE
But sooth pley quade pley / as the Flemyng seith	quaad flemyng
And therfore herry Bailly / by thy feith	therfore / Herry feitħ
Be thou nat wrooth / er we departen heer	na
Thogh þat my tale / be of an hostiler	Though that Hostileer
But nathelees / I wol nat telle it yit	yit
But er we parte / ywis thow shalt be quyt	thou quit /
And ther with al / he lough / and made cheere	lougħ
And seyde his tale / as ye shal after heere	shul

¶Here bigynneth the Cook his tale

¶Heere bigynneth the Cookes tale

A Prentis / whilom dwelled in oure Citee	Prentys dwelled /
And of a craft of vitaillers was he	vitailliers hee
Gaillard he was / as goldfynch in the shawe	Goldfyncħ
Broun as a berye / a p*ro*pre short felawe	2 propre short felwe
With lokkes blake / ykembd ful fetisly	
Dauncen he koude / so wel and iolily	
That he / was clepyd Perkyn Reuelour	he cleped
He was / as ful / of loue and p*ar*amour	ful
As is the hyue / ful of hony swete	hyve / sweete
Wel was the wenche / þat w*ith* hym myghte meete	wenche / with mygħte
At euery bridale / wolde he synge *and* hoppe	and
He loued bet the Tauerne / than the shoppe	bet Tau*er*ne
For / whan ther any ridyng was in Chepe	ther / ridyng
Out of the shoppe / thider wolde he lepe	
Til þat he hadde / al the sighte yseyn	that sigħte
And daunced wel / he wolde noght come ageyn	nat ayeyn
And gadred hym / a meynee of his sort	gadered
To hoppe and synge / and maken swich disport	
And ther / they setten steuene / for to meete	ther steuene
To pleyen at the dees / in swich a Streete	pleyen / dys
For in the town / nas ther no Prentys	toun / p*re*ntys
That fairer / koude caste a paire of dys	fairer caste /
Than Perkyn koude / and ther to he was free	therto
Of his dispense / in place of pryuetee	
That foond his maister wel / in his chaffare	fond wel
For ofte tyme / he foond his box ful bare	often
For sikerly / a prentys reuelour	p*re*ntys Reuelour
That haunteth dees / ryot or p*ar*amour	dys / Riot

[2] Miniature of the Cook in right margin.

But sooth pley quade pley / as the fflemyng seith
And ther fore herry Baily / by thy feith
Be thou nat wrooth / er we departen heer
Though þt my tale / be of an hostiler
But nathelees / I wol nat telle it yit
But er we parte / ywis thow shalt be quyt
And ther with al / he lough / and made cheere
And seyde his tale / as ye shal after heere

Heere bigynneth the Cook his tale

A Prentis / whilom dwelled in oure Citee
And of a craft / of vitaillers was he
Gaillard he was / as goldfynch in the shawe
Broun as a berye / a propre short felawe
With lokkes blake / ykembd ful fetisly
Dauncen he koude / so wel and iolily
That he / was clepyd Perkyn Reueloun
He was / as ful of loue and paramour
As is the hyue / ful of hony swete
Wel was the wenche / þt with hym myghte meete
At euery brydale / wolde he synge & hoppe
He loued bet the Tauerne / than the shoppe
ffor whan ther any rydyng / was in Chepe
Out of the shoppe / thider wolde he lepe
Til þt he hadde / al the sighte yseyn
And daunced wel / he wolde noght come ageyn
And gadered hym / a meynee of his sort
To hoppe and synge / and maken swich disport
And ther / they setten steuene / for to meete
To pleyen at the dees / in swich a streete
ffor in the town / nas ther no prentys
That fairer / koude caste a paire of dys
Than Perkyn koude / and ther to he was free
Of his dispense / in place of pryuetee
That foond his maister / wel in his chaffare
ffor ofte tyme / he foond his box ful bare
ffor sikerly / a prentys reuelour
That haunteth dees / ryot or paramour

His maister / shal it in his shope abye
Al haue he no part of the mynstralcye
For thefte and riot / they been conuertible
Al konne he pleye / on Gyterne / or Ribible
Reuel and trouthe / as in a lowe degree
They been ful wrothe al day / as men may see
This ioly prentys / with his maister bood
Til he were neigh / out of his prentishood
Al were he snybbed / bothe erly and late
And som tyme / lad with reuel to Newegate
But atte laste / his maister hym bithoghte
Vp on a day / whan he his papir soghte
Of a prouerbe / that seith this same word
Wel bet is roten appul / out of hoord
Than þt it rotte / al the remenaunt
So fareth it / by a riotous seruaunt
It is ful lasse harm / to lete hym pace
Than he shende / alle the seruantz in the place
Ther fore / his maister yaf hym acquitaunce
And bad hym go / with sorwe / and wt meschaunce
And thus this ioly prentys / hadde his leue
Now lat hym riote / al the nyght / or leue
And for ther nys no theef / with oute a lowke
That helpeth hym to wasten and to sowke
Of that he brybe kan / or borwe may
Anon / he sente his bed / and his array
Vn to a compeer / of his owene sort
That loued dees / and reuel / and disport
And hadde a wyf / that heeld for contenaunce
A shoppe / and swyued for hir sustenaunce

Of this Cokes tale
maked Chaucer na
moore

	ELLESMERE
His maister / shal it in his shoppe abye	
Al haue he / no part of the Minstralcye	part' Mynstralcye
For thefte and riot / they been conue*r*tible	Riot'.
Al konne he pleye / on Giterne / or Rubible	pleye gyterne / Ribible
Reuel and trouthe / as in a lowe degree	3
They been ful wrothe al day / as men may see	
¶This ioly Prentys / with his Maister bood	p*re*ntys / maister
Til he were neigh / out of his p*re*ntishood	ny /
Al were he snybbed / bothe erly and late	
And som tyme / lad with reuel to Newgate	somtyme / Newegate
But atte laste / his maister hym bithoghte·	
Vp on a day / whan he his papir soghte	
Of a p*ro*uerbe / that seith this same word	p*ro*ue*r*be /
Wel bet is roten Appul / out of hoord	
Than þ*at* it rotte / al the remenaunt'	þ*at* / rotie remenau*n*t'
So fareth it' by a riotous seruaunt'	¶So seruau*n*t'
It is ful lasse harm / to lete hym pace	is wel lasse
Than he shende / alle the seruantz in the place	
Ther fore / his maister gaf hym acquitaunce	Therfore / maister' yaf Acquitance
And bad hym go / with sorw / and wi*th* meschaunce	wi*th* sorwe / meschance
And thus this ioly p*re*ntys / hadde his leeue	leue
Now lat hym riote / al the nyght' or leeue	riote nyght / leue
And for ther nys no theef' with oute a lowke	ther is no theef /
That helpeth hym / to wasten and to sowke	
Of that he brybe kan / or borwe may	
Anon / he sente his bed / and his array	Anon
Vn to a compeer / of his owene sort'	compier / ⟨sort⟩
That loued dees / and reuel / and disport'	louede dys / Reuel
And hadde a wyf / that heeld for contenaunce	contenance
A shoppe / and swyued for hir sustenaunce	sustenance

⟨Of this Cokes tale maked Chaucer na moore⟩[4]

[3] ¶Cook' *47v*

[4] This editorial note does not occur in El.

.The Wyf of Bathe.

¶Here bigynneth the prologe of the tale of the Wyf of Bathe

EXperience / thogh noon Auctoritee
Were in this world / is right ynogh for me
To speke of wo / that is in mariage
For lordynges / sith þat I twelf yeer was of age
Thonked be god / that is eterne on lyue
Housbondes atte chirche dore / I haue had fyue
If I so ofte / myghte han wedded be
And alle were worthy men / in hir degree
But me was told certeyn / noght longe agon is
That sith þat Crist ne wente neu*er*e but onys
To weddyng in the Cane of Galilee
That by the same ensample / taughte he me
That I ne sholde / wedded be but ones
¶Herke eek / lo / which a sharp word for the nones
Bisyde a welle / Ie*s*us / god and man
Spak / in repreeue of the Samaritan
¶Thow hast yhad / fyue housbondes quod he
And that ilke man / which that now hath thee
Is nat thyn housbonde / thus he seyde c*er*teyn
What that he mente ther by / I kan nat seyn
But þat I axe / why þat the fifthe man
Was noon housbonde / to the Samaritan
How manye / myghte she han in mariage
Yet herde I neuere / tellen in myn age
Vp on this nombre / diffynycioun
Men may dyuyne / and glosen vp *and* doun
But wel I woot exp*res* / with outen lye
God bad vs / for to wexe and multiplye
That gentil text kan I wel vnderstonde
¶Eek wel I woot he seyde þat myn housbonde
Sholde lete / fader and moder and take to me
But of ⟨no⟩ nombre / menciou*n* made he
Of Bigamye / or of Octogamye
Why sholde men thanne speke of it vileynye
¶Lo here / the wise kyng daun Salomon
I trowe / he hadde wyues many oon

¶The Prologe / of the Wyues tale of Bathe[1]

though
world / were right ynogh to me
sith I .xij. Age
Ythonked
at chirche dore
For I ofte / haue ywedded bee
alle / men
toold c*er*teyn / nat agoon
that onis
By the ensample / thoughte me
Herkne eek / which a sharp*e*
Biside Ie*s*us
¶Thou
that man / the which þat hath now thee
noght seyde he
why that
housbonde samaritan
haue
neuere
Vpon nombre diffiniciou*n*
deuyne / vp and
woot expres oute
I vnderstonde
Eek seyde myn
lete mooder take me
no
2 bigamye /
men / speke
audi
heere /
wyues / mo than oon

11 In Cana Galilee El

13 Qui enim semel iuit ad nupcias docuit semel esse nubendum El

23 Non est vxorum numerum diffinitum quia secundum Paulum Qui habent vxores sic sint tanquam non habentes El

28 Crescite et multiplicamini El

[1] ¶of lawe on *63r*

[2] ¶Wyf *63v*

Here bigynneth the prologe of the tale of the Wyf of Bathe

Experience though noon auctoritee
Were in this world is right ynogh for me
To speke of wo that is in mariage
ffor lordynges sith þt I twelf yeer was of age
Thonked be god that is eterne on lyue
Housbondes atte chirche dore I haue had fyue
If I so ofte myghte han wedded be
And alle were worthy men in hir degree
But me was told certeyn noght longe agon is
That sith þt Crist ne wente neuere but onys
To weddyng in the Cane of Galilee
That by the same ensample taughte he me
That I ne sholde wedded be but ones
Herke eek lo which a sharp word for the nones
Bisyde a welle Ihesus god and man
Spak in repreeue of the Samaritan
Thow hast yhad fyue housbondes quod he
And that ilke man which that now hath thee
Is nat thyn housbonde thus he seyde certeyn
What that he mente ther by I kan nat seyn
But þt I axe why þt the fifthe man
Was noon housbonde to the Samaritan
How manye myghte she han in mariage
Yet herde I neuere tellen in myn age
Vp on this nombre diffynycioun
Men may dyuyne and glosen vp & doun
But wel I woot expres with outen lye
God bad vs for to wexe and multiplye
That gentil text kan I wel vnderstonde
Eek wel I woot he seyde þt myn housbonde
Sholde lete fader and moder and take to me
But of no nombre mencion made he
Of Bigamye or of Octogamye
Why sholde men thanne speke of it vileynye
Lo here the wise kyng daun Salomon
I trowe he hadde wyues many oon

As wolde god / it leueful were to me
To be refresshed / half so ofte as he
Which yifte of god hadde he / for alle hise wyuys
No man hath swich / that in this world alyue is
God woot this noble kyng / as to my wit
The firste nyght / hadde many a murye fit
With ech of hem / so wel was hym on lyue
Blessed be god / that I haue wedded fyue
Wel come the syxte / whan þt eue he shal
ffor sith I wol nat kepe me chaast in al
Whan myn housbonde / is fro the world agon
Som cristen man / shal wedde me anon
ffor thanne thapostle seith / þt I am free
To wedde a goddes half / where it liketh me
He seith / that to be wedded is no synne
Bet is to be wedded / than to brynne
What rekketh me / theigh folk seye vileynye
Of shrewed lameth / and his bigamye
I woot wel / Abraham was an holy man
And Iacob eek / as fer as eue I kan
And ech of hem / hadde wyues mo than two
And many another holy man also
Where kan ye seye / in any manere age
That heighe god / defended mariage
By expres word / I pray yow telleth me
Or where comanded he virgynytee
I woot as wel as ye / it is no drede
Thapostle whan he speketh of maydenhede
He seyde / that precept ther of hadde he noon
Men may conseille a womman / to be oon
But conseillyng / nys no comandement
He put it / in oure owene Iuggement
ffor hadde god / comanded maydenhede
Thanne hadde he dampned weddyng / wt the dede
And certes / if ther were no seed ysowe
Virgynytee thanne / wher of sholde it growe
Poul dorste nat comanden / at the leeste
A thyng / of which his maister yaf noon heeste
The dart is set vp for virgynytee
Cacche who so may / who renneth best lat se

	ELLESMERE
As wolde god / it leueful were to me	were leueful vn to
To be refresshed / half so ofte as he	refresshed /
Which yifte of god hadde he / for alle hise wyuys	god /
No man hath swich / that in this world alyue is	þat
God woot this noble kyng as to my wit	woot /
The firste nyght hadde many a murye fit	nyght had myrie
With ech of hem / so wel was hym on lyue	
Blessed be god / that I haue wedded fyue[3]	Yblessed
Wel come the sixte / whan þat euere he shal	whan euere
For sith I wol nat kepe ⟨me⟩ / chaast in al	For sothe / I me
Whan myn housbonde / is fro the world agon	ygon
Som cristen man / shal wedde me anon	
For thanne thapostle seith / þat I am free	thanne / seith / I
To wedde a goddes half / where it liketh me	half where
He seith / that to be wedded is no synne	seith / to wedded /
Bet is to be wedded / than to brynne	is /
What rekketh me / theigh folk / seye vileynye	thogh folk
Of shrewed Lameth / and his bigamye	and of bigamye
I woot wel / Abraham was an holy man	Abraham / hooly
And Iacob eek as fer as euere I kan	eek / as ferforth as I
And ech of hem / hadde wyues mo than two	
And many another / holy man also	another man
¶Where kan ye seye / in any maner age	Whanne saugh ye euere / in manere Age
That heighe god / defended mariage	hye
By expres word / I pray yow telleth me	
Or where comanded he virgynytee	where / virginitee
I woot as wel as ye / it is no drede	
Thapostle / whan he speketh of maydenhede	Whan thapostel / speketh
He seyde / that precept ther of / hadde he noon	precept of
Men may conseille a womman / to be oon	conseille / womman been
But conseillyng nys no comandement	conseillyng is nat comandement
He put it in oure owene Iuggement	putte
For hadde god / comanded maydenhede	
Thanne hadde he dampned weddyng with the dede	with
And certes / if ther were no seed ysowe	certein / were /
Virgynytee thanne / wher of sholde it growe	Virginitee / wher of thanne sholde
Poul dorste nat comanden / at the leeste	Poul / ne dorste nat / comanden atte leeste
A thyng of which / his mayster yaf noon heeste	which maister
The dart / is set vp for virgynytee	dart vp / of virginitee
Cacche who so may / who renneth best lat se	see

46 Si autem non continent nubant El

50 Quod si dormierit vir eius liberata est cui vult nubat in Domino El

52 Si acceperis vxorem non peccasti et si nupserit virgo non peccauit set hij qui domino se vouerunt Ita idem et cetera El

54 Melius est nubere quam vri El

55 Lameth qui primus intrauit bigamiam sanguinarius et homicida est et cetera El

56 Abraham trigamus Iacob quatrigamus El

73 Paulus de virginibus preceptum non habeo consilium autem do et cetera El

75 Inuitat ad cursum tenet in manu virginitatis brauium qui potest capere capiat et cetera El

[3] *Out* Hg El 44 a-f. Dd reads:

44a Of whiche / I haue pyked out the beste
Bothe of here nether purs / and of here cheste
Diuerse scoles / maken parfyt clerkes
And diuerse practyk in many sondry werkes
Maken / the werkman parfyt / sekirly
f Of fyue husbondes scoleiyng / am I

.The Wyf of Bathe.	ELLESMERE
But this word / is noght take of euery wightꝭ	¶But nat taken wight
But ther as god / list yeue it of his myghtꝭ	therꝭ god lustꝭ gyue mightꝭ
I woot wel / that thapostle was a mayde	wel / the Apostel
But nathelees / thogh þ*at* he wrootꝭ or sayde	thogh / that wroot and sayde
He wolde / that euery wightꝭ were swich as he	4 þ*at* eu*er*y wight /
Al nys but conseil / to virgynytee	nys / conseil virginitee
And for to been a wyf / he yaf me leue	
Of Indulgence / so nys it no repreue	so it is no
To wedde me / if that my make dye	if my
With outen excepciou*n* of bigamye	outen / Bigamye
Al were it good / no womman for to touche	wo*m*man
He mente / as in his bed / or in his couche	
For p*er*il is / bothe fyr and tow tassemble	
Ye knowe / what this ensample may resemble	
This al and som / he heeld virgynytee	This is al som / that virginitee
Moore p*ar*fitꝭ than weddyng in freletee	Moore profiteth / than weddyng /
Freletee clepe I / but if þ*at* he and she	that
Wolde leden / al hir lyfꝭ in chastitee	lede / lyf
I graunte it wel / I haue noon enuye	¶I envie
Thogh maydenhede / p*re*ferre bigamye	maydenhede Bigamye
It liketh hem to be clene / in body and goostꝭ	Hem liketh to be clene / body
Of myn estatꝭ ne wol I make no boostꝭ	estaatꝭ I nyl nat make
For wel ye knowe / a lord in his houshold	houshold
Ne hath nat euery vessel / al of gold	He nath nat gold
So*m*me been of tree / and doon hir lord s*er*uyse	seruyse
God clepeth folk to hym / in sondry wyse	
And euerich / hath of god a p*ro*pre yifte	euerich
Som this / som thatꝭ as hym liketh shifte	this
Virgynytee / is greet p*er*feccioun	¶Virginitee /
And continence eekꝭ with deuociou*n*	
But Cristꝭ that of p*er*feccion / is welle	crist / p*er*feccio*n*
Bad nat euery wight / he sholde go selle	wight / sholde
Al that he hadde / and yeue it to the poore	gyue
And in swich wise / folwe hym and his foore	.i. steppes foore
He spak to hem / that wol lyue p*ar*fitly	wolde
And lordynges / by youre leue / that am nat I	lordynges
I wol bistowe / the flour of al myn age	of myn
In thactes / and in fruyt of mariage	In the Actes /
questio ¶Telle me also / to what conclusiou*n*	¶questio
Were membres maad / of generaciou*n*	ymaad /

4¶of Bathe *64r*

81 Volo autem omnes homines esse sicut me ipsum El

87 Bonum est homini mulierem non tangere El

103 Vnusquisque proprium habet donum ex deo alius quidem sic alius autem sic El

105 Qui cantant sequentur Agnum xliiij[or] Millia El

But this word is noght take of euery wight
But ther as god list yeue it of his myght
I woot wel that thapostle was a mayde
But nathelees thogh þt he wroot or sayde
He wolde that euery wight were swich as he
Al nys but conseil to virgynytee
And for to been a wyf he yaf me leue
Of Indulgence so nys it no repreue
To wedde me if that my make dye
With outen excepcion of bigamye
Al were it good no womman for to touche
He mente as in his bed or in his couche
ffor peril is bothe fyr and tow tassemble
Ye knowe what this ensample may resemble
This al and som he heeld virginitee
Moore ꝑfit than weddyng in freletee
ffreletee clepe I but if þt he and she
Wolde leden al hir lyf in chastitee
I graunte it wel I haue noon envye
Thogh maydenhede ꝑferre bigamye
It liketh hem to be clene in body and goost
Of myn estat ne wol I make no boost
ffor wel ye knowe a lord in his houshold
He hath nat euery vessel al of gold
Somme been of tree and doon hir lord seruyse
God clepeth folk to hym in sondry wyse
And euerich hath of god a ꝓpre yifte
Som this som that as hym liketh shifte
Virgynytee is greet ꝑfeccion
And continence eek with deuocion
But crist that of ꝑfeccion is welle
Bad nat euery wight he sholde go selle
Al that he hadde and yeue it to the poore
And in swich wise folwe hym and his foore
He spak to hem that wol lyue ꝑfitly
And lordynges by youre leue that am nat I
I wol bistowe the flour of al myn age
In thactes and in fruyt of mariage
questio Telle me also to what conclusion
Were membres maad of generacion

And of so pfit / wys a wight ywroght /
Trusteth right wel / they were nat maad for noght /
Glose who so wole / and seye bothe vp and doun
That they were maad / for purgacioun
Of vryne / and oure bothe thynges smale
Was eek to knowe / a femelle from a male
And for noon oother cause / sey ye no!
Thexpience woot wel it is noght so
So that the clerkes / be nat with me wrothe
I sey this / þt they maked been for bothe
That is to seyn / for office and for ese
Of engendrure / ther we nat god displese
Why sholde men ellis / in hir bokes sette
That man shal yelde / to his wyf hir dette
Now wher with / sholde he make his paiement
If he ne vsed his sely instrument /
Thanne were they maad / vp on a creature
To purge vryne / and eek for engendrure
But I seye noght / þt euery wight is holde
That hath swich harneys / as I to yow tolde
To goon and vsen hem in engendrure
Thanne sholde men take / of chastitee no cure
Crist was a mayde / and shapen as a man
And many a seynt / sith that the world bigan
Yet lyued they euere / in pfit chastitee
I nyl envie / no virginitee
Lat hem be breed / of pured whete seed
And lat vs wyues / hote barly breed
And yet wt barly breed / Mark telle kan
Oure lord Ihu / refresshed many a man
In swich estat / as god hath clepyd vs
I wol pseuere / I nam nat precius
In wifhode wol I vse myn instrument /
As frely as my makere hath it sent /
If I be daungerous / god yeue me sorwe
Myn housbonde / shal it han / bothe eue and morwe
Whan that hym list / com forth and paye his dette
And housbonde / wol I haue / I wol nat lette
Which shal be bothe / my dettour and my thral
And haue his tribulacion / with al

	ELLESMERE
And of so p*ar*fit wys a wight ywroght	And for what p*ro*fit was a wight ywroght
Trusteth right wel / they were nat maad for noght	right noght
Glose who so wole / and seye bothe vp and doun	
That they were maad / for purgacioun	
⟨Of⟩ Vryne / and oure bothe thynges smale	Of vryne bothe / and thynges
Was eek to knowe / a femelle / from a male	And eek femele
And for noon oother cause / sey ye / no	ye
Thexp*er*ience / woot wel it is noght so	The exp*er*ience / noght
So that the Clerkes / be nat with me wrothe	clerkes / *with*
I sey this / *þa*t they maked been for bothe	sey yis / that they beth maked
That is to seyn / for office and for ese	seye /
Of engendrure / ther we nat god displese	
Why sholde men ellis / in hir bokes sette	5 elles / bookes
That man shal yelde / to his wyf hir dette	That a man hir*e*
Now wherwith / sholde he make his paiement	wher with / paiement
If he ne vsed / his sely Instrument	Instrument
Thanne were they maad / vp on a creature	
To purge vryne / and eek for engendrure	and for
¶But I seye noght *þa*t euery wight is holde	noght
That hath swich harneys / as I to yow tolde	I of tolde
To goon / and vsen hem in engendrure	goon
Thanne sholde men take / of Chastitee no cure	They shul nat take / chastitee
Crist was a mayde / and shapen as a man	
And many a Seynt sith that the world bigan	seint sith the
Yet lyued they euere / in p*ar*fit Chastitee	chastitee
I nyl envie / no virgynytee	nyl nat enuye / virginitee
Lat hem be breed / of pured whete seed	
And lat vs wyues / hote Barlybreed	hoten barly breed
And yet *with* Barly breed / Mark telle kan	yet with barly
Oure lord Ie*su* / refresshed many a man	lord / refresshed
In swich estat as god hath clepyd vs	estaat cleped
I wol p*er*seuere / I nam nat p*re*cius	
In wifhode / wol I vse myn Instrument	wyfhode / I wol Instrument /
As frely / as my makere hath it sent	
If I be daungerous / god yeue me sorwe	
Myn housbonde / shal it han / bothe eue and morwe	housbonde haue / *and*
Whan that hym list com forth and paye his dette	*þa*t *and*
And housbonde / wol I haue / I wol nat lette	An housbonde I wol I nyl nat
Which shal be / bothe / my dettour and my thral	bothe dettour /
And haue / his tribulacion / with al	tribulaciou*n*

147 Ea vocacione qua vocati estis et cetera El

155 Qui vxorem habet et debitor dicitur et esse in prepucio et seruus vxoris et quod malorum seruorum est alligatus El

5¶Wyf *64v*

Vp on his flessħ / whil that I am his wyf
I haue the power / duryng al my lyf
Vp on his p*ro*pre body / and nat he
Right thus / thapostle / tolde it vn to me
And bad oure housbondes / for to loue vs wel
Al this sentence / me liketh euery del
Up stirte the Pardoner / and that anon
Now dame quod he / by god and by Seint Ioħn
Ye been a noble Prechour in this cas
I was aboute / to wedde a wyf allas
What sholde I bye ⟨it⟩ / on my flessh so deere
Yet hadde I leuere / wedde no wyf to yeere
¶Abyd quod she / my tale is nat bigonne
Nay / thow shalt drynken / of another tonne
Er *pat* I go / shal sauoure wors than Ale
And whan that I / haue toold thee forth my tale
Of tribulacion / in maryage
Of which I am expert in al myn age
This is to seye / my self hath been the whippe
Thanne maystow / chese / wheither *pat* thow wolt sippe
Of thilke tonne / that I shal abroche
Be war of it / er thow to neigh approche
For I shal telle ensamples / mo than ten
Who so *pat* nyle / be war by othere men
By hym / shal othere men corrected be
Thise same wordes / writeth Protholome
Rede in his Almageste / and take it there
¶Dame I wolde pray yow / if youre wyl it were
Seyde this Pardoner / as ye bigan
Telle forth youre tale / spareth for no man
And techeth vs yonge men / of youre praktyke
¶Gladly quod she / syn it may yow lyke
But that I praye / to al this compaignye
If that I speke / after my fantasye
As taketh nat agrief / of that I seye
For myn entente / nys but for to pleye
Now sire / thanne wol I telle yow forth my tale
As euere / moot I drynke / wyn or Ale
I shal seye sooth / tho housbondes *pat* I hadde
As three of hem were goode / and two were badde

158 Et iterum seruus vxoris es noli propter hoc habere tristiciam Item si acceperis vxorem non peccasti tribulacionem tamen carnis habebunt huiusmodi et cetera Item vir corporis sui non habet potestatem set vxor Item viri diligite vxores vestras El

193 Bihoold how this goode wyf serued hir iij firste housbondes whiche were goode olde men El

ELLESMERE

whil I wyf /
durynge lyf
Vpon noght
Right the Apostel /
weel
deel
P*ar*doner /
and seint
prechour

What it flessħ

¶Abyde
thou drynken
that sauour*e*
pat toold forth
tribulaciou*n* / that is in mariage
which /
This to seyn / self haue
Than maystow wheither thou
6 Of that tonne /
it thou ny

so / *pat* wol nat be war /
shul
The same Protholomee
Rede it in
¶Dame / praye / if
P*ar*doner /

teche youre praktike
¶Gladly sires / sith like
But yet I

taketh it nat agrief / that
entente / is but
NOw sire / now wol telle forth
eu*er*e / moote drynken
sooth / of tho
thre

6 ¶of Bathe *65r*

The Wyf of Bathe

Vp on his flessh / whil that I am his wyf
I haue the power / durynge al my lyf
Vp on his propre body / and nat he
Right thus thapostle / tolde it vn to me
And bad oure housbondes / for to loue vs wel
Al this sentence / me liketh euery del
Vp stirte the Pardoner / and that anon
Now dame quod he / by god and by Seint Iohn
Ye been a noble prechour / in this cas
I was aboute / to wedde a wyf allas
What sholde I bye it / on my flessh so deere
Yet hadde I leuere / wedde no wyf to yeere
Abyde quod she / my tale is nat bigonne
Nay thow shalt drynken / of another tonne
Er þt I go / shal sauoure wors than ale
And whan that I / haue toold thee forth my tale
Of tribulacion / in mariage
Of which I am expert / in al myn age
This is to seye / my self hath been the whippe
Thanne maystow chese / wheither þt thow wolt sippe
Of thilke tonne / that I shal abroche
Be war of it / er thow to neigh approche
ffor I shal telle ensamples / mo than ten
Who so þt nyle be war / by othere men
By hym / shal othere men corrected be
This same wordes writeth Protholomee
Rede in his almageste / and take it there
Dame I wolde pray yow / if youre wyl it were
Seyde this Pardoner / as ye bigan
Telle forth youre tale / spareth for no man
And techeth vs yonge men / of youre praktyke
Gladly quod she / syn it may yow lyke
But that I praye / to al this compaignye
If that I speke / after my fantasye
As taketh nat agrief / of that I seye
ffor myn entente / nys but for to pleye
Now sire thanne wol I telle yow forth my tale
As euere moot I drynke wyn or ale
I shal seye sooth / tho housbondes þt I hadde
As thre of hem were goode / and two were badde

Tho thre men were goode and ryche and olde
Vnnethe myghte they the statut holde
In which that they were bounden vn to me
Ye woot wel what I mene of this pardee
As help me god I laughe whan I thynke
How pitously a nyght I made hem swynke
And by my fey I tolde of it no stoor
They hadde me yeuen hir land and hir tresoor
Me neded nat do lenger diligence
To wynne hir loue or doon hem reuerence
They loued me so wel by god aboue
That I ne tolde no deyntee of hir loue
A wys womman wol bisye hir euere in oon
To gete hir loue ye ther as she hath noon
But sith I hadde hem hoolly in myn hond
And sith that they hadde yeuen me al hir lond
What sholde I take kepe hem for to plese
But it were for my profit and myn ese
I sette hem so awerke by my fey
That many a nyght they songen weylawey
The bacon was nat fet for hem I trowe
That som men han in Essex at Donmowe
I gouerned hem so wel after my lawe
That ech of hem ful blisful was and fawe
To brynge me gaye thynges fro the ffeyre
They were ful glad whan I spak to hem feyre
ffor god it woot I chidde hem spitously
Now herkneth how I bar me proprely
Ye wise wyues that konne vnderstonde
Thus sholde ye speke and bere hem wrong on honde
ffor half so boldely kan ther no man
Swere and lye as a womman kan
I sey nat this by wyues þt ben wyse
But if it be whan they hem mysauyse
A wys wyf if that she kan hir good
Shal bere hym an hond the cow is wood
And take witnesse of hir owene mayde
Of hire assent but herkneth how I sayde
Sire olde kaynard is this thyn array
Why is my neighebores wyf so gay

	ELLESMERE
The thre men / were goode / and ryche / and olde	riche /
Vnnethe myghte they / the Statut holde	Vnnethe / mygħte statut
In which / that they were bounden vn to me	were /
Ye woot wel / what I mene of this p*ar*dee	meene
As help me god / I laughe whan I thynke	
How pitously / a nyght I made hem swynke	anyght
And by my fey / I tolde of it no stoor	
They hadde me yeuen / hir land and hir tresoor	had yeuen hir gold / and
Me neded nat do lenger diligence	nat /
To wynne hir loue / or doon hem reu*er*ence	
They loued me so wel / by god aboue	
That I ne tolde / no deyntee of hir loue	
A wys womman / wol bisye hir*e* / eu*er*e in oon	wo*m*man / wol sette hir*e*
To gete hir loue / ye ther as she hath noon	hir*e* loue / ther
But sith I hadde hem / hoolly in myn hond	hond
And sith that they / hadde yeuen me al hir lond	sith / they hadde / me yeuen / lond
What sholde I take kepe / hem for to plese	taken heede / hem
But it were / for my p*ro*fit and myn ese	But if it profit
I sette hem awerk by my fey	hem so a werk /
That many a nyght they songen weylawey	nygħt / weilawey
The bacon / was nat fet for hem I trowe	bacou*n* / fet
That som men han / in Essex*e* at Donmowe	Dunmowe
I gou*er*ned hem / so wel after my lawe	
That ech of hem / ful blisful was and fawe	hem / was ful blisful and
To brynge me / gaye thynges fro the Feyre	thynges / Fayre
They were ful glad / whan I spak to hem feyre	faire
For god it woot I chidde hem spitously	woot /
¶Now herkneth / how I bar me p*ro*prely	hou baar
Ye wise wyues / that konne vnderstonde	7 kan
Thus sholde ye speke / and bere hem wrong on honde	¶Thus shul beren hem on
For half so boldely / kan ther no man	
Swere and lye / as a womman kan	as kan a womman |
I sey nat this / by wyues þ*at* ben wyse	been
But if it be / whan they hem mysauyse	
A wys wyf / if that she kan hir good	
Shal bere hym an hond / the Cow is wood	hym on hond /
And take witnesse / of hir owene mayde	
Of hire assent but herkneth how I sayde	hir
¶Sire olde kaynard / is this thyn array	¶Sir*e* kaynard /
Why is / my Neghebores wyf so gay	neighebores

199 Ierophancias quoque Atheniencium vsque hodie cicute sorbicione castrari El

7 ¶Wyf / 65*v*

The Wyf of Bathe.ſ

	ELLESMERE
She is honou*ur*ed / ouer al ther she goth	honoured / ou*er* gooth
I sitte at hoom / I haue no thrifty cloth	clooth
What dostow / at my neghebores hous	neighebores
Is she so fair / artow so amorous	
What rowne ye with oure mayde / benedicite	mayde
Sire olde lechour / lat thy Iapes be	Sir*e* Lecchour /
And if I haue / a gossib / or A freend	gossib a
With outen gilt⁊ ye chiden as a feend	gilt⁊ thou chidest
If that I walke / or pleye vn to his hous	
Thow comest hoom / as dronken as a mous	Thou Mous
And p*re*chest on thy bench / with yuel preef	bencħ /
Thow seyst to me / it is a greet mescheef	Thou seist meschief
To wedde a poure womman / for costage	wo*m*man
And if that she be ryche / of heigh parage	if she riche / and of heigħ
Thanne seistow / that it is a tormentrye	seistow / it tormentrie
To suffre / hir pryde / and hir malencolye	suffren hir*e* pride / hir*e* malencolie
And if þ*at* she be fair / thow verray knaue	if she fair⁊ thou
Thow seist⁊ that euery holour wol hir*e* haue	Thou seyst⁊
She may no while / in chastitee abyde	
That is assayled / vp on ech a syde	assailled /
¶Thow seyst⁊ som folk / desiren vs for richesse	¶Thou seyst⁊ that som vs /
So*m*me for oure shap*e* / and so*m*me for oure fairnesse	shap*e* / so*m*me
And so*m*me / for she kan outher synge / or daunce	som / kan synge and daunce
And so*m*me / for gentillesse / and dalyaunce	som and som for daliaunce
So*m*me for hir handes / and hir armes smale	Som Armes
Thus goth al to the deuel / by thy tale	
Thow seyst / men may nat kepe a Castel wal	Thou seyst⁊
It may so longe / assaylled been ouer al	assailled
And if that she be foul / thow seyst þ*at* she	¶And thou seist that
Coueiteth euery man / that she may se	
For as a Spaynel / she wol on hym lepe	
Til that she fynde / som man hir to chepe	þ*at* hire
Ne noon so grey goos / goth ther in the lake	gooth in
As seistow / wol be with oute make	been
And seyst⁊ it is an hard thyng / for to wolde	to welde
A thyng / that no man wol his thankes holde	thyng⁊ þ*at* wole helde
Thus seistow lorel / whan thow goost to bedde	8 goost⁊
And that no wys man / nedeth for to wedde	þ*at*
Ne no man / that entendeth vn to heuene	
With wilde thonder dynt⁊ and firy leuene	

8 ¶of Bathe *66r*

She is honoured ouer al ther she goth
I sitte at hoom I haue no thrifty cloth
What dostow at my neghebores hous
Is she so fair art thow so amorous
What rowne ye with oure mayde benedicite
Sire olde lechour lat thy Iapes be
And if I haue a gossib or a freend
With outen gilt ye chiden as a feend
If that I walke or pleye vn to his hous
Thow comest hoom as dronken as a mous
And prechest on thy bench with yuel preef
Thow seyst to me it is a greet meschief
To wedde a poure womman for costage
And if that she be ryche of heigh parage
Thanne seistow that it is a tormentrye
To suffre hir pryde and hir malencolye
And if þt she be fair thow verray knaue
Thow seist that euery holour wol hir haue
She may no while in chastitee abyde
That is assayled vp on ech a syde
Thow seyst som folk desiren vs for richesse
Somme for oure shap and somme for oure fairnesse
And somme for she kan outher synge or daunce
And somme for gentillesse and dalyaunce
Somme for hir handes and hir armes smale
Thus goth al to the deuel by thy tale
Thow seyst men may nat kepe a castel wal
It may so longe assayled been ouer al
And if that she be foul thow seyst þt she
Coueiteth euery man that she may se
For as a Spaynel she wol on hym lepe
Til that she fynde som man hir to chepe
Ne noon so grey goos goth ther in the lake
As seistow wol be with oute make
And seyst it is an hard thyng for to wolde
A thyng that no man wol his thankes holde
Thus seistow lorel whan thow goost to bedde
And that no wys man nedeth for to wedde
Ne no man that entendeth vn to heuene
With wilde thonder dynt and firy leuene

Moote thy welked nekke be to broke
Thow seyst that droppyng houses and eek smoke
And chidyng wyues / maken men to flee
Out of hir owene houses / a benedicitee
What eyleth swich an old man for to chide
Thow seyst we wyues / wil oure vices hyde
Til we be fast / and thanne we wol hem shewe
Wel may that be a prouerbe of a shrewe
Thow seist þt oxen / asses hors / and houndes
They been assayed at dyuerse stoundes
Bacynes lauours / er that men hem bye
Spoones stooles / and al swich housbondrye
And so be pottes / clothes / and array
But folk of wyues / maken noon assay
Til they be wedded / olde dotard shrewe
And thanne seistow / we wil oure vices shewe
Thow seist also / that it displeseth me
But if that thow wolt preyse my beautee
And but thow poure alwey vp on my face
And clepe me faire dame / in euery place
And but thow make a feeste / on thilke day
That I was born / and make me fressh and gay
And but thow do to my norice honour
And to my chambrere / withinne my bour
And to my fadres folk / and his allyes
Thus seistow olde barel ful of lyes
And yet of oure apprentice Iankyn
ffor his crisp heer / shynyng as gold so fyn
And for he squyereth me bothe vp and doun
Yet hastow caught / fals suspecioun
I wil hym nat / thogh thow were deed tomorwe
But tel me this / why hidestow with sorwe
The keyes of thy cheste / awey fro me
It is my good / as wel as thyn pardee
What wenestow / make an ydiote of oure dame
Now by that lord / that called is Seint Iame
Thow shalt noght bothe / thogh þt thow were wood
Be maister of my body / and my good
That oon thow shalt forgo / maugree thyne eyen
What helpeth it of me enquere and spyen

	ELLESMERE
Moote thy welked nekke / be to broke	Moote / nekke
Thow seyst⁊ that droppyng houses / and eek smoke	¶Thow *and*
And chidyng wyues / maken men to flee	chidyng⁊
Out of hir owene houses / a be*ne*dicitee ∫	benedicitee
What eyleth / swich an old man for to chide	
Thow seyst⁊ we wyues / wil oure vices hyde	¶Thow seyst⁊ þ*at* we wol hide
Til we be fast⁊ and thanne we wol hem shewe	
Wel may that be / a prouerbe of a shrewe	p*rouer*be
Thow seist⁊ þ*at* Oxen / Asses / hors / and houndes	¶Thou
They been assayed / at dyu*er*se stoundes	assayd / diuerse
Bacynes / lauours / er that men hem bye	Bacyns /
Spoones / stooles / and al swich housbondrye	Spoones and stooles /
And so be pottes / clothes / and array	been / pottes
But folk / of wyues / maken noon assay	folk⁊
Til they be wedded / olde dotard shrewe	
And thanne seistow / we wil oure vices shewe	Thanne wol
Thow seist also / that it displeseth me	¶Thou seist⁊
But if that thow / wolt preise my beautee	thou / preyse
And but thow powre / alwey vp on my face	thou poure alwey /
And clepe me faire dame / in eu*er*y place	dame euery
And but thow make a feeste / on thilke day	thou
That I was born / and make me fressh and gay	fressħ *and*
And but thow do / to my norice honour	thou
And to my chambrere / with Inne my bour	
And to my fadres folk / and his allyes	hise
Thus seistow / olde barel ful of lyes	
And yet⁊ of oure App*re*ntice / Iankyn	¶And Ianekyn
For his crisp*e* heer / shynyng⁊ as gold so fyn	heer⁊ shynynge
And for he squyereth me / bothe vp and doun	squiereth
Yet hastow caught⁊ fals suspecioun	caught⁊ a fals
I wil hym nat⁊ thogh thow were deed to morwe	wol noghŧ⁊ thou tomorwe
¶But tel me this / why hidestow with sorwe	me / why hydestow
The keyes of thy Cheste / awey fro me	of my cheste /
It is my good / as wel as thyn pardee	p*ar*dee
What wenestow / make an ydiote of oure dame	wenestow / to make ydiot⁊
Now by that lord / that called is Seint Iame	
Thow shalt noght bothe / thogh þ*at* thow were wood	Thou nat thogh thou
Be maister / of my body / and my good	and of my
That oon thow shalt forgo / maugree thyne eyen	thou
What helpeth it⁊ of me enquere and spyen	What nedeth thee / of me / to enquere or spyen

303 Et procurator calamistratus et cetera El

I trowe / thow woldest' lok me in thy chiste	thou loke
Thow sholdest seye / wyf / go wher thee liste	Thou wyf
Taak youre disport' I nyl leue no talis	I wol leue talys
I knowe yow / for a trewe wyf / Dame Alis	wyf Alys
We loue no man / that taketh kepe / or charge	9
Wher þ*at* we goon / we wol been at oure large	that ben
Of alle men / yblessed moote he be	¶Of blessed moot
The wise Astrologen / Daun Protholome	Astrologien /
That seith this prouerbe / in his Almageste	prou*er*be /
Of alle men / his wisdom is hyeste	wysdom is the hyeste
That rekketh nat' who hath the world in honde	rekketh neu*er*e / who
By this p*rouer*be / thow shalt vnderstonde	prou*er*be / thou
Haue thow ynogh / what thar thee rekke / or care	thou ynogħ / recche
How myrily / that othere folkes fare	
For c*er*tes / olde dotard / by youre leue	c*er*teyn / dotard
Ye shal han queynte / right ynogh at eue	shul haue rigħt ynogħ
He is to greet a nygard / that wil werne	that wolde werne
A man to lighte a candle / at his lanterne	man / lighte his candle lant*er*ne
He shal han / neuer the lasse light pardee	haue / p*ar*dee
Haue thow ynogh / thee thar nat pleyne thee	thou
¶Thow seist also / that if we make vs gay	¶Thou seyst þ*at*
With clothyng' and with p*re*cious array	
That it is peril / of oure chastitee	That' p*er*il
And yet with sorwe / thow most enforce thee	thou
And seye thise wordes / in thapostles name	in the Apostles
In habit' maad with chastitee and shame	habit maad /
Ye wo*m*men / shal apparaille yow quod he	wommen / shul
And nat in tressed heer / and gay perree	noght'
As perlys / ne with gold / ne clothes ryche	perles / riche
After thy text' ne after thy rubryche	Rubriche
I wol nat werke / as muche / as is a gnat'	wirche / muchel as a
Thow seydest this / þ*at* I was lyk a Cat'	¶Thou that lyk'
For who so wolde senge / a Cattes skyn	wolde / senge
Thanne wolde the Cat' wel dwellen in his In	
And if the Cattes skyn / be slyk' and gay	slyk
She wol nat dwelle in house / half a day	
But forth she wole / er any day be dawed	
To shewe hir skyn / and goon a Caterwawed	Cat*er*wawed
This is to seye / if I be gay sir*e* shrewe	
I wol renne out' my borel for to shewe	out /

327 Intra omnes ulcior existit qui non curat in cuius manu sit mundus El

341 Similiter et mulieres in habitu ornato cum verecundia et castitate ornent se non in tortis crinibus aut auro aut margaritis siue veste preciosa et cetera hec Paulus El

9 ¶Wyf' *66v*

The wif of Bathe

I trowe thow woldest lok me in thy chiste
Thow sholdest seye / wyf go wher thee liste
Taak youre disport / I wyl leue no talis
I knowe yow / for a trewe wyf dame Alis
We loue no man / that taketh kepe or charge
Wher þt we goon / we wol been at oure large
Of alle men / yblessed moote he be
The wise Astrologen / daun Protholome
That seith this prouerbe / in his Almageste
Of alle men his wisdom is hyeste
That rekketh nat / who hath the world in honde
By this prouerbe / thow shalt vnderstonde
Haue thow ynogh / what thar thee rekke / or care
How myrily / that othere folkes fare
ffor certes / olde dotard by youre leue
Ye shal han queynte / right ynogh at eue
He is to greet a nygard / that wil werne
A man to lighte a candle / at his lanterne
He shal han neuer the lasse light pardee
Haue thow ynogh / thee thar nat pleyne thee
Thow seist also / that if we make vs gay
With clothyng / and with precious array
That it is peril / of oure chastitee
And yet with sorwe / thow most enforce thee
And seye thise wordes / in thapostles name
In habit maad with chastitee and shame
Ye women shal apparaille yow quod he
And nat in tressed heer / and gay perree
As perlys / ne with gold / ne clothes ryche
After thy text / ne after thy rubryche
I wol nat werke / as muche as is a gnat
Thow seydest this / þt I was lyk a Cat
ffor who so wolde senge a cattes skyn
Thanne wolde the cat wel dwellen in his In
And if the cattes skyn / be slyk and gay
She wol nat dwelle in house / half a day
But forth she wole / er any day be dawed
To shewe hir skyn / and goon a caterwawed
This is to seye / if I be gay sir shrewe
I wol renne out / my borel for to shewe

Sire olde fool / what helpeth thee tespyen
Thogh thow preye Argus / wt his hundred eyen
To be my wardecorps / as he kan best
In feith / he shal nat kepe me / but me lest /
Yet koude I make his berd / as mote I thee
Thow seydest eek / þt ther ben thynges three
The whiche thynges / troublen al this erthe
And that no wight / may endure the ferthe
O leeue sire shrewe / Ihu shorte thy lyf
Yet prechestow / and seist an hateful wyf
Yrekened is / for oon of thise myschaunces
Been ther / noone othere resemblaunces
That ye may likne / youre parables to
But if a sely wyf / be oon of tho
Thow liknest eek / wommanes loue to helle
To bareyne lond / ther water may nat dwelle
Thow liknest it also / to wilde fyr
The moore it brenneth / the moore it hath desyr
To consumen euery thyng / þt brent wol be
Thow seist / right as wormes shende a tree
Right so a wyf / destroyeth hir housbonde
This knowen they / that been to wyues bonde
Lordynges / right thus / as ye han vnderstonde
Baar I stifly / myne olde housbondes on honde
That thus they seyden / in hir dronkenesse
And al was fals / but that I took witnesse
On Iankyn / and on my Nece also
O lord / the pyne I dide hem / and the wo
fful giltlees / by goddes swete pyne
ffor as an hors / I koude byte and whyne
I koude pleyne / and I was in the gilt
Or ellis / often tyme / I hadde been spilt /
Who so that first to mille comth / first grynt /
I pleyned first / so was oure werre stynt /
They were ful glad / to excusen hem ful blyue
Of thyng / of which they neuere agilte hir lyue
Of wenches / wolde I beren hem on honde
Whan that for syk / they myghte vnnethe stonde
Yet tikled I his herte / for that he
Wende that I hadde had of hym / so greet chiertee

62v

Sire olde fool / what helpeth thee tespyen
Thogh thow preye Argus / w*ith* his hundred eyen
To be my warde corps / as he kan best
In feith / he shal nat kepe me / but me lest
Yet koude I make his berd / as mote I thee
¶Thow seydest eek þat ther ben thynges three
The whiche thynges / troublen al this erthe
And that no wight may endure the ferthe
O leeue sire shrewe / Ie*s*u shorte thy lyf
Yet p*re*chestow / and seist an hateful wyf
Yrekened is / for oon of thise myschaunces
Been ther / noone othere resemblaunces
That ye may likne / youre p*ar*ables to
But if a sely wyf be oon of tho
¶Thow liknest eek / wo*m*manes loue to helle
To bareyne lond / ther water may nat dwelle
Thow liknest it also / to wilde fyr
The moore it brenneth / the moore it hath desyr
To consumen euery thyng þat brent wol be
Thow seist right as wormes shende a tree
Right so a wyf / destroyeth hir housbonde
This knowen they / that been to wyues bonde
¶Lordynges / right thus / as ye han vnderstonde
Bar I stifly / myne olde housbondes on honde
That thus they seyden / in hir dronkenesse
And al was fals / but that I took witnesse
On Iankyn / and on my Nece also
O lord / the pyne I dide hem / and the wo
Ful giltlees / by goddes swete pyne
For as an hors / I koude byte and whyne
I koude pleyne / and I was in the gilt
Or ellis / often tyme / I hadde been spilt
Who so that first to Mille comth / first grynt
I pleyned first so was oure werr*e* stynt
They were ful glad / to excusen hem ful blyue
Of thyng of which they neuere agilte hir lyue
Of wenches / wolde I bern hem on honde
Whan that for syk they myghte vnnethe stonde
Yet tikled I his herte / for that he
Wende that I hadde had of hym / so greet chiertee

362 eciam odiosa vxor si habeat virum bonum et cetera El

371 Amor illius inferno et urenti terre et incendio comparatur vnde illud et cetera Infernus et amor mulieris et terra que non saciatur aqua et ignis non dicent satis et cetera El

376 Sicut in ligno vermis ita perdet virum suum vxor El

379 Nemo melius scire potest quid sit vxor vel mulier nisi ille qui passus est El

ELLESMERE

¶Sire what eyleth thee to spyen
thou hise
wardecors / best
me but lest
berd / so moot
¶Thou eek / that been thre

þat wight /
sire Ie*s*u / lyf /
seyst and hateful wyf
meschances
ther none resemblances
10 parables
if / wyf /
¶Thou liknest wommenes

¶Thou
desir
wole
Thou seyst. right shendeth
Right hir*e* housbond
knowe
LOrdynges / right haue
Baar

On Ianekyn /

sweete

pleyne / thogh I were in gilt
elles / tyme / Hadde I been
Who so comth first to Mille / first grynt
first / werre ystynt
excuse hem blyue
thyng / neuer*e*
¶Of beren hym
syk vnnethes myghte he stonde
tikled it his
Wende / þat I hadde of hym

10 ¶of Bathe 67*r*

The Wif of Bathe	ELLESMERE
I swoor / that my walkyng⁊ out by nyghte	þ*at* al my walkynge nygħte
Was for to espye / wenches that he dighte	Was / for tespye þ*at* digħte
Vnder that colour / hadde I many a myrthe	
For al swich wit⁊ is yeuen vs in oure birthe	swich thyng⁊ was yeuen byrthe
Deceite / wepyng⁊ spynnyng⁊ god hath yeue	
To wommen kyndely / whil they may lyue	wo*m*men whil that they
And thus / of o thyng⁊ I auante me	auaunte
At ende / I hadde the bet in ech degree	Atte ende / bettre
By sleighte / or force / or by som maner thyng⁊	sleigħte /
As by continuel murmur / or grucchyng⁊	continueel murmur*e*
Namely abedde / hadden they meschaunce	Namely /
Ther wolde I chide / and do hem no plesaunce	
I wolde no lenger / in the bed abyde	wolde / lenger
If that I felte his arm / ouer my syde	Arm
Til he hadde maad / his raunceon vn to me	he / had raunsou*n*
Thanne wolde I suffre hym / do his nycetee	
And ther fore / euery man / this tale I telle	
Wynne who so may / for al is for to selle	
With empty hond / men may none haukes lure	hand /
For wynnyng⁊ wolde I al his lust endure	
And make me / a feyned appetit⁊	11
And yet in bacou*n* / hadde I neu*er*e delit	yet⁊ delit⁊
That made me / that euere I wolde hem chyde	eu*er*e chide
For thogh the Pope / hadde seten hem bisyde	pope / biside
I wolde noght spare hem / at hir owene bord	nat bordʾ
For by my trouthe / I quytte hem / word for word	quitte hem for wordʾ
As help me / verray god omnipotent	help*e* omnipotent⁊
Togh I right now / sholde make my testament⁊	Though rigħt
I ne owe hem nat a word / that it nys quyt⁊	þ*at* quit
I broghte it so aboute / by my wit	aboute wit /
That they moste yeue it vp / as for the beste	
Or ellis / hadde we neu*er*e been in reste	elles /
For thogh he looked / as a wood leou*n*	
Yet sholde he faille / of his conclusiou*n*	
¶Thanne wolde I seye / good lief taak keep*e*	lief⁊
How mekely / looketh Wilkyn oure sheep*e*	
Com neer my spouse / lat me ba thy cheke	
Ye sholden be / al pacient / and meke	sholde been / pacient
And han / a swete spyced conscience	sweete spiced
Sith ye so p*re*che / of Iobes pacience	

11 ¶Wyf⁊ *67v*

The Wif of Bathe

I swoor that my walkyng out by nyghte
Was for to espye wenches that he dighte
Vnder that colour hadde I many a myrthe
ffor al swich wit is yeuen vs in oure byrthe
Deceite wepyng spynnyng god hath yeue
To wommen kyndely whil they may lyue
And thus of o thyng I auante me
At ende I hadde the bet in ech degree
By sleighte or force or by som maner thyng
As by continuel murmur or grucchyng
Namely abedde hadden they meschaunce
Ther wolde I chide and do hem no plesaunce
I wolde no lenger in the bed abyde
If that I felte his arm ouer my syde
Til he hadde maad his raunceon vn to me
Thanne wolde I suffre hym do his nycetee
And therfore euery man this tale I telle
Wynne who so may for al is for to selle
With empty hond men may none haukes lure
ffor wynnyng wolde I al his lust endure
And make me a feyned appetit
And yet in bacon hadde I neuere delit
That made me that euere I wolde hem chyde
ffor thogh the pope hadde seten hem bisyde
I wolde noght spare hem at hir owene bord
ffor by my trouthe I quytte hem word for word
As help me verray god omnipotent
Togh I right now sholde make my testament
I ne owe hem nat a word that it nys quyt
I broghte it so aboute by my wit
That they moste yeue it vp as for the beste
Or ellis hadde we neuere been in reste
ffor thogh he looked as a wood leon
Yet sholde he faille of his conclusion
Thanne wolde I seye good lief taak keep
How mekely looketh wilkyn oure sheep
Com neer my spouse lat me ba thy cheke
Ye sholden be al pacient and meke
And han a swete spyced conscience
Sith ye so preche of Iobes pacience

Suffiseth alwey syn ye so wel kan preche
And but ye do certeyn we shal yow teche
That it is fair / to han a wyf in pees
Oon of vs two / moste bowen doutelees
And sith a man / is moore resonable
Than womman is / ye moste been suffrable
What eyleth yow / to grucche thus and grone
Is it / for ye wolde haue my queynte allone
Wy taak it al lo haue it euery del
Peter I shrewe yow / but ye loue it wel
ffor if I wolde selle my bele chose
I koude walke / as fressh as is a rose
But I wol kepe it / for youre owene tooth
Ye be to blame / by god I sey yow sooth
Swiche manere wordes / hadde we on honde
Now wol I speke of my ferthe housbonde
My ferthe housbonde was a reuelour
This is to seyn / he hadde a paramour
And I was yong / and ful of ragerye
Stibourne and strong / and ioly as a pye
How koude I daunce to an harpe smale
And synge ywys as any nyghtyngale
Whan I hadde dronke / a draghte of swete wyn
Metellyus / the foule cherl the swyn
That with a staf / birafte his wyf hir lyf
ffor she drank wyn / though I hadde been his wyf
He sholde nat / han daunted me fro drynke
And after wyn / on Venus moste I thynke
ffor also siker / as cold engendreth hayl
A likerous mouth / moste han a likerous tayl
In womman vynolent / is no defence
This knowen lechours / by experience
But lord crist / whan þt it remembreth me
Vp on my youthe / and on my iolitee
It tikeleth me / aboute myn herte roote
Vn to this day / it dooth myn herte boote
That I haue had my world / as in my tyme
But age allas / that al wole envenyme
Hath me biraft / my beautee and my pith
Lat go farwel / the deuel go ther with

	ELLESMERE
Suffreth alwey / syn ye so wel kan p*re*che	
And but ye do / *cer*teyn we shal yow teche	certein
That it is fair / to han a wyf in pees	haue
Oon of vs two / moste bowen doutelees	
And sith a man / is moore resonable	
Than womman is / ye mosten been suffrable	wo*m*man moste
What eyleth yow / to grucche thus and grone	
Is it for ye wolde haue / my queynte allone	haue
Wy taak it al / lo haue it euery del	deel
Peter I shrewe yow / but ye loue it wel	weel
For if I wolde selle / my bele chose	wolde / selle
I koude walke / as fressh as is a rose	fressh
But I wol kepe it for youre owene tooth	kepe /
Ye be to blame / by god I sey yow sooth	god /
Swiche manere wordes / hadde we on honde	¶Swiche maner*e* wordes
Now wol I speke / of my ferthe housbonde	speken / fourthe
My ferthe housbonde / was a reuelour	fourthe
This is to seyn / he hadde a pa*ra*mour	
And I was yong and ful of ragerye	
Stibourne and strong and ioly as a pye	
How koude I daunce / to an harpe smale	Wel koude
And synge ywys / as any nyghtyngale	ywis /
Whan I hadde dronke / a draghte of swete wyn	had draughte sweete
Metellyus / the foule cherl the swyn	Metellius /
That with a staf / birafte his wyf hir lyf	lyf
For she drank wyn /. though I hadde been his wyf	drank wyn / thogh
Ne sholde nat han daunted me fro drynke	He sholde
And after wyn / on Venus moste I thynke	
For also siker / as coold engendreth hayl	12 al so cold
A likerous mouth / moste han a likerous tayl	
In womman vynolent / is no defence	wommen vinolent /
This knowen lechours / by experience	lecchours exp*er*ience
But lord crist whan þat it remembreth me	¶But crist / that
Vp on my youthe / and on my iolytee	yowthe / Iolitee
It tikeleth me / aboute myn herte roote	tikleth
Vn to this day / it dooth myn herte boote	
That I haue had my world / as in my tyme	
But age allas / that al wole enuenyme	Age
Hath me biraft my beautee / and my pith	biraft /
Lat go farwel / the deuel go ther with	farewel / therwith

453 Of the condicioun of the fourthe housbonde of this goode wyf And how she serued hym El

460 Valerius libro 6° capitulo 3° Metellius vxorem suam eo quod vinum bibisset fuste percussam interemit El

12 ¶of Bathe *68r*

The flour is goon / ther is namoore to telle	
The bren as I best kan / now moste I selle	
But yet⁊ to be right murye / wol I fonde	riħt myrie /
Now wol I tellen / of my ferthe housbonde	fourthe
¶I seye I hadde in herte gret despit	seye / greet
That he / of any oother had delit	delit⁊
But he was quyt⁊ by god and by Seint Ioce	quit⁊ god /
I made hym / of the same wode a troce	a croce |
Nat of my body / in no foul manere	
But c*er*teynly / I made folk swich chiere	c*er*tein / cheere
That in his owene grece / I made hym frye	
For angre / and for verray Ialousye	Angre /
By god / in erthe / I was his purgatorie	erthe
For which I hope / his soule be in glorie	
For god it woot⁊ he sat ful ofte and soong /	song /
Whan *þa*t his shoo / ful bitterly hym wroong⁊	wrong⁊
Ther was no wight⁊ saue god and he / *þa*t wiste	wiħt⁊ he
In many wise / how soore I hym twiste	
He deyde / whan I cam fro Ier*usa*l*e*m	Ierusalem
And lyth ygraue / vnder the roode beem	lith
Al is his toumbe / noght so curyus	tombe /
As was the sepulcre / of hym Daryus	
Which that Appellus / wroghte subtilly	Appelles / wroħte
It nys but wast⁊ to burye hym p*re*ciously	
Lat hym fare wel / god gyue his soule reste	yeue
⟨He is now / in his g*ra*ue / and in his cheste⟩	graue /
Now / of my fifthe housbonde / wol I telle	**N**Ow / housbonde
God lat his soule / neuere come in helle	lete neu*er*e
And yet was he to me / the mooste shrewe	
That feele I / on my rybbes al by rewe	ribbes
And euere shal / vn to myn endyng day	eu*er*e
But in oure bed / he was so fressħ and gay	was / ful fressħ
And ther with al / so wel koude he me glose	
Whan that he wolde / han my bele chose	that⁊ wolde
That thogh he hadde me bet⁊ on euery bon	thogh /
He koude wynne agayn / my loue anon	wynne / agayn
I trowe I loued hym best⁊ for that he	13
Was of his loue / daungerous to me	
We wommen han / if that I shal nat lye	
In this matere / a queynte fantasye	

499 Appelles fecit mirabile opus in tumulo darij vide in Alexandro libro 6°
El

503 Of the fifthe housbonde of this wyf and hou she bar hire ayens hym
El

13 ¶Wyf / *68v*

The flour is goon / ther is namoore to telle
The bren as I best kan / now moste I selle
But yet to be right murye / wol I fonde
Now wol I tellen / of my ferthe housbonde
I seye I hadde in herte gret despit
That he / of any oother hadde delit
But he was quyt / by god and by Seint Ioce
I made hym / of the same wode a croce
Nat of my body / in no foul manere
But certeinly / I made folk swich cheere
That in his owene grece / I made hym frye
For angre / and for verray Ialousye
By god / in erthe / I was his purgatorie
For which I hope / his soule be in glorie
For god it woot / he sat ful ofte and soong
Whan þt his sho / ful bitterly hym wroong
Ther was no wight / saue god and he þt wiste
In many wise / how soore I hym twiste
He deyde / whan I cam fro Ierusalem
And lyth ygraue / vnder the roode beem
Al is his tombe / noght so curyus
As was the sepulcre / of hym Daryus
Which that Appellus / wroghte subtilly
It nys but wast / to burye hym preciously
Lat hym fare wel / god yeue his soule reste +
+ He is now in his graue and in his cheste
Now of my fifthe housbonde / wol I telle
God lat his soule / neuere come in helle
And yet was he to me / the mooste shrewe
That feele I / on my rybbes al by rewe
And euere shal / vn to myn endyng day
But in oure bed / he was so fressh and gay
And ther with al / so wel koude he me glose
Whan that he wolde / han my bele chose
That thogh he hadde me bet / on euery bon
He koude wynne agayn / my loue anon
I trowe I loued hym best / for that he
Was of his loue / daungerous to me
We wommen han / if that I shal nat lye
In this matere / a queynte fantasye

Wayte what thyng we may nat lightly haue
Ther after wol we crie al day and craue
fforbede vs thyng and that desiren we
Preesse on vs faste and thanne wol we fle
With daunger oute we al oure chaffare
Greet prees at market maketh deere ware
And to greet cheep is holden at litel prys
This knoweth euery womman that is wys
¶ My fifthe housbonde god his soule blesse
Which þt I took for loue and no richesse
He som tyme was a clerk of Oxenford
And hadde left scole and wente at hom to bord
With my gossyb dwellyng in oure town
God haue hir soule hir name was Alisoun
She knew myn herte and eek my pryuetee
Bet than oure parisshe preest as mote I thee
To hire biwreyed I my conseil al
ffor hadde myn housbonde pissed on a wal
Or doon a thyng that sholde haue cost his lyf
To hire and to another worthy wyf
And to my Nece which þt I loued wel
I wolde han toold his conseil euery del
And so I dide ful often god it woot
That made his face often reed and hoot
ffor verray shame and blamed hym self for he
Hadde toold to me so greet a pryuetee
¶ And so bifel that ones in a lente
So often tymes I to my gossyb wente
ffor euere yet I loued to be gay
And for to walke in March Aueryll and May
ffrom hous to hous to heere sondry tales
That Iankyn clerk and my gossyb dame Alys
And I my self in to the feeldes wente
Myn housbonde was at london al that lente
I hadde the bettre leyser for to pleye
And for to se and eek for to be seye
Of lusty folk what wiste I wher my grace
Was shapen for to be or in what place
Ther fore I made my visitacions
To vigilies and to processions

	ELLESMERE
Wayte what thyng' we may nat lightly haue	
Ther after / wol we crye al day / and craue	crie / day
Forbede vs thyng' and that desiren we	
Preesse on vs faste / and thanne wol we fle	
With daunger / oute we / al oure chaffare	we
Greet prees at Market / maketh deere ware	Market'
And to greet cheep*e* / is holden at litel prys	holde
This knoweth euery womman / that is wys	knoweth / wo*m*man
¶My fifthe housbonde / god his soule blesse	
Which p*a*t I took for loue / and no rychesse	richesse
He som tyme / was a clerk of Oxenford	Oxenford'
And hadde laft scole / and wente at hom to bord	left bord'
With my gossyb / dwellyng in oure town	gossib / dwellynge toun
God haue hir soule / hir name was Alisoun	
She knew myn herte / and eek my pryuetee	p*ri*uetee
Bet than oure parysshe preest' as mote I thee	parissħe moot
To hire biwreyed I / my conseil al	hir*e* /
For hadde myn housbonde / pissed on a wal	
Or doon a thyng' that sholde haue cost his lyf	p*a*t han lyf /
To hire / and to another worthy wyf	hire / wyf /
And to my Nece / which p*a*t I loued wel	weel
I wolde han toold / his conseil euery del	deel
And so I dide / ful often / god it woot'	often
That made his face / often reed and hoot	face / ful often hoot'
For verray shame / and blamed hym self' for he	he'
Hadde toold to me / so greet a pryuetee	Had
¶And so bifel / that ones in a lente	
So often tymes / I to my gossyb wente	
For euere yet' I louede to be gay	loued
And for to walke / in March / Aueryƚƚ / and May	Aueriƚƚ
From hous to hous / to here sondry tales	Fro heere talys
That Iankyn Clerk / and my gossyb dame Alys	Clerk'
And I my self / in to the feeldes wente	
Myn housbonde was at londou*n* / al that lente	housbonde / Londou*n* al the lente
I hadde / the bettre leyser for to pleye	
And for to se / and eek for to be seye	eek'
Of lusty folk' what wiste ⟨I⟩ wher my g*ra*ce	I / grace
Was shapen for to be / or in what place	
Ther fore / I made my visitacions	Therfore / visitaciou*n*s
To vigilies / and to processions	vigiles / processiou*n*s

The Wif of Bathe./	ELLESMERE
To p*re*chyng eek / and to thise pilgrymages	eek pilg*ri*mages
To pleyes of myracles / and to mariages	
And wered vp on / my gaye scarlet gytes	
Thise wormes / ne thise moththes / ne thise Mytes	Motthes / mytes
Vp on my peril / frete hem neuer a del	[14] Vpon pe*r*il / neue*r* deel
And wostow / why / for they were vsed wel	wostow why ./ weel
¶Now wol I tellen forth / what happed me	NOw
I seye / that in the feeldes walked we	
Til trewely / we hadde swich daliaunce	daliance
This clerk / and I / that of my p*ur*ueiaunce	clerk p*ur*ueiance
I spak to hym / and seyde hym / how that he	þat he./
If I were wydewe / sholde wedde me	wydwe /
For certeynly / I seye for no bobau*n*ce	ce*r*teinly / sey bobance
Yet was I neuere / with outen purueiau*n*ce	neue*re* / p*ur*ueiance
Of mariage / nof othere thynges eek /	eek
I holde a mouses herte / noght worth a leek	Mouses nat leek /
That hath but oon hole / for to sterte to	
And if that faille / thanne is al ydo[15]	þat
But now sire / lat me se / what shal I seyn	¶But sire / I shal
A .ha. by god / I haue my tale ageyn	A / ha /
¶Whan that my fourthe housbonde / was a beere	þat was on beere
I weep algate / and made sory cheere	weep*e*
As wyues mooten / for it is vsage	
And with my cou*er*chief / coueréd my visage	cou*er*ed
But for that I was / purueyed of a make	þat I / was
I wepte but smal / and that I vndertake	
¶To chirche was myn housbonde / born a morwe	chirche / amorwe
With neghebores / that for hym maden sorwe	neighebores /
And Iankyn oure clerk / was oon of tho	Clerk
As help me god / whan that I saw hym go	þat saugh
After the beere / me thoughte he hadde a payre	thoughte paire./
Of legges / and of feet so clene and fayre	feet / faire
That al myn herte / I yaf vn to his hoold	
He was I trowe / twenty wynter oold	trowe / a twenty
And I was fourty / if I shal seye sooth	
But yet I hadde alwey / a coltes tooth	And yet /
Gat tothed I was / *and* that bicam me weel	and
I hadde the preente / of Seynt Venus seel	prente / Seint
As help me god / I was a lusty oon	
And fayr and ryche / and yong and wel bigoon	faire riche / bigon

[14] ¶of Bathe *69r*

[15] *Out* Hg 575-84. El reads:

¶I bar hym on honde / he hadde enchanted me
My dame taughte me that soutiltee
And eek I seyde / I mette of hym al nyght
He wolde han slayn me / as I lay vp right
And al my bed / was ful of verray blood
But yet I hope / that he shal do me good
For blood / bitokeneth gold / as me was taught
And al was fals / I dremed of it right naught
But I folwed ay / my da*m*mes loore
As wel of this / as othere thynges moore

To prechyng eek / and to thise pilgrymages
To pleyes of myracles / and to mariages
And wered vp on / my gaye scarlet gytes
Thise wormes / ne thise motthes / ne thise mytes
Vp on my peril / frete hem neuere a del
And wostow why / for they were vsed wel
Now wol I tellen forth / what happed me
I seye that in the feeldes walked we
Til trewely / we hadde swich daliaunce
This clerk and I / that of my purueiaunce
I spak to hym / and seyde hym / how that he
If I were wydwe / sholde wedde me
For certeynly / I seye for no bobance
Yet was I neuere / withouten purueiance
Of mariage / nof othere thynges eek
I holde a mouses herte / noght worth a leek
That hath but oon hole / for to sterte to
And if that faille / thanne is al ydo
But now sire lat me se / what shal I seyn
A ha / by god / I haue my tale ageyn
Whan that my fourthe housbonde / was a beere
I weep algate / and made sory cheere
As wyues mooten / for it is vsage
And with my couerchief / couered my visage
But for that I was / purueyed of a make
I wepte but smal / and that I vndertake
To chirche was myn housbonde / born amorwe
With neghebores / that for hym maden sorwe
And Iankyn oure clerk / was oon of tho
As help me god / whan that I saugh hym go
After the beere / me thoughte he hadde a paire
Of legges and of feet / so clene and faire
That al myn herte / I yaf vn to his hoold
He was I trowe / twenty wynter oold
And I was fourty / if I shal seye sooth
But yet I hadde alwey / a coltes tooth
Gat tothed I was / and that bicam me weel
I hadde the preente / of seynt Venus seel
As help me god / I was a lusty oon
And fayr / and ryche / and yong / and wel bigoon

And trewely / as myne housbondes tolde me
I hadde the beste quoniam myghte be
Myn ascendent was Taur / and Mars ther Inne
Allas / allas / that euere loue was synne
I folwed ay myn Inclinacion
By vertu of my constellacion
That made me / I koude noght withdrawe
My chambre of Venus / from a good felawe
What sholde I seye / but at the monthes ende
This ioly clerk Iankyn þt was so hende
Hath wedded me / with greet solempnytee
And to hym yaf I / al the lond and fee
That euere was me yeuen / ther bifore
But afterward / repented me ful sore
He nolde suffre / no thyng of my list
By god / he smoot me ones / on the lyst
ffor that I rente / out of his book leef
That of the strook / myn ere wex al deef
Stibourne I was / as is a leonesse
And of my tonge / a verray Iangleresse
And walke I wolde / as I hadde doon biforn
ffrom hous to hous / al thogh he hadde it sworn
ffor which / he often tymes wolde preche
And me / of olde Romayn gestes teche
How he Symplicius Gallus / lafte his wyf
And hire forsook / for terme of al his lyf
Noght but for open heueded / he hir say
Lokynge out at his dore / vp on a day
Another Romayn / tolde he me by name
That for his wyf / was at a somers game
With outen his wityng / he forsook hire eke
And thanne wolde he / vp on his Bible seke
That ilke prouerbe of Ecclesiaste
Where he comandeth / and forbedeth faste
Man shal nat suffre his wyf / go roule aboute
Thanne wolde he seye right thus / with outen doute
Who so þt buyldeth his hous / al of salwes
And priketh his blynde hors / ouer the falwes
And suffreth his wyf / to go seken halwes
Is worthy / to ben hanged on the galwes

	ELLESMERE
And trewely / as myne housbondes tolde me	
I hadde the beste quonyam / myghte be[16]	Quonyam myghte
Myn ascendent' was Taur / and Mars ther Inne	Ascendent Taur therInne
Allas / allas / that eu*er*e loue was synne	þ*at* euere
I folwed ay / myn Inclinaciou*n*	
By vertu / of my constellaciou*n*	ve*r*tu /
That made me / I koude noght withdrawe	
My chambre of Venus / from a good felawe[18]	
¶What sholde I seye / but at the Monthes ende	
This ioly clerk / Iankyn þ*at* was so hende	
Hath wedded me / with greet solempnytee	
And to hym yaf I / al the lond and fee	
That euere was me yeuen / ther bifore	euere / yeuen bifoore
But afterward / repented me ful sore	soore
He nolde suffre / no thyng of my list'	
By god / he smoot me ones / on the lyst'	ones
For that I rente / out of his book ⟨a⟩ leef	þ*at* book' a leef /
That of the strook' myn ere weex al deef	strook / wax deef /
Stibourne I was / as is a leonesse	Leonesse
And of my tonge / a verray Iangleresse	
And walke I wolde / as I hadde doon biforn	had
From hous to hous / al thogh he hadde it sworn	though had
For which / he often tymes / wolde p*re*che	tymes
And me / of olde Romayn gestes teche	geestes
How he Symplicius Gallus / lafte his wif	lefte wyf'
And hire forsook' for terme of al his lif'	hir*e* forsook / *ter*me lyf'
Noght' but for open heueded he hir say	heueded /
Lokynge out at his dore / vp on a day	Lookynge vpon
¶Another Romayn / tolde he me by name	
That for his wyf / was at a som*er*es game	someres
With outen his wityng' he forsook hir*e* eke	Wit*h*
And thanne wolde he / vp on his Bible seke	vpon
That ilke p*rouer*be / of Ecclesiaste	prou*er*be /
Where he comandeth / and forbedeth faste	Wher*e*
Man shal nat suffre his wyf / go roule aboute	wyf
Thanne wolde he seye right thus / with outen doute	right / wit*h*
Who so þ*at* buyldeth his hous / al of salwes	¶No*ta*] Who so / that
And priketh his blynde hors / ouer the falwes	
And suffreth his wyf / to go seken halwes	19 ¶And
Is worthy / to ben hanged on the galwes	been hanged /

no*ta* (bracketing the last four lines)

[But al for] noght'

609 Mansor Amphorisoun 14 Cumque in Ascendente fuerint infortune turpem notam in facie pacietur In natiuitatibus mulierum cum fuerit ascendens aliqua de domibus Veneris Marte existente in eis vel e contrario erit mulier inpudica Idem erit si habuerit capricornum in ascendente He Hermes in libro fiducie Amphoriso 25° El

643 Valerius libro 6° folio 14° El

657 Ne des mulieri nequam veniam prodeundi ecclesiastici 25° El

[16] *Out* Hg 609-12. El reads:

For certes / I am al Venerien[17]
610 In feelynge / and myn herte ⟨is⟩ Marcien
Venus me yaf my lust' my likerousnesse
And Mars yaf me / my sturdy hardynesse

[17] ¶Wyf 69*v*

66r Quire 10^{8} (begins)

.The Wyf of Bathe.

	ELLESMERE
But al for noght7 I sette noght an hawe	noght7 noght
Of his p*rouer*be / nof his olde sawe	prouerbes / olde lawe
Ny wolde nat7 of hym corrected be	Ne I wolde
I hate hym / *þa*t my vices telleth me	that
And so doon mo / god woot of vs than I	doo vs /
This made hym / with me wood al outrely	
I nolde noght forbere hym / in no cas	noght / hym
¶Now wol I sey yow sooth / by Seint Thomas	seye
Why *þa*t I rente / out of his book a leef	
For which / he smoot me so / *þa*t I was deef	
He hadde a book / *þa*t gladly nyght and day	¶He nyght
For his disport7 he wolde rede alway	desport7
He clepyd it7 Valerie and Theofraste	cleped Valerie /
At which book / he logh alwey ful faste	lough
And eek ther was / som tyme a clerk at Rome	¶And eek / was tyme /
A Cardynal / that highte Seint Ierome	Cardinal /
That made a book7 agayn Iovinian	Iouinian
In which book7 eek ther was Tertulan	eek7
Crisippus / Trotula / and Helowys	
That was Abbesse / nat fer fro Parys	
And eek the parables / of Salomon	eek7 Parables
Ouydes art7 and bokes many on	Ouides Art7 bookes
And alle thise were bounden / in o volume	thise /
And euery nyght and day / was his custume	nyght
Whan he hadde leyser / and vacaciou*n*	leyser7
From oother / worldly ocupaciou*n*	oother7 worldly / occupaciou*n*
To reden in this book7 of wikked wyues	reden on this
He knew of hem / mo legendes and lyues	
Than been of goode wyues in the Bible	been /
For trusteth wel / it is an inpossible	
That any clerk7 wol speke good of wyues	
But if it be / of holy seintes lyues	hooly Seintes
Nof noon oother womman / neuer the mo	Ne noon wo*m*man / neue*r*
Who peynted the leou*n* / tel me who	Leou*n* / who./
By god / if wo*m*men / hadden writen stories	hadde
As clerkes han / with Inne hir oratories	hir*e*
They wolde han writen of men / moore wikkednesse	writen / men
Than al the mark of Adam may redresse	mark7
The children / of Mercurie and Venus	
Been in hir wirkyng / ful contrarius	wirkyng7

692 Quis pinxit leonem El

[18] *Out* Hg 619-26. El reads:

Yet haue I / Martes Mark vp on my face
And also / in another p*ri*uee place
For god so wys / be my sauaciou*n*
I ne loued neuere / by no discreciou*n*
But euere / folwed myn appetit
Al were he / short7 or long7 or blak / or whit
I took no kepe / so that he liked me
How poore he was / ne eek7 of what degree

[19] ¶of Bathe *70r*

But al for noght / I sette noght an hawe
Of his prouerbe / nof his olde sawe
Ny wolde nat / of hym corrected be
I hate hym / þt my vices telleth me
And so doon mo / god woot of vs than I
This made hym / with me wood al outrely
I nolde noght forbere hym in no cas
Now wol I seye yow sooth / by Seint Thomas
Why þt I rente / out of his book a leef
ffor which / he smoot me so / þt I was deef
He hadde a book / þt gladly nyght and day
ffor his disport / he wolde rede alway
He clepyd it / Valerie and Theofraste
At which book he logh alwey ful faste
And eek ther was / som tyme a clerk at Rome
A Cardynal / that highte Seint Jerome
That made a book / agayn Jovinian
In which book eek ther was Tertulan
Crisippus / Trotula / and Helowys
That was Abbesse / nat fer fro Parys
And eek the parables / of Salomon
Ovydes art / and bokes many on
And alle thise were bounden / in o volume
And euery nyght and day / was his custume
Whan he hadde leyser / and vacacion
ffrom oother worldly ocupacion
To reden in this book / of wikked wyues
He knew of hem / mo legendes and lyues
Than been of goode wyues in the Bible
ffor trusteth wel / it is an impossible
That any clerk / wol speke good of wyues
But if it be / of holy seintes lyues
Ne of noon oother womman / neuer the mo
Who peynted the leon / tel me who
By god / if wommen / hadden writen stories
As clerkes han / with Inne hir oratories
They wolde han writen of men / moore wikkednesse
Than al the mark of Adam may redresse
The children / of Mercurie and Venus
Been in hir wirkyng / ful contrarius

Mercurie loveth / wysdam and science
And Venus loveth / riot and dispence
And for hir diuerse / disposicion
Ech falleth / in otheres exaltacion
And thus god woot / Mercurie is desolat
In pisces / wher Venus is exaltat /
And Venus falleth / ther Mercurie is reysed
Ther fore no womman / of no clerk is preysed
The clerk / whan he is old / and may noght do
Of Venus werkes / worth his olde sho
Thanne sit he doun / and writ in his dotage
That wommen / kan nat kepe hir mariage
But now to purpos / why I tolde thee
That I was beten / for a book pardee
Vp on a nyght / Jankyn þt was oure sire
Redde on his book / as he sat by the fire
Of Eua first / þt for hir wikkednesse
Was al mankynde / broght to wrecchednesse
Tho redde he me / how Sampson loste his heres
Slepynge his lemman kitte it wt hir sheres
Thurgh which treson / loste he bothe hise eyen
Tho redde he me / if that I shal nat lyen
Of Hercules / and of his Dianyre
That caused hym / to sette hym self afyre
No thyng forgat he the sorwe and wo
That Socrates / hadde with hise wyues two
How Xantippa / caste pisse vp on his heed
This sely man sat stille / as he were deed
He wipte his heed / namoore dorste he seyn
But er that thonder stynte / comth a reyn
Of Phasipha / that was the queene of Crete
ffor shrewednesse / hym thoughte the tale swete
ffy spek namoore / it is a grisly thyng /
Of hir horrible lust / and hir likyng /
Of Clitermystra / for hir lecherye
That falsly made hir housbonde for to dye
He redde it / with ful good deuocion
He tolde me eek / for what occasion
Amphiorax / at Thebes loste his lyf
Myn housbonde / hadde a legende of his wyf

Hengwrt	ELLESMERE
Mercurie loueth / wysdam and science	Mercurie / loueth
And Venus loueth / Riot and dispence	Venus / loueth ryot'
And for hir diu*er*se / disposiciou*n*	hir*e* diu*er*se
Ech faileth / in ootheres exaltaciou*n*	Ech falleth / in otheres
And thus god woot' Mercurie is desolat	desolat'
In pisces / wher Venus is exaltat'	In Pisces /
And Venus faileth / ther Mercurie is reysed	20 Venus falleth / ther Me*r*curie reysed .i. i*n* Virgine
Ther fore no wo*m*man / of no clerk is preysed	Therfore womman /
The clerk' whan he is old / and may noght do	oold /
Of Venus werkes / worth his olde sho	
Thanne sit he doun / and writ in his dotage	
That wommen / kan nat kepe hir mariage	wo*m*men /
¶But now to purpos / why I tolde thee	**B**ut
That I was beten / for a book pardee	p*ar*dee
Vp on a nyght' Iankyn þ*at* was oure sire	nygħt'
Redde on his book / as he sat by the fire	
Of Eua first / þ*at* for hir wikkednesse	first' that
716 Was al man kynde / broght to wrecchednesse[21]	mankynde / brogħt
721 ¶Tho redde he me / how Sampson loste his herys	hise heres
Slepynge / his lemman kitte it w*ith* hir sherys	lemman / sheres
Thurgh which tresou*n* / loste he bothe hise eyen	Thurgħ
¶Tho redde he me / if that I shal nat lyen	
Of Hercules / and of his Dianyre	hercules /
That caused hym / to sette hym self afyre	
¶No thyng forgat he / the sorwe and wo	thyng /
That Socrates / hadde with his wyues two	w*ith* hise
How Xantippa / caste pisse vp on his heed	
This sely man sat stille / as he were deed	man / stille
He wipte his heed / namoore dorste he seyn	wiped
But er that thonder stynte / comth a reyn	But' þ*at*
¶Of Phasifpha / that was the queene of Crete	
For shrewednesse / hym thoughte the tale swete	
Fy spek namoore / it is a grisly thyng'	
Of hir*e* horrible lust' and hir likyng'	hir*e* / horrible
¶Of Clitermystra / for hir lecherye	hir*e*
That falsly / made hir housbonde for to dye	hir*e*
He redde it' with ful good deuociou*n*	it /
¶He tolde me eek / for what occasiou*n*	eek'
Amphiorax / at Thebes loste his lyf	lyf'
Myn housbonde / hadde a legende of his wyf	wyf /

702 Vtraque cadit vbi alia exaltatur El

705 In libro Mansor primo Vniuscuiusque planetarum 7 Exaltacio illo in loco fore dicitur in quo subito patitur ab alio contrarium et cetera Velut Mercurius in virgine quod est casus Veneris Alter scilicet Mercurius significat scientiam et philosophiam Alter vero cantus et alacritates et quicquid est sapiferum corpori El

733 Quid referam Phasifphen Clitermistram et Eriphilem quarum prima delicijs fluens quippe vt Regis vxor Tauri dicitur adpetisse concubitus Alia occidisse virum suum ob amorem Adulterij Tercia perdidisse Amphiorax et saluti viri monile Aureum pertulisse et cetera Hec Metellius Marrio secundum Valerium El

20 ¶Wyf' *70v*

21 *Out* Hg 717-20. El reads:

For which crist' hym self / was slayn
That boghte vs / with his herte blood agayn
Lo heere exp*res* / of wo*m*man may ye fynde
That wo*m*man / was the los / of al mankynde

¶Exiphilem / that for an Ouch of gold
Hath p*ri*uely / vn to the grekys told
Wher *pat* hir housbonde / hidde hym in a place
For which / he hadde at Thebes sory grace
¶Of lyma tolde he me / and of lucie
They bothe / made hir housbondes for to dye
That oon for loue / that oother was for hate
Lyma hir housbonde / on an euen late
Empoysoned hath / for *pat* she was his fo
Lucya likerous / loued hir housbonde so
That for he sholde alwey / vp on hir thynke
She yaf hym / swich a manere loue drynke
That he was deed / er it were by the morwe
And thus algates / housbondes han sorwe
¶Thanne tolde he me / how *pat* oon latumyus
Compleyned / vn to his felawe Arrius
That in his gardyn / growed swich a tree
On which he seyde / how *pat* hise wyues thre
Honged hem self / for hertes despitus
¶O leeue brother / quod this Arrius
Yif me a plante / of thilke blessed tree
And in my gardyn / planted shal it be
¶Of latter date of wyues / hath he red
That so*m*me han slayn / hir housbondes in hir bed
And lete hir Lechour / dighte hir*e* al the nyght
Whan *pat* the corps / lay in the floor vp ryght
¶And so*m*me / han dryuen nayles in hir brayn
Whil *pat* they sleepe / and thus they han hem slayn
¶So*m*me han hem yeuen poysou*n* / in hir drynke
He spak moore harm / than herte may bithynke
And ther with al / he knew of mo p*ro*uerbes
Than in this world / ther growen gras or herbes
Bet is quod he / thyn habitaciou*n*
Be with a leou*n* / or a foul dragou*n*
Than w*ith* a womman / vsyng for to chide
Bet is quod he / hye in the roof abyde
Than with an angry wyf / down in the hous
They been so wikked / and contrarious
They haten / that hir housbondes loueth ay
He seyde / a womman / cast hir shame away

ELLESMERE

¶Eriphilem / Ouche
grekes
that
Lyma Lucye
housbonde / vp on
Lucia hir*e*
22 THat sholde / alwey hir*e*
Latumyus
that
Hanged self herte
blissed
planted it shal bee
so*m*me / slayn
Lecchour / nyght
that right
dryue nayles /
slepte /
yeue / poysou*n* hir*e*
world /.
with vsynge chyde
w*ith* doun
wikked
housbondes /
womman

22 ¶Wyf / *71r*

The wyf of Bathe.

Eryphilem / that for an Ouche of gold
Hath priuely / vn to the grekys told
Wher þt hir housbonde / hidde hym in a place
For which / he hadde at Thebes sory grace
Of lyma tolde he me / and of lucie
They bothe / made hir housbondes for to dye
That oon for loue / that oother was for hate
Lyma hir housbonde / on an euen late
Empoysoned hath / for þt she was his fo
Lucya likerous / loued hir housbonde so
That for he sholde alwey / vp on hir thynke
She yaf hym / swich a manere loue drynke
That he was deed / er it were by the morwe
And thus algates / housbondes han sorwe
Thanne tolde he me / how þt oon latumyus
Compleyned / vn to his felawe arrius
That in his gardyn / growed swich a tree
On which he seyde / how þt hise wyues thre
Honged hem self / for hertes despitus
O leeue brother / quod this arrius
Yif me a plante / of thilke blessed tree
And in my gardyn / planted shal it be
Of latter date of wyues / hath he red
That somme han slayn / hir housbondes in hir bed
And lete hir lechour / dighte hir al the nyght
Whan þt the corps / lay in the floor vp right
And somme / han dryuen nayles in hir brayn
Whil þt they sleepe / and thus they han hem slayn
Somme han hem yeuen poyson / in hir drynke
He spak moore harm / than herte may bithynke
And ther with al / he knew of mo prouerbes
Than in this world / ther growen gras or herbes
Bet is quod he / thyn habitacion
Be with a leoun / or a foul dragon
Than with a womman / vsyng for to chide
Bet is quod he / hye in the roof abyde
Than with an angry wyf / down in the hous
They been so wikked / and contrarious
They haten / that hir housbondes loueth ay
He seyde / a womman cast hir shame away

whan she cast of hir smok / and forther mo
A fair womman / but she be chaast also
Is lyk a gold ryng / in a sowes nose
Who wolde wene / or who wolde suppose
The wo / that in myn herte was and pyne
¶ And whan I say / he wolde neuere fyne
To reden / on this cursed book al nyght /
Al sodeynly thre leues / haue I plyght /
Out of his book / right as he radde / and eke
I with my fist / so took on the cheke
That in oure fyr / he fil bakward adown
And he vp stirte / as dooth a wood leoun
And with his fest / he smoot me on the heed
That in the floor / I lay as I were deed
And whan he say / how stille þt I lay
He was agast / and wolde haue fled his way
Til atte laste / out of my swowgh I brayde
O hastow slayn me / false theef I sayde
And for my land / thus hastow mordred me
Er I be deed / yet wol I kisse thee
¶ And neer he cam / and kneled faire adown
And seyde / deere suster Alisoun
As help me god / I shal thee neuere smyte
That I haue doon / it is thy self to wyte
fforyeue it me / and that I thee biseke
And yet eft sones / I hitte hym on the cheke
And seyde theef / thus muchel am I wreke
Now wol I dye / I may no lenger speke
¶ But at the laste / with muchel care and wo
We fille acorded / by vs seluen two
He yaf me / al the brydel in myn hond
To han the gouernance / of hous and lond
And of his tonge / and his hond also
And made hym brenne his book / anon right tho
And whan that I hadde geten vn to me
By maistrye / al the soueraynetee
And þt he seyde / myn owene trewe wyf
Do as thee lust / the terme of al thy lyf
Keep thyn honour / and keep eek myn estaat
After that day / we hadden neuere debaat

Whan she cast of hir smokꝫ and forther mo
A fair wo*m*man / but she be chaast also
Is lyk a gold ryngꝫ in a sowes nose
Who wolde wene / or who wolde suppose
The wo / that in myn herte was and pyne
¶And whan I say / he wolde neu*er*e fyne
To reden / on this cursed book al nyghtꝫ
Al sodeynly / thre leues / haue I plyghtꝫ
Out of his bookꝫ right as he radde / and eke
I with my fistꝫ so took on the cheke
That in oure fyr / he fil bakward adown
And he vp stirte / as dooth a wood leoun
And with his fest / he smoot me on the heed
That in the floor / I lay as I were deed
And whan he say / how stille *þat* I lay
He was agastꝫ and wolde haue fled his way
Til atte laste / out of my swowgh I brayde
O hastow slayn me / false theef I sayde
And for my land / thus hastow mordred me
Er I be deed / yet wol I kisse thee
¶And neer he cam / and kneled faire adown
And seyde / deere suster Alisoun
As help me god / I shal thee neu*er*e smyte
That I haue doon / it is thy self to wyte
Foryeue it me / and that I thee biseke
And yet eft soones / I hitte hym on the cheke
And seyde theef / thus muchel am I wreke
Now wol I dye / I may no lenger speke
¶But at the laste / with muchel care and wo
We fille acorded / by vs seluen two
He yaf me / al the brydel in myn hond
To han the gouernance / of hous and lond
And of his tonge / and his hond also
And made hym brenne his bookꝫ anon right tho
And whan that I hadde / geten vn to me
By maistrye / al the souerayneteе
And *þat* he seyde / myn owene trewe wyf
Do as thee lustꝫ the t*er*me of al thy lyf
Keepe thyn honour / and keepe eek myn estaat
After that day / we hadden neu*er*e debaat /

ELLESMERE

womman /	
goldryngꝫ	
wolde leeue / or	
saugħ /	
reden	nyghtꝫ
leues	plyghtꝫ
rigħt	
festꝫ	took hym on
adoun	
festꝫ	
lay /	
saugħ /	
han	
swogh	breyde
seyde	
23	
adoun	
But atte laste /	
bridel	hond'
gou*er*nance /	lond'
rigħt	
I / hadde	
maistrie /	
that	wyf /
lustꝫ to t*er*me	lyfꝫ
estaatꝫ	
neu*er* debaatꝫ	

785 Circulus aureus in naribus Suis Mulior formosa et fatua id est impudica El

23 ¶Wyf *71v*

⸝The Wyf of Bathe.⸝	ELLESMERE
God help me so / I was to hym as kynde	help*e*
As any wyf / from Denmark' vn to Inde	wyf' Denmark Ynde
And also trewe / and so was he to me	
I pray to god / that sit in magestee	prey
So blesse his soule / for his m*er*cy deere	
Now wol I seye my tale / if ye wol heere[24]	25
The frere logh / whan he hadde herd al this	lough /
Now dame quod he / so haue I ioye / or blys	ioye blis
This is a long p*re*amble / of a tale	is / p*re*amble
And whan the Somnour / herde the frere gale	Somonour /
¶Lo quod the Somnour / goddes armes two	Somonour / Armes
A frere / wol entremette hym eu*er*e mo	eueremo
Loo goode men / a flye / and eek a frere	Lo flye
Wol falle in euery dyssħ and matere	falle / mateere
What spekestow / of preambulacioun	
What amble / or trotte / or pees / or go sit doun	
Thow lettest oure disport' in this manere	Thou disport /.
¶Ye woltow so / sir Somnour / quod the frere	sir*e* Somonour
Now by my feith / I shal er that I go	
Telle of a Somnour / swich a tale / or two	Somono*ur* / tale
That al the folk / shal laughen in this place	alle
¶Now ellis frere / I wol bishrewe thy face	elles I bishrewe
Quod this Somnour / and I bishrewe me	26 Somono*ur* /
But if I telle tales / two or thre	
Of freres / er I come to Sydyngborne	Sidyngborne
That I shal make / thyn herte for to morne	
For wel I woot' thy pacience is gon	
¶Oure hoost' cryde pees / and that anon	hoost cride
And seyde / lat the womman / telle hir tale	womman hir*e*
Ye fare as folk / that dronken ben of Ale	dronken were of
Do dame / tel forth youre tale / and that is best'	telle
¶Al reddy sire quod she / right as yow lest'	redy sir*e* rigħt
If I haue licence / of this worthy frere	
¶Yis dame quod he / tel forth / and I wol heere	

¶Here endeth the prologe of the Wyf of Bathe

¶Heere endeth the Wyf of Bathe hir Prologe / And bigynneth Hir tale

[24] No break in Hg.

[25] After 828 El reads:
¶Biholde the wordes bitwene the Somono*ur* / and the Frere

[26] ¶of Bathe *72r*

God help me so / I was to hym as kynde
As any wyf / from Denmark / vn to Ynde
And also trewe / and so was he to me
I pray to god / that sit in magestee
So blesse his soule / for his mercy deere
Now wol I seye my tale / if ye wol heere
The frere logh / whan he hadde herd al this
Now dame quod he / so haue I ioye / or blys
This is a long preamble / of a tale
And whan the Somnour / herde the frere gale
Lo quod the Somnour / goddes armes two
A frere / wol entremette hym euere mo
Loo goode men / a flye / and eek a frere
Wol falle in euery dyssh / and matere
What spekestow / of preambulacioun
What amble / or trotte / or pees / or go sit doun
Thow lettest oure disport / in this manere
Ye woltow so / sire Somnour / quod the frere
Now by my feith / I shal er that I go
Telle of a Somnour / swich a tale / or two
That al the folk / shal laughen in this place
Now elles frere / I wol bishrewe thy face
Quod this Somnour / and I bishrewe me
But if I telle tales / two or thre
Of freres / er I come to Sydyngborne
That I shal make / thyn herte for to morne
ffor wel I woot / thy pacience is gon
Oure hoost cryde pees / and that anon
And seyde / lat the womman telle hir tale
Ye fare as folk / that dronken ben of ale
Do dame / tel forth youre tale / and that is best
Al redy sire quod she / right as yow lest
If I haue licence / of this worthy frere
Yis dame quod he / tel forth / and I wol heere

Heere endeth the prologe of the wyf of Bathe

Here bigynneth the tale / of the Wyf of Bathe

In tholde dayes / of the kyng Arthour
Of which that Britouns / speken greet honour
Al was this land / fulfild of ffayrye
The Elf queene / with hir ioly compaignye
Daunced ful ofte / in many a grene mede
This was / the olde opynyon / as I rede
I speke / of many hundred yeris ago
But now kan no man / se none Elues mo
ffor now the grete charitee / and prayeres
Of lymytours / and othere holy freres
That serchen / euery lond and euery streem
As thikke / as motes in the sonne beem
Blessynge halles / chambres / kichenes / boures
Citees / Burghes / Castels / hye Toures
Thropes / Bernes / Shipnes / Dayeryes
This maketh yt ther been no fayryes
ffor ther as wont / to walken was an Elf
Ther walketh now / the lymytour hym self
In vndermelys and in morwenynges
And seith his matyns / and his holy thynges
As he gooth / in his lymytacioun
Wommen may go saufly vp and doun
In euery bussh / or vnder euery tree
Ther is noon oother Incubus / but he
And he ne wol doon hem / but dishonour
And so bifel / that this kyng Arthour
Hadde in his hous a lusty Bacheler
That on a day / cam ridyng fro Ryuer
And happed that allone / as he was born
He say a mayde walkynge hym biforn
Of which mayde / anoon maugree hir heed
By verray force / he rafte hir maydenhed
ffor which oppressioun / was swich clamour
And swich pursuyte vn to the kyng Arthour
That dampned was this knyght / for to be deed
By cours of lawe / and sholde han lost his heed

¶Here bigynneth the tale / of the Wyf of Bathe

IN tholde dayes / of the kyng Arthour	of kyng
Of which that Britons / speken greet honour	
Al was this land / fulfild of Fairye	27
The Elf queene / with hir ioly compaignye	
Daunced ful ofte / in many a grene mede	
This was / the olde opynyou*n* / as I rede	was opinion
I speke / of many hundred yerys ago	manye yeres
But now kan no man / se none Elues mo	
For now the grete charitee / and prayeres	
Of lymytours / and othere holy freres	hooly
That serchen / euery lond and euery streem	lond /
As thikke / as motes in the sonne beem	motes /
Blessynge halles / chambres / kichenes boures	
Citees / Burghes / Castels / hye Toures	
Thropes / Bernes / Shipnes / Dayeryes	
This maketh / *þat* ther been no fairyes	that Fairyes
For ther as wont to walken was an Elf	Elf
Ther walketh now / the lymytour hym self	self
In vndermelys / and in morwenynges	vndermeles /
And seith his matyns / and his holy thynges	seyth hooly
As he gooth / in his lymytacioun	
Wommen / may go saufly vp and down	Wo*m*men / doun
In euery bussh / or vnder euery tree	bussħ /
Ther is noon oother **Incubus** / but he	is /
And he ne wol doon hem / but dishonour	he /
¶And so bifel / that this kyng Arthour	kyng
Hadde in his hous / a lusty Bachiler	in hous / Bacheler
That on a day / cam ridyng fro Ryuer	ridynge
And happed that allone / as he was born	
He say a mayde / walkynge hym biforn	saugh
Of which mayde / anoon maugree hir hed	28 anon heed
By verray force / he rafte hir maydenhed	force / birafte hir*e*
For which opp*re*ssiou*n* / was swich clamour	
And swich pursuyte / vn to the kyng Arthour	pursute /
That dampned was this knyght / for to be deed	knygħt
By cours of lawe / and sholde han lost his heed	

27 Miniature of the Wife of Bath in right margin.

28 ¶Wyf *72v*

	ELLESMERE
Par auenture / swich was the statut tho	P*ar*auenture /
But that the queene / and othere ladyes mo	
So longe preyden / the kyng of grace	
Til he his lyf / hym graunted in the place	he /
And yaf hym to the queene / al at hir wille	
To chese / wheither she wolde / hym saue or spille[29]	wheither / wolde
And after this / thus spak she to the knyght	knygħt
Whan that she saw / hir tyme vp on a day	p*at* / saugh
Thow standest yet quod she / in swich array	Thou
That of thy lyf / yet hastow no suretee	
I graunte thee lyf / if thow kanst tellen me	grante thou
What thyng is it p*at* wommen moost desiren	that wo*m*men
Be war / and keep*e* thy nekke boon from Iren	
And if thow kanst nat / tellen me anon	thou / nat tellen it anon
Yet wol I yeue thee leue / for to gon	Yet shal I
A twelf monthe and a day / to seche and lere	montħ leere
An answere suffisant in this matere	suffisant mateere
And seuretee wol I han / er that thow pace	suretee p*at* thou
Thy body / for to yelden / in this place	yelden
¶Wo was this knyght and sorwefully he siketh	Wo knygħt
But what he may nat doon / al as hym liketh	But he do /
And atte laste / he chees hym for to wende	at the laste /
And come agayn / right at the yeres ende	
With swich answere / as god wolde hym p*ur*ueye	
And taketh his leue / and wendeth forth his weye	
He seketh euery hous / and euery place	¶He seketh /
Where as he hopeth / for to fynde grace	
To lerne / what thyng wommen loue moost	wo*m*men louen
But he ne koude / arryuen in no coost	
Where as he myghte fynde / in this matere	Wher mygħte mateere
Two creatures / acordyng in feere	accordynge
¶So*m*me seyden / wommen louen best richesse	seyde / wo*m*men /
So*m*me seyde honour / so*m*me seyde Iolifnesse	Iolynesse
So*m*me riche array / so*m*me lust abedde	so*m*me seyden lust
And ofte tyme / to be widwe and wedde	wydwe
So*m*me seyde / that oure herte / is moost esed	¶So*m*me p*at* hertes / been moost
Whan that we been / yflatered and yplesed	¶Titus liueus]
He gooth ful ny the sothe / I wol nat lye	¶He
A man shal wynne vs best / with flaterye	man / best

[29] *Out* Hg 899. El reads:
¶The queene / thanketh the kyng w*ith* al hir mygħt

Par auenture / swich was the statut tho
But that the queene / and othere ladyes mo
So longe preyden / the kyng of grace
Til he his lyf / hym graunted in the place
And yaf hym to the queene / al at hir wille
To chese / wheither she wolde hym saue or spille
And after this / thus spak she to the knyght
Whan that she saugh hir tyme vp on a day
Thow standest yet quod she in swich array
That of thy lyf / yet hastow no suretee
I graunte thee lyf / if thow kanst tellen me
What thyng is it / þt wommen moost desiren
Be war / and keep thy nekke boon from iren
And if thow kanst nat / tellen me anon
Yet wol I yeue thee leue / for to gon
A twelf monthe and a day / to seche and lere
An answere suffisant / in this matere
And suretee wol I han / er that thow pace
Thy body / for to yelden in this place
Wo was this knyght / and sorwefully he siketh
But what / he may nat doon / al as hym liketh
And atte laste / he chees hym for to wende
And come agayn / right at the yeres ende
With swich answere / as god wolde hym purueye
And taketh his leue / and wendeth forth his weye
He seketh euery hous / and euery place
Where as he hopeth / for to fynde grace
To lerne / what thyng wommen loue moost
But he ne koude / arryuen in no coost
Where as he myghte fynde in this matere
Two creatures / acordyng in feere
Somme seyden / wommen louen best richesse
Somme seyde honour / somme seyde iolynesse
Somme riche array / somme lust abedde
And ofte tyme / to be wydwe and wedde
Somme seyde / that oure herte is moost esed
Whan that we been yflatered and yplesed
He gooth ful ny the sothe / I wol nat lye
A man shal wynne vs best / with flaterye

And with attendaunce and with bisynesse
Been we ylymed bothe moore and lesse
¶ And somme seyn þt we louen best
ffor to be free and do right as vs lest
And that no man repreue vs of oure vice
But seye þt we be wise and no thyng nyce
ffor trewely ther is noon of vs alle
If any wight wolde clawe vs on the galle
That we nyl kike for he seith vs sooth
Assay and he shal fynde it that so dooth
ffor be we neuer so vicious withinne
We wol be holden wise and clene of synne
¶ And somme seyn that greet delit han we
ffor to be holden stable and eek secree
And in o purpos stedefastly to dwelle
And nat biwreye thyng that men vs telle
But that tale is nat worth a rake stele
Pardee we wommen konne no thyng hele
Witnesse on Myda wol ye heere the tale
¶ Ouyde amonges othere thynges smale
Seyde Myda hadde vnder his longe herys
Growynge vp on his heed two asses erys
The which vice he hydde as he best myghte
fful subtilly from euery mannes sighte
That saue his wyf ther wiste of it na mo
He loued hire moost and trusted hire also
He preyed hire that to no creature
She sholde tellen of his disfigure
¶ She swoor hym nay for al this world to wynne
She nolde do that vileynye or synne
To make hir housbonde han so foul a name
She nolde nat telle it for hir owene shame
But nathelees hir thoughte þt she dyde
That she so longe sholde a conseil hyde
Hir thoughte it swal so sore aboute hir herte
That nedely som word hir moste asterte
And sith she dorste telle it to no man
Doun to a marys faste by she ran
Til she cam there hir herte was afyre
And as a bitore bombleth in the myre

And with attendaunce / and with bisynesse
Been we ylymed / bothe moore and lesse
¶And so*m*me seyn / þ*at* we louen best
For to be free / and do right as vs lestꝭ
And that no man / repreue vs of oure vice
But seye þ*at* we be wise / and no thyng nyce
For trewely / ther is noon of vs alle
If any wightꝭ wolde clawe vs on the galle
That we nyl kike / for he seith vs sooth
Assay / and he shal fynde itꝭ that so dooth
For be we / neu*er* so vicious / with Inne
We wol be holden wise / and clene of synne
¶And so*m*me seyn / that greet delit han we
For to be holden / stable and eek secree
And in o purpos / stedefastly to dwelle
And nat biwreye thyngꝭ that men vs telle
But that tale / is nat worth a Rake stele
Pardee / we wommen / konne no thyng hele
Witnesse on Mida / wol ye heere the tale
¶Ouyde / amonges othere thynges smale
Seyde / Mida / hadde vnder his longe herys
Growynge vp on his heed / two Asses erys
The which vice he hidde / as he best myghte
Ful sotilly / from euery mannes sighte
That saue his wyf / ther wiste of it na mo
He loued hir*e* moostꝭ and trusted hir*e* also
He preyed hir*e* / that to no creature
She sholde tellen / of his diffigure
¶She swoor hym nay / for al this world to wynne
She nolde do / that vileynye / or syn
To make hir housbonde / han so foul a name
She nolde nat telle itꝭ for hir owene shame
But nathelees / hir thoughte þ*at* she dyde
That she so longe / sholde a conseil hyde
Hir thoughte / it swal so soore aboute hir herte
That nedely / som word / hir moste asterte
And sith / she dorste nat telle it to no man
Doun to a Marys / faste by she ran
Til she cam there / hir herte was a fyre
And as a Bitore / bombleth in the Myre

ELLESMERE

attendance /
[30] that bestꝭ
righ̄t
wigh̄t / wol
nel
it þ*at*
vicious
been
been holden stable /
rake
Pardee wo*m*men / thyngꝭ
Myda /
Myda heres
eres
hydde /
subtilly / eu*ery*
namo
triste
preyde
disfigure
vileynye synne
soore /
word hir*e*
sith dorste / telle
Mareys /
Til ⁄ she

[30] ¶of Bathe *73r*

The Wyf of Bathe.⸗	ELLESMERE
She leyde hir mouth / vn to the water down	doun
Biwrey me nat' thow water with thy sown	Biwreye thou *with* soun
Quod she / to thee I telle it and namo	
Myn housbonde / hath longe Asses erys two	
Now is myn herte al hool / now it is oute	now is it oute
I myghte no lenger / kepe it out of doute	it'
Heere may ye see / thogh we a tyme abyde	se / thogħ
Yet out it moot' we kan no conseil hyde	
The remenant of the tale / if ye wol heere	
Redeth Ouyde / and ther ye may it leere	
¶This knyght' of which my tale is specially	31 THis knyghť / which /
Whan that he say / he myghte nat come ther by	saugħ / therby
This is to seye / what wommen louen moost'	loue
With Inne his brest' ful sorweful was the goost /	
But hom he gooth / he myghte nat soiorne	hoom myghte soio*ur*ne
The day was come / that homward moste he torne	*þat* to*ur*ne
And in his wey / it happed hym to ryde	
In al this care / vnder a Forest syde	
Wher as he say / vp on a daunce go	saugħ /
Of ladyes .xxiiij. and yet mo	ladyes / foure and twenty /
Toward the whiche daunce / he drow ful yerne	which
In hope / that som wisdom sholde he lerne	wysdom /
But *cer*teynly / er he cam fully there	certeinly /
Vanysshed was this daunce / he nyste where	Vanysshed
No creature say he / that bar lyf	saugħ
Saue on the grene / he say sittynge a wyf	saugħ
A fouler wight' ther may no man deuyse	wighť
Agayn the knyght' this olde wyf gan ryse	knyghť
And seyde sire knyght' heer forth ne lyth no wey	si*re* knyghť / lith
Tel me / what *þat* ye seken by youre fey	that seken / you*re*
Par auenture / it may the bettre be	P*ar*auenture /
This olde folk' konne muchel thyng quod she	Thise kan thyng'
¶My leeue moder / quod this knyght *cer*teyn	mooder' knyght
I nam but deed / but if that I kan seyn	nam ⁏ but
What thyng it is / that wommen moost desire	wo*m*men
Koude ye me wisse / I wolde wel quyte youre hyre	quite hire
¶Plight me thy trouthe / here in myn hand quod she	¶Plighť heere
The nexte thyng' that I requere thee	
Thow shalt it do / if it lye in thy myght'	Thou myghť
And I wol telle it yow / er it be nyght'	nyghť

[31] ¶Wyf *73v*

She leyde hir mouth / vn to the water doun
Biwrey me nat / thou water with thy soun
Quod she / to thee I telle it and namo
Myn housbonde / hath longe asses erys two
Now is myn herte al hool / now it is oute
I myghte no lenger / kepe it out of doute
Heere may ye se / thogh we a tyme abyde
Yet out it moot / we kan no conseil hyde
The remenant of the tale / if ye wol heere
Redeth Ovyde / and ther ye may it leere
This knyght / of which my tale is specially
Whan that he say / he myghte nat come ther by
This is to seye / what wommen louen moost /
With Inne his brest / ful sorweful was the goost /
But hom he gooth / he myghte nat soiorne
The day was come / that homward moste he torne
And in his wey / it happed hym to ryde
In al this care / vnder a fforest syde
Wher as he say / vp on a daunce go
Of ladyes .xxiiij. and yet mo
Toward the whiche daunce / he drow ful yerne
In hope / that som wysdom sholde he lerne
But certeinly / er he cam fully there
Vanysshed was this daunce / he nyste where
No creature say he / that bar lyf
Saue on the grene / he say sittynge a wyf
A fouler wight / ther may no man deuyse
Agayn the knyght / this olde wyf gan ryse
And seyde sire knyght / heer forth no lyth no wey
Tel me / what y^{t} ye seken by youre fey
Par auenture / it may the bettre be
Thise olde folk / konne muchel thyng quod she
My leue moder / quod this knyght certeyn
I nam but deed / but if that I kan seyn
What thyng it is / that wommen moost desire
Koude ye me wisse / I wolde wel quyte youre hyre
Plight me thy trouthe / heere in myn hand quod she
The nexte thyng / that I requere thee
Thou shalt it do / if it lye in thy myght /
And I wol telle it yow / er it be nyght /

haue here my trouthe quod the knyght I graunte
Thanne quod she I dar me wel auaunte
Thy lyf is sauf / for I wol stonde ther by
Vp on my lyf / the queene wol seye as I
Lat see / which is the proudeste of hem alle
That wereth on / a couerchief / or a calle
That dar seye nay / of that I shal thee teche
Lat vs go forth / with outen lenger speche
Tho rowned she / a pistel in his ere
And bad hym to be glad / and haue no fere
Whan they be comen to the court / this knyght
Seyde / he hadde holde his day / as he had hight
And redy was his answere / as he sayde
Ful many a noble wyf / and many a mayde
And many a wydwe / for þt they ben wise
The queene hir self / sittyng as Iustise
Assembled been / this answere for to here
And afterward / this knyght was bode appere
To euery wight / comanded was silence
And that the knyght / sholde telle in audience
What thyng / that worldly wommen louen best /
This knyght / ne stood nat stille as dooth a best /
But to his question / anon answerde
With manly voys / that al the court it herde
My lige lady / generally quod he
Wommen desire / to haue souereyntee
As wel ouer hir housbonde / as hir loue
And for to been in maistrie / hym aboue
This is youre mooste desir / though ye me kille
Dooth as yow list / I am here at youre wille
In al the court / ne was ther wyf ne mayde
Ne wydwe / that contraryed that he sayde
But seyden / he was worthy han his lyf
And with that word / vp stirte that olde wyf
Which that the knyght / say sittyng on the grene
Mercy quod she / my souereyn lady queene
Er that youre court departe / do me ryght /
I taughte this answere / vn to the knyght /
For which he plighte me his trouthe there
The firste thyng / I wolde hym requere

[¶Haue here my trouthe / quod the knyght I graunte
¶Thanne quod she / I dar me wel auaunte
Thy lyf is sauf / for I wole stonde ther by
Vp on my lyf / the queene wol seye as I
Lat see / which is the prouddeste of hem alle
That wereth on / a coue*r*chief / or a calle
That dar seye nay / of that I shal thee teche
Lat vs go forth / with outen lenger speche
Tho rowned she / a pistel in his ere
And bad hym to be glad / and haue no fere
¶When they be comen to the Courtꝭ this knyghtꝭ
Seyde / he hadde holde his day / as he had hightꝭ
And redy was his answere / as he sayde
Ful many a noble wyfꝭ and many a mayde
And many a widwe / for þ*at* they ben wise
The queene hir self / sittyng as Iustise
Assembled been / this answere for to here
And afterward / this knyght was bode appere
To euery wightꝭ comanded was silence
And that the knyghtꝭ sholde telle in audience
What thyngꝭ that worldly wommen louen bestꝭ
This knyghtꝭ ne stood nat stille as dooth a bestꝭ
But to his question / anon answerde
With manly voys / that al the court it herde
¶My lige lady / generally quod he
Wommen desire / to haue souereyntee
As wel / ouer hir housbonde / as hir loue
And for to been in maistrie / hym aboue
This is youre mooste desir / thogh ye me kille
Dooth as yow listꝭ I am here at youre wille
¶In al the Courtꝭ ne was ther wyf ne mayde
Ne wydwe / that contraryed that he sayde
But seyden / he was worthy han his lyf
¶And with that word / vp stirte that olde wyf
Which that the knyghtꝭ say sittyng on the grene
Mercy quod she / my soue*r*eyn lady queene
Er that youre Court departe / do me rightꝭ
I taughte this answere / vn to the knyghtꝭ
For which / he plighte me his trouthe there
The firste thyngꝭ I wolde hym requere

heer knyght grante
auante
wol therby

se / proudeste
coue*r*chiefꝭ

court / knyghtꝭ
had holde hadde hightꝭ

wyf /
wydwe / been
selfꝭ sittynge
been / his answere heere
afterward / knyghtꝭ appeere
32 ¶To wight /
knyght / Audience
wo*m*men
knyghtꝭ stille / doth best
questiou*n* /
W*ith*
generally /
desiren haue souereynetee
housbond
been / maistrie

am at
courtꝭ
contraried

stirte the olde
knyghtꝭ / saugh sittynge in the
she soueréyn
court rightꝭ
knyghtꝭ
me /

32 ¶of Bathe 74r

ꟷThe Wyf of Batheꟷ

ELLESMERE

He wolde it do / if it laye in his myght	lay myghꞇt
Bifore the court thanne preye I thee sire knyght	s*ir* knyghꞇt
Quod she / that thow me take vn to thy wyf	thou wyf
For wel thow woost that I haue kept thy lyf	thou lyf
If I seye fals / sey nay vp on thy fey	
¶This knyght answerde / allas and weilawey	knyghꞇt weylawey
I woot right wel / that swich was my biheste	
For goddes loue / as chees a newe requeste	
Taak al my good / and lat my body go	
¶Nay thanne quod she / I shrewe vs bothe two	
For thogh þ*at* I be foul / old / and poore	that oold
I nolde for al the metal / ne for oore	
That vnder erthe is graue // or lith aboue	
But if thy wyf I were / and eek thy loue	
¶My loue quod he / nay my dampnaciou*n*	he ꟷ
Allas / that any of my naciou*n*	
Sholde euere / so foule disp*ar*aged be	eu*er*e foule / disparaged
But al for noght thende is this / that he	noghꞇt
Constreyned was / he nedes moste hir wedde	hir*e*
And taketh his olde wyf / and goth to bedde	gooth
¶Now wolden som men / seye p*ar* auenture	p*ar*auenture
That for my necligence / I do no cure	
To tellen yow / the ioye / and al tharray	
That at the feste / was that ilke day	feeste was /
To which thyng shortly / answere I shal	thyng /. shortly
I seye / ther nas no ioye / ne feste at al	feeste
Ther nas but heuynesse / and muche sorwe	33
For p*ri*uely / he wedded hir*e* on morwe	on a morwe
And al day after hidde hym as an Owle	after /
So wo was hym / his wyf looked so foule	
¶Greet was the wo / the knyght hadde in his thoght	knyghꞇt thoghꞇt
Whan he was with his wyf / a bedde ybroght	wyf abedde ybroghꞇt /
He walweth / and he turneth to and fro	
His olde wyf / lay smylyng eu*er*e mo	smylynge eu*er*emo
And seyde / o deere housbonde benedicite	benedicitee
Fareth euery knyght thus with his wyf / as ye	eu*er*y knyghꞇt / w*ith* ye ꟷ
Is this the lawe / of kyng Arthures hous	kyng hous ꟷ
Is euery knyght of his / thus daungerous	knyghꞇt his so dangerous ꟷ
I am youre owene loue / and youre wyf	your*e* wyf /
I am she / which that saued hath youre lyf	þ*at* lyf /

33 ¶Wyf *74v*

He wolde it do / if it laye in his myght/
Bifore the court / thanne preye I thee sire knyght/
Quod she / that thow me take vn to thy wyf
ffor wel thow woost / that I haue kept thy lyf
If I seye fals / sey nay vp on thy fey
This knyght answerde / allas and weilawey
I woot right wel / that swich was my biheste
ffor goddes loue / as chees a newe requeste
Taak al my good / and lat my body go
Nay thanne quod she / I shrewe vs bothe two
ffor thogh þt I be foul / old / and poore
I nolde for al the metal / ne for oore
That vnder erthe is graue / or lith aboue
But if thy wyf I were / and eek thy loue
My loue quod he / nay my dampnacion
Allas / that any of my nacion
Sholde euere so foule disparaged be
But al for noght / the ende is this / that he
Constreyned was / he nedes moste hir wedde
And taketh his olde wyf / and goth to bedde
Now wolden som men seye parauenture
That for my necligence I do no cure
To tellen yow / the ioye and al tharray
That at the feste was that ilke day
To which thyng shortly answere I shal
I seye ther nas no ioye / ne feste at al
Ther nas but heuynesse / and muche sorwe
ffor priuely he wedded hire on morwe
And al day after / hidde hym as an owle
So wo was hym / his wyf looked so foule
Greet was the wo / the knyght hadde in his thoght/
Whan he was with his wyf / a bedde ybroght/
He walweth / and he turneth to and fro
His olde wyf lay smylyng eueremo
And seyde / o deere housbonde benedicite
ffareth euery knyght thus with his wyf / as ye
Is this the lawe of kyng Arthures hous
Is euery knyght of his / thus daungerous
I am youre owene loue / and youre wyf
I am she / which that saued hath youre lyf

And eek / yet ne dide I yow neuere vnright /
Why fare ye thus with me / this firste nyght /
Ye faren lyk a man / hadde lost his wit
What is my gilt / for goddes loue tel it
And it shal ben amended / if I may
¶ Amended quod this knyght / allas nay nay
It wol nat ben amended neuere mo
Thow art so loothly / and so old also
And ther to comen / of so lowe a kynde
That litel wonder is / thogh I walwe and wynde
So wolde god / myn herte wolde breste
¶ Is this quod she / the cause of youre vnreste
¶ Ye certeinly quod he / no wonder is
¶ Now sire quod she / I koude amende al this
If that me liste / er it were dayes thre
So wel ye myghte / bere yow vn to me

Nota bene ¶ But for ye speken / of swich gentillesse
As is descended / out of old richesse
That therfore / sholden ye be gentil men
Swich arrogance / is nat worth an hen
Looke who þt is / moost vertuous alway
Pryuee and apert / and moost entendeth ay
To do the gentil dedes þt he kan
Taak hym / for the gentileste man
Crist wol we clayme of hym oure gentillesse
Nat of oure eldres / for hir old richesse
ffor thogh they yeue vs / al hir heritage
ffor which we claime / to been of hir parage
Yet may they nat biquethe / for no thyng /
To noon of vs / hir vertuous lyuyng /
That made hem / gentil men ycalled be
And bad vs / folwen hem in swich degree
¶ Wel kan / the wise poete of fflorence
That highte Dant / speken in this sentence
Lo / in swich maner rym / is Dantes tale
fful selde vp riseth / by his branches smale
Prowesse of man / for god of his prowesse
Wole /. that of hym / we clayme oure gentillesse
ffor of oure eldres / may we no thyng clayme
But temporel thyng / that man may hurte and mayme

	ELLESMERE
And c*er*tes / yet ne dide I yow neu*er*e vnright	vnright /
Why fare ye thus with me / this firste nyght	nyght / /
Ye faren lyk a man / hadde lost his wit	had wit
What is my gilt / for goddes loue tel it	gilt /
And it shal ben amended / if I may	been
¶Amended quod this knyght allas nay / nay	knyght / allas / nay / nay /
It wol nat ben amended neu*er*e mo	been
Thow art so loothly / and so old also	Thou oold
And ther to comen / of so lowe a kynde	lough
That litel wonder is / thogh I walwe and wynde	
So wolde god / myn herte wolde breste	
¶Is this quod she / the cause of youre vnreste	vnreste /
¶Ye c*er*teynly quod he / no wonder is	certeinly
¶Now sire quod she / I koude amende al this	
If that me liste / er it were dayes thre	
So wel ye myghte / bere yow vn to me	myghte /
¶No*ta* bene ¶But for ye speken / of swich gentillesse	¶De gen*er*ositate] Bvt
As is descended / out of old richesse	
That therfore / sholden ye be gentil men	
Swich errogau*n*ce / is nat worth an hen	arrogance /
Looke who þ*at* is / moost v*er*tuous alway	Looke / that
Pryuee and apert and moost entendeth ay	
To do / the gentil dedes / þ*at* he kan	dedes that
Taak hym / for the gentileste man	the grettest ⟨gentil man⟩
Crist / wol we clayme of hym oure gentilesse	Crist wole / gentillesse
Nat of oure eldres / for hir old richesse	hir*e*
For thogh they yeue vs / al hir heritage	
For which we clame / to been of hir parage	clayme / of heigh parage
Yet may they nat biquethe / for no thyng	
To noon of vs / hir vertuous lyuyng	
That made hem / gentil men ycalled be	
And bad vs / folwen hem in swich degree	
¶Wel kan / the wise poete of Florence	Poete
That highte Dant speken in this sentence	
Lo / in swich maner rym / is Dantes tale	34 ¶Lo /
Ful selde vp riseth / by his brau*n*ches smale	branches
Prowesse of man / for god of his prowesse	his goodnesse |
Wole /. that of hym / we clayme oure gentilesse	Wole / gentillesse
For of oure eldres / may we no thyng clayme	
But temporel thyng that man may hurte and mayme	þ*at* *and*

34 ¶of Bathe *75r*

The Wyf of Bathe.∫	ELLESMERE
Eek eu*er*y wight⁊ woot this as wel I	¶Eek euery wigħt⁊ wel as I
If gentilesse / were planted naturelly	gentillesse / natureelly
Vn to a c*er*teyn lynage / doun the lyne	certeyn
Pryuee and apert⁊ thanne wolde they neu*er*e fyne	Pryuee nor apert⁊
To doon / of gentilesse / the faire office	doon gentillesse /
They myghte do / no vileynye or vice	mygħte
¶Taak fyr / and bere it in the derkeste hous	ber it⁊
Bitwix this / and the mount of kaukasous	mount⁊
And lat men shette the dores / and go thenne	men / dores
Yet wol the fyr / as faire lye and brenne	wole
As twenty thousand men / myghte it biholde	
His office naturel / ay wol it holde	natureel /
Vp p*er*il of my lyf⁊ til that it dye	lyf /
Here may ye se wel / how *þat* genterye	¶Heere [¶exemplum]
Is nat annexed / to possessiou*n*	annexed
Sith folk⁊ ne doon hir op*er*aciou*n*	
Alwey / as dooth the fyr lo in his kynde	Alwey fyr /
For god it woot⁊ men may wel often fynde	
A lordes sone / do shame and vileynye	
And he *þat* wol han prys / of his gentrye	wole / pris
For he was born / of a gentil hous	
And hadde hise eldres / noble and v*er*tuous	eldres
And nyl hym seluen / do no gentil dedis	nel
Ne folwen his gentil Auncestre / that deed is	Auncestre *þat*
He nys nat gentil / be he Duc⁊ or Erl	
For vileynes synful dedes / maken a cherl	vileyns make
For gentilesse / nys but renomee	gentillesse /
Of thyne Auncestres / for hir hye bou*n*tee	hir*e* heigħ
Which is straunge thyng⁊ for thy p*er*sone	is a strange thyng⁊ to thy
Thy gentilesse / cometh fro god allone	gentillesse /
Thanne comth / oure verray gentilesse of g*ra*ce	gentillesse
It was no thyng⁊ biquethe vs / with oure place	thyng / vs
¶Thenketh how noble / as seith Valerius	hou
Was thilke / Tullius hostillius	
That out of pouerte / roos to heigh noblesse	pou*er*te / heigħ
Redeth Senek⁊ and redeth eek Boece	Reed Senek /
Ther shul ye seen expres / *þat* no drede is	
That he is gentil / that dooth gentil dedis	
And ther fore / leue housbonde / I thus conclude	therfore leeue
Al were it⁊ that myne Auncestres weren rude	it /

The Wyf of Bathe :

Eek eu(er)y wight / woot this as wel I
If gentilesse / were planted natureelly
Vn to a certeyn lynage / doun the lyne
Pryuee and apert / thanne wolde they neu(er)e fyne
To doon of gentilesse / the faire office
They myghte do / no vileynye or vice
Taak fyr / and bere it in the derkeste hous
Bitwix this / and the mount of kaukasous
And lat men shette the dores / and go thenne
yet wol the fyr / as faire lye and brenne
As twenty thousand men / myghte it biholde
His office natureel / ay wol it holde
Vp peril of my lyf / til that it dye
Heere may ye se wel / how þt genterye
Is nat annexed / to possessioun
Sith folk ne doon hir operacioun
Alwey / as dooth the fyr / lo in his kynde
ffor god it woot / men may wel often fynde
A lordes sone / do shame and vileynye
And he þt wol han prys / of his gentrye
ffor he was born / of a gentil hous
And hadde hise eldres / noble and v(er)tuous
And nyl hym seluen / do no gentil dedis
Ne folwen his gentil auncestre / that deed is
He nys nat gentil / be he duc or Erl
ffor vileynes synful dedes / maken a cherl
ffor gentilesse / nys but renomee
Of thyne auncestres / for hir heye bountee
Which is straunge thyng / for thy p(er)sone
Thy gentilesse / cometh fro god allone
Thanne comth oure verray gentilesse of grace
It was no thyng / biquethe vs / with oure place
Thenketh how noble / as seith Valerius
Was thilke / Tullius hostillius
That out of pouerte / roos to heigh noblesse
Reedeth Senek / and redeth eek Boece
Ther shul ye seen expres / þt no drede is
That he is gentil / that dooth gentil dedis
And therfore leue housbonde / I thus conclude
Al were it / that myne auncestres weren rude

yet may the hye god / and so hope I
Grante me grace / to lyuen vertuously
Thanne am I gentil / whan þt I bigynne
To lyuen vertuously / and weyue synne
And ther as ye / of pouerte me repreue
The hye god / on whom þt we bileue
In wilful pouerte / chees to lyue his lyf
And certes euery man / mayden or wyf
May vnderstonde / þt Ihesus heuene kyng
Ne wolde nat chese / a vicious lyuyng
Glad pouerte / is an honeste thyng certeyn
This wol Senek / and othere clerkes seyn
Who so þt halt hym payd / of his pouerte
I holde hym riche / al hadde he nat a sherte
He that coueiteth / is a poure wight
ffor he wolde han / that is nat in his myght
But he þt noght hath / ne coueiteth haue
Is riche / al thogh we holde hym but a knaue
Verray pouerte / is synne proprely
Iuuenal seith / of pouerte myrily
The poure man / whan he gooth by the weye
Biforn the theues / he may synge and pleye
Pouerte is hateful good / and as I gesse
A ful greet bryngere / out of bisynesse
A greet amendere eek of Sapience
To hym / that taketh it in pacience
Pouerte is thyng / al thogh it seme elenge
Possessioun / that no wight wol chalenge
Pouerte ful ofte / whan a man is lowe
Maketh hym self / and eek his god to knowe
Pouerte a spectacle is / as thynketh me
Thurgh which he may / his verray freendes se
And ther fore sire / syn þt I noght yow greue
Of my pouerte / namoore ye me repreue
Now sire of elde / ye repreue me
And certes sire / thogh noon auctoritee
Were in no book / ye gentils of honour
Seyn þt men an old wight / sholde doon fauour
And clepe hym fader / for youre gentilesse
And auctours / shal I fynden / as I gesse

	ELLESMERE
Yet may the hye god / and so hope I /	.I.
Graunte me grace / to lyuen v*er*tuously	Grante
Thanne am I gentil / whan þ*a*t I bigynne	35 that
To lyuen v*er*tuously / and weyue synne	
¶And ther as ye / of pou*er*te me repreue	¶De paup*er*tate] ANd pouerte repreeue
The hye god / on whom þ*a*t we bileue	bileeue
In wilful pou*er*te / chees to lyue his lyf	pouerte / lyf'
And certes euery man / mayden / or wyf	certes / mayden wyf /
May vnderstonde / þ*a*t Ie*s*us heuene kyng'	that
Ne wolde nat chese / a vicious lyuyng'	chesen vicious
Glad pou*er*te / is an honeste thyng c*er*teyn	certeyn
This wol Senek' and othere clerkes seyn	wole Senec'
Who so þ*a*t halt hym payd / of his pouerte	payd
I holde hym riche / al hadde he nat a sherte	
He that coueiteth / is a poure wight'	þ*a*t pouere wiħt'
For he wolde han / that is nat in his myght'	myħt'
But he þ*a*t noght hath / ne coueiteth haue	noħt
Is riche / al thogh we holde hym but a knaue	though ye holde
Verray pouerte / is synne p*ro*prely	¶Verray pou*er*te / it syngeth p*ro*prely
Iuuenal seith / of pouerte myrily	Iuuenal / seith pou*er*te
¶The poure man / whan he gooth by the weye	The goth
Biforn the theues / he may synge and pleye	Bifore
Pouerte is hateful good / and as I gesse	Pou*er*te
A ful greet bryngere / out of bisynesse	
A greet amendere eek' of Sapience	amender*e* eek sapience
To hym / that taketh it in pacience	
Pouerte is thyng' al thogh it seme elenge	is this / al though alenge
Possessiou*n* / that no wight wol chalenge	wiħt'
Pouerte ful often / whan a man is lowe	Pou*er*te ofte /
Maketh hym self / and eek his god to knowe	Maketh his god / and eek hym self to
Pouerte / a spectacle is / as thynketh me	Pou*er*te /
Thurgh which he may / his verray freendes se	Thurħ hise see
And ther fore sire / syn þ*a*t I noght yow greue	therfore noħt
Of my pouerte / namoore ye me repreue	
¶Now sire / of elde ye repreue me	¶De senectute] NOw elde /
And c*er*tes sire / thogh noon auctoritee	certes Auctoritee
Were in no book / ye gentils of honour	
Seyn / þ*a*t men an old wight' sholde doon fauour	men sholde / an oold wiħt doon fauo*ur*
And clepe hym fader / for youre gentilesse	fader' gentillesse
And Auctours / shal I fynden / as I gesse	fynden

1182 Seneca in epistola
Honesta res est leta paupertas El

1186 Pauper est qui eget eo quod non habet sed qui non habet nec appetit habere ille diues est de quo intelligitur id Apocalypsis 3° dicis quia diues sum El

1193 Cantabit vacuus coram latrone viator et nocte ad lumen trepidabit Arundinis vmbram El

1195 Secundus Philosophus Paupertas est odibile bonum sanitatis mater curarum remocio sapientie reparatrix possessio sine calumpnia El

1202 Vnde et Crates ille Thebanus Proiecto in mari non perno auri pondere Abite inquit pessime male cupiditates ego vos mergam ne ipse mergar a vobis El

[35] ¶Wyf *75v*

	ELLESMERE
¶Now ther ye seye / that I am foul and old	¶De t*ur*pitudine] NOw þ*a*t old
Thanne drede yow noght to been a Cokewold	Than you noght / Cokewold
For filthe and elde / al so mote I thee	eelde / moot
Been grete wardeyns / vp on chastitee	
But nathelees / syn I knowe youre delit /	delit
I shal fulfille / youre worldly appetit	
¶Chees now quod she / oon of thise thynges tweye	¶Chese
To han me foul and old / til that I deye	old /
And be to yow / a trewe humble wyf	wyf
And neu*er*e yow displese / in al my lyf	lyf /
Or ellis / ye wol han me / yong and fair	36 elles / me
And take youre auenture / of the repair	
That shal be to youre hous / by cause of me	
Or in som oother place / may wel be	
Now chees your seluen / wheither þ*a*t yow liketh	chese
¶This knyght auyseth hym / and soore siketh	knyght hym sore
But atte laste / he seyde in this manere	
My lady and my loue / and wyf so deere	
I putte me / in youre wise gouernau*n*ce	put gouernance
Cheseth your*e* self which þ*a*t may be moost plesau*n*ce	self / which may plesance
And moost honour to yow / and me also	honour yow
I do no fors / the wheither of the two	wheither
For as yow liketh / it suffiseth me	
¶Thanne haue I gete / of yow maistrye / quod she	gete yow / maistrie
Syn I may chese / and gouerne as me lest	gou*er*ne
¶Ye c*er*tes wyf quod he / I holde it best	certes
¶Kys me quod she / we be no lenger wrothe	
For by my trouthe / I wol be to yow bothe	
This is to seyn / ye bothe fair and good	
I pray to god / that I mote steruen wood	prey þ*a*t moote
But I to yow / be al so good and trewe	also
As euere was wyf / syn þ*a*t the world was newe	eu*er*e
And but I be to morn / as fair to sene	tomorn / seene
As any lady / Emperice / or Queene	Emperice queene
That is bitwix the Est and eek the West	bitwixe eke West
Do with my lyf and deth / right as yow lest	Dooth wit*h* lyf / right
Cast vp the Curtyn / looke how þ*a*t it is	curtyn / that
And whan the knyght say verraily al this	¶And knyght saugh ve*r*raily
That she so fair was / and so yong ther to	
For ioye he hente hir*e* / in his armes two	ioye / hise

36 ¶of Bathe 76*r*

The Wif of Bathe·

Now ther ye seye that I am foul and old
Thanne drede yow noght to been a Cokewold
For filthe and elde also moot I thee
Been grete wardeyns vp on chastitee
But nathelees syn I knowe youre delit
I shal fulfille youre worldly appetit
Chese now quod she oon of thise thynges tweye
To han me foul and old til that I deye
And be to yow a trewe humble wyf
And neuere yow displese in al my lyf
Or ellis ye wol han me yong and fair
And take youre auenture of the repair
That shal be to youre hous by cause of me
Or in som oother place may wel be
Now chese your seluen wheither þt yow liketh
This knyght auyseth hym and sore siketh
But atte laste he seyde in this manere
My lady and my loue and wyf so deere
I putte me in youre wise gouernance
Cheseth youre self which þt may be moost plesance
And moost honour to yow and me also
I do no fors the wheither of the two
For as yow liketh it suffiseth me
Thanne haue I gete of yow maistrie quod she
Syn I may chese and gouerne as me lest
Ye certes wyf quod he I holde it best
Kys me quod she we be no lenger wrothe
For by my trouthe I wol be to yow bothe
This is to seyn ye bothe fair and good
I pray to god that I mote steruen wood
But I to yow be also good and trewe
As euere was wyf syn þt the world was newe
And but I be to morn as fair to seene
As any lady Emperice or Queene
That is bitwix the Est and eek the West
Do with my lyf and deth right as yow lest
Cast vp the curtyn looke how þt it is
And whan the knyght say verraily al this
That she so fair was and so yong therto
For ioye he hente hire in his armes two

his herte bathed in a bath of blisse
A thousand tyme a rewe he gan hir kisse
And she obeyed hym in euery thyng
That myghte do hym plesance or likyng
And thus they lyue vn to hir lyues ende
In parfit ioye and Ihesu crist vs sende
Housbondes meke yonge and fressh a bedde
And grace to ouerbyde hem that we wedde
And eek I praye Ihesu shorte hir lyues
That noght wol be gouerned by hir wyues
And olde and angry nygardes of dispence
God sende hem soone verray pestilence

Here endeth the Wyues tale of Bathe

The prologe of the ffreres tale

This worthy lymytour this noble frere
He made alwey a maner louryng chiere
Vp on the Somonour but for honestee
No vileyns word as yet to hym spak he
But atte laste he seyde vn to the wyf
Dame quod he god yeue yow right good lyf
Ye han heer touched also moote I thee
In scole matere greet difficultee
Ye han seyd muche thyng right wel I seye
But dame heere as we ryden by the weye
Vs nedeth nat to speken but of game
And lete auctoritees on goddes name
To prechyng and to scole of clergye
But if it like to this compaignye
I wol yow of a Somonour telle a game
Pardee ye may wel knowe by the name
That of a Somonour may no good be sayd
I praye that noon of yow be yuele apayd
A Somonour is a rennere vp and doun
With mandementz for fornicacioun
And is ybet at euery townes ende
Oure hoost tho spak a sire ye sholde be hende

His herte bathed / in a bath of blisse	
A thousand tyme a rewe / he gan hir kisse	arewe / hir*e*
And she obeyed hym / in euery thyng	hym
That myghte do hym plesance / or likyng	doon plesance
And thus they lyue / vn to hir lyues ende	¶And
In p*ar*fit ioye / and Ies*u* crist vs sende	
Housbondes meke / yonge / and fressħ a bedde	meeke /
And grace / tou*er*byde hem that we wedde	þ*a*t
And eek / I praye Ies*u* shorte hir lyues	pray
That noght wol be gou*er*ned / by hir wyues	nat gou*er*ned
And olde / and angry nygardes of dispence	
God sende hem soone / verray pestilence	
¶Here endeth the Wyues tale of Bathe	¶Heere endeth / the Wyues tale of Bathe
¶The prologe of the Freres tale	¶The prologe of the freres tale[1]
This worthy lymytour / this noble frere	
He made alwey / a manere louryng cheere	maner chiere
Vp on the Somnour / but for honestee	Somono*ur* /
No vileyns word / as yet to hym spak he	
But atte laste / he seyde vn to the wyf	
¶Dame quod he god yeue yow right good lyf	Dame he / right
Ye han heer touched / al so mote I thee	also moot
In scole matere / greet difficultee	
Ye han seyd muche thyng right wel I seye	right
But dame / here as we ryden by the weye	heere ryde
Vs nedeth nat to speken / but of game	nat. speken
And lete Auctoritees / on goddes name	lete /
To prechyng and to scole of clergye	pr*e*chyng Scole
But if it like / to this compaignye	And if lyke /
I wol yow / of a Somnour telle a game	Somono*ur*
Pardee / ye may wel knowe by the name	
That of a Somno*ur* / may no good be sayd	Somono*ur* / sayd
I praye / that noon of yow / be ypayd	þ*a*t you / be yuele apayd
A somnour / is a rennere vp and doun	Somono*ur* / renner*e*
With mandementz / for fornicacioun	
And is ybet at euery townes ende	
¶Oure hoost tho spak / a sire ye sholde be hende	

And curteys

[1] ¶Frere *76v*

74r Quire 11[8] (begins)

.The Frere.

And curteys / as a man of youre estaat
In compaignye / we wol no debaat
Telleth youre tale / and lat the Somno*ur* be
¶Nay quod the Somno*ur* / lat hym seye to me
What so hym list when it comth to my lot
By god / I shal hym quyten euery grot
I shal hym telle / which a gret honour
It is / to be a flaterynge lymytour
And of / many another maner*e* cryme
Which nedeth nat rehercen / for this tyme
And his office / I shal hym telle ywys
¶Oure hoost answerde / pees namoore of this
And after this / he seyde vn to the frere
Tel forth youre tale / leeue maister deere

¶Here endeth the prologe of the Frere and bigynneth his tale

WHilom / ther was dwellynge in my contree
An Erchedekne / a man of hy degree
That boldely / dide execuciou*n*
In punysshynge of Fornicaciou*n*
Of wicchecraft and eek of Bawderye
Of diffamaciou*n* / and auoutrye
Of chirche Reues / and of testamentz
Of contractes / and eek of lakke of sacramentz
Of vsure / and of Symonye also
But c*er*tes / lecchours / dide he grettest wo
They sholde synge⟨n if that they were hent⟩
And smale tyth⟨eres were foule yschent⟩
If any p*er*sou*n* / ⟨wold vp on hem pleyne⟩
Ther myghte ⟨asterte hym no pecunial peyne⟩
For smale ⟨tithes *and* for smal offryng⟩
He made the ⟨peple ful pitusly to syng⟩
For er the ⟨bysschop caght hem w*ith* hys hooc⟩
They were ⟨in the erchdeknys book / ⟩
And thanne ⟨had he thurgh hys Iurisdiccion⟩
Power / to ⟨do on hem correccion⟩

ELLESMERE

youre estaat
wol haue no
Somono*ur*
Somono*ur* /

quiten
tellen / greet

of
nat rehercen
ywis

¶Heere bigynneth the Freres tale

2 WHilom dwellynge /
Erchedekene / heigh

punysshynge / fornicaciou*n*
3 bawderye
Auowtrye

cont*ra*ctes / eek

lecchours
syngen / if þ*at* they were hent
tytheres / weren foule yshent
p*er*sou*n* / wolde vp on hem pleyne
myghte asterte hym / no pecunyal peyne
tithes / and smal offrynge
peple / pitously to synge
bisshop*e* / caughte hym with his hook
in the Erchedeknes book
thanne / hadde he / thurgh his Iurisdicciou*n*
doon on hem correcciou*n*

[2] Miniature of the Friar in left margin.

[3] ¶Frere 77*r*

And curteys as a man of youre estaat
In compaignye we wol no debaat
Telleth youre tale and lat the Somnour be
Nay quod the Somnour lat hym seye to me
What so hym list whan it comth to my lot
By god I shal hym quyten euery grot
I shal hym telle which a greet honour
It is to be a flaterynge lymytour
And of many another manere cryme
Which nedeth nat reherten for this tyme
And his office I shal hym telle ywys
Oure hoost answerde pees namoore of this
And after this he seyde vn to the frere
Tel forth youre tale leeue maister deere

Here endeth the prologe of the ffrere and bigynneth his tale

Whilom ther was dwellynge in my contree
An erchedekne a man of hy degree
That boldely dide execucion
In punysshynge of fornicacion
Of wicchecraft and eek of bawderye
Of diffamacion and auoutrye
Of chirche reues and of testamentz
Of contractes and eek of lakke of sacramentz
Of vsure and of Symonye also
But certes lecchours dide he grettest wo
They sholde syngen if that they were hent
And smale tytheres were foule yshent
If any person wolde vpon hem pleyne
Ther myghte asterte hym no pecunial peyne
ffor smale tithes and for smal offrynge
He made the peple ful pitously to synge
ffor er the bysshop caughte hem with his hook
They were in the erchedeknes book
And thanne hadde he thurgh his iurisdiccion
Power to doon hem correccion

He hadde a Somnour / redy to his hond
A slyer boy / nas noon in Engelond
ffor subtilly / he hadde his espiaille
That taughte hym / wher hym myghte auaille
He koude spare / of lecchours / oon or two
To techen hym / to foure and twenty mo
ffor though this Somnour / wood were as an hare
To telle his harlotrye / I wol nat spare
ffor we been / out of his correccioun
They han of vs / no Iurisdiccioun
Ne neuere shullen / terme of hir lyues
Peter / so been wommen of the Styues
Quod the Somonour / yput out of my cure
Pees with myschaunce and with mysauenture
Thus seyde oure hoost / and lat hym telle his tale
Now telleth forth / though þt the Somnour gale
Ne spareth nat / myn owene maister deere
This false theef / this Somnour / quod the frere
Hadde alwey / baudes redy to his hond
As any hauk to lure in Engelond
That tolde hym / al the secree þt they knewe
ffor hire aqueyntance was nat come of newe
They weren hise approwours pryuely
He took hym self / a greet profit ther by
His maister knew nat alwey / what he wan
With outen mandement / a lewed man
He koude somne / on peyne of Cristes curs
And they were glade / for to fille his purs
And make hym / grete festes atte nale
And right as Iudas / hadde purses smale
And was a theef / right swich a theef was he
His maister / hadde but half his duetee
He was / if I shal yeuen hym his laude
A theef / and eek a Somnour / and a baude
He hadde eek wenches / at his retenue
That wheither þt Sir Robert / or Sir Huwe
Or Iakke / or Rauf / or who so that it were
That lay by hem / they tolde it in his ere
Thus was the wenche and he / of oon assent
And he wolde fecche / a feyned mandement /

	ELLESMERE
He hadde a Somno*ur* / redy to his hond	Somono*ur* / hondꝭ
A slyer boy / nas noon in Engelond	boye / Engelondꝭ
For subtilly / he hadde his espiaille	
That taughte hym / wher hym myghte auaille	mygħte
He koude spare / of lecchours / oon or two	spare
To techen hym / to foure and twenty mo	
For theigh this Somno*ur* / wood were as an hare	thogh Somono*ur* / was
To telle his harlotrye / I wol nat spare	
For we been / out of his correcciou*n*	
They han of vs / no Iurisdicciou*n*	vs
Ne neu*er*e shullen / terme of hir lyues	
¶Peter / so been wommen of the Styves	been / wo*m*men
Quod the Somnour / yput out of my cure	Somono*ur* /
¶Pees with myschaunce / and with mysauenture	myschance / *with* mysauenture
Thus seyde oure hoost / and lat hym telle his tale	hoost⁊
Now telleth forth / thogh *þat* the Somno*ur* gale	somono*ur*
Ne spareth nat⁊ myn owene mayster deere	maister
¶This false theef⁊ this Somno*ur* / quod the frere	Somono*ur*
Hadde alwey / baudes redy to his hond	bawdes hondꝭ
As any hauk⁊ to lure in Engelond	Engelondꝭ
That tolde hym / al the secree *þat* they knewe	
For hire aqueyntance / was nat come of newe	hir*e*
They weren / hise Approwours pryuely	approwours p*ri*uely
He took hym self / a greet p*ro*fit ther by	therby
His maister knew nat alwey / what he wan	nat /
With outen mandement⁊ a lewed man	mandement /
He koude somne / on peyne of cristes curs	Cristes
And they were glade / for to fille his purs	
And make hym / grete festes atte nale	feestes
And right as Iudas / hadde purses smale	rigħt
And was a theef⁊ right swich a theef was he	rigħt⁊
His maister / hadde but half his duetee	maister⁊ hadde /
He was / if I shal yeuen hym his laude	[4]
A theef / and eek a somnour / and a baude	eek / Somnour /
He hadde eek wenches / at his retenue	
That wheither *þat* sir Rob*er*t / or sir*e* hewe	wheither / Rob*er*t sir Huwe
Or Iakke / or Rauf⁊ or who so that it were	Rauf / *þat*
That lay by hem / they tolde it in his ere	
Thus was the wenche and he / of oon assent⁊	¶Thus
And he wolde fecche / a feyned mandement⁊	

[4] ¶Frere *77v*

./The Frere./	ELLESMERE
And somne hem to Chapitre / bothe two	
And pile the man / and lete the wenche go	
¶Thanne wolde he seye / freend I shal for thy sake	
Do stryke hir*e* / out of oure lettres blake	striken
Thee thar namoore / as in this cas t*ra*uaille	
I am thy freend / ther I thee may auaille	
Certeyn / he knew of bryberyes mo	bribryes
Than possible is / to telle in yeres two	
For in this world / nys dogge for the bowe	
That kan an hurt deer / from an hool knowe	
Bet than this Somno*ur* / knew a sly lecchour	Bet / Somnour /
Or an Auouter / or a p*ar*amour	Auowtier /
And for that was / the fruyt of al his rente	fruyt
Ther fore on it / he sette al his entente	Therfore it
¶And so bifel / that ones on a day	
This Somnour / eu*er*e waityng on his pray	Somno*ur* / waityng
For to somne an old wydewe / a Ribibe	wydwe
Feynynge a cause / for he wolde brybe	
Happed / that he say / bifore hym ryde	saugh
A gay yeman / vnder a Forest syde	
A bowe he bar / and arwes brighte *and* kene	Arwes and
He hadde vp on / a courtepy of grene	
An hat vp on his heed / with frenges blake	
¶Sir*e* quod this Somno*ur* / hayl / and wel atake	hayl
¶Wel come quod he / and euery good felawe	
Wher*e* ridestow / vnder this grene shawe	Wher rydestow / grene wode shawe./
Seyde this yeman / wiltow fer to day	day./
¶This Somnour hym answerde / and seyde nay	Somno*ur*
Here faste by quod he / is myn entente	Heere
To ryden / for to reysen vp a rente	
That longeth / to my lordes duetee	
¶Artow thanne a Bailly./ / ye quod he	bailly./ he./
He dorste nat for verray filthe and shame	
Seye *pa*t he was a Somno*ur* / for the name	somono*ur* /
¶Dep*ar*dieux quod this yeman / deere brother	broother
Thow art a bailly / and I am another	Thou
I am vnknowen / as in this contree	
Of thyn aqueyntance / I wolde praye thee	
And eek of bretherhede / if *pa*t yow leste	
I haue gold / and siluer in my cheste	siluer

And somne hem to chapitre / bothe two
And pile the man / and lete the wenche go
Thanne wolde he seye / ffreend I shal for thy sake
Do stryke hire out of oure lettres blake
Thee thar namoore / as in this cas trauaille
I am thy freend / ther I thee may auaille
Certeyn / he knew of bryberyes mo
Than possible is / to telle in yeres two
ffor in this world / nys dogge for the bowe
That kan an hurt deer / from an hool knowe
Bet than this Somnour / knew a sly lecchour
Or an Auouter / or a paramour
And for that was / the fruyt of al his rente
Ther fore on it he sette al his entente
And so bifel / that ones on a day
This Somnour / euer waityng on his pray
ffor to somne an old wydwe / a ribibe
ffeynynge a cause / for he wolde brybe
Happed that he say / bifore hym ryde
A gay yeman / vnder a fforest syde
A bowe he bar / and arwes brighte & kene
He hadde vp on / a courtepy of grene
An hat vp on his heed / with frenges blake
Sire quod this Somnour / hayl and wel atake
Wel come quod he / and euery good felawe
Wher rydestow / vnder this grene shawe
Seyde this yeman / wiltow fer to day
This Somnour hym answerde / and seyde nay
Heere faste by quod he / is myn entente
To ryden / for to reysen vp a rente
That longeth / to my lordes duetee
Artow thanne a Bailly / ye quod he
He dorste nat / for verray filthe and shame
Seye that he was a Somnour / for the name
Depardieux quod this yeman / deere brother
Thow art a Bailly / and I am another
I am vnknowen / as in this contree
Of thyn aqueyntance / I wolde praye thee
And eek of bretherhede / if that yow leste
I haue gold / and siluer in my cheste

If that thee happe to come in oure shire
Al shal be thyn right as thow wolt desire
¶ Grauntmercy quod this Somonour by my feith
Everich in otheres hond his trouthe leith
For to be sworn bretheren til they deye
In daliaunce they ryden forth and pleye
¶ This Somonour which that was as ful of jangles
As ful of venym been thise waryangles
And evere enqueryng upon every thyng
Brother quod he where is now youre dwellyng
Another day if that I sholde yow seche
This yeman hym answerde in softe speche
¶ Brother quod he fer in the North contree
Wher as I hope som tyme I shal thee see
Er we departe I shal thee so wel wisse
That of myn hous ne shaltow nevere mysse
¶ Now brother quod this Somonour I yow preye
Teche me whil that we ryden by the weye
Syn that ye been a Baillyf as am I
Som subtiltee and tel me feithfully
In myn office how I may moost wynne
And spareth nat for conscience ne synne
But as my brother tel me how do ye
¶ Now by my trouthe brother deere seyde he
As I shal tellen thee a feithful tale
My wages been ful streyte and ful smale
My lord is hard to me and daungerous
And myn office is ful laborous
And therfore by extorcions I lyve
For sothe I take al that men wol me yeve
Algate by sleighte or by violence
Fro yeer to yeer I wynne al my dispence
I kan no bettre tellen feithfully
¶ Now certes quod this Somonour so fare I
I spare nat to taken god it woot
But it be to hevy or to hoot
What I may gete in conseil prively
No maner conscience of that have I
Nere myn extorcion I myghte nat lyven
Ne of swiche japes wol I nat be shryven

	ELLESMERE
If that thee happed / to come in oure shire	[5] happe / comen
Al shal be thyn / right as thow wolt desire	thou
¶Graunt m*er*cy quod this Somno*ur* / by my feith	¶Grantm*er*cy Somono*ur* /
Euerich in ootheres hond / his trouthe leyth	Eu*er*ych hand / leith
For to be sworn bretheren / til they deye	
In daliaunce / they ryden forth and pleye	daliance / forth hir weye
¶This Somno*ur* / which þ*at* was / as ful of Iangles	Somono*ur* / that was
As ful of venym / been thise waryangles	venym
And eu*er*e enqueryng vp on euery thyng	
Brother quod he / wher*e* is now youre dwellyng	where youre
Another day / if þ*at* I sholde yow seche	
This yeman hym answerde / in softe speche	
¶Brother quod he / fer in the North contree	
Wher*e* as I hope / som tyme I shal thee see	somtyme
Er we departe / I shal thee so wel wisse	
That of myn hous / ne shaltow neu*er*e mysse	
¶Now brother quod this Somno*ur* / I yow preye	Somono*ur* /
Teche me / whil þ*at* we ryden by the weye	
Syn þ*at* ye been a Baillyf / as am I	been / baillif
Som subtiltee / and tel me feithfully	
In myn office / how I may moost wynne	
And spareth nat for conscience ne synne	
But as my brother / tel me how do ye	me /
¶Now by my trouthe / brother deere / seyde he	deere
As I shal tellen thee / a feithful tale	
My wages been / ful streyte / and ful smale	wages / been streite
My lord is hard to me / and daungerous	
And myn office / is ful laborous	
And therfore / by extorcions I lyue	
For sothe I take / al that men wol me yeue	sothe / take that
Algate / by sleighte / or by violence	sleyghte /
Fro yeer to yeer / I wynne al my dispence	
I kan no bettre tellen / feithfully	telle /
¶Now certes quod this Somno*ur* / so fare I	Somono*ur* /
I spare nat to taken / god it woot	
But it be to heuy / or to hoot	But if it be / heuy
What I may gete / in conseil p*ri*uely	
No manere conscience / of that haue I	maner
Nere myn extorciou*n* / I myghte nat lyuen	myghte
Ne of swiche Iapes / wol I nat be shryuen	Nor of

[5] ¶Frere *78r*

./The Frere./	ELLESMERE
Stomak' ne Conscience / ne knowe I noon	Stomak / ne conscience /
I sherewe / thise Shryftesfadres eu*er*ychon	shrewe shriftefadres eu*er*ychoon
Wel be we met' by god / and by seint Iame	
But leeue brother / tel me thanne thy name	brother'
Quod this Somnour / in this mene whyle	Somonou*r* / meene while
This yeman / gan a litel for to smyle	
¶Brother quod he / woltow *þ*at I thee telle	wiltow /
I am a feend / my dwellyng' is in helle	
And here I ryde / aboute my purchasyng'	6 heere pu*r*chasyng'
To wite / wher men wolde yeue me any thyng'	wolde me yeuen thyng
My p*ur*chas / is theffect of al my rente	purchas / theffect'
Looke how thow rydest' for the same entente	Looke / thou
To wynne good / thow rekkest neu*er*e how	thou
Right so fare I / for ryde wold I now	Right ryde I wolde right now
Vn to the worldes ende / for a preye	
¶A quod this Somno*ur* / benedicite what sey ye	Somono*ur* / be*n*edicite ye./
I wende / ye were a yeman trewely	
Ye han a mannes shap*e* / as wel as I	
Han ye a figure thanne / det*er*mynat	ye figure thanne determinat'
In helle ther ye been / in youre estat	helle / been estat' ./
¶Nay c*er*teynly quod he / ther haue we noon	c*er*teinly
But whan vs liketh / we kan take vs oon	
Or ellis make yow seme / we ben shape	elles been
Som tyme / lyk a man / or lyk an Ape	man
Or lyk an Aungel / kan I ryde or go	Angel /
It is no wonder thyng' theigh it be so	thogh
A lousy Iogelour / kan deceyue thee	lowsy
And pardee yet kan I / moore craft than he	p*ar*dee / I
¶Whi quod this Somnour / ryde ye thanne or goon	¶Why Somonour /
In sondry shap*e* / and nat alwey in oon	oon./
¶For we quod he / wol vs swiche formes make	
As moost able is / oure preyes for to take	
¶What maketh yow / to han al this labour	
¶Ful many a cause / leue sire Somnour	leeue Sir*e* Somonour
Seyde this feend / but alle thyng hath tyme	
The day is short / and it is passed pryme	short'
And yet' ne wan I no thyng' in this day	
I wol entende / to wynnyng / if I may	wynnen
And nat entende / oure wittes to declare	entende / hir wittes
For brother myn / thy wit is al to bare	

6 ¶Frere *78v*

The ffrere:

Stomak ne Conscience / ne knowe I noon
I shrewe / thise Shryftes fadres euerychon
Wel be we met / by god / and by Seint Iame
But leue brother / tel me thanne thy name
Quod this Somonour / in this mene whyle
This yeman / gan a litel for to smyle
Brother quod he / woltow þt I thee telle
I am a feend / my dwellyng is in helle
And here I ryde / aboute my purchasyng/
To wite / wher men wolde yeue me any thyng/
My purchas / is theffect of al my rente
Looke how thow rydest / for the same entente
To wynne good / thow rekkest neuere how
Right so fare I / for ryde wolde I now
Vn to the worldes ende / for a preye
A quod this Somno' / benedicite what sey ye
I wende ye were a yeman trewely
Ye han a mannes shap / as wel as I
Han ye a figure thanne / determinat
In helle ther ye been / in youre estat
Nay certeinly quod he / ther haue we noon
But whan vs liketh / we kan take vs oon
Or ellis make yow seme / we ben shape
Som tyme / lyk a man / or lyk an ape
Or lyk an Angel / kan I ryde or go
It is no wonder thyng / theigh it be so
A lowsy Iogelour / kan deceyue thee
And pardee yet kan I / moore craft than he
Why quod this Somonour / ryde ye thanne or goon
In sondry shap / and nat alwey in oon
ffor we quod he / wol vs swiche formes make
As moost able is / oure preyes for to take
What maketh yow / to han al this labour
fful many a cause / leue sire Somonour
Seyde this feend / but alle thyng hath tyme
The day is short / and it is passed pryme
And yet ne wan I no thyng / in this day
I wol entende / to wynnyng / if I may
And nat entende oure wittes to declare
ffor brother myn / thy wit is al to bare

To vnderstonde / al thogh I tolde hem thee
But for thow axest / why labouren we
ffor som tyme / we been goddes Instrumentz
And meenes / to doon his comandementz
Whan that hym list / vp on his creatures
In diuers art / and in diuerse figures
With outen hym / we han no myght certayn
If that hym lyst / to stonde ther agayn
And som tyme / at oure prayere / han we leue
Oonly the body / and nat the soule greue
Witnesse on Iob / whom þt we diden wo
And som tyme / han we myght of bothe two
This is to seyn / of soule and body eke
And som tyme / be we suffred for to seke
Vp on a man / and do his soule vnreste
And nat his body / and al is for the beste
Whan he withstandeth oure temptacion
It is a cause / of his sauacion
Al be it / that it was nat oure entente
He sholde be sauf / but þt we wolde hym hente
And som tyme / be we seruant / vn to man
As to the Erchebisshop / Seint Dunstan
And to the apostles / seruant eek was I
Yet tel me / quod the Somnour / feithfully
Make ye yow newe bodyes thus alway
Of Elementz / the feend answerde nay
Som tyme we feyne / and som tyme we aryse
With dede bodyes / in ful sondry wyse
And speke as renably / and faire and wel
As to the Phitonissa / dide Samuel
And yet wol som men seye / it was nat he
I do no fors / of youre dyuynytee
But o thyng warne I thee / I wol nat Iape
Thow wolt algates wite / how we be shape
Thow shalt her afterwardes / my brother deere
Come there / thee nedeth nat of me to leere
ffor thow shalt / by thyn owene experience
Konne in a chayer / rede of this sentence
Bet than Virgile / whil he was on lyue
Or Dant also / now lat vs ryde blyve

	ELLESMERE
To vnderstonde / al thogh I tolde hem thee	
But for thow axestꝭ why labouren we	thou
For som tyme / we been goddes Instrumentz	
And meenes / to doon his comandementz	hise
Whan that hym list / vp on his creatures	listꝭ
In diu*er*s artꝭ and in diu*er*se figures	
With outen hym / we han no myght *cer*tayn	haue myght
If that hym lystꝭ to stonde ther agayn	listꝭ stonden
And som tyme / at oure preyere / han we leue	prayere /
Oonly the body / and nat the soule greue	
Witnesse on Iob / whom *þ*at we diden wo	that
And som tyme / han we myght of bothe two	myghtꝭ
This is to seyn / of soule and body eke	
And som tyme / be we suffred for to seke	somtyme /
Vp on a man / and do his soule vnreste	doon
And nat his body / and al is for the beste	his soule / and
Whan he with standeth / oure temptaciou*n*	7 withstandeth
It is / a cause / of his sauaciou*n*	is / cause /
Al be itꝭ that it was / nat oure entente	was
He sholde be saufꝭ but *þ*at we wolde hym hente	
And som tyme / be we *ser*uantꝭ vn to man	seruant
As to the Erchebisshop*e* / Seint Dunstan	Bisshop*e* /
And to the Apostles / seruant eek was I	*ser*uant .I.
¶Yet tel me / quod the Somno*ur* feithfully	Somono*ur*
Make ye yow newe bodyes / thus alway	bodies /
Of Elementz ∫ / the feend answerde nay	Elementz ∫ nay ∫
Som tyme we feyne / and som tyme we aryse	
With dede bodyes / in ful sondry wyse	
And speke as renably / and faire and wel	
As to the Phitonissa / dide Samuel	
And yet wol som men seye / it was nat he	
I do no fors / of youre dyuynytee	
But o thyng warne I thee / I wol nat Iape	
Thow wolt algates wite / how we be shape	Thou algates / wite been
Thow shalt her afterwardes / my brother deere	Thou
Come there / thee nedeth nat of me to lere	natꝭ leere
For thow shaltꝭ by thyn owene experience	thou
Konne in a chayer / rede of this sentence	
Bet than Virgile / whil he was on lyue	while
Or Dant also / now lat vs ryde blyue	

7 ¶Frere *79r*

For I wol holde / compaignye with thee	wole / holde
Til it be so / that thow forsake me	thou
¶Nay quod this Somno*ur* / that shal nat bityde	Somonour /
I am a yeman / knowen is ful wyde	
My trouthe wol I holde / as in this cas	
For theigh thow were / the deuel Sathanas	though thou
My trouthe wol I holde / to thee my brother	to my
As I am sworn / and ech of vs til oother	
For to be trewe brother / in this cas	
And bothe we goon / abouten oure purchas	p*ur*chas
Taak thow thy part' what þ*at* men wol thee yeue	thou
And I shal myn / thus may we bothe lyue	myn / and thus
And if that any of vs / haue moore than oother	þ*at*
Lat hym be trewe / and parte it with his brother	wi*th*
¶I graunte quod the deuel / by my fey	
And with that word / they ryden forth hir wey	
And right at the entryng' of the townes ende	
To which this Somnour / shoop hym for to wende	Somonour / shoop*e*
They saye a Cart' that charged was wi*th* hey	saugħ with
Which that a Cartere / droof forth in his wey	þ*at* Cartere /
Deep was the wey / for which the Carte stood	Deep*e*
This Carter*e* smoot' and cryde as he were wood	cryde /
Hayt Brok' hayt Scot' what spare ye for the stones	Brok /
The feend quod he / yow fecche body and bones	
As ferforthly / as euere were ye foled	[8] eu*ere*
So muchel wo / as I haue with yow tholed	muche
The deuel haue al / bothe hors / and Cart' and hey	hors Cart
¶This Somno*ur* seyde / heer shul we han a pley	Somono*ur* heere shal haue
And neer the feend he drogh / as noght ne were	droughħ /
Ful pryuely / and rowned in his ere	pr*i*uely /
Herkne my brother / herkne by thy feith	brother'
Herestow nat' how þ*at* the Cartere seith	Carter*e*
Hent it anon / for he hath yeue it thee	
Bothe hey / and Cart' and eek his caples thre	hey hise
¶Nay quod the deuel / god woot' neuer a del	woot neu*er* deel
It is nat his entente / trust thow me wel	thou weel
Axe hym thy self / if thow nat trowest me	self' thou
Or ellys stynt a while / and thow shalt se	elles thou see
¶This Cartere / taketh his hors ⟨vp⟩ on the croupe	Carter*e* / hors on
And they bigonne / drawen and to stoupe	bigonne

[8] ¶Frere 79*v*

ffor I wol holde / compaignye with thee
Til it be so / that thow forsake me
Nay quod this Somnour / that shal nat bityde
I am a yeman / knowen is ful wyde
My trouthe wol I holde / as in this cas
ffor though thow were / the deuel Sathanas
My trouthe wol I holde / to thee my brother
As I am sworn / and ech of vs til oother
ffor to be trewe brother / in this cas
And bothe we goon / abouten oure purchas
Taak thow thy part / what þt men wol thee yeue
And I shal myn / thus may we bothe lyue
And if that any of vs / haue moore than oother
Lat hym be trewe / and parte it with his brother
I graunte quod the deuel / by my fey
And with that word / they ryden forth hir wey
And right at the entryng / of the townes ende
To which this Somnour / shoop hym for to wende
They saye a Cart / that charged was with hey
Which that a Cartere / droof forth in his wey
Deep was the wey / for which the Carte stood
This Cartere smoot / and cryde as he were wood
Hayt Brok / hayt Scot / what spare ye for the stones
The feend quod he / yow fecche body and bones
As ferforthly / as euere were ye foled
So muchel wo / as I haue with yow tholed
The deuel haue al / bothe hors / and cart and hey
This Somnour seyde / heere shal we han a pley
And neer the feend he drogh / as noght ne were
ffUl pryuely / and rowned in his ere
Herkne my brother / herkne by thy feith
Herestow nat / how þt the Cartere seith
Hent it anon / for he hath yeue it thee
Bothe hey and cart / and eek his caples thre
Nay quod the deuel / god woot neuer a del
It is nat his entente / trust thow me wel
Axe hym thy self / if thow nat trowest me
Or ellys stynt a while / and thow shalt se
This Cartere / taketh his hors on the croupe
And they bigonne / drawen and to stoupe

76

Heyt now quod he / ther Ihu crist yow blesse
And al his handes werk / bothe moore and lesse
That was wel twight / myn owene lyard boy
I pray god saue thee / and Seint loy
Now is my cart / out of the slow pardee
Lo brother quod the feend / what tolde I thee
Heere may ye se / myn owene deere brother
The carl spak o thyng / but he thoghte another
Lat vs go forth / abouten oure viage
Heere wynne I no thyng / vp on cariage
Whan that they comen / som what out of towne
This Somonour / to his brother gan to rowne
Brother quod he / heer woneth an old rebekke
That hadde almoost / as leef to lese hir nekke
As for to yeue a peny / of hir good
I wol han ·xij· pens / though that she be wood
Or I wol somne hire / vn to oure office
And yet god woot / of hire knowe I no vice
But for thow kanst nat / as in this contree
Wynne thy cost / taak heer ensample of me
This Somonour / clappeth at the wydwes gate
Com out quod he / thow olde viritrate
I trowe thow hast / som frere / or preest with thee
Who clappeth / seyde this wyf / benedicitee
God saue yow sire / what is youre swete wille
I haue quod he / of somonce a bille
Vp peyne of cursyng / looke that thow be
To morn / bifore the Erchedeknes knee
Tanswere to the court / of certeyn thynges
Now lord quod she / crist Ihu kyng of kynges
So wisly helpe me / as I ne may
I haue been syk / and that ful many a day
I may nat go so fer quod she / ne ryde
But I be deed / so priketh it in my syde
May I nat axe a libel / sire Somonour
And answere there / by my procutour
To swich thyng / as men wole opposen me
Yis quod this Somonour / pay anon lat se
Twelf pens to me / and I wol thee acquyte
I shal no profit han ther by / but lyte

	ELLESMERE
Heyt now quod he / ther I*es*u crist yow blesse	
And al his handes werkꝭ bothe moore and lesse	handwerkꝭ
That was wel twightꝭ myn owene lyard boy	
I pray god saue thee / and Seint loy	pray to god seint
Now is my Cartꝭ out of the slow pardee	p*ar*dee
¶Lo brother quod the feend / what tolde I thee	
Heere may ye se / myn owene deere brother	
The Carl spak o thyngꝭ but he thoghte another	carl oon / but
Lat vs go forth / abouten oure viage	
Heere wynne I no thyng vp on cariage	Heere / thyngꝭ
¶Whan that ⟨they⟩ coomen / som what out of towne	they
This Somnour / to his brother gan to rowne	Somono*ur* /
Brother quod he / here woneth an old rebekke	heere
That hadde almoostꝭ as leef to lese hir nekke	liefꝭ hir*e*
As for to yeue a peny / of hir good	yeue / peny
I wol han .xij. pens / thogh that she be wood	wole though þ*a*t
Or I wol somne hire / vn to oure office	sompne
And yet god wootꝭ of hir*e* knowe I no vice	woot /
But for thow canst natꝭ as in this contree	thou kanst
Wynne thy costꝭ taak heer ensample of me	taakꝭ
This Somnour / clappeth at the wydwes gate	¶This Somono*ur* /
Com out quod he / thow olde viritrate	thou virytrate
I trowe thow hastꝭ som frere / or preest with thee	thou wit*h*
¶Who clappeth seyde this wyf / benedicitee	
God saue yow sire / what is youre swete wille	sweete wille ./
¶I haue quod he / of somonce a bille	
Vp peyne of cursyngꝭ looke that thow be	Vp on peyne þ*a*t thou
To morn / bifore the Erchedeknes knee	Tomorn /
Tanswere to the courtꝭ of c*er*teyn thynges	certeyn
¶Now lord quod she / crist I*es*u kyng of kynges	
So wisly helpe me / as I ne may	help*e*
I haue been sykꝭ and that ful many a day	syk /
I may nat go so fer quod she / ne ryde	9 she
But I be deed / so priketh it in my syde	
May I nat axe a libel / sire Somnour	Somonour
And answere there / by my procutour	p*ro*cutour
To swich thyngꝭ as men wole opposen me	me ./
¶Yis quod this Somnour / pay anon lat see	Somono*ur* / se
Twelf pens to me / and I wol thee acquyte	acquite
I shal no p*ro*fit han ther by / but lyte	profitꝭ therby / lite

9 ¶Frere *80r*

	ELLESMERE
My Maister hath the profit / and nat I	maister profit'
Com of / and lat me ryden hastily	
Yif me .xij. pens / I may no lenger tarye	
¶Twelf pens quod she / now lady Seinte Marie	she / /
So wisly help me god / out of care and synne	
This wyde world / thogh that I sholde wynne	thogħ þ*at*
Ne haue I nat .xij. pens / with Inne myn hoold	pens w*ith* hoold'
Ye knowen wel / that I am poure and oold	oold'
Kythe youre almesse / on me poure wrecche	Kithe Almesse /
¶Nay thanne quod he / the foule feend me fecche	
If I thexcuse / theigh thow shul be spilt'	though thou
¶Allas quod she / god woot I haue no gilt'	woot'
¶Pay me quod he / or by the swete Seinte Anne	sweete seinte
As I wol bere awey / thy newe panne	I / awey
For dette / which thow owest me of oold	which that thou old'
Whan þ*at* thow madest / thyn housbonde cokewold	thou madest' cokewold'
I payde at hom / for thy correcciou*n*	hoom /
¶Thow lyxt quod she / by my sauaciou*n*	¶Thou lixt
Ne was I neu*er*e er now / wydwe ne wyf'	
Somoned vn to youre court' in al my lyf /	lyf'
Ne neu*er*e I nas / but of my body trewe	
Vn to the deuel / blak' and row of hewe	rougħ
Yeue I thy body / and my panne also	
¶And whan the deuel / herde hir*e* cursen so	
Vp on hir knees / he seyde in this manere	
Now Mabely / myn owene moder deere	mooder
Is this youre wyl in ernest / þ*at* ye seye	wyl / ernest seye /
¶The deuel quod she / so fecche hym er he deye	
And panne and al / but he wol hym repente	
¶Nay olde stot' that is nat myn entente	Stot'
Quod this Somnour / for to repente me	Somono*ur* /
For any thyng' that I haue had of thee	
I wolde I hadde thy smok / and euery clooth	smok cloothħ
¶Now brother quod the deuel / be noght wrooth	nat wroothħ
Thy body and this panne / been myne by right	right'
Thow shalt w*ith* me to helle / yet to nyght'	Thou with nyghħt'
Wher thow shalt knowen / of oure pryuetee	Wher*e* / thou p*ri*uetee
Moore / than a maister of dyuynytee	than /
And with that word / this foule feend hym hente	w*ith*
Body and soule / he with the deuel wente	

My maister hath the profit / and nat I
Com of / and lat me ryden hastily
Yif me .xij. pens / I may no lenger tarye
Twelf pens quod she / now lady Seinte Marie
So wisly help me god / out of care and synne
This wyde world / thogh that I sholde wynne
Ne haue I nat .xij. pens / with Inne myn hold
Ye knowen wel / that I am poure and old
Kythe youre almesse / on me poure wrecche
Nay thanne quod he / the foule feend me fecche
If I thexcuse / theigh thow shul be spilt /
Allas quod she / god woot I haue no gilt /
Pay me quod he / or by the swete Seinte Anne
As I wol bere awey / thy newe panne
For dette / which thow owest me of old
Whan þt thow madest / thyn housbonde cokewold
I payde at hom / for thy correccion
Thow lyxt quod she / by my sauacion
Ne was I neuere er now / wydwe ne wyf
Somoned vn to youre court / in al my lyf /
Ne neuere I nas / but of my body trewe
Vn to the deuel / blak and rough of hewe
Yeue I thy body / and my panne also
And whan the deuel / herde hire cursen so
Vp on hir knees / he seyde in this manere
Now Mabely / myn owene moder deere
Is this youre wyl in ernest / þt ye seye
The deuel quod she / so fecche hym er he deye
And panne and al / but he wol hym repente
Nay olde stot / that is nat myn entente
Quod this Somonour / for to repente me
For any thyng / that I haue had of thee
I wolde I hadde thy smok / and euery clooth
Now brother quod the deuel / be noght wrooth
Thy body and this panne / been myne by right
Thow shalt with me to helle / yet to nyght /
Where thow shalt knowen / of oure pryuetee
Moore than a maister of dyuynytee
And with that word / this foule feend hym hente
Body and soule / he with the deuel wente

Ther as that Somnours han hir heritage
And god that maked after his ymage
Mankynde saue and gyde vs alle and some
And leue thise Somnours goode men to bicome
Lordynges I koude han told yow quod this frere
Hadde I had leyser for this Somnour heere
After the text of crist Poul and John
And of oure othere doctours many oon
Swiche peynes that youre hertes myghte agryse
Al be it so no tonge may deuyse
Thogh that I myghte a thousand wynter telle
The peynes of thilke cursed hous of helle
But for to kepe vs fro that cursed place
Waketh and preyeth Ihesu for his grace
So kepe vs fro the temptour Sathanas
Herketh this word beth war as in this cas
The leon sit in his awayt alway
To sle the innocent if that he may
Disposeth ay youre hertes to withstonde
The feend that yow wolde maken thral and bonde
He may nat tempte yow ouer youre myght
For crist wol be youre champion and knyght
And prayeth that thise Somnours hem repente
Of hir mysdedes er that the feend hem hente

Heere endeth the freres tale

The Prologe of the Somnours tale

This Somnour in his styropes hye he stood
Vp on this frere his herte was so wood
That lyk an aspen leef he quook for ire
Lordynges quod he but o thyng I desire
I yow biseke that of youre curteisye
Syn ye han herd this false frere lye
As suffreth me I may my tale telle
This frere bosteth that he knoweth helle
And god it woot that it is litel wonder
Freres and feendes been but lyte a sonder

Wher as that Somnours / han hir heritage
And god / that made after his ymage
Mankynde / saue / and gyde vs alle and some
And leue thise Somno*urs* / goode men to bicome
¶Lordynges / I koude han told yow / quod this frere
Hadde I had leyser / for this Somno*ur* heere
After the text / of crist Poul and Iohn
And of oure othere doctours / many oon
Swiche peynes / that youre hertes myghte agryse
Al be it so / no tonge may ⟨it⟩ deuyse
Thogh that I myghte / a thousand wynter telle
The peynes / of thilke cursed hous of helle
But for to kepe vs / fro that cursed place
Waketh / and preyeth I*es*u for his grace
So kepe vs / fro the temptour Sathanas
Herketh this word / beth war as in this cas
The leou*n* sit in his awayt alway
To sle the Innocent if that he may
Disposeth ay youre hertes / to withstonde
The feend / that yow wolde maken thral and bonde
He may nat tempte yow / ouer your*e* myght /
For crist wol be youre champion and knyght
And prayeth / that this Somno*urs* hem repente
Of hir mysdedes / er that the feend hem hente

¶Here endeth / the freres tale

¶The Prologe / of the Somnours tale

This Somnour in his Stiropes / hye he stood
Vp on this frere / his herte was so wood
That lyk an Aspen lief / he quook for Ire
¶Lordynges quod he / but o thyng I desire
I yow biseke / that of youre curteisye
Syn ye han herd / this false frere lye
As suffreth me / I may my tale telle
This frere bosteth / that he knoweth helle
And god it woot that it is litel wonder
Freres and feendes / been but lyte a sonder

1656 Sedet in insidiis cum diuitibus El

ELLESMERE

10 Wher*e* Somono*urs* /
þ*a*t made /
saue
Somonours / men bicome
LOrdynges / toold yow q*uod*
Somnour
text Crist Poul /
doctours
h*er*te
may it
Thogh þ*a*t
war
Innocent /
ay / hertes
feend / þ*a*t make / *and*
myght
crist be /
þ*a*t thise Somonours
þ*a*t

¶Heere endeth the Freres tale

¶The prologe / of the Somono*urs* tale

Somono*ur* / Styropes hye stood
wood
leef /

10 ¶Frere *80v*

.ſThe So*m*nour.ſ

For pardee / ye han ofte tyme herd telle
How that a frere / ⟨ra⟩uysshed was to helle
In Spirit ones / by avisioun
And as an Aungel / ladde hym vp and down
To shewen hym / the peynes *þ*at ther were
In al the place / say he nat a frere
Of oother folk / he say ynowe in wo
Vn to this Aungel / spak the frere tho
¶Now Sire quod he / han freres swich a g*ra*ce
That noon of hem / shal come to this place
¶Yis quod this Aungel / many a Milioun
And vn to Sathanas / he ladde hym doun
And now hath Sathanas / seith he a tayl
Brodder / than of a Carryk is the sayl
Hold vp thy tayl / thow Sathanas quod he
Shewe forth thyn ers / and lat the frere se
Where is the nest of freres / in this place
And er *þ*at / half a furlong wey of space
Right so as bees / out swarmen from an hyue
Out of the deueles ers / ther gonne dryue
Twenty thousand freres / on a route
And thurgh out helle / swarmeden aboute
And comen again / as faste as they may gon
And in his ers / they crepten euerychon
He clapte his tayl agayn / and lay ful stille
This frere / whan he looked hadde his fille
Vp on the tormentz / of this sory place
His spiritꝭ god restored of his grace
Vn to his body agayn / and he awookꝭ
But nathelees / for fere yet he quookꝭ
So was the deueles ers / ay in his mynde
That is his heritage / of verray kynde
God saue yow alle / saue this cursed frere
My prologe / wol I ende / in this manere

¶Here endeth the prologe of the Somno*ur*s tale

ELLESMERE

p*ar*dee /
frere / vanysshed was
spirit by a visioun
Angel / doun

saugh
1 otherꝭ folkꝭ saugh
Angel /
sir*e* grace
place.ſ
Angel / Millioun

Brodderꝭ Carryk /
Hoold thou Sathnas

Wher*e*
erꝭ
Rigħt

freres / in a
thurgħ
agayn /
eu*er*ychon

he hadde looke al his
Vpon

natheles /

2

[1]¶Somonou*r* *81r*
[2]Rubric *Out* El.

ffor pardee / ye han ofte tyme herd telle
How that a frere / rauysshed was to helle
In spirit ones / by a visioun
And as an Angel / ladde hym vp and doun
To shewen hym / the peynes þt ther were
In al the place / saugh he nat a frere
Of oother folk / he saugh ynowe in wo
Vn to this Angel / spak the frere tho
Now sire quod he / han freres swich a grace
That noon of hem / shal come to this place
Yis quod this Angel / many a millioun
And vn to Sathanas / he ladde hym doun
And now hath Sathanas / seith he a tayl
Brodder than of a Carryk / is the sayl
Hold vp thy tayl / thow Sathanas quod he
Shewe forth thyn ers / and lat the frere se
Where is the nest of freres / in this place
And er þt half a furlong wey of space
Right so as bees / out swarmen from an hyue
Out of the deueles ers / ther gonne dryue
Twenty thousand freres / on a route
And thurgh out helle / swarmeden aboute
And comen agayn / as faste as they may gon
And in his ers / they crepten euerychon
He clapte his tayl agayn / and lay ful stille
This frere / whan he looked hadde his fille
Vp on the tormentz / of this sory place
His spirit / god restored of his grace
Vn to his body agayn / and he awook
But nathelees / for fere yet he quook
So was the deueles ers / ay in his mynde
That is his heritage / of verray kynde
God saue yow alle / saue this cursed frere
My prologe / wol I ende in this manere

Rs

Heere endeth the prologe of the Somnours tale

Here bygynneth the Somonours tale

Lordynges ther is in yorkshire as I gesse
A mersssh contree called holdernesse
In which ther wente a lymytour aboute
To preche and eek to begge it is no doute
And so bifel that on a day this frere
Hadde preched at a chirche in his manere
And specially abouen euery thyng
Excited he the peple in his prechyng
To trentals and to yeue for goddes sake
Wher with men myghte holy houses make
Ther as dyuyne seruice is honoured
Nat ther as it is wasted and deuoured
Ne ther it nedeth nat to be yeue
As to possessioners that mowen lyue
Thanked be god in wele and habundaunce
Trentals seyde he deliuereth from penaunce
Hir freendes soules as wel olde as yonge
Ye whan that they been hastily ysonge
Nat for to holde a preest joly and gay
He syngeth nat but o masse in a day
Deliuereth out quod he anon the soules
fful hard it is wt flessh hook or wt oules
To been yclawed or to brenne or bake
Now spede yow hastily for cristes sake
And whan this frere hadde seyd al his entente
With qui cum patre forth his wey he wente
Whan folk in chirche hadde yeue hym what hem leste
He wente his wey no lenger wolde he reste
With scrippe and tipped staf ytukked hye
In euery hous he gan to poure and prye
And beggeth mele and chese or ellis corn
His felawe hadde a staf tipped with horn
A peyre of tables al of yuory
And a poyntel polysshed fetisly
And wroot the names alwey as he stood
Of alle folk that yaf hem any good

¶Here bygynneth the Somnours tale	¶Heere bigynneth the Somono*ur* his tale
LOrdynges / ther is in Yorkshire / as I gesse	[3]
A Merssh contree / called holdernesse	Mersshcontree / Holdernesse
In which / ther wente a lymytour aboute	
To p*re*che / and eek to begge / it is no doute	
And so bifel / that on a day this frere	day /
Hadde p*re*ched at a chirche / in his manere	preched chirche
And specially / abouen eu*er*y thyng	euery thyng /
Excyted he the peple / in his p*re*chyng	Excited prechyng
To trentals / and to yeue for goddes sake	
Wher with men myghte / holy houses make	with / myghte hooly
Ther as dyuyne seruice / is honoured	diuine s*er*uyce
Nat ther / as it is wasted and deuoured	ther ⟨as⟩
Ne ther / it nedeth nat to be yeue	ther nat for to
As to possessioners / that mowen lyue	
Thanked be god / in wele and habundaunce	[4]
Trentals seyde he / deliu*er*eth from penaunce	deliueren fro
Hir freendes soules / as wel olde as yonge	
Ye / whan that they / been hastily ysonge	þ*a*t they
Nat for to holde a preest Ioly and gay	preest
He syngeth nat but o masse in a day	
Deliuereth out quod he / anon the soules	
Ful hard it is / w*ith* flessh hook / or w*ith* oules	flesshhook
To been y clawed / or to brenne / or bake	yclawed / brenne
Now spede yow hastily / for cristes sake	
And whan this frere / hadde seyd al his entente	had
With **qui cum patre** / forth his wey he wente	With / cu*m*
Whan folk in chirche / hadde yeue hym / what hem leste	¶Whan had hi*m* /
He wente his wey / no lenger wolde he reste	
With scryppe and typped staf / y tukked hye	Scrippe tipped ytukked
In euery hous / he gan to poure and prye	
And beggeth Mele / and chese / or ellis corn	mele / elles
His felawe hadde a staf / typped with horn	tipped
A peyre of tables / al of yuory	
And a poyntel / polysshed fetisly	polysshed
And wroot the names / alwey as he stood	
Of alle folk / that yaf hem any good	hym

[3] Miniature of the Summoner in right margin.

[4] ¶Somono*ur* *81v*

	ELLESMERE
Ascaunces / that he wolde for hem preye	prey
Yif vs a busshel whete / Maltꝭ or Reye	Yif hym a bussħel
A goddes kechyl / or a tryp*e* of cheese	chese
Or ellis what yow lystꝭ we may nat chese	elles cheese
A goddes half peny / or a masse peny	halfpeny /
Or yif vs of youre brawn / if ye haue eny	your*e*
A dagon of youre Blanketꝭ leeue dame	dagou*n* blanketꝭ
Oure suster deere / lo heere I write your*e* name	Lo youre
Bacou*n* / or boef / or swich thyng as ye fynde	boefꝭ thyngꝭ
A sturdy harlotꝭ wente ay hem bihynde	¶A
That was hir hostes man / and baar a sakꝭ	bar sak /
And what men yaf hem / leyde it on his bakꝭ	
And whan þ*at* he was out at dore anon	he /
He planed awey / the names euerichon	
That he biforn / hadde writen in his tables	had
He serued hem / with nyfles and w*ith* fables	s*er*ued with fables
¶Nay ther thow lixtꝭ thow Somno*ur* quod the frere	thou lixtꝭ thou Somono*ur* q*uod*
¶Pees quod oure hoostꝭ for cristes moder deere	c*ri*stes mooder
Tel forth thy tale / and spare it nat at al	
¶So thryue I quod this Somno*ur* / so I shal	Somono*ur* /
So longe he wente / hous by hous / til he	¶So wente
Cam til an hous / ther he was wont to be	
Refresshed moore / than in an hundred placis	Refressħed
Syk lay the goode man / whos the place is	
Bedrede vp on a couche / lowe he lay	couche
Deus hicꝭ quod he / o Thomas freend good day	q*uod*
Seyde this frere / curteisly and softe	[5]
Thomas quod he / god yelde yow ful ofte	yow /
Haue I vp on this bench / faren ful wel	I / vpon weel
Heere haue I eten / many a murye mel	myrie meel
And fro the bench / he droof awey the catꝭ	cat
And leyde adoun / his potente and his hatꝭ	
And eek his scrippe / and sette hym softe adown	adoun
His felawe / was go walked in to town	toun
Forth with his knaue / in to that hostelrye	
Wher as he shoop*e* hym / thilke nyght to lye	Wher*e* nygħt
¶O deere maister / quod this syke man	sike
How han ye fare / sith that March bigan	þ*at* Marcħ bigan
I say yow noghtꝭ this fourtnyghtꝭ or moore	saugħ nogħt / fourtnygħtꝭ
¶God woot quod he / laboured I haue ful soore	God

[5] ¶Somono*ur* *82r*

Ascaunces / that he wolde for hem preye
yif vs a busshel whete / malt / or reye
A goddes kechyl / or a tryp of cheese
Or ellis what yow lyst / we may nat chese
A goddes half peny / or a masse peny
Or yif vs of youre brawn / if ye haue eny
A dagon of youre blanket / leue dame
Oure suster deere / lo heere I write youre name
Bacon / or beef / or swich thyng as ye fynde
A sturdy harlot / wente ay hem bihynde
That was hir hostes man / and bar a sak
And what men yaf hem / leyde it on his bak
And whan þt he was out at dore anon
He planed awey the names euerychon
That he biforn / hadde writen in his tables
He serued hem / with nyfles and wt fables
Nay ther thow lixt / thow Somnour quod the frere
Pees quod oure hoost / for cristes mooder deere
Tel forth thy tale / and spare it nat at al
So thryue I quod this Somnour / so I shal
So longe he wente / hous by hous / til he
Cam til an hous / ther he was wont to be
Refresshed moore / than in an hundred placis
Syk lay the goode man / whos the place is
Bedrede vp on a couche / lowe he lay
Deus hic / quod he / o Thomas freend good day
Seyde this frere / curteisly and softe
Thomas quod he / god yelde yow / ful ofte
Haue I vp on this bench / faren ful wel
Heere haue I eten / many a murye mel
And fro the bench / he droof awey the cat
And leyde adoun / his potente and his hat
And eek his scrippe / and sette hym softe adoun
His felawe was go walked in to toun
Forth with his knaue / in to that hostelrye
Wher as he shoop hym / thilke nyght to lye
O deere maister / quod this syk man
How han ye fare / sith that march bigan
I say yow noght / this fourtnyght / or moore
God woot quod he / laboured I haue ful soore

And specially for thy saluacion
Haue I seyd many a precious oryson
And for oure othere freendes god hem blesse
I haue to day been at youre chirche at messe
And seyd a sermon after my symple wit
Nat al after the text of holy writ
ffor it is hard to yow as I suppose
And therfore wol I teche yow al the glose
Glosyng is a glorious thyng certeyn
ffor lettre sleeth so as we clerkes seyn
Ther haue I taught hem to be charitable
And spende hir good ther it is resonable
And ther I say oure dame a wher is she
Yond in the yerd I trowe þt she be
Seyde this man and she wol come anon
Ey maister wel come be ye by seint Iohn
Seyde this wyf how fare ye hertely
The frere ariseth vp ful curteisly
And hire embraceth in hise armes narwe
And kiste hir swete and chirketh as a sparwe
With his lippes dame quod he right wel
As he that is youre seruant euery del
Thanked be god that yow yaf soule and lyf
Yet say I nat this day so fair a wyf
In al the chirche god so saue me
Ye god amende defautes sire quod she
Algates wel come be ye by my fey
Graunt mercy dame this haue I founde alwey
But of youre grete goodnesse by youre leue
I wolde pray yow that ye nat yow greue
I wol with Thomas speke a litel throwe
Thise curatz been ful necligent and slowe
To grope tendrely a conscience
In shrift in prechyng is my diligence
And studie in Petres wordes and in Poules
I walke and fisshe cristen mennes soules
To yelden Ihu crist his propre rente
To sprede his word is set al myn entente
Now by youre leue o deere sire quod she
Chideth hym wel for seinte Trinitee

	ELLESMERE
And specially / for thy sauaciou*n*	
Haue I seyd / many a p*re*cious orisou*n*	
And for oure othere freendes / god hem blesse	
I haue to day / been at youre chirche ⟨at messe⟩	your*e* at messe
And seyd a sermon / after my symple wit	se*r*mou*n* / wit
Nat al / after the text of holy writ	Nat al after hooly writ
For it is hard to yow / as I suppose	
And ther fore / wol I teche yow al the glose	therfore /
Glosyng is a glorious thyng c*er*teyn	Glosynge / certeyn
For lettre sleeth / so as we clerkes seyn	as thise clerkes
Ther haue I taught hem / to be charitable	Ther*e* taught hem
And spende hir good / ther it is resonable	
And ther I say oure dame / a wher*e* is she	ther*e* saugh she
¶Yond in the yerd / I trowe þ*at* she be	yerd/
Seyde this man / and she wol come anon	
¶Ey maister / wel come be ye / by Seint Iohn	seint
Seyde this wyf / how fare ye hertely	hertely
¶The frere ariseth vp / ful curteisly	vp
And hir*e* embraceth / in hise armes narwe	embraceth his Armes
And kiste hir swete / and chirteth as a Sparwe	hir*e* sweete /
With his lippes / dame quod he / right wel	lyppes /. right weel
As he / that is youre seruant euery del	seruant deel
Thanked be god / that yow yaf soule and lyf	þ*at* lyf
Yet say I nat this day / so fair a wyf	saugh wyf
In al the chirche / god so saue me	
¶Ye god amende defautes / sire quod she	¶Ye /
Algates / wel come be ye / by my fey	
¶Graunt m*er*cy dame / this haue I founde alwey	
But of youre grete goodnesse / by youre leue	But
I wolde pray yow / that ye nat yow greue	prey þ*at*
I wol with Thomas / speke a litel throwe	wole Thomas
Thise Curatz / been ful necligent and slowe	curatz / necligent
To grope tendrely / a conscience	tendrely
In shrift in p*re*chyng is my diligence	
And studie / in Petres wordes / and in Poules	6
I walke / and fisshe / cristen mennes soules	fisshe
To yelden I*es*u crist. his p*ro*pre rente	crist /
To sprede his word / is set al myn entente	
¶Now by youre leeue / o deere sire quod she	leue / sir*e*
Chideth hym wel / for Seinte Trinitee	weel / seinte

1794 Litera occidit et cetera El

6¶Somono*ur* *82v*

He is as angry / as a Pissemyre	pissemyre
Thogh that he haue / al that he kan desire	Though þat
Thogh I hym wrye a nyght and make hym warm	Though nyght / and
And on hym leye / my leg outher myn arm	leye Arm
He groneth lyk oure boor / lyth in oure Sty	lith sty
Oother disport right noon of hym haue I	desport right
I may nat plese hym / in no maner cas	
¶O Thomas Ie vous dy / Thomas / Thomas	¶O Thomas /
This maketh the feend / this moste been amended	ben
Ire is a thyng that hye god defended	
And ther of / wol I speke / a word / or two	speke word
¶Now maister quod the wyf / er þat I go	wyf
What wol ye dyne / I wol go ther aboute	dyne /
¶Now dame quod he / now Ie vous dy sanz doute	
Haue I nat of a Capoun / but the lyuere	capoun /
And of youre softe breed / nat but a Shyuere	shyuere
And after that a rosted pigges heed	
But þat I nolde / no beest for me were deed	that
Thanne hadde I with yow / homly suffisaunce	yow hoomly suffisaunce
I am a man / of litel sustenaunce	sustenaunce
My spirit hath his fostryng in the bible	Bible
The body is ay / so redy and penyble	
To wake / that my stomak is destroyed	stomak
I pray yow dame / ye be nat anoyed	prey
Thogh I so freendly / yow my conseil shewe	Though
By god / I wolde nat telle it but a fewe	
¶Now sire quod she / but o word / er I go	sire word
My child is deed / with Inne thise wykes two	
Soone after that ye wente / out of this town	after / þat wente toun
¶His deeth say I / by reuelacioun	deeth / saugh I
Seith this frere / at hom in oure dortour	hoom
I dar wel seyn / that er þat half an hour	
After his deeth / I say hym born to blisse	saugh
In myn avisioun / so god me wisse	Avisioun /
So dide oure Sexteyn / and oure Fermerer	
That han been trewe freres fifty yeer	freres /
They may now / god be thanked / of his lone	thanked loone
Maken hir Iubilee / and walke allone	
And vp I roos / and al oure Couent eke	
With many a teere / triklyng on my cheke	triklyng /

He is as angry / as a pissemyre
Thogh that he haue / al that he kan desire
Thogh I hym wrye a nyght / and make hym warm
And on hym leye / my leg / outher myn arm
He groneth lyk oure boor / lyth in oure sty
Oother desport / right noon of hym haue I
I may nat plese hym / in no maner cas
O Thomas je vous dy Thomas Thomas
This maketh the feend / this moste ben amended
Ire is a thyng / that hye god defended
And ther of wol I speke / a word or two
Now maister quod the wyf / er þt I go
What wol ye dyne / I wol go ther aboute
Now dame quod he / now je vous dy sanz doute
Haue I nat of a capon / but the lyuere
And of youre softe breed / nat but a shyuere
And after that / a rosted pigges heed
But þt I nolde / no beest for me were deed
Thanne hadde I with yow / homly suffisaunce
I am a man / of litel sustenaunce
My spirit / hath his fostryng in the bible
The body is ay / so redy and penyble
To wake / that my stomak is destroyed
I pray yow dame / ye be nat anoyed
Thogh I so freendly / yow my conseil shewe
By god / I wolde nat telle it / but a fewe
Now sire quod she / but o word / er I go
My child is deed / with Inne thise wykes two
Soone after that / ye wente / out of this town
His deeth saugh I / by reuelacioun
Seith this frere / at hom in oure dortour
I dar wel seyn / that er þt half an hour
After his deeth / I saugh hym born to blisse
In myn avision / so god me wisse
So dide oure sexteyn / and oure fermerer
That han been trewe freres fifty yeer
They may now / god be thanked of his lone
Maken hir Iubilee / and walke allone
And vp I roos / and al oure couent eke
With many a teere / trikelyng on my cheke

With outen noyse / or claterynge of belles
Te deum was oure song / and no thyng elles
Saue that to crist / I seyde an orison
Thankynge hym / of his reuelacion
ffor sire and dame / trusteth me right wel
Oure orisons / been wel moore effectuel
And moore we seen / of cristes secree thynges
Than burel folk / al thogh þt they weere kynges
We lyue in pouerte / and in abstinence
And burell folk / in richesse and despence
Of mete and drynke / and in hir foul delit /
We han this worldes lust / al in despit
Lazar and Diues / lyueden diuersly
And diuerse gerdon / hadde they ther by
Who so wol preye / he moot faste and be clene
And fatte his soule / and make his body lene
We fare as seith thapostle / clooth and foode
Suffiseth vs / thogh they be nat ful goode
The clennesse and the fastyng of vs freres
Maketh that crist accepteth oure preyeres
Lo Moyses / fourty dayes / and fourty nyght /
ffasted / er that the heighe god of myght /
Spak with hym / in the mountayne of Synay
With empty wombe / fastynge many a day
Receyued he the lawe / that was writen
With goddes fynger / and Elye wel ye witen
In mount Oreb / er he hadde any speche
With hye god / that is oure lyues leche
He fasted longe / and was in contemplaunce
Aaron / that hadde the temple in gouernaunce
And eek that othere preestes euerichon
In to the temple / whan they sholde gon
To preye for the peple / and do seruyse
They nolden drynken / in no maner wyse
No drynke / which that myghte hem dronke make
But there in abstinence / preye and wake
Lest that they deyden / tak hede what I seye
But they be sobre / that for the peple preye
War that I seye namoore / for it suffiseth
Oure lord Ihu / as holy writ deuyseth

yaf vs ensample

	ELLESMERE
With outen noyse / or clateryng of belles	Withouten claterynge
Te deum was oure song and no thyng elles	deu*m*
Saue that to crist / I seyde an orisou*n*	7 Saue / crist
Thankynge hym / of his reuelaciou*n*	
For sire and dame / trusteth me right wel	sir*e* right weel
Oure orisons / been wel moore effectuel	effectueel
And moore we seen / of cristes secree thynges	
Than burell folk al thogh *þat* they were kynges	burel folk / though they weren
We lyue in pouerte / and in abstinence	pou*er*te /
And burell folk in richesse and dispence	folk / despence
Of mete and drynke / and in hir foul delit	
We han this worldes lust al in despit	despit /
Lazar and Diues / lyueden diuersly	diues /
And diu*er*se gerdou*n* / hadde they ther by	hadden
Who so wol praye / he moot faste and be clene	preye /
And fatte his soule / and make his body lene	
We fare as seith thapostle / clooth and foode	
Suffiseth vs / thogh they be nat ful goode	Suffisen though
The clennesse / and the fastyng of vs freres	clennesse fastynge
Maketh / that crist accepteth oure prayeres	*þa*t preyeres
¶Lo Moyses / fourty dayes / and fourty nyght	nyght
Fasted / er that the heighe god of myght	*þa*t myght
Spak with hym / in the mountayne of Synay	mount
With empty wombe / fastynge many a day	
Receyued he the lawe / that was writen	
With goddes fynger / and Elye wel ye witen	
In Mount Oreb / er he hadde any speche	mount
With hye god / that is oure lyues leche	
He fasted longe / and was in contemplaunce	contemplau*n*ce
Aaron / that hadde the temple in gouernaunce	¶Aaron / gou*er*nau*n*ce
And eek that othere preestes euerichon	eek / euerichon
In to the temple / whan they sholde gon	
To preye for the peple / and do seruyse	
They nolden drynken / in no maner wyse	
No drynke / which that myghte hem dronke make	*þa*t
But there in abstinence / preye and wake	there / abstinence
Lest that they deyden / tak hede what I seye	taak heede
But they be sobre / that for the peple preye	
War that I seye namoore / for it suffiseth	that /.
Oure lord Ies*u* / as holy writ deuyseth	¶Oure hooly

Yaf vs ensample

1880 Melius est animam saginare quam corpus El

1881 Victum et vestitum hiis contenti sumus et cetera El

1884 de oracionibus et Ieiunijs El

7¶Somono*ur* *83r*

∫ The Somnour ∫

	ELLESMERE
Yaf vs ensample / of fastyng / and prayeres	fastynge preyeres
Ther fore / we mendynantz / we sely freres	Therfore /
Been wedded / to pouerte and continence	
To charitee / humblesse and abstinence	charite / humblesse /
To p*er*secuciou*n* / for rightwisnesse	rightwisnesse
To wepyng misericorde and clennesse	wepynge / Misericorde
And ther fore may ye se / that oure prayeres	therfore *þat* preyeres
I speke of vs / we mendinantz / we freres	mendynantz
Be to the hye god / moore acceptable	Been
Than youres / with youre festes at the table	*with* feestes
Fro Paradys first if I shal nat lye	8
Was man out chaced / for his glotonye	
And chaast was man / in Paradys certeyn	*cer*teyn
¶But herkne Thomas / what I shal seyn	
I ne haue no text of it as I suppose	text
But I shal fynde it in a maner glose	
That specially / oure swete lord I*es*us	sweete
Spak this by freres / whan he seyde thus	
Blessed be they / that poure in spirit been	¶Blessed pouere
And so forth / al the gospel / may ye seen	
Wher it be likker / oure professiou*n*	
Or hire / that swymmen in possessiou*n*	hirs /
Fy on hir pompe / and hir glotonye	hir*e* hir*e*
And for hir lewednesse / I hem diffye	
Me thynketh / they been lyk Iouynyan	¶Me Iovinyan
Fat as a whale / and walkyng as a swan	walkynge
Al vynolent as Botel in the Spence	vinolent
Hir preyere is / of ful greet reu*er*ence	preyere / is reuerence
Whan they for soules / seye the psalm of Dauit	psalm
Lo buf they seye / **cor meum eructauit**	Lo / but **cor meum eructauit**
Who folweth cristes gospel / and his foore	folweth / foore ∫
But we that hu*m*ble been / and chaast / and poore	*þat* humble chaast
Werkers of goddes word / nat Auditours	Werkeris
Ther fore / right as an hauk / vp at a sours	Therfore / right hauk
Vp spryngeth in to theyr / right so prayeres	their / right
Of charitable / and chaste bisy freres	
Maken hir sours / to goddes erys two	eres
Thomas / Thomas / so mote I ryde or go	Thomas Thomas / moote
And by that lord / that clepid is Seint yue	*þat* clepid
Nere thow oure brother / sholdestow nat thryue	thou sholdestou

8 ¶Somono*ur* *83v*

yaf vs ensample / of fastyng and prayeres
Ther fore we mendyuantz / we sely freres
Been wedded / to pouerte and continence
To charitee / humblesse and abstinence
To persecucion / for rightwisnesse
To wepyng / misericorde and clennesse
And ther fore may ye se / that oure prayeres
I speke of vs / we mendinantz we freres
Be to the hye god / moore acceptable
Than youres / with youre festes at the table
ffro paradys first / if I shal nat lye
Was man out chaced / for his glotonye
And chaast was man in paradys certeyn
But herkne Thomas / what I shal seyn
I ne haue no text of it / as I suppose
But I shal fynde it / in a maner glose
That specially / oure swete lord Ihesus
Spak this by freres / whan he seyde thus
Blessed be they / that poure in spirit been
And so forth / al the gospel may ye seen
Wher it be likker / oure profession
Or hire that swymmen in possession
ffy on hir pompe / and hir glotonye
And for hir lewednesse / I hem diffye
Me thynketh they been lyk Iouynyan
ffat as a whale / and walkyng as a swan
Al vynolent / as botel in the spence
Hir preyere is / of ful greet reuerence
Whan they for soules / seye the psalm of Dauit
Lo buf they seye / cor meum eructauit
Who folweth cristes gospel / and his foore
But we that humble been / and chaast / and poore
Werkers of goddes word / nat auditours
Ther fore right as an hauk vp at a sours
Vp spryngeth in to their / right so prayeres
Of charitable / and chaste bisy freres
Maken hir sours / to goddes erys two
Thomas / Thomas / so mote I ryde or go
And by that lord / that clepid is seint yue
Nere thow oure brother / sholdestow nat thryue

oure chapitre / praye we day and nyght /
To crist / that he thee sende heele and myght /
Thy body / for to welden hastily
God woot quod he / no thyng ther of feele I
As help me crist / as I in fewe yeres
Haue spended / vp on diuerse maneres freres
Ful many a pound / yet fare I neuer the bet
Certeyn / my good haue I almoost biset /
Farwel my gold / for it is al ago
The frere answerde / o Thomas dostow so
What nedeth yow / diuerse freres seche
What nedeth hym / that hath a parfit leche
To sechen othere leches in the town
Youre inconstance / is youre confusioun
Holde ye thanne me / or elles oure couent /
To preye for yow / been insufficient /
Thomas that Iape / nys nat worth a myte
Youre maladye / is for we han to lyte
A yif that couent / half a quarter otes
A yif that couent / ·xxiiij· grotes
A yif that frere a peny / and lat hym go
Nay nay Thomas / it may no thyng be so
What is a ferthyng worth / parted in twelue
Lo ech thyng / that is oned in hym selue
Is moore strong / than whan it is to scatered
Thomas of me / thow shalt nat been yflatered
Thow woldest han oure labour / al for noght /
The hye god / that al this world hath wroght /
Seith / that the werkman worthy is his hyre
Thomas / noght of youre tresor I desire
As for my self / but that al oure couent
To preye for yow / is ay so diligent /
And for to buylden / cristes owene chirche
Thomas / if ye wol lernen for to wirche
Of buyldyng vp of chirches / may ye fynde
If it be good / in Thomas lyf of Inde
Ye lye heere / ful of anger and of Ire
With which the deuel set youre herte afire
And chiden heere / the sely Innocent /
Youre wyf / that is so meke and pacient /

	ELLESMERE
[In o]ure chapitre / praye we day and nyght	In oure Chapitre / nyght
To crist that he thee sende / heele and myght	crist / þat myght
Thy body / for to welden hastily	weelden
¶God woot quod he / no thyng ther of feele I	woot
As help me crist as I in fewe yeres	as in a fewe
Haue spended / vp on diu*er*se manere freres	I han spent /
Ful many a pound / yet fare I neu*ere* the bet	pound / neuer bet
Certeyn / my good haue I almoost biset	Certeyn good / .I. haue almoost
Farwel my gold / for it is al ago	
¶The frere answerde / o Thomas doostow so	dostow so
What nedeth yow / diu*er*se freres seche	
What nedeth hym / that hath a p*ar*fit leche	þat
To sechen / othere leches in the town	toun
Youre inconstance / is youre confusioun	
Holde ye thanne me / or ellis oure Couent	elles
To preye for yow / been insufficient	praye insufficient
Thomas / that Iape / nys nat worth a myte	Thomas nat
Youre maladye / is for we han to lyte	
A yif that Couent / half a quarter otes	9 Couent quart*er*
A yif that Couent .xxiiij. grotes	
A yif that frere a peny / and lat hym go	
Nay nay Thomas / it may no thyng be so	
What is a ferthyng worth / parted in twelue	ferthyng
Lo / ech thyng / that is oned in hym selue	Lo oned / in it selue
Is moore strong than whan it is to scatered	toscatered
Thomas / of me / thow shalt nat been yflatered	thou
Thow woldest han oure labour / al for noght	Thou labour noght
The hye god / that al this world hath wroght	wroght
Seith / that the werkman / worthy is his hire	Seith hyre
Thomas / noght of youre tresor I desire	noght youre
As for my self / but that al oure Couent	self Couent
To praye for yow / is ay so diligent	preye
And for to buylden / cristes owene chirche	
Thomas / if ye wol lernen for to wirche	
Of buyldyng vp of chirches / may ye fynde	buyldynge
If it be good / in Thomas lyf of Inde	
Ye lye heere / ful of Anger and of Ire	Anger of
With which / the deuel set youre herte afire	youre afyre
And chiden heere / the sely Innocent /	Innocent
Youre wyf / that is so meke and pacient	

1968 Omnis virtus vnita forcior est seipsa dispersa El

1973 Dignus est operarius mercede et cetera El

9¶Somono*ur* *84r*

The So*m*nour

	ELLESMERE
And ther fore Thomas / trowe me if thee leste	therfore
Ne stryue nat with thy wyf as for thy beste	wyf /
And bere this word awey / now by thy feith	ber feitħ
Touchynge swich thyng lo what the wise man seith	Touchynge this thyng wise seith
¶With Inne thyn hous / ne be thow no leou*n*	thou Leou*n*
To thy subgitz / do noon opp*re*ssiou*n*	
Ne make thyne aqueyntances / nat for to flee	
And Thomas / yet eft soones I charge thee	
Be war from hire / that in thy bosom slepeth	hire / þat
War fro the serpent that so sleighly crepeth	Be war / serpent / slily crepetħ
Vnder the gras / and styngeth subtilly	
Be war my sone / and herkne paciently	
That twenty thousand men / han lost hir lyues	
For stryuyng with hir lemmans and hir wyues	*with* le*m*mans
Now sith ye han / so holy meke a wyf	hooly
What nedeth yow Thomas / to maken stryf	
Ther nys ywis / no serpent so cruel	ywys /
Whan man tret on his tayl / ne half so fel	What man tret
As womman is / whan she hath caught an Ire	wo*m*man caught
Vengeance is thanne / al that they desire	
Ire is a synne / oon of the grete of seuene	
Abhomynable / vn to the god of heuene	
And to hym self / it is destrucciou*n*	
This euery lewed viker / or p*er*sou*n*	viker
Kan seye / how Ire engendreth homicide	homycide
Ire is in sooth / executour of pryde	
I koude of Ire / seye so muche sorwe	10
My tale / sholde laste til to morwe	laste / tomorwe
And ther fore praye I god / bothe day and nyght	therfore / preye *and* nyght
An Irous man / god sende hym litel myght	myght
It is greet harm / and c*er*tes greet pitee	and eek greet
To sette an Irous man in heigh degree	man / heigħ
Whilom / ther was an Irous potestat	potestat /
As seith Senek that durynge his estat	estaat
Vp on a day / out ryden knyghtes two	knyghtes
And as Fortune wolde / that it were so	Fortune / wolde
That oon of hem cam hom / that oother noght	hoom / noght
Anon the knyght bifore the Iuge is broght	knyght broght
That seyde thus / thow hast thy felawe slayn	thou
For which / I deme thee to the deeth certayn	c*er*tayn

1989 Noli esse sicut leo in domo tua euertens domesticos tuos opprimens subiectos tibi El

2017 De quodam potestate Iracundo El

19 ¶Somono*ur* *84v*

And therfore Thomas trowe me if thee leste
Ne stryue nat with thy wyf as for thy beste
And bere this word awey now by thy feith
Touchynge swich thyng lo what the wise man seith
Withinne thyn hous ne be thow no leon
To thy subgitz do noon oppressioun
Ne make thyne aqueyntances nat for to flee
And Thomas yet eft soones I charge thee
Be war from hire that in thy bosom slepeth
War fro the serpent that so slyly crepeth
Vnder the gras and styngeth subtilly
Be war my sone and herkne paciently
That twenty thousand men han lost hir lyues
ffor stryuyng with hir lemmans and hir wyues
Now sith ye han so holy meke a wyf
What nedeth yow Thomas to maken stryf
Ther nys ywis no serpent so cruel
Whan man tret on his tayl ne half so fel
As womman is whan she hath caught an Ire
Vengeance is thanne al that they desire
Ire is a synne oon of the grete of seuene
Abhomynable vn to the god of heuene
And to hym self it is destruccion
This euery lewed viker or persoun
Kan seye how Ire engendreth homicide
Ire is in sooth executour of pryde
I koude of Ire seye so muche sorwe
My tale sholde laste til to morwe
And therfore praye I god bothe day and nyght
An Irous man god sende hym litel myght
It is greet harm and eek greet pitee
To sette an Irous man in heigh degree
Whilom ther was an Irous potestat
As seith Senek that durynge his estat
Vp on a day out ryden knyghtes two
And as ffortune wolde that it were so
That oon of hem cam hoom that oother noght
Anon the knyght bifore the Iuge is broght
That seyde thus thow hast thy felawe slayn
ffor which I deme thee to the deeth certayn

… to another knyght/ comanded he
Go lede hym to the deeth/ I charge thee
And happed/ as they wente by the weye
Toward the place/ ther he sholde deye
The knyght cam/ which men wenden had be deed
Thanne thoghten they/ it were the beste reed
To lede hem bothe/ to the Iuge agayn
They seyden lord/ the knyght ne hath nat slayn
His felawe/ heere he stant hool alyue
¶ Ye shul be deed quod he/ so moot I thryue
This is to seyn/ bothe oon and two and thre
And to the firste knyght/ right thus spak he
¶ I dampned thee/ thou most algate be deed
And thow also/ most nedes lese thyn heed
ffor thow art cause/ why thy felawe deyth
And to the thridde knyght/ right thus he seith
Thow hast nat doon/ that I comanded thee
And thus he dide/ do sleen hem alle thre
¶ Irous Cambyses/ was eek dronkelewe
And ay delited hym/ to been a shrewe
And so bifel/ a lord of his meynee
That louede/ vertuous moralitee
Seyde on a day/ bitwix hem two right thus
¶ A lord is lost if he be vicius
And dronkenesse is eek a foul record
Of any man/ and namely in a lord
Ther is ful many an eighe/ and many an ere
Awaityng on a lord/ he noot nat where
ffor goddes loue/ drynk moore attemprely
Wyn maketh man/ to lesen wrecchedly
His mynde/ and eek his lymes euerychon
¶ The reuers shaltow se/ quod he anon
And preue it by thyn owene experience
That wyn ne dooth to folk/ no swich offence
Ther is no wyn/ bireueth me my myght/
Of hond ne foot/ ne of myne eyen sight/
And for despit he drank ful muchel moore
An hundred part/ than he hadde doon bifore
And right anon/ this yrous cursed wrecche
6· Leet this knyghtes sone/ bifore hym fecche

	ELLESMERE
[An]d to another knyght comanded he	And knyght
Go leed hym to the deeth / I charge thee	lede
And happed / as they wente by the weye	
Toward the place / ther he sholde deye	
The knyght cam / which men wenden had be deed	knyght
Thanne thoghten they / it were the beste reed	thoughte was
To lede hem bothe / to the Iuge agayn	
They seyden / lord / the knyght ne hath nat slayn	seiden knyght
His felawe / heere he stant hool alyue	standeth
¶Ye shul be deed quod he / so moot I thryue	Ye
This is to seyn / bothe oon and two and thre	That is oon / two /
And to the firste knyght right thus spak / he	knyght right spak
¶I dampned thee / thou most algate be deed	I most
And thow also / most nedes lese thyn heed	thou
For thow art cause / why thy felawe deyth	thou
And to the thridde knyght right thus he seith	knyght
Thow hast nat doon / that I comanded thee	Thou
And thus he dide / do sleen hem alle thre	thus / dide doon
¶Irous Cambyses / was eek dronkelewe	Irous Cambises / eek
And ay delited hym / to been a shrewe	
And so bifel / a lord of his meynee	
That louede / vertuous moralitee	loued
Seyde on a day / bitwix hem two right thus	bitwene right
¶A lord is ⟨lost if he be vicius⟩	lost if he be vicius
And dronkenesse / is eek a foul record	eek / record
Of any man / and namely in a lord	lord
Ther is ful many an eighe / and many an ere	eye
Awaityng on a lord / he noot nat where	lord / and he noot where
For goddes loue / drynk moore attemprely	drynk
Wyn maketh man / to lesen wrecchedly	
His mynde / and eek his lymes eu*er*ychon	and hise euerichon
¶The reuers shaltow se / quod he anon	shaltou anon
And preue it by thyn owene experience	preeue exp*er*ience
That wyn ne dooth to folk no swich offence	wyn /
Ther is no wyn / bireueth me my myght	11 myght
Of hond ne foot ne of myne eyen sight	hand sight
And for despit he drank ful muchel moore	drank
An hundred part than he hadde doon bifore	hondred hadde bifoore
And right anon / this Irous cursed wrecche	right
⟨.b.⟩ Leet this knyghtes sone / bifore hym fecche	Leet /
⟨.a.⟩	

11¶Somono*ur* *85r*

	ELLESMERE
Comandynge hym / he sholde bifore hym stonde	
And sodeynly / he took his bowe in honde	
And vp the streng he pulled to his ere	
And with an arwe / he slow the child right there	riħt
Now / wheither haue I / a siker hand or noon	
Quod he / is al my myght and mynde agoon	myħt agon
Hath wyn byreued me / myn eye sight	bireft me myne eyen siħt
¶What sholde I telle / thanswere of the knyght	knyħt
His sone was slayn / ther is namoore to seye	
Beth war ther fore / with lordes how ye pleye	therfore /
Syngeth **Placebo** / and I shal if I kan	
But if it / be / vn to a poure man	it
To a poure man / men sholde his vices telle	hise
But nat to a lord / thogh he sholde go to helle	thoħ
¶Lo Irous Syrus / thilke Percien	LO Cirus / Pe*r*cien
How he destroyed / the ryuer of Gysen	
For that an hors of his / was dreynt ther Inne	his
Whan that he wente / Babiloyne to wynne	þ*a*t Babiloigne
He made / that the Ryuer was so smal	Ryuer /
That wommen / myghte wade it ou*er* al	wo*m*men /
Lo what seyde he / that so wel teche kan	
Ne be no felawe / to an Irous man	felawe
Ne with no wood man / walke by the weye	wit*h*
Lest thee repente / I wol no ferther seye	repente / ther is namoore to seye
¶Now Thomas leeue brother / lef thyn Ire	NOw
Thow shalt me fynde / as Iust as is a Squyre	Thou Iust /
Hoold nat the deueles knyf / ay at thyn herte	knyf
Thyn angre dooth thee / al to soore smerte	
But shewe to me / al thy confessiou*n*	
¶Nay quod the sike man / by Seint Symou*n*	
I haue be shryuen this day / at my Curat	curat
I haue hym toold / hoolly al myn estat	toold
Nedeth namoore to speke of it seith he	namoore / speken
But if me list of myn humylitee	
¶Yif me thanne of thy gold / to make oure cloystre	
Quod he / for many a Muscle / and many an Oystre	oystre
Whan othere men / han been ful wel ateyse	other*e* ben
Hath been oure foode / oure Cloystre for to reyse	cloystre
And yet god woot vnnethe the fundement /	fundement
Parfourned is / ne of oure pauement	Pa*r*fourned

Comandynge hym / he sholde bifore hym stonde
And sodeynly / he took his bowe in honde
And vp the streng / he pulled to his ere
And with an arwe / he slow the child right there
Now / wheither haue I / a siker hand or noon
Quod he / is al my myght and mynde agoon
Hath wyn byreued me / myn eye sight
What sholde I telle / thanswere of the knyght /
His sone was slayn / ther is namoore to seye
Beth war ther fore / with lordes how ye pleye
Syngeth Placebo / and I shal if I kan
But if it be / vn to a pouere man
To a pouere man / men sholde his vices telle
But nat to a lord / thogh he sholde go to helle
Lo irous Cirus / thilke Percien
How he destroyed / the ryuer of Gysen
ffor that an hors of his / was dreynt ther inne
Whan that he wente / Babiloyne to wynne
He made / that the ryuer was so smal
That wommen / myghte wade it ouer al
lo what seyde he / that so wel teche kan
Ne be no felawe / to an irous man
Ne with no wood man / walke by the weye
lest thee repente / I wol no ferther seye
Now Thomas leeue brother / lef thyn ire
Thow shalt me fynde / as iust as is a squyre
Hoold nat the deueles knyf / ay at thyn herte
Thyn angre dooth thee / al to soore smerte
But shewe to me / al thy confessioun
Nay quod the sike man / by Seint Symoun
I haue be shryuen this day / at my Curat /
I haue hym toold / hoolly al myn estat /
Nedeth namoore to speke of it seith he
But if me list / of myn humylitee
Yif me thanne of thy gold / to make oure cloystre
Quod he / for many a muscle / and many an oystre
Whan othere men / han been ful wel at eyse
Hath been oure foode / oure cloystre for to reyse
And yet god woot / vnnethe the fundement /
Parfourned is / ne of oure pauement /

ys nat a tyle / yet with inne oure wones
By god / we owen fourty pound for stones
Now help Thomas / for hym þt harwed helle
Or ellis mote we / oure bookes selle
And if yow lakke / oure predicacion
Thanne gooth the world / al to destruccion
ffor who so / fro this world wolde vs byreue
So god me saue / Thomas by youre leue
he wolde byreue / out of the world the sonne
ffor who kan teche / and werchen as we konne
And that is nat / of litel tyme quod he
But sith Elie was / or Elize
Han freres been / that fynde I of record
In charitee / thonked be oure lord
Now Thomas / help for seinte charitee
And doun anon / he set hym on his knee
¶ This sike man / wax wel neigh wood for ire
he wolde that the frere / hadde been afire
With his false dissimulacion
Swich thyng / as is in my possession
Quod he / that may I yeue and noon oother
ye sey me thus / how that I am youre brother
¶ ye certes quod the frere / trusteth wel
I took oure dame / oure lettre with oure seel
¶ Now wel quod he / and som what / shal I yeue
Vn to youre holy couent / whil I lyue
And in thyn hand / thow shalt it han anon
On this condicion / and oother noon
That thow departe it so / my deere brother
That euery frere / haue as muche as oother
This shaltow swere / on thy p̄fession
With outen fraude / or cauelacion
¶ I swere it quod this frere / vp on my feith
And ther with al / his hand in his he leith
lo here my feith / in me shal be no lak
¶ Now thanne put thyn hand / doun by my bak
Seyde this man / and grope wel bihynde
Bynethe my buttok / there shaltow fynde
A thyng / that I haue hyd in pryuetee
¶ A thoghte this frere / that shal go with me

	ELLESMERE
[N]ys nat a tyle / yet⁊ with Inne oure wones	Nys tyl yet /
By god / we owen fourty pound for stones	
Now help Thomas / for hym þat harwed helle	12 ¶Now that
Or ellis mote we / oure bookes selle	For elles / moste we
And if yow lakke / oure predicacioun	ye
Thanne gooth the world / al to destruccioun	goth
For who so / fro this world / wolde vs bireue	so wolde / vs fro this world bireue
So god me saue / Thomas by youre leue	youre
He wolde bireue / out of the world the sonne	of this world
For who kan teche / and werchen as we konne	
And that is nat⁊ of litel tyme quod he	
But sith Elie was / or Elize	syn Ennok was / Elise
Han freres been / that fynde I of record	record
In charitee / thonked be oure lord	ythanked lord
Now Thomas / help for Seinte charitee	helpe seinte
And down anon / he set hym on his knee	doun sette
¶This sike man / weex wel neigh wood for Ire	THis wax ny
He wolde / that the frere / hadde been afire	þat had been on fire
With his false dissimulacioun	dissymulacioun
Swich thyng / as is in my possessioun	thyng⁊
Quod he / ∫ that may I yeue and noon oother	he / yeuen /
Ye sey me thus / how that I am youre brother	thus / that
¶Ye certes quod the frere / trusteth wel	weel
I took oure dame / oure lettre with oure sel	lettre and oure seel
¶Now wel quod he / and som what⁊ shal I yeue	
Vn to youre holy Couent⁊ whil I lyue	hooly
And in thyn hand / thow shalt it han anon	thou haue
On this condicioun / and oother noon	
That thow departe it so / my deere brother	thou my leeue brother
That euery frere / haue as muche as oother	haue also muche
This shaltow swere / on thy professioun	shaltou professioun
With outen fraude / or cauelacioun	cauillacioun
¶I swere it quod this frere / vp on my feith	frere / by my
And ther with al / his hand in his he leith	
Lo here my feith / in me / shal be no lak	heer me lak⁊
¶Now thanne put thyn hand / down by my bak⁊	put In thyn hand doun
Seyde this man / and grope wel bihynde	
Bynethe my buttok⁊ there shaltow fynde	ther
A thyng⁊ that I haue hyd in pryuetee	
¶A thoghte this frere / that shal go with me	frere / this shal with

12 ¶Somonour 85v

	ELLESMERE
And down his hand / he launcheth to the clifte	doun
In hope / for to fynde there a yifte	
And whan this sike man / felte this frere	
Aboute his tuwel / grope there and heere	
Amydde his hand / he leet the frere a fartꝭ	
Ther is no capul / drawyng in a Cartꝭ	Ther nys no drawynge
That myghte han late a fartꝭ of swich a sown	haue lete soun
¶The frere vp stirte / as dooth a wood leoun	
A false cherl quod he / for goddes bones	fals
This hastow for despitꝭ doon for the nones	
Thow shalt abye this fartꝭ if *þat* I may	13 Thou that
His meynee / which that herden this affray	¶His whiche
Cam lepyng In / and chaced out the frere	lepynge
And forth he gooth / with a ful angry cheere	Angry
And fette his felawe / ther as lay his stoor	
He looked / as he were a wilde boor	as it were
He grynt with his teeth / so was he wrooth	grynte
A sturdy paas / doun to the court he gooth	the lordes co*ur*t
Wher as ther woned / a man of greet honour	Where as woned a man /
To whom / that he was alwey confessour	
This worthy man / was lord of that village	
This frere cam / as he were in a rage	
Where as this lord / sat etyngꝭ at his boord	Wher*e* bordꝭ
Vnnethe / myghte the frere speke a woord	Vnnethes / myghte frere / wordꝭ
Til atte laste / he seyde / god yow see	
¶This lord gan looke / and seyde benedicitee	lord bigan to looke / seide
What frere Ioħn / what manere world is this	maner this ⸗
I se wel / that som thyngꝭ ther is amys	I trowe / som maner thyngꝭ
Ye looken / as the wode were ful of theuys	wode /
Sit doun anon / and tel me what youre grief is	your*e*
And it shal been amended / if I may	if that .I.
¶I haue quod he / had a despit to day	despit this day
God yelde yow / adown in youre village	adoun your*e*
That in this world / ther nys so poure a page	world / is noon so
That he nolde haue / abhomynacioun	haue abhomynaciou*n*
Of thatꝭ I haue receyued in youre toun	
And yetꝭ ne greueth me / no thyng so soore	yet greueth
As that this olde cherl / with lokkes hoore	
Blasphemed hath / oure hooly Couent eke	Blasphemed Hath /
¶Now maister quod this lord / I yow biseke	

13 ¶Somono*ur* *86r*

And down his hand / he launcheth to the clifte
In hope / for to fynde there a yifte
And whan this sike man / felte this frere
Aboute his tuwel / grope there and heere
Amydde his hand / he leet the frere a fart /
Ther is no capul / drawyng in a cart /
That myghte han lete a fart / of swich a sown
¶ The frere up stirte / as dooth a wood leoun
A false cherl quod he / for goddes bones
This hastow for despit / doon for the nones
Thow shalt abye this fart / if þat I may
His meynee / which that herden this affray
Cam lepyng In / and chaced out the frere
And forth he gooth / with a ful angry cheere
And fette his felawe / ther as lay his stoor
He looked / as he were a wilde boor
He grynt with his teeth / so was he wrooth
A sturdy paas / doun to the court he gooth
Wher as ther woned / a man of greet honour
To whom / that he was alwey confessour
This worthy man / was lord of that village
This frere cam / as he were in a rage
Where as this lord / sat etyng / at his boord
Unnethe / myghte the frere speke a word
Til atte laste / he seyde / god yow see
¶ This lord gan looke / and seyde benedicitee
What frere John / what manere world is this
I se wel / that som thyng ther is amys
Ye looken / as the wode were ful of thevys
Sit doun anon / and tel me what youre grief is
And it shal been amended / if I may
¶ I haue quod he / had a despit to day
God yelde yow / adown in youre village
That in this world / ther nys so poure a page
That he nolde haue / abhomynacioun
Of that / I haue receyued in youre toun
And yet / ne greueth me / no thyng so soore
As that this olde cherl / with lokkes hoore
Blasphemed hath / oure holy couent eke
¶ Now maister quod this lord / I yow biseke

No maister sire quod he / but seruitour
Thogh I haue had in scole / that honour
God liketh nat / that Raby men vs calle
Neither in market / nyn youre large halle
No force quod he / but tel me al youre grief
Sire quod this frere / an odious meschief
This day bityd is / to myn ordre and me
And so per consequens / to ech degree
Of holy chirche / god amende it soone
Sire quod the lord / ye woot what is to doone
Distempre yow noght / ye be my confessour
Ye been the salt of therthe / and the sauour
ffor goddes loue / youre pacience ye holde
Tel me youre grief / And he anon hym tolde
As ye han herd biforn / ye woot wel what
The lady of the hous / ay stille sat
Til she hadde herd / what the frere sayde
Ey goddes moder quod she / blisful mayde
Is ther aught ellis / tel me feithfully
Madame quod he / how thynketh yow ther by
How þt me thynketh quod she / so god me spede
I seye a cherl / hath doon a cherles dede
What sholde I seye / god lat hym neuere thee
His sike heed is ful of vanytee
I holde hym in a manere frenesye
Madame quod he / by god I shal nat lye
But I on oother wise may be wreke
I shal diffame hym ouer al wher I speke
The false blasphemour / that charged me
To parte / that wol nat departed be
To euery man yliche / with meschaunce
The lord sat stille / as he were in a traunce
And in his herte / he rolled vp and doun
How hadde this cherl / ymaginacioun
To shewe swich a probleme / to the frere
Neuere erst er now / herde I swich matere
I trowe the deuel / putte it in his mynde
In arsmetrik / shal ther no man fynde
Biforn this day / of swich a question
Who sholde make a demonstracion

	ELLESMERE
[¶]No maister sire quod he / but seruytour	¶No maister quod seruitour
Thogh I haue had in scole / that honour	Thogħ scole swich honour
God liketh nat' that Raby men vs calle	
Neither in Market' nyn youre large halle	Market' ne in youre
¶No force quod he / but tel me al youre grief	fors grief'
¶Sire quod this frere / an odious meschief	quod he an meschief /
This day bityd is / to myn ordre and me	
And so ***par* consequens** / to ech degree	***par* consequens** / in ech
Of holy chirche / god amende it soone	hooly
¶Sire quod the lord / ye woot what is to doone	¶Sir*e*
Distempre yow noght' ye be my confessour	nogħt / Confessour
Ye been the salt of therthe / and the sauour	the erthe /
For goddes loue / youre pacience ye holde	
Tel me youre grief / and he anon hym tolde	your*e*
As ye han herd biforn / ye woot wel what	what'
The lady of the hous / ay stille sat'	¶The hous / al stille sat /
Til she hadde herd / what the frere sayde	had
¶Ey goddes moder quod she / blisful mayde	Ey mooder
Is ther aught ellis / tel me feithfully	14 oght elles / telle
¶Madame quod he / how thynketh yow ther by	thynke ye her by //
¶How þ*at* me thynketh quod she / so god me spede	that she // speede
I seye / a cherl / hath doon a cherles dede	cherl doon /
What sholde I seye / god lat hym neu*er*e thee	shold'
His sike heed / is ful of vanytee	
I holde hym / in a manere frenesye	
¶Madame quod he / by god I shal nat lye	
But I / on oother wise / may be wreke	But I on hym / oother weyes be
I shal diffame hym / ouer al wher I speke	shal disclaundre hym / ou*er* al ther I
The false blasphemour / that charged me	This false blasphemo*ur* /
To parte / that wol nat departed be	
To euery man yliche / with meschaunce	eu*er*y
¶The lord sat stille / as he were in a traunce	
And in his herte / he rolled vp and down	doun
How hadde this cherl / ymaginacioun	hadde the cherl / this ymaginacioun //
To shewe swich a probleme / to the frere	p*ro*bleme / to a frere
Neu*er*e erst er now / herde I swich matere	Neuere erst' I of swich mateere
I trowe the deuel / putte it in his mynde	trowe /
In Arsmetrik' shal ther no man fynde	Ars Metrik'
Bifore this day / of swich a questiou*n*	Biforn
Who sholde / make a demonstraciou*n*	Certes / it was a shrewed conclusiou*n*

14 ¶Somono*ur* *86v*

⸗The So*m*nour⸗	ELLESMERE
That euery man sholde han / ylike his part /	eu*er*y man / haue yliche partꝭ
As of a soun / or sauour / of a fartꝭ	of the soun /
O nyce prowde cherl / I shrewe his face	O vile proude
¶Lo sires quod the lord / with harde grace	Lo
Who euere herde / of swich a thyngꝭ er now	herde eu*er*e /
To euery man ylike / tel me how	eu*er*y how ⸗
It is an inpossible / it may nat be	
Ey nyce cherl / god lat hym neu*er*e thee	lete thee neu*er*e thee
The rumblyng of a fartꝭ and euery soun	rumblynge fart / eu*er*y
Nys but of Eyr / reuerberacioun	Nis Eir reue*r*beracioun
And ther it wasteth / lite and lite awey	And eu*er*e it litel and litel
Ther nys no man / kan deme by my fey	Ther is no deemen
If that it were / departed equally	
What lo my cherl / lo yet how shrewedly	
Vn to my confessour / to day he spak /	spakꝭ
I holde hym certeynly / demonyakꝭ	certeyn / a demonyak /
Now ete youre mete / and lat the cherl go pleye	your*e*
Lat hym go hange hym selfꝭ a deuel weye[15]	honge self[16]
¶Now stood / the lordes Squyer at the boord	NOw stood Squier bord'
That carf his mete / and herde word by woord	karfꝭ word' by word'
Of alle thyngꝭ of which I haue yow sayd	thynges / whiche that I haue sayd'
¶My lord quod he / be ye nat yuele apayd	My beth nat apayd'
I koude telle / for a gowne clooth	17 ¶I clootħ
To yow sire frere / so ye be nat wrooth	sir*e* wrootħ
How that this fartꝭ sholde euene ydeled be	fartꝭ euene delt shal be
Among youre Couentꝭ if it liked me	your*e* lyked
¶Tel quod the lord / and thow shalt haue anon	thou
A gowne clooth / by god and by Seint Ioħn	god /
¶My lord quod he / whan that the weder is fair	*pat*
With outen wynd / or p*er*turbynge of Air	wynd' /
Lat brynge a Cartwheel / heere in to this halle	Cartwheel in
But looke that it haue / his spokes alle	looke / haue
Twelf spokes / hath a Cartwheel comunly	Twelue
And brynge me thanne twelf freres / woot ye why	bryng .xij. why ⸗
For thrittene / is a Couentꝭ as I gesse	For twelue is Couent /
Youre confessour heere / for his worthynesse	The Confessour
Shal p*ar*fourne vp / the nombre of this Couentꝭ	of his Couentꝭ
Thanne shal they knele adown / by oon assentꝭ	knele doun /
And to euery spokes ende / in this manere	
Ful sadly / leye his nose / shal a frere	nose

[15] No break in Hg.

[16] Break in El followed by:

¶The wordes of the lordes Squier and his keru*er*e / for departynge of the fartꝭ on twelue

[17] ¶Somono*ur* *87r*

That euery man sholde han ylike his part
As of a soun / or sauour / of a fart /
O nyce proude cherl / I shrewe his face
Lo sires quod the lord / with harde grace
Who euere herde / of swich a thyng er now
To euery man ylike / tel me how
It is an inpossible / it may nat be
Ey nyce cherl / god lat hym neuere thee
The rumblynge of a fart / and euery soun
Nys but of Eyr / reuerberacioun
And ther it wasteth / lite and lite awey
Ther nys no man / kan deme by my fey
If that it were / departed equally
What lo my cherl / lo yet how shrewedly
Vn to my confessour / to day he spak /
I holde hym certeynly / demonyak /
Now ete youre mete / and lat the cherl go pleye
Lat hym go hange hym self / a deuel weye
Now stood / the lordes squyer at the bord
That carf his mete / and herde word by word
Of alle thyng / of which I haue yow sayd
My lord quod he / be ye nat yuele apayd
I koude telle / for a gowne clooth
To yow sire frere / so ye be nat wrooth
How that this fart / sholde euene ydeled be
Among youre Couent / if it lyked me
Tel quod the lord / and thow shalt haue anon
A gowne clooth / by god and by Seint John
My lord quod he / whan that the weder is fair
With outen wynd / or perturbynge of air
Lat brynge a cartwheel / heere in to this halle
But looke that it haue / his spokes alle
Twelf spokes hath a cartwheel comunly
And brynge me thanne twelf freres woot ye why
ffor thrittene / is a Couent / as I gesse
Youre confessour heere / for his worthynesse
Shal parfourne vp / the nombre of this Couent /
Thanne shal they knele adoun / by oon assent /
And to euery spokes ende / in this manere
fful sadly leye his nose / shal a frere

Youre noble Confessour / ther god hym saue
Shal holde his nose / vp right vnder the naue
Thanne shal this cherl / with bely / stif and toght /
As any tabour / hyder been ybroght /
And sette hym on the wheel / right of this cart /
Vp on the naue / and make hym lete a fart /
And ye shal seen / on peril of my lyf
By preue / which that is demonstratif
That equally / the soun of it wol wende
And eek the stynk / vn to the spokes ende
Saue / that this worthy man / youre Confessour
By cause he is a man of greet honour
Shal han the firste fruyt / as reson is
The noble vsage of freres / yet is this
The worthy men of hem / shul first be serued
And certeynly / he hath it wel disserued
He hath to day / taught vs so muchel good
With prechyng in the pulpit ther he stood
That I may vouche sauf / I seye for me
He hadde the firste smel / of fartes thre
And so wolde / al his Couent hardily
He bereth hym / so faire and holily
The lord / the lady / ech man saue the frere
Seyden / that Jankyn spak in this matere
As wel as Euclyde / or Protholomee
Touchynge the cherl / they seyde subtiltee
And hy wit / made hym speke as he spak
He nys no fool / ne no demonyak
And Jankyn hath ywonne a newe gowne
My tale is doon / we been almoost at towne

Here endeth the Somnours tale

	ELLESMERE
[Y]oure noble Confessour / ther god hym saue	Your*e* Confessourꝛ ther*e*
Shal holde his nose / vp right vnder the Naue	vprigħt /
Thanne shal this cherl / with baly / stif and toghtꝛ	wit*h* bely toghħt
As any tabour / hider been ybroghtꝛ	Tabour / been hyder ybroghħtꝛ
And sette hym on the wheel / right of this Cartꝛ	righħt
Vp on the Naue / and make hym lete a fartꝛ	
And ye shal seen / on pe*r*il of my lyf	shul seen / vp pe*r*il lyf /
By proue / which that is demonstratyf	preeue / demonstratifꝛ
That equally / the soun of it wol wende	
And eek the stynk / vn to the spokes ende	eke stynkꝛ
Saue / that this worthy man / youre Confessour	Saue þ*at* your*e*
By cause / he/is a man of greet honour	he is
Shal han the firste fruytꝛ as reson is	haue fruytꝛ / resou*n*
The noble vsage of freres / yet is this	As yetꝛ the noble vsage / of freres is |
The worthy men of hem / shul first be serued	
And certeynly / he hath it wel disserued	c*er*teinly / weel
He hath to day / taughtꝛ vs so muchel good	day muche
With p*re*chyngꝛ in the pulputꝛ ther he stood	pulpitꝛ
That I may vouche sauf / I seye for me	sey
He hadde the firste smel / of fartes thre	
And so wolde / al his Couent hardily	al the Couentꝛ
He bereth hym / so faire and holily	hoolily
¶The lord / the lady / ech man / saue the frere	lady / and alle men
Seyden / that Iankyn / spak in this matere	Seyde / þ*at* Iankyn spak /
As wel / as Euclyde / or Protholomee	wel Euclude /
Touchynge the cherl / they seyde subtiltee	Touchynge this cherl /
And hy witꝛ made hym speke / as he spak	heigh spak /
He nys no fool / ne no demonyakꝛ	
And Iankyn hath ywonne / a newe gowne	Iankyn / ywonne
My tale is doon / we been almoost at towne	
¶Here endeth the Somnours tale[18]	¶Heere endeth the Somonours tale

[18] A blank leaf follows in Hg.

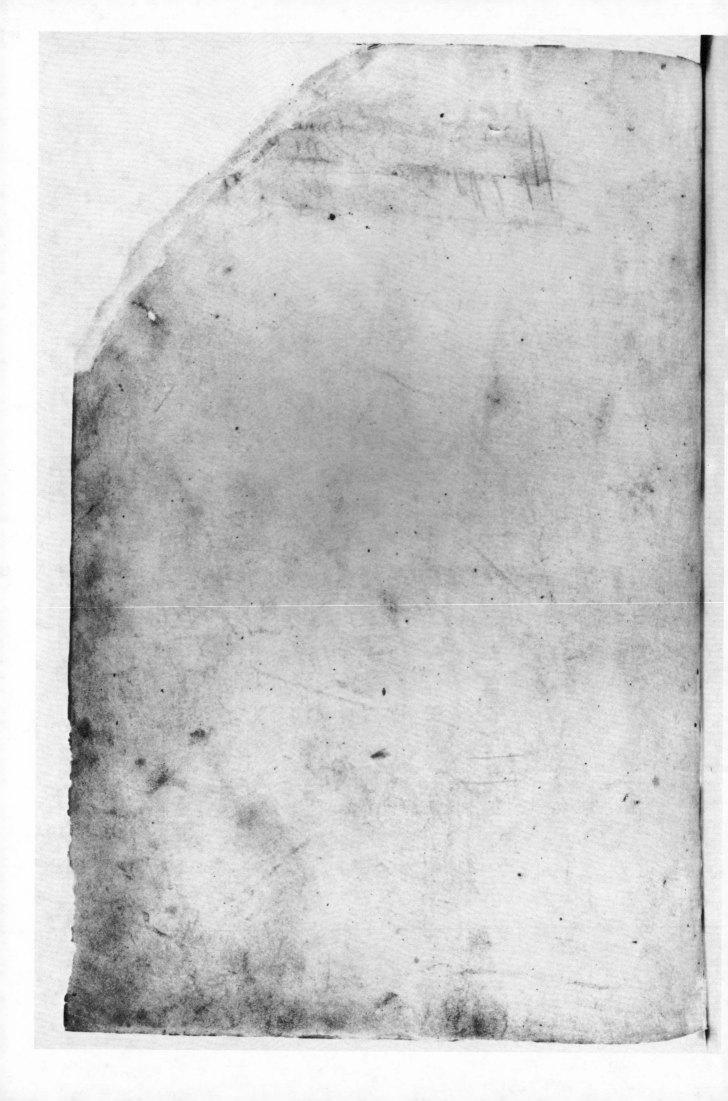

¶Here bigynneth the prologe of the Monkes [tale]

WHan ended was my tale / of Melibee
And of Prudence / and hir*e* benygnitee
Oure hoost seyde / as I am feithful man
And by / that precious corpus Madrian
I hadde leu*ere* / than a barel Ale
That goode lief my wyf / hadde herd this tale
She nys no thyng of swich pacience
As was / this Melibeus wif Prudence
By goddes bones / whan I bete my knaues
She bryngeth me / the grete clobbed staues
And crieth / slee the dogges euerichon
And breke hem / bothe bak and euery bon
And if *þat* / any neighebore / of myne
Wol nat in chirche / to my wyf enclyne
Or be so hardy / to hir*e* to trespace
Whan she cometh / she raumpeth in my face
And crieth / false coward wrek thy wyf
By corpus bones / I wol haue thy knyf
And thow shalt haue my distaf / and go spynne
Fro day to nyght right thus she wol bigynne
Allas she seith / *þat* euere *þat* I was shape
To wedden a Milksop*e* / or a coward Ape
That wol been ouerlad / of euery wight
Thow darst nat stonden / by thy wyues right
This is my lif / but if *þat* I wol fighte
And out at dore / anoon I moot me dighte
Or ellis I am but lost but if *þat* I
Be lyk a wilde leou*n* / fool hardy
I woot wel / she wol do me sle som day
Som neighebore / and thanne go my way
For I am p*er*ilous / with knyf in honde
Al be it that I dar nat hir*e* withstonde
For she is big in armes / by my feith
That shal he fynde / *þat* hir*e* mysdooth / or seith
But lat vs passe awey / fro this matere
¶My lord the Monk quod he / be myrie of cheere

¶The murye wordes of the Hoost / to the Monk[1]

ended /
benignytee
by pr*e*cious
leuere /
good
thyng /
was wyf
me forth / the
euerichoon
brek / boon
¶And that neighebore
comth / rampeth
coward / wyf /
knyf /
thou distaf
nyght / right
that eu*ere*
ou*er*lad with eu*er*y wight
Thou nat stonden right
¶This lif that fighte
anon dighte
elles that
lik Leou*n*
slee
hir*e* nat
is / byg Armes feith
mysdooth
mateere

[1] ¶Monk *168r*

Heere bigynneth the prologe of the Monkes

Whan ended was my tale of Melibee
And of Prudence / and hir benygnytee
Oure hoost seyde / as I am feithful man
And by that precious corpus Madrian
I hadde leuere / than a barel ale
That goode lief my wyf / hadde herd this tale
She nys no thyng / of swich pacience
As was / this Melibeus wyf Prudence
By goddes bones / whan I bete my knaues
She bryngeth me / the grete clobbed staues
And crieth / slee the dogges euerichon
And breke hem / bothe bak and euery bon
And if þt any neighebore of myne
Wol nat in chirche / to my wyf enclyne
Or be so hardy / to hire to trespace
Whan she cometh / she rampeth in my face
And crieth / false coward / wrek thy wyf
By corpus bones / I wol haue thy knyf
And thow shalt haue my distaf / and go spynne
Fro day to nyght / right thus she wol bigynne
Allas she seith / þt euere þt I was shape
To wedden a milksop / or a coward ape
That wol been ouerlad / of euery wight
Thow darst nat stonden / by thy wyues right
This is my lif / but if þt I wol fighte
And out at dore / anoon I moot me dighte
Or ellis I am but lost / but if þt I
Be lyk a wilde leon / fool hardy
I woot wel / she wol do me sle som day
Som neighebore / and thanne go my way
ffor I am perilous / with knyf in honde
Al be it that I dar nat hire withstonde
ffor she is byg in armes / by my feith
That shal he fynde / þt hire mysdooth or seith
But lat vs passe awey / fro this matere
Oure lord the Monk quod he / be myrie of cheere

Or ye shul telle a tale trewely
Lo Rouchestre / stant heer faste by
Ryde forth myn owene lord / brek nat oure game
But by my trouthe / I knowe nat youre name
Wher shal I calle yow / my lord daun John
Or daun Thomas / or ellis daun Albon
Of what hous be ye / by youre fader kyn
I vowe to god / thow hast a ful fair skyn
It is a gentil pasture / ther thow goost
Thow art nat lyk / a penaunt or a goost /
Vp on my feith / thow art som officer
Som worthy sexteyn / or som celerer
ffor by my fader soule / as to my doom
Thow art a maister / whan thou art at hoom
No poure cloystrer / ne no nouys
But a gouernour / wily and wys
And therwith al of brawnes & of bones
A wel farynge persone / for the nones
I prey to god / yeue hym confusion
That first thee broghte vn to religion
Thow woldest han been a tredefoul aright /
Haddestow / as greet a leue as thow hast myght /
To parfourne / al thy lust in engendrure
Thow haddest bigeten ful many a creature
Allas / why werestow so wyd a cope
God yeue me sorwe / but and I were a Pope
Nat oonly thow / but euery myghty man
Thogh he were shore / ful hye vp on his pan
Sholde haue a wyf / for al the world is lorn
Religion hath take vp al the corn
Of tredyng / and we borel men been shrympes
Of feble trees / they comen wrecched ympes
This maketh þt oure heires beth so sklendre
And feble / þt they may nat wel engendre
This maketh þt oure wyues wole assaye
Religious folk / for ye mowe bettre paye
Of Venus paiementz / than may we
God woot / no lussheburgh payen ye
But be nat wrooth my lord / thogh þt I pleye
Ful ofte in game / a sooth I haue herd seye

	ELLESMERE
[Fo]r / ye shul telle a tale trewely	For
Lo / Rouchestre / stant heer fasteby	Loo faste by
Ride forth myn owene lord / brek nat oure game	Ryde
But by my trouthe / I knowe nat youre name	
Wher shal I calle yow / my lord Daun Iohn	daun
Or Daun Thomas / or ellis Daun Albon	daun elles daun
Of what hous be ye / by youre fader kyn	
I vow to god / thow hast a ful fair skyn	vowe thou
It is a gentil pasture / ther thow goost	2
Thow art nat lyk a penaunt or a goost	Thou penant
Vp on my feith / thow art som Officer	Vpon thou
Som worthy Sexteyn / or som Celerer	
For by my fader soule / as to my doom	
Thow art a maister / whan thou art at hom	Thou maister hoom
No poure Cloistrer / ne no novys	cloystrer Novys
But a gou*er*nour / wily and wys	
And ther with al / of brawnes *and* of bones	therw*ith* and
A wel farynge p*er*sone / for the nones	
I prey to god / yeue hym confusiou*n*	pray
That first thee broghte / vn to Religiou*n*	broghte /
Thow woldest han been a tredefoul aright	Thou been / tredefowel aright
Haddestow / as greet a leue as thow hast myght	leeue / thou myght
To p*ar*fourne / al thy lust in engendrure	p*ar*fourne lust /
Thow haddest bigeten / ful many a creature	Thou haddest
Allas / why werestow so wyd a cope	werestow / Cope
God yeue me sorwe / but and I were a Pope	pope
Nat oonly thow / but euery myghty man	thou /
Thogh he were shore / ful hye vp on his pan	Though shorn /
Sholde haue a wyf for al the world is lorn	wyf /
Religion / hath take vp al the corn	Religiou*n* /
Of tredyng and we borel men been shrympes	tredyng
Of feble trees / ther comen wrecched ympes	fieble
This maketh / þ*at* oure heires beth so sklendre	3
And feble / þ*at* they may nat wel engendre	
This maketh / þ*at* oure wyues wole assaye	that
Religious folk / for ye mowe bettre paye	folk
Of Venus paiementz / than may we	mowe
God woot no lussheburgh payen ye	Lussheburgh
But be nat wrooth my lord / thogh þ*at* I pleye	wrooth / lord for þ*at*
Ful ofte in game / a sooth I haue herd seye	

2 ¶Monk *168v*

3 *Out* El 3147-48.

	ELLESMERE
¶This worthy Monk / took al in pacience	
And seyde / I wol doon al my diligence	
As fer / as sowneth in to honestee	fer sowneth /
To telle yow a tale / or two / or three	
And if yow list' to herkne hiderward	hyderward'
I wol yow seyn / the lyf of Seint Edward	wol seyn lyf / seint Edward'
Or ellis first' tragedies wol I telle	ellis / Tragedies
Of whiche / I haue an hundred in my Celle	I /
Tragedie is to seyn / a certeyn storie	¶Tragedie
As olde bokes / maken vs memorie	bookes /
Of hym / þ*at* stood in greet p*ro*sp*er*itee	that stood /
And is yfallen / out of heigh degree	heigħ
In to myserie / and endeth wrecchedly	
And they been / versified comunly	been co*m*munely
Of .vj. feet' whiche men clepyn Exametron	feet' · which clepen Exametrou*n*
In prose eek' been endited many oon	eek /
And eek in metre / in many a sondry wise	meetre / wyse
Lo this declaryng' oghte ynogh suffise	Lo / ogħte ynogħ
¶Now herkneth / if yow liketh for to heere	[4] Now herknetħ / liketħ
But first' I yow biseke / in this matere	first / biseeke / mateere
Though I by ordre / telle nat thise thynges	Thougħ
Be it of Popes / Emp*er*ours / or kynges	
After hir ages / as men writen fynde	
But telle hem / som bifore / and som bihynde	tellem hem / bifore *and*
As it now cometh / vn to my remembrance	comth / remembrau*n*ce
Haueth me excused / of myn ignorance	Haue excused ignorau*n*ce
	¶Explicit'
¶Here bigynneth / the Monkes tale	¶Heere bigynneth / the Monkes tale / de casib*us* viror*um* Illustrium
I Wol biwaille / in manere of Tragedie	[5] wol
The harm of hem / that stoode in heigh degree	heigħ
And fillen so / that ther nas no remedie	
To brynge hem / out of hir*e* Aduersitee	adu*er*sitee
For certeyn / whan þ*at* Fortune list to flee	certein /
Ther may no man / the cours of hir*e* withholde	hire
Lat no man triste / on blynd p*ro*speritee	truste / prosp*er*itee
Beth war / by thise ensamples / trewe and olde	Be war of thise

[4] ¶Monk' *169r*

[5] Miniature of the Monk and two hounds in right margin.

This worthy monk / took al in pacience
And seyde / I wol doon al my diligence
As fer / as souneth in to honestee
To telle yow a tale / or two / or three
And if yow list / to herkne hyderward
I wol yow seyn the lyf of Seint Edward
Or ellis first / tragedies wol I telle
Of whiche / I haue an hundred in my celle
Tragedie is to seyn / a certeyn storie
As olde bokes / maken vs memorie
Of hym / þt stood in greet prosperitee
And is yfallen / out of heigh degree
In to myserie / and endeth wrecchedly
And they been / versified communly
Of vi. feet / whiche men clepyn Exametron
In prose eek been endited many oon
And eek in metre / in many a sondry wise
Lo this declaryng / oghte ynogh suffise
Now herkneth / if yow liketh for to heere
But first I yow biseke / in this mateere
Though I by ordre / telle nat thise thynges
Be it of Papes / Emperours / or kynges
After hir ages / as men writen fynde
But telle hem som bifore / and som bihynde
As it now cometh / vn to my remembrance
Haueth me excused / of myn ignorance

Here bigynneth the Monkes tale

I Wol biwaille / in manere of Tragedie
The harm of hem / that stode in heigh degree
And fillen so / that ther nas no remedie
To brynge hem out / of hir aduersitee
For certeyn / whan þt Fortune list to flee
Ther may no man / the cours of hir withholde
Lat no man truste / on blynd prosperitee
Beth war / by thise ensamples trewe and olde

At Lucifer though he an Angel were
And nat a man at hym I wol bigynne
For though Fortune may noon Angel dere
From heigh degree yet fil he for his synne
Doun in to helle where as he yet is inne
O Lucifer brightest of Angels alle
Now artow Sathanas that mayst nat twynne
Out of myserie in which þt thou art falle

Sampson

Lo Sampson which that was annunciat
By the Angel longe er his natiuitee
And was to god almyghty consecrat
And stood in noblesse whil he myghte see
Was neuere swich another as was he
To speke of strengthe and ther wt hardynesse
But to hise wyues tolde he his secree
Thurgh which he slow hym self for wrecchednesse

Sampson this noble almyghty champion
With outen wepne saue hise handes tweye
He slow and al to rente the leon
Toward his weddyng walkynge by the weye
His false wyf koude hym so plese and preye
Til she his conseil knew and she vntrewe
Vn to his foos his conseil gan biwreye
And hym forsook and took another newe

Thre hundred foxes took Sampson for Ire
And alle hir tayles he togydre bond
And sette the foxes tayles alle on fire
For he on euery tayl hadde knyt a brond
And they brende alle the cornes in that lond
And alle hir Olyueres and vynes eke
A thousand men he slow eek with his hond
And hadde no wepne but an asses cheke

Whan they were slayn so thursted hym þt he
Was wel ny lorn for which he gan to preye
That god wolde on his peyne haue som pitee
And sende hym drynke or elles moste he deye
And of this asses cheke that was dreye
Out of a wang tooth sprang anon a welle
Of which he drank ynogh shortly to seye
Thus heelp hym god as Iudicum kan telle

Lo Adam in the feld of damyss[...]
Wt goddes owene fynger wro[...]
he And nat bigeten of mannes sp[...]
vnclene And welte al paradys
sauynge o tree Hadde neuere wo[...]
man so hey degree As Adam til
for mysgouernance Was dryue[...]
of his hey prospitee To labour
to helle and to meschaunce

AT lucifer / thogh he an Aungel were
And nat a man / at hym I wol bigynne
For thogh Fortune / may noon Aungel dere
From heigh degree / yet fil he for his synne
Doun in to helle / where as he yet is Inne
O Lucifer / brightest of Aungels alle
Now artow Sathanas / that mayst nat twynne
Out of Miserie / in which *þat* thou art falle

⟨Lo Adam in the feld of Damysse[ne]
W*ith* godes owne fynger wrowt [was] he
And nat bygeten of mannes sper[me] vnclene
And welte al paradiis sauyng o tree
Had neuere word[ly] man so hey degre
As Adam til [he] for mysgou*er*nance
Was dryue o[wt] of his hey prosp*er*itee
To labour [and] to helle and to meschance⟩

Sampson LO Sampson / which that was anunciat'
By the Aungel / longe er his natiuitee
And was / to god almyghty consecrat'
And stood in noblesse / whil he myghte see
Was neuere swich another / as was he
To speke of strengthe / and ther w*ith* hardynesse
But to hise wyues / tolde he his secree
Thurgh which / he slow hym self for wrecchednesse

¶Sampson / this noble almyghty champiou*n*
With outen wepne / saue hise hondes tweye
He slow / and al to rente the leou*n*
Toward his weddyng' walkynge by the weye
His false wyf / koude hym so plese and preye
Til she his conseil knew / and she vntrewe
Vn to his foos / his conseil gan biwreye
And hym forsook / and took another newe

¶Thre hundred foxes / took Sampson for Ire
And alle hir tayles / he togydre bond
And sette the foxes tayles / alle on fire
For he on euery tayl / hadde knyt a brond
And they brende / alle the cornes in that lond
And alle hir*e* Olyueris / and Vynes eke
A thousand men / he slow with his hond
And hadde no wepne / but an Asses cheke

¶Whan they were slayn / so thursted hym / *þat* he
Was wel ny lorn / for which he gan to preye
That god / wolde on his peyne / haue som pitee
And sende hym drynke / or ellis moste he deye
And of this Asses cheke / that was dreye
Out of a wang' tooth / sprang anon a welle
Of which he drank ynogh / shortly to seye
Thus heelp hym god / as Iudicum kan telle

AT Lucifer / though / Angel ⌈¶Lucifer⌉
wol I
though Angel
heigh fel
where he
Lucifer' brightest'. Angels
þat
miserie / art'

Loo Adam / in the feeld of Damyssene ⌈¶Adam⌉
With goddes owene fynger' wroght was he
And nat bigeten / of mannes sp*er*me vnclene
And welte al Paradys / sauynge o tree
Hadde neu*er*e worldly man so heigh degree
As Adam / til he for mysgouernau*n*ce
Was dryuen / out of hys hye prosp*er*itee
To labour and to helle / and to meschau*n*ce

Loo Sampsou*n* / Annunciat' ⌈¶Sampson⌉
By Angel / Natiuitee
myghte
neu*er*e / another hee
toolde
Thurgh self /

6 Sampsou*n* / almyghty Champiou*n*
wepene / handes tweyne
torente
Toward'
hise foos /
forsook'.

Thre
bond'
he / had knyt' brond'
lond'
Olyueres / vynes
slow eek w*ith* hond'
wepene /

Whan that
god wolde / peyne han
elles
asses
drank anon / shortly
heelp*e* can

[6] ¶Monk / 169*v*

The Monkes tale

¶By verray force / at Gazan / on a nyght
Maugree Philistiens / of that Citee
The gates of the toun / he hath vp plight
And on his bak ycaried hem hath he
Hye on an hiƚ / wher*e* as men myghte hem se
O noble almyghty Sampsou*n* / leef and deere
Had thow nat toold / to wommen thy secree
In al this world / ne hadde been thy peere

¶This Sampsou*n* / neu*er*e Ciser drank ne wyn
Ne on his heed / cam Rasour noon ne shere
By p*re*cept of the Messager deuyn
For alle his strengthes / in his herys were
And fully .xx. wynter / yeer by yere
He hadde of Israel / the gouernance
But soone / shal he wepe many a teere
For wommen / shul hym bryngen to meschaunce

¶Vn to his lemman Dalida / he tolde
That in his herys / al his strengthe lay
And falsly / to his fomen she hym solde
And slepynge in hir barm / vp on a day
She made to clippe / or shere his heer away
And made his fomen / al this craft espien
And whan þat they / hym fond in this array
They bounde hym faste / and putten out his eyen

¶But / er his heer / was clipped or yshaue
Ther was no bond / with which / men myghte hym bynde
But now is he / in prisone in a Caue
Wher*e* as they made hym / at the querne grynde
O noble Sampsou*n* / strengest of mankynde
O whilom / Iuge in glorie / and in richesse
Now / maystow wepen / w*ith* thyne eyen blynde
Sith thow fro wele / art falle in wrecchednesse

¶The ende of this caytif was as I shal seye
His fomen / made a feste vp on a day
And made hym as hir*e* fool / bifore hem pleye
And this was / in a temple of greet array
But atte laste / he made a foul affray
For he two pilers shook / and made hem falle
And doun fil temple and al / and there it lay
And slow hym self / and eek his fomen alle

ELLESMERE

By v*er*ray nyght
Philistiens
plyght
bak . ycaryed hee
hiƚ / þ*at* men myghte see
almyghty lief
thou
world /

This Sampson /
rasour sheere
precept diuyn
hise hise heeres weere
twenty by yeere
He / Israel gouernau*n*ce

shal meschance

Vn Dalida
hise heeris /
falsly hise foomen /
7 ¶And
shere / hise heres
hise foomen / espyen
foond
hise

But heer were
boond / w*ith* which myghte hi*m*
p*ri*son
Where Queerne
strongest
glorie
Now
thou

The caytyf
Hise foomen / feeste
as a fool / biforn

he / the pilers
Temple ther
self foomen

7 ¶Monk *170r*

The Monkes tale

By verray force at Gazan on a nyght
Maugree Philistiens of that Citee
The gates of the toun he hath vp plight
And on his bak ycaried hem hath he
Hye on an hill wher as men myghte hem se
O noble almyghty Sampson leef and deere
Hadstow nat tolde to wommen thy secree
In al this world ne hadde been thy peere

This Sampson neuere Ciser drank ne wyn
Ne on his heed cam rasour noon ne sheere
By precept of the messager dyuyn
For alle his strengthes in his heeris weere
And fully .xx. wynter yeer by yeere
He hadde of Israel the gouernaunce
But soone shal he wepe many a teere
For wommen shul hym bryngen to meschaunce

Vn to his lemman Dalida he tolde
That in his heeris al his strengthe lay
And falsly to his fomen she hym solde
And slepynge in hir barm vp on a day
She made to clippe or shere his heer away
And made his fomen al this craft espien
And whan þt they hym fond in this array
They bounde hym faste and putten out his eyen

But er his heer was clipped or yshaue
Ther was no bond with which men myghte hym bynde
But now is he in prisone in a Caue
Ther as they made hym at the querne grynde
O noble Sampson strengest of mankynde
O whilom Iuge in glorie and in richesse
Now maystow wepen with thyne eyen blynde
Sith thow fro wele art falle in wrecchednesse

The ende of this caytif was as I shal seye
His fomen made a feste vp on a day
And made hym as hir fool bifore hem pleye
And this was in a temple of greet array
But atte laste he made a foul affray
For he two pilers shook and made hem falle
And down fil temple and al and ther it lay
And slow hym self and eek his fomen alle

This is to seyn / the Prynces euerichon
And eek thre thousand bodyes / were ther slayn
With fallyng / of the grete temple of stoon
Of Sampson / now wol I namoore sayn
Beth war by this ensample / old and playn
That no men telle hir conseil / til hir wyues
Of swich thyng / as they wolde han secree fayn
If þ^t^ it touche / hir lymes / or hir lyues

Hercules

Of Hercules / the souereyn conquerour
Syngen hise werkes / laude and heigh renoun
ffor in his tyme / of strengthe he was the flour
He slow / and rafte the skyn fro the leoun
He of Centauros / leyde the boost adoun
He Arpies slow / the cruel bryddes felle
He golden apples / rafte of the dragoun
He drow out Cerberus / the hound of helle

He slow the cruel tyrant / Busirus
And made his hors / to frete hym flessh and bon
He slow the firy serpent venymus
Of Achilois two hornes / he brak oon
And he slow Cakus / in a Caue of stoon
He slow the geant / Antheus the stronge
He slow the grisly boor / and that anon
And bar the heuene / on his nekke longe

Was neuere wight / sith þ^t^ this world bigan
That slow so manye monstres / as dide he
Thurgh out this wyde world / his name ran
What for his strengthe / and for his heigh bountee
And euery Reawme / wente he for to se
He was so strong / þ^t^ no man myghte hym lette
At bothe the worldes endes / seith Trophee
In stede of boundes / he a piler sette — Ille vates Caldeorum Tropheus

A lemman / hadde this noble champioun
That highte Dianyra / fressh as May
And as thise clerkes / maken mencioun
She hath hym sent a sherte / fressh and gay
Allas this sherte / allas and weylaway
Enuenymed was / so subtilly with alle
That er þ^t^ he / hadde wered it half a day
It made his flessh / al from hise bones falle

[¶T]his is to seyn / the Prynces eu*er*ychon
And eek thre thousand bodies / were ther slayn
With fallyngꝫ of the grete temple of stoon
Of Sampson / now wol I namoore sayn
Beth war by this ensample / old and playn
That no men / telle hir conseil / til hir wyues
Of swich thyngꝫ as they wolde han secree fayn
If þ*at* it touche / hir lymes / or hir lyues

Hercules Of hercules / the souereyn conquerour
Syngen hise werkes / laude and heigh renoun
For in his tyme / of strengthe he was the flour
He slow / and rafte the skyn fro the leoun
He of Centauros / leyde the boost adown
He Arpies slow / the cruel briddes felle
He golden Apples / rafte of the dragoun
He drow out Cerberus / the hound of helle

¶He slow the cruel tyrantꝫ Busirus
And made his hors / to frete hym flessh and bon
He slow the firy serpent venymus
Of Achilois two hornes / he brak oon
And he slow Cakus / in a Caue of stoon
He slow the geantꝫ. Anthe*us* the stronge
He slow the grisly boor / and that anon
And bar the heuene / on his nekke longe

¶Was neuere wightꝫ sith þ*at* this world bigan
That slew so manye monstres / as dide he
Thurgh out this wide world / his name ran
What for his strengthe / and for his heigh bou*n*tee
And euery Reawme / wente he for to se
He was so strongꝫ þ*at* no man myghte hym lette
At bothe the worldes endes / seith Trophee
In stede of boundes / he a piler sette

¶A lemman / hadde this noble champiou*n*
That highte Dianra / fressh as May
And as thise clerkes / maken menciou*n*
She hath hym sent a sherte / fressh and gay
Allas this sherte / allas and weylaway
Enuenymed was / so subtilly with alle
That er þ*at* he / hadde wered it half a day
It made his flessh / al from hise bones falle

3307 Ille vates Caldeorum Tropheus Hg El
Variant: Caldeorum) Chaldeorum El

ELLESMERE

This euerichoon
eek / thousand bodyes
fallynge / Temple

war ensample oold
conseil

lymes

OF sou*er*eyn Conquerour ⌈¶hercules⌉
heigħ

skyn of the
adoun
crueel bryddes
refte

He crueel tyrant
flessħ boon
slow /
Acheloys hornes two / brakꝫ
Cacus /
geantꝫ Antheus
8

Was neu*er*e wighꝫ that
slow Monstres /
Thurgħ wyde
heigħ
see
stroongꝫ myghte

stide pileer

A lemman hadde / Champiou*n*
highte Dianira / fressħ

sentꝫ. sherte fressħ

Euenymed
had
flessħ /

8 ¶Monkꝫ *170v*

The Monkes tale .ſ

¶But natheles / somme clerkes hire excusen
By oon þat highte Nessus / þat it maked
Be as be may / I wol hire noght accusen
But on his bak the sherte he wered al naked
Til þat his flessh / was for the venym blaked
And whan he say / noon oother remedie
In hote coles / he hath hym seluen raked
For with no venym / deigned hym to dye

¶Thus starf / this worthy myghty Hercules
Lo who may truste on Fortune / any throwe
For hym þat folweth / al this world of prees
Er he be war / is ofte yleyd ful lowe
Ful wys is he / þat kan hym seluen knowe
Beth war / for whan þat Fortune list to glose
Thanne waiteth she / hir man to ouerthrowe
By swich a wey / as he wolde leest suppose

Nabugo-donosor

The myghty trone / the precious tresor
The glorious ceptre / and roial maiestee
That hadde / the kyng Nabugodonosor
With tonge / vnnethe / may discryued be
He twies / wan Ierusalem the Citee
The vessel of the temple / he with hym ladde
At Babiloigne / was his souereyn see
In which / his glorie / and his delit he hadde

¶The faireste children / of the blood roial
Of Israel / he leet do gelde anon
And maked ech of hem / to been his thral
Amonges othere / Danyel was oon
That was / the wiseste child of euerychoon
For he the dremes / of the kyng expowned
Ther as in Chaldeye / clerk / ne was ther noon
That wiste / to what fyn his dremes sowned

¶This proude kyng leet make a Statue of gold
Sixty cubites long and Seuene in brede
To which ymage / he bothe yong and old
Comanded to loute / and haue in drede
Or in a fourneys / ful of flambes rede
He shal be brend / that wolde noght obeye
But neuere / wolde assente to that dede
Danyel / ne hise yonge felawes tweye

ELLESMERE

But nathelees /
highte Nessus that
noght
bak this sherte
flessh /
saugh / remedye
hoote
with venym

Thus worthy /
Lo / truste / Fortune

that
war / that
wayteth ouerthrowe

¶Nabugodonosor] precious
Roial magestee
hadde kyng
vnnethe bee
twyes /
with
souereyn
which

9 The Roial
anoon

Daniel
was euerychon
he / dremes
Where as clerk
fyn / hise

This maken statue gold
seuene
The which yonge oold

Fourneys /
brent noght
neuere assente /
Daniel /

9 ¶Monk 171r

The Monkes tale

But natheles somme clerkes hym excusen
By oon yt highte Nessus yt it maked
Be as be may I wol hym noght accusen
But on his bak this sherte he wered al naked
Til yt his flessh was for the venym blaked
And whan he say noon oother remedie
In hote coles he hath hym seluen raked
ffor with no venym deigned hym to dye

Thus starf this worthy myghty Hercules
Lo who may truste on ffortune any throwe
ffor hym yt folweth al this world of prees
Er he be war is ofte yleyd ful lowe
ffull wys is he yt kan hym seluen knowe
Beth war for whan yt ffortune list to glose
Thanne waiteth she hir man to ouerthrowe
By swich a wey as he wolde leest suppose

Nabugodonosor The myghty trone the precious tresor
The glorious ceptre and roial maiestee
That hadde the kyng Nabugodonosor
With tonge vnnethe may discryued be
He twies wan Ierusalem the Citee
The vessel of the temple he with hym ladde
At Babiloigne was his souereyn see
In which his glorie and his delit he hadde

The faireste children of the blood roial
Of Israel he leet do gelde anon
And maked ech of hem to been his thral
Amonges othere Daniel was oon
That was the wiseste child of euerychoon
ffor he the dremes of the kyng expowned
Ther as in Chaldeye clerk ne was ther noon
That wiste to what fyn his dremes sowned

This proude kyng leet make a statue of gold
Sixty cubites long and seuene in brede
To which ymage he bothe yong and old
Comanded to loute and haue in drede
Or in a fourneys ful of flambes rede
He shal be brend that wolde noght obeye
But neuere wolde assente to that dede
Daniel ne hise yonge felawes tweye

This kyng of kynges proud was and elaat
He wende that god that sit in mageste
Ne myghte hym nat bireue of his estaat
But sodeynly he loste his dignytee
And lyk a beest hym semed for to be
And eet hey as an oxe and lay ther oute
In reyn with wilde beestes walked he
Til certeyn tyme was ycome aboute

And lyk an egles fetheres wax hise heres
Hise nayles lyk a briddes clawes weere
Til god relessed hym a certeyn yeres
And yaf hym wit and thanne with many a teere
He thanked god and euere his lyf in feere
Was he to doon amys or moore trespace
And til that tyme he leyd was on his beere
He knew that god was ful of myght and grace

Balthasar

His sone which that highte Balthasar
That heeld the regne after his fader day
He by his fader koude noght be war
ffor proud he was of herte and of array
And eek an ydolastre was he ay
His hye estaat assured hym in pryde
But ffortune caste hym doun and ther he lay
And sodeynly his regne gan dyuyde

A feste he made vn to hise lordes alle
Vp on a tyme and made hem blithe be
And thanne hise Officers gan he calle
Gooth bryngeth forth the vessels quod he
Whiche that my fader in his prosperitee
Out of the temple of Jerusalem birafte
And to oure hye goddes thanke we
Of honour that oure eldres with vs lafte

This wyf hise lordes and hise concubynes
Ay dronken whil hir appetites laste
Out of thise noble vessels sondry wynes
And on a wal this kyng hise eyen caste
And saugh an hand armlees that wroot ful faste
ffor feere of which he quook and siked soore
This hand that Balthasar so soore agaste
Wroot mane techel phares and namoore

	ELLESMERE
[¶]This kyng of kynges / proud was and elat'	This elaat'
He wende / that god / that sit in magestee	þ*at* god
Ne myghte hym nat bireue / of his estat	myġħte / bireue estaat
But sodeynly / he loste his dignytee	And sodeynly /
And lyk a beest' hym semed for to be	beest / bee
And eet hey as an Oxe / and lay ther oute	
In reyn / with wilde beestes walked he	hee
Til certeyn tyme / was ycome aboute	certein
¶And lyk an Egles fetheres / wax hise herys	And lik / his heres
Hise nayles / lyk a briddes clawes weere	
Til god relessed hym / a c*er*teyn yerys	certeyn yeres
And yaf hym wit' and thanne *with* many a teere	wit /
He thanked god / and euere his lyf in feere	
Was he to doon amys / or moore trespace	he /
And til that tyme / he leyd was on his beere	
He knew / that god / was ful of myght *and gra*ce	god was / myġħt grace
Balthasar **H**is sone / which that highte Balthasar	hiġħte [¶Balthasar]
That heeld the regne / after his fader day	
He by his fader / koude noght be war	noġħt
For proud he was / of herte and of array	
And eek an ydolastre / was he ay	eek / he was
His hye estat / assured hym in pryde	estaat'
But Fortune caste hym down / and ther he lay	Fortune / doun /
And sodeynly / his regne gan dyuyde	diuide
¶A feste he made / vn to hise lordes alle	A feeste
Vp on a tyme / and made hem blithe be	and bad hem bee
And thanne hise Officers / gan he calle	thanne / Officers
Gooth bryngeth forth / the vessels quod he	10 Gooth bryngeth forth /
Whiche that my fader / in his prosp*er*itee	fader' p*ro*sp*er*itee
Out of the temple / of Ierusalem / birafte	Ierusalem
And to oure hye goddes / thanke we	
Of honour / that oure eldres / *with* vs lafte	honou*r* / eldres
¶His wyf / hise lordes / and hise concubynes	His wyf'
Ay dronken / whil hir*e* appetites laste	
Out of thise noble vessels / sondry wynes	
And on a wal / this kyng' hise eyen caste	
And say an hand armlees / that wroot ful faste	saugħ Armlees / þ*at*
For feere of which / he quook / and siked soore	quook'
This hand / þ*at* Balthasar so soore agaste	hand / that
Wroot' Mane techel phares / and namoore	Mane techel phares /

10 ¶Monk' *171v*

ELLESMERE

¶In al that land / Magicien was noon
That koude expounde / what that lettre mente
But Danyel / expowned it anoon
And seyde / kyng god to thy fader lente
Glorie / and honour / regne / tresor / rente
And he was proud / and no thyng god ne dradde
And therfore / god greet wreche vp on hym sente
And hym birefte / the regne þ*at* he hadde

¶He was out cast of mannes compaignye
With Asses / was his habitaciou*n*
And eet hey as a beest in weet and drye
Til þ*at* he knew / by gr*a*ce / and by resou*n*
That god of heuene / hath domynaciou*n*
Ouer euery regne / and euery creature
And thanne / hadde god of hym compassiou*n*
And hym restored / his regne and his figure

¶Eke / thow that art his sone / art proud also
And knowest alle thise thynges verraily
And art rebel to god / and art his fo
Thow drank eek / of his vessel boldely
Thy wyf eke / and thy wenches synfully
Dronke of the same vessels / sondry wynys
And heriest false goddes cursedly
Therfore to thee / yshapen ful greet pyne is

¶This hand was sent fro god / that on the wal
Wroot Mane techel phares / truste me
Thy regne is doon / thow weyest noght at al
Dyuyded is thy regne / and it shal be
To Medes and to Perses / yeuen quod he
And thilke same nyght this kyng was slawe
And Darius / occupieth his degree
Though he ther to / hadde neither right ne lawe

¶Lordynges / ensample heer by may ye take
How that in lordshipe / is no sikernesse
For whan Fortune / wol a man forsake
She bereth awey / his regne and his richesse
And eke hise freendes / bothe moore and lesse
For what man / þ*at* hath freendes thurgh Fortune
Mishap*e* / wol make hem enemys I gesse
This p*ro*uerbe / is ful sooth / and ful co*m*mune

In land /
what this lettre
Daniel /
seyde fader sente
Glorie tresour /
proud / thyng

birafte /

He
asses /

that grace

Eek / thou art his
knowest /
foo
Thou hise vessels
eek /

heryest
ys

This from
Wroot Mane techel phares /
thou weyest noght

Perses quod
nyght kyng
11
Thogh therto right

Lordynges / ensample /
that
wole

eek
freendes / thurgh
maken enemys as I
prouerbe / sooth

11 ¶Monk *172r*

The monkes tale

In al that land / Magicien was noon
That koude expounde / what that lettre mente
But Daniel / expowned it anoon
And seyde kyng / god to thy fader lente
Glorie and honour / regne / tresor / rente
And he was proud / and no thyng god ne dradde
And therfore / god greet wreche up on hym sente
And hym birafte / the regne þt he hadde

He was out cast / of mannes compaignye
With asses / was his habitacioun
And eet hey as a beest / in weet and drye
Til þt he knew / by grace / and by resoun
That god of heuene / hath domynacioun
Ouer euery regne / and euery creature
And thanne / hadde god of hym compassioun
And hym restored / his regne and his figure

Eke thow that art his sone / art proud also
And knowest alle thise thynges verraily
And art rebel to god / and art his fo
Thow drank eek / of his vessel boldely
Thy wyf eke / and thy wenches synfully
Dronke of the same vessels / sondry wynys
And heriest false goddes cursedly
Therfore to thee / yshapen ful greet pyne is

This hand was sent fro god / that on the wal
Wroot mane techel phares / truste me
Thy regne is doon / thow weyest noght at al
Dyuyded is thy regne / and it shal be
To Medes and to Perses / yeuen quod he
And thilke same nyght this kyng was slawe
And Darius / occupieth his degree
Though he therto / hadde neither right ne lawe

Lordynges / ensample heer by may ye take
How that in lordshipe is no sikernesse
For whan Fortune / wol a man forsake
She bereth awey / his regne and his richesse
And eke hise freendes / bothe moore and lesse
For what man / þt hath freendes thurgh Fortune
Mishap wol make hem enemys I gesse
This prouerbe / is ful sooth / and ful commune

Cenobia of Palymerie queene
As writen Persiens of hir noblesse
So worthy was in armes and so keene
That no wight passed hire in hardynesse
Ne in lynage ne oother gentillesse
Of kynges blood of Perce is she descended
I sey nat þt she hadde moost fairnesse
But of hir shap she myghte nat been amended

¶ Ffrom hire childhede I fynde þt she fledde
Office of wommen and to wode she wente
And many a wilde hertes blood she shedde
With arwes brode that she to hem sente
She was so swift þt she anoon hem hente
And whan þt she was elder she wolde kille
Leons leopardes and beres al torente
And in hir armes welde hem at hir wille

¶ She dorste wilde beestes dennes seke
And rennen in the montaynes al the nyght
And slepen vnder the bussh and she koude eke
Wrastlen by verray force and verray myght
With any yong man were he neuer so wight
Ther myghte no thyng in hir armes stonde
She kepte hir maydenhede from euery wight
To no man deigned hire for to be bonde

¶ But atte laste hir freendes han hire maryed
To Onedake a prynce of that contree
Al were it so that she hem longe taryed
And ye shal vnderstonde how þt he
Hadde swiche fantasies as hadde she — Simil
But natheles whan they were knyt in feere
They lyued in ioye and in felicitee
ffor ech of hem hadde oother lief and deere

¶ Saue o thyng that she wolde neuere assente
By no wey that he sholde by hire lye
But ones for it was hir pleyn entente
To haue a child the world to multiplye
And also soone as that she myghte espye
That she was nat with childe with that dede
Thanne wolde she suffren hym doon his fantasye
Eft soone and noght but ones out of drede

ELLESMERE

CEnobia / of Palymerie queene
As writen Persiens / of hir noblesse
So worthy was in Armes / and so keene
That no wight passed hir*e* in hardynesse
Ne in lynage / ne oother gentilesse
Of kynges blood of Perce / is she descended
I sey nat þ*at* she hadde moost fairnesse
But of hir shap*e* / she myghte nat been amended

¶From hir*e* childhede / I fynde þ*at* she fledde
Office of wommen / and to wode she wente
And many / a wilde hertes blood she shedde
With Arwes brode / that she to hem sente
She was so swift þ*at* she anoon hem hente
And whan þ*at* she was elder / she wolde kille
Leons / Leopardes / and Beres al to rente
And in hir Armes / welde hem at hir wille

¶She dorste / wilde beestes dennes seke
And rennen in the montaynes / al the nyght
And slepen vnder the bussh / and she koude eke
Wrastlen / by v*er*ray force / and verray myght
With any yong man / were he neuer so wight
Ther myghte no thyng in hir armes stonde
She kepte hir maydenhede / from euery wight.
To no man / deigned hir*e* for to be bonde

¶But atte laste / hir freendes han hir*e* maryed
To Onedake / a prynce of that contree
Al were it so / that she hem longe taryed
And ye shal vnderstande / how þ*at* he
Hadde swiche fantasies / as hadde she
But nathelees / whan they weere knyt in feere [simul]
They lyued / in ioye / and in felicitee
For ech of hem / hadde oother lief and deere

¶Saue o thyng that she wolde neu*er*e assente
By no wey / that he sholde by hir*e* lye
But ones / for it was hir pleyn entente
To haue a child / the world to multiplye
And also soone / as that she myghte espye
That she was nat with childe / with that dede
Thanne wolde she suffren hym doon his fantasye
Eft soone / and noght but ones / out of drede

Queene ⌈¶Cenobia⌉
P*er*siens /
wight
lynage / nor in oother gentillesse
P*er*ce /
seye that
myghte
From that
wo*m*men /
many
swift / anon
Leou*n*s /
weelde
She
montaignes nyght
myght /
wight
myghte / Armes
maydenhod / eu*er*y wight
But maried
Prynce
taried
shul vnderstonde / that he
were infeere [simul]
12 Saue
child /
þ*at* myghte
wi*th* that
suffre hym /
nat oones

12 ¶Monk *172v*

The Monkes tale.ſ

¶And if she were with childe / at thilke cast'
Namoore / sholde he pleyen thilke game
Til fully / .xl. dayes weren past'
Thanne wolde she ones / suffre hym do the same
Al were this Onedake / wilde / or tame
He gat namoore of hire / for thus she seyde
It was to wyues / lecherie and shame
In oother cas / if *þ*at men with hem pleyde

¶Two sones / by this Onedake hadde she
The whiche she kepte / in v*er*tu and lettrure
But now / vn to oure tale turne we
I seye / so worshipful a creature
And wys ther with / and large w*ith* mesure
So penyble in the werre / and curteis eke
Ne moore labour / myghte in werre endure
Was noon / thogh al this world men sholde seke

¶Hir riche array / ne myghte nat be toold
As wel in vessel / as in hire clothyng'
She was al clad / in perree and in gold
And eek she lafte noght' for noon huntyng'
To haue / of sondry tonges ful knowyng'
Whan *þ*at she leyser hadde / and for to entende
To lerne bookes / was al hir likyng'
How she in vertu / myghte hir lyf despende

¶And shortly / of this storie for to trete
So doughty was hir*e* housbonde / and eek she
That they conquered / manye regnes grete
In thorient' with many a fair Citee
App*er*tenant' vn to the magestee
Of Rome / and w*ith* strong hond / heeld hem ful faste
Ne neu*er*e myghte / hir fomen / doon hem flee
Ay / whil that Onedakes dayes laste

¶Hir batailles / who so list hem for to rede
Agayn Sapor the kyng / and othere mo
And how / *þ*at al this p*ro*ces / fil in dede
Why she conquered / and what title ther to
And after / of hir*e* meschief and hir*e* wo
How that she was / biseged and ytake
Lat hym / vn to my maister Petrak go
That writ ynow of this / I vndertake

ELLESMERE

And

fourty dayes /

wilde
hir*e* /

caas / with

Two by Onedake
v*er*tu
tale /

Nemoore mygħte
thougħ men wolde seke

Hir told'
hir*e*
gold'
eek / nogħt /
haue tonges /

hir*e*
v*er*tu / mygħte dispende

And this proces for
doghty hir housbonde

the Orient'
Ap*er*tenaunt'
and hond held
mygħte / foo men

Hir
kyng'
how al
13 therto
after' hir meschief'
*þ*at
Lat'
ynougħ this

[13] ¶Monk' *173r*

And if she were with childe / at thilke cast/
Namoore sholde he pleyen thilke game
Til fully . xl . dayes weren past/
Thanne wolde she ones / suffre hym do the same
Al were this Odenake / wilde or tame
He gat namoore of hire / for thus she seyde
It was to wyues / lecherie and shame
In oother cas / if þt men with hem pleyde

Two sones / by this Odenake hadde she
The whiche she kepte / in vertu and lettrure
But now / vn to oure tale turne we
I seye / so worshipful a creature
And wys therwith / and large with mesure
So penyble in the werre / and curteis eke
Ne moore labour / myghte in werre endure
Was noon / though al this world men sholde seke

Hir riche array / ne myghte nat be told
As wel in vessel / as in hire clothyng/
She was al clad / in perree and in gold
And eek she lafte noght / for noon huntyng/
To haue / of sondry tonges ful knowyng/
Whan þt she leyser hadde / and for to entende
To lerne bookes / was al hir likyng/
How she in vertu / myghte hir lyf despende

And shortly / of this storie for to trete
So doughty was hir housbonde / and eek she
That they conquered / manye regnes grete
In thorient / with many a fair Citee
Appertenant / vn to the magestee
Of Rome / and with strong hond heeld hem ful faste
Ne neuere myghte hir foomen doon hem flee
Ay whil that Odenakes dayes laste

Hir batailles / who so list hem for to rede
Agayn Sapor the kyng / and othere mo
And how þt al this proces fil in dede
Why she conquered / and what title ther to
And after / of hir meschief and hire wo
How that she was / biseged and ytake
Lat hym / vn to my maister Petrak go
That writ ynow of this / I vndertake

Whan Odenake was ded she myghtily
The regnes heeld and with hir propre hond
Agayns hir foos she faught so cruelly
That ther nas kyng ne prynce in al that lond
That he nas glad if he þt grace fond
That she ne wolde vp on his land werreye
With hir they made alliance by bond
To been in pees and lete hir ryde and pleye

¶ The Emperour of Rome Claudius
Ne hym biforn the Romayn Galien
Ne dorsten neuere been so corageus
Ne noon Ermyn ne noon Egipcien
Ne Surryen ne noon Arabien
With inne the feeldes þt dorste wt hir fighte
Lest þt she wolde hem wt hir handes slen
Or with hir meynee putten hem to flighte

¶ In kynges habit wenten hir sones two
As heires of hir fadres regnes alle
And Hermanno and Thymalao
Hir names were as Persiens hem calle
But ay ffortune hath in hir hony galle
This myghty queene may no while endure
ffortune out of hir regne made hir falle
To wrecchednesse and to mysauenture

¶ Aurelian whan þt the gouernance
Of Rome cam in to hise handes tweye
He shoop vp on this queene to doon vengeance
And with his legions he took his weye
Toward Cenobie and shortly for to seye
He made hire flee and atte laste hir hente
And fettred hir and eek hir children tweye
And wan the land and hoom to Rome he wente

¶ Amonges othere thynges that he wan
Hir chaar þt was wt gold wroght & perree
This grete Romayn this Aurelian
Hath with hym lad for þt men sholde it se
Biforn his triumphe walketh she
With gilte cheynes on hir nekke hangynge
Corowned was she as after hir degree
And ful of perree charged hir clothynge

	ELLESMERE
[¶]Whan Onedake was deed / she myghtily	Whan
The regnes heeld / and with hir*e* pro*pre* hond	wi*th* hondʼ
Agayns hir foos / she faught so cruelly	Agayn faughħt
That ther nas kyng⁊ ne Prynce in al that lond	prynce / londʼ
That he nas glad / if he þ*at* grace fond	that fondʼ
That she ne wolde / vp on his land werreye	lond
With hir*e* / they made alliance by bond	bondʼ
To been in pees / and lete hir*e* ryde and pleye	ride *and*
¶The Emp*er*our of Rome / Claudius	The Rome
Ne hym biforn / the Romayn Galien	bifore /
Ne dorsten neu*ere* / been so corageus	dorste
Ne noon Ermyn / ne noon Egipcien	
Ne Surryen / ne noon Arabien	Ne Surrien / Arabyen
With Inne the feeldes / þ*at* dorste w*ith* hir*e* fighte	that fighħte
Lest þ*at* she wolde / hem w*ith* hir handes slen	that
Or with hir*e* meynee / putten hem to flighte	hir meignee / flighħte
¶In kynges habit⁊ wenten hir*e* sones two	In habit / wente hir
As heires / of hir fadres regnes alle	
And Hermanno / and Thymalao	
Hir names weere / as Persiens hem calle	were / P*er*siens
But ay Fortune / hath in hir*e* hony galle	
This myghty queene / may no while endure	
Fortune / out of hir regne made hir*e* falle	
To wrecchednesse / and to mysauenture	
¶Aurelian / whan þ*at* the gou*er*nance	Aurelian / that gou*er*naunce
Of Rome / cam in to hise handes tweye	
He shoop*e* / vp on this queene / to doon vengeance	queene vengeau*n*ce
And with his legions / he took his weye	hise legions /
Toward Cenobie / and shortly for to seye	
He made hir*e* flee / and atte laste hir*e* hente	hir*e* flee /
And fettred hir*e* / and eek hir*e* children tweye	
And wan the land / and hoom to Rome he wente	
¶Amonges othere thynges / that he wan	Amonges
His Chaar / þ*at* was w*ith* gold wroght *and* perree	Hir Chaar⁊ þ*at*⁊ wroghħt and
This grete Romayn / this Aurelian	
Hath with hym lad /. for þ*at* men sholde it see	w*ith* lad / that
Biforn his triumphe / walketh she	shee
With gilte cheynes / on hir*e* nekke hangynge	
Corowned was she / as after hir*e* degree	[14] Coroned she / after hir
And ful of perree / charged hir clothynge	hir*e*

[14] ¶Monk⁊ *173v*

		Ellesmere
	¶Allas Fortune / she that whilom was	Allas
	Dredeful / to kynges / and to Emp*er*oures	kynges
	Now gawreth al the peple / on hir*e* allas	gaureth
	And she that helmed was / in starke stoures	she / was starke shoures
	And wan by force / townes stronge and toures	*and*
	Shal on hir*e* heed / now were a vitremyte	hir
	And she þ*a*t bar / the Ceptre ful of floures	that bar ceptre
	Shal bere a distaf hir*e* cost for to quyte[15]	distaf / costes
De Nerone	Al though / that Nero were vicius	¶Nero] AL
	As any feend / that lyth ful lowe adown	lith in helle adoun
	Yet he / as telleth vs Swetonius	
	This wide world / hadde in subieccioun	wyde
	Bothe Est and West North / and Septemtrioun	Est *and* Septemtriou*n*
	Of Rubies / Saphires / and of p*er*les white	saphires / peerles
	Were alle hise clothes / browded vp and doun	brouded
	For he in gemmes / greetly gan delite	
	¶Moore delicat moore pompous of array	Moore delicaat
	Moore proud / was neuere Emp*er*our than he	neu*er*e
	That ilke clooth / that he hadde weryd o day	þ*a*t he wered
	After that tyme / he nolde it neuere see	neu*er*e
	Nettes of gold threed / hadde he greet plentee	
	To fisshen in Tybre / whan hym liste pleye	fisshe
	Hise lustes were al lawe / in his decree	
	For Fortune / as his freend / hym wolde obeye	freend
	¶He Rome brende / for his delicacie	He delicasie
	The Senatours / he slow vp on a day	
	To heere / how þ*a*t men wolde wepe *and* crye	how men and crie
	And slow his brother / and by his suster lay	brother
	His moder he made / in pitous array	mooder made he /
	For he hir*e* wombe slytte / to biholde	he / slitte /
	Where he conceyued was / so weilaway	Wher*e* was
	That he so litel / of his moder tolde	mooder
	¶No teere out of hise eyen / for that sighte	No sighte
	Ne cam / but seyde / a fair womman was she	wo*m*man
	Greet wonder is / how þ*a*t he koude / or myghte	myghte
	Be domesman / of hir*e* dede beautee	
	The wyn to bryngen hym / comanded he	hym
	And drank anoon / noon oother wo he made	drank / anon /
	Whan myght is ioyned / vn to crueltee	myght ioyned
	Allas to depe / wol the venym wade	

[15] In Hg El the Modern Instances are placed after the episode of Croesus.

The Monkes tale .

Allas ffortune / she that whilom was
Dredeful / to kynges / and to Emperoures
Now gaureth al the peple on hir allas
And she that helmed was / in starke stoures
And wan by force / townes stronge and toures
Shal on hir heed / now were a vitremyte
And she þt bar / the ceptre ful of floures
Shal bere a distaf / hir cost / for to quyte

De Nerone

Al though / that Nero were vicius
As any feend / that lyth ful lowe adoun
Yet he / as telleth vs Swetonius
This wyde world / hadde in subieccioun
Bothe Est / and West / North / and Septemtrioun
Of Rubies / Saphires / and of perles white
Were alle hise clothes / brouded vp and doun
ffor he in gemmes / gretly gan delite

Moore delicat / moore pompous of array
Moore proud / was neuere Emperour than he
That ilke cloth / that he hadde wered o day
After that tyme / he nolde it neuere se
Nettes of gold threed / hadde he greet plentee
To fisshen in Tybre / whan hym liste pleye
Hise lustes were al lawe / in his decree
ffor ffortune / as his freend / hym wolde obeye

He Rome brende / for his delicacie
The Senatours / he slow vp on a day
To heere / how þt men wolde wepe and crie
And slow his brother / and by his suster lay
His moder he made / in pitous array
ffor he hir wombe slitte / to biholde
Where he conceyued was / so weilaway
That he so litel / of his moder tolde

No teere out of hise eyen / for that sighte
Ne cam / but seyde a fair womman was she
Greet wonder is / how þt he koude or myghte
Be domesman / of hir dede beautee
The wyn to bryngen hym / comanded he
And drank anoon / noon oother wo he made
Whan myght is ioyned / vn to crueltee
Allas to depe / wol the venym wade

In youthe a maister hadde this Emperour
To teche hym lettrure and curteisye
ffor of moralitee he was the flour
As in his tyme but if bookes lye
And whil this maister hadde of hym maistrye
He maked hym so louyng and so souple
That longe tyme it was er tirannye
Or any vice dorste in hym vncouple

This Seneca of which pt I deuyse
By cause Nero hadde of hym swich drede
ffor he fro vices wolde hym ay chastise
Discreetly as by word and nat by dede
Sire wolde he seyn an Emperour moot nede
Be vertuous and hate tirannye
ffor which he in a bath made hym to blede
On bothe hise armes til he moste dye

This Nero hadde eek of acustumance
In youthe agayns his maister for to rise
Which afterward hym thoughte a greet greuance
Ther fore he made hym dyen in this wise
But natheles this Seneca the wise
Chees in a bath to dye in this manere
Rather than han another tormentyse
And thus hath Nero slayn his maister deere

Now fil it so that ffortune liste no lenger
The hye pryde of Nero to cherice
ffor though pt he was strong yet was she strenger
She thoughte thus by god I am to nyce
To sette a man that is fulfild of vice
In heigh degree and Emperour hym calle
By god out of his sete I wol hym trice
Whan he leest weneth sonnest shal he falle

The peple roos vp on hym on a nyght
ffor his defaute and whan he it espied
Out of his dores anon he hath hym dight
Allone and ther he wende han been allyed
He knokked faste and ay the moore he cryed
The faster shette they the dores alle
ffor drede of this hym thoughte pt he dyed
And wente his wey no lenger dorste he calle

	ELLESMERE
[¶I]n youthe / a maister hadde this Emp*er*our	16 In yowthe /
To teche hym lettrure / and curteisye	
For of moralitee / he was the flour	moraltee /
As in his tyme / but if bookes lye	
And whil this maister / hadde of hym maistrye	maisterꝰ
He maked hym / so louyngꝰ and so souple	so konnyngꝰ and sowple
That longe tyme it was / er tirannye	
Or any vice / dorste in hym vncouple	dorste on hym vncowple
¶This Seneca / of which þ*at* I deuyse	This that
By cause Nero / hadde of hym swich drede	
For he fro vices / wolde hym ay chastise	hym chastise
Discretly / as by word / and nat by dede	Discreetly /
Sire wolde he seyn / an Emp*er*our moot nede	
Be v*er*tuous / and hate tirannye	
For which he in a bath / made hym to blede	which /
On bothe hise armes / til he moste dye	Armes /
¶This Nero / hadde eek / of acustumance	This acustumau*n*ce
In youthe / agayns his maister for to rise	ryse
Which afterward / hym thoughte a greet greuance	afterward' / thoughħte greet greuau*n*ce
Ther fore / he made hym dyen in this wise	Therfore /
But nathelees / this Seneca the wise	
Chees / in a bath / to dye in this manere	Chees Bath dye /
Rather than han / another tormentrise	han / any oother tormentise
And thus hath Nero / slayn his maister deere	
¶Now fil it so / that Fortune liste no lenger	Now
The hye pride of Nero / to cherice	pryde Nero
For thogh þ*at* he was strongꝰ yet was she strenger	though
She thoghte thus / by god I am to nyce	thoughte
To sette a man / that is fulfild of vice	
In heigh degree / and Emp*er*our hym calle	heigħ
By god / out of his sete / I wol hym trice	
Whan he leest weneth / sonnest shal he falle	leestꝰ
¶The peple roos / vp on hym / on a nyghtꝰ	The roos nyghħtꝰ
For his defaute / and whan he it espied	
Out of his dores / anon he hath hym dightꝰ	hise dighħtꝰ
Allone / and there he wende han been allyed	ther allied
He knokked faste / and ay the moore he cryed	cried
The faster shette they / the dores alle	fasterꝰ
For drede of this / hym thoughte þ*at* he dyed	
And wente his wey / no lenger dorste he calle	

16 ¶Monkꝰ *174r*

ELLESMERE

¶The peple cryde / and rombled vp and doun
That *with* hise erys / herde he / how they seyde
What is this false tirant this Neroun
For fere almoost out of his wit he breyde
And to hise goddes / pitously he preyde
For socour / but it myghte noght bityde
For drede of this / hym thoughte þ*at* he deyde
And ran in to a gardyn / hym to hyde

¶And in this gardyn /. foond he cherles tweye
That seten by a fyr / greet and reed
And to thise cherlis two / he gan to preye
To sleen hym / and to girden of his heed
That to his body / whan þ*at* he were deed
Were no despit ydoon / for his defame
Hym self he slow / he koude no bettre reed
Of which / Fortune / lough and hadde a game

De Oloferno **W**as neuere Capitayn / vnder a kyng
That regnes mo / putte in subieccioun
Ne strenger was in feeld / of alle thyng
As in his tyme / ne gretter of renoun
Ne moore pompous / in heigh p*re*sumpcioun
Than Oloferne / which Fortune ay kiste
So likerously / and ladde hym vp and doun
Til þ*at* his heed was of / er that he wiste

¶Nat oonly / that this world hadde hym in awe
For lesynge / of richesse / or libertee
But made euery man / reneyen his lawe
Nabugodonosor / was god seyde he
Noon oother god / sholde adoured be
Agayns this heste / no wight dorste trespace
Saue in Bethulia / a strong Citee
Where Eliachym / a preest was of that place

¶But tak kepe / of the deeth of Oloferne
Amydde his oost he dronke lay a nyght
With Inne his tente / large as is a berne
And yet / for al his pompe / and al his myght
Iudith a womman / as he lay vpright
Slepynge / his heed of smoot and from his tente
Ful pryuely she stal / from euery wight
And with his heed / vn to hir toun she wente

The cride /
tiraunt
17 fere /
myghte nat
thoughte
gardyn

And gardyn /
greet reed
cherles
heed
deed
reed
Fortune lough /

¶De Oloferno] neu*ere* kyng /
subiecciou*n*
p*re*sumpciou*n*
er þ*at*

Nat world / Awe
eu*ery*
hee
bee
Agayns his heeste / wight
Eliachim /

But taak kepe of
hoost / nyght
yet pomp*e* / myght
wo*m*man / vpright
pryuely / stal eu*ery* wight

3755 Et fecerunt filij Israel secundum quod constituerat eis sacerdos domini Eliachym Hg El

17 ¶Monk / *174v*

The Monkes tale

The peple cryde and rombled vp and doun
That with hise erys herde he how they seyde
Where is this false tirant this Neroun
ffor fere almoost out of his wit he breyde
And to hise goddes pitously he preyde
ffor socour but it myghte noght bityde
ffor drede of this hym thoughte þt he deyde
And ran in to a gardyn hym to hyde

And in this gardyn foond he cherles tweye
That seten by a fyr greet and reed
And to thise cherlis two he gan to preye
To sleen hym and to girden of his heed
That to his body whan þt he were deed
Were no despit ydoon for his defame
Hym self he slow he koude no bettre reed
Of which ffortune lough and hadde a game

De Oloferno

Was neuere Capitayn vnder a kyng
That regnes mo putte in subieccioun
Ne strenger was in feeld of alle thyng
As in his tyme ne gretter of renoun
Ne moore pompous in heigh presumpcioun
Than Oloferne which ffortune ay kiste
So likerously and ladde hym vp and doun
Til þt his heed was of er that he wiste

Nat oonly that this world hadde hym in awe
ffor lesynge of richesse or libertee
But made euery man reneyen his lawe
Nabugodonosor was god seyde he
Noon oother god sholde adoured be
Agayns his heste no wight dorste trespace
Saue in Bethulia a strong Citee
Where Eliachym a preest was of that place

Et fecerunt filij Israel secundum quod constituerat eis sacerdos domini Eliachym

But tak kepe of the deeth of Oloferne
Amydde his oost he dronke lay a nyght
With Inne his tente large as is a berne
And yet for al his pompe and al his myght
Iudith a womman as he lay vpright
Slepynge his heed of smoot and from his tente
fful pryuely she stal from euery wight
And with his heed vn to hir toun she wente

What nedeth it of kyng Anthiochus
To telle his hye Roial mageste
His hye pryde hise werkes venymus
ffor swich another / was ther noon as he
Rede which that he was in Machabe
And rede the proude wordes / þt he seyde
And why he fil fro heigh prosperitee
And in an hill / how wrecchedly he deyde

ffortune hym hadde enhaunced so in pride
That verraily / he wende he myghte attayne
Vn to the sterres / vp on euery syde
And in balance weyen ech montayne
And alle the flodes / of the see restrayne
And goddes peple hadde he moost in hate
Hem wolde he sleen in torment and in payne
Wenynge that god ne myghte his pryde abate

And for that Nichanore / and Thymothe
Of Iewes weren venquysshed myghtily
Vn to the Iewes / swich an hate hadde he
That he bad greithe his chaar ful hastily
And swoor / and seyde ful despitously
Vn to Ierusalem he wolde eft soone
To wreken his Ire on it ful cruelly
But of his purpos / he was let ful soone

God for his manace / hym so soore smoot
With inuisible wounde / ay incurable
That in hise guttes / carf it so and boot
That hise peynes weren importable
And certeinly the wreche was resonable
ffor many a mannes guttes / dide he peyne
But from his purpos cursed and dampnable
ffor al his smert / he wolde hym nat restreyne

But bad anon apparaillen his hoost
And sodeynly er he was of it war
God daunted al his pryde and al his boost
ffor he so soore fil out of his char
[illegible]
That it hise lymes and his skyn totar
So þt he neither myghte go ne ryde
But in a chayer men aboute hym bar
Al forbrused bothe bak and syde

What nedeth it' of kyng Anthiochus
To telle / his hye Roial magestee
His hye pryde / hise werkes venymus
For swich another / was ther noon as he
Reed which that he was / in Machabee
And reed / the proude wordes / þat he seyde
And why he fil / fro heigh prosperitee
And in an hiƚƚ / how wrecchedly he deyde

¶Fortune / hym hadde enchaunted so in pride
That verraily / he wende he myghte attayne
Vn to the sterres / vp on euery syde
And in balance / weyen ech montayne
And alle the floodes / of the See restrayne
And goddes peple / hadde he moost in hate
Hem wolde he sleen / in torment' and in payne
Wenynge / that god ne myghte / his pryde abate

¶And for that Nichanore / and Thymothe
Of Iewes / weren venquysshed myghtily
Vn to the Iewes / swich an hate hadde he
That he bad greithe his Chaar ful hastily
And swoor / and seyde ful despitously
Vn to Ierusalem / he wolde eft soone
To wreken his Ire on it ful cruelly
But of his purpos / he was let ful soone

¶God for his manace / hym so soore smoot'
With invisible wounde / ay incurable
That in hise guttes / carf it so and boot'
That hise peynes / weren inportable
And certeinly / the wreche was resonable
For many a mannes guttes / dide he peyne
But from his purpos / cursed and dampnable
For al his smert' he wolde hym nat restreyne

¶But bad anon / apparaillen his hoost
And sodeynly / er he was of it war
God daunted / al his pride / and al his boost'
For he / so soore fil / out of his char
That it hise lymes / and his skyn totar (lacerauit/)
So þat / he neither myghte go ne ryde
But in a chayer / men aboute hym bar
Al forbrused / bothe bak and syde

[The wreche of god]

ELLESMERE

¶De Rege Anthiocho illustri] WHat
pride /
Rede þat
rede / wordes that
18 heigħ
Fortune / hadde enhaunced so
verraily / myghte
moost'
þat myghte pride
And for Thymothee
venquysshed
bad / greithen
Ire /
God ⟨so⟩
importable
certeinly /
But
pride
he soore / fil Char
lemes / lacerauit / totar
that' neyther' myghte
chayer' men /

18 ¶Monk' 175r

The Monkes tale.

¶The wreche of god / hym smoot so cruelly
That thurgh his body / wikked wormes crepte
And ther with al / he stank so horribly
That noon / of al his meynee þ*a*t hym kepte
Wheither so he wook / or ellis slepte
Ne myghte noght for stynk of hym endure
In this meschief / he wayled and eek wepte
And knew god / lord of euery creature

¶To al his hoost and to hym self also
Ful wlatsom / was the stynk / of his careyne
No man / ne myghte hym bere to ne fro
And in this stynk and this horrible peyne
He starf ful wrecchedly / in a monteyne
Thus hath this Robbour / and this homycide
That many a man / made to wepe and pleyne
Swich gerdon / as bilongeth vn to pryde

De Alexandro

The Storie of Alisandre / is so co*m*mune
That euery wight þ*a*t hath discreciou*n*
Hath herd som what or al / of his fortune
This wide world / as in conclusiou*n*
He wan by strengthe / or for hys hye renou*n*
They were glad / for pees vn to hym sende
The pryde / of man and beest he leyde adoun
Where so he cam / vn to the worldes ende

¶Comparison / myghte neu*ere* yet ben maked
Bitwixe hym / and another Conquerour
For al this world / for drede of hym hath quaked
He of knyghthod / and of fredom flour
Fortune hym made / the heir of hir*e* honour
Saue wyn and wommen / no thyng myghte aswage
His hye entente / in armes and labour
So was he ful / of Leonyn corage

¶What prys were it to hym / thogh I yow tolde
Of Darius / and an hundred thousand mo
Of kynges / Prynces / Dukes / Erles bolde
Whiche he conquered / and broghte hem in to wo
I seye / as fer / as man may ride or go
The world was his / what sholde I moore deuyse
For thogh I write / or tolde yow euere mo
Of his knyghthode / it myghte nat suffise

ELLESMERE

The
thurgh
stank horriblely
noon meynee /
wook
myghte noght stynk

19 To
wlatsom was / stynk
myghte bere /

Monteyne

gerdou*n* /

¶De Alexandro] THe storie Alisaundre /
wight that
Fortune
wyde
his
weren
pride / beest /

Comparisou*n* / myghte been
Bitwixen

knyghthod

wo*m*men / no man myghte
entente Armes
leonyn

What pris though

p*ri*nces / Erles / Dukes / bolde

fer ryde

though eu*er*emo
knyghthode / myghte

19 ¶Monk *175v*

The Monkes tale

The wreche of god / hym smoot so cruelly
That thurgh his body / wikked wormes crepte
And ther with al / he stank so horribly
That noon of al his meynee þt hym kepte
Wheither so he wook / or ellis slepte
Ne myghte noght / for stynk of hym endure
In this meschief / he wayled and eek wepte
And knew god / lord of euery creature

To al his hoost / and to hym self also
ffull wlatsom was the stynk of his careyne
No man / ne myghte hym bere to ne fro
And in this stynk / and this horrible peyne
He starf ful wrecchedly / in a monteyne
Thus hath this robbour / and this homycide
That many a man / made to wepe and pleyne
Swich gerdon / as bilongeth vn to pryde

De Alexandro

The storie of Alisaundre / is so commune
That euery wight þt hath discrecion
Hath herd som what / or al of his fortune
This wyde world / as in conclusion
He wan by strengthe / or for his hye renon
They were glad / for pees vn to hym sende
The pryde of man and beest / he leyde adoun
Where so he cam / vn to the worldes ende

Comparison myghte neuere yet ben maked
Bitwixe hym and another conquerour
ffor al this world / for drede of hym hath quaked
He of knyghthod / and of fredom flour
ffortune hym made / the heir of hir honour
Saue wyn and wommen / no thyng myghte aswage
His hye entente / in armes and labour
So was he ful of leonyn corage

What prys were it to hym / thogh I yow tolde
Of Darius / and an hundred thousand mo
Of kynges / princes / dukes / erles bolde
Whiche he conquered / and broghte hem in to wo
I seye / as fer as man may ryde or go
The world was his / what sholde I moore deuyse
ffor thogh I write / or tolde yow euere mo
Of his knyghthode / it myghte nat suffise

Twelf yeer he regned as seith Machabee
Philippes sone of Macidoyne he was
That first was kyng in Grece the contree
O worthy gentil Alisandre allas
That euere sholde fallen swich a cas
Empoysoned of thyn owene folk thow weere
Thy sys ffortune hath turned in to aas
And for thee ne weep she neuere a teere

Who shal me yeue teeris to compleyne
The deth of gentilesse and of franchise
That al this world weelded in his demeyne
And yet hym thoughte it myghte nat suffise
So ful was his corage of heigh emprise
Allas who shal me helpe to endite
ffalse ffortune and poyson to despise
The whiche two of al this wo I wyte

De Julio Cesare

By wisdom manhede and by greet labour
ffrom humble bed to roial magestee
Vp roos he Julius the Conquerour
That wan al the Occident by land and see
By strengthe of hond or ellis by tretee
And vn to Rome made hem tributarie
And sith of Rome the Emperour was he
Til that ffortune weex his aduersarie

O myghty Cesar that in Thessalie
Agayn Pompeus fader thyn in lawe
That of thorient hadde al the chiualrie
As fer as yt the day bigynneth dawe
Thow thurgh thy knyghthod hast hem take & slawe
Saue fewe folk yt with Pompeus fledde
Thurgh which thow puttest al thorient in awe
Thanke ffortune that so wel thee spedde

But now a litel while I wol biwaille
This Pompeus this noble gouernour
Of Rome which yt fleigh at this bataille
I seye oon of hise men a fals traitour
His heed of smoot to wynnen hym fauour
Of Julius and hym the heed he broghte
Allas Pompeie of thorient conquerour
That ffortune vn to swich a fyn thee broghte

		ELLESMERE
	[¶T]welf yeer he regned / as seith Machabee	Twelf
	Philippes sone of Macidoyne / he was	Macidoyne
	That first was kyngꝫ in Grece the contree	
	O worthy / gentil Alisandre allas	worthy
	That euere / sholde fallen swich a cas	euere
	Empoysoned / of thyn owene folkꝫ thow weere	folk thou
	Thy sys / Fortune hath turned in to Aas	Sys / Fortune /
	And for thee / ne weep she neuer a teere	weep*e* neu*er*
	¶Who shal me yeue teeris / to compleyne	Who yeuen teeris
	The deeth / of gentilesse / and of franchise	deeth gentillesse / Franchise
	That al this world / weldid in his demeyne	Thatꝫ al the world / weelded
	And yet hym thoughte / it myghte nat suffise	20 thoughte / myghte
	So ful was his corage / of heigh emprise	heigh
	Allas / who shal me helpe to endite	
	False Fortune / and poyson to despise	
	The whiche two / of al this wo I wyte	
De Iulio Cesare	By wisdom / manhede / and by greet labour	wisedom / by labour [¶De Iulio Cesare]
	From humble bed / to Roial magestee	roial
	Vp roos / he Iulius the Conquerour	roos
	That wan al the Occidentꝫ by land and see	thoccidentꝫ land' See
	By strengthe of hond / or ellis by tretee	hand / elles
	And vn to Rome / made hem tributarie	
	And sith of Rome / the Emp*er*our was he	sitthe
	Til that Fortune / weex his Adu*er*sarie	
	¶O myghty Cesar / that in Thessalie	O
	Agayn Pompeus / fader thyn in lawe	
	That of thorientꝫ hadde al the chiualrie	the Orientꝫ Chiualrie
	As fer / as *þat* the day bigynneth dawe	ferꝫ
	Thow / thurgh thy knyghthod / hast hem take *and* slawe	Thou thurgh knyghthod' and
	Saue fewe folkꝫ *þat* with Pompeus fledde	folk / that w*ith*
	Thurgh which / thow puttest al Thorient in awe	Thurgh which thou puttestꝫ thorientꝫ Awe
	Thanke Fortune / that so wel thee spedde	
	¶But now a litel while / I wol biwaille	[¶No*ta* de Pompeyo]
	This Pompeus / this noble gouernour	gou*er*nour
	Of Rome / which *þat* fleigh at this bataille	that fleigh
	I seye / oon of hise men / a fals traitour	
	His heed of smoot / to wynnen hym fauour	smootꝫ
	Of Iulius / and hym the heed he broghte	broghte
	Allas Pompeie / of Thorient conquerour	Pompeye / Conquerour
	That Fortune / vn to swich a fyn thee broghte	broghte

20 ¶Monkꝫ *176r*

ELLESMERE

¶To Rome agayn / repaireth Iulius
With his triumphe / lauriat ful hye
But on a tyme / Brutus Cassius
That euere hadde / of his heighe estat enuye
Ful pryuely / hath maad conspiracie
Agayns this Iulius / in subtil wise
And caste the place / in which he sholde dye
With Boydekyns / as I shal yow deuyse

¶This Iulius / to the Capitolie wente
Vp on a day / as he was wont to goon
And in the Capitolie / anon hym hente
This false Brutus / and hise othere foon
And stiked hym / with Boydekyns anon
With many a wounde / and thus they lete hym lye
But neuere gronte he / at no strook but oon
Or ellis at two / but if his storie lye

¶So manly / was this Iulius of herte
And so wel / louede estatly honestee
That thogh hise deedly woundes / so sore sm*er*te
His mantel ouer his hipes / caste he
For no man / sholde seen his pryuetee
And as he lay / of dyyng in a traunce
And wiste verraily / that deed was he
Of honestee / yet hadde he remembraunce

¶Lucan ./ to thee this storie I recomende
And to Sweton / and to Valerius also
That of this storie / writen word *and* ende
How that to thise grete Conquerours two
Fortune / was first freend / and siththe a foo
No man ne triste / vp on hir*e* fauour longe
But haue hire / in awayt for euere mo
Witnesse / on alle thise Conquerours stronge

Cresus This riche Cresus / whilom kyng of Lyde
Of which Cresus / Cirus soore hym dradde
Yet was he caught amyddes al his pryde
And to be brent / men to the fyr hym ladde
But swich a reyn / doun fro the welkne shadde
That slow the fyr / and made hym to escape
But to be war / no grace yet he hadde
Til Fortune / on the galwes made hym gape

eu*er*e hye estaat envye
p*ri*uely / conspiracye

This
Vpon

boydekyns anoon

21 neu*er*e strook
elles but

So
wel louede / estaatly
That though woundes soore
Mantel / ouer hise hypes
p*ri*uetee
diyng
ve*r*raily / hee
remembrau*n*ce

Lucan / thee /
Swetou*n* /
and
þat /
Fortune sitthe foo
truste /
hire / moo

¶Cresus] kyng

caught /

galwes /

21 ¶Monk *176v*

The Monkes tale

To Rome agayn / repaireth Iulius
With his triumphe / lauriat ful hye
But on a tyme / Brutus Cassius
That euere hadde / of his heighe estat enuye
fful pryuely / hath maad conspiracie
Agayns this Iulius / in subtil wise
And caste the place / in which he sholde dye
With boydekyns / as I shal yow deuyse

This Iulius / to the Capitolie wente
Vp on a day / as he was wont to goon
And in the Capitolie / anon hym hente
This false Brutus / and hise othere foon
And stiked hym / with boydekyns anon
With many a wounde / and thus they lete hym lye
But neuere gronte he / at no strook but oon
Or ellis at two / but if his storie lye

So manly / was this Iulius of herte
And so wel / louede estatly honestee
That thogh hise deedly woundes / so sore smerte
His mantel ouer hise hipes / caste he
ffor no man / sholde seen his pryuetee
And as he lay / of dyyng in a traunce
And wiste verraily / that deed was he
Of honestee / yet hadde he remembraunce

Lucan / to thee this storie I recomende
And to Swetoun / and to Valerius also
That of this storie / writen word and ende
How that to thise grete conquerours two
ffortune was first freend / and sitthe a foo
No man ne truste / vp on hire fauour longe
But haue hire in awayt / for euere mo
Witnesse / on alle thise conquerours stronge

Cresus

This riche Cresus / whilom kyng of Lyde
Of which Cresus / Cirus soore hym dradde
Yet was he caught / amyddes al his pryde
And to be brent / men to the fyr hym ladde
But swich a reyn / doun fro the welkne shadde
That slow the fyr / and made hym to escape
But to be war / no grace yet he hadde
Til ffortune / on the galwes made hym gape

Whanne he escaped was / he kan nat stente
ffor to bigynne / a newe werre agayn
He wende wel / for þt ffortune hym sente
Swich hap / that he escaped thurgh the rayn
That of his foos / he myghte nat be slayn
And eek a swevene / vp on a nyght he mette
Of which / he was so proud / and eek so fayn
That in vengeance / he al his herte sette

Vp on a tree he was / as þt hym thoughte
Ther Iuppiter hym wessh / bothe bak and syde
And Phebus eek a fair towaille hym broughte
To drye hym with / and ther fore wax his pryde
And to his doghter / that stood hym bisyde
Which that he knew / in heigh sentence habounde
He bad hire telle hym / what it signyfide
And she his dreem / bigan right thus expounde

The tree quod she / the galwes is to mene
And Iuppiter / bitokneth snow and reyn
And Phebus / with his towaille so clene
Tho been / the sonnes stremes for to seyn
Thow shalt an hanged be / fader certeyn
Reyn shal thee wasshe / and sonne shal thee drye
Thus warned hym / ful plat and ful pleyn
His doghter / which þt called was Phanye

Anhanged was Cresus the proude kyng
His roial trone / myghte hym nat availle
Tragedies noon oother maner thyng
Ne kan in syngyng / crye ne biwaille
But þt ffortune / alwey wole assaille
With vnwar strook / the regnes þt been proude
ffor whan men trusteth hire / thanne wol she faille
And couere hire brighte face / with a clowde

De Petro Ispanie

O noble o worthy Petro / glorie of Spayne
Whom ffortune heeld / so heighe in magestee
Wel oghten men / thy pitouse deeth complayne
Out of thy land / thy brother made thee flee
And after / at a sege / by subtiltee
Thow were bitraysed / and lad vn to his tente
Wher as he with his owene hand slow thee
Succedynge in thy regne and in thy rente

	ELLESMERE
[¶Wh]anne he escaped was / he kan nat stente	Whanne
For to bigynne / a newe werre agayn	
He wende wel / for þ*at* Fortune hym sente	
Swich hap*e* / that he escaped thurgh the rayn	thurgħ
That of his foos / he myghte nat be slayn	hise
And eek a sweuene / vp on a nyght he mette	nyghť
Of which / he was so proud / and eek so fayn	proud' /
That in vengeance / he al his herte sette	
¶Vp on a tree he was / as þ*at* hym thoughte	Vp tree / that
Ther Iuppiter hym wessħ / bothe bak and syde	bak'
And Phebus eek / a fair towaille hym broughte	Phеb*us* eek' broughte
To drye hym with / and ther fore wax his pryde	dryen Hym with / therfore' wax
And to his doghter / that stood hym bisyde	doghter'
Which that he knew / in heigh sentence habounde	þ*at* heigh Science habounde
He bad hir*e* telle hym / what it signyfide	signyfyde
And she his dreem / bigan right thus expounde	right'
¶The tree quod she / the galwes is to mene	22 The meene
And Iuppiter / bitokneth snow and reyn	Iuppiter'
And Phebus / with his towaille so clene	*with*
Tho been / the sonnes stremes for to seyn	sonne bemes for
Thow shalt an hanged be / fader certeyn	Thou anhanged
Reyn shal thee wasshe / and sonne shal thee drye	wasshe /
Thus warned hym / ful plat and ful pleyn	plat'
His doghter / which þ*at* called was Phanye	that
¶An hanged was Cresus / the proude kyng'	An
His Roial trone / myghte hym nat auaille	roial Trone / myghte
Tragedies noon oother maner*e* thyng'	Tragedies / maner thyng /
Ne kan in syngyng' crye ne biwaille	crie
But þ*at* Fortune / alwey wole assaille	that
With vnwar strook / the regnes þ*at* been proude	*With* strook' / Regnes
For whan men trusteth hire / thanne wol she faille	hire /
And couere hir*e* brighte face / with a clowde	cou*ere* brighte
De Petro Ispanni*e* O noble / o worthy Petro / glorie of Spayne	o. worthy [¶De Petro Rege Ispanni*e*]
Whom Fortune heeld / so heighe in magestee	heeld' / hye
Wel oghten men / thy pitous deeth complayne	
Out of thy land / thy brother made thee flee	land'
And after at a sege / by subtiltee	after' seege
Thow were bitraysed / and lad vn to his tente	Thou
Wher*e* as he / with his owene hand slow thee	Where
Succedynge / in thy regne and in thy rente	

22 ¶Monk' *177r*

¶The feeld of snow / with thegle of blak ther Inne
Caught with the lymrod / coloured as the glede
He brew this cursednesse / and al this synne
The wikked nestʼ was werkere of this nede
Noght Charles Olyuer / þ*a*t took ay hede
Of trouthe and honour / but of Armorike
Genylon Olyuer / corrupt for mede
Broghte this worthy kyngʼ in swich a brike

De Petro de Cipr*o*

O worthy Petro / kyng of Cipre also
That Alisaundre wan / by heigh maistrie
Ful many an hethen / wroghtestow ful wo
Of which / thyne owene liges hadde envie
And for no thyngʼ but for thy chiualrie
They in thy bed / han slayn thee by the morwe
Thus kan Fortune / hire wheel gouerne and gye
And out of ioye / brynge men to sorwe

De Barnabo

Of Melan / grete Barnabo Viscounte
God of delitʼ and scourge of Lumbardye
Why sholde I noghtʼ thyn Infortune acounte
Sith in estatʼ thow clombe were so hye
Thy brother sone / that was thy double allye
For he thy Nevew was / and sone in lawe
With Inne his prisou*n* / made thee to dye
But why ne how / noot .I. that thow were slawe

De hugelyn*o* Comite de Pize

Of the Erl hugelyn of Pize / the langour
Ther may no tonge / tellen for pitee
But litel out of Pize / stant a tour
In which tour / in prisou*n* put was he
And with hym been / hise litel children thre
The eldeste scarsly / fyue yeer was of age
Allas Fortune / it was greet crueltee
Swiche briddes / for to putte in swich a cage

¶Dampned was he / to dyen in that prisou*n*
For Roger / which þ*a*t bisshop*e* was of Pize
Hadde on hym maad / a fals suggestiou*n*
Thurgh which the peple / gan vp on hym rise
And putten hym to prison / in swich wise
As ye han herd / and mete and drynke he hadde
So smal / thatʼ wel vnnethe it may suffise
And ther with al / it was ful poure and badde

The
Caugħt lymerod / gleede
werker*e*
Nogħt that heede
honourʼ
Genylou*n* corruptʼ meede
Brogħte
[¶De Petro Rege de Cipr*o*]
Alisandre heigħ
wrogħtestow
Chiualrie
hir gou*er*ne
Ioye /
Of [¶De Barnabo de Lumbard*ia*]
delitʼ.
natʼ
23 estaatʼ cloumbe
I þ*a*t thou
¶De Hugelino Comite de Pize] Of Pyze /
telle
Butʼ
tourʼ
hym / been
eldeste / fyf Age
putte / Cage
Dampned
Rogerʼ Bissħop*e*
Thurgħ which / vpon
prisou*n* /
mete /
that vnnethe
therwith

[23] ¶Monkʼ *177v*

The Monkes tale

The feeld of snow / with thegle of blak ther Inne
Caught with the lymrod / coloured as the glede
He brew this cursednesse / and al this synne
The wikked nest / was werker of this nede
Noght Charles Olyuer / pt took ay heede
Of trouthe and honour / but of Armorike
Genylon Olyuer / corrupt for meede
Broghte this worthy kyng / in swich a brike

De petro de Cipr — O worthy Petro / kyng of Cipre also
That Alisaundre wan / by heigh maistrie
ffule many an hethen / wroghtestow ful wo
Of which thyne owene liges / hadde envie
And for no thyng / but for thy chiualrie
They in thy bed / han slayn thee by the morwe
Thus kan ffortune / hir wheel gouerne and gye
And out of ioye / brynge men to sorwe

De Barnabo — Of Melan / grete Barnabo viscounte
God of delit / and scourge of lumbardye
Why sholde I noght / thyn infortune acounte
Sith in estat / thow clomben were so hye
Thy brother sone / that was thy double allye
ffor he thy nevew was / and sone in lawe
With Inne his prison / made thee to dye
But why ne how / noot I / that thow were slawe

De hugelyno Comite de Pize — Of the Erl Hugelyn of Pize / the langour
Ther may no tonge tellen / for pitee
But litel out of Pize / stant a tour
In which tour / in prison put was he
And with hym been / hise litel children thre
The eldeste scarsly / fyue yeer was of age
Allas ffortune / it was greet crueltee
Swiche briddes / for to putte in swich a cage

Dampned was he / to dyen in that prison
ffor Roger / which pt bisshop was of Pize
Hadde on hym maad / a fals suggestion
Thurgh which the peple / gan vp on hym rise
And putten hym to prison / in swich wise
As ye han herd / and mete and drynke he hadde
So smal / that wel vnnethe it may suffise
And ther with al / it was ful poure and badde

[..]d on a day bifel / yt in that hour
Whan yt his mete / wont was to be broght
The Gayler / shette the dores of the tour
He herde it wel / but he spak / right noght
And in his herte / anon ther fil a thoght
That they for hunger / wolde doon hym dyen
Allas quod he / allas yt I was wroght
Ther with / the teeris fillen from hise eyen

This yonge sone / yt thre yeer was of age
Un to hym seyde / fader / fader why do ye wepe
Whanne wol the Gayler / bryngen oure potage
Is ther no morsel breed / yt ye do kepe
I am so hungry / that I may nat slepe
Now wolde god / yt I myghte slepen euere
Thanne sholde noght hunger / in my wombe crepe
Ther is no thyng but breed / yt me were leuere

Thus day by day / this child bigan to crye
Til in his fadres barm / adoun it lay
And seyde / ffarewel fader / I moot dye
And kiste his fader / and deyde the same day
And whan the woful fader / deed it say
ffor wo hise armes two / he gan to byte
And seyde / allas ffortune / and weylaway
Thy false wheel / my wo al may I wyte

Hise children wende / that it for hunger was
That he hise armes gnow / and nat for wo
And seyden fader / do nat so allas
But rather / ete the flessh vp on vs two
Oure flessh thow yaf / taak oure flessh vs fro
And ete ynow / right thus they to hym seyde
And after that / with Inne a day / or two
They leyde hem in his lappe adoun / and deyde

Hym self despeyred / eek for hunger starf
Thus ended is this myghty Erl of Pize
ffrom heigh estat / ffortune awey hym carf
Of this tragedie it oghte ynogh suffise
Who so wol heere it / in a lenger wise
Redeth the grete Poete of ytaille
That highte Dant / for he kan al deuyse
ffro point to point / nat o word wol he faille

Here is ended the monkes tale

	ELLESMERE
[¶An]d on a day bifel / þat in that hour	And day / bifil /
Whan þat his mete / wont was to be broght	broght
The Gayler / shette the dores of the tour	Gayler
He herde it wel / but he spak / right noght	spak right noght
And in his herte / anon ther fil a thoght	thoght /
That they for hunger / wolde doon hym dyen	hunger
Allas quod he / allas þat I was wroght	that wroght
Ther with / the teeris fillen from hise eyen	
¶His yonge sone / þat thre yeer was of age	His that
Vn to hym seyde / fader / fader / why do ye wepe	fader / fader
Whanne wol the Gayler / bryngen oure potage	
Is ther no morsel breed / þat ye do kepe	that
I am so hungry / that I may nat slepe	
Now wolde god / þat I myghte slepen euere	that myghte
Thanne sholde noght hunger / in my wombe crepe	nat
Ther is no thyng but breed / þat me were leuere	thyng that
¶Thus day by day / this child bigan to crye	Thus
Til in his fadres barm / adoun it lay	
And seyde / farewel fader / I moot dye	fare wel fader moot
And kiste his fader / and deyde the same day	fader dyde
And whan the woful fader / deed it say	fader
For wo / hise armes two / he gan to byte	
And seyde / allas Fortune and weylaway	24 Allas
Thy false wheel / my wo al may I wyte	
¶Hise children wende / that it for hunger was	Hise
That he hise armes gnow / and nat for wo	
And seyden / fader / do nat so allas	seyde fader
But rather / ete the flessh vp on vs two	rather flessh
Oure flessh thow yaf taak oure flessh vs fro	flessh thou yaf /. take
And ete ynow / right thus they to hym seyde	ynogh / right
And after that with Inne a day / or two	day
They leyde hem / in his lappe adoun / and deyde	adoun
¶Hym self despeired / eek for hunger starf	Hym eek starf
Thus ended is / this myghty Erl of Pize	
From heigh estat. Fortune awey hym carf	heigh estaat
Of this tragedie / it oghte ynogh suffise	Tragedie / oghte ynough
Who so wole heere it in a lenger wise	wol here
Redeth / the grete Poete of Ytaille	
That highte Dant. for he kan al deuyse	highte
Fro point to point nat o word wol he faille	to point.
	¶Explicit Traged*ia*
Here is ended the Monkes tale	¶Heere stynteth the Knyght the Monk / of his tale

[24] ¶Monk *178r*

¶This is the prologe / of the Nonnes p[reestes] tale

HO quod the knyght good sire namoore of this
That ye han seyd / is right ynow ywis
And muchel moore / for litel heuynesse
Is right ynow / to muche folk I gesse[1]
Youre tales / doon vs no desport ne game
Wher fore sir*e* Monk / o. Daun Piers by youre name
I prey yow hertely / telle vs som what ellis
For sikerly / nere clynkyng of youre bellis
That on youre bridel hange / on euery syde
By heuene kyng þ*at* for vs alle dyde
I sholde er this / haue fallen doun for sleep*e*
Al thogh the slow / hadde neu*er*e ben so deep*e*
Thanne hadde youre tale / al be toold in veyn
For certeynly / as þ*at* thise clerkes seyn
Where as a man / may haue noon audience
Naught helpeth it to tellen his sentence
And wel I woot the substau*n*ce is in me
If any thyng shal wel reported be
Sire / sey som what of huntyng I yow preye
¶Nay quod this Monk I haue no lust to pleye
Now lat another telle / as I haue toold
¶Thanne spak oure hoost with rude speche *and* boold
And seyde / vn to the Nonnes preest anon
Com neer thow preest com hider thow s*ir* Iohn
Telle vs swich thyng as may oure hertes glade
Be blythe / though thow ryde vp on a Iade
What though thyn hors / be bothe foul and lene
If he wol serue thee / rekke nat a bene
Looke / that thyn herte / be murye euere mo
¶Yis sire quod he / yis hoost so mote I go
But I be murye / ywis I wol be blamed
And right anon / his tale he hath attamed
And thus he seyde / vn to vs euerichon
This sweete preest this goodly man s*ir* Iohn

Explicit

¶The Prologe of the Nonnes preestes tale[1]

Hoo knyght / namoore this
right ynough

right ynough /
[2] For therInne / is ther no desport ne game
¶Wherfore Sir*e* Monk Daun
pray somwhat elles
clynkyng belles
your*e*
kyng /. that
han
thogh slough / had neu*er* been
toold
certeinly / that
Audience
Noght
substance

Sir*e* / somwhat huntyng
Monk / lust
toold
Thanne boold

thou preest. hyder thou

blithe / though thou
What thogh

murie eu*er*emo
sir*e* hoost moot
myrie /
right

preest.

¶Explicit

[1] On *178r*

[2] *Out* Hg 3961-80. The two stages in which the Mk-NP Link has come down to us are exemplified here in the short Hg and the long El version which effectively relates the NP Prol to the MkT by reference to the tragedy of Croesus in 3972. The short form (34 lines) is found in fourteen MSS, the long form (54 lines) in thirty-three MSS. El reads:

I seye for me / it is a greet disese
Where as men han been / in greet welthe and ese
To heeren / of hir*e* sodeyn fal allas
And the contrarie / is ioye and greet solas
As whan a man / hath been in poure estaat
And clymbeth up / and wexeth fortunat

This is the prologe of the Nonnes p[re]estes tale

Ho quod the knyght good sire namoore of this
That ye han seyd is right ynow ywis
And muchel moore for litel heuynesse
Is right ynow to muche folk I gesse
Youre tales doon vs no desport ne game
Wherfore sire Monk o daun Piers by youre name
I preye yow hertely telle vs som what ellis
For sikerly nere clynkyng of youre bellis
That on youre bridel hange on euery syde
By heuene kyng þt for vs alle dyde
I sholde er this haue fallen doun for sleep
Al thogh the slow hadde neuere ben so deep
Thanne hadde youre tale al be told in veyn
For certeynly as þt thise clerkes seyn
Where as a man may haue noon audience
Naught helpeth it to tellen his sentence
And wel I woot the substance is in me
If any thyng shal wel reported be
Sire sey som what of huntyng I yow preye
Nay quod this Monk I haue no lust to pleye
Now lat another telle as I haue told
Thanne spak oure hoost with rude speche and bold
And seyde vn to the Nonnes preest anon
Com neer thow preest com hider thow sir John
Telle vs swich thyng as may oure hertes glade
Be blythe though thow ryde vp on a Iade
What though thyn hors be bothe foul and lene
If he wol serue thee rekke nat a bene
Looke that thyn herte be murye euere mo
Yis sire quod he yis hoost so mote I go
But I be murye ywis I wol be blamed
And right anon his tale he hath attamed
And thus he seyde vn to vs euerychon
This sweete preest this goodly man sir John

Explicit

Heere bigynneth the Nonnes preestes tale
of the Cok and Hen, Chauntecleer & Pertelote

A poore wydwe somdel stape in age
Was whilom dwellynge in a narwe cotage
Biside a greve stondyng in a dale
This wydwe of which I telle yow my tale
Syn thilke day þt she was last a wyf
In pacience ladde a ful symple lyf
ffor litel was hir catel and hir rente
By housbondrye of swich as god hir sente
She foond hir self and eek hir doghtren two
Thre large sowes hadde she and namo
Thre kyn and eek a sheep þt highte malle
ffull sooty was hir bour and eek hir halle
In which she eet ful many a sklendre meel
Of poynaunt sauce hir neded neu a deel
No deyntee morsel passed thurgh hir throte
Hir diete was acordant to hir cote
Repleccion ne made hir neuere syk
Attempree diete was al hir phisyk
And exercise and hertes suffisaunce
The goute lette hir no thyng for to daunce
Napoplexie shente nat hir heed
No wyn ne drank she neither whit ne reed
Hir bord was serued moost wt whit and blak
Milk and broun breed in which she foond no lak
Seynd bacoun and somtyme an Ey or tweye
ffor she was as it were a maner deye
A yeerd she hadde enclosed al aboute
With stikkes and a drye dych wt oute
In which she hadde a cok heet Chauntecleer
In al the land of crowyng nas his peer
His voys was murier than the myrie orgon
On messedayes þt in the chirche gon
Wel sikerer was his crowyng in his logge
Than is a clokke or any Abbey orlogge
By nature he knew ech Ascention
Of equinoxial in thilke toun

¶Here bigynneth the Nonnes preestes tale of the Cok / and Hen / Chauntecler *and* Pertelote

A poore widwe / som del stape in age
Was whilom dwellynge / in a narwe cotage
Biside a groue / stondyng in a dale
This widwe / of which I telle yow my tale
Syn thilke day / *þa*t she was last a wyf
In pacience / ladde a ful symple lyf
For / litel was hire catel and hir*e* rente
By housbondrye / of swich as god hir*e* sente
She foond hir*e* self / and eek hir*e* doghtren two
Thre large sowes / hadde she and namo
Thre kyn / and eek a sheep*e* / *þa*t highte Malle
Ful sooty was hir*e* bour / and eek hir*e* halle
In which she eet ful many a sklendre meel
Of poynau*n*t sawce / hir neded neu*er* a deel
No deyntee morsel / passed thurgh hir throte
Hir diete / was acordant to hir cote
Replecciou*n* / ne made hir*e* neuere syk
Attempree diete / was al hir*e* phisyk
And excercise / and hertes suffisaunce
The gowte / lette hir*e* no thyng for to daunce
Napoplexie / shente nat hir*e* heed
No wyn ne drank she / neither whit ne reed
Hir*e* bord was serued / moost w*ith* whit and blak
Milk and broun breed / in which she foond no lak
Seynd bacou*n* / and som tyme an Ey / or tweye
For she was / as it were / a maner deye
A yeerd she hadde / enclosed al aboute
With stikkes / and a drye dych w*ith* oute
In which she hadde a cok heet Chau*n*tecler
In al the land / of crowyng nas his peer
His voys was murier / than the myrie Orgon
On massedayes / *þa*t in the chirche gon
Wel sikerer / was his crowyng in his logge
Than is a Clokke / or any Abbey Orlogge
By nature / he krew ech ascenciou*n*
Of equinoxial / in thilke town

¶Heere bigynneth / the Nonnes Preestes tale of the Cok and Hen Chauntecleer and Pertelote[4]

poure wydwe / somdeel Age
dwellyng.
greue / stondynge
wydwe / which
that wyf /
lyf /
For litel / hir hir
housbondrie /
hir hir

keen / sheep*e* highte
sooty / hir bour hir
Meel
poynaunt Sauce /
thurgh
accordant Cote
neu*er*e sik /
hir Phisik

goute / thyng
hir heed
drank / reed
Hir serued moost
Milk lak
Bacou*n* / somtyme Ey

¶A yeerd

which / Cok / heet Chauntecleer
land /
murier murie
Messedayes / that
sikerer crowyng
or an Abbey
crew Ascenciou*n*
Of the equynoxial toun

And there abideth / in prosp*er*itee
Swich thyng is gladsom / as it thynketh me
And of swich thyng. were goodly for to telle
Ye quod oure hoost by seint Poules belle
Ye seye right sooth / this Monk / he clappeth lowde
He spak /. how Fortune / coue*r*ed with a clowde
¶I noot neu*er*e what and also of a Tragedie[3]
Right now ye herde / and pardee no remedie
It is / for to biwaille / ne compleyne
That *þa*t is doon / and als it is a peyne
As ye han seyd / to heere of heuynesse
¶Sire monk. namoore of this / so god yow blesse
Youre tale / anoyeth al this compaignye
Swich talkyng is nat worth a boterflye

[3] ¶Nonnes preest *178v*

	ELLESMERE
For whan degrees .xv. / were ascended	fiftene weren
Thanne krew he / þ*at* it myghte nat ben amended	crew that been
His komb / was redder / than the fyn coral	Coomb
And batayled / as it were a Castel wal	batailled /
His byle was blak' and as the Ieet' it shoon	Ieet
Lyk asure / were hise legges and his toon	
Hise nayles whitter / than the lylye flour	nayles / whitter Lylye
And lyk the burned gold / was his colour	lyk'
This gentil cok / hadde in his gou*er*nau*n*ce	[6] Cok'.
Seuene hennes / for to doon ⟨A⟩l his plesau*n*ce	al
Whiche were hise sustres / and his p*ar*amours	were /
And wonder lyke to hym / as of colours	lyk'
Of whiche / the faireste hewed on hire throte	hewed / hir
Was clepid / faire damoysele Pertelote	cleped /
Curteys she was / discret and debonaire	discreet
And compaignable / and bar hir self so faire	hyr
Syn thilke day / þ*at* she was seuen nyght oold	nyght oold'
That trewely / she hath the herte in hoold	hoold'
Of Chau*n*tecler' loken in euery lyth	Chauntecleer' lith
He loued hir*e* so / þ*at* wel was hym ther with	therwith
But swich a ioye was it' to here hem synge	And swich
Whan þ*at* / the brighte sonne gan to sprynge	sonne / bigan
In swete acord / my leef / is faren in londe	sweete accord' My lief'
For thilke tyme / as I haue vnderstonde	
Beestes / and briddes / kouden speke and synge	Beestes koude
And so bifel / þ*at* in a dawenynge	¶And that in the dawenynge
As Chau*n*tecler / among hise wyues alle	Chauntecleer /
Sat on his perche / that was in the halle	p*er*che /
And next hym sat' this faire Pertelote	hym / sat P*er*telote
This Chau*n*tecler / gan gronen in his throte	Chauntecleer /
As man / þ*at* in his dreem / is drecched soore	man
¶And whan þ*at* Pertelote / thus herde hym rore	that P*er*telote / roore
She was agast / and seyde herte deere	agast' seyde o herte
What eyleth yow / to grone in this manere	
Ye ben a verray sleper*e* / fy for shame	been
¶And he answerde / and seyde thus / madame	thus' /
I prey yow / þ*at* ye take it nat agrief'	pray that
By god me mette / I was in swich meschief'	god / me thoughte / I
Right now / þ*at* yet myn herte is soore afright'	Right afright'
Now god quod he / my sweuene recche aright'	aright'

[4] *179r*

[5] Miniature of the Nun's Priest in right margin.

[6] ¶Nonnes *179v*

ffor whan degrees .xv. were ascended
Thanne crew he þt it myghte nat ben amended
His comb was redder / than the fyn coral
And batayled as it were a castel wal
His byle was blak / and as the jeet it shoon
lyk asure were hise legges and his toon
hise nayles whitter / than the lylye flour
And lyk the burned gold / was his colour
This gentil cok hadde in his gouernaunce
Seuene hennes for to doon al his plesaunce
Whiche were hise sustres and his paramours
And wonder lyke to hym as of colours
Of whiche the fayreste hewed on hire throte
Was cleped faire damoysele Pertelote
Curteys she was discreet and debonaire
And compaignable and bar hir self so faire
Syn thilke day þt she was seuen nyght old
That trewely she hath the herte in hoold
Of Chauntecler loken in euery lith
He loued hire so þt wel was hym therwith
But swich a ioye was it / to here hem synge
Whan þt the brighte sonne gan to sprynge
In swete acord / my leef is faren in londe
ffor thilke tyme as I haue vnderstonde
Beestes and briddes kouden speke and synge
And so bifel þt in a dawenynge
As Chauntecler among hise wyues alle
Sat on his perche that was in the halle
And next hym sat this faire Pertelote
This Chauntecler gan gronen in his throte
As man þt in his dreem is drecched soore
And whan þt Pertelote thus herde hym roore
She was agast and seyde herte deere
What eyleth yow to grone in this manere
ye ben a verray sleper fy for shame
And he answerde and seyde thus / madame
I prey yow þt ye take it nat agrief
By god me mette I was in swich meschief
Right now þt yet myn herte is soore afright
Now god quod he my sweuene recche aright

And kepe my body out of foul prisoun
Me mette how that I romed up and doun
With inne oure yeerd / where as I say a beest
Was lyk an hound / and wolde han maad arest
Up on my body and han had me ded
His colour was bitwixe yelow and red
And tipped was his tayl / and bothe hise erys
With blak / unlik the remenant of hise herys
His snowte smal / wt glowyng eyen tweye
Yet of his look for fere almoost I deye
This caused me my gronyng doutelees
Avoy quod she / fy on yow hertelees
Allas quod she / for by that god aboue
Now han ye lost / myn herte and al my loue
I kan nat loue a coward / by my feith
ffor certes / what so any womman seith
We alle desiren / if it myghte be
To han housbondes / hardy / wise and fre
And secree and no nygard / ne no fool
Ne hym þt is agast of euery tool
Ne noon auauntour / by that god aboue
How dorste ye seyn for shame / vn to youre loue
That any thyng / myghte make yow aferd
Haue ye no mannes herte / and han a berd
Allas / and konne ye ben agast of sweuenys
No thyng god woot / but vanytee in sweuene is
Sweuenes engendren of replexions
And ofte of fume / and of complexions
Whan humours ben to habundant in a wight
Certes this dreem / which ye han met to nyght
Cometh of the grete superfluitee
Of youre rede colera pardee
Which causeth folk to dreden in hir dremes
Of arwes and of fyr wt rede lemes
Of rede bestes / that they wol hem byte
Of contek and of whelpes grete and lyte
Right as the humour of malencolie
Causeth ful many a man in sleep to crie
ffor fere of blake beres or boles blake
Or ellis blake deueles wol hem take

[Th]e Nonnes preestes tale	ELLESMERE
[A]nd kepe my body / out of foul p*ri*soun	And prisoun
Me mette / how that I romed vp and doun	thatꝛ
With Inne oure yeerd / where as I say a beestꝛ	W*ith* yeerdꝫ wheer saugħ
Was lyk an hound / and wolde han maad arestꝛ	lykꝛ arestꝛ
Vp on my body / and han had me ded	Vpon deedꝭ
His colour / was bitwixe yelow and red	colourꝛ reedꝭ
And tipped was his tayl / and bothe hise erys	eeris
With blakꝛ vnlik the remenau*n*t of hise herys	vnlyk / remenantꝛ heeris
His snowte smal / w*ith* glowyng eyen tweye	with glowynge
Yet of his lookꝛ for fere almoost I deye	feere
This caused me / my gronyng doutelees	gronyngꝛ
¶Avoy quod she / fy on yow hertelees	
Allas quod she / for by that god aboue	
Now han ye lostꝛ myn herte and al my loue	
I kan nat loue a Coward / by my feith	I/ Cowardꝫ feitħ
For certes / what so any wo*m*man seith	seitħ
We alle desiren / if it myghte be	7 myghte bee
To han housbondes / hardy / wise and fre	hardy free
And secree / and no nygard / ne no fool	Nygardꝫ
Ne hym / *þa*t is agast of euery tool	
Ne noon auauntour / by that god aboue	
How dorste ye seyn / for shame / vn to youre loue	seyn
That any thyngꝛ myghte make yow aferd	myghte aferdꝭ
Haue ye no mannes herte / and han a berd	berdꝭ
Allas / and konne ye ben agast of sweuenys	¶Allas / been agastꝛ
No thyng god wootꝛ but vanytee in sweuene is	thyng / wootꝛ / vanitee
Sweuenes / engendren of replexions	repleccioun*s*
And ofte / of fume / and of co*m*plexions	ofte complexioun*s*
Whan humours / ben to habundant in a wightꝛ	been habundantꝛ wightꝛ
Certes this dreem / which ye han met to nyghtꝛ	¶Certes nyghtꝛ
Comth / of the grete sup*er*fluitee	Cometh / of greet sup*er*fluytee
Of youre rede Colera pardee	
Which causeth folk / to dreden in hir dremes	
Of Arwes / and of fyr w*ith* rede lemes	with
Of rede bestes / that they wol hem byte	Of grete beestes /
Of contek / and of whelpes grete and lyte	contek*es* whelpes /
Rightꝛ as the humour / of Malencolie	Right humourꝛ
Causeth ful many a man / in sleep*e* to crie	
For fere of blake beres / or boles blake	feere
Or ellis / blake deueles wol hem take	elles / deueles / wole

[7] ¶Preestꝛ *180r*

Of othere humours / koude I telle also	¶Of
That werken many a man / in sleep ful wo	sleep*e*
But I wol passe / as lightly as I kan	ligħtly
Lo Catou*n* / which þ*at* was so wys a man	Lo
Seyde he nat thus / ne do no fors of dremes	
Now sire quod she / whan we fle fro thise bemes	¶Now whan ye flee fro the bemes
For goddes loue / as taak som laxatif	taak' laxatyf'
Vp p*er*il of my soule / and of my lif	lyf'
I conseile yow the beste / I wol nat lye	conseille I. wol
That bothe of Coler*e* / and of Malencolye	Colere /
Ye purge yow / and for ye shal nat tarye	tarie
Thogh / in this town / is noon Apothecarye	Though toun / Apothecarie
I shal my self / to herbes techen yow	self'.
That shul ben / for youre heele and for youre prow	been / your*e* heele / *and* your*e*
And in oure yerd / tho herbes shal I fynde	yeerd' /
The whiche han / of hir*e* p*ro*pretee by kynde	
To purge yow / bynethe and eek' aboue	eek
Foryet nat this / for goddes owene loue	
Ye ben ful colerik' of complexiou*n*	been coleryk' complecciou*n*
Ware the sonne / in his Ascenciou*n*	
Ne fynde yow nat replet' of humo*ur*s hote	repleet' hoote
And if it do / I dar wel leye a grote	
That ye shul haue / a feuere terciane	Feuere
Or an Agew / þ*at* may be youre bane	Agu / that
A day / or two / ye shul han degestyues	8 day haue digestyues
Of wormes / er ye take youre laxatyues	
Of Lauriol / Centaur*e* / and Fumetere	lawriol /
Or ellis of Ellebor / that groweth there	elles
Of Katapuce / or of Gaytrys beryis	Gaitrys
Of herbe yue growyng in oure yerd / ther merye is	he*r*be growyng' yeerd' mery
Pekke hem vp right as they growe / and ete hem In	right' growe yn
Be myrie housbonde / for youre fader kyn	
Dredeth no dreem / I kan sey yow namoore	
¶Madame quod he / grant mercy of youre loore	Madame graunt' m*er*cy
But nathelees / as touchyng' Daun Catoun	
That hath of wisdom / swich a gret renoun	wysdom / greet
Thogh þ*at* he bad / no dremes for to drede	Thougħ that
By god men may / in olde bokes rede	god / bookes
Of many a man / moore of auctoritee	Auctorite
Than euere Caton was / so mote I thee	moot

[8] ¶Nonnes *180v*

Of othere humours / koude I telle also
That werken many a man / in sleep ful wo
But I wol passe / as lightly as I kan
Lo Caton / which þt was so wys a man
Seyde he nat thus / ne do no fors of dremes
Now sire quod she / whan we fle fro thise bemes
ffor goddes loue / as taak som laxatif
Vp peril of my soule / and of my lif
I conseille yow the beste / I wol nat lye
That bothe of colere / and of malencolye
Ye purge yow / and for ye shal nat tarye
Though in this town / is noon apothecarye
I shal my self / to herbes techen yow
That shul ben / for youre heele and for youre prow
And in oure yerd / tho herbes shal I fynde
The whiche han / of hire propretee by kynde
To purge yow / bynethe and eek / aboue
fforyet nat this / for goddes owene loue
Ye ben ful coleryk of complexion
Ware the sonne in his ascention
Ne fynde yow nat repleet / of humors hote
And if it do / I dar wel leye a grote
That ye shul haue / a feuere terciane
Or an agu / þt may be youre bane
A day or two / ye shul han degestyues
Of wormes / er ye take youre laxatyues
Of lauriol / Centaure / and ffumetere
Or ellis of Ellebor / that groweth there
Of katapuce / or of Gaytres berys
Of herbe yue growyng in oure yerd / ther merye is
Pekke hem vp right as they growe / and ete hem In
Be myrie housbonde / for youre fader kyn
Dredeth no dreem / I kan sey yow namoore
Madame quod he / graunt mercy of youre loore
But natheles / as touchyng daun Catoun
That hath of wysdom / swich a greet renoun
Though þt he bad / no dremes for to drede
By god men may / in olde bokes rede
Of many a man / moore of auctoritee
Than euere Caton was / so mote I thee

[Th]at al the reuers seyn / of his sentence
And han wel founden / by experience
That dremes ben significaciouns
As wel of ioye / as tribulaciouns
That folk enduren / in this lyf present
Ther nedeth / make of this noon argument
The verray preue / sheweth it in dede
¶ Oon of the gretteste auctour / þt men rede
Seith thus / þt whilom two felawes wente
On pilgrymage / in a ful good entente
And happed so / they comen in a toun
Where as ther was / swich congregacioun
Of peple / and eek so streit of herbergage
That they ne founde / as muche as o cotage
In which they bothe / myghte ylogged be
Wherfore / they mosten of necessitee
As for that nyght / departe compaignye
And ech of hem / gooth to his hostelrye
And took his loggyng / as it wolde falle
That oon of hem / was logged in a stalle
Fer in a yeerd / with oxen of the plow
That oother man / was logged wel ynow
As was his auenture / or his fortune
That vs gouerneth alle / as in commune
And so bifel / þt longe / er it were day
This man mette in his bed / ther as he lay
How þt his felawe / gan vp on hym calle
And seyde allas / for in an oxes stalle
This nyght / I shal be mordred ther I lye
Now help me deere brother / or I dye
In alle haste / com to me / he sayde
¶ This man out of his sleep / for feere abrayde
But whan þt he was wakned / of his sleep
He turned hym / and took of this no keep
Hym thoughte / his dreem nas but a vanytee
Thus twies in his slepyng dremed he
And atte thridde tyme / yet his felawe
Cam as hym thoughte / and seyde I am now slawe
Bihoold my blody woundes / depe and wyde
Arys vp erly / in the morwe tyde

	ELLESMERE
[Th]at al the reuers seyn / of his sentence	That of this sentence
And han wel founden / by experience	That han founden
That dremes / ben signyficaciou*n*s	been signifaciou*n*s
As wel / of ioye / as tribulaciou*n*s	wel Ioye / as of tribulaciou*n*s
That folk enduren / in this lyf p*re*sent⁊	lif
Ther nedeth / make of this noon argument⁊	Argument⁊
The verray preue / sheweth it in dede	v*er*ray preeue /
¶Oon of the gretteste Auctour / *þa*t men rede	¶Oon /
Seith thus / *þa*t whilom two felawes wente	
On pilgrymage / in a ful good entente	pilg*ri*mage /
And happed so / they coomen in a town	toun
Where as ther was / swich congregacioun	Wher
Of peple / and eek⁊ so streit of herbergage	streit⁊
That they ne founde / as muche as o cotage	
In which they bothe / myghte ylogged be	myghte logged bee
Wherfore / they mosten of necessitee	
As for that nyght⁊ departe compaignye	that⁊ nyght⁊ departen
And ech of hem / gooth to his hostelrye	
And took his loggyng⁊ as it wolde falle	took⁊
That oon of hem / was logged in a stalle	
Fer in a yeerd / with oxen of the plow	yeerd / Oxen plough
That oother man / was logged wel ynow	ynough
As was his auenture / or his fortune	Auenture /
That vs gou*er*neth alle / as in co*m*mune	
And so bifel / *þa*t longe / er it were day	¶And that longe
This man mette in his bed / ther as he lay	.i. dremed mette bed
How *þa*t his felawe / gan vp on hym calle	
And seyde allas / for in an Oxes stalle	
This nyght⁊ I shal be mordred ther I lye	nyght mordred /
Now help me deere brother⁊ or I dye	help*e* brother /
In alle haste / com to me / he sayde	me
¶This man / out of his sleep*e* / for feere abrayde	man
But whan *þa*t he was wakned / of his sleep	9 that wakened / sleep*e*
He turned hym / and took of this no keep*e*	of it no
Hym thoughte / his dreem nas but a vanytee	but⁊ vanitee
Thus twies / in his slepyng dremed he	slepyng⁊ hee
And atte thridde tyme / yet his felawe	
Cam as hym thoughte / and seyde I am now slawe	thoughte / seide
Bihoold my blody woundes / depe and wyde	bloody woundes
Arys vp erly / in the morwe tyde	

4174 Nota de sompnio El

[9] ¶Preest⁊ *181r*

ELLESMERE

And atte Westgate / of the town quod he
A Carte ful of donge / ther shaltow se
In which / my body is hyd ful p*ri*uely
Do thilke Cart aresten boldely
My gold caused my mordre / sooth to seyn
And tolde hym euery poynt how he was sleyn
With a ful pitous face / pale of hewe
And truste wel / his dreem he fond ful trewe
For on the morwe / as soone as it was day
To his felawes In / he took the way
And whan þat he cam / to this Oxes stalle
After his felawe / he bigan to calle
¶The hostiler / answerde hym anon
And seyde / sire / youre felawe is agon
As soone as day / he wente out of the town
¶This man / gan fallen in suspecioun
Remembrynge / on hise dremes þat he mette
And forth he goth / no lenger wolde he lette
Vn to the westgate of the town / and fond
A dong Carte / wente as it were to donge lond
That was arrayed / in that same wise
As ye han herd / the dede man deuyse
And w*ith* an hardy herte / he gan to crye
Vengeau*n*ce / and Iustice / of this felonye
My felawe / mordred is / this same nyght
And in this Cart heere / he lyth gapyng vpright
I crye / on the Mynystres / quod he
That sholde kepe / and rulen this Citee
Harrow / allas / heere lyth my felawe slayn
What sholde ⟨.I.⟩ moore / vn to this tale sayn
The peple vp sterte / and caste the Cart to grounde
And in the myddel of the dong they founde
The dede man / þat mordred was al newe
¶O blisful god / þat art so Iust and trewe
Lo / how þat thow biwreyest mordre alway
Mordre wol out that se we day by day
Mordre / is so wlatsom / and abhomynable
To god / that is so Iust and resonable
That / he / ne wol nat suffre it helyd be
Though it abyde / a yeer / or two / or thre

at the West gate / toun
Carte /
hid /
Carte / arresten
sayn
point slayn
foond
seyde youre
toun
dremes /
gooth /
toun / fond
Carte / as lond
herd /
with
Vengeance
nyght
Carte / heere lith vpright
crye out / on Ministres
sholden reulen
Harrow lith
I
peple out sterte / *and* Cart
that
O that Iust [¶Auctor]
thou
out /
Iust
That nat / heled
Though

And atte West gate of the town quod he
A carte ful of donge ther shal tow se
In which my body is hyd ful priuely
Do thilke cart arresten boldely
My gold caused my mordre / sooth to seyn
And tolde hym euery poynt / how he was slayn
With a ful pitous face / pale of hewe
And truste wel / his dreem he fond ful trewe
For on the morwe / as soone as it was day
To his felawes In / he took the way
And whan pt he cam / to this Oxes stalle
After his felawe / he bigan to calle
The hostiler / answerde hym anon
And seyde sire / youre felawe is agon
As soone as day / he wente out of the town
This man gan fallen in suspecioun
Remembrynge on hise dremes pt he mette
And forth he goth / no lenger wolde he lette
Vn to the West gate of the town / and fond
A dong carte / wente as it were to donge lond
That was arrayed / in that same wise
As ye han herd / the dede man deuyse
And wt an hardy herte / he gan to crye
Vengeance and Iustice / of this felonye
My felawe mordred is / this same nyght /
And in this cart heere / he lyth gapyng vp right /
I crye on the mynystres / quod he
That sholde kepe / and rulen this Citee
Harrow / allas / heere lyth my felawe slayn
What sholde I / moore vn to this tale sayn
The peple vp sterte / and caste the cart to grounde
And in the myddel of the dong they founde
The dede man / pt mordred was al newe
O blisful god / pt art so Iust and trewe
Lo how pt thow biwreyest / mordre alway
Mordre wol out / that se we day by day
Mordre is so wlatsom / and abhomynable
To god / that is so Iust and resonable
That he ne wol nat suffre it heled be
Though it abyde / a yeer / or two / or thre

rdre wol out/ this my conclusioun
And right anon mynistres of that toun
Han hent the Carter/ and so soore hym pyned
And eek the hostiler/ so sore engyned
That they biknewe hir wikkednesse anon
And were an hanged by the nekke bon
Heere may men seen/ þt dremes ben to drede
¶ And certes in the same book I rede
Right in the nexte chapitre after this
I gabbe nat/ so haue I ioye or blys
Two men þt wolde han passed ouer see
ffor certeyn cause in to a fer contree
If þt the wynd ne hadde ben contrarie
That made hem in a Citee for to tarie
That stood ful myrie vp on an hauen syde
But on a day agayn the euen tyde
The wynd gan chaunge and blew right as hem leste
Iolif and glad they wenten vn to reste
And casten hem ful erly for to sayle
But herkneth to that o man fil a gret meruaille
¶ That oon of hem in slepyng as he lay
Hym mette a wonder dreem agayn the day
Hym thoughte a man stood by his beddes syde
And hym comanded þt he sholde abyde
And seyde hym thus if thow tomorwe wende
Thow shalt be dreynt my tale is at an ende
¶ He wook and tolde his felawe what he mette
And preyde hym his viage to lette
As for that day he preyde hym to byde
¶ His felawe þt lay by his beddes syde
Gan for to laughe and scorned hym ful faste
No dreem quod he may so myn herte agaste
That I wol lette for to do my thynges
I sette nat a straw by thy dremynges
ffor sweuenes ben but vanytees and Iapes
Men dreme alday of Owles or of apes
And of many a maze ther with al
Men dreme of thyng þt neuere was ne shal
But sith I see þt thow wolt here abyde
And thus forslewthen wilfully thy tyde

	ELLESMERE
[M]ordre wol out this my conclusioun	10 Mordre conclusiou*n*
[¶]And right anon / Ministres of that town	And toun
Han hent the Cartere / and so soore hym pyned	Carter*e* /
And eek the hostiler / so sore engyned	eek soore
That they biknewe / hir*e* wikkednesse anon	
And were an hanged / by the nekke bon	
Heere may men sen / *þ*at dremes ben to drede	¶Heere seen / been
¶And c*er*tes / in the same book I rede	And book /
Right in the nexte Chapitre / after this	Right Chapitre
I gabbe nat so haue I ioye or blys	nat. blis
Two men / *þ*at wolde han passed ouer see	Two that ou*er*
For certeyn cause / in to a fer contree	c*er*teyn
If *þ*at the wynd / ne hadde ben cont*ra*rie	that been contrarie
That made hem / in a Citee for to tarie	
That stood ful myrie / vp on an hauen syde	vpon hauen/syde
But on a day / agayn the euen tyde	
The wynd gan chaunge / and blew right as hem leste	right
Iolif and glad / they wenten vn to reste	wente to hir reste
And casten hem / ful erly for to sayle	saille
But herkneth / to that o man / fil a gret m*er*uaille	¶But greet
¶That oon of hem / in slepyng as he lay	That
Hym mette a wonder dreem / agayn the day	
Hym thoughte / a man stood / by his beddes syde	stood
And hym comanded / *þ*at he sholde abyde	
And seyde hym thus / if thow tomorwe wende	thou
Thow shalt be dreynt my tale is at an ende	
¶He wook / and tolde his felawe what he mette	
And preyde hym / his viage to lette	
As for that day / he preyde hym to byde	
¶His felawe / *þ*at lay / by his beddes syde	that lay /.
Gan for to laughe / and scorned hym ful faste	laughe /
No dreem quod he / may so myn herte agaste	
That I wol lette / for to do my thynges	
I sette nat a straw / by thy dremynges	
For sweuenes ben / but vanytees and Iapes	sweuenes / been
Men dreme alday / of Owles / or of Apes	
And of many a maze / ther with al	therwithal
Men dreme of thyng *þ*at neuere was ne shal	neu*e*re
But sith I see / *þ*at thow wolt here abyde	sith that thou wolt heere
And thus forslewthen / wilfully thy tyde	

4257 Adhuc de sompnio El

10 ¶Nonnes 181*v*

The Nonnes preest	ELLESMERE
God woot it reweth me / and haue good day	woot
And thus / he took his leue / and wente his way	
But er *pat* he / hadde half his cours yseyled	he hadde /
Noot I nat why / ne what meschaunce it eyled	myschaunce
But casuelly / the shippes botme rente	
And ship*e* and man / vnder the water wente	
In sighte of othere shippes / it bisyde	sighte
That w*ith* hem seyled / at the same tyde	with
And therfore / faire Pertelote so deere	11
By swiche ensamples olde / maystow leere	olde / yet maistow
That no man / sholde ben to recchelees	been recchelees
Of dremes / for I sey thee doutelees	seye
That many a dreem / ful soore is for to drede	
¶Lo / in the lyf of Seint kenelm I rede	Lo / lyf kenelm /
That was kenulphus sone / the noble kyng	
Of Mertenrike / how kenelm mette a thyng	
Alite / er he was mordred / on a day	Alite
His mordre / in his auysion he say	Auysiou*n*
His norice / hym expowned euery del	Norice / eu*er*y deel
His sweuene / and bad hym for to kepe hym wel	weel
For traysou*n* / but he nas but .vij. yeer old	traisou*n* / oold
And therfore / litel tale hath he told	toold
Of any dreem / so holy was his herte	hooly is his
By god / I hadde leuere than my sherte	leu*er*e /
That ye hadde rad his legende / as haue I	I.
Dame Pertelote / I sey yow trewely	P*er*telote /
Macrobeus / that writ the Auysiou*n*	Avisiou*n*
In Affrike / of the worthy Cipiou*n*	
Affermeth dremes / and seith *pat* they ben	been
Warnynge of thynges / *pat* men after sen	seen
¶And forther moore / I pray yow looketh wel	
In the olde testament of Danyel	Daniel
If he heeld dremes / any vanytee	he / dremes vanitee
¶Rede eek of Ioseph / and there shul ye see	¶Reed eek Ioseph / ther
Wher dremes be som tyme / I sey nat alle	somtyme /
Warnynge of thynges / *pat* shul after falle	Warnynge /
¶Looke of Egipte / the kyng Daun Pharao	kyng
His bakere / and his butiller also	Bakere / Butiller
Wher they ne felte / noon effect in dremes	felte effect
Who so wol seke / Actes of sondry Remes	seken Actes /

4300 De sompnio sancti kenelmi El

4317 Adhuc de sompnijs El

11 ¶Preest *182r*

God woot it reweth me and haue good day
And thus he took his leue and wente his way
But er þt he hadde half his cours yseyled
Noot I nat why ne what meschaunce it eyled
But casuelly the shippes botme rente
And ship and man vnder the water wente
In sighte of othere shippes it bisyde
That wt hem seyled at the same tyde
And therfore faire Pertelote so deere
By swiche ensamples olde maystow leere
That no man sholde been to recchelees
Of dremes for I sey thee doutelees
That many a dreem ful sore is for to drede
Lo in the lyf of Seint kenelm I rede
That was kenulphus sone the noble kyng
Of Mercenrike how kenelm mette a thyng
A lite er he was mordred on a day
His mordre in his auysion he say
His norice hym expowned euery del
His sweuene and bad hym for to kepe hym wel
For traysoun but he nas but .vij. yeer old
And therfore litel tale hath he told
Of any dreem so holy was his herte
By god I hadde leuere than my sherte
That ye hadde rad his legende as haue I
Dame Pertelote I sey yow trewely
Macrobeus that writ the auysion
In Affrike of the worthy Cipion
Affermeth dremes and seith þt they ben
Warnynge of thynges þt men after seen
And forther moore I pray yow looketh wel
In the olde testament of Danyel
If he heeld dremes any vanytee
Rede eek of Joseph and there shul ye see
Wher dremes be somtyme I sey nat alle
Warnynge of thynges þt shul after falle
Looke of Egipte the kyng daun Pharao
His bakere and his butiller also
Wher they ne felte noon effect in dremes
Who so wol seke actes of sondry remes

[...] rede of sweuenes many a wonder thyng/
[...] Cresus which þt was of lyde kyng/
Mette he nat/ þt he satt vp on a tree
Which signyfide/ he sholde an hanged be
And here Andromacha Ettores wyf
That day that Ettor sholde lese his lyf
She dremed on the same nyght biforn
How þt the lyf of Ettor sholde be lorn
If thilke day/ he wente in to bataille
She warned hym/ but it myghte nat auaille
He wente for to fighte natheles
But he was slayn anon of Achilles
But thilke tale is al to long to telle
And eek it is ney day/ I may nat dwelle
Shortly I seye as for conclusion
That I shal han of this Avysion
Aduersitee and I seye forther moor
That I ne telle of laxatyues no stoor
ffor they ben venymes/ I woot it wel
I hem deffie/ I loue hem neuer a del
Now lat vs speke of myrthe and stynte al this
Madame Pertelote/ so haue I blys
Of o thyng/ god hath sent me large grace
ffor whan I se the beautee of youre face
ye ben so scarlet reed aboute youre eyen
It maketh al my drede for to dyen
ffor also siker as In principio
Mulier est hominis confusio
Madame the sentence of this latyn is
Womman is mannes ioye and al his blys
ffor whan I feele a nyght youre softe syde
Al be it/ þt I may nat on yow ryde
ffor þt oure perche is maad so narwe allas
I am so ful of ioye and of solas
That I deffie bothe swevene and dreem
And with that word he fley doun fro the beem
ffor it was day/ and eke hise hennes alle
And with a chuk/ he gan hem for to calle
ffor he hadde founde a corn/ lay in the yerd
Real he was/ he was namoore aferd

	ELLESMERE
[M]ay rede of dremes / many a wonder thyng	May
[¶]Lo Cresus / which þ*at* was of Lyde kyng	¶Lo
Mette he nat þ*at* he sat vp on a tree	nat / that
Which signyfide / he sholde an hanged be	signified / bee
¶Lo here Andromacha / Ectores wyf	heere Adromacha / wyf
That day that Ector / sholde lese his lyf	day / lyf
She dremed / on the same nyght biforn	nyght
How þ*at* the lyf of Ector sholde be lorn	Ector /
If thilke day / he wente in to bataille	
She warned hym / but it myghte nat auaille	but myghte
He wente for to fighte nathelees	wente / natheles
But he was slayn anon / of Achilles	anon
But thilke tale / is al to long to telle	thilke is longe for to
And eek / it is ney day / I may nat dwelle	eek ny
Shortly I seye / as for conclusiou*n*	
That I shal han / of this Auysiou*n*	Avisiou*n*
Adu*er*sitee / and I seye forther moor	12 Adu*er*sitee /. forthermoor
That I ne telle / of laxatyues no stoor	
For they ben venymes / I woot it wel	been weel
I hem deffie / I loue hem neuer a del	diffye / neu*er* deel
¶Now lat vs speke of myrthe and stynte al this	myrthe /
Madame Pertelote / so haue I blys	blis
Of o thyng god hath sent me large g*ra*ce	grace
For whan I se / the beautee / of youre face	beautee
Ye ben so scarlet reed / aboute youre eyen	been scarlet your*e*
It maketh / al my drede for to dyen	
For also siker / as **In principio**	
Mulier / est hominis confusio	**Mulier est**
Madame / the sentence / of this latyn is	¶Madame /
Womman / is mannes ioye and al his blys	Wo*m*man Ioye / blis
For whan I feele a nyght youre softe syde	nyght your*e*
Al be it þ*at* I may nat on yow ryde	that nat
For þ*at* oure p*er*che / is maad so narwe allas	
I am so ful / of Ioye and of solas	ful ioye /
That I deffie / bothe sweuene and dreem	diffye /
And with that word / he fley doun fro the beem	fly
For it was day / and eke hise hennes alle	eek
And with a chuk he gan hem for to calle	chuk /
For he hadde founde a corn / lay in the yerd	yerd
Real he was / he was namoore aferd	aferd

He fethered Pertelote

12 ¶Nonnes *182v*

		ELLESMERE
He fethered Pertelote / twenty tyme		And fethered
And trad as ofte / er it was pryme		
He looketh as it were a grym leoun		looketh / were / Leoun
And on hise toos / he rometh vp and doun		
Hym deyned nat / to sette his foot to grounde		deigned nat
And chukketh / whan he hath a corn yfounde		He chukketh /
And to hym rennen thanne / hise wyues alle		
Thus real / as a Prince is in his halle		Thus roial / as prince in an halle
Leue I this Chauntecler / in his pasture		Chauntecleer /
And after / wol I telle his auenture		telle /
¶Whan that the Monthe / in which the world bigan		**W**han *þat*
That highte March / whan god first maked man		higħte Marcħ /
Was complet and passed were also		compleet
Syn March bigan / 30. dayes and two		Marcħ thritty
Bifel / *þat* Chauntecler / in al his pryde		that Chauntecleer
Hise seuene wyues / walkyng hym bisyde		walkynge by his syde
Caste vp hise eyen / to the brighte sonne		brigħte
That in the signe of Taurus / hadde yronne		
xx. degrees and oon / and som what moore		Twenty
And knew by kynde / and by noon oother loore		
That it was pryme / and krew w*ith* blisful steuene		Pryme / crew
The sonne he seyde / is clomben vp on heuene		
40. degrees and oon / and moore ywis		Fourty
Madame Pertelote / my worldes blys		P*er*telote / blis
Herkneth thyse blisful bryddes / how they synge		13 thise briddes /
And se the fresshe floures / how they sprynge		se / fressħe
Ful is myn herte / of reuel and solas		
But sodeynly / hym fil a sorweful cas		
For euere the latter ende of ioye / is wo		eu*er*e / ioye
God woot *þat* worldly ioye / is soone ago		
And if a Rethor / koude faire endite		
He in a Cronycle / saufly myghte it write		mygħte
As for a souereyn notabilitee	Petrus Comestor	[¶Petrus Comestor]
Now euery wys man / lat hym herkne me		
This storie / is also trewe I vndertake		trewe /
As is the book of Launcelot de Lake		book / Launcelot
That wommen holde / in ful gret reu*er*ence		wo*m*men greet
Now wol I / torne agayn to my sentence		I / come / agayn
¶A Colfox / ful of sley Iniquitee		**A** sly
That in the groue / hadde woned yeres thre		three

13 ¶Preest / *183r*

He fethered Pertelote twenty tyme
And trad as ofte er it was pryme
He looketh as it were a grym leoun
And on hise toos he rometh vp and doun
Hym deyned nat to sette his foot to grounde
And chukketh whan he hath a corn yfounde
And to hym rennen thanne hise wyues alle
Thus real as a prince is in his halle
Leue I this Chauntecleer in his pasture
And after wol I telle his auenture
Whan that the monthe in which the world bigan
That highte March whan god first maked man
Was complet and passed were also
Syn March bigan 30. dayes and two
Bifel þt Chauntecleer in al his pryde
Hise seuene wyues walkyng hym bisyde
Caste vp hise eyen to the brighte sonne
That in the signe of Taurus hadde yronne
xx. degrees and oon and som what moore
And knew by kynde and by noon oother loore
That it was pryme and krew with blisful steuene
The sonne he seyde is clomben vp on heuene
xl. degrees and oon and moore ywis
Madame Pertelote my worldes blis
Herkneth thise blisful briddes how they synge
And se the fresshe floures how they sprynge
Ful is myn herte of reuel and solas
But sodeynly hym fil a sorweful cas
For euere the latter ende of ioye is wo
God woot þt worldly ioye is soone ago
And if a rethor koude faire endite
He in a cronycle saufly myghte it write
As for a souereyn notabilitee — Petrus Comestor
Now euery wys man lat hym herkne me
This storie is also trewe I vndertake
As is the book of Launcelot de lake
That wommen holde in ful greet reuerence
Now wol I torne agayn to my sentence
A colfox ful of sley iniquitee
That in the groue hadde woned yeres thre

heigh ymaginacion forncast/
The same nyght/ thurgh out the hegges brast/
In to the yerd ther Chauntecler the faire
Was wont/ and eek hise wyues to repaire
And in a bed of wortes stille he lay
Til it was passed vndren of the day
Waitynge his tyme on Chauntecler to falle
As gladly doon thise homycides alle
That in awayt liggen to mordre men
O false mordrour lurkynge in thy den
O newe Scariot/ newe Genyloun
ffalse dissimulour o greek Synon
That broghtest Troye al outrely to sorwe
O Chauntecler acursed be that morwe
That thow in to the yerd/ flaugh fro the bemys
Thow were ful wel ywarned by thy dremys
That thilke day was perilous to thee
But what þt god forwoot/ moot nedes be
After the opynyon of certeyn clerkis
Witnesse on hym þt any pfit clerk is
That in scole is greet altercacion
In this mater and greet disputisoun
And hath ben of an hundred thousand men
But I ne kan nat bulte it to the bren
As kan the holy doctour Augustyn
Or Boece or the Bisshop Bradwardyn
Wheither þt goddes worthy forwityng/
Streyneth me nedely for to doon a thyng/
Nedely clepe I symple necessitee
Or ellis if free choys be graunted me
To do that same thyng/ or do it noght/
Though god forwoot it er þt I was wroght/
Or if his wityng/ streyneth neuer a del
But by necessitee condicionel
I wol nat han to do of swich matere
My tale is of a cok/ as ye may heere
That took his conseil of his wyf wt sorwe
To walken in the yerd vp on that morwe
That he hadde met the dreem þt I yow tolde
Wommens conseils been ful ofte colde

	ELLESMERE
[By] heigh ymaginaciou*n* / forncast	By heigh forn cast
[T]he same nyght thurgh out the hegges brast	The nyght / thurgh
In to the yerd / ther Chauntecler the faire	Chauntecleer
Was wont and eek hise wyues to repaire	
And in a bed of wortes / stille he lay	
Til it was passed / vndren of the day	
Waitynge his tyme / on Chauntecler to falle	Chauntecleer
As gladly doon / thise homycides alle	gladly / doon
That in awayt liggen / to mordre men	await
O false mordrour / lurkynge in thy den	
O newe Scariot newe Genylou*n*	
False dissimilour / o greek Synou*n*	dissymulour greek
That broghtest Troye / al outrely to sorwe	
O Chauntecler / acursed be that morwe	Chauntecleer
That thow in to the yerd / flaugh fro the bemys	thou to that yerd / flaugh bemes
Thow were / ful wel ywarned by thy dremys	Thou dremes
That thilke day / was pe*r*ilous to thee	
But what *pa*t god forwoot moot nedes be	But bee
After the opynyou*n* / of certeyn clerkis	opiniou*n* / certein
Witnesse on hym / *pa*t any pa*r*fit clerk is	that clerk
That in scole / is gret altercaciou*n*	greet
In this matere / and gret disputisou*n*	mateere / greet
And hath ben / of an hundred thousand men	been /
But I ne kan / nat bulte it to the bren	kan nat
As kan / the holy doctour Augustyn	kan hooly
Or Boece / or the Bisshop*e* Bradwardyn	Bisshop*e*
Wheither / *pa*t goddes worthy forewityng	that goddes / forwityng
Streyneth me nedely / for to doon a thyng /	me / nedefully to thyng
Nedely clepe I / symple necessitee	Nedely /
Or ellis / if fre choys / be graunted me	elles / free choys
To do that same thyng or do it noght	thyng. noght
Though god forwoot it / er *pa*t I was wroght	Though forwoot it *pa*t it was wroght
Or if his wityng streyneth neuer a del	14 wityng. neu*er* deel
But by necessitee / condicionel	But necessitee condicioneel
I wol nat han to do / of swich matere	mateere
My tale is of a Cok as ye may heere	Cok.
That took his conseil / of his wyf / w*ith* sorwe	wyf
To walken in the yerd / vp on that morwe	yerd / vpon
That he hadde met the dreem / *pa*t I yow tolde	met that dreem / I of tolde
Wommens conseils / be ful ofte colde	Wo*m*mennes been

14 ¶Nonnes *183v*

The Nonnes preest	ELLESMERE
Wo*m*mannes conseil / broghte vs first to wo	broghte
And made Adam / fro Paradys to go	Adam / out of Paradys
Ther as he was / ful myrie and wel atese	was myrie /
But for I noot to whom it myghte displese	myght
If I conseil of wommen / wolde blame	I / wo*m*men
Passe ouer / for I seyde it in my game	seye
Rede Auctours / where they trete of swich matere	wher*e* trete / mateere
And what they seyn of wommen heere	wo*m*men / ye may heere
Thise ben the Cokkes wordes and nat myne	been wordes /
I kan noon harm / on no womman deuyne	harm / of no wo*m*man diuyne
¶Faire in the Sond / to bathe hir*e* myrily	**F**aire soond
Lyth Pertelote / and alle hir*e* sustres by	Lith
Agayn the sonne / and Chauntecler so free	Chauntecleer
Song myrier than the Mermayde in the see	Soong murier /
For Phisiologus / seith sikerly	
How *þa*t they syngen / wel and myrily	
¶And so bifel / that as he caste his eye	
Among the wortes / on a Boterflye	Among
He was war of this fox / *þa*t lay ful lowe	
No thyng ne liste hym thanne for to crowe	
But cryde anon / cok cok and vp he sterte	cride anon cok / cok /
As man / *þa*t was affrayd in his herte	that affrayed
For naturelly / a beest desireth flee	natureelly / beest
Fro his contrarie / if he may it see	contrarie /.
Though he neuere erst hadde seye it wi*th* his eye	Though neu*er* erst · seyn
This Chauntecler whan he gan hym espye	¶This Chauntecleer /
He wolde han fled / but *þa*t the fox anon	that
Seyde gentil sire / allas wher wol ye gon	
Be ye affrayd / of me *þa*t am youre freend	affrayed me / that freend
Now certes / I were worse than a feend	feend
If I to yow / wolde harm / or vileynye	
I am nat come / youre conseil for tespye	
But trewely / the cause of my comynge	
Was oonly / for to herkne how *þa*t ye synge	that
For trewely / ye han as myrie a steuene	haue
As any Angel hath / *þa*t is in heuene	Aungel / that
Ther with / ye han in Musyk moore feelynge	with
Than hadde Boece / or any *þa*t kan synge	
My lord youre fader / god his soule blesse	fader
And eek youre moder / of hir*e* gentillesse	mooder

Wommannes conseil broghte us first to wo
And made Adam fro Paradys to go
Ther as he was ful myrie and wel at ese
But for I noot to whom it myghte displese
If I conseil of wommen wolde blame
Passe ouer for I seyde it in my game
Rede auctours where they trete of swich matere
And what they seyn of wommen heere
Thise ben the cokkes wordes and nat myne
I kan noon harm on no womman deuyne
Faire in the sond to bathe hir myrily
Lyth Pertelote and alle hir sustres by
Agayn the sonne and Chaunteclere so free
Song myrier than the mermayde in the see
For Phisiologus seith sikerly
how þt they syngen wel and myrily
And so bifel that as he caste his eye
Among the wortes on a boterflye
He was war of this fox þt lay ful lowe
No thyng ne liste hym thanne for to crowe
But cryde anon cok cok and up he sterte
As man þt was affrayd in his herte
For naturelly a beest desireth flee
Fro his contrarie if he may it see
Though he neuere erst hadde seye it wt his eye
This Chaunteclere whan he gan hym espye
He wolde han fled but þe fox anon
Seyde gentil sire allas wher wol ye gon
Be ye affrayd of me þt am youre freend
Now certes I were worse than a feend
If I to yow wolde harm or vileynye
I am nat come youre conseil for tespye
But trewely the cause of my comynge
Was oonly for to herkne how þt ye synge
For trewely ye han as myrie a steuene
As any angel hath þt is in heuene
Ther with ye han in musyk moore feelynge
Than hadde Boece or any þt kan synge
My lord youre fader god his soule blesse
And eek youre moder of hir gentillesse

[Ha]n in myn hous yben to my gret ese
And certes sire ful fayn wolde I yow plese
But for men speke of syngynge I wol seye
So mote I brouke wel myn eyen tweye
Saue ye I herde neuere man so synge
As dide youre fader in the morwenynge
Certes it was of herte al that he song
And for to make his voys the moore strong
He wolde so peyne hym þt with bothe hise eyen
He moste wynke so loude he wolde cryen
And stonden on his tipton ther with al
And streeche forth his nekke long and smal
And eek he was of swich discrecion
That ther nas no man in no region
That hym in song or wisdom myghte passe
I haue wel rad in daun Burnell the asse
Among hise vers how þt ther was a cok
ffor a preestes sone yaf hym a knok
Vp on his leg whil he was yong and nyce
He made hym for to lese his benefice
But certeyn ther nys no comparison
Bitwix the wisdom and discrecion
Of youre fader and of his subtiltee
Now syngeth sire for seinte charitee
Lat se konne ye youre fader countrefete
This Chauntecleer hise wynges gan to bete
As man þt koude his traysoun nat espie
So was he rauysshed with his flaterie
Allas ye lordes many a fals flatour
Is in youre court and many a losengeour
That plesen yow wel moore by my feith
Than he þt soothfastnesse vn to yow seith
Redeth Ecclesiaste of flaterye
Beth war ye lordes of hir trecherye
This Chauntecleer stood hye vp on his toos
Strecchynge his nekke and heeld hise eyen cloos
And gan to crowe loude for the nones
And daun Russell the fox stirte vp atones
And by the gargat hente Chauntecleer
And on his bak toward the wode hym beer

	ELLESMERE
[Ha]n in myn hous yben / to my gret ese	15 Han ybeen greet
And certes sire / ful fayn wolde I yow plese	c*er*tes
¶But for men speke of syngynge / I wol seye	syngyngꝰ wol yow seye
So mote I browke wel / myne eyen tweye	16 moote brouke
Saue ye / I herde neuere man so synge	yow / herde I neu*er*e man yet synge
As dide youre fader / in the morwenynge	
Certes / it was of herte / al that he songꝰ	
And for to make his voys / the moore strongꝰ	make /
He wolde so peyne hym / þ*at* w*ith* bothe hise eyen	that
He moste wynke / so loude he wolde cryen	
And stonden on his typton / ther with al	tiptoon / therwith
And strecche forth his nekke / long and smal	longꝰ
And eek / he was of swich discreciou*n*	eek was /
That ther nas no man / in no Regiou*n*	nas / man
That hym in song / or wisdom myghte passe	hym / songꝰ wisedom mygħte
I haue wel rad / in daun Burneƚƚ the Asse	Burnel
Among hise vers / how þ*at* ther was a cokꝰ	Amongꝰ v*er*s / that Cokꝰ
For a preestes sone / yaf hym a knokꝰ	For that a
Vp on his legꝰ whil he was yong and nyce	
He made hym / for to lese his benefice	
But certeyn / ther nys no comparisou*n*	c*er*teyn /
Bitwix the wisdom / and discreciou*n*	Bitwixe / wisedom /
Of youre faderꝰ and of his subtiltee	fader /
Now syngeth sire / for seynte charitee	seinte
Lat se / konne ye youre fader countrefete	
¶This Chauntecler / hise wynges gan to bete	Chauntecleer /
As man þ*at* koude / his trayson nat espie	man / koude traysou*n*
So was he rauysshed / with his flaterie	rauyssħed
¶Allas ye lordes / many a fals flatour	Allas
Is in youre courtꝰ and many a losengeour	Co*ur*tes /
That plesen yow wel moore / by my feyth	yow / moore feith
Than he / þ*at* soothfastnesse vn to yow seith	that soothfastnesse /
Redeth Ecclesiaste / of flaterye	Flaterye
Beth war ye lordes / of hir trecherye	
¶This Chauntecler / stood hye vp on his toos	Chauntecleer /
Strecchynge his nekke / and heeld hise eyen cloos	
And gan to crowe / lowde for the nones	loude
And daun Russeƚƚ the fox / stirte vp atones	Daun
And by the gargatꝰ hente Chauntecler	Chauntecleer
And on his bak / toward the wode hym beer	

15 ¶Preestꝰ *184r*

16 The El scribe writes 4490 twice:

So moote I brouke wel / myne eyen tweye
So moot I / brouke wel myne eyen tweye

The second line is clearly marked by the scribe for removal.

For yet ne was ther no man / þ*at* hym sewed	
¶O destynee / þ*at* mayst nat ben eschewed	destinee / that been
Allas þ*at* Chauntecler / fly fro the bemes	Allas / Chauntecleer / fleigħ
Allas / his wif / ne roghte nat of dremes	wyf /
And on a friday / fil al this meschau*n*ce	meschaunce
¶O Venus / þ*at* art goddesse of plesau*n*ce	that plesaunce
Syn þ*at* thy seruant was this Chauntecler	17 that seruant. Chauntecleer
And in thy seruyce / dide al his power	poweer
Moore for delit than world to multiplie	multiplye
Why woldestow suffre hym / on thy day to dye	
¶O Gaufred / deere maister souerayn	¶O Gaufred Maister
That whan / thy worthy kyng Richard was slayn	That whan kyng Richard
With shot compleynedest his deth so soore	shot. deeth
Why ne hadde I now / thy sentence and thy loore	sentence /
The friday for to chide / as diden ye	
For on a Friday / soothly slayn was he	friday /
Thanne wolde I shewe yow / how þ*at* I kowde pleyne	koude
For Chaunteclerys drede / and for his peyne	Chauntecleres
¶Certes / swich cry / ne lamentaciou*n*	
Was neuere of ladyes maad / whan yliou*n*	neu*ere* /
Was wonne / and Pirr*us* / *with* his streite swerd	wo*n*ne / Pirrus swerd
Whanne he hadde hent kyng Priam by the berd	Whan Priam / berd
And slayn hym / as seith vs Eneydos	
As maden / alle the hennes in the cloos	clos
Whan they hadde seyn / of Chauntecler the sighte	had Chauntecleer sighte
But souereynly / dame Pertelote shrighte	But sodeynly / dame shrighte
Ful louder / than dide Hasdrubales wyf	louder **Hasdrubales**
Whan þ*at* hire housbonde / hadde ylost his lyf	hir lost lyf
And þ*at* the Romayns / hadden brend Cartage	hadde
She was / so ful of torment and of rage	
That wilfully / vn to the fyr she sterte	wilfully / in to
And brende hir seluen / *with* a stedefast herte	with
¶O woful hennes / right so cryden ye	right criden
As / whan þ*at* Nero / brende the Citee	As that
Of Rome / cryden the senatours wyues	cryden Senatours
For þ*at* hir housbondes / losten alƚ hir*e* lyues	alle hir
With outen gilt this Nero hath hem slayn	
Now wol I turne / to my tale agayn	Now turne I wole /. to
¶The sely widwe / and eek hire doghtres two	This sely wydwe / eek hir
Herden thise hennes crye / and maken wo	crie /

[17] ¶Nonnes *184v*

Ffor yet ne was ther no man þt hym sewed
O destynee þt mayst nat ben eschewed
Allas þt Chauntecleer fley fro the bemes
Allas his wyf ne roghte nat of dremes
And on a Friday fil al this meschance
O Venus þt art goddesse of plesance
Syn þt thy seruant was this Chauntecleer
And in thy seruyce dide al his power
Moore for delit than world to multiplie
Why woldestow suffre hym on thy day to dye
O Gaufred deere maister souerayn
That whan thy worthy kyng Richard was slayn
With shot compleynedest his deth so soore
Why ne hadde I now thy sentence and thy loore
The Friday for to chide as diden ye
Ffor on a Ffriday soothly slayn was he
Thanne wolde I shewe yow how þt I koude pleyne
Ffor Chauntecleres drede and for his peyne
Certes swich cry ne lamentacion
Was neuere of ladyes maad whan Ylion
Was wonne and Pirrus wt his streite swerd
Whanne he hadde hent kyng Priam by the berd
And slayn hym as seith vs Eneydos
As maden alle the hennes in the clos
Whan they hadde seyn of Chauntecleer the sighte
But souereynly dame Pertelote shrighte
Ful louder than dide Hasdrubales wyf
Whan þt hire housbonde hadde ylost his lyf
And þt the Romayns hadden brend Cartage
She was so ful of torment and of rage
That wilfully vn to the fyr she sterte
And brende hir seluen wt a stedefast herte
O woful hennes right so cryden ye
As whan þt Nero brende the Citee
Of Rome cryden the senatours wyues
Ffor þt hir housbondes losten alle hir lyues
With outen gilt this Nero hath hem slayn
Now wol I turne to my tale agayn
The sely wydwe and eek hir doghtres two
Herden thise hennes crye and maken wo

[...]o out at dores / stirten they anon
And seyen the fox / toward the groue gon
And bar vp on his bak / the cok awey
And cryden out / harrow and weilaway
Ha / ha / the fox / and after hym they ran
And eek with staues / many another man
Ran Colle oure dogge / and Talbot / and Gerland
And Malkyn / with a distaf in hir hand
Ran cow and calf / and eek the verray hogges
So fered for berkynge of the dogges
And showtynge of the men / and wommen eek
They ronne so / hem thoughte hir herte breek
They yelleden / as feendes doon in helle
The dokes cryden / as men wolde hem quelle
The gees for feere / flowen ouer the trees
Out of the hyue / cam the swarm of bees
So hydous was the noyse / a benedicite
Certes / he Iakke Straw / and his meynee
Ne made neuere shoutes / half so shrille
Whan þt they wolden / any Flemyng kille
As thilke day / was maad vp on the fox
Of bras they broghten bemys / and of box
Of horn / of boon / in whiche they blewe and powped
And ther with al / they skryked and they howped
It semed / as þt heuene sholde falle
Now goode men / I prey yow herkneth alle
Lo / how fortune / turneth sodeynly
The hope and pryde eek of hir enemy
This cok / þt lay vp on the foxes bak
In al his drede / vn to the fox he spak
And seyde sire / if þt I were as ye
Yit sholde I seyn / as wys god helpe me
Turneth agayn ye proude cherles alle
A verray pestilence / vp on yow falle
Now I am come / vn to this wodes syde
Maugree youre heed / the cok shal heere abyde
I wol hym ete in feith / and that anon
The fox answerde / in feith it shal be don
And he spak that word / al sodeynly
This cok brak from his mouth delyuerly

ELLESMERE

[And] out at dores / stirten they anon
[A]nd seyen the fox / toward the groue gon
And bar vp on his bak / the cok / away
And criden / out harrow and weilaway
Ha / ha. the fox / and after hym they ran
And eek with staues / many another man
Ran Colle oure dogge / and Talbot and Gerland
And Malkyn / with a distaf in hir*e* hand
Ran Cow and calf / and eek the v*er*ray hogges
So fered / for berkynge of the dogges
And showtynge of the men / and wo*m*men eek
They ronne so / hem thoughte hir*e* herte breek /
They yelleden / as fendes doon in helle
The dokes cryden / as men wolde hem quelle
The gees for feere / flowen ouer the trees
Out of the hyue / cam the swarm of bees
So hydous was the noyse / a benedicite
Certes / he Iakke Straw / and his meynee
Ne made neuere showtes / half so shrille
Whan p*at* they wolden / any flemyng kille
As thilke day / was maad vp on the fox
Of bras / they broghten bemys / and of box
Of horn / of boon / in whiche they blewe and powped
And ther with al / they skryked and they howped
It semed / as p*at* heuene sholde falle
Now goode men / I prey yow herkneth alle
¶Lo / how Fortune / turneth sodeynly
The hope / and pryde eek of hire enemy
This cok p*at* lay vp on the foxes bak
In al his drede / vn to the fox he spak
And seyde sire / if p*at* I were as ye
Yit sholde I seyn / as wys god helpe me
Turneth ayein ye proude cherles alle
A verray pestilence / vp on yow falle
Now I am come / vn to this wodes syde
Maugree youre heed / the cok shal here abyde
I wol hym ete in feith / and that anon
¶The fox answerde / in feith it shal be don
And he spak that word / al sodeynly
This cok / brak from his mouth delyuerly

And
And syen
Cok
cryden harrow / weylaway
Ha. ha /
eek

dystaf / hir
Calf and the verray
berkyng
shoutyng men
The ronne thoughte hir breek
yolleden / feendes

18 ou*er*
hyve /
benedicitee

neu*er*e / shoutes / so shille

bemes

withal / skriked /
that

Lo /
pryde / of hir
Cok / that vpon bak

that
Yet wolde I
agayn /
v*er*ray
to the wodes
Cok heere

And as he
Cok /

[18] ¶Preest *185r*

And hye vp on a tree / he fley anon
¶And whan the fox say / þat he was gon
Allas quod he / o Chauntecler Allas
I haue to yow quod he / ydon trespas
In as muche / as I maked yow aferd
Whan I yow hente / and broghte in to this yerd
But sire / I dide it in no wikke entente
Com doun / and I shal telle yow what I mente
I shal seye sooth to yow / god help me so
¶Nay thanne quod he / I shrewe vs bothe two
And first I shrewe my self / bothe blood and bones
If thow bigile me / any ofter than ones
Thow shalt namoore / thurgh thy flaterye
Do me to synge / and wynken *with* myn eye
For he þat wynketh / whan he sholde see
Al wilfully / god lat hym neuere thee
¶Nay quod the fox / but god yeue hym meschau*n*ce
That is / so vndiscret / of gouernau*n*ce
That Iangleth / whan he sholde holde his pees
¶Lo / swich it is / for to be recchelees
And necligent and truste on flaterye
But ye / þat holden this tale a folye
As of a fox / or of a cok and hen
Taketh the moralitee / goode men
For Seint Poul seith / þat al that writen is
To oure doctryne / it is ywrite ywis
Taketh the fruyt and lat the chaf be stille
Now goode god / if þat it be thy wille
As seith my lord / so make vs alle goode men
And brynge vs / to his heye blisse Amen[20]

¶Here is ended / the Nonnes preestes tale
¶And here folweth the prologe of the Manciples tale

Woot ye nat where / ther stant a litel town
Which / þat clepid is / Bobbe vpanddown
Vnder the Blee / in Caunterbury weye
Ther gan oure hoost for to iape and pleye
And seyde sires / what / Don is in the Myre
Is ther no man / for preyere ne for hyre

ELLESMERE

heighe fleigh
And saugh /
¶Allas Chauntecleer allas
ydoon
aferd
broghte yerd
sire it. of no
first *and*
thou bigyle
Thou thurgh
wynke with
that
neu*er*e
meschaunce
is so / vndiscreet gou*er*naunce
¶But that holden /
19 Cok
moralite /
Paul
doctrine /
that
lord
heighe

¶Heere is ended / the Nonnes preestes tale
¶Heere folweth the Prologe / of the Mauncipies tale[1]

Woot nat / where stant / toun
Which ycleped is Bobbeup and doun
Iape
what Dun

4635 dominus Archiepiscopus Cantuariensis Hg El
Variant: silicet d. A. C. El

[19] ¶Seconde *185v*

[20] *Out* Hg El 4637-52. Only nine MSS, including Ch, Dd, and En[1], contain 4637-52, which include a view of the Priest absorbed in the Monk's Prol. Dd reads:

Sire Nonnes Preest / oure hoost seide a noon
I blissed be thy breche / *and* eu*er*y ston
This was a murie tale / of Chauntecleer
But by my trouthe / if þou were seculer
Thow woldest ben a tredfoul / a right
For if þou haue corage / as þou hast myght
The were nede of hennes / as I wene
Ȝa / moo than seuene tymes / seuentene
Se which braunes / hath this gentil Preest
So gret a nekke / *and* swich a large breest

And hye vp on a tree he fley anon
And whan the fox say þt he was gon
Allas quod he o Chauntecleer allas
I haue to yow quod he ydon trespas
In as muche as I maked yow aferd
Whan I yow hente and broghte in to this yerd
But sire I dide it in no wikke entente
Com doun and I shal telle yow what I mente
I shal seye sooth to yow god help me so
Nay thanne quod he I shrewe vs bothe two
And first I shrewe my self bothe blood and bones
If thow bigile me any ofter than ones
Thow shalt namoore thurgh thy flaterye
Do me to synge and wynken wt myn eye
For he þt wynketh whan he sholde see
Al wilfully god lat hym neuere thee
Nay quod the fox but god yeue hym meschance
That is so vndiscreet of gouernance
That iangleth whan he sholde holde his pees
Lo swich it is for to be rechelees
And necligent and truste on flaterye
But ye þt holden this tale a folye
As of a fox or of a cok and hen
Taketh the moralitee goode men
For seint Poul seith þt al that writen is
To oure doctryne it is ywrite ywis
Taketh the fruyt and lat the chaf be stille
Now goode god if þt it be thy wille
dns archiepus As seith my lord so make vs alle goode men
Cantuarien And brynge vs to his heye blisse Amen

Heer is ended the Nonnes preestes tale
And heere folweth the Prologe of the Maunciples tale

Woot ye nat where ther stant a litel town
Which þt cleped is Bobbe vp and doun
Vnder the Blee in Caunterbury weye
Ther gan oure hoost for to iape and pleye
And seyde sires what Dun is in the myre
Is ther no man for preyere ne for hyre

at wole awake oure felawe al bihynde
A theef myghte hym ful lightly robbe and bynde
See how he nappeth see how for cokkes bones
That he wol falle from his hors atones
Is that a cook of londoun with meschance
Do hym come forth he knoweth his penaunce
ffor he shal telle a tale by my fey
Al though it be nat worth a botel hey
Awake thow cook quod he god yeue thee sorwe
What eyleth thee to slepe by the morwe
Hastow had flees al nyght or artow dronke
Or hastow with som quene al nyght yswonke
So that thow mayst nat holden vp thyn heed
This cook þt was ful pale and no thyng reed
Seyde to oure hoost so god my soule blesse
As ther is falle on me swich heuynesse
Noot I nat why þt me were leuere slepe
·ix Than the beste galon wyn in Chepe
Wel quod the Manciple if it may don ese
To thee sire cook and to no wight displese
Which þt here rideth in this compaignye
And þt oure hoost wole of his curteisye
I wole as now excuse thee of thy tale
ffor in good feith thy visage is ful pale
Thyne eyen daswen eek as þt me thynketh
And wel I woot thy breeth ful soure stynketh
That sheweth wel thow art nat wel disposed
Of me certeyn thow shalt nat ben yglosed
See how he ganeth lo this dronken wight
As though he wolde swolwe vs anon right
Hoold cloos thy mouth man by thy fader kyn
The deuel of helle sette his foot ther yn
Thy cursed breeth infecte wol vs alle
ffy stynkynge swyn fy foule mote thee falle
A taketh hede sires of this lusty man
Now swete sire wol ye justen atte ffan
Ther to me thynketh ye ben wel yshape
I trowe þt ye dronken han wyn ape
And that is whan men pleyen with a straw
And with his speche the cook wax wroth and wraw

	ELLESMERE
[Tha]t wole awake / oure felawe al bihynde	That
[A] theef myghte hym / ful lightly robbe and bynde	A theef / hym
Se how he nappeth / se how for Cokkes bones	See see
That he wol falle / from his hors atones	fro
Is that a Cook of londou*n* / with meschau*n*ce	Londou*n* / meschaunce
Do hym come forth / he knoweth his penau*n*ce	penaunce
For he shal telle a tale / by my fey	
Al thogh / it be nat worth a botel hey	though / nat Botel
Awake thow Cook quod he / god yeue thee sorwe	thou Cook
What eyleth thee / to slepe by the morwe	morwe /
Hastow had fleen al nyght or artow dronke	nyght dronke /
Or hastow w*ith* som quene / al nyght yswonke	hastow / with nyght yswonke /
So / that thow mayst nat holden vp thyn heed	So nat heed
¶This Cook þ*at* was ful pale / and no thyng reed	Cook / pale reed
Seyde to oure hoost so god my soule blesse	hoost / .
As ther is / falle / on me swich heuynesse	is falle
Noot I nat why / þ*at* me were leuere slepe	why / leu*er*e
⟨ye⟩ Than / the beste galou*n* wyn in Chepe	galon
¶Wel quod the Manciple / if it may don ese	Mau*n*ciple / doon
To thee *sir* Cook and to no wight displese	Sire Cook / wight
Which þ*at* here rideth / in this compaignye	heere
And þ*at* oure hoost wole of his curteisye	that hoost /
I wole as now / excuse thee of thy tale	wol now / thee /
For in good feith / thy visage is ful pale	
Thyne eyen daswen eek as þ*at* me thynketh	2 that
And wel I woot thy breth ful soure stynketh	woot / breeth /
That sheweth wel / thow art nat wel disposed	thou disposed
Of me certeyn / thow shalt nat ben yglosed	c*er*teyn / thou been yglosed
Se how he ganeth / lo this dronken wight	See wight
As though he wolde / swolwe vs anon right	though anonright
Hoold cloos thy mouth / man by thy fader kyn	mouth man /
The deuel of helle / sette his foot ther yn	In
Thy cursed breeth / infecte wol vs alle	breeth / wole
Fy stynkynge swyn / fy / foule mote thee falle	stynkyng moote thou
A taketh hede sires / of this lusty man	heede
Now swete sire / wol ye Iusten atte Fan	sweete
Ther to me thynketh / ye ben wel yshape	Therto been
I trowe / þ*at* ye dronken han wyn ape	that
And that is / whan men pleyen w*ith* a straw	with
And with his speche / the Cook wax wroth *and* wraw	with this speche / Cook wrooth

He loketh as a sp*ar*hauke / w*ith* hise eyen
Hi*m* nedeth nat / his colour for to dyghen
W*ith* brasile / ne with greyn of Portyngale
Now sire / faire falle ȝow / for ȝoure tale
And after that / he w*ith* ful merie chere
Seide vn to a nother / as ȝe shuln heere

[1] ¶Yeman̄ on *202r*

[2] ¶Mau*n*ciple *202v*

The Manciple tale of the [Crowe]	ELLESMERE
And on the Manciple / bigan he nodde faste	Manciple / he gan nodde
For lakke of speche / and doun the hors hym caste	
Wher as he lay / til þ*at* men vp hym took	Where took
This was / a fair chyuachee of a Cook	chyuachee /
Allas / he nadde yholde hym / by his ladel	nadde / holde hym
And er þ*at* he / agayn were in his sadel	
Ther was gret showuyng bothe to and fro	greet
To lifte hym vp / and muchel care and wo	
So vnweldy / was this sory palled goost	vnweeldy /
And to the Manciple / thanne spak oure hoost	hoost /
¶By cause // drynke hath domynaciou*n*	cause / drynke / dominaciou*n*
Vp on this man / by my sauaciou*n*	Vpon
I trowe he lewedly / telle wolde his tale	trowe / lewedly / he wolde telle
For were it wyn / or old / or moisty Ale	oold / moysty
That he hath dronke / he speketh in his nose	
And fneseth faste / and eek he hath the pose	eek
He hath also to do / moore than ynow	¶He also / do ynougħ
To kepen hym / and his capil / out of the slow	hym Capul of slougħ
And if he falle / from his capil eft soone	capul eftsoone
Than shal we alle / haue ynow to doone	Thanne ynogħ
In liftynge vp / his heuy dronken cors	liftyng
Telle on thy tale / of hym make I no fors	
But yet Manciple / in feith thow art to nyce	¶But thou art /
Thus openly / repreue hym of his vice	
Another day / he wole p*ar* Auenture	
Reclayme thee / and brynge thee to lure	
I mene / he speke wole / of smale thynges	meene /
As for to pynchen / at thy rekenynges	
That were nat honeste / if it cam to preef	preef /
¶No quod the Manciple / that were a gret mescheef	greet mescheef
So myghte he lightly / brynge me in the snare	mygħte ligħtly /
Yet hadde I leuere / payen for the Mare	
Which he rit on / than he sholde w*ith* me stryue	3 Whicħ that he sholde / witħ
I wol nat wrathe hym / also mote I thryue	wratthen moot
That þ*at* I spak I seyde it in my bourde	That that / I speke /
And wite what I haue here in a gourde	wite ye what heer
A draughte of wyn / ye of a rype grape	draghte ripe
And right anon / ye shul seen a good Iape	rigħt
This Cook / shal drynke ther of if I may	Cook of / if þ*at* I
Vp peyne of deeth / he wol nat seye me nay	

[3] ¶Mau*n*ciple *203r*

And on the manciple bigan he nodde faste
ffor lakke of speche and doun the hors hym caste
Wher as he lay til þt men up hym took
This was a fair chyuachee of a cook
Allas he nadde yholde hym by his ladel
And er þt he agayn were in his sadel
Ther was gret showuyng bothe to and fro
To lifte hym up and muchel care and wo
So unweldy was this sory palled goost
And to the manciple thanne spak oure hoost
By cause drynke hath dominacion
Upon this man by my saluacion
I trowe he lewedly telle wolde his tale
ffor were it wyn or old or moisty ale
That he hath dronke he speketh in his nose
And fneseth faste and eek he hath the pose
He hath also to do moore than ynowh
To kepen hym and his capil out of the slowh
And if he falle from his capil eft soone
Than shal we alle haue ynowh to doone
In liftynge up his heuy dronken cors
Telle on thy tale of hym make I no fors
But yet manciple in feith thow art to nyce
Thus openly repreue hym of his vice
Another day he wole parauenture
Reclayme thee and brynge thee to lure
I mene he speke wole of smale thynges
As for to pynchen at thy rekenynges
That were nat honeste if it cam to preef
No quod the manciple that were a gret mescheef
So myghte he lightly brynge me in the snare
Yet hadde I leuere payen for the mare
Which he rit on than he sholde with me stryue
I wol nat wrathe hym also mote I thryue
That þt I spak I seyde it in my bourde
And wite what I haue here in a gourde
A draughte of wyn ye of a rype grape
And right anon ye shul seen a good Iape
This cook shal drynke ther of if I may
Up peyne of deeth he wol nat seye me nay

[An]d shortly to tellen as it was
Of this vessel / the cook drank faste / allas
What neded it / he drank ynogh biforn
And whan he hadde pouped in this horn
To the Manciple / he took the gourde agayn
And of that drynke the cook was wonder fayn
And thanked hym in which wise as he kowde
Thanne gan oure hoost / to laughen wonder lowde
And seyde I se wel it is necessarie
Where yt we goon good drynke we wt us carye
ffor that wol turne / rancour and disese
Tacord and loue / a many a wrong apese
O Bacus / yblessed be thy name
That so kanst turnen / ernest in to game
Worship and thank / be to thy deitee
Of that matere / ye gete namoore for me
Telle on thy Manciple / I the preye
Wel sire quod he / now herkneth what I seye

Here bigynneth the Manciples tale of the Crowe

Whan Phebus dwelled here in this erthe adoun
As olde bokes / maken mencioun
He was / the mooste lusty bachiler
In al this world / and eek the beste archer
He slow Phiton the serpent / as he lay
Slepynge agayn the sonne vp on a day
And many another / noble worthy dede
He wt his bowe wroghte / as men may rede
Pleyen he koude on euery mynstralcye
And syngen yt it was a melodye
To heren of his clere voys the soun
Certes the kyng of Thebes Amphioun
That wt his syngyng / walled that Citee
Koude neuere syngen / half so wel as he
Therto he was the semelieste man
That is or was / sith yt the world bigan
What nedeth it / hise fetures to discryue
ffor in this world / was noon so fair on lyue
He was ther with / fulfild of gentillesse
Of honour / and of parfit worthynesse

[An]d *cer*teynly / to tellen as it was
Of this vessel / the Cook drank faste / allas
What neded it he drank ynow biforn
And whan he hadde / powped in this horn
To the Manciple / he took the gourde agayn
And of that drynke / the Cook was wonder fayn
And thanked hym / in swich wise as he kowde
¶Thanne gan oure hoost to laughen wonder lowde
And seyde / I se wel it is necessarie
Where *pat* we goon / good drynke we *with* vs carye
For that wol turne / rancour and disese
Tacord and loue / a many a wrong appese
¶O Bacus / yblessed be thy name
That so kanst turnen / ernest in to game
Worship*e* and thank be to thy deitee
Of that matere / ye gete namoore for me
Telle on thy Manciple / I the preye
Wel *sir* quod he / now herkneth what I seye

¶Here bigynneth the Manciples tale / of the Crowe

Whan Phebus / dwelled here / in this erthe adoun
As olde bokes / maken mencioun
He was / the mooste lusty bachiler
In al this world / and eek the beste Archer
He slow Phitou*n* the serpent as he lay
Slepynge agayn the sonne vp on a day
And many another noble worthy dede
He *with* his bowe wroghte / as men may rede
Pleyen he koude / on euery Mynstralcye
And syngen / *pat* it was a melodye
To heren / of his clere voys / the soun
Certes / the kyng of Thebes Amphioun
That *with* his syngyng walled that Citee
Koude neuere syngen / half so wel as he
Therto / he was the semelieste man
That is / or was / sith *pat* the world bigan
What nedeth it hise fetures to discryue
For in this world / was noon so fair on lyue
He was ther with / fulfild of gentillesse
Of honour and of parfit worthynesse

ELLESMERE

¶And certeynly /
Cook allas
neded hym / he ynough
pouped
koude
laughen loude
wel /
Wher*e* goon / *pat* drynke carie
loue / and many wrong apese
ernest
mateere / namoore of me
thy tale / Manciple thee
¶Wel sire

¶Heere bigynneth the Mau*n*ciples tale / of the Crowe[4]

WHan heere / this world adoun
bookes /
Bachiler
Phitou*n* /
Slepynge /
another /
with wroghte /
¶Pleyen Mynstralcie
that melodie
heeren / cleere voys
kyng
with
neu*ere* hee
Therto was /
is
[5] with / fulfild
p*ar*fit

[4] Miniature of the Manciple in right margin.

[5] ¶Mau*n*ciple *203v*

	ELLESMERE
¶This Phebus / *pat* was flour of Bachelrye	that was / Bachilrie
As wel / in fredom as in Chiualrye	fredom / Chiualrie
For his desport in signe eek of victorie	desport. Signe
Of Phitoun / so as telleth vs the storie	
Was wont to beren / in his hand a bowe	wont beren
Now hadde this Phebus / in his hous a Crowe	¶Now crowe
Which in a Cage / he fostred many a day	
And taughte it speke / as men teche a Iay	taughte
Whit was this Crowe / as is a snow whit swan	
And contrefete / the speche of euery man	countrefete
He kowde / whan he sholde telle a tale	koude /
Ther with in al this world / no nyghtyngale	nyghtyngale
Ne koude / by an hondred thousand deel	thousand
Syngen / so wonder myrily and weel	
¶Now hadde this Phebus / in his hous a wyf/	
Which *pat* he louede / moore than his lyf	lyf
And nyght / and day / dide euere his diligence	nyght
Hire for to plese / and doon hire reuerence	Hir ⟨for⟩
Saue oonly / that the sothe / if I shal sayn	oonly / the sothe that I
Ialous he was / and wolde han kept hire fayn	haue hire
For hym were looth / byiaped for to be	
And so is euery wight in swich degree	euery wight
But al for naught / for it auaileth noght	al in ydel / for auailleth noght
A good wyf that is clene in werk and thoght	wyf / clene / of werk *and* thoght
Sholde nat be kept in noon awayt certayn	been certayn
And trewely / the labour is in vayn	
To kepe a shrewe / for it wol nat be	bee
This holde I / for a verray nycetee	
To spille labour / for to kepe wyues	
Thus writen olde clerkes in hir lyues	clerkes /
¶But now to purpos / as I first bigan	Bvt
This worthy Phebus / dooth al that he kan	
To plesen hire / wenynge for swich plesaunce	plesen hire / wenynge that swich
And for his manhode / and his gouernaunce	manhede / gouernaunce
That no man / sholde han put hym from hire grace	hir
But god it woot ther may no man embrace	woot.
As to destreyne a thyng which *pat* nature	thyng.
Hath naturelly / set in a creature	natureelly /
¶Take any bryd / and put it in a Cage	¶Taak
And do al thyn entente / and thy corage	

147 Verum quid prodest diligens custodia
cum vxor impudica seruari non possit
pudica non debeat feda enim custos
est castitatis necessitas pulcra
adamatur feda facile concupiscit
difficile custoditur quod plures amant Hg

163 Exemplum de volucre El

This Phebus þt was flour of bachelrye
As wel in fredom as in chiualrye
ffor his desport in signe eek of victorie
Of Phiton so as telleth vs the storie
Was wont to beren in his hand a bowe
Now hadde this Phebus in his hous a Crowe
Which in a cage he fostred many a day
And taughte it speke as men teche a Iay
Whit was this Crowe as is a snow whit swan
And contrefete the speche of euery man
He koude whan he sholde telle a tale
Ther with in al this world no nyghtyngale
Ne koude by an hondred thousand deel
Syngen so wonder myrily and weel
Now hadde this Phebus in his hous a wyf
Which þt he louede moore than his lyf
And nyght and day dide euere his diligence
Hire for to plese and doon hire reuerence
Saue oonly that the sothe if I shal sayn
Ialous he was and wolde han kept hire fayn
ffor hym were looth byiaped for to be
And so is euery wight in swich degree
But al for naught for it auailleth noght
A good wyf that is clene in werk and thoght
Sholde nat be kept in noon awayt certayn
And trewely the labour is in vayn
To kepe a shrewe for it wol nat be
This holde I for a verray nycetee
To spille labour for to kepe wyues
Thus writen olde clerkes in hir lyues
But now to purpos as I first bigan
This worthy Phebus dooth al that he kan
To plesen hire wenynge for swich plesance
And for his manhode and his gouernance
That no man sholde han put hym from hir grace
But god it woot ther may no man embrace
As to destreyne a thyng which þt nature
Hath naturelly set in a creature
Take any bryd and put it in a cage
And do al thyn entente and thy corage

Quid enim prodest diligens custodia
cum uxor impudica seruari non possi
pudica non debeat ffeda enim custos
est castitatis necessitas pulcra
adamatur ffeda facile concupis
difficile custoditur quod plures ama

fostre it tendrely with mete and drynke
Of alle deyntees þt thou kanst bithynke
And kepe it also clenly as thou may
Al though his cage of gold be neuer so gay
yet hath this brid by .xx. thousand fold
Leuere in a fforest þt is rude and cold
Gon ete wormes and swich wrecchednesse
ffor euere this brid wol doon his bisynesse
To eschape out of his cage if he may
his libertee this brid desireth ay
Lat take a cat and fostre hym wel wt milk
And tendre flessh and make his couche of silk
And lat hym seen a mous go by the wal
Anon he weyueth milk and flessh and al
And euery deyntee þt is in that hous
Swich appetit hath he to ete a mous
lo heere hath lust his domynacion
And appetit flemeth discrecion
A she wolf hath also a vileyns kynde
The lewedeste wolf þt she may fynde
And leest of reputacion that wol she take
In tyme whan hir lust to han a make
Alle thise ensamples speke I by thise men
That ben vntrewe but no thyng by wommen
ffor men han euere a likerous appetit
On lower thyng to pformen hir delit
Than on hire wyues be they neuer so faire
Ne neuer so trewe ne so debonaire
fflessh is so newfangel with meschance
That we ne konne in no thyng han plesance
That sowneth in to vertu any while
This Phebus which þt thoughte vp on no gile
Deceyued was for al his iolitee
ffor vnder hym another hadde she
A man of litel reputacion
Nat worth to Phebus in comparison
The moore harm is it happeth ofte so
Of which ther cometh muchel harm and wo
And so bifel whan Phebus was absent
his wyf anon hath for hire lemman sent

	ELLESMERE
[To] fostre it tendrely / with mete and drynke	To
Of alle deyntees / þ*at* thow kanst bithynke	thou
And kepe it al so clenly as thow may	keepe also clenly / thou
Al though his Cage / of gold / be neuer so gay	thougħ gold neu*er*
Yet hath this bryd / by .xx. thousand fold	brid / twenty foold
Leuere in a Forest þ*at* is rude and cold	Leu*er*e Forest / that coold
Gon ete wormes / and swich wrecchednesse	6 Goon
For euere this bryd / wol doon his bisynesse	eu*er*e brid /
To eschape out of his Cage / if he may	escape
His libertee / this bryd desireth ay	brid
¶Lat take a Cat and fostre hym wel w*ith* Milk	
And tendre flessh / and make his couche of silk	flessħ /
And lat hym seen a Mous / go by the wal	seen / Mous
Anon he weyueth / Milk / and flessh and al	flessħ
And euery deyntee / þ*at* is in that hous	that
Swich appetit hath he / to ete a Mous	he hath /
Lo / heere hath lust his domynaciou*n*	lust dominaciou*n*
And appetit flemeth discreciou*n*	Appetit fleemeth
¶A she wolf hath also / a vileyns kynde	wolf /
The lewedeste wolf þ*at* she may fynde	
And leest of reputaciou*n* / that wol she take	Or leest
In tyme / whan hire lust to han a make	hir lust
¶Alle thise ensamples / speke I by thise men	
That ben vntrewe / but no thyng by wo*m*men	been vntrewe / and no thyng
For men han euere / a likerous appetit	eu*er*e / Appetit
On lower thyng / to p*ar*formen hir delit	thyng p*ar*fourne hir*e* delit
Than on hire wyues / be they neuer so faire	hir*e* neu*er*
Ne neuer so trewe / ne so debonaire	neu*er*
Flessħ is so newfangel / with meschau*n*ce	newefangel meschaunce
That we ne konne / in no thyng han plesau*n*ce	plesaunce
That sowneth in to v*er*tu / any while	vertu /
¶This Phebus / which þ*at* thoughte vp on no gile	thoghte vpon
Deceyued was / for al his iolitee	Iolitee
For vnder hym / another hadde she	shee
A man / of litel reputaciou*n*	
Nat worth to Phebus in comparisou*n*	Phebus / co*m*parisou*n*
The moore harm is / it happeth ofte so	
Of which ther cometh / muchel harm and wo	*and*
And so bifel / whan Phebus was absent	¶And
His wyf anon / hath for hire lemman sent	hir

175 Exemplum de Murelego El

183 Exemplum de lupo El

6 ¶Mau*n*ciple *204r*

The Manciple.//	ELLESMERE
Hir lemman / certes this a knauyssh speche	le*m*man /*cer*tes this is a knauyssħ
Foryeueth it me / and that I yow biseche	
The wise Plato seith / as ye may rede	¶The
The word moot nede / acorde w*ith* the dede	word / nede accorde with
If men shal telle / *pro*prely a thyng'	telle
The word / moot cosyn be to the werkyng'	
I am a boystous man / right thus seye I	am am[7] a riħt
Ther nys no difference / trewely	difference
Bitwix a wyf / þ*a*t is of heigh degree	Bitwixe wyf'
If of hire body / deshoneste she be	hir dishoneste bee
And a poore wenche / oother than this	poure wenche / /
If it so be / they werke bothe amys	
But þ*a*t the gentile / in estat aboue	in hir*e* estaat
She shal be clepid his lady / as in loue	cleped / lady
And for that oother / is a poore womman	8 poure
She shal be clepid / his wenche / or his lemman	cleped /
And god it woot / myn owene deere brother	woot'
Men leyn þ*a*t oon / as lowe as lyth that oother	lith þ*a*t
¶Right so / bitwix a titlelees tirau*n*t' (sine titulo)	¶Riħt bitwixe titlelees tirau*n*t /
And an Outlawe / or a theef errau*n*t'	
The same I seye / ther is no difference	
To Alisandre / was told this sentence	Alisaundre / toold
That for the tirau*n*t / is of gretter myght'	tirant' myħt'
By force of meyne / for to sleen doun right'	meynee / riħt'
And brennen hous and hoom / and make al playn	*and* *and*
Lo / ther fore / is he clepid a Capitayn	therfore / cleped
And for the Outlawe / hath but smal meynee	
And may nat doon / so gret an harm as he	greet
Ne brynge a contree / to so gret meschief	greet mescheef /
Men clepen hym / an Outlawe or a theef /	Outlawe /
But for I am a man / noght textuel	noħt textueel
I wol noght telle of textes / neuer a del	noħt telle / textes deel
I wol go to my tale / as I bigan	go /
¶Whan Phebus wyf / hadde sent for hire lemman	Whan had hir le*m*man
Anon they wroghte / al hire lust volage	wroghten / hir*e*
The white Crowe / þ*a*t heng ay in the Cage	¶The crowe / that heeng
Biheld hir werk / and seyde neuer a word	Biheeld hir*e* werk' neu*er* word'
And whan that hoom was come / Phebus the lord	þ*a*t come lord'
This Crowe sang' Cokkow / Cokkow Cokkow	sang / Cokkow / Cokkow / Cokkow /
¶What bryd / quod Phebus / what song' syngestow	byrd syngestow /

[7] The second 'am' marked for deletion.

[8] ¶Mau*n*ciple *204v*

hir lemman certes this a knavyssh speche
fforyeueth it me and that I yow biseche
The wise Plato seith as ye may rede
The word moot nede acorde wt the dede
If men shal telle proprely a thyng
The word moot cosyn be to the werkyng
I am a boystous man right thus seye I
Ther nys no difference trewely
Bitwix a wyf þt is of heigh degree
If of hire body deshoneste she be
And a poore wenche oother than this
If it so be they werke bothe amys
But þt the gentile in estat above
She shal be cleped his lady as in love
And for that oother is a poore womman
She shal be cleped his wenche or his lemman
And god it woot myn owene deere brother
Men leyn þt oon as lowe as lyth that oother
sine titulo
Right so bitwix a titlelees tirant
And an Outlawe or a theef erraunt
The same I seye ther is no difference
To Alisandre was told this sentence
That for the tirant is of gretter myght
By force of meyne for to sleen doun right
And brennen hous and hoom and make al playn
lo therfore is he cleped a Capitayn
And for the Outlawe hath but smal meynee
And may nat doon so gret an harm as he
Ne brynge a contree to so gret meschief
Men clepen hym an Outlawe or a theef
But for I am a man noght textuel
I wol noght telle of textes neuer a del
I wol go to my tale as I bigan
Whan Phebus wyf hadde sent for hire lemman
Anon they wroghte al hire lust volage
The white crowe þt heng ay in the cage
Biheld hir werk and seyde neuer a word
And whan that hoom was come Phebus the lord
This crowe sang Cokkow Cokkow Cokkow
What bryd quod Phebus what song syngestow

[W]ere thow wont so myrily to synge
[Th]at to myn herte it was a reioysynge
To here thy voys allas what song is this
By god quod he I synge nat amys
Phebus quod he for al thy worthynesse
ffor al thy beautee and thy gentillesse
ffor al thy song and al thy mynstralcye
ffor al thy waityng blered is thyn eye
With oon of litel reputacion
Nat worth to thee in comparison
The montance of a gnat so mote I thryve
ffor in thy bed thy wif I sey hym &c
What wol ye moore the crowe anon hym tolde
By sadde toknes and by wordes bolde
How þt his wyf hadde doon hire lecherye
Hym to greet shame and to greet vileynye
And tolde hym ofte he say it wt hise eyen
This Phebus gan aweyward for to wryen
And thoughte his sorweful herte brast atwo
His bowe he bente and sette ther inne a flo
And in his Ire his wyf thanne hath he slayn
This is theffect ther nys namoore to sayn
ffor sorwe of which he brak his mynstralcye
Bothe harpe and lute and gyterne and sautrye
And eek he brak hise arwes and his bowe
And after that thus spak he to the crowe
Traytour quod he wt tonge of scorpion
Thow hast me broght to my confusion
Allas þt I was wroght why nere I ded
O deere wyf o gemme of lustihed
That were to me so sad and eek so trewe
Now lystow ded wt face pale of hewe
ffull giltlees that dorste I swere ywys
O rakel hand to doon so foule amys
O troubled wit o Ire recchelees
That vnavysed smytest giltlees
O wantrust ful of fals suspecion
Where was thy wit and thy discrecion
O euery man be war of rakelnesse
Ne trowe ye no thyng wt outen strong witnesse

[N]e were thow wont so myrily to synge	Ne
That to myn herte / it was a reioysynge	
To here thy voys / allas what song is this	heere this ./
¶By god quod he / I synge nat amys	
Phebus quod he / for al thy worthynesse	
For al thy beautee / and thy gentillesse	gentilesse
For al thy song and al thy Mynstralcye	and thy
For al thy waityng blered is thyn eye	
With oon / of litel reputacioun	
Nat worth to thee / in comparisoun	Noght
The montaunce of a gnat so mote I thryue	montance moote
For in thy bed / thy wif I sey hym *etcetera*	For on thy wyf / saugh hym swy *etcetera*
What wol ye moore / the Crowe anon hym tolde	¶What
By sadde toknes / and by wordes bolde	tokenes /
How *þat* his wyf hadde doon hire lecherye	had hire
Hym to gret shame / and to gret vileynye	greet / shame / greet
And tolde hym / ofte he say it *with* hise eyen	hym ofte / saugh
¶This Phebus / gan aweyward for to wryen	
And thoughte / his sorweful herte brast atwo	thoughte /
His bowe he bente / and sette ther Inne a flo	therInne
And in his Ire / his wyf thanne hath he slayn	wyf /
This is theffect ther nys namoore to sayn	theffect. ther is namoore
For sorwe of which / he brak his Mynstralcye	9 which / Mynstralcie
Bothe harpe / and Lute / and Gyterne / and Sawtrye	lute / Gyterne / Sautrie
And eek he brak / hise arwes / and his bowe	eek brak Arwes /
And after that thus spak he to the Crowe	crowe
¶Traytour quod he / *with* tonge of Scorpioun	¶Traitour with
Thow hast me broght to my confusioun	Thou broght /
Allas *þat* I was wroght why nere I ded	that wroght / deed
O deere wyf / o gemme of lustihed	wyf lustiheed
That were to me / so sad / and eek so trewe	eek
Now lystow ded / *with* face pale of hewe	listow deed /
Ful giltlees / that dorste I swere ywys	
O rakel hand / to doon so foule amys	
O trouble wit o Ire recchelees	
That vnauysed / smytest giltlees	smyteth
O wantrust ful of fals suspecioun	wantrust.
Where was thy wit and thy discrecioun	
O euery man / be war of rakelnesse	euery
Ne trowe ye no thyng *with* outen strong witnesse	trowe no

256 Nota malum quid El

9 ¶Maunciple *205r*

The Manciple

	ELLESMERE
Smyt nat to soone / er þat ye witen why	
And beth auysed / wel and sobrely	beeth
Er ye do / any execuciou*n*	doon /
Vp on youre Ire / for suspeciou*n*	
¶Allas / a thousand folk / hath rakel Ire	Allas / folk
Fully fordoon / or broght hem in the Myre	fordoon / and broght Mire
Allas / for sorwe / I wol my seluen sle	sorwe slee
¶And to the Crowe / o false theef seyde he	
I wol thee quyte anon / thy false tale	quite
Thow songe whilom / lyk a nyghtyngale	Thou lyk
Now shaltow false theef thy song forgon	song
And eek thy white fetheres euerichon	eek
Ne neuere in al thy lyf ne shaltow speke	neu*er*e lyf shaltou
Thus shal men / on a traytour ben awreke	been
Thow and thyn ofspryng euere shul be blake	Thou / of spryng /
Ne neuere / swete noyse shul ye make	neu*er*e / sweete voys shul
But euere crye / agayn tempest and rayn	eu*er*e crie /
In tokenynge / þat thurgh thee my wyf is slayn	thurgħ thee /
And to the Crowe he stirte / and that anon	Crowe /
And pulled / hise white fetheres euerichon	eu*er*ychon
And made hym blak and refte hym al his song	
And eek his speche / and out at dore hym slong	
Vn to the deuel / which I hym bitake	
And for this cas / ben alle Crowes blake	caas / been
¶Lordynges / by this ensample / I yow preye	LOrdynges / ensample
Beth war and taketh kepe what I seye	war /
Ne telleth neu*er*e / no man in youre lyf	neuere /
How þat another man / hath dight his wyf	digħt wyf /
He wol yow haten / mortally certeyn	
¶Daun Salomon / as wise clerkes seyn	Daun
Techeth a man / to kepen his tonge wel	10 Techetħ weel
But as I seyde / I nam nat textuel	I am nogħt textueel
But nathelees / thus taughte me my Dame	
My sone / thenk on the Crowe agoddes name	thenk / Crowe on goddes
My sone / keep wel thy tonge / and kepe thy freend	keepe *and* keepe freend
A wikke tonge / is worse than a feend	wikked feend
My sone / from a feend / men may hem blesse	
My sone / god / of his endelees goodnesse	god
Walled a tonge / with teeth / and lippes eke	*with* teeth *and*
For man sholde hym auyse / what he speeke	

10 ¶Mau*n*ciple *205v*

Smyt nat to soone / er pt ye witen why
And beth avysed / wel and sobrely
Er ye do any execucion
Vp on youre Ire / for suspecion
Allas / a thousand folk hath rakel Ire
ffully fordoon / or broght hem in the myre
Allas / for sorwe / I wol my seluen sle
And to the Crowe / o false theef seyde he
I wol thee quyte anon / thy false tale
Thow songe whilom / lyk a nyghtyngale
Now shaltow false theef / thy song forgon
And eek thy white fetheres euerychon
Ne neuere in al thy lyf / ne shaltow speke
Thus shal men / on a traytour ben awreke
Thow and thyn ofspryng / euere shul be blake
Ne neuere / swete noyse shul ye make
But euere crye / agayn tempest / and rayn
In tokenynge / pt thurgh thee my wyf is slayn
And to the Crowe he styrte / and that anon
And pulled hise white fetheres euerychon
And made hym blak / and refte hym al his song
And eek his speche / and out at dore hym slong
Vn to the deuel / which I hym bitake
And for this cas / ben alle Crowes blake
Lordynges / by this ensample / I yow preye
Beth war / and taketh kepe what I seye
Ne telleth neuere no man in youre lyf
how pt another man hath dight his wyf
he wol yow haten mortally certeyn
Daun Salomon / as wise clerkes seyn
Techeth a man / to kepen his tonge wel
But as I seyde / I nam nat textuel
But nathelees / thus taughte me my dame
My sone / thenk on the Crowe a goddes name
My sone / keep wel thy tonge / and kepe thy freend
A wikke tonge / is worse than a feend
My sone / from a feend men may hem blesse
My sone / god of his endelees goodnesse
Walled a tonge / with teeth and lippes eke
ffor man sholde hym avyse / what he speeke

ne ful ofte for to muche speche
hath many a man ben spilt as clerkes teche
But for litel speche avysely
Is no man shent to speke generally
My sone thy tonge sholdestow restreyne
At alle tymes but whan thow dost thy peyne
To speke of god in honour and prayere
The firste vertu sone if thow wolt lere
Is to restreyne and kepe wel thy tonge
Thus lernen children whan þt they ben yonge
My sone of muchel spekyng yvele avysed
Ther lasse spekyng hadde ynow suffised
Comth muchel harm thus was me told & taught
In muchel speche synne wanteth naught
Wostow wher of a rakel tonge serveth
Right as a swerd forkutteth and forkerveth
An arm atwo my dere sone right so
A tonge kutteth frendship al atwo
A jangler is to god abhomynable
Rede Salomon so wys and honurable
Rede David in his psalmes rede Senekke
My sone spek noght but wt thyn hed thow bekke
Dissimule as thow were deef if þt thow here
A jangler speke of perilous matere
The Flemyng seith and lerne it if thee leste
That litel janglyng causeth muchel reste
My sone if thow no wikked word hast seyd
Thee thar nat drede for to be biwreyd
But he þt hath mysseyd I dar wel sayn
He may by no wey clepe his word agayn
Thyng that is sayd is seyd and forth it gooth
Though hym repente or be hym leef or looth
He is his thral to whom þt he hath sayd
A tale of which he is now yvele apayd
My sone be war and be noon auctour newe
Of tydynges wher they ben false or trewe
Wher so thow come amonges heye or lowe
Kepe wel thy tonge and thynk up on the crowe

Here is ended the maunciples tale of the crowe

	ELLESMERE
[My s]one ful ofte / for to muche speche	My sone /
[H]ath many a man ben spilt as clerkes teche	Hath been
But for litel speche auysely	speche /
Is no man shent to speke gen*er*ally	shent.
My sone / thy tonge sholdestow restreyne	
At alle tymes / but whan thow doost thy peyne	thou
To speke of god / in honour and prayere	preyere
The firste v*er*tu sone / if thow wolt leere	vertu thou
Is to restreyne / and kepe wel thy tonge	
Thus lernen children / whan *þa*t they ben yonge	lerne been
My sone / of muchel spekyng yuele auysed	
Ther lasse spekyng hadde ynow suffised	ynough
Comth muchel harm / thus was me told *and* taught	toold *and* taught
In muchel speche / synne wanteth naught	
Wostow / wher of a rakel tonge serueth	serueth
Right as a swerd / forkitteth and forkerueth	Right forkutteth forkerueth
An arm atwo / my deere sone right so	right
A tonge / kitteth frendship al atwo	kutteth freendshipe
A Ianglere / is to god abhomynable	Ianglere /
Rede Salomon / so wys and honurable	Reed
Rede Dauid in his psalmes / rede Senekke	Reed hise reed
My sone / spek noght but w*ith* thyn hed thow bekke	sone nat heed thou
Dissimule as thow were deef / if *þa*t thow heere	thou that thou
A Ianglere speke / of p*er*ilous matere	Ianglere /. speke mateere
¶The flemyng seith and lerne it if thee leste	The flemyng seith / it
That litel Ianglyng causeth muchel reste	
My sone / if thow no wikked word hast seyd	thou seyd
Thee thar nat drede / for to be biwreyd	biwreyd
But he *þa*t hath mysseyd / I dar wel sayn	
He may by no wey / clepe his word agayn	
Thyng that is sayd / is seyd / and forth it gooth	seyd is seyd /
Though hym repente / or be hym leef or looth	Though leef /
He is his thral / to whom *þa*t he hath sayd	sayd
A tale / of which he is now yuele apayd	apayd
My sone be war / and be noon Auctour newe	
Of tidynges wher they ben false or trewe	tidynges / wheither they been
Wher so thow come / amonges heye or lowe	Where thou hye
Kepe wel thy tonge / and thynk vp on the Crowe	thenk
¶Here is ended / the Manciples tale / of the Crowe	¶Heere is ended / the Mau*n*ciples tale of the Crowe

The Man of Lawe

¶The p*ro*hemie of the Mannes tale of La[we]

Ovre hoost saw wel that the brighte sonne
The ark of his artificial day hath ronne
The ferthe part and half an hour and moore
And thogh he were nat depe ystert in loore
He wiste / it was the xviij.the day
Of April / that is messager to May
And saw wel / *pat* the shadwe of eu*er*y tree
Was as in lengthe / the same quantitee
That was the body erect that caused it
And therfore by the shadwe / he took his wit
That Phebus / which *pat* shoon so cleer and brighte
Degrees was .xlv. clombe on highte
And for that day / as in that latitude
It was ten at the Clokke he gan conclude
And sodeynly / he plighte his hors aboute
¶Lordynges quod he I warne yow al this route
The ferthe party of this day is goon
Now for the loue of god / and of Seint Ioħn
Leseth no tyme / as ferforth as ye may
Lordynges the tyme / it wasteth nyght and day
And steleth from vs / what pryuely slepynge
And what thurgh necligence / in oure wakynge
As dooth the streem *pat* turneth neuere agayn
Descendynge / fro the montaigne in to playn
Wel kan Senec and many a Philosophre
Biwaillen tyme / moore than gold in cofre
For los of catel may recou*er*ed be
But los of tyme shendeth vs quod he
It wol nat come agayn / with outen drede
Namoore / than wol Malkyns maydenhede
Whan she hath lost it / in hir wantownesse
Lat vs nat / mowlen thus in ydelnesse
¶Sire man of lawe quod he / so haue ye blys
Tel vs a tale anon / as forward is
Ye been submitted / thurgh youre free assent
To stonden in this cas / at my Iuggement

¶The wordes of the Hoost to the compaignye[1]

saugh wel /
Ark Artificial
houre
though /
eighte and twentithe
Aprill /
saugh that
ther fore / wit
shoon / clere brighte
Degrees / fyue and fourty highte
clokke /
he /
fourthe gon
Lordynges / tyme wasteth nyght
streem / that neu*er*e
¶Wel philosophre
losse catel / recouered
losse tyme /
wole Malkynes
it
nat
¶Sir*e* blis
Telle
submytted /

[1] *49r*

The prohemie of the mannes tale of lawe

Oure hoost saugh wel that the brighte sonne
The ark of his artificial day hath ronne
The ferthe part and half an hour and moore
And though he were nat depe ystert in loore
He wiste it was the .xviij.the day
Of Aprill that is messager to May
And saugh wel þt the shadwe of euery tree
Was as in lengthe the same quantitee
That was the body erect that caused it
And therfore by the shadwe he took his wit
That Phebus which þt shoon so cleer and brighte
Degrees was .xlv. clomben on highte
And for that day as in that latitude
It was ten at the clokke he gan conclude
And sodeynly he plighte his hors aboute
Lordynges quod he I warne yow al this route
The ferthe party of this day is goon
Now for the loue of god and of Seint Iohn
Leseth no tyme as ferforth as ye may
Lordynges the tyme it wasteth nyght and day
And steleth from vs what pryuely slepynge
And what thurgh necligence in oure wakynge
As dooth the streem þt turneth neuere agayn
Descendynge fro the montaigne in to playn
Wel kan Senec and many a philosophre
Biwaillen tyme moore than gold in cofre
For los of catel may recouered be
But los of tyme shendeth vs quod he
It wol nat come agayn withouten drede
Namoore than wol Malkyns maydenhede
Whan she hath lost it in hir wantownesse
Lat vs nat mowlen thus in ydelnesse
Sire man of lawe quod he so haue ye blys
Tel vs a tale anon as forward is
Ye been submytted thurgh youre free assent
To stonden in this cas at my juggement

quiteth yow now of youre biheste
Thanne haue ye don youre deuoir atte leeste
Hoost quod he depardieux ich assente
To breken forward is nat myn entente
Biheste is dette and I wol holde fayn
Al my biheste I kan no bettre sayn
ffor swich lawe as a man yeueth another wight
He sholde hym self vsen it by right
Thus wol oure text but natheles certeyn
I kan right now no thrifty tale seyn
That Chaucer thogh he kan but lewedly
On metres and on rymyng craftily
Hath seyd hem in swich englissh as he kan
Of olde tyme as knoweth many a man
And if he ne haue nat seyd hem leue brother
In o book he hath seyd hem in another
ffor he hath told of loueris vp and doun
Mo than Ouide made of mencioun
In his epistles þt been ful olde
What sholde I tellen hem syn they been tolde
In youthe he made of Ceys and Alcione
And sithen hath he spoke of euerychone
Thise noble wyues and thise loueres eke
Who so þt wole his large volum seke
Cleped the Seintes legende of Cupide
Ther maystow seen the large woundes wyde
Of lucresse and of Babilan Tisbee
The swerd of Dido for the false Enee
The tree of Phillis for hir Demophon
The pleinte of Dianire and of Hermyon
Of Adriane and of ysiphilee
The bareyne Ile stondynge in the see
The dreynte leandre for his Erro
The teerys of Eleyne and eke the wo
Of Brysseyde and of the ladomea
The crueltee of the queene Medea
The litel children hangyng by the hals
ffor thy Iason that was of loue so fals
O ypermystra penolopee Alceste
Youre wifhod he comendeth with the beste

	ELLESMERE
[A]quiteth yow now / of youre biheste	Acquiteth biheeste
Thanne haue ye doon youre deuoir atte leeste	do
¶Hoost quod he dep*ar*dieux ich assente	¶Hoost he /
To breken forward / is nat myn entente	breke
Biheste is dette / and I wol holde fayn	wole
Al my biheste / I kan no bettre sayn	
For swich lawe / as a man yeueth another wight /	2 wigħt
He sholde hym self / vsen it by right	seluen / righ̄t
Thus wol oure text / but nathelees c*er*tein	wole text c*er*teyn
I kan right now / no thrifty tale seyn	righ̄t
That Chaucer / thogh he kan but lewedly	
On metres / and on rymyng craftily	
Hath seyd hem / in swich englissħ as he kan	englissħ /
Of olde tyme / as knoweth many a man	
And if he ne haue nat seyd hem / leeue brother	he haue noght hem leue
In o book he hath seyd hem in another	book /
For he hath toold / of louers vp and doun	loueris doun /
Mo than Ouide / made of mencioun	
In his epistles / *þa*t been ful olde	hise that
What sholde I tellen hem / syn they been tolde	telle ben
In yowthe he made / of Ceys and Alcione	¶In youthe /
And sithen / hath he spoke of eu*er*ychone	sitthe / spoken euerichone
Thise noble wyues / and thise loueres eke	loueris
Who so *þa*t wole / his large volum seke	that volume
Clepyd the Seintes legende of Cupide	Cleped /
Ther maystow seen /. the large woundes wyde	may he seen /
Of Lucresse / and of Babilan Tisbee	Tesbee
The swerd of Dido / for the false Enee	
The tree of Phillis / for hir Demophon	hir*e*
The pleinte of Dianire / and of hermyon̄	Diane / Hermyon̄
Of Adriane / and of ysiphilee	Isiphilee
The barayne Ile / stondynge in the See	bareyne ⟨yle⟩ /
The dreynte leandre / for his Erro	Leandre /
The terys of Eleyne / and eke the wo	teeris and the
Of Brixseyde / and of the Ladomea	and the Ladomya
The crueltee / of the queene Medea	
The litel children / hangyng by the hals	Thy litel hangynge
For thy Iasou*n* / that was of loue so fals	Iason / was in loue
O Yp*er*mystra / Penolopee / Alceste	
Youre wifhod / he comendeth with the beste	wifhede /

[2] ¶Man *49v*

	ELLESMERE
But *cer*teinly / no word ne writeth he	¶But certeinly /
Of thilke wikke ensample / of Canacee	ensample
That loued / hir owene brother synfully	That
Of swiche cursed stories / I sey fy	
Or ellis / of Tyro Appollonius	
How *þa*t / the cursed kyng Antiochus	that kyng /
Birafte his doghter / of hir maydenhede	
That is / so horrible a tale for to rede	
Whan he hir threw / vp on the pauement	pauement
And ther fore / he of ful auisement	therfore he / auysement
Nolde neu*er*e write / in noon of his *ser*mons	neuere none
Of swiche / vnkynde abhominacions	abhomynacions
Ne I wol noon reherce / if *þa*t I may	that
But of my tale / how shal I doon this day	¶But
Me were looth / be likned doutelees	3
To Muses / *þa*t been clepyd Pierides	that men clepe
Methamorphosios / woot what I mene	
But nathelees / I recche noght a bene	
Thogh I come after hym / with hawe bake	Though hawebake
I speke in prose / and lat hym rymes make	
And with that word / he with a sobre cheere	
Bigan his tale / as ye shal after heere	

¶Here bigynneth the tale	¶The prologe of the mannes tale of Lawe
O hateful harm / condicion of pou*er*te	pouerte
With thurst with cold / w*ith* hunger so confoundid	coold / with
To axen help / thee shameth in thyn herte	asken
If thou noon axe / with nede artow so woundid	aske / so soore artow ywoundid
That verray nede / vnwrappeth al thy wounde hid	
Maugree thyn heed / thou most for Indigence	
Or stele / or begge / or borwe thy despence	
¶Thou blamest Crist and seist ful bitterly	Thow crist
He mysdeparteth / richesse temporal	
Thy neghebore / thow witest synfully	neighebore / thou wytest
And seist thow hast to lite / and he hath al	thou
P*ar*fay seistow / som tyme he rekne shal	somtyme rekene
Whan *þa*t his tayl / shal brennen in the gleede	that
For he noght helpeth / nedefulle in hir nede	noght needfulle / neede

[3]¶of Lawe *50r*

But certeinly no word ne writeth he
Of thilke wikke ensample of Canacee
That loued hir owene brother synfully
Of swiche cursed stories I sey fy
Or ellis of Tyro Appollonius
How þt the cursed kyng Antiochus
Birafte his doghter of hir maydenhede
That is so horrible a tale for to rede
Whan he hir threw vp on the pauement
And therfore he of ful auisement
Nolde neuere write in noon of his sermons
Of swiche vnkynde abhominacions
Ne I wol noon reherce if þt I may
But of my tale how shal I doon this day
Me were looth be likned doutelees
To Muses þt been clepyd Pierides
Methamorphosios woot what I mene
But nathelees I recche noght a bene
Though I come after hym with hawe bake
I speke in prose and lat hym rymes make
And with that word he with a sobre cheere
Bigan his tale as ye shal after heere

Here bigynneth the tale

O hateful harm condicion of pouerte
With thurst with cold with hunger so confoundid
To axen help thee shameth in thyn herte
If thou noon axe with nede artow so woundid
That verray nede vnwrappeth al thy wounde hid
Maugree thyn heed thou most for indigence
Or stele or begge or borwe thy despence

Thou blamest crist and seist ful bitterly
He mysdepartith richesse temporal
Thy neghebore thow witest synfully
And seist thow hast to lite and he hath al
Parfay seistow som tyme he rekne shal
Whan þt his tayl shal brennen in the gleede
ffor he noght helpeth nedefulle in hir nede

rke / What is the sentence of the wise
Bet is to dyen / than haue indigence
Thy selue neghebor / wol thee despise
If thow be poure / farwel thy reuerence
Yet of the wise man / take this sentence
Alle the dayes of poure men been wikke
Be war therfore / er thow come to that prikke

If thou be poure / thy brother hateth thee
And alle thy freendes / fleen from thee allas
O riche marchauntz / ful of wele been ye
O noble / o prudent folk / as in this cas
Youre bagges / been noght filled wt ambes as
But with sys cynk / that renneth for youre chaunce
At Cristemasse / murye may ye daunce

Ye seken lond and see / for youre wynnynges
As wise folk / ye knowen al thestaat /
Of regnes / ye been fadres of tidynges
And tales / bothe of pees and of debaat /
I were right now / of tales desolaat
Nere þt a marchaunt / goon is many a yeere
Me taughte a tale / which þt ye shal heere

In Surrye whilom / dwelte a compaignye
Of chapmen riche / and ther to sadde and trewe
That wyde where / senten hir spicerye
Clothes of gold / and Satyns riche of hewe
Hir chaffare / was so thrifty and so newe
That euery wight / hath deyntee to chaffare
With hem / and eek to sellen hem hir ware

Now fil it / that the maistres of that sort /
Han shapen hem / to Rome for to wende
Were it for chaphod / or for desport /
Noon oother message / wolde they thider sende
But comen hem self to Rome / this is the ende
And in swich place / as thoughte hem auantage
ffor hir entente / they take hir herbergage

	ELLESMERE
[¶He]rke / what is the sentence of the wise	¶Herke /
Bet is to dyen / than haue Indigence	
Thy selue neghebor / wol thee despise	neighebor /
If thow be poue*re* / fare wel thy reue*re*nce	thou poure / farwel reuerence
Yet of the wise man / tak⁊ this sentence	Yet⁊ take
Alle the dayes / of poue*re* men been wikke	Alle dayes poure
Be war ther fore / er thow come to that prikke	therfore / thou
¶If thou be poue*re* / thy brother hateth thee	If poure /
And alle thy freendes / fleen from thee allas	
O riche Marchauntz / ful of wele been ye	marchauntz / yee
O noble / o prudent folk⁊ / as in this cas	folk /
Youre bagges / been noght filled w*ith* ambes as	nat fild with Ambes As
But with sys cynk⁊. that renneth for youre chaunce	cynk /
At Cristemasse / murye may ye daunce	myrie
¶Ye seken lond and see / for youre wynnynges	4 Ye yowre
As wise folk⁊ ye knowen al thestat⁊	thestaat⁊
Of regnes / ye been fadres of tidynges	
And tales / bothe of pees and of debat⁊	pees / debaat⁊
I were right now / of tales desolat⁊	desolaat⁊
Nere *þat* a Marchaunt⁊ goon is many a yere	that Marchant⁊ yeere
Me taughte a tale / which *þat* ye shal heere	Me / that 5
¶In Surrye whilom / dwelte a compaignye	6 In whilom
Of chapmen riche / and ther to sadde and trewe	therto
That wyde where / senten hir Spicerye	spicerye
Clothes of gold / and Satyns riche of hewe	
Hir cheffare / was so thrifty and so newe	chaffare /
That euery wight⁊ hath deyntee to cheffare	wight / chaffare
With hem / and eek to sellen hem hir ware	eek / hire
¶Now fil it / that the maistres of that sort⁊	Now it⁊ maistres /
Han shapen hem / to Rome for to wende	
Were it⁊ for chaphod / or for desport⁊	it chapmanhode / disport
Noon oother message / wolde they thider sende	
But coomen hem self to Rome / this is the ende	comen
And in swich place / as thoughte hem auauntage	auantage
For hir entente / they take hir herbergage	For hire

4 ¶Man *50v*

5 Break in El followed by:

¶Heere bigynneth the man of Lawe his tale

6 Miniature of the Man of Law in left margin.

¶Soio*ur*ned han thise Marchauntz / in that town
A *cer*tein tyme / as fil to hir plesaunce
But so bifel / *þat* the excellent renoun
Of the Emp*er*ours doghter / dame Custaunce
Reported was / with euery circumstaunce
Vn to thise Surryen Marchauntz / in swich wise
Fro day / to day / as I shal yow deuyse

¶This was the co*mm*une voys / of euery man
Oure Emp*er*our of Rome / god hym se
A doghter hath / *þat* syn the world bigan
To rekne as wel / hir goodnesse as beautee
Nas neu*ere* swich another / as is she
I pray to god / in honour hir sustene
And wolde she were / of al Europe the queene

¶In hire is heigh beautee / with oute pryde
Youthe / with outen grenehede / or folye
To alle hir werkes / *ver*tu is hir gyde
Humblesse / hath slayn in hir*e* al tirannye
She is Mirour / of al curteisye
Hir herte / is verray chambre of holynesse
Hir hand Ministre / of fredam / for almesse

¶And al this voys was sooth / as god is trewe
But now to purpos / lat vs come agayn
Thise Marchauntz / han doon fraught hir shippes newe
And whan they han / this blisful mayden sayn
Hom to Surrye / been they went ful fayn
And doon hir nedes / as they han doon yoore
And lyuen in wele / I kan sey yow namoore

¶Now fil it7 that thise Marchauntz stode in g*ra*ce
Of hym / that was the Sowdan of Surrye
For whan they coome / from any straunge place
He wolde / of his benygne curteisye
Maken hem good cheere / and bisily espye
Tidynges / of sondry regnes for to leere
The wondres / that they myghte seen or heere

161 Europa est tercia pars mundi Hg El

ELLESMERE

¶Soiourned Marchantz / toun
certein hire plesance
And so that thexcellent
Dame Custance
circumstance
Marchantz / swich a wyse
Fro day

was / voys
see
that
rekene
neuere / another shee
prey hir*e* susteene

7 In hir*e* / pride
Yowthe / oute
hir*e* werkes / vertu

alle
hoolynesse
hand / Ministre fredam Almesse

And
vs turne agayn
Marchantz / fraught /

Hoom

Marchantz / grace

cam / strange
benigne
Make chiere /

myghte

7 ¶of Lawe *51r*

The man of lawe

¶ Soiorned han thise marchauntz / in that toun
A certeyn tyme / as fil to hir plesaunce
But so bifel / þt the excellent renoun
Of the Emperours doghter / dame Custaunce
Reported was / with euery circumstaunce
Vn to thise Surryen marchauntz / in swich wise
ffro day to day / as I shal yow deuyse

¶ This was the commune voys / of euery man
Oure Emperour of Rome / god hym se
A doghter hath / þt syn the world bigan
To rekne as wel / hir goodnesse as beautee
Nas neuere swich another / as is she
I pray to god / in honour hir sustene
And wolde she were / of al Europe the queene — ¶ Europa est tercia pars mundi

¶ In hire is heigh beautee / with oute pride
Youthe / with outen grenehede or folye
To alle hir werkes / vertu is hir gyde
Humblesse / hath slayn in hire al tirannye
She is mirour / of al curteisye
Hir herte / is verray chambre of holynesse
Hir hand ministre / of fredam for almesse

¶ And al this voys was sooth / as god is trewe
But now to purpos / lat vs come agayn
Thise marchauntz / han doon fraught hir shippes newe
And whan they han / this blisful mayden sayn
Hoom to Surrye / been they went ful fayn
And doon hir nedes / as they han doon yoore
And lyuen in wele / I kan sey yow namoore

¶ Now fil it / that thise marchauntz stode in grace
Of hym / that was the Sowdan of Surrye
ffor whan they come / from any straunge place
He wolde / of his benygne curteisye
Maken hem good cheere / and bisily espye
Tidynges of sondry regnes for to lere
The wondres / that they myghte seen or heere

Amonges othere thynges specially
Thise marchantz han hym toold of dame Custaunce
So greet noblesse in ernest ceriously (pitously)
That this Sowdan hath caught so greet plesaunce
To han hir figure in his remembraunce
And al his lust and al his bisy cure
Was for to loue hire whil his lyf may dure

Parauenture in thilke large book
Which þt men clepe the heuene ywriten was
With sterres whan þt he his birthe took
That he for loue sholde han his deeth allas
ffor in the sterres clerer than is glas
Is writen god woot who so koude it rede
The deeth of euery man with outen drede

In sterres many a wynter ther biforn
Was writen the deeth of Ector Achilles
Of Pompei Iulius er they were born
The stryf of Thebes and of Hercules
Of Sampson Turnus and of Socrates
The deeth but mennes wittes been so dulle
That no wight kan wel rede it atte fulle

Cepit phoronei fatum [illegible]
fflamma phetontis declinis aque
In stellis priami species audacia turni
Sensus vlixei herculeusque rigor

This Sowdan for his priuee conseil sente
And shortly of this matere for to pace
He hath to hem declared his entente
And seyde hem certein but he myghte haue grace
To han Custaunce with inne a litel space
He nas but deed and charged hem in hye
To shapen for his lyf som remedye

Diuerse men diuerse thynges seyden
They argumenten casten vp and doun
Many a subtil reson forth they leyden
They speken of magyk and abusioun
But finally as in conclusioun
They kan nat seen in that noon auauntage
Ne in noon oother wey saue mariage

	ELLESMERE
[¶Am]onges othere thynges specially	Amonges
Thise Marchauntz han hym told / of dame Custaunce	Marchantz / toold / Custance
.i. ceriose	
So greet noblesse / in ernest ceriously	
That this Sowdan / hath caught so greet plesaunce	caught⁊ plesance
To han hir figure / in his remembraunce	remembrance
And al his lust / and al his bisy cure	That al lust⁊
Was for to loue hir*e* / whil his lyf may dure	
¶P*ar* auenture / in thilke large book⁊	P*ar*auenture / book /
Which þat men clepe the heuene / ywriten was	clipe
With sterres / whan þat he his birthe took /	that
That he for loue / sholde han his deth allas	deeth
For in the sterres / clerer than is glas	
Is writen god woot⁊ who so koude it⁊ rede	it
The deeth of euery man / with outen drede	
¶In sterres / many a wynter / ther biforn	In
Was writen the deeth / of Ector / Achilles	
Of Pompei / Iulius / er they were born	Pompei
The stryf of Thebes / and of Hercules	strif Ercules
Of Sampson / Turnus / and of Socrates	
The deeth / but mennes wittes been so dulle	ben
That no wight⁊ kan wel rede it atte fulle	wight⁊
¶This Sowdan / for his p*ri*uee conseil sente	8
And shortly / of this matere for to pace	matiere
He hath to hem / declared his entente	
And seyde hem *cer*tein / but he myghte haue g*ra*ce	myghte
To han Custaunce / with Inne a litel space	Custance /
He nas but deed / and charged hem in hye	
To shapen / for his lyf som remedye	shapen lyf /
¶Diu*er*se men / diu*er*se thynges seyden	¶Diuerse diuerse
They argumenten / casten vp and doun	
Many a subtil reson / forth they leyden	resou*n* /
They speken of Magyk / and Abusioun	of / Magyk⁊ Abusiou*n*
But finally / as in conclusioun	conclusiou*n*
They kan nat seen / in that noon Auauntage	Auantage
Ne in noon oother wey / saue mariage	wey

197 Ceptra phoronei fratrum discordia Thebe
Flammam Phetontis Decalionis Aque
In stellis Priami species Audacia Turni
Sensus Vlixeus Herculeusque vigor
Hg El
Variants: phoronei] Phorenei El Decalionis] Deucalionis El

8 ¶Man *51v*

The Man of Lawe.

	ELLESMERE
¶Thanne sawe they ther Inne / swich difficultee	Thanne Inne
By wey of reson / for to speke al playn	
By cause / þ*at* ther was swich diu*er*sitee	that diuersitee
Bitwene hir bothe lawes / þ*at* they sayn	that
They trowe / þ*at* no cristen Prince wolde fayn	cristene prince
Wedden his child / vnder oure lawes swete	sweete
That vs was taught by Mahoun oure *pro*phete	were taught
¶And he answerde / rather than I lese	
Custaunce / I wol be cristned doutelees	Custance./
I moot ben hires / I may noon oother chese	been
I pray yow / hold youre argumentz in pees	prey hoold Argumentz
Saueth my lyf / and beth noght recchelees	
To geten hire / þ*at* hath my lyf in cure	hire / that
For in this wo / I may nat longe endure	
¶What nedeth / gretter dilatacioun	
I seye / by tretys / and embassadrye	Embassadrie
And by the Popes[9] mediacioun	by / Popes
And al the chirche / and al the chiualrie	
That in destruccioun of Mawmetrie	That Mawmettrie
And in encrees / of Cristes lawe deere	cristes
They been acorded / so as ye shal heere	
¶How þ*at* the Sowdan / and his Baronage	How that sowdan /
And alle his liges / sholde ycristned be	hise
And he shal han / Custaunce in mariage	Custance /
And c*er*teyn gold / I noot what quantitee	c*er*tein
And heer to / founden sufficient seuretee	to founden / suretee
This same acord / was sworn on either syde	accord / eyther
Now faire Custaunce / al myghty god thee gyde	Custance / almyghty
¶Now wolde som men / waiten as I gesse	[10]
That I sholde tellen / al the purueiaunce	p*ur*ueiance
That Themp*er*our / of his grete noblesse	themp*er*our /
Hath shapen for his doghter / dame Custaunce	shapen / doghter Custance
Wel may men knowen / þ*at* so greet ordinaunce	ordinance
May no man tellen / in a litel clause	
As was arrayed / for so heigh a cause	

[9] Word inked out in Hg and 'byshop' written above it in later hand.

[10] ¶of Lawe *52r*

Thanne sawe they ther inne swich difficultee
By wey of reson for to speke al playn
By cause pt ther was swich diuersitee
Bitwene hir bothe lawes pt they sayn
They trowe pt no cristen Prince wolde fayn
Wedden his child vnder oure lawes swete
That vs was taught by Mahoun oure prophete

And he answerde rather than I lese
Custaunce I wol be cristned doutelees
I moot ben hires I may noon oother chese
I pray yow hold youre argumentz in pees
Saueth my lyf and beth noght rechelees
To geten hire pt hath my lyf in cure
ffor in this wo I may nat longe endure

What nedeth gretter dilatation
I seye by tretys and embassadrye
And by the popes mediation
And al the chirche and al the chiualrie
That in destruction of Maumetrie
And in encrees of Cristes lawe deere
They been acorded so as ye shal heere

How pt the Sowdan and his Baronage
And alle his liges sholde ycristned be
And he shal han Custaunce in mariage
And certeyn gold I noot what quantitee
And heer to founden sufficient suretee
This same acord was sworn on either syde
Now faire Custaunce almyghty god thee gyde

Now wolde som men waiten as I gesse
That I sholde tellen al the purueiaunce
That Themperour of his grete noblesse
Hath shapen for his doghter dame Custaunce
Wel may men knowen pt so greet ordinaunce
May no man tellen in a litel clause
As was arrayed for so heigh a cause

Shippes been shapen / with hir for to wende
Lordes / ladies / knyghtes of renoun
And oother folk ynowe / this is thende
And notified is / thurgh out the town
That euery wight / with greet deuocioun
Sholde preyen crist / þt he this mariage
Receyue in gree / and spede this viage

The day is comen / of hir departynge
I seye / the woful day fatal / is come
That ther may be / no lenger tariynge
But forthward they hem dresse / alle and some
Custaunce / that was with sorwe al ouercome
Ful pale arist / and dresseth hire to wende
For wel she seeth / ther nys noon oother ende

Allas / what wonder is it / thogh she wepte
That shal be sent / to straunge nacion
Fro freendes / þt so tendrely hir kepte
And to be bounden / vnder subieccion
Of oon / she knoweth noght his condicion
Housbondes been alle goode / and han been yoore
That knowen wyues / I dar sey yow namoore

Fader she seyde / thy wrecched child Custaunce
Thy yonge doghter / fostred vp so softe
And ye my mooder / my souereyn plesaunce
Ouer alle thyng / outtaken crist on lofte
Custaunce youre child / hir recomaundeth ofte
Vn to youre grace / for I shal to Surrye
Ne shal I neuere / seen yow moore with eye

Allas / vn to the Barbre nacion
I moste anon / syn þt it is youre wille
But crist that starf for oure redempcion
So yeue me grace / hise heestes to fulfille
I wrecche womman / no fors thogh I spille
Wommen are born / to thraldom and penaunce
And to been / vnder mannes gouernaunce

	ELLESMERE	
[¶Biss]hopes been shapen / with hir*e* for to wende	Bisshopes	
Lordes / ladies / knyghtes of renoun		
And oother folk ynowe / this is thende	ynogh /	
And notified is / thurgh out the town	thurgh	toun
That euery wight with greet deuocioun	wight /	
Sholde preyen crist þ*at* he this mariage	that	
Receyue in gree / and spede this viage		
¶The day is comen / of hir departynge		
I seye / the woful day fatal / is come	fatal	
That ther may be / no lenger taryynge	tariynge	
But forthward they hem dresse / alle and some	forthward /	dressen /
Custaunce / that was with sorwe al ou*er*come	Custance / þ*at*	
Ful pale arist and dresseth hire to wende	hir*e*	
For wel she seeth / ther nys noon oother ende	ther is noon	
¶Allas / what wonder is it thogh she wepte	Allas /	
That shal be sent to straunge naciou*n*	sent /	strange
Fro freendes / þ*at* so tendrely hir kepte	freendes	hir*e*
And to be bounden / vnder subiecciou*n*		
Of oon / she knoweth noght his condiciou*n*	nat	
Housbondes been alle goode / and han been yoore	han ben	
That knowen wyues / I dar sey yow namoore		
¶Fader she seyde / thy wrecched child Custaunce	Custance	
Thy yonge doghter / fostred vp so softe	doghter /	
And ye my moder / my souereyn plesaunce	mooder /	souerayn plesance
Ouer alle thyng outtaken crist on lofte	out taken	
Custaunce youre child / hir recomaundeth ofte	Custance	hir*e* recomandeth
Vn to youre grace / for I shal to Surrye		
Ne shal I neu*er*e / seen yow moore with eye		
¶Allas / vn to the Barbre naciou*n*	Allas /	
I moste anon / syn þ*at* it is youre wille	moste goon / syn that	
But crist that starf for oure redempciou*n*	starf /	oure sauaciou*n* ǀ
So yeue me g*ra*ce / hise hestes to fulfille	grace /	heestes
I wrecche womman / no fors thogh I spille	wo*m*man / nofors / though	
Wommen are born / to thraldom and penaunce	Wo*m*men	penance
And to been / vnder mannes gou*er*naunce	gouernance	

¶I trowe at Troye / whan Pirrus brak the wal
Or Ylion / brent hadde Thebes the Citee
Nat Rome / for the harm thurgh Hanybal
That Romayns / hath venquysshed tymes thre
Nas herd / swich tendre wepyng for pitee
As in the chambre was / for hir dep*ar*tynge
But forth she moot wher so she wepe or synge

¶O firste moeuer / cruel firmament
With thy diurnal sweigh / *þa*t crowdest ay
And hurlest al / fro Est / til Occident
That naturelly / wolde holde another way
Thy crowdyng / set the heuene in swich array
At bigynnyng of this fiers viage
That cruel Mars / hath slayn this mariage

¶Infortunat ascendent tortuous
Of which the lord / is helplees falle allas
Out of his angle / in to the derkest hous
O. Mars / o. Atazir / as in this cas
O fieble Moone / vnhappy been thy pas
Thow knyttest thee / ther thow nart nat receyued
Ther thow were wel / fro thennes artow weyued

¶Inprudent Emp*er*our of Rome / allas
Was ther no Philosophre / in al thy town
Is no tyme bet than oother / in swich cas
Of viage / is ther noon eleccioun
Namely / to folk of heigh condicioun
Nat whan a roote / is of a burthe yknowe
Allas / we been / to lewed or to slowe

¶To ship*e* is broght this woful faire mayde
Solempnely / with euery circumstaunce
Now I*es*u crist be with yow alle / she seyde
Ther nys namoore / but fare wel faire Custaunce
She peyneth hire / to make good contenaunce
And forth I lete hir Sayle / in this manere
And turne I wole / agayn to my matere

295 Vnde Protholomeus libro .i.° capitulo 8° [Primi] motus celi duo sunt quorum vnus est qui [mouet] celum semper ab Oriente in Occidentem vno [modo] super orbes et cetera Item aliter vero motus est qui mo[uet] orbem stellarum currencium contra motum primum videlicet ab Occidente in Orientem super alios duos polos et cetera. Hg (defective) El
Variants: Protholomeus) Pthολομeus El celum) totum El aliter) alter El

309 Omnes concordati sunt quod elecciones sint debiles nisi in diuitibus habent enim isti licet debilitentur eorum elecciones radicem .i. natiuitates eorum que confortat omnem planetam debilem in itinere et cetera. Hg El

ELLESMERE

11 brak /
Ilion / brende Thebes
thurgh
venquysshed
wepyng
was hir*e* departynge

¶O. firste moeuyng / crueel firmament
sweigh / that
from Est Occident

At the bigynnyng
crueel

Infortunat Ascendent
which / lord
Angle / derkeste
o Atazir /
O. paas
Thou thou art nat
thou weel /

Inprudent Emp*er*our Rome
ther philosophre / toun

eleccíou*n*
folk / condiciou*n*
Noght

is come / this
circumstance
alle sayde
farewel / Custance
hir*e* / contenance
forth / hir*e* saille /

11 ¶Man *52v*

I trowe at Troye whan Pirrus brak the wal
Or ylion brent hadde Thebes the Citee
Nat Rome for the harm thurgh Hanybal
That Romayns hath venquysshed tymes thre
Nas herd swich tendre wepyng for pitee
As in the chambre was for hir departynge
But forth she moot wher so she wepe or synge

O firste moeuyng cruel firmament
With thy diurnal sweigh þt crowdest ay
And hurlest al fro Est til Occident
That naturelly wolde holde another way
Thy crowdyng set the heuene in swich array
At bigynnyng of this fiers viage
That cruel Mars hath slayn this mariage

Unde Ptholomeus libro .1º. capitulo .8.
motus celi duo sunt quorum vnus est pri[mi]
celi semper ab Oriente in Occidente uno m[odo]
super orbes &c. Alius uero motus est qui mo[uet]
orbem stellarum currencium contra motum primum
videlicet ab Occidente in Orientem super alios duos
polos &c.

Infortunat ascendent tortuous
Of which the lord is helplees falle allas
Out of his angle in to the derkest hous
O mars o Atazir as in this cas
O fieble moone vnhappy been thy pas
Thow knyttest thee ther thow nat art receyued
Ther thow were wel fro thennes artow weyued

Inprudent Emperour of Rome allas
Was ther no Philosophre in al thy town
Is no tyme bet than oother in swich cas
Of viage is ther noon eleccioun
Namely to folk of heigh condicioun
Nat whan a roote is of a burthe yknowe
Allas we been to lewed or to slowe

Omnes concordati sunt quod electiones sunt
debiles nisi in diuitibus habent enim isti
licet debilitentur electiones radicem
.i. natiuitates eorum que confortat omnem
planetam debilem in itinere &c.

To ship is broght this woful faire mayde
Solempnely with euery circumstaunce
Now Ihesu crist be with yow alle she seyde
Ther nys namoore but fare wel faire Custaunce
She peyneth hire to make good contenaunce
And forth I lete hire saille in this manere
And turne I wole agayn to my matere

[illegible]oder of the Sowdan / welle of vices
Espied hath / hir sones pleyn entente
How he wol lete / his olde sacrifices
And right anon / she for hir conseil sente
And they ben come / to knowen what she mente
And whan assembled was / this folk in feere
She sette hir down / and seyde as ye shal heere

Lordes quod she / ye knowen euerichon
How þt my sone / in point is for to lete
The holy lawes / of oure Alkaron
Yeuen by goddes message Makomete
But oon auow / to grete god I hete
The lyf shal rather / out of my body sterte
Than Makometes lawe / out of myn herte

What sholde vs tyden / of this newe lawe
But thraldom to oure bodies / and penance
And afterward / in helle to be drawe
ffor we reneyed / Mahoun oure creance
But lordes / wol ye maken assurance
As I shal seyn / assentyng to my loore
And I shal make vs sauf / for euere moore

They sworen / and assenten euery man
To lyue with hire and dye / and by hir stonde
And euerich / in the beste wise he kan
To strengthen hire / shal alle hise freendes fonde
And she hath / this emprise ytake on honde
Which ye shal heren / þt I shal deuyse
And to hem alle / she spak right in this wise

We shul first feyne vs / cristendom to take
Cold water / shal nat greue vs but alite
And I shal swich a feste / and reuel make
That as I trowe / I shal the Sowdan quyte
ffor thogh his wyf / be cristned neuer so whyte
She shal haue nede / to wasshe awey the rede
Thogh she a font ful water / with hir lede

[¶The] moder of the Sowdan / welle of vices
[E]spied hath / hir sones pleyn entente
How he wol lete / his olde sacrifices
And right anon / she for hir conseil sente
And they ben come / to knowen what she mente
And whan assembled was / this folk in feere
She sette hir down / and seyde as ye shal heere

¶Lordes quod she / ye knowen eu*er*ychon
How þ*at* my sone / in point is for to lete
The holy lawes / of oure Alkaron
Yeuen by goddes message[13] Makomete
But oon avow / to grete god I hete
The lyf shal rather / out of my body sterte
Than Makometes lawe / out of myn herte

¶What sholde vs tiden / of this newe lawe
But thraldom to oure bodies / and penaunce
And afterward / in helle to be drawe
For we reneyed / Mahoun oure creaunce
But lordes / wol ye maken assuraunce
As I shal seyn / assentyng to my loore
And I shal make vs sauf / for eue*re* moore

¶They sworen / and assenten euery man
To lyue w*ith* hir*e* and dye / and by hir stonde
And euerich / in the beste wise he kan
To strengthen hir*e* / shal alle hise freendes fonde
And she hath / this emprise ytake on honde
Which ye shal heren / þ*at* I shal deuyse
And to hem alle / she spak right in this wise

¶We shul first feyne vs / cristendom to take
Coold water / shal nat greue vs but alite
And I shal / swich a feste / and reuel make
That as I trowe / I shal the sowdan quyte
For thogh his wyf / be cristned neu*er* so whyte
She shal haue nede / to wasshe awey the rede
Thogh she / a font ful[14] water with hir lede

ELLESMERE

The mooder /
Espied
hise
right
been knowe
folk /
hir*e* doun /

12 ¶Lordes she seyde / ye euerichon
that
hooly
Yeuen / message
auow / heete

What tyden /
bodies penance

creance
assurance
assentynge
sauf eue*r*emoore

with by hir*e*

frendes

that
right wyse

first
feeste
quite
white
wasshe
Thogh ful water / hir*e*

12 ¶of Lawe *53r*

[13] A signal for 'er' is written over the 'g' in a late hand.

[14] The word 'of' inserted over a caret by later hand.

¶O Sowdanesse / roote of Iniquitee
Virago / thow Semyrame the secounde
O Serpentꝛ vnder femynynytee
Lyk to the Serpentꝛ depe in helle ybounde
O feyned womman / al that may confounde
Vertu and Innocence / thurgh thy malice
Is bred in thee / as nest of euery vice

¶O Sathan enuyous / syn thilke day
That thow were chaced / from oure heritage
Wel knowestow to wommen / the olde way
Thow madest Eua / brynge vs in seruage
Thow wolt fordoon / this cristen mariage
Thyn Instrumentꝛ so weylawey the while
Makestow of wommen / whan thou wolt bigile

¶This Sowdanesse / whom I thus blame and warye
Leet pryuely hir conseil / goon his way
What sholde I in this tale / lenger tarye
She rideth to the Sowdan / on a day
And seyde hym / *þa*t she wolde reneye hir lay
And cristendom / of preestes handes fonge
Repentynge hire / she hethen was so longe

¶Bisekyng hym / to doon hir*e* that honour
That she moste han / the cristen folk to feste
To plesen hem / I shal do my labour
The Sowdan seith / I wol doon at youre heste
And knelynge / thanketh hir*e* of that requeste
So glad he was / he nyste what to seye
She kiste hir sone / and hom she gooth hir weye

¶Arryued been this cristen folk to londe
In Surrye / with a gret solempne route
And hastily / this Sowdan sente his sonde
First to his moder / and al the regne aboute
And seyde / his wyf / was comen out of doute
And preyde hir*e* / for to ryde agayn the queene
The honour / of his regne to sustene

ELLESMERE

O [¶Auctor]
thou
serpent /
Lik serpentꝛ
wo*m*man /
thurgħ
nestꝛ

O enuious /
thou
knowestow / wo*m*men
Thou
Thou

wo*m*men /

15
pr*i*uely / hire conseil goon hir*e* way
I. tale
rydeth
that

hir*e* /

Bisechynge
feeste
I wol do
heeste

whatꝛ
hoom 16

Arryued been /
greet
hastifliche /
mooder /
wyf

honour regne / susteene

[15] ¶Man *53v*

[16] Break in El followed by:
¶Explicitꝛ p*ri*ma pars
¶Sequitꝛ*ur* pars secunda

The Man of lawe

O Sowdanesse / roote of Iniquitee
Virago / thow Semyrame the secounde
O serpent / vnder femynynytee
Lyk to the serpent / depe in helle ybounde
O feyned womman / al that may confounde
Vertu and Innocence / thurgh thy malice
Is bred in thee / as nest of euery vice

O Sathan enuyous / syn thilke day
That thow were chaced / from oure heritage
Wel knowestow to wommen / the olde way
Thow madest Eua / brynge vs in seruage
Thow wolt fordoon / this cristen mariage
Thyn Instrument / so weylawey the while
Makestow of wommen / whan thou wolt bigile

This Sowdanesse / whom I thus blame and warye
Leet priuely hir conseil / goon his way
What sholde I in this tale / lenger tarye
She rydeth to the Sowdan / on a day
And seyde hym / þt she wolde reneye hir lay
And cristendom / of preestes handes fonge
Repentynge hire / she hethen was so longe

Bisekyng hym / to doon hire that honour
That she moste han / the cristen folk to feste
To plesen hem / I shal do my labour
The Sowdan seith / I wol doon at youre heste
And knelynge / thanketh hire of that requeste
So glad he was / he nyste what to seye
She kiste hir sone / and hom she gooth hir weye

Arryued been this cristen folk to londe
In Surrye / with a gret solempne route
And hastily / this Sowdan sente his sonde
ffirst to his moder / and al the regne aboute
And seyde his wyf / was comen out of doute
And preyde hire / for to ryde agayn the queene
The honour / of his regne to susteene

Greet was the prees / and riche was tharay
Of Surryens / and Romayns met yfeere
The moder of the Sowdan / riche and gay
Receyueth hire / with also glad a cheere
As any moder / myghte hir doghter deere
And to the nexte citee / ther bisyde
A softe paas / solempnely they ryde

¶ Naught trowe I / the triumphe of Julius
Of which þt Lucan / maketh swich a boost
Was roiallere / ne moore curyus
Than was the assemblee / of this blisful oost
But this scorpion / this wikked goost
The Sowdanesse / for al hir flaterynge
Caste vnder this / ful mortally to stynge

¶ The Sowdan cometh hym self / soone after this
So roially / þt wonder is to telle
He welcometh hire / with alle ioye and blys
And thus in myrthe and Joye / I lete hem dwelle
The fruyt of this matere / is þt I telle
Whan tyme cam / men thoughte it for the beste
That reuel stynte / and men go to hir reste

¶ The tyme cam / this olde Sowdanesse
Ordeyned hath this feste / of which I tolde
And to the feste / cristen folk hem dresse
In general / ye bothe yonge and olde
Heer may men feste / and roialtee biholde
And deyntees mo / than I kan yow deuyse
But al to deere / they boghte it er they ryse

¶ Auctor de inopinato dolore

¶ O sodeyn wo / that eue art Successour
To worldly blisse / spreynd with bitternesse
The ende of the ioye / of oure worldly labour
Wo occupieth / the fyn of oure gladnesse
Herke this conseil / for thy sikernesse
Vp on thy glade day / haue in thy mynde
The vnwar wo or harm / þt comth bihynde

¶ Semp mundane leticie tristicia
repentina succedit / mundana
igitur felicitas multis amaritu
dinibz est respsa extrema gau
dij luctus occupat / Audi ergo
salubre consiliu in die bono
ne immemor sis malor

ELLESMERE

[¶G]reet was the prees / and riche was tharray
Of Surryens / and Romayns met yfeere
The moder of the Sowdan / riche and gay
Receyueth hire / with also glad a cheere
As any moder / myghte hir doghter deere
And to the nexte Citee / ther bisyde
A softe paas / solempnely they ryde

¶Naught trowe I / the triumphe of Iulius
Of which þat lucan / maketh swich a boost
Was roiallour / ne moore curyus
Than was the assemblee / of this blisful oost
But this scorpion / this wikked goost
The Sowdanesse / for al hir flaterynge
Caste vnder this / ful mortally to stynge

¶The Sowdan cometh hym self / soone after this
So roially / þat wonder is to telle
He welcometh hire / with alle ioye and blys
And thus in myrthe and Ioye / I lete hem dwelle
The fruyt of this matere / is þat I telle
Whan tyme cam / men thoughte it for the beste
That reuel stynte / and men go to hir reste

¶The tyme cam / this olde Sowdanesse
Ordeyned hath this feste / of which I tolde
And to the feste / cristen folk hem dresse
In general / ye bothe yonge and olde
Heer may men feste / and roialtee biholde
And deyntees mo / than I kan yow deuyse
But al to deere / they boghte it er they ryse

¶O sodeyn wo / that eu*er*e art Successour
To worldly blisse / spreynd with bitt*er*nesse
The ende of the ioye / of oure worldly labour
Wo ocupieth / the fyn of oure gladnesse
Herke this conseil / for thy sikernesse
Vp on thy glade day / haue in thy mynde
The vnwar wo / or harm / þat comth bihynde

421 Nota de inopinato dolore

Semper mundane leticie tristicia
repentina succedit Mundana
igitur felicitas multis amaritudinibus
est respersa extrema gaudij
luctus occupat Audi ergo salubre consilium in die bonorum
ne inmemor sis malorum. Hg (defective) El
Variant: amaritudinibus) amaritudibus El

Greet
Surryens
mooder
hire /
mooder /

¶Nogħt
which / that Lucan
roialler / or moore curius
thassemblee / hoost
scorpiou*n* / goost
hir*e*

17 comth self
that
hir*e* / blis
thus / murthe ioye he*m*
matiere / that

The reuel goon

feeste /
feeste /

Heere men / feeste /

bogħte

O euere [¶Auctor]
wi*th*

occupieth /

harm

17¶of Lawe *54r*

¶For shortly / for to tellen / at a word	For soothly / at o word
The Sowdan / and the cristen eu*er*ychone	euerichone
Been al to hewe / and stiked at the bord	
But it were oonly / dame Custaunce allone	Custance
This olde sowdanesse / cursed krone	
Hath with hir freendes / doon this cursed dede	w*ith*
For she hir self / wolde al the contree lede	
¶Ne ther nas Surryen noon / þ*at* was conu*er*ted	Ne was Surryen that
That of the conseil / of the Sowdan woot	
That he nas al tohewe / er he asterted	
And Custaunce / han they take anon foot hoot	Custance /
And in a ship / al sterelees / god woot	Ship*e* / steerelees
They han hir set and bidde hir lerne Sayle	biddeth hir*e* saille
Out of Surrye / agaynward to Itaille	ytaille
¶A c*er*tein tresor / that she thider ladde	A she with hir*e* ladde
And sooth to seyn / vitaille gret plentee	greet
They han hir yeuen / and clothes eek she hadde	hir*e*
And forth she sayleth / in the salte see	sailleth /
O my Custaunce / ful of benygnytee	Custance / benignytee
O Emp*er*ours / yonge doghter deere	Emp*er*ours
He þ*at* is lord of Fortune be thy steere	that
¶She blisseth hire / and w*ith* ful pitous voys	18 She blesseth hir*e* / with
Vn to the cros of Crist thus seyde she	croys
O clere / of weleful Auter / holy croys	cleere / o woful Auter / hooly
Reed of the lambes blood / ful of pitee	Lambes
That wesshe the world / fro the olde Iniquitee	wesshe
Me fro the feend / and fro his clawes kepe	
That day / þ*at* I shal drenchen in the depe	that I
¶Victorious tree / p*ro*teccion of trewe	Victorious protecciou*n*
That oonly / worthy were for to bere	
The kyng of heuene / with his woundes newe	w*ith* hise
The white lamb / that hurt was w*ith* a spere	þ*at* w*ith* the spere
Flemere of feendes / out of hym and here	Flemer*e*
On which thy lymes / feithfully extenden	which /
Me kepe / and yeue me myght my lyf tamenden	Me helpe / and yif myght /

18 ¶Man *54v*

For shortly for to tellen at a word
The Sowdan and the cristen euerychone
Been al tohewe and stiked at the bord
But it were oonly dame Custance allone
This olde Sowdanesse cursed krone
Hath with hir freendes doon this cursed dede
ffor she hir self wolde al the contree lede

Ne ther nas Surryen noon þt was conuerted
That of the conseil of the Sowdan woot
That he nas al tohewe er he asterted
And Custance han they take anon foot hoot
And in a ship al sterelees god woot
They han hir set and bidde hir lerne sayle
Out of Surrye agaynward to Itaille

A certeyn tresor that she thider ladde
And sooth to seyn vitaille gret plentee
They han hir yeuen and clothes eek she hadde
And forth she sayleth in the salte see
O my Custance ful of benygnytee
O Emperours yonge doghter deere
He þt is lord of ffortune be thy steere

She blesseth hire and wt ful pitous voys
Vn to the crois of Crist thus seyde she
O cleere o welful auter holy croys
Reed of the lambes blood ful of pitee
That wesshe the world fro the olde iniquitee
Me fro the feend and fro his clawes kepe
That day þt I shal drenchen in the depe

Victorious tree proteccion of trewe
That oonly worthy were for to bere
The kyng of heuene with his woundes newe
The white lamb that hurt was wt a spere
fflemere of feendes out of hym and here
On which thy lymes feithfully extenden
Me kepe and yeue me myght my lyf tamenden

res and dayes fleet this creature
Thurgh out the See of Grece / vn to the Strayte
Of Marrok / as it was hir auenture
O many a sory meel / now may she bayte
After hir deth / ful often may she wayte
Er þt the wilde wawes / wol hir dryue
Vn to the place / ther she shal arryue

Men myghten axen / why she was noght slayn
Eek at the feste / who myghte hir body saue
And I answere / to that demaunde agayn
Who saued Danyel / in the horrible caue
Ther euery wight saue he / maister and knaue
Was with the leon frete / er he asterte
No wight but god / þt he bar in his herte

God liste to shewe / his wonderful myracle
In hir / for we sholde seen / his myghty werkes
Crist which þt is / to euery harm triacle
By certein menes ofte / as knowen clerkes
Dooth thyng for certein ende / þt ful derk is
To mannes wit / þt for oure ignorance
Ne konne noght knowe / his prudent purueiaunce

Now sith she was nat / at the feste yslawe
Who kepte hire / fro the drenchyng in the see
Who kepte Jonas / in the fisshes mawe
Til he was spouted vp at Nynyuee
Wel may men knowe / it was no wight but he
That kepte peple Ebrayk / from hir drenchyng /
With drye feet / thurgh out the see passyng /

Who bad / the foure spirits of tempest /
That power han / tanoyen lond and see
Bothe North and South / and also West and Est /
Anoyeth neither / see ne land / ne tree
Soothly the comaundour of that was he
That fro the tempest / ay this womman kepte
As wel whan she wook / as whan she slepte

	ELLESMERE
[¶Ye]res and dayes / fleet this creature	¶Yeres fleteth
Thurgh out the see of Grece / vn to the Strayte	Thurghout See
Of Marrok7 as it was hir auenture	Marrok7. hir*e* Auenture
O many a sory meel / now may she bayte	On many
After hir deth / ful often may she wayte	deeth /
Er þ*at* the wilde wawes / wol hir dryue	that hir*e*
Vn to the place / ther she shal arryue	
¶Men myghten axen / why she was noght slayn	Men asken / nat7
Eek at the feste / who myghte hir body saue	feeste /
And I answere / to that demaunde agayn	demande
Who saued Danyel / in the horrible Caue	
Ther euery wight saue he / maister and knaue	wigħt
Was with the Leou*n* frete / er he asterte	leou*n*
No wight but god / þ*at* he bar in his herte	wigħt7 that
¶God liste to shewe / his wonderful miracle	God myracle
In hir*e* / for we sholde seen / his myghty werkes	mygħty werkis
Crist / which þ*at* is / to euery harm triacle	Crist7 that
By c*er*tein menes ofte / as knowen clerkes	certeine meenes clerkis
Dooth thyng for c*er*tein ende / þ*at* ful derk is	thyng7 certein that
To mannes wit7 þ*at* for oure ignoraunce	wit /. that ignorance
Ne konne noght knowe / his prudent p*ur*ueiaunce	p*ur*ueiance
¶Now sith she was nat / at the feste yslawe	feeste
Who kepte hire / fro the drenchyng in the see	hir*e* / drenchyng / See./
Who kepte Ionas / in the fisshes mawe	
Til he / was spowted vp at Nynyuee	spouted Nynyuee./
Wel may men knowe / it was no wight but hee	wigħt he
That kepte peple Ebrayk7 / from hir drenchyng7	Ebrayk7 drenchynge
With drye feet7 thurgh out the see passyng7	passynge
¶Who bad / the foure Spiritz of tempest7	19 bad spirites tempest
That power han / tanoyen lond and see	
Bothe North and South / and also West and Est7	West7
Anoyeth neither / see / ne land / ne tree	land
Soothly / the comaundour of that was hee	Comandour he
That fro the tempest7 ay this womman kepte	tempest / wom*m*an
As wel / whan she wook7 as whan she slepte	

19 ¶of Lawe *55r*

The Man of Lawe ⸗	ELLESMERE
¶Wher myghte this womma*n* / mete and drynke haue	¶Where womman / haue⸗
Thre yeer and moore / how lasteth hir vitaille	hir*e* vitaille⸗
Who fedde the Egipcien Marie / in the Caue	fedde / Marie Caue⸗
Or in desert / no wight but cristꝭ sanz faille	desert⸗ /
Fyue thousand folkꝭ / it was as greet m*er*uaille	
With loues fyue / and fisshes two to fede	fissħes feede
God sente his foyson / at hir grete nede	neede
¶She dryueth forth / in to oure Occian	
Thurgh out the wilde see / til at the laste	out oure wilde til atte laste
Vnder an hoold / þ*at* nempnen I ne kan	that
Fer in Northumberlandꝭ / the wawe hir caste	Northhumberlondꝭ hire
And in the sond / hir ship*e* stiked so faste	Sond / ship*e* /
That thennes wolde it noghtꝭ of al a tyde	nogħtꝭ
The wyl of cristꝭ was þ*at* she sholde abyde	cristꝭ
¶The Constable of the Castel / down is fare	doun
To seen this wrakꝭ and al the ship*e* he soghte	seen his wrakꝭ sogħte
And foond this wery womman ful of care	foond /
He foond also / the tresor þ*at* she broghte	brogħte
In hir langage / mercy she bisoghte	m*er*cy
The lyf / out of hir body for to twynne	
Hir to deliu*er*e / of wo that she was Inne	Hir*e* wo /
¶A manere latyn corruptꝭ was hir speche	A maner corrupt /
But algates / ther by was she vnderstonde	
The Constable / whan hym liste no lenger seche	lystꝭ
This woful womman / broghte he to the londe	
She kneleth doun / and thanketh goddes sonde	
But what she was / she wolde no man seye	
For foul ne fair / thogh þ*at* she sholde deye	thogħ
¶She seyde / she was so mazed in the see	She she was /
That she forgat hir mynde / by hir trouthe	
The Constable / hath of hir*e* so greet pitee	
And eek his wyf / that they wepten for routhe	wepen
She was so diligentꝭ with outen slouthe	
To serue and plese / euerich in that place	
That alle hir louen / that looken on hir face	looken in hir

The man of lawe.

Wher myghte this womman / mete and drynke haue
Thre yeer and moore / how lasteth hir vitaille
Who fedde the Egipcien Marie / in the Caue
Or in desert / no wight but crist / sanz faille
ffyue thousand folk / it was as greet merueille
With loues fyue / and fisshes two to fede
God sente his foyson / at hir grete nede

She dryueth forth / in to oure Occian
Thurgh out the wilde see / til at the laste
Vnder an hoold / þt nempnen I ne kan
ffer in Northumberland / the wawe hir caste
And in the sond / hir ship stiked so faste
That thennes wolde it noght / of al a tyde
The wyl of crist / was þt she sholde abyde

The Constable of the Castel / doun is fare
To seen this wrak / and al the ship he soghte
And foond this wery womman ful of care
He foond also / the tresor þt she broghte
In hir langage / mercy she bisoghte
The lyf out of hir body for to twynne
Hir to delyuere / of wo that she was inne

A manere latyn corrupt / was hir speche
But algates / ther by was she vnderstonde
The Constable / whan hym liste no lenger seche
This woful womman / broghte he to the londe
She kneleth doun / and thanketh goddes sonde
But what she was / she wolde no man seye
ffor foul ne fair / thogh þt she sholde deye

She seyde / she was so mazed in the see
That she forgat hir mynde / by hir trouthe
The Constable / hath of hire so greet pitee
And eek his wyf / that they wepten for routhe
She was so diligent / with outen slouthe
To serue and plese / euerych in that place
That alle hir louen / that looken on hir face

This Constable and dame Hermengyld his wyf
Were payens and that contree euery where
But Hermengyld loued hire right as hir lyf
And Custance hath so longe soiorned there
In orisons with many a bitter teere
Til Ihu hath conuerted thurgh his grace
Dame Hermengyld Constablesse of thilke place

In al that land no cristen dorste route
Alle cristen folk been fled fro that contree
Thurgh payens þt conquereden al aboute
The plages of the North by land and See
To Walys fledde the cristianytee
Of olde Britons dwellyng in this Ile
Ther was hir refut for the mene while

But yet nere cristen Britons so exiled
That ther nere somme þt in hir pryuetee
Honoured crist and hethen folk bigiled
And neigh the Castel swiche ther dwelten thre
That oon of hem was blynd and myghte nat se
But it were with thilke eyen of his mynde
With whiche men seen after þt they been blynde

Bright was the sonne as in that someres day
ffor which the Constable and his wyf also
And Custance han ytake the righte way
Toward the See a furlong wey or two
To pleyen and to romen to and fro
And in hir walk this blynde man they mette
Croked and old with eyen faste yshette

In name of crist cryde this blynde Britoun
Dame hermengyld yif me my sighte agayn
This lady weex affrayed of the soun
lest þt hir housbonde shortly for to sayn
Wolde hire for Ihu cristes loue han slayn
Til Custance made hire boold and bad hire wirche
The wyl of crist as doghter of his chirche

The Constable

[¶T]his Constable / and dame Hermengyld his wyf
Were payens / and that contree euery where
But hermengyldꝭ / loued hir*e* right as hir lyf
And Custaunce / hath so longe soio*ur*ned there
In orisons / with many a bitter teere
Til Ie*s*u / hath conu*er*ted thurgh his grace
Dame hermengyldꝭ / Constablesse of thilke place

¶In al that land / no cristen dorste route
Alle cristen folk / been fled fro that contree
Thurgh Payens / *þa*t conquereden al aboute
The plages of the North / by land and see
To Walys / fledde the cristianytee
Of olde Britons / dwellyng in this Ile
Ther was hir refutꝭ for the mene while

¶But yetꝭ nere cristen Britons / so exiled
That ther nere so*m*me / *þa*t in hir pryuetee
Honoured cristꝭ and hethen folk bigiled
And neigh the Castel / swiche ther dwelten thre
That oon of hem / was blynd and myghte nat se
But it were / with thilke eyen of his mynde
With whiche men seen / after *þa*t they been blynde

¶Bright was the sonne / as in that Som*er*es day
For which the Constable / and his wyf also
And Custaunce / han ytake the righte way
Toward the see / a furlong wey / or two
To pleyen / and to romen to and fro
And in hir walkꝭ this blynde man they mette
Croked and old / with eyen faste yshette

¶In name of Cristꝭ cryde this blynde Britoun
Dame hermengyld / yif me my sighte agayn
This lady / weex affrayed of the sown
Lest *þa*t hir housbonde / shortly for to sayn
Wolde hire / for Ie*s*u cristes loue han slayn
Til Custaunce made hir boold / and bad hir wirche
The wyl of Cristꝭ as doghter of his chirche

ELLESMERE

20 ¶This Hermengyldꝭ wyf /
hermengyldꝭ / right
Custance / soiourned
conu*er*ted /
Hermengyldꝭ / of that place
In lond /
Thurgh that
North
Cristyanytee
dwellynge
meene
But yet cristene Britons
that in p*ri*uetee
Hono*ur*ed
ny three
hem blynd / see
seen / whan *þa*t ben
Bright
Custance /
wey
to romen to romen to
oold /
In cride this olde Britou*n*
Hermengyldꝭ / me / sighte
soun
that
hire /
Custance hir*e* hir*e*

20 ¶Man *55v*

. The Man of Lawe .

	ELLESMERE
¶The Constable / weex abasshed of that sight	sigħt
And seide / what amounteth al this fare	seyde /
Custaunce answerde / sire it is Cristes myght	Custance sire / cristes mygħt
That helpeth folk / out of the feendes snare	folk /
And so ferforth / she gan oure lay declare	
That she the Constable / er *þa*t it was eue	that it
Conu*er*teth / and on Crist made hym bileue	Crist maketh
¶This Constable / was no thyng lord of this place	21 This thyng Lord
Of which I speek ther he Custaunce fond	speke / Custance fond
But kepte it strongly / many wynter space	wyntres
Vnder Alla / kyng of al Northumberlond	kyng Northhumbrelond
That was ful wys / and worthy of his hond	
Agayn the Scottes / as men may wel heere	
But turne I wole / agayn to my matere	mateere
¶Sathan / *þa*t eu*er*e vs waiteth to bigile	that
Saugh of Custaunce / al hir p*er*feccioun	Saugħ Custance / hir*e*
And caste anon / how he myghte quite hir while	mygħte
And made a yong knyght *þa*t dwelte in that town	yong knygħt / toun
Loue hir*e* hote / of foul affeccioun	hir*e* so hoote
That verraily / hym thoughte he sholde spille	ver*r*aily /
But he of hir*e* / myghte ones haue his wille	mygħte
¶He woweth hire / but it auailleth noght	He hir*e* / nogħt /
She wolde do no synne / by no weye	
And for despit he compassed in his thoght	thogħt
To maken hir*e* / on shameful deeth to deye	
He wayteth / whan the Constable was aweye	
And p*ri*uely / vp on a nyght he crepte	pryuely / nygħt
In Hermengildes chambre / whil she slepte	Hermengyldes
¶Wery for waked / in hir orisons	¶Wery / hir*e* orisou*n*s
Slepeth Custaunce / and hermengild also	Custance / Hermengyld
This knyght thurgh Sathans temptacions	knygħt thurgħ temptaciou*n*s
Al softely / is to the bed ygo	
And kitte the throte / of hermengild atwo	Hermengyld
And leyde the blody knyf / by dame Custaunce	Custance
And wente his wey / ther god yeue hym meschaunce	meschance

21 ¶of Lawe *56r*

The Constable wex abasshed of that sight
And seide what amounteth al this fare
Custaunce answerde Sire it is Cristes myght
That helpeth folk out of the feendes snare
And so ferforth she gan oure lay declare
That she the Constable er þt it was eue
Conuerteth and on Crist made hym bileue

This Constable was no thyng lord of this place
Of which I speke ther he Custaunce fond
But kepte it strongly many wynter space
Vnder Alla kyng of al Northumberlond
That was ful wys and worthy of his hond
Agayn the Scottes as men may wel heere
But turne I wole agayn to my matere

Sathan þt euere vs waiteth to bigile
Saugh of Custaunce al hir pfeccion
And caste anon how he myghte quite hir while
And made a yong knyght þt dwelte in that town
Loue hire so hote of foul affeccioun
That verraily hym thoughte he sholde spille
But he of hire myghte ones haue his wille

He woweth hire but it auailleth noght
She wolde do no synne by no weye
And for despit he compassed in his thoght
To maken hire on shameful deeth to deye
He wayteth whan the Constable was aweye
And pryuely vp on a nyght he crepte
In hermengildes chambre whil she slepte

Wery forwaked in hir orisons
Slepeth Custaunce and hermengild also
This knyght thurgh Sathans temptacions
Al softely is to the bed ygo
And kitte the throte of hermengild atwo
And leyde the blody knyf by dame Custaunce
And wente his wey ther god yeue hym meschaunce

[...]ne after cometh this Constable hom agayn
And eek Alla that kyng was of that lond
And sauh his wyf despitously yslayn
ffor which ful ofte he weep and wrong his hond
And in the bed the blody knyf he fond
By dame Custaunce allas what mighte she seye
ffor verray wo hir wit was al aweye

¶ To kyng Alla was told al this meschaunce
And eek the tyme and where and in what wyse
That in a ship was founde this Custaunce
As her bifore þt ye han herd deuyse
The kynges herte of pitee gan agryse
Whan he sauh so benygne a creature
ffalle in disese and in mysauenture

¶ ffor as the lomb toward his deeth is broght
So stant this innocent bifore the kyng
This false knyght þt hath this treson wroght
Bereth hir on hond þt she hath doon this thyng
But natheles ther was greet moornyng
Among the peple and seyn they kan nat gesse
That she had doon so greet a wikkednesse

¶ ffor they han seyn hir euere so vertuous
And louyng Hermengild right as hir lyf
Of this bar witnesse euerich in that hous
Saue he þt Hermengild slow with his knyf
This gentil kyng hath caught a gret motyf
Of this witnesse and thoghte he wolde enquere
Depper in this a trouthe for to lere

¶ Allas Custaunce thow hast no champion
Ne fighte kanstow noght so weilawey
But he þt starf for oure redempcion
And bond Sathan and yet lith ther he lay
So be thy stronge champion this day
ffor but if Crist open miracle kythe
With outen gilt thow shalt been slayn as swythe

	ELLSMERE
[¶Soon]e after / cometh this Constable hom agayn	¶Soone hoom
[A]nd eek Alla / that kyng was of that lond	And *pa*t
And saw his wyf / despitously yslayn	saugh
For which ful ofte / he weep*e* and wrong his hond	ofte weep*e* / wroong
And in the bed / the blody knyf he fond	
By Dame Custaunce / allas what myghte she seye	Custance / mygħte
For verray wo / hir wit was al aweye	ve*r*ray witꝭ
¶To kyng Alla / was told al this meschaunce	toold meschance
And eek the tyme / and where / and in what wise	
That in a ship*e* / was founde this Custaunce	founden Dame Custance
As her biforn / *pa*t ye han herd deuyse	heer that
The kynges herte / of pitee gan agryse	
Whan he saw / so benygne a creature	saugh / benigne
Falle in disese / and in mysauenture	
¶For as the lomb / toward his deeth is broghtꝭ	22 For brogħtꝭ
So stant this Innocentꝭ bifore the kyngꝭ	
This false knyghtꝭ *pa*t hath this treson wroghtꝭ	knygħtꝭ tresou*n* wrogħtꝭ
Bereth hir*e* on hond / *pa*t she hath doon this thyngꝭ	Berth thys
But nathelees / ther was greet moornyngꝭ	
Among the peple / and seyn they kan nat gesse	seyn /
That she had doon / so greet a wikkednesse	
¶For they han seyn hir*e* / eu*er*e so v*er*tuous	For they / hir*e* euere
And louyng Hermengild / right as hir lyf	louynge Hermengyldꝭ rigħt lyf /
Of this baar witnesse / euerich in that hous	
Saue he *pa*t hermengild / slow with his knyfꝭ	he / hermengyldꝭ / wi*th*
This gentil kyngꝭ hath caught a gret motyf	kyng / greet
Of this witnesse / and thoghte he wolde enquere	
Depper in this / a trouthe for to lere	
¶Allas Custaunce / thow nast no champiou*n*	Custance / thou hast
Ne fighte kanstow noghtꝭ so weilawey	weylaway
But he *pa*t starf / for oure redempciou*n*	he / that starf
And bond Sathan / and yet lyth ther he lay	boond lith
So be thy stronge champion this day	be /
For but if Crist / open miracle kythe	cristꝭ myracle kithe
With outen giltꝭ thow shalt been slayn as swythe	Wi*th*outen thou be swithe

22 ¶Man *56v*

The Man of Lawe .	ELLESMERE
¶She sette hir down on knees / and thus she sayde	She sit hir*e* doun
Inmortal god / that sauedest Susanne	
Fro fals blame / and thow m*er*ciful mayde	thou
Marie I mene / doghter to Seint Anne	meene /
Biforn whos child / Aungels synge Osanne	Bifore Angeles
If I be giltlees / of this felonye	
My socour be / for ellis shal I dye	
¶Haue ye nat seyn som tyme / a pale face	Haue seyn / somtyme
Among a prees / of hym *þa*t hath be lad	Amongꝭ
Toward his deeth / wher as hym gat no g*ra*ce	grace
And swich a colour / in his face hath had	
Men myghte knowe his face / *þa*t was bistad	mygħte knowe / face that
Amonges alle the faces / in that route	
So stant Custance / and looketh hir*e* aboute	
¶O Queenes / lyuynge in p*ro*sp*er*itee	O p*ro*speritee
Duchesses / and ye ladies euerichon*e*	and ladyes euerichone
Haueth som reuthe / on hir adu*er*sitee	routhe / hir*e* Adu*er*sitee
An Emp*er*ours doghter / stant allone	
She hath no wightꝭ / to whom to make hir mone	wigħtꝭ /
O blood roial / that stondest in this drede	
Fer be thy freendes / at thy grete nede	been
¶This Alla kyngꝭ hath swich compassioun	23 This compassiou*n*
As gentil herte / is fulfild of pitee	
That from his eyen / ran the water doun	hise
Now hastily / do fecche a book / quod he	bookꝭ
And if this knyghtꝭ. wol sweren how *þa*t she	knygħtꝭ
This wo*m*man slow / yet wol we vs auyse	womman
Whom *þa*t we wole / that shal been oure Iustise	
¶A Briton bookꝭ writen with Eu*a*ngiles	A Briton*n* book /
Was fetꝭ and on this book he swoor anon	bookꝭ anoon
She gilty was / and in the mene whiles	meene
An hand hym smootꝭ vp on the nekke bon	boon
That doun he fel / atones / as a stoon	fil / atones
And bothe hise eyen / broste out of his face	
In sighte / of euery body in that place	sigħte /

[23] ¶of Lawe *57r*

She sette hir doun on knees and thus she sayde
Immortal god that sauedest Susanne
ffro fals blame and thow merciful mayde
Marie I mene doghter to Seint Anne
Bifore whos child Aungels synge Osanne
If I be giltlees of this felonye
My socour be for ellis shal I dye

Haue ye nat seyn som tyme a pale face
Among a prees of hym þt hath be lad
Toward his deeth wher as hym gat no grace
And swich a colour in his face hath had
Men myghte knowe his face þt was bistad
Amonges alle the faces in that route
So stant Custance and looketh hire aboute

O Queenes lyuynge in prosperitee
Duchesses and ye ladies euerichon
Haueth som routhe on hir aduersitee
An Emperours doghter stant allone
She hath no wight to whom to make hir mone
O blood roial that stondest in this drede
ffer be thy freendes at thy grete nede

This Alla kyng hath swich compassioun
As gentil herte is fulfild of pitee
That from his eyen ran the water doun
Now hastily do fecche a book quod he
And if this knyght wol sweren how þt she
This womman slow yet wol we vs auyse
Whom þt we wole that shal been oure Iustise

A Bryton book writen with Euangiles
Was fet and on this book he swoor anon
She gilty was and in the mene whiles
An hand hym smoot vp on the nekke bon
That doun he fel atones as a stoon
And bothe hise eyen broste out of his face
In sighte of euery body in that place

...ys was herd in general audience
And seyde thow hast disclaundred giltlees
The doghter of holy chirche in heigh presence
Thus hastow doon and yet I holde my pees
Of this merueille agast was al the prees
As mazed folk they stoden euerychone
ffor drede of wreche saue Custance allone

Greet was the drede and eek the repentaunce
Of hem þt hadden wrong suspecion
Vp on this sely Innocent Custaunce
And for this miracle in conclusion
And by Custaunces mediacion
The kyng and many another in that place
Conuerted was thanked be Cristes grace

This false knyght was slayn for his vntrouthe
By Iuggement of Alla hastily
And yet Custaunce hadde of his deeth greet routhe
And after this Ihesus of his mercy
Made Alla wedden ful solempnely
This holy mayden þt is so bright and sheene
And thus hath Crist maad Custance a queene

But who was woful if I shal nat lye
Of this weddyng but Donegild and namo
The kynges moder ful of tirannye
Hir thoughte hir cursed herte brast atwo
She wolde noght hir sone had doon so
Hir thoughte a despit þt he sholde take
So straunge a creature vn to his make

Me list nat of the chaf or of the stree
Maken so long a tale as of the corn
What sholde I tellen of the realtee
At mariages or which cours gooth biforn
Who bloweth in trompe or in an horn
The fruyt of euery tale is for to seye
They ete and drynke and daunce and synge and pleye

	ELLESMERE
[¶A vo]ys was herd / in general audience	¶A voys Audience
[A]nd seyde / thow hast disclaundred giltlees	And thou hast’ desclaundred
The doghter of holy chirche / in heigh p*re*sence	hooly
Thus hastow doon / and yet I holde my pees	hastou holde I
Of this m*er*uaille / agast was al the prees	
As mazed folk / they stoden eu*er*ychone	folk’ euerichone
For drede of wreche / saue Custance allone	
¶Greet was the drede / and eek the repentaunce	eek’ repentance
Of hem / *þa*t hadden wrong suspeciou*n*	that
Vp on / this sely Innocent Custaunce	Vpon / Custance
And for this miracle / in conclusiou*n*	miracle
And by Custaunces mediaciou*n*	Custances
The kyng’ and many another in that place	
Conuerted was / thanked be Cristes grace	cristes
¶This false knyght was slayn for his vntrouthe	knygħt
By Iuggement of Alla hastily	hastifly
And yet Custaunce / hadde of his deeth greet routhe	Custance /
And after this / I*es*us of his mercy	this
Made Alla / wedden ful solempnely	Alla
This holy mayden / *þa*t is so bright and shene	hooly that brigħt sheene
And thus hath Crist’ maad Custance a queene	crist’ ymaad
¶But who was woful / if I shal nat lye	But
Of this weddyng’ but Donegild and namo	Donegild
The kynges moder’ ful of tirannye	mooder /
Hir thoughte / hir cursed herte brast atwo	
She wolde noght’ hir sone had doon so	noghħt do
Hir thoughte a despit’ *þa*t he sholde take	that
So straunge a creature / vn to his make	strange creature
¶Me list nat’ of the chaf / or of the stree	24 nat
Maken so long a tale / as of the corn	
What sholde I tellen / of the realtee	roialtee
At mariages / or which cours gooth biforn	goth
Who bloweth in trompe / or in an horn	in the trumpe /
The fruyt of euery tale / is for to seye	fruyt’
They ete and drynke / and daunce / *and* synge *and* pleye	ete / *and* drynke / *and*

24 ¶Man *57v*

The Man of Lawe

	ELLESMERE
¶They goon to bedde as it was skile and right'	They bedde / rigħt'
For though þ*at* wyues / been ful holy thynges	thogh be hooly
They moste take / in pacience at nyght'	nygħt'
Swiche manere necessaries / as been plesynges	man*ere*
To folk / that han ywedded hem with rynges	þ*at*
And leye alite / hir holynesse asyde	hoolynesse aside
As for the tyme / it may noon oother bityde	may no bet bitide
¶On hire / he gat a knaue child anon	On hir*e* gat' a man[25] child
And to a bisshop*e* / and his Constable eke	bissħop*e* /
He took his wyf to kepe / whan he is gon	
To Scotlond'ward / his foomen for to seke	Scotlondward /
Now faire Custaunce / þ*at* is so hu*m*ble *and* meke	Custance / that and
So longe is goon with childe / til þ*at* stille	that'
She halt hir chambre / abidyng' cristes wille	
¶The tyme is come / a knaue child she beer	The a man[26] child
Mauricius at the font stoon / they hym calle	fontstoon /
This Constable / dooth forth come a Messager	Messageer
And wroot vn to his kyng' þ*at* clepyd was Alle	that cleped
How þ*at* / this blisful tidynge is bifalle	that tidyng'
And othere tidynges / speedful for to seye	spedeful
He tath the lettre / and forth he goth his weye	He taketh the gooth
¶This Messager / to doon his auauntage	auantage
Vn to the kynges moder / rideth swithe	Vnto mooder
And salueth ful faire / in his langage	salueth hir*e* ful faire
Madame quod he / ye may be glad and blithe	
And thanketh god / an hundred thousand sithe	anhundred
My lady queene / hath child with outen doute	
To ioye and blisse / of al this regne aboute	blisse / to al
¶Lo here the lettres / seled of this thyng'	Lo heere
That I moot bere / with al the haste I may	
If ye wol aught' vn to youre sone the kyng'	kyng /
I am youre seruaunt' bothe nyght and day	*ser*uant' nygħt
Donegild answerde / as now at this tyme nay	
But here al nyght' I wol thow take thy reste	heere nygħt / thou
To morwe / wol I seye thee what me leste	Tomorwe / thee /

[25] 'man' altered from 'knaue.'

[26] 'man' altered from 'knaue.'

They goon to bedde as it was skile and right /
For though þt wyues been ful holy thynges
They moste take in pacience at nyght /
Swiche manere necessaries / as been plesynges
To folk that han ywedded hem with rynges
And leye a lite hir holynesse asyde
As for the tyme / it may noon oother bityde

On hire / he gat a knaue child anon
And to a bisshop / and his Constable eke
He took his wyf to kepe / whan he is gon
To Scotland ward / his foomen for to seke
Now faire Custaunce / þt is so humble & meke
So longe is goon with childe / til þt stille
She halt hir chambre / abidyng cristes wille

The tyme is come / a knaue child she beer
Mauricius at the font stoon / they hym calle
This Constable dooth forth come a messager
And wroot vn to his kyng / þt clepid was Alle
How þt this blisful tidynge is bifalle
And othere tidynges speedful for to seye
He taith the lettre / and forth he goth his weye

This messager / to don his auauntage
Vn to the kynges moder rideth swithe
And salueth ful faire in his langage
Madame quod he ye may be glad and blithe
And thanketh god / an hundred thousand sithe
My lady queene hath child with outen doute
To ioye and blisse / of al this regne aboute

Lo here the lettres / seled of this thyng /
That I moot bere / with al the haste I may
If ye wol aught / vn to youre sone the kyng /
I am youre seruaunt / bothe nyght and day
Donegild answerde / as now at this tyme nay
But here al nyght / I wol thow take thy reste
To morwe wol I seye thee what me leste

This messager drank sadly ale and wyn
And stolen were his lettres pryuely
Out of his box whil he sleep as a swyn
And countrefeted was ful subtilly
Another lettre wroght ful synfully
Vn to the kyng direct of this matere
ffro his Constable as ye shal after heere

The lettre spak the queene delyuered was
Of so horrible a feendlich creature
That in the Castel noon so hardy was
That any while dorste ther endure
The moder was an Elf by auenture
ycomen by charmes or by sorcerye
And euerich hateth hir compaignye

Wo was this kyng whan he this lettre hadde seyn
But to no wight he tolde his sorwes soore
But of his owene hond he wroot ageyn
Welcome the sonde of Crist for eueremoore
To me þt am now lerned in his loore
lord welcome be thy lust and thy plesaunce
My lust I putte al in thyn ordinaunce

Kepeth this child al be it foul or feir
And eek my wyf vn to myn hom comynge
Crist whan hym list may sende me an heir
Moore agreable than this to my likynge
This lettre he seleth pryuely wepynge
Which to the messager was take soone
And forth he goth ther is namoore to doone

O messager fulfild of dronkenesse
Strong is thy breeth thy lymes faltren ay
And thow biwreyest al secreenesse
Thy mynde is lorn thow ianglest as a Iay
Thy face is turned in a newe array
Ther dronkenesse regneth in any route
Ther is no conseil hid with outen doute

Quid turpius ebrioso cui fetor in […]
ore tremor in corpore qui pr[…]
stulta prodit occulta cui men[…]
alienatur facies transformat[…]
nullum enim latet secretum u[…]
regnat ebrietas

[¶This] Messager / drank sadly ale and wyn
[A]nd stolen were / his lettres pryuely
Out of his box / whil he sleep as a swyn
And countrefeted / was ful subtilly
Another lettre / wroght ful synfully
Vn to the kyng direct' of this matere
Fro his Constable / as ye shal after heere

¶The lettre spak / the queene deliu*er*ed was
Of so horrible / a fendlich creature
That in the Castel / noon so hardy was
That any while / dorste ther endure
The moder was an Elf / by auenture
Ycomen / by charmes / or by sorcerye
And euerich / hateth hir compaignye

¶Wo was this kyng' whan he this lettre hadde seyn
But to no wight' he tolde his sorwes soore
But of his owene hond / he wroot ageyn
Wel come the sonde of Crist / for eu*er*e moore
To me / *þ*at am now lerned in his loore
Lord / wel come be thy lust' and thy plesaunce
My lust' I putte al in thyn ordinaunce

¶Kepeth this child / al be it foul or feir
And eek my wyf / vn to myn hom comynge
Crist whan hym list' may sende me an heir
Moore agreable than this / to my likynge
This lettre he seleth / pryuely wepynge
Which to the Messager / was take soone
And forth he goth / ther is namoore to doone

¶O. Messager / fulfild of dronkenesse
Strong is thy breeth / thy lymes faltren ay
And thow biwreyest' al secrenesse
Thy mynde is lorn / thow ianglest as a Iay
Thy face is turned / in a newe array
Ther dronkenesse regneth / in any route
Ther is no conseil hid / with outen doute

771 Quid turpius ebrioso cui fetor in ore tremor in corpore qui prom[it] stulta prodit occulta cui men[s] alienatur facies transformat[ur] nullum enim latet secretum vb[i] regnat ebrietas Hg (defective) El
Variant: cui mens) cuius m. El

ELLESMERE

27 ¶This Messager' Ale
And were hise
sleep*e*
countrefeted
wroght'
mateere

The spak'
horrible feendly

mooder Elf
sorcerie

had sayn

hand / agayn
crist' eu*er*emoore
that
plesau*n*ce
ordinau*n*ce

Kepeth
hoom

seleth

gooth /

¶Auctor] O

thou biwreyest / alle secreenesse
thou

dronkenesse / regneth
hyd /

27 ¶of Lawe *58r*

	ELLESMERE
ꝗO. Donegild / I ne haue noon englissħ digne	O donegild /
Vn to thy malice / and thy tirannye	
And ther fore / to the feend I thee resigne	therfore /
Lat hym enditen / of thy traitorie	
Fy mannyssh fy / o nay by god I lye	mannyssħ
Fy fendlich spiritꝛ for I dar wel telle	feendlych
Thogh thow heere walke / thy spirit is in helle	thou
ꝗThis Messager / comth fro the kyng agayn	28
And at the kynges modres Court he lighte	moodres court
And she was / of this Messager ful fayn	
And plesed hym / in al that eu*er*e she myghte	eu*er* mygħte
He drank / and wel his girdel vnder pighte	drankꝛ / vnderpigħte
He slepeth / and he fnorteth in his gyse	
Al nyghtꝛ til the sonne gan aryse	nygħtꝛ
ꝗEft were his l*ett*res / stolen euerichon	Eftꝛ hise lettres eu*er*ychon
And countrefeted lettres / in this wyse	
The kyng comaundeth / his Constable anon	⟨kingꝛ⟩ comandeth /
Vp peyne of hangyngꝛ and on heigh Iuyse	
That he ne sholde suffren / in no wyse	sholde / suffren
Custance / in with his regne for tabyde	inwith his Reawme for
Thre dayes / and a quarter of o tyde	and o quarter of a tyde
ꝗBut in the same Ship*e* / as he hir fond	But ship*e* / hir*e* fond'
Hire and hir yonge sone / and al hir geere	Hir*e* and
He sholde putte / and crowde hir fro the lond	croude hir*e* lond'
And charge hire / *þa*t she neu*er*e eft coome there	chargen hir*e* / she neu*er* eftꝛ theere
O my Custaunce / wel may thy goost haue fere	Custance / feere
And slepyng in thy dreem / been in penaunce	slepynge penance
Whan Donegild / caste al this ordinaunce	Donegild' / cast ordinance
ꝗThis Messager / on morwe whan he wookꝛ	Messagerꝛ morwe /
Vn to the Castel / halt the nexte wey	way
And to the Constable / he the lettre tookꝛ	
And whan *þa*t he / this pitous lettre sey	say
Ful ofte / he seyde allas and weilawey	ofte seyde / Allas weylaway
Lord crist quod he / how may this world endure	
So ful of synne / is many a creature	

[28] ꝗMan *58v*

O. Donegild I ne haue noon englissh digne
Vn to thy malice / and thy tirannye
And ther-fore to the feend I thee resigne
Lat hym enditen / of thy traitorie
ffy mannyssh fy / o nay by god I lye
ffy feendlich spirit / for I dar wel telle
Though thow heere walke / thy spirit is in helle

This messager / comth fro the kyng agayn
And at the kynges moodres court he lighte
And she was / of this messager ful fayn
And plesed hym / in al that euere she myghte
He drank / and wel his girdel vnderpighte
He slepeth / and he fnorteth in his gyse
Al nyght / til the sonne gan aryse

Eft were his lettres stolen euerichon
And countrefeted lettres / in this wyse
The kyng comaundeth his Constable anon
Vp peyne of hangyng / and on heigh Iuyse
That he ne sholde suffren / in no wyse
Custance / inwith his regne for tabyde
Thre dayes / and a quarter of o tyde

But in the same ship / as he hir fond
Hire and hir yonge sone / and al hir gere
He sholde putte / and crowde hir fro the lond
And charge hire / þt she neuere eft come there
O my Custance / wel may thy goost haue fere
And slepyng in thy dreem / been in penaunce
Whan Donegild / caste al this ordinaunce

This messager / on morwe whan he wook
Vn to the Castel halt the nexte wey
And to the Constable / he the lettre took
And whan þt he / this pitous lettre sey
ffful ofte he seyde allas and weylawey
Lord crist quod he / how may this world endure
So ful of synne / is many a creature.

[O] myghty god if that it be thy wille
Sith thow art rightful Iuge / how may it be
That thow wolt suffren / Innocentz to spille
And wikked folk / regnen in prosperitee
O goode Custaunce / allas so wo is me
That I moot be thy tormentour / or deye
On shames deeth / ther nys noon oother weye

Wepen bothe yonge and olde in al that place
Whan þt the kyng this cursed lettre sente
And Custaunce / with a dedly pale face
The ferthe day / toward hir ship she wente
But nathelees / she taketh in good entente
The wyl of Crist / and knelyng on the stronde
She seyde lord / ay wel come be thy sonde

He þt me kepte fro the false blame
Whil I was on the lond amonges yow
He kan me kepe fro harm and eek fro shame
In salte see al thogh I se noght how
As strong as euere he was he is yet now
In hym triste I and in his moder deere
That is to me my sayl and eek my steere

Hir litel child lay wepyng in hir arm
And knelyng / pitously to hym she seyde
Pees litel sone I wol do thee noon harm
With that hir couerchief / ouer hir heed she breyde
And ouer his litel eyen / she it leyde
And in hir arm she lulleth it ful faste
And in to heuene / hir eyen vp she caste

Moder quod she / and mayden bright Marie
Sooth is þt thurgh wommanes eggement /
Mankynde was lorn and dampned ay to dye
ffor which thy child was on a croys yrent /
Thy blisful eyen / sawe al his torment /
Thanne is ther no comparison bitwene
Thy wo and any wo man may sustene

	ELLESMERE
[¶O] myghty god / if that it be thy wille	¶O
Sith thow art rightful Iuge / how may it be	thou
That thow wolt suffren / Innocentz to spille	thou
And wikked folk / regnen in p*ro*sp*er*itee	prosp*er*itee
O goode Custaunce / allas so wo is me	Custance / Allas
That I moot be thy tormentour / or deye	tormentour
On shames deeth / ther nys noon oother weye	ther is noon
¶Wepen bothe yonge and olde / in al that place	
Whan þ*at* the kyngꝭ this cursed lettre sente	
And Custaunce / with a dedly pale face	Custance / deedly
The ferthe day / toward hir ship*e* she wente	
But nathelees / she taketh in good entente	
The wyl of Crist / and knelyng on the Stronde	Cristꝭ knelynge
She seyde lord / ay wel come be thy sonde	
¶He þ*at* me kepte / fro the false blame	29 He that
Whil I was on the lond / amonges yow	was / lond
He kan me kepe / fro harm and eek fro shame	from harm /
In salte see / al thogh I se noght how	
As strong as eu*er*e he was / he is yet now	
In hym triste I / and in his moder deere	mooder
That is to me / my sayl and eek my steere	seyl /
¶Hir litel child / lay wepyng in hir arm	Hir wepyngꝭ Arm
And knelyngꝭ pitously / to hym she seyde	knelynge /
Pees litel sone / I wol do thee noon Harm	harm
With that hir couerchiefꝭ / ouer hir hed she breyde	Wi*th* cou*er*chief / ou*er* heed
And ouer his litel eyen / she it leyde	ou*er* hise
And in hir arm / she lulleth it ful faste	Arm /
And in to heuene / hir eyen vp she caste	hir*e*
¶Moder quod she / and mayden bright Marie	¶Mooder mayde
Sooth is / þ*at* thurgh wommans eggementꝭ	that wommanes
Man kynde was lorn / and dampned ay to dye	
For which thy child / was on a croys yrentꝭ	yrent
Thy blisful eyen / sawe al his tormentꝭ	
Thanne is therꝭ no comparisou*n* bitwene	ther / comparison
Thy wo / and any wo man may sustene	wo / man

29 ¶of Lawe *59r*

	ELLESMERE
¶Thow saw thy child / yslayn bifor thyne eyen	Thow sawe child bifore
And yet now / lyueth my litel child *par*fay	my child
Now lady brightꝰ to whom alle woful cryen	bright /
Thow glorie of wommanhod / thow faire may	wommanhede /
Thow hauen of refutꝰ brighte sterre of day	brighte
Rewe on my child / that of thy gentillesse	
Rewestꝰ on euery rewful in distresse	Ruestꝰ reweful
¶O litel child / allas what is thy giltꝰ	
That neuere wroghtest synne / as yet *par*dee	neu*ere*
Why wil thyn harde fader / han thee spiltꝰ	
O mercy deere Constable / quod she	Constable
As lat my litel child / dwelle here with thee	heer
And if thow darst noghtꝰ sauen hym for blame	thou natꝰ
So kys hym ones / in his fader name	Yet kys fadres
¶Ther with she looketh / bakward to the londe	Ther with / looked
And seyde / fare wel housbonde routhelees	
And vp she ristꝰ and walketh doun the Stronde	rist / stronde
Toward the ship*e* / hir folweth al the prees	
And euere / she prayeth hir child / to holde his pees	eu*ere* preyeth hir*e*
And taketh hir leue / and with an holy entente	hooly
She blesseth hire / and in to ship*e* she wente	blissed hir*e* /
¶Vitailled was the ship*e* / it is no drede	30 Vitailled
Habundantly for hire / ful longe space	Habundantly / hir*e*
And othere necessaries / þ*at* sholde nede	that
She hadde ynow / heryed be goddes grace	ynogh /
For wynd and weder / almyghty god purchace	almyghty *pur*chace
And brynge hir hom / I kan no bettre seye	hir*e* hoom /
But in the see / she dryueth forth hir weye	See / 31
¶Alla the kyngꝰ comth hom soone after this	Alla hoom
Vn to his Castel / of the which I tolde	
And axeth / wher*e* his wyf / and his child is	asketh / wh*e*re
The Constable / gan aboute his herte colde	
And pleynly / al the manere he hym tolde	
As ye han herd / I kan telle it no bettre	
And sheweth the kyngꝰ his seel and his lettre	

30 ¶Man *59v*

31 Break in El followed by:
¶Explicit secunda pars
¶Sequitur pars tercia

Thow sawe thy child / yslayn bifor thyne eyen
And yet now lyveth my litel child parfay
Now lady bright / to whom alle woful cryen
Thow glorie of wommanhod / thow faire may
Thow hauen of refut / brighte sterre of day
Rewe on my child / that of thy gentillesse
Rewest / on euery rewful in distresse

O litel child / allas what is thy gilt /
That neuere wroghtest synne / as yet pardee
Why wil thyn harde fader / han thee spilt /
O mercy deere Constable / quod she
As lat my litel child / dwelle here with thee
And if thow darst noght / sauen hym for blame
So kys hym ones / in his fader name

Ther with she looketh / bakward to the londe
And seyde farewel housbonde routhelees
And vp she rist / and walketh doun the stronde
Toward the ship / hir folweth al the prees
And euere she prayeth hir child / to holde his pees
And taketh hir leue / and with an holy entente
She blesseth hire / and in to ship she wente

Vitailled was the ship / it is no drede
Habundantly for hire / ful longe space
And othere necessaries / þt sholde nede
She hadde ynow / heryed be goddes grace
ffor wynd and weder / almyghty god purchace
And brynge hir hom / I kan no bettre seye
But in the see / she dryueth forth hir weye

Alla the kyng / comth hom soone after this
Vn to his castel / of the which I tolde
And axeth wher his wyf / and his child is
The Constable / gan aboute his herte colde
And pleynly / al the manere he hym tolde
As ye han herd / I kan telle it no bettre
And sheweth the kyng / his seel and his lettre

And seyde lord / as ye comanded me
Up peyne of deeth / so haue I do certein
This messager tormented was til he
Moste biknowe / and tellen plat and pleyn
ffro nyght to nyght / in what place he had leyn
And thus by wit / and subtil enquerynge
Ymagined was by whom this harm gan sprynge

¶ The hond was knowe þt the lettre wroot /
And al the venym of this cursed dede
But in what wise / certeinly I noot /
Theffect is this þt Alla out of drede
His moder slow that may men pleynly rede
ffor that she traytour was to hir ligeaunce
Thus endeth olde Donegild wt meschaunce

¶ The sorwe þt this Alla / nyght and day
Maketh for his wyf / and for his child also
Ther is no tonge / that it telle may
But now wol I vn to Custaunce go
That fleteth in the see / in peyne and wo
ffyue yeer and moore / as liked Cristes sonde
Er þt hir ship / approched vn to londe

¶ Under an hethen castel atte laste
Of which the name / in my text noght I fynde
Custaunce and eek hir child / the see vp caste
Almyghty god / that saueth al mankynde
Haue on Custaunce and on hir child som mynde
That fallen is / in hethen hand eft soone
In point to spille / as I shal telle yow soone

¶ Doun fro the castel / comth ther many a wight /
To gauren on this ship / and on Custaunce
But shortly from the castel / on a nyght /
The lordes styward god yeue hym meschaunce
A theef that hadde reneyed oure creaunce
Cam in to ship allone / and seyde he sholde
Hir lemman be / wher so she wolde or nolde

[¶A]nd seyde lord / as ye comaunded me
Vp peyne of deeth / so haue I do c*er*tein
This Messager / tormented was / til he
Moste biknowe / and tellen plat and pleyn
Fro nyght to nyght in what place he had leyn
And thus by wit and subtil enquerynge
Ymagined was / by whom this harm gan sprynge

¶The hond was knowe / þ*a*t the lettre wroot
And al the venym / of this cursed dede
But in what wise / c*er*teynly I noot
Theffect is this / þ*a*t Alla out of drede
His moder slow / that may men pleynly rede
For that she traytour was / to hir ligeaunce
Thus endeth olde Donegild w*ith* meschaunce

¶The sorwe þ*a*t this Alla / nyght and day
Maketh for his wyf / and for his child also
Ther is no tonge / that it telle may
But now wol I / vn to Custaunce go
That fleteth in the see / in peyne and wo
Fyue yeer and moore / as liked Cristes sonde
Er þ*a*t hir ship*e* / approched vn to londe

¶Vnder an hethen Castel / atte laste
Of which the name / in my text noght I fynde
Custaunce and eek hir child / the see vp caste
Almyghty god / that saueth al mankynde
Haue on Custaunce / and on hir child som mynde
That fallen is / in hethen hand eft soone
In point to spille / as I shal telle yow soone

¶Down fro the Castel / comth ther many a wight
To gauren on this Ship*e* / and on Custaunce
But shortly from the Castel / on a nyght
The lordes Styward / god yeue hym meschaunce
A theef / that hadde reneyed oure creaunce
Cam in to ship*e* allone / and seyde he sholde
Hir lemman be / wher so she wolde or nolde

ELLESMERE

And comanded
doon
was he /
nyght to nyght /
sotil

hand that
c*er*teinly
mooder
þ*a*t traitour*e* was hir*e* ligeance
Donegild with meschance

The that nyght
Custance
cristes
that to the londe

32
Custance /
Almyghty saued
Custance /

¶Doun wight
Custance
shortly / nyght
Styward / meschance
creance
to the ship*e*

32 ¶of Lawe *60r*

The Man of Lawe ꝭ	ELLESMERE
¶Wo was this wrecched womman / tho bigon	womman
Hir child cryde / and she cryde pitously	cride / she cride
But blisful Marie / heelp hir*e* right anon	riħt
For with hir strogelyngꝰ wel and myghtily	struglyngꝰ
The theef / fil ouer bord / al sodeynly	theef
And in the see / he dreynte for vengeaunce	vengeance
And thus hath Cristꝰ vnwemmed kept Custaunce	cristꝰ Custance
¶O. foule lust of luxurie / lo thyn ende	¶Auctor] O
Nat oonly / *þa*t thou fayntest mannes mynde	that feyntest ma*n*nes
But v*er*raily / thow wolt his body shende	verraily / thou
Thende of thy werk / or of thy lustes blynde	werkꝰ
Is compleynyngꝰ how many oon may men fynde	co*m*pleynyngꝰ hou
That noght for werk som tyme / but for thentente	
To doon this synne / been outher slayn or shente	
¶How may this wayke womman / han this strengthe	How wo*m*man /
Hir to defende / agayn this renegatꝰ	Hir*e*
O. Golias / vnmesurable of lengthe	O
How myghte Dauid / make thee so maat	Hou myħte maatꝰ
So yongꝰ and of armure so desolatꝰ	Armure desolaat
How dorste he looke / vp on thy dredful face	Hou
Wel may men seen / it was but goddes gr*a*ce	it nas but grace
¶Who yaf Iudith / corage / or hardynesse	Who corage
To sleen hym Olofernus / in his tente	Oloferne /
And to delieuren / out of wrecchednesse	
The peple of god / I sey for this entente	seye
That right as god / spirit of vigour sente	riħt
To hem / and saued hem / out of meschaunce	meschance
So sente he myghtꝰ and vigour to Custaunce	myħtꝰ Custance
¶Forth gooth hir ship*e* / thurgh out the narwe mouth	33 thurħ
Of Iubaltar*e* / and Septe / dryuyng ay	Iubaltar*e* Septe dryuynge alway |
Som tyme Westꝰ and som tyme North and South	Norħ Souħ
And som tyme Estꝰ ful many a wery day	estꝰ
Til Cristes moder / blissed be she ay	cristes mooder / blessed
Hath shapen / thurgh hir endelees goodnesse	thurħ
To make an ende / of al hir heuynesse	

925 O extrema libidinis turp[itudo]
que non solum mentem effemi[nat]
set eciam corpus eneruat se[mper]
sequntur dolor et penitencia post et [cetera]
Hg (defective) El

33 ¶Man *60v*

Tho was this wrecched womman tho bigon
Hir child cryde and she cryde pitously
But blisful Marie heelp hir right anon
For with hir strogelyng / wel and myghtily
The theef fil ouer bord / al sodeynly
And in the See he dreynte for vengeaunce
And thus hath Crist / vnwemmed kept Custaunce

125

O foule lust of luxurie lo thyn ende
Nat oonly þt thou faynt est mannes mynde
But verraily thow wolt his body shende
Thende of thy werk / or of thy lustes blynde
Is compleynyng / how many oon may men fynde
That noght for werk som tyme / but for thentente
To doon this synne / been outher slayn or shente

O extrema libidinis turp.
que non solu mente effemi.
set etiam corpus eneruat &c.
sequitur dolor et penitentia post &c

How may this wayke womman / han this strengthe
Hir to defende / agayn this renegat
O Golias / vnmesurable of lengthe
How myghte Dauid / make thee so maat
So yong / and of armure so desolat
How dorste he looke / vp on thy dredful face
Wel may men seen / it was but goddes grace

Who yaf Iudith / corage or hardynesse
To sleen hym Olofernus / in his tente
And to deliueren / out of wrecchednesse
The peple of god / I sey for this entente
That right as god / spirit of vigour sente
To hem / and saued hem / out of meschaunce
So sente he myght / and vigour / to Custaunce

Forth gooth hir ship / thurgh out the narwe mouth
Of Iubaltar and Septe / dryuyng ay
Som tyme west / and som tyme North and South
And som tyme Est / ful many a wery day
Til Cristes moder / blissed be she ay
Hath shapen thurgh hir endelees goodnesse
To make an ende / of al hir heuynesse

[…]at vs stynte of Custaunce but a throwe
[…]nd speke we / of the Romayn Emperour
That out of Surrye / hath by lettres knowe
The slaughtre of cristen folk / and dishonour
Doon to his doghter / by a fals traytour
I mene / the cursed wikked Sowdanesse
That at the feeste / leet sleen bothe moore and lesse

For which this Emperour / hath sent anon
His Senatour / with roial ordinaunce
And othere lordes / god woot many oon
On Surryens / to taken heigh vengeaunce
They brennen sleen / and brynge hem to meschaunce
Ful many a day / but shortly this is thende
Homward to Rome / they shapen hem to wende

This Senatour / repaireth with victorie
To Romeward / saillynge ful roially
And mette the ship dryuynge / as seith the storie
In which Custaunce / sit ful pitously
No thyng ne knew he / what she was ne why
She was in swich array / ne she nyl seye
Of hir estaat / thogh she sholde deye

He bryngeth hire to Rome / and to his wyf
He yaf hire / and hir yonge sone also
And with the Senatour / she ladde hir lyf
Thus kan oure lady / bryngen out of wo
Woful Custaunce / and many another mo
And longe tyme / dwelled she in that place
In holy werkes euere / as was hir grace

Maria mater omni virtutum

The Senatours wyf / hir aunte was
But for al that / she knew hir neuer the moore
I wol no lenger / tarien in this cas
But to kyng Alla / which I spak of yoore
That for his wyf / wepeth and siketh soore
I wol retourne / and lete I wole Custaunce
Vnder the Senatours gouernaunce

	ELLESMERE
[¶Now] lat vs stynte of Custaunce / but a throwe	Now stynte / Custance
[A]nd speke we / of the Romayn Emp*er*our	And
That out of Surrye / hath by lettres knowe	
The slaughtre of cristen folk / and dishonour	
Doon to his doghter / by a fals traytour	
I mene / the cursed wikked Sowdanesse	
That at the feeste / leet sleen bothe moore and lesse	*and*
¶For which this Emp*er*our / hath sent anon	For
His Senatour / with Roial ordinaunce	roial ordinance
And othere lordes / god woot many oon	
On Surryens / to taken heigh vengeaunce	heigh vengeance
They brennen / sleen / and brynge hem to meschaunce	meschance
Ful many a day / but shortly this is thende	shortly /
Homward to Rome / they shapen hem to wende	
¶This Senatour / repaireth with Victorie	victorie
To Romeward / saylynge ful Roially	Romeward saillynge
And mette the ship dryuynge / as seith the storie	ship*e*
In which Custaunce / sit ful pitously	Custance /
No thyng ne knew he / what she was / ne why	thyng knew why /
She was in swich array / ne she nyl seye	
Of hir estaat thogh she sholde deye	hir*e* thogh
¶He bryngeth hir*e* to Rome / and to his wyf	He wyf /
He yaf hire / and hir yonge sone also	hir*e* / and
And with the Senatour / she ladde hir lyf	lyf
Thus kan oure lady / bryngen out of wo	
Woful Custaunce / and many another mo	Custance /
And longe tyme / dwelled she in that place	
In holy werkes eu*er*e / as was hir grace	hooly euere /
¶The Senatours wyf / hir Aunte was	The
But for al that she knew hir neu*er* the moore	hir*e*
I wol no lenger taryen in this cas	lenger / tarien
But to kyng Alla / which I spak of yoore	
That for his wyf / wepeth and siketh soore	That wepeth for his wyf / and
I wol retourne / and lete I wole Custaunce	wol Custance
Vnder the Senatours gouernaunce	Vnder / gou*er*nance

977 Maria mater omnium virtutum Hg (in a later hand)

980 R Wryne Hg (in same hand as gloss in 977)

The Man of Lawe ⸗	ELLESMERE
¶Kyng Alla / which þ*at* hadde his moder slayn	34 **K**yng that mooder
Vp on a day / fil in swich repentaunce	repentance
That if I shortly / tellen shal and playn	I /
To Rome he cometh / to receyuen his penaunce	comth / penance
And putte hym / in the Popes ordinaunce	popes ordinance
In heigh and logh / and Ie*s*u Crist bisoghte	loghħ / crist bisoghħte
Foryeue / his wikked werkes þ*at* he wroghte	hise wroghħte
¶The fame anon / thurgh Rome town is born	thurgh out the toun
How Alla kyng’ shal comen in pilgrymage	kyng / comen on pilgrymage
By herbergeours / that wenten hym biforn	
For which the Senatour / as was vsage	which /
Rood hym agayns / and many of his lynage	
As wel to shewen / his heighe magnyficence	heighħe magnificence
As to doon / any kyng a reuerence	
¶Greet cheere / dooth this noble Senatour	
To kyng Alla / and he to hym also	
Euerich of hem / dooth oother greet honour	
And so bifel / þ*at* in a day / or two	that in with a day
This Senatour / is to kyng Alla go	
To feste / and shortly / if I shal nat lye	
Custaunces sone / wente in his compaignye	Custances
¶Som men wolde seyn / at requeste of Custaunce	Custance
This Senatour / hath lad this child to feste	Senatour’ feeste
I may nat tellen / euerich circumstaunce	euery circumstance
Be as be may / ther was he atte leste	at the leeste
But sooth is this / þ*at* at his modres heste	that moodres heeste
Biforn Alla / duryng’ the metes space	durynge
The child stood / lookynge in the kynges face	
¶This Alla kyng’ hath of this child greet wonder	
And to the senatour / he seyde anon	
Whos is that faire child / that stondeth yonder	yonder ⸗
I noot quod he / by god and by Seint Ioħn	god / seint
A moder he hath / but fader hath he non	mooder noon
That I of woot’ and shortly in a stounde	woot / but shortly /
He tolde Alla / how þ*at* this child was founde	that’

34 ¶of Lawe *61r*

Kyng Alla which þt hadde his moder slayn
Vp on a day fil in swich repentaunce
That if I shortly tellen shal and playn
To Rome he cometh to receyuen his penaunce
And putte hym in the popes ordinaunce
In heigh and logh and Ihu Crist bisoghte
fforyeue his wikked werkes þt he wroghte

The fame anon thurgh Rome town is born
How Alla kyng shal comen in pilgrymage
By herbergeours that wenten hym biforn
ffor which the Senatour as was vsage
Rood hym agayns and many of his lynage
As wel to shewen his heighe magnyficence
As to doon any kyng a reuerence

Greet cheere dooth this noble Senatour
To kyng Alla and he to hym also
Euerich of hem dooth oother greet honour
And so bifel þt in a day or two
This Senatour is to kyng Alla go
To feste and shortly if I shal nat lye
Custaunces sone wente in his compaignye

Som men wolde seyn at requeste of Custaunce
This Senatour hath lad this child to feste
I may nat tellen euerich circumstaunce
Be as be may ther was he atte leeste
But sooth is this þt at his modres heeste
Biforn Alla durynge the metes space
The child stood lookynge in the kynges face

This Alla kyng hath of this child greet wonder
And to the Senatour he seyde anon
Whos is that faire child that stondeth yonder
I noot quod he by god and by seint John
A moder he hath but fader hath he non
That I of woot and shortly in a stounde
He tolde Alla how þt this child was founde

[.]r god woot vpon this Senatour also
So vertuous a lyuere in my lyf
Ne sawh I neue as she ne herde of mo
Of worldly wommen mayde ne of wyf
I dar wel seyn hir hadde leu a knyf
Thurgh out hir brest than been a womman wikke
Ther is no man koude brynge hire to that prikke

Now was this child as lyk vn to Custaunce
As possible is a creature to be
This Alla hath the face in remembraunce
Of dame Custaunce and ther on mused he
If þt the childes moder were aught she
That is his wyf and pryuely he sighte
And spedde hym fro the table that he myghte

Parfay thoughte he fantome is in myn heed
I oghte deme of skilful iugement
That in the salte see my wif is deed
And afterward he made his argument
What woot I if þt Crist hath hider sent
My wif by see as wel as he hir sente
To my contree from thennes þt she wente

And after noon hom with the Senatour
Goth Alla for to seen this wonder chaunce
This Senatour dooth Alla greet honour
And hastily he sente after Custaunce
But trusteth wel hir liste noght to daunce
Whan that she wiste wher fore was that sonde
Unnethe vp on hir feet she myghte stonde

Whan Alla saugh his wyf faire he hir grette
And weep that it was routhe for to se
For at the firste look he on hir sette
He knew wel verraily þt it was she
And she for sorwe as doumb stant as a tree
So was hir herte shet in hir distresse
Whan she remembred his vnkyndenesse

	ELLESMERE
[¶But] god woot quod this Senatour also	But
[S]o vertuous a lyuere / in my lyf	So lyuere lyf
Ne saw I neu*er*e as she / ne herde of mo	saugh neuere
Of worldly wommen / mayde ne of wyf	wyf
I dar wel seyn / hir hadde leu*er*e a knyf	leuere
Thurgh out hir brest than been a womman wikke	ben wo*m*man
Ther is no man / koude brynge hire to that prikke	hir*e*
¶Now was this child / as lyk vn to Custaunce	35 child / lyk Custance
As possible is / a creature to be	
This Alla / hath the face in remembraunce	remembrance
Of dame Custaunce / and ther on mused he	Custance /
If *pat* the childes moder / were aught she	that mooder /
That is his wyf / and pryuely he sighte	
And spedde hym fro the table that he myghte	table / mygħte
¶P*ar*fay thoughte he / fantome is in myn heed	P*ar*fay thoghte
I oghte deme / of skilful Iugement	Iuggement
That in the salte see / my wif is deed	wyf
And afterward / he made his argument	Argument
What woot I / if *pat* Crist hath hider sent	that haue hyder ysent
My wif by see / as wel as he hir sente	wyf hir*e*
To my contree / from thennes *pat* she wente	fro that
¶And after noon / hom with the Senatour	And Noon / hoom
Goth Alla / for to seen this wonder chaunce	
This Senatour / dooth Alla greet honour	Senatour
And hastily / he sente after Custaunce	hastifly /
But tristeth wel / hir liste noght to daunce	trusteth weel / hir*e* nat
Whan that she wiste / wher fore was that sonde	*pat* she wherfore
Vnnethe / vp on hir feet she myghte stonde	
¶Whan Alla saugh his wyf / faire he hir grette	saugħ wyf hir*e*
And weep*e* / that it was routhe for to se	see
For at the firste look / he on hir sette	look hir*e*
He knew wel verraily / *pat* it was she	that
And she for sorwe / as domb stant as a tree	doumb
So was hir herte shet in hir distresse	
Whan she remembred / his vnkyndenesse	

35 ¶Man *61v*

The Man of Lawe ſ	ELLESMERE
¶Twies she swowneth / in his owene sighte	Twyes swowned /
He weep*e* / and hym excuseth pitously	
Now god quod he / and his halwes brighte	hise brigħte
So wisly on my soule / as haue m*er*cy	mercy
That of youre harm / as giltlees am I.	I
As is Maurice my sone / so lyk youre face	
Ellis the feend / me fecche out of this place	Elles
¶Long was the sobbyng⁊ and the bitter peyne	sobbyng⁊
Er þ*at* / hir woful hertes myghte cesse	that / mygħte
Greet was the pitee / for to heere hem pleyne	
Thurgh whiche pleintes / gan hir wo encresse	Thurgħ
I pray yow / al my labour to relesse	yow alle /
I may nat telle hir wo / vn til to morwe	
I am so wery / for to speke of sorwe	
¶But finally / whan þ*at* the sooth is wist /	36 But that sothe wist
That Alla / giltlees was of hir wo	Alla giltlees /
I trowe / an hundred tymes been they kist⁊	tymes /
And swich a blisse / is ther bitwix hem two	
That saue the ioye / þ*at* lasteth eu*er*emo	that lasteth
Ther is noon lyk / þ*at* any creature	that
Hath seyn / or shal / whil þ*at* the world may dure	seyn or /
¶Tho preyde she / hir housbond mekely	Tho she housbonde
In relief / of hir longe pitous pyne	
That he wolde praye / hir fader specially	preye /
That of his magestee / he wolde enclyne	
To vouche sauf / som day with hym to dyne	w*ith*
She preyde hym eek⁊ he sholde by no weye	eek / he wolde by
Vn to hir fader / no word of hir seye	fader⁊ hir*e*
¶Som men wolde seyn / how þ*at* the child Mauryce	Maurice
Dooth this message / vn to this Emp*er*our	Message /
But as I gesse / Alla was noght so nyce	nat
To hym þ*at* was / of so souereyn honour	that hono*ur*
As he þ*at* is / of cristen folk the flour	that
Sente any child / but it is bet to deme	deeme
He wente hym self / and so it may wel seme	seeme

[36]¶of Lawe *62r*

Whies she swowneth / in his owene sighte
He weep / and hym excuseth pitously
Now god quod he / and his halwes brighte
So wisly on my soule / as haue mercy
That of youre harm / as giltlees am I.
As is Maurice my sone / so lyk youre face
Ellis the feend / me fecche out of this place

Long was the sobbyng / and the bitter peyne
Er yt / hir woful hertes myghte cesse
Greet was the pitee / for to heere hem pleyne
Thurgh whiche pleintes / gan hir wo encresse
I pray yow / al my labour to relesse
I may nat telle hir wo / vn til to morwe
I am so wery / for to speke of sorwe

But finally / whan yt the sooth is wist
That Alla / giltlees was of hir wo
I trowe / an hundred tymes been they kist /
And swich a blisse / is ther bitwix hem two
That saue the ioye / yt lasteth eueremo
Ther is noon lyk / yt any creature
Hath seyn / or shal / whil yt the world may dure

Tho preyde she / hir housbond mekely
In relief / of hir longe pitous pyne
That he wolde praye / hir fader specially
That of his magestee / he wolde enclyne
To vouche sauf / som day with hym to dyne
She preyde hym eek / he sholde by no weye
Vn to hir fader / no word of hir seye

Som men wolde seyn / how yt the child Maurice
Dooth this message / vn to this Emperour
But as I gesse / Alla was noght so nyce
To hym / yt was / of so souereyn honour
As he yt is / of cristen folk the flour
Sente any child / but it is bet to deme
He wente hym self / and so it may wel seme

[...]s Emperour hath graunted gentilly
[.]o come to dyner as he hym bisoghte
And wel rede I he looked bisily
Vp on this child and on his doghter thoghte
Alla gooth to his In and as hym oghte
Arrayed for this feste in euery wise
As ferforth as his konnyng may suffise

¶ The morwe cam and Alla gan hym dresse
And eek his wyf this Emperour to meete
And forth they ryde in ioye and in gladnesse
And whan she say hir fader in the Strete
She lighte doun and falleth hym to feete
ffader quod she youre yonge child Custaunce
Is now ful clene out of youre remembraunce

¶ I am youre doghter Custance quod she
That whilom ye han sent vn to Surrye
It am I fader that in the salte see
Was put allone and dampned for to dye
Now goode fader mercy I yow crye
Sende me namoore vn to noon hethenesse
But thonke my lord heere of his kyndenesse

¶ Who kan the pitous ioye tellen al
Bitwix hem thre syn they be thus ymette
But of my tale make an ende I shal
The day goth faste I wol no lenger lette
This glade folk to dyner they hem sette
In ioye and blisse at mete I lete hem dwelle
A thousand fold wel moore than I kan telle

¶ This child Maurice was sithen Emperour
Maad by the Pope and lyued cristenly
To cristes chirche he dide greet honour
But I lete al this storie passen by
Of Custaunce is my tale specially
In the olde Romayn gestes may men fynde
Maurices lyf I bere it noght in mynde

This kyng Alla

	ELLESMERE
[¶Thi]s Emp*er*our / hath graunted gentilly	¶This
[T]o come to dyner / as he hym bisoghte	To dyner⁊ bisoughte
And wel rede I / he looked bisily	
Vp on this child / and on his doghter thoghte	
Alla gooth to his In / and as hym oghte	goth ogħte
Arrayed for this feste / in euery wise	
As ferforth / as his konnyng may suffise	konnyng⁊
¶The morwe cam / and Alla gan hym dresse	
And eek his wyf / this Emp*er*our to meete	
And forth they ryde / in Ioye and in gladnesse	ioye
And whan she say / hir fader in the Streete	saugħ / Strete
She lighte doun / and falleth hym to feete	
Fader quod she / youre yonge child Custaunce	Custance
Is now ful clene / out of youre remembraunce	remembrance
¶I am youre doghter Custance / quod she	I doghter / Custance
That whilom ye han sent⁊ / vn to Surrye	whilom / sent /
It am I fader / that in the salte See	see
Was put allone / and dampned for to dye	
Now goode fader / m*er*cy I yow crye	mercy
Seend me namoore / vn to noon hethenesse	Sende
But thonke my lord heere / of his kyndenesse	thonketh lord /
¶Who kan the pitous Ioye / tellen al	37 kan / ioye
Bitwix hem thre / syn they be thus ymette	Bitwixe been
But of my tale / make an ende I shal	
The day goth faste / I wol no lenger lette	
This glade folk⁊ to dyner they hem sette	folk /
In ioye and blisse / at mete I lete hem dwelle	
A thousand fold / wel moore than I kan telle	foold /
¶This child Maurice / was sithen Emp*er*our	
Maad by the Pope / and lyued cristenly	pope /
To cristes chirche / he dide greet honour	greet⁊
But I lete / al this storie passen by	lete al his storie
Of Custaunce / is my tale specially	Custance /
In the olde Romayn gestes / may men fynde	geestes /
Maurices lyf / I bere it noght in mynde	

This kyng⁊ Alla

[37] ¶Man *62v*

. The Man of Lawe .

	ELLESMERE
¶This kyng Alla / whan he his tyme say	
With his Custaunce / his holy wif so swete	Custance / hooly wyf sweete
To Engelond / been they come the righte way	Engelond /
Wher as they lyue / in ioye and in quiete	
But litel while it lasteth I yow heete	lasteth /
Ioye of this world / for tyme wol nat abyde	
Fro day to nyght it chaungeth as the tyde	nygħt / changeth
¶Who lyued eu*er*e / in swich delit / a day	Who euere / delit o day
That hym ne moeued / outher Conscience	conscience
Or Ire / or talent or som kyn affray	kynnes
Enuye / or pryde / or passion / or offence	pride /
I ne seye / but for this ende this sentence	
That litel while / in ioye / or in plesaunce	plesance
Lasteth the blisse of Alla with Custaunce	Custance
¶For deeth that taketh / of heigh and logh his rente	For deeth / heigħ logh /
Whan passed was a yeer / euene as I gesse	
Out of this world / this kyng Alla he hente	
For whom Custance / hath ful greet heuynesse	whom /
Now lat vs prayen god / his soule blesse	praye to god /
And dame Custance / fynally to seye	finally
Toward the town of Rome / gooth hir weye	toun goth
¶To Rome is come / this holy creature	hooly
And fyndeth hir freendes / hoole and sownde	hir*e* sounde
Now is she scaped / al hir auenture	hir*e*
And whan that she / hir fader hath yfownde	þ*a*t yfounde
Doun on hir knees / falleth [s]he to grownde	she grounde
Wepynge for tendrenesse / in herte blythe	blithe
She herieth god / an hondred thousand sythe	heryeth hundred sithe
¶In vertue / and holy alm*us*dede	[38] vertu hooly Almus
They lyuen alle / and neuere asonder wende	neu*er*e a sonder
Til deeth departeth hem / this lyf they lede	departed
And fareth now wel / my tale is at an ende	weel /
Now I*es*u crist that of his myght may sende	Crist mygħt
Ioye after wo / gouerne vs in his *gr*ace	gou*er*ne grace
And kepe vs alle / that been in this place Amen[39]	

¶Here is ended / the tale / of the man of Lawe

¶Heere endeth the tale / of the man of Lawe

1132 A mane vsque [ad vesperam mu]tabitur tempus t[enent tympan]um et gaudent ad so[num organi et cetera] Hg (defective) El

1136 Quis vnquam vnicam diem tota[m duxit] in sua dileccione iocundam quem [in ali]qua parte diei reatus consciencie [vel] impetus ire vel motus concupiscen[cie] non turbauerit quem liuor Inuidi[e] vel ardor auaricie vel tumor super[bie] non vexauerit quem aliqua iactura vel offensa vel passio non commonuerit et [cetera] Hg (defective) El

[38] ¶of Lawe *63r*

[39] *Out* Hg El 1163-1190. The Man of Law's Endlink is out in a number of MSS besides Hg and El, including Ad[3], En[1], Dd, and Gg. The Hg scribe left a blank verso (128v) for the lines when they were to become available. In all but two of the thirty-five MSS that contain the endlink, it occurs after the MLT. The following text is taken from Cp:

This kyng Alla whan he his tyme say
With his Custaunce his holy wif so swete
To Engelond been they come the righte way
Wher as they lyue in ioye and in quiete
But litel whil it lasteth I yow heete
Ioye of this world for tyme wol nat abyde
ffro day to nyght it chaungeth as the tyde

Who lyued euere in swich delit a day
That hym ne moeued outher conscience
Or Ire or talent or som kyn affray
Enuye or pryde or passion or offence
I ne seye but for this ende this sentence
That litel while in ioye or in plesaunce
Lasteth the blisse of Alla with Custaunce

ffor deeth that taketh of heigh and logh his rente
Whan passed was a yeer euene as I gesse
Out of this world this kyng Alla he hente
ffor whom Custance hath ful greet heuynesse
Now lat vs prayen god his soule blesse
And dame Custance fynally to seye
Toward the town of Rome gooth hir weye

To Rome is come this holy creature
And fyndeth hir freendes hoole and sounde
Now is she scaped al hir auenture
And whan that she hir fader hath yfounde
Doun on hir knees falleth she to grounde
Wepynge for tendrenesse in herte blythe
She heryeth god an hundred thousand sythe

In vertu and holy almus dede
They lyuen alle and neuere asonder wende
Til deeth departeth hem this lyf they lede
And fareth now wel my tale is at an ende
Now Ihu crist that of his myght may sende
Ioye after wo gouerne vs in his grace
And kepe vs alle that been in this place Amen

Here is ended the tale of the man of lawe

12[illegible]

A mane vsq[ue] [illegible]
tabit tempus [illegible]
in gaudent ad [illegible]

Quis vnq[ua]m vnica diem tot[am]
in sua delectac[i]o[n]e iocundam quem [illegible]
aliqua p[ar]te diei reat[us] conscientie [illegible]
impet[us] ire vel mot[us] concupiscen[tie]
no[n] turbauerit quem liuor inuid[ie]
vel ardor auaricie vel tumor sup[er]
bie non vexauerit quem aliqua iac
tura vel offensa vel passio non
commouerit &c

age
.an In tender, hath most In lore:
.th alwas to keepe he
in
..t:: Wherfore, age who greatly longes
.rnt to mowe: In youth he must aplye
.u self good seed to sowe ::: :

P. Ellen: Banester the grandmother
of the under named Children

Ellen Brereton was borne the 24 of Julij
beinge on wensday betwixt 4 & 5 of the clocke
In the after noone and in the year of
the Lords god 1605. And in the raigne
of Kinge James of England the thirde
Shee was borne at Newington beyond london

2 John Brereton was borne the fifte day
of desember on a fryday att tenn of
the clocke in the nyght in the yeare
of the lord 1606. Christened att
St Olloffes church in Chester

3 Francis Brereton Borne the 19 of
Jun on monday 2 of the clocke
in the after nowne att Llanbor
neare carnarvon 1609

Richard Brereton was born the 19 of August
on a monday att 3 of the clocke in the
after nowne att Llanbor — 1611

5 Ann Brereton borne the 14 of marche on
a Monday att eleven of the clocke in the
morninge in Llanbire — 1612

[. . . m]an In tender ⟨age⟩, hath most in v[e]re
[. . . d]eth alwas to keepe he [sh]
[. . .]re : : wherfore ⟨in⟩ age who greatly longes
[. . . f]rut to mowe: In youth he must aplye
[. . . y]m self good seed to sowe : : :

per Ellenor Banestor the graundmother
of this vndernamed ⟨Children⟩

[1] Ellen Brereton was Borne. the 24. of Julij
Beinge on wensday Betwixt 4. & .5. of the Clocke
In the after noown and in the year of
the Lord god. 1605. And in the rainge.
of Kinge James of England the threed.
Shee was Borne at Newington. Behond London.

John Brereton was borne the fifte day
2 of desember on a fryday att tenn of
the clocke in the nighte in the yeare
of the Lord. 1606. Christened att
St Petteres Churche in Chester

Frances Brereton Borne the 19 of
3 Jun on monday 2 of the cloke
in the after nowne. att llanver
neare carnarvon. 1609

Richard Brereton was born the 19 of August
4 on a mondey att 3. of the Cloke in the
after nown att llanver—1611

5 Ann Brereton: borne the 14 of marche on
a Sonday att seven of the cloke in the
morninge in llanvire—1612

Owre oost vpon his stiropes stood anoon
And seyde goode men herkeneþ eu*er*ych on
This was a thrifty tale for þe nones
Sire parissche prest q*uo*d he for goddes boones
Telle vs a tale as was þi forward yore
I se wel þ*a*t ye lerned men in loore
Can moche good by goddes dignete
The p*er*sou*n* him answerde benedicite
What eyleþ þe man so synfully to swere /
Oure ost answerde. O Ianekyn be ye þere
I smelle a lollere in þe wynd quod he
How goode men q*uo*d oure host herkeneþ me
Abydeþ for goddes digne passiou*n*
For we schal han a predicaciou*n*
This lollere heer wil prechen vs som what
Nay by my fader soule þ*a*t schal he nat
Seyde þe Esquier heer schal he nat preche
He schal no gospel glosen here ne teche
He leueþ att in þe grete god he
He wolde sowen som difficulte
Or springen Cokkel in oure clene corn
And þ*er*fore oost I warne þe biforn /
My Ioly body schal a tale telle
And I schal clynken ȝou so mery a belle
That I schal waken al þis compaignie
But it schal not ben of philosophie
Ne Phislyas ne termes queinte of lawe
Ther is but litel latyn in my mawe

1179 Esquier) sompnour Ha^{4}; Shipman Se

¶Here bigynneth / the Squiers tale[1]	¶Heere bigynneth / the Squieres tale[2]
AT Sarray / in the land of Tartarye	
Ther dwelte a kyngꝭ that werreyed Russye	
Thurgh which / ther deyde many a doghty man	Thurgħ which dyde / doughty
This noble kyngꝭ was clepid Kambyuskan	cleped Cambyuskan
Which in his tyme / was of so greet renoun	renou*n*
That ther nas nowher in no Regioun	ther was / nowher Regiou*n*
So excellent a lord / in alle thyngꝭ	
Hym lakked noghtꝭ þ*at* longed to a kyngꝭ	noghtꝭ that longeth
As of the secte / of which þ*at* he was born	And of
He kepte his lay / to which þ*at* he was sworn	
And ther to / he was hardy / wys / and riche	wys
Pietous and Iustꝭ and eu*er*emoore yliche	And pitous Iustꝭ alwey yliche
Sooth of his word / benigne and honurable	hon*ur*able
Of his corage / as any Centre stable ¶Centru*m* circuli	¶Centru*m* circuli]
Yongꝭ fressħ / and strongꝭ in armes desirous	fressħ / strongꝭ and in Armes
As any Bachilerꝭ of al his hous	Bacheler /
A fair p*er*sone he was / and fortunatꝭ	
And kepte alwey / so wel Roial estatꝭ	roial
That ther nas no wher / swich another man	ther was nowher /
¶This noble kyng / this Tartre Cambyuskan	kyngꝭ
Hadde two sones / on Elfeta his wyfꝭ	Elpheta wyf
Of whiche / the eldeste highte Algarsyf /	highte Algarsyfꝭ
That oother sone / was clepid Cambalo	cleped
A doghter hadde / this worthy kyng also	
That yongestꝭ was / and highte Canacee	highte
But for to telle yow / al hir beautee	
It lyth nat in my tonge / nyn my konnyngꝭ	
I dar nat vndertake / so heigh a thyngꝭ	natꝭ heigħ
Myn englyssħ eek / is insufficientꝭ	englissħ eekꝭ
It moste been / a Rethor excellentꝭ	I moste
That koude his colours / longyngꝭ for that Artꝭ	hise longynge
If he sholde hir*e* / discryuen euery partꝭ	he / hir*e*
I am noon swich / I moot speke as I kan	
And so bifel / that whan this Kambyuskan	¶And Cambyuskan
Hath .xx. wynter / born his dyademe	twenty diademe
As he was wontꝭ fro yeer to yeer I deme	

[1] That Chaucer clearly intended the SqT to follow immediately after the MerT is evident in El, Ad[3], Ch, Dd, Ha[4], and others. A long form of the Mer-Sq Link occurs in El; however, in Hg the link is placed between the Mer-FrankT with minor emendations to accommodate this placement, e.g., in fragment F-1 Hg reads "Sire Frankeleyn" instead of "Squier." See below, *153r*.

[2] On *115v*. Miniature of the Squire in left margin.

Heere bigynneth the Squyers tale

At Sarray in the land of Tartarye
Ther dwelte a kyng that werreyed Russye
Thurgh which ther dyde many a doghty man
This noble kyng was clepyd Cambyuskan
Which in his tyme was of so greet renoun
That ther nas nowher in no regioun
So excellent a lord in alle thyng
Hym lakked noght þt longed to a kyng
As of the secte of which þt he was born
He kepte his lay to which þt he was sworn
And ther to he was hardy wys and riche
Pitous and Iust and euere moore yliche
Sooth of his word benigne and honurable
Of his corage as any centre stable — Centrum circuli
Yong fressh and strong in armes desirous
As any bacheler of al his hous
A fair persone he was and fortunat
And kepte alwey so wel roial estat
That ther nas nowher swich another man
This noble kyng this Tartre Cambyuskan
Hadde two sones on Elpheta his wyf
Of whiche the eldeste highte Algarsyf
That oother sone was cleped Camballo
A doghter hadde this worthy kyng also
That yongest was and highte Canacee
But for to telle yow al hir beautee
It lyth nat in my tonge nyn my konnyng
I dar nat vnder take so heigh a thyng
Myn englissh eek is insufficient
It moste been a rethor excellent
That koude his colours longyng for that art
If he sholde hire discryuen euery part
I am noon swich I moot speke as I kan
And so bifel that whan this Cambyuskan
Hath .xx. wynter born his dyademe
As he was wont fro yeer to yeer I deme

[illegible] the feste of his Natiuitee
[illegible] cryen thurgh out Sarray his Citee
The laste Idus of March / after the yeer
Phebus the sonne ful Ioly was and cleer
ffor he was nygh his exaltacioun
In Martes face / and his mansioun
In Aries the Colerik hote signe
fful lusty was the weder and benygne
ffor which the foweles agayn the sonne shene
What for the seson / and the yonge grene
fful loude songen / hir affeccions
Hem semed / han geten hem proteccions
Agayn the swerd of wynter / kene and cold
This Cambynskan / of which I haue yow told
In Roial vestyment / sit on his deys
With dyademe / ful hye in his paleys
And halt his feste / so solempne and so riche
That in this world / ne was ther noon it liche
Of which / if I shal tellen al tharay
Thanne wolde it occupie / a somers day
And eek it nedeth nat to deuyse
At euery cours / the ordre of hir seruyse
I wol nat tellen / of hir straunge sewes
Ne of hir swannes / ne of hir heron sewes
Eek in that land / as tellen knyghtes olde
Ther is som mete / þt is ful deyntee holde
That in this land / men recche of it but smal
Ther nys no man / þt may reporten al
I wol nat taryen yow / for it is pryme
And for it is no fruyt / but los of tyme
Vn to my firste / I wol haue my recours
And so bifel / þt after the thridde cours
Whil þt this kyng / sit thus / in his nobleye
Herkynge his mynstrals / hir thynges pleye
Biforn hym at the bord / deliciously
In at the halle dore / al sodeynly
Ther cam a knyght / vp on a steede of bras
And in his hand / a brood myrour of glas
Vp on his thombe / he hadde of gold a ryng /
And by his syde / a naked swerd hangyng /

	ELLESMERE
[He leet] the feste / of his Natiuitee	He leet' feeste /
[Don] crien / thurgh out Sarray his Citee	Doon cryen / thurgħ Sarray
The laste Idus of Marcħ / after the yeer	
Phebus the sonne / ful iolyf was and cleer	Sonne / ioly
For he was ny his exaltaciou*n*	was / neigħ
In Martes face / and his mansiou*n*	and in his
In Aries / the Coleryk hote signe	3 colerik / hoote
Ful lusty was the weder / and benygne	was / weder benigne
For which the foweles / agayn the sonne shene	sheene
What for the sesou*n* / and the yonge grene	
Ful loude songen / hir affeccions	loude / songen hir*e* affecciou*n*s
Hem semed / han geten hem p*ro*teccions	protecciou*n*s
Agayn the swerd of wynter / kene and cold	keene coold'
¶This Cambyuskan / of which I haue yow told	toold'
In Roial vestyment' sit on his deys	roial vestiment'
With dyademe / ful hye in his paleys	diademe / heighe
And halt his feste / solempne and so riche	feeste ⟨so⟩ solempne / ryche
That in this world / ne was ther noon it liche	world / was lyche
Of which / if I shal tellen al tharray	
Thanne wolde it ocupie / a som*er*es day	it' occupie
And eek' it nedeth nat' to deuyse	eek / nat' for to
At eu*ery* cours / the ordre of hir seruyse	hir*e*
I wol nat tellen / of hir straunge sewes	strange
Ne of hir swannes / ne of hir herou*n* sewes	swannes / nor of hir*e* heronsewes
Eek in that land / as tellen knyghtes olde	Eek / lond / knygħtes
Ther is som mete / þ*at* is ful deyntee holde	deynte
That in this land / men recche of it but smal	lond /
Ther nys no man / þ*at* may reporten al	that
I wol nat tarien yow / for it is pryme	¶I taryen
And for it is no fruyt' but los of tyme	
Vn to my firste / I wol haue my recours	wole
¶And so bifel / þ*at* after the thridde Cours	that cours
Whil þ*at* this kyng' sit thus / in his nobleye	thus
Herknynge his Mynstrals / hir thynges pleye	hise
Biforn hym at the bord / deliciously	
In at the halle dore / al sodeynly	
Ther cam a knyght' vp on a steede of bras	knygħt'
And in his hand / a brood Mirour of glas	
Vp on his thombe / he hadde / of gold a ryng'	Vpon hadde ryng /
And by his syde / a naked swerd hangyng'	

[3] ¶Squier *116r*

ELLESMERE

And vp he rydeth / to the heighe bord
In al the halle / ne was ther spoke a word
For m*er*ueille of this knyght hym to biholde
Ful bisily / they wayten / yonge and olde
¶This straunge knyght that cam thus sodeynly
Al armed saue his heed / ful richely
Salueth kyng and queene / and lordes alle
By ordre / as they seten in the halle
With so heigh reue*r*ence / and obeisau*n*ces
As wel in his speche / as in his contenau*n*ces
That Gawayn / with his olde curteisye
Thogh he were come agayn / out of Fairye
Ne koude hym nat amende / with a word
And after this / biforn the hye bord
He with a manly voys / seyde his message
After the forme / vsed in his langage
With outen vice / of silable / or of lettre
And for his tale / sholde seme the bettre
Acordant to his wordes / was his cheere
As techeth art of speche / hem þ*at* it leere
Al be / þ*at* I kan nat sowne / his style
Ne kan nat clymben / ouer so heigh a style
Yet seye I this / þ*at* as to co*m*mune entente
Thus muche amounteth / al that eu*er*e he mente
If it so be / þ*at* I haue it in my mynde
¶He seyde / the kyng of Arabe / and of Inde
My lige lord / on this solempne day
Salueth yow / as he best kan and may
And sendeth yow / in honour of youre feste
By me / that am al redy / at youre heste
This Steede of bras / that esily and weel
Kan in the space / of o day naturel
This is to seyn / in .xxiiij. houres
Wher so yow list / in droghte / or ellis shoures
Beren youre body / in to euery place
To which youre herte / wilneth for to pace
With outen wem of yow / thurgh foul or fair
Or if yow list to flee as hye in the Ayr
As dooth an Egle / whan hym list to soore
This same Steede / shal bere yow eu*er*emoore

rideth / heighe bord
spoken word

bisily / ther wayten
strange knyght
armed /
Saleweth

heigh reuerence / obeisau*n*ce
in speche / in contenau*n*ce

Though were / comen ayeyn
amende word
heighe bord
4 seith

Accordant hise wordes /
art
that sowne stile
ou*er* heigh
this / as
þ*at*
in mynde
Arabe

Saleweth
youre feeste
redy youre heeste

natureel
foure and twenty
lyst droghte elles

thurgh
lyst fleen / Air
whan þ*at* hym
eu*er*e moore

115 Of the vertu of the steede of bras El

[4] ¶Squier *116v*

And vp he rydeth to the heighe bord
In al the halle ne was ther spoke a word
ffor merueille of this knyght / hym to biholde
Ful bisily they wayten yonge and olde
This straunge knyght / that cam thus sodeynly
Al armed saue his heed / ful richely
Salueth kyng and queene / and lordes alle
By ordre as they seten in the halle
With so heigh reuerence and obeisaunce
As wel in his speche as in his contenaunce
That Gawayn with his olde curteisye
Though he were come agayn / out of ffayrye
Ne koude hym nat amende with a word
And after this biforn the hye bord
He with a manly voys seyde his message
After the forme vsed in his langage
With outen vice of sillable or of lettre
And for his tale / sholde seme the bettre
Acordant to his wordes was his cheere
As techeth art / of speche / hem þt it leere
Al be þt I kan nat sowne his style
Ne kan nat clymben ouer so heigh a style
Yet seye I this þt as to commune entente
Thus muche amounteth / al that euere he mente
If it so be þt I haue it in my mynde
He seyde / the kyng of Arabe and of Inde
My lige lord / on this solempne day
Salueth yow / as he best kan and may
And sendeth yow in honour of youre feste
By me that am al redy / at youre heste
This steede of bras / that esily and weel
Kan in the space of o day natureel
This is to seyn / in ·xxiiij· houres
Wher so yow list in droghte / or ellis shoures
Beren youre body / in to euery place
To which youre herte wilneth for to pace
With outen wem of yow / thurgh foul or fair
Or if yow list / to flee as hye in the air
As dooth an Egle / whan hym list to soore
This same steede / shal bere yow euere moore

outen harm / til ye be ther yow leste
ough þt ye slepen / on his bak or reste
And turne agayn / with writhyng of a pyn
He þt it wroghte / koude many a gyn
He wayted / many a constellacion
Er he hadde doon / this operacion
And knew ful many a seel / and many a bond
¶ This mirour eek / that I have in myn hond
Hath swich a myght / þt men may in it see
Whan ther shal fallen / any adversitee
Un to youre regne / or to your self also
And openly / who is youre freend or fo
¶ And over al this / if any lady bright
Hath set hir herte / on any maner wight
If he be fals / she shal his trayson see
His newe love / and al his subtiltee
So openly / þt ther shal no thyng hyde
Wher fore / agayn this lusty somers tyde
This mirour and this ryng / þt ye may see
He hath sent / to my lady Canacee
Youre excellente doghter / þt is heere
¶ The vertu of the ryng / if ye wol heere
Is this / þt if hir list it for to were
Up on hir thombe / or in hir purs it bere
Ther nys no fowel / þt fleeth under the hevene
That she ne shal wel / understonde his stevene
And knowe his menyng / openly and pleyn
And answere hym / in his langage ageyn
And every gras / þt groweth up on roote
She shal eek knowe / and whom it wol doon boote
Al be his woundes / never so depe and wyde
¶ This naked swerd / þt hangeth by my syde
Swich vertu hath / þt what man so ye smyte
Thurgh out his armure / it wol kerve and byte
Were it as thikke / as is a braunched ook
And what man / þt is wounded wt the strook
Shal nevere be hool / til þt yow list of grace
To stroke hym with the platte / in thilke place
Ther he is hurt / this is as muche to seyn
Ye moote / with the platte swerd ageyn

	ELLESMERE
[With] outen harm / til ye be ther yow leste	With
[Th]ough *pat* ye slepen / on his bak / or reste	Though that bak
[A]nd turne agayn / with writhyng of a pyn	And ayeyn / writhyng
He *pat* it wroghte / koude many a gyn	koude ful many
He wayted / many a constellacioun	
Er he hadde doon / this op*er*aciou*n*	he / had
And knew ful many a seel / and many a bond	bond
¶This Mirour eek / that I haue in myn hond	*pat* hond
Hath swich a myght *pat* men may in it see	myght /
Whan ther shal fallen / any adu*er*sitee	
Vn to youre regne / or to your sel also	your*e* youre self
And openly / who is youre freend / or fo	youre freend foo
¶And ouer al this / if any lady bright	ou*er* bright
Hath set hir herte / on any maner wight	hir*e* herte / in any wight
If he be fals / she shal his trayson see	tresou*n*
His newe loue / and al his subtiltee	
So openly / *pat* ther shal no thyng hyde	
Wher fore / agayn this lusty som*er*es tyde	Wherfore / ageyn
This Mirour and this ryng / *pat* ye may see	Mirour / ryng
He hath sent to my lady Canacee	sent vn to
Youre excellente doghter / *pat* is heere [hic]	Your*e* doghter that
¶The v*er*tu of the ryng if ye wol heere [audire]	
Is this / *pat* if hir list it for to were	5 that hire lust
Vp on hir thombe / or in hir purs it bere	
Ther nys no fowel / *pat* fleeth vnder the heuene	Ther is no
That she ne shal wel / vnderstonde his steuene	she / shal / wel
And knowe his menyng openly and pleyn	
And answere hym / in his langage ageyn	
And euery gras / *pat* groweth vp on roote	eu*er*y that
She shal eek knowe / and whom it wol doon boote	do
Al be his woundes / neuer so depe and wyde	hise neu*er*
¶This naked swerd / *pat* hangeth by my syde	swerd /
Swich v*er*tu hath / *pat* what man so ye smyte	
Thurgh out his armure / it wol kerue and byte	Thurgh Arm*ure* / wole hym kerue
Were it as thikke / as is a braunched ook	branched
And what man / *pat* is wounded w*ith* the strook	that w*ith* a strook
Shal neuere be hool / til *pat* yow lust of grace	neu*er* list
To stroke hym with the platte / in thilke place	w*ith* plat in that place
Ther he is hurt this is as muche to seyn	hurt /
Ye moote / with the platte swerd ageyn	plat

132 Of the vertu of the Mirour El
146 Of the vertu of the ryng El
156 Of the vertu of the swerd El

[5] ¶Squier *117r*

	ELLESMERE
Stroke hym in the wounde / and it wol close	Strike hym
This is a verray sooth / with outen glose	v*er*ray
It failleth nat / whiles it is in youre hold	nat whils hoold
And whan this knyght hath thus his tale ytold	¶And knyght toold
He rideth out of halle / and doun he lighte	lighte
¶His Steede which *þat* shoon / as sonne brighte	His steede / brighte
Stant in the Court stille as any stoon	court
This knyght is to his chambre lad anon	knyght anoon
And is vnarmed / and to mete yset	and vn to
The pr*es*entz / been ful realliche yfet	¶The pr*es*entes / been / roially
This is to seyn / the swerd and the Mirour	
And born anon / in to the heighe tour	heighe Tour
With c*er*tein Officers / ordeyned ther fore	c*er*teine officers / therfore
And vn to Canacee / the ryng is bore	Canacee / this ryng was bore
Solempnely / ther she sit at the table	sit /
But sikerly / with outen any fable	
The hors of bras / *þat* may nat been remewed	be remewed
It stant as it were / to the ground yglewed	yglewed
Ther may no man / out of the place it dryue	
For noon engyn / of wyndas or polyue	wyndas ne polyue
And cause why / for they kan nat the craft	why∫ /
And ther fore / in the place / they han it laft	therfore / it laft /
Til *þat* the knyght hath taught hem the manere	knyght taught
To voyden hym / as ye shal after heere	
¶Greet was the prees / that swarmeth to and fro	Greet *þat*
To gauren on this hors / that stondeth so	
For it so heigh was / and so brood and long	heigh
So wel p*ro*porcioned / for to ben strong	been
Right as it were / a Steede of lumbardye	Right Lumbardye
Ther with so horsly / and so quyk of eye	
As it a gentil Poyleys courser weere	6 Poilleys Courser were
For c*er*tes / fro his tayl / vn to his eere	ere
Nature / ne art ne koude hym nat amende	Nature Art
In no degree / as al the peple wende	
¶But eu*er*e moore / hir mooste wonder was	But eu*er*emoore /
How *þat* it koude goon / and was of bras	go /
It was a Fairye / as the peple semed	as al the
Dyuerse folk dyu*er*sely han demed	Diu*er*se folk / diuersely they demed
As many heuedes / as many wittes ther been	heddes / manye wittes
They murmured / as dooth a swarm of been	murm*ur*eden / Been

6 ¶Squier *117v*

Smyte hym in the wounde / and it wol close
This is a verray sooth / with outen glose
It failleth nat / whiles it is in youre hold
And whan this knyght / hath thus his tale ytold
He rideth out of halle / and doun he lighte
His steede which þt shoon / as sonne brighte
Stant in the court / stille as any stoon
This knyght / is to his chambre lad anon
And is vnarmed / and to mete yset /
The presentz / been ful realliche yfet /
This is to seyn / the swerd and the mirour
And born anon / in to the heighe tour
With certein officers / ordeyned ther fore
And vn to Canacee / the ryng is bore
Solempnely / ther she sit / at the table
But sikerly / with outen any fable
The hors of bras / þt may nat been remewed
It stant / as it were / to the ground yglewed
Ther may no man / out of the place it dryue
For noon engyn / of wyndas or polyue
And cause why / for they kan nat the craft /
And ther fore / in the place / they han it laft /
Til þt the knyght / hath taught hem the manere
To voyden hym / as ye shal after heere
Greet was the prees / that swarmeth to and fro
To gauren on this hors / that stondeth so
For it so heigh was / and so brood and long /
So wel proporcioned / for to ben strong /
Right as it were / a steede of lumbardye
Ther with so horsly / and so quyk of eye
As it a gentil Poilleys courser were
For certes / fro his tayl / vn to his ere
Nature / ne art / ne koude hym nat amende
In no degree / as al the peple wende
But euere moore / hir mooste wonder was
How þt it koude goon / and was of bras
It was a fairye / as the peple semed
Diuerse folk / diuersely han demed
So many heuedes / as manye wittes ther been
They murmured / as dooth a swarm of been

They maden skiles after hir fantasies
Rehersynge of thise olde poetries
And seyden it was lyk the Pegasee .i. equus pegaseus.
The hors þt hadde wynges for to flee
Or ellis it was the Grekys hors Synon
That broghte Troye to destruccion
As men in thise olde gestes rede
Myn herte quod oon is euere moore in drede
I trowe som men of armes been ther Inne
That shapen hem this Citee for to wynne
It were right good þt al swich thyng were knowe
Another rowned to his felawe lowe
And seyde he lyeth for it is rather lyk
An apparence ymaad by som magyk
As Iogelours pleyen at thise festes grete
Of sondry doutes thus they Iangle and trete
As lewed peple demeth comunly
Of thynges þt been moore maad subtilly
Than they kan in hir lewednesse comprehende
They demen gladly to the badder ende
And somme of hem wondren on the mirour
That born was vp in to the maister tour
How men myghte in it swiche thynges se
Another answerde and seyde it myghte wel be
Naturelly by composiciouns
Of anglis and of sly reflexiouns
And seiden þt in Rome was swich oon
They speke of Alocen and Vitulon
Of Aristotle þt writen in hir lyues
Of queynte mirours and of perspectiues
As knowen they þt han hir bookes herd
And oother folk han wondred on the swerd
That wolde percen thurgh out euery thyng
And fille in speche of Thelophus the kyng
And of Achilles for his queynte spere
For he koude with it bothe heele and dere
Right in swich wise as men may with the swerd
Of which right now ye han youre seluen herd
They speke of sondry hardyng of metal
And speke of medicynes ther with al

[And] maden skiles / after hir fantasies	And
[R]ehersynge / of thise olde Poetries	Rehersynge / poetries
And seyden / it was lyk the Pegasee .i. equs Pegaseus	seyde / that it [¶.i. equs Pegaseus]
The hors / *pa*t hadde wynges for to flee	
Or ellis it was / the Grekys hors Synou*n*	elles / was Grekes
That broghte Troye / to destruccciou*n*	broghte Troie
As men / in thise olde gestes rede	geestes
¶Myn herte quod oon / is eu*er*e moore in drede	eu*er*emoore
I trowe / som men of armes been ther Inne	Armes therInne
That shapen hem / this Citee for to wynne	
It were right good / *pa*t al swich thyng were knowe	right
¶Another rowned / to his felawe lowe	
And seyde he lyeth / for it is rather lyk	lyeth / it
An apparence / ymaad by som magyk	Magyk
As Iogelours pleyen / at thise festes grete	feestes
Of sondry doutes / thus they iangle and trete	Iangle *and*
As lewed peple / demeth comunly	
Of thynges / *pa*t been moore maad subtilly	been maad / moore subtilly
Than they kan / in hir lewednesse co*m*p*re*hende	
They demen gladly / to the badder ende	
¶And so*m*me of hem / wondren on the Mirour	wondred
That born was vp / vn to the maister tour	vp / in to the hye tour
How men myghte in it / swiche thynges se	Hou
¶Another answerde / and seyde it myghte wel be	myghte
Naturelly / by composicions /	composiciou*n*s
Of Anglis / and of sly reflexions	slye reflexiou*n*s
And seiden / *pa*t in Rome was swich oon	seyden /
They speke of Alocen / and Vitulon	speken / Alocen Vitulon
Of Aristotle / *pa*t writen in hir lyues	And Aristotle / that
Of queynte Mirours / and of p*er*spectyues	p*er*spectiues
As knowen they / *pa*t han hir bookes herd	that herd
¶And oother folk / han wondred on the swerd	folk swerd
That wolde p*er*cen / thurgh out eu*er*y thyng	thurgh euery
And fille in speche / of Thelophus the kyng	
And of Achilles / for his queynte spere	Achilles / with his
For he koude with it / bothe heele and dere	it
Right in swich wise / as men may / with the swerd	Right may wi*th* swerd
Of which right now / ye han your seluen herd	right youre herd
¶They speeke / of sondry hardyng of metal	7 They speken / hardyng
And speke of medicynes / ther with al	

7 ¶Squier *118r*

	ELLESMERE
And how / and whanne / it sholde yharded be	how
Which is vnknowe / algates vn to me	vnto
¶Tho speeke they / of Canacees ryng⁊	
And seyden alle / þ*at* swich a wonder thyng⁊	
Of craft of rynges / herde they neu*er*e non	craft⁊ noon
Saue þ*at* he Moyses / and kyng Salomon	kyng⁊ Salomon̄
Hadde a name of konnyng⁊ in swich art⁊	Art⁊
Thus seyn the peple / and drawen hem a part⁊	apart⁊
¶But nathelees / somme seyden þ*at* it was	seiden
Wonder / to maken of fern asshen glas	maken / Asshen
And yet is glas / nat lyk asshen of fern	yet nys glas / lyk⁊ Asshen
But for they han / knowen it so fern	
Therfore / cesseth hir Ianglyng and hir wonder	cesseth / Ianglyng⁊ *and*
¶As soore wondren so*m*me / on cause of thonder	
On ebbe and flood / on gossom*er* / and on myst⁊	ebbe / on flood /
And alle thyng⁊ til þ*at* the cause is wist⁊	wyst⁊
Thus Ianglen they / and demen and deuyse	Iangle
Til that the kyng⁊ gan fro the bord aryse	þ*at*
¶Phebus hath laft⁊ the angle Meridional	**P**hebus / Angle meridional
And yet⁊ ascendyng is / the beest roial	yet ascendynge / was the
The gentil leon / with his Aldiran	leou*n* / Aldrian[8]
Whan þ*at* this tartre kyng Cambyuskan	Tartre kyng⁊ Cambyuskan̄
Roos fro his bord / ther as he sat ful hye	ther that he
Biforn hym gooth / the loude Mynstralcye	Toforn hym
Til he cam / to his chambre of parementz	
There as ther sownen / diu*er*se Instrumentz	Ther as they sownen /
That it is lyk / an heuene for to heere	is / lyk
Now dauncen / lusty Venus children deere	
For in the fissħ / hir lady sat ful hye	fyssħ /
And looketh on hem / with a freendly eye	
¶This noble kyng⁊ is set vp on his trone	vp in his Trone
This straunge knyght⁊ is fet to hym ful soone	strange
And on the daunce he gooth / with Canacee	daunce / gooth
Here is / the reuel / and the Iolitee	Heere is
That is nat able / a dul man to deuyse	
He moste han knowe / loue and his seruyse	knowen /
And been a festlich man / as fressħ as May	feestlych
That sholde yow deuysen / swich array	yow / deuysen
¶Who koude telle yow / the forme daunces	forme of daunces
So vnkouthe / and swiche fresshe contenaunces	and so fressħe

[8]'aldiran': in another hand in right margin of El.

And how and whanne / it sholde yharded be
Which is vnknowe / algates vn to me
¶ Tho speeke they / of Canacees ryng/
And seyden alle / þt swich a wonder thyng/
Of craft of rynges / herde they neuere non
Saue þt he Moyses / and kyng Salomon
Hadde a name of konnyng / in swich art/
Thus seyn the peple / and drawen hem apart/
¶ But nathelees / somme seyden þt it was
Wonder / to maken of fern asshen glas
And yet is glas / nat lyk asshen of fern
But for they han / knowen it so fern
Therfore / cesseth hir Janglyng and hir wonder
¶ As soore wondren somme / on cause of thonder
On ebbe and flood / on gossomer / and on myst/
And alle thyng / til þt the cause is wist/
Thus janglen they / and demen and deuyse
Til that the kyng / gan fro the bord aryse
¶ Phebus hath laft / the angle meridional
And yet / ascendyng is / the beest roial
The gentil leon / with his Aldyran
Whan þt this tartre kyng Cambyuskan
Roos fro his bord / ther as he sat ful hye
Biforn hym gooth / the loude mynstralcye
Til he cam / to his chambre of parementz
Ther as they sownen / diuerse instrumentz
That it is lyk / an heuene for to heere
Now dauncen / lusty Venus children deere
ffor in the fissh / hir lady sat ful hye
And looketh on hem / with a freendly eye
¶ This noble kyng / is set vp on his trone
This straunge knyght / is fet to hym ful soone
And on the daunce he gooth / with Canacee
Heere is the reuel / and the Iolitee
That is nat able / a dul man to deuyse
He moste han knowe / loue and his seruyse
And been a festlich man / as fressh as May
That sholde yow deuysen / swich array
¶ Who koude telle yow / the forme of daunces
So vnkouthe / and swiche fresshe contenaunces

Swich subtil lookyng and dissimulynges
ffor drede of Jalous mennes aperceyuynges
No man but launcelot and he is deed
Ther fore I passe of al this lustiheed
I sey namoore but in this Iolynesse
I lete hem til men to the soup dresse
¶ The Styward byt Spices for to hye
And eek the wyn in al this melodye
The usshers and the Squyers been ygon
The Spices and the wyn is come anon
They ete and drynke and whan this hadde an ende
Vn to the temple as reson was they wende
¶ The seruyce doon they soupen al by day
What nedeth yow rehercen hir array
Ech man woot wel þt at a kynges feste
Hath plentee to the meeste and to the leeste
And deyntees mo than been in my knowyng
At after soup gooth this noble kyng
To seen this hors of bras with al a route
Of lordes and of ladyes hym aboute
¶ Swich wondryng was ther on this hors of bras
That syn the grete sege of Troye was
Ther as men wondreden on an hors also
Ne was ther swich a wondryng as was tho
But fynally the kyng axeth this knyght
The vertu of this courser and the myght
And preyed hym to telle his gouernaunce
¶ This hors anon gan for to trippe and daunce
Whan þt this knyght leyde hand vp on his reyne
And seyde sire ther nys namoore to seyne
But whan yow list to ryden any where
Ye moten trille a pyn stant in his ere
Which I shal yow telle bitwixe vs two
Ye mote nempne hym to what place also
Or to what contree þt yow list to ryde
And whan ye come ther as yow list abyde
Byd hym descende and trille another pyn
ffor ther Inne lyth theffect of al the gyn
And he wol doun descende and doon youre wille
And in that place he wol abiden stille

	ELLESMERE
[Sw]ich subtil lookyngʼ and dissimulynges	Swich dissymulynges
For drede / of Ialous mennes ap*er*ceyuynges	Ialouse ap*er*ceyuynges /
No man but launcelotʼ and he is deed	
Ther fore I passe / of al this lustiheed	Therfore lustiheedʼ
I sey namoore / but in this Iolynesse	
I lete hem / til men / to the soup*er* dresse	men soper
¶The Styward / byt Spices for to hye	9 Stywardʼ bitʼ
And eek the wyn / in al this melodye	
The Vsshers / and the Squyers / been ygon	Vsshers / Squiers ygoon
The Spices and the wyn / is come anon	wyn anoon
They ete and drynke / and whan this hadde an ende	
Vn to the temple / as reson was they wende	
¶The seruyce doon / they soupen al by day	seruice
What nedeth yow / rehercen hir array	nedeth me / rehercen hir*e*
Ech man woot wel / þ*at* at a kynges feste	þ*at* a feeste
Hath plentee / to the meeste / and to the leeste	mooste
And deyntees / mo than been in my knowyngʼ	mo /
At after soup*er* / gooth this noble kyngʼ	soper /
To seen this hors of bras / with al a route	w*ith* al the route
Of lordes / and of ladyes / hym aboute	ladyes
¶Swich wondryng was ther / on this hors of bras	wondryngʼ ther
That syn the grete sege / of Troye was	Troie
Ther as men wondreden / on an hors also	10
Ne was ther / swich a wondryngʼ as was tho	ther
But finally / the kyng axeth this knyghtʼ	fynally / kyngʼ knyghtʼ
The v*er*tu of this Courser / and the myghtʼ	vertu myghtʼ
And preyed hym / to telle his goue*r*naunce	preyde goue*r*nau*n*ce
¶This hors anon / gan for to trippe and daunce	anoon / bigan to dau*n*ce
Whan þ*at* this knyghtʼ leyde hand vp on his reyne	that knyghtʼ
And seyde sire / ther nys namoore to seyne	ther is namoore
But whan yow listʼ to ryden any where	
Ye moten trille a pyn / stant in his ere	mooten
Which I shal yow telle / bitwixe vs two	bitwix
Ye mote nempne hym / to what place also	moote
Or to what contree / þ*at* yow list to ryde	
And whan ye come / ther as yow list abyde	
Byd hym descende / and tryl another pyn	Bidde trille
For ther Inne lyth / theffect of al the gyn	ther lith / theffectʼ
And he wol doun descende / and doon youre wille	
And in that place / he wol abiden stille	wol stonde stille

[9] ¶Squier *118v*

[10] In El, 307-308 reversed, labeled .b. and .a. in left margin.

	ELLESMERE
Theigh al the world / the cont*ra*rie hadde yswore	Thougħ
He shal nat thennes / be ydrawe nor ybore	been
Or if yow list / bidde hym thennes gon	list goon
Trille this pyn / and he wol vanysshe anon	vanysshe anoon
Out of the sighte / of euery maner wight	sighte / wight
And come agayn / be it day or nyght	nyght
Whan *pa*t yow list to clepen hym ageyn	⟨to⟩
In swich a gyse / as I shal to yow seyn	
Bitwixen yow and me / and that ful soone	Bitwixe
Ryd whan yow lust ther is namoore to doone	Ride list
¶Enformed / whan the kyng was of that knyght	was / knyght
And hath conceyued / in his wit aright	aright
The manere / and the forme / of al this thyng	
Ful glad and blythe / this noble doghty kyng	Thus glad blithe / noble kyng
Repeireth to his reuel / as biforn	11
The brydel is / vn to the tour yborn	¶The brydel /
And kept among his Iewels / lief and deere	among hise Iueles / leeue *and*
The hors vanysshed / I noot in which manere	vanysshed / I noot / in what manere
Out of hir sighte / ye gete namoore for me	namoore of me
But thus I lete / in lust and Iolitee	lust
This Cambyuskan / his lordes festeyynge	hise festeiynge
Til wel neigh / the day bigan to sprynge	ny /
¶Explicit prima pars	¶Explicit prima pars
¶Incipit pars secunda	¶Sequit*ur* pars secunda
The norice of digestiou*n* / the sleep*e*	The Norice
Gan on hem wynke / and bad hem take keep*e*	taken
That muche drynke and labour / wol haue reste	muchel drynke / lab*our* wolde han
And with a galpyng mouth / hem alle he keste	galpyng
And seyde / that it was tyme / to lye adoun	seyde / it tyme
For blood / was in his domynacioun	domynaciou*n*
Cherisseth blood / natures freend quod he	
They thanken hym galpynge / by two / by thre	
And euery wight gan drawe hym to his reste	eu*er*y wight /
As sleep*e* hem bad / they take it for the beste	tooke
¶Hir dremes / shul nat now be toold for me	¶Hir*e* nat been ytoold
Ful were hir heuedes / of fumositee	hir*e* heddes /

11 ¶Squier *119r*

Theigh al the world / the contrye hadde yswore
He shal nat thennes / be ydrawe nor ybore
Or if yow list / bidde hym thennes gon
Trille this pyn / and he wol vanysshe anon
Out of the sighte / of euery maner wight
And come agayn / be it day or nyght
Whan yt yow list / to clepen hym ageyn
In swich a gyse / as I shal to yow seyn
Bitwixen yow and me / and that ful soone
Ryd whan yow list / ther is namoore to doone
Enformed / whan the kyng was of that knyght
And hath conceyued / in his wit aright
The manere / and the forme / of al this thyng
ffful glad and blythe / this noble doghty kyng
Repeyreth to his reuel / as biforn
The brydel is / vn to the tour yborn
And kept among his iewels / lief and deere
The hors vanysshed / I noot in which manere
Out of hir sighte / ye gete namoore for me
But thus I lete / in lust and Iolitee
This Cambyuskan / his lordes festeyynge
Til wel neigh / the day bigan to sprynge

Explicit prima pars

Incipit pars secunda

[...] norice of digestioun / the sleep
[...] on hem wynke / and bad hem take keep
That muche drynke and labour / wol haue reste
And with a galpyng mouth / hem alle he keste
And seyde / that it was tyme to lye adoun
ffor blood / was in his domynacioun
Cherisseth blood / natures freend quod he
They thanken hym galpynge / by two by thre
And euery wight / gan drawe hym to his reste
As sleep hem bad / they take it for the beste
Hir dremes / shul nat now be toold for me
ffful were hir heuedes / of fumositee

…useth dreem / of which ther nys no charge
…y slepen til that it was pryme large
The mooste part / but it were Canacee
She was ful mesurable / as wommen be
ffor of hir fader / hadde she take leue
To goon to reste / soone after it was eue
Hir liste nat / apalled for to be
Nor on the morwe / vnfestlich for to se
And slepte hir firste sleep / and awook
ffor swich a ioye / she in hir herte took
Bothe of hir queynte ryng / and hir myrour
That .xx. tyme / she chaunged hir colour
And in hir sleep / right for impression
Of hir myrour / she hadde a vision
Wher fore / er þt the sonne gan vp glyde
She cleped / vp on hir maistresse / hir bisyde
And seyde / þt hir liste for to ryse
Thise olde wommen / þt been gladly wyse
As is hir maystresse / answerde hir anon
And seyde / madame / whider wolde ye gon
Thus erly / for the folk been alle on reste
I wol quod she aryse / for me leste
No lenger for to slepe / and walke aboute
Hir maistresse clepith wommen / a gret route
And vp they rysen / wel an .x. or .xij.
Vp riseth / fresshe Canacee hir selue
As rody and bright / as dooth the yonge sonne
That in the ram / is .4. degrees vp ronne
Noon hyere was he / whan she redy was
And forth she walketh / esily a pas
Arrayed / after the lusty seson soote
Lightly for to pleye / and walke on foote
Nat but with .v. or .vj. of hir meynee
And in a trench / forth in the park goth she
The vapour which þt fro the erthe glood
Made the sonne / to seme rody and brood
But nathelees / it was so fair a sighte
That it made / al hir hertes for to lighte
What for the seson / and the morwenynge
And for the foweles / that she herde synge

	ELLESMERE
[That cau]seth dreem / of which ther nys no charge	That causeth
[They] slepen / til that it was pryme large	They
The mooste part⁊ but it were Canacee	
She was ful mesurable / as wommen be	
For of hir fader / hadde she take leue	
To goon to reste / soone after it was eue	
Hir liste nat⁊ apalled for to be	appalled
Nor on the morwe / vnfestlich for to se	Ne on vnfeestlich
And slepte hir firste sleep / and awook⁊	hir*e* sleep*e* / and thanne awook /
For swich a ioye / she in hir herte took⁊	took
Bothe of hir queynte ryng⁊ and hir Mirour	hir*e* Mirour
That .xx. tyme / she chaunged hir colour	twenty changed
And in hir sleep*e* / right for imp*re*ssiou*n*	hir*e* rigħt impressiou*n*
Of hir Mirour / she hadde a visiou*n*	hir*e* Mirour⁊ hadde Avisiou*n*
Wher fore / er þat the sonne gan vp glyde	Wherfore /
She clepyd / vp on hir maistresse / hir bisyde	cleped / on Maistresse / hir*e*
And seyde / þat hir liste for to ryse	that hir*e*
¶Thise olde wommen / þat been gladly wyse	wo*m*men /
As is hir maystresse / answerde hir anon	As hir*e* Maistresse / hir*e*
And seyde / madame / whider wolde ye gon	seyde whider wil ye goon
Thus erly / for the folk been alle on reste	folk /
¶I wol quod she aryse / for me leste	arise /
No lenger for to slepe / and walke aboute	12
Hir maistresse / clepith wommen / a gret route	¶Hir*e* Maistresse / clepeth greet
And vp they rysen / wel an .x. or .xij.^{e}	ten / twelue
Vp riseth / fresshe Canacee hir selue	fressħe Canacee /
As rody and bright⁊ as dooth the yonge sonne	brigħt /
That in the ram / is .4. degrees vp ronne	Ram / foure
Noon hyere was he / whan she redy was	hyer
And forth she walketh / esily a pas	
Arrayed / after the lusty seson soote	sesou*n*
Lightly for to pleye / and walke on foote	Ligħtly
Nat but with .v. or .vj. of hir meynee	wi*th* fyue sixe /
And in a trench / forth in the park⁊ goth she	gooth
¶The vapour / which þat fro the erthe glood	
Made the sonne / to seme rody and brood	
But nathelees / it was so fair a sighte	sigħte
That it made / al hir hertes for to lighte	alle hir*e* ligħte
What for the seson / and the morwenynge	sesou*n* /
And for the fowles / that she herde synge	foweles /

[12]¶Squier *119v*

For right anon / she wiste what they mente	riħt
Right by hir songꝭ and knew al hir entente	Riħt hir*e* entente
¶The knotte / why / that eu*er*y tale is told	why þ*at* tooldꝰ
If it be taryed / til þatꝭ lust be cold	taried / that cooldꝰ
Of hem / þ*at* han it after herkned yoore	hem han /
The sauour passeth / euer lenger the moore	eu*er*
For fulsomnesse / of his p*ro*lixitee	prolixitee
And by this same reson / thynketh me	by the same resou*n* /
I sholde / to the knotte condescende	knotte /
And maken of hir walkyngꝭ soone an ende	
¶Amydde a tree / for drye as whit as chalk /	Amydde fordryed / chalkꝭ
As Canacee / was pleyynge in hir walkꝭ	pleyyngꝭ
Ther sat a Fawkon / ouer hir heed ful hye	Faucou*n* / ou*er* hire
And with a pitous voys / so gan to crye	That with
That al the wode / resowned of hir cry	resouned hir*e*
Ybeten hadde she hir self / so pitously	hath
With bothe hir wynges / til the rede blood	
Ran endelong the tree / ther as she stood	ther she
And eue*re* in oon / she cryde alwey and shrighte	shriħte
And with hir beekꝭ hir seluen so she prighte	beek / priħte
That ther nys tygre / ne so cruel beestꝭ	Tygre / ne noon so crueel
That dwelleth / outher in wode / or in Forestꝭ	wode
That nolde han weptꝭ / if þ*at* he wepe koude	weptꝭ þ*at* she wepe
For sorwe of hire / she shrighte alwey so loude	hire /
¶For ther nas neuere man / yet on lyue	For neu*ere*
If þ*at* I koude / a Faukon wel discryue	Faucou*n*
That herde of swich another / of fairnesse	another
As wel of plumage / as of gentillesse	
Of shap*e* / of al that myghte yrekened be	shap*e* / and al
A Faukon P*er*egryn / thanne semed she	Faucou*n* peregryne /
Of fremde land / and eue*re* moore as she stood	13 landꝰ / eu*er*emoore stoodꝰ
She swowned now and now / for lakke of blood	swowneth bloodꝰ
Til wel neigh / is she fallen / fro that tree	neiħ / fallen fro the tree
¶This faire kynges doghter Canacee	doħter
That on hir fynger / baar the queynte ryngꝭ	
Thurgh which / she vnderstood wel euery thyngꝭ	Thurħ eu*er*y
That any fowl / may in his ledne sayn	fowel / leden seyn
And koude answere hym / in his ledne agayn	answeren ledene ageyn
Hath vnderstonden / what this Faukon seyde	vnderstonde / Faucou*n*
And wel neigh for the routhe / almoostꝭ she deyde	neiħ / almoost

[13] ¶Squier *120r*

ffor right anon she wiste what they mente
Right by hir song / and knew al hir entente
The knotte why that euery tale is told
If it be taryed / til pt lust be cold
Of hem pt han it after herkned yoore
The sauour passeth euer lenger the moore
ffor fulsomnesse of his plixitee
And by this same resoun thynketh me
I sholde to the knotte condescende
And maken of hir walkyng / soone an ende
Amydde a tree for drye as whit as chalk
As Canacee was pleyynge in hir walk
Ther sat a ffaukon ouer hir heed ful hye
And with a pitous voys so gan to crye
That al the wode / resowned of hir cry
ybeten hadde she hir self / so pitously
With bothe hir wynges til the rede blood
Ran endelong the tree / ther as she stood
And euere in oon / she cryde alwey and shrighte
And with hir beek hir seluen so she prighte
That ther nys tygre ne so cruel beest
That dwelleth outher in wode or in fforest
That nolde han wept / if pt he wepe koude
ffor sorwe of hire she shrighte alwey so loude
ffor ther nas neuere man yet on lyue
If pt I koude a ffaukon wel discryue
That herde of swich another of fairnesse
As wel of plumage / as of gentillesse
Of shap of al that myghte yrekened be
A ffaukon peregryn thanne semed she
Of fremde land / and euere moore as she stood
She swowned now and now / for lakke of blood
Til wel neigh is she fallen fro that tree
This faire kynges doghter Canacee
That on hir fynger baar the queynte ryng
Thurgh which / she vnderstood wel euery thyng
That any fowel / may in his ledne sayn
And koude answere hym / in his ledne agayn
Hath vnderstonden / what this ffaukon seyde
And wel neigh for the routhe almoost she deyde

[...] the tree / she goth ful hastily
[...] on this ffaukon / looketh pitously
[...] held hir lappe abrood / for wel she wiste
The ffaukon moste fallen fro the twiste
Whan þt it swowneth next / for lakke of blood
A long while to wayten hir she stood
Til at the laste / she spak in this manere
Vn to the hauk / as ye shal after heere
What is the cause / if it be for to telle
That ye been / in this furial pyne of helle
Quod Canacee / Vn to this hauk aboue
Is this for sorwe of deeth / or los of loue
ffor as I trowe / thise been causes two
That causen moost / a gentil herte wo
Of oother harm / it nedeth nat to speke
ffor ye youre self / vp on yow self yow wreke
Which proueth wel / þt outher ire or drede
Moot been enchesoun / of youre cruel dede
Syn þt I se / noon oother wight yow chace
ffor loue of god / as dooth youre seluen grace
Or what may been youre help / for west nor est
Ne saugh I neuere er now / no bryd ne beest
That ferde / with hym self so pitously
Ye sleen me / with youre sorwe verraily
I haue of yow / so greet compassioun
ffor goddes loue / com fro the tree adoun
And as I am / a kynges doghter trewe
If þt I verraily / the cause knewe
Of youre disese / if it laye in my myght
I wolde amende it / er that it were nyght
As wisly help me / grete god of kynde
And herbes shal I right ynowe fynde
To heele with youre hurtes hastily
Tho shrighte this ffaukon / yet moore pitously
Than euer she dide / and fil to grounde anon
And lyth aswowne deed / and lik a ston
Til Canacee / hath in hir lappe hir take
Vn to that tyme / she gan of swowne awake
And after / that she of swowe gan abreyde
Right in hir haukes ledne / thus she seyde

	ELLESMRE
[And t]o the tree / she goth ful hastily	And to gooth
[An]d on this Faukon / looketh pitously	And Faukou*n* /
[A]nd heeld hir lappe abrood / for wel she wiste	And abroodʼ /
The Faukon / moste fallen fro the twiste	
Whan þ*at* it swowneth next⁊ for lakke of blood	swowned bloodʼ
A long while / to wayten hir she stood	longe hir*e* stoodʼ
Til at the laste / she spak / in this manere	Til atte laste / spak⁊
Vn to the hauk⁊ / as ye shal after heere	hauk⁊
¶What is the cause / if it be for to telle	
That ye been / in this furial pyne of helle	be /
Quod Canacee / vn to this hauk aboue	to the hauk /
Is this for sorwe of deeth / or los of loue	
For as I trowe / thise been causes two	
That causen moost / a gentil herte wo	causeth moost⁊
Of oother harm / it nedeth nat to speke	
For ye your self⁊ / vp on yow self yow wreke	your*e* self / vpon your self
Which proeueth wel / þ*at* outher Ire or drede	proueth that outher loue or
Moot been encheson / of youre cruel dede	enchesou*n* / your*e*
Syn þ*at* I se / noon oother wight yow chace	see / wigħt
For loue of god / as dooth your seluen g*ra*ce	your*e* grace
Or what may been youre help / for West nor Est⁊	your*e* help*e* / West⁊
Ne saw I neuere er now / no bryd ne beest⁊	saugħ neu*ere*
That ferde / with hym self so pitously	ferde self /
Ye sleen me / with youre sorwe v*er*raily	sle me your*e* verraily
I haue of yow / so greet compassioun	greet passiou*n* |
For goddes loue / com fro the tree adoun	
And as I am / a kynges doghter trewe	dogħter
If þ*at* I v*er*raily / the cause knewe	verraily /
Of youre disese / if it laye in my mygħt	your*e* lay mygħt⁊
I wolde amende it⁊ er that it were nyght⁊	amenden þ*at* nygħt⁊
As wisly help me / grete god of kynde	help*e* me / the grete
And herbes / shal I right ynowe fynde	rigħt yfynde
To heele with / youre hurtes hastily	
¶Tho shrighte this Faukon / yet moore pitously	Faucou*n* / moore yet
Than euer she dide / and fil to ground anon	eu*er* grounde
And lyth aswowne deed / and lik a ston	lith lyk stoon
Til Canacee / hath in hir lappe hir take	hir*e* hir*e*
Vn to that tyme / she gan of swowne awake	to the tyme / of swougħ awake
And after / that she of swow / gan abreyde	14 ¶And after that⁊ of hir swougħ gan breyde
Right in hir haukes ledne / thus she seyde	Rigħt ledene /

14¶Squier *120v*

¶That pitee renneth soone / in gentil herte
Feelynge his similitude / in peynes smerte
Is proued al day / as men may it see
As wel by werk / as by auctoritee
For gentil herte / kitheth gentilesse
I se wel / *þat* ye han of my distresse
Compassion / my faire Canacee
Of verray / wommanly benygnitee
That nature / in youre p*ri*nciples hath set /
But for noon hope / for to fare the bet7
But for to obeye / vn to youre herte free
And for to maken othere / ywar by me
As by the whelp*e* / chasted is the leou*n*
Right for that cause / and for that conclusiou*n*
Whil *þat* I haue / a leyser and a space
Myn harm / I wol confessen / er I pace
And euere / whil *þat* oon / hir sorwe tolde
That oother weep / as she to water wolde
Til *þat* the Faukon / bad hir to be stille
And with a syk7 right thus she seyde hir wille
¶Ther I was bred / allas that ilke day
And fostred in a Roch / of Marbul gray
So tendrely / *þat* no thyng eyled me
I nyste nat7 what was aduersitee
Til I koude fle / ful hye vnder the sky
Tho dwelte a tercelet7 me faste by
That semed welle / of alle gentillesse
Al were he ful / of trayson and falsnesse
It was so wrapped / vnder humble cheere
And vnder hewe of trouthe / in swich manere
.b.That no wight wolde han wend / he koude feyne
.a.Vnder plesaunce / and vnder bisy peyne
So depe in greyn / he dyed his colours
Right as a serpent7 hit hym vnder floures
Til he may se his tyme / for to byte
Right so / this god of loues ypocrite
Dooth so his cerymonijs / and obeysau*n*ces
And kepeth in semblant7 alle hise obseruau*n*ces
That sownen / in to gentilesse of loue
As on a Tombe / is al the faire aboue

ELLESMERE

That pitee / soone
preued alday / may see
werk7 Auctoritee
gentillesse
wel / ye
Compassiou*n* /
v*er*ray benignytee
your*e* yset7
for obeye / your*e*
othere / be war by
Right
confessen
¶And eu*er*e / oon
weep*e* /
that Faucou*n* / hir*e*
wit*h* syk7 / right
¶That I that harde day
Roche /
that
Aduersitee
flee hye /
dwelte / Tercelet7
he / ful tresou*n* /
[15] That I ne koude han wend /
plesance /
Right
seen /
Right so loue / this ypocryte
hise cerymonyes obeisau*n*ces
semblau*n*t7 obs*er*uau*n*ces
sowneth / gentillesse
As in a toumbe /

[15] Order of 509-510 correct in El.

That pitee renneth soone in gentil herte
ffeelynge his similitude in peynes smerte
Is preued al day as men may it se
As wel by werk as by auctoritee
ffor gentil herte kitheth gentilesse
I se wel pt ye han of my distresse
Compassion my faire Canacee
Of verray wommanly benygnitee
That nature in youre principles hath set
But for noon hope for to fare the bet
But for to obeye vn to youre herte free
And for to maken othere ywar by me
As by the whelp chasted is the leon
Right for that cause and for that conclusion
Whil pt I haue a leyser and a space
Myn harm I wol confessen er I pace
And euere whil pt oon hir sorwe tolde
That oother weep as she to water wolde
Til pt the ffaukon bad hir to be stille
And with a syk right thus she seyde hir wille
Ther I was bred allas that ilke day
And fostred in a roch of marbul gray
So tendrely pt no thyng eyled me
I nyste nat what was aduersitee
Til I koude flee ful hye vnder the sky
Tho dwelte a tercelet me faste by
That semed welle of alle gentillesse
Al were he ful of trayson and falsnesse
It was so wrapped vnder humble cheere
And vnder hewe of trouthe in which manere
b That no wight wolde han wend he koude feyne
a Vnder plesaunce and vnder bisy peyne
So depe in greyn he dyed his colours
Right as a serpent hit hym vnder floures
Til he may se his tyme for to byte
Right so this god of loues ypocrite
Dooth so his cerymonyes and obeysaunces
And kepeth in semblant alle hise obseruaunces
That sownen in to gentilesse of loue
As on a tombe is al the faire aboue

[...]nd vnder is the cors swich as ye woot
Swich was this ypocrite bothe cold and hoot
And in this wise he serued his entente
That saue the feend noon wiste what he mente
Til he so longe hadde wopen and compleyned
And many a yeer his seruice to me feyned
Til that myn herte to pitous and to nyce
Al innocent of his crowned malice
fforfered of his deeth as thoughte me
Vpon his othes and his seuretee
Graunted hym loue vp on this condicioun
That euere mo myn honour and renoun
Were saued bothe pryuee and apert
This is to seyn that after his desert
I yaf hym al myn herte and my thoght
God woot and he þt oother wise noght
And took his herte in chaunge of myn for ay
But sooth is seyd goon sithen many a day
A trewe wight and a theef thynketh nat oon
¶ And whanne he sauh the thyng so fer ygon
That I hadde graunted hym fully my loue
In swich a gise as I haue seyd aboue
And yeuen hym my trewe herte as fre
As he swoor he yaf his herte to me
Anoon this tygre ful of doublenesse
ffil on his knees with so deuout humblesse
With so heigh reuerence and as by his cheere
So lyk a gentil louere of manere
So rauysshed as it semed for the ioye
That neuere Iason ne Parys of Troye
Iason certes ne noon oother man
Syn Lameth was þt alderfirst bigan
To louen two as writen folk biforn
Ne neuere syn the firste man was born
Ne koude man by twenty thousand part
Countrefete the sophymes of his art
Ne were worthy vnbokele his galoche
Ther doublenesse or feynyng sholde approche
Ne so koude thanke a wight as he dide me
His manere was an heuene for to see

Til any womman

	ELLESMERE
[An]d vnder is the cors / swich as ye woot	And corps /
[S]wich was this ypocrite / bothe cold and hoot	Swich was the ypocrite / cold
And in this wise / he serued his entente	
That saue the feend / noon wiste what he mente	
Til he so longe / hadde wopen and compleyned	compleyned
A many a yeer / his seruice to me feyned	And many yeer seruice feyned
Til that myn herte / to pitous and to nyce	16
Al Innocent of his crowned malice	corouned
For fered of his deeth / as thoughte me	ferd thoughte
Vp on his othes / and his seuretee	Vpon hise
Graunted hym loue / vp on this condicioun	vpon condicioun
That euere mo / myn honour and renoun	eueremoore / honour renoun
Were saued / bothe pryuee and apert	priuee
This is to seyn / that after his desert	
I yaf hym al myn herte / and my thoght	thoght
God woot and he / þat oother wise noght	ootherwise noght
And took his herte / in chaunge of myn for ay	chaunge for myn
But sooth is seyd / goon sithen many a day	
A trewe wight and a theef / thynketh nat oon	wight theef thenken
¶And whanne he saw the thyng so fer ygon	And whan saugh / thyng ygoon
That I hadde graunted hym fully my loue	hym /
In swich a gise / as I haue seyd aboue	gyse /
And yeuen hym / my trewe herte as fre	free
As he swoor / he yaf his herte to me	
Anoon this tygre / ful of doublenesse	Anon Tigre /
Fil on his knees / with so deuout humblesse	hise
With so heigh reuerence / and as by his cheere	heigh
So lyk a gentil louere / of manere	lyk louere /
So rauysshed / as it semed for the ioye	rauysshed / Ioye
That neuere Iason / ne Parys of Troye	neuere Troilus / ne
Iason certes / ne noon oother man	Iasoun certes /
Syn Lameth was / þat alderfirst bigan	
To louen two / as writen folk biforn	
Ne neuere / syn / the firste man was born	syn
Ne koude man / by twenty thousand part	
Countrefete / the Sophymes of his art	Art
Ne were worthy / vnbokele his galoche	vnbokelen
Ther doublenesse / or feynyng sholde approche	feynyng
Ne so koude thanke a wight as he did me	thonke wight / dide
His manere / was an heuene for to see	manere /

Til any womman

16 ¶Squier *121r*

. The Squyer .

	ELLESMERE
Til any womman / were she neu*er* so wys	wom*m*an /
So peynted he / and kembde at poynt deuys	point
As wel his wordes / as his contenaunce	hise wordes / contenau*n*ce
And I so loued hym / for his obeisaunce	I loued obeisau*n*ce
And for the trouthe / I demed in his herte	
That if so weere / that any thyng hym sm*er*te	were / smerte
Al were it neuer so litel / and I it wiste	neu*er* lite /
Me thoughte / I felte deeth myn herte twiste	thougħte /
And shortly / so ferforth this thyng is went	ferforth /
That my wyl / was his willes Instrument	
This is to seyn / my wyl obeyed his wil	obeyed his wyl
In alle thyng / as fer as reson fil	thyng resou*n*
Kepynge the boundes / of my worship eu*ere*	worship*e*
Ne neuere hadde I thyng so lief ne leu*ere*	neu*ere*
As hym god woot ne neuere shal namo	17 neu*ere*
¶This laste lenger / than a yeer / or two	This lasteth yeer
That I supposed of hym nat but good	hym / nogħt
But finally / thus a the laste it stood	thus atte laste
That Fortune wolde / þ*at* he moste twynne	
Out of that place / which þ*at* I was Inne	
Wher me was wo / that is no questiou*n*	
I kan nat make of it descripsiou*n*	discripsiou*n*
For o thyng dar I tellen boldely	thyng
I knowe what is / the peyne of deeth ther by	knowe / is
Swich harm I felte / for he ne myghte bileue	for I ne mygħte
So on a day / of me he took his leue	
So sorwefully eek / that I wende v*er*raily	eek
That he hadde feelyd / as muche harm as I	had felt
Whan that I herde hym speke / and saw his hewe	þ*at* *and* saugħ
But nathelees / I thoughte he was so trewe	thoughte /
And eek / that he repeyre sholde agayn	eek þ*at* he / repaire ageyn
With Inne a litel while / sooth to sayn	seyn
And reson wolde eek þ*at* he moste go	resou*n* that
For his honour / as ofte happeth so	honour ofte it happeth
That I made / vertu of necessitee	made v*er*tu /
And took it wel / syn þ*at* it moste be	
As I best myghte / I hidde from hym my sorwe	fro
And took hym by the hand / Seint Ioħn to borwe	hond / seint
And seyde thus / lo I am youres al	seyde hym thus /
Beeth swich / as I to yow haue been and shal	Beth yow /

17 ¶Squier *121v*

Til any womman / were she neu so wys
So peynted he / and kembde at poynt deuys
As wel his wordes / as his contenaunce
And I so loued hym / for his obeisaunce
And for the trouthe / I demed in his herte
That if so were / that any thyng hym smerte
Al were it neuer so litel / and I it wiste
Me thoughte / I felte deeth myn herte twiste
And shortly / so ferforth this thyng is went
That my wyl / was his willes instrument
This is to seyn / my wyl obeyed his wil
In alle thyng / as fer as reson fil
Kepynge the boundes / of my worship euere
Ne neuere hadde I thyng / so lief ne leuere
As hym god woot / ne neuere shal namo
This laste lenger / than a yeer / or two
That I supposed of hym nat but good
But finally / thus at the laste it stood
That Fortune wolde / þt he moste twynne
Out of that place / which þt I was inne
Wher me was wo / that is no question
I kan nat / make of it descripsion
For o thyng / dar I tellen boldely
I knowe what is / the peyne of deeth ther by
Swich harm I felte / for he ne myghte bileue
So on a day / of me he took his leue
So sorwefully eek / that I wende verraily
That he hadde feelyd / as muche harm as I
Whan that I herde hym speke / and saw his hewe
But natheles / I thoughte he was so trewe
And eek / that he repeire sholde agayn
With Inne a litel while / sooth to seyn
And reson wolde eek / þt he moste go
For his honour / as ofte happeth so
That I made / vertu of necessitee
And took it wel / syn þt it moste be
As I best myghte / I hidde from hym my sorwe
And took hym by the hand / Seint John to borwe
And seyde thus / lo I am youres al
Beth swich / as I to yow haue been and shal

...answerde / it nedeth nat reherse
... kan seyn bet than he / who kan doon werse
... han he hath al wel seyd / thanne hath he doon
Therfore bihoued hire / a ful long spoon
That shal ete with a feend / thus herde I seye
So at the laste / he moste forth his weye
And forth he fleeth / til he cam ther hym leste
Whan it cam hym / to purpos for to reste
I trowe he hadde thilke text in mynde
That alle thyng / repeirynge to his kynde
Gladeth hym self / thus seyn men as I gesse — Reditu suo singula gaudent
Men louen of propre kynde / newefangelnesse
As briddes doon / that men in cages fede
For theigh thow nyght and day / take of hem hede
And strawe hir cage faire and softe as silk
And yeue hem sugre / hony / breed / and milk
Yet right anon / as that his dore is vppe
He with his feet / wol sporne doun his cuppe
And to the wode he wole / and wormes ete
So newefangel / been they of hir mete
And louen nouelries / of propre kynde
No gentillesse of blood / may hem bynde
So ferde this gentil tercelet / allas the day
Though he were gentil born / and fressh and gay
And goodlich for to seen / and humble and free
He saugh vp on a tyme / a kyte flee
And sodeynly / he loued this kyte so
That al his loue / is clene fro me ago
And hath his trouthe / falsed in this wise
Thus hath the kyte / my loue in hir seruyse
And I am lorn / withouten remedye
And with that word / this faucon gan to crye
And swowned eft / in Canacees barm
Greet was the sorwe / for the haukes harm
That Canacee / and alle hir wommen made
They nyste how / that they myghte the faucon glade
But Canacee / hom bereth hire / in hir lappe
And softely / in plastres gan hir wrappe
Ther as she with hir beek / hadde hurt hir selue
Now kan nat Canacee / but herbes delue

	ELLESMERE
[What he a]nswerde / it nedeth nat reherse	What he answerde nedeth noghħt reherce
[Who] kan seyn bet than he / who kan doon werse	Who sey do
[W]han he hath al wel seyd / thanne hath he doon	Whan al seyd /
Ther fore bihoued hir*e* / a ful long spoon	Therfore bihoueth
That shal ete with a feend / thus herde I seye	feend' /
So at the laste / he moste forth his weye	atte laste /
And forth he fleeth / til he cam ther hym leste	
¶Whan it⁊ cam hym / to purpos for to reste	Whan it cam / hym p*ur*pos /
I trowe he hadde / thilke text in mynde	trowe /
That alle thyng⁊ repeiryng to his kynde	repeirynge
Gladeth hym self / thus seyn men as I gesse	self⁊
Men louen of p*ro*pre kynde / Newfangelnesse	kynde newefangelnesse
As bryddes doon / that men in Cages feede	briddes cages fede
For theigh thow / nyght and day / take of hem hede	though thou nyghħt *and*
And strawe hir Cages / faire / and softe as sylk⁊	Cage / faire silk⁊
And yeue hem sugre / hony / breed / and Milk	breed Milk⁊
Yet right anon / as *þat* his dore is vppe	righħt that
He with his feet⁊ wol sporne doun his cuppe	*with* spurne adoun
And to the wode he wole / and wormes ete	wole
So newfangel / been they of hir mete	newefangel / hir*e*
And louen nouelries / of p*ro*pre kynde	nouelrie / propre
No gentilesse of blood / may hem bynde	gentillesse
¶So ferde this gentil tercelet⁊ allas the day	18 this Tercelet⁊
Thogh he were gentil born / and fresshħ and gay	Thoughħ born / fresshħ
And goodlich for to seen / and humble and free	seen / humble
He saw vp on a tyme / a kyte flee	saughħ tyme
And sodeynly / he loued this kyte so	
That al his loue / is clene fro me ago	
And hath his trouthe / falsed in this wise	wyse
Thus hath the kyte / my loue in hir seruyse	hir*e* se*r*uyse
And I am lorn / with outen remedye	remedie
And with that word / this Faukon gan to crye	word' Faucou*n* crie
And swowned eft / in Canacees barm	
¶Greet was the sorwe / for the haukes harm	
That Canacee / and alle hir wommen made	wo*m*men
They nyste / how *þat* they myghte the Faukon glade	hou they myghħte Faucou*n*
But Canacee / hom bereth hire / in hir lappe	bereth hir*e*
And softely / in plastres gan hir wrappe	hir*e*
Ther as she with hir beek / hadde hurt hir selue	she / hir*e* beek
¶Now kan nat Canacee / but herbes delue	Now

608 reditu suo singula gaudent Hg El (609)

18 ¶Squier *122r*

	ELLESMERE
Out of the grownd / and maken saues newe	Out ground / make
Of herbes p*re*ciouse / and fyn of hewe	fyne
To heelen with this hauk / fro day to nyght	this / fro nyght
She dooth hir bisynesse / and al hir myght	hir*e* and hir*e* fulle myght
And by hir beddes heed / she made a Muwe	hir*e* Mewe
And couered it / with veluettes blue	it blewe
In signe of trouthe / that is in wommen sene	wo*m*men
And al with oute / the Muwe is peynted grene	wit*h* oute Mewe /
In which were peynted / alle thise false fowles	which ther were ypeynted /
As been thise tydyues / terceletz / and Owles	beth tidyues / tercelettes
Right for despit were peynted hem bisyde	Right
And Pyes / on hem / for to crye / and chyde	pyes crie
¶Thus lete I Canacee / hir hauk kepyng	
I wol namoore as now / speke of hir ryng	
Til it come eft to purpos for to seyn	
How that this Faukon / gat hir loue ageyn	Faucou*n* / hir*e*
Repentant / as the storie telleth vs	Repentant
By mediacion / of Cambalus	mediaciou*n*
The kynges sone / of which I to yow tolde	I yow
But hennes fort I wol my p*ro*ces holde	forth /
To speke of auentures / and of batailles	speken
That neu*ere* yet was herd / so greet m*er*uailles	grete
¶First wol I telle yow / of Cambyuskan	
That in his tyme / many a Citee wan	
¶And after / wol I speke / of Algarsyf	And after speke Algarsif
How that he wan / Theodora to his wyf	wan Theodera wif
For whom ful ofte / in gret p*er*il he was	greet
Ne hadde he been holpen / by the Steede of bras	be steede
¶And after / wol I speke of Cambalo	And
That faught in lystes / with the bretheren two	wit*h*
For Canacee / er that he myghte hir wynne	[19] myghte hir*e*
And ther I lefte / I wol ayein bigynne	An ther ayeyn

¶Explicit secunda pars	¶Explicit secunda pars

[19] ¶Squier *122v*

Out of the grownd / and maken salues newe
Of herbes preciouse / and fyn of hewe
To heelen with this hauk / fro day to nyght /
She dooth hir bisynesse / and al hir myght /
And by hir beddes heed / she made a mewe
And couered it / with veluettes blewe
In signe of trouthe / that is in wommen sene
And al with oute / the mewe is peynted grene
In which were peynted / alle thise false fowles
As been thise tydyues / tercelettz / and Owles
Right for despit / were peynted hem bisyde
And pyes / on hem / for to crye and chyde
Thus lete I Canacee / hir hauk kepyng /
I wol namoore as now / speke of hir ryng /
Til it come eft to purpos for to seyn
How that this ffaukon / gat hir loue ageyn
Repentant / as the storie telleth vs
By mediacion / of Cambalus
The kynges sone / of which I to yow tolde
But hennes forth / I wol my proces holde
To speke of auentures / and of batailles
That neuere yet / was herd so greet meruailles
First wol I telle yow / of Cambynskan
That in his tyme / many a Citee wan
And after wol I speke / of Algarsyf
How that he wan Theodora to his wyf
ffor whom ful ofte / in greet peril he was
Ne hadde he been holpen / by the Steede of bras
And after / wol I speke of Camballo
That faught in lystes with the bretheren two
ffor Canacee / er that he myghte hir wynne
And ther I lefte / I wol ayein bigynne

Explicit secunda pars

...pit tercia pars

Appollo whirleth vp his chaar so hye
Til that the god Mercuries hous the slye

The prologe of the Marchauntes tale

In feith Squyer thow hast thee wel yquyt
And gentilly I preise wel thy wit
Quod the marchaunt considerynge thy youthe
So feelyngly thow spekest sire I allowe the
As to my doom ther is noon þt is heere
Of eloquence þt shal be thy peere
If þt thow lyue god yeue thee good chaunce
And in vertu sende thee continuaunce
ffor of thy speche I haue greet deyntee
I haue a sone and by the Trinitee
I hadde leuere than .xx.ti pound worth lond
Though it right now were fallen in myn hond
He were a man of swich discrecion
As þt ye ben fy on possession
But if a man be vertuous wt al
I haue my sone snybbed and yit shal
ffor he to vertu listeth nat entende
But for to pleye at dees and to despende
And lese al that he hath is his vsage
And he hath leuere talken wt a page
Than to commune with any gentil wight
Where he myghte lerne gentillesse aright
Straw for youre gentillesse quod oure hoost
What marchaunt pardee sire wel thow woost
That ech of yow moot tellen atte leste
A tale or two or breken his biheste
That knowe I wel sire quod the marchaunt certeyn
I prey yow haueth me nat in desdeyn
Though to this man I speke a word or two
Telle on thy tale with outen wordes mo
Gladly sire hoost quod he I wol obeye
Vn to youre wyl now herkneth what I seye
I wole yow nat contrarien in no wise
As fer as þt my wittes wole suffise
I prey to god that it may plesen yow
Thanne woot I wel that it is good ynow

Explicit

[¶Incip]it tercia pars

[A]ppollo whirleth vp / his Char so hye
Til that / the god Mercuries hous the slye

¶The prologe / of the Marchau*n*tes tale

IN feith Squyer / thow hast thee wel yquyt
And gentilly / I preise wel thy wit
Quod the Marchant considerynge thy youthe
So feelyngly thow spekest sire I allowthe
As to my doom / ther is noon þ*at* is heere
Of eloquence / þ*at* shal be thy peere
If þ*at* thow lyue / god yeue thee good chaunce
And in vertu / sende thee continuaunce
For of thy speche / I haue gret deyntee
I haue a sone / and by the Trinitee
I hadde leuere / than .xx.[ti] pound worth lond
Thogh it right now ./ were fallen in myn hond
He were a man / of swich discreciou*n*
As þ*at* ye ben / fy on possessiou*n*
But if a man / be v*er*tuous w*ith* al
I haue my sone snybbed / and yit shal
For he to vertu / lusteth nat entende
But for to pleye at dees / and to despende
And lese al that he hath / is his vsage
And he hath leuere / talken w*ith* a page
Than to co*m*mune / with any gentil wight
Wher*e* he myghte lerne / gentillesse aright
¶Straw for youre gentillesse / quod oure hoost
What Marchau*n*t / pardee sire wel thow woost
That ech of yow / moot tellen atte leeste
A tale / or two / or breken his biheste
¶That knowe I wel sire / quod the Marchant c*er*teyn
I prey yow / haueth me nat in desdeyn
Thogh to this man / I speke a word or two
¶Telle on thy tale / with outen wordes mo
¶Gladly sire hoost quod he / I wol obeye
Vn to youre wyl / now herkneth what I seye
I wole yow nat cont*ra*rien / in no wise
As fer / as þ*at* my wittes wole suffise
I prey to god / that it may plesen yow
Thanne woot I wel / that it is good ynow

Explicit

¶Incipit pars tercia

Chaar
that god / M*er*curius
[20]¶Heere folwen the wordes of the Frankeleyn to the Squier and the wordes of the hoost to the Frankeleyn
Squier / yquit
wit
the Frankeleyn / considerynge yowthe
thou allowethe
that
that
that thou

greet

leu*ere* / twenty lond
Though right now / hond

that been /
with
yet
vertu / listneth nat

with
comune / wight
Where myghte lerne aright /
your*e* hoost
What Frankeleyn / p*ar*dee thou woost
leste
tale
quod the Frankeleyn |

Though speke or two [21]

hoost wole

wol contrarien wyse
that wittes / wol suffyse

¶Explicit

[20] *123r*

[21] 'a word': in another hand in right margin of El.

¶Here bigynneth / the Marchantes tale[1]	¶Heere bigynneth the Marchantes tale[2]
WHilom / ther was dwellynge in Lumbardye	
A worthy knyght' / that born was of Pauye	knygħt' þ*at* Pavye
In which he lyuede / in greet p*ros*p*er*itee	lyued / prosp*er*itee
And .lx. yeer / a wiflees man was he	sixty wyflees hee
And folwed ay / his bodily delit'	ay delyt'
On wommen / ther as was his appetit	wo*m*men / appetyt'
As doon thise fooles / that been seculer	3 seculeer
And whan that he / was passed .lx. yeer	sixty
Were it for holynesse / or for dotage	it' hoolynesse /
I kan nat seye / but swich a greet corage	
Hadde this knyght' to been a wedded man	knygħt'
That day and nyght' / he dooth al that he kan	nygħt /
Tespien / where he myghte wedded be	mygħte
Preyynge oure lord / to graunten hym / þ*at* he	Preyinge hi*m* he ⸍
Mighte ones knowe / of thilke blisful lyf	Mighte
That is / bitwix an housbonde and his wyf	is bitwixe / housbonde / wyf /
And for to lyue / vnder that holy bond	hooly boond'
With which / þ*at* god / man and womman boond	which þ*at* first' god / wo*m*man bond'
Noon oother lyf seyde he / is worth a bene	
For wedlok' is so esy / and so clene	wedlok /
That in this world / it is a Paradys	
Thus seyde this olde knyght' þ*at* was so wys	knygħt /
¶And c*er*teynly / as sooth as god is kyng'	c*er*teinly / sooħ /
To take a wyf / it is a glorious thyng'	wyf'
And namely / whan a man is old and hoor	man / oold
Thanne is a wyf / the fruyt of his tresor	wyf' fruyt'
Thanne sholde he take / a yong wyf and a feir	*and*
On which he myghte / engendren hym an heir	which /
And lede his lyf' in ioye / and in solas	ioye
Wher' as thise Bachilers / synge allas	Wher*e* bacheleris /
Whan þ*at* that they fynde / any adu*er*sitee	Whan that they fynden /
In loue / which nys but childissh vanytee	nys / childyssħ
And trewely / it sit wel to be so	
That Bachilers / haue ofte peyne and wo	bacheleris / often
On brotil ground they bilde / and brotilnesse	brotel ground' buylde / brotelnesse
They fynde / whan they wene sikernesse	

[1] *Out* Hg 1213-1244. The MerT Prol occurs in only 23 MSS including El Ad[3] Dd Ha[4] and He. El 102v reads:

¶The prologe of the Marchantes tale

Wepyng' and waylyng' care and oother sorwe
I knowe ynogħ / on euen and amorwe
Quod the Marchant' and so doon othere mo
That wedded been / I trowe that it be so
For wel I woot' it fareth so with me
I haue a wyf / the worste that may be
For thogh the feend / to hire ycoupled were
She wolde hym ou*er*macche / I dar wel swere
What sholde I yow reherce in special
Hir hye malice / she is a shrewe at al
Ther is a long' and large difference
Bitwix Grisildis grete pacience

Here bigynneth the Marchantes tale

Whilom ther was dwellynge in lumbardye
A worthy knyght / that born was of Pauye
In which he lyuede / in greet prosperitee
And lx yeer / a wyflees man was he
And folwed ay / his bodily delit
On wommen / ther as was his appetit
As doon thise fooles / that been seculer
And whan that he / was passed .lx. yeer
Were it for holynesse / or for dotage
I kan nat seye / but swich a greet corage
Hadde this knyght / to been a wedded man
That day and nyght / he dooth al that he kan
Tespien where he myghte wedded be
Preyynge oure lord / to graunten hym þt he
Mighte ones knowe / of thilke blisful lyf
That is / bitwix an housbonde and his wyf
And for to lyue / vnder that holy bond
With which þt god / man and womman bond
Noon oother lyf seyde he / is worth a bene
For wedlok / is so esy / and so clene
That in this world / it is a paradys
Thus seyde this olde knyght / þt was so wys
And certeinly / as sooth as god is kyng
To take a wyf / it is a glorious thyng
And namely / whan a man is old and hoor
Thanne is a wyf / the fruyt of his tresor
Thanne sholde he take / a yong wyf and a feir
On which he myghte / engendren hym an heir
And lede his lyf / in ioye / and in solas
Ther as thise bachilers / synge allas
Whan þt that they fynde / any aduersitee
In loue / which nys but childissh vanytee
And trewely / it sit wel to be so
That bachilers / haue ofte peyne and wo
On brotil ground they bilde / and brotilnesse
They fynde / whan they wene sikernesse

[...]e/ but as bryd/ or as a beest/
[...]bertee and vnder noon arest/
[...]her as a wedded man/ in his estat/
[...]yueth a lyf/ blisful and ordynat/
Vnder this yok of mariage ybounde
Wel may his herte/ in ioye and blisse habounde
ffor who kan be/ so buxom as a wyf
Who is so trewe/ and eek so ententyf
To kepe hym syk and hool/ as is his make
ffor wele or wo/ she wol hym nat forsake
She nys nat wery/ hym to loue and serue
Though þt he ly bedrede/ til he sterue
And yet som clerkes seyn/ it is nat so
Of whiche he Theofraste/ is oon of tho
What force/ though Theofraste liste lye
Ne take no wyf quod he/ for housbondrye
As for to spare in housholde thy dispence
A trewe seruant/ dooth moore diligence
Thy good to kepe/ than thyn owene wyf
ffor she wol clayme/ half part al hir lyf
And if thow be syk/ so god me saue
Thy verray freendes/ or a trewe knaue
Wol kepe thee bet than she/ that wayteth ay
After thy good/ and hath do many a day
And if thow take a wyf/ she wole destroye
Thy good substance and thy body annoye
This sentence/ and an hundred thynges worse
Writeth this man/ ther god his bones curse
But take no kepe/ of al swich vanytee
Diffye Theofraste/ and herke me
A wyf is goddes yifte verraily
Alle othere manere yiftes hardily
As londes/ rentes/ pasture/ or commune
Or moebles/ alle been yiftes of fortune
That passen/ as a shadwe vp on the wal
But drede nat/ if pleynly speke I shal
A wyf wol laste/ and in thyn hous endure
Wel lenger than thee lyst/ parauenture
Mariage is a ful greet sacrament/
He which þt hath no wyf/ I holde hym shent/

Vxor est diligenda/ q[uia] donum de[i]
[...] filij Sirach/ Domus et diuicie
dantur a parentibus/ a deo autem
[pro]prie/ uxor bona vel prudens

[They ly]ue / but as bryd / or as a beest⁊
[In lib]ertee / and vnder noon arest⁊
[T]her as a wedded man / in his estat⁊
Lyueth a lyf / blisful and ordynat⁊
Vnder this yok⁊ of mariage ybounde
Wel may his herte / in ioye and blisse habounde
For who kan be / so buxom as a wyf
Who is so trewe / and eek so ententyf⁊
To kepe hym syk and hool / as is his make
For wele or wo / she wol hym nat forsake
She nys nat wery / hym to loue / and serue
Thogh *pat* he ly bedrede / til he sterue
And yet⁊ som clerkes seyn / it is nat so
Of whiche / he Theofraste / is oon of tho
What force / thogh Theofraste liste lye
¶Ne tak no wyf quod he / for housbondrye
As for to spare / in houshold thy dispence
A trewe seruant⁊ dooth moore diligence
Thy good to kepe / than thyn owene wyf
For she wol clayme / half part al hir lyf
And if thow be syk / so god me saue
Thy verray freendes / or a trewe knaue
Wol kepe thee bet than she / that wayteth ay
After thy good / and hath do many a day
And if thow take a wyf / ⟨she wole destroye⟩
⟨Thy good substance / and thy body annoye⟩
¶This sentence / and an hundred thynges worse
Writeth this man / ther god his bones curse
But tak no kepe / of al swich vanytee
Diffye Theofraste / and herke me
¶A wyf⁊ is goddes yifte verraily
Alle othere manere yiftes hardily
As londes / rentes / pasture / or comune
Or moebles / alle been yiftes of fortune
That passen / as a shadwe vp on the wal
But dreed nat⁊ if pleynly speke I shal
A wyf wol laste / and in thyn hous endure
Wel lenger than thee lyst⁊ p*ar*auenture
¶Mariage / is a ful greet sacrament⁊
He / which *pat* hath no wyf⁊ I holde hym shent⁊

1311 Vxor est diligenda quia donum dei [est]
Iesus filius Syrac domus et diuicie
dantur a parentibus a domino autem
proprie vxor bona vel prudens Hg El

ELLESMERE

They lyue / as a bryd /
In libertee / arreest⁊
Ther estaat⁊
lyf⁊ ordinaat⁊
wyf⁊
syk⁊
wole
loue
Thogħ lye
som*m*e it nys nat
Theofraste
thougħ
Ne take
houshold'
4 wyf⁊
lyf⁊
thou syk⁊
ve*r*ray
bet⁊ she *pat* waiteth
doon
thou wyf / vn to thyn hoold' |
Ful lightly / maystow been a Cokewold' |
This
corse
take swicħ
Deffie
wyf /
otherere
co*m*mune
Fortune
dona fortune] on a wal
dredelees / if
list⁊
¶Mariage is / sacrement⁊
wyf /

And of my wyf / the passyng⁊ crueltee
Were I vnbounden / also moot I thee
I wolde neu*er*e eft⁊ comen in the snare
We wedded men / lyue in sorwe and care
Assaye who so wole / and he shal fynde
I seye sooth / by Seint Thomas of ynde
As for the moore part⁊ I sey nat alle
God shilde / that it sholde so bifalle
¶A goode sire hoost / I haue ywedded bee
Thise Monthes two / and moore nat p*ar*dee
And yet I trowe / he that al his lyue
Wyflees hath been / thougħ *pat* men wolde hi*m* ryue
Vn to the herte / ne koude in no manere
Tellen so muchel / sorwe / as I now heere
Koude tellen / of my wyues cursednesse

He lyueth helplees / and al desolat
I speke of folk / in seculer estat
¶And herke why / I sey nat this for noght
That womman is / for mannes help*e* ywroght.
The hye god / whan he hadde Adam maked
And seigh hym allone / bely naked
God of his grete goodnesse / seyde than
Lat vs now make an help / vn to this man
Lyk to hym self and thanne he made hym Eue
Here may ye see / and here may ye preeue
That wyf is mannes help*e* / and his confort
His Paradys terrestre / and his disport
So buxom / and so *ver*tuous is she
They moste nedes / lyue in vnytee
¶no*ta* { O flessh they been / and o flessh as I gesse
Hath but oon herte / in wele and in distresse }
¶A wyf / a Seinte Marie benedicitee
How myghte a man / han any adu*er*sitee
That hath a wyf / certes / I kan nat seye
The blisse / which þ*at* is bitwix hem tweye
Ther may no tonge telle / or herte thynke
If he be poure / she helpeth hym to swynke
She kepeth his good / and wasteth neuer a del
Al that hir housbonde lust hir liketh wel
She seith nat ones nay / whan he seith yee
Do this seith he / al redy sire seith she
¶O blisful ordre / o wedlok p*re*cious
Thou art so murye / and eek so *ver*tuous
And so co*m*mended / and approued eek
That any man / that halt hym worth a leek
Vp on his bare knees / oghte al his lyf
Thanken his god / that hym hath sent a wyf
Or ellis preye to god / hym for to sende
A wyf / to laste vn to his lyues ende
For thanne his lyf / is set in sikernesse
He may nat be / deceyued / as I gesse
So that he werke / after his wyues reed
Thanne may he boldely / kepen vp his heed
They been so trewe / and ther with al so wyse
For which / if thow wolt werken as the wyse

ELLESMERE

folk estaat
And noght
womman ywroght
saugh hym al allone /
help*e*
hi*m* Eue
Heer*e* se / heer by may preue
vertuous
vnitee
flessh as
wyf / marie benedicite
myghte
c*er*tes
bitwixe
neu*er* deel
hir*e* hir*e* weel
ye
5 O ordre of wedlok
appreued
That eu*er*y man / þ*at* leek /
oughte lyf /
þ*at* wyf /
elles
laste /
nat be deceyued
þ*at* reede
6

1327 Faciamus ei adiutorium et ex[tracta costa de] corpore Ade fecit Euam et dix[it propter hec] relinquet homo patrem et matrem et [adherebit et cetera] et erunt duo in carne vna Hg (defective) El

1335 Vna caro vnum Animum in omni Adversitate cogitat Hg (in a later hand)

1240 ¶Now quod our hoost. Marchau*n*t so god yow blesse
Syn ye so muchel / knowen of that Art
Ful hertely / I pray yow telle vs part
¶Gladly quod he / but of myn owene soore
1244 For soory herte / I telle may namoore

[2] ¶Marchant on *102v*. Miniature of the Merchant in left margin.

[3] ¶Marchant *103r*

[4] ¶Marchant *103v*

[5] ¶Marchant *104r*

[6] *Out* El 1358-61.

He lyueth helplees and al desolat
I speke of folk in seculer estat
And herke why I sey nat this for noght
That womman is for mannes help ywroght
The hye god whan he hadde Adam maked
And saugh hym allone bely naked
God of his grete goodnesse seyde than
Lat vs now make an help vn to this man
Lyk to hym self and thanne he made hym Eue
Heere may ye se and heere may ye preeue
That wyf is mannes help and his confort
His paradys terrestre and his disport
So buxom and so vertuous is she
They moste nedes lyue in vnytee
Auc. O flessh they been and o flessh as I gesse
Hath but oon herte in wele and in distresse
A wyf a Seinte Marie benedicitee
How myghte a man han any aduersitee
That hath a wyf certes I kan nat seye
The blisse which þt is bitwix hem tweye
Ther may no tonge telle or herte thynke
If he be poure she helpeth hym to swynke
She kepeth his good and wasteth neuer a del
Al that hir housbonde lust hir liketh wel
She seith nat ones nay whan he seith ye
Do this seith he al redy sire seith she
O blisful ordre o wedlok precious
Thou art so murye and eek so vertuous
And so comended and approued eek
That any man that halt hym worth a leek
Vp on his bare knees oghte al his lyf
Thanken his god that hym hath sent a wyf
Or ellis preye to god hym for to sende
A wyf to laste vn to his lyues ende
For thanne his lyf is set in sikernesse
He may nat be deceyued as I gesse
So that he werke after his wyues reed
Thanne may he boldely beren vp his heed
They been so trewe and ther with al so wyse
For which if thow wolt werken as the wyse

Ffaciamus ei adiutorium et ex corpore ade fecit Euam et dixit relinquet homo patrem et matrem et erunt duo in carne vna

Vna caro unum animum in omni aduersitate cogitant

…y so as wommen wol thee rede
…ow that Iacob / as thise clerkes rede
…y good conseil / of his moder Rebekke
Boond the kydes skyn / aboute his nekke
ffor which / his fadres benyson he wan
Lo Iudith / as the storie eek telle kan
By good conseil / she goddes peple kepte
And slowh hym Olofernus / whil he slepte
Lo Abigayl / by good conseil how she
Saued hir housbonde Nabal / whan þ[t] he
Sholde han ben slayn / and looke Ester also
By good conseil / delyuered out of wo
The peple of god / and made hym Mardochee
Of Assuere / enhaunced for to be
Ther nys no thyng in gree superlatyf
As seith Senec / aboue an humble wyf
Suffre thy wyues tonge / as Caton byt
She shal comande / and thow shalt suffren it
And yet / she wol obeye of curteisye
A wyf / is keper of thyn housbondrye
Wel may the sike man / biwaille and wepe
Ther as ther is no wyf / the hous to kepe
I warne thee / if wisly thow wolt wirche
Loue wel thy wyf / as Crist loued his chirche
If thow louest thy self / thow louest thy wyf
No man hateth his flessh / but in his lyf
He fostreth it / and ther fore bidde I thee
Cherisse thy wyf / or thow shalt neuere thee
Housbonde and wyf / what so men Iape or pleye
Of worldly folk / holden the siker weye
They been so knyt / ther may noon harm bityde
And namely / vp on the wyues syde
ffor which this Ianuarie / of whom I tolde
Considered hath / inwith his dayes olde
The lusty lyf / the vertuous quyete
That is in mariage / hony swete
And for his freendes / on a day he sente
To tellen hem / theffect of his entente
With face sad / this tale he hath hem told
He seyde freendes / I am hoor and old

Iacob enim per consilium matris sue Rebecce

Iudith etc. de manibus Olofernis

Et Abigail per suum bonum consilium virum suum Nabal ab ira David liberauit

Ester etc. Iudeos per bonum consilium simul cum Mardocheo in regno Assueri

Seneca Sicut nichil est superius benigna coniuge ita nichil est crudelius infesta muliere

Cato Uxoris linguam si frugi est ferre memento

Apostolus ad Ephesios Diligite uxores vestras sicut Christus dilexit ecclesiam etc.

Apostolus Ita viri debent diligere uxores suas ut corpora sua qui suam uxorem diligit seipsum diligit nemo unquam carnem suam odio habuit set nutrit et fouet eam etc.

Postea Unusquisque suam uxorem sicut seipsum diligat

[Do alwe]y so / as wommen wol thee rede
[Lo h]ow that Iacob / as thise clerkes rede
[B]y good conseil / of his moder Rebekke
Boond the kydes skyn / aboute his nekke
For which / his fadres benyson he wan
¶Lo Iudith / as the storie eek telle kan
By good conseil / she goddes peple kepte
And slow hym Olofernus / whil he slepte
¶Lo Abigayl / by good conseil / how she
Saued hir housbonde Nabal / whan þ*a*t he
Sholde han ben slayn / and looke Ester also
By good conseil / delyu*er*ed out of wo
The peple of god / and made hym Mardochee
Of Assuere / enhaunced for to be
¶Ther nys no thyng in gree sup*er*latyf
As seith Senec / aboue an humble wyf /
¶Suffre thy wyues tonge / as Caton byt
She shal comaunde / and thow shalt suffren it /
And yet she wol obeye of curteisye
¶A wyf / is kepere of thyn housbondrye
Wel may the sike man / biwaille and wepe
Ther as ther is no wyf / the hous to kepe
I warne thee / if wisly thow wolt wirche
Loue wel thy wyf / as Crist loued his chirche
If thow louest thy self / thow louest thy wif
No man hateth his flessh / but in his lyf /
He fostreth it and ther fore bidde I thee
Cherisse thy wyf / or thow shalt neu*er*e thee
Housbonde and wyf what so men Iape or pleye
Of worldly folk / holden the siker weye
They been so knyt / ther may noon harm bityde
And namely / vp on the wyues syde
For which this Ianuarie / of whom I tolde
Considered hath / inwith his dayes olde
The lusty lyf / the v*er*tuous quyete
That is in mariage / hony swete
And for his freendes / on a day he sente
To tellen hem / theffect of his entente
¶With face sad / this tale he hath hem told
He seyde freendes / I am hoor and old

ELLESMERE

¶Lo how þ*a*t
By mooder
Thurgh which / benysou*n*
By wys conseil /
he /
be
delyuered
Assuer*e* /
thyng / sup*er*latyf
Senek
Catou*n* bit
comande / thou it
yet / wole
A kepere /
and
ther nys no
wisely / thou
wel thy wyf crist
thou self thou wyf /
lyf /
therfore
thou
iape
knyt
hise
vertuous
sweete
hise
hem theffect
7 With sad / his tale toold
oold

7 ¶Marchant *104v*

1362 Iacob enim per consilium matris sue Rebecce et cetera Hg El
Variant: enim) *om.* El

1368 Iudith et cetera de manibus Oloferni Hg El (1366)
Variants: Iudith et cetera) I. El Oloferni) O. et cetera El

1369 Et Abigail per suum bonum consilium virum suum Nabal ab ira Dauid liberauit Hg El Variant: Et) *om.* El

1372 Ester et cetera Iudeos per bonum consilium simul cum Mardocheo in regno Assueri et cetera Hg El (1371) Variant: Assueri et cetera) A. El

1376 Seneca sicut nichil est superius benigna coniug[e] ita nichil est crudelius infesta muliere Hg El (1375) Variants: superius) *om.* El est crudelius) c. e. El

1378 Cato vxoris linguam si frugi est ferre memento Hg El (1377)

And almoost god woot on my pittes brynke	
Vp on my soule / som what moste I thynke	on the soule / somwhat
I haue my body / folily despended	
Blissed be god / þ*at* it shal been amended	Blessed that
For I wol be c*er*teyn / a wedded man	be / certeyn
And that anon / in al the haste I kan	anoon /
Vn to som mayde / fair and tendre of age	fair /
I pray yow / shapeth for my mariage	prey
Al sodeynly / for I wol nat abyde	
And I wol fonde / tespien on my syde	
To whom I may / be wedded hastily	whom / may
But for as muche / as ye been mo than I.	I
Ye shullen rather / swich a thyng espien	espyen
Than I / and where me best were to allien	allyen
¶But o thyng warne I yow / my freendes deere	thyng
I wol noon old wyf han / in no manere	oold
She shal nat passe / .xx. yeer certeyn	twenty certayn
Old fissh / and yong flessh / wol I haue feyn	Oold fissh yong / wolde fayn
Bet is quod he / a Pyk / than a Pykerel	pyk pykerel
And bet than old boef / is the tendre vel	olde boef veel
I wol no womman / xxx.ti yeer of age	wo*m*man / thritty
It is but bene straw / and greet forage	benestraw /
And eek thise olde widwes / god it woot	eek / wydwes /
They konne so muche craft on Wades boot	konne / muchel
So muchel broken harm / whan hem leste	whan þ*at* hem
That with hem / sholde I neu*ere* lyue in reste	wit*h*
For sondry scoles / maketh subtile clerkis	maken sotile
Womman of many scoles / half a clerk is	Wo*m*man manye clerk
But c*er*teinly / a yong thyng may men gye	certeynly / yong thyng
Right as men may warm wex / wit*h* handes plye	Right may / wex
Wherfore / I sey yow pleynly in a clause	pleynly /
I wol noon old wyf han / right for this cause	oold han / for
For if so were / I hadde swich meschaunce	were / þ*at* I myschau*n*ce
That I in hire / ne koude han no plesaunce	hir*e* / plesau*n*ce
Thanne sholde I lede my lyf / in avoutrye	lyf Auoutrye
And ⟨go⟩ straight to the deuel / whan I dye	And streight vn to
Ne children sholde I none / vp on hir geten	children / none hir*e*
Yet were me leuere / houndes hadde me eten	leu*ere* / þ*at* houndes had
Than that myn heritage sholde falle	þ*at*
In straunge hand / and this I telle yow alle	

1380 Bona mulier fidelis custos est et bona domus El

1383 Apostolus Paulus Ad Ephesianos Diligite vxores vestras sicut christus dilexit ecclesiam et cetera Hg El

1385 Apostolus Ita viri debent diligere vxores su[as] vt corpora sua quia qui suam vxorem dilig[it] seipsum diligit nemo vnquam carnem suam odio habuit set nutrit et fouet eam et postea vnusquisque suam vxorem sicut se ipsum diligat Hg El Variant: sicut se ipsum) sicut i. El

And almoost god woot on my pittes brynke
Vp on my soule som what moste I thynke
I haue my body folily despended
Blissed be god þt it shal been amended
ffor I wol be certeyn a wedded man
And that anon in al the haste I kan
Vn to som mayde fair and tendre of age
I pray yow shapeth for my mariage
Al sodeynly for I wol nat abyde
And I wol fonde tespien on my syde
To whom I may be wedded hastily
But for as muche as ye been mo than I.
Ye shullen rather swich a thyng espien
Than I and where me best were to allien
But o thyng warne I yow my freendes deere
I wol noon old wyf han in no manere
She shal nat passe .xx. yeer certeyn
Old fissh and yong flessh wol I haue feyn
Bet is quod he a Pyk than a Pykerel
And bet than old boef is the tendre veel
I wol no womman xxx.ti yeer of age
It is but bene straw and greet forage
And eek thise olde wydwes god it woot
They konne so muche craft on wades boot
So muchel broken harm whan hem leste
That with hem sholde I neuere lyue in reste
ffor sondry scoles maketh subtile clerkis
Womman of many scoles half a clerk is
But certeynly a yong thyng may men gye
Right as men may warm wex wt handes plye
Wher fore I sey yow pleynly in a clause
I wol noon old wyf han right for this cause
ffor if so were I hadde swich meschaunce
That I in hire ne koude han no plesaunce
Thanne sholde I lede my lyf in auoutrye
And streight to the deuel whan I dye
Ne children sholde I none vp on hir geten
Yet were me leuere houndes hadde me eten
Than that myn heritage sholde falle
In straunge hand and this I telle yow alle

ote nat I woot the cause why
Men sholde wedde / and forther moore woot I
Ther speketh many a man of mariage
That woot namoore of it / than woot my page
ffor whiche causes / man sholde take a wyf
If he ne may nat lyue chaast his lyf
Take hym a wyf with greet deuocion
By cause of leueful procreacion
Of children / to thonour of god aboue
And nat oonly / for paramour or loue
And for they sholde lecherye eschue
And yelde hir dette whan þt it is due
Or for þt ech of hem sholde helpen oother
In meschief / as a suster shal the brother
And lyue in chastitee ful holily
But sires by youre leue that am nat I
ffor god be thanked / I dar make auaunt
I feele my lymes / stark and suffisant
To do / al that a man bilongeth to
I woot my self best / what I may do
¶ [illegible] Thogh I be hoor / I fare as dooth a tree
That blosmeth / er the fruyt ywoxen be
And blosmy tree / nys neither drye ne deed
I feele me nowher hoor / but on myn heed
Myn herte / and alle my lymes / been as grene
As laurer thurgh the yeer is for to sene
And syn þt ye han herd / al myn entente
I pray yow / to my wyl ye wol assente
¶ Dyuerse men / diuersely hym tolde
Of mariage / manye ensamples olde
Somme blamed it / somme preysed it certeyn
But at the laste / shortly for to seyn
As alday / falleth altercacion
Bitwixe freendes / in disputison
Ther fil a stryf / bitwix his bretheren two
Of whiche / that oon was cleped Placebo
Iustinus soothly / called was that oother
¶ Placebo seyde / o Ianuarie brother
ffful litel nede / hadde ye my lord so deere
Conseil to axe / of any that is heere

	ELLESMERE
[I do]te nat / I woot the cause why	I dote nat why ⁄
Men sholde wedde / and ferther moore woot I	forthermoore
Ther speketh many a man of mariage	speketh /
That woot namoore of it / than woot my page	it
For whiche causes / man sholde take a wyf	
If he ne may nat lyue / chast his lyf	Siththe / he may nat lyuen chaast lyf /
Take hym a wyf / with greet deuociou*n*	8 wyf with
By cause / of leueful p*ro*creaciou*n*	procreaciou*n*
Of children / to thonour of god aboue	
And nat oonly / for p*ar*amour or loue	
And for they sholde / lecherye eschue	leccherye
And yelde hir dette / whan þ*at* it is due	dettes / þ*a*t they ben due
Or for þ*at* ech of hem / sholde helpen oother	that
In meschief as a Suster shal the brother	meschief / suster
And lyue in chastitee / ful holily	
But sires by youre leue / that am nat I	
For god be thanked / I dar make auant	auau*n*t
I feele my lymes / stark and suffisant	stark / suffisau*n*t
To do / al that a man bilongeth to	
I woot my self best what I may do	seluen
¶No*ta* Thogh I be hoor / I fare as dooth a tree	Though
That blosmeth / er the fruyt ywoxen be	er þ*a*t fruyt bee
And blosmy tree / nys neither drye ne deed	
I feele me nowher hoor / but on myn heed	me / nowher*e*
Myn herte / and alle my lymes / been as grene	lymes
As laurer thurgh the yeer is for to sene	laurer / thurgh yeer /
And syn þ*at* ye han herd / al myn entente	ye / herd
I pray yow / to my conseil ye wol assente	prey my wyl / ye wole
¶Dyu*er*se men / diu*er*sely hym tolde	**D**iu*er*se diuersely
Of mariage / manye ensamples olde	
Som*m*e blamed it som*m*e preised it c*er*teyn	it / preysed certeyn
But at the laste / shortly for to seyn	atte laste /
As alday / falleth altercaciou*n*	al day /
Bitwixe freendes / in disputisou*n*	Bitwixen freendes
Ther fil a stryf bitwix his bretheren two	stryf / bitwixe hise
Of whiche / that oon was clepid Placebo	cleped
Iustinus soothly / called was that oother	
¶Placebo seyde / o Ianuarie brother	⌈¶Placebo⌉
Ful litel nede / hadde ye my lord so deere	
Conseil to axe / of any that is heere	

[8] ¶Marchant *105r*

	ELLESMERE
But þ*at* ye been / so ful of Sapience	sapience
That yow ne liketh / for youre heigh prudence	your*e* heighe
To weyuen / fro the word of Salomon	
This word seyde he / vn to vs euerichon	eu*er*ychon
Werk alle thyng by conseil / thus seyde he	Wirk thyng
And thanne shaltow nat repenten thee	thanne / repente
But thogh þ*at* Salomon / spak swich a word	though word
Myn owene deere brother / and my lord	
So wisly / god my soule brynge at reste	wysly /
I holde / your owene conseil is the beste	your*e*
For brother myn / of me tak this motyf	taak
I haue now been / a Court man al my lyf	lyf
And god it woot thogh I vnworthy be	though
I haue stonden / in ful greet degree	
Abouten lordes / in ful greet estat	9 lordes / of ful heigh estaat
Yet hadde I neu*er*e / with noon of hem debat	wit*h* debaat
I neu*er*e hem contraryed / trewely	neuere contraried
I woot wel / þ*at* my lord kan moore than I	that
What that he seith / I holde it ferm and stable	ferme
I seye the same / or ellis thyng semblable	elles
A ful greet fool / is any conseillour	conseill*our*
That serueth any lord / of heigh honour	*ser*ueth hono*ur*
That dar p*re*sume / or ellis thenken it	elles it
That his conseil / sholde passe his lordes wit	
Nay / lordes be no fooles by my fay	been
Ye han your seluen / shewed heer to day	your*e* seluen / seyd heer
So heigh sentence / so holily and weel	
That I consente / and conferme eu*er*y deel	eu*er*ydeel
Youre wordes alle / and youre opynyoun	opiniou*n*
By god / ther nys no man in al this toun	man /
Ne in ytaille / koude bet han ysayd	Nyn ytaille / that koude sayd
Crist halt hym of this conseil / ful wel apayd	hym / conseil
And trewely / it is an heigh corage	heigh
Of any man / that stapen is in age	
To take a yong wyf / by my fader kyn	wyf
Youre herte hangeth / on a iolyf pyn	Your*e* ioly
Dooth now in this matere / right as yow leste	matiere / right
For fynally / I holde it for the beste	finally /
¶Iustinus / that ay stille sat and herde	¶Iustinus] ¶Iustinus / þ*at*
Right in this wise / he to Placebo answerde	Right

9 ¶Marchant *105v*

But þt ye been / so ful of sapience
That yow ne liketh / for youre heigh prudence
To weyuen / fro the word of Salomon
This word seyde he / vn to vs euerychon
Werk alle thyng by conseil / thus seyde he
And thanne shaltow nat repenten thee
But though þt Salomon / spak swich a word
Myn owene deere brother / and my lord
So wisly / god my soule brynge at reste
I holde / youre owene conseil is the beste
ffor brother myn / of me tak this motyf
I haue now been / a court man al my lyf
And god it woot / though I vnworthy be
I haue stonden / in ful greet degree
Abouten lordes / in ful greet estat
Yet hadde I neuere / with noon of hem debat
I neuere hem contraryed trewely
I woot wel / þt my lord kan moore than I
What that he seith / I holde it ferm and stable
I seye the same / or ellis thyng semblable
A ful greet fool / is any conseillour
That serueth any lord / of heigh honour
That dar presume / or ellis thenken it
That his conseil / sholde passe his lordes wit
Nay / lordes be no fooles by my fay
Ye han youre seluen / shewed heer to day
So heigh sentence / so holily and weel
That I consente / and conferme euery deel
Youre wordes alle / and youre opynyoun
By god / ther nys no man in al this toun
Ne in ytaille / koude bet han ysayd
Crist halt hym of this conseil ful wel apayd
And trewely / it is an heigh corage
Of any man / that stapen is in age
To take a yong wyf / by my fader kyn
Youre herte hangeth / on a ioly pyn
Dooth now in this matere / right as yow leste
ffor fynally / I holde it for the beste
Justinus that ay stille sat and herde
Right in this wise / he to Placebo answerde

[...]s brother myn / be pacient I preye
[...]yn ye han seyd / and herkneth what I seye
Senec / amonges othere wordes wise
Seith þt a man / oghte hym right wel avyse
To whom / he yeveth his lond / or his catel
And syn I oghte / avysen me right wel
To whom I yeeve my good / awey fro me
Wel muchel moore / I oghte avysed be
To whom I yeeve my body / for alwey
I warne yow wel / it is no childes pley
To taken a wyf / withouten avysement /
Men moste enquere / this is myn assent /
Wher she be wys and sobre / or dronkelewe
Or proud / or ellis oother weys a shrewe
A chidester / or wastour of thy good
Or riche / or poure / or ellis mannyssh wood
Al be it so / þt no man fynden shal
Noon in this world / that trotteth hool in al
Ne man ne beest / swich as men koude devyse
But nathelees / it oghte ynogh suffise
With any wyf / if so were þt she hadde
Mo goode thewes / than hir vices badde
And al this axeth leyser / for tenquere
ffor god it woot / I have wept many a teere
fful pryvely / syn þt I hadde a wyf
Preyse who so wole / a wedded mannes lyf
Certeyn I fynde in it / but cost and care
And observances / of alle blisses bare
And yet god woot / my neghebores aboute
And namely / of wommen many a route
Seyn þt I have / the mooste stedefast wyf
And eek the mekeste / that bereth lyf
But I woot best / where wryngeth me my sho
Ye mowe for me / right as yow liketh do
Avyseth yow / ye been a man of age
How þt ye entren / in to mariage
And namely with a yong wyf and a fair
By hym þt made water / erthe and eyr
The yongest man / þt is in al this route
Is bisy ynow to bryngen it aboute

	ELLESMERE
[Now] brother myn / be pacient I preye	Now
[S]yn ye han seyd / and herkneth what I seye	Syn
Senec amonges othere wordes wise	¶Senek among hise othere wyse
Seith / þat a man / oghte hym right wel auyse	man rigħt
To whom / he yeueth his lond / or his catel	
And syn I oghte / auysen me right wel	ogħte / auyse rigħt
To whom I yeeue my good / awey fro me	yeue
Wel muchel moore / I oghte auysed be	ogħte
To whom I yeeue my body / for alwey	yeue
I warne yow wel / it is no childes pley	
To taken a wyf withouten auysement	take with outen
Men moste enquere / this is myn assent	
Wher she be wys and sobre / or dronkelewe	wys / or sobre /
Or proud / or ellis oother weys a shrewe	elles ootherweys
A chidester / or wastour of thy good	chidestere /
Or riche / or poure / or ellis mannyssħ wood	poore / elles
Al be it so / þat no man fynden shal	that
Noon in this world / that trotteth hool in al	
Ne man ne beest swich as men koude deuyse	beest / which as
But nathelees / it oghte ynogh suffise	ogħte ynougħ
With any wyf if so were þat she hadde	wyf / that
Mo goode thewes / than hir vices badde	hire
And al this axeth leyser / for tenquere	[10] this /
For god it woot I haue wept many a teere	
Ful pryuely / syn þat I hadde a wyf	syn I haue had a
Preyse who so wole / a wedded mannes lyf	lyf
Certeyn I fynde in it but cost and care	Certein
And obseruances / of alle blisses bare	
And yet god woot my neghebores aboute	neighebores
And namely / of wommen many a route	wommen
Seyn þat I haue / the mooste stedefast wyf	wyf
And eek the mekeste / that bereth lyf	eek / mekeste oon / that
But I woot best where wryngeth me my sho	where
Ye mowe for me / right as yow liketh do	rigħt
Auyseth yow / ye been a man of age	
How þat ye entren / in to mariage	that
And namely / with a yong wyf and a feir	wyf / fair
By hym þat made water / erthe and Eir	erthe / Air
The yongest man / þat is in al this route	yongeste
Is bisy ynow / to bryngen it aboute	ynougħ /

[10] ¶Marchant *106r*

	ELLESMERE
To han his wyf allone / trusteth me	
Ye shul nat plesen hir*e* / fully yeres thre	
This is to seyn / to doon hir*e* ful plesance	plesau*n*ce
A wyf axeth / ful many an obs*er*uance	obseruaun*ce*
I pray yow / þ*at* ye be nat yuele apayd	prey apayd
¶Wel quod this Ianuarie / and hastow ysayd	ysayd
Straw for thy Senec and for thy p*ro*uerbes	Senek / prouerbes
I counte nat a panyer ful of herbes	
Of scole t*er*mes / wiser man than thow	t*er*mes / / wyser men
As thow hast herd / assenteden right now	thou right
To my purpos / Placebo what sey ye	Placebo / ye
¶I seye / it is a cursed man quod he	
That letteth matrymoigne sikerly	matrimoigne
And with that word / they risen sodeynly	rysen
And been assented fully / that he sholde	assented / fully þ*at*
Be wedded whan hym liste / and wher he wolde	wedded / whanne liste wher*e*
¶Heigh fantasie / and curious bisynesse	Heigh fantasye /
Fro day to day / gan in the soule impresse	imp*re*sse
Of Ianuarie / aboute his mariage	
Many fair shap*e* / and many a fair visage	
Ther passeth thurgh his herte / nyght by nyght	thurgh nyght nyght
As who so tooke a Miro*ur* / polisshed bright	Mirour polisshed bryght
And sette it in a co*m*mune Market place	
Thanne sholde he se / ful many a figure pace	
By his Mirour / and in the same wise	wyse
Gan Ianuarie / inwith his thoght deuyse	thoght
Of maydens / whiche þ*at* dwelten hym bisyde	dwellen
He wiste nat wher þ*at* he myghte abyde	myghte
For if þ*at* oon / haue beautee in hir face	beaute /
Another stant so / in the peples g*ra*ce	grace
For hir sadnesse / and hir benygnytee	11 hir*e* hir*e* benyngnytee
That of the peple / grettest voys hath she	
And som*m*e were riche / and hadden badde name	
But nathelees / bitwene ernest and game	bitwixe ernest
He atte laste / apoynted hym on oon	
And leet alle othere / from his herte goon	
And chees hir*e* / of his owene auctoritee	
For loue is blynd alday / and may nat see	
And whan that he / was in his bed ybroght	he was / ybroght
He purtreyde / in his herte / and in his thoght	p*ur*treyed / herte thoght

11¶Marchant *106v*

Do han his wyf allone / trusteth me
Ye shul nat plesen hire / fully yeres thre
This is to seyn / to doon hire ful plesance
A wyf axeth / ful many an obseruance
I pray yow / þt ye be nat yuele apayd
Wel quod this Januarie / and hastow ysayd
Straw for thy Senec / and for thy prouerbes
I counte nat a panyer ful of herbes
Of scole termes / wiser man than thow
As thow hast herd / assenteden right now
To my purpos / Placebo what sey ye
I seye / it is a cursed man quod he
That letteth matrymoigne sikerly
And with that word they rysen sodeynly
And been assented fully / that he sholde
Be wedded whan hym liste / and wher he wolde
Heigh fantasie / and curious bisynesse
ffro day to day / gan in the soule impresse
Of Januarie / aboute his mariage
Many fair shap / and many a fair visage
Ther passeth thurgh his herte / nyght by nyght /
As who so tooke a mirour / polisshed bryght /
And sette it / in a commune market place
Thanne sholde he se / ful many a figure pace
By his mirour / and in the same wise
Gan Januarie / inwith his thoght deuyse
Of maydens / whiche þt dwelten hym bisyde
He wiste nat wher þt he myghte abyde
ffor if þt oon / haue beautee in hir face
Another stant so / in the peples grace
ffor hir sadnesse / and hir benygnytee
That of the peple / grettest voys hath she
And somme were riche / and hadden badde name
But nathelees / bitwixe ernest and game
He atte laste / apoynted hym on oon
And leet alle othere / from his herte goon
And chees hire / of his owene auctoritee
ffor loue is blynd alday / and may nat see
And whan that he was in his bed ybroght /
He purtreyde / in his herte / and in his thoght /

fresshe beautee and hir age tendre
Hir myddel smal hir armes longe and sklendre
Hir wise gouernance hir gentilesse
Hir wommanly beryng and hir sadnesse
And whan þt he on hire was condescended
Hym thoughte his choys myghte nat ben amended
ffor whan þt he hym self concluded hadde
Hym thoughte ech oother mannes wit was badde
That inpossible it were to replye
Agayn his choys this was his fantasie
His freendes sente he to at his instance
And preyde hem to doon hym that plesance
That hastily they wolden to hym come
He wolde abregge hir labour alle and some
Nedeth namoore for hym to go ne ryde
He was apoynted ther he wolde abyde
Placebo cam and eek his freendes soone
And alderfirst he bad hem alle a boone
That noon of hem none argumentz make
Agayn the purpos which þt he hath take
Which purpos was plesant to god seyde he
And verray ground of his prosperitee
He seyde ther was a mayden in the toun
Which þt of beautee hadde greet renoun
Al were it so she were of smal degree
Suffiseth hym hir youthe and hir beautee
Which mayde he seyde he wolde han to his wyf
To lede in ese and holynesse his lyf
And thanked god þt he myghte han hire al
That no wight his blisse parten shal
And preyde hem to labouren in this nede
And shapen þt he faille nat to spede
ffor thanne he seyde his spirit was at ese
Thanne is quod he no thyng may me displese
Saue o thyng priketh in my conscience
The which I wol reherce in youre presence
I haue quod he herd seyd ful yoore ago
Ther may no man han parfite blisses two
This is to seye in erthe and eek in heuene
ffor though he kepe hym fro the synnes seuene

	ELLESMERE
[Hir] fresshe beautee / and hir age tendre	Hir fressħe
[H]ir myddel smal / hir armes longe and sklendre	Hir hir*e* armes
Hir wise gou*er*nance / hir gentilesse	gou*er*nau*n*ce / gentillesse
Hir wommanly beryng' and hir sadnesse	wo*m*manly berynge / hir*e*
And whan þ*at* he on hire / was condescended	that he / hir*e*
Hym thoughte / his choys myghte nat ben amended	thougħte / mygħte
For whan þ*at* he hym self / concluded hadde	
Hym thoughte / ech oother mannes wit' was badde	thougħte / wit so badde
That impossible / it weere to replye	inpossible / were repplye
Agayn his choys / this was his fantasie	fantasye
¶His freendes sente he to / at his instance	Hise instau*n*ce
And preyde hem / to doon hym that plesance	preyed plesau*n*ce
That hastily / they wolden to hym come	
He wolde abregge hir labour alle and some	
Nedeth namoore / for hym to go ne ryde	
He was apointed / ther he wolde abyde	apoynted /
¶Placebo cam / and eek his freendes soone	hise
And alderfirst' he bad hem alle a boone	
That noon of hem / none argumentz make	Argumentz
Agayn the purpos / which þ*at* he hath take	
Which purpos / was plesant to god / seyde he	plesant' god
And verray ground / of his p*ro*sp*er*itee	prosp*er*itee
¶He seyde / ther was a mayden in the toun	
Which þ*at* of beautee / hadde greet renoun	
Al were it so / she were of smal degree	were / of
Suffiseth hym / hir youthe and hir beautee	yowthe /
Which mayde he seyde / he wolde han to his wyf	wyf'
To lede in ese / and holynesse his lyf	hoolynesse lyf'
And thanked god / þ*at* he myghte han hir*e* al	mygħte
That no wight' his blisse parten shal	wigħt /
And preyde hem / to labouren in this nede	laboure
And shapen / þ*at* he faille nat to spede	
For thanne he seyde / his Spirit was atese	spirit
Thanne is quod he / no thyng may me displese	thyng'
Saue o thyng' priketh in my conscience	
The which I wol reherce / in youre p*re*sence	
¶I haue quod he herd seyd / ful yoore ago	he / seyd
Ther may no man / han p*ar*fite blisses two	
This is to seye / in erthe and eek in heuene	12 eek'
For thogh he kepe hym / fro the synnes seuene	though

12 ¶Marchanť *107r*

	ELLESMERE
And eek from euery branche / of thilke tree	eek / branche
Yet is ther / so p*ar*fit felicitee	ther' parfit
And so greet ese / and lust in mariage	
That euere I am agast' now in myn age	agast /
That I shal lede now / so murye a lyf	myrie lyf'
So delicat' with outen wo and stryf	stryf'
That I shal han myn heuene / in erthe heere	haue / heuene
For sith *þa*t verray heuene / is boght so deere	boghħt
With tribulacions / and greet penance	tribulaciou*n* /
How sholde I thanne / that lyue in swich plesance	*þa*t swicħ plesau*n*ce
As alle wedded men / doon with hir wyuys	wit*h* hire
Come to the blisse / that Crist eterne on lyue is	blisse / ther crist et*er*ne ys
This is my drede / and ye my bretheren tweye	
Assoileth me / this question I preye	Assoilleth questiou*n*
¶Iustinus / which *þa*t hated his folye	Iustinus / [¶Iustinus]
Answerde anon / right in his iaperye	righħt
And for he wolde / his longe tale abregge	
He wolde / noon auctoritee allegge	Auctoritee
But seide sire / so ther be noon obstacle	seyde
Oother than this / god of his hye myracle	hyghħ
And of his mercy / may so for yow werche	his hyghħ mercy / wirche
That er ye haue / your right' of holy cherche	haue youre righħt' hooly chirche
Ye may repente / of wedded mannes lyf	lyf'
In which ye seyn / ther is no wo ne stryf	stryf'
And ellis god forbede / but he sente	elles
A wedded man / hym g*ra*ce to repente	grace
Wel ofte / rather than a sengle man	
And ther fore sire / the beste reed I kan	therfore
Dispeire yow noght' but haue in youre memorie	noghħt'
P*ar*aunter / she may be youre purgatorie	
She may be goddes mene / and goddes whippe	meene /
Thanne shal your soule / vp to heuene skippe	your*e*
Swifter / than dooth an arwe / out of a bowe	Swifter' Arwe / of the bowe
I hope to god / heer after ye shul knowe	her shul ye
That' ther nys / noon so greet felicitee	That nys / no so
In mariage / ne neuere mo shal be	neueremo bee
That yow shal lette / of your*e* saluaciou*n*	your*e* sauaciou*n*
So that ye vse / as skile is and resou*n*	
The lustes of your*e* wyf / attemprely	wyf
And *þa*t / ye plese hir*e* / nat to amorously	*þa*t hir*e*

And eek from euery braunche / of thilke tree
yet is ther / so parfit felicitee
And so greet ese / and lust in mariage
That euere I am agast / now in myn age
That I shal lede now / so myrie a lyf
So delicat / with outen wo and stryf
That I shal han myn heuene / in erthe heere
ffor sith þt verray heuene / is boght so deere
With tribulaciouns / and greet penance
How sholde I thanne / that lyue in swich plesance
As alle wedded men / doon with hir wyuys
Come to the blisse / ther Crist eterne on lyue is
This is my drede / and ye my bretheren tweye
Assoilleth me / this question I preye
Justinus / which þt hated his folye
Answerde anon / right in his iaperye
And for he wolde / his longe tale abregge
He wolde / noon auctoritee allegge
But seyde sire / so ther be noon obstacle
Oother than this / god of his hye myracle
And of his mercy / may so for yow werche
That er ye haue / youre right of holy chirche
Ye may repente / of wedded mannes lyf
In which ye seyn / ther is no wo ne stryf
And ellis god forbede / but he sente
A wedded man / hym grace to repente
Wel ofte / rather than a sengle man
And ther fore sire / the beste reed I kan
Dispeire yow noght / but haue in youre memorie
Parauenture / she may be youre purgatorie
She may be goddes meene / and goddes whippe
Thanne shal youre soule / vp to heuene skippe
Swifter than dooth an arwe / out of a bowe
I hope to god / heer after ye shul knowe
That ther nys noon so greet felicitee
In mariage / ne neuere mo shal be
That yow shal lette / of youre saluacion
So that ye vse / as skile is and reson
The lustes of youre wyf / attemprely
And þt ye plese hire nat to amorously

that ye kepe yow eek from oother synne
My tale is doon for my wit is thynne
Beth nat agast her of my brother deere
But lat vs waden out of this mateere
The wyf of Bathe if ye han vnderstonde
Of mariage which we han on honde
Declared hath ful wel in litel space
Fareth now wel god haue yow in his grace
¶ And with that word this Iustyn and his brother
Han take hir leue and ech of hem of oother
For whan they saughe þt it moste nedes be
They wroghten so by sly and wys tretee
That she this mayden which that Mayus highte
As hastily as euere þt she myghte
Shal wedded be vn to this Ianuarie
¶ I trowe it were to longe yow to tarye
If I yow tolde of euery scrit and bond
By which þt she was feffed in his lond
Or for to herknen of hir riche array
But finally ycomen is that day
That to the chirche bothe be they went
For to receyue the holy sacrament
¶ Forth comth the preest with stole aboute his nekke
And bad hire be lyk Sarra and Rebekke
In wisdom and in trouthe of mariage
And seyde his orisons as is vsage
And crouched hem and bad god sholde hem blesse
And made al siker ynow with holynesse
¶ Thus been they wedded with solempnitee
And at the feste sitteth he and she
With oother worthy folk vp on the deys
Al ful of ioye and blisse is the paleys
And ful of instrumentz and of vitaille
The mooste deyntenous of al ytaille
Biforn hem stoode swiche instrumentz of swich soun
That Orpheus ne of Thebes Amphioun
Ne maden neuere swich a melodye
At euery cours thanne cam loud mynstralcye
That neuere tromped Ioab for to heere
Ne he Theodomas yet half so cleere

At Thebes

	ELLESMERE
[And] that ye kepe yow eek / from oother synne	And þ*at*
[M]y tale is doon / for my wit is thynne	My
Beth nat agast her of / my brother deere	agast'
But lat vs waden / out of this matere	mateere
The wyf of Bathe / if ye han vnderstonde	
Of mariage / which we han on honde	which ye haue
Declared hath ful wel / in litel space	13
Fareth now wel / god haue yow in his *gra*ce	
¶And with that word / this Iustyn and his brother	And with this word /
Han take hir leue / and ech of hem of oother	
For whan they sawe / þ*at* it moste nedes be	saugħ that' moste be
They wroghten so / by sly / and wys tretee	sly
That she this mayden / which that Mayus highte	þ*at* higħte
As hastily / as euer þ*at* she myghte	euere that mygħte
Shal wedded be / vn to this Ianuarie	
¶I trowe / it were to longe yow to tarye	I trowe tarie
If I yow tolde / of euery scrit and bond	bond'
By which / þ*at* she was feffed in his lond	lond'
Or for to herknen / of hir riche array	
But finally / ycomen is that day	is the day
That to the chirche / bothe be they went	went'
For to receyue / the holy sacrament	hooly sacrement'
¶Forth comth the preest' with stoole aboute his nekke	Forth wit*h* stole
And bad hire be lyk / Sarra and Rebekke	hir*e* lyk' to Sarra
In wisdom / and in trouthe of mariage	wysdom
And seyde his orisons / as is vsage	seyde hir orisons /
And croucheth hem / and bad / god sholde hem blesse	bad he*m* blesse
And made al siker ynow / with holynesse	ynogħ / hoolynesse
¶Thus been they wedded / with solempnitee	
And at the laste / sitteth he and she	the feeste / sitteth
With oother worthy folk / vp on the deys	other*e* folk'
Al ful of ioye and blisse / is the paleys	blisse
And ful of Instrumentz / and of vitaille	
The mooste deynteuous / of al Ytaille	
Biforn hem stoode swiche Instrumentz of swich soun	hem / stooden Instrumentz
That Orpheus / nof Thebes Amphioun	ne of Thebes Amphiou*n*
Ne maden neuere / swich a melodye	neu*er*e /
At euery cours / thanne cam loud mynstralcye	¶At eu*ery* Mynstralcye
That neuere tromped / Ioab / for to heere	neu*er*e tromped
Ne he Theodomas / yet half so cleere	Nor he

At Thebes

13¶Marcħant' *107v*

	ELLESMERE
At Thebes / whan the Citee was in doute	
Bacus / the wyn hem shenketh al aboute	skynketh
And Venus laugheth / vp on euery wight	Venus / laugheth wight
For Ianuarie / was bicome hir knyght	knyght
And wolde / bothe assayen his corage	wolde bothe /
In libertee / and eek in mariage	
And with hir firbrond / in hir hand aboute	*with* hir*e* fyrbrond/ hir*e* hand
Daunceth bifore the bryde / and al the route	Daunceth / biforn bryde
And c*er*teinly / I dar right wel seye this	certeinly / right seyn
Ymeneus / that god of weddyng is	
Say neuere his lyf / so murye a wedded man	Saugh neu*ere* lyf myrie
Hoold thow thy pees / thou poete Marcian	thou thy
That writest vs / that ilke weddyng murye	weddyng murie
Of hir*e* Philologie / and he Mercurie	and hym Mercurie
And of the songes / that the Muses songe	14
To smal / is bothe thy penne / and eek thy tonge	smal
For to discryuen / of this mariage	
Whan tendre youthe / hath wedded stoupyng age	
Ther is swich murthe / that it may nat be writen	myrthe / þ*a*t
Assayeth it your self than may ye witen	your*e* self / thanne
If that I lye or noon / in this matere	matiere
¶Mayus that sit with so benygne a cheere	sit / *with* benyngne chiere
Hir to biholde / it semed Fairye	Hir*e* fairye
Queene Ester / looked neu*ere* *with* swich an eye	
On Assuer / so meke a look hath she	
I may yow nat deuyse / al hir beautee	
But thus muche / of hir beautee / telle I may	muche hir*e* beautee
That she was lyk the brighte morwe of May	lyk /
Fulfild / of alle beautee and plesau*n*ce	
¶This Ianuarie / is rauysshed in a traunce	trau*n*ce
At euery tyme / he looked on hir face	
But in his herte / he gan hir to manace	hir*e*
That he that nyght in armes wolde hir streyne	nyght Armes hir*e*
Harder than euere / Parys dide Eleyne	Harder / euere
But nathelees / yet hadde he gret pitee	greet
That thilke nyght offenden hir*e* moste he	
And thoghte allas / o tendre creature	thoughte
Now wolde god / ye myghte wel endure	
Al my corage / it is so sharp*e* and kene	keene
I am agast ye shul it nat sustene	susteene

14¶Marchant *108r*

At Thebes whan the Citee was in doute
Bacus the wyn hem shenketh al aboute
And Venus laugheth vp on euery wight
ffor Ianuarie was bicome hir knyght
And wolde bothe assayen his corage
In libertee and eek in mariage
And with hir fyrbrond in hir hand aboute
Daunceth bifore the bryde and al the route
And certeinly I dar right wel seye this
Ymeneus that god of weddyng is
Say neuere his lyf so murye a wedded man
Hoold thow thy pees thou poete Marcian
That writest vs that ilke weddyng murye
Of hire Philologie and he Mercurie
And of the songes that the Muses songe
To smal is bothe thy penne and eek thy tonge
ffor to discryuen of this mariage
Whan tendre youthe hath wedded stoupyng age
Ther is swich myrthe that it may nat be writen
Assayeth it youre self than may ye witen
If that I lye or noon in this matere
Mayus that sit with so benygne a cheere
Hir to biholde it semed ffayerye
Queene Ester looked neuere wt swich an eye
On Assuer so meke a look hath she
I may yow nat deuyse al hir beautee
But thus muche of hir beautee telle I may
That she was lyk the brighte morwe of May
ffulfild of alle beautee and plesance
This Ianuarie is rauysshed in a traunce
At euery tyme he looked on hir face
But in his herte he gan hir to manace
That he that nyght in armes wolde hir streyne
Harder than euere Parys dide Eleyne
But nathelees yet hadde he greet pitee
That thilke nyght offenden hire moste he
And thoghte allas o tendre creature
Now wolde god ye myghte wel endure
Al my corage it is so sharp and kene
I am agast ye shul it nat sustene

god forbede that I dide al my myght
Now wolde god that it were woxen nyght
And pt the nyght wolde laste eue mo
I wolde that al this peple were ago
And fynally he doth al his labour
As he best myghte sauyng his honour
To haste hem fro the mete in subtil wise
The tyme cam pt reson was to rise
And after that men daunce and drynken faste
And spices al aboute the hous they caste
And ful of ioye and blisse is euery man
Al but a Squyer highte Damyan
Which carf biforn the knyght ful many a day
He was so rauysshed on his lady may
That for the verray peyne he was ny wood
Almoost he swelte and swowned as he stood
So sore hath venus hurt hym with hir brond
As that she bar it dauncyng in hir hond
And to his bed he wente hym hastily
Namoore of hym at this tyme speke I
But ther I lete hym wepe ynow and pleyne
Til fresshe may wol rewen on his peyne
Auctor O perilous fyr that in the bedstraw bredeth
O famulier foo that his seruice bedeth
O seruant traytour false homly hewe
Lyk to the neddre in bosom sly vntrewe
God shilde vs alle from youre aqueyntance
O Januarie dronken in plesance
In mariage se how thy Damyan
Thyn owene Squyer and thy born man
Entendeth for to do thee vileynye
God graunte thee thyn homly fo espye
For in this world nys worse pestilence
Than homly fo alday in thy presence
Parfourned hath the sonne his ark diurne
No lenger may the body of hym soiurne
On thorisonte as in that latitude
Night with his mantel that is derk and rude
Gan ouersprede the hemysperie aboute
For which departed is this lusty route

ELLESMERE

[But] god forbede / that I dide al my myght
[N]ow wolde god / that it were woxen nyght
[A]nd þ*at* the nyght wolde laste eue*re* mo
I wolde / that al this peple were ago
And fynally / he dooth al his labour
As he best myghte / sauyng his honour
To haste hem fro the mete / in subtil wise
The tyme cam / þ*at* reson was to rise
And after that men daunce / and drynken faste
And Spices / al aboute the hous they caste
And ful of ioye and blisse / is euery man
Al but a Squyer / highte Damyan
Which carf biforn the knyght ful many a day
He was so rauysshed / on his lady May
That for the verray peyne / he was ny wood
Almoost he swelte / and swowned as he stood
So sore hath Venus / hurt hym with hir brond
As that she baar it dauncyng in hir hond
And to his bed / he wente hym hastily
Namoore of hym / as this tyme speke .I
But ther I lete hym / wepe ynow and pleyne
Til fresshe May / wol rewen on his peyne
Auctor ¶O. pe*r*ilous fyr / that in the bed straw bredeth
O. famulier foo / that his se*r*uice bedeth
O. se*r*uant traytour / false homly hewe
Lyk to the Neddre in bosom / sly vntrewe
God shilde vs alle / from youre aqueyntance
O Ianuarie / dronken in plesance
In mariage / se how thy Damyan
Thyn owene Squyer / and thy born man
Entendeth / for to do thee vileynye
God grante thee / thyn homly fo espye
For in this world / nys worse pestilence
Than homly fo / alday in thy p*re*sence
¶P*ar*fourned hath the sonne / his Ark diurne
No lenger / may the body of hym soiurne
On thorisonte / as in that latitude
Night with his mantel / that is derk and rude
Gan ouersprede / Themysperies aboute
For which / dep*ar*ted is / this lusty route

But myght
Now þ*at* nyght
And that nyght / lasten eue*re*mo

finally /
myghte / sauynge
wyse
¶The that resou*n* ryse
daunce

blisse eue*r*y
highte
knyght

ve*r*ray
swowned ther he
soore / venus wi*th* hire brond
þ*a*t bar daunsynge hir*e* hond

speke |
ther*e* hym ynogh
fresshe
15 ¶Auctor] O bedstraw
O seruyce
O seruant hoomly
naddre / bosom
aqueyntau*n*ce

Squier /

graunte hoomly tespye

hoomly foo /

wi*th* Mantel þ*a*t derk
oue*r*sprede the hemyspe*r*ie
which / departed

1795 [Ar]ke diurne . . . quidam circulus . . . mento vocatus Zodiacus . . . quam sol cotidie currit Hg (in another hand)

[15] ¶Marchant *108v*

	ELLESMERE
Fro Ianuarie / with thank on eu*er*y syde	euery
Hom to hir houses / lustily they ryde	Hoom hous /
Wher as they doon hir thynges / as hem leste	Wher*e*
And whan they say hir tyme / go to reste	they sye hir goon
¶Soone after þ*at* this hasty Ianuarie	Soone that hastif
Wol go to bedde / he wol no lenger tarie	Wolde wolde tarye
He drynketh Ypocras / Clarree and Vernage	
Of Spices hoote / tencressen his corage	spices tencreessen
And many a letuarie / hadde he ful fyn	Letuarie / hath he
Swich as the cursed Monk / daun Constantyn	Swiche the Monk
Hath writen / in his book **De coitu**	book **de coitu**
To eten hem alle / he nas no thyng eschu	
And to his pryuee freendes / thus seyde ⟨he⟩	hise p*ri*uee he
For goddes loue / as soone as it may be	
Lat voyden al this hous / in curteis wise	curteys wyse
And they han doon / right as he wol deuyse	right
Men drynken / and the trauers drawe anon	
The bryde was broght a bedde / as stille as stoon	bryde / broght
And whan the bed / was with the preest yblessed	
Out of the chambre / hath euery wight hym dressed	wight
And Ianuarie / hath faste in armes take	Armes
His fresshe May / his Paradys / his make	fresshe Paradys
He lulleth hir*e* / he kisseth hire / ful ofte	hir*e* ful
With thilke bristles / of his berd vnsofte	brustles /
Lyk to the Skyn of houndfyssh / sharp*e* as brere	skyn
For he was shaue al newe / in his manere	
He rubbeth hir*e* / aboute hir tendre face	
And seyde thus / allas I moot trespace	
To yow my Spouse / and yow gretly offende	spouse / greetly
Er tyme come / þ*at* I wol doun descende	wil
But natheles / considereth this quod he	16 nathelees /
Ther nys no werkman / what so eu*er*e he be	
That may bothe / werke wel and hastily	
This wol be doon / at leyser p*ar*fitly	doon
It is no fors / how longe þ*at* we pleye	
In trewe wedlok coupled be we tweye	wedlok / wedded be
And blessed be the yok / þ*at* we been Inne	yok
For in actes / we mow do no synne	Actes / mowe
A man / may do no synne with his wyf	*with*
Ne hurte hym seluen / with his owene knyf	*with*

16 ¶Marchant *109r*

ffro Ianuarie / with thank on euery syde
Hom to hir houses / lustily they ryde
Where as they doon hir thynges / as hem leste
And whan they say hir tyme / go to reste
Soone after p^t this hasty Ianuarie
Wol go to bedde / he wol no lenger tarie
He drynketh ypocras / clarree and vernage
Of spices hoote / tencreessen his corage
And many a letuarie / hadde he ful fyn
Swich as the cursed monk / daun Constantyn
Hath writen / in his book / de coitu
To eten hem alle / he nas no thyng eschu
And to his pryuee freendes / thus seyde he
ffor goddes loue / as soone as it may be
Lat voyden al this hous / in curteis wyse
And they han doon / right as he wol deuyse
Men drynken / and the trauers drawe anon
The bryde was broght a bedde / as stille as stoon
And whan the bed / was with the preest yblessed
Out of the chambre / hath euery wight hym dressed
And Ianuarie / hath faste in armes take
His fresshe May / his Paradys / his make
He lulleth hire / he kisseth hire / ful ofte
With thikke brustles / of his berd vnsofte
Lyk to the skyn of houndfyssh / sharp as brere
ffor he was shaue al newe / in his manere
He rubbeth hire / aboute hir tendre face
And seyde thus / allas I moot trespace
To yow my spouse / and yow gretly offende
Er tyme come / p^t I wol doun descende
But nathelees / considereth this quod he
Ther nys no werkman / what so euere he be
That may bothe / werke wel and hastily
This wol be doon / at leyser parfitly
It is no fors / how longe p^t we pleye
In trewe wedlok / coupled be we tweye
And blessed be the yok / p^t we been inne
ffor in actes / we mowe do no synne
A man may do no synne with his wyf
Ne hurte hym seluen / with his owene knyf

we han leue / to pleye vs by the lawe
Thus laboureth he / til that the day gan dawe
And thanne / he taketh a sop in fyn clarree
And vp right in his bed / thanne sitteth he
And after that / he song ful loude and cleere
And kiste his wyf / and made wantowen cheere
He was al coltyssh / ful of ragerye
And ful of Iargon as a flekked pye
The slakke skyn / aboute his nekke shaketh
Whil þt he song / so chaunteth he and craketh
But god woot / what þt May thoghte in hir herte
Whan she hym saugh / vp sittyng in his sherte
In his nyght cappe / and with his nekke lene
She preiseth nat his pleyyng worth a bene
Thanne seyde he thus / my reste wol I take
Now day is come / I may no lenger wake
And doun he leyde his heed / and sleep til pryme
And afterward / whan þt he saugh his tyme
Vp riseth Ianuarie / but fresshe May
Heeld hir chambre / vn to the fourthe day
As vsage is of wyues / for the beste
ffor euery labour / som tyme moot han reste
Or ellis / longe may he nat endure
This is to seyn / no lyues creature
Be it fissh / or brid / or beest / or man
Now wol I speke / of woful Damyan
That langwissheth for loue / as ye shul heere
Ther fore I speke to hym / in this manere
Auctor I seye / o sely Damyan allas
Answere to my demaunde / as in this cas
How shaltow to thy lady fresshe May
Telle thy wo / she wol alwey seye nay
Eek if thow speke / she wol thy wo biwreye
God be thyn help / I kan no bettre seye
This sike Damyan / in Venus fyr
So brenneth / that he dyeth for desyr
ffor which he putte his lyf in auenture
No lenger myghte he / in this wise endure
But priuely a penner gan he borwe
And in a lettre / wroot he al his sorwe

	ELLESMERE
[For] we han leue / to pleye vs by the lawe	For
[Th]us laboureth he / til that the day gan dawe	Thus *pat*
And thanne / he taketh a sope in fyn Clarree	thanne sope / clarree
And vp right in his bed / thanne sitteth he	vpright
And after that he song ful loude and clere	sang cleere
And kiste his wyf / and made wantown cheere	wantowne
He was al coltyssħ / ful of ragerye	coltissħ /
And ful of Iargon / as a flekked pye	
The slakke skyn / aboute his nekke shaketh	shaketħ
Whil *pat* he song so chaunteth he and craketh	sang / crakeħ
But god woot what *pat* may thoghte in hir herte	May thoughte
Whan she hym saw / vp sittyng in his sherte	saugħ / sittynge
In his nyght cappe / and with his nekke lene	nyght *with*
She preiseth nat his pleyyng worth a bene	preyseth nat pleyyng
Thanne seyde he thus / my reste wol I take	seide
Now day is come / I may no lenger wake	
And doun he leyde his heed / and sleepe til pryme	
And afterward / whan *pat* he saw his tyme	saugh
Vp riseth Ianuarie / but fresshe May	ryseth
Heeld hir chambre / vn to the fourthe day	hir*e*
As vsage is of wyues / for the beste	is /
For euery labour / som tyme moot han reste	
Or ellis / longe may he nat endure	elles /
This is to seyn / no lyues creature	
Be it fissħ / or bryd / or beest or man	it of fyssħ /
Now wol I speke / of woful Damyan	
That langwissheth for loue / as ye shul heere	langwissħetħ
Ther fore / I speke to hym / in this manere	Therfore / hym
Auctor ¶I seye / o sely Damyan allas	[¶Auctor]
Answere to my demaunde / as in this cas	Andswere
How shaltow / to thy lady fresshe May	fresshe
Telle thy wo / she wol alwey sey nay	wole seye
Eek if thow speke / she wol thy wo biwreye	thou
God be thyn help*e* / I kan no bettre seye	
This syke Damyan / in Venus fyr	¶This sike
So brenneth / that he dyeth for desyr	
For which / he putte his lyf in auenture	
No lenger myghte he / in this wise endure	myghte
But pr*i*uely / a penner gan he borwe	17
And in a lettre / wroot he al his sorwe	

1875 Venus God of loue Hg (in a later hand)

[17] ¶Marchant *109v*

In manere of a compleynt or a lay	
Vn to his faire / fresshe lady May	fresshe
And in a purs of sylk heng on his sherte	
He hath it put and leyd it at his herte	leyde
¶The moone *pat* at Noon / was thilke day	The moone / that Noon
That Ianuarie / hath wedded fresshe May	fresshe
In two of Taur / was in to Cancre gliden	Tawr / glyden
So longe hath Mayus / in hir chambre abyden	cha*m*bre byden
As custume is / vn to thise nobles alle	
A bryde / shal nat eten in the halle	
Til dayes foure / or thre dayes atte leeste	or .iij. dayes
Ypassed ben / thanne lat hir go to feste	been / hir*e* feeste
¶The fourthe day complet fro noon to noon	The compleet Noon Noon
Whan *pat* the heighe masse / was ydoon	*pat* / masse
In halle / sit this Ianuarie and May	
As fressħ / as is the brighte Someres day	brighte Som*er*es
And so bifel / how that this goode man	
Remembred hym / vp on this Damyan	vpon
And seyde / Seynte Marie how may it be	Marie / may this be
That Damyan / entendeth nat to me	
Is he ay syk / or how may this bityde	syk /
¶Hys Squyers / whiche *pat* stooden ther bisyde	Hise squieres / that
Excused hym / by cause of his siknesse	
Which letted hym / to doon his bisynesse	
Noon oother cause / myghte make hym tarye	
¶That me forthynketh / quod this Ianuarye	Ianuarie
He is a gentil Squyer / by my trouthe	squier /
If *pat* he deyde / it were harm and routhe	that
He is as wys / discret and eek secree	discreet / and as secree
As any man / I woot of his degree	
And ther to manly / and eek *ser*uysable	seruysable
And for to be a thrifty man / right able	been man
But after mete / as soone as euere I may	
I wol my self visite hym / and eek May	hym
To do hym / al the confort *pat* I kan	doon confort that
And for that word / hym blessed euery man	
That of his bou*n*tee / and his gentilesse	gentillesse
He wolde so / conforten in siknesse	so
His squyer / for it was a gentil dede	squier
¶Dame quod this Ianuarie / tak good hede	Dame taak

In manere of a compleynt / or a lay
Vn to his faire / fresshe lady May
And in a purs of sylk / heng on his sherte
He hath it put / and leyd it at his herte
¶ The moone þt at noon / was thilke day
That Januarie / hath wedded fresshe May
In two of Tawr / was in to Cancre gliden
So longe hath Mayus / in hir chambre abyden
As custume is / vn to thise nobles alle
A bryde / shal nat eten in the halle
Til dayes foure / or thre dayes atte leeste
Ypassed ben / thanne lat hir go to feeste
¶ The fourthe day complet / fro noon to noon
Whan þt the heighe masse / was ydoon
In halle / sit this Januarie and May
As fressh / as is the brighte someres day
And so bifel / how that this goode man
Remembred hym / vp on this Damyan
And seyde / Seynte Marie how may it be
That Damyan / entendeth nat to me
Is he ay syk / or how may this bityde
¶ Thise Squyers / whiche þt stooden ther bisyde
Excused hym / by cause of his siknesse
Which letted hym / to doon his bisynesse
Noon oother cause / myghte make hym tarye
¶ That me forthynketh / quod this Januarye
He is a gentil Squyer / by my trouthe
If þt he deyde / it were harm and routhe
He is as wys / discreet / and eek secree
As any man / I woot of his degree
And ther to manly / and eek seruysable
And for to be a thrifty man / right able
But after mete / as soone as euere I may
I wol my self visite hym / and eek May
To do hym / al the confort þt I kan
And for that word / hym blessed euery man
That of his bountee / and his gentilesse
He wolde so conforten in siknesse
His Squyer / for it was a gentil dede
¶ Dame quod this Januarie / tak good heede

[At af]ter mete / ye with youre wommen alle
[Wh]an ye han ben in chambre / out of this halle
[T]hat alle ye go / to this Damyan
Dooth hym disport / he is a gentil man
And telleth hym / þt I wol hym visite
Have I no thyng / but rested me a lite
And spede yow faste / for I wol abide
Til that ye slepe / faste by my syde
And with that word / he gan to hym to calle
A Squier / that was marchal of his halle
And tolde hym certein thynges / what he wolde
This fresshe may / hath streight hir wey yholde
With alle hir wommen / vn to Damyan
Doun by his beddes syde / sit she than
Confortyng hym / as goodly as she may
This Damyan / whan þt his tyme he say
In secree wyse / his purs and eek his bille
In which þt he ywriten hadde his wille
Hath put in to hir hand / with oute moore
Save þt he siketh / wonder depe and soore
And softely to hire / right thus seyde he
Mercy / and þt ye nat discouere me
ffor I am deed / if þt this thyng be kyd
This purs hath she / inwith hir bosom hyd
And wente hir wey / ye gete namoore of me
But vn to Januarie / ycomen is she
That on his beddes syde / sit ful softe
And taketh hire / and kisseth hire ful ofte
And leyde hym doun to slepe / and that anon
She feyned hire / as þt she moste gon
Ther as ye woot / that euery wight moot nede
And whan she of this bille / hath taken hede
She rente it al to cloutes / at the laste
And in the pryuee / softely it caste
Who studieth now / but faire fresshe may
Adoun by olde Januarie she lay
That sleep / til þt the coghe hath hym awaked
Anon he preyde / strepen hire al naked
He wolde of hire he seyde / han som plesance
He seyde hir clothes / dide hym encombrance

	ELLESMERE
[At af]ter mete / ye with your*e* wommen alle	At after Noon / ye wit*h* youre wo*m*men
[Wh]an ye han ben in chambre / out of this halle	Whan been
[T]hat alle ye go / to this Damyan	That ye / go se this
Dooth hym disport⁊ he is a gentil man	
And telleth hym / *þat* I wol hym visite	that
Haue I no thyng⁊ but rested me alite	
And spede yow faste / for I wol abide	[18] wole abyde
Til that ye slepe / faste by my syde	
And with that word / he gan to hym to calle	wit*h*
A Squier / that was Marchal of his halle	
And tolde hym c*er*tein thynges / what he wolde	c*er*teyn
¶This fresshe May / hath streight hir wey yholde	fressħe streighħt
With alle hir wommen / vn to Damyan	wo*m*men /
Doun by his beddes syde / sit she than	
Confortyng hym / as goodly as she may	Confortynge
¶This Damyan / whan *þat* his tyme he say	This that
In secree wise / his purs and eek his bille	
In which / *þat* he ywriten hadde his wille	which he /
Hath put in to hir hand / with oute moore	hir*e* outen
Saue *þat* he siketh / wonder depe and soore	
And softely to hir*e* / right thus seyde he	rigħt
Mercy / and *þat* ye nat discouere me	that
For I am deed / if *þat* this thyng be kyd	that thyng /
This purs hath she / in with hir bosom hyd	inwith
And wente hir wey / ye gete namoore of me	hir*e*
But vn to Ianuarie / ycomen is she	
That on his beddes syde / sit ful softe	
And taketh hir*e* / and kisseth hir*e* ful ofte	
And leyde hym doun to slepe / and that anon	
She feyned hir*e* / as *þat* she moste gon	that
Ther as ye woot⁊ that euery wight moot nede	*þat* wigħt neede
And whan she of this bille / hath taken hede	heede
She rente it al to cloutes / at the laste	it / cloutes atte laste
And in the pryuee / softely it caste	
¶Who studieth now / but faire fresshe May	Who
Adoun / by olde Ianuarie she lay	
That sleep*e* / til *þat* the coghe hath hym/awaked	cougħe / hym awaked
Anon he preyde / strepen hir*e* al naked	preyde hir*e* / strepen hir*e*
He wolde of hir*e* he seyde / han som plesau*n*ce	
He seyde / hir clothes / dide hym encombrance	encombrau*n*ce

[18]¶Marcħant⁊ *110r*

	ELLESMERE
And she obeyeth / be hir lief or looth	hire looth
But lest þ*at* p*re*cious folk / be w*ith* me wrooth	lest ye p*re*cious with
How þ*at* he wroghte / I dar nat to yow telle	that
Or wheither / it thoughte Paradys / or helle	wheither / þ*a*t hire thoughte it Paradys
But heere I lete hem werken / in hir wise	hem / werken wyse
Til euensong rong and þ*at* they moste arise	aryse
Were it by destynee / or by auenture	
Were it by Influence / or by nature	
Or constellaciou*n* / that in swich estat	estaat
The heuene stood / that tyme fortunat	heuene / stood fortunaat
As for to putte a bille / of Venus werkes	Was for
For alle thyng hath tyme / as seyn thise clerkes	
To any womman / for to gete hir loue	wom*m*an / hire
I kan nat seye / but grete god aboue	
That knoweth / þ*a*t noon Act is causelees	19 that noon
He deme of al / for I wol holde my pees	wole
¶But sooth is this / how þ*a*t this fresshe May	But that fresshe
Hath taken / swich imp*re*ssiou*n* that day	take /
Of pitee / on this syke Damyan	For pitee / of this sike
That from hir herte / she ne dryue kan	hire
The remembrance / for to doon hym ese	
Certeyn thoghte she / whom þ*a*t this thyng displese	thoghte
I rekke nat for here I hym assure	noght / heere
To loue hym best of any creature	
Thogh he namoore hadde / than his sherte	Though hadde
Loo / pitee renneth soone / in gentil herte	Lo pitee / soone
¶Heere may ye se / how excellent franchise	
In wommen is / whan they hem narwe auyse	wom*m*en
Som tirau*n*t is / as ther be many oon	tyrant
That hath an herte / as hard as is a stoon	hard / as any stoon
Which wolde / han leten steruen / in the place	han lat hym storuen in
Wel rather / than han graunted hym hir gr*a*ce	hire
And hem reioysen / in hir cruel pryde	hire crueel
And rekke nat to been an homycide	
¶This gentil May / fulfilled of pitee	
Right of hir hand / a lettre maked she	Right hire made
In which she graunteth hym / hir ve*r*ray gr*a*ce	hym hire
Ther lakketh noght oonly / but day and place	noght /
Wher that she myghte / vn to his lust suffise	þ*a*t myghte /
For it shal be / right as he wol deuyse	right wole

[19] ¶Marchant *110v*

And she obeyeth / be hir lief or looth
But lest pt precious folk / be wt me wrooth
How pt he wroghte / I dar nat to yow telle
Or wheither / it thoughte Paradys / or helle
But heere I lete hem werken in hir wise
Til euensong rong / and pt they moste arise
Were it by destynee / or by auenture
Were it by Influence / or by nature
Or constellacion / that in swich estat
The heuene stood / that tyme fortunat
As for to putte a bille / of Venus werkes
ffor alle thyng hath tyme / as seyn thise clerkes
To any womman / for to gete hir loue
I kan nat seye / but grete god aboue
That knoweth / pt noon act / is causelees
He deme of al / for I wol holde my pees
¶ But sooth is this / how pt this fresshe May
Hath taken / swich impression that day
Of pitee / on this sike Damyan
That from hir herte / she ne dryue kan
The remembrance / for to doon hym ese
Certeyn thoghte she / whom pt this thyng displese
I rekke nat / for heere I hym assure
To loue hym best / of any creature
Though he namoore hadde / than his sherte
Lo / pitee renneth soone in gentil herte
¶ Heere may ye se / how excellent franchise
In wommen is / whan they hem narwe auyse
Som tirant is / as ther be many oon
That hath an herte / as hard as is a stoon
Which wolde han leten steruen / in the place
Wel rather / than han graunted hym hir grace
And hem reioysen / in hir cruel pryde
And rekke nat / to been an homycide
¶ This gentil May / fulfilled of pitee
Right of hir hand / a lettre maked she
In which she graunteth hym / hir verray grace
Ther lakketh noght oonly / but day and place
Wher that she myghte / vn to his lust suffise
ffor it shal be / right as he wol deuyse

Whan she sauh hir tyme vp on a day
To visite this Damyan goth May
And subtilly this lettre doun she threste
Vnder his pilwe rede it if hym leste
She taketh hym by the hand and harde hym twiste
So secrely that no wight of it wiste
And bad hym be al hool and forth she wente
To Januarie whan þt he for hir sente
¶ Vp riseth Damyan the nexte morwe
Al passed was his siknesse and his sorwe
He kembeth hym he prayneth hym and pyketh
He dooth al that his lady lust and lyketh
And eek to Januarie he goth as lowe
As euere dide a dogge for the bowe
He is so plesant vn to euery man
ffor craft is al who so þt do it kan
That euery wight is fayn to speke hym good
And fully in his ladyes grace he stood
Thus lete I Damyan aboute his nede
And in my tale forth I wol procede
¶ Somme clerkes holden þt felicitee
Stant in delit and ther fore certeyn he
This noble Januarie with al his myght
In honeste wise as longeth to a knyght
Shoop hym to lyue ful deliciously
His housyng his array as honestly
To his degree was maked as a kynges
Amonges othere of his honeste thynges
He made a gardyn walled al with stoon
So fair a gardyn woot I nowher noon
ffor out of doute I verraily suppose
That he þt wroot the Romance of the Rose
Ne koude of it the beautee wel deuyse
Ne Priapus ne myghte nat suffise
Though he be god of gardyns for to telle
The beautee of the gardyn and the welle
That stood vnder a laurer alwey grene
fful ofte tyme he Pluto and his queene
Proserpina and al hir ffayrye
Disporten hem and maken melodye

	ELLESMERE
[And] whan she saw hir tyme / vp on a day	And saugħ tyme
[To] visite this Damyan / goth May	To gooth
And subtilly / this lettre doun she threste	sotilly le*tt*re /
Vnder his pilwe / rede it if hym leste	
She taketh hym by the hand / and harde hym twiste	
So secrely / that no wight of it wiste	wigħt
And bad hym be al hool / and forth she wente	been forth he wente
To Ianuarie / whan þ*a*t he for hir sente	for hym sente
¶Vp riseth Damyan / the nexte morwe	Up
Al passed was / his siknesse and his sorwe	
He kembeth hym / he prayneth hym and pyketh	preyneth
He dooth / al that his lady lust and lyketh	
And eek to Ianuarie / he goth as lowe	gooth
As euere dide / a dogge for the bowe	eue*re*
He is so plesant vn to euery man	
For craft is al / who so þ*a*t do it kan	that
That euery wight is fayn to speke hym good	wigħt
And fully / in his ladyes g*ra*ce he stood	lady grace
Thus lete I Damyan / aboute his nede	
And in my tale / forth I wol p*ro*cede	procede
¶So*m*me clerkes / holden þ*a*t felicitee	that
Stant in delit and therfore c*er*teyn he	he /
This noble Ianuarie / with al his myght	20 mygħt
In honeste wise / as longeth to a knyght	wyse / knygħt
Shoop*e* hym to lyue / ful deliciously	
His housyng his array / as honestly	housynge /
To his degree / was maked / as a kynges	maked
Amonges othere / of his honeste thynges	hise
He made a gardyn / walled al with stoon	
So fair a gardyn / woot I nowher noon	
For out of doute / I v*er*raily suppose	verraily
That he / þ*a*t wroot the Romance of the Rose	romance
Ne koude of it the beautee wel deuyse	
Ne Priapus / ne myghte nat suffise	mygħte
Thogh he be god of gardyns / for to telle	Though
The beautee / of the gardyn and the welle	beautee gardyn /
That stood vnder a laurer / alwey grene	Laurer /
Ful ofte tyme / he Pluto and his queene	
Proserpina / and al hir Fairye	hir*e* fairye
Disporten hem / and maken melodye	

20¶Marchant *111r*

Aboute that welle / and daunced as men tolde	
This noble knyght this Ianuarie the olde	¶This knyght
Swich deyntee hath / in it to walke and pleye	
That he wol no wight suffre bere the keye	wight suffren
Saue he hym self for of the smal wyket	self / smale
He bar alwey / of siluer a Clyket	baar
With which / whan þat hym leste / he it vnshette	leste
And whan he wolde / paye his wyf hir dette	
In somer seson / thider wolde he go	sesoun /
And May his wyf and no wight but they two	wyf /
And thynges / whiche þat were nat doon abedde	
He in the gardyn / parfourned hem and spedde	
And in this wise / many a murye day	wyse /
Lyued this Ianuarie / and fresshe May	fresshe
But worldly ioye / may nat alwey dure	Ioye /
To Ianuarie / ne to no creature	
Auctor ¶O. sodeyn hape / o. thow Fortune vnstable	O o thou fortune Instable ⌈¶Auctor⌉
Lyk to the Scorpion / so deceyuable	
That flaterest with thyn heed / whan thow wolt stynge	thou wolt synge |
Thy tayl is deeth / thurgh thyn enuenymynge	thurgh
O. brotil ioye / o. swete venym queynte	O Ioye / o sweete
O. Monstre / that so subtilly kanst peynte	O
Thy yiftes / vnder hewe of stedefastnesse	stidefastnesse
That thow deceyuest bothe moore and lesse	thou
Why hastow Ianuarie / thus deceyued	
That haddest hym / for thy fulle freend receyued	ful
And now thow hast biraft hym / bothe his eyen	thou hast biraft hym hise
For sorwe of which / desireth he to dyen	
Allas / this noble Ianuarie free	¶Allas /
Amydde his lust and his prosperitee	prosperitee
Is woxen blynd / and that al sodeynly	21
He wepeth / and he waileth pitously	wepeth wayleth
And ther with al / the fyr of Ialousye	Ialousie
Lest that his wyf sholde falle in som folye	þat wyf / in swich folye
So brente his herte / þat he wolde fayn	that
That som man / bothe hire and hym had slayn	hym and hire
For neither after his deeth / ne in his lyf	deeth / nor in lyf
Ne wolde he / þat she were loue ne wyf	wyf
But euere lyue as wydwe / in clothes blake	euere wydwe
Soul as the turtle / that lost hath hir make	þat hire

21 ¶Marchant 111v

Aboute that welle and daunced as men tolde
This noble knyght / this Januarie the olde
Swich deyntee hath in it to walke and pleye
That he wol no wight / suffre bere the keye
Saue he hym self / for of the smal wyket /
He bar alwey of siluer a clyket
With which / whan þt hym leste / he it vnshette
And whan he wolde / paye his wyf hir dette
In somer seson / thider wolde he go
And May his wyf / and no wight but they two
And thynges / whiche þt were nat don abedde
He in the gardyn / pfourned hem and spedde
And in this wise / many a murye day
Lyued this Januarie / and fresshe May
But worldly ioye / may nat alwey dure
To Januarie / ne to no creature
Auctor O · sodeyn hap / o · thow ffortune vnstable
Lyk to the scorpion / so deceyuable
That flaterest wt thyn heed / whan thow wolt stynge
Thy tayl is deeth / thurgh thyn envenymynge
O · brotil ioye / o · swete venym queynte
O · monstre that so subtilly kanst peynte
Thy yiftes / vnder hewe of stedefastnesse
That thow deceyuest / bothe moore and lesse
Why hastow Januarie thus deceyued
That haddest hym for thy fulle freend receyued
And now thow hast biraft hym / bothe his eyen
ffor sorwe of which / desireth he to dyen
Allas / this noble Januarie free
Amydde his lust / and his prosperitee
Is woxen blynd / and that al sodeynly
He wepeth / and he waileth pitously
And ther with al / the fyr of jalousye
Lest that his wyf / sholde falle in som folye
So brente his herte / þt he wolde fayn
That som man / bothe hire and hym had slayn
ffor neither after his deeth / ne in his lyf
Ne wolde he / þt she were loue ne wyf
But euere lyue as wydwe / in clothes blake
Soul as the turtle / that lost hath hir make

…t atte laste / after a monthe or tweye
…is sorwe gan aswage / sooth to seye
ffor whan he wiste / it may noon oother be
He paciently / took his aduersitee
Saue out of doute / he may nat forgoon
That he nas Ialous / eueremoore in oon
Which Ialousye / it was so outrageous
That neither in halle / ne in noon oother hous
Ne in noon oother place / neuer the mo
He nolde suffre hire / for to ryde or go
But if þt he hadde hond on hire alway
ffor which ful ofte / wepeth fresshe May
That loueth Damyan / so benyngnely
That she moot outher dyen sodeynly
Or ellis / she moot han hym as hir leste
She wayteth / whan hir herte wolde breste
Vp on that oother syde / Damyan
Bicomen is the sorwefulleste man
That euere was / for neither nyght ne day
Ne myghte he speke a word to fresshe May
As to his purpos / of no swich matere
But if þt Ianuarie moste it heere
That hadde an hand / vp on hire eueremo
But nathelees / by writyng to and fro
And pryuee signes / wiste he what she mente
And she knew eek / the fyn of his entente
O Ianuarie / what myghte it thee auaille
Thow myghtest se / as fer as shippes saille
ffor as good / is blynd deceyued be
As to be deceyued / whan a man may se
Lo Argus / which þt hadde an hundred eyen
ffor al that euere / he koude poure or pryen
Yet was he blent / and god woot so been mo
That wenen wisly / that it be nat so
Passe ouer is an ese / and sey namoore
This fresshe May / that I spak of so yoore
In warm wex / hath prented the clyket
That Ianuarie bar / of that smale wyket /
By which in to his gardyn / ofte he wente
And Damyan that knew al his entente

	ELLESMERE
[Bu]t atte laste / after a Monthe or tweye	But
[H]is sorwe gan aswage / sooth to seye	His
For whan he wiste / it may noon oother be	
He paciently / took his aduersitee	took Aduersitee
Saue out of doute / he may nat forgoon	
That he nas Ialous / eu*er*e moore in oon	eu*er*emoore
Which Ialousye / it was so outrageous	
That neither in halle / ne in noon oother hous	halle / nyn noon
Ne in noon oother place / neu*er* the mo	Nyn noon neu*er*themo
He nolde suffre hir*e* / for to ryde or go	
But if þ*at* he / hadde hond on hir alway	had hir*e*
For which ful ofte / wepeth fresshe May	fressħe
That loueth Damyan / so benygnely	benyngnely
That she moot outher dyen sodeynly	
Or ellis / she moot han hym as hir leste	elles /
She wayteth / whan hir herte wolde breste	
¶Vp on that oother syde / Damyan	syde
Bicomen is / the sorwefulleste man	
That euere was / for neither nyght ne day	eu*er*e nygħt
Ne myghte he speke a word to fresshe May	mygħte fressħe
As to his purpos / of no swich matere	mateere
But if þ*at* Ianuarie / moste it heere	that
That hadde an hand / vp on hir*e* eu*er*e mo	eu*er*emo
But nathelees / by writyng to and fro	
And pryuee signes / wiste he what she mente	p*ri*uee
And she knew eek / the fyn of his entente	
¶O. Ianuaire / what myghte it thee auaille (	¶Auctor] O Ianuarie / mygħte
Thow myghtest se / as fer as shippes saille	Thogh thou mygħtest
For as good / is blynd deceyued be	good is /
As to be deceyued / whan a man may se	
Lo Argus / which þ*at* hadde an hundred eyen	¶Lo hadde / hondred
For al that eu*er*e / he koude poure or pryen	þ*at*
Yet was he blent and god woot so been mo	
That weneth wisly / that it be nat so	wenen
Passe ouer is an ese / and sey namoore	ese / I sey
¶This fresshe May / that I spak of so yoore	fressħe þ*at* spak
In warm wex / hath p*ri*nted the Clyket	emp*ri*nted clyket
That Ianuarie bar / of that smale wyket	of the smale
By which / in to his gardyn / ofte he wente	22 whicħ / gardyn
And Damyan / that knew al his entente	al hir*e* entente

[22] ¶Marcħant *112r*

The Clyket countrefeted pryuely	cliket
Ther nys namoore to seye / but hastily	
Som wonder / by this Cliket shal bityde	clyket
Which ye shal heren / if ye wol abyde	shul heeren / wole
¶O noble Ouyde / wel sooth seistow god woot	Ouyde / ful sooth seystou ⌈¶Auctor⌉
What sleighte is it / thogh it be long and hoot	it
That he nel fynde it out in som manere	he nyl fynde out /
By Pyram*us* and Thesbe / may men lere	Piramus / Tesbee / leere
Thogh they were kept ful longe / streyte ou*er* al	Thogħ kept longe streite ou*er*al
They been acorded / rownyng thurgh a wal	accorded / rownynge thurgħ
Ther no wight koude / han founde out swich a sleighte	wigħt / koude swicħ sleigħte
But now to purpos / er that dayes eighte	¶But þ*a*t eigħte
Were passed / er the Monthe of Iuyl bifille	
That Ianuarie / hath caught so greet a wille	caugħt
Thurgh eggyng of his wyf / hym for to pleye	wyf
In his gardyn / and no wight but they tweye	wigħt
That in a morwe / vn to his May seith he	to this May
Rys vp my wyf my loue / my lady free	wyf /
The Turtles voys is herd / my dowue swete	turtle sweete
The wynter is goon / with reynes wete	with ⟨his⟩ reynes weete
Com forth now / with thyne eyen Colu*m*byn	columbyn
How fairer been thy brestes / than is wyn	
The gardyn / is enclosed al aboute	
Com forth my white spouse / out of doute	
Thow hast me wounded in myn herte / O wyf	Thou wounded / o wyf
No spot of thee / ne knew I al my lyf	
Com forth / and lat vs taken oure desport	taken som disport
I chees thee / for my wyf and my confort	
¶Swiche olde lewed wordes / vsed he	wordes
On Damyan / a signe made she	
That he sholde go biforn / with his Clyket	cliket
This Damyan thanne / hath opned the wyket	opened
And in he stirte / and that in swich manere	And In he
That no wight myghte it se / neither yheere	wigħt mygħte
And stille he sit / vnder a bussh anon	bussħ
¶This Ianuarie / as blynd as is a stoon	
With Mayus in his hand / and no wight mo	wigħt
In to his fresshe gardyn / is ago	fressħe gardyn
And clapte to / the wyket sodeynly	
Now wyf quod he / here nys but thow and .I.	¶Now heere thou I

The clyket/ countrefeted pryuely
Ther nys namoore to seye/ but hastily
Som wonder/ by this clyket shal bityde
Which ye shal heeren/ if ye wol abyde
O noble Ouyde/ wel sooth seistow god woot/
What sleighte is it/ thogh it be long and hoot/
That he nel fynde it out/ in som manere
By Pyramus and Thesbe/ may men leere
Thogh they were kept ful longe/ streyte ouer al
They been acorded/ rownyng thurgh a wal
Ther no wight koude/ han founde out swich a sleighte
But now to purpos/ er that dayes eighte
Were passed/ er the monthe of Iuyl bifille
That Ianuarie hath caught so greet a wille
Thurgh eggyng of his wyf/ hym for to pleye
In his gardyn/ and no wight but they tweye
That in a morwe/ vn to his May seith he
Rys vp my wyf/ my loue/ my lady free
The turtles voys is herd/ my dowue swete
The wynter is goon/ with reynes wete
Com forth now/ with thyne eyen Columbyn
How fairer been thy brestes/ than is wyn
The gardyn is enclosed al aboute
Com forth my white spouse/ out of doute
Thow hast me wounded in myn herte/ o wyf
No spot of thee/ ne knew I al my lyf
Com forth/ and lat vs taken oure desport/
I chees thee for my wyf/ and my confort/
Swiche olde lewed wordes/ vsed he
On Damyan/ a signe made she
That he sholde go biforn/ with his clyket/
This Damyan thanne/ hath opned the wyket
And in he stirte/ and that in swich manere
That no wight myghte it se/ neither yheere
And stille he sit/ vnder a bussh anon
This Ianuarie/ as blynd as is a stoon
With Mayus in his hand/ and no wight mo
In to his fresshe gardyn/ is ago
And clapte to/ the wyket sodeynly
Now wyf quod he/ heere nys but thow and I

[Th]at art the creature that I best loue
ffor by that lord that sit in heuene aboue
leuere ich hadde to dyen on a knyf
Than thee offende / trewe deere wyf
ffor goddes sake / thenk how I thee chees
Noght for no coueitise doutelees
But oonly for the loue I hadde to thee
And thogh þt I be old / and may nat see
Beth to me trewe / and I wol telle yow why
Thre thynges certes / shal ye wynne ther by
¶ ffirst loue of crist / and to your self honour
And al myn heritage / toun and tour
I yeue it yow / maketh chartres as ye leste
This shal be doon to morwe / er sonne reste
So wisly god my soule brynge in blisse
I pray yow first / in couenant ye me kisse
And thogh þt I be Ialous / wyt me noght
Ye been so depe / emprinted in my thoght
That whan þt I / considere youre beautee
And ther with al / the vnlikly elde of me
I may noght certes / thogh I sholde dye
fforbere / to been out of youre compaignye
ffor verray loue / this is with outen doute
Now kys me wyf / and lat vs rome aboute
¶ This fresshe May / whan she thise wordes herde
Benyngnely / to Ianuarie answerde
But first and forward / she bigan to wepe
I haue quod she / a soule for to kepe
As wel as ye / and also myn honour
And of my wifhod / thilke tendre flour
Which þt I haue / assured in youre hond
Whan þt the preest / to yow my body bond
Wher fore / I wol answere in this manere
By the leue of yow / my lord so deere
I pray to god / þt neuere dawe the day
That I ne sterue / as foule as womman may
If euere I do / vn to my kyn that shame
Or ellis / I empeyre so my name
That I be fals / and if I do that lakke
Do strepe me / and put me in a sakke

	ELLESMERE
[Th]at art the creature / that I best loue	That art
For by that lord / that sit in heuene aboue	*þat* sit
Leuere ich hadde / to dyen on a knyf	Leu*ere* knyf
Than thee offende / trewe deere wyf	wyf
For goddes sake / thenk how I thee chees	thenk
Noght for no coueitise doutelees	
But oonly / for the loue I hadde to thee	23 loue / had
And thogh *þat* I be old / and may nat see	though oold /
Beth to me trewe / and I wol telle yow why	I shal telle why
Thre: thynges certes / shal ye wynne ther by	Thre thynges /
¶First loue of Crist and to your self honour	First your*e*
And al myn heritage / toun and tour	
I yeue it yow / maketh chartres as ye leste	as yow leste
This shal be doon to morwe / er sonne reste	tomorwe
So wisly / god my soule / brynge in blisse	soule
I pray yow first in couenant ye me kisse	prey first / couenat
And thogh *þat* I be Ialous / wyt me noght	though Ialous wyte noght /
Ye been so depe / emp*ri*nted in my thoght	enp*ri*nted thoght
That whan *þat* I / considere your*e* beautee	whan I youre
And ther with al / the vnlikly elde of me	
I may noght *cer*tes / thogh I sholde dye	nat certes / though
Forbere / to been out of your*e* compaignye	youre
For verray loue / this is with outen doute	ve*rr*ay
Now kys me wyf and lat vs rome aboute	
¶This fresshe May / whan she thise wordes herde	fresshe
Benygnely / to Ianuarie answerde	Benyngnely /
But first and forward / she bigan to wepe	first forward
I haue quod she / a soule for to kepe	
As wel as ye / and also myn honour	
And of my wifhod / thilke tendre flour	wyfhod /
Which *þat* I haue / assured in your*e* hond	hond
Whan *þat* the preest to yow my body bond	bond
Wher fore / I wol answere in this manere	Wherfore / wole answere /
By the leue of yow / my lord so deere	
I pray to god / *þat* neu*ere* dawe the day	prey neuere
That I ne sterue / as foule as womman may	wo*m*man
If euere I do / vn to my kyn that shame	
Or ellis / I empeyre so my name	elles /
That I be fals / and if I do that lakke	
Do strepe me / and put me in a sakke	

23 ¶Marchant *112v*

The Marchaunt

ELLESMERE

And in the nexte Ryuer / do me drenche
I am a gentil womman / and no wenche
Why speke ye thus / but men been eu*er*e vntrewe
And wommen haue reproue / of yow ay newe
Ye han / noon oother contenance I leue
But speke to vs / of vntrust and repreue
¶And with that word / she saw wher Damyan
Sat in the bussħ / and coghen/she bigan
And with hir fynger / signes made she
That Damyan / sholde clymbe vp on a tree
That charged was with fruyt and vp he wente
For verraily / he knew al hir entente
And euery signe / þ*at* she koude make
Wel bet than Ianuarie / hir owene make
For in a lettre / she hadde told hym al
Of this matere / how he werken shal
And thus I lete hym sitte / vp on the purye
And Ianuarie and May / romynge murye
¶Bright was the day / and blew the firmament
Phebus hath of gold / his stremys doun ysent
To gladen euery flour / with his warmnesse
He was that tyme / in Geminis as I gesse
But litel / fro his declynaciou*n*
Of Cancer / Iouis exaltaciou*n*
And so bifel / that brighte morwe tyde
That in that gardyn / in the ferther syde
Pluto / that is ⟨the⟩ kyng of Fairye
And many a lady / in his compaignye
Folwynge his wyf / the queene Proserpyne
⟨Whos answer*e* hath doon many a man pyne⟩
¶Whil that she gadrede / floures in the mede
In Claudyan / ye may the stories rede
How in his grysly Carte / he hir sette
This kyng of Fairye / thanne adown hym sette
Vp on a bench of turues / fressh and grene
And right anon / thus seyde he to his queene
¶My wyf quod he / ther may no wight sey nay
Thexp*er*ience / so proueth euery day
The treson / which þ*at* womman dooth to man
Ten hundred thousand / tellen I kan

ryuer
wo*m*man
thus /
wo*m*men / repreue
han leeue
repreeue
saugħ
coughen she

wit*h*
hir*e*

24 toold
werchen
pyrie
May myrie
Bright
hise stremes
flour

morwetyde

that is kyng

Ech after oother / right as a lyne
Whil þ*at* gadered /
stories
And in grisly hir*e*
adoun
fressħ
right
wight seye
preueth
tresons / whiche wo*m*men doon
hondred

[24]¶Marchant *113r*

And in the nexte tree / do me drenche
I am a gentil womman / and no wenche
Why speke ye thus / but men been eue vntrewe
And wommen haue repreue / of yow ay newe
Ye han noon oother contenance I leue
But speke to vs of vntrust and repreue
And with that word / she saugh wher Damyan
Sat in the bussh / and coghen she bigan
And with hir fynger / signes made she
That Damyan / sholde clymbe vp on a tree
That charged was with fruyt / and vp he wente
ffor verraily / he knew al hir entente
And euery signe / þt she koude make
Wel bet than Januarie / hir owene make
ffor in a lettre / she hadde told hym al
Of this matere / how he werken shal
And thus I lete hym sitte / vp on the pyrie
And Januarie and May / romynge myrie
Bright was the day / and blew the firmament
Phebus hath of gold / his stremys down ysent
To gladen euery flour / with his warmnesse
He was that tyme / in Geminis as I gesse
But litel / fro his declynacion
Of Cancer / Jouis exaltacion
And so bifel / that brighte morwe tyde
That in that gardyn / in the ferther syde
Pluto that is the kyng / of ffairye
And many a lady / in his compaignye
ffolwynge his wyf / the queene Proserpyne
Whos answere hath doon many a man pyne
Whil that she gadrede floures in the mede
In Claudyan / ye may the stories rede
How in his grisly carte / he hir sette
This kyng of ffairye / thanne adoun hym sette
Vp on a bench of turues / fressh and grene
And right anon / thus seyde he to his queene
My wyf quod he / ther may no wight sey nay
Thexperience / so preueth euery day
The tresoun / which þt womman dooth to man
Ten hundred thousand / tellen I kan

…table of youre vntrouthe and brotelnesse
O Salomon wys and richest of richesse
ffulfild of Sapience and of worldly glorie
fful worthy been thy wordes to memorie
To euery wight that wit and reson kan
Thus preyseth he yet the bountee of man
¶ Amonges a thousand men yet foond I oon
But of wommen alle foond I noon
¶ Thus seith the kyng pt knoweth youre wikkednesse
And Ihc filius Syrak as I gesse
Ne speketh of yow but selde reuerence
A wilde fyr and corrupt pestilence
So falle vp on youre bodyes yet to nyght
Ne se ye noght this honurable knyght
By cause allas pt he is blynd and old
His owene man shal make hym cokewold
lo where he sit the lechour in the tree
Now wol I graunten of my magestee
Vn to this olde blynde worthy knyght
That he shal haue ayein his eyen syght
Whan pt his wyf wolde doon hym vileynye
Thanne shal he knowen al hir harlotrye
Bothe in repreue of hire and othere mo
¶ Ye shal quod Proserpyne wol ye so
Now by my modres sires soule I swere
That I shal yeuen hire suffisant answere
And alle wommen after for hir sake
That though they be in any gilt ytake
With face bold they shul hem self excuse
And bere hem doun that wolde hem accuse
ffor lakke of answere noon of hem shal dyen
Al hadde man seyn a thyng with bothe his eyen
yet shal we wommen visagen it hardily
And wepe and swere and chide subtilly
So that ye men shul been as lewed as gees
What rekketh me of youre auctoritees
¶ I woot wel pt this Iew this Salomon
ffand of vs wommen foles many oon
But though pt he ne fand no good womman
yet hath ther founde many another man

Hengwrt	Ellesmere
[N]otable / of your*e* vntrouthe and brotelnesse	Notable / youre brotilnesse
[O] Salomon / wys / and richest of richesse	O
Fulfild of Sapience / and of worldly glorie	sapience /
Ful worthy been thy wordes / to memorie	wordes
To euery wight that wit and reson kan	eu*er*y wight þ*at*
Thus preyseth he yet the bou*n*tee of man	preiseth
¶Amonges a thousand men / yet foond I oon	
But of wommen alle / foond I noon	wo*m*men
¶Thus seith the kyng þ*at* knoweth youre wikkednesse	your*e*
And I*esus* filius Syrak as I gesse	I*es*us
Ne speketh of yow / but selde reu*er*ence	seelde
A wilde fyr / and corrupt pestilence	wylde
So falle vp on youre bodyes / yet to nyght	bodyes nyght
Ne se ye noght this honurable knyght	nat knyght
By cause allas / þ*at* he is blynd and old	that old
His owene man / shal make hym Cokewold	Cokewold
Lo where he sit the lechour in the tree	Lo heere he Lechour
Now wol I graunten / of my magestee	
Vn to this olde / blynde worthy knyght	olde knyght
That he shal haue ayein / his eyen syght	ayeyn hise syght
Whan þ*at* his wyf wolde doon hym vileynye	wyf / wold
Thanne shal he knowen / al hir harlotrye	hir*e*
Bothe in repreue of hir*e* / and othere mo	25
¶Ye shal quod Proserpyne / wol ye so	so /
Now by my modres sires soule / I swere	moodres soule
That I shal yeuen hire / suffisant answere	hir*e*
And alle wommen after / for hir sake	
That thogh they be / in any gilt ytake	though
With face bold / they shul hem self excuse	boold / shulle
And bere hem doun / that wolde hem accuse	wolden
For lakke of answer*e* / noon of hem shal dyen	
Al hadde man seyn a thyng with bothe his eyen	*with* hise
Yet shal we wommen / visagen it hardily	Yit shul wo*m*men / visage
And wepe and swere / and chide subtilly	wepe / swere / and visage it subtilly
So that ye men / shul been as lewed as gees	þ*at* been /
What rekketh me / of youre auctoritees	Auctoritees
¶I woot wel / þ*at* this Iew / this Salomon	that
Fand of vs wommen / folyes many oon	Foond wo*m*men / fooles
But thogh þ*at* he / ne fand no good womman	though he foond / wo*m*man
Yet hath ther founde / many another man	

[25] ¶Marchant *113v*

	ELLESMERE
Wommen ful trewe / ful goode and vertuous	Wommen
Witnesse on hem / that dwelle in Cristes hous	pat
With martirdom / they proued hir constaunce	preued hire constance
The Romayn geestes / eek maken remembraunce	eek remembrance
Of many a verray / trewe wyf also	
But sire ne be nat wrooth / al be it so	
Thogh pat he seyde / he foond no good womman	Though womman
I pray yow / taak the sentence of the man	prey take
He mente thus / pat in souerayn bountee	that souereyn bontee
Nys noon but god / but neither he ne she	Nis noon / god pat sit in Trinitee |
¶Ey for verray god / that nys but oon	
What make ye / so muche of Salomon	
What thogh / he made a temple goddes hous	What though
What thogh he were riche and glorious	though were /
So made he eek / a temple / of false goddys	temple goddis
How myghte he do a thyng pat moore forbode is	
Pardee / as faire / as ye his name emplastre	
He was a lechour / and an ydolastre	Lecchour /
And in his elde / he verray god forsook	
And if god ne hadde / as seith the book	
Yspared hym / for his fadres sake / he sholde	Yspared for
Haue lost his regne / rather than he wolde	
I sette right noght of al the vileynye	right noght
That ye of wommen write / a Boterflye	wommen
I am a womman / nedes moot I speke	womman /
Or ellis swelle / til myn herte breke	elles
For sithen he seyde / pat we been Iangleresses	that
As euere hool / I mote brouke my tresses	euere moote
I shal nat spare / for no curteisye	
To speke hym harm / pat wolde vs vileynye	
¶Dame quod this Pluto / be no lenger wrooth	26 Dame wrooth
I yeue it vp / but sith I swoor myn ooth	
That I wolde graunten hym / his sighte ayein	wolde / hym ageyn
My word shal stonde / I warne yow certeyn	certeyn
I am a kyng it sit me noght to lye	noght
¶And I quod she / a queene of Fairye	Queene
Hir answere shal she haue / I vndertake	haue
Lat vs namoore wordes / her of make	wordes heer
For sothe / I wol no lenger yow contrarie	lenger
¶Now lat vs / turne agayn to Ianuarie	

26 ¶Marchant 114r

Wommen ful trewe / ful goode and vertuous
Witnesse on hem / that dwelle in Cristes hous
With martirdom / they preued hir constaunce
The Romayn geestes / eek maken remembraunce
Of many a verray / trewe wyf also
But sire ne be nat wrooth / al be it so
Though pt he seyde / he foond no good womman
I pray yow / taak the sentence of the man
He mente thus / pt in souereyn bontee
Nis noon but god / but neither he ne she
Ey for verray god / that nys but oon
What make ye / so muche of Salomon
What though he made a temple goddes hous
What though he were riche and glorious
So made he eek / a temple of false goddys
How myghte he do a thyng / pt moore forbode is
Pardee as faire / as ye his name emplastre
He was a lechour / and an ydolastre
And in his elde / he verray god forsook
And if god ne hadde / as seith the book
Yspared hym for his fadres sake / he sholde
Haue lost his regne / rather than he wolde
I sette right noght / of al the vileynye
That ye of wommen write / a boterflye
I am a womman / nedes moot I speke
Or elles swelle / til myn herte breke
For sithen he seyde / pt we been iangleresses
As euere hool / I mote brouke my tresses
I shal nat spare / for no curteisye
To speke hym harm / pt wolde vs vileynye
Dame quod this Pluto / be no lenger wrooth
I yeue it vp / but sith I swoor myn ooth
That I wolde graunten hym / his sighte ageyn
My word shal stonde / I warne yow certeyn
I am a kyng / it sit me noght to lye
And I quod she / a queene of Fairye
Hir answere shal she haue / I vndertake
Lat vs namoore wordes / her of make
For sothe I wol no lenger yow contrarie
Now lat vs turne agayn to Januarie

..at in the gardyn with his faire may
..yngeth ful murier than the Papeiay
yow loue I best and shal and oother noon
So longe aboute the aleyes is he goon
Til he was come agaynes thilke pyrie
Wher as this Damyan sitteth ful myrie
An heigh among the fresshe leues grene
¶ This fresshe may that is so bright and shene
Gan for to syke and seyde allas my syde
Now sire quod she for aught pt may bityde
I moste han of the perys pt I se
Or I moot dye so sore longeth me
To eten of the smale perys grene
Help for hir loue pt is of heuene queene
I telle yow wel a womman in my plit
May han to fruyt so gret an appetit
That she may dyen but she of it haue
¶ Allas quod he pt I ne hadde here a knaue
That koude clymbe allas allas quod he
ffor I am blynd ye sire no fors quod she
¶ But wolde ye vouche sauf for goddes sake
The pyrie inwith youre armes for to take
ffor wel I woot pt ye mystruste me
Thanne sholde I clymbe wel ynow quod she
So I my foot myghte sette vp on youre bak
¶ Certes quod he ther on shal be no lak
Myghte I yow helpen with myn herte blood
He stoupeth doun and on his bak she stood
And caughte hir by a twiste and vp she goth
Ladys I pray yow pt ye be nat wroth
I kan nat glose I am a rude man
And sodeynly anon this Damyan
Gan pullen vp the smok and in he throng
¶ And whan pt Pluto saugh this grete wrong
To Ianuarie he yaf agayn his sighte
And made hym see as wel as euere he myghte
And whan that he hadde caught his sighte agayn
Ne was ther neuere man of thyng so fayn
But on his wyf his thoght was euere mo
Vn to the tree he caste his eyen two

And say pt Damyan

	ELLESMERE
[Th]at in the gardyn / with his faire May	That
[S]yngeth ful murier / than the Papeiay	Syngeth
Yow loue I best and shal and oother noon	
So longe / aboute the Aleyes is he goon	
Til he was come / agayns thilke pirye	pyrie
Wher as this Damyan / sitteth ful myrye	Wher*e* myrie
Anheigh / among the fresshe leues grene	Anheighħ / among fressħe
¶This fresshe May / that is so bright and shene	fressħe brigħt sheene
Gan for to syke / and seyde allas my syde	seyde /
Now sire quod she / for aught þ*at* may bityde	sir*e* augħt
I moste han / of the perys þ*at* I se	peres that see
Or I moot dye / so sore longeth me	soore
To eten / of the smale perys grene	peres
Help for hir loue / þ*at* is of heuene queene	
I telle yow wel / a womman in my plit	wo*m*man plit
May han to fruyt so gret an appetit	greet Appetit
That she may dyen / but she of it haue	
¶Allas quod he / þ*at* I ne hadde here a knaue	had heer
That koude clymbe / allas allas quod he	
For I am blynd / ye sire nofors quod she	That I blynd / sir*e*
¶But wolde ye / vouche sauf / for goddes sake	ye sauf
The pirye inwith youre armes / for to take	pyrie / Armes
For wel I woot þ*at* ye mystruste me	woot / that
Thanne sholde I clymbe / wel ynow quod she	ynogħ
So I my foot myghte sette vp on your*e* bak	myghte youre bak /
¶Certes quod he / ther on shal be no lak	
Mighte I yow helpen / with myn herte blood	Migħte wi*th*
He stoupeth doun / and on his bak she stood	
And caughte hir by a twiste / and vp she goth	caugħte hir*e* gootħ
Ladys I pray yow / þ*at* ye be nat wroth	Ladyes / prey wrootħ
I kan nat glose / .I a rude man	glose / I am a
And sodeynly / anon this Damyan	
Gan pullen vp the smok / and in he throng	In
¶And whan þ*at* Pluto / saugh this grete wrong	saugħ
To Ianuarie / he yaf agayn his sighte	gaf sigħte
And made hym see / as wel as euere he myghte	se / eu*er*e mygħte
And whan that he / hadde caught his sighte agayn	þ*at* caugħt sigħte
Ne was ther neuere man / of thyng so fayn	neu*er*e / man thyng
But on his wyf his thoght was euere mo	27 wyf / thogħt eu*er*emo
Vn to the tree / he caste his eyen two	Vp to hise

And say þ*at* Damyan

[27] ¶Marchanħ *114v*

.The Marchaunt' / .

And say *pat* Damyan / his wyf had dressed
In swich manere / it may nat ben expressed
But if I wolde speken / vncurteisly
And vp he yaf' a roryng and a cry
As dooth the moder / whan the child shal dye
Out help / allas / harrow / he gan to crye
O. stronge lady stoore / . what dostow
¶And she answerde / sire what eyleth yow
Haue pacience and reson / in youre mynde
I haue yow holpe / on bothe you*re* eyen blynde
Vp pe*r*il of my soule / .I shal nat lyen
As me was taught' to heele with you*re* eyen
Was no thyng bet' to make yow to se
Than strugle *with* a man / vp on a tree
God woot' I dide it in ful good entente
¶Strugled quod he / ye algate In it wente
God yeue yow bothe / on shames deth to dyen
He swyued thee / I saw it *with* myne eyen
And ellis / be I hanged by the hals
¶Thanne is quod she / my medicyne al fals
For ce*r*teinly / if *pat* ye myghte se
Ye wolde nat seyn / thise wordes vn to me
Ye han som glymsynge / and no pa*r*fit sighte
¶I se quod he / as wel as eu*er*e I myghte
Thonked be god / with bothe myne eyen two
And by my trouthe / me thoughte he dide thee so
¶Ye maze maze / goode sire quod she
This thank haue I / for I haue maad yow se
Allas quod she / *pat* euere I was so kynde
¶Now dame quod he / lat al passe out of mynde
Com doun my lief' and if I haue myssayd
God help me so / as I am yuele apayd
But by my fadres soule / I wende haue seyn
How *pat* this Damyan / hadde by thee leyn
And *pat* thy Smok / hadde leyn vp on his bryst'
¶Ye sire quod she / ye may,' wene as yow lyst'
But sire / a man that waketh out of his sleep*e*
He may nat sodeynly / wel taken keep*e*
Vp on a thyng' ne seen it pa*r*fitly
Til that he be / adawed verraily

ELLESMERE

saugħ
man*ere* / been
wolde / speke
yaf / roryng'
mooder /
help*e* / harrow
O stoore / dostow ./
sire yow ./
pacience / resou*n* you*re*
youre
I
taughħt / youre
see
it /
¶Strugle he ./
saugħ it. withħ
elles /
medicyne fals
certeinly / that myghħte
glymsyng' sighħte
myghħte
with
thoughħte
maze / maze /
see
that eu*ere*
myssayd'
help*e* apayd'
fader han
that
smok' brest'
may wene lest'
man / *pat*
parfitly
pat

And say þt Damyan his wyf had dressed
In swich manere it may nat ben expressed
But if I wolde speken vncurteisly
And vp he yaf a roryng and a cry
As doth the moder whan the child shal dye
Out help allas harrow he gan to crye
O stronge lady stoore what dostow
And she answerde sire what eyleth yow
Haue pacience and resoun in youre mynde
I haue yow holpe on bothe youre eyen blynde
Vp peril of my soule I shal nat lyen
As me was taught to heele with youre eyen
Was no thyng bet to make yow to se
Than strugle with a man vp on a tree
God woot I dide it in ful good entente
Strugled quod he ye algate in it wente
God yeue yow bothe on shames deth to dyen
He swyued thee I saugh it wt myne eyen
And ellis be I hanged by the hals
Thanne is quod she my medicyne al fals
For certeinly if þt ye myghte se
Ye wolde nat seyn thise wordes vn to me
Ye han som glymsynge and no parfit sighte
I se quod he as wel as euere I myghte
Thonked be god with bothe myne eyen two
And by my trouthe me thoughte he dide thee so
Ye maze maze goode sire quod she
This thank haue I for I haue maad yow se
Allas quod she þt euere I was so kynde
Now dame quod he lat al passe out of mynde
Com doun my lief and if I haue myssayd
God help me so as I am yuele apayd
But by my fadres soule I wende haue seyn
How þt this Damyan hadde by thee leyn
And þt thy smok hadde leyn vp on his brest
Ye sire quod she ye may wene as yow lyst
But sire a man that waketh out of his sleep
He may nat sodeynly wel taken keep
Vp on a thyng ne seen it parfitly
Til that he be adawed verraily

..ot so a man that longe hath blynd ybe
..e may nat sodeynly so wel yse
ffyrst whan his sighte is newe come ageyn
As he þt hath a day or two yseyn
Til þt youre sighte ysatled be a while
Ther may ful many a sighte yow bigile
Beth war I pray yow for by heuene kyng
fful many a man weneth to se a thyng
And it is al another than it semeth
He þt mysconceyueth he mysdemeth
And with that word she lepte doun fro the tree
This Januarye who is glad but he
He kisseth hyr and clippeth hyr ful ofte
And on hyr wombe he stroketh hyr ful softe
And to his palays hom he hath hyr lad
Now goode men I pray yow to be glad
Thus endeth here my tale of Januarye
God blesse vs and his moder Seinte Marie Amen

Here is ended the marchantes tale of Januarye

Memorandum that I Andrew Brereton of Llanvair
isvaird in the countie of Carnarvon yeoman doe owe
and stand duly indebted unto William ap Robert
servant unto the said Andrew Brereton in
the some of twentie shillings to bee paid
to the said William ap Robert the twentith
daye of November 1625 :

Memorandum that I Andrew Brereton

Andrew Brereton
of [illegible]

[Righ]t so a man / that longe hath blynd ybe
[N]e may nat sodeynly / so wel yse
First whan his sighte / is newe come ageyn
As he þ*at* hath / a day or two yseyn
Til þ*at* your*e* sighte / ysatled be a while
Ther may ful many a sighte yow bigile
Beth war I pray yow / for by heuene kyng7
Ful many a man / weneth to se a thyng7
And it is al another / than it semeth
He þ*at* mysconceyueth / he mysdemeth
And with that word / she lepte doun fro the tree
¶This Ianuarie / who is glad but he
He kisseth hir*e* / and clippeth hir*e* ful ofte
And on hir wombe / he stroketh hire ful softe
And to his Palays / hom he hath hir*e* lad
Now goode men / I pray yow to be glad
Thus endeth here / my tale of Ianuarie
God blesse vs / and his moder Seinte Marie   Amen

¶Here is ended the Marchantes tale / of Ianuarie

ELLESMERE

¶Rigħt   þ*at*
Ne
First7   sigħte /

that youre sigħte /
may /
28   Betħ   prey
seen
is /   semetħ
mysdemetħ
leep*e*

hir*e*   hir*e*
palays / hoom
yow be
heere /
⟨vs⟩ /   mooder   Marie |

¶Heere is ended / the Marcħantes tale of Ianuarie

[28] ¶Marcħant7 *115r*

Memmorandum that I Andrew Brereton of llanvair
iscaire in the Countie of Carnarvon gent dow owe
and stand duly indepted vnto william ap Robeart
searvant vnto the said Andrew Brereton in
the some of Twentie shillings to bee paid
to the said william ap Robeart the Twentieth
daye of december 1625: :—

Memorandum that I Andrew Brereton

Andrew Brereton
of llan[vair?]

¶Here folwen the wordes of the worthy Hoost to the Frankeleyn[29]	¶The Prologe of the Squieres tale[30]
BY goddes m*er*cy / seyde oure hoost tho	mercy / Hoost
Now swich a wyf / I prey god kepe me fro	pray
Lo which sleightes / and subtiltees	
In wommen ben / for ay as bisy as bees	wo*m*men been /
Ben they / vs sely men for to [de]ceyue	Been deceyue
And from a sooth / euere wol they weyue	
By this Marchantes tale / it preueth weel	Marchau*n*tes
But doutelees / as trewe as any steel	
I haue a wyf / thogh þ*a*t she poore be	though poure
But of hir tonge / a labbyng shrewe is she	labbyng
And yit she hath / an heep of vices mo	yet heep*e*
Ther of no fors / lat alle swiche thynges go	nofors /
But wite ye what in conseil be it seyd	wyte seyd
Me reweth soore / I am vn to hire teyd	hir*e* teyd
For and I sholde / rekenen euery vice	
Which þ*a*t she hath / ywis I were to nyce	
And cause why / it sholde reported be	
And toold to hire / of so*m*me of this meynee	hire /
Of whom / it nedeth nat for to declare	whom / nat
Syn wo*m*men / konnen oute swich chaffare	outen
And eek my wit suffiseth nat ther to	
To tellen al / wherfore my tale is do	
¶Sire Frankeleyn / com neer / if it your*e* wille be	¶Squier com
And sey vs a tale / for certes ye	sey somwhat of loue / for ce*r*tes ye
Konnen ther on / as muche as any man	
¶Nay sire quod he / but I wol seye as I kan	sir*e*

[29] The endlink of the Merchant's Tale (Mer-SqL) is always conjoined with the Squire's Prologue or Headlink making them a single unit regardless of the tales which they join. The Hengwrt scribe, however, while attaching fragment F 1–8 to fragment E 2419–2440, reads 'Frankeleyn' for 'Squier' in F 1 and uses the link to introduce the Franklin's Tale. The entire passage, E 2419–40 + F 1–8, forms the Squire's Prologue in Ellesmere.

[30] On *115r* ¶Marchant

Here folweth the wordes of the worthy hoost to the ffrankeleyn

Ey goddes mercy seyde oure hoost tho
Now swich a wyf I prey god kepe me fro
Lo whiche sleightes and subtiltees
In wommen ben for ay as bisy as bees
Ben they vs sely men for to deceyue
And from a sooth euere wol they weyue
By this Marchauntes tale it preueth weel
But doutelees as trewe as any steel
I haue a wyf though þt she poore be
But of hir tonge a labbyng shrewe is she
And yit she hath an heep of vices mo
Ther of no fors lat alle swiche thynges go
But wite ye what in conseil be it seyd
Me reweth soore I am vn to hire teyd
ffor and I sholde rekenen euery vice
Which þt she hath ywis I were to nyce
And cause why it sholde reported be
And toold to hire of somme of this meynee
Of whom it nedeth nat for to declare
Syn wommen konnen oute swich chaffare
And eek my wit suffiseth nat ther to
To tellen al wher fore my tale is do
Sire ffrankeleyn com neer if it youre wille be
And sey vs a tale for certes ye
Konnen ther on as muche as any man
Nay sire quod he but I wol seye as I kan

Gentilly wyl for I wol nat rebelle
Agayns youre wyl a tale wol I telle
Haue me excused if yt I speke amys
My wyl is good and lo my tale is this

Explicit

Here bigynneth the ffrankeleyns tale

Thise olde gentil Britons in hir dayes
Of diuse auentures maden layes
Rymeyed in hir firste Briton tonge
Whiche layes with hir instrumentz they songe
Or ellis redden hem for hir plesance
And oon of hem haue I in remembrance
Which I shal seyn wt good wyl as I kan
But sires by cause I am a burel man
At my bigynnyng first I yow biseche
Haue me excused of my rude speche
I lerned neuere Rethorik certeyn
Thyng yt I speke it moot be bare and pleyn

	ELLESMERE
[Wi]th hertly wyl / for I wol nat rebelle	With
[A]gayns youre wyl / a tale wol I telle	Agayn your*e* lust⁊ ⸍ a
Haue me excused / if þ*at* I speke amys	[31] if I
My wyl is good / and lo my tale is this	
¶Explicit⁊	[32]
¶Here bigynneth the Frankeleyns tale[1]	¶The Prologe / of the Frankeleyns tale[2]
THise olde gentil Britons / in hir dayes	Britou*n*s /
Of diu*er*se auentures / maden layes	diuerse
Rymeyed / in hir firste Briton tonge	
Whiche layes / with hir Instrumentz they songe	
Or ellis redden hem / for hir*e* plesau*n*ce	elles hir
And oon of hem / haue I in remembrau*n*ce	
Which I shal seyn / w*ith* good wyl as I kan	with
¶But sires / by cause I am a burel man	
At my bigynnyng⁊ first I yow biseche	first⁊
Haue ⟨me⟩ excused / of my rude speche	me
I lerned neuere / Rethorik⁊ certeyn	neuere Rethorik
Thyng þ*at* I speke / It moot be bare and pleyn	it

[31] ¶Squier *115v*

[32] Rubric *Out* El.

[1] See above, pp. xxx–xxxi.

[2] ¶Frankeleyn *123v*

I sleep*e* neu*er*e / in the Mount of P*ar*naso	neu*er*e / on the Pernaso
Ne lerned / Marcus Tullius Scithero	
Colours ne knowe I none / with outen drede	none
But swiche colours / as growen in the mede	Mede
Or ellis swiche / as men dye / or peynte	elles dye
Colours of Rethoryk' they ben to queynte	Rethoryk / been
My Spirit' feeleth nat of swich matere	spirit' noght' mateere
But if yow list' my tale shul ye heere	3
¶Narrat' IN Armorik' that called is Britayne	Armorik /
Ther was a knyght' þ*at* louede *and* dide his payne	knyght / loued
To serue a lady / in his beste wise	
And many a labour / many a gret emprise	greet
He for his lady wroghte / er she were wonne	wroghte /
For she was / oon the faireste vnder Sonne	sonne
And eek ther to / come of so heigh kynrede	therto / comen heigh
That wel vnnethes / dorste this knyght for drede	knyght
Telle hir*e* his wo / his peyne / and his distresse	
But atte laste / she for his worthynesse	
And namely / for his meke obeysance	obeysau*n*ce
Hath swich a pitee caught' of his penance	penau*n*ce
That pr*i*uely / she fel of his acord	pryuely / fil accord
To taken hym / for hir housbonde *and* hir lord	take and lord
Of swich lordshipe / as men han ouer hir wyues	ou*er*
And for to lede / the moore in blisse hir lyues	
Of his fre wyl / he swoor hir*e* as a knyght	free knyght'
That neu*er*e in al his lyf' he day ne nyght'	nyght'
Ne sholde vp on hym take / no maistrye	hym / take maistrie
Agayn hir wyl / ne kithe hir*e* Ialousye	Ialousie
But hir*e* obeye / and folwe hir wyl in al	4
As any louere / to his lady shal	
Saue / þ*at* the name of souerayneteе	that
That wolde he haue / for shame of his degree	
¶She thonked hym / and w*ith* ful gret hu*m*blesse	thanked with greet humblesse
She seyde sire / sith of youre gentilesse	gentillesse
Ye pr*o*fre me / to haue so large a reyne	profre
Ne wolde neuere god / bitwix vs tweyne	neu*er*e bitwixe
As in my gilt / were outher werre / or stryf	gilt' werre stryf /
Sire I wol be / you*re* hu*m*ble trewe wyf	Sir*e* / humble wyf'
Haue heer my trouthe / til that myn herte breste	þ*at*
Thus been they bothe / in quiete and in reste	they / bothe

721 Vnde Persius Nec fr[onte labra prolui] caballino [nec in bicipite] parnaso me mem[ini sompniasse] Hg (defective) El Variants: Nec) *om.* El fronte) fonte El

[3] Miniature of the Franklin in left margin. Break in El followed by:

¶Heere bigynneth / the Frankeleyns tale

[4] ¶Frankeleyn *124r*

The ffrankeleyn

I sleep neue in the mount of Pnaso
Ne lerned Marcus Tullius Scithero
Colours ne knowe I none withouten drede
But swiche colours as growen in the mede
Or ellis swiche as men dye or peynte
Colours of Rethoryk they ben to queynte
My spirit feeleth nat of swich mateere
But if yow list my tale shul ye heere
Narratio
In Armoryk that called is Britayne
Ther was a knyght þt louede & dide his payne
To serue a lady in his beste wise
And many a labour many a gret emprise
He for his lady wroghte er she were wonne
ffor she was oon the faireste vnder sonne
And eek ther to come of so heigh kynrede
That wel vnnethes dorste this knyght for drede
Telle hire his wo his peyne and his distresse
But atte laste she for his worthynesse
And namely for his meke obeysance
Hath swich a pitee caught of his penance
That priuely she fel of his accord
To taken hym for hir housbonde & hir lord
Of swich lordshipe as men han ouer hir wyues
And for to lede the moore in blisse hir lyues
Of his free wyl he swoor hire as a knyght
That neue in al his lyf he day ne nyght
Ne sholde vp on hym take no maistrie
Agayn hir wyl ne kithe hire Ialousye
But hire obeye and folwe hir wyl in al
As any louere to his lady shal
Saue þt the name of souereynetee
That wolde he haue for shame of his degree
She thanked hym and with ful gret humblesse
She seyde sire sith of youre gentilesse
Ye pfre me to haue so large a reyne
Ne wolde neuere god bitwix vs tweyne
As in my gilt were outher werre or stryf
Sire I wol be youre humble trewe wyf
Haue heer my trouthe til that myn herte breste
Thus been they bothe in quiete and in reste

[...] thyng ones saufly dar I seye
[..]at freendes euerych oother moote obeye
If they wol longe holden compaignye
loue wol nat be constreyned by maistrye
Whan maistrie comth / the god of loue anon
Beteth his wynges / and farwel he is gon
loue is a thyng / as any spirit free
Wommen of kynde / desiren libertee
And nat to been constreyned / as a thral
And so doon men / if I sooth seyn shal
looke / who þt moost / is pacient in loue
he is at his auantage al aboue
Pacience / is an heigh vertu certeyn
ffor it venquyssheth / as thise clerkes seyn
Thynges / that rigour sholde neuere atteyne
ffor euery word / men may nat chide or pleyne
lerneth to suffre / or ellis so moot I gon
ye shul it lerne / wher so ye wole or non
ffor in this world / certeyn ther no wight is
That he ne dooth / or seith som tyme amys
Ire / siknesse / or constellacion
Wyn / wo / or chaungynge of compleccion
Causeth ful ofte / to doon amys or speken
On euery wrong / a man may nat be wreken
After the tyme / moste be temperaunce
To euery wight / þt kan on gouernaunce
And therfore / hath this wise worthy knyght /
To lyue in ese / suffraunce hir bihight /
And she to hym / ful wisly gan to swere
That neuere / sholde ther be defaute in here
Here may men seen / an humble wys acord
Thus hath she take / hir seruant and hir lord
Seruant in loue / and lord in mariage
Thanne was he bothe / in lordshipe & seruage
Seruage nay / but in lordshipe aboue
Sith he hath bothe his lady and his loue
his lady certes / and his wyf also
The which / þt lawe of loue acordeth to
And whan he was / in this prosperitee
hom with his wyf / he gooth to his contree

[For o] thyng sires / saufly dar I seye
[Th]at freendes / euerich oother moote obeye
If they wol longe holden compaignye
Loue wol nat⁊ be constreyned by maistrye
Whan maistrie comth / the god of loue anon
Beteth his wynges / and farwel he is gon
Loue is a thyng⁊ as any spirit free
Wommen of kynde / desiren libertee
And nat to been constreyned / as a thral
And so doon men / if I sooth seyn shal
Looke / who þ*at* moost⁊ is pacient in loue
He is / at his auantage al aboue
Pacience / is an heigh v*er*tu c*er*teyn
For it venquysseth / as thise clerkes seyn
Thynges / that rigour sholde neu*er*e atteyne
For euery word / men may nat chide or pleyne
Lerneth to suffre / or ellis so moot I gon
Ye shul it lerne / wher so ye wole or non
For in this world / c*er*teyn ther no wight is
That he ne dooth / or seith som tyme amys
Ire / siknesse / or constellaciou*n*
Wyn / wo / or chaungyng of co*m*plexiou*n*
Causeth ful ofte / to doon amys or speken
On euery wrong⁊ a man may nat be wreken
After the tyme / moste be temp*er*aunce
To euery wight⁊ þ*at* kan on gouernaunce
And therfore / hath this wise worthy knyght /
To lyue in ese / suffrau*n*ce hir*e* bihight⁊
And she to hym / ful wisly gan to swere
That neu*ere* / sholde ther be / defaute in here
¶Here may men seen / an humble wys acord
Thus hath she take / hir seruant and hir lord
Seruant in loue / and lord in mariage
Thanne was he bothe / in lordshipe *and ser*uage
Seruage nay / but in lordshipe aboue
Sith he hath / bothe his lady and his loue
His lady certes / and his wyf also
The which / þ*at* lawe of loue acordeth to
And whan he was / in this p*ro*sp*er*itee
Hom with his wyf⁊ he gooth to his contree

ELLESMERE

¶For o
That euerych moot
longe /
Loue / nat been
hise farewel
Spirit
Wo*m*men
nat⁊ constreyned
seyen
þ*a*t is moost pacient
his auantate al
certeyn
þ*a*t rigour /
nat⁊
elles goon
noon
world c*er*tein / wight
dooth seith /
chaungynge complexiou*n*
wrong /
temperau*n*ce
eu*er*y wight⁊ gou*er*nau*n*ce
knyght⁊
suffrance bihight⁊
be
¶Heere accord
seruant⁊ lord
he / bothe lordship*e* and seruage
Seruage
5
prosp*er*itee
Hoom wit*h* wyf /

5¶Frankeleyn *124v*

The Frankeleyn	ELLESMERE
Nat fer fro Pedmark ther his dwellyng was	Nat
Wher as he lyueth / in blisse and in solas	Where
¶Who koude telle / but he hadde wedded be	
The ioye / the ese / and the p*ro*sp*er*itee	prosp*er*itee
That is / bitwix an housbonde / and his wyf	bitwixe
A yeer and moore / lasted this blisful lyf	
Til *þat* the knyght of which I speke of thus	knyght
That of kairrud / was clepid Arueragus	kayrrud / cleped
Shoop*e* hym to goon / and dwelle a yeer or twayne	tweyne
In Engelond / that clepid was ek Britayne	Engelond cleped eek Briteyne
To seke in armes / worship*e* and honour	Armes /
For al his lust he sette in swich labour	
And dwelled ther two yeer / the book seith thus	there book
¶Now wol I stynte / of this Arueragus	stynten /
And speke I wole / of Dorigene his wyf	speken wyf
That loueth hir housbonde / as hir hertes lyf	hir*e* hir*e* lyf
For his absence / wepeth she and siketh	Absence /
As doon thise noble wyues / whan hem liketh	
She moorneth / waketh / waileth / fasteth / pleyneth	wayleth /
Desir of his p*re*sence / hir so destreyneth	hir*e*
That al this wide world / she set at noght	wyde sette noght
Hir freendes whiche *þat* knowe / hir heuy thoght	Hir*e* freendes / knewe thoght
Conforten hire / in al that euer they may	hir*e* / *þat* eu*er*
They p*re*chen hire / they telle hir*e* nyght and day	p*re*chen hir*e* / nyght
That causelees / she sleeth hir self allas	
And euery confort possible in this cas	
They doon to hire / with al hir bisynesse	hire / hir*e*
Al for to make hire / leue hir heuynesse	Al / hir*e* / hir*e*
¶By p*ro*ces / as ye knowen euerichoon	
Men may so longe / grauen in a stoon	
Til som figure / ther Inne emp*ri*nted be	
So longe / han they conforted hir*e* / til she	longe
Receyued hath / by hope and by resou*n*	
The emp*ri*ntyng of hir consolaciou*n*	hir*e*
Thurgh which / hir grete sorwe gan aswage	
She may nat alwey / duren in swich rage	
¶And eek Arueragus / in al this care	
Hath sent hir*e* lettres hom / of his welfare	hoom /
And that he wole / come hastily agayn	*þat* wol
Or ellis hadde this sorwe / hir herte slayn	elles

The ffrankeleyn

Nat fer fro Pedmark ther his dwellyng was
Ther as he lyueth in blisse and in solas
Who koude telle / but he hadde wedded be
The ioye the ese / and the prosperitee
That is bitwix an housbonde and his wyf
A yeer and moore / lasted this blisful lyf
Til þt the knyght / of which I speke of thus
That of Kayrrud / was cleped Arueragus
Shoop hym to goon / and dwelle a yeer or tweyne
In Engelond / that cleped was ek Britayne
To seke in armes / worshipe and honour
ffor al his lust / he sette in swich labour
And dwelled ther two yeer / the book seith thus
Now wol I stynte / of this Arueragus
And speke I wole / of Dorigene his wyf
That loueth hir housbonde as hir hertes lyf
ffor his absence wepeth she and siketh
As doon thise noble wyues / whan hem liketh
She moorneth waketh / waileth / fasteth / pleyneth
Desir of his presence / hir so destreyneth
That al this wyde world / she set at noght
Hir freendes whiche þt knowe / hir heuy thoght
Conforten hire / in al that euere they may
They prechen hire / they telle hire nyght and day
That causelees / she sleeth hir self allas
And euery confort / possible in this cas
They doon to hire / with al hir bisynesse
Al for to make hire / leue hir heuynesse
By proces as ye knowen euerichoon
Men may so longe grauen in a stoon
Til som figure ther inne emprented be
So longe han they conforted hire til she
Receyued hath by hope and by resoun
The emprentyng of hir consolacioun
Thurgh which hir grete sorwe gan aswage
She may nat alwey / duren in swich rage
And eek Arueragus / in al this care
Hath sent hire lettres hom / of his welfare
And that he wole / come hastily agayn
Or ellis hadde this sorwe / hir herte slayn

[..]reendes sawe hir sorwe gan to slake
[..]t preyde hir on knees for goddes sake
To come and romen hire in compaignye
Awey to dryve hir derke fantasye
And finally she graunted that requeste
ffor wel she saw þ[t] it was for the beste
Now stood hir castel faste by the see
And often with hir freendes walketh she
Hir to disporte up on the bank anheigh
Wher as she many a ship and barge seigh
Seillynge hir cours wher as hem liste go
But thanne was that a parcel of hir wo
ffor of hir self ful ofte allas seith she
Is ther no ship of so manye as I se
Wol bryngen hom my lord thanne were myn herte
Al warisshed of hise bittre peynes smerte
Another tyme there wolde she sitte and thynke
And caste hir eyen dounward fro the brynke
But whan she seigh the grisly rokkes blake
ffor verray fere so wolde hir herte quake
That on hir feet she mighte hir noght sustene
Thanne wolde she sitte adoun up on the grene
And pitously in to the see biholde
And seyn right thus with sorweful sikes colde
Eterne god that thurgh thy purueiance
ledest the world by certeyn gouernance
In ydel as men seyn ye no thyng make
But lord thise grisly feendly rokkes blake
That semen rather a foul confusioun
Of werk than any fair creacioun
Of swich a parfit wys god and a stable
Why han ye wroght this werk unresonable
ffor by this werk south north ne west ne est
Ther nys yfostred man ne bryd ne beest
It doth no good to my wit but anoyeth
Se ye nat lord how mankynde it destroyeth
An hundred thousand bodies of mankynde
Han rokkes slayn al be they nat in mynde
Which mankynde is so fair part of thy werk
That thow it madest lyk to thyn owen merk

	ELLESMERE
[Hire f]reendes sawe / hir sorwe gan to slake	¶Hir*e* freendes
[An]d preyde hir*e* on knees / for goddes sake	And
To come / and romen hire in compaignye	hir*e*
Awey to dryue / hir derke fantasye	hir*e*
And finally / she graunted that requeste	6
For wel she saw / þ*a*t it was for the beste	saugħ / that
¶Now stood hir Castel / faste by the See	hir*e* fasteby
And often / with hir freendes walketh she	hir*e* shee
Hir to disporte / vp on the bank anheigh	Hir*e* anheigħ
Wher as she / many a Ship*e* and Barge seigh	Where / ship*e* barge seigħ
Seillynge hir cours / wher as hem liste go	wher*e*
But thanne was that a p*ar*cel of hir wo	hir*e*
For of hir self / ful ofte allas seith she	For to hir self
Is ther no ship*e* / of so manye as I se	
Wol bryngen hom my lord / thanne were myn herte	
Al warisshed / of hise bittre peynes smerte	
¶Another tyme / there wolde she sitte and thynke	ther
And caste hir eyen / downward fro the Brynke	dounward brynke
But whan she seigh / the grisly Rokkes blake	saugħ /
For verray fere / so wolde hir herte quake	feere /
That on hir feet she myghte hir noght sustene	hir*e* myghte hir*e* noght
Thanne wolde she / sitte adoun vp on the grene	
And pitously / in to the See biholde	
And seyn right thus / with sorweful sikes colde	right *with*
¶Eterne god / that thurgh thy purueiance	¶Et*er*ne thurgħ p*ur*ueiaunce
Ledest the world / by certeyn gou*er*nance	certein gou*er*nau*n*ce
In ydel as men seyn / ye no thyng make	thyng
But lord / thise grisly / feendly Rokkes blake	
That semen rather / a foul confusiou*n*	
Of werk / than any fair creaciou*n*	werk
Of swich a p*ar*fit wys god and a stable	
Why han ye wroght this werk vnresonable	wroght
For by this werk South / North / ne West ne Est	werk / South / North / Est
Ther nys yfostred / man / ne bryd / ne beest	yfostred bryd
It doth no good to my wit but anoyeth	dooth
Se ye nat lord / how mankynde it destroyeth	lord destroyetħ
An hundred thousand bodies / of mankynde	bodyes
Han Rokkes slayn / al be they nat in mynde	
Which mankynde / is so fair part of thy werk	part
That thow it madest lyk to thyn owen merk	thou owene

6 ¶Frankeleyn *125r*

The Frankeleyn.⸗	ELLESMERE
Thanne semed it ye hadde a greet chiertee	¶Thanne
Toward mankynde / but how thanne may it be	bee
That ye swiche menes make / it to destroyen	meenes
Whiche menes do no good / but eu*er*e anoyen	meenes
I woot wel / clerkes wol seyn as hem leste	
By argumentz / that al is for the beste	Argumentz /
Thogh I ne kan / the causes nat yknowe	Thougħ I kan /
But thilke god / ꝥ*at* made wynd to blowe	that
As kepe my lord / this my conclusiou*n*	lord
To clerkes / lete I al disputisou*n*	clerkes I / al this disputisou*n*
But wolde god / ꝥ*at* alle thise Rokkes blake	that
Were sonken in to helle / for his sake	helle
Thise Rokkes sleen myn herte / for the feere	⁊ Rokkes / herte
Thus wolde she seyn / w*ith* many a pitous teere	
¶Hir freendes sawe / that it was no disport	¶Hir*e*
To romen by the See / but disconfort	
And shopen / for to pleyen / som wher ellys	shopen somwher elles
They leden hir*e* / by Ryuers and by wellys	Ryueres welles
And eek in othere places delitables	eek /
They dauncen / and they pleyen at Ches *and* tables	pleyen / ches and
¶So on a day / right in the morwe tyde	rigħt
Vn to a gardyn / that was ther bisyde	
In which / that they hadde maad hir ordinance	ordinau*n*ce
Of vitaille / and of oother purueiance	purueiau*n*ce
They goon and pleye hem / al the longe day	
And this was / on the sixte morwe of May	was / in the
Which may hadde peynted / with his softe shoures	May w*ith*
This gardyn / ful of leues / and of floures	leues
And craft of mannes hond / so curiously	craft hand
Arrayed hadde / this gardyn trewely	
That neuere was ther gardyn / of swich prys	neu*er*e / gardyn
But if it were / the verray Paradys	
The odour of floures / and the fresshe sighte	fressħe sigħte
Wolde han maked / any herte lighte	ligħte
That euere was born / but if to greet siknesse	eu*er*e
Or to greet sorwe / helde it in destresse	distresse
So ful it was / of beautee with plesaunce	plesau*n*ce
At after dyner / gonne they to daunce	dyner
And synge also / saue Dorigen allone	
Which made alwey / hir compleynt and hir mone	co*m*pleint *and* moone

[7]¶Frankeleyn *125v*

The ffrankeleyn

Thanne semed it ye hadde a greet chiertee
Toward mankynde / but how thanne may it be
That ye swiche menes make / it to destroyen
Whiche menes do no good / but euere anoyen
I woot wel / clerkes wol seyn as hem leste
By argumentz / that al is for the beste
Though I ne kan / the causes nat yknowe
But thilke god / þt made wynd to blowe
As kepe my lord / this my conclusion
To clerkes / lete I al disputison
But wolde god / þt alle thise rokkes blake
Were sonken in to helle / for his sake
Thise rokkes sleen myn herte / for the feere
Thus wolde she seyn / wt many a pitous teere
Hir freendes sawe / that it was no disport /
To romen by the see / but disconfort /
And shopen for to pleyen som wher ellys
They leden hire / by ryuers and by wellys
And eek in othere places delitables
They dauncen / and they pleyen at ches & tables
So on a day / right in the morwe tyde
Vn to a gardyn / that was ther bisyde
In which that they hadde maad hir ordinaunce
Of vitaille / and of oother purueiaunce
They goon and pleye hem / al the longe day
And this was / on the sixte morwe of may
Which may hadde peynted / with his softe shoures
This gardyn / ful of leues and of floures
And craft of mannes hond / so curiously
Arrayed hadde this gardyn trewely
That neuere was ther gardyn / of swich prys
But if it were / the verray Paradys
The odour of floures / and the fresshe sighte
Wolde han maked / any herte lighte
That euere was born / but if to greet siknesse
Or to greet sorwe / helde it in destresse
So ful it was / of beautee with plesaunce
At after dyner / gonne they to daunce
And synge also / saue Dorigen allone
Which made alwey / hir compleynt and hir mone

…e she ne saugh hym / on the daunce go
That was hir housbonde / and hir loue also
But nathelees she moste a tyme abyde
And with good hope / lete hir sorwe slyde
Up on this daunce / amonges othere men
Daunced a Squier / bifore Dorigen
That fressher was / and iolyer of array
As to my doom / than is the monthe of May
He syngeth / daunceth / passyng any man
That is or was / sith þt the world bigan
Ther with he was / if men sholde hym discryue
Oon of the beste farynge man / on lyue
Yong / strong / right vertuous / and riche and wys
And wel biloued / and holden in greet prys
And shortly / if the sothe I tellen shal
Unwityng of this Dorigen at al
This lusty Squier / seruant to Venus
Which that ycleped was Aurelius
Hadde loued hire / best of any creature
Two yeer and moore / as was his auenture
But neuere dorste he tellen hire / his greuance
With outen coppe / he drank al his penance
He was despeyred / no thyng dorste he seye
Saue in his songes / som what wolde he wreye
His wo / as in a general compleynyng
He seyde he louede / and was biloued no thyng
Of which matere / made he many layes
Songes / compleyntes / roundels / vyrelayes
How þt he dorste nat / his sorwe telle
But langwissheth / as a furye dooth in helle
And dye he moste he seyde / as dide Ekko
For Narcisus / that dorste nat telle hir wo
In oother manere / than ye heere me seye
Ne dorste he nat to hire / his wo biwreye
Saue that p(ar)auenture / som tyme at daunces
Ther yong folk / kepen hir obseruaunces
It may wel be / he looked on hir face
In swich a wise / as man þt asketh g(ra)ce
But no thyng wiste she / of his entente
Nathelees it happed / er they thennes wente

	ELLESMERE
[For] she ne saugh hym / on the ďaunce go	For saugħ
That was hir housbonde / and hir loue also	
But nathelees / she moste a tyme abyde	
And with good hope / lete hir sorwe slyde	
¶Vp on this daunce / amonges othere men	
Daunced a Squier / bifore Dorigen	biforn
That fressher was / and Iolier of array	fressħer Iolyer
As to my doom / than is the Monthe of May	
He syngeth / daunceth / passyng any man	passynge
That is / or was / sith þ*at* the world bigan	is / /
Ther with he was / if men sholde hym discryue	wit*h*
Oon of the beste farynge man / on lyue	Oon / man
Yong' strong' right v*er*tuous / and riche and wys	Yong / righ̄t *and* wys
And wel biloued / and holden in gret prys	greet
And shortly / if the sothe I tellen shal	
Vnwityng' of this Dorigen at al	
This lusty Squier / seruant to Venus	
Which / that yclepid was Aurelius	Which ycleped
Hadde loued hir*e* / best of any creature	
Two yeer and moore / as was his auenture	
But neu*ere* dorste he tellen hir*e* / his greuance	8 neu*ere* / hir*e* greuau*n*ce
With outen coppe / he drank al his penance	penau*n*ce
He was despeyred / no thyng dorste he seye	
Saue in his songes / som what wolde he wreye	somwhat
His wo / as in a general compleynyng'	
He seyde he louede / and was biloued no thyng'	
Of which matere / made he many layes	Of swich matere / manye
Songes / compleyntes / roundels / vyrelayes	compleintes / virelayes
How þ*at* he dorste nat' his sorwe telle	that / nat /
But langwissheth / as a furye dooth in helle	langwissħetħ /
And dye he moste he seyde / as dide Ekko	[¶Methamorphosios]
For Narcisus / that dorste nat telle hir wo	
In oother manere / than ye heere me seye	
Ne dorste he nat to hire / his wo biwreye	nat'. hir*e*
Saue that p*ar*auenture / som tyme at daunces	
Ther yong folk / kepen hir obseruaunces	
It may wel be / he looked on hir face	
In swich a wise / as man þ*at* asketh g*ra*ce	grace
But no thyng wiste she / of his entente	thyng'
Nathelees it happed / er they thennes wente	Nathelees / happed

8 ¶Frankeleyn *126r*

	ELLESMERE
¶By cause / that he was / hir neghebour	By was hir*e* Neighebour
And was a man / of worship*e* and honour	
And hadde yknowen hym / of tyme yoore	
They fille in speche / and forth moore and moore	forth
Vn to this purpos / drough Aurelius	drough
And whan he saugh his tyme / he seyde thus	saugh
¶Madame quod he / by god that this world made	þ*a*t
So þ*a*t I wiste / it myghte your*e* herte glade	that
I wolde that day / þ*a*t youre Arueragus	that youre
Wente ouer the See / that I Aurelius	ou*er* see /
Hadde went / ther neuere I sholde haue come agayn	went neu*er*e
For wel I woot my seruyce is in vayn	
My gerdon is / but brestyng of myn herte	gerdou*n*
Madame reweth / vp on my peynes smerte	Madame / reweth vpon
For with a word / ye may me sle or saue	word sleen
Here at youre feet god wolde þ*a*t I were graue	Heere your*e* feet /
I ne haue as now / no leyser moore to seye	
Haue m*er*cy swete / or ye wol do me deye	sweete /
¶She gan to looke / vp on Aurelius	
Is this youre wil quod she / and sey ye thus	your*e* wyl thus.
Neuere erst quod she / ne wiste I what ye mente	Neu*er*e erst
But now Aurelie / I knowe youre entente	
By thilke god / that yaf me soule and lyf	
Ne shal I neuere / been vntrewe a wyf	neu*er*e / vntrewe wyf
In word ne werk as fer as I haue wyt	werk / wit /
I wol been hys / to whom þ*a*t I am knyt	his /
Taak this for fynal / as of me	fynal answer*e* / as
But after that in pleye thus seyde she	pley
¶Aurelie quod she / by heighe god aboue	9 heighe
Yet wolde I graunte yow / to been your*e* loue	
Syn I yow se / so pitously complayne	
Looke what day / þ*a*t endelong Britayne	that
Ye remoeue alle the Rokkes / stoon by stoon	
That they ne lette / ship*e* ne Boot to goon	boot
I seye / whan ye han maad / the coost so clene	
Of Rokkes / that ther nys no stoon ysene	
Thanne wol I loue yow / best of any man	I / yow
Haue heer my trouthe / in al that euere I kan	þ*a*t eu*er*e
¶Is ther noon oother grace / in yow quod he	gr*a*ce / he.
¶No by that lord quod she / that maked me	¶No / she

9 ¶Frankeleyn *126v*

The ffrankeleyn

By cause that he was hir neghebour
And was a man of worship and honour
And hadde yknowen hym of tyme yoore
They fille in speche and forth moore and moore
Vn to this purpos drough Aurelius
And whan he saugh his tyme he seyde thus
Madame quod he by god that this world made
So þt I wiste it myghte youre herte glade
I wolde that day þt youre Arueragus
Wente ouer the see that I Aurelius
Hadde went ther neuere I sholde haue come agayn
For wel I woot my seruyce is in vayn
My gerdon is but brestyng of myn herte
Madame reweth vp on my peynes smerte
For with a word ye may me sle or saue
Here at youre feet god wolde þt I were graue
I ne haue as now no leyser moore to seye
Haue mercy swete or ye wol do me deye
She gan to looke vp on Aurelius
Is this youre wil quod she and sey ye thus
Neuere erst quod she ne wiste I what ye mente
But now Aurelie I knowe youre entente
By thilke god that yaf me soule and lyf
Ne shal I neuere been vntrewe wyf
In word ne werk as fer as I haue wyt
I wol been hys to whom þt I am knyt
Taak this for fynal as of me
But after that in pleye thus seyde she
Aurelie quod she by heighe god aboue
Yet wolde I graunte yow to been youre loue
Syn I yow se so pitously complayne
Looke what day þt endelong Britayne
Ye remoeue alle the rokkes stoon by stoon
That they ne lette ship ne boot to goon
I seye whan ye han maad the coost so clene
Of rokkes that ther nys no stoon ysene
Thanne wol I loue yow best of any man
Haue heer my trouthe in al that euere I kan
Is ther noon oother grace in yow quod he
No by that lord quod she that maked me

Wel I woot/ that it shal neuere bityde
Lat swiche folies/ out of youre herte slyde
What deyntee/ sholde a man han in his lyf
ffor to loue/ another mannes wyf
That hath hir body/ whan so that hym liketh
Aurelius/ ful ofte soore siketh
Wo was Aurelie/ whan pt he this herde
And wt a sorweful herte/ he thus answerde
Madame quod he/ this were an inpossible
Thanne moot I dye/ of sodeyn deth horrible
And with that word/ he turned hym anon
Tho coome hir othere freendes many oon
And in the aleyes/ romeden vp and doun
And no thyng wiste/ of this conclusioun
But sodeynly/ bigonne reuel newe
Til that the brighte sonne/ loste his hewe
ffor thorisonte/ hath reft the sonne his light/
This is as muche to seye/ as it was nyght/
And hoom they goon/ in ioye and in solas
Saue oonly/ wrecched Aurelius allas
He to his hous is goon/ with sorweful herte
He seeth he may nat from his deeth asterte
Hym semed that he felte/ his herte colde
Vp to the heuene/ hise hondes he gan holde
And on his knowes bare/ he sette hym doun
And in his rauynge/ seyde his orisoun
ffor verray wo/ out of his wit he breyde
He nyste what he spak/ but thus he seyde
Wt pitous herte/ his pleynt hath he bigonne
Vn to the goddes/ and first vn to the sonne
He seyde Appollo/ god and gouernour
Of euery plaunte/ herbe/ tree/ and flour
That yeuest/ after thy declynacioun
To ech of hem/ his tyme and his sesoun
As thyn herberwe/ chaungeth/ lowe or heighe
Lord Phebus/ cast thy merciable eighe
On wrecche Aurelie/ which pt am but lorn
Lo lord/ my lady/ hath my deeth yswoorn
With outen gilt/ but thy benygnytee
Vp on my dedly herte/ haue som pitee

	ELLESMERE
[For] wel I woot⁊ that it shal neu*er*e bityde	For p*at* neu*er*
[La]t swiche folies / out of youre herte slyde	Lat youre
What deyntee / sholde a man han his lyf	deyntee man / han in his
For to loue / another mannes wyf	to go loue /
That hath hir body / whan so that hym liketh	p*at* hym
¶Aurelius / ful ofte soore siketh	
Wo was Aurelie / whan p*at* he this herde	
And w*ith* a sorweful herte / he thus answerde	with
¶Madame quod he / this were an inpossible	
Thanne moot I dye / of sodeyn deth horrible	
And with that word / he turned hym anon	
Tho coome / hir othere freendes many oon	
And in the Aleyes / romeden vp and doun	
And no thyng wiste / of this conclusioun	
But sodeynly / bigonne reuel newe	sodeynly ./
Til that the brighte sonne / loste his hewe	that⁊
For thorisonte / hath reft the Sonne his light⁊	For Thorisonte/ reft⁊ lygħt⁊
This is as muche to seye / as it was nyght⁊	nygħt⁊
And hom they goon / in ioye and in solas	hoom
Saue oonly / wrecched Aurelius allas	wrecche
He to his hous is goon / with sorweful herte	
He seeth / he may nat from his deeth asterte	nat⁊ fro
Hym semed / that he felte his herte colde	
Vp to the heuene / hise hondes he gan holde	handes
And on his knowes bare / he sette hym doun	hise
And in his rauynge / seyde his orisoun	rauyng⁊
For v*er*ray wo / out of his wit he breyde	
He nyste what he spak⁊ but thus he seyde	
W*ith* pitous herte / his pleynt hath he bigonne	With
Vn to the goddes / and first vn to the sonne	first⁊
¶He seyde Appollo / god and gouernour	gou*er*nour
Of euery plaunte / herbe / tree / and flour	eu*er*y tree
That yeuest⁊ after thy declynaciou*n*	declinaciou*n*
To ech of hem / his tyme and his sesou*n*	
As thyn herberwe / chaungeth / lowe or heighe	chaungeth heighe
Lord Phebus / cast thy merciable eighe	eighe
On wrecche Aurelie / which p*at* am but lorn	10 whicħ am
Lo lord / my lady hath my deeth ysworn	
With outen gilt⁊ but thy benygnytee	oute benignytee
Vp on my dedly herte / haue som pitee	

1031 The compleint of Aurelius to the goddes and to the sonne El

[10] ¶Frankeleyn *127r*

The Frankeleyn.	ELLESMERE
For wel I woot lord Phebus / if yow lest /	woot / lest
Ye may me helpen / saue my lady best	
Now voucheth sauf / þat I may yow deuyse	
How þat I may been holpe / and in what wyse	holpen /
¶Youre blisful Suster / lucyna [i. luna] the shene	¶Your*e* Lucina [.i. luna] sheene
That of the See / is chief goddesse and queene	
Thogh Neptim*us* / haue deitee in the See	Though Neptimus /
Yet Empiresse / abouen hym is she	Yet Emperisse /
Ye knowen wel lord / that right as hir desir	right
Is / to be quyked / and lighted of youre fyr	Is lightned fir
For which / she folweth yow / ful bisily	
Right so the See / desireth naturelly	Right / so / See
To folwen hire / as she þat is goddesse	hir*e* / that
Bothe in the See / and Ryuers moore and lesse	Ryueres
Wher fore lord Phebus / this is my requeste	Wherfore
Do this myracle / or do myn herte breste	miracle /
That now next at this opposiciou*n*	
Which in the signe / shal be of the liou*n*	leou*n*
As preyeth hire / so greet a flood to brynge	preieth hir*e* /
That fyue fadme at the leeste / it ouer sprynge	leeste ou*er*sprynge
The hyeste Rok in Armoryk Britayne	Rokke / Armorik / Briteyne
And lat this flood / endure yeris twayne	yeres tweyne
Thanne certes / to my lady / may I seye	c*er*tes / lady
Holdeth youre heste / the Rokkes been aweye	
¶Lord Phebus / dooth this myracle for me	miracle
Pray hire / she go no faster cours than ye	Preye hir*e* /
I seye this / prayeth youre Suster þat she go	seye / preyeth suster that
No faster cours than ye / thise yeris two	yeres
Thanne shal she been euene / at the fulle alway	been / euene atte fulle
And spryng flood lasten / bothe nyght and day	flood / laste nyght
And but she vouche sauf in swich manere	sauf /
To graunte me / my souerayn lady deere	sou*er*eyn
Pray hire / to synken euery Rok / adown	Prey hir*e* / Rok adoun
In to / hir owene dirke Regioun	
Vnder the ground / ther Pluto dwelleth Inne	
Or neu*ere* mo / shal I my lady wynne	neu*er*emo /
Thy temple in Delphos / wol I barfoot seke	Temple barefoot
Lord Phebus / se the teerys on my cheke	teeris
And of my peyne / haue som compassioun	
And w*ith* that word / in swowne he fil adoun	with

The ffrankeleyn.

ffor wel I woot lord Phebus if yow lest
Ye may me helpen saue my lady best
Now vouchesauf þt I may yow deuyse
How þt I may been holpe / and in what wyse
Youre blisful suster / Lucyna the shene
That of the See / is chief goddesse and queene
Though Neptunus / haue deitee in the See
Yet Emperesse / abouen hym is she
Ye knowen wel lord / that right as hir desir
Is to be quyked / and lighted of youre fyr
ffor which / she folweth yow ful bisily
Right so the See / desireth naturelly
To folwen hire / as she þt is goddesse
Bothe in the See / and Ryuers moore and lesse
Wher fore lord Phebus / this is my requeste
Do this miracle / or do myn herte breste
That now next / at this opposicion
Which in the signe / shal be of the lion
As preyeth hire / so greet a flood to brynge
That fyue fadme at the leeste / it ouer sprynge
The hyeste rok / in Armoryk Briteyne
And lat this flood / endure yeres tweyne
Thanne certes / to my lady / may I seye
Holdeth youre heste / the rokkes been aweye
Lord Phebus / dooth this miracle for me
Pray hire / she go no faster cours than ye
I seye this / preyeth youre suster þt she go
No faster cours than ye thise yeres two
Thanne shal she been euene / at the fulle alway
And spryng flood laften / bothe nyght and day
And but she vouche sauf / in which manere
To graunte me / my souerayn lady deere
Pray hire to synken euery rok adown
In to hir owene dirke regioun
Vnder the ground / ther Pluto dwelleth Inne
Or neuere mo / shal I my lady wynne
Thy temple in Delphos / wol I barfoot seke
Lord Phebus / se the teerys on my cheke
And of my peyne / haue som compassioun
And with that word / in swowne he fil adoun

[...]onge tyme he lay forth in a traunce
[...]s brother / which that knew of his penaunce
[...]p caughte hym / and to bedde he hath hym broght /
Despeired / in this torment / and this thoght
Lete I this woful creature lye
Chese he for me / wher he wol lyve or dye
Arueragus / with heele / and greet honour
As he þt was / of chiualrie the flour
Is comen hom / and othere worthy men
O blisful artow now / thow dorigen
That hast thy lusty housbonde / in thyn armes
The fresshe knyght / the worthy man of armes
That loueth thee / as his owene hertes lyf
No thyng list hym to been ymaginatyf
If any wight hadde spoke / whil he was oute
To hire of loue / he ne hadde of it no doute
He noght entendeth / to no swich matere
But daunceth / iusteth / maketh hir good cheere
And thus in ioye and blisse / I lete hem dwelle
And of the syke Aurelius / wol I telle
In langour / and in torment furyus
Two yeer and moore / lay wrecche Aurelius
Er any foot / he myghte on erthe gon
Ne confort in this tyme / hadde he non
Saue of his brother / which þt was a clerk
He knew of al this wo / and al this werk
ffor to noon oother creature certeyn
Of this matere / he dorste no word seyn
Vnder his brest / he baar it moore secree
Than euere dide Panfilus / for Galathee
His brest was hool / with oute for to sene
But in his herte ay was the arwe kene
And wel ye knowe / þt of a sursanure
In surgerye / is perilous the cure
But men myghte touche the arwe / or come therby
His brother / weep and wayled pryuely
Til at the laste / hym fil in remembrance
That whils he was / at Orliens in ffrance
As yonge clerkes / that been lykerous
To reden artz / that been curious

	ELLESMERE
[And l]onge tyme / he lay forth in a traunce	And longe
[Hi]s brother / which that knew of his penaunce	¶His ' *pat* penau*n*ce
Vp caughte hym / and to bedde he hath hym broght	broght
Despeired / in this torment and this thoght	Dispeyred / thoght
Lete I / this woful creature lye	11
Chese he for me / wher he wol lyue or dye	me / wheither he
¶Arueragus / with heele / and greet honour	Arueragus / heele hono*ur*
As he *pat* was / of Chiualrie the flour	he / chiualrie
Is comen hom / and othere worthy men	hoom /
O blisful artow now / thow Dorigen	blisful / thou
That hast thy lusty housbonde / in thyn armes	That hast housbonde thyne Armes
The fresshe knyght the worthy man of armes	fresshe knyght Armes
That loueth thee / as his owene hertes lyf	lyf
No thyng list hym / to been ymagynatyf	thyng ymaginatyf
If any wight hadde spoke / whil he was oute	wight
To hire of loue / he ne hadde of it no doute	he hadde
He noght entendeth / to no swich matere	noght swich mateere
But daunceth / Iusteth / maketh hir good cheere	hir*e*
And thus in ioye and blisse / I lete hem dwelle	thus /
And of the Syke Aurelius / wol I telle	sike I wol yow telle
¶In langour / and in torment furyus	IN
Two yeer and moore / lay wrecche Aurelius	Aurelyus
Er any foot he myghte on erthe gon	foot. myghte
Ne confort in this tyme / hadde he non	noon
Saue of his brother / which *pat* was a Clerk	clerk
He knew of al this wo / and al this werk	werk
For / to noon oother creature *cer*teyn	For certeyn
Of this matere / he dorste no word seyn	
Vnder his brist he baar it moore secree	brest
Than euere dide Panfil*us* / for Galathee	eu*e*re Pamphilus
His brist was hool / with oute for to sene	brest
But in his herte / ay was the arwe kene	Arwe
And wel ye knowe / *pat* of a Sursanure	As wel that
In Surgerye / is *per*ilous the cure	
But men myghte touche the arwe / or come therby	myghte Arwe /
His brother / weep*e* and wayled pryuely	weep*e* /
Til at the laste / hym fil in remembrance	atte laste / remembrau*n*ce
That whils he was / at Orliens in France	whiles Frau*n*ce
As yonge clerkes / that been lykerous	
To reden Artz / that been curious	

1110 Pamphilus ad Galatheam vulneror et clausum porto sub pectore telum et cetera El

[11] ¶Frankeleyn *127v*

The Frankeleyn.

Seken / in eu*er*y halke / and euery herne
Particuler sciences / for to lerne
He hym remembred / þ*at* vp on a day
At Orliens in Studie / a book he say
Of Magyk naturel / which his felawe
That was that tyme / a Bachiler of lawe
Al were he ther / to lerne another craft
Hadde p*ri*uely / vp on his desk ylaft
Which book spak muchel / of the op*er*aciou*n*s
Touchynge / the .xxviij. mansiou*n*s
That longen to the Moone / and swich folye
As in oure dayes / is nat worth a flye
For holy chirches feith / in oure bileue
Ne suffreth / noon illusiou*n* vs to greue
And whan this book was in his remembrau*n*ce
Anon for ioye / his herte gan to dau*n*ce
And to hym self / he seyde pryuely
My brother / shal be warisshed hastily
For I am siker / þ*at* ther be sciences
By whiche / men make diu*er*se apparences
Swiche / as thise subtile / Tregettours pleye
For ofte at festes / haue I wel herd seye
That Tregettours / wi*th* Inne an halle large
Haue maad come In / a water / and a barge
And in the halle / rowen vp and doun
Som tyme hath semed / come a grym leoun
And som tyme floures sprynge / as in a mede
Som tyme a vyne / and grapes white and rede
Som tyme a Castel / al of lym and stoon
And whan hem lyked / voyded it anoon
Thus semed it to euery mannes sighte
¶Now thanne conclude I thus / þ*at* if I myghte
At Orliens / som old felawe yfynde
That hadde / this Moones mansions in mynde
Or oother Magyk naturel aboue
He sholde wel / make my brother han his loue
For with an apparence / a clerk may make
To mannes sighte / þ*at* alle the Rokkes blake
Of Britaigne / were yvoyded euerichon
And shippes / by the brynke / comen and gon

ELLESMERE

euery
P*ar*ticuler
that vpon

Magyk / natureel /
Bacheler

vpon desk ylaft /
book
eighte and twenty
moone /

12 hooly feith /
suffreth
book /
daunce
self

By whce /
subtile tregetours
feestes /
tregetours /
water

Somtyme / semed
somtyme Mede
Somtyme
Somtyme
whan hym lyked / anon
eu*er*y sighte

oold
moones
natureel
wel make /
clerk

weren
brynke

[12]¶Frankeleyn *128r*

The ffrankeleyn

Seken in euery halke / and euery herne
Particuler sciences / for to lerne
He hym remembred / þt vp on a day
At Orliens in studie / a book he say
Of magyk naturel / which his felawe
That was that tyme / a bachiler of lawe
Al were he ther to lerne another craft
Hadde priuely vp on his desk ylaft
Which book spak muchel / of the operacions
Touchynge the xxviij · mansiouns
That longen to the moone / and swich folye
As in oure dayes / is nat worth a flye
For holy chirches feith / in oure bileue
Ne suffreth / noon illusion vs to greue
And whan this book / was in his remembrance
Anon for ioye / his herte gan to daunce
And to hym self / he seyde pryuely
My brother / shal be warisshed hastily
For I am siker / þt ther be sciences
By whiche / men make diuerse apparences
Swiche / as thise subtile tregettours pleye
For ofte at festes / haue I wel herd seye
That tregettours / wᵗ inne an halle large
Haue maad come in / a water and a barge
And in the halle / rowen vp and doun
Som tyme hath semed / come a grym leoun
And som tyme floures sprynge / as in a mede
Som tyme a vyne / and grapes white and rede
Som tyme a castel / al of lym and stoon
And whan hem lyked / voyded it anoon
Thus semed it / to euery mannes sighte
Now thanne conclude I thus / þt if I myghte
At Orliens / som old felawe yfynde
That hadde thise moones mansions in mynde
Or oother magyk naturel aboue
He sholde wel / make my brother han his loue
For with an apparence / a clerk may make
To mannes sighte / þt alle the rokkes blake
Of Britaigne / were yvoyded euerichon
And shippes / by the brynke / comen and gon

[Th]e in swich forme / endwyen a day or two
Thanne were my brother / warisshed of his wo
Thanne moste she nedes / holden hir biheste
Or ellis / he shal shame hir / at the leeste
¶ What sholde I make / a lenger tale of this
Vn to his brotheres bed / he comen is
And swich confort / he yaf hym for to gon
To Orliens / that he vp stirte anon
And on his wey forthward / thanne he is fare
In hope / for to been lissed of his care
¶ Whan they were come / almoost to that Citee
But if it were / a two furlong or thre
A yong clerk / romynge by hym self they mette
Which þt in latyn / thriftily hem grette
And after that / he seyde a wonder thyng
I knowe quod he / the cause of youre comyng
And er they ferther / any foote wente
He tolde hem / al that was in hir entente
¶ This Briton clerk / hym asked of felawes
The whiche þt he hadde knowe / in olde dawes
And he answerde hym / þt they dede were
ffor which / he weep ful ofte many a tere
¶ Doun of his hors / Aurelius lighte anon
And with this magicien / forth he is gon
Hom to his hous / and maden hem wel at ese
Hem lakked no vitaille / þt myghte hem plese
So wel arrayed hous / as ther was oon
Aurelius in his lyf / saw neuere noon
¶ He shewed hym / er he wente to soper
fforestes parkes / ful of wilde deer
Ther saw he hertes / with hir hornes hye
The gretteste / þt euere were seyn wt eye
He say of hem / an hundred slayn wt houndes
And somme with arwes blede / of bittre woundes
¶ He saw / whan voyded were thise wilde deer
Thise ffauconers / vp on a fair Ryuer
That with hir haukes / han the heron slayn
¶ Tho saugh he knyghtes / Iustyng in a playn
And after this / he dide hym this plesaunce
That he hym shewed / his lady on a daunce

	ELLESMERE
[And] in swich forme / enduren a day or two	And a wowke or
Thanne were my brother / warisshed of his wo	brother// warissħed
Thanne moste she nedes / holden hir biheste	hir*e*
Or ellis / he shal shame hir*e* / at the leeste	elles / hir*e* atte leeste
¶What sholde I make / a lenger tale of this	
Vn to his brotheres bed / he comen is	
And swich confort' he yaf hym for to gon	
To Orliens / that he vp stirte anon	
And on his wey forthward / thanne he is fare	wey / forthward is he
In hope / for to been lissed of his care	
¶Whan they were come / almoost to that Citee	almoost'
But if it were / a two furlong or thre	furlong'
A yong clerk'/ romynge by hym self they mette	clerk'
Which þ*a*t in latyn / thriftily hem grette	
And after that / he seyde a wonder thyng'	that'
I knowe quod he / the cause of youre comyng'	
And er they ferther / any foote wente	ferther'
He tolde hem / al that was in hir entente	hir*e*
¶This Britou*n* clerk' hym asked of felawes	Briton
The whiche þ*a*t he hadde knowe / in olde dawes	had
And he answerde hym / þ*a*t they dede were	13 that
For which / he weep*e* ful ofte many a teere	weep
¶Doun of his hors / Aurelius lighte anon	ligħte
And with this Magicien / forth he is gon	is he
Hom to his hous / and maden hem wel atese	Hoom
Hem lakked no vitaille / þ*a*t myghte hem plese	mygħte
So wel arrayed hous / as ther was oon	
Aurelius / in his lyf / saw neuere noon	Aurelius saugħ neu*er*e
¶He shewed hym / er he wente to soper	Sopeer
Forestes / Parkes / ful of wilde deer	
Ther saw he hertes / with hir hornes hye	saugħ wit*h*
The gretteste / þ*a*t eu*er*e were seyn wit*h* eye	that
He say of hem / an hundred slayn wit*h* houndes	saugħ hondred with
And so*m*me with arwes blede / of bittre woundes	Arwes
¶He saw / whan voyded were thise wilde deer	saugħ /
Thise Fawconers / vp on a fair Ryuer	Fauconers / vpon
That with hir hawkes / han the heron slayn	wit*h* haukes / herou*n*
¶Tho saugh he knyghtes / Iustyng in a playn	saugħ knygħtes / iustyng'
And after this / he dide hym this plesaunce	hym swich plesaunce
That he hym shewed / his lady on a daunce	

[13] ¶Frankeleyn *128v*

On which hym self / he daunced as hym thoughte
And whan this maister⁊ þat this magyk wroughte
Saugh it was tyme / he clapte his handes two
And farwel / al oure reuel was ago
And yet remoeued they neu*er*e / out of the hous
Whil they sawe / al this sighte m*er*ueillous
But in his studie / ther as his bookes be
They sitten stille / and no wight⁊ but they thre
¶To hym this maister / called his Squyer
And seide hym thus / is redy oure soper
Almoost⁊ an houre it is / I vndertake
Sith I yow bad / oure soper for to make
Whan that thise worthy men / wenten w*ith* me
In to my studie / ther as my bookes be
¶Sire quod this Squyer / whan it liketh yow
It is al redy / thogh ye wol right now
Gowe thanne soupe quod he / as for the beste
This amorous folk⁊ som tyme mote han hir reste
¶At after soper / fille they in tretee
What so*m*me sholde / this Maistres gerdou*n* be
To remoeuen / alle the Rokkes of Britayne
And eek from Geronde / to the mouth of Sayne
He made it straunge / and swoor so god hym saue
Lasse than a thousand pound / he wolde nat haue
Ne gladly for that somme / he wolde nat gon
¶Aurelius / with blisful herte anon
Answerde thus / fy on a thousand pound'
This wyde world / which þat men seye is round'
I wolde it yeue / if I were lord of it⁊
This bargayn is ful dryue / for we ben knyt⁊
Ye shal be payed trewely / by my trouthe
But looketh now / for no necligence or slouthe
Ye tarie vs heer / no lenger than tomorwe
¶Nay quod this clerk⁊ haue heer my feith to borwe
¶To bedde is goon Aurelius / whan hym leste
And wel neigh al that nyght⁊ he hadde his reste
What for his labour / and his hope of blisse
His woful herte / of penaunce hadde a lisse
¶Vp on the morwe / whan þat it was day
To Britayne / tooke they the righte way

ELLESMERE

daunced / thoughte
Maister / Magyk wroughte
hise
farewel /

saugħ / sighte
hise
seten wight⁊
hym / Maister Squier
seyde
is

Studie /
Squier /
though right

moote

so*m*me / sholde

mouth
¶He swoor /
thousand' pound' /
gladly / so*m*me goon
anoon

world' that
14 ¶I
been
payed / trewely

heere / to morwe

ny / nyght

¶Vpon
Britaigne / righte

[14] ¶Frankeleyn *129r*

In which hym self he daunced as hym thoughte
And whan this maister þt this magyk wroughte
Saugh it was tyme / he clapte his handes two
And farwel / al oure revel was ago
And yet remoeued they neuere out of the hous
Whil they saugh / al this sighte merueillous
But in his studie / ther as his bookes be
They seten stille / and no wight but they thre
To hym this maister called his Squyer
And seide hym thus / is redy oure soper
Almoost an houre it is I undertake
Sith I yow bad / oure soper for to make
Whan that thise worthy men / wenten wt me
In to my studie ther as my bookes be
Sire quod this Squyer / whan it liketh yow
It is al redy / though ye wol right now
Go we thanne soupe quod he / as for the beste
This amorous folk som tyme mote han hir reste
At after soper / fille they in tretee
What somme sholde this maistres gerdon be
To remoeuen / alle the rokkes of Britayne
And eek from Gerounde to the mouth of Sayne
He made it straunge / and swoor so god hym saue
Lasse than a thousand pound / he wolde nat haue
Ne gladly for that somme / he wolde nat gon
Aurelius with blisful herte anon
Answerde thus / fy on a thousand pound
This wyde world / which þt men seye is round
I wolde it yeue / if I were lord of it
This bargayn is ful dryue / for we ben knyt
Ye shal be payed trewely / by my trouthe
But looketh now / for no necligence or slouthe
Ye tarie us heer / no lenger than tomorwe
Nay quod this clerk / haue heer my feith to borwe
To bedde is goon Aurelius / whan hym leste
And wel neigh al that nyght / he hadde his reste
What for his labour / and his hope of blisse
His woful herte / of penaunce hadde a lisse
Vp on the morwe / whan þt it was day
To Britaigne / tooke they the righte way

[Aure]lius and this magicien bisyde
[B]ind been descended ther they wolde abyde
And this was as thise bookes me remembre
The colde frosty seson of Decembre
Phebus wax old / and hewed lyk laton
That / in his hote declynacion
Shoon as the burned gold / with stremys brighte
But now in Capricorn / adoun he lighte
Wher as he shoon ful pale / I dar wel seyn
The bittre frostes / with the sleet and reyn
Destruyed hath the grene / in euery yerd

Janus biceps — Janus sit by the fyr / with double berd
And drynketh / of his bugle horn the wyn
Biforn hym stant brawen / of the tusked swyn
And Nowel / crieth euery lusty man
Aurelius / al þt euere he kan
Dooth to this maister / chiere & reuerence
And preyeth hym / to doon his diligence
To bryngen hym / out of his peynes smerte
Or with a swerd / þt he wolde slitte his herte
This subtil clerk swich routhe hadde of this man
That nyght and day / he spedde hym that he kan
To wayten a tyme / of his conclusion
This is to seyn / to make illusion
By swich an apparence / or Iogelrye
I ne kan no termes of Astrologye
That she and euery wight / sholde wene and seye
That of Britayne / the rokkes were aweye
Or ellis / were sonken vnder grounde
So at the laste / he hath his tyme yfounde
To maken his Iapes / and his wrecchednesse
Of swich a supersticious cursednesse
His tables Tolletanes / forth he broght /
ffful wel corrected / ne ther lakked noght /
Neither his collect / ne his expans yeris
Ne hise rootes / ne hise othere geris
As been his centris / and hise argumentz
And hise proporcioneles conuenientz
ffor hise equacions / in euery thyng
And by his .8. speere / in his werkyng /

& he knew ful wel

[Aur]elius / and this Magicien bisyde
[A]nd been descended / ther they wolde abyde
And this was / as thise bookes me remembre
The colde / frosty seson of decembre
¶Phebus wax old / and hewed lyk latou*n*
That⁊ in his hote declynaciou*n*
Shoon as the burned gold / w*ith* stremys brighte
But now in Capricorn / adoun he lighte
Wher*e* as he shoon ful pale / I dar wel seyn
The bittre frostes / with the sleet and reyn
Destruyed hath the grene / in euery yerdˡ
¶Ianus biceps Ianus sit by the fyr / with double berdˡ
And drynketh / of his bugle horn the wyn
Biforn hym stant brawen / of the tusked swyn
And Nowel / crieth euery lusty man
¶Aurelius / al þat eue*r*e he kan
Dooth to this maister / cheere *and* reue*r*ence
And preyeth hym / to doon his diligence
To bryngen hym / out of his peynes smerte
Or with a swerd / þat he wolde slytte his herte
¶This subtil clerk⁊ swich routhe hadde of this man
That nyght and day / he spedde hym that he kan
To wayten a tyme / of his conclusiou*n*
This is to seyn / to make illusiou*n*
By swich an apparence / or Iogelrye
I ne kan / no termes of Astrologye
That she and euery wight⁊ sholde wene and seye
That of Britayne / the Rokkes were aweye
Or ellis / were sonken vnder grounde
So at the laste / he hath his tyme yfounde
To maken his Iapes / and his wrecchednesse
Of swich / a sup*er*sticious cursednesse
His tables tolletanes / forth he broght⁊
Ful wel corrected / ne ther lakked noght⁊
Neither his collect⁊ ne his expans yeris
Ne hise rootes / ne hise othere geris
As been his centris / and hise argumentz
And hise p*ro*porcionels conuenientz
For hise equacions / in euery thyng
And by his . 8 . speere / in his wirkyng⁊

He knew ful wel

ELLESMERE

Aurelius /
And
sesou*n*
Phebus
That hoote
with stremes brigħte
ligħte
Destroyed
[¶Ianus biceps]
hym /
¶Aurelius / in al that euere
to his Maister / chiere and
swerdˡ / slitte
had
nygħt þat
seye / maken
swich a apparence of Iogelrye
kan termes /
eu*ery* wigħt⁊ *and*
Britaigne /
ellis / they were
So atte laste /
hise Iapes /
swich ⟨a⟩ /
Hise brougħt
nougħt
hise expans yeeris
geeris
15 Hise Argumentz
p*ro*porcioneles
eu*ery* thyng⁊
speere

[15] ¶Frankeleyn *129v*

. The Frankeleyn .

HENGWRT	ELLESMERE	
He knew ful wel / how fer Alnath was shoue		
Fro the heed / of thilke fixe Aries aboue		
That in the . 9 . speere / considered is	speere	
Ful subtilly / he kalkuled al this	he hadde kalkuled	
¶Whan he hadde founde / his firste mansiou*n*		
He knew the remenaunt' by p*ro*porciou*n*	remenau*n*t'	
And knew the arisyng' of his Moone wel	moone weel	
And in whos face / and t*er*me / and euerydel	t*er*me	eu*er*ydeel
And knew ful wel / the Moones mansiou*n*	weel /	moones
Acordaunt / to his operaciou*n*	Acordaunt'	
And knew also / hise othere obseruaunces	obs*er*uau*n*ces	
For swiche illusions / and swiche meschau*n*ces	illusiou*n*s /	
As hethen folk vseden / in thilke dayes	folk / vseden	
For which no lenger / maked he delayes	which /	lenger
But thurgh his magyk' for a wyke or tweye	thurgħ	magik /
It semed / that alle the Rokkes were aweye		
¶Aurelius / which þ*at* yet despeired is		
Wher he shal han his loue / or fare amys		
Awaiteth nyght and day / on this myracle	nygħt	
And whan he knew / that ther was noon obstacle	þ*at*	
That voyded were / thise Rokkes euerichon	eu*er*ychon	
Doun to his maistres feet' he fil anon	Doun /	hise Maistres
And seyde / I woful wrecche Aurelius		
Thonke yow lord / and lady myn Venus	Thanke	
That me han holpen / fro my cares colde		
And to the temple / his wey forth hath he holde		
Wher as he knew / he sholde his lady se	Wher*e*	see
And whan he saw his tyme / anon right he	saugħ	rigħt hee
With dredful herte / and with ful humble cheere	hu*m*ble	
Salued hath / his sou*er*ayn lady deere	Salewed	souereyn
¶My righte lady / quod this woful man	My rigħte	
Whom I moost drede / and loue as I best kan	drede	
And lothest were / of al this world displese		
Nere it' þ*at* I for yow haue swich disese	yow /	
That I moste dyen heer / at youre foot anon	heere /	
Noght wolde I telle yow / how me is wo bigon	telle / how	
But c*er*tes / outher moste I dye / or pleyne	certes /	dye
Ye sleen me giltlees / for verray peyne	sle	
But of my deeth / thogh þ*at* ye haue no routhe	thogħ	
Auyseth yow / er that ye breke your trouthe	þ*at*	youre

1281 Alnath dicitur prima mansio lune El

1283 In nona spera El

He knew ful wel / how fer Alnath was shoue
ffro the heed / of thilke fixe Aries aboue
That in the .9. speere / considered is
fful subtilly / he kalkuled al this
Whan he hadde founde / his firste mansion
He knew the remenaunt / by proporcion
And knew the arysyng / of his moone wel
And in whos face / and terme / and euerydel
And knew ful wel / the moones mansion
Acordaunt / to his operacion
And knew also / hise othere obseruaunces
ffor swiche illusions / and swiche meschaunces
As hethen folk vseden / in thilke dayes
ffor which no lenger / maked he delayes
But thurgh his magyk / for a wyke or tweye
It semed / that alle the rokkes weere aweye
Aurelius / which þt yet despeyred is
Wher he shal han his loue / or fare amys
Awaiteth nyght and day / on this myracle
And whan he knew / that ther was noon obstacle
That voyded weere / thise rokkes euerichon
Doun to his maistres feet / he fil anon
And seyde / I woful wrecche Aurelius
Thanke yow lord / and lady myn Venus
That me han holpen / fro my cares colde
And to the temple / his wey forth hath he holde
Wher as he knew / he sholde his lady se .
And whan he saugh his tyme / anon right he
With dredful herte / and with ful humble cheere
Salued hath / his souereyn lady deere
My righte lady / quod this woful man
Whom I moost drede / and loue as I best kan
And lothest weere / of al this world displese
Nere it / þt I for yow haue swich disese
That I moste dyen heer / at youre foot anon
Noght wolde I telle yow / how me is wo bigon
But certes / outher moste I dye / or pleyne
Ye sleen me giltlees / for verray peyne
But of my deeth / thogh þt ye haue no routhe
Auyseth yow / er that ye breke youre trouthe

[...]uteth yow / for thilke god above
[E]r ye me sleen / by cause that I yow love
Ffor madame wel ye woot / what ye han hight
Nat þt I chalange / any thyng of right
Of yow my sovereyn lady / but youre grace
But in a gardyn yond / at swich a place
Ye woot right wel / what ye bihighten me
And in myn hand / youre trouthe plighten ye
To love me best / god woot ye seyden so
Al be þt I unworthy am therto
Madame I speke it / for the honour of yow
Moore than to save myn hertes lyf right now
I have do so / as ye comanded me
And if ye vouche sauf / ye may go se
Dooth as yow list / have youre biheste in mynde
Ffor quyk or deed / right ther ye shal me fynde
In yow lyth al / to do me lyve or deye
But wel I woot the rokkes been aweye
He taketh his leve / and she astoned stood
In al hir face nas a drope of blood
She wende nevere han come in swich a trappe
Allas quod she / þt evere this sholde happe
Ffor wende I nevere / by possibilitee
That swich a monstre or merveille myghte be
It is agayns the proces of nature
And hom she gooth a sorweful creature
Ffor verray feere / unnethe may she go
She wepeth wailleth / al a day or two
And swowneth / that it routhe was to se
But why it was / to no wight tolde she
Ffor out of towne was goon Arveragus
But to hir self she spak and seyde thus
With face pale / and with ful sorweful cheere
In hir compleinte / as ye shal after heere
Allas quod she / on thee ffortune I pleyne
That unwar wrapped hast me in thy cheyne
Ffor which tescape / woot I no socour
Save oonly / deeth or deshonour
Oon of thise two / bihoveth me to chese
But nathelees yet have I levere to lese

	ELLESMERE
[Repen]teth yow / for thilke god aboue	Repenteth
[E]r ye me sleen / by cause that I yow loue	Er *þat*
For madame / wel ye wootꝰ what ye han hightꝰ	hiħtꝰ
Nat *þat* I chalange / any thyng of rightꝰ	riħtꝰ
Of yow my souereyn lady / but youre *gra*ce	16 sou*er*eyn grace
But in a gardyn yond / at swich a place	
Ye woot right wel / what ye bihighten me	riħt bihiħten
And in myn hand / your trouthe plighten ye	handʼ / youre pliħten
To loue me bestꝰ god woot ye seyden so	seyde
Al be / *þat* I vnworthy am ther to	therto
Madame I speke it / for the hono*ur* of yow	
Moore than to saue / myn hertes lyf right now	riħt
I haue do so / as ye comaunded me	comanded
And if ye vouche sauf / ye may go se	see
Dooth as yow listꝰ haue youre biheste in mynde	your*e*
For quyk / or deed / right ther ye shal me fynde	quykꝰ ther*e*
In yow lyth al / to do me lyue or deye	lith
But wel I wootꝰ the Rokkes been aweye	
¶He taketh his leue / and she astoned stood	stoodʼ
In al hir face / nas a drope of blood	bloodʼ
She wende neu*er*e haue come / in swich a trappe	neu*er*e / han come
Allas quod she / *þat* eu*er*e this sholde happe	
For wende I neuere / by possibilitee	neu*er*e /
That swich a Monstre / or m*er*ueille myghte be	myħte bee
It is agayns / the proces of nature	is / agayns
And hom she gooth / a sorweful creature	hoom goth /
For verray feere / vnnethe may she go	*ver*ray
She wepeth / wayleth / al a day or two	wailleth /
And swowneth / that it routhe was to se	see
But why it was / to no wight tolde she	wiħt shee
For out of towne / was goon Arueragus	
But to hir self / she spak and seyde thus	spakꝰ
With face pale / and with ful sorweful cheere	*with* ful
In hir compleinte / as ye shal after heere	hir*e* compleyntꝰ
¶Allas quod she / on thee Fortune I pleyne	
That vnwar / wrapped hast me in thy cheyne	
For which tescape / woot I no socour	scour |
Saue oonly / deeth / or deshonour	deeth dishonour
Oon of thise two / bihoueth me to chese	
But nathelees / yet haue I leu*er*e to lese	

1355 The compleynt of Dorigene ayeyns Fortune El

16¶Frankeleyn *130r*

	ELLESMERE
My lyf / than of my body to haue a shame	lif / body haue
Or knowen my seluen fals / or lese my name	knowe
And with my deeth / I may be quyt ywis	deth / quyt
Hath ther nat many a noble wyf er this	
And many a mayde / yslayn hir self allas	
Rather / than with hir body doon trespas	Rather *with*
¶Yis certes / lo thise stories beren witnesse	ce*r*tes /
Whan . xxx . tirauntz / ful of cursednesse	
Hadde slayn Phidon / in Atthenes atte feste	Phidou*n* / at feste
They comaunded / his doghtren for tareste	comanded / hise doghtres
And bryngen hem / biforn hem in despit	despit
Al naked / to fulfille hir foul delit	delit
And in hir fadres blood / they made hem daunce	17 Hem
Vp on the pauement god yeue hem meschaunce	Vpon myschaunce
For which / thise woful maydens / ful of drede	which / maydens
Rather / than they wolde lese hir maydenhede	
They pryuely / been stirt in to a welle	p*ri*uely / stirt /
And dreynte hem seluen / as the bokes telle	bookes
¶They of Mecene / leete enquere and seke	They
Of Lacedomye / fifty maydens eke	lacedomye /
On whiche / they wolden doon hir lecherye	
But was ther noon / of al that compaignye	
That she nas slayn / and with a good entente	*with*
Chees rather for to dye / than assente	Chees / dye
To been opp*re*ssed / of hir maydenhede	
Why sholde I thanne / to dye been in drede	
¶Loo eek / the tiraunt Aristoclides	Lo
That loued a mayden / highte Stymphalides	heet
Whan *þ*at hir fader / slayn was on a nyght	that nyght
Vn to Dianes temple / gooth she right	goth right
And hente the ymage / in hir handes two	
Fro which ymage / wolde she neu*er*e go	
No wight ne myghte / hir handes of it arace	wight myghte
Til she was slayn / right in the selue place	right
Now sith *þ*at maydens / hadden swich despit	¶Now despit
To been defouled / with mannes foul delit	
Wel oghte a wyf / rather hir seluen sle	oghte slee
Than be defouled / as it thynketh me	
¶What shal I seyn / of hasdrubales wyf	What
That at Cartage / birafte hir self hir lyf	

[17]¶Frankeleyn *130v*

1369 30. a Atheniensium tiranni [cum Phidonem] necassent in conuiuio filia[s eius virgi]nes ad se venire iusserunt et s[cortorum mo]re nudari ac super pauimenta [patris] sanguine cruentatas inpudicis ge[stibus] ludere que paulisper dissimulato [dolo]re cum tumulentos conuiuas cernere[nt] quasi ad requisita nature egredientes inuicem se complexe precipitauer[unt] in puteum vt virginitatem morte seruare[nt]. Hg (defective) El (1364) Variants: tumulentos) timulentos El complexe) complexere El

1379 Cum .50. virgines lacedomoniorum Messeni violare temptassent El

1387 Aristoclides Orcomeni tirannus adamauit virginem stymphalidem que cum patre occiso ad templum diane et cetera El

1395 Singulas has historias et plur[es] hanc materiam concernentes reci[tat] beatus Ieronimus contra Iouinia[num] in primo suo libro capitulo .39. Hg El (1462)

1399 Nam hasdrubalis vxor capta et incensa vrbe cum se cerneret a Romanis

My lyf / than of my body to haue a shame
Or knowen my seluen fals / or lese my name
And with my deeth I may be quyt ywis
Hath ther nat many a noble wyf er this
And many a mayde / yslayn hir self allas
Rather / than with hir body doon trespas
¶ Yis certes / lo thise stories beren witnesse
Whan .xxx. tirauntz / ful of cursednesse
Hadde slayn Phidon / in Athenes atte feste
They comanded / his doghtren for tareste
And bryngen hem / biforn hem in despit
Al naked / to fulfille hir foul delit
And in hir fadres blood / they made hem daunce
Vp on the pauement / god yeue hem meschaunce
ffor which / thise woful maydens / ful of drede
Rather / than they wolde lese hir maydenhede
They pryuely been stirt / in to a welle
And dreynte hem seluen / as the bokes telle
¶ They of Messene / lete enquere and seke
Of Lacedomye fifty maydens eke
On whiche / they wolden doon hir lecherye
But was ther noon / of al that compaignye
That she nas slayn / and with a good entente
Chees rather for to dye / than assente
To been oppressed / of hir maydenhede
Why sholde I thanne / to dye been in drede
¶ Loo eek the tiraunt Aristoclides
That loued a mayden / highte Stymphalides
Whan þt hir fader / slayn was on a nyght
Vn to Dianes temple / gooth she right
And hente the ymage / in hir handes two
ffro which ymage / wolde she neuere go
No wight ne myghte / hir handes of it arace
Til she was slayn / right in the selue place
Now sith þt maydens / hadden swich despit
To been defouled / with mannes foul delit
Wel oghte a wyf / rather hir seluen sle
Than be defouled / as it thynketh me
¶ What shal I seyn / of Hasdrubales wyf
That at Cartage / birafte hir self hir lyf

¶ xxx^o. Atheniensium tyranni
ne cum essent in conuiuio filia
nes ad se venire iusserunt et sc
re nudari ac super pauimenta
sanguine cruentatas impudicis ge
ludere que paulisper dissimulato
re cum temulentos conuiuas cerner
quasi ad requisita nature egredien
tes inuicem se complexe precipitauer
in puteum ut virginitatem morte seruare

¶ Singulas has historias et plur
hanc materiam concernentes reci
beatus Jeronimus contra Jouinian
in primo suo libro capitulo 39.

Whan she saw, that Romayns wan the toun
She took hir children alle, and skipte adoun
In to the fyr, and chees rather to dye
Than any Romayn, dide hir vileynye
¶ Hath nat lucresse, yslayn hir self allas
At Rome, whan she oppressed was
Of Tarquyn, for hir thoughte it was a shame
To lyuen, whan she hadde lost hir name
¶ The .vij. maydens, of Milesie also
Han slayn hem self, for verray drede and wo
Rather than folk of Gawle, hem sholde oppresse
Mo than a thousand stories, as I gesse
Koude I now telle, as touchyng this matere
¶ Whan habradace was slayn, his wyf so deere
Hir seluen slow, and leet hir blood to glyde
In habradaces woundes, depe and wyde
And seyde my body, at the leeste way
Ther shal no wight, defoulen if I may
¶ What sholde I mo ensamples, her of sayn
Sith that so manye, han hem seluen slayn
Wel rather, than they wolde defouled be
I wol conclude, that it is bet for me
To sleen my self than ben defouled thus
I wol be trewe, vn to Arueragus
Or rather sle my self in som manere
As dide demociennis doghter deere
By cause, þt she wolde nat defouled be
¶ O Cedasus, it is ful greet pitee
To reden, how thy doghtren deyde allas
That slowe hem self, for swich manere cas
¶ As greet a pitee was it, or wel moore
The Theban mayden, that for Nychanore
Hir seluen slow, right for swich manere wo
¶ Another Theban mayden, dide right so
For oon of Macedonye, hadde hir oppressed
She wt hir owene deeth, hir maydenhed redressed
¶ What shal I seyn, of Nyceratis wyf
That for swich cas, birafte hir self hir lyf
¶ How trewe eek was to Alcebiades
His loue, that rather for to dyen chees

	ELLESMERE
[For] whan she saw / that Romayns wan the town	For saugh / toun
[S]he took hir children alle / and skipte adown	She adoun
In to the fyr / and chees rather to dye	
Than any Romayn / dide hir*e* vileynye	
¶Hath nat Lucresse / yslayn hir self allas	Hath lucresse /
At Rome / whan she opp*re*ssed was	
Of Tarquyn / for hir thoughte it was a shame	hir*e*
To lyuen / whan she hadde lost hir name	had
¶The . vij . maydens / of Milesie also	The seuene Melesie
Han slayn hem self for verray drede and wo	self / for drede
Rather than folk / of Gawle / hem sholde opp*re*sse	folk
Mo than a thousand stories / as I gesse	
Koude I now telle / as touchyng this matere	touchynge mateere
¶Whan habradace was slayn / his wyf so deer*e*	Whan habradate
Hir seluen slow / and leet hir blood to glyde	
In habradaces woundes / depe and wyde	habradates woundes
And seyde / my body / at the leeste way	seyde
Ther shal no wight defoulen if I may	wight /
¶What sholde I mo ensamples / her of sayn	I / ensamples heer
Sith that so manye / han hem seluen slayn	
Wel rather / than they wolde defouled be	18
I wol conclude / that it is bet for me	
To sleen my self than ben defouled thus	self / been
I wol be trewe / vn to Arueragus	
Or rather sle my self in som manere	rather / sleen self
As dide / Democienis doghter deere	As Demociones doghter
By cause / *þ*at she wolde nat defouled be	
¶O Cedasus / it is ful gret pitee	O greet
To reden / how thy doghtren deyde allas	
That slowe hem self for swich maner cas	self / manere
¶As greet a pitee was it or wel moore	As it /
The Theban mayden / that for Nychanore	Nichanore
Hir seluen slow / right for swich manere wo	right
¶Another Theban mayden / dide right so	Another right
For oon of Macedonye / hadde hir*e* opp*re*ssed	Macidonye /
She w*ith* hir owene deeth / hir maydenhed redressed	with hir*e* deeth / maydenhede
¶What shal I seyn / of Nyceratis wyf	What seye Nicerates
That for swich cas / birafte hir self hir lyf	lyf /
¶How trewe eek / was to Alcebiades	How eek was /
His loue / that rather for to dyen chees	loue / rather

1405 primo ponam lucreciam que violate pudicie nolens superuiuere maculam corporis cruore deleuit El

1409 Quis valet silencio preterire vij. Milesias virgines que Gallorum et cetera El

1414 Senapho in Ciri maioris scribit infancia occiso habradate et cetera El

1426 Democionis Ariopagitarum principis virgo filia et cetera El

1428 Quo ore laudande sunt Cedasij filie et cetera El

1432 Nichanor victis Thebis vnius captiue virginis amore superatus est El

1434 Narrant scriptores Grecie et aliam Thebanam virginem et cetera El

1437 Quid loquar Nicerati coniugem pie impaciens iniurie viri mortem et cetera El

1439 Alcebiades ille socraticus victus et cetera El

18 ¶Frankeleyn *131r*

	ELLESMERE
Than for to suffre / his body vnburyed be	
¶Lo which a wyf / was Alceste quod she	Lo
¶What Omer / of goode Penolopee	What seith Omer / Penalopee
Al Grece / knoweth of hir chastitee	hir*e*
¶P*ar*dee of Laodomya / is writen thus	Pardee / Lacedomya /
That whan at Troye / was slayn Prothesel*aus*	Troie /
No lenger wolde she lyue / after his day	lenger /
¶The same / of noble Porcia telle I may	The
With oute Brutus / koude she nat lyue	
To whom she hadde / al hool hir herte yeue	
¶The p*ar*fit wifhod / of Arthemesye	The wyfhod Arthemesie
Honoured is / thurgh al the Barbarye	Honured thurgh Barbarie
¶O Teuta queene / thy wifly chastitee	O wyfly
To alle wyues / may a Mirour bee[19]	
¶Thus pleyned Dorigene / a day or tweye	pleyne
Purposynge euere / þat she wolde deye	eu*er*e / that
¶But nathelees / vp on the thridde nyght	vpon nyght
Hom cam Arueragus / this worthy knyght	Hoom knyght
And asked hire / why þat she weep*e* so soore	hir*e* / that
And she gan wepen / eu*er* lenger the moore	eu*er*lenger
¶Allas quod she / þat eu*er*e was I born	that I was
Thus haue I seyd quod she / thus haue I sworn	
And tolde hym al / as ye han herd bifore	toold
It nedeth nat reherce it yow namoore	
¶This housbond w*ith* glad cheere / in frendly wise	housbonde / with chiere freendly wyse
Answerde and seyde / as I shal yow deuyse	
¶Is ther oght ellis Dorigen / but this	20 Is oght elles this
¶Nay nay quod she / god help me so as wys	help*e*
This is to muche / and it were goddes wille	
¶Ye wyf quod he / lat slepen that is stille	
It may be wel p*ar* auenture / yet to day	wel / p*ar*auenture
Ye shul youre trouthe holden / by my fay	your*e* trouthe / holden
For god so wisly / haue mercy vp on me	m*er*cy
I hadde wel leuere / ystiked for to be	
For verray loue / which þat I to yow haue	v*er*ray that
But if ye sholde / youre trouthe kepe and saue	your*e* *and*
Trouthe is the hyeste thyng þat man may kepe	Trouthe /
But w*ith* that word / he brast anon to wepe	
And seyde I yow forbede / vp peyne of deeth	seyde / peyne deeth
That neuere whil thee lasteth / lyf ne breeth	neu*er*e / breeth

1442 Alcesten fabule ferunt pro marito Adameto sponte defunctam et Penolopes pudicia Omeri carmen est El

1445 Lacedomia quoque poetarum ore cantatur occiso apud Troiam Protheselao et cetera El

1448 Porcia sine Bruto viuere non potuit El

1451 Arthemesia quoque vxor Mauseoli insignis pudicicjs fuisse perhibetur et cetera El

1453 Teuta Illiricorum Regina et cetera El

1455 Memorandum Strato regulus El

1456 Vidi et omnes pene Barbares capitulo xxvj° primi El

1458 Item Cornelia et cetera El

[19] *Out* Hg 1455-56. The lines occur only in Ad[3] and El; El reads:

The same thyng I seye of Bilyea
Of Rodogone / and eek Valeria

[20] ¶Frankeleyn *131v*

Than for to suffre his body vnburyed be
Lo which a wyf / was Alceste quod she
What Omer / of goode Penolopee
Al Grece knoweth of hir chastitee
Pardee of Laodomya / is writen thus
That whan at Troye / was slayn Protheselau
No lenger wolde she lyue / after his day
The same / of noble Porcia telle I may
With oute Brutus / koude she nat lyue
To whom she hadde / al hool hir herte yeue
The ꝑfit wyfhod / of Arthemesye
Honoured is / thurgh al the Barbarye
O Teuta queene / thy wifly chastitee
To alle wyues / may a myrour bee
Thus pleyned Dorigene / a day or tweye
Purposynge euere / þt she wolde deye.
But nathelees / vp on the thridde nyght /
Hom cam Arueragus / this worthy knyght
And asked hire / why þt she weep so soore
And she gan wepen / eu lenger the moore
Allas quod she / þt eue was I born
Thus haue I seyd quod she / thus haue I sworn
And tolde hym al / as ye han herd bifore
It nedeth nat / reherce it yow namoore
This housbond wt glad cheere / in frendly wise
Answerde and seyde / as I shal yow deuyse
Is ther oght ellis Dorigen / but this
Nay nay quod she / god help me so as wys
This is to muche / and it were goddes wille
Ye wyf quod he / lat slepen that is stille
It may be wel ꝑauenture / yet to day
Ye shul youre trouthe holden / by my fay
ffor god so wisly / haue mercy vp on me
I hadde wel leuere / ystiked for to be
ffor verray loue / which þt I to yow haue
But if ye sholde / youre trouthe kepe and saue
Trouthe is the hyeste thyng / þt man may kepe
But wt that word / he brast anon to wepe
And seyde I yow forbede / vp peyne of deeth
That neuere whil thee lasteth / lyf ne breeth

... wight tel thow of this auentyre
... I may best I wol my wo endure
Ne make no contenance of heuynesse
That folk of yow may demen harm or gesse
¶ And forth he clepyd a Squyer and a mayde
Goth forth anon with Dorigen he sayde
And bryngeth hir to swich a place anon
They toke hir leue and on hir wey they gon
But they ne wiste why they thider wente
He nolde no wight tellen his entente
¶ This Squyer which yt highte Aurelius
On Dorigen yt was so amorus
Of auenture happed hir to meete
Amydde the town right in the quykkest strete
As she was bown to goon the wey forth right
Toward the gardyn ther as she had hight
And he was to the gardynward also
ffor wel he spyed whan she wolde go
Out of hir hous to any maner place
But thus they meete of auenture or grace
And he salueth hir with glad entente
And asked of hir whiderward she wente
¶ And she answerde half as she were mad
Vn to the gardyn as myn housbond bad
My trouthe for to holde allas allas
¶ Aurelius gan wondren on this cas
And in his herte hadde greet compassion
Of hir and of hir lamentacion
And of Arueragus the worthy knyght
That bad hir holden al that she had hight
So looth hym was his wyf sholde breke hir trouthe
And in his herte he caughte of this greet routhe
Considerynge the beste on euery syde
That fro his lust yet were hym leuer abyde
Than doon so heigh a cherlyssh wrecchednesse
Agayns franchise and alle gentillesse
ffor which in fewe wordes seyde he thus
¶ Madame seyeth to youre lord Arueragus
That sith I se his grete gentillesse
To yow and eek I se wel youre distresse

	ELLESMERE
[To no] wight tel thow / of this auenture	To no wight telle thou
[As] I may best / I wol my wo endure	As best
Ne make / no contenance of heuynesse	
That folk of yow / may demen harm or gesse	folk /
¶And forth he clepyd / a Squyer and a mayde	forth / cleped / Squier
Goth forth anon with Dorigen / he sayde	Gooth anon / Dorigen
And bryngeth hir*e* / to swich a place anon	
They toke hir leue / and on hir wey they gon	take
But they ne wiste / why they thider wente	why she thider
1492 He nolde to no wight tellen his entente[21]	nolde / no wight
1499 ¶This Squyer / which þ*at* highte Aurelius	This squier /
On Dorigen / þ*at* was so amorus	that
Of auenture / happed hir to meete	hir*e*
Amydde the town / right in the quykkest strete	toun / right
As she was boun / to goon the wey forth right	bown / right
Toward the gardyn / ther as she had hight	hight
And he was / to the gardynward also	
For wel he spyed / whan she wolde go	
Out of hir hous / to any maner place	
But thus they meete / of auenture or gr*a*ce	mette / grace
And he salueth hir*e* / with glad entente	saleweth
And asked of hir*e* / whiderward she wente	
¶And she answerde / half as she were mad	mad
Vn to the gardyn / as myn housbond bad	housbonde bad
My trouthe for to holde / allas / allas	
¶Aurelius / gan wondren on this cas	
And in his herte / hadde greet co*m*passiou*n*	
Of hir*e* / and of hir lamentaciou*n*	hir*e* lamentaciou*n*
And of Arueragus / the worthy knyght	22 ¶And Arueragus knyght
That bad hir holden / al that she had hight	hir*e* þ*at* hight
So looth hym was / his wyf sholde breke hir trouthe	
And in his herte / he caughte of this greet routhe	
Considerynge the beste / on euery syde	Considerynge / beste eu*e*ry
That fro his lust yet were hym leu*er*e abyde	
Than doon so heigh / a cherlyssh wrecchednesse	doon / heigh cherlyssh
Agayns franchise / and alle gentillesse	
For which in fewe wordes / seyde he thus	which / wordes
¶Madame / seyeth to youre lord Arueragus	your*e*
That sith I se / his grete gentillesse	se
To yow / and eek I se wel youre distresse	your*e*

1459 Imitentur ergo nupte Theanam Cleobiliam Gorgim Thymodiam Claudias atque Cornelias in fine libri primi El

1462 See Hg 1395.

[21] *Out* Hg 1493-98. These lines occur only in Ad[3] and El; El reads:

¶P*ar*auenture / an heep*e* of yow ywis
Wol holden hym / a lewed man in this
That he wol putte / his wyf in Iup*ar*tie
Herkneth the tale / er ye vp on hir*e* crie
She may haue bettre Fortune / than yow semeth
And whan þ*at* ye han herd the tale / demeth

[22] ¶Frankeleyn *132r*

That hym were leu*ere* han shame / and that were routhe
Than ye to me / sholde breke thus your trouthe
I haue wel leu*ere* / euere to suffre wo
Than I departe the loue / bitwix yow two
I yow relesse madame / in to youre hond
Quyt euery serement and euery bond
That ye han maad to me / as her biforn
Sith thilke tyme / which *þ*at ye were born
My trouthe I plighte / I shal you neu*er* repreue
Of no biheeste / and here I take my leue
As of the treweste / and the beste wyf
That euere yet I knew / in al my lyf
But euery wyf / be war of hir biheste
On Dorigene / remembreth at the leste
Thus kan a Squyer / doon a gentil dede
As wel as kan a knyght with outen drede
¶She thonketh hym / vp on hir knees al bare
And hom vn to hir housbond / is she fare
And tolde hym al / as ye han herd me sayd
And be ye siker / he was so wel apayd
That it were inpossible / me to write
What sholde I lenger / of this cas endite
¶Arueragus / and Dorigene his wyf
In souereyn blisse / leden forth hir lyf
Neu*ere* eft ne was ther angre hem bitwene
He cherisseth hir*e* / as thogh she were a queene
And she was to hym trewe / for euere moore
Of thise two folk / ye gete of me namoore
¶Aurelius / that his cost hath al forlorn
Curseth the tyme / that euere he was born
Allas quod he / allas that I bihighte
Of pured gold / a thousand pound of wighte
Vn to this Philosophre / how shal I do
I se namoore / but that I am for do
Myn heritage / moot I nedes selle
And been a beggere / here may I nat dwelle
And shamen al my kynrede / in this place
But I of hym / may gete bettre grace
But nathelees / I wol of hym assaye
At c*er*teyn dayes / yeer by yeer to paye

hi*m* *þ*at
youre
leuere /
departe / loue
your*e* hond
Quyt eu*er*y s*er*ement bond
heer

plighte / yow
biheste / heere
wyf /
eu*er*e yet knew lyf /
eu*er*y hir*e* biheeste
remembreth / atte leeste
Squier /
knyght

hoom / housbonde
sayd
weel apayd
wryte
endyte

Angre
though
hym / trewe eu*er*emoore
thise folk /
Aurelius /
*þ*at eu*er*e
bihighte
wighte

fordo

beggere / heere
23 shamen / kynrede

wole

[23] ¶Frankeleyn *132v*

The ffrankeleyn

That hym were leue han shame / and that were routhe
Than ye to me sholde breke thus youre trouthe
I haue wel leue / euere to suffre wo
Than I departe the loue / bitwix yow two
I yow relesse madame / in to youre hond
Quyt euery serement / and euery bond
That ye han maad to me / as heer biforn
Sith thilke tyme / which þt ye were born
My trouthe I plighte / I shal yow neuere repreue
Of no biheeste / and heere I take my leue
As of the treweste / and the beste wyf
That euere yet I knew / in al my lyf
But euery wyf / be war of hir biheeste
On Dorigene / remembreth at the leeste
Thus kan a Squyer / doon a gentil dede
As wel as kan a knyght / withouten drede
She thonketh hym / vp on hir knees al bare
And hom vn to hir housbond / is she fare
And tolde hym al / as ye han herd me sayd
And be ye siker / he was so wel apayd
That it were inpossible / me to write
What sholde I lenger / of this cas endite
Arueragus / and Dorigene his wyf
In souereyn blisse / leden forth hir lyf
Neuere eft ne was ther angre hem bitwene
He cherisseth hir / as thogh she were a queene
And she was to hym trewe / for euere moore
Of thise two folk / ye gete of me namoore
Aurelius / that his cost / hath al forlorn
Curseth the tyme / that euere he was born
Allas quod he allas that I bihighte
Of pured gold / a thousand pound of wighte
Vn to this Philosophre / how shal I do
I se namoore / but that I am fordo
Myn heritage / moot I nedes selle
And been a beggere / heere may I nat dwelle
And shamen al my kynrede / in this place
But I of hym / may gete bettre grace
But nathelees / I wol of hym assaye
At certeyn dayes / yeer by yeer / to paye

... thonke hym of his grete curteisye
...y trouthe wol I kepe I wol nat lye
¶ With herte soor he gooth vn to his cofre
And broghte gold vn to this Philosophre
The value of fyue hundred pound I gesse
And hym bisecheth of his gentillesse
To graunten hym dayes of the remenant
And seyde maister I dar wel make auant
I fayled neuere of my trouthe as yit
ffor sikerly my dette shal be quyt
Towardes yow how euere þt I fare
To goon abegged in my kirtel bare
But wolde ye vouche sauf vp on seuretee
Two yeer or thre for to respiten me
Thanne were I wel for ellis moot I selle
Myn heritage ther is namoore to telle
¶ This Philosophre sobrely answerde
And seyde thus whan he thise wordes herde
Haue I nat holden couenant vn to thee
¶ Yis certes wel and trewely quod he
¶ Hastow nat had thy lady as thee liketh
¶ No no quod he and sorwefully he siketh
¶ What was the cause tel me if thow kan
¶ Aurelius his tale anon bigan
And tolde hym al as ye han herd biforе
It nedeth nat to yow reherce it moore
¶ He seyde Arueragus of gentillesse
Hadde leuere dye in sorwe and in distresse
Than þt his wyf were of hir trouthe fals
The sorwe of Dorigen he tolde hym als
How looth hir was to ben a wikked wyf
And þt she leuere had lost that day hir lyf
And þt hir trouthe she swoor thurgh Innocence
She neuere erst hadde herd speke of apparence
That made me han of hire so greet pitee
And right as frely as he sente hir me
As frely sente I hire to hym agayn
This al and som ther is namoore to sayn
¶ This Philosophre answerde leeue brother
Euerich of yow dide gentilly til oother

	ELLESMERE
[And] thonke hym / of his grete curteisye	And thanke
[M]y trouthe wol I kepe / I nel nat lye	My I wol nat lye
¶With herte soor / he gooth vn to his cofre	
And broghte gold / vn to this Philosophre	broghte
The value / of fyue hundred pound I gesse	
And hym bisecheth / of his gentillesse	bisecheth
To graunten hym dayes / of the remenant	graunte dayes remenau*nt*
And seyde Maister / I dar wel make auant	maister / auau*nt*
I fayled neuere / of my trouthe as yit	failled neu*er*e /
For sikerly / my dette shal be quyt	
Towardes yow / how euere *þat* I fare	eu*er*e that
To goon abegged / in my kirtel bare	a begged /
But wolde ye vouche sauf vp on seuretee	sauf /
Two yeer or thre / for to respiten me	
Thanne were I wel / for ellis moot I selle	elles
Myn heritage / ther is namoore to telle	
¶This Philosophre / sobrely answerde	THis
And seyde thus / whan he thise wordes herde	
Haue I nat holden couenant vn to thee	thee./
¶Yis c*er*tes / wel and trewely quod he	¶Yes certes /
¶Hastow nat had / thy lady as thee liketh	lady / liketh./
¶No no quod he / and sorwefully he siketh	
¶What was the cause / tel me if thow kan	thou kan./
¶Aurelius / his tale anon bigan	
And tolde hym al / as ye han herd bifore	as he han bifoore
It nedeth nat to yow reherce it moore	
¶He seyde / Arueragus / of gentillesse	seide / Arueragus
Hadde leu*er*e dye / in sorwe and in distresse	sorwe /
Than *þat* his wyf were of hir trouthe fals	wyf /
The sorwe of Dorigen / he tolde hym als	
How looth hir was / to ben a wikked wyf	hir*e* been wyf /
And *þat* she leu*er*e had lost that day hir lyf	
And *þat* hir trouthe / she swoor thurgh Innocence	thurgh
She neu*er*e erst hadde herd speke of apparence	Apparence
That made me han of hir*e* / so greet pitee	hir*e*
And right as frely / as he sente hir me	right hir*e*
As frely sente I hire / to hym agayn	frely / hir*e* ageyn
This al and som / ther is namoore to sayn	seyn
¶This Philosophre answerde / leeue brother	
Euerich of yow / dide gentilly til oother	

Thow art a Squyer / and he is a knyght
But god forbede / for his blisful myght
But if a clerk koude doon a gentil dede
As wel as any of yow / it is no drede
¶Sire I relesse thee / thy thowsand pound
As thow right now / were cropen out of the ground
Ne neuere er now / ne haddest knowen me
For sire / I wol nat take a peny of thee
For al my craft ne noght for my t*ra*uaille
Thow hast ypayed wel / for my vitaille
It is ynogh / and fare wel haue good day
And took his hors / and forth he goth his way
¶Lordynges / this questiou*n* / than wol I aske now
Which was the mooste free / as thynketh yow
Now telleth me / er that ye ferther wende
I kan namoore / my tale is at an ende

¶Here endeth the Frankeleyns tale

ELLESMERE

Thou Squier / knyght
myght
clerk /

24 ¶Sire / releesse thousand pound
thou right ground
neu*er*e
taken
noght trauaille
Thou hast
ynogh / farewel

Lordynges / questiou*n* thanne wolde I
fre

¶Heere is ended the Frankeleyns tale

24 ¶Frankeleyn *133r*

Richard Banestar was borne the xxj daye of ceptember beynge
⟨venus⟩
Saynt mathews daye vpon a fryday betwext x and xj of the
cloke before noone in ⟨the⟩ xiij ⟨yere⟩ of quene Elezabeth. 1571.
⟨having one tothe at his byrth⟩

Elenor banestar was borne the xix daye of novembar beynge the
⟨Jubter(?)⟩
xvi yere of quene Elezabeth vpon a thorsday at fowr of the cloke
aftar noone 1573 [oct matyn martyn] Elyzabeth mat[er?]*

Frauncis Banestar was borne the xixth daye of aprell beynge
⟨mars⟩
twesdaye between j and ij of the clok before daye the [ij]
yere of the rayn of quene Elyzabeth 1575

Ellyzabeth Bannester was borne the xxviijth of August being
Thursday betwyxt twelue & one of the clock at mydnight th[e]
Eightyne yeare of the Quenes raygne. 1576

Anno domini 1576

martha Banester was borne the xijth
January between iiij and v of th[e clock]
⟨soulle⟩†
a sunday in the mornyng in [the]
xx year of qene Elyzabeth
⟨And her doug(hter?)⟩

**xix* was originally written as the day, then erased and *xvii* written over, only to be erased and *xix* written again in yellower ink, which was also used to cancel *oct matyn martyn* (November 18 being the Octave of Saint Martin) and to add *Elyzabeth mat*[*er?*].

†I.e., *sol.*

Thow art a Squyer and he is a knyght
But god forbede for his blisful myght
But if a clerk koude don a gentil dede
As wel as any of yow it is no drede
Sire I relesse thee thy thowsand pound
As thow right now were cropen out of the ground
Ne neuere er now ne haddest knowen me
ffor sire I wol nat take a peny of thee
ffor al my craft ne noght for my trauaille
Thow hast ypayed wel for my vitaille
It is ynogh and farewel haue good day
And took his hors and forth he goth his way
Lordynges this question than wol I aske now
Which was the mooste free as thynketh yow
Now telleth me er that ye ferther wende
I kan namoore my tale is at an ende

Here endeth the ffrankeleyns tale

martha Banester was borne the xij th of
January between iiij and v of
a sunday in the mornyng
xx year of quene Elyzabeth

Richard Banestar was borne the xxj daye of ceptember beynge
saynt mathews daye vpon a fryday betweyt x and xj of the
cloke before noone in the xiij yere of quene Elezabeth ·1571· havinge one tothe
at his byrth

Elenor banestar was borne the xix daye of novembar beynge the
xvj yere of quene Elezabeth vpon a thorsday at fowr of the cloke
aftar noone 1573 Elyzabeth mat

francis Banestar was borne the xix th daye of aprell beynge
wednesday betweene j and ij of the clok before daye the
yere of the rayne of quene Elyzabeth 1575

Ellyzabeth Bannester was borne the xxviij th of August beinge
Thursday betwyxt twelue & one of the clocke at mydnight
Eighteene yeere of the Quenes raygne 1576
Ano dni 1576

The Nonne

The ministre and the norice vn to vices
Which that men clepeth in englissh ydelnesse
That porter at the gate is of delices
To eschuen and by hir contrarie hir oppresse
That is to seyn by leueful bisynesse
Wel oghte we to doon al oure entente
Lest that the feend thurgh ydelnesse vs hente

For he that with his thousand cordes slye
Continuelly vs wayteth to biclappe
Whan he may man in ydelnesse espye
He kan so lightly cacche hym in his trappe
Til that a man be hent right by the lappe
He nys nat war the feend hath hym in honde
Wel oghte vs werche and ydelnesse withstonde

And thogh men dradden neuere for to dye
Yet seen men wel by resoun doutelees
That ydelnesse is roten slogardye
Of which ther neuere comth no good nencrees
And seen that slouthe hir holdeth in a lees
Oonly for to slepe and ete and drynken
And to deuouren al that othere swynken

And for to putte vs from swich ydelnesse
That cause is of so greet confusion
I haue heer doon my feithful bisynesse
After the legende in translacion
Right of thy glorious lyf and passion
Thow with thy gerland wroght of rose and lilie
Thee meene I mayde and martir Seinte Cecilie

Invocacio ad Mariam
And thow that flour of virgines art alle
Of whom that Bernard list so wel to write
To thee at my bigynnyng first I calle
Thow confort of vs wrecches do me endite
Thy maydens deeth that wan thurgh hir merite
The eternal lyf and of the feend victorie
As man may after reden in hir storie

The Nonne.

The Ministre / and the norice vn to vices
Which that men clepeth in englissh ydelnesse
That porter at the gate is / of delices
To eschuen / and by hir cont*ra*rie hir*e* opp*re*sse
That is to seyn / by leueful bisynesse
Wel oghte we / to doon al oure entente
Lest that the feend / thurgh ydelnesse vs hente

¶For he / that with his thousand cordes slye
Continuelly / vs wayteth to biclappe
Whan he may man / in ydelnesse espye
He kan so lightly / cacche hym in his trappe
Til that a man / be hent right by the lappe
He nys nat war / the feend hath hym in honde
Wel oghte vs werche / and ydelnesse withstonde

¶And thogh men dradden / neu*er*e for to dye
Yet seen men wel / by reson doutelees
That ydelnesse / is roten slogardye
Of which ther neu*er*e comth / no good nencrees
And seen that slouthe / hir holdeth in a lees
Oonly for to slepe / and ete and drynken
And to deuouren / al that othere swynken

¶And for to pu[tte] vs / from swich ydelnesse
That cause is / of so greet confusiou*n*
I haue here doon / my feithful bisynesse
After the legende / in translaciou*n*
Rightꝫ of thy glorious lyf / and passiou*n*
Thow with thy gerland / wroght of rose *and* lilie
Thee mene I / mayde and martir Seinte Cecilie

And thow / that flour of virgines art alle
Of whom that Bernard / list so wel to write
To thee / at my bigynnyngꝫ I first calle
Thow confort of vs wrecches / do mendite
Thy maydens deeth / that wan thurgh hir merite
The eternal lyf / and of the feend victorie
As man may after / reden in hir Storie

29 [In]uocacio ad mariam Hg (defective) El

1 ¶The prologe of the Seconde Nonnes tale
Ministre Norice /
clepe Englissħ
Porter of the
eschue / hir*e* contrarie /

oghten
feendꝫ thurgħ vs shente |

For thatꝫ hise /
waiteth

p*at* hentꝫ righ̄t

oghte

And though
resoun*n*

seen / p*at* slouthe / it holdeth
Oonly to and for to ete drynke
swynke

And putte fro

heer

Right lif
Thou *with* gerlandꝫ wroght *with* rose
meene and mooder Cecilie

2 ANd
Bernardꝫ
first I
Thou do me endite
thurgħ hir*e* m*er*ite
ete*r*neel
hir*e*

[1] ¶Seconde on *185v*
[2] ¶Nonne *186r*

166r

./The [Nonne] ELLESMERE

¶Thow mayde and moder / doghter of thy sone	Thow	mooder / doghter
Thow welle of m*er*cy / synful soules cure		
In whom / that god / for bou*n*tee chees to wone	god	bou*n*tee /
Thow humble and heigh / ouer euery creature	heigh̄ / oue*r*	
Thow nobledest' so ferforth oure nature	ferforth /	
That no desdaign / the makere hadde of kynde	desdeyn /	
His sone / in blood *and* flessh̄ / to clothe *and* wynde	and	and
¶With Inne the Cloistre blisful / of thy sydis	With	blisful
Took mannes shap*e* / the eternal loue and pees	eterneel	
That of the tryne compas / lord and gyde is		
Whom erthe and see / and heuene out of relees		
Ay heryen / and thow virgyne wemmelees	thou virgine	
Bar of thy body / and dweltest mayde pure	Baar	mayden
The creatour / of euery creature		
¶Assembled is in thee Magnificence	Assembled	thee / magnificence
With mercy / goodnesse / and swich pitee	m*er*cy /	and w*ith* swich
That thow that art' the sonne of excellence	That' thou /	art
Nat oonly / helpest hem *þat* prayen thee	that preyen	
But ofte tyme / of thy benygnytee	often	
Ful frely / er that men / thyn help*e* biseche	help	
Thow goost biforn / and art hir lyues leche	Thou	
¶Now help thow meke / and blisful faire mayde	Now	meeke /
Me flemed wrecche / in this desert of galle		
Thynk on the womman Cananee / that sayde	Thynk'	wo*m*man
That whelpes eten / so*m*me of the crommes alle	cro*m*mes	
That from hir lordes table / been yfalle	That'	
And thogh that I / vnworthy sone of Eue	though̄	
Be synful / yet accepte my bileue		
¶And for that feith is deed / with outen werkis	And	
So for to werken / yif me wit and space		
That I be quyt' from thennes / that moost derk is	quit' fro	*þat* moost
O thow / that art so fair / and ful of grace	thou /	
Be myn Aduocate / in that heighe place	Aduocat'	heigh̄e
Ther as with outen ende / is songe Osanne	Theras	
Thow cristes moder / doghter deere of Anne	Cristes mooder'	

Thow mayde and moder doghter of thy sone
Thow welle of mercy synful soules cure
In whom that god for bountee chees to wone
Thow humble and heigh ouer euery creature
Thow nobledest so ferforth oure nature
That no desdeyn the makere hadde of kynde
His sone in blood & flessh to clothe & wynde

Withinne the cloistre blisful of thy sydis
Took mannes shap the eternal loue and pees
That of the tryne compas lord and gyde is
Whom erthe and see and heuene out of relees
Ay heryen and thow virgyne wemmelees
Bar of thy body and dweltest mayde pure
The creatour of euery creature

Assembled is in thee magnificence
With mercy goodnesse and with swich pitee
That thow that art the sonne of excellence
Nat oonly helpest hem þt preyen thee
But ofte tyme of thy benygnytee
fful frely er that men thyn help biseche
Thow goost biforn and art hir lyues leche

Now help thow meke and blisful faire mayde
Me flemed wrecche in this desert of galle
Thynk on the womman Cananee that sayde
That whelpes eten somme of the crommes alle
That from hir lordes table been yfalle
And thogh that I vnworthy sone of Eue
Be synful yet accepte my bileue

And for that feith is deed with outen werkis
So for to werken yif me wit and space
That I be quyt from thennes that moost derk is
O thow that art so fair and ful of grace
Be myn aduocate in that heighe place
Ther as with outen ende is songe Osanne
Thow cristes moder doghter deere of Anne

[..]d of thy light my soule in prison lighte
That troubled is by the contagion
Of my body and also by the wighte
Of erthely lust and fals affection
O hauene o refut o saluacion
Of hem that been in sorwe and in distresse
Now help for to my werk I wol me dresse

Yet praye ich yow þt reden that I write
Forgeue me that I do no diligence
This ilke storie subtilly to endite
For bothe haue I the wordes and sentence
Of hym that at the seintes reuerence
The storie wroot and folwen hir legende
And pray yow that ye wol my werk amende

Interpretacio nominis Cecilie
quam ponit frater Jacobus
Januensis in legenda
aurea

First wolde I yow the name of seinte Cecilie
Expowne as men may in hir storie se
It is to seyn in englissh heuenes lilie
For pure chastnesse of virginitee
Or for she whitnesse hadde of honestee
And grene of conscience and of good fame
The swote sauour lilie was hir name

Or Cecile is to seyn the wey to blynde
For she ensample was by good techynge
Or ellis Cecile as I writen fynde
Is ioyned by a manere conioignynge
Of heuene and Lia and here in figurynge
The heuene is set for thoght of holynesse
And Lia for hir lastynge bisynesse

Cecile may eek be seyd in this manere
Wantynge of blyndnesse for hir grete light
Of sapience and for hir thewes clere
Or ellis lo this maydenes name bright
Of heuene and leos comth for which by right
Men myghte hire wel the heuene of peple calle
Ensample of goode and wise werkes alle

	ELLESMERE
[¶An]d of thy light my soule in p*ri*son lighte	3 And ligħt prison ligħte
[T]hat troubled is by the contagiou*n*	That is /
Of my body / and also by the wighte	wigħte
Of erthely lust and fals affecciou*n*	
O · hauene / o · refut o · sauaciou*n*	O hauene of refut o saluaciou*n*
Of hem / that been in sorwe and in distresse	þ*a*t sorwe / *and*
Now help / for to my werk I wol me dresse	help*e* /
¶Yet praye ich yow / þ*a*t reden that I write	Yet preye I
Foryeue me / that I do no diligence	
This ilke storie / subtilly tendite	to endite
For bothe haue I / the wordes and sentence	
Of hym / that at the Seintes reu*er*ence	seintes
The storie wroot and folwen hir legende	hir*e*
And pray yow / that ye wol my werk amende	I pray wole werk
First wolde I yow / the name of Seinte Cecilie	I / the Cecile
Expowne / as men may in hir storie se	see
It is to seyn on englissh / heuenes lilie	seye in englissħ /
For pure chastnesse / of virginitee	chaastnesse
Or for she whitnesse hadde of honestee	Or /
And grene of conscience / and of good fame	Conscience /
The swote sauour lilie / was hir name	soote
¶Or Cecile is to seyn / the wey to blynde	Or Cecilie seye /
For she ensample was / by good techynge	
Or ellis Cecile / as I writen fynde	elles
Is ioyned / by a manere conioignynge	conioynynge
Of heuene / and lia / and here in figurynge	heuene heere
The heuene is set for thoght of holynesse	thogħt hoolynesse
And lia / for hir lastynge bisynesse	Lia / hir*e*
¶Cecile may eek be seyd in this manere	Cecile / seyd /
Wantynge of blyndnesse / for hir grete light	ligħt
Of sapience / and for hir thewes clere	hir*e* cleere
Or ellis lo / this maydenes name bright	elles loo / maydens brigħt
Of heuene and leos comth / for which by right	rigħt /
Men myghte hir*e* wel / the heuene of peple calle	mygħte
Ensample of goode / and wise werkes alle	Ensample /

85 Interpretacio nominis Cecilie quam ponit frater Iacobus Ianuensis in legenda aurea Hg El
Variant: aurea) *om.* El

[3] ¶Seconde *186v*

¶For leos / peple in englissħ is to seye
And right as men may / in the heuene see
The sonne and moone / and sterres euery weye
Right so men goostly / in this mayden free
Sayen / of feith / the magnanymytee
And eek the cleernesse hool of sapience
And sondry werkes / brighte of excellence

¶And right so / as thise Philosophres write
That heuene is swift and round / *and* eek brennynge
Right so / was faire Cecile the white
Ful swift and bisy / eu*er*e in good werkynge
And round *and* hool / in good p*er*seuerynge
And brennyng⁊ eu*er*e in charite / ful brighte
Now haue I yow declared / what she highte

This mayde bright Cecilie / as hir lyf seith
Was come of Romayns / and of noble kynde
And from hir Cradel / vp fostred in the feith
Of crist⁊ and baar his gospel in hir mynde
She neuere cessed / as I writen fynde
Of hir prayere / and god to loue and drede
Bisekyng hym / to kepe hir maydenhede

¶And whan this mayden sholde / vn til a man
Ywedded be / that was ful yong of age
Which that ycleped was Valerian
And day was comen / of hir mariage
She ful deuout⁊ and humble in hir corage
Vnder hir robe of gold / that sat ful faire
Hadde next hir flessħ / yclad hir*e* in an haire

¶And whil that the Organs / maden melodie
To god allone / in hir herte / thus soong she
O · lord my soule / and eek my body gye
Vnwemmed / lest that I confounded be
And for his loue / that deyde vp on the tree
Euery seconde / and thridde day she faste
Ay biddyng⁊ in hir orisons ful faste

ELLESMERE

For
right⁊
eu*er*y
Right
Syen
eek⁊ hool /
brighte /

[4] And right /
swift⁊ and eek
Right Cecilie
swift⁊
and hool p*er*seu*er*ynge
brennynge eu*er*e / charite brighte
declared highte [5]

mayden bright⁊ lif
comen

Crist⁊ bar

preyere /
Bisekynge

And mayden / sholde vn to a

hir*e* flessħ /

And whil the Orgnes /
in herte sang
O lord /
that it confounded
dyde / vp on a tree
Eu*er*y
biddynge / hir*e*

120 Cecilia virgo clarissima Hg

gregorius in registro libro .10. ad Eulogium patriarcham scribit Iudicamus preterea quia grauem hic interpretum difficultatem patimur dum enim non sunt qui sensum de sensu exprimant set transferre semper verborum proprietatem volunt omnem dictorum sensum confundunt et cetera. Hg

[4] ¶Nonne *187r*

[5] Break in El followed by:
¶Explicit⁊
¶Heere bigynneth / the Seconde Nonnes tale / of the Lyf⁊ of Seinte Cecile
Miniature of the Nun in right margin.

The [illegible]

Or leos peple in englissh is to seye
And right as men may in the heuene see
The sonne and moone and sterres euery weye
Right so men goostly in this mayden free
Seyen of feith the magnanymytee
And eek the cleernesse hool of sapience
And sondry werkes brighte of excellence

And right so as thise Philosophres write
That heuene is swift and round and eek brennynge
Right so was faire Cecile the white
Ful swift and bisy euere in good werkynge
And round and hool in good perseuerynge
And brennyng euere in charite ful brighte
Now haue I yow declared what she highte

Cecilia virgo clarissima

[illegible] mayde bright Cecile as hir lyf seith
[illegible] was come of Romayns and of noble kynde
And from hir cradel vp fostred in the feith
Of crist and bar his gospel in hir mynde
She neuere cessed as I writen fynde
Of hir prayere and god to loue and drede
Bisekyng hym to kepe hir maydenhede

And whan this mayden sholde vn til a man
Ywedded be that was ful yong of age
Which that ycleped was Valerian
And day was comen of hir mariage
She ful deuout and humble in hir corage
Vnder hir robe of gold that sat ful faire
Hadde next hir flessh yclad hir in an haire

And whil that the Orgnes maden melodie
To god allone in hir herte thus song she
O lord my soule and eek my body gye
Vnwemmed lest that I confounded be
And for his loue that deyde vp on the tree
Euery seconde and thridde day she faste
Ay biddyng in hir orisons ful faste

Gre^go in registro li^o. io. ad Eulogium
patriarcham scribit. Indicamus pre[illegible]
quia [illegible] hic nimium difficultate[illegible]
patimur, quia enim non sunt qui [illegible]
[illegible] exprimant [illegible]
[illegible] [illegible] voluntatem [illegible]
[illegible] [illegible] confundunt [illegible]

. nyght cam / and to bedde moste she gon
With hir housbonde / as ofte is the manere
And priuely / to hym she seyde anon
O swete and wel biloued spouse deere
Ther is a conseil / and ye wolde it heere
Which that right fayn / I wolde vn to yow seye
So that ye swere / ye shul it nat biwreye

Valerian gan faste / vn to hir swere
That for no cas ne thyng þt myghte be
He sholde neuere mo biwreyen here
And thanne at erst / to hym seyde she
I haue an Aungel which that loueth me
That with greet loue / wher so I wake or slepe
Is redy ay / my body for to kepe

And if that he / may feelen out of drede
That ye me touche / or loue in vileynye
He right anon / wol sleen yow with the dede
And in youre youthe / thus ye shullen dye
And if that ye / in clene loue me gye
He wol yow loue as me / for youre clennesse
And shewe to yow / his ioye and his brightnesse

This Valerian / corrected as god wolde
Answerde agayn / if I shal trusten thee
Lat me that Aungel seen / and hym biholde
And if that it / a verray Aungel be
Thanne wol I doon / as thow hast prayed me
And if thow loue another man / for sothe
Right with this swerd / than wol I sle yow bothe

Cecile answerde / right in this wise
If that yow list / the Aungel shal ye se
So that ye trowe on crist / and yow baptise
Goth forth to Via Apia · quod she
That fro this town / ne stant but myles thre
And to the poure folkes / that ther dwellen
Sey hem right thus / as that I shal yow tellen

	ELLESMERE
[¶Th]e nyght cam / and to bedde moste she gon	The nyght
With hir*e* housbonde / as ofte is the manere	
And p*ri*uely / to hym she seyde anon	pryuely /
O swete / and wel bilo‍ued spouse deere	sweete /
Ther is a conseil / and ye wolde it heere	
Which that right fayn / I wolde vn to yow seye	right
So that ye swere / ye shul it nat biwreye	that shul me nat
¶Valerian gan faste / vn to hir swere	6 ¶Valerian / faste hir*e*
That for no cas / ne thyng þ*a*t myghte be	thyng / that myghte
He sholde neuere mo biwreyen here	neu*er*e mo /
And thanne at erst to hym seyde she	hym thus seyde
I haue an Aungel which that loueth me	Aungel /
That with gret loue / wher so I wake or slepe	greet sleepe
Is redy ay / my body for to kepe	
¶And if that he / may feelen out of drede	And if he /
That ye me touche / or loue in vileynye	touche / /
He right anon / wol sleen yow with the dede	right sle
And in youre youthe / thus ye shullen dye	yowthe / sholden
And if that ye / in clene loue me gye	
He wol yow loue as me / for youre clennesse	louen
And shewe to yow / his ioye and his brightnesse	shewen yow / brightnesse
¶This Valerian / corrected as god wolde	¶Valerian / corrected /
Answerde agayn / if I shal trusten thee	
Lat me that Aungel seen / and hym biholde	se /
And if that it / a verray Aungel be	it Angel bee
Thanne wol I doon / as thow hast prayed me	thou
And if thow loue another man / for sothe	thou loue /
Right with this swerd / than wol I sle yow bothe	Right w*ith* swerd / thanne
¶Cecile answerde / right in this wise	Cecile answerde anon / right
If that yow list the Aungel shal ye se	That if list· Angel shul see
So that ye trowe on crist and yow baptise	þ*a*t trowe in Crist baptize
Goth forth / to **Via Apia** · quod she	Gooth **Apia** / shee
That fro this town / ne stant but Milys thre	toun / Miles three
And to the poure folkes / that ther dwellen	þ*a*t dwelle
Sey hem right thus / as that I shal yow tellen	right telle

6 ¶Seconde *187v*

¶Telle hem / that I Cecile / yow to hem sente
To shewen yow / the goode Vrban the olde
For secree nedes / and for good entente
And whan that ye / Seint Vrban han biholde
Telle hym the wordes / which I to yow tolde
And whan that he / hath purged yow fro synne
Thanne shal ye seen that Aungel / er we twynne

¶This Valerian / is to the place gon
And right as hym was taught by his lernynge
He foond / this holy olde Vrban anon
Among the Seintes buryels lotynge [.i. latitante*m*]
And he anon / with outen tariynge
Dide his message / and whan that he it tolde
Vrban for ioye / hise handes gan vp holde

¶The teerys from hise eyen / leet he falle
Almyghty lord / o I*es*u crist quod he
Sower*e* of chaast conseil / hierde of vs alle
The fruyt of thilke seed / of chastitee
That thow hast sowe in Cecilie / taak to thee
Lo lyk a bisy bee / with outen gyle
Thee serueth ay / thyn owene thral Cecile

¶For thilke spouse / that she took but now
Ful lyk a fiers leou*n* /. she sendeth heere
As meke / as euere was any lamb to yow
And with that word / anon ther gan appeere
An old man / clad in white clothes cleere
That hadde a book with l*ett*re of gold in honde
And gan / biforn Valerian to stonde

¶Valerian as deed / fil doun for drede
Whan he hym say / and he vp hente hym tho
And on his book right thus he gan to rede
O · lord / o · feith / o · god with oute mo
O · cristendom / and fader of aƚƚ also
Abouen alle / and oueral euery where
Thise wordes / al with gold ywriten were

ELLESMERE

Telle
secree thynges / and
whiche *þat* I
þat
shul se / Angel er ye twynne
¶Valerian / ygon
right taught /
foond hooly /
buryeles lotynge [.i. latitantem]
þat
7 The teeris / eyen
Crist
seed Chastitee
thou Cecile /
Lo / gile
For took right · now
leoun / she
eu*er*e / lomb
oold
wi*th* lettre
bifore
Valerian
saugh /
book / right
O· lord· / o· feith ·o· outen
O· Cristendom / alle
alle / ouer alle / euerywhere

[7] ¶Nonne *188r*

Telle hem that I Cecile / yow to hem sente
To shewen yow / the goode Vrban the olde
ffor secree nedes / and for good entente
And whan that ye / Seint Vrban han biholde
Telle hym the wordes / whiche I to yow tolde
And whan that he / hath purged yow fro synne
Thanne shal ye seen that Angel / er ye twynne

This Valerian / is to the place gon
And right as hym was taught / by his lernynge
He foond this holy olde Vrban anon
i. latitante
Among the seintes buryels lotynge
And he anon / with outen taryynge
Dide his message / and whan that he it tolde
Vrban for ioye / hise handes gan vp holde

The teerys from hise eyen / leet he falle
Almyghty lord / o Ihu crist quod he
Sowere of chaast conseil / hierde of vs alle
The fruyt of thilke seed of chastitee
That thow hast sowe in Cecilie / taak to thee
Lo lyk a bisy bee / with outen gyle
Thee serueth ay / thyn owene thral Cecile

ffor thilke spouse / that she took but now
ffull lyk a fiers leon / she sendeth heere
As meke as euere was any lamb to yow
And with that word / anon ther gan appeere
An old man / clad in white clothes cleere
That hadde a book / with lettre of gold in honde
And gan biforn Valerian to stonde

Valerian as deed / fil doun for drede
Whan he hym saugh / and he vp hente hym tho
And on his book / right thus he gan to rede
O lord / o feith / o god with oute mo
O cristendom / and fader of alle also
Abouen alle / and ouer al euery where
Thise wordes / al with gold ywriten were

Whan this was rad / thanne seyde this olde man
Leuestow this thyng / or no / sey ye / or nay
I leue al this thyng / quod Valerian
For sother thyng than this / I dar wel say
Vnder the heuene / no wight thynke may
Tho vanysshed this olde man / he nyste where
And [illegible] Vrban / hym cristned right there

Valerian goth hom / and fynt Cecilie
In with his chambre / with an Angel stonde
This Angel hadde / of Roses and of lilie
Corones two / the whiche he bar in honde
And first to Cecile / as I vnderstonde
He yaf that oon / and after gan he take
That oother / to Valerian hir make

With body clene / and with vnwemmed thoght
Kepeth ay wel / thise corones quod he
Fro paradys to yow / haue I hem broght
Ne neuere mo / ne shal they roten be
Ne lese hir swote sauour / trusteth me
Ne neue wight / shal seen hem with his eye
But he be chaast / and hate vileynye

And thow Valerian / for thow so soone
Assentedest / to good conseil also
Sey what thee list / and thow shalt han thy boone
I haue a brother / quod Valerian tho
That in this world I loue no man so
I pray yow / that my brother may han grace
To knowe the trouthe / as I do in this place

The Angel seyde / god liketh thy requeste
And bothe / with the palm of martirdom
Ye shullen come vn to his blisful feste
And with that word Tiburce his brother coom
And whan that he / the sauour vndernoom
Which yt the Roses / and the lilies caste
With inne his herte / he gan to wondre faste

[¶W]han this was rad / thanne seyde this olde man
Leuestow this thyng' or no / sey ye / or nay
I leue al this thyng' quod Valerian
For sother thyng than this / I dar wel say
Vnder the heuene / no wight thynke may
Tho vanysshed this olde man / he nyste where
And [Pope] Vrban / hym cristned right there

¶Valerian goth hom / and fynt Cecilie
In with his chambre / with an Aungel stonde
This Aungel hadde / of Roses and of lilie
Corones two / the whiche he bar in honde
And first to Cecile / as I vnderstonde
He yaf that oon / and after gan he take
That oother / to Valerian hir make

¶With body clene / and with vnwemmed thoght'
Kepeth ay wel / thise corones quod he
Fro Paradys / to yow / haue I hem broght'
Ne neuere mo / ne shal they roten be
Ne lese hir swote sauour / trusteth me
Ne neu*ere* wight' shal seen hem w*ith* his eye
But he be chaast / and hate vileynye

¶And thow Valerian / for thow so soone
Assentedest' to good conseil also
Sey what thee list' and thow shalt han thy boone
I haue a brother / quod Valerian tho
That in this world / I loue no man so
I pray yow / that my brother may han g*ra*ce
To knowe the trouthe / as I do in this place

¶The Aungel seyde / god liketh thy requeste
And bothe / with the palm of martirdom
Ye shullen come / vn to his blisful feste
And with that word / Tiburce his brother coom
And whan that he / the sauour vndernoom
Which þ*a*t the Roses / and the lilies caste
With Inne his herte / he gan to wondre faste

ELLESMERE

Whan
Leeuestow no' / ye nay'
leeue thyng /
For oother thyng'
wight'
vanysshed
And Pope right

gooth hoom /
With Inne his Angel
Angel / ⟨of lilie⟩

first'

With body thoght'
corones three |
Paradys broght'
bee
soote sauour'
neuere
chaast'

8 And

thou

grace

Angel

with word' /

that

[8] ¶Seconde *188v*

The Nonne	ELLESMERE
¶And seyde / I wondre this tyme of the yere	And wondre / yeer
Whennes / that swote sauour / cometh so	soote sauour
Of Rose and lilies / that I smelle heere	heer
For thogh I hadde hem / in myne handes two	thougħ
The sauour mygħte in me / no depper go	sauour / mygħte me
The swete smel / that in myn herte I fynde	sweete þ*at*
Hath chaunged me / al in another kynde	
¶Valerian seyde / two corones han we	corones /
Snow white and Rose reed / þ*at* shynen clere	that cleere
Which þ*at* thyne eyen / han no myght to se	Whiche mygħt see
And as thow smellest hem / thurgh my prayere	thou preyere
So shaltow seen hem / leue brother deere	leeue
If it so be / thow wolt′ with outen slouthe	thou wi*th*
Bileue aright′ and knowen verray trouthe	arigħt′
¶Tiburce answerde / seystow this to me	seistow
In soothnesse / or in dreem I herkne this	
In dremes quod Valerian / han we be	
Vn to this tyme / brother myn ywys	ywis
And now at erst′ in trouthe oure dwellyng is	
How wostow this quod Tiburce / in what wyse	woostow Tiburce / and in wyse./
Quod Valerian / that shal I thee deuyse	
¶The Aungel of god / hath me the trouthe ytaught	me trouthe ytaugħt′
Which thow shalt seen / if that thow wolt reneye	thou thou
The ydoles / and be clene / and ellis n⟨a⟩ught′	ydoles elles naugħt′
And of the myracle / of thise corones tweye	
Seint Ambrose / in his p*re*face / list to seye	preface
Solempnely / this noble doctour deere	
Co*m*mendeth it′ and seith in this manere	Co*m*mendeth hym / and
¶The palme of martirdom / for to receyue	9 palm
Seinte Cecile / fulfild of goddes yifte	
The world / and eek hir chambre gan she weyue	hir*e* chambre /
Witnesse Tiburces / and Cecilies shrifte	Witnesse / Tyburces /
To whiche / god of his bou*n*tee wolde shifte	
Corones two / of floures wel smellynge	
And made his Aungel / hem the corones brynge	Angel /

9 ¶Nonne *189r*

And seyde / I wondre this tyme of the yere
Whennes that swete sauour / cometh so
Of Rose and lilies / that I smelle heere
For thogh I hadde hem / in myne handes two
The sauour myghte in me / no depper go
The swete smel / that in myn herte I fynde
Hath chaunged me / al in another kynde

Valerian seyde / two corones han we
Snow white and Rose reed / þt shynen cleere
Which þt thyne eyen / han no myght to se
And as thow smellest hem / thurgh my prayere
So shaltow seen hem / leue brother deere
If it so be / thow wolt with outen slouthe
Bileue aright / and knowen verray trouthe

Tiburce answerde / seistow this to me
In soothnesse / or in dreem I herkne this
In dremes quod Valerian / han we be
Vn to this tyme / brother myn ywis
And now at erst / in trouthe oure dwellyng is
How wostow this quod Tiburce / in what wyse
Quod Valerian / that shal I thee deuyse

The Aungel of god / hath me the trouthe ytaught
Which thow shalt seen / if that thow wolt reneye
The ydoles / and be clene / and ellis naught
And of the myracle / of thise corones tweye
Seint Ambrose / in his preface / list to seye
Solempnely / this noble doctour deere
Commendeth it / and seith in this manere

The palme of martirdom / for to receyue
Seinte Cecile / fulfild of goddes yifte
The world / and eek hir chambre gan she weyue
Witnesse Tiburces / and Cecilies shrifte
To whiche / god of his bountee wolde shifte
Corones two / of floures wel smellynge
And made his Aungel / hem the corones brynge

..e mayde hath broght men / to blisse aboue
The world hath wist / what it is worth certeyn
Deuotion / of chastitee to loue
Tho shewed hym Cecile / al open and pleyn
That alle ydoles / nys but a thyng in veyn
ffor they been dombe / and ther to they been deue
And charged hym / hise ydoles for to leue

Who so þt troweth nat this / a beest he is
Quod tho Tiburce / if that I shal nat lye
And she gan kisse his brest / that herde this
And was ful glad / he koude trouthe espye
This day I take thee / for myn allye
Seyde this blisful faire mayde deere
And after that / she seyde as ye may heere

Lo right so / as the loue of Crist quod she
Made me thy brotheres wyf / right in that wise
Anon for myn allie / heere take I thee
Syn that thow wolt / thyne ydoles despise
Go with thy brother now / and thee baptise
And make thee clene / so þt thow mowe biholde
The aungeles face / of which thy brother tolde

Tiburce answerde / and seyde brother deere
ffirst tel me whider that I shal / and to what man
To whom quod he / com forth with right good cheere
I wol thee lede / vn to the ~~pope~~ Vrban
Til Vrban / brother myn Valerian
Quod tho Tiburce / woltow me thider lede
Me thynketh / that it were a wonder dede

Ne menestow nat Vrban / quod he tho
That is so ofte / dampned to be deed
And woneth in halkes / alwey to and fro
And dar nat ones / putte forth his heed
Men sholde hym brennen / in a fyr so reed
If he were founde / or þt men myghte hym espye
And we also / to bere hym compaignye

	ELLESMERE
[¶Th]e mayde hath broght men / to blisse aboue	The broght
The world hath wist what it is worth c*er*teyn	wist /
Deuocion / of chastitee to loue	Deuociou*n* Chastitee
Tho shewed hym Cecile / al open and pleyn	
That alle ydoles / nys but a thyng in veyn	thyng
For they been dowmbe / and ther to they been deue	dombe / therto
And charged hym / hise ydoles for to leue	
¶Who so þ*at* troweth nat this / a beest he is	Who so / that
Quod tho Tiburce / if that I shal nat lye	þ*at*
And she gan kisse his brest that herde this	brest ·
And was ful glad / he koude trouthe espye	
This day I take thee / for myn allye	day / Allye
Seyde this blisful / faire mayde deere	
And after that she seyde as ye may heere	that ·
¶Lo right so / as the loue of Crist quod she	¶Lo / right Crist
Made me thy brotheres wyf / right in that wise	wyf · right
Anon for myn allie / heere take I thee	Allyee / heer
Syn that thow wolt thyne ydoles despise	thou
Go with thy brother now / and thee baptise	wit*h*
And make thee clene / so þ*at* thow mowe biholde	thou
The Aungeles face / of which thy brother tolde	Angeles
¶Tiburce answerde / and seyde brother deere	
First tel me whider that I shal / and to what man	me / þ*at* man
To whom quod he / com forth with right good cheere	he forth / wit*h* right
Bishop	
I wol thee lede / vn to the [pope] Vrban	Pope
Til Vrban / brother myn Valerian	Vrban /
Quod tho Tiburce / woltow me thider lede	Tiburce /.
Me thynketh / that it were a wonder dede	
¶Ne menestow nat Vrban / quod he tho	Ne
That is so ofte / dampned to be deed	deed
And woneth in halkes / alwey to *and* fro	and fro
And dar nat ones / putte forth his heed	heed
Men sholde hym brennen / in a fyr so reed	reed
If he were founde / or þ*at* men myghte hym spye	
And we also / to bere hym compaignye	

In left margin: [Elizabe]th dei gratia Anglie Francie et Hibernie Regina fidei defensor &c. Custodi eiusdem Castri et Gaole nostre ibidem salutem cum Radulphum Hot Cestrensis generosus iudicatus Existit de quibusdam felonijs et murdres per ipsum in Gaolam nostram Castri nostri Cestrie sub custodia tua detentus tibi prec[ipimus] per indenturam inter te et latorem presencium debite conficiendam latoribus prese custodi Et usque Gaolam nostram Apud lancastriam in Comitatu lancastrie predicto duci faciendus secundum legem et consuetudinem Regni nostri Anglie coram Justiciis nostris ad Gaolam n[ostram] in Comitatu predicto deliberandum assignatis alias inde legitimo modo deliberatus fuerat Et hoc(?) incumbenti T R H Apud

The Nonn[e]	ELLESMERE
¶And whil we seken / thilke diuinytee	10 And diuinitee
That is yhyd / in heuene pr*i*uely	yhid / pryuely
Algate / ybrend in this world shul we be	
To whom Cecile / answerde boldely	
Men myghten dreden / wel and skilfully	mygħten
This lyf to lese / myn owene deere brother	
If thys were lyuyng oonly / and noon oother	this lyuynge oonly
¶But ther is bettre lyf / in oother place	But lifꝰ
That neu*er*e shal be lostꝰ ne drede thee noghtꝰ	nogħtꝰ
Which goddes sone / vs tolde thurgh his grace	thurgħ
That fadres sone / hath alle thynges wroghtꝰ	thyngꝫ wrogħtꝰ
And al that wroght is / with a skilful thoghtꝰ	w*ith* thogħtꝰ
The goost that fro the fader / gan procede	goostꝰ· fader
Hath souled hem / with outen any drede	sowled
¶By word and by myracle / he goddes sone	By myracle / goddes
Whan he was / in this world / declared heere	was world
That ther was oother lyf / ther men may wone	
To whom answerde Tiburce / o suster deere	
Ne seydestow right now / in this manere	rigħt
Ther nys but o god / lord in sothfastnesse	soothfastnesse
And now of thre / how maystow bere witnesse	three /
¶That shal I telle quod she / er I go	
Right as a man / hath sapiences thre	Rigħt three
Memorie / engyn / and intellect also	Engyn / Intellectꝰ
So in o beynge / of diuinytee	So / in beynge / diuinitee
Thre p*er*sones / may ther right wel be	rigħt bee
Tho gan she hym / ful bisily to p*re*che	
Of cristes come / and of his peynes teche	Cristes hise
¶And manye pointes / of his passiou*n*	And
How goddes sone / in this world was w*ith*holde	withholde
To doon mankynde / pleyn remyssiou*n*	remissiou*n*
That was ybounde / in synne / and cares colde	ybounde synne
Al this thyngꝫ she vn to Tiburce tolde	thyngꝫ·
And after this / Tiburce in good entente	
With Valerian / to [Pope] (byshop) Vrban he wente	Pope

10 ¶Seconde *189v*

And whil we seken / thilke diuinytee
That is yhyd / in heuene pryuely
Algate ybrend in this world shul we be
To whom Cecile / answerde boldely
Men myghten dreden / wel and skilfully
This lyf to lese / myn owene deere brother
If this were lyuyng oonly / and noon oother

But ther is bettre lyf / in oother place
That neuere shal be lost / ne drede thee noght
Which goddes sone / vs tolde thurgh his grace
That fadres sone / hath alle thynges wroght
And al that wroght is / with a skilful thoght
The goost that fro the fader / gan procede
Hath souled hem / with outen any drede

By word and by myracle / he goddes sone
Whan he was in this world / declared heere
That ther was oother lyf / ther men may wone
To whom answerde Tiburce / o suster deere
Ne seydestow right now / in this manere
Ther nys but o god / lord in soothfastnesse
And now of thre / how maystow bere witnesse

That shal I telle quod she / er I go
Right as a man / hath sapiences thre
Memorie / engyn / and intellect also
So in o beynge of diuinytee
Thre persones / may ther right wel be
Tho gan she hym / ful bisily to preche
Of cristes come / and of his peynes teche

And manye pointes / of his passion
How goddes sone / in this world was withholde
To doon man kynde / pleyn remyssion
That was ybounde in synne and cares colde
Al this thyng / she vn to Tiburce tolde
And after this / Tiburce in good entente
With Valerian / to pope Vrban he wente

[...]t thankes god and with glad herte and light
He cristned hym and made hym in that place
Parfit in his lernyng goddes knyght
And after this Tiburce gat swich grace
That euery day he say in tyme and space
The Aungel of god and euery maner boone
That he god axed it was sped ful soone

It were ful hard by ordre for to seyn
How many wondres Ihus for hem wroghte
But at the laste to tellen short and pleyn
The sergeantz of the town of Rome hem soghte
And hem biforn Almache the prefect broghte
Which hem opposed and knew al hir entente
And to the ymage of Iubiter hem sente

And seyde who so wol nat sacrifise
Swap of his heed this is my sentence heer
Anon thise martirs that I yow deuyse
Oon Maximus that was an Officer
Of the prefectes and his Corniculer
Hem hente and whan he forth the seintes ladde
Hym self he weep for pitee that he hadde

Whan Maximus hadde herd the seintes loore
He gat hym of the tormentours leue
And ladde hem to his hous with oute moore
And with hir prechyng er that it were eue
They gonnen fro the tormentours to reue
And fro Maxime and fro his folk echone
The false feith to trowe in god allone

Cecile cam whan it was woxen nyght
With preestes that hem cristned alle yfeere
And afterward whan day was woxen light
Cecile hym seyde with a ful stedefast cheere
Now cristes owene knyghtes leue and deere
Cast al awey the werkes of derknesse
And armeth yow in armure of brightnesse

	ELLESMERE
[¶Tha]t [vrbanus] thanked god / and with glad herte and light	qui .s. vrbanus That thanked
[H]e cristned hym / and made hym in that place	He
Parfit in his lernyng goddes knyght	P*ar*fit lernynge / knyghħt
And after this / Tiburce gat swich gr*a*ce	Tiburce / grace
That euery day / he say in tyme and space	saugħ
The Aungel of god / and euery maner boone	
That he god axed / it was sped ful soone	axed //
¶It were ful hard / by ordre for to seyn	11
How many wondres / I*es*us for hem wroghte	manye wroghħte
But at the laste / to tellen short / and pleyn	atte laste / short
The sergeantz / of the town of Rome hem soghte	toun soghħte
And hem biforn Almache / the Prefect broghte	hem / Almache broghħte
Which hem opposed / and knew al hir entente	hir*e*
And to the ymage of Iubiter hem sente	ymage / Iuppiter
¶And seyde / who so wol nat sacrifise	And
Swap*e* of his heed / this is my sentence heer	this my
Anon thise martirs / that I yow deuyse	*pa*t
Oon Maxim*us* / that was an Officer	
Of the Prefectes / and his Corniculer	
Hem hente / and whan he forth the Seintes ladde	
Hym self he weep / for pitee that he hadde	weep*e* /
¶Whan Maxim*us* / hadde herd the Seintes loore	Whan had
He gat hym / of the tormentours leue	
And ladde hem to his hous / with oute moore	wit*h*
And with hir p*re*chyng er that it were eue	
They gonnen / fro the tormentours to reue	
And fro Maxime / and fro his folk echone	
The false feith / to trowe in god allone	
¶Cecile cam / whan it was woxen nyght	nyghħt
With preestes / that hem cristned alle yfeere	
And afterward / whan day was woxen light	afterward lighħt
Cecile hym seyde / with a ful stedefast cheere	Cecile hem seyde /
Now cristes owene knyghtes / leue and deere	Cristes knyghħtes / leeue
Cast al awey / the werkes of derknesse	alle
And armeth yow / in armure of brightnesse	And Armeth Armure brighħtnesse

[11] ¶Nonne *190r*

	ELLESMERE
¶Ye han for sothe / ydoon a greet bataille	Ye
Youre cours is doon / youre feith han ye conserued	your*e* feith
Goth to the corone of lyf / that may nat faille	Gooth lif
The rightful Iuge / which that ye han serued	rightful þ*at*
Shal yeue it yow / as ye han it disserued	deserued
And whan this thyng was seyd / as I deuyse	
Men ledde hem forth / to doon the sacrifise	sacrefise
¶But whan they weren / to the place broght	But broght
To tellen shortly / the conclusioun	
They nolde encense / ne sacrifise right noght	right noght
But on hir knees / they setten hem adoun	
With humble herte / and sad deuocioun	
And losten / bothe hir heuedes / in the place	heuedes
Hir soules wenten / to the kyng of grace	kyng
¶This Maxim*us* / that say this thyng bityde	12 This Maximus / saugh thyng
With pitous teerys / tolde it anon right	teeris / right
That he hir soules / saugh to heuene glyde	saugh
With Aungeles / ful of cleernesse / and of light	Aungels / cleernesse light
And with his word / conu*er*ted many a wight	with this word / wight
For which Almachius / dide hym so bete	
With whippe of leed / til he his lyf gan lete	he the lif
¶Cecile hym took / and buryed hym anon	toook
By Tiburce and Valerian softely	Tiburce /
With Inne hir buryyng place / vnder the stoon	hir*e* buriyng place
And after this / Almachius hastily	
Bad hise Ministres / fecchen openly	
Cecilie / so þ*at* she myghte in his p*re*sence	Cecile / that myghte
Doon sacrifice / and Iubiter encense	Iuppiter
¶But they conu*er*ted / at hir wise loore	.s. Ministres But they
Wepten ful sore / and yauen ful credence	soore /
Vn to hir word / and cryden moore *and* moore	hir*e* word and moore
Crist goddes sone / with outen difference	
Is verray god / this is al oure sentence	v*er*ray is oure
That hath so good a seruant / hym to serue	seruant
This with o voys / we trowen / thogh we st*er*ue	thogh sterue

12 ¶Seconde *190v*

Ye han for sothe / ydoon a greet bataille
Youre cours is doon / youre feith han ye conserued
Goth to the corone of lyf / that may nat faille
The rightful Iuge / which that ye han serued
Shal yeue it yow / as ye han it disserued
And whan this thyng was seyd / as I deuyse
Men ledde hem forth / to doon the sacrifise

But whan they weren / to the place broght
To tellen shortly / the conclusioun
They nolde encense / ne sacrifise right noght
But on hir knees / they setten hem adoun
With humble herte / and sad deuocioun
And losten bothe hir heuedes / in the place
Hir soules wenten / to the kyng of grace

This Maximus / that say this thyng bityde
With pitous teerys / tolde it anon right
That he hir soules / saugh to heuene glyde
With Aungeles ful of cleernesse / and of light
And with his word / conuerted many a wight
ffor which Almachius / dide hym so bete
With whippe of leed / til he his lyf gan lete

Cecile hym took / and buryed hym anon
By Tiburce and Valerian softely
With inne hir buryyng place / vnder the stoon
And after this / Almachius hastily
Bad hise mynistres / fecchen openly
Cecile / so þt she myghte in his presence
Doon sacrifice / and Iubiter encense

But they conuerted / at hir wise loore
Wepten ful soore / and yauen ful credence
Vn to hir word / and cryden moore & moore
Crist goddes sone / withouten difference
Is verray god / this is al oure sentence
That hath so good a seruant / hym to serue
This with o voys / we trowen / thogh we sterue

…achius that herde of this doynge
Bad fecchen Cecilie that he myghte hir se
And alderfirst lo this was his axynge
What maner womman artow quod he
I am a gentil womman born quod she
I axe thee quod he though it the greue
Of thy religioun and of thy bileue

¶ Ye han bigonne youre questioun folily
Quod she that wolden two answeres conclude
In o demaunde ye axed lewedly
Almachius answerde vn to that similitude
Of whennes comth thyn answeryng so rude
Of whennes quod she whan that she was freyned
Of conscience and of good feith vnfeyned

¶ Almachius seyde ne takestow noon hede
Of my power and she answerde hym this
Youre myght quod she ful litel is to drede
ffor euery mortal mannes power nys
But lyk a bladdre ful of wynd ywys
ffor with a nedles poynt whan it is blowe
May al the boost of it be leyd ful lowe

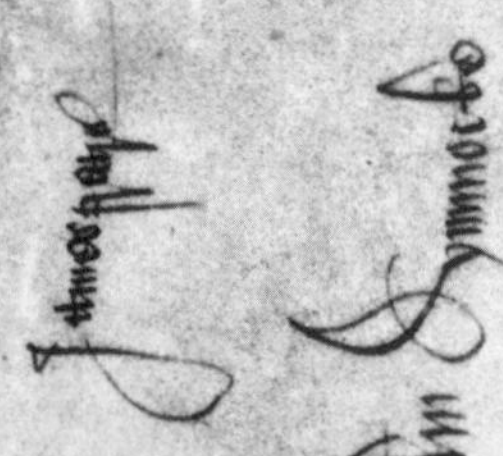

¶ ffful wrongfully bigonne thow quod he
And yet in wrong is al thy perseuerance
Wostow nat how oure myghty princes free
Han thus comanded and maad ordinaunce
That euery cristen wight shal han penaunce
But if that he his cristendom withseye
And goon al quyt if he wol it reneye

¶ Youre princes erren as youre nobleye dooth
Quod tho Cecile and with a wood sentence
Ye make vs gilty and it is nat sooth
ffor ye þt knowen wel oure Innocence
ffor as muche as we doon a reuerence
To crist and for we bere a cristen name
Ye putte on vs a cryme and eek a blame

ELLESMERE

[¶Alm]achius / that herde of this doynge
[B]ad fecchen Cecilie / that he myghte hir se
And alderfirst lo / this was his axynge
What maner womman / artow quod he
I am a gentil womman born / quod she
I axe thee quod he / thogh it the greue
Of thy religiou*n* / and of thy bileue

¶Ye han bigonne / youre question folily
Quod she / that wolden two answeres conclude
In o demande / ye axed lewedly
Almachie answerde / vn to that similitude
Of whennes comth / thyn answeryng so rude
Of whennes quod she / whan that she was freyned
Of conscience / and of good feith vnfeyned

¶Almachius seyde / ne takestow noon hede
Of my power / and she answerde hym / this
Youre myght quod she / ful litel is to drede
For euery / mortal mannes power nys
But lyk a bladdre / ful of wynd ywys
For with a nedles pointꝛ whan it is blowe
May al the boost of itꝛ be leyd ful lowe

¶Ful wrongfully / bigonne thow quod he
And yet in wrongꝛ is al thy pe*r*seue*r*au*n*ce
Wostow natꝛ how / oure myghty p*ri*nces free
Han thus comanded / and maad ordinau*n*ce
That euery cristen wightꝛ shal han penau*n*ce
But if that he / his cristendom withseye
And goon al quytꝛ if he wol it reneye

¶Youre Prynces erren / as youre nobleye dooth
Quod tho Cecile / and with a wood sentence
Ye make vs gilty / and is nat sooth
For ye þ*at* knowen wel / oure Innocence
For as muche / as we doon a reuerence
To crist / and for we bere a cristen name
Ye putte on vs / a cryme / *and* eek a blame

ELLESMERE

¶Almachius /
Bad Cecile / hir*e* see
alderfirstꝛ · lo
wo*m*man / he.
wo*m*man born
thougħ thee greeue
Religou*n* / bileeue

questiou*n*

Almache
answeryngꝛ rude.
quod she / . þ*at*
Of Conscience /

heede
power / answerde hym |
mygħtꝛ dreede
eu*ery* / mortal /

poyntꝛ

[13]
is thy pe*r*seuerau*n*ce
how

eu*ery* wigħtꝛ

quit / wole

¶Yowre p*ri*nces

ye / that wel

cristꝛ
and

13 ¶Nonne *191r*

	ELLESMERE
¶But we that knowen / thilke name so	But
For ve*r*tuous / we may it nat withseye	
Almache answerde / chees oon of thise two	
Do sacrifice / or cristendom reneye	
That thow mowe now / escapen by that weye	thou
At which / this holy / blisful faire mayde	which / the hooly
Gan for to laughe / and to the Iuge she sayde	laughe / Iuge sayde
¶O Iuge confus / in thy nycetee	¶O Iuge / confus
Wiltow / that I reneye Innocence	Woltow /
To maken me / a wikked wight quod she	make wight shee
Lo / he dissimuleth heere in audience	dissymuleth heer*e* / Audience
He stareth and woodeth / in his adu*er*tence	stareth / and he woodeth Adu*er*tence
To whom Almachius / vnsely wrecche	
Ne wostow nat how fer my myght may strecche	woostow myght
¶Han noght oure myghty p*ri*nces / to me yeuen	Han noght myghty
Ye bothe power and auctoritee	power / Auctoritee
To maken folk / to dyen or to lyuen	
Why spekestow so prowdly / thanne to me	spekestow / proudly
I speke noght but stedefastly quod she	noght / stedfastly
Nat proudly / for I seye / as for my syde	I speke as
We haten dedly / thilke vice of pryde	deedly /
¶And if thow drede nat a sooth to here[audir*e*]	And thou .i. audire heere
Thanne wol I shewe / al openly by right	right
That thow hast maad / a ful greet lesyng here[hic]	thou lesyng heere[hic]
Thow seist thy p*ri*nces / han thee yeuen myght	Thou seyst P*ri*nces / myght
Bothe for to sleen / and for to quyken a wight	wight
Thow that ne mayst but oonly lyf byreue	Thou bireue
Thow hast noon oother power / ne no leue	Thou hast power
¶But thow mayst seyn / thy p*ri*nces han thee maked	14 But thou
Ministre of deeth / for if thow speke of me	thou of mo|
Thow lyest for thy power is ful naked	Thou
Do wey thy boldnesse / seyde Almachius tho	booldnesse /
And sacrifice / to ⟨oure⟩ goddes / er thow go	sacrifie to oure goddes thou
I recche nat what wrong that thow me p*ro*fre	*pa*t thou profre
For I kan suffre it / as a Philosophre	

14 ¶Seconde *191v*

But ye that knowen thilke name so
For vertuous / ye may it nat withseye
Almache answerde / chees oon of thise two
Do sacrifice / or cristendom reneye
That thow mowe now / escapen by that weye
At which / this holy / blisful faire mayde
Gan for to laughe / and to the Juge she sayde

O Juge confus / in thy nycetee
Wiltow / that I reneye innocence
To maken me / a wikked wight / quod she
Lo / he dissimuleth heere in audience
He stareth and woodeth / in his advertence
To whom Almachius / unsely wrecche
Ne woostow nat / how fer my myght may strecche

Han noght oure myghty princes / to me yeuen
Ye bothe power / and auctoritee
To maken folk / to dyen or to lyuen
Why spekestow so proudly / thanne to me
I speke noght / but stedefastly / quod she
Nat proudly / for I seye / as for my syde
We haten deedly / thilke vice of pryde

And if thow drede nat / a sooth to heere
Thanne wol I shewe / al openly by right /
That thow hast maad / a ful greet lesyng heere
Thow seist / thy princes / han thee yeuen myght /
Bothe for to sleen / and for to quyken a wight /
Thow that ne mayst / but oonly lyf byreue
Thow hast noon oother power / ne no leue

But thow mayst seyn / thy princes han thee maked
Mynistre of deeth / for if thow speke of mo
Thow lyest / for thy power is ful naked
Do wey thy boldnesse / seyde Almachius tho
And sacrifice / to oure goddes / er thow go
I recche nat / what wrong / that thow me profre
For I kan suffre it / as a Philosophre

Thilke wronges may I nat endure
That thow preisest of oure goddes here quod he
Cecilie answerde / o nyce creature
Thow seydest no word / syn thow spak to me
That I ne knew ther with thy nycetee
And that thow were / in euery maner wise
A lewed officer / a veyn Iustise

Ther lakketh no thyng / to thyne outter eyen exterioribz oculis
That thow nart blynd / for thyng þt we seen alle
That is a stoon / that men may wel espien
That ilke stoon / a god thow wolt it calle
I rede thee / lat thyn hand vp on it falle
And taste it wel / and stoon thow shalt it fynde
Syn that thow seest nat / with thyne eyen blynde

It is a shame / that the peple shal
So scornen thee / and laughe at thy folye
ffor comly men woot it wel ouer al
That myghty god / is in hise heuenes hye
And thise ymages / wel thow mayst espye
To thee ne to hem self / mowe noght profite
ffor in effect / they be nat worth a myte

Thise / and swiche othere / seyde she
And he weex wrooth / and bad men sholde hir lede
Hoom til hir hous / and in hir hous quod he
Bren hire / right in a bath of flambes rede
And as he bad / right so was doon the dede
ffor in a bath / they gonne hire faste shetten
And nyght and day / greet fyr they vnder betten

The longe nyght / and eek a day also
ffor al the fyr / and eek the bathes hete
She sat al cold / and feelede no wo
It made hir nat / a drope for to swete
But in that bath / hir lyf she moste lete
ffor he Almachius / with a ful wikke entente
To sleen hire in the bath / his sonde sente

	ELLESMERE
[⁋But] thilke wronges may I nat endure	⁋But wronges /
[T]hat thow spekest⁊ of oure goddes here quod he	That thou heere
Cecilie answerde / o nyce creature	Cecile
Thow seydest no word / syn thow spak to me	Thou thou
That I ne knew ther with thy nycetee	with /
And that thow were / in euery maner wise	thou
A lewed Officer / a veyn Iustise	Officer / and a
⁋Ther lakketh no thyng⁊ to thyne outter eyen (ext*er*iorib*us* oculis)	Ther thyng⁊. outter eyen (ext*er*iorib*us* ocul*is*)
That thow nart blynd / for thyng þ*at* we seen alle	thou blynd' / thyng⁊
That is a stoon / that men may wel espien	That it is stoon / þ*at* espyen
That ilke stoon / a god thow wolt it calle	
I rede thee / lat thyn hand vp on it falle	
And taste it wel / and stoon thow shalt it fynde	thou
Syn that thow seest⁊ nat⁊ / with thyne eyen blynde	thou nat⁊
⁋It is a shame / that the peple shal	It
So scornen thee / and laughe at thy folye	scorne
For com*en*ly / men woot it wel ouer al	com*m*unly / ou*er*al
That myghty god / is in hise heuenes hye	
And thise ymages / wel thow mayst espye	thou
To thee / ne to hem self / mowe noght p*ro*fite	self⁊ ne mowen noħt
For in effect⁊ they be nat worth a myte	been
⁋Thise / and swiche othere / seyde she	⁋Thise wordes / and othere
And he weex wrooth / and bad men sholde hir lede	
Hoom til hir hous / and in hir hous quod he	Hom in hir*e*
Bren hir*e* / right in a Bath of flambes rede	Brenne bath
And as he bad / right so was doon the dede	riħt doon in dede
For in a Bath / they gonne hir*e* faste shetten	
And nyght and day / greet fyr they vnder betten	
⁋The longe nyght⁊ and eek a day also	nyħt / eek⁊
For al the fyr / and eek the Bathes hete	fyr⁊ bathes heete
She sat al coold / and feeled no wo	
It made hir nat⁊ o drope for to swete	hir*e* / nat⁊ a drope sweete
But in that Bath / hir lyf she moste lete	
For he Almachius / with a ful wikke entente	w*ith*
To sleen hir*e* in the Bath / his sonde sente	Bath

¶Thre strokes in the nekke / he smoot hir*e* tho	15 Thre
The tormentour / but for no maner chaunce	tormentour
He myghte noght smyte al hir nekke atwo	myghte noght smyte /
And for ther was / that tyme an ordinaunce	
That no man / sholde doon man swich penaunce	doon men swich
The ferthe strook to smyten / softe or soore	strook / smyten
This tormentour / ne dorste do namoore	
¶But half deed / with hir nekke ycoruen there	But
He lefte hir lye / and on his wey he went	
The cristen folk whiche þ*at* aboute hir*e* were	folk / which that
With shetes / han the blood ful faire yhent	sheetes / blood /
Thre dayes / lyued she in this torment	dayes she /
And neuere cessed / hem the feith to teche	
That she hadde fostred / hem she gan to p*re*che	
¶And hem she yaf / hir moebles / and hir thyng	And
byshop And to the [Pope] Vrban / bitook hem tho	Pope
And seyde / I axed þis of heuene kyng	this at heuene
To han respit thre dayes / and namo	respit · dayes
To reco*m*mende to yow / er that I go	recomende
Thise soules / lo / and þ*at* I myghte do werche	soules
Here of myn hous / p*er*petuelly a cherche	Heere
¶Seint Vrban / with hise deknes pryuely	p*ri*uely
The body fette / and buryed it by nyghte	This body
Among hise othere Seintes honestly	Among seintes /
Hir hous / the chirche of Seinte Cecilie highte	chirche / seinte highte
Seint Vrban halwed it as he wel myghte	
In which / in to this day / in noble wyse	
Men doon to crist and to his Seinte seruyse.	Crist · seinte seruyse

¶Here is ended / the Nonnes tale

¶Heere is ended / the Seconde Nonnes tale

15 ¶Nonne *192r*

Thre strokes in the nekke / he smoot hir tho
The tormentour / but for no maner chaunce
He myghte noght / smyte al hir nekke atwo
And for ther was / that tyme an ordinaunce
That no man / sholde doon man swich penaunce
The ferthe strook to smyten / softe or soore
This tormentour / ne dorste do namoore

But half deed / with hir nekke ycoruen there
He lefte hir lye / and on his wey he wente
The cristen folk / which þt aboute hir were
With shetes / han the blood ful faire yhent
Thre dayes / lyued she in this torment
And neuere cessed / hem the feith to teche
That she hadde fostred / hem she gan to preche

And hem she yaf / hir moebles / and hir thyng
And to the Pope Vrban / bitook hem tho
And seyde / I axed this of heuene kyng
To han respit / thre dayes / and namo
To recomende to yow / er that I go
Thise soules / lo / and þt I myghte do werche
Heere of myn hous / perpetuelly a cherche

Seint Vrban / with hise deknes pryuely
The body fette / and buryed it by nyghte
Among hise othere seintes honestly
Hir hous / the chirche of Seinte Cecilie highte
Seint Vrban halwed it / as he wel myghte
In which / in to this day / in noble wyse
Men doon to Crist and to his seinte seruyse

Heere is ended the Seconde Nonnes tale

¶ The prohemie of the Clerkys tale of Oxenford

Sire clerk of Oxenford oure hoost sayde
Ye ryde as coy and stille as dooth a mayde
Were newe spoused sittyng at the bord
This day ne herde I of youre tonge a word
I trowe ye studie aboute som sophyme
But Salomon seith euery thyng hath tyme
¶ For goddes sake as beth of bettre cheere
It is no tyme for to studien heere
Tel vs som murye tale by youre fey
For what man that is entred in a pley
He nedes moot vn to the pley assente
But precheth nat as freres doon in lente
To maken vs for oure olde synnes wepe
Ne that thy tale make vs nat to slepe
¶ Tel vs som murye thyng of auentures
Youre termes youre colours and youre figures
Kepe hem in stoor til so be ye endite
Heigh stile as whan þt men to kynges write
Speketh so pleyn at this tyme we yow preye
That we may vnderstonde what ye seye
¶ This worthy clerk benygnely answerde
Hoost quod he I am vnder youre yerde
Ye han of vs as now the gouernance
And ther fore wol I do yow obeisance
As fer as reson axeth hardily
I wol yow telle a tale which that I
Lerned at Padwe of a worthy clerk
As preued by his wordes and his werk
He is now deed and nayled in his cheste
I prey to god so yeue his soule reste
¶ Fraunceys Petrak the lauriat poete
Highte this clerk whos rethoryk swete
Enlumyned al ytaille of poetrie
As lynyan dide of philosophie
Or lawe or oother art particuler
But deeth þt wol nat suffre vs dwellen heer

¶The p*ro*hemie of the Clerkys tale of Oxenford	[1] ¶Heere folweth the Prologe of the clerkes tale of Oxenford
Sire clerk of Oxenford / oure Hoost sayde	Sire clerk / Oxenford Hoost
Ye ride as coy / and stille as dooth a mayde	ryde stille /
Were newe spoused / sittyng at the bord	sittynge
This day ne herde I / of your*e* tonge a word	day / youre
I trowe ye studie / aboute som Sophyme	
But Salomon seith / euery thyng hath tyme	⌈¶pausacio⌉[2]
¶For goddes sake / as beth of bettre cheere	
It is no tyme / for to studien heere	
Tel vs som murie tale / by youre fey	Telle myrie
For what man / that is entred in a pley	
He nedes moot vn to the pley assente	
But p*re*cheth nat as freres doon in lente	
To maken vs / for oure olde synnes wepe	make
Ne that thy tale / make vs nat to slepe	⌈¶pausacio⌉
¶Tel vs / som murye thyng of auentures	¶Telle murie thyng /
Youre t*er*mes / youre colours / and your*e* figures	youre colours / youre figures
Kepe hem in stoor / til so be ye endite	Keep*e* be that ye
Heigh stile / as whan þ*a*t men to kynges write	style /
Speketh so pleyn at this tyme / we yow preye	pleyn / tyme
That we may vnderstonde / what ye seye	vnderstonde ⌈¶pausacio⌉
¶This worthy clerk benygnely answerde	benignely
Hoost quod he / I am vnder your*e* yerde	youre
Ye han of vs / as now the gou*er*nau*n*ce	gouernance
And therfore / wol I do yow obeisau*n*ce	obeisance
As fer / as reson asketh hardily	fer resou*n* axeth
I wol yow telle a tale / which that I	that I/
Lerned at Padwe / of a worthy Clerk	clerk
As proued / by his wordes and his werk	preued /
He is now deed / and nayled in his Cheste	cheste
I pray to god / so yeue his soule reste	prey ⌈¶pausacio⌉
¶Fraunceys Petrak / the lauryat poete	Perak lauriat
Highte this clerk whos Rethoryk swete	Rethorik sweete
Enlumyned al Ytaille / of Poetrie	Ytaille poetrie
As Lynyan dide / of Philosophie	
Or lawe / or oother art p*ar*ticuler	Art
But deth / þ*a*t wol nat suffre vs dwellen her	deeth / nat dwellen heer

[1] ¶Clerk *87v*

[2] In El the Prologue of the Clerk's Tale is in stanzas marked off by the marginal gloss ¶pausacio.

But as it were / a twynklyng of an eye
Hem bothe hath slayn / and alle shul we dye
¶But forth to tellen / of this worthy man
That taughte me this tale / as I bigan
I seye *þat* first with heigh stile he enditeth
Er he / the body of his tale writeth
A prohemie / in which discryueth he
Pemond / and of Saluces the contree
And speketh of Appenyn / the hilles hye
That been the boundes / of westlumbardye
And of Mount Vesulus / in special
Wher as the Poo / out of a welle smal
Taketh his firste spryngyng / and his cours
That Estward / ay encresseth in his cours
To Emeleward / to Ferare / and Venyse
The which / a long thyng were to deuyse
And trewely / as to my Iuggement
Me thynketh it a thyng inp*er*tinent
Saue *þat* he wole / convoien his matere
But this his tale / which *þat* ye shal heere

¶Here bigynneth the tale

Ther is / at the west syde of Ytaille
Doun at the roote / of vesulus the colde
[g]rata planicies A lusty playne / habundant of vitaille
Wher many a tour and town / thow mayst biholde
That founded were / in tyme of fadres olde
And many another / delitable sighte
And Saluces / this noble contree highte

¶A Markys whilom / lord was of that lond
As were / his worthy eldres hym bifore
And obeysant ay redy to his hond
Were alle his liges / bothe lasse and moore
Thus in delit he lyueth / and hath doon yoore
Biloued and drad / thurgh fauour of Fortune
Bothe of his lordes / and of his co*m*mune

44 Est ad ytalie latus occiduum vesulus [ex appenini] Iugis mons altissimus qui vertice nu[bula super]ans liquido sese ingerit etheri Mons [suapte] nobilis natura padi ortu nobilissimus q[ui latere] fonte lapsus exiguo orientem contra solem fertur [et cetera] Hg (defective) El (40) Variant: nubula) nebula El

58 Inter cetera ad radicem Vesuli terra Saluciarum vicis et castellis Hg El (57)

ELLESMERE

twynklyng
[¶pausacio]
3 ¶But
taughte
seye / that heigh
prohemye / in the which
Pemond
[¶pausacio]
¶And
Where poo /
spryngyng his sours
Emeleward / Ferrare
which long thyng
thyng
that conuoyen mateere
that ye may heere [¶pausacio]

¶Heere bigynneth the tale of the Clerk / of Oxenford

THer
Vesulus
[¶grata planicies]
Where toun / thou
tyme /
sighte
Saluces highte
A Markys / whilom 4
hise
obeisant and redy hond
hise
thurgh fauo*ur*
hise lordes /

[3] **¶of Oxenford** *88r*

[4] Miniature of the Clerk in right margin.

But as it were a twynklyng of an ye
Hem bothe hath slayn and alle shul we dye
But forth to tellen of this worthy man
That taughte me this tale as I bigan
I seye þt first with heigh stile he enditeth
Er he the body of his tale writeth
A prohemie in which discryveth he
Pemond and of Saluces the contree
And speketh of Appenyn the hilles hye
That been the boundes of West lumbardye
And of mount Vesulus in special
Wher as the Poo out of a welle smal
Taketh his firste spryngyng and his cours
That estward ay encresseth in his cours
To Emeleward to fferare and Venyse
The which a long thyng were to devyse
And trewely as to my juggement
Me thynketh it a thyng inpertinent
Save þt he wole conveien his matere
But this his tale which þt ye shal heere

Est ad ytalie latus occiduum Vesulus ... pugis mons altissimus qui ... ans liquido sese ingerit ethera ... nobilis natura padi ortu nobilissimus ... fonte lapsus exiguo orientem contra solem ...

Here bigynneth the tale

Ther is at the west syde of ytaille
Doun at the roote of Vesulus the colde
(planiness) A lusty playne habundant of vitaille
Wher many a tour and toun thow mayst biholde
That founded were in tyme of fadres olde
And many another delitable sighte
And Saluces this noble contree highte

Est ... ad radices Vesuli ... castell...

A markys whilom lord was of that lond
As were his worthy eldres hym bifore
And obeysant ay redy to his hond
Were alle his liges bothe lasse and moore
Thus in delit he lyveth and hath doon yoore
Biloued and drad thurgh fauour of ffortune
Bothe of his lordes and of his commune

with he was to speke as of lynage
e gentileste yborn of lumbardye
A fair persone and strong and yong of age
And ful of honour and of curteisye
Discret ynogh his contree for to gye
Saue in some thynges þt he was to blame
And walter was this yonge lordes name

I blame hym thus that he considered noght
In tyme comynge what myghte hym bityde
But on his lust present was al his thoght
As for to hauke and hunte on euery syde
Wel neigh alle othere cures leet he slyde
And eek he nolde and that was worst of alle
Wedde no wyf for noght þt may bifalle

Oonly that point his peple bar so soore
That flokmele on a day they to hym wente — catervatim
And oon of hem þt wisest was of loore
Or ellis þt the lord best wolde assente
That he sholde telle hym what his peple mente
Or ellis koude he shewe wel swich matere
He to the markys seyde as ye shal heere

O noble markys youre humanitee — tua inquid humanitas optime marchio
Assureth vs and yeueth vs hardynesse
As ofte as tyme is of necessitee
That we to yow mowe telle oure heuynesse
Accepteth lord now of youre gentillesse
That we with pitous herte vn to yow pleyne
And lat youre eres noght my voys disdeyne

Al haue I noght to doone in this matere
Moore than another man hath in this place
Yet for as muche as ye my lord so deere
Han alwey shewed me fauour and grace
I dar the bettre aske of yow a space
Of audience to shewen oure requeste
And ye my lord to doon right as yow leste

[¶The]r with he was to speke as of lynage
[Th]e gentileste / yborn of Lumbardye
[A] fair p*er*sone / and strong⁊ and yong of age
And ful of hono*ur* / and of curteisye
Discret ynogh / his contree for to gye
Saue in some thynges / þ*at* he was to blame
And Walter / was this yonge lordes name

¶I blame hym thus / that he considered noght⁊
In tyme comynge / what myghte hym bityde
But on his lust p*re*sent⁊ was al his thoght⁊
As for to hauke / and hunte on euery syde
Wel neigh / alle oothere cures leet he slyde
And eek he nolde / and that was worst of alle
Wedde no wyf⁊ for noght þ*at* may bifalle

¶Oonly that point⁊ his peple bar so soore
cateruatim That flokmele on a day / they to hym wente
And oon of hem / þ*at* wisest was of loore
Or ellis / þ*at* the lord / best wolde assente
That he sholde telle hym / what his peple mente
Or ellis koude he / shewe wel swich matere
He to the Markys seyde / as ye shal heere

¶O noble Markys / your*e* humanitee
Assureth vs / and yeueth vs hardynesse
As ofte / as tyme is of necessitee
That we to yow / mowe telle oure heuynesse
Accepteth lord / now of your*e* gentillesse
That we with pitous herte / vn to yow pleyne
And lat youre erys / noght my voys disdeyne

¶Al haue I noght to doone / in this matere
Moore than another man / hath in this place
Yet for as muche / as ye my lord so deere
Han alwey shewed me / fauour and g*ra*ce
I dar the bettre / aske of yow a space
Of audience / to shewen oure requeste
And ye my lord / to doon right as yow leste

92 tua inquid humanitas optime Marchio Hg El

was /
The gentilleste / lumbardye
A p*er*sone
ful honour /
Discreet ynogh /
Saue that in so*m*me

5 considereth noght⁊
hym myghte
But in his thoght⁊
hauke hunte / eu*er*y
ny / othere cures /
eek⁊
wyf / noght

Oonly
¶Cat*er*uatim] flokmeele
that
elles / that

elles / he mateere
Markys / seyde shul

youre
Asseureth vs / to yeue hardinesse

now for your*e*
id
That
eres / nat desdeyne

Al mateere

alwey / grace

Audience /
right⁊

5 ¶Clerk⁊ *88v*

The Clerk of Oxenforde

¶For c*er*tes lord / so wel vs liketh yow
And al youre werk and eu*er*e han doon / þ*at* we
Ne kouden nat vs self / deuysen how
We myghte lyuen / in moore felicitee
Saue o thyng lord / if it your*e* wille be
That for to been a wedded man / yow leste
Thanne were your*e* peple / in sou*er*eyn hertes reste

¶Boweth your*e* nekke / vnder that blisful yok
Of souereyntee / noght of seruyse
Which that men clepe / spousaille / or wedlok
And thenketh lord / among your*e* thoghtes wyse
How þ*at* oure dayes passe / in sondry wyse
For thogh we slepe / or wake / or renne / or ryde
Ay fleeth the tyme / it nel no man abyde

¶And thogh youre grene youthe / floure as yit
In crepeth age alwey / as stille as stoon
And deth / manaceth euery age and smyt
In ech estat for ther escapeth noon
And also certeyn / as we knowe echon
That we shal dye / as vnc*er*teyn we alle
Been of that day / whan deth shal on vs falle

¶Accepteth thanne of vs / the trewe entente
That neu*er*e yet refuseden thyn heste
And we wol lord / if þ*at* ye wol assente
Chese yow a wyf in short tyme at the leeste
Born of the gentileste / and of the meeste
Of al this lond / so þ*at* it oghte seme
Honour / to god and yow / as we kan deme

¶Delyu*er*e vs / out of al this bisy drede
And tak a wyf / for heighe goddes sake
For if so bifelle / as god forbede
That thurgh youre deeth / youre ligne sholde slake
And that a straunge Successour / sholde take
Youre heritage / o. wo were vs alyue
Wher fore / we pray yow / hastily to wyue

ELLESMERE

For certes
werk / we
koude self how
myghte
if youre
man
youre souereyn

Boweth youre yok /
soueraynetee / noght
þ*at* clepeth / spousaille
youre

thogh or rome / or ryde
nyl

6 And thogh

deeth manaceth /
estaat escapeth
c*er*tein / echoon
shul deye / vnc*er*teyn / alle
deeth

Accepteth
heeste
that wole
wyf / atte leeste
gentilleste /
land that oghte
Honour deeme

Deliu*er*e
taak wyf hye
if it so
thurgh youre youre lyne
Successour
o
Wherfore / yow

6 ¶of Oxenford *89r*

The clerk of Oxenforde

For certes lord so wel vs liketh yow
And al youre werk and euere han doon þt we
Ne kouden nat vs self deuysen how
We myghte lyuen in moore felicitee
Saue o thyng lord if it youre wille be
That for to been a wedded man yow leste
Thanne were youre peple in souereyn hertes reste

Boweth youre nekke vnder that blisful yok
Of souereyntee noght of seruyse
Which that men clepe spousaille or wedlok
And thenketh lord among youre thoghtes wyse
How þt oure dayes passe in sondry wyse
ffor thogh we slepe or wake or rome or ryde
Ay fleeth the tyme it nel no man abyde

And thogh youre grene youthe floure as yit
In crepeth age alwey as stille as stoon
And deth manaceth euery age and smyt
In ech estat for ther escapeth noon
And also certeyn as we knowe echon
That we shal dye as vncerteyn we alle
Been of that day whan deth shal on vs falle

Accepteth thanne of vs the trewe entente
That neuere yet refuseden thyn heste
And we wol lord if þt ye wol assente
Chese yow a wyf in short tyme at the leeste
Born of the gentileste and of the meeste
Of al this lond so þt it oghte seme
Honour to god and yow as we kan deme

Delyuere vs out of al this bisy drede
And tak a wyf for heighe goddes sake
ffor if so bifelle as god forbede
That thurgh youre deeth youre lyne sholde slake
And that a straunge Successour sholde take
Youre heritage o wo were vs alyue
Wher fore we pray yow hastily to wyue

meke prayere and hir pitous cheere
Made the markys herte han pitee
Ye wol quod he myn owene peple deere
To that I neuere erst thoghte streyne me
I me reioysed of my libertee
That selde tyme is founde in mariage
Ther I was free I moot ben in seruage

But nathelees I se youre trewe entente
And truste vp on youre wit and haue doon ay
Wher fore of my free wyl I wol assente
To wedde me as soone as euere I may
But ther as ye han profred me to day
To chese me a wyf I yow relesse
That choys and pray yow of that profre cesse

For god it woot þt children ofte been
Vnlyk hir worthy eldres hem bifore
Bountee comth al of god nat of the streen
Of which they been engendred and ybore
I truste in goddes bountee and ther fore
My mariage and myn estat and reste
I hym bitake he may doon as hym leste

Lat me allone in chesyng of my wyf
That charge vp on my bak I wol endure
But I pray yow and charge vp on youre lyf
That what wyf þt I take ye me assure
To worshipe hire whil þt hir lyf may dure
In word and werk bothe heere and euerywheere
As she an Emperours doghter weere

And ferther moore this shal ye swere þt ye
Agayn my choys shal neither grucche ne stryue
For sith I shal forgoon my libertee
At youre requeste as euere moot I thryue
Ther as myn herte is set ther wol I wyue
And but ye wol assente in swich manere
I pray yow speketh namoore of this matere

	ELLESMERE
[¶Hir] meke prayere / and hir pitous cheere	¶Hir meeke preyere /
[M]ade the Markys herte / han pitee	Made
Ye wol quod he / myn owene peple deere	
To that I neu*er*e erst thoghte / streyne me	thoughte /
I me reioysed / of my libertee	liberte
That selde tyme / is founde in mariage	seelde
Ther I was free / I moot ben in seruage	been
¶But nathelees / I se your*e* trewe entente	But youre
And truste vp on youre wit and haue doon ay	vpon your*e* wit /
Wher fore / of my free wyl / I wol assente	Wherfore / wole
To wedde me / as soone as eu*er*e I may	
But ther as ye / han p*ro*fred me to day	profred me this day
To chese me a wyf I yow relesse	wyf /
That choys / and pray yow of that p*ro*fre cesse	prey of profre
¶For god it woot *þat* children ofte ben	For that been
Vnlyk hir worthy eldres hem bifore	Vnlyk
Bountee comth al of god / nat of the stren	Bou*n*tee streen
Of which / they been engendred and ybore	
I triste in goddes bou*n*tee / and ther fore	truste bontee / therfore
My mariage / and myn estat and reste	estaat
I hym bitake / he may doon as hym leste	
¶Lat me allone / in chesyng of my wyf	7 Lat chesynge wyf
That charge vp on my bak I wol endure	charge / bak / wole
But I pray yow / and charge vp on your*e* lyf	yow preye / youre lyf
That what wyf *þat* I take / ye me assure	What wyf that
To worshipe hire / whil *þat* hir lyf may dure	hire / that
In word and werk / bothe here and eu*er*ywhere	werk / heere euerywheere
As she / an Emp*er*ours doghter were	Emp*er*oures weere
¶And ferther moore / this shal ye swere / *þat* ye	And forthermoore / that ye
Agayn my choys / shal neither grucche ne stryue	shul
For sith / I shal forgoon my libertee	shal /
At your requeste / as euere mote I thryue	youre eu*er*e moot
Ther as myn herte is set ther wol I wyue	
And but ye wol assente / in swich manere	wole assente in this manere
I pray yow / speketh namoore of this matere	prey

7 ¶Clerk *89v*

¶With hertly wyl / they sworen and assenten
To al this thyng ther seyde no wight nay
Bisekynge hym of *gra*ce / er þ*a*t they wenten
That he wolde / graunten hem a *cer*tein day
Of his spousaille / as soone as eu*er*e I may
For yet alwey / the peple som what dredde
Lest that the Markys / no wyf wolde wedde

¶He graunted hem a day / swich as hym leste
On which / he wolde be wedded sikerly
And seyde / he dide al this at hir requeste
And they / with humble entente buxomly
Knelynge vp on hir knees / ful reuerently
Hym thanken alle / and thus they han an ende
Of hir entente / and hom agayn they wende

¶And her vp on / he to his officers
Comaundeth / for the feste to purueye
And to his pryuee knyghtes and Squyers
Swich charge yaf / as hym liste on hem leye
And they / to his comandement obeye
And ech of hem / dooth al his diligence
To doon / vn to the feste reuerence

¶Explicit prima pars

¶Incipit pars secunda

NOght fer / fro thilke paleys hon*ur*able
Wher as this Markys / shoope his mariage
Ther stood a Throop*e* / of site delitable
In which þ*a*t poure folk / of that village
Hadden hir bestes / and hir herbergage
And of hir labour token hir sustenance
After that the erthe / yaf hem habundance

197 Fuit haut procul a palacio et cetera El

ELLESMERE

hertely
wight
that
he / wolde certein
soone / eu*er*e he may

þ*a*t wyf /

entente /
knees
thonken
hir*e* hoom

heer hise officeres
purveye
hise p*ri*uee knyghtes Squieres

feeste

¶Explicit / prima pars

[8] ¶Incipit / secunda pars

NOght honurable
Ther as
There throop*e* /
which / that
beestes /
hir*e* labour / tooke

[8] ¶of Oxenford *90r*

With hertly wyl they sworen and assenten
To al this thyng ther seyde no wight nay
Bisekynge hym of grace er þt they wenten
That he wolde graunten hem a certein day
Of his spousaille as soone as eue[r] he may
For yet alwey the peple som what dredde
Lest that the markys no wyf wolde wedde

He graunted hem a day swich as hym leste
On which he wolde be wedded sikerly
And seyde he dide al this at hir requeste
And they with humble entente buxomly
Knelynge vp on hir knees ful reuerently
Hym thanken alle and thus they han an ende
Of hir entente and hom agayn they wende

And her vp on he to his officers
Comaundeth for the feste to purueye
And to his pryuee knyghtes and squyers
Swich charge yaf as hym liste on hem leye
And they to his comandement obeye
And ech of hem dooth al his diligence
To doon vn to the feste reuerence

Explicit prima pars

Incipit pars secunda

Noght fer fro thilke paleys honurable
Wher as this markys shoop his mariage
Ther stood a throop of site delitable
In which þt poure folk of that village
Hadden hir beestes and hir herbergage
And of hir labour token hir sustenance
After that the erthe yaf hem habundance

Amonge this poure folk ther dwelte a man
Which þt was holden pourest of hem alle
But heighe god som tyme senden kan
His grace in to a litel oxes stalle
Ianicula men of that thorp hym calle
A doghter hadde he fair ynogh to sighte
And Grisildis this yonge mayden highte

But for to speke of vertuous beautee
Thanne was she oon the faireste vnder the sonne
ffor pouerliche yfostred vp was she
No likerous lust was thurgh hir herte yronne
Wel ofter of the welle than of the tonne
She drank and for she wolde vertu plese
She knew wel labour but noon ydel ese

But thogh this mayde tendre were of age
Yet in the brest of hir virginitee
Ther was enclosed rype and sad corage
And in greet reuerence and charitee
Hir olde poure fader fostred she
A fewe sheep spynnynge on feld she kepte
She wolde noght been ydel til she slepte

And whan she homward cam she wolde brynge
Wortes or othere herbes tymes ofte
The whiche she shredde and seeth for hir lyuynge
And made hir bed ful harde and no thyng softe
And ay she kepte hir fadres lyf on lofte
With euery obeisaunce and diligence
That child may doon to fadres reuerence

Vp on Grisilde this poure creature
ffui ofte sithe this markys sette his eye
As he on huntyng rood parauenture
And whan it fil þt he myghte hire espye
He noght with wantowne lookyng of folye
Hise eyen caste on hir but in sad wyse
Vp on hir chiere he wolde hym ofte auyse

Commendynge in his

	ELLESMERE
[¶A]mong this poure folk / ther dwelte a man	Amonges thise
Which þ*at* was holden / pourest of hem alle	
But heighe god / som tyme senden kan	hye
His g*ra*ce / in to a litel Oxes Stalle	grace / oxes
Ianicula / men of that Throop*e* hym calle	**Ianicula** throop*e*
A doghter hadde he / fair ynogh to sighte	doghter ynogh sighte
And Grisildis / this yonge mayden highte	highte
¶But for to speke / of v*er*tuous beautee	But v*er*tuous bou*n*tee
Thanne was she / oon the faireste vnder the sonne	vnder sonne
For poureliche / yfostred vp was she	
No likerous lust7 was thurgh hir herte yronne	lust7 / thurgh hir*e*
Wel ofter of the welle / than of the tonne	ofter /
She drank7 and for she wolde v*er*tu plese	drank /
She knew wel labour / but noon ydel ese	labour7
¶But thogh this mayde / tendre were of age	But
Yet in the brest7 of hir virginitee	Yet7 hir*e*
Ther was enclosed / rype and sad corage	
And in gret reuerence / and charitee	greet reu*e*rence /
Hir olde poure fader / fostred she	fader7 shee
A fewe sheep*e* / spynnynge / on feld she kepte	spynnynge feeld
She wolde noght been ydel / til she slepte	noght7 ydel
¶And whan she homward cam / she wolde brynge	And
Wortes / or othere herbes / tymes ofte	
The whiche she shredde / and seeth for his lyuynge	for hir lyuynge
And made hir bed ful harde / and no thyng softe	bed / harde
And ay she kepte / hir fadres lyf on lofte	
With euery obeysance / and diligence	euerich obeisaunce
That child may doon / to fadres reuerence	reu*e*rence
¶Vp on Grisilde / this poure creature	
Ful ofte sithe / this Markys sette his eye	Markys caste his
As he / on huntyng rood p*ar* auenture	p*ar*auenture
And whan it fil / þ*at* he myghte hir*e* espie	when þ*at* it myghte espye
He noght7 wit wantowne lookyng of folye	noght / with
Hise eyen caste on hir*e* / but in sad wyse	
Vp on hir cheere / he wolde hym ofte auyse	Vpon chiere / he gan hym

Co*mm*endynge in his

177r Quire 23[8] (begins)

· The Clerk of Oxenforde ·

	ELLESMERE
¶Commendynge in his herte / hir wommanhede	9 Com*m*endynge
And eek hir vertu / passyng any wight	v*er*tu / passynge wight
Of so yong age / as wel in cheere as dede	chiere
For thogh the peple / hath no greet insight	hadde greet insight
In v*er*tue / he considered ful right	v*er*tu / right /
Hir bou*n*tee / and disposed þ*at* he wolde	that
Wedde hir*e* oonly / if eu*er*e he wedden sholde	euere wedde
¶The day of weddyng cam / but no wight kan	wight
Telle what womman / þ*at* it sholde be	Telle / that
For which m*er*ueille / wondred many a man	
And seyden / whan they were in p*ri*uetee	whan that they
Wol nat oure lord / yet leue his vanytee	vanytee.
Wol he nat wedde / allas the while	allas allas the while.
Why wol he thus / hym self and vs bigyle	wole bigile.
¶But nathelees / this Markys hath doon make	
Of gemmes / set in gold and in Asure	
Broches and rynges / for Grisildis sake	Brooches
And of hir clothyng took he the mesure	
Of a mayde / lyk to hir stature	By a lyk hir*e* stature.
And eek of othere / aournementes alle	eek othere aornementz
That vn to swich a weddyng sholde falle	
¶The tyme of vndren / of the same day	The time
Approcheth / þ*at* this weddyng sholde be	that weddyng
And al the palays / put was in array	paleys /
Bothe halle and chambres / ech in his degree	
Houses of office / stuffed with plentee	
Ther maystow seen / of deynteuous vitaille	
That may be founde / as fer as last Ytaille	
¶This Roial Markys / richeliche arrayed	This roial richely
Lordes and ladys / in his compaignye	ladyes /
The whiche / þ*at* to the feste were yprayed	that feeste weren
And of his retenue / the Bachilrye	bachelrye
With many a sown / of sondry melodye	soun /
Vn to the village / of the which I tolde	
In this array / the righte wey han holde	

9 ¶Clerk *90v*

Commendynge in his herte hir wommanhede
And eek hir vertu passyng any wight/
Of so yong age as wel in cheere as dede
ffor thogh the peple hath no greet insight/
In vertu he considered ful right/
Hir bontee and disposed þt he wolde
Wedde hir oonly if eue he wedden sholde

The day of weddyng cam but no wight kan
Telle what womman þt it sholde be
ffor which merueille wondred many a man
And seyden whan they were in priuetee
Wol nat oure lord yet leue his vanytee
Wol he nat wedde allas the while
Why wol he thus hym self and vs bigyle

But nathelees this markys hath doon make
Of gemmes set in gold and in asure
Broches and rynges for Grisildis sake
And of hir clothyng/ took he the mesure
Of a mayde lyk to hir stature
And eek of othere aournementes alle
That vn to swich a weddyng/ sholde falle

The tyme of vndren of the same day
Approcheth þt this weddyng sholde be
And al the paleys put was in array
Bothe halle and chambres ech in his degree
Houses of office stuffed with plentee
Ther maystow seen of deyntevous vitaille
That may be founde as fer as last ytaille

This roial markys richeliche arrayed
Lordes and ladys in his compaignye
The whiche þt to the feste were yprayed
And of his retenue the bachilrye
With many a sown / of sondry melodye
Vn to the village of the which I tolde
In this array the righte wey han holde

[Gris]ilde of this god woot ful innocent
[Th]at for hir shapen was al this array
To fecchen water at a welle is went
And cometh hom as sone as eu[er] she may
ffor wel she hadde herd seyd þt thilke day
The markys sholde wedde and if she myghte
She wolde fayn han seyn som of that sighte

She thoghte I wole wt othere maydens stonde
That been my felawes in oure dore and se
The markisesse and therfore wol I fonde
To doon at hom as soone as it may be
The labour which þt longeth vn to me
And thanne I may at leyser hir biholde
yf she this wey vn to the castel holde

Ut expeditis tamen aliis ad visendum dni sui sponsam cum puellis comitibus properet

And as she wolde ouer the thresshfold gon
The markys cam and gan hir for to calle
And she sette doun hir water pot anon
Bisyde the thresshfold in an oxes stalle
And doun vp on hir knees she gan to falle
And with sad contenance kneleth stille
Til she hadde herd what was the lordes wille

This thoghtful markys spak vn to this mayde
ffull sobrely and seyde in this manere
Where is youre fader o Grisildis he sayde
And she with reuerence in humble cheere
Answerde lord he is al redy heere
And she goth with outen lenger lette
And to the markys she hir fader fette

Cui Walterus cogitabundus incedens eamque compellans vbi

He by the hand than took this olde man
And seyde thus whan he hym hadde asyde
Janicula I neither may ne kan
Lenger the plesance of myn herte hyde
If that thow vouche sauf what so bityde
Thy doghter wol I take er that I wende
As for my wyf vn to my lyues ende

¶[Gris]ilde of this / god woot ful Innocent
[Th]at for hire shapen was / al this array
To fecchen water / at a welle / is went
And cometh hom / as soone as eu*er* she may
For wel she hadde herd seyd / þ*at* thilke day
The Markys sholde wedde / and if she myghte
She wolde fayn han seyn / som of that sighte

¶She thoghte / I wole w*ith* othere maydens stonde
That been my felawes / in oure dore and se
The Markisesse / and therfore wol I fonde
To doon at hom / as soone as it may be
The labour / which þ*at* longeth vn to me
And thanne I may / at leyser hir biholde
Yf she this wey / vn to the Castel holde

¶And as she wolde / ouer the thresshfold gon
The Markys cam / and gan hir*e* for to calle
And she sette doun / hir water pot anon
Bisyde the thresshfold / in an Oxes Stalle
And doun vp on hir knees / she gan to falle
And with sad contenance / kneleth stille
Til she hadde herd / what was the lordes wille

¶This thoghtful Markys / spak vn to this mayde
Ful sobrely / and seyde in this manere
Where is youre fader / o. Grisildis he sayde
And she with reu*er*ence / in humble cheere
Answerde / lord he is al redy heere
And she goth / with outen lenger lette
And to the Markys / she hir fader fette

¶He by the hand / than took this olde man
And seyde thus / whan he hym hadde asyde
Ianicula / I neither may ne kan
Lenger / the plesance of myn herte hyde
If that thow vouche sauf / what so bityde
Thy doghter wol I take / er that I wende
As for my wyf vn to my lyues ende

282 vt expeditis curis alijs ad visendum domini sui sponsam cum puellis comitibus propararet Hg El (281) Variant: visendum) videndum El

295 quam Walterus cogitabundus incedens eamque compellans nomine Hg El Variant: incedens) cedens El

ELLESMERE

¶Grisilde
That hir*e* / was
water welle
comth hoom /
that
myghte
fayn / sighte

10 She wole / with

Markysesse /
hoom /
that
hir*e*
If

And ou*er* hir thresshfold

set
Biside thresshfold
knes
w*ith*
had

thoghtful

o

Answerde · lord /
And In she gooth /

He thanne

thou sauf
þ*at*
to hir lyues

10 ¶of Oxenford 91r

// The Clerk / of Oxenforde //	ELLESMERE
¶Thow louest me / I woot it wel certeyn	Thou
And artꝛ my feithful lige man ybore	art feithful /
And al that liketh me / I dar wel seyn	that /
It liketh thee / and specially ther fore	therfore
Tel me that pointꝛ that I haue seyd bifore	poynt /
If that thow woltꝛ vn to that purpos drawe	thou pu*r*pos
To take me / as for thy sone in lawe	
¶The sodeyn cas / this man astoneyd so	¶This astonyed
That reed he weex abaystꝛ and al quakyngꝛ	wax
He stood / vnnethe seyde he wordes mo	vnnethes
But oonly this / lord quod he / my willyngꝛ	oonly thus / lord willynge//
Is as ye wole / ne ayeins youre likyngꝛ	ayeyns / likynge//
I wol no thyngꝛ ye be my lord so deere	
Right as yow list / gou*er*neth this matere	Rigħt lustꝛ mateere
¶Yet wol I / quod this Markys / softely	11 Markys
That in thy chambre / I. and thow . and she	thou /
Haue a collaciou*n* / and wostow why	why //
For .I wol aske / if it hir wille be	I axe / hir*e*
To be my wyf / and rule hir*e* after me	reule
And al this shal be doon / in thy p*re*sence	
I wol noght speke / out of thyn audience	noghtꝛ Audience
¶And in the chambre / whil they were aboute	
Hir tretys / which as ye shal after heere	
The peple cam / vn to the hous with oute	
And wondred hem / in how honeste manere	
And tentifly / she kepte hir fader deere	
But outrely / Grisildis wondre myghte	myghte
For neu*er*e eft / ne saw she swich a sighte	neu*er*e erstꝛ ne saugħ sighte
¶No wonder is / thogh þ*at* she were astoned	No thogh she
To seen so greet a gestꝛ come in to place	in that place
She neu*er*e was / to swiche gestes woned	
For which she looked / with ful pale face	which / *with*
But shortly / forth this matere for to chace	this tale for
Thise arn the wordes / þ*at* this Markys sayde	þ*at* the Markys
To this benygne / verray feithful mayde	benigne /

337 Et insolito tanti hospitis aduentu stupidam inuenit Hg El

11 ¶Clerk / *91v*

Thow louest me / I woot it wel certeyn
And art my feithful lige man ybore
And al that liketh me / I dar wel seyn
It liketh thee / and specially therfore
Tel me that poynt / that I haue seyd bifore
If that thow wolt / vn to that purpos drawe
To take me / as for thy sone in lawe

This sodeyn cas / this man astoneyd so
That reed he weex abayst / and al quakyng
He stood / vnnethe seyde he wordes mo
But oonly this / lord quod he my willyng
Is as ye wole / ne ayeins youre likyng
I wol no thyng / ye be my lord so deere
Right as yow list / gouerneth this matere

Yet wol I / quod this markys softely
That in thy chambre / I and thow / and she
Haue a collacion / and wostow why
ffor I wol aske / if it hir wille be
To be my wyf / and rule hir after me
And al this shal be doon in thy presence
I wol noght speke / out of thyn audience

And in the chambre / whil they were aboute
Hir tretys / which as ye shal after heere
The peple cam / vn to the hous with oute
And wondred hem / in how honeste manere
And tentifly / she kepte hir fader deere
But outrely / Grisildis wondre myghte
ffor neuere erst / ne saugh she swich a sighte

No wonder is / thogh þt she were astoned
To seen so greet a gest / come in to place
She neuere was / to swiche gestes woned
ffor which she looked / with ful pale face
But shortly / forth this matere for to chace
Thise arn the wordes / þt this markys sayde
To this benygne / verray feithful mayde

Et insolito tanti hospit' aduentu
stupidam inuenit

…ilde he seyde / ye shal wel vnderstonde
[I]t liketh to youre fader / and to me
That I yow wedde / and eek it may so stonde
As I suppose / ye wol þt it so be
But thise demandes / aske I first quod he
That sith it shal be doon / in hastif wyse
Wol ye assente / or ellis yow avyse

Et patri tuo placet inquit et michi vt vxor mea sis / et credo idem tibi placeat / set habeo ex te querere …

I sey this / be ye redy / with good herte
To al my lust / and þt I frely may
As me best thynketh / do yow laughe or smerte
And neuere ye to grucche it / nyght ne day
And eek whan I sey ye / ne sey nat nay
Neither by word / ne frownyng contenance
Swere this / and here I swere oure alliance

Sine vlla frontis aut verbi impugnacione

Wondrynge vp on this word / quakyng for drede
She seyde lord / vndigne / or vnworthy
I am to thilke honour / þt ye me bede
But as ye wol your self / right so wol I
And here I swere / that neuere willyngly
In werk ne thoght / I nel yow disobeye
ffor to be deed / thogh me were loth to deye

Nil ego inquit sciens nedum faciam set etiam cogitabo quod contra animum tuum sit / nec tu aliquid facies / etsi me mori iusseris quod moleste feram

This is ynough / Grisilde myn quod he
And forth he goth / with a ful sobre cheere
Out at the dore / and after that cam she
And to the peple / he seyde in this manere
This is my wyf quod he / that standeth heere
Honoureth hire / and loueth hire I preye
Who so me loueth / ther is namoore to seye

And for þt no thyng / of hir olde geere
She sholde brynge in to his hous / he bad
That wommen sholde despoylen hir right there
Of which thise ladys were noght right glad
To handle hir clothes / wher inne she was clad
But natheles / this mayde bright of hewe
ffro foot to heed / they clothed han al newe

Et hinc ne quid reliquiarum fortune veteris nouam inferat in domum nudari eam iussit

[¶Gris]ilde he seyde / ye shal wel vnderstonde
[It] liketh to youre fader / and to me
That I yow wedde / and eek it may so stonde
As I suppose / ye wol *þat* it so be
But thise demandes / aske I first quod he
That sith it shal be doon / in hastif wyse
Wol ye assente / or ellis yow auyse

¶I sey this / be ye redy / with good herte
To al my lust' and *þat* I frely may
As me best thynketh / do yow laughe or sm*er*te
And neu*er*e ye to grucche it / nyght ne day
And eek whan I sey ye / ne sey nat nay
Neither by word / ne frownyng contenance
Swere this / and heere I swere oure alliance

¶Wondrynge vp on this word / quakyng for drede
She seyde lord / vndigne / or vnworthy
I am / to thilke honour / *þat* ye me bede
But as ye wol your self' right so wol I
And heere I swere / that neu*er*e willyngly
In werk ne thoght' I nel yow disobeye
For to be deed / thogh me were looth to deye

¶This is ynough / Grisilde myn quod he
And forth he goth / with a ful sobre cheere
Out at the dore / and after that cam she
And to the peple / he seyde in this manere
This is my wyf quod he / that standeth heere
Honureth hire / and loueth hire I preye
Who so me loueth / ther is namoore to seye

¶And for *þat* no thyng' of hir olde gere
She sholde brynge in to his hous / he bad
That wommen / sholde dispoylen hir right there
Of which / thise ladys / were noght right glad
To handle hir clothes / wher Inne she was clad
But nathelees / this mayde bright of hewe
Fro foot to heed / they clothed han al newe

344 Et patri tuo placet inquid et michi vt vxor mea sis et credo idipsum tibi placeat set habeo ex te querere et cetera Hg El

356 Sine vlla frontis aut verbi impugnacione Hg El Variant: impugnacione) inpugnacione El

358 Nil ego vnquam sciens ne dum faciam set eciam cogitabo quod contra animum tuum sit nec tu aliquid facies et si me mori iusseris quod moleste feram Hg El Variant: feram) f. et cetera El

372 De hinc ne quid reliquiarum fortune veteris nouam inferat in domum nudari eam iussit Hg El Variant: iussit) iusserit El

¶Grisilde
It fader
yow /
that
axe

elles

I seye redy
that
smerte
it' nyght
eek'
frownyng'
swere yow alliance

quakynge
vndigne and vnworthy
Am I / honour' beede
wole your*e* right .I.
neuere
nyl
though

12 ynogh /
gooth /

þat
Honoureth hir*e* / hir*e*

And that geere
bad
wo*m*men / dispoillen hir*e* right theere
which ladyes / nat right
wherInne
bright

[12] ¶of Oxenford *92r*

¶Hir herys han they kembdꝭ / that laye vntressed
Ful rudely / and with hir fyngres smale
A coroune on hir heed / they han ydressed
And sette hir*e* ful Nowches grete and smale
Of hir array / what sholde I make a tale
Vnnethe the peple hir knew / for hir fairnesse
Whan she translated was / in swich richesse

¶This Markys / hath hire spoused with a ryngꝭ
Broght for the same cause / and thanne hir sette
Vp on an hors snow whytꝭ and wel amblyngꝭ
And to his palays / er he lenger lette
With ioyful peple / þ*at* hir ledde and mette
Convoied hire / and thus / the day they spende
In reuel / til the sonne gan descende

¶And shortly / forth this tale for to chace
I seye / þ*at* to this newe Markysesse
God hath / swich fauour sent hire of his *gra*ce
That it ne semed natꝭ by liklynesse
That she / was born and fed in rudenesse
As in a cote / or in an Oxes Stalle
But norissed / in an Emp*er*ours halle

¶To eu*er*y wightꝭ she woxen is so deere
And worshipful / þ*at* folkꝭ ther she was bore
That from hir burthe / knewe hir*e* yeer by yeere
Vnnethe trowed they / but dorste han swore
That to Ianicle / of which I spak bifore
She doghter were / for as by coniecture
Hem thoughte / she was another creature

¶For thogh þ*at* euere / v*er*tuous was she
She was encressed / in swich excellence
Of thewes goode / yset in heigh bou*n*tee
And so discreetꝭ and fair of eloquence
So benygne / and so digne of reu*er*ence
And koude so / the peples herte embrace
That ech hir louede / that looked on hir face

ELLESMERE

Hir heris kembd / lay
corone hir*e*
hir*e* / ful of Nowches
hir*e*
hir*e* fairnesse
was

hir*e* w*ith*
Broħt hir*e*
whitꝭ
paleys /
peple hir*e* ladde
Conuoyed hir*e* / thus

And
that
hath fauo*ur* / hir*e*
she was /
Oxe
Emp*er*oures

wiħt /
folk
And from hir*e* birthe /
That she to
doħter

13 For thouħ that eu*er*e
ysetꝭ heiħ
benigne /
hir*e* louede /

400 Atque apud omnes supra fidem cara et venerabilis facta est vix quod hijs ipsis qui illius originem nouerant persuaderi posset Ianicule natam esse tantus vite tantus morum decor ea verborum grauitas atque dulcedo quibus omnium animos nexu sibi magni amoris astrinxerat Hg El

13 ¶Clerkꝭ *92v*

Hir heris han they kembd / that laye vntressed
Ful rudely / and with hir fyngres smale
A coroune on hir heed / they han ydressed
And sette hir ful of nowches grete and smale
Of hir array / what sholde I make a tale
Vnnethe the peple hir knew / for hir fairnesse
Whan she translated was / in swich richesse

This markys / hath hire spoused with a ryng /
Broght for the same cause / and thanne hir sette
Vp on an hors snow whyt / and wel amblyng /
And to his paleys / er he lenger lette
With ioyful peple / þt hir ledde and mette
Conuoyed hire / and thus the day they spende
In reuel / til the sonne gan descende

And shortly / forth this tale for to chace
I seye / þt to this newe markysesse
God hath / swich fauour sent hire of his grace
That it ne semed nat / by liklynesse
That she was born and fed in rudenesse
As in a cote / or in an Oxes stalle
But norissed / in an Emperours halle

To euery wight / she woxen is so deere
And worshipful / þt folk ther she was bore
That from hir birthe / knewe hire yeer by yeere
Vnnethe trowed they / but dorste han swore
That to Ianicle / of which I spak bifore
She doghter were / for as by coniecture
Hem thoughte / she was another creature

For thogh þt euere vertuous was she
She was encressed / in swich excellence
Of thewes goode / yset in heigh bountee
And so discreet / and fair of eloquence
So benygne / and so digne of reuerence
And koude so / the peples herte embrace
That ech hir louede / that looked on hir face

atque apud omnes supra fidem cara et venerabilis facta
est vix ut ulli qui illius originem
nouerant persuaderi posset Ianicule natam esse
tantus vite tantus morum decor ea verborum grauitas
atque dulcedo quibus omnium animos nexu
sibi magni amoris astrinxerat

Noght oonly of Saluce in the town
Publissed was the bountee of hir name
But eek bisyde in many a regioun
If oon seyde wel another seyde the same
So spradde of hir heighe bountee the fame
That men and wommen as wel yonge as olde
Goon to Saluce on hire to biholde

Thus Walter lowely nay but roially
Wedded with fortunat honestetee
In goddes pees lyueth ful esily
At hom and outward grace ynogh hath he
And for he saugh that vnder lowe degree
Was ofte vertu hyd the peple hym helde
A prudent man and that is seyn ful selde

Sic Walterus humili quidem set insigni ac prospero matrimonio honestatis summa dei in pace etc.

Quod eximia virtute tanta sub inopia latitantem tam perspicaciter deprehendisset vulgo prudentissimus habebatur

Noght oonly this Grisildis thurgh hir wit
Koude al the feet of wifly humblenesse
But eek whan that the cas required it
The commune profit koude she redresse
Ther nas discord rancour ne heuynesse
In al that land that she ne koude apese
And wisly brynge hem alle in reste and ese

Neque vero solers sponsa muliebria tantum ac domestica set ubi res posceret publica etiam subibat officia

Though that hir housbonde absent were anon
If gentil men or othere of hir contree
Were wrothe she wolde bryngen hem aton
So wise and rype wordes hadde she
And iuggementz of so greet equitee
That she from heuene sent was as men wende
Peple to saue and euery wrong tamende

Viro absente lites patrie nobilium discordias dirimens atque componens tam grauibus responsis tantaque maturitate et iudicii equitate ut omnes ad salutem publicam demissam celo feminam predicarent

Nat longe tyme after that this Grisild
Was ywedded she a doghter hath ybore
Al hadde hir leuere haue born a knaue child
Glad was the markys and the folk therfore
For though a mayde child coome al bifore
She may vn to a knaue child atteyne
By liklyhede syn she nys nat bareyne

Explicit secunda pars

	ELLESMERE
[¶No]ght oonly / of Saluce in the town	¶Noght oonly Saluces toun
Publissed was / the bou*n*tee of hir name	Publiced the beautee of
But eek bisyde / in many a Regioun	biside / regioun
If oon seyde wel / another seyde the same	seide wel /
So spradde / of hir heighe bou*n*tee the fame	hir*e* heigħe bou*n*tee the name |
That men and wommen / as wel yonge as olde	wo*m*men /
Goon to Saluce / on hir*e* to biholde	Saluce / vpon
¶Thus Walter lowely / nay but roially	lowely ⁄ nay /
Wedded / with fortunat honestetee	
In goddes pees / lyueth ful esily	
At hom / and outward grace ynow hath he	hoom / outward / gr*a*ce ynogħ had he
And for he saugh / þat vnder lowe degree	saugħ / that vnder heigh degree
Was ofte vertu hyd / the peple hym helde	Was v*er*tu hid / heelde
A prudent man / and that is seyn ful selde	seelde
¶Noght oonly / this Grisildis / thurgh hir wit	¶Nat oonly thurgħ wit’
Koude al the feet’ of wifly humblenesse	wyfly
But eek’ whan þat the cas required it	that it’
The co*m*mune p*ro*fit’ koude she redresse	
Ther nas discord / rancour’ ne heuynesse	rancour /
In al that land / þat she ne koude apese	that she
And wisly / brynge hem alle in reste and ese	wisely / *and*
¶Thogh þat hir housbond absent were / anon	Though that hir*e* housbonde anon ⁄
If gentil men / or othere of hir contree	hir*e*
Were wrothe / she wolde bryngen hem aton	
So wise / and rype wordes / hadde she	wordes
And Iuggementz / of so greet equytee	Iuggementz equitee
That she from heuene sent was / as men wende	heuene / was
Peple to saue / and euery wrong tamende	
¶Nat longe tyme after that’ this Grisild’	tyme / after / that
Was ywedded / she a doghter hath ybore	wedded /
Al hadde hir leuere / haue had a knaue child	had hir*e* leu*er*e / haue born a man[14] child’
Glad was the Markys / and the folk ther fore	was this Markys / folk’ therfore
For thogh a mayde child / coome al bifore	though
She may / vn to a knaue child atteyne	a man child
By liklyhede / syn she nys nat bareyne	liklihede /
Explicit secunda pars	¶Explicit’ secunda pars

421 Sic Walterus humili quidem set insigni ac prospero matrimonio honestatis summa dei in pace et cetera Hg El

425 Quodque eximiam virtutem tanta sub inopia latitantem tam perspicaciter deprendisset vulgo prudentissimus habebatur Hg El

428 Neque vero solers sponsa muliebria tantum ac domestica set vbi res posceret publica eciam subibat officia Hg El

435 viro absente lites patrie nobilium discordias dirimens atque componens tam grauibus responsis tantaque maturitate et Iudicij equitate vt omnes ad salutem publicam demissam celo feminam predicarent Hg El

[14] Here, as in 447 and 612, the word ‘knaue’ has been erased, and the word ‘man’ substituted for it.

Incipit pars tercia The Cler[k of Oxenforde]	15 ¶Incipit tercia pars
Ther fil / as it bifalleth tymes mo	mo
Whan þat this child / hath souked but a throwe	had
This Markys / in his herte longeth so	
To tempte his wyf / hir sadnesse for to knowe	wyf
That he ne myghte / out of his herte throwe	
This m*er*ueilous desir / his wyf tassaye	m*er*ueilous desir
Nedelees god woot he thoghte hir*e* for tafraye	woot / thoghte / taffraye
¶He hadde assayed hir*e* / ynow bifore	He ynogħ
And fond hir eu*er*e good / what neded it	foond hir*e* it
Hir for to tempte / and alwey moore *and* moore	Hir*e* alwey / moore and
Thogh som men preyse it for a subtil wit	Thougħ preise wit /
But as for me / I seye þat yuele it sit	that
Tassaye a wyf / whan þat it is no nede	To assaye wyf
And putten hir*e* / in angwyssħ and in drede	Angwyssħ
¶For which / this Markys / wroghte in this manere	For
He cam allone a nyght ther as she lay	allone / nyght /
With steerne face / and with ful trouble cheere	stierne *with*
And seyde thus / Grisilde quod he that day	
That I yow took out of your*e* poure array	pouere
And putte yow in estat of heigh noblesse	yow / estaat heigħ
Ye haue nat that forgeten as I gesse	haue / nat that
¶I seye Grisilde / this p*re*sent dignitee	I
In which þat I haue put yow / as I trowe	that yow /. trowe
Maketh yow / nat foryetful for to be	yow nat
That I yow took in poure estat ful lowe	took / estaat
For any wele / ye mote your seluen knowe	moot your*e*
Tak hede of euery word / þat I yow seye	Taak heede / eu*ery* that y yow
Ther is no wight þat hereth it but we tweye	wight / that it
¶Ye woot your self wel / how þat ye cam heere	Ye your*e*
In to this hous / it is nat longe ago	
And thogh to me / þat ye be lief and deere	thougħ
Vn to my gentils / ye be no thyng so	
They seyn / to hem / it is greet shame *and* wo	and
For to be subgitz / and been in seruage	subgetz / and to been
To thee / that born art of a smal village	

449 cep[erit vt fit interdum Walterum cum] iam a[blactata esset infantula] mirabilis q[uedam quam laudabilis] cupiditas sa[tis expertam care fidem] coniugis experien[di altius et iterum] atque iterum rete[mptandi] Hg (defective) El

15 ¶of Oxenford *93r*

Ther fil / as it bifalleth tymes mo
Whan pt this child / hath souked but a throwe
This markys / in his herte longeth so
To tempte his wyf / hir sadnesse for to knowe
That he ne myghte / out of his herte throwe
This merueillous desir / his wyf tassaye
Nedelees god woot / he thoghte hire for taffraye

Cepit[...]
iam ut[...]
mirabilis[...]
cupiditas[...]
coniugis experien[...]
atque iterum seten[...]

He hadde assayed hire / ynowh bifore
And foond hire euere good / what neded it
Hire for to tempte / and alwey moore & moore
Thogh som men preyse it / for a subtil wit
But as for me / I seye pt yuele it sit
Tassaye a wyf / whan pt it is no nede
And putten hire / in angwyssh and in drede

For which / this markys / wroghte in this manere
He cam allone a nyght / ther as she lay
With steerne face / and with ful trouble cheere
And seyde thus / Grisilde quod he that day
That I yow took / out of youre poure array
And putte yow in estat / of heigh noblesse
Ye haue nat / that forgeten as I gesse

I seye Grisilde / this present dignitee
In which pt I haue put yow / as I trowe
Maketh yow / nat foryetful for to be
That I yow took / in poure estat ful lowe
For any wele / ye mote youre seluen knowe
Tak hede of euery word / pt I yow seye
Ther is no wight / pt hereth it / but we tweye

Ye woot youre self wel / how pt ye cam heere
In to this hous / it is nat longe ago
And thogh to me / pt ye be lief and deere
Vn to my gentils / ye be no thyng so
They seyn / to hem / it is greet shame & wo
For to be subgitz / and been in seruage
To thee / that born art / of a smal village

. . namely sith thy doghter was ybore
Thise wordes han they spoken doutelees
But I desire as I haue doon bifore
To lyue my lyf wt hem in reste and pees
I may nat in this cas be recchelees
I moot doon wt thy doghter for the beste
Nat as I wolde but as my peple leste

And yet god woot this is ful looth to me
But nathelees with outen youre wityng
I wol nat doon but this wol I quod he
That ye to me assente as in this thyng
Shewe now youre pacience in youre werkyng
That ye me highte and swore in youre village
That day þt maked was oure mariage

Whan she hadde herd al this she noght ameued
Neither in word or cheere or contenaunce — Nec vbo mota nec vultu
For as it semed she was nat agreued
She seyde lord al lith in youre plesaunce
My child and I with hertly obeisaunce
Been youres al and ye mowe saue or spille
Youre owene thyng werketh after youre wille

Ther may no thyng god so my soule saue
Liken to yow þt may displesen me
Ne I ne desire no thyng for to haue
Ne drede for to lese saue oonly thee — vel ye
This wyl is in myn herte and ay shal be
No lengthe of tyme or deth may this deface
Ne chaunge my corage to oother place

Glad was this markys of hir answeryng
But yet he feyned as he were nat so
Al drery was his cheere and his lookyng
Whan þt he sholde out of the chambre go
Soone after this a furlong wey or two
He pryuely hath told al his entente
Vn to a man and to his wyf hym sente

[¶And] namely / sith thy doghter was ybore
[T]hise wordes / han they spoken doutelees
But I desire / as I haue doon bifore
To lyue my lyf w*ith* hem / in reste and pees
I may nat⁊ in this cas be recchelees
I moot doon w*ith* thy doghter / for the beste
Nat as I wolde / but as my peple leste

¶And yet god woot⁊ this is ful looth to me
But nathelees / with outen your*e* wityng⁊
I wol nat doon / but this wol I quod he
That ye to me assente / as in this thyng⁊
Shewe now youre pacience / in your*e* wirkyng⁊
That ye me highte / and swore in youe village
That day / þ*at* maked was oure mariage

¶Whan she hadde herd al this / she noght ameued
Neither in word / or cheere / or contenance
For as it semed / she was nat agreued
She seyde lord / al lith in your*e* plesance
My child and I / with hertly obeisance
Been youres al / and ye mowe saue or spille
Youre owene thyng⁊ werketh after your*e* wille

¶Ther may no thyng⁊ god so my soule saue
Liken to yow / þ*at* may displesen me
Ne I ne desire / no thyng for to haue
Ne drede for to lese / saue oonly thee / vel ye
This wyl is in myn herte / and ay shal be
No lengthe of tyme / or deth may this deface
Ne chaunge my corage / to oother place

¶Glad was this Markys / of hir answeryng⁊
But yet he feyned / as he were nat so
Al drery was his cheere / and his lookyng⁊
Whan þ*at* he sholde / out of the chambre go
Soone after this / a furlang wey or two
He pryuely / hath told al his entente
Vn to a man / and to his wyf hym sente

ELLESMERE

And
Thise
nat caas /
doghter⁊
16 And
oute youre
youre werkyng⁊
highte / in youre village
that maked
had
chiere contenau*n*ce
lyth plesau*n*ce
hertely obeisau*n*ce
saue *and* spille
Your*e* youre
Ther thyng /
that displese
thyng⁊
leese / thee / . vel yee
deeth
to another place
hir*e*
out /
furlong
p*ri*uely / toold

499 Nec verbo mota nec vultu Hg El Variants: mota) *om.* El vultu) v. et cetera El

[16] ¶Clerk / *93v*

¶A maner sergeant / was this p*ri*uee man	A sergeantꝰ
The which *þat* feithful ofte / he founden hadde	
In thynges grete / and eek swich folk wel kan	
Doon execuciou*n* / in thynges badde	execuciou*n* on thynges
The lord knew wel / that he m loued and dradde	he hym loued *and*
And whan this sergeantꝰ wiste his lordes wille	s*er*geantꝰ wiste the lordes
In to the chambre / he stalked hym ful stille	
¶Madame he seyde / ye mote foryeue it me	moote
Thogh I do thyngꝰ to which I am constreyned	Though
Ye ben so wys / *þat* ful wel knowe ye	been that
That lordes hestes / mowe nat ben yfeyned	heestes / been
They mowe wel been / biwailled / or compleyned	biwailled and compleyned
But men mote nede / vn to hir lust obeye	moote hir*e*
And so wol I. / ther is namoore to seye	I /
¶This child / I am comaunded for to take	17 This child' / comanded
And spak namoore / but out the child he hente	
Despitously / and gan a cheere make	
As thogh he wolde / han slayn it er he wente	though
Grisildis moot al suffre / and al consente	Grisildis / suffren and consente
And as a lamb / she sitteth meke and stille	
And leet this crewel sergeantꝰ doon his wille	leetꝰ crueel s*er*geant
¶Suspecious was / the diffame of this man	¶Suspecious / was
Suspectꝰ his face / suspect his word also	suspectꝰ his word
Suspect / the tyme / in which he this bigan	Suspectꝰ
Allas hir doghter / *þat* she loued so	doghterꝰ that
She wende / he wolde / han slayn it right tho	wolde slawen rigħt
But nathelees / she neither weep*e* ne syked	
Conformynge hire / to that the Markys liked	Consentynge hir*e* / lyked
¶But at the laste / speken she bigan	But atte laste / to speken
And mekely / she to the sergeant preyde	
So as he was / a worthy gentil man	
That she moste kisse hir child / er *þat* it deyde	
And on hir barm / this litel child she leyde	And in hir
With ful sad face / and gan the child to blesse	child to kisse |
And lulled itꝰ and after gan it kesse	gan it blisse |

540 Suspecta viri fama Hg El

541 Suspecta facies Hg El

542 Suspecta hora Hg El

543 Suspecta erat oracio Hg El

17 ¶of Oxenford' *94r*

The clerk of Oxenford

A maner sergeant / was this pryuee man
The which þt feithful ofte / he founden hadde
In thynges grete / and eek swich folk wel kan
Doon execucion / in thynges badde
The lord knew wel / that he hym loued and dradde
And whan this sergeant / wiste his lordes wille
In to the chambre / he stalked hym ful stille

Madame he seyde / ye mote foryeue it me
Though I do thyng / to which I am constreyned
Ye ben so wys / þt ful wel knowe ye
That lordes hestes / mowe nat ben yfeyned
They mowe wel been biwailled / or compleyned
But men mote nede / vn to hir lust obeye
And so wol I / ther is namoore to seye

This child / I am comanded for to take
And spak namoore / but out the child he hente
Despitously / and gan a cheere make
As though he wolde / han slayn it er he wente
Grisildis moot al suffre / and al consente
And as a lamb / she sitteth meke and stille
And leet this cruel sergeant / doon his wille

Suspecious was / the diffame of this man — Suspecta viri fama
Suspect his face / suspect his word also — Suspecta facies
Suspect the tyme / in which he this bigan — Suspecta hora
Allas hir doghter / þt she loued so — Suspecta erat oracio
She wende / he wolde han slayn it right tho
But nathelees / she neither weep ne syked
Conformynge hire / to that the markys lyked

But at the laste / speken she bigan
And mekely / she to the sergeant preyde
So as he was / a worthy gentil man
That she moste kisse hir child / er þt it deyde
And in hir barm / this litel child she leyde
With ful sad face / and gan the child to blesse
And lulled it / and after gan it kesse

And thus she seyde in hir benygne voys
ffare wel my child I shal thee neuere see
But sith I thee haue marked with the croys
Of thilke fader blessed moote he be
That for vs deyde vp on a croys of tree
Thy soule litel child I hym bitake
ffor this nyght shaltow dyen for my sake

I trowe that to a norice in this cas
It hadde been hard this routhe for to se
Wel myghte a moder thanne han cryd allas
But nathelees so sad stedefast was she
That she endured al aduersitee
And to the sergeant mekely she sayde
Haue heer agayn youre litel yonge mayde

Goth now quod she and dooth my lordes heste
But o thyng wol I pray yow of youre grace
That but my lord forbad yow at the leeste
Burieth this litel body in som place
That beestes ne no briddes it torace
But he no word wol to that purpos seye
But took the child and wente vp on his weye

This sergeant cam vn to his lord agayn
And of Grisildis wordes and hir cheere
He tolde hym poynt for poynt in short and playn
And hym presenteth with his doghter deere
Som what this lord hadde routhe in his manere
But nathelees his purpos heeld he stille
As lordes doon whan they wol han hir wille

And bad this sergeant þt he pryuely
Sholde this child softe wynde and wrappe
With alle circumstances tendrely
And carie it in a cofre or in a lappe
But vp on peyne his heed of for to swappe
That no man sholde knowe of his entente
Ne whennes he cam ne whider þt he wente

	ELLESMERE
[¶A]nd thus she seyde / in hir benygne voys	And hir*e* benigne
Fare wel my child / I shal thee neu*er*e see	weel
But sith I thee / haue marked with the croys	sith / w*ith*
Of thilke fader / blessed mote he be	faderꝛ moote
That for vs deyde / vp on a croys of tree	
Thy soule litel child / I hym bitake	
For this nyghtꝛ shaltow dyen for my sake	nyghtꝛ
¶I trowe / that ⟨to⟩ a Norice in this cas	to norice
It hadde been hard / this routhe for to se	had reuthe
Wel myghte a moder / haue cryd allas	mooderꝛ thanne han
But nathelees / so sad stedefast was she	sad and stidefast
That she endured / al aduersitee	Aduersitee
And to the Sergeantꝛ mekely she sayde	s*er*geantꝛ
Haue here agayn / youre litel yonge mayde	heer your*e*
¶Goth now quod she / and doth my lordes heste	Gooth dooth heeste
But o thyngꝛ wol I pray yow / of youre grace	thyng / prey yow
That but my lord / forbad yow at the leeste	atte leeste
Burieth this litel body / in som place	
That bestes / ne no bryddes / it to race	beestes briddes /
But he no word / wol to that purpos seye	p*ur*pos
But took the child / and wente vp on his weye	vpon
¶This sergeantꝛ cam / vn to his lord agayn	18 cam ageyn
And of Grisildis wordes / and hir cheere	hir*e*
He tolde hym poynt for poyntꝛ in short and playn	pointꝛ for pointꝛ pleyn
And hym p*re*senteth / with his doghter deere	
Som what this lord / hadde routhe in his manere	Somwhat hath
But nathelees / his purpos held he stille	p*ur*pos heeld
As lordes doon / whan they wol han hir wille	Lordes
¶And bad this Sergeantꝛ *þ*at he pryuely	And bad his sergeantꝛ that
Sholde this child / softe wynde and wrappe	
With alle circumstances tendrely	circumstances /
And carie it in a cofre / or in a lappe	
But vp on peyne / his heed of for to swappe	
That no man sholde knowe / of this entente	of his entente
Ne whennes he cam / ne whider *þ*at he wente	vnde whenne / ne that

[18] ¶Clerkꝛ *94v*

	ELLESMERE
¶But at Boloigne / he to his suster deere	But Boloigne / to Suster
That thilke tyme / of Pauyk was Countesse	Pavik
He sholde it take / and shewe hir*e* this matere	mateere
Bisekynge hir*e* / to doon hir bisynesse	hir*e* bisynesse
This child to fostre / in alle gentilesse	gentillesse
And whos child ꝥ*at* it was / he bad hir*e* hyde	that bad hym hyde
From euery wight for aught ꝥ*at* may bityde	wight oght
¶The Sergeant goth / and hath fulfild this thyng	sergeant gooth /
But to this Markys / now retourne we	
For now goth he / ful faste ymagynyng	gooth ymaginyng
If by his wyues cheere / he myghte se	
Or by hir word ap*er*ceyue / that she	hire she
Were chaunged / but he neuere hir koude fynde	neu*e*re hire
But euere in oon / ylike sad and kynde	eu*e*re
¶As glad / as humble / as busy in seruyse	As glad / bisy
And eek in loue / as she was wont to be	eek
Was she to hym / in euery maner wise	eu*e*ry wyse
Ne of hir doghter / noght a word spak she	doghter
Noon accident for noon adu*er*sitee	Accident Adu*er*sitee
Was seyn in hir*e* / ne neu*e*re hir doghter name	doghter
Ne nempned she / in ernest ne in game	ernest / nor in
¶Explicit tercia pars	¶Explicit tercia pars
¶Incipit pars quarta	[19] ¶Sequit*ur* pars quarta
IN this estat / ther passed ben .4. yeer	estaat / been four
Er she with childe was / but as god wolde	
A knaue child she bar / by this Walter	A man[20] child
Ful gr*a*cious / and fair for to biholde	gracious /
And whan ꝥ*at* folk / it to his fader tolde	that folk
Nat oonly he / but al his contree merye	
Was for this child / and god they thanke and herye	

603 Par alacritas atque sedalitas solitum obsequium idem amor nulla filie mencio Hg El Variant: obsequium) obsquium El

610 transiuerant hoc in statu anni .4. dum ecce grauida et cetera Hg El Variant: .4.) iiij.or El

[19] ¶of Oxenford 95*r*

[20] Here, as in 444 and 447, the word 'knaue' has been erased, and the word 'man' substituted for it.

But at Bologne / he to his suster deere
That thilke tyme / of Pavyk was Countesse
He sholde it take / and shewe hire this matere
Bisekynge hire / to doon hir bisynesse
This child to fostre / in alle gentilesse
And whos child þt it was / he bad hire hyde
ffrom euery wight / for aught þt may bityde

The sergeant goth / and hath fulfild this thyng /
But to this markys / now retourne we
ffor now goth he / ful faste ymagynyng /
If by his wyues cheere / he myghte se
Or by hir word aperceyue / that she
Were chaunged / but he neuere hir koude fynde
But euere in oon / ylike sad and kynde

As glad / as humble / as bisy in seruyse
And eek in loue / as she was wont to be
Was she to hym / in euery maner wise
Ne of hir doghter / noght a word spak she
Noon accident / for noon aduersitee
Was seyn in hire / ne neuere hir doghter name
Ne nempned she / in ernest / ne in game

Erat alacritas atque sedulitas solita obsequium idem amor nulla filie mentio

Explicit tercia pars

Sequitur pars quarta

In this estat ther passed ben · 4 · yeer
Er she with childe was / but as god wolde
A knaue child she bar / by this Walter
fful gracious / and fair for to biholde
And whan þt folk it to his fader tolde
Nat oonly he / but al his contree merye
Was for this child / and god they thanke and herye

Continuant hoc in statu anni · 4 · dum ecce grauida &c

Whan it was two yeer old / and fro the brest /
Departed of his Norice / on a day
This markys / caughte yet another lest /
To tempte his wyf / yet ofter / if he may
O nedelees / was she tempted in assay
But wedded men / ne knowe no mesure
Whan þt they fynde / a pacient creature

Wyf quod this markys / ye han herd er this
My peple sikly berth this mariage
And namely / sith my sone yborn is
Now is it worse / than eue in al oure age
The murmur sleeth myn herte / and my corage
For to myne erys / comth the voys so smerte
That it wel neigh / destroyed hath myn herte

Now sey they thus / Whan Walter is agon
Thanne shal the blood of Janycle succede
And been oure lord / for oother haue we noon
Swiche wordes / seith my peple out of drede
Wel oghte I / of swich murmur taken hede
For certeinly / I drede swich sentence
Though they nat pleyn / speke in myn audience

I wolde lyue in pees / if þt I myghte
Wher fore / I am disposed outrely
As I his suster / serued by nyghte
Right so thenke I / to serue hym pryuely
This warne I yow / þt ye nat sodeynly
Out of youre self / for no wo sholde outraye
Beth pacient / and ther of I yow praye

I haue quod she seyd thus / and eue shal
I wol no thyng / ne nyl no thyng certeyn
But as yow list / noght greueth me at al
Though that my doghter / and my sone be sleyn
At youre comandement / this is to seyn
I haue nat had no part / of children tweyne
But first siknesse / and after wo and peyne

// Et olim ait audisti popu[...]
egre nostrum ferre connubi[...]

	ELLESMERE
[¶W]han it was two yeer old / and fro the brest'	Whan old'
Departed of his Norice / on a day	norice /
This Markys / caughte yet another lest'	
To tempte his wyf / yet ofter / if he may	ofter
O nedelees / was she tempted in assay	
But wedded men / ne knowe no mesure	
Whan þ*at* they fynde / a pacient creature	
¶Wyf quod this Markys / ye han herd er this	
My peple / sikly berth this mariage	berth oure mariage
And namely / sith my sone yborn is	
Now is it worse / than eu*er*e in al oure age	
The murmur sleeth myn herte / and my corage	m*ur*mure herte
For to myne erys / comth the voys so smerte	eres / sm*er*te
That it wel neigh / destroyed hath myn herte	ny /
¶Now sey they thus / whan Walter is agon	
Thanne shal / the blood of Ianycle succede	Ianicle
And been oure lord / for oother haue we noon	
Swiche wordes / seith my peple out of drede	
Wel oghte I / of swich murmur taken hede	oughte murm*ur* heede
For certeinly / I drede swich sentence	
Though they nat pleyn / speke in myn audience	Thougħ Audience
¶I wolde lyue in pees / if þ*at* I myghte	I wolde that mygħte
Wherfore / I am disposed outrely	
As I his suster / serued by nyghte	nygħte
Right so thenke I / to serue hym p*ri*uely	Rigħt pryuely
This warne I yow / þ*at* ye nat sodeynly	
Out of your self / for no wo sholde outraye	youre self' outreye
Beth pacient' and ther of I yow praye	preye
¶I haue quod she seyd thus / and eu*er*e shal	
I wol no thyng' ne nyl no thyng certeyn	certayn
But as yow list' noght greueth me at al	naugħt
Thogh that my doghter / and my sone be sleyn	Thougħ þ*at* dougħter / slayn
At youre comandement' this is to seyn	sayn
I haue nat had no part' of children tweyne	noght
But first siknesse / and after wo and peyne	

624 Et olim ait audisti populum meum egre nostrum ferre connubium et cetera Hg El   Variant: ait) *om.* El

The Clerk of Oxenforde ∫	ELLESMERE
¶Ye ben oure lord / dooth w*ith* youre owene thyngꝫ	21 Ye been with
Right as yow listꝫ axeth no reed of me	Riħt reed at me
For as I lefte at hom / al my clothyngꝫ	hoom /
Whan I first cam to yow / right so quod she	yow / ∕riħt
Lefte I my wyl / and al my libertee	
And took youre clothyngꝫ wherfore I yow preye	your*e*
Dooth your*e* plesance / I wol youre lust obeye	youre plesau*n*ce /
¶And c*er*tes / if I hadde prescience	And certes /
Youre wyl to knowe / er ye your*e* lust me tolde	Your*e* youre
I wolde it doon / with outen necligence	
But now I woot youre lust / and what ye wolde	your*e* lustꝫ
Al your*e* plesance / ferm and stable I holde	ferme
For wiste I / *þ*at my deeth / wolde doon yow ese	that do
Right gladly wolde I dyen / yow to plese	gladly / dyen
¶Deeth may nat make / no comparisou*n*	Deth noghtꝫ make
Vn to youre loue / and whan this Markys say	
The constance of his wyf / he caste adoun	
Hise eyen two / and wondreth *þ*at she may	
In pacience / suffre al this array	
And forth he goth / with drery contenance	
But to his herte / it was ful gret plesance	greet
¶This vggly s*er*geantꝫ in the same wyse	vgly sergeantꝫ
That he hir doghter caughte / right so he	hir*e* riħt
Or worse / if men worse kan deuyse	
Hath hent hir sone / *þ*at ful was of beautee	hir*e*
And euere in oon / so pacient was she	eue*r*e
That she / no cheere made of heuynesse	she chiere maade /
But kiste hir sone / and after gan it blesse	
¶Saue this she prayde hym / *þ*at if he myghte	Saue this / preyde that myħte
Hir litel sone / he wolde in erthe graue	
His tendre lymes / delicat to sighte	delicaat siħte
Fro foweles / and fro bestes / hem to saue	foweles beestes for to
But she noon answere / of hym myghte haue	myħte
He wente his wey / as hym no thyng roghte	thyng ne roħte
But to Boloigne / he tendrely it broghte	

660 Fac senciam tibi placere quod moriar volens moriar Hg El (663)

[21] ¶Clerk / *95v*

The clerk of Oxenforde

Ye ben oure lord / dooth wt youre owene thyng /
Right as yow list / axeth no reed of me
ffor as I lefte at hom / al my clothyng /
Whan I first cam to yow / right so quod she
lefte I my wyl / and al my libertee
And took youre clothyng / wher fore I yow preye
dooth youre plesance / I wol youre lust obeye

And certes / if I hadde prescience
youre wyl to knowe / er ye youre lust me tolde
I wolde it doon / with outen necligence
But now I woot youre lust / and what ye wolde
Al youre plesance / ferm and stable I holde
ffor wiste I / pt my deeth / wolde doon yow ese
Right gladly wolde I dyen / yow to plese

Ffac senciam tibi placere
Sy moriar volens moriar

Deeth may nat make / no comparison
vn to youre loue / and whan this markys say
The constance of his wyf / he caste adoun
hise eyen two / and wondreth pt she may
In pacience / suffre al this array
And forth he goth / with drery contenance
But to his herte / it was ful gret plesance

This vggly sergeant / in the same wyse
That he hir doghter caughte / right so he
Or worse / if men worse kan deuyse
Hath hent hir sone / pt ful was of beautee
And euere in oon / so pacient was she
That she / no cheere made of heuynesse
But kiste hir sone / and after gan it blesse

Saue this she prayde hym / pt if he myghte
hir litel sone / he wolde in erthe graue
His tendre lymes / delicat to sighte
ffro foweles / and fro beestes / for to saue
But she noon answere / of hym myghte haue
He wente his wey / as hym no thyng roghte
But to Bologne / he tendrely it broghte

This markys wondreth / euer lenger the moore
Up on hir patience / and if þt he
Ne hadde soothly / knowen ther biforre
That parfitly / hir children loued she
He wolde haue wend / þt of som subtiltee
And of malice / or of cruel corage
That she hadde suffred this / with sad visage

But wel he knew / þt next hym self certayn
She loued hir children best in euery wise
But now of wommen / wolde I asken fayn
If thise assayes / myghte nat suffise
What koude a sturdy housbond / moore deuyse
To preue hir wifhod / and hir stedfastnesse
And he contynuynge / eue in sturdynesse

But ther ben folk / of swich condicion
That whan they haue / a certeyn purpos take
They kan nat stynte / of hir entencion
But right / as they were bounden to that stake
They wol nat / of that firste purpos slake
Right so this markys / fulliche hath purposed
To tempte his wyf / as he was first disposed

He wayteth / if by word / or contenance
That she to hym / was chaunged of corage
But neuer / koude he fynde variance
She was ay oon / in herte and in visage
And ay the ferther / þt she was of age
The moore trewe / if þt it were possible
She was to hym in loue / and moore penyble

For which it semed thus / þt of hem two
Ther nas but o wyl / for as Walter leste
The same lust / was hir plesance also
And god be thanked / al fyl for the beste
She shewed wel / for no worldly unreste
A wif as of hir self / no thyng ne sholde
Wille in effect / but as hir housbond wolde

	ELLESMERE
[¶T]his Markys wondreth / euer lenger the moore	This Markys / wondred eu*er*e
Vp on hir pacience / and if þat he	that
Ne hadde soothly / knowen ther bifoore	
That p*ar*fitly / hir children loued she	
He wolde haue wend / þat of som subtiltee	
And of malice / or of cruel corage	or for crueel
That she hadde suffred this / with sad visage	this w*ith*
¶But wel he knew / þat next hym self c*er*tayn	22 But that certayn
She loued hir children best in euery wise	best wyse
But now of wommen / wolde I asken fayn	wo*m*men / axen
If thise assayes / myghte nat suffise	
What koude a sturdy housbond / moore deuyse	housbonde
To proue hir wifhod / and hir stedfastnesse	preeue wyfhod / or hir stedefastnesse
And he contynuynge / eu*er*e in sturdynesse	continuynge euere sturdinesse
¶But ther ben folk / of swich condiciou*n*	But been
That whan they haue / a certeyn purpos take	certein p*ur*pos
They kan nat stynte / of hir ententiou*n*	stynte hir*e*
But right as they were bounden to that stake	right
They wol nat of that firste purpos slake	
Right so this Markys / fulliche hath purposed	p*ur*posed
To tempte his wyf / as he was first disposed	
¶He wayteth / if by word / or contenance	He waiteth /
That she to hym / was chaunged of corage	changed
But neu*er*e / koude he fynde variance	
She was ay oon / in herte and in visage	
And ay the ferther / þat she was of age	forther / was in age
The moore trewe / if þat it were possible	
She was to hym in loue / and moore penyble	
¶For which it semed thus / þat of hem two	For
Ther nas but o wyl / for as Walter leste	
The same lust was hir plesance also	hir*e*
And god be thanked / al fyl for the beste	fil
She shewed wel / for no worldly vnreste	
A wif as of hir self no thyng ne sholde	wyf thyng
Wille in effect but as hir housbond wolde	housbonde
	22 ¶of Oxenford 96*r*

¶The sclaundre of Walter / ofte and wyde spradde
That of a cruel herte / he wikkedly
For he / a poure womman / wedded hadde
Hath mordred / bothe his children pryuely
Swich murmur / was among hem comunly
No wonder is / for to the peples ere
Ther cam no word / but *þat* they mordred were

¶For which / wher as his peple ther bifore
Hadde loued hym wel / the sclaundre of his diffame
Made hem / that they hym hated therfore
To ben a mordrer*e* / is an hateful name
But natheles / for ernest⁊ ne for game
He / of his cruel purpos nolde stente
To tempte his wyf / was set al his entente

¶Whan that this doghter / .xij. yer was of age
He to the court of Rome / in subtil wise
Enformed of his wil / sente his message
Comaundynge hem / swiche bulles to deuyse
As to his cruel purpos / may suffise
How *þat* the pope / as for his peples reste
Bad hym to wedde / another if hym leste

¶I seye / he bad they sholde contrefete
The popes bulles / makyng menciou*n*
That he hath leue / his firste wyf to lete
As by the popes dispensaciou*n*
To stynte rancour / and dissenciou*n*
Bitwix his peple and hym / thus seyde the bulle
The which / they han publissed at the fulle

¶The rude peple / as it no wonder is
Wenden ful wel / *þat* it hadde ben right so
But whan thise tidynges / cam to Grisildis
I deme / that hir herte was ful wo
But she / ylike sad for euere mo
Disposed was / this humble creature
Thaduersitee of Fortune / al tendure

crueel
he womman
p*ri*uely
m*ur*mure /

For where*e*
been mordrere
nathelees /
He crueel

23 that his doghter yeer
Rome wyse
wyl /
crueel purpos suffyse

I countrefete
makynge
rancour
Bitwixe
publiced atte fulle

that be righ̄t
tidynges
deeme / hir*e*
eu*er*emo

The Adu*er*sitee Fortune

722 ceperit sensi[m de Waltero] decolor fama cr[ebescere] Hg (defective) El

23 ¶Clerk *96v*

The sclaundre of Walter ofte and wyde spradde
That of a cruel herte he wikkedly
For he a povre womman wedded hadde
Hath mordred bothe his children prively
Swich murmur was among hem comunly
No wonder is for to the peples ere
Ther cam no word but pt they mordred were

Cepit sini[...]
de eo fama [...]

For which wher as his peple ther bifore
Hadde loved hym wel the sclaundre of his diffame
Made hem that they hym hated therfore
To ben a mordrer is an hateful name
But nathelees for ernest ne for game
He of his cruel purpos nolde stente
To tempte his wyf was set al his entente

Whan that his doghter .xij. yeer was of age
He to the court of Rome in subtil wyse
Enformed of his wil sente his message
Comaundynge hem swiche bulles to devyse
As to his cruel purpos may suffise
How pt the pope as for his peples reste
Bad hym to wedde another if hym leste

I seye he bad they sholde contrefete
The popes bulles makyng mencion
That he hath leve his firste wyf to lete
As by the popes dispensacion
To stynte rancour and dissencion
Bitwix his peple and hym thus seyde the bulle
The which they han publissed at the fulle

The rude peple as it no wonder is
Wenden ful wel pt it hadde ben right so
But whan thise tidynges cam to Grisildis
I deme that hir herte was ful wo
But she ylike sad for evere mo
Disposed was this humble creature
Thadversitee of Fortune al tendure

Abidynge after his lust and his plesance
To whom þt she was yeuen / herte and al
As to hire / verray worldly suffisance
But shortly / if this storie I tellen shal
This markys / writen hath in special
A lettre / in which he sheweth his entente
And secrely / he to Boloigne it sente

To the Erl of Panyk / which þt hadde tho
Wedded his suster / preyde he specially
To bryngen hom agayn / his children two
In honurable estat / al openly
But o thyng / he hym preyde outrely
That he to no wight / though men wolde enquere
Sholde nat tellen / whos children þt they were

But seye / the mayden sholde ywedded be
Vn to the markys of Saluce / anon
And as this Erl was preyd / so dide he
ffor at day set / he on his wey is gon
Toward Saluce / and lordes many oon
In riche array / this mayden for to gyde
Hir yonge brother / rydyng hir bisyde

Arrayed was / toward hir mariage
This fresshe mayde / ful of gemmes clere
Hir brother / which þt seuen yeer was of age
Arrayed eek / ful fressh in his manere
And thus in gret noblesse / and with glad cheere
Toward Saluces / shapyng hir iourney
ffro day. to day / they ryden in hir wey

Explicit quarta pars

Among al this

[¶A]bidynge eu*er*e / his lust' and his plesance
To whom *þ*at she was yeuen / h̄erte and al
As to hir*e* / verray worldly suffisance
But shortly / if this storie I tellen shal
This Markys / writen hath in special
A lettre / in which / he sheweth his entente
And secrely / he to Boloigne it sente

¶To the Erl of Pavyk' which *þ*at hadde tho
Wedded his suster / prayde he specially
To bryngen hom agayn / his children two
In honurable estat' al openly
But o thyng' he hym prayde outrely
That he to no wight' thgh men wolde enquere
Sholde nat tellen / whos children *þ*at they were

¶But seye / the mayden sholde ywedded be
Vn to the Markys of Saluce / anon
And as this Erl was prayd / so dide he
For at day set' he on his wey is gon
Toward Saluce / and lordes many oon
In riche array / this mayden for to gyde
Hir yonge brother / ridyng hir bisyde

¶Arrayed was / toward hir mariage
This fresshe mayde / ful of gemmes clere
Hir brother / which *þ*at seuen yeer was of age
Arrayed eek' ful fressh in his manere
And thus in gret noblesse / and with glad cheere
Toward Saluces / shapyng hir iourney
Fro day to day / they ryden in hir wey ∫

¶Explicit quarta pars

Among al this

ELLESMERE

Abidynge lust
hir*e*
which
secreely

To Pavyk /
suster' preyde
hoom agayn hise
estaat'
preyde
wigh̄t' though
telle /

But mayden /
Markys / Saluce
preyd /
goon
array
ridynge hir*e*

24 was
ge*m*mes cleere
.vij.
eek / fressh̄
greet *with*
shapynge
wey

¶Explicit' quarta pars

24 ¶of Oxenford' *97r*

	ELLESMERE
¶Incipit pars quinta ¶The [Clerk of Oxenforde]	¶Sequitur pars quinta
Among al this / after his wikke vsage	
This Markys yet his wif to tempte moore	wyf
To the outreste preue / of hir corage	outtreste preeue /
Fully to han / experience and loore	Fully / han
If that she were / as stedefast as bifore	stidefast bifoore
He on a day / in open audience	udience
Ful boystously / hath seyd hire this sentence	boistously / haþ
¶Certes Grisilde / I hadde ynogh plesance	ynogh
To han yow to my wyf / for youre goodnesse	
As for youre trouthe / and for youre obeysance	obeisance
Noght for youre lynage / ne for youre richesse	youre richesse
But now knowe I / in verray sothfastnesse	soothfastnesse
That in gret lordshipe / if I wel auyse	greet
Ther is gret seruitute / in sondry wyse	greet
¶I may nat do / as euery Plowman may	I doon / euery
My peple / me constreyneth for to take	
Another wyf / and cryen day by day	crien
And eek the pope / rancour for to slake	
Consenteth it that dar I vndertake	
And trewely / thus muche I wol yow seye	treweliche /
My newe wif / is comynge by the weye	wyf
¶Be strong of herte / and voyde anon hir place	Be
And thilke dowere / þat ye broghten me	that
Tak it agayn / I graunte it of my grace	Taak grace
Retourneth / to youre fadres hous quod he	
No man may / alwey han prosperitee	man / may prosperitee
With euene herte / I rede yow tendure	
The strook / of Fortune / or of auenture	This strook Auenture
¶And she agayn / answerde in pacience	25 answerde agayn
My lord quod she / I woot and wiste alway	woot
How þat bitwixen / youre magnificence	þat / bitwixen
And my pouerte / no wight kan ne may	wight
Maken comparisoun / it is no nay	
I ne heeld me neuere digne / in no manere	digne
To be youre wyf no / ne youre chambrere	wyf / youre Chambrere

25 ¶Clerk *97v*

Incipit pars quinta ¶ [illegible]

Among al this / after his wikke vsage
This markys yet / his wif to tempte moore
To the outtreste preeue / of hir corage
ffully to han / experience and loore
If that she were / as stedefast as bifore
He on a day / in open audience
fful boystously / hath seyd hire this sentence

¶ Certes Grisilde / I hadde ynogh plesance
To han yow to my wyf / for youre goodnesse
As for youre trouthe / and for youre obeysance
Noght for youre lynage / ne for youre richesse
But now knowe I / in verray soothfastnesse
That in greet lordshipe / if I wel avyse
Ther is greet seruitute / in sondry wyse

¶ I may nat do / as euery plowman may
My peple / me constreyneth for to take
Another wyf / and crien day by day
And eek the pope / rancour for to slake
Consenteth it / that dar I vndertake
And trewely / thus muche I wol yow seye
My newe wyf / is comynge by the weye

¶ Be strong of herte / and voyde anon hir place
And thilke dower / that ye broghten me
Tak it agayn / I graunte it of my grace
Retourneth to youre fadres hous quod he
No man may / alwey han prosperitee
With euene herte / I rede yow tendure
The strook of ffortune / or of auenture

¶ And she agayn / answerde in pacience
My lord quod she / I woot and wiste alway
How that bitwixen / youre magnificence
And my pouerte / no wight kan ne may
Maken comparison / it is no nay
I ne heeld me neuere digne / in no manere
To be youre wyf / no ne youre chambrere

And in this hous ther ye me lady made
The heighe god take I for my witnesse
And also wisly he my soule glade
I neuere heeld me lady ne maistresse
But humble seruant to youre worthynesse
And euere shal whil þt my lyf may dure
Abouen euery worldly creature

¶ That ye so longe of youre benygnytee
Han holden me in honour and nobleye
Where as I was noght worthy for to be
That thonke I god and yow to whom I preye
fforyelde it yow ther is namoore to seye
Vn to my fader gladly wol I wende
And with hym dwelle vn to my lyues ende

¶ Ther I was fostred of a child ful smal
Til I be deed my lyf ther wol I lede
A wydewe clene in body herte and al
ffor sith I yaf to yow my maydenhede
And am youre trewe wyf it is no drede
God shilde swich a lordes wyf to take
Another man to housbonde or to make

¶ And of youre newe wyf god of his grace
So graunte yow wele and prosperitee
ffor I wol gladly yelden hire my place
In which þt I was blisful wont to be
ffor sith it liketh yow my lord quod she
That whilom weren al myn hertes reste
That I shal goon I wol goon whan yow leste

¶ But ther as ye me profre swich dowaire
As I first broghte it is wel in my mynde
It were my wrecched clothes no thyng faire
The whiche to me were hard now for to fynde
O goode god how gentil and how kynde
Ye semed by youre speche and youre visage
The day that maked was oure mariage

	ELLESMERE
[¶A]nd in this hous / ther ye me lady made	And maade
The heighe god take I / for my witnesse	god / I
And also wisly / he my soule glade	wysly / glaade
I neu*er*e heeld me lady / ne maistresse	neu*er*e /
But humble seruantꝭ to youre worthynesse	your*e*
And eu*er*e shal / whil þat my lyf may dure	
Abouen / euery worldly creature	
¶That ye so longe / of youre benygnytee	That benignitee
Han holden me / in honour and nobleye	
Where as I was / noght worthy for to be	Wher*e* nogħt worthy bee
That thonke I god and yow / to whom I preye	god / yow / .
Foryelde it yow / ther is namoore to seye	
Vn to my fader / gladly wol I wende	
And with hym dwelle / vn to my lyues ende	
¶Ther I was fostred / of a child ful smal	Ther
Til I be deed / my lyf ther wol I lede	
A wydewe clene / in body / herte / and al	wydwe herte
For sith / I yaf to yow / my maydenhede	sith yaf / yow
And am youre trewe wyf / it is no drede	
God shilde / swich a lordes wyf to take	
Another man / to housbond / or to make	housbonde /
¶And of youre newe wyf / god of his *gra*ce	And grace
So graunte yow / wele and p*ro*sp*er*itee	yow prosp*er*itee
For I wol gladly / yelden hir*e* my place	
In which / þat I was blisful wont to be	which that bee
For sith it liketh yow / my lord quod she	shee
That whilom weren / al myn hertes reste	
That I shal goon / I wol goon whan yow leste	
¶But ther as ye / me p*ro*fre swich dowaire	But ye profre /
As I first broghte / it is wel in my mynde	brogħte /
It were my wrecched clothes / no thyng faire	clothes
The whiche to me / were hard now for to fynde	
O goode god / how gentil / and how kynde	gentil
Ye semed / by your*e* speche / and your*e* visage	youre youre
The day / that maked was oure mariage	

ELLESMERE

¶But sooth is seyd / algate I fynde it trewe
For in effect it proued is on me
Loue is noght old / as whan þat it is newe
But c*er*tes lord / for noon adu*er*sitee
To dyen in this cas / it shal nat be
That eu*er*e in word or werk / I shal repente
That I yow yaf myn herte / in hool entente

¶My lord ye woot þat in my fadres place
Ye dide me strepe / out of my poure wede
And richely / me cladden of youre grace
To yow broghte I / noght ellis out of drede
But feith / and nakednesse / and maydenhede
And here agayn / my clothyng I restore
And eek my weddyng ryng for euere moore

¶The remenant of your*e* Iewels / redy be
Inwith your*e* chambre / dar I saufly sayn
Naked / out of my fadres hous quod she
I cam / and naked moot I turne agayn
Al youre plesance / wol I folwen fayn
But yet I hope / it be nat youre entente
That I smoklees / out of your*e* palays wente

¶Ye koude nat doon / so dishoneste a thyng
That thilke wombe / in which youre children leye
Sholde biforn the peple / in my walkyng
Be seyn al bare / wher fore I yow preye
Lat me / nat lyk a worm / go by the weye
Remembre yow / myn owene lord so deere
I was youre wyf / thogh I vnworthy weere

¶Wher fore / in gerdou*n* of my maydenhede
Which þat I broghte / and noght agayn I bere
As voucheth sauf to yeue me to my mede
But swich a smok as I was wont to were
That I ther with / may wrye the wombe of here
That was youre wyf / and here I take my leeue
Of yow myn owene lord / lest I yow greeue

Ellesmere variants:

26 But
preeued
noght oold /
certes Adu*er*sitee
in the cas / bee
eu*er*e /
herte

My woot / that
streepe / weede

I elles /
feith
heere restoore
eek / ryng / eu*er*emoore

The Iueles
In with

your*e*
your*e*
paleys

Ye thyng /
your*e*
walkyng /
wherfore

your*e* though

Wherfore /
noght
sauf / me/ meede
wit*h* .i. cou*er*e wrye
your*e* heer take I
greue

[26] ¶of Oxenford *98r*

But sooth is seyd, algate I fynde it trewe
For in effect, it preued is on me
Loue is noght old, as whan þt it is newe
But certes lord, for noon aduersitee
To dyen in this cas, it shal nat be
That euere in word or werk, I shal repente
That I yow yaf myn herte, in hool entente

My lord ye woot, þt in my fadres place
Ye dide me strepe, out of my poure wede
And richely, me cladden of youre grace
To yow broghte I, noght ellis out of drede
But feith, and nakednesse, and maydenhede
And here agayn, my clothyng I restore
And eek, my weddyng ryng, for euere more

The remenant of youre jewels, redy be
Inwith youre chambre, dar I saufly sayn
Naked, out of my fadres hous quod she
I cam, and naked moot I turne agayn
Al youre plesance, wol I folwen fayn
But yet I hope, it be nat youre entente
That I smoklees, out of youre paleys wente

Ye koude nat doon, so dishoneste a thyng
That thilke wombe in which youre children leye
Sholde biforn the peple, in my walkyng
Be seyn al bare, wher fore I yow preye
Lat me nat lyk a worm, go by the weye
Remembre yow myn owene lord so deere
I was youre wyf, though I vnworthy weere

Wher fore, in gerdon of my maydenhede
Which þt I broghte, and noght agayn I bere
As voucheth sauf, to yeue me to my mede
But swich a smok, as I was wont to were
That I therwith may wrye the wombe of here
That was youre wyf, and here I take my leue
Of yow myn owene lord, lest I yow greue

The smok quod he / that thow hast on thy bak
Lat it be stille / and bere it forth with thee
But wel vnnethes / thilke word he spak
But wente his wey / for routhe and for pitee
Biforn the folk / hir seluen strepeth shee
And in hir smok / with heued & feet al bare
Toward hir fader hous / forth is she fare

¶ The folk hir folwen / wepynge in hir weye
And ffortune / ay they cursen as they goon
But she fro wepyng / kepte hir eyen dreye
Ne in this tyme / word ne spak she noon
Hir fader / that this tidynge herde anon
Curseth the day and tyme / þt nature
Shoop hym / to been a lyues creature

¶ ffor out of doute / this olde poure man
Was euere / in suspect / of hir mariage
ffor euere he demed / sith þt it bigan
That whan the lord / fulfild hadde his corage
Hym wolde thynke / it were a disparage
To his estat / so lowe for talighte
And voyden hire / as soone as euere he myghte

¶ Agayns his doghter / hastiliche goth he
ffor he by noyse of folk / knew hir comynge
And with hir olde cote / as it myghte be
He couered hire / ful sorwefully wepynge
But on hir body / myghte he it nat brynge
ffor rude was the clooth / and she moore of age
By dayes fele / than at hir mariage

¶ Thus with hir fader / for a certeyn space
Dwelleth this flour / of wyfly pacience
That neyther / by hir wordes / ne hir face
Biforn the folk / ne eek in hir absence
Ne shewed she / þt hir was doon offence
Ne of hir heighe estat / no remembrance
Ne hadde she / as by hir contenance

	ELLESMERE
[¶T]he smok quod he / that thow hast on thy bak	¶The thou bak
Lat it be stille / and bere it forth with thee	
But wel vnnethes / thilke word he spak	
But wente his wey / for routhe and for pitee	
Biforn the folk / hir seluen strepeth shee	she
And in hir smok / with heued *and* feet al bare	wi*th* heed / and foot al
Toward hir fader hous / forth is she fare	
¶The folk hir folwen / wepynge in hir weye	27 folk hir*e* folwe /
And Fortune / ay they cursen as they goon	Fortune cursen /
But she fro wepyng kepte hir eyen dreye	hir*e*
Ne in this tyme / word ne spak she noon	
Hir fader / that this tidynge herde anon	anoon
Curseth the day and tyme / þat nature	day / tyme that
Shoop*e* hym / to been a lyues creature	
¶For out of doute / this olde poure man	For
Was euere / in suspect of hir mariage	eu*ere* /
For eu*er*e he demed / sith þat it bigan	that
That whan the lord / fulfild hadde his corage	
Hym wolde thynke / it were a disp*ar*age	disparage
To his estat so lowe for talighte	estaat / talighte
And voyden hir*e* / as soone as eu*er*e he myghte	eu*er* myghte
¶Agayns his doghter / hastiliche goth he	Agayns
For he by noyse of folk / knew hir comynge	hir*e*
And with hir olde cote / as it myghte be	hir*e* coote /
He coue*re*d hire / ful sorwefully wepynge	hir*e* /
But on hir body / myghte he it nat brynge	hir*e* myghte
For rude was the clooth / and she moore of age	
By dayes fele / than at hir mariage	hir*e*
¶Thus with hir fader / for a c*er*tein space	hir*e* certeyn
Dwelleth this flour / of wifly pacience	wyfly
That neyther / by hir wordes / ne hir face	neither hir*e* hir*e*
Biforn the folk / ne eek in hir absence	hir*e*
Ne shewed she / þat hir was doon offence	that hir*e*
Ne of hir heighe estat no remembrance	hir*e* heighe estaat. remembrau*n*ce
Ne hadde she / as by hir contenance	hir*e* contenau*n*ce

27 ¶Clerk / *98v*

The Clerk of Oxenforde	ELLESMERE
¶No wonder is / for in hir grete estat	No hir*e* estaat
Hir goost was euere / in pleyn humylitee	Hir*e*
No tendre mouth / noon herte delicat	delicaat
No pompe / no semblant of realtee	roialtee
But ful / of pacient benygnytee	But benyngnytee
Discreet and pridelees / ay honurable	
And to hir housbonde / euere meke *and* stable	hir*e* and
¶Men speke of Iob / and moost for his hu*m*blenesse	moost humblesse
As clerkes whan hem lest konne wel endite	list /
Namely of men / but as in soothfastnesse	
Thogh clerkes / preyse wommen but alite	Though preise wo*m*men
Ther kan no man / in humblesse hym acquite	
As wommen kan / ne kan be half so trewe	wo*m*man ne been half
As wommen been / but it be falle of newe	wo*m*men
¶Fro Bologne / is this Erl of Pavyk come	28 Pavyk
Of which the fame vp sprong to moore *and* lesse	sprang and
And to the peples erys / alle and some	And in the eres /
Was kouth eek / þ*at* a newe Markisesse	that Markysesse
He w*ith* hym broghte / in swich pomp*e* *and* richesse	broghte / and
That neuere was ther seyn / w*ith* mannes eye	neu*e*re with
So noble array / in al westlumbardye	
¶The Markys / which þ*at* shoop*e* / and knew al this	that shoop*e*
Er that this Erl was come / sente his message	
For thilke / sely / poure Grisildis	sely
And she with humble herte / and glad visage	
Nat w*ith* no swollen thoght in hir corage	with hir*e*
Cam at his heste / and on hir knees hir sette	hir*e* hir*e*
And reuerently / and wysly she hym grette	reu*e*rently / wisely
¶Grisilde quod he / my wyl is outrely	
This mayden / þ*at* shal wedded been to me	that
Receyued be tomorwe / as really	Receiued be / to morwe roially
As it possible is / in myn hous to be	
And eek / that euery wight in his degree	wight
Haue his estat in sittyng and seruyse	estaat sittyng
And heigh plesance / as I kan best deuyse	heigh plesau*n*ce /

[28] ¶of Oxenford *99r*

No wonder is / for in hir grete estat
Hir goost was euere / in pleyn humylitee
No tendre mouth / noon herte delicat
No pompe / no semblant of realtee
But ful / of pacient benyngnytee
Discreet and pridelees / ay honurable
And to hir housbonde / euere meke & stable

Men speke of Iob / and moost for his humblenesse
As clerkes whan hem list / konne wel endite
Namely of men / but as in soothfastnesse
Thogh clerkes preyse wommen but a lite
Ther kan no man / in humblesse hym acquite
As wommen kan / ne kan be half so trewe
As wommen been / but it be falle of newe

Ffro Boloigne / is this Erl of Pavyk come
Of which the fame vp sprong / to moore & lesse
And to the peples erys / alle and some
Was kouth eek / þt a newe markisesse
He with hym broghte / in swich pomp & richesse
That neuere was ther seyn / with mannes eye
So noble array / in al westlumbardye

The markys / which þt shoop and knew al this
Er that this Erl was come / sente his message
ffor thilke / sely poure Grisilde
And she with humble herte / and glad visage
Nat with no swollen thoght / in hir corage
Cam at his heste / and on hir knees hir sette
And reuerently / and wysly she hym grette

Grisilde quod he / my wyl is outrely
This mayden / þt shal wedded been to me
Receyued be tomorwe / as really
As it possible is / in myn hous to be
And eek that euery wight / in his degree
Haue his estat / in sittyng and seruyse
And heigh plesance / as I kan best deuyse

haue no wommen suffisant certayn
The chambres for tarraye in ordinance
After my lust / and therfore wolde I fayn
That thyn were / al swich manere gouernance
Thow knowest eek of old al my plesance
Though thyn array be badde / and yuel biseye
Do thow thy deuoir / at the leeste weye

Nat oonly lord / that I am glad / quod she
To doon youre lust / but I desire also
Yow for to serue / and plese in my degree
With outen feyntyng / and shal euere mo
Ne neuere for no wele / ne no wo
Ne shal the goost / with inne myn herte stente
To loue yow best / with al my trewe entente

And with that word / she gan the hous to dighte
And tables for to sette / and beddes make
And peyned hire / to doon al that she myghte
Preyynge the chambreres / for goddes sake
To hasten hem / and faste swepe and shake
And she / the mooste seruysable of alle
Hath euery chambre arrayed / and his halle

Abouten vndren / gan this Erl alighte
That wt hym broghte / thise noble children tweye
ffor which the peple / ran to seen the sighte
Of hire array / so richely biseye
And thanne at erst / amonges hem they seye
That Walter was no fool / though þt hym leste
To chaunge his wyf / for it was for his beste

ffor she is fairer / as they demen alle
Than is Grisilde / and moore tendre of age
And fairer fruyt / bitwene hem sholde falle
And moore plesant / for hir heigh lynage
Hir brother eek / so fair was of visage
That hem to seen / the peple hath caught plesance
Comendynge now / the markys gouernance

	ELLESMERE
[¶I] haue no wommen suffisant c*er*tayn	I wom*m*en / suffisau*n*t certayn
The chambres for taraye / in ordynance	chambres / tarraye ordinau*n*ce
After my lust⁊ and ther fore wolde I fayn	therfore
That thyn were / al swich manere gouernance	man*ere* gou*er*nau*n*ce
Thow knowest⁊ eek of old al my plesance	knowest eek⁊ plesau*n*ce
Though thyn array be badde / and yuel biseye	Thogh badde
Do thow thy deuoir / at the leeste weye	thou
¶Nat oonly lord / that I am glad / quod she	.I. glad
To doon youre lust⁊ but I desire also	your*e* .I.
Yow for to serue / and plese in my degree	
With outen feyntyng⁊ and shal euere mo	eu*er*emo
Ne neuere / for no wele / ne no wo	
Ne shal the goost⁊ with Inne myn herte stente	w*ith*
To loue yow best⁊ with al my trewe entente	w*ith*
¶And with that word / she gan the hous to dighte	And digħte
And tables for to sette / and beddes make	
And peyned hir*e* / to doon al that she myghte	mygħte
Preyynge the chambreres / for goddes sake	
To hasten hem / and faste swepe and shake	
And she / the mooste seruysable of alle	
Hath euery chambre arrayed / and his halle	eu*ery*
¶Abouten vndren / gan this Erl alighte	29 aligħte
That w*ith* hym broghte / thise noble children tweye	
For which the peple / ran to seen the sighte	sigħte
Of hire array / so richely biseye	hir*e*
And thanne at erst⁊ amonges hem they seye	
That Walter was no fool / thogh þ*at* hym leste	thogħ
To chaunge his wyf⁊ for it was for his beste	wyf / for the beste
¶For she is fairer / as they demen alle	For deemen
Than is Grisilde / and moore tendre of age	
And fairer fruyt⁊ bitwene hem sholde falle	
And moore plesant⁊ for hir*e* heigh lynage	plesant⁊. heigħ
Hir brother eek / so fair was of visage	
That hem to seen / the peple hath caught plesance	plesau*n*ce
Co*m*mendynge now / the Markys gouernance	gouernau*n*ce

[29] ¶Clerk⁊ *99v*

The Clerk of Oxenforde	ELLESMERE
¶O. stormy peple vnsad / and eu*er*e vntrewe	¶Auctor] O peple /
Ay vndiscreet and chaungynge as a vane	
Delitynge eu*er*e in rumbel / þ*at* is newe	euere / rumbul that
For lyk the moone / ay wexe ye and wane	
Ay ful of clappyng deere ynow a Iane	ynogħ
Youre doom is fals / youre constance yuele preueth	preeueth
A ful greet fool is he / that on yow leueth	fool / þ*at* leeueth
¶Thus seyden sadde folk / in that Citee	Thus
Whan that the peple / gazed vp and doun	
For they were glad / right for the noueltee	rigħt
To han / a newe lady / of hir town	lady toun
Namoore of this / make I now mencioun	
But to Grisilde agayn / wol I me dresse	
And telle hir constance / and hir bisynesse	telle /
¶Ful bisy was Grisilde / in euery thyng	thyng
That to the feste / was ap*er*tinent	feeste /
Right noght was she abayst of hir clothyng	Rigħt noght hir*e*
Thogh it were rude / and somdel eek to rent	Thogħ somdeel
But w*ith* glad cheere / to the yate is she went	
With oother folk to greete the Markysesse	
And after that dooth forth hir bisynesse	hir*e*
¶With so glad cheere / his gestes she receyueth	With chiere / hise
And so konnyngly / euerich in his degree	
That no defaute / no man aparceyueth	ap*er*ceyueth
But ay they wondren / what she myghte be	bee
That in so poure array / was for to se	array see
And koude swich honour / and reu*er*ence	koude / honour
And worthily / they preysen hir prudence	preisen hir*e*
¶In al this mene while / she ne stente	30 In meene
This mayde / and eek hir brother to co*m*mende	
With al hir herte / in ful benygne entente	benyngne
So wel / þ*at* no man koude hir prys amende	pris
But at the laste / whan þ*at* thise lordes wende	atte laste /
To sitten doun to mete / he gan to calle	
Grisilde / as she was bisy in his halle	

30 ¶of Oxenford *100r*

O stormy peple vnsad / and eue vntrewe
Ay vndiscreet / and chaungynge as a vane
Delitynge eue in rumbel / þt is newe
ffor lyk the moone / ay wexe ye and wane
Ay ful of clappyng / deere ynogh a Iane
Youre doom is fals / youre constance yuele preueth
A ful greet fool is he / that on yow leueth

Thus seyden sadde folk / in that Citee
Whan that the peple / gazed vp and doun
ffor they were glad / right for the noueltee
To han / a newe lady / of hir toun
Namoore of this / make I now mencioun
But to Grisilde agayn / wol I me dresse
And telle hir constance / and hir bisynesse

fful bisy was Grisilde / in euery thyng /
That to the feste / was apertinent /
Right noght was she abayst / of hir clothyng /
Though it were rude / and somdel eek to rent /
But wt glad cheere / to the yate is she went /
With oother folk / to greete the markysesse
And after that / dooth forth hir bisynesse

With so glad cheere / his gestes she receyueth
And so konnyngly / euerich in his degree
That no defaute / no man aperceyueth
But ay they wondren / what she myghte be
That in so poure array / was for to se
And koude swich honour / and reuerence
And worthily / they preysen hir prudence

In al this meene while / she ne stente
This mayde / and eek hir brother to commende
With al hir herte / in ful benyngne entente
So wel / þt no man koude hir prys amende
But at the laste / whan þt thise lordes wende
To sitten doun to mete / he gan to calle
Grisilde / as she was bisy in his halle

Grisilde quod he / as it were in his pley
How liketh thee my wyf / and hir beautee
Right wel quod she my lord / for in good fey
A fairer / saugh I neuere noon / than she
I prey to god / yeue hire prosperitee
And so hope I / þt he wol to yow sende
Plesance ynogh / vn to youre lyues ende

O thyng / biseke I yow / and warne also
That ye ne prike / with no tormentynge
This tendre mayden / as ye han do mo
ffor she is fostred / in hir norisshynge
Moore tendrely / and to my supposynge
She koude nat / aduersitee endure
As koude / a pouere fostred creature

Unum bona fide precor ac moneo / ne hanc illis aculeis agites / quibus alteram agitasti namque et iunior et delicacius nutrita est pati quantum ego vt reor non valeret

And whan this Walter / saugh hir pacience
Hir glade chiere / and no malice at al
And he so ofte / had doon to hire offence
And she ay sad / and constant as a wal
Continuynge euere / hir innocence ouer al
This sturdy markys / gan his herte dresse
To rewen / vp on hir wyfly stedfastnesse

This is ynogh / Grisilde myn quod he
Be now namoore agast / ne yuele apayed
I haue thy feith / and thy benygnytee
As wel as euere womman was · assayed
In greet estat / and pouerliche arrayed
Now knowe I deere wyf / thy stedfastnesse
And hire in armes took / and gan hir kesse

And she for wonder / took of it no keep
She herde nat / what thyng he to hir seyde
She ferde / as she hadde stirt / out of a sleep
Til she / out of hir mazednesse abreyde
Grisilde quod he / by god þt for vs deyde
Thow art my wyf / noon oother I haue
Ne neuere hadde / as god my soule saue

	ELLESMERE
[¶]Grisilde quod he / as it were in his pley	¶Grisilde
How liketh thee my wyf / and hir beautee	hir*e* beautee /
Right wel quod she my lord / for in good fey	Rigħt
A fairer saw I neu*er*e noon / than she	saugħ noon
I prey to god / yeue hire p*ro*sp*er*itee	hir*e* prosperitee
And so Hope I / ꝥ he wol to yow sende	hope that
Plesance ynogh / vn to youre lyues ende	ynogħ /
¶O thyng biseke I yow / and warne also	O thyng
That ye ne prike / with no tormentynge	prikke /
This tendre mayden / as ye han do mo	doon
For she is fostred / in hir norissynge	hir*e*
Moore tendrely / and to my supposynge	
She koude nat adu*er*sitee endure	nat / Aduersitee
As koude / a poure fostred creature	
¶And whan this Walter / saw hir pacience	saugħ hir*e*
Hir glad cheere / and no malice at al	chiere /
And he so ofte / had doon to hir*e* offence	hir*e* /
And she ay sad / and constant as a wal	
Continuynge eu*er*e / hir Innocence ouer al [vbiq*ue*]	hir*e* oueral [.i. ubiq*ue*]
This sturdy Markys / gan his herte dresse	
To rewen / vp on hir wifly stedfastnesse	hir*e* wyfly
¶This is ynogh / Grisilde myn quod he	ynogħ /
Be now namoore agast ne yuele apayed	
I haue thy feith / and thy benygnytee	benyngnytee
As wel / as euere womman . was / assayed	eu*er*e womman was
In greet estat and poureliche arrayed	estaat.
Now knowe I deere wyf / thy stedfastnesse	I goode wyf /
And hire in armes took / and gan hir kesse	hir*e* hir*e*
¶And she for wonder / took of it no keep*e*	
She herde nat what thyng he to hir seyde	nat / hir*e*
She ferde / as she hadde stirt out of a sleep*e*	had stert out
Til she / out of hir mazednesse abreyde	
Grisilde quod he / by god ꝥ for vs deyde	that
Thow art my wyf / noon oother I haue	Thou
Ne neuere hadde / as god my soule saue	neu*er*e

1037 Vnum bona fide precor ac moneo ne hanc illis aculeis agites quibus alteram agitasti namque et iunior et delicacius nutrita est pati quantum ego vt reor non valeret Hg El

	ELLESMERE
¶This is thy doghter / which thow hast supposed	31 doghter / thou
To be my wyf / that oother feithfully	
Shal be myn heir / as I haue ay supposed	
Thow bare hym / in thy body trewely	Thou
At Boloigne / haue I kept⁊ hem pr*i*uely	kept
Tak hem agayn / for now maistow nat seye	Taak maystow
That thow hast lorn / noon of thy children tweye	thou
¶And folk / þ*at* oother weys / han seyd of me	And that ootherweys /
I warne hem wel / þ*at* I haue doon this dede	deede
For no malice / ne for no crueltee	
But for tassaye in thee / thy wommanhede	tassaye / thee wommanheede
And nat to sleen my children / god forbede	nat⁊ forbeede
But for to kepe hem / pryuely and stille	
Til I thy purpos knewe / and al thy wille	
¶Whan she this herde / / aswowne doun she falleth	herde /
For pitous ioye / and after hir swownynge	Ioye / hir*e*
She bothe hir yonge children / vn to hir*e* calleth	hir*e* yonge
And in hir armes / pitously wepynge	hir*e* Armes /
Embraceth hem / and tendrely kissynge	
Ful lyk a moder / with hir salte terys	mooder⁊ hir*e* teeres
She batheth / bothe hir visage and hir herys	bathed / hir*e* hir*e* heeres
¶O which a pitous thyng⁊ it was to se	
Hir swownyng⁊ and hir humble voys to heere	swownyng⁊. hir*e*
Grant m*er*cy lord / god thanke it yow / quod she	Grauntm*er*cy lord / that thanke I yow
That ye han saued me / my children deere	me
Now rekke I neu*ere* / to been ded right heere	deed right
Sith I stonde in your*e* loue / and in youre g*ra*ce	your*e* grace
No fors of deeth / ne whan my spirit pace	Nofors Spirit
¶O tendre / o deere / o yonge children myne	O tendre /
Youre woful moder / wende stedefastly	Your*e* mooder / stedfastly
That cruel houndes / or som foul v*er*myne	crueel
Hadde eten yow / but god of his mercy	
And youre benygne fader / tendrely	benyngne
Hath doon yow kept⁊ and in that same stounde	
Al sodeynly / she swapte adoun to grounde	

[31] ¶Clerk⁊ *100v*

This is thy doghter / which thow hast supposed
To be my wyf / that oother feithfully
Shal be myn heir / as I haue ay supposed
Thow bare hym / in thy body trewely
At Boloigne / haue I kept hem priuely
Tak hem agayn / for now maistow nat seye
That thow hast lorn / noon of thy children tweye

And folk / þt oother weys / han seyd of me
I warne hem wel / þt I haue doon this dede
ffor no malice / ne for no crueltee
But for tassaye in thee thy wommanhede
And nat to sleen my children / god forbede
But for to kepe hem pryuely and stille
Til I thy purpos knewe / and al thy wille

Whan she this herde / aswowne doun she falleth
ffor pitous ioye / and after hir swownynge
She bothe hir yonge children / vn to hire calleth
And in hir armes / pitously wepynge
Embraceth hem / and tendrely kissynge
fful lyk a moder / with hir salte terys
She batheth bothe hir visage and hir herys

O which a pitous thyng / it was to se
Hir swownyng / and hir humble voys to heere
Grant mercy lord / god thanke it yow / quod she
That ye han saued me / my children deere
Now rekke I neuere / to been deed right heere
Sith I stonde in youre loue / and in youre grace
No fors of deeth / ne whan my spirit pace

O tendre / o deere / o yonge children myne
Youre woful moder / wende stedefastly
That cruel houndes / or som foul vermyne
Hadde eten yow / but god of his mercy
And youre benygne fader / tendrely
Hath doon yow kept / and in that same stounde
Al sodeynly / she swapte adoun to grounde

And in hir swough / so sadly holdeth she
Hir children two / whan she gan hem tembrace
That with greet sleighte / and greet difficultee
The children from hir arm / they gonne arace
O many a teer / o many a pitous face
Doun ran / of hem þt stoden hir bisyde
Unnethe aboute hire / myghte they abyde

¶ Walter hir gladeth / and hir sorwe slaketh
She riseth up abaysed / from hir traunce
And every wight / hir joye and feste maketh
Til she / hath caught agayn hir contenaunce
Walter hir dooth / so feithfully plesaunce
That it was deyntee / for to seen the cheere
Bitwix hem two / now they ben met yfeere

¶ Thise ladies / whan þt they hir tyme say
Han taken hire / and in to chambre goon
And strepen hire / out of hir rude array
And in a clooth of gold / þt brighte shoon
With a coroune / of many a riche stoon
Up on hir hed they in to halle hire broghte
And ther she was / honured as hir oghte

¶ Thus hath this pitous day / a blisful ende
ffor every man and womman / dooth his myght /
This day / in murthe and revel to dispende
Til on the welkne / shoon the sterres lyght /
ffor moore solempne / in every mannes syght /
This feste was / and gretter of costage
Than was / the revel of hir mariage

¶ fful many a yeer / in heigh prosperitee
Lyven thise two / in concord and in reste
And richely / his doghter maried he
Un to a lord / oon of the worthieste
Of al ytaille / and thanne in pees and reste
His wyves fader / and his court he kepeth
Til that the soule / out of his body crepeth

[¶]And in hir swogħ / so sadly holdeth she
Hir children two / whan she gan hem tembrace
That with greet sleghte / and greet difficultee
The children from hir arm / they gonne arace
O· many a teer / o many a pitous face
Doun ran / of hem *þat* stoden hir bisyde
Vnnethe aboute hir*e* / myghte they abyde

¶Walter hir gladeth / and hir sorwe slaketh
She riseth vp abaysed / from hir traunce
And euery wight hir ioye and feste maketh
Til she / hath caught agayn hir contenau*n*ce
Walter hir dooth / so feithfully plesau*n*ce
That it was deyntee / for to seen the cheere
Bitwix hem two / now they ben met yfeere

¶Thise ladies / whan *þat* they / hir tyme say
Han taken hir*e* / and in to chambre goon
And strepen hir*e* / out of hir rude aray
And in a clooth of gold / *þat* brighte shoon
With a coroune / of many a riche stoon
Vp on hir hed / they in to halle hir broghte
And ther she was / honured as hir oghte

¶Thus hath this pitous day / a blisful ende
For euery man and womman / dooth his myght
This day / in murthe and reuel to dispende
Til on the welkne / shoon the sterres lyght
For moore solempne / in euery mannes syght
This feste was / and gretter of costage
Than was / the reuel of hir mariage

¶Ful many a yeer / in heigh p*ro*sp*er*itee
Lyuen thise two / in concord and in reste
And richely / his doghter maried he
Vn to a lord / oon of the worthyeste
Of al Ytaille / and thanne in pees and reste
His wyues fader / and his court he kepeth
Til that the soule / out of his body crepeth

ELLESMERE

And hir*e* swougħ /
Hir*e*
with sleighte /
children / hir*e*
O teere / on many
stooden hir*e*
abouten myghte

32 hir*e* hir*e* slakethħ
hir*e* trau*n*ce
wighħt / hir*e* feeste makethħ
hir*e*
hir*e*

Bitwixe been

ladyes / that they
gon
hir*e* rude array
brighte
richħe
hir*e* heed / hir*e* broghte
hir*e* oghte

Thus day
eu*er*y wo*m*man myght
lyght
syght
reuel / hir*e*

maryed
worthieste
fader / in his kepethħ
that crepethħ

[32] ¶of Oxenford *101r*

	ELLESMERE
¶His sone / succedeth in his heritage	His sone /
In reste and pees / after his fader day	
And fortunat was eek his mariage	eek in mariage
Al putte he nat his wyf in gret assay	wyf / greet
This world is nat so strong it is no nay	
As it hath been / in olde tymes yore	been / of olde yoore
And herkneth / what this Auctour seith therfore	ther foore
¶This storie is seyd / nat for *þat* wyues sholde	that
Folwen Grisilde / as in humylitee	
For it were inportable / thogh they wolde	though
But for *þat* euery wight in his degree	that wight
Sholde be constant in aduersitee	Aduersitee
As was Grisilde / therfore Petrak writeth	petrak
This storie / which he with heigh stile enditeth /	which *with* heigh stile he enditeth
¶For sith a womman / was so pacient	33 For
Vn to a mortal man / wel moore vs oghte	oghte
Receyuen al in gree / that god vs sent	sent
For gret skile is / he preue that he wroghte	greet preeue wroghte
But he ne tempteth / no man *þat* he boghte	he / tempteth man / that boghte
As seith Seint Iame / if ye his pistel rede	
He preueth folk al day / it is no drede	preeueth
¶And suffreth vs / as for oure excercise	And
With sharpe scourges / of aduersitee	Aduersitee
Ful ofte to be bete / in sondry wise	ofte / bete
Nat for to knowe oure wyl / for *cer*tes he	he
Er we were born / knew al oure freletee	knew oure
And for oure beste / is al his gouernance	gou*er*nau*n*ce
Lat vs thanne lyue / in v*er*tuous suffrance	suffra*un*ce
¶But o word lordynges / herkneth er I go	
It were ful hard / to fynde now a dayes	
In al a town / Grisildis thre or two	toun / Grisildis /
For if *þat* they were put to swiche assayes	
The gold of hem / hath now so badde alayes	
With bras / that thogh the coigne / be fair at eye	*þat* thogh coyne
It wolde rather / breste atwo than plye	

1142 hanc historiam stilo nunc alto retexere v[isum fuit] non tum ideo vt matronas nostri temporis [ad] imitandam huius vxoris pacienciam que mich[i] inimitabilis videtur quam vt legentes ad imitandam saltem femine constanciam excitarentur Vt quod hec viro suo prestitit hoc prestare deo nostro audeat quilibet Vt Iacobus ait Apostolus Intemptator sit malorum et ipse neminem temptat probat tum et sepe nos multis ac grauibus flagellis excerceri sinit non vt animum nostrum sciat quem sciuit antequam crearemur et cetera Hg (defective) El Variant: excitarentur) excitarent El

33 ¶Clerk *101v*

This sone succedeth in his heritage
In reste and pees / after his fader day
And fortunat / was eek his mariage
Al putte he nat his wyf in gret assay
This world is nat so strong / it is no nay
As it hath been in olde tymes yore
And herkneth / what this Auctour seith therfore

This storie is seyd / nat for þt wyues sholde
ffolwen Grisilde / as in humylitee
ffor it were inpor-table / thogh they wolde
But for þt euery wight / in his degree
Sholde be constant / in aduersitee
As was Grisilde / ther fore Petrak writeth
This storie / which he with heigh stile enditeth

Hanc historiam stilo nunc alto retexere visum
non tamen ideo ut matronas nostri temporis
imitanda huius uxoris paciencia que michi
inimitabilis videtur / quam ut legentes ad
imitandam saltem femine constanciam excitarentur
Ut quod hec viro suo prestitit / hoc prestare deo nostro
audeat quilibet / ut Iacobus ait apostolus / Intemptator sit malorum et ipse neminem temptat / probat tamen
et sepe nos multis ac grauibus flagellis exerceri
sinit / non ut animum nostrum sciat / quem sciuit antequam
crearemur etc

ffor sith a womman / was so pacient /
Vn to a mortal man / wel moore vs oghte
Receyuen al in gree / that god vs sent
ffor gret skile is / he preue that he wroghte
But he ne tempteth / no man þt he boghte
As seith seint Iame / if ye his pistel rede
He preueth folk al day / it is no drede

And suffreth vs / as for oure excercise
With sharpe scourges / of aduersitee
fful ofte to be bete / in sondry wise
Nat for to knowe oure wyl / for certes he
Er we were born / knew al oure freletee
And for oure beste / is al his gouernaunce
lat vs thanne lyue / in vertuous suffraunce

But o word lordynges / herkneth er I go
It were ful hard / to fynde now a dayes
In al a town / Grisildis thre or two
ffor if þt they were put / to swiche assayes
The gold of hem / hath now so badde alayes
With bras / that thogh the coyne be fair at eye
It wolde rather / breste atwo than plye

For which heere for the wyues loue of Bathe
Whos lyf and al hir secte god mayntene
In heigh maistrye or ellis were it scathe
I wol with lusty herte fressh and grene
Seyn yow a song to glade yow I wene
And lat vs stynte of ernestful matere
Herkneth my song that seith in this manere

Here is ended the tale of the clerk of Oxenford

Lenuoy de Chaucer

Grisilde is deed and eek hir pacience
And bothe atones buryed in ytaille
For which I crye in open audience
No wedded man so hardy be tassaille
His wyues pacience in trust to fynde
Grisildis for in certein he shal faille

O noble wyues ful of heigh prudence
Lat noon humilitee youre tonge nayle
Ne lat no clerk haue cause or diligence
To write of yow a storie of swich meruaille
As of Grisildis pacient and kynde
Lest Chichyuache yow swelwe in hir entraille

Folweth Ekko that holdeth no silence
But euere answereth at the countretaille
Beth nat bidaffed for youre Innocence
But sharply tak on yow the gouernaille
Emprenteth wel this lesson in youre mynde
For commune profit sith it may auaille

[¶]For which heere / for the wyues loue of Bathe
Whos lyf7 / and al hir secte / god mayntene
In heigh maistrie / or ellis were it scathe
I wol with lusty herte / fressħ and grene
Seye yow a song7 to glade yow I wene
And lat vs stynte / of ernestful matere
Herkneth my song7 that seith in this manere

¶Here is ended the tale / of the clerk of7 Oxenfordˡ [34]

¶Lenuoy de Chaucer

GRisilde is deed / and eek hir pacience
And bothe atones / buryed in Ytaille
For which I cryė / in open audience
No wedded man / so hardy be tassaille
His wyues pacience / in trust to fynde
Grisildis / for in c*er*tein he shal faille

¶O noble wyues / ful of heigh prudence
Lat noon humilitee / youre tonge nayle
Ne lat no clerk / haue cause or diligence
To write of yow / a storie of swich m*er*uaile
As of Grisildis / pacient and kynde
Lest Chichyuache / yow swelwe in hir entrayle

¶Folweth Ekko / that holdeth no silence
But eu*er*e answereth / at the countretaile
Beth nat bidaffed / for youre Innocence
But sharply / tak on yow the gouernaile
Emp*ri*nteth wel / this lessou*n* in your*e* mynde
For com*m*une p*ro*fit7 sith it may auaile

For
lyf7 hir*e* secte
maistrie / and elles

Seyn

34

¶Lenuoy de Chaucer

Grisilde hir*e*

crie /

in hope to
certein

O ful / heigħ
humylitee / naille

m*er*uaille

Chichiuache / hir*e* entraille

35 Folweth
countretaille
bidaffed
taak gou*er*naille
wel youre
auaille

[34] Rubric *Out* El
[35] ¶of Oxenfordˡ *102r*

	ELLESMERE
¶Ye Archewyues / stondeth at defense	Ye Archiwyues /
Syn ye be strong as is a gret Camaile	greet Camaille
Ne suffreth nat þ*at* men yow doon offense	nat /
And sklendre wyues / fieble as in bataile	bataille
Beth egre / as is a tigre yond in Ynde	Tygre
Ay clappeth as a Mille / I yow consaile	consaille
¶Ne dreed hem nat dooth hem no reue*re*nce	Ne doth
For thogh thyn housbond / armed be in maile	though housbonde / maille
The arwes / of thy crabbed eloquence	
Shal p*er*ce his brest and eek his auentaile	eek auentaille
In Ialousie / I rede eek thow hym bynde	eek thou
And thow shalt make hym couche / as dooth a Quaile	thou couche doth quaille
¶If thow be fair / ther folk ben in p*re*sence	If thou fair been
Shewe thow thy visage / and thyn aparaile	thou app*ar*aille
If thow be foul / be fre of thy dispence	thou
To gete thee freendes / ay do thy trauaile	*tra*uaille
Be ay of cheere / as light as leef on lynde	chiere / light
And lat hym care and wepe / and wrynge *and* wayle	care *and* wepe / waille
¶Explicit	¶Bihoold the murye wordes of the Hoost
¶This worthy Clerk whan ended was his tale	This clerk /
Oure hoost seyde / and swoor by goddes bones	
Me were leuere / than a barel ale	
My wyf at hom / had herd this legende ones	hoom /
This is / a gentil tale for the nones	is tale /
As to my purpos / wiste ye my wille	p*ur*pos /
But thyng that wol nat be / lat it be stille	thyng þat
	¶Heere endeth the tale / of the Clerk of Oxenford

Ye archewyues / stondeth at defense
Syn ye be strong / as is a greet Camaille
Ne suffreth nat / þt men yow doon offense
And sklendre wyues / fieble as in bataille
Beth egre / as is a tygre yond in Ynde
Ay clappeth as a Mille / I yow consaille

Ne drede hem nat / doth hem no reuerence
For thogh thyn housbond / armed be in maille
The arwes / of thy crabbed eloquence
Shal perce his brest / and eek his auentaille
In Ialousie / I rede eek thow hym bynde
And thow shalt make hym couche / as doth a Quaille

If thow be fair / ther folk ben in presence
Shewe thow thy visage and thyn apparaille
If thow be foul / be fre of thy dispence
To gete thee freendes / ay do thy trauaille
Be ay of cheere / as light as leef on lynde
And lat hym care and wepe / and wrynge & wayle

Explicit

This worthy Clerk / whan ended was his tale
Oure hoost seyde / and swoor by goddes bones
Me were leuere / than a barel ale
My wyf at hoom / had herd this legende ones
This is a gentil tale for the nones
As to my purpos / wiste ye my wille
But thyng that wol nat be / lat it be stille

Heere bigynneth the Phisitiens tale

Ther was as telleth Titus liuius
A knyght that called was Virginius
ffulfild of honour and of worthynesse
And strong of freendes and of greet richesse
This knyght a doghter hadde by his wif
No children hadde he mo in al his lif
ffair was this mayde in excellent beautee
Abouen euery wight þt man may see
ffor nature hath with souereyn diligence
yformed hire in so greet excellence
As though she wolde seyn lo I nature
Thus kan I forme and peynte a creature
Whan þt me list who kan me countrefete
Pigmalion noght though he ay forge and bete
Or graue or peynte for I dar wel seyn
Apelles zanzis sholde werche in veyn
Outher to graue or peynte or forge or bete
If they presumeden me to countrefete
ffor he that is the formere principal
Hath maked me his vicaire general
To forme and peynten erthely creaturis
Right as me list and ech thyng in my cure is
Vnder the moone that may wane and waxe
And for my werk right no thyng wol I axe
My lord and I been ful of oon acord
I made hire to the worship of my lord
So do I alle myne othere creatures
What colour þt they han or what figures
Thus semeth me that nature wolde seye
This mayde of age xij yeer was and tweye
In which þt nature hadde swich delit
ffor right as she kan peynte a lilie whit
And reed a rose right with swich peynture
She peynted hath this noble creature
Er she were born vp on hir lymes free
Ther as by right swiche colours sholden be

Quere in methamorphosios

Apelles fecit mirabile opus in tumulo Darij vide in Alexandri lio. 6o. de zanz in lo. Tullij

¶Here bigynneth / the Phisiciens tale

Ther was / as telleth Titus Liuius
A knyght that called was Virginius
Fulfild of honour / and of worthynesse
And strong of freendes / and of greet richesse
¶This knyght a doghter hadde by his wif
No children hadde he mo / in al his lif
Fair was this mayde / in excellent beautee
Abouen euery wight þat man may see
For Nature ⟨hath⟩ / with souereyn diligence
Yformed hir*e* / in so greet excellence
As thogh she wolde seyn / lo I nature
Thus kan I forme / and peynte a creature
Whan þat me list / who kan me countrefete
Pigmalion noght thogh he ay forge and bete
Or g*ra*ue / or peynte / for I dar wel seyn
Apelles zanzis / sholde werche in veyn
Outher to graue / or peynte / or forge / or bete
If they p*re*sumeden / me to countrefete
For he that is / the former*e* principal
Hath maked me / his vicaire general
To forme and peynten / erthely creaturis
Right as me list and ech thyng in my cure is
Vnder the Moone / that may wane and waxe
And for my werk right no thyng wol I axe
My lord and I / been ful of oon acord
I made hire / to the worship*e* of my lord
So do I / alle myne othere creatures
What colour þat they han / or what figures
Thus semeth me / that nature wolde seye
This mayde of age / xij. yeer was and tweye
In which þat nature / hadde swich delit
For / right as she kan peynte a lilye whit
And reed a Rose / right with swich peynture
She peynted hath / this noble creature
Er she were born / vp on hir lymes free
Wher as by right swiche colours sholden be

14 Quere in Methamorphosios Hg El

16 Apelles fecit mirabile opus in tumulo darij Vide in Alexandro libro .6°. de Zanze in libro Tullij Hg El Variant: .6°.) .1°. El

¶Heere folweth / the Phisiciens tale[1]

Ther
knyght was called
Fulfild /

knyght doghter wyf / [2]
mo lyf

euery wight that
Nature / hath soue*r*eyn

though Nature

that list
noght / though
graue /

p*re*sumed /
he / is p*ri*ncipal

peynten
Right thyng
þat
right
accord
hire / lord

that
[3] Nature
¶This mayde / Age .xij.
Nature / delit
For right lilie
right *with*
hath
fre
Where right / sholde

[1] ¶Frankeleyn on *133r*
[2] Miniature of the Physician in right margin.
[3] ¶Phisicien *133v*

	ELLESMERE
And Phebus / dyed hath hir tresses grete	And Phebus hath / hir*e* treses
Lyk to the stremys / of his burned hete	stremes / heete
And if þ*a*t excellentꝭ was hir beautee	hir*e*
A thousand fold / moore v*er*tuous was she	thousandꝭ fooldꝭ
In hire / ne lakked no condiciou*n*	
That is to preyse / as by discreciou*n*	
As wel in goostꝭ as body / chaast was she	chast
For which / she floured in virginitee	
With aƚƚ humilitee / and abstinence	alle humylitee / Abstinence
With aƚƚ atemp*er*ance / and pacience	alle attemp*er*aunce
With mesure eek / of beryngꝭ and array	
Discreet she was / in answeryng alway	
Thogh she were wise Pallas / dar I seyn	Thougħ Pallas
Hir facound eek / ful wommanly and pleyn	facoundꝭ wo*m*manly a pleyn
No countrefeted termes / hadde she	
To seme wys / but after hir degree	
She spak / and alle hir wordes / moore and lesse	hir*e* wordes *and* lesse
Sownynge in v*er*tu / and in gentilesse	vertu / gentillesse
Shamefast she was / in maydens shamefastnesse	was / maydens
Constant in herte / and euere in bisynesse	
To dryue hir*e* outꝭ of ydel slogardye	hir*e* / out
Bacus hadde of hir mouth / right no maistrye	moutħ / rigħt maistrie
For wyn and youthe / dooth Venus encreesse	encresse
As men in fyr / wol casten oille / or gresse	man wol wasten oille greesse
And of hir owene v*er*tu / vnconstreyned	
She hath ful ofte tyme / syk hir feyned	hir*e*
For þ*a*t she wolde / fleen the compaignye	that / wolde
Where likly was / to treten of folye	Wher*e*
As is at festes / reuels / and at daunces	feestes /
That been occasions / of daliaunces	been / occasions
Swich thyngꝭ maken children for to be	thyng /
To soone rype / and boold / as men may se	rype
Which is ful p*er*ilous / and hath be yoore	been
For al to soone / may they lerne loore	
Of boldnesse / whan she woxe[n] is a wyfꝭ	booldnesse / woxen
¶And ye Maistresses / in youre olde lyf	maistresses / lyf /
That lordes doghtres / han in gou*er*nance	gou*er*nau*n*ce
Ne taketh of my wordes / no displesance	wordes displesau*n*ce
Thenketh / þ*a*t ye been setꝭ in gouernynges	that set gou*er*nynges
Of lordes doghtres / oonly for two thynges	

And phebus dyed hath hir tresses grete
Lyk to the stremys / of his burned hete
And if pt excellent / was hir beautee
A thousand fold / moore vertuous was she
In hire / ne lakked no condicion
That is to preyse / as by discrecion
As wel in goost as body / chaast was she
ffor which / she floured in virginitee
With all humilitee / and abstinence
With all atemprance / and pacience
With mesure eek / of beryng and aray
Discreet she was / in answeryng alway
Thogh she were wise pallas / dar I seyn
Hir facound eek / ful wommanly and pleyn
No countrefeted termes / hadde she
To seme wys / but after hir degree
She spak / and alle hir wordes / moore and lesse
Sownynge in vertu / and in gentilesse
Shamefast she was / in maydens shamefastnesse
Constant in herte / and euere in bisynesse
To dryue hir out / of ydel slogardye
Bacus hadde of hir mouth / right no maistrye
ffor wyn and youthe / dooth venus encreesse
As men in fyr / wol casten oille or greesse
And of hir owene vertu / unconstreyned
She hath ful ofte tyme / syk hir feyned
ffor pt she wolde / fleen the compaignye
Where likly was / to treten of folye
As is at festes / reuels / and at daunces
That been occasions / of daliaunces
Swich thyngs / maken children for to be
To soone rype / and boold / as men may se
Which is ful perilous / and hath be yoore
ffor al to soone / may they lerne loore
Of boldnesse / whan she woxe / is a wyf
And ye maistresses / in youre olde lyf
That lordes doghtres / han in gouernance
Ne taketh of my wordes / no displesance
Thenketh / pt ye been set / in gouernynges
Of lordes doghtres / oonly for two thynges

Outher for ye han kept youre honestee
Or ellis ye han falle in freletee
And knowen wel ynough the olde daunce
And han forsaken fully swich meschaunce
For euere mo therfore for cristes sake
To teche hem vertu looke þt ye ne slake
A theef of venysoun that hath forlaft
His likerousnesse and al his olde craft
Kan kepe a fforest best of any man
Now kepeth wel for if ye wole ye kan
Looke wel þt ye vn to no vice assente
Lest ye be dampned for youre wikke entente
ffor who so dooth a traytour is certeyn
And taketh kepe of that þt I shal seyn
Nota Of alle treson souereyn pestilence
Is whan a wight bitrayseth Innocence
Ye fadres and ye modres eek also
Though ye han children be it oon or mo
Youre is the charge of al hir surueiaunce
Whil þt they been vnder youre gouernaunce
Beth war þt by ensample of youre lyuynge
Or by youre necligence in chastisynge
That they perisse for I dar wel seye
If þt they doon ye shul it deere abeye
Vnder a shepherde softe and necligent
The wolf hath many a sheep and lamb to rent
Suffiseth oon ensample now as heere
ffor I moot turne agayn to my matere
This mayde of which I wol this tale expresse
So kepte hir self hir neded no maistresse
ffor in hir lyuyng maydens myghten rede
As in a book euery good word or dede
That longeth to a mayden vertuous
She was so prudent and so bounteuous
ffor which the fame out sprong on euery syde
Bothe of hir beautee and hir bountee wyde
That thurgh that land they preysed hire echone
That loued vertu saue enuye allone
Augustinus. That sory is of oother mennes wele
And glad is of his sorwe and his vnheele

The doctour maketh

	ELLESMERE
[¶]Owther / for ye han kept' youre honestee	4 Outher /
Or ellis / ye han falle in freletee	elles /
And knowen wel ynow / the olde daunce	ynougħ
And han forsaken fully / swich meschaunce	forsaken / fully
For eu*er*e mo / therfore / for Cristes sake	eu*er*emo / therfore
To teche hem v*er*tu / looke þ*at* ye ne slake	
¶A theef of venyson / that hath forlaft'	venysou*n* /
His likerousnesse / and al his olde craft'	
Kan kepe a Forest' best of any man	
Now kepeth wel / for if ye wole ye kan	
Looke wel þ*at* ye / vn to no vice assente	wel /
Lest ye be dampned / for youre wikke entente	your*e*
For who so dooth / a traytour is c*er*teyn	traitour certeyn
And taketh kepe / of that' þ*at* I shal seyn	that þ*at*
¶no*ta* Of alle tresou*n* / souerayn pestilence	No*ta*] tresons / souereyn
Is / whan a wight' bitrayseth Innocence	wighħ'
¶Ye fadres / and ye modres eek also	fadres moodres /
Thogh ye han cħildren / be it oon or mo	Thougħ or two |
Youre is the charge / of al hir surueau*n*ce	surueiau*n*ce
Whil þ*at* they been / vnder youre gou*er*nau*n*ce	
Beth war / if by ensample of youre lyuynge	ensample /
Or by youre necligence / in chastisynge	
That they p*er*isse / for I dar wel seye	
If þ*at* they doon / ye shul it deere abeye	
Vnder a Shepherde / softe and necligent'	shepherde / necligent
The wolf' hath many a sheep*e* / and lomb to rent'	wolf / sheep*e* lamb
Suffiseth oon ensample / now as heere	5
For I moot' turne agayn to my matere	
¶This mayde / of which / I wol this tale exp*re*sse	This which
So kepte hir self' hir neded no maistresse	
For in hir lyuyng' maydens myghten rede	lyuyng /
As in a book' euery good word / or dede	book / word
That longeth / to a mayden vertuous	v*er*tuous
She was so prudent' and so bou*n*teuous	
For which the fame out sproong on eu*er*y syde	which / fame / sprong
Bothe of hir beautee / and hir bou*n*tee / wyde	bou*n*tee
That thurgh that land / they preysed hir*e* echone	thurgħ preised
That loued vertu / saue enuye allone	Enuye
¶Augustinus That sory is / of oother mennes wele	¶Augustinus]
And glad is / of his sorwe / and his vnheele	is

The doctor maketh

[4] ¶Phisicien *134r*
[5] *Out* El 103-4.

· The phisicien ·

	ELLESMERE
The doctor / maketh this discripcioun	doctour / descripciou*n*
This mayde / vp on a day / wente in the toun	mayde
Toward a temple / with hir moder deere	hir*e* mooder
As is / of yonge maydens the manere	
¶Now was ther thanne / a Iustice in that toun	
That gou*er*nour was / of that Regioun	
And so bifel / this Iuge hise eyen caste	Iuge /
Vp on this mayde / auysynge hym ful faste	
As she cam forby / ther as this Iuge stood	stood
Anoon his herte chaunged / and his mood	Anon / chaunged mood
So was he caught with beautee of this mayde	6 caught
And to hym self / ful pryuely he sayde	
This mayde shal be myn / for any man	mayde /
Anon the feend / in to his herte ran	
And taughte hym sodeynly / þ*at* he by slyghte	taughte slyghte
This mayden / to his purpos wynne myghte	The mayden / myghte
For c*er*tes / by no force / ne by no meede	certes
Hym thoughte / he was nat able for to speede	thoughte / nat
For she was strong of freendes / and eek she	strong
Confermed was / in swich souer*a*yn bou*n*tee	
That wel he wiste / he myghte hir neu*ere* wynne	myghte hir*e*
As for to make hir*e* / with hir body synne	maken
For which / by greet deliberacioun	deliberaciou*n*
He sente after a cherl / was in the town	toun
Which þ*at* he knew / for subtil and for bold	boold
This Iuge vn to this cherl / his tale hath told	Iuge / toold
In secree wise / and made hym to ensure	
He sholde telle it to no creature	
And if he dide / he sholde lese his heed	heed
Whan þ*at* assented was / this cursed reed	reed
Glad was this Iuge / and maked hym gret cheere	*and* hi*m* greet
And yaf hym yiftes / p*re*ciouse and deere	
¶Whan shapen was / al hir conspiracie	hir*e*
Fro point to point how þ*at* his lecherie	point to point
P*ar*fourned sholde been / ful subtilly	been
As ye shul heere it after openly	ye / it
¶Hom goth the cherl / that highte Claudius	Hoom gooth þ*at* highte Claudius
This false Iuge / that highte Apius	highte Apius
So was his name / for this is no fable	
But knowen / for historial thyng notable	

6 ¶Phisicien *134v*

The phisicien

The dottor / maketh this disicripcioun
This mayde / vp on a day / wente in the toun
Toward a temple / with hir mooder deere
As is of yonge maydens the manere
Now was ther thanne / a Iustice in that toun
That gouernour / was of that Regioun
And so bifel / this Iuge hise eyen caste
Vp on this mayde / auysynge hym ful faste
As she cam forby / ther as this Iuge stood
Anoon his herte chaunged / and his mood
So was he caught / with beautee of this mayde
And to hym self / ful pryuely he sayde
This mayde shal be myn / for any man
Anon the feend / in to his herte ran
And taughte hym sodeynly / þt he by slyghte
This mayden / to his purpos wynne myghte
For certes / by no force / ne by no meede
Hym thoughte / he was nat able for to speede
For she was strong of freendes / and eek she
Confermed was / in swich souerayn bontee
That wel he wiste / he myghte hir neuere wynne
As for to make hire / with hir body synne
For which / by greet deliberacioun
He sente after a cherl / was in the toun
Which þt he knew / for subtil and for bold
This Iuge vn to this cherl / his tale hath told
In secree wise / and made hym to ensure
He sholde telle it / to no creature
And if he dide / he sholde lese his heed
Whan þt assented was / this cursed reed
Glad was this Iuge / and maked hym greet cheere
And yaf hym yiftes / preciouse and deere
Whan shapen was / al hir conspiracie
Fro point to point / how þt his lecherie
Parfourned sholde been / ful subtilly
As ye shul heere it / after openly
Hoom gooth the cherl / that highte Claudius
This false Iuge / that highte Apius
So was his name / for this is no fable
But knowen / for historial thyng notable

The sentence of it sooth is out of doute
This false Iuge gooth now faste aboute
To hasten his delit / al that he may
And so bifel / soone after on a day
This false Iuge / as telleth vs the storie
As he was wont / sat in his Consistorie
And yaf his domes / vp on sondry cas
This false cherl cam forth / a ful gret pas
And seyde lord if þt it be youre wille
As dooth me right / vp on this pitous bille
In which / I pleyne vp on Virginius
And if þt he wol seyn / it is nat thus
I wol it preeue / and fynde good witnesse
That sooth is / that my bille wol expresse
This Iuge answerde / of this in his absence
I may nat yeue / diffynytif sentence
Lat do hym calle / and I wol gladly heere audire
Thow shalt haue al right / and no wrong heere hic
Virginius cam to wite / the Iuges wille
And right anon / was rad this cursed bille
The sentence of it / was as ye shul heere
To yow my lord / sire Apius so deere
Sheweth / youre poure seruant Claudius
How þt a knyght / called Virginius
Agayns the lawe / agayn al equitee
Holdeth expres / agayn the wyl of me
My seruant / which þt is my thral by right
Which fro myn hous / was stole vp on a nyght
Whil that she was ful yong / this wol I preeue
By witnesse lord / so þt it nat yow greue
She nys his doghter nat / what so he seye
Wher to yow / my lord the Iuge I preye
Yeld me my thral / if þt it be youre wille
Lo this was al the sentence of his bille
Virginius gan vp on the cherl biholde
But hastily / er he his tale tolde
And wolde haue preued it / as sholde a knyght
And eek by witnessynge / of many a wight
That it was fals / that seyde his aduersarie
This cursed Iuge / wolde no thyng tarie

The sentence of itꝫ sooth is out of doute	
This false Iuge / gooth now faste aboute	
To hasten his delitꝫ al that he may	
And so bifel / soone after on a day	
This false Iuge / as telleth vs the storie	
As he was wontꝫ sat in his Consistorie	
And yaf his domes / vp on sondry cas	doomes /
¶This false cherl cam forth / a ful gret pas	This cherl / greet
And seyde / lord if þ*at* it be youre wille	seyde lord /
As dooth me rightꝫ vp on this pitous bille	rigħt /
In which / I pleyne vp on Virginius	which pleyne /
And if þ*at* he wol seyn / it is nat thus	
I wol it preue / and fynde good witnesse	preeue /
That sooth is / that my bille wol exp*re*sse	
¶This Iuge answerde / of this in his absence	¶The Iuge
I may nat yeue / diffynytif sentence	diffynyue
Lat do hym calle / and I wol gladly heere [audire]	
Thow shalt haue al rightꝫ and no wrong heere [hic]	Thou rigħtꝫ
¶Virginius cam to wite / the Iuges wille	7 ¶Virginius / wite
And right anon / was rad this cursed bille	rigħt
The sentence of itꝫ was as ye shul heere	it /
¶To yow my lord / sire Apius so deere	lordꝭ Apius
Sheweth / youre poure seruant Claudius	Sheweth Claudius
How þ*at* a knyghtꝫ called Virginius	that knygħt / Virginius
Agayns the lawe / agayn al equitee	
Holdeth expres / agayn the wyl of me	
My seruantꝫ which þ*at* is my thral by rightꝫ	seruantꝫ. rigħtꝫ
Which fro myn hous / was stole vp on a nyghtꝫ	nygħtꝫ
Whil that she was ful yongꝫ this wol I preue	þ*at* preeue
By witnesse lord / so þ*at* it nat yow greue	greeue
She nys his doghter natꝫ what so he seye	dogħter
Wher to yow / my lord the Iuge I preye	Wherfore / to
Yeld me my thral / if þ*at* it be youre wille	
Lo / this was al the sentence / of his bille	was / sentence
¶Virginius / gan vp on the cherl biholde	¶Virginius /
But hastily / er he his tale tolde	
And wolde haue proued itꝫ as sholde a knyghtꝫ	preeued knygħtꝫ
And eekꝫ by witnessynge / of many a wightꝫ	witnessyngꝫ wigħtꝫ
That it was fals / that seyde his Adu*er*sarie	
This cursed Iuge / wolde no thyng tarie	

7 ¶Phisicien *135r*

The Phisicien	ELLESMERE
Ne here a word / moore of Virginius	heere word Virginius
But yaf his Iuggement and seyde thus /	thus
¶I deme anon / this cherl / his seruant haue	deeme cherl s*er*uant
Thou shalt no lenger / in thyn hous hir saue	
Go bryng hir forth / and put hir*e* in oure warde	hir*e* forth /
The cherl shal han his thral / this I awarde	haue
¶And whan / this worthy knyght Virginius	whan knyght Virginius
Thurgh sentence / of this Iustice Apius	Apius
Moste by force / his deere doghter yeuen	
Vn to the Iuge / in lecherie to lyuen	
He goth hym hom / and sette hym in his halle	gooth hoom / hi*m* in
And leet anoon / his deere doghter calle	leet anon /
And with a face deed / as asshen colde	
Vp on hir humble face / he gan biholde	Vpon
With fadres pitee / stikyng thurgh his herte	stikynge
Al wolde he / from his purpos nat conuerte	
¶Doghter quod he / Virginia by thy name	Doghter Virginia /
Ther been two weyes / outher deeth / or shame	deeth
That thow most suffre / allas *þat* I was bore	thou most /
For neu*er*e / thow deseruedest wherfore	thou
To dyen / with a swerd / or with a knyf	knyf
O deere doghter / endere of my lyf	doghter / ender*e*
Which I haue fostred vp / with swich plesance	swich plesau*n*ce
That thow were neuere / out of my remembrance	thou neu*er*e / remembrau*n*ce
O doghter / which that art my laste wo	*þat*
And in my lyf my laste ioye also	
O gemme of chastitee / in pacience	8 ge*m*me o Chastitee
Tak thow thy deeth / for this is my sentence	Take thou
For loue / and nat for hate / thow most be deed	loue thou deed
My pitous hand / moot smyten of thyn heed	heed
Allas / *þat* euere Apius thee say	that Apius the
Thus hath he falsly / Iugged thee to day	the today
And tolde hir*e* al the cas / as ye bifore	
Han herd / nat nedeth for to telle it moore	herd
¶O m*er*cy deere fader / quod this mayde	
And with that word / she bothe hir armes layde	wit*h* Armes
Aboute his nekke / as she was wont to do	
The teeris borste / out of hir eyen two	teeris / bruste
And seyde / goode fader / shal I dye	fader
Is ther no grace / is ther no remedye	

[8] ¶Phisicien *135v*

Ne here a word moore of Virginius
But yaf his Juggement / and seyde thus /
¶ Deme anon / this cherl / his seruant hano
Thou shalt no lenger / in thyn hous hir saue
Go bryng hir forth / and put hir in oure warde
The cherl shal han his thral / this I awarde
¶ And whan / this worthy knyght Virginius
Thurgh sentence / of this Justice Apius
Moste by force / his deere doghter yeuen
Vn to the Juge / in lecherye to lyuen
He goth hym hom / and sette hym in his halle
And leet anoon / his deere doghter calle
And with a face deed / as asshen colde
Vp on hir humble face / he gan biholde
With fadres pitee / stikyng thurgh his herte
Al wolde he / from his purpos nat conuerte
¶ Doghter quod he / Virginia by thy name
Ther been two weyes / outher deeth / or shame
That thow most suffre / allas þt I was bore
ffor neuere thow deseruedest / wherfore
To dyen / with a swerd / or with a knyf
O deere doghter / endere of my lyf
Which I haue fostred vp / with swich plesance
That thow were neuere / out of my remembrance
O doghter / which that art my laste wo
And in my lyf / my laste ioye also
O gemme of chastitee / in pacience
Tak thow thy deeth / for this is my sentence
ffor loue / and nat for hate / thow most be deed
My pitous hand / moot smyten of thyn heed
Allas / þt euere Apius thee say
Thus hath he falsly / Jugged thee to day
And tolde hir al the cas / as ye bifore
Han herd / nat nedeth for to telle it moore
¶ O mercy deere fader / quod this mayde
And with that word / she bothe hir armes layde
Aboute his nekke / as she was wont to do
The teeris borste / out of hir eyen two
And seyde / goode fader / shal I dye
Is ther no grace / is ther no remedye

No certes / deere doghter myn quod he
¶ Thanne yif me leyser / fader myn quod she
My deeth for to compleyne / a litel space
ffor pardee Jepte / yaf his doghter grace
ffor to compleyne / er he hir slowe allas
And god it woot / no thyng was hir trespas
But for she ran hir fader for to se
To welcome hym / with greet solempnytee
And with that word / she fil aswowne anon
And after / whan hir swownyng is agon
She riseth up / and to hir fader sayde
Blissed be god / þt I shal dye a mayde
Yif me my deeth / er þt I haue a shame
Dooth with youre child / youre wyl a goddes name
And wt that word / she preyed hym ful ofte
That with his swerd / he sholde smyte softe
And with that word / aswowne doun she fil
¶ Hir fader / with ful sorweful herte and wil
Hir heed of smoot / and by the top it hente
And to the Juge / he gan it to presente
As he sat yet / in doom / in Consistorie
¶ And whan the Juge it saw / as seith the storie
He bad to take hym / and anhange hym faste
But right anon / a thousand peple in thraste
To saue the knyght / for routhe and for pitee
ffor knowen was / the false iniquitee
¶ The peple anon / hadde suspect in this thyng
By manere of the cherles chalangyng
That it was by the assent of Apius
They wisten wel / þt he was lecherus
ffor which / vn to this Apius they gon
And caste hym in a prison / right anon
Ther as he slow hym self / and Claudius
That seruant was / vn to this Apius
Was demed / for to hange vp on a tree
But that Virginius / of his pitee
So preyde for hym / that he was exiled
And ellis certes / he hadde been bigyled
The remenant were anhanged / moore and lesse
That were consentant / of this cursednesse

¶ Iudicum cap. xjo. fuit illo tempore Jepte Galaaditis

	ELLESMERE
¶No certes / deere doghter myn quod he	dogħter
¶Thanne yif me leyser / fader myn quod she	
My deeth for to compleyne / a litel space	
For p*ar*dee Iepte / yaf his doghter grace	p*ar*dee / Iepte
For to compleyne / er he hir slowe allas	slow
And god it woot' no thyng was hir trespas	
But for she ran / hir fader for to se	see
To wel come hym / with greet solempnytee	solempnitee
And with that word / she fil aswowne anon	w*ith*
And after / whan hir swownyng is agon	after' swownyng'
She riseth vp / and to hir fader sayde	
Blessed be god / þat I shal dye a mayde	Blissed that
Yif me my deeth / er þat I haue a shame	that
Dooth with your*e* child / youre wyl agoddes name	w*ith* child'
And w*ith* that word / she preyed hym ful ofte	¶And with
That with his swerd / he wolde smyte softe	swerd' /
And with that word / aswowne doun she fil	w*ith* word' /
¶Hir fader / with ful sorweful herte and wil	Hir w*ith*
Hir heed of smoot' and by the top*e* it hente	
And to the Iuge / he gan it to p*re*sente	
As he sat yet' in doom / in Consistorie	doom
¶And whan the Iuge it saw / as seith the storie	And saugħ /
He bad to take hym / and anhange hym faste	
But right anon / a thousand peple In thraste	rigħt thousand' in
To saue the knyght' for routhe and for pitee	knygħt'
For knowen was / the false Iniquitee	
¶The peple anon / hadde suspect' in this thyng'	The hath suspect' of this
By manere / of the cherles chalangyng'	
That it was / by the assent of Apius	**Apius**
They wisten wel / þat he was lecherus	that
For which / vn to this Apius they gon	**Apius**
And caste hym in a p*ri*son / right anon	p*ri*sou*n* rigħt
Ther as he slow hym self' / and Claudius	self / **Claudius**
That seruant was / vn to this Apius	**Apius**
Was demed / for to hange vp on a tree	9 And demed / vpon
But that Virginius / of his pitee	**Virginius** /
So preyde for hym / that he was exiled	exiled'
And ellis certes / he hadde been bigyled	elles had bigyled'
The remenant were anhanged / moore and lesse	anhanged *and*
That were consentant' of this cursednesse	

240 Iudicum capitulo .xj°. fuit illo tempore Iepte Galaandes Hg El

9 ¶Phisicien *136r*

	ELLESMERE
¶Heere may men seen / how synne hath his merite	Heere merite
Beth war / for no man woot whom god wol smyte	
In no degree / ne in which manere wise	manere wyse
The worm of conscience / may agrise	agryse
Of wikked lyf / thogh it so pryuee be	lyf though
That no man woot ther of but god and he	man / of /
For be ⟨he⟩ lewed man / or ellis lered	he lered
He noot how soone / that he shal been afered	þat afered
Ther fore I rede yow / this conseil take	Therfore /
Forsaketh synne / er synne yow forsake	
¶Here endeth the Phisiciens tale	¶Heere endeth / the Phisiciens tale
¶The myry talkyng of the hoost to the Phisicien and the P*ar*doner	¶The wordes of the Hoost to the Phisicien and the P*ar*don*er*
Oure hoost gan to swere / as he were wood	Ovre Hoost wood
Harrow quod he / by nayles and by blood	blood
This was a fals cherl / and a fals Iustise	cherl and and[10] a
As shameful deeth / as herte may deuyse	
Come to thise Iuges / and hir Aduocatz	thise false Iuges / hir*e*
Algate this sely mayde / is slayn allas	Algate /
Allas / to deere boghte she beautee	boughte
Wherfore I seye alday / þat men may se	seye / alday / as men see
That yiftes of Fortune / and of nature	Fortune Nature
Been cause of deeth / to many a creature[11]	
Of bothe yiftes / þat I speke of now	that
Men han ful ofte / moore for harm than prow	
¶But trewely / myn owene maister deere	
This is a pitous tale / for to heere	is / tale
But nathelees passe ouer is no fors	nathelees / ouer /
I pray to god / so saue thy gentil cors	
And eek thyne Vrynals / and thy Iurdones	eek
Thyn Ypocras / and eek thy galyones	Galiones
And euery boyste / ful of thy letuarie	
God blesse hem / and oure lady Seinte Marie	Seint
So mote I then / thow art a pr*o*pre man	moot theen / thou
And lyk a pr*e*lat / by Seint Ronyan	pr*e*lat

[10] Second 'and' marked for deletion.

[11] *Out* Hg El 297–8. Ad[3] reads:
Hir beaute was hir deth I dar wel sayn
Allas so pitously as she was slayn

Heere may men seen how synne hath his merite
Beth war for no man woot whom god wol smyte
In no degree ne in which manere wyse
The worm of conscience may agryse
Of wikked lyf though it so pryuee be
That no man woot ther of but god and he
ffor be he lewed man or ellis lered
He noot how soone that he shal been afered
Ther fore I rede yow this conseil take
fforsaketh synne er synne yow forsake

Heere endeth the Phisiciens tale

The myrie talkyng of the hoost to the Phisicien and the Pardoner

Oure hoost gan to swere as he were wood
Harrow quod he by nayles and by blood
This was a fals cherl and a fals Iustise
As shameful deeth as herte may deuyse
Come to thise Iuges and hir aduocatz
Algate this sely mayde is slayn allas
Allas to deere boghte she beautee
Wher fore I seye alday þt men may se
That yiftes of ffortune and of nature
Been cause of deeth to many a creature
Of bothe yiftes þt I speke of now
Men han ful ofte moore for harm than prow
But trewely myn owene maister deere
This is a pitous tale for to heere
But nathelees passe ouer is no fors
I pray to god so saue thy gentil cors
And eek thyne vrynals and thy Iurdones
Thyn ypocras and eek thy galyones
And euery boyste ful of thy letuarie
God blesse hem and oure lady Seinte marie
So moote I theen thow art a propre man
And lyk a prelat by Seint Ronyan

Seyde I nat wel / I kan nat speke in terme
But wel I woot / thow doost myn herte to erme
That I almoost / haue caught a cardynacle
By corpus bones / but if I haue triacle
Or elles a draghte / of moyste and corny ale
Or but I heere anon / a myrie tale
Myn herte is lost / for pitee of this mayde
Thow beel amy / thow Pardoner he sayde
Telle vs som myrthe / or Iapes right anon
It shal be doon quod he / by Seint Ronyon
But first quod he / heere at this ale stake
I wol bothe drynke / and eten of a cake
And right anon / thise gentils gonne to crye
Nay lat hym telle vs of no ribawdye
Telle vs som moral thyng / þt we may leere
Som wit / and thanne wol we gladly heere
I graunte ywis quod he / but I moot thynke
Vp on som honeste thyng / whil þt I drynke

Radix omnium malorum est Cupiditas Ad Thimotheum 6°.

Here bigynneth the prologe of the Pardoners tale

Lordynges quod he in chirches whan I preche
I peyne me to han an hauteyn speche
And rynge it out / as round as gooth a belle
For I kan al by rote / that I telle
My theme is alwey oon / and euere was
Radix malorum est Cupiditas
First I pronounce / whennes þt I come
And thanne my bulles / shewe I alle and some
Oure lige lordes seel / on my patente
That shewe I first / my body to warente
That no man be so boold / ne preest ne clerk
Me to destourbe / of Cristes holy werk
And after that / thanne telle I forth my tales
Bulles of Popes / and of Cardynales

	ELLESMERE
Seyde I nat wel / I kan nat speke in terme	kan nat *ter*me
But wel I woot thow doost myn herte to erme	thou
That I almoost haue caught a Cardynacle	12
By corpus bones / but if I haue triacle	but I
Or ellis a draghte / of moyste and corny ale	elles draughte / Ale
Or but I heere anon / a murye tale	myrie
Myn herte is lost for pitee of this mayde	
¶Thow beel amy / thow Pardoner he sayde	Thou thou P*ar*doner
Tel vs som myrthe / or Iapes right anon	Telle right
¶It shal be doon quod he / by Seint Ronyon	Ronyou*n*
But first quod he / heere at this ale stake	Ale
I wol bothe drynke / and eten of a Cake	
¶And right anon / thise gentils gonne to crye	right anon / the gentils
Nay lat hym telle vs / of no ribawdye	Nay / vs ribaudye
Tel vs som moral thyng / *þat* we may leere	Telle thyng
Som wit / and thanne wol we gladly heere	wit
¶I graunte ywis quod he / but I moot thynke	
Vp on som honeste thyng whil *þat* I drynke	

¶Radix om*nium* malor*um* / est Cupiditas // Ad Thimotheu*m* . 6°.	¶Heere folweth the Prologe / of the P*ar*doners tale
¶Here bigynneth / the ⟨p*ro*loge of the⟩ Pardon*er*s tale	¶Radix malor*um* est Cupiditas Ad Thimotheum .6°.

LOrdynges quod he / in chirches whan I p*re*che	He / chirches /
I peyne me / to han an hauteyn speche	
And rynge it out as round as gooth a belle	
For I kan / al by rote that I telle	
My theme is alwey oon / and eu*er*e was	
Radix malor*um* / est cupiditas	**malor*um*** **Cupiditas**
¶First I p*ro*nounce / whennes *þat* I come	First pronounce /
And thanne my bulles / shewe I alle *and* some	
Oure lige lordes seel / on my patente	
That shewe I first my body to warente	
That no man be so boold / ne preest ne clerk	
Me to destourbe / of Cristes holy werk	hooly
And after that thanne telle I forth my tales	
Bulles of Popes / and of Cardynales	⟨Bulles of popes⟩

[12] ¶P*ar*doner *136v*

	ELLESMERE
Of Patriarkes / and Bisshopes I shewe	bisshopes
And in latyn / I speke a wordes fewe	
To saffron with / my p*re*dicaciou*n*	with
And for to stire hem / to deuociou*n*	
¶Thanne shewe I forth / my longe c*ri*stal stones	Thanne
Ycrammed ful / of cloutes and of bones	ful
Relikes been they / as wenen they echon	echoon
Thanne haue I in a latou*n* / a shulder bon	haue in latou*n* sholder boon
Which þ*at* was / of an holy Iewes sheep*e*	that hooly
Goode men I seye / tak of my wordes keep*e*	taak
If þ*at* this boon be wasshe / in any welle	[1] that boon / wassħe
If cow / or calf or sheep*e* / or Oxe swelle	Cow / Calf Sheep*e* /
That any worm hath ete / or worm ystonge	
Taak water of that welle / and wassħ his tonge	
And it is hool anoon / and forther moor	anon / forthermoor
Of pokkes / and of Scabbe / and eu*er*y soor	
Shal eu*er*y sheep*e* be hool / þ*at* of this welle	
Drynketh a draughte / taak kepe eek what I telle	draughte /
¶If þ*at* the goode man / þ*at* the bestes oweth	that that beestes
Wol euery wike / er þ*at* the cok hym croweth	wyke / that Cok
Fastynge / drynken of this welle a draghte	Fastynge drynke / draughte
As thilke holy Iew / oure eldres taghte	hooly taughte
Hise bestes and his stoor / shal multiplie	beestes stoor
And sire also / it heeleth Ialousie	¶And sire /
For thogh a man / be falle in Ialous rage	though
Lat maken with this water / his potage	maken / water
And neuere shal he moore / his wyf mystriste	neu*er*e
Thogh he the soothe / of hir defaute wiste	Though
Al hadde she / taken preestes / two or thre	had
¶Heere is a Miteyn eek / þ*at* ye may se	that
He þ*at* his hand / wol putte / in this Mitayn	hand putte
He shal haue / multiplyyng of his grayn	multipliyng
Whan he hath sowen / be it whete or Otes	
So þ*at* / he / offre pens / or ellis grotes	þ*at* he offre / elles
¶Goode men and wommen / o thyng warne I yow	wo*m*men /
If any wight be in this chirche now	wight /
That hath doon synne horrible / that he	horrible þ*at* he
Dar nat for shame / of it yshryuen be	
Or any womman / be she yong or old	wo*m*man /
That hath ymaked / hir housbond Cokewold	housbonde

[1] ¶P*ar*doner *137r*

Of patriarkes and bisshopes I shewe
And in latyn I speke a wordes fewe
To saffron with my p̄dicacion
And for to stire hem to deuocioū
Thanne shewe I forth my longe c̄stal stones
Ycrammed ful of cloutes and of bones
Relikes been they as wenen they echon
Thanne haue I in a latoun a sholder bon
Which þt was of an holy Iewes sheep
Goode men I seye tak of my wordes keep
If þt this boon be wasshe in any welle
If cow or calf or sheep or oxe swelle
That any worm hath ete or worm ystonge
Taak water of that welle and wassh his tonge
And it is hool anoon and forther moor
Of pokkes and of scabbe and eūy soor
Shal eūy sheep be hool þt of this welle
Drynketh a draughte taak kepe eek what I telle
If þt the goode man þt the bestes oweth
Wol euery wike er þt the cok hym croweth
ffastynge drynken of this welle a draughte
As thilke holy Iewe oure eldres taughte
Hise bestes and his stoor shal multiplie
And sire also it heleth Ialousie
ffor thogh a man be falle in Ialous rage
lat maken with this water his potage
And neuere shal he moore his wyf mystriste
Thogh he the soothe of hir defaute wiste
Al hadde she taken preestes two or thre
Heere is a miteyn eek þt ye may se
He þt his hand wol putte in this mitayn
He shal haue multiplyyng of his grayn
Whan he hath sowen be it whete or otes
So þt he offre pens or ellis grotes
Goode men and wommen o thyng warne I yow
If any wight be in this chirche now
That hath doon synne horrible that he
Dar nat for shame of it yshryuen be
Or any womman be she yong or old
That hath ymaked hir housbond cokewold

Swich folk shal haue no power / ne no grace
To offren to my relikes / in this place
And who so fyndeth hym / out of swich blame
He wol come vp / and offre a goddes name
And I assoille hym / by the auctoritee
Which þt by bulle / ygraunted was to me
¶ By this gaude haue I wonne / yeer by yeer
An hundred mark / sith I was Pardoner
I stonde lyk a clerk / in my pulpet
And whan þt lewed peple / is doun yset
I preche so / as ye han herd bifore
And telle / an hundred false iapes moore
Thanne peyne I me / to strecche forth the nekke
And est and west / vp on the peple I bekke
As dooth a dowue / sittyng on a berne
Myne handes / and my tonge goon so yerne
That it is ioye / to se my bisynesse
Of auarice / and of swich cursednesse
Is al my prechyng / for to make hem free
To yeuen hir pens / and namely vn to me
ffor myn entente is nat / but for to wynne
And no thyng / for correccion of synne
I rekke neue / whan þt they been beryed
Though þt hir soules / goon a blakeberyed
ffor certes / many a predicacion
Comth ofte tyme / of yuel entencion
¶ Som for plesance of folk / and flaterye
To been auanced / by ypocrisie
And som for veyne glorie / and som for hate
ffor whan I dar / noon oother weyes debate
Thanne wol I stynge hym / with my tonge smerte
In prechyng / so þt he shal nat asterte
To been diffamed falsly / if þt he
Hath trespased to my bretheren / or to me
ffor though I telle noght / his propre name
Men shal wel knowe / that it is the same
By signes and by othere circumstances
Thus quyte I folk / that doon vs displesances
Thus spete I out / my venym vnder hewe
Of holynesse / to semen holy and trewe

ELLESMERE

Swich folk / shal haue no power / ne no g*ra*ce
To offren to my Relikes / in this place
And who so fyndeth hym / out of swich blame
He wol come vp / and offre a goddes name
And I assoille hym / by the auctoritee
Which þ*at* by bulle / ygraunted was to me
¶By this gaude / haue I wonne / yeer by yeer
An hundred markꝭ sith I was Pardoner
I stonde lyk a Clerk / in my pulpetꝭ
And whan þ*at* lewed peple / is doun ysetꝭ
I p*re*che so / as ye han herd bifore
And telle / an hundred false Iapes more
Thanne peyne I me / to strecche forth the nekke
And Est and Westꝭ vp on the peple I bekke
As dooth a dowue / sittyng on a berne
Myne handes / and my tonge goon so yerne
That it is ioye / to se my bisynesse
Of Auarice / and of swich cursednesse
Is al my p*re*chyngꝭ for to make hem free
To yeuen hir pens / and namely vn to me
For myn entente is natꝭ but for to wynne
And no thyngꝭ for correcciou*n* of synne
I rekke neu*er*e / whan þ*at* they been beryed
Thogh þ*at* hir soules / goon a blakeberyed
For certes / many a p*re*dicaciou*n*
Comth ofte tyme / of yuel ent*en*ciou*n*
¶Som for plesance of folkꝭ and flaterye
To been auanced / by ypocrisie
And som for veyne glorie / and som for hate
For whan I dar / noon oother weyes debate
Thanne wol I styngе hym / wit*h* my tonge sm*er*te
In p*re*chyngꝭ so þ*at* he shal nat asterte
To been diffamed falsly / if þ*at* he
Hath trespased / to my bretheren / or to me
For though I telle noghtꝭ his p*ro*pre name
Men shal wel knowe / that it is the same
By signes / and by othere circumstances
Thus quyte I folkꝭ that ⟨doon⟩ vs displesances
Thus spete I outꝭ my venym vnder hewe
Of holynesse / to seme holy and trewe

folkꝭ power grace
offren / relikes
swich famel
They wol offre on goddes
assoille hem / by Auctoritee
that

P*ar*doner
clerk /
whan the lewed yset /
preche bifoore
moore

And Est *and*
sittynge /
handes

2

entente / nat

neuere / when they beryed
Though

Som folk /
auaunced / ypocrisye

whan / dar
smerte
p*re*chyng / that
defamed that he
though / noght /

doon
spitte out venym /
hoolynesse / semen hooly

[2] ¶P*ar*doner *137v*

But shortly / myn entente I wol deuyse
I p*re*che of no thyng but for coueitise
Ther fore my theme is yet and eu*er*e was
Radix malor*um* / est Cupiditas
¶Thus kan I p*re*che / agayn that same vice
Which þat I vse / and that is Auarice
But though my self be gilty in that synne
Yet kan I make / oother folk to twynne
From Auarice / and soore to repente
But that is nat my principal entente
I p*re*che no thyng but for coueitise
Of this matere / it oghte ynow suffise
¶Thanne telle I hem / ensamples many oon
Of olde stories / longe tyme agoon
For lewed peple / louen tales olde
Swiche thynges / kan they wel reporte *and* holde
What trowe ye / þat whiles I may p*re*che
And wynne / gold and siluer / for I teche
That I wol lyue in pouerte / wilfully
Nay nay / I thoghte it neu*er*e trewely
For I wol p*re*che / and begge / in sondry landes
I wol nat do no labour / w*ith* myne handes
Ne make baskettes / and lyue ther by
By cause / I wol nat beggen ydelly
I wol / none of the Apostles countrefete
I wol haue moneye / wolle / chese / and whete
Al were it yeuen / of the pouerest page
Or of the poueres te widwe / in a village
Al sholde hir children / sterue for famyne
Nay I wol drynke / licour of the vyne
And haue a ioly wenche / in euery toun
But herkneth lordynges / in conclusioun
¶Youre likyng is / þat I shal telle a tale
Now haue I dronke / a draghte of corny Ale
By god I hope / I shal yow telle a thyng
That shal by resou*n* / been at youre likyng
For thogh my self be / a ful vicious man
A moral tale / yet I yow telle kan
Which I am wont to p*re*che / for to wynne
Now holde youre pees / my tale I wol bigynne

ELLESMERE

¶But
coueityse
Therfore /. euere
malor*um*
Thus
self /
maken / folk
mateere / oghte ynogh
ye / the whiles
pou*er*te
thoghte
begge
nat with
therby
wol noon /
moneie / wolle chese
3 pou*er*este
pou*er*este wydwe /
children sterue /
Nay /
lordynges
¶Your*e* that
Now / dronke draughte
god /
though self be
preche /
hoold your*e*

3 ¶P*ar*doner *138r*

The Pardoner.

But shortly myn entente I wol devyse
I preche of no thyng / but for coveitise
Therfore my theme is yet / and euere was
Radix malorum est Cupiditas
Thus kan I preche / agayn that same vice
Which þt I use / and that is Avarice
But though my self be gilty in that synne
Yet kan I make / oother folk to twynne
ffrom Avarice / and soore to repente
But that is nat / my principal entente
I preche no thyng / but for coveitise
Of this matere / it oghte ynow suffise
Thanne telle I hem / ensamples many oon
Of olde stories / longe tyme agoon
ffor lewed peple / loven tales olde
Swiche thynges / kan they wel reporte & holde
What trowe ye / þt whiles I may preche
And wynne gold and silver / for I teche
That I wol lyve in poverte / wilfully
Nay nay / I thoghte it neue trewely
ffor I wol preche / and begge in sondry landes
I wol nat do no labour / wt myne handes
Ne make baskettes / and lyve ther by
By cause / I wol nat beggen ydelly
I wol none of the Apostles countrefete
I wol have moneye / wolle / chese / and whete
Al were it yeuen / of the poverest page
Or of the povereste wydwe / in a village
Al sholde hir children / sterve for famyne
Nay I wol drynke / licour of the vyne
And have a joly wenche / in every toun
But herkneth lordynges / in conclusioun
Youre likyng is / þt I shal telle a tale
Now have I dronke / a draghte of corny ale
By god I hope / I shal yow telle a thyng /
That shal by reson / been at youre likyng /
ffor though my self be / a ful vicious man
A moral tale / yet I yow telle kan
Which I am wont to preche / for to wynne
Now holde youre pees / my tale I wol bigynne

ere bigynneth the pardons tale

In fflaundres whilom was a compaignye
Of yonge folk that haunteden folye
As riot hasard stewes and tauernes
Where as with harpes lutes and gyternes
They daunce and pleyen at dees bothe day & nyght
And ete also and drynke ouer hir myght
Thurgh which they doon the deuel sacrifise
With Inne that deueles temple in cursed wise
By superfluytee abhomynable
Hir othes been so grete and so dampnable
That it is grisly for to heere hem swere
Oure blissed lordes body they to tere
Hem thoughte that Iewes rente hym noght ynough
And ech of hem at otheres synne lough
And right anon thanne comen tombesteres
ffetys and smale and yonge ffrutesteres
Syngeres with harpes baudes wafereres
Whiche been the verray deueles officeres
To kyndle and blowe the fyr of lecherye
That is annexed vn to glotonye
The holy writ take I to my witnesse
That luxurie is in wyn and dronkenesse — Nolite inebriari vino in quo est luxuri
Lo how þt dronken Loth vnkyndely
Lay by his doghtres two vnwityngly
So dronke he was he nyste what he wroghte
Herodes who so wel the stories soghte
Whan he of wyn was replet at his feste
Right at his owene table he yaf his heste
To sleen the Baptist John ful giltelees
Seneca seith a good word doutelees
Sen° He seith he kan no difference fynde
Bitwix a man that is out of his mynde
And a man which þt is dronkelewe
But that woodnesse yfallen in a shrewe
Perseuereth lenger than dooth dronkenesse
O glotonye ful of cursednesse
O cause first of oure confusion
O original of oure dampnacion
Til crist hadde boght vs with his blood agayn
Lo how deere shortly for to sayn

	ELLESMERE
[¶H]ere bigynneth / the Pardon*er*s tale	¶Heere bigynneth the P*ar*doners tale
IN Flandres / whilom was a compaignye	Flaundres
Of yonge folk' that haunteden folye	
As Riot' hasard / Stewes / and Tauernes	hasard' Stywes /
Where as with harpes / lutes / and gyternes	Wher*e* / Harpes / Lutes Gyt*er*nes
They daunce / and pleyen at dees / bothe day *and* nyght'	and nyght' 4
And ete also and drynke / ou*er* hir myght'	eten also / drynken ouer myght /
Thurgh which / they doon the deuel sacrifise	
With Inne that deueles temple / in cursed wise	temple
By sup*er*fluytee / abhomynable	superfluytee
Hir othes been so grete / and so dampnable	othes / grete
That it is grisly / for to heere hem swere	
Oure blissed lordes body / they to tere	
Hem thoughte / that Iewes / rente hym noght ynougħ	þ*a*t noght
And eech of hem / at otheres synne lougħ	ech
And right anon / thanne coomen Tombesteres	right comen
Fetys and smale / and yonge Frutesteres	
Syngeris with harpes / Baudes / waufereres	Syngeres w*ith* Harpes / Wafereres
Whiche been / the verray deueles Officers	Officeres
To kyndle and blowe / the fyr of lecherye	
That is annexed / vn to glotonye	annexed
The holy writ take I / to my witnesse	hooly writ / I
That luxure / is in wyn / and dronkenesse	Luxurie / wyn
¶Lo how þ*a*t dronken loth / vnkyndely	Lo Looth
Lay by his doghtres two / vnwityngly	hise two
So dronke he was / he nyste what he wroghte	wroghte
Herodes / who so wel the stories soghte	¶Herodes / so / Stories soghte
Whan he of wyn was replet' at his feste	wyn / repleet' feeste
Right at his owene table / he yaf his heste	Right' heeste
To sleen the Baptist' Iohn / ful giltelees	Baptist
Senec' seith a good word doutelees	¶Senec'
¶No*ta* ¶He seith / he kan no difference fynde	5 ¶Seneca] He seith /
Bitwix a man / that is out of his mynde	that is
And a man / which þ*a*t is dronkelewe	which that
But that woodnesse / yfallen in a sherewe	fallen shrewe
P*er*seuereth lenger / than dooth dronkenesse	P*er*seu*er*eth
O glotonye / ful of cursednesse	
O cause first' of oure confusiou*n*	
O original / of oure dampnaciou*n*	
Til Crist hadde boght vs / with his blood agayn	Crist / boght w*ith*
Lo how deere / shortly for to sayn	Lo /

485 Nolite inebriari vino in quo est luxuria Hg El
Of Glotonye and of leccherye El

[4] Miniature of the Pardoner in right margin.
[5] ¶P*ar*doner 138*v*

	ELLESMERE
Aboght was / thilke cursed vileynye	Aboght
Corrupt was al this world for glotonye	Corrupt / world
Adam oure fader and his wyf also	¶Adam
Fro Paradys / to labour and to wo	
Were dryuen for that vice / it is no drede	
For whil þat Adam fasted / as I rede	
He was in Paradys / and whan þat he	he
Eet of the frut defended on a tree	fruyt deffended on the tree
Anon he was out cast to wo and peyne	
O glotonye / on thee wel oghte vs pleyne	oghte
¶O wiste a man / how manye maladies	O maladyes
Folwen of excesse / and of glotonyes	
He wolde been / the moore mesurable	
Of his diete / sittyng at his table	sittynge
Allas the shorte throte / the tendre mouth	Allas / tendre mouth
Maketh / þat Est and West and North and South	Maketh *and* West *and* South
In erthe / in Eyr / in Water / men to swynke	In Erthe / Eir / man
To gete a gloton / deyntee mete and drynke	glotoun /
Of this matere / o Paul / wel kanstow trete	matiere / Paul
Mete vn to wombe / and wombe eek vn to mete	wombe eek
Shal god destroyen bothe / as Paulus seith	seith
Allas a foul thyng is it by my feith	Allas / thyng it / feith
To seye this word / and fouler is the dede	
Whan man so drynketh / of the white *and* rede	and
That of his throte / he maketh his pryuee	
Thurgh / thilke cursed sup*er*fluite	Thurgh sup*er*fluitee
¶The Apostle wepyng seith ful pitously	¶The Apostel
Ther walken manye / of whiche yow toold haue I	
I seye it now wepyng with pitous voys	
Ther been enemys / of Cristes croys	enemys
Of whiche the ende is deth / wombe is hir god	deeth /
O wombe / o bely / o stynkyng cod	o·bely / o· Cod
Fulfilled of dong and of corrupcioun	donge /
At either ende of thee / foul is the soun	
How greet labour / and cost is thee to fynde	
Thise Cokes / how they stampe / *and* streyne / *and* grynde	Cookes / and streyne and
And turnen substance / in to accident	substaunce Accident
To fulfillen al / the likerous talent	fulfillen / al thy likerous
Out of the harde bones / knokke they	6 bones
The mary / for they caste nat awey	noght

508 Ieronimus contra Iouinianum Quam diu Ieiuna[uit Adam] in paradiso fuit comedit et eiectus est st[atim] duxit vxorem Hg (defective) El

522 esca ventri et venter escis deus autem et hunc et illam destruet Hg El

529 Ad Philipenses capitulo .3°. Hg El

[6] ¶P*ar*doner *139r*

Abought was thilke cursed vileynye
Corrupt was al this world for glotonye
Adam oure fader and his wyf also
ffro Paradys to labour and to wo
Were dryuen for that vice it is no drede
ffor whil þt Adam fasted as I rede
He was in Paradys and whan þt he
Eet of the fruyt defended on a tree

Ieron' contra Iouinianum // Quamdiu ieiunauit in paradiso fuit / comedit et eiectus est · statim duxit uxorem

Anon he was out cast to wo and peyne
O glotonye on thee wel oghte vs pleyne
O wiste a man how manye maladies
ffolwen of excesse and of glotonyes
He wolde been the moore mesurable
Of his diete sittyng at his table
Allas the shorte throte the tendre mouth
Maketh þt Est and West and North and South
In erthe in Eyr in water men to swynke
To gete a glotoun deyntee mete and drynke
Of this matere o Paul wel kanstow trete
Mete vn to wombe and wombe eek vn to mete
Shal god destroyen bothe as Paulus seith

// Esca ventri et venter escis / deus autem et hunc et illa destruet

Allas a foul thyng is it by my feith
To seye this word and fouler is the dede
Whan man so drynketh of the white & rede
That of his throte he maketh his pryuee
Thurgh thilke cursed superfluitee
The Apostle wepyng seith ful pitously
Ther walken manye of whiche yow toold haue I

// Ad Philipenses ca° 3°.

I seye it now wepyng with pitous voys
They been enemys of Cristes croys
Of whiche the ende is deth wombe is hir god
O wombe o bely o stynkyng cod
ffulfilled of dong and of corrupcioun
At either ende of thee foul is the soun
How greet labour and cost is thee to fynde
Thise cokes how they stampe & streyne & grynde
And turnen substance in to accident
To fulfillen al the likerous talent
Out of the harde bones knokke they
The mary for they caste nat awey

That may go thurgh the golet / softe and soote
Of Spicerie of leef and bark and roote
Shal been his sauce ymaked by delit
To make hym yet a newer appetit
But certes he that haunteth swiche delices — Qui autem in deliciis est viuens mortuus est
Is deed / whil þt he lyueth in tho vices
A lecherous thyng is wyn / and dronkenesse — Luxuriosa res vinum
Is ful of stryuyng / and of wrecchednesse — Et contumeliosa ebrietas
O dronke man / disfigured is thy face
Sour is thy breeth / foul artow to embrace
And thurgh thy dronke nose / semeth the soun
As thogh thou seydest ay / Sampson Sampsoun
And yet god woot / Sampson drank neuere no wyn
Thou fallest / as it were a stiked swyn
Thy tonge is lost / and al thyn honeste cure
ffor dronkenesse is verray sepulture
Of mannes wit / and his discrecion
In whom þt drynke / hath dominacion
He kan no conseil kepe / it is no drede
Now kepe yow / fro the white and fro the rede
And namely / fro the white wyn of Lepe
That is to selle / in ffisshstrete / or in Chepe
This wyn of Spaigne / crepeth subtilly
In othere wynes / growynge faste by
Of which ther ryseth swich fumositee
That whan a man / hath dronken draghtes thre
And weneth þt he be / at hom in Chepe
He is in Spaigne / right at the toune of Lepe
Nat at the Rochel / ne at Burdeux toun
And thanne wol he seyn / Sampson Sampsoun
But herkneth lordynges / o word I yow preye
That alle the souereyn actes / dar I seye
Of victories / in the olde testament
Thurgh verray god / that is omnipotent
Were doon in abstinence / and in prayere
Looketh the Bible / and ther ye may it leere
Looke Attilla / the grete conquerour
Deyde in his sleep / with shame and dishonour
Bledyng at his nose / in dronkenesse
A capitayn / sholde lyue in sobrenesse

	ELLESMERE
That may go thurgh the golet softe and soote	thurgħ swoote
Of Spicerie / of lief / and bark / and roote	spicerie / leef // bark
Shal been his Sauce / ymaked by delit	sauce delit
To make hym yet a newer appetit	Appetit
But c*er*tes / he that haunteth swiche delices	
Is deed / whil *þ*at he lyueth in tho vices	
¶A lecherous thyng is wyn // and dronkenesse	thyng wyn
Is ful of stryuyng and of wrecchednesse	
O dronke man / disfigured is thy face	
Sour is thy breeth / foul artow to embrace	breetħ /
And thurgh thy dronke nose / semeth the soun	thurgħ
As thogh thou seydest ay / Sampsou*n* Sampsoun	thougħ seydest ay Sampsou*n* Sampsou*n*
And yet god woot Sampson drank neu*er*e no wyn	Sampsou*n*
Thou fallest as it were a stiked swyn	styked
Thy tonge is lost and al thyn honest cure	lost / honeste
For dronkenesse / is verray sepulture	
Of mannes wit and his discreciou*n*	
In whom *þ*at drynke / hath domynaciou*n*	drynke dominaciou*n*
He kan no conseil kepe / it is no drede	
Now kepe yow / fro the white and fro the rede	
And namely / fro the white wyn of lepe	
That is to selle / in Fisshstrete / or in Chepe	Fysshstrete /
This wyn of Spaigne / crepeth subtilly	
In othere wynes / growynge faste by	
Of which / ther riseth swich fumositee	ryseth
That whan a man / hath dronken draghtes thre	man draughtes
And weneth *þ*at he be / at hom in Chepe	weneth / that be hoom
He is in Spaigne / right at the toune of lepe	rigħt
Nat at the Rochel / ne at Burdeux toun	Rochele /
And thanne wol he seyn / Sampson Sampsoun	seye / Sampsou*n* Sampsou*n*
¶But herkneth lordynges / o word I yow preye	lordes /
That alle the souereyn actes / dar I seye	sou*er*eyn Actes
Of victories / in the olde testament	
Thurgh verray god / that is om*n*ipotent	Thurgħ *þ*at omnipotent
Were doon in abstinence / and in prayere	Abstinence / preyere
Looketh the Bible / and ther ye may it leere	
¶Looke Attilla / the grete conquerour	Attilla Conquerour
Deyde in his sleep*e* / with shame and dishono*ur*	w*ith* dishonour
Bledyng at his nose / in dronkenesse	Bledynge ay at nose
A Capitayn / sholde lyue in sobrenesse	

547 qui autem in delicijs est viuens mortuus est Hg El

549 luxuriosa res vinum et contumeliosa ebrietas Hg El

¶And ou*er* al this / auyseth yow right wel	And right
What was comaunded / vn to Lamwel	
Nat Samuel / but Lamwel seye I	
Redeth the Bible / and fynd it exp*re*sly	fynde
Of wyn yeuynge / to hem þ*a*t han Iustise	yeuyng
Namoore of this / for it may wel suffise	
¶And now / that I haue spoken of glotonye	7 ¶Of hasardrye] ANd now I Glotonye
Now wol I / yow defende hasardrye	I yow / deffenden
Hasard / is verray moder of lesynges	mooder
And of deceite / and cursed forswerynges	
Blaspheme of Crist manslaughtre / and wast also	Blasphemyng *crist* manslaughtre *and*
Of catel / and of tyme / and forthermo	catel
It is reproue / and contrarie of honour	repreeue / hono*ur*
For to ben holden / a co*m*mune hasardour	holde /
And euere the hyer / he is of estaat	euer
The moore is he holden desolat	moore / desolaat
If þ*a*t a Prynce / vseth hasardrye	that
In alle gouernance / and policye	gouernau*n*ce
He is / as by co*m*mune opynyou*n*	opiniou*n*
Yholde / the lasse in reputaciou*n*	Yholde lasse /
¶Stilbon / that was a wys Embassadour	¶Stilbou*n* / embassadour
Was sent to Corynthe / in ful gret honour	greet hono*ur*
Fro lacedomye / to make hir*e* alliau*n*ce	Lacidomye / maken
And whan he cam / hym happed p*ar* chaunce	
That alle the gretteste / þ*a*t were of that lond	that were lond
Pleiynge at the hasard / he hem fond	Pleyynge atte hasard / fond
For which as soone / as it myghte be	which /
He stal hym hom agayn / to his contree	hoom
And seyde / ther wol I nat lese my name	
Ny wol nat take on me / so greet defame	Ne I wol me
Yow for to allie / vn to none hasardours	
Sendeth / othere wise Embassadours	
For by my trouthe / me were leu*er*e dye	
Than I yow sholde / to hasardours allye	Hasardours
For ye that been / so glorious in honours	
Shal nat allye yow / with hasardours	Shul allyen
As by my wyl / ne as by my tretee	
This wise Philosophre / thus seyde he	hee
¶Looke eek / that to the kyng Demetrius	eek that the kyng
The kyng of Parthes / as the book seith vs	

584 Noli vinum dare et cetera Hg El Variant: et cetera) *om.* El

591 Policratici libro .1°. Mendaciorum et periuriarum mater est Alea Hg El

7 ¶Pardoner *139v*

The Pardoner

And over al this / avyseth yow right wel
What was comaunded / vn to Lamuel
Nat Samuel / but Lamuel seye I
Redeth the Bible / and fynd it expresly
Of wyn yevynge / to hem þt han Iustise
Namoore of this / for it may wel suffise
And now that I haue spoken of glotonye
Now wol I / yow deffende hasardrye
Hasard / is verray moder of lesynges
And of deceite / and cursed forswerynges
Blasphemé of Crist / manslaughtre / and wast also
Of catel / and of tyme / and forther mo
It is repreve / and contrarie of honour
ffor to ben holden / a commune hasardour
And euere the hyer / he is of estaat
The moore is he holden desolat
If þt a Prynce / vseth hasardrye
In alle gouernance / and policye
He is / as by commune opynyon
Yholde the lasse in reputacion
Stilbon / that was a wys Embassadour
Was sent to Corynthe / in ful gret honour
ffro Lacedomye / to make hir alliance
And whan he cam / hym happed par chaunce
That alle the grettest / þt were of that lond
Pleyynge at the hasard / he hem fond
ffor which as soone / as it myghte be
He stal hym hoom agayn / to his contree
And seyde / ther wol I nat lese my name
Ny wol nat take on me / so greet defame
Yow for to allie / vn to none hasardours
Sendeth / othere wise Embassadours
ffor by my trouthe / me were leuere dye
Than I yow sholde / to hasardours allye
ffor ye that been / so glorious in honours
Shal nat allye yow / with hasardours
As by my wyl / ne as by my tretee
This wise Philosophre / thus seyde he
Looke eek / that to the kyng Demetrius
The kyng of Parthes / as the book seith vs

Noli vinum dare &c.

Policr' li. 1o. Mendaciorum et periuriorum mater est alea

Sente hym a paire of dees / of gold in scorn
ffor he hadde vsed hasard ther biforn
ffor which he heeld his glorie / or his renoun
At no value / or reputacioun
lordes may fynden oother maner pley
Honeste ynow / to dryue the day awey
Now wol I speke of othes false and grete
A word or two / as olde bokes trete
Greet sweryng / is a thyng abhomynable
And fals sweryng / is yet moore repreuable
The heighe god / forbad sweryng at al
Witnesse on Mathew / but in special — Nolite iurare omnino / mathei
Of sweryng / seith the holy Jeremye — Jeremie .4o. Jurabis in veritate in iudicio & iusticia
Thow shalt swere sooth thyne othes / & nat lye
And swere in doom / and eek in rightwisnesse
But ydel sweryng / is a cursednesse
Bihoold and se / þt in the firste table
Of heighe goddes hestes honurable
How þt the seconde heste of hym / is this
Take nat my name / in ydel or amys
lo rather he forbedeth swich sweryng /
Than homycide / or many a cursed thyng /
I seye þt as by ordre / thus it stondeth
This knoweth / that hise hestes vnderstondeth
How that the seconde heste of god / is that /
And forther ouer / I wol thee telle al plat /
That vengeance shal nat parten from his hous
That of hise othes / is to outrageous
By goddes precious herte / and by his nayles
And by the blood of Crist / that is in hayles
Seuene is my chaunce / and thyn is cynk & treye
By goddes armes / if thow falsly pleye
This daggere / shal thurgh out thyn herte go
This fruyt cometh / of the bicche bones two
fforsweryng / Ire / falsnesse / homycide
Now for the loue of Crist / that for vs dyde
lete youre othes / bothe grete and smale
But sires now wol I telle forth my tale
Thise Riotours thre / of whiche I telle
longe erst er prime / rong of any belle

Sente hym a paire of dees / of gold in scorn	him / dees
For he hadde vsed / hasard ther biforn	hasard
For which / he heeld his glorie / or his renoun	
At no value / or reputacioun	
Lordes may fynden / oother man*er*e pley	maner
Honeste ynow / to dryue the day awey	ynough /
¶Now wol I speke / of oothes false and grete	Now othes
A word or two / as olde bokes trete	bookes
¶Greet sweryng is a thyng abhomynable	Greet thyng abhominable
And fals sweryng is yet moore repreuable	
The heighe god / forbad sweryng at al	heighe sweryng
Witnesse on Mathew / but in special	
Of sweryng seith the holy Ieremye	hooly
Thow shalt swere sooth thyne othes / *and* nat lye	Thou shalt seye sooth othes and
And swere in doom / and eek in rightwisnesse	8 in doom in doom /9 rightwisnesse
But ydel sweryng is a cursednesse	
¶Bihoold and se / þat in the firste table	Bihoold that
Of heighe goddes hestes honurable	heighe heestes
How þat the seconde heste of hym / is this	Hou / that heeste /
Take nat my name / in ydel or amys	
Lo rather he forbedeth / swich sweryng	forbedeth
Than homycide / or many a cursed thyng	or any cursed
I seye / þat as by ordre / thus it standeth	that stondeth
This knoweth / that hise hestes vnderstandeth	knowen / heestes vnderstondeth
How that the seconde heste of god / is that	þat / the heeste god
And forther ouer I wol thee telle al plat	ou*er* /
That vengeance / shal nat parten from his hous	p*ar*ten
That of hise othes / is to outrageous	
By goddes p*re*cious herte / and by his nayles	
And by the blood of Crist that is in hayles	
Seuene is my chance / and thyn is cynk *and* treye	chaunce / cynk
By goddes armes / if thow fa[ls]ly pleye	Armes / thou falsly
This dagger / shal thurgh out thyn herte go	daggere / thurgh
This frut cometh / of the bicche bones two	fruyt bicched
Forsweryng / Ire / falsnesse / homycide	Forsweryng
Now for the loue of Crist that for vs dyde	þat
Lete youre othes / bothe grete and smale	
But sires / now wol I / telle forth my tale	I forth
¶Thise Riotours thre / of whiche I telle	Thise
Longe erst er Pryme ronge of any belle	p*ri*me rong

629 Of sweryng and forsweryng El

633 Nolite iurare omnino Mathei .5. Hg El Variants: iurare omnino) o.i. El Mathei .5°.) *om.* El

635 Ieremie .4°. Iurabis in veritate in Iudicio et Iusticia Hg El

8 ¶P*ar*doner *140r*

9 Second 'in doom' marked for deletion.

Were set hem / in a Tau*er*ne to drynke
And as they sat they herde a belle klynke
Biforn a cors / was caryed to his graue
That oon of hem / gan callen to his knaue
Go bet quod he / and axe redily
What cors is this / that passeth heer forby
And looke / *þ*at thow reporte his name wel
¶Sire quod this boy / it nedeth neu*er* a del
It was me told / er ye cam heer two houres
He was p*ar*dee / an old felawe of youres
And sodeynly / he was yslayn to nyght
Fordronke / as he sat on his bench vp right
Ther cam a p*ri*uee theef / men clepeth deeth
That in this contree / al the peple sleeth
And with his spere / he smoot his herte atwo
And wente his wey / with outen wordes mo
He hath / a thousand slayn this pestilence
And maister / er ye come in his p*re*sence
Me thynketh / that it were necessarie
For to be war / of swich an Adu*er*sarie
Beeth redy / for to meete hym eu*er*e moore
Thus taughte me my dame / I sey namoore
¶By Seinte Marie / seyde this Tauerner
The child seith sooth / for he hath slayn this yer
Henne ouer a myle / with Inne a greet village
Bothe man and womman / child and hyne *and* page
I trowe / his habitacIou*n* be there
To been auysed / greet wisdom it were
Er that he dide / a man a dishonour
¶Ye goddes armes / quod this Riotour
Is it swich pe*r*il / with hym for to meete
I shal hym seke / by wey / and eek by Strete
I make avow / to goddes digne bones
Herkneth felawes / we thre been al ones
Lat ech of vs / holde vp his hand to oother
And ech of vs / bicome ootheres brother
And we wol sleen / this false traytour deeth
He shal be slayn / he *þ*at so manye sleeth
By goddes dignytee / er it be nyght
¶Togidres han thise thre / hir trouthes plyght

ELLESMERE

Tauerne
clynke
caried /
*þ*at
thou weel
¶Si*re* neu*er*adeel
toold /
old
nyght
For dronke / right
theef / deeth
sleeth
with
Beth eu*er*emoore
taughte
[10] Tau*er*ner
yeer
ou*er* Mile /
wom*m*an / child *and* hyne /
wysdom
that dide man /
Armes /
meete ⸗
wey
auow /
hand til oother
bicomen otheres
trayto*ur* deeth
slayn / which *þ*at sleeth
dignitee / nyght /
plight

[10] ¶P*ar*doner *140v*

Were set hem / in a tauerne to drynke
And as they sat / they herde a belle clynke
Biforn a cors / was caried to his graue
That oon of hem / gan callen to his knaue
Go bet quod he / and axe redily
What cors is this / that passeth heer forby
And looke þt thow reporte his name wel
Sire quod this boy / it nedeth neuer a del
It was me told / er ye cam heer two houres
He was pardee / an old felawe of youres
And sodeynly / he was yslayn to nyght
ffordronke / as he sat on his bench vp ryght
Ther cam a priuee theef / men clepeth deeth
That in this contree / al the peple sleeth
And with his spere / he smoot his herte atwo
And wente his wey / with outen wordes mo
He hath a thousand slayn this pestilence
And maister / er ye come in his presence
Me thynketh / that it were necessarie
ffor to be war / of swich an aduersarie
Beth redy / for to meete hym eueremoore
Thus taughte me my dame / I sey namoore
By seinte marie / seyde this tauerner
The child seith sooth / for he hath slayn this yeer
Henne ouer a myle / with inne a greet village
Bothe man and womman / child and hyne & page
I trowe / his habitacion be there
To been auysed / greet wysdom it were
Er that he dide / a man a dishonour
Ye goddes armes / quod this Riotour
Is it swich peril / with hym for to meete
I shal hym seke / by wey and eek by strete
I make avow / to goddes digne bones
Herkneth felawes / we thre been al ones
Lat ech of vs / holde vp his hand to oother
And ech of vs / bicome otheres brother
And we wol sleen / this false traytour deeth
He shal be slayn / he þt so manye sleeth
By goddes dignytee / er it be nyght
Togidres han thise thre / hir trouthes plyght

To lyue and dyen / ech of hem with oother
As though he were / his owene ybore brother
And vp they stirte al dronken in this rage
And forth they goon towardes that village
Of which the Tauerner / hadde spoke biforn
And many a grisly ooth / thanne han they sworn
And Cristes blessed body / they torente
Deeth shal be deed / if they may hym hente
Whan they han goon / nat fully half a myle
Right as they wolde / han treden ouer a style
An old man and a poure / with hem mette
This olde man / ful mekely hem grette
And seyde thus / now lordes god yow se
The proudeste / of thise Riotours thre
Answerde agayn / what carl with sory grace
Why artow al forwrapped / saue thy face
Why lyuestow so longe / in so greet age
This olde man / gan looke in his visage
And seyde thus / for I ne kan nat fynde
A man / though þt I walked in to Ynde
Neither in Citee / ne in no village
That wolde chaunge / his youthe for myn age
And therfore moot I han / myn age stille
As longe tyme / as it is goddes wille
Ne deeth allas / ne wol nat haue my lyf
Thus walke I / lyk a restelees caytyf
And on the ground / which is my modres gate
I knokke with my staf / bothe erly and late
And seye / leeue moder leet me in
Lo how I vanysshe / flessh and blood and skyn
Allas whan shal my bones / been at reste
Moder with yow / wolde I chaunge my cheste
That in my chambre / longe tyme hath be
Ye for an heyre clowt / to wrappe me
But yet to me / she wol nat do that grace
For which ful pale / and welked is my face
But sires to yow / it is no curteisye
To speken / to an old man vileynye
But he trespase in word / or elles in dede
In holy writ / ye may your self wel rede

Agayns an old man

	ELLESMERE
To lyue and dyen / ech of hem with oother	hem for oother
As thogh he were / his owene ybore brother	thoughħ yborn
And vp they stirte / al dronken / in this rage	stirte / and dronken
And forth they goon / towardes that village	
Of which the Tau*er*ner / hadde spoke biforn	
And many a grisly ooth / thanne han they sworn	
And Cristes blessed body / they to rente	
Deeth shal be deed / if they may hym hente	if that they
¶When they han goon / nat fully half a myle	Mile
Right as they wolde / han treden ou*er* a style	Rigħt troden stile
An old man and a poure / with hem mette	oold w*ith*
This olde man / ful mekely hem grette	
And seyde thus / now lordes god yow se	lordes / see
¶The proudeste / of thise Riotours thre	three
Answerde agayn / what carl w*ith* sory gr*a*ce	
Why artow al forwrapped / saue thy face	artow / forwrapped face./
Why lyuestow so longe / in so greet age	age./
¶This olde man / gan looke in his visage	
And seyde thus / for I ne kan nat fynde	
A man / thogh *þat* I walked in to Inde	thoughħ ynde
Neither in Citee / ne in no village	Citee / nor in
That wolde chaunge / his youthe for myn age	Age
And ther fore moot I han / myn age stille	therfore / han Age
As longe tyme / as it is goddes wille	
¶Ne deeth allas / ne wol nat haue my lyf	han lyf /
Thus walke I / lyk a restelees caytyf'	lyk' kaityf'
And on the ground / which is my modres gate	ground' / moodres
I knokke with my staf / bothe erly and late	
And seye / leeue moder leet me In	mooder'
Lo how I vanysshe / flesshħ *and* blood *and* skyn	vanysshħe / and blood' and
Allas / whan shal my bones / been at reste	11 shul / bones
Moder / with yow / wolde I chaunge my cheste	Mooder /
That in my chambre / longe tyme hath be	
Ye for an heyre clowt' to wrappe me	
But yet to me / she wol nat' do that gr*a*ce	nat
For which ful pale / and welked is my face	which /
But sires / to yow / it is no curteisye	¶But sires
To speken / to an old man vileynye	
But he trespase in word / or ellis in dede	trespasse / elles
In holy writ' ye may your self wel rede	hooly

Agayns an old man

11 ¶P*ar*doner *141r*

	ELLESMERE
¶Agayns an old man / hoor vp on his heed	Agayns oold vpon heedꝭ
Ye shal arise / wher fore I yeue yow reed	Ye sholde arise wherfore reedꝭ
Ne dooth vn to an old man / noon harm now	oold
Namoore than *þ*at ye wolde /. men dide to yow	wolde / did
In age // if *þ*at ye so longe abyde	age / that
And god be with yow / wher ye go or ryde	wi*th* wher*e*
I moot go thider / as I haue to go	
¶Nay olde cherl / by god thow shalt nat so	thou
Seyde / this oother hasardour anon	Seyde
Thow p*ar*test nat so lightly / by Seint Ioħn	Thou partest lighħtly /
Thow speeke right now / of thilke traytour deeth	Thou spak⁊ righħt / trayt*our*
That in this contree / alle oure freendes sleeth	
Haue here my trouthe / as thow art his espye	heer thou
Tel wher he is / or thow shalt it abye	Telle wher*e* thou
By god / and by the holy sacrament	hooly sacrement⁊
For soothly / thow art oon of his assent⁊	thou
To sleen vs yonge folk⁊ thow false theef /	folk / thou
¶Now sires quod he / if *þ*at yow be so leef⁊	ye
To fynde deeth / turn vp this croked wey	turne
For in that groue / I lafte hym by my fey	
Vnder a tree / and ther he wol abyde	there wole
Nat for youre boost⁊ he wol hym no thyng hyde	Noght your*e* wole hi*m*
Se ye that ook⁊ right ther ye shal hym fynde	righħt ther*e*
God saue yow / that boghte agayn man kynde	yow *þ*at mankynde
And yow amende / thus seyde this olde man	
¶And euerich / of thise Riotours ran	And
Til he cam to that tree / and ther they founde	
Of floryns fyne / of gold / ycoyned rounde	fyne goldꝭ
Wel ny an .viij. busshels / as hem thoughte	busshħels / thoughħte
No lenger thanne / after deeth they soughte	soughħte
But ech of hem / so glad was of the sighte	of that sighħte
For *þ*at the floryns / been so faire and brighte	brighħte
That doun they sette hem / by this p*re*cious hoord	hoordꝭ
The worste of hem / he spak the firste word	wordꝭ
¶Bretheren quod he / taak kepe / what *þ*at I seye	kepe what I
My wit is greet⁊ thogh *þ*at I bourde and pleye	thoughħ
This tresor hath Fortune / vn to vs yeuen	tresor / Fortune
In myrthe and iolitee / oure lyf to lyuen	Ioliftee /
And lightly as it cometh / so wol we spende	12 lighħtly comthħ /
Ey goddes precious dignytee / who wende	p*re*cious dignitee /

743 coram canuto capite consurg[e] Hg (defective) El

[12] ¶P*ar*doner *141v*

Agayns an old man / hoor vp on his heed — Coram canuto capite consurge
Ye shal aryse / wherfore I yeue yow reed
Ne dooth vn to an old man / noon harm now
Namoore than þt ye wolde / men dide to yow
In age / if þt ye so longe abyde
And god be with yow / wher ye go or ryde
I moot go thider / as I haue to go
Nay olde cherl / by god thow shalt nat so
Seyde this oother hasardour anon
Thow partest nat so lightly / by Seint John
Thow speeke right now / of thilke traytour deeth
That in this contree / alle oure freendes sleeth
Haue heer my trouthe / as thow art his espye
Tel wher he is / or thow shalt it abye
By god / and by the holy sacrament
For soothly / thow art oon of his assent /
To sleen vs yonge folk / thow false theef /
Now sires quod he / if þt yow be so leef /
To fynde deeth / turne vp this croked wey
For in that groue / I lafte hym by my fey
Vnder a tree / and ther he wol abyde
Nat for youre boost / he wol hym no thyng hyde
Se ye that ook / right ther ye shal hym fynde
God saue yow / that boghte agayn man kynde
And yow amende / thus seyde this olde man
And euerich of thise Riotours ran
Til he cam to that tree / and ther they founde
Of floryns fyne of gold / ycoyned rounde
Wel ny an .viij. busshels / as hem thoughte
No lenger thanne / after deeth they soughte
But ech of hem / so glad was of the sighte
For þt the floryns / been so faire and brighte
That down they sette hem / by this precious hoord
The worste of hem / he spak the firste word
Bretheren quod he / taak kepe what þt I seye
My wit is greet / though þt I bourde and pleye
This tresor hath Fortune / vn to vs yeuen
In myrthe and iolitee / oure lyf to lyuen
And lightly as it cometh / so wol we spende
Ey goddes precious dignytee / who wende

To day / that we sholde han / so fair a grace
But myghte this gold / be caried fro this place
Hoom to myn hous / or ellis vn to youres
For wel ye woot / that al this gold is oures
Thanne were we / in heigh felicitee
But trewely / by daye it may nat be
Men wolde seyn / þt we were theues stronge
And for oure owene tresor / doon vs honge
This tresor / moste ycaried be by nyghte
As wisly / and as sleyly / as it myghte
Ther fore I rede / that cut amonges vs alle
Be drawe / and lat se / wher the cut wol falle
And he þt hath the cut / with herte blithe
Shal renne to towne / and that ful swithe
And brynge vs breed / and wyn / ful priuely
And two of vs / shal kepen subtilly
This tresor wel / and if he wol nat tarie
Whan it is nyght / we wol this tresor carie
By oon assent / wher as vs thynketh best /
That oon of hem / the cut broghte in his fest /
And bad hem drawe / and looke wher it wol falle
And it fel / on the yongeste of hem alle
And forth toward the town / he wente anon
And also soone / as þt he was agon
That oon of hem / spak thus vn to that oother
Thow knowest wel / thow art my sworn brother
Thy profit / wol I telle thee anon
Thow woost wel / þt oure felawe is agon
And heere is gold / and that ful greet plentee
That shal departed been / among vs thre
But nathelees / if I kan shape it so
That it departed were / among vs two
Hadde I nat doon / a freendes torn to thee
That oother answerde / I noot how that may be
He woot þt the gold / is with vs tweye
What shal we doon / what shal we to hym seye
Shal it be conseil / seyde the firste shrewe
And I shal telle / in a wordes fewe
What we shul doon / and brynge it wel aboute
I graunte quod that oother / out of doute

To day / that we sholde han / so fair a g*ra*ce	han grace
But myghte this gold / be caried fro this place	myghte
Hoom to myn hous / or ellis vn to youres	elles
For wel ye woot that al this gold is oures	þ*at*
Thanne were we / in heigh felicitee	heigh
But trewely / by daye it may nat be	bee
Men wolde seyn / þ*at* we were theues stronge	⟨we⟩
And for oure owene tresor / doon vs honge	
This tresor / moste ycaried be by nyghte	nyghte
As wisly / and as sleyly / as it myghte	wisely / slyly / myghte
Ther fore I rede / that cut amonges vs alle	Wherfore I þ*at* Cut among
Be drawe / and lat se / wher the cut wol falle	the Cut
And he þ*at* hath the cut with herte blithe	Cut
Shal renne to towne / and that ful swithe	
And brynge vs / breed / and wyn / ful p*ri*uely	vs breed
And two of vs / shal kepen subtilly	shul
This tresor wel / and if he wol nat tarye	tarie
Whan it is nyght we wol this tresor carye	nyght carie
By oon assent wher as vs thynketh best	assent / where
That oon of hem / the cut broghte in his fest	Cut broghte
And bad hem drawe / and looke wher it wol falle	bad hym drawe / where
And it fel / on the yongeste of hem alle	fil /
And forth toward the town / he wente anon	forth toun /
And also soone / as þ*at* he was agon	that gon
That oon of hem / spak thus vn to that oother	oon spak thus /
Thow knowest wel / thow art my sworn brother	wel / thou
Thy p*ro*fit wol I telle thee anon	
Thow woost wel / þ*at* oure felawe is agon	Thou that
And heere is gold / and that ful greet plentee	
That shal departed been / among vs thre	
But nathelees / if I kan shape it so	
That it departed were / among vs two	
Hadde I nat doon / a freendes torn to thee	thee
¶That oother answerde / I noot how that may be	noot hou
He woot þ*at* the gold / is with vs tweye	woot how that gold
What shal we doon / what shal we to hym seye	Whal we seye
¶Shal it be conseil / seyde the firste shrewe	shrewe
And I shal telle / in a wordes fewe	tellen /
What we shul doon / and brynge it wel aboute	shal bryngen
¶I graunte quod that oother / out of doute	

⸗The Pardoner⸗	ELLESMERE
That by my trouthe / I wol thee nat biwreye	I shal thee
¶Now quod the firste / thow woost wel we be tweye	thou
And two of vs / shul strenger be than oon	
Looke whan þat he is set that right anon	riħt anoon
Arys / as though thow woldest with hym pleye	thouġh thou *with*
And I shal ryue hym / thurgh the sydes tweye	shal / thurgħ
Whil that thow strogelest with hym / as in game	13 thou
And with thy daggere / looke thow do the same	dagger*e* / thou
And thanne shal / al this gold departed be	thanne / shal gold /
My deere freend / bitwixe thee and me	freend / bitwixen me and thee
Thanne may we bothe / oure lustes al fulfille	we / bothe aƚƚ
And pleye at dees / right at oure owene wille	riħt
And thus acorded been / thise sherewes tweye	thus / been shrewes
To sleen the thridde / as ye han herd me seye	
¶This yongeste / which that wente to the toun	þ*a*t wente vn to
Ful ofte in herte / he rolleth vp and doun	
The beautee of thise floryns / newe *and* brighte	and briġħte
O lord quod he / if so were þat I myghte	myġħte
Haue al this tresor / to my self allone	
Ther is no man / þat lyueth vnder the trone	
Of god / that sholde lyue / so myrie as I	lyue murye
And at the laste / the feend oure enemy	atte laste /
Putte in his thoght þat he sholde poyson beye	thouġħt
With which he myghte sleen / his felawes tweye	which / myġħte / sleen hise
For why / the feend foond hym / in swich lyuynge	hym
That he hadde leue / hym to sorwe brynge	leue / hem to
For this was outrely / his ful entente	fulle
To sleen hem bothe / and neuere to repente	neu*er*e
¶And forth he goth / no lenger wolde he tarye	And gooth / tarie
In to the toun / vn to Apothecarye	Apothecarie
And preyed hym / þat he hym wolde selle	preyde
Som poysou*n* / that he myghte his rattes quelle	þ*a*t myġħte hise
And eek ther was / a polcat in his hawe	
That as he seyde / his capons hadde yslawe	hise capou*n*s
And fayn he wolde / wreke hym if he myghte	hym / myġħte
On v*er*myn / that destroyed hym by nyghte	þ*a*t nyġħte
¶The Pothecarie answerde / and thow shalt haue	thou
A thyng that also god / my soule saue	god
In al this world / ther is no creature	world /
That ete / or dronke / hath of this confiture	eten dronken hath /

13 ¶P*ar*doner *142r*

That by my trouthe I wol thee nat biwreye
¶ Now quod the firste / thow woost wel we be tweye
And two of vs / shul strenger be than oon
Looke whan þt he is set / that right anon
Arys / as though thow woldest / with hym pleye
And I shal ryue hym / thurgh the sydes tweye
Whil that thow strogelest with hym / as in game
And with thy daggere / looke thow do the same
And thanne shal al this gold departed be
My deere freend / bitwixe thee and me
Thanne may we bothe / oure lustes al fulfille
And pleye at dees / right at oure owene wille
And thus acorded been / thise sherewes tweye
To sleen the thrydde / as ye han herd me seye
¶ This yongeste / which that wente to the toun
fful ofte in herte / he rolleth vp and doun
The beautee of thise floryns / newe and brighte
O lord quod he / if so were þt I myghte
Haue al this tresor / to my self allone
Ther is no man / þt lyueth vnder the trone
Of god / that sholde lyue so murye as I
And at the laste / the feend oure enemy
Putte in his thoght / þt he sholde poyson beye
With which he myghte sleen / his felawes tweye
ffor why / the feend foond hym / in swich lyuynge
That he hadde leue / hym to sorwe brynge
ffor this was outrely / his ful entente
To sleen hem bothe / and neuere to repente
¶ And forth he goth / no lenger wolde he tarye
In to the toun / vn to a pothecarye
And preyed hym / þt he hym wolde selle
Som poyson / that he myghte his rattes quelle
And eek ther was / a polcat / in his hawe
That as he seyde / his capouns hadde yslawe
And fayn he wolde / wreke hym if he myghte
On vermyn / that destroyed hym by nyghte
¶ The pothecarye answerde / and thow shalt haue
A thyng / that also god / my soule saue
In al this world / ther is no creature
That ete or drunke / hath of this confiture

Ete but the montance / of a corn of whete
That he ne shal his lyf / anoon forlete
Ye sterue he shal / and that in lasse while
Than thow wolt goon a paas / nat but a myle
The poyson / is so strong / and violent /
This cursed man / hath in his hand yhent /
This poyson in a box / and sith he ran
In to the nexte strete / vn to a man
And borwed hym / large botels thre
And in the two / his poyson poured he
The thridde / he kepte clene for his drynke
ffor al the nyght / he shoop hym for to swynke
In caryyng / of the gold / out of that place
And whan this Riotour / with sory grace
Hadde filled with wyn / hise grete botels thre
To hise felawes / agayn repaireth he
¶ What nedeth it / to sermone of it moore
ffor right as they / hadde cast his deeth bifore
Right so they han hym slayn / and that anon
And whan this was doon / thus spak that oon
Now lat vs sitte and drynke / and make vs merye
And afterward / we wol his body berye
And with that word / it happed hym par cas
To take the botel / ther the poyson was
And drank / and yaf his felawe drynke also
ffor which anon / they storuen bothe two
¶ But certes I suppose / that Auycen
Wroot neuere in no Canon / ne in no fen
Mo wonder signes / of empoysonyng /
Than hadde thise wrecches two / er hir endyng /
Thus ended been / thise homicides two
And eek / the false empoysoner also
¶ O · cursed synne / of alle cursednesse
O · traytours homicide / o wikkednesse
O · glotonye / luxurie / and hasardrye
Thou blasphemour of Crist / with vileynye
And othes grete / of vsage / and of pryde
Allas mankynde / how may it bitide
That to thy creatour / which that thee wroghte
And with his precious herte blood / thee boghte

ELLESMERE

Nat but the montau*n*ce / of a corn of whete
That he ne shal his lyf / anoon for lete
Ye sterue he shal / and that in lasse while
Than thow wolt goon a paas / nat but a myle
The poyson / is so strong / and violentꝛ
This cursed man / hath in his hand yhentꝛ
This poyson in a box / and sith he ran
In to the nexte Strete / vn to a man
And borwed hym / large Botels thre
And in the two / his poison poured he
The thridde / he kepte clene for his drynke
For al the nyghtꝛ he shoop*e* hym for to swynke
In cariyngꝛ of the gold / out of that place
And whan this Riotour / with sory *gra*ce
Hadde filled with wyn / hise grete Botels thre
To hise felawes / agayn repaireth he
¶What nedeth itꝛ to sarmone of it moore
For right as they / hadde cast his deeth bifore
Right so / they han hym slayn / and that anon
And whan this was doon / thus spak that oon
Now lat vs sitte and drynke / and make vs merye
And afterward / we wol his body berye
And with that word / it happed hym p*ar* cas
To take the Botel / ther the poyson was
And drank / and yaf his felawe drynke also
For which anon / they storuen bothe the two
¶But certes I suppose / that Auycen
Wroot neuere in no Canon / ne in no fen
Mo wonder signes / of empoysonyngꝛ
Than hadde thise wrecches two / er hir endyngꝛ
Thus ended been / thise homicides two
And eek / the false empoysoner*e* also
¶O · cursed synne / of alle cursednesse
O · traytours homicide / o wikkednesse
O · glotonye / luxure / and hasardrye
Thou blasphemour of Cristꝛ with vileynye
And othes grete / of vsage / and of pryde
Allas mankynde / how may it bityde
That to thy Creatour / which þ*a*t thee wroghte
And with his p*re*cious herte blood / the boghte

Noħt / montance
shal / lif anon forlete

thou Mile
poysou*n* / strong
¶This hond
poysou*n*

botels
poyson
thridde clene / his owene drynke
nyħt /
cariynge
grace
14 botels

sermone
riħt so / as they bifoore
Riħt so
whan þ*a*t this
merie
afterward / berie

botel / poysou*n*
drankꝛ

Auycen̄
neu*ere* Canou*n* / fen̄
empoisonyngꝛ
homycides
eekꝛ
¶Auctor] ¶O
O homycide .o.
O luxurie /
blasphemo*ur*
pride
bitide
creatour / the wroħte
blood thee boħte

[14] ¶P*ar*doner *142v*

	ELLESMERE
Thow art so fals / and so vnkynde allas	Thou
¶Now goode men / god foryeue yow youre t*re*spas	your*e* trespas
And ware yow / fro the synne of Auarice	
Myn holy pardou*n* / may yow alle warisse	hooly p*ar*dou*n* / warice
So that ye offre nobles / or starlynges	þ*at* offre / Sterlynges
Or ellis siluer broches / spones / rynges	elles spoones /
Boweth your*e* heed / vnder this holy bulle	hooly
Cometh vp ye wyues / offreth of youre wolle	Com
Youre name I entre / ⟨here⟩ in my rolle anon	names / entre heer
In to the blisse of heuene / shul ye gon	
I yow assoille / by myn heigh power	heigħ
Ye þ*at* wol offre / as clene and eek as cler	Yow cleer
As ye were born / and lo sires thus I p*re*che	
And Ie*s*u crist that is oure soules leche	
So graunte yow / his pardou*n* to receyue	
For that is best I wol yow nat deceyue	nat
¶But sires / o word / forgat I in my tale	But o· forgat
I haue Relikes / and pardon in my male	pardou*n*
As faire / as any man in Engelond	fair*e* Engelond
Whiche were me yeuen / by the Popes hond	⟨popes⟩ hond
If any of yow / wol of deuociou*n*	wole
Offren / and han myn absolucioun*n*.	Absolucio*un*
Com forth anon / and kneleth here adoun	15 forthħ heer*e*
And mekely / receyueth my pardoun	p*ar*doun
Or ellis / taketh p*ar*dou*n* as ye wende	elles / pardou*n* /
Al newe and fressħ / at euery myles ende	Miles
So þ*at* ye offren alwey / newe and newe	offren / alwey
Nobles / or pens / whiche þ*at* been goode *and* trewe	Nobles be and
It is an honour / to euerich that is heer	
That ye mowe haue / a suffisant p*ar*doner	P*ar*doneer
Tassoille yow / in contree as ye ryde	
For auentures / whiche þ*at* may bityde	
P*ar*auenture / ther may falle oon or two	fallen /
Doun of his hors / and breke his nekke atwo	
Looke which a seuretee is it to yow alle	seuretee /
That I am / in your*e* felaweship yfalle	felaweship*e*
That may assoille yow / bothe moore *and* lasse	and
Whan þ*at* the soule / shal fro the body passe	
I rede / that oure hoost shal bigynne	þ*at* hoost heere shal
For he is moost envoluped in synne	is / moost

[15] ¶P*ar*doner *143r*

The pardoner

Thow art so fals, and so vnkynde allas
Now goode men, god foryeue yow youre trespas
And ware yow, fro the synne of Auarice
Myn holy pardoun, may yow alle warisse
So that ye offre nobles, or starlynges
Or ellis siluer broches, spones, rynges
Boweth youre heed, vnder this holy bulle
Cometh vp ye wyues, offreth of youre wolle
Youre name I entre heer in my rolle anon
In to the blisse of heuene, shul ye gon
I yow assoille, by myn heigh power
Ye that wol offre, as clene and eek as cleer
As ye were born, and lo sires thus I preche
And Ihesu crist, that is oure soules leche
So graunte yow, his pardoun to receyue
ffor that is best, I wol yow nat deceyue
But sires o word, forgat I in my tale
I haue relikes, and pardoun in my male
As faire, as any man in Engelond
Whiche were me yeuen, by the popes hond
If any of yow, wol of deuocion
Offren, and han myn absolucion.
Com forth anon, and kneleth heere adoun
And mekely, receyueth my pardoun
Or ellis taketh pardoun as ye wende
Al newe and fressh, at euery myles ende
So that ye offren alwey, newe and newe
Nobles, or pens, whiche that been goode and trewe
It is an honour, to euerich that is heer
That ye mowe haue, a suffisant Pardoner
Tassoille yow, in contree as ye ryde
ffor auentures, whiche that may bityde
Parauenture, ther may falle oon or two
Doun of his hors, and breke his nekke atwo
Looke which a seuretee is it to yow alle
That I am, in youre felaweshipe yfalle
That may assoille yow, bothe moore and lasse
Whan that the soule, shal fro the body passe
I rede, that oure hoost, shal bigynne
ffor he is moost, envoluped in synne

Com forth oure hoost / and offre fyrst anon
And thow shalt kisse / the relikes euerychon
Ye for a grote / vnbokeled anon thy purs
¶ Nay nay quod he / thanne haue I Cristes curs
Lat be quod he / it shal nat be so theech
Thow woldest make me kisse thyn olde breech
And swere it were / a relyk of a seint /
Thogh it were / with thy fondement depeynt /
But by the croys / which þt Seint Eleyne fond
I wolde I hadde / thy coylons in myn hond
In stide of relikes / or of seintuarie
Lat cutte hem of / I wol thee hem carie
They shul be shryned / in an hogges toord
¶ This pardoner / answerde nat a word
So wrooth he was / no word ne wolde he seye
¶ Now quod oure hoost / I wol no lenger pleye
With thee / ne with noon oother angry man
¶ But right anon / the worthy knyght bigan
Whan þt he saugh / þt al the peple lough
Namoore of this / for it is right ynough
Sire Pardoner be glad / and murye of cheere
And sire hoost / that been to me so deere
I pray yow / þt ye kisse the Pardoner
And Pardoner / I pray thee / drawe thee neer
And as we diden / lat vs lawe and pleye
Anon they kiste / and ryden forth hir weye

Here is ended the Pardoners tale

	ELLESMERE
Com forth sire hoost / and offre first anon	sir*e* hoost
And thow shalt kisse / the Relikes eu*er*ychon	thou shalt kisse / my Relikes
Ye for a grote / vnbokele anon thy purs	
¶Nay nay quod he / thanne haue I Cristes curs	Nay nay cr*i*stes
Lat be quod he / it shal nat be so thee ich	so theechħ
Thow woldest make me kisse thyn olde breech	Thou woldest me / breechħ
And swere it were / a Relyk of a Seint	swere / were relyk
Thogh it were / with thy fondement depeynt	Thoughħ *with* fundement depeint
But by the croys / which þ*at* Seint Eleyne foond	fond
I wold I hadde / thy coylons in myn hond	wolde / coillons hond
In stide of Relikes / or of Seintuarie	
Lat cutte hem of / I wol thee hem carie	kutte wol with thee
They shul be shryned / in an hogges toord	toord
¶This pardoner / answerde nat a word	P*ar*doner word
So wrooth he was / no word ne wolde he seye	
¶Now quod oure hoost I wol no lenger pleye	
With thee / ne with noon oother angry man	*with* noon
¶But right anon / the worthy knyght bigan	But knyght
Whan þ*at* he saugh / þ*at* al the peple loughħ	saughħ /
Namoore of this / for it is right ynoughħ	rightħ
Sire Pardoner be glad / and murye of cheere	Sir*e* p*ar*doner / glad myrie
And sire hoost that been to me so deere	And ye Sir*e* hoost / þ*at*
I pray yow / þ*at* ye kisse the Pardoner	prey
And Pardoner / I pray thee / drawe thee neer	P*ar*doner / prey
And as we diden / lat vs lawe and pleye	laughħe
Anon they kiste / and ryden forþ hir weye	forth hir

¶Here is ended the Pardoners tale	¶Heere is ended the P*ar*doners tale

## ¶Here bigynneth the Shipmannes tale	1 ¶Heere bigynnetħ the Shipmannes tale
A Marchant whilom / dwelled at Seint Denys	2 whilom
That riche was / for which men helde hym wys	
A wyf he hadde / of excellent beautee	
And compaignable / and reuelous was she	
Which is a thyng⁊ that causeth moore dispence	more
Than worth / is al the cheere and reuerence	worth is / chiere
That men hem doon / at festes and at daunces	
Swiche salutacions / and contenances	salutaciou*n*s / contenaunces
Passen / as dooth a shadwe vp on the wal	
But wo is hym / that payen moot for al	
The sely housbonde / algate he moot paye	moste
He moot vs clothe / and he moot vs arraye	
Al for his owene worship*e* / richely	worship*e*
In which array / we dauncen iolily	daunce
And if þ*at* he noght may / p*ar*auenture	⟨he⟩ nogħt p*ar* auenture
Or ellis / list no swich dispense endure	dispence
But thynketh / it is wasted and ylost⁊	wasted /
Thanne moot another / payen for oure cost⁊	moot⁊ another⁊
Or lene vs gold / and that is pe*r*ilous	
This noble Marchant⁊ heeld a worthy hous	¶This Marchau*nt*⁊
For which / he hadde alday / so greet repair	alday
For his largesse / and for his wyf was fair	
That wonder is / but herkneth to my tale	
Amonges alle hise gestes / grete and smale	
¶Ther was a Monk⁊ a fair man and a bold	Ther boold'
I trowe / a thritty wynter / he was old	trowe / of thritty wynter oold'
That euere in oon / was drawyng⁊ to that place	eue*r*e was comynge to
This yonge Monk⁊ that was so fair of face	Monk / þ*at*
Aqueynted was so / with the goode man	
Sith that⁊ hir firste knewliche bigan	knoweliche
That in his hous / as famulier was he	
As it is possible / any freend to be	
And for as muchel / as this goode man	¶And
And eek this Monk / of which þ*at* I bigan	Monk⁊
Were bothe two yborn / in o village	two / yborn
The Monk⁊ hym claymeth / as for cosynage	Monk /

1 ¶Shipman *143v*

2 Miniature of the Shipman in left margin.

Here bigynneth the Shipmannes tale

A Marchant whilom / dwelled at Seint Denys
That riche was / for which men helde hym wys
A wyf he hadde / of excellent beautee
And compaignable / and reuelous was she
Which is a thyng / that causeth moore dispence
Than worth / is al the cheere and reuerence
That men hem doon / at festes and at daunces
Swiche salutacions / and contenaunces
Passen / as dooth a shadwe vp on the wal
But wo is hym / that payen moot for al
The sely housbonde / algate he moot paye
He moot vs clothe / and he moot vs arraye
Al for his owene worshipe / richely
In which array / we daunceen iolily
And if p^{t} he noght may / par auenture
Or ellis / list no swich dispense endure
But thynketh / it is wasted and ylost /
Thanne moot another / payen for oure cost /
Or lene vs gold / and that is perilous
This noble marchant / heeld a worthy hous
ffor which / he hadde alday / so greet repair
ffor his largesse / and for his wyf was fair
That wonder is / but herkneth to my tale
Amonges alle hise gestes / grete and smale
Ther was a monk / a fair man and a bold
I trowe a thritty wynter / he was old
That euere in oon / was drawyng to that place
This yonge monk / that was so fair of face
Aqueynted was so / with the goode man
Sith that hir firste knoweliche bigan
That in his hous / as famulier was he
As it is possible / any freend to be
And for as muchel / as this goode man
And eek this monk / of which p^{t} I bigan
Were bothe two yborn / in o village
The monk hym clayneth / as for cosynage

And he agayn / he seith nat ones nay
But was as glad ther of / as fowel of day
ffor to his herte / it was a greet plesance
Thus been they knyt / with eterne alliance
And ech of hem / gan oother / for tassure
Of bretherhede / whil þt hir lyf may dure
¶ ffree was daun Iohn / and manly of dispence
As in that hous / and ful of diligence
To doon plesance / and also greet costage
He nat forgat / to yeue the leeste page
In al that hous / but after hir degree
He yaf the lord / and sith al his meynee
Whan þt he cam / som manere honeste thyng
ffor which / they were as glad of his comyng
As fowel is fayn / whan þt the sonne vp riseth
Namoore of this as now / for it suffiseth
¶ But so bifel / this marchant on a day
Shoop hym / to make redy his array
Toward the town of Brugges / for to fare
To byen there / a porcion of ware
ffor which he hath / to Parys sent anon
A messager / and preyed hath daun Iohn
That he sholde come / to Seint Denys and pleye
With hym / and with his wyf / a day or tweye
Er he to Brugges wente / in alle wise
¶ This noble monk / of which I yow deuyse
Hath of his Abbot / as hym list licence
By cause he was a man / of heigh prudence
And eek an Officer / out for to ryde
To seen hir granges / and hir bernes wyde
And vn to Seint Denys / he comth anon
Who was so welcome / as my lord daun Iohn
Oure deere cosyn / ful of curteisye
With hym broghte he / a Iubbe of Maluesye
And eek another / ful of fyn vernage
And volatil / as ay was his vsage
And thus I lete hem / ete and drynke and pleye
This marchant / and this monk / a day or tweye
¶ The thridde day / this marchant vp ariseth
And on his nedes / sadly hym auyseth

	ELLESMERE
And he agayn / he seith nat ones nay	
But was as glad ther of / as fowel of day	as glad
For to his herte / it was a gret plesance	greet plesau*n*ce
Thus been they knytꝰ with eterne alliance	*with* ete*r*ne alliau*n*ce
And ech of hem / gan ootherꝰ for tassure	oother
Of bretherhede / whil *þ*at hir lyf may dure	
¶Free was daun Ioħn / and manly of dispence	3 and namely of
As in that hous / and ful of diligence	
To doon plesance / and also greet costage	plesau*n*ce /
He nat forgatꝰ to yeue the leeste page	noghtꝰ
In al that hous / but after hir degree	al the hous /
He yaf the lord / and sith al his meynee	sitthe
Whan *þ*at he cam / som manere honeste thyngꝰ	that honest
For which / they were as glad of his comyngꝰ	
As fowel is fayn / whan *þ*at the sonne vp riseth	
Namoore of this as now / for it suffiseth	
¶But so bifel / this Marchantꝰ on a day	**B**ut Marchant
Shoop*e* hym / to make redy his array	
Toward the town of Brugges / for to fare	Toward / toun Brugges
To byen there / a porcion of ware	porciou*n*
For which he hath / to Parys sent anon	which / hath
A messager / and preyed hath daun Ioħn	Messager /
That he sholde come / to Seint Denys and pleye	Denys to pleye
With hym / and with his wyfꝰ a day or tweye	hym *with* his wyf /
Er he to Brugges wente / in alle wise	
¶This noble Monkꝰ of which I yow deuyse	
Hath of his Abbotꝰ as hym list licence	
By cause he was a man / of heigh prudence	cause / heiħ
And eek an Officer / out for to ryde	eekꝰ
To seen hir granges / and hir bernes wyde	graunges / and hir*e*
And vn to Seint Denys / he comth anon	
Who was so welcome / as my lord Daun Ioħn	
Oure deere cosyn / ful of curteisye	
With hym broghte he / a Iubbe of Maluesye	he
And eek anotherꝰ ful of fyn vernage	ve*r*nage
And volatil / as ay was his vsage	volatyl /
And thus I lete hem / ete and drynke and pleye	thus / hem drynke and pleye
This Marchantꝰ and this Monk / a day or tweye	Monkꝰ
¶The thridde day / this Marchant vp ariseth	
And on his nedes / sadly hym auyseth	hise

[3] ¶Shipman *144r*

And vp / in to his Countour hous goth he	gooth
To rekene with hym self / wel may be	*with*
Of thilke yeer / how þ*at* it with hym stood	
And how þ*at* he / despended hadde his good	
And if that he / encressed were or noon	þ*at*
Hise bokes / and his bagges / many oon	bookes / bagges
He leyth biforn hym / on his Countyng bord	leith countyng bord
Ful riche was his tresor / and his hord	riche / tresor hord
For which ful faste / his Countour dore he shette	
And eek he nolde / þ*at* no man sholde hym lette	
Of his acountes / for the mene tyme	hise meene
And thus he sit / til it was passed p*ri*me	sit pryme
¶Daun Ioħn was risen / in the morwe also	rysen /
And in the gardyns / walketh to and fro	gardyn /
And hath his thynges seyd / ful curteisly	4 hise
¶This goode wyf / cam walkyng p*ri*uely	wyf walkynge pryuely
In to the gardyn / ther he walketh softe	ther*e*
And hym salueth / as she hath doon ofte	saleweth /
A mayde child / cam in hir compaignye	hir*e*
Which as hir list she may gouerne and gye	gou*er*ne
For yet vnder the yerde was the mayde	
¶O deere cosyn myn / Daun Ioħn she sayde	O
What eyleth yow / so rathe for to ryse	
¶Nece quod he / it oghte ynow suffise	ogħte ynougħ
Fyue houres / for to slepe / vp on a nyght	houres nygħt
But it were / for an old apalled wight	But old appalled wigħt
As been thise wedded men / þ*at* lye and dare	
As in a forme / sit a wery hare	fourme /
Were al forstraught w*ith* houndes grete *and* smale	forstraugħt /
But deere Nece / why be ye so pale	But
I trowe c*er*tes / that oure goode man	
Hath yow laboured / sith the nyght bigan	nygħt
That yow were nede / to resten hastily	
And with that word / he lough ful myrily	*with* lougħ murily
And of his owene thoght he weex al reed	thougħt wax reed
¶This faire wyf / gan for to shake hir heed	wyf heed
And seyde thus / ye god woot al quod she	
Nay cosyn myn / it stant nat so with me	Nay nay cosyn *with*
For by that god / that yaf me soule and lyf	lyf /
In al the Reawme of France / is ther no wyf	wyf

4 ¶Shipman *144v*

The Shipman .

And vp / in to his countour hous goth he
To rekene with hym self / wel may be
Of thilke yeer / how pt it with hym stood
And how pt he / despended hadde his good
And if that he / encressed were or noon
Hise bokes / and his bagges / many oon
He leyth biforn hym / on his countyng bord
fful riche was his tresor / and his hord
ffor which ful faste / his countour dore he shette
And eek he nolde / pt no man sholde hym lette
Of his acountes / for the mene tyme
And thus he sit / til it was passed pryme
¶ Daun Iohn was rysen / in the morwe also
And in the gardyn / walketh to and fro
And hath his thynges seyd / ful curteisly
¶ This goode wyf / cam walkyng pryuely
In to the gardyn / ther he walketh softe
And hym salueth / as she hath doon ofte
A mayde child / cam in hir compaignye
Which as hir list / she may gouerne and gye
ffor yet vnder the yerde was the mayde
¶ O deere cosyn myn / daun Iohn she sayde
What eyleth yow / so rathe for to ryse
¶ Nece quod he / it oghte ynow suffise
ffyue houres / for to slepe / vp on a nyght /
But it were / for an old apalled wight /
As been thise wedded men / pt lye and dare
As in a forme / sit a wery hare
Were al forstraught / wt houndes grete & smale
But deere nece / why be ye so pale
I trowe certes / that oure goode man
Hath yow laboured / sith the nyght bigan
That yow were nede / to resten hastily
And with that word / he lough ful murily
And of his owene thoght / he wax al reed
¶ This faire wyf / gan for to shake hir heed
And seyde thus / ye god woot al quod she
Nay cosyn myn / it stant nat so with me
ffor by that god / that yaf me soule and lyf
In al the Reawme of ffrance / is ther no wyf

That lasse lust hath / to that sory pley
ffor I may synge / allas and weilawey
That I was born / but to no wight quod she
Dar I nat telle / how þt it stant with me
Wher fore I thynke / out of this land to wende
Or ellis / of my self / to make an ende
So ful am I / of drede / and eek of care
¶ This monk bigan / vp on this wyf to stare
And seyde / allas / my nece god forbede
That ye / for any sorwe / or any drede
ffordo youre self / but telleth me youre grief
Parauenture / I may in youre meschief
Conseille / or helpe / and ther fore telleth me
Al youre anoy / for it shal been secree
ffor on my Porthors / I make an oth
That neuere in my lif / for lief / or loth
Ne shal I / of no conseil / yow biwreye
¶ The same agayn to yow / quod she I seye
By god / and by this Porthors I swere
Though men me wolde / al in to peces tere
Ne shal I neuere / for to gon to helle
Biwreye a word / of thyng þt ye me telle
Nat for no cosynage / ne alliance
But verraily / for loue and affiance
Thus been they sworn / and her vp on they keste
And ech of hem / tolde oother what hem leste
¶ Cosyn quod she / if þt I hadde a space
As I haue noon / and namely in this place
Thanne wolde I telle / a legende of my lyf
What I haue suffred / sith I was a wyf
With myn housbonde / al be he youre cosyn
¶ Nay quod this monk / by god and Seint Martin
He is namoore / cosyn vn to me
Than is this leef / þt hangeth on the tree
I clepe hym so / by Seint Denys of ffrance
To han / the moore cause of aqueyntance
Of yow / which I haue loued specially
Abouen alle wommen / sikerly
This swere I yow / on my professiou
Telleth youre grief / lest þt he come adoun

	ELLESMERE
That lasse lust hath / to that sory pley	
For I may synge / allas and weilawey	weylawey
That I was born / but to no wight quod she	wight
Dar I nat telle / how þat it stant with me	that with
Wher fore I thynke / out of this land to wende	Wherfore land
Or ellis / of my self / to make an ende	elles / self
So ful am I / of drede / and eek of care	
¶This Monk bigan / vp on this wyf to stare	Monk bigan
And seyde / allas / my Nece god forbede	And / allas
That ye / for any sorwe / or any drede	
Fordo your self / but telleth me your*e* grief	your*e* self tel me of your*e* grief
P*ar*auenture / I may in youre meschief	I yow may / your*e*
Conseille / or helpe / and therfore telleth me	Conseille
Al youre anoy / for it shal been secree	your*e*
For on my Porthors / I make an oth	ooth
That neu*er*e in my lif / for lief / or loth	lyf / lief ne looth
Ne shal I / of no conseil / yow biwreye	conseil
¶The same agayn to yow / quod she I seye	agayn / . yow
By god / and by this Porthors / I swere	Porthors I yow swere
Thogh men me wolde / al in to peces tere	Though pieces
Ne shal I neu*er*e / for to gon to helle	neuere / goon
Biwreye a word / of thyng þat ye me telle	thyng
Nat for no cosynage / ne alliance	5 Alliance
But verraily / for loue and affiance	ve*r*raily /
Thus been they sworn / and her vp on they keste	heer kiste
And ech of hem / tolde oother what hem leste	liste
¶Cosyn quod she / if þat I hadde a space	
As I haue noon / and namely in this place	
Thanne wolde I telle / a legende of my lyf	
What I haue suffred / sith I was a wyf	
With myn housbonde / al be he youre cosyn	he of youre kyn |
¶Nay quod this Monk by god and Seint Martin	god / and by Seint Martyn
He is namore / cosyn vn to me	is / namoore
Than is this leef þat hangeth on the tree	lief
I clepe hym so / by Seint Denys of France	Frau*n*ce
To han / the moore cause of aqueyntance	haue / Aqueyntau*n*ce
Of yow / which I haue loued specially	
Abouen alle wommen / sikerly	wommen
This swere I yow / on my p*ro*fessiou*n*	
Telleth youre grief / lest þat he come adoun	

5 ¶Shipman *145r*

	ELLESMERE
And hasteth yow / and goth awey anon	gooth your*e* wey
¶My deere loue quod she / o my daun Ioħn	
Ful lief were me / this conseil for to hyde	
But out it moot I may namoore abyde	
¶Myn housbonde is to me / the worste man	Myn housbonde / me
That euere was / sith þ*a*t the world bigan	eu*er*e
But sith I am a wyf / it sit nat me	wyf
To tellen no wight of oure p*ri*uetee	wight /
Neither abedde / ne in noon oother place	a bedde /
God shilde / I sholde it tellen for his g*ra*ce	
A wyf ne shal nat seyn / of hir housbonde	wyf / seyn
But al honour / as I kan vnderstonde	
Saue vn to yow / thus muche I tellen shal	
As help me god / he is noght worth at al	help*e* noght
In no degree / the value of a flye	
But yet me greueth moost his nygardye	moost
And wel ye woot þ*a*t wommen naturelly	wo*m*men
Desiren thynges .vj. as wel as I	sixe /
They wolde / þ*a*t hir housbondes sholde be	that
¶no*ta* ¶Hardy and wise / and riche / and ther to free	Hardy *and* riche *and* therto
And buxom vn to his wyf / and fressh abedde	wyf fressħ
But by that ilke lord / that for vs bledde	
For his honour / my self for to arraye	honour
A sonday next I moot nedes paye	moste
An hundred frankes / or ellis am I lorn	I am
Yet were me leu*er*e / þ*a*t I were Vnborn	that vnborn
Than me were doon / a sclaundre / or vileynye	sclaundre
And if myn housbonde eek / myghte it espye	housbonde / eek it myghte
I nere but lost and ther fore I yow preye	therfore
Lene me this so*m*me / or ellis moot I deye	
Daun Ioħn I seye / lene me thise hundred frankes	6
Pardee / I wol noght faile yow my thankes	P*ar*dee / nat faille
If þ*a*t yow list to doon / that I yow praye	If that doon
For at a c*er*teyn day / I wol yow paye	certeyn
And doon to yow / what plesance and seruyse	s*er*uice
That I may doon / right as yow list deuyse	right deuise
And but .I. do / god take on me vengeance	I
As foul / as eu*er*e hadde Geneloun of France	Genylou*n*
¶This gentil Monk answerde in this manere	Monk /
Now trewely / myn owene lady deere	
I haue quod he / on yow so gret a routhe	greet
That I yow swere / and plighte yow my trouthe	plighte

1363 A womman wolld haue her husband to be hardye wyse Ryche free buxom that is to saye gentell and to be freshe in bed these syxe things a woman dothe desyre as Mr. Chaucer dothe wryte Hg (in sixteenth-century hand)

6 ¶Shipman *145v*

And hasteth yow / and goth awey anon
Nay dere loue quod she / o my daun John
ffful lief were me / this conseil for to hyde
But out it moot / I may namoore abyde
Myn housbonde is to me / the worste man
That euere was / sith pt the world bigan
But sith I am a wyf / it sit nat me
To tellen no wight / of oure priuetee
Neither abedde / ne in noon oother place
God shilde I sholde it tellen for his grace
A wyf ne shal nat seyn / of hir housbonde
But al honour / as I kan vnderstonde
Saue vn to yow / thus muche I tellen shal
As help me god / he is noght worth at al
In no degree / the value of a flye
But yet me greueth moost his nygardye
And wel ye woot / pt wommen naturelly
Desiren thynges .vj. as wel as I
They wolde / pt hir housbondes sholde be
Hardy and wise / and riche / and ther to free
And buxom vn to his wyf / and fressh abedde
But by that ilke lord / that for vs bledde
ffor his honour / my self for to araye
A sonday next / I moot nedes paye
An hundred frankes / or ellis am I lorn
yet were me leuere / pt I were vnborn
Than me were doon / a sclaundre or vileynye
And if myn housbonde eek / myghte it espye
I nere but lost / and ther fore I yow preye
Lene me this somme / or ellis moot I deye
Daun John I seye / lene me thise hundred frankes
Pardee I wol noght / faille yow my thankes
If pt yow list / to doon that I yow praye
ffor at a certeyn day / I wol yow paye
And doon to yow / what plesance and seruyse
That I may doon / right as yow list deuyse
And but I do / god take on me vengeance
As foul / as euere hadde Genelon of ffrance
This gentil monk / answerde in this manere
Now trewely / myn owene lady deere
I haue quod he / on yow so gret a routhe
That I yow swere / and plighte yow my trouthe

That whan youre housbonde / is to fflaundres fare
I wol deliuere yow / out of this care
ffor I wol brynge yow / an hundred frankes
And with that word / he caughte hir by the flankes
And hir embraceth harde / and kiste hir ofte
Goth now youre wey quod he / al stille and softe
And lat vs dyne / as sone / as pt ye may
ffor by my chilyndre / it is pryme of day
Goth now / and beth as trewe as I shal be
¶ Now ellis / god forbede sire quod she
And forth she goth / as iolif as a pye
And bad the Cokes / pt they sholde hem hye
So pt men myghte dyne / and that anon
Vp to hir housbonde / is his wyf ygon
And knokketh at his Countour / boldely
·xi· la· ¶ Who ther quod he / Peter it am I
Quod she / what sire / how longe wol ye faste
How longe tyme / wol ye rekene and caste
Youre sommes / and youre bokes / and youre thynges
The deuel haue part / on alle swiche rekenynges
Ye haue ynogh pardee / of goddes sonde
Com doun to day / and lat youre bagges stonde
Ne be ye nat ashamed / that daun John
Shal fastynge / al this day elenge gon
What lat vs heere a masse / and go we dyne
¶ Wyf quod this man / litel kanstow deuyne
The curious bisynesse / that we haue
ffor of vs chapmen / also god me saue
And by that lord / that clepid is Seint yue
Scarsly amonges · xij · ij · shul thryue
Continuelly / lastyng vn to oure age
We may wel make chere / and good visage
And dryue forth the world / as it may be
And kepen oure estat / in pryuetee
Til we be dede / or ellis that we pleye
A pilgrymage / or goon out of the weye
And therfore / haue I gret necessitee
Vp on this queynte world / tauyse me
ffor euere mo / we mote stonde in drede
Of hap and ffortune / in oure chapmanhede

	ELLESMERE
That whan youre housbonde / is to Flandres fare	youre Flaundres
I wol deliuere yow / out of this care	delyuere
For I wol brynge yow / an hundred frankes	
And with that word / he caughte hire by the flankes	with caughte
And hire embraceth harde / and kiste hire ofte	
Goth now youre wey quod he / al stille and softe	Gooth and
And lat vs dyne / as soone / as þat ye may	soone
For by my chilyndre / it is Pryme of day	pryme
Goth now / and beth as trewe as I shal be	Gooth beeth
¶Now ellis / god forbede sire quod she	elles /
And forth she goth / as iolif as a pye	gooth / Iolif
And bad the Cokes / þat they sholde hem hye	cookes /
So þat men myghte dyne / and that anon	myghte
Vp to hir housbonde / is his wyf ygon	is this wyf
And knokketh at his Countour boldely	knokketh / Countour
.qi la. ¶Who ⟨ys⟩ ther quod he / Peter it am I	¶qi la ./] ¶Who ther ./ I.
Quod she / what sire / how longe wol ye faste	sire / faste./
How longe tyme / wol ye rekene and caste	caste./
Youre sommes / and youre bokes / and youre thynges	Youre sommes / and youre bookes / and youre thynges./
The deuel haue part on alle swiche rekenynges	
Ye haue ynogh pardee / of goddes sonde	ynough pardee /
Com doun to day / and lat youre bagges stonde	youre
Ne be ye nat ashamed / that daun Iohn	ashamed Daun
Shal fastynge / al this day elenge gon	fasting alenge goon
What lat vs heere a masse / and go we dyne	Lat vs messe /
¶Wyf quod this man / litel kanstow deuyne	
The curious bisynesse / that we haue	
For of vs chapmen / also god me saue	Chapmen /
And by that lord / that clepid is Seint Yue	þat clepid Yve
Scarsly amonges .xij. x. shul thryue	.xij. ten
Continuelly / lastyng vn to oure age	lastynge
We may wel make cheere / and good visage	wel / chiere /
And dryue forth the world / as it may be	
And kepen oure estat in pryuetee	kepen / estaat
Til we be dede / or ellis that we pleye	deed / elles
A pilgrymage / or goon out of the weye	
And ther fore / haue I gret necessitee	7 therfore / greet
Vp on this queynte world / tauyse me	world
For euere mo / we mote stonde in drede	eueremoore / moote
Of hap and Fortune / in oure chapmanhede	hape

7 ¶Shipman 146r

∫ The Shipman ∫

	ELLESMERE
¶To Flandres wol I go / tomorwe at day	¶To Flaundres / to morwe
And come agayn / as soone as eu*er*e I may	
For which my deere wyf / I thee biseke	wyf
As be to euery wight' buxom and meke	wighħ'
And for to kepe oure good / be curious	
And honestly / gouerne wel oure hous	gou*er*ne
Thow hast ynow / in euery maner*e* wise	Thou ynougħ / eu*er*y maner
That to a thrifty houshold / may suffise	That / houshold
Thee lakketh noon array / ne no vitaille	
Of siluer in thy purs / shaltow nat faille	
And with that word / his Countour dore he shette	word' / Count*our*
And doun he goth / no lenger wolde he lette	gooth /
But hastily / a masse was ther seyd	messe seyd'
And spedily / the tables were yleyd	yleyd'
And to the dyner / faste they hem spedde	dyner'
And richely this Monk' the chapman fedde	richely / Monk /
¶At after dyner / daun Ioħn sobrely	
This chapman took a part' and p*ri*uely	Chapman took'
He seyde hym thus / cosyn it standeth so	
That wel I se / to Brugges wol ye go	Brugges /
God and Seint Austyn / spede yow and gyde	
I pray yow cosyn / wysly þ*at* ye ryde	prey wisely that
Gouerneth yow also / of youre diete	Gou*er*neth
Atemprely / and namely / in this hete	namely
Bitwix vs two / nedeth no strange fare	
Farewel cosyn / god shilde yow fro care	Fare wel
And if þ*at* any thyng' by day or nyght	nyghħ'
If it lye in my power' and my myght'	myghħ'
That ye me wol comande / in any wise	comande wyse
It shal be doon / right as ye wol deuyse	righħ
¶O thyng er þ*at* ye goon / if it may be	thyng'
I wold' preye yow / for to lene me	wolde prey
An hundred frankes / for a wyke or tweye	
For c*er*teyn bestes / þ*at* I moste beye	c*er*tein beestes /
To store with a place / that is oures	stoore place þ*at*
God help me so / I wolde it were youres	help*e*
I shal nat faille / seurely of my day	surely at my
Nat for a thousand frankes / a myle way	thousand' frankes Mile
But lat this thyng be secree / I yow preye	
For yet to nyght' thise bestes moot I beye	nyghħ' beestes

The Shipman 2

To fflaundres wol I go / tomorwe at day
And come agayn / as soone as euere I may
ffor which my deere wyf / I thee biseke
As be to euery wight / buxom and meke
And for to kepe oure good / be curious
And honestly / gouerne wel oure hous
Thow hast ynow / in euery maner wise
That to a thrifty houshold / may suffise
Thee lakketh noon array / ne no vitaille
Of siluer in thy purs / shaltow nat faille
And with that word / his Countour dore he shette
And doun he goth / no lenger wolde he lette
But hastily / a masse was ther seyd
And spedily / the tables were yleyd
And to the dyner / faste they hem spedde
And richely this monk / the chapman fedde
At after dyner / daun John sobrely
This chapman took apart / and priuely
He seyde hym thus / cosyn it standeth so
That wel I se / to Brugges wol ye go
God and seint Austyn / spede yow and gyde
I pray yow cosyn / wisly þt ye ryde
Gouerneth yow also / of youre diete
Atemprely / and namely / in this hete
Bitwix vs two / nedeth no strange fare
ffare wel cosyn / god shilde yow fro care
And if þt any thyng / by day or nyght
If it lye in my power / and my myght
That ye me wol comande / in any wise
It shal be doon / right as ye wol deuyse
O thyng er þt ye goon / if it may be
I wolde preye yow / for to lene me
An hundred frankes / for a wyke or tweye
ffor certeyn beestes / þt I moste beye
To store with a place / that is oures
God help me so / I wolde it were youres
I shal nat faille / seurely of my day
Nat for a thousand frankes / a myle way
But lat this thyng be secree / I yow preye
ffor yet to nyght / thise beestes moot I beye

And fare now wel / myn owene cosyn deere
Graunt mercy / of youre cost / and of youre cheere
¶ This noble marchaunt / gentilly anon
Answerde and seyde / o cosyn myn daun John
Now sikerly / this is a smal requeste
My gold is youres / whan þt it yow leste
And nat oonly my gold / but my chaffare
Tak what yow list / god shilde þt ye spare
But o thyng is / ye knowe it wel ynow
Of chapmen / that hir moneye is hir plow
We may creance / whil we han a name
But goldlees for to been / it is no game
Pay it agayn / whan it lyth in youre ese
After my myght / ful fayn wol I yow plese
¶ Thise hundred frankes / he sette forth anon
And priuely / he took hem to daun John
No wight in al this world / wiste of this loone
Sauyng this marchaunt / and daun John allone
They drynke and speke / and rome a while & pleye
Til that daun John / rideth to his abbeye
¶ The morwe cam / and forth this marchaunt rideth
To fflaundres ward / his prentys wel hym gydeth
Til he cam in to Brugges myrily
Now goth this marchaunt / faste and bisily
Aboute his nede / and byeth and creaunceth
He neither / pleyeth at the dees / ne daunceth
But as a marchaunt / shortly for to telle
He let his lyf / and ther I lete hym dwelle
¶ The sonday next / the marchaunt was agon
To Seint Denys / ycomen is daun John
With crowne and berd / al fressh & newe shaue
In al the hous / ther nas so litel a knaue
Ne no wight ellis / þt he nas ful fayn
That my lord daun John / was come agayn
And shortly / to the poynt / right for to gon
This faire wyf / acorded with daun John
That for thise hundred frankes / he sholde al nyght /
Haue hire in his armes / bolt upright /
And this acord / parfourned was in dede
In myrthe al nyght / a bisy lyf they lede

And fare now wel / myn owene cosyn deere	
Grant m*er*cy / of youre costꝰ and of youre cheere	Grauntm*er*cy /
¶This noble Marchantꝰ gentilly anon	
Answerde and seyde / o cosyn myn daun Ioħn	Answerde / seyde
Now sikerly / this is a smal requeste	8
My gold is youres / whan þ*at* it yow leste	
And nat oonly my gold / but my chaffare	
Tak what yow listꝰ god shilde þ*at* ye spare	Take
But o thyng is / ye knowe it wel ynow	¶But ynogħ
Of Chapmen / that hir moneye is hir plow	moneie plogħ
We may creance / whil we han a name	creau*n*ce / haue
But goldlees for to been / it is no game	be /
Pay it agayn / whan it lyth in youre ese	Paye lith
After my myghtꝰ ful fayn wol I yow plese	myghtꝰ / wolde
¶Thise hundred frankes / he fette forth anon	fette hym forth
And p*ri*uely / he took hem to daun Ioħn	
No wight in al this world / wiste of this lone	wightꝰ loone
Sauyngꝰ this Marchantꝰ and daun Ioħn allone	Sauynge
They drynke / and speke / and rome a while *and* pleye	
Til that daun Ioħn / rideth to his Abbeye	þ*at*
¶The morwe cam / and forth this Marchant rydeth	The ridetħ
To Flandres ward / his Prentys wel hym gydeth	Flaundresward / p*re*ntys gydetħ
Til he cam / in to Brugges murily	
Now goth this Marchantꝰ faste and bisily	gooth
Aboute his nede / and byeth and creau*n*ceth	creaunceth
He neither / pleyeth at the dees / ne daunceth	neitherꝰ at dees dauncetħ
But as a Marchantꝰ shortly for to telle	Marchau*n*tꝰ
He let his lyf / and ther I lete hym dwelle	there
¶The sonday next / the Marchant was agon	The nextꝰ this Marchant
To Seint denys / ycomen is daun Ioħn	Denys /
With crowne and berd / al fressħ *and* newe shaue	berd fressħ and yshaue
In al the hous / ther nas so litel a knaue	
Ne no wight ellis / þ*at* he nas ful fayn	wight elles /
That my lord daun Ioħn / was come agayn	
And shortly / to the poyntꝰ right for to gon	shortly / rigħt to the point for
This faire wyfꝰ acorded with daun Ioħn	
That for thise hundred frankes / he sholde al nyghtꝰ	nygħtꝰ
Haue hire in his armes / bolt vprightꝰ	hire hise Armes / vprigħt
And this acord / p*ar*fourned was in dede	
In myrthe al nyghtꝰ a bisy lyf they lede	alnygħtꝰ

8 ¶Shipman *146v*

Text	ELLESMERE
Til it was day / that daun Iohn wente his way	þ*at*
And bad the meynee / fare wel haue good day	
For noon of hem / ne no wight in the town	wight toun
Hath of daun Iohn / right no suspecioun	right
And forth he rydeth hom / til his Abbeye	forth rydeth / hoom to
Or where hym list namoore of hym I seye	list .
¶This Marchant whan þ*at* ended was the faire	This
To Seint Denys / he gan for to repaire	
And with his wyf / he maketh feste and cheere	wyf feeste
And telleth hir*e* / that chaffare is so deere	Chaffare
That nedes / moste he make a cheuyssance	cheuyssau*n*ce
For he was bounden / in a reconyssance	reconyssau*n*ce
To paye / twenty thousand sheeld anon	[9] paye thousand
For which / this Marchant is to Parys gon	
To borwe / of *cer*teyne freendes / that he hadde	*cer*teine freendes þ*at*
A *cer*teyn frankes / and so*mm*e w*ith* hym he ladde	hi*m*
And whan þ*at* he was come / in to the town	toun
For greet chiertee / and greet affeccioun	greet chiertee / Affecciou*n*
Vn to daun Iohn / he first goth / hym to pleye	he gooth hym first to
Nat for to axe / or borwe of hym moneye	
But for to wite / and seen of his welfare	
And for to tellen hym / of his chaffare	
As freendes doon / whan they been met yfeere	
Daun Iohn / hym maketh feste / and murye cheere	feeste
And he hym tolde agayn / ful specially	
How he hadde / wel yboght and *gra*ciously	hadde yboght
Thanked be god / al hool his marchandise	
Saue þ*at* he moste / in alle maner wyse	wise
Maken a cheuyssance / as for his beste	cheuyssau*n*ce /
And thanne / he sholde been / in ioye and reste	
¶Daun Iohn answerde / certes I am fayn	
That ye in heele / ar comen hom agayn	come*n*
And if þ*at* I were riche / as haue I blisse	
Of twenty thousand sheeld / sholde ye nat mysse	thousand
For ye so kyndely / this oother day	ye /
Lente me gold / and as I kan and may	
I thanke yow / by god / and by Seint Iame	god
But nathelees / I took vn to oure dame	
Yowre wyf at hom / the same gold agayn	Your*e* wyf / ageyn
Vp on youre bench / she woot it wel certayn	your*e* bench / certeyn

[9] ¶Shipman *147r*

Til it was day / that daun Iohn wente his way
And bad the meynee / fare wel haue good day
ffor noon of hem / ne no wight in the town
Hath of daun Iohn / right no suspecioun
And forth he rydeth hom / til his abbeye
Or where hym list / namoore of hym I seye
This marchant / whan þt ended was the faire
To Seint Denys / he gan for to repaire
And with his wyf / he maketh feste and cheere
And telleth hir / that chaffare is so deere
That nedes / moste he make a cheuyssance
ffor he was bounden / in a reconyssance
To paye / twenty thousand sheeld anon
ffor which this marchant / is to Parys gon
To borwe / of certeyne freendes / that he hadde
A certeyn frankes / and somme wt hym he ladde
And whan þt he was come / in to the town
ffor greet chiertee / and greet affeccioun
Vn to daun Iohn / he first goth hym to pleye
Nat for to axe / or borwe of hym moneye
But for to wite / and seen of his welfare
And for to tellen hym / of his chaffare
As freendes doon / whan they been met yfeere
Daun Iohn / hym maketh feste / and murye cheere
And he hym tolde agayn / ful specially
How he hadde wel yboght / and graciously
Thanked be god / al hool his marchandise
Saue þt he moste / in alle maner wyse
Maken a cheuyssance / as for his beste
And thanne he sholde been / in ioye and reste
Daun Iohn answerde / certes I am fayn
That ye in heele / ar comen hom agayn
And if þt I were riche / as haue I blisse
Of twenty thousand sheeld / sholde ye nat mysse
ffor ye so kyndely / this oother day
Lente me gold / and as I kan and may
I thanke yow / by god / and by Seint Iame
But nathelees / I took vn to oure dame
Youre wyf at hom / the same gold agayn
Vp on youre bench / she woot it wel certayn

By certeyn tokenes / that I kan yow telle
Now by youre leue / I may no lenger dwelle
Oure Abbot / wol out of this town anon
And in his compaignye / moot I gon
Greet wel oure dame / myn owene nece swete
And fare wel deere cosyn / til we meete
¶ This marchant / which þt was ful war and wys
Creanced hath / and payed eek in Parys
To certeyn lombardes / redy in hir hond
The somme of gold / and gat of hem his bond ¶ .i. obligacionem
And hoom he gooth / murye as a Papejay
ffor wel he knew / he stood in swich array
That nedes moste he wynne / in that viage
A thousand frankes / abouen al his costage
¶ His wyf ful redy / mette hym at the gate
As she was wont / of old vsage algate
And al that nyght / in myrthe they bisette
ffor he was riche / and cleerly out of dette
¶ Whan it was day / this marchant gan embrace
His wyf al newe / and kiste hir on hir face
And vp he goth / and maketh it ful tough
¶ Namoore quod she / by god ye haue ynough
And wantownely agayn / with hym she pleyde
Til at the laste / this marchant seyde
¶ By god quod he / I am a litel wroth
With yow my wyf / al thogh it be me looth
And woot ye why / by god as þt I gesse
That ye han maad / a manere straungenesse
Bitwyxen me and my cosyn daun John
Ye sholde han warned me / er I had gon
That he yow hadde / a hundred frankes payed
By redy tokne / and heeld hym yuele apayed
ffor that I to hym / spak of cheuyssance
Me semed so / as by his contenance
But natheles / by god oure heuene kyng
I thoghte nat / to axe of hym no thyng
I pray thee wyf / ne do namoore so
Tel me alwey / er that I fro thee go
If any dettour / hath in myn absence
Ypayed thee / lest thurgh thy necligence

I myghte hym axe

	ELLESMERE
By c*er*teyn toknes / that I kan yow telle	tokenes /
Now by youre leue / I may no lenger dwelle	
Oure Abbot⁊ wol out of this town anon	wole toun
And in his compaignye / moot I gon	goon
Greet wel oure dame / myn owene Nece swete	Grete sweete
And fare wel deere cosyn / til we meete	
¶This Marchant⁊ which þ*at* was ful war and wys	This *and*
Creanced hath / and payed eek in Parys	payd
To c*er*teyn lombardes / redy in hir hond	certeyn lumbardes / hond
The somme of gold / and gat of hem his bond ¶.i. obligacionem	so*m*me and hadde of bond .i. obligac*ion*em
And hoom he gooth / murye as a Papyniay	murie / Papeiay
For wel he knew / he stood in swich array	
That nedes moste he wynne / in that viage	wynne
A thousand frankes / abouen al his costage	thousand
¶His wyf ful redy / mette hym at the gate	atte gate
As she was wont⁊ of old vsage algate	oold
And al that nyght⁊ in myrthe they bisette	
For he was riche / and cleerly out of dette	
¶Whan it was day / this Marchant gan embrace	Whan
His wyf al newe / and kiste hir*e* on hir face	wyf /
And vp he goth / and maketh it ful tougħ	10 gooth /
Namoore quod she / by god ye haue ynougħ	¶Namoore
And wantownely agayn / with hym she pleyde	*with*
Til at the laste / this Marchant seyde	¶Til atte laste /
¶By god quod he / I am alitel wroth	By wrootħ
With yow my wyf / al thogh it be me looth	al thougħ it were me
And woot ye why / by god as þ*at* I gesse	
That ye han maad / a manere strangenesse	straungenesse
Bitwixen me / and my cosyn Daun Iohn	
Ye sholde han warned me / er I had gon	
That he yow hadde / a hundred frankes payed	hadde / an hundred
Be redy tokne / and heeld hym yuele apayed	tokene /
For that I to hym / spak of cheuyssance	þ*at* hym cheuyssau*n*ce
Me semed so / as by his conten[ance]	contenau*n*ce
But nathelees / by god oure heuene kyng⁊	
I thoghte nat⁊ to axe of hym no thyng⁊	thoughte axen hym
I pray thee wyf⁊ ne do namoore so	prey wyf / as do
Tel me alwey / er that I fro thee go	Telle
If any dettour / hath in myn absence	dettour⁊
Ypayed thee / lest thurgh thy necligence	thurgħ

I myghte hym axe

[10] ¶Shipman *147v*

· The Shipman ·

	ELLESMERE
I myghte hym axe / a thyng þ*at* he hath payed	myghte thing that payed
¶This wyf / was nat afered ne afrayed	wyf afered / nor affrayed
But boldely she seyde / and that anon	
Marie I diffye / the false Monk daun Ioħn	Marie / deffie / Monk / Daun
I kepe nat of his toknes / neu*er* a del	hise tokenes / deel
He took me c*er*teyn gold / this woot I wel	certeyn gold / that woot weel
What yuel thedam / on his Monkes snowte	
For god it woot I wende with outen dowte	wit*h* doute
That he hadde yeue it me / by cause of yow	
To doon ther with / myn honour / and my prow	hono*ur*
For cosynage / and eek for bele cheere	beele
That he hath had / ful ofte tymes heere	
¶But sith I se / it stant in this disioynt	But I se / I stonde in
I wole answere yow / shortly to the poynt	wol
Ye han mo slakker dettours / than am I	¶Ye slakker*e*
For I wol paye yow / wel and redily	
Fro day to day / and if so be I fayle	faille
I am youre wyf / score it vp on my tayle	wyf taille
And I shal paye / as soone as euere I may	eu*er*
For by my trouthe / I haue on myn array	
And nat in wast bistowed eu*er*y del	nat on wast deel
And for I haue / bistowed it so wel	weel
For youre honour / for goddes sake I seye	your*e* hono*ur* /
As be nat wrooth / but lat vs laughe *and* pleye	laughe and
Ye shal / my ioly body han to wedde	body / haue
By god / I wol noght paye yow but abedde	god nat a bedde
Forgyue it me / myn owene spouse deere	
Turn hiderward / and maketh bettre cheere	Turne hiderward /
¶This Marchant saugh / ther was no remedye	11 Marchant saugh / remedie
And for to chide / it nere but folye	but greet folie
Syn that the thyng may nat amended be	Sith
Now wyf he seyde / and I foryeue it thee	
But by thy lyf ne be namoore so large	
Keep*e* bet thy good / this yeue ⟨I⟩ thee in charge	bet oure good / that yeue I
Thus endeth my tale / and god vs sende	
Taillynge ynough / vn to oure lyues ende	ynough / ende Amen
¶Here endeth / the Shipmannes tale	¶Heere endeth / the Shipmannes tale

[11] ¶Shipman *148r*

The Shipman

I myghte hym axe / a thyng þt he hath payed
This wyf / was nat afered ne affrayed
But boldely she seyde / and that anon
Marie I deffye / the false monk daun John
I kepe nat of his tokenes / neuere a del
He took me certeyn gold / this woot I wel
What yuel thedam / on his monkes snowte
ffor god it woot / I wende with outen doute
That he hadde yeue it me / by cause of yow
To doon ther with / myn honour and my prow
ffor cosynage / and eek for bele cheere
That he hath had / ful ofte tymes heere
But sith I se / it stant in this disioynt /
I wol answere yow / shortly to the poynt /
Ye han mo slakker dettours / than am I
ffor I wol paye yow / wel and redily
ffro day to day / and if so be I fayle
I am youre wyf / score it vp on my tayle
And I shal paye / as soone as euere I may
ffor by my trouthe / I haue on myn array
And nat in wast / bistowed euery del
And for I haue / bistowed it so wel
ffor youre honour / for goddes sake I seye
As be nat wrooth / but lat vs laughe & pleye
Ye shal / my ioly body han to wedde
By god / I wol noght paye yow but a bedde
fforgyue it me / myn owene spouse deere
Turn hiderward / and maketh bettre cheere
This marchant saugh / ther was no remedye
And for to chide / it nere but folye
Syn that the thyng / may nat amended be
Now wyf he seyde / and I foryeue it thee
But by thy lyf / ne be namoore so large
Keep bet thy good / this yeue I thee in charge
Thus endeth my tale / and god vs sende
Taillynge ynough / vn to oure lyues ende .

Here endeth the Shipmannes tale

Here the myrye wordes of the worthy Hoost

Wel seyd by corpus dominus quod oure hoost
Now longe moote thow saille by the coost
Thow gentil maister gentil maryner
God yeue the monk a thousand last quaad yeer
A ha. felawes beth war of swich a iape
The monk putte in the mannes hood an ape
And in his wyues eek by seint Austyn
Draweth no monkes moore in to youre In
But now passe ouer and lat vs seke aboute
Who shal now telle first of al this route
Another tale and with that word he sayde
As curteisly as it hadde been a mayde
My lady Prioresse by youre leue
So that I. wiste I sholde yow nat greue
I wolde demen that ye telle sholde
A tale next if so were that ye wolde
Now wol ye vouche it sauf my lady deere
Gladly quod she and seyde as ye shal heere

The prohemie of the Prioresse tale

Domine dominus noster

O lord oure lord thy name how merueillous
Is in this large world ysprad quod she
For nat oonly thy laude precious
Parfourned is by men of dignytee
But by the mouth of children thy bountee
Parfourned is for on the brest soukynge
Somtyme shewen they thyn heryynge

Wher fore in laude as I best kan or may
Of thee and of the white lilye flour
Which þt the bar and is a mayde alway
To telle a storie I wol do my labour
Nat that I may encreessen hir honour
ffor she hir self is honour and the roote
Of bountee next hir sone and soules boote

¶Herke the myrie wordes / of the worthy Hoost

WEl seyd / by corpus dominus / quod oure hoost
Now longe / moote thow saille by the coost
Thow gentil Maister gentil Maryner
God yeue the Monk / a thousand last quaad yeer
A .ha. felawes / beth war of swich a Iape
The Monk putte / in the mannes hood an Ape
And in his wyues eek / by Seint Austyn
Draweth no Monkes / moore in to youre In
¶But now passe ouer / and lat vs seke aboute
Who shal now telle first of al this route
Another tale / and with that word he sayde
As curteisly / as it hadde been a mayde
My lady Prioresse / by youre leue
So that .I. wiste / I sholde yow nat agreue
I wolde demen / that ye telle sholde
A tale next if so were that ye wolde
Now wol ye vouche it sauf my lady deere
¶Gladly quod she / and seyde as ye shal heere

¶The proheme of the Prioresse tale

Domine dominus noster

O lord oure lord / thy name how me*r*ueilous
Is in this large world / ysprad quod she
For nat oonly / thy laude precious
P*ar*fourned is / by men of dignytee
But by the mouth of children / thy bou*n*tee
Parfourned is / for on the brest soukynge
Som tyme / shewen they thyn heryynge

¶Wher fore in laude / as I best kan or may
Of thee / and of the white lilye flour
Which *þ*at the bar / and is a mayde alway
To telle a storie / I wol do my labour
Nat that I may / encressen hir honour
For she hir self / is honour and the Roote
Of bou*n*tee next hir sone / and soules boote

1 ¶Bihoold the murie wordes of the Hoost to the Shipman and to the lady / Prioresse

Wel seyd dominus
thou cost
Sir*e* gentil maister Maryneer
yeue this Monk / thousand last quade
A ha
Monk
eek
moore vn to your*e*
ou*er* /
now /
with
had

I wiste / greue
tellen

vouche sauf

¶Explicit

¶The prologe of the Prioresses tale

Domine dominus noster

me*r*ueillous
world /
noght p*re*cious
dignitee

P*ar*fourned
Somtyme / heriynge

2 Wherfore Laude /
the lylye
that

Nat encreessen
hon*our* roote
next

[1] ¶Shipman on *148r*
[2] ¶Prioresse *148v*

¶O. moder mayde / o mayde moder free
O. bussħ vnbrentꝭ brennyng in Moyses sighte
That rauysedestꝭ doun / fro the deitee
Thurgh thyn humblesse / the goost / *þ*at in thalighte
Of whos v*er*tu / whan he thyn herte lighte
Conceyued was / the fadres sapience
Help me / to telle it in thy reuerence

¶Lady thy bou*n*tee / thy magnificence
Thy vertu / and thy grete humylitee
Ther may no tonge ex*pre*sse / in no science
For som tyme lady / er men praye to thee
Thow goost biforn / of thy benygnytee
And getestꝭ vs / the light of thy prayere
To gyden vs / vn to thy sone so deere

¶My konnyng is so waykꝭ o blisful queene
For to declare / thy grete worthynesse
That I ne may / the weighte nat sustene
But as a child / of twelue monthħ old / or lesse
That kan vnnethe / any word ex*pre*sse
Right so fare I / and ther fore I yow preye
Gideth my songꝭ that I shal of yow seye

¶Explicit prohemium

¶Here bigynneth / the Prioresse tale ofꝭ

¶Alma redemptoris mater

Ther was in Asye / in a greet Citee
Amonges cristen folkꝭ a Iewerye
Sustened / by a lord / of that contree
For foul vsure / and lucre of vileynye turpe lucrum
Hateful / to Cristꝭ and to his compaignye
And thurgh this strete / me[n myghte ri]de *and* wen[de]
For it was free / an[d open at eyther ende]

ELLESMERE

O mooder mooder
O brennynge sighte
doun
Thurgħ hu*m*blesse / goostꝭ thalighte
vertu / lighte

Help*e* reu*er*ence

Lady /
v*er*tu /

somtyme
Thou benyngnytee
getest vs / thurgħ lyght / preyere

My konnyngꝭ

susteene
twelf / monthe oold

Right therfore
Gydeth *þ*at

¶Explicitꝭ

¶Heere bigynneth the Prioresses tale

3

4
cristene folk /

[¶*tur*pe lucrum]

thurgħ men myghte ride or wende
and open at eyther ende

[3] Latin rubric *Out*.

[4] Miniature of the Prioress in left margin.

O moder mayde / o mayde moder free
O bussh vnbrent / brennyng in moyses sighte
That rauysedest doun / fro the deitee
Thurgh thyn humblesse / the goost yt in thalighte
Of whos vertu / whan he thyn herte lighte
Conceyued was / the fadres sapience
Help me / to telle it in thy reuerence

Lady thy bountee / thy magnificence
Thy vertu / and thy grete humylitee
Ther may no tonge expresse / in no science
ffor som tyme lady / er men praye to thee
Thow goost biforn / of thy benygnytee
And getest vs / the light of thy prayere
To gyden vs / vn to thy sone so deere

My konnyng is so wayk / o blisful queene
ffor to declare / thy grete worthynesse
That I ne may / the weighte nat sustene
But as a child / of twelue month old or lesse
That kan vnnethe / any word expresse
Right so fare I / and ther fore I yow preye
Gydeth my song / that I shal of yow seye

Explicit prohemium

Here bigynneth the Prioresses tale of
Alma redemptoris mater

Ther was in Asye / in a greet Citee
Amonges cristen folk / a Iewerye
Sustened by a lord / of that contree — turpe lucrum
ffor foul vsure / and lucre of vileynye
Hateful to crist / and to his compaignye
And thurgh this strete / [illegible] a wend[illegible]
ffor it was free an[illegible]

¶ A litel scole of cristen folk ther stood
Doun at the ferther ende / in which ther were
Children an heep / ycomen of cristen blood
That lerned in that scole / yeer by yere
Swich manere doctrine / as men used there
This is to seyn / to syngen and to rede
As smale children doon / in hir childhede ·

¶ Among thise children / was a wydwes sone
A litel clergeon / ·vij· yeer of age
That day by day / to scole was his wone
And eek also / wher as he say thymage
Of cristes moder / hadde he in usage
As hym was taught / to knele adoun and seye
His Aue marie / as he goth by the weye

¶ Thus hath this wydwe / hir litel sone ytaught /
Oure blisful lady / cristes moder deere
To worshipe ay / and he forgat it naught /
ffor sely child / wol alwey soone lere
But ay / whan I remembre / on this matere
Seint Nicholas / stant euere in my presence
ffor he so yong / to crist dide reuerence

¶ This litel child / his litel book lernynge
As he sat in the scole / at his prymer
He Alma redemptoris / herde synge
As children lerned hir Antiphoner
And as he dorste / he drow hym ner and ner
And herkned ay / the wordes and the note
Til he the firste vers / koude al by rote

¶ Nat wiste he / what this latyn was to seye ·
ffor he so yong / and tendre was of age
But on a day / his felawe gan he preye
Texpounden hym this song / in his langage
Or telle hym why / this song was in usage
This praide he hym [...]men and declare
[...]e

	ELLESMERE
¶A litel scole / of cristen folk ther stood	5 A folk' stood'
Doun at the ferther ende / in which ther weere	were
Children an heep*e* / ycomen of cristen blood	c*ri*sten blood'
That lerned in that scole / yeer by yere	
Swich manere doctrine / as men vsed there	man*ere*
This is to seyn / to syngen and to rede	syngen /
As smale children doon / in hir childhede	hir*e*
¶Among thise children / was a wydwes sone	Among'
A litel clergeon / .vij. yeer of age	clergeou*n* / seuen
That day by day / to scole was his wone	
And eek also / wher as he say thymage	wher*e* saugħ
Of Cristes moder / hadde he in vsage	mooder / he hadde
As hym was taught' to knele adoun and seye	taught'
His Aue Marie / as he goth by the weye	
¶Thus hath this wydwe / hir litel sone ytaught'	Thus ytaught'
Oure blisful lady / Cristes moder deere	lady cristes mooder
To worshipe ay / and he forgat it naught'	naught'
For sely child / wol alwey soone lere	wol alday soone leere
But ay / whan I remembre / on this matere	remembre mateere
Seint Nicholas / stant euere in my p*re*sence	
For he so yong' to Crist dide reuerence	Crist' reu*er*ence
¶This litel child / his litel book lernynge	This child' book' ·
As he sat in the scole / at his prymer	
He **Alma redemptoris** / herde synge	He /
As children / lerned hir Antiphoner	hir*e* Anthiphoner
And as he dorste / he drow hym ner and ner	drougħ
And herkned ay / the wordes and the note	noote
Til he the firste vers / koude al by rote	
¶Nat wiste he / what this latyn was to seye.	Noght seye
For he so yong' and tendre was of age	
But on a day / his felawe gan he preye	
Texpounden hym this song' in his langage	
Or telle hym why / this song was in vsage	hym / why song'
This prayde he hym / [to constr]uen and declare	preyde to construe
[Ful often tyme / vpon hise knowes bar]e	Ful often tyme / vpon hise knowes bare

5 ¶Prioresse *149r*

¶His felawe / which *pat* elder was than he
Answerde hym thus / this song⁊ I haue herd seye
Was maked / of oure blisful lady free
Hir to salue / and eek hir*e* for to preye
To been oure help*e* / and socour⁊ whan we deye
I kan namoore / expounde in this matere
I lerne song⁊ I kan but smal gramere

¶And is this song⁊ maked in reuerence
Of Cristes moder / seyde this Innocent⁊
Now certes / I wol do my diligence
To konne it al / er Cristemasse is went⁊
Thogh *pat* I / for my Prymer shal be shent⁊
And shal be beten / thries in an houre
I wol it konne / oure lady for to honoure

¶His felawe taughte hym / homward p*ri*uely
Fro day to day / til he koude it by rote
And thanne he soong⁊ it / wel and boldely
Fro word to word / acordyng with the note
Twyes a day / it passed thurgh his throte
To scoleward / and homward / whan he wente
On Cristes moder / set was his entente

¶As I haue seyd / thurgh out the Iuerye
This litel child / as he cam to and fro
Ful murily / wolde he synge and crye
O Alma redemptoris / euere mo
The swetnesse / his herte p*er*ced so
Of Cristes moder / that to hir to preye
He kan nat stynte / of syngyng by the weye

¶Oure firste foo / the Serpent Sathanas
That hath in Iewes herte / his waspes nest⁊
Vp swal and seyde / o hebrayk peple allas
Is this to yow / a thyng⁊ that is honest⁊
That swich a boy / shal walken As hym lest⁊
In youre despit⁊ and synge [of swich] sentence
Which is agayns / oure l[awes reuerence]

ELLESMERE

His that
song

Hir*e* to
socour
mateere
grammeere

6 reue*r*ence
cristes mooder⁊ seyde /

Thougħ *pat* / I prymer

His felawe / taugħte hym

thanne / song⁊ it
word to word' to word' acordynge *with*
Twies thurgħ
scoleward' homward
cristes mooder /

thurgħ Iuerie
child'
crie
eueremo

cristes mooder / hir*e*
syngyng⁊

¶Auctor] Ovre serpent
hath / Iues herte
swal / seide / o. Hebrayk⁊
pat
as
of swich
is / agayn lawes reuerence

[6] ¶Prioresse *149v*

His felawe / which þt elder was than he
Answerde hym thus / this song I haue herd seye
Was maked / of oure blisful lady free
Hir to salue / and eek hir for to preye
To been oure help / and socour / whan we deye
I kan namoore / expounde in this matere
I lerne song / I kan but smal grammere

And is this song / maked in reuerence
Of cristes moder / seyde this Innocent /
Now certes / I wol do my diligence
To konne it al / er cristemasse is went /
Though þt I / for my prymer shal be shent /
And shal be beten / thries in an houre
I wol it konne / oure lady for to honoure

His felawe taughte hym / homward priuely
Fro day to day / til he koude it by rote
And thanne he song it / wel and boldely
Fro word to word / acordyng with the note
Twies a day / it passed thurgh his throte
To scoleward / and homward / whan he wente
On cristes moder / set was his entente

As I haue seyd / thurgh out the Iuerie
This litel child / as he cam to and fro
Ful murily / wolde he synge and crie
O Alma redemptoris / euere mo
The swetnesse / his herte perced so
Of cristes moder / that to hir to preye
He kan nat stynte / of syngyng by the weye

Oure firste foo / the serpent Sathanas
That hath in Iewes herte / his waspes nest /
Vp swal and seyde / o hebrayk peple allas
Is this to yow / a thyng / that is honest /
That swich a boy / shal walken as hym lest /
In youre despit / and synge o[...] sentence
Which is agayns oure l[...]

Ffro thennes forth / the Iewes han conspired
This Innocent / out of this world to chace
An homycide ther to han they hyred
That in an Aleye / at a pryuee place
And as the child / gan forby for to pace
This cursed Iew / hym hente / and heeld hym faste
And kitte his throte / and in a pit hym caste

I seye / that in a wardrobe / they hym threwe
Wher as thise Iewes / purgen hir entraille
O cursed folk of Herodes / al newe
What may / youre yuel entente yow auaille
Mordre wol out / certeyn it wol nat faille
And namely / ther as thonour of god shal sprede
The blood out crieth / on youre cursed dede

O martir souded to virginitee
Now maystow syngen / folwyng euere in oon
The white lamb celestial quod she
Of which / the grete Euangelist Seint Iohn
In Pathmos wroot / which seith þ[t] they þ[t] gon
Biforn this lamb / and synge a song al newe
That neuere fflesshly (carnaliter) / wommen they ne knewe

Secundum Apocalipsim Iohannis et vi[di]
[illegible] agnum supra montem Syon et
cum illo . cxliiij . milia signatorum etc
qui cantant canticum nouum etc
Isti sunt qui cum mulieribus non
coinquinauerunt virgines enim
permanserunt . hij sunt qui sequntur
agnum quocumque vadit etc

This poure wydwe / awaiteth al that nyght /
After hir litel child / but he cam noght /
ffor which as soone / as it was dayes lyght /
With face pale / of drede and bisy thoght /
She hath at scole / and ellis where hym soght
Til fynally / she gan so fer espie
That he last seyn was / in the Iewerie

With modres pitee / in hir brest enclosed
She goth / as she were half out of hir mynde
To euery place / wher as she hath supposed
By liklyhede / hir litel child to fynde
And euere / on Cristes mooder / meke and kynde
She cryde / and at the la… …thoghte
…

¶Fro thennes forth / the Iewes han conspired
This Innocent out of this world to chace
An homycide / ther to han they hired
That in an Aleye / at a p*ri*uee place
And as the child / gan for by for to pace
This cursed Iew / hym hente / and heeld hym faste
And kitte his throte / and in a pit hym caste

¶I seye / that in a wordrobe / they hym threwe
Wher as thise Iewes / purgen hir entraille
O cursed folk of herodes / al newe
What may / youre yuel entente yow auaille
Mordre wol out c*er*teyn it wol nat faille
And namely / ther as thonour of god shal sprede
The blood out cryeth / on youre cursed dede

¶O martir souded to virginitee
Now maystow syngen / folwyng eu*er*e in oon
The white lamb celestial quod she
Of which / the grete Eu*a*ngelist Seint Ioħn
In Pathmos wroot which seith *þ*at they *þ*at gon
Biforn this lamb / and synge a song al newe
carnaliter
That neuere Flesshly / womman they ne knewe

¶This poure wydwe / awaiteth al that nyght
After hir litel child / but he cam noght
For which as soone / as it was dayes lyght
With face pale / of drede and bisy thoght
She hath at scole / and ellis where hym soght
Til fynally / she gan so fer espie
That he last seyn was / in the Iewerie

¶With modres pitee / in hir brest enclosed
She goth / as she were half out of hir mynde
To euery place / wher as she hath supposed
By liklyhede / hir litel child to fynde
And euere / on Cristes moder meke and kynde
She cryde / and at the la[ste thus she] wroghte
[Among the cursed Iues / she hym sog]hte

1770 Legamus Apocalipsim Iohannis et ibi reperimus agnum super montem Syon et cum illo .Cxliiij. Milia signatorum et cetera qui cantant canticum nouum et cetera Hg

1773 Isti sunt qui cum mulieribus se non coinquinauerunt virgines autem permanserunt hij sunt qui secuntur agnum quocumque vadit et cetera Hg

ELLESMERE

Fro Iues
to / hyred
Aleye / hadde a
child forby
Iew *and*

I ⟨a⟩ wardrobe /
Where hir*e*
folk / herodes
may your*e*
certeyn /
ther thonour
crieth /

7 martir / sowded
folwynge

Eu*a*ngelist
seith / goon
.i. carnalit*er*
neu*er*e flesshly / wom*m*en

nyght.
noght
lyght
pale drede / thoght
elles soght
finally /
he / was Iuerie

With moodres
gooth / half /
where she
liklihede /
eu*er*e / mooder / meeke
cride / atte laste / thus she wroghte
Among the cursed Iues / she hym soghte

[7] ¶Prioresse *150r*

¶She frayneth / and she prayeth pitously
To euery Iew / that dwelte in thilke place
To telle hir*e* / if hir child / wente oght forby
They seyde nay / but I*es*u of his grace
Yaf in hir thought in with a litel space
That in that place / after hir sone she cryde
Wher he was casten / in a pit bisyde

¶O grete god / that p*ar*fournest thy laude
By mouth of Innocentz / lo here thy myght
This gemme of chastitee / this Emeraude
And eek of martirdom / the Ruby bright
Ther he with throte ycoruen / lay vpright
He **Alma redemptoris** / gan to synge
So loude / that al the place gan to rynge

¶The cristen folk that thurgh the strete wente
In coomen / for to wondre vp on this thyng
And hastily / they for the Prouost sente
He cam anon / with outen tariyng
And herieth Crist that is of heuene kyng
And eek his moder / honour of mankynde
And after that the Iewes leet he bynde

¶This child / with pitous lamentaciou*n*
Vp taken was / syngynge his song alway
And with honour / of greet p*ro*cessiou*n*
They carien hym / vn to the nexte Abbay
His moder swownyng by his beere lay
Vnnethe myghte / the peple that was there
This newe Rachel / bryngen fro his beere

¶With torment and with shameful deth echon
This Prouost dooth thise Iewes for to sterue
That of this mordre wiste / and that anon
He nolde / no swich cursednesse obserue
Yuel shal haue / that yuel wol disserue
Ther fore with wilde ho[rs he dide] hem drawe
And after that he [heng hem by the lawe]

1817 Rachel plorans filios suos noluit consolari et cetera Hg

ELLESMERE

She preyeth
þ*at*
ogħt

thogħt inwith

Wher*e*

¶Auctor O
heer*e* myghŧ
chastite /
brighŧ
ykoruen vprighŧ

þ*at*

cristene folk / thurgħ

mooder /
that /

8

honour

mooder swownynge /
Vnnethe / myghte þ*at* theere
brynge

wi*th* shameful deeth echon
dooth the Iewes
anon

Yuele shal he haue / þ*at* yuele wol deserue
Therfore / hors / he dide
heng hem by the lawe

8 ¶Prioresse *150v*

The Prioresse.

She frayneth / and she prayeth pitously
To every Jew / that dwelte in thilke place
To telle hir / if hir child wente oght forby
They seyde nay / but Jhesu of his grace
Yaf in hir thoughte / inwith a litel space
That in that place / after hir sone she cryde
Wher he was casten / in a pit bisyde

O grete god / that parfournest thy laude
By mouth of Innocentz / lo here thy myght /
This gemme of chastitee / this Emeraude
And eek of martirdom / tho Ruby bright /
Ther he with throte ykorven / lay upright /
He Alma redemptoris / gan to synge
So loude / that al the place gan to rynge

The Cristen folk / that thurgh the strete wente
In comen / for to wondre up on this thyng /
And hastily / they for the Provost sente
He cam anon / withouten tariyng /
And heryeth Crist / that is of hevens kyng /
And eek his moder / honour of mankynde
And after that / the Jewes leet he bynde

This child / with pitous lamentacion
Up taken was / syngynge his song alway
And with honour / of greet processioun
They caryen hym / un to the nexte abbay
His moder swownyng / by his bere lay
Unnethe myghte / the peple that was there
This newe Rachel / bryngen fro his bere

With torment / and with shameful deth echon
This Provost / dooth thise Jewes for to sterve
That of this mordre wiste / and that anon
He nolde / no swich cursednesse observe
Yvel shal have / that yvel wol deserve
Ther fore with wilde hors [illegible] hem drawe
And after that / he [illegible]

Rachel plorans filios suos
noluit consolari &c.

De puero qui cantauit de gloriosa virgine

De Maria quicquid sciuit
puer cantans enunciauit — Marian inop[illegible]
Hunc Iudeus necari strauit
Domo sua quem humauit — Quam p Iundi[illegible]
Mater queres hunc vocauit
Hic in terra recantauit — Solita preconia
Puer liber mox exiuit
Mortis reos lex puniuit — Iudeos &c

Vp on his beere ay lyth this Innocent
Biforn the chief auter whil the masse laste
And after that the Abbot wt his Couent
Han sped hem for to buryen hym ful faste
And whan they holy water on hym caste
Yet spak this child whan spreynd was holy water
And song O alma redemptoris mater

This Abbot which pt was an holy man
As monkes ben or ellis oghten be
This yonge child to coniure he bigan
And seyde o deere child I halse thee
In vertu of the holy Trinitee
Tel me what is thy cause for to synge
Sith pt thy throte is kit to my semynge

My throte is kit vn to my nekke boon
Seyde this child and as by wey of kynde
I sholde haue dyed ye longe tyme agoon
But Ihu crist as ye in bokes fynde
Wol pt his glorie laste and be in mynde
And for the worship of his moder deere
Yet may I synge O alma loude and cleere

This welle of mercy Cristes moder swete
I loued alwey as after my konnynge
And whan pt I my lyf sholde forlete
To me she cam and bad me for to synge
This Antheme verraily in my deiynge
As ye han herd and whan pt I had songe
Me thoughte she leyde a greyn vp on my tonge

Wher fore I synge and synge moot certeyn
In honour of that blisful mayden free
Til fro my tonge of taken is the greyn
And after that thus seyde she to me
My litel child now wol I fecche thee
Whan pt the greyn [illegible] tonge y take

	ELLESMERE
¶Vp on his beere / ay lyth this Innocent	on this beere / lith
Biforn the chief Auter / whil the masse laste	
And after that the Abbot w*ith* his Couent	with
Han sped hem / for to buryen hym ful faste	burien
And whan they / holy water on hym caste	hooly water
Yet spak this child / whan spreynd was holy water	hooly
And song O **alma redemptoris mater**	**Alma**
¶This Abbot which þ*at* was an holy man	hooly
As monkes ben / or ellis oghten be	As Monkes been / elles oghte
This yonge child / to coniure he bigan	
And seyde / o deere child I halsen thee	
In vertu / of the holy Trinitee	hooly
Tel me / what is thy cause for to synge	cause /
Sith þ*at* thy throte is kit to my semynge	kut
¶My throte is kit .vn to my nekke boon	kut
Seyde this child / and as by wey of kynde	child
I sholde haue dyed / ye longe tyme agoon	agon
But I*es*u crist as ye in bokes fynde	crist / bookes
Wol þ*at* his glorie laste / and be in mynde	Wil glorie /
And for the worship*e* / of his moder deere	mooder
Yet may I synge / **O alma** / loude and clere	**Alma** / cleere
¶This welle of m*er*cy / Cristes moder swete	mercy mooder sweete
I loued alwey / as after my konnynge	
And whan þ*at* I my lyf sholde forlete	lyf /
To me she cam / and bad me for to synge	
This Antheme / v*er*raily in my deiynge	This Anthephen*e* / verraily / deyynge
As ye han herd / and whan þ*at* I had songe	herd hadde
Me thoughte / she leyde a greyn vp on my tonge	
¶Wher fore I synge / and synge moot c*er*teyn	9 Wherfore synge I moot
In honour / of that blisful mayden free	
Til fro my tonge / of taken is the greyn	
And after that thus seyde she to me	And afterward / thus
My litel child / now wol I fecche thee	
Whan þ*at* the greyn / [is fro thy ton]ge ytake	is fro thy tonge
[Be nat agast I wol thee nat forsake]	Be nat agast I wol thee nat forsake

1825 de puero qui cantauit de gloriosa virgine
de maria quicquid sciuit / puer cantans enutriuit } Maternam inopiam
hunc Iudeus nequam strauit / domo sua quem humauit } Diram per Inuidiam
Mater querens hunc vocauit / hic in terra recantauit } Solita preconia
Puer liber mox exiuit / Mortis reos lex puniuit } Iudeos et cetera
Hg

9 ¶Prioresse *151r*

	ELLESMERE
¶This holy monk⁊ this Abbot⁊ hym mene I	hooly Monk⁊ Abbot meene
His tonge out caughte / and took awey the greyn	a wey
And he / yaf vp the goost ful softely	he goost⁊
And whan this Abbot⁊ hadde this wonder seyn	
His salte teerys / trikled doun as reyn	Hise teeris /
And gruf he fil / al flat vp on the grounde	plat
And stille he lay / as he hadde leyn ybounde	had
¶The Couent eek / lay on the pauement	The Couent⁊ pauement⁊
Wepynge / and heryen cristes moder deere	mooder
And after that they ryse / and forth been went⁊	that⁊ ryse
And toke awey this martir / from his beere	tooken awey / martir
And in a toumbe / of Marbilstones cleere	a temple / of Marbulstones
Enclosen they / this litel body swete	they / his litel sweete
Ther he is now / god leue vs for to meete	vs alle for
¶O yonge Hugħ of lyncoln / slayn also	Lyncoln̄
With cursed Iewes / as it is notable	
For it is / but alitel while ygo	a litel ago
Preye eek for vs / we synful folk vnstable	eek /
That of his mercy / god so merciable	
On vs / his grete mercy multiplie	
For reuerence / of his moder Marie Amen	mooder
¶Here endeth / the Prioresse tale	¶Heere is ended / the Prioresses tale
¶Bihoold the myrie talkyng⁊ of the hoost⁊. to Chaucer	¶Bihoold the murye wordes of the Hoost⁊ to Chaucer
WHan seyd was al this myracle / eu*er*y man	miracle /
As sobre was / that wonder was to se	
Til that oure hoost⁊ iapen to bigan	Iapen
And thanne at erst⁊ he looked vp on me (.i. Chaucer)	on me (.s. Chaucer)
And seyde thus / what man artow quod he	he ∫
Thow lookest⁊ as thow woldest fynde an hare	Thou thou
For eu*er*e vp on the ground / I se thee stare	eu*er*e / ground' /

This holy monk this Abbot hym mene I
His tonge out caughte and took awey the greyn
And he yaf up the goost ful softely
And whan this Abbot hadde this wonder seyn
His salte teerys trikled doun as reyn
And gruf he fil al flat up on the grounde
And stille he lay as he hadde leyn ybounde

The couent eek lay on the pauement
Wepynge and heryen cristes moder deere
And after that they ryse and forth been went
And toke awey this martir from his beere
And in a tombe of marbilstones cleere
Enclosen they this litel body swete
Ther he is now god leue us for to meete

O yonge Hugh of Lyncoln slayn also
With cursed Iewes as it is notable
For it is but a litel while ygo
Preye eek for us we synful folk unstable
That of his mercy god so merciable
On us his grete mercy multiplie
For reuerence of his moder Marie Amen

Here endeth the Prioresse tale

Bihoold the murye talkyng of the hoost to Chaucer

Whan seyd was al this miracle euery man
As sobre was that wonder was to se
Til that oure hoost iapen to bigan
And thanne at erst he looked up on me Chaucer
And seyde thus what man artow quod he
Thow lookest as thow woldest fynde an hare
For euere up on the ground I se thee stare

Approche neer and looke vp myrily
Now war yow sires and lat this man haue place
He in the waast is shape as wel as I
This were a popet in an arm tenbrace
For any womman smal and fair of face
He semeth eluyssh by his contenance
For vn to no wight dooth he no daliance

Sey now som what syn oother folk han sayd
Telle vs a tale of myrthe and that anon
Hoost quod I ne beth nat yuele apayd
For oother tale certes kan I noon
But of a rym I lerned longe agoon
Ye that is good quod he now shul we heere
Som deyntee thyng me thynketh by his cheere

Here bigynneth Chaucers tale of Thopas

Listeth lordes in good entent
And I wol telle verrayment
Of myrthe and of solas
Al of a knyght was fair and gent
In bataille and in tornament
His name was sir Thopas
Yborn he was in fer contree
In Flaundres al biyonde the see
At Poperyng in the place
His fader was a man ful free
And lord he was of that contree
As it was goddes grace
Sire Thopas wax a doghty swayn
Whit was his face as payndemayn
His lippes reed as rose
His rode is lyk scarlet in grayn
As I yow telle in good certayn
He hadde a semely nose
His heer his berd was lyk saffroun
That to his girdel raughte adoun
His shoon of cordewane
Of Brugges were his hosen broun
His robe was of syklatoun
That coste many a Iane
He koude hunte at wilde deer
And ryde an haukyng for ryuer
With grey goshauk on honde
Ther to he was a good archer
Of wrastlyng was ther noon his peer
Ther any ram shal stonde

¶Approche neer / and looke vp myrily
Now war yow sires / and lat this man haue place
He in the wastꝛ is shape as wel as I
This were a popetꝛ in an arm tenbrace
For any womman / smal and fair of face
He semeth eluyssħ / by his contenance
For vn to no wightꝛ dooth he no daliance

¶Sey now som whatꝛ syn oother folk han sayd
Telle vs a tale / of myrthe / and that anon
Hoost quod I / ne beth nat yuele ypayd
For oother tale / c*er*tes kan I noon
But of a rym / I lerned longe agoon
Ye that is good quod he / now shul we heere
Som deyntee thyngꝛ me thynketh by his cheere

¶Here bigynneth Chaucers tale of Thopas

Listeth lordes / in good ententꝛ
And I wil telle v*er*raymentꝛ
} Of myrthe / and of solas
Al of a knyghtꝛ was fair and gentꝛ
In bataille / and in tornamentꝛ
} his name / was sir Thopas
¶Yborn he was / in fer contree
In Flaundres / al biyonde the see
} At Poperyngꝛ in the place
His fader was / a man ful free
And lord he was / of that contree
} As it was / goddes g*ra*ce
¶Sire Thopas wax / a doghty swayn
Whit was his face / as Payndemayn
} his lippes reed as Rose
His rode is lyk / Scarlet in grayn
As I yow telle / in good certayn
} he hadde a semely nose
¶His heerꝛ his berd / was lyk Safrown
That to his girdel / raughte adown
} his shoon / of Cordewane
Of Brugges / were his hosen brown
His Robe was / of Syklatown
} That coste many a Iane
¶He koude hunte / at wilde deer
And ride an hawkyngꝛ for Ryuer
} With grey goshauk on honde
Ther to he was / a good Archier
Of wrastlyngꝛ was ther noon his pier
} Ther any Ram shal stonde

ELLESMERE

1 Approche murily
waastꝛ shape / .I. .i. henry Bailly
Arm
wo*m*man smal /
contenau*n*ce
wigħt / he daliau*n*ce

Sey folkꝛ sayd
Hoostꝛ apayd
certes
.i. hoost he / shul ye heere

¶Explicitꝛ

¶Heere bigynneth Chaucers tale of Thopas

Listeth lordes
myrthe
wol
knygħt /
sire
tourneymentꝛ
flaundres /
was grace
¶Sir*e* Thopas / wax doghty
Hise rede rose
face
scarlet
hadde /
And I
heer / berd / saffroun
Hise shoos
girdel raugħte adoun
broun
Robe / was Syklatoun
W*ith*
haukyngꝛ Riuer
Archeer
peer

[1] ¶Chaucer *151v*

⸗Chaucer of sire Topas⸗

ELLESMERE

¶Ful many mayde / bright in bour
They moorne for hym / *par*amour
When hem / were bet to sle[pe]
But he was chaast and no lechour
And swete / as is the brambel flour
That bereth the rede hepe
¶And so it fel / vp on a day
For sothe / as I yow telle may
Sire Thopas / wolde out ryde
He warth vp on / his Steede gray
And in his hand / a launcegay
A long swerd / by his syde
¶He priketh thurgh / a fair Forest
Ther Inne / is many a wilde best
Ye bothe / bukke and hare
And as he priketh / North *and* Est
I telle it yow / hym hadde almest
bitydde / a sory care
¶There spryngen herbes / grene *and* smale
The Licorys / and Cetewale
And many a clowe Gylofre
And notemuge / to putte in Ale
Wheither it be / moyste or stale
Or / for to leye in cofre
¶The bryddes synge / it is no nay
The Sp*ar*hauk and the Popyniay
That ioye / it was to here
The Thurstelcok / made eek his lay
The wodedowue / vp on the spray
She sang ful loude *and* clere
¶Sire Thopas fil / in loue longynge
Al whan he herde / the thrustel synge
And pryked / as he were wood
His fayre Steede / in his p*ri*kynge
So swatte / þ*at* men myghte hym wrynge
hys sydes / were al blood
¶Sire Thopas eek / so wery was
For prikyng on the softe gras
So fiers / was his corage
That doun he leyde hym / in the plas
To make his Steede / som solas
And yaf hym / good forage
¶O Seinte Marie / benedicite
What eyleth / this loue at me
To bynde me / so soore
Me dremed / al this nyght *par*dee
An Elf queene / shal my lemman be
And slepe / vnder my gore
¶An Elf queene / wol I haue ywys
For in this world / no womman is
Worthy to be my make // in towne ⸗
Alle othere wommen / I forsake
And to an Elf queene / I me take
by dale / and eek by downe
¶In to his Sadel / he clamb anoon
And priketh ouer / style and stoon
An Elf queene / for tespye
Til he so longe / hath riden *and* goon
That he foond / in a pryuee woon
The contree of Fairye // So wylde⸗

many a mayde / bright
hem slepe
hym
sweete / Brembul
so bifel
Sir*e* ride
worth / vpon
side
hand Launcegay
2 priketh / thurgh forest
bothe
Bitidde /
¶Ther herbes / grete *and*
gylofre
lycorys
Notemuge /
Or
it be moyste /
briddes
ioye heere
papeiay
thrustelcok / eek hir lay
cleere
vp on a spray
¶Sir*e* fil
wood
faire steede / prikynge
his blood
hi*m*
¶Sir*e*
fiers
hi*m* in that plas
hym
Steede
seinte Marie
me
nyght
slepe goore
elf le*m*man
I loue ywis
make⸗ In towne
wo*m*man
¶Alle wo*m*men /
By dale *and*
Elf queene
sadel / anon
Elf queene
ouer stile
hadde and
Fairye wilde
pryue

[2]¶Thopas *152r*

Chaucer of Sire Topas.

¶ Ful many mayde bright in bour
They moorne for hym paramour
Whan hem were bet to slepe
But he was chaast and no lechour
And sweete as is the brambel flour
That bereth the rede hepe

¶ And so it fel vp on a day
ffor sothe as I yow telle may
Sire Thopas wolde out ryde
He worth vp on his steede gray
And in his hand a launcegay
A long swerd by his syde

¶ He priketh thurgh a fair forest
Ther Inne is many a wilde best
Ye bothe bukke and hare
And as he priketh North & Est
I telle it yow hym hadde almest
Bitydde a sory care

¶ Ther springen herbes grene & smale
The lycorys and cetewale
And many a clowe gylofre
And notemuge to putte in ale
Whether it be moyste or stale
Or for to leye in cofre

¶ The briddes synge it is no nay
The sparhauk and the papyniay
That ioye it was to here
The thrustelcok made eek his lay
The wodedowue vp on the spray
She sang ful loude & clere

¶ Sire Thopas fil in loue longynge
Al whan he herde the thrustel synge
And pryked as he were wood
His faire steede in his prikynge
So swatte þt men myghte hym wrynge
His sydes were al blood

¶ Sire Thopas eek so wery was
ffor prikyng on the softe gras
So fiers was his corage
That doun he leyde hym in the plas
To make his steede som solas
And yaf hym good forage

¶ O seinte marie benedicite
What eyleth this loue at me
To bynde me so sore
Me dremed al this nyght pardee
An elf queene shal my lemman be
And slepe vnder my gore

¶ An elf queene wol I haue ywys
ffor in this world no womman is
Worthy to be my make // in towne
Alle othere wommen I forsake
And to an elf queene I me take
By dale and eek by downe

¶ In to his sadel he clamb anoon
And priketh ouer style and stoon
An elf queene for tespye
Til he so longe hath riden & goon
That he foond in a pryuee woon
The contree of ffairye so wylde

ffor in that contree was ther noon
Neither wyf ne childe
Til þt ther cam a greet geaunt
His name was sire Olifaunt
A perilous man of dede
He seyde child by Termagaunt
But if thow pryke out of myn haunt
Anon I sle thy steede
With mace
Here is the queene of ffairye
With harpe & pipe & Symphonye
Dwellyng in this place
The child seyde als mote I thee
Tomorwe wol I meete thee
Whan I haue myn armowre
And yet I hope par ma fay
That thow shalt with this launcegay
Abyen it ful sowre
Thy mawe
Shal I percen if I may
Er it be fully pryme of day
ffor here shaltow ben slawe
Sire Thopas drow abak ful faste
This geaunt at hym stones caste
Out of a fel staf slynge
But faire escapeth child Thopas
And al it was thurgh goddes gras
And thurgh his fair berynge
Yet lesteth lordes to my tale
Murier than the nyghtyngale
I wol yow rowne
How sire Thopas with sydes smale
Prikyng ouer hill and dale
Is come agayn to towne
His murye men comanded he
To make hym bothe game and glee
ffor nedes moste he fighte
With a geaunt with heuedes thre
ffor paramour and Iolitee
Of oon that shoon ful brighte
Do come he seyde my mynstrales
And Gestours for to tellen tales
Anon in myn armynge
Of romances that been reales
Of Popes and of Cardynales
And eek of loue likyng
They sette hym first swete wyn
And mede eek in a maselyn
And real Spicerye
Of gyngebred that was ful fyn
And lycorys and eek Comyn
With sugre that is trye
He dide next his white leer
Of clooth of lake fyn & cleer
A breech and eek a sherte
And next his sherte an aketoun
And ouer that an haubergeon
ffor percyng of his herte
And ouer that a fyn hawberk
Was al ywroght of Iewes werk
ffull strong it was of plate

For in that contree / was ther noon
Neither wyf ne childe
} [3]

¶Til þat ther cam / a greet geaunt
His name was / sire Olifaunt
} A p*er*ilous man of dede

He seyde child / by Termagaunt
But if thow pryke / out of myn haunt
} Anon I sle thy Steede
} ¶With Mace

¶Heere is this queene / of Fairye
With harpe *and* pipe / *and* Symphonye
} dwellyng in this place

¶The child seyde / als mote I thee
Tomorwe / wol I meete thee
} Whan I haue myn Armowre

¶And yet I hope / *par* ma fay
That thow shalt w*ith* this launcegay
} Abyen it ful sowre
} ¶Thy Mawe

Shal I percen / if I may
Er it be fully pryme of day
} For here shaltow ben slawe

¶Sire Thopas / drow abak ful faste
This geant at hym stones caste
} Out of a fel staf slynge

¶But faire escapeth / child Thopas
And al it was / thurgh goddes graas
} And thurgh his fair berynge

Ȝet lesteth lordes / to my tale
Murier than the nyghtyngale
} I wol yow rowne

How sire Thopas / with sydes smale
Prikyng ouer hyll and dale
} Is come agayn to towne

¶Hys murye men / comanded he
To make hym / bothe game and glee
} For nedes moste he fighte

With a geant with heuedes thre
For p*ar*amour / and Iolitee
} Of oon / that shoon ful brighte

¶Do come he seyde / my Mynstrales
And Gestours / for to tellen tales
} Anon / in myn Armyng

Of romances / that been reales
Of Popes / and of Cardynales
} And eek / of loue likyng

¶They fette hym first swete wyn
And Mede eek in a Maselyn
} And real Spicerye

Of gyngebred / that was ful fyn
And lycorys / and eek Comyn
} With Sugre / that is trye

¶He dide next his white leer
Of clooth of Lake / fyn *and* cleer
} A breech / and eek a Sherte

And next his Sherte / an Aketou*n*
And ouer that an haubergeou*n*
} For p*er*cyng of his herte

¶And ouer that a fyn hauberk
Was al ywroght of Iewes werk
} Ful strong it was of plate

contree noon
wyf childe
cam
sir*e*
Termagaunt / with Mace thou prike /
is / the queene dwellynge harpe / and pipe and symphonye
Also moote Armour*e* meete w*ith* thee
Thy Mawe thou
Thyn hauberk / shal I p*er*cen / heere thow shalt be
¶Sir*e*
escapeth sir*e* Thopas thurgh was thurgh gras
[4] Yet listeth /
Nightyngale
sir comen hill
¶His myrie nedes / fighte
geaunt three
p*ar*amour
Anon Armynge geestours /
Romances / Roiales eek likynge Cardinales
sweete Roial Mazelyn
And Gyngebreed / þat sugre þat is so trye lycorys
dide / next leere
and cleere
sherte percynge
ou*er* that / hawberk
ywroght

[3] *Out* Hg El 1995. Dd[1] reads: That to hi*m* durst ride or goon

[4] ¶Chaucer *152v*

./Chaucer of sire Topas./

And ouer that / his cote Armour
As whit as is / a lilie flour
In which / he wol debate
¶His sheeld was al / of gold so reed
And ther Inne was / a bores heed
A Charbocle / by his syde
And there he swoor / on Ale and breed
How þat the geant / shal be deed
Bityde / what bityde
¶Hise Iambeux were / of quyrboily
His swerdes shethe / of Yuory
his helm / of laton bright
His Sadel was / of Rewel bon
His brydel / as the Sonne shon
Or as the moone light
¶His spere was / of fyn Cipres
That bodeth werre / and no thyng pes
The heed / ful sharpe ygrounde
His Steede was / al dappel gray
It goth an Ambel / in the way
Ful softely / and rounde
// In londe./
¶Lo lordes myne / here is a fit
If ye wole / any moore of it
To telle it wol I fonde
⟨n⟩Ow hoold youre mouth par charitee
Bothe knyght and lady free
And herkneth / to my spell
Of bataille / and of chiualry
And of ladyes / loue drury
Anon / I wol yow tell
¶Men speken / of Romances of pris
Of Hornchild / and of Ypotys
of Beves and Sir Gy
Of Sire lybeux / and playn damo*ur*
But sire Thopas / he bereth the flo*ur*
Of real Chiualry
¶His goode Steede / al he bystrood
And forth vp on his wey he glood
As Sparcle / out of the bronde
Vp on his Creest he bar a tour
And ther Inne stiked / a lilie flour
God shilde / his cors fro shonde
¶And for he was / a knyght auntrous
He nolde slepen / in noon hous
But liggen in his hode
His brighte helm / was his wonger
And by hym / bayteth his destrer
Of herbes / fyne and goode
¶Hym self / drank water of the well
As dide the knyght Sire Percyuell
So worly vnder wede
Til on a day

¶here the hoost stynteth Chaucer of his tale of Thopas / and biddeth hym / telle another tale

Namoore of this / for goddes dignytee
Quod oure hoost for thow makest me

that
whit lilye
sheeld / reed
Charbocle bisyde
Inne / was heed
breed
Bityde
geaunt deed
were quyrboilly
helm latou*n* bright
shethe yuory
was boon
light
shoon
spere it was / Ciprees
thyng pees
¶His dappull
softely // rounde londe
gooth Ambil
¶Loo heere
it /
wol
NOw holde your*e* mouth
herkneth spelle
knyght
¶Of batailles / Chiualry
Anon telle
speken prys
Of Beves and of *sir*
Hornchild
¶Of *sir* lybeux pleyn
Roial
sir
bistrood
sparcle /
forth / vpon he rood
5 ¶Vp on
shilde
Inne / stiked
knyght Auntrous
hoode
¶His brighte
herbes
baiteth dextrer
knyght Percyuell
¶Til

¶Heere the Hoost stynteth Chaucer / of his tale of Thopas

dignitee
thou me./

5 ¶Thopas *153r*

Chaucer of sire Topas

And ouer that his cote armour
As whit as is a lilie flour
In which he wol debate
His sheeld was al of gold so reed
And ther Inne was a bores heed
A charbocle by his syde
And there he swoor on ale and breed
How þt the geant shal be deed
Bityde what bityde
Hise Iambeux were of quyrboily
His swerdes shethe of yuory
His helm of laton bright
His sadel was of rewel bon
His brydel as the sonne shon
Or as the moone light
His spere was of fyn Cipres
That bodeth werre and no thyng pees
The heed ful sharp ygrounde
His steede was al dappel gray
It goth an ambel in the way
fful softely and rounde // In londe
Lo lordes myne heere is a fit
If ye wole any moore of it
To telle it wol I fonde
Now hoold youre mouth par charitee
Bothe knyght and lady free
And herkneth to my spelle
Of bataille and of chiualry
And of ladyes loue drury
Anon I wol yow telle
Men speken of romances of pris
Of Hornchild and of Ypotys
Of Beves and sir Gy
Of sir Lybeux and Playndamour
But sir Thopas he bereth the flour
Of real chiualry
His goode steede al he bistrood
And forth vp on his wey he glood
As sparcle out of the bronde
Vp on his creest he bar a tour
And ther Inne stiked a lilie flour
God shilde his cors fro shonde
And for he was a knyght auntrous
He nolde slepen in noon hous
But liggen in his hoode
His brighte helm was his wonger
And by hym baiteth his destrer
Of herbes fyne and goode
Hym self drank water of the well
As dide the knyght sir Percyuell
So worly vnder wede
Til on a day

Here the hoost stynteth Chaucer of his tale of
Thopas and biddeth hym telle another tale

Namoore of this for goddes dignitee
Quod oure hoost for thow makest me

So wery —— of thy verray lewednesse
That also wisly god my soule blesse
Myne erys aken of thy drasty speche
Now swich a rym the deuel I biteche
This may wel be rym dogerel quod he
¶ Why so quod I why wiltow lette me
Moore of my tale than another man
Syn that it is the beste rym I kan
¶ By god quod he for pleynly at o word
Thy drasty rymyng is nat worth a tord
Thow doost noght ellis but despendest tyme
Sire at o word thow shalt no lenger ryme
Lat se wher thow kanst tellen aught in geste
Or tel in prose somwhat at the leeste
In which ther be som myrthe or som doctryne
¶ Gladly quod I by goddes swete pyne
I wol yow telle a litel thyng in prose
That oghte liken yow as I suppose
Or ellis certes ye be to daungerous
It is a moral tale vertuous
Al be it told som tyme in sondry wise
Of sondry folk as I shal yow deuyse
¶ As thus ye woot þt euery Euangelist
That telleth vs the peyne of Ihu crist
Ne seith nat alle thyng as his felawe dooth
But nathelees hir sentence is al sooth
And alle acorden as in hir sentence
Al be ther in hir tellyng difference
ffor somme of hem seyn moore & somme seyn lesse
Whan they his pitous passion expresse
I mene of Mark Mathew Luk and Iohn
But doutelees hir sentence is al oon
¶ Therfore lordynges alle I yow biseche
If þt ye thynke I varie as in my speche
As thus though þt I telle somwhat moore
Of prouerbes than ye han herd bifore
Comprehended in this litel tretys heere
To enforcen with theffect of my matere
And though I nat the same wordes seye
As ye han herd yet to yow alle I preye

So wery—— / of thy verray lewednesse	wery /
That also wisly / god my soule blesse	
Myne erys aken / of thy drasty speche	eres
Now swich a rym / the deuel I biteche	Rym /
This may wel be / rym dogerel quod he	wel / be Rym
¶Why so quod I / why wiltow lette me	me ./
Moore of my tale / than another man	
Syn that it is / the beste rym I kan	beste tale I
¶By god quod he / for pleynly at o word	at a worđ
Thy drasty rymyngꝭ is nat worth a tord	rymyng / toorđ
Thow doost noght ellis / but despendest tyme	Thou doostꝭ elles /
Sire at o word / thow shalt no lenger ryme	Sir*e* thou
Lat se / wher thow kanst tellen aught in geste	thou aughŧ geeste
Or tel in prose / som what atꝭ the leeste	telle somwhat at
In which ther be som myrthe / or som doctrine	murthe / doctryne
¶Gladly quod I / by goddes swete pyne	sweete
I wol yow telle / a litel thyng in prose	thyng /
That oghte like yow / as I suppose	oghte liken
Or ellis certes / ye be to daungerous	elles c*er*tes / been
It is a moral tale v*er*tuous	vertuous
Al be it toold som tyme in sondry wise	it take somtyme / wyse
Of sondry folk / as I shal yow deuyse	folkꝭ
¶As thus / ye wootꝭ *þat* euery Eu*a*ngelistꝭ	Eu*a*ngelist /
That telleth vs / the peyne of I*es*u Cristꝭ	cristꝭ
Ne seith nat alle thyngꝭ as his felawe dooth	dooħ
But nathelees / hir sentence is al sooth	sooħ
And alle acorden / as in hir sentence	hir*e*
Al be ther / in hir tellyng difference	tellyngꝭ
For som*m*e of hem seyn moore / *and* som*m*e seyn lesse	he*m* and
Whan they / his pitous passion exp*re*sse	passiou*n*
I mene / of Mark / Mathew / Lukꝭ and Ioħn	meene Markꝭ Lucꝭ
But doutelees / hir sentence is al oon	
¶Therfore / lordynges alle / I yow biseche	6 ¶Therfore Lordynges
If *þat* ye thynke / I varie / as in my speche	yow varie
As thus / thogh *þat* I telle somwhat moore	thouġ that som what
Of p*ro*uerbes / than ye han herd bifore	bifoore
Comp*re*hended / in this litel tretys heere	
To enforcen with / theffect of my matere	enforce theffectꝭ mateere
And thogh I natꝭ the same wordes seye	thouħ I / nat
As ye han herd / yet to yow alle I preye	herđ /

[6] ¶Chaucer *153v*

Blameth me nat / for as in my sentence
Shul ye / nowher / fynden difference
Fro the sentence / of this tretys lite
After the which / this myry tale I write
And therfore herkneth / what þat I shal seye
And lat me tellen / al my tale I preye

¶Here bigynneth Chaucers tale of Melibeus*

A yongꝛ man whilom / called Melibeus myghty and riche / bigat vp on his wif / þat called was Prudence / a doghter / which þat called was Sophie / vp on a day bifel / þat he for his desportꝛ is went in to the feeldes / hym to pleye / his wif *and* eek his doghter / hath he laft inwith his hous / of which the dores weren faste yshette / thre of his olde foos / han it espied / *and* setten laddres / to the walles of his hous / and by wyndowes ben entred / *and* betten his wif / *and* wounded his doghter / w*it*h fyue mortal woundes in fyue sondry places / this is to seyn / in hir feetꝛ in hir handes / in hir erys / in hir nose / and in hir mouth / and leften hir*e* for deed *and* wenten awey ¶Whan Melibeus retourned was in to his hous / *and* seigh al this meschief / he lyk a mad man / rentyne his clothes / gan to wepe / and crye //
¶Prudence his wyf / as ferforth as she dorste / bisoughte hym / of his wepyngꝛ for to stynte / but nat for thy / he gan to crye *and* wepen euere lenger the moore ¶This noble wif Prudence remembred hire / vp on the sentence of Ouyde / in his bookꝛ þat cleped is / the remedie of loue / wher as he seith / he is a fool / that destourbeth the moder / to wepe / in the deth of hir child' til she haue weptꝛ hir fille / as for ⟨a⟩ c*er*teyn tyme / and thanne shal man doon his diligence w*it*h amyable wordes / hir*e* to reconforte / and preye hir*e* / of hir wepyng for to stynte / for which reson / this noble wyf Prudence / suffred hir housbonde / for to wepe *and* crye / as for a certeyn space / and whan she say hir tyme / she seyde hym in this wise ¶Allas my lord quod she / why make ye your selfꝛ for to be lyk a fool / for sothe / it ap*er*teneth nat to a wys man / to maken swich a sorwe / yowre doghter / with the g*ra*ce of god / shal warisshe and escape

ELLESMERE

natꝛ
nowherꝛ
lyte
murye
therfore /

¶Explicitꝛ

¶Heere bigynneth Chaucers tale of Melibee

17 Ouidius de remedio amoris Hg El (2166)

*Ellesmere variants for MelT on pages 999–1011.

Blameth me nat / for as in my sentence
Shul ye nowher / fynden difference
ffro the sentence / of this tretys lite
After the which / this murye tale I write
And therfore herkneth / what þt I shal seye
And lat me tellen / al my tale I preye

Here bigynneth Chaucers tale of Melibeus

[A y]oung man whilom called Melibeus myghty and
[r]iche bigat vp on his wif / þt called was Prudence a
doghter / which þt called was Sophie / vp on a day bifel þt
he for his desport / is went in to the feeldes hym to pleye / his
wif & eek his doghter / hath he laft inwith his hous / of which
the dores weren faste yshette / thre of his olde foos / han it espi
ed & setten laddres to the walles of his hous / and by wyndo
wes ben entred / & betten his wif / & wounded his doghter / wt
fyue mortal woundes in fyue sondry places / this is to seyn
in hir feet / in hir handes / in hir erys / in hir nose / and in hir
mouth / and leften hir for deed & wenten awey ¶ Whan me
libeus retourned was in to his hous & sigh al this meschief / he
lyk a mad man rentynge his clothes / gan to wepe and crye
¶ Prudence his wyf as ferforth as she dorste / bisoughte hym / of
his wepyng for to stynte / but nat for thy he gan to crye &
wepen euere lenger the moore ¶ This noble wif Prudence
remembred hire vp on the sentence of Ouyde in his book þt
cleped is the remedie of loue / wher as he seith / he is a fool
that destourbeth the moder to wepe in the deth of hir child
til she haue wept hir fille / as for a certeyn tyme / and thanne
shal man doon his diligence wt amyable wordes hire to re
conforte and preye hire / of hir wepyng for to stynte / for which
reson / this noble wyf Prudence suffred hir housbonde for to
wepe & crye / as for a certeyn space / and whan she say hir
tyme / she seyde hym in this wise ¶ Allas my lord quod she
why make ye youre self for to be lyk a fool / for sothe it aperte
neth nat to a wys man to maken swich a sorwe / youre
doghter with the grace of god / shal warisshe and escape.

¶ Ouid' de remedio amoris

Seneca

And al were it so þt she right now were deed / ye ne oghte nat as
for hir deth youre self to destroye ¶ Senec seith / the wise man
shal nat take to greet disconfort / for the deth of his children / but
certes he sholde suffren it in pacience as wel as he abideth the
deth of his owene ppre psone ¶ This Melibeus answerde anon
& seyde ¶ What man quod he sholde of his wepyng stynte ·
that hath so gret a cause for to wepe / Jhu crist / oure lord hym
self wepte for the deth of lazarus his freend ¶ Prudence
answerde ¶ Certes wel I woot / attempree wepynge is no thyng
defended to hym þt sorweful is amonges folk in sorwe · but
it is rather graunted hym to wepe ¶ The Apostle Poul vn to
the Romayns writeth / man shal reioysse wt hem þt maken ioye
and wepen / wt swich folk as wepen / but thogh attempree we
pyng be graunted / outrageous wepyng certes is defended / mesure
of wepyng sholde be considered / after the loore þt techeth vs
Senec ¶ Whan þt thy freend is deed quod he / lat nat thyne eyen
to moyste ben of terys / ne to muche drye / al thogh the terys
come to thyne eyen / lat hem nat falle / and whan thou hast
forgoon thy freend / do diligence to geten another freend and
this is moore wysdom / than for to wepe for thy freend which
þt thou hast lorn / for ther Inne is no boote and ther fore if ye
gouerne yow by sapience / put awey sorwe out of youre herte /
¶ Remembre yow þt Jhc Syrak seith / A man þt is ioyous and
glad in herte / it hym conserueth florisshynge in his age / but
soothly sorweful herte maketh his bones drye / he seith eek
thus / þt sorwe in herte / sleeth ful many a man / Salomon
seith that right as moththes in the shepes flees anoyen
to the clothes and the smale wormes to the tree / right so anoy
eth sorwe to the herte / wher fore vs oghte as wel in the deth
of oure children as in the losse of oure goodes temporels haue
pacience / Remembre yow vp on the pacient Job whan he
hadde lost his children and his temporel substance and in his body
endured & receyued ful many a greuous tribulacion / yet seyde
he thus / Oure lord hath biraft it me right so as oure lord
hath wold right so it is doon / yblessed be the name of oure
lord ¶ To thise forseyde thynges answerde Melibeus vn to
his wif Prudence / Alle thy wordes quod he been sothe &
ther to pfitable but trewely myn herte is troubled wt this
sorwe so greuously þt I noot what to doon ¶ Lat calle quod
Prudence thy trewe freendes alle & thy lynage whiche þt

Jhc flevit ppter mortem lazari

Epistola ad Romanos

...en wise

And al were it so / þ*at* she right now were deed ⸍ ye ne oghte nat as [S]eneca for hir deth / your*e* self to destroye ¶Senec seith / the wise man shal nat take to greet disconfort for the deth of his children / but c*er*tes / he sholde suffren it in pacience / as wel / as he abideth the deth / of his owene p*ro*pre p*er*sone ¶This Melibeus / answerde anon *and* seyde ¶What man quod he / sholde of his wepyng stynte that hath so gret a cause for to wepe // Ies*u* c*ris*t oure lord hym self / wepte / for the deth / of lazarus his freend ¶Prudence answerde ¶Certes wel I woot attempree wepynge / is no thyng defended / to hym þ*at* sorweful is / amonges folk in sorwe /⸍ but it is rather / graunted hym to wepe ¶The Apostle Poul / vn to the Romayns writeth // Man shal reioysse w*ith* hem þ*at* maken ioye / and wepen / w*ith* swich folk as wepen // but thogh attempree wepyng be graunted / out*ra*geous wepyng c*er*tes is defended // Mesure of wepyng sholde be considered / after the loore þ*at* techeth vs Senec ¶Whan þ*at* thy freend is deed quod he / lat nat thyne eyen / to moyste ben of terys / ne to muche drye / al thogh the teerys come to thyne eyen / lat hem nat falle / And whan thou hast forgoon thy freend / do diligence / to geten another freend / and this is moore wysdom / than for to wepe for thy freend / which þ*at* thou hast lorn / for ther Inne / is no boote / And therfore / if ye gou*er*ne yow by Sapience / put awey sorwe / out of youre herte / ¶Remembre yow / þ*at* I*esus* Syrak seith // A man þ*at* is ioyous and glad in herte /· it hym conserueth florisshynge in his age / but soothly / sorweful herte / maketh his bones drye // he seith eek thus /· þ*at* sorwe in herte / sleeth ful many a man // Salomon seith / that right as Moththes in the Shepes flees / anoyeþ to the clothes / and the smale wormes to the tree . right so anoyeth sorwe to the herte / wher fore / vs oghte as wel in the deth of oure children / as in the losse of oure goodes temporels / haue pacience // Remembre yow / vp on the pacient Iob / whan he hadde lost his children / and his temporel substance / and in his body endured *and* receyued ful many a greuous tribulacion ⸍ yet seide he thus // Oure lord / hath biraft it me / right so as oure lord hath wold / right so it is doon / yblessed be / the name of oure lord ¶To thise forseyde thynges / answerde Melibeus / vn to his wif Prudence // Alle thy wordes quod he been sothe / *and* ther to p*ro*fitable / but trewely / myn herte is troubled w*ith* this sorwe / so greuously / þ*at* I noot what to doon ¶lat calle quod Prudence / thy trewe freendes alle / *and* thy lynage / whiche þ*at*

ben wise

36 qualiter Iesus Christus fleuit propter mortem lazari Hg El (2177)

39 Apostolus ad Romanos Hg (2179)

ben wise / telleth youre cas / *and* herkneth what they seye in conseylynge / *and* yow gouerne / after hir sentence ¶Salomon seith / Werk alle thy thynges by conseil / *and* thow shalt neu*er*e repente // Thanne by the conseil of his wyf Prudence / this Melibeus leet callen a greet congregaciou*n* of folk / as Sirurgiens / Phisiciens / olde folk and yonge / *and* som*m*e of hise olde enemys reconsiled / as by hir semblant to his loue / *and* in to his *gra*ce / And ther with al / þer coomen som*m*e of hise neghebores / þ*at* diden hym reu*er*ence / moore for drede than for loue / as it happeth ofte / Ther coomen also / ful manye subtile flaterers / and wise Aduocatz lerned in the lawe / And whan this folk togydre assembled weren / this Melibeus in sorweful wise / shewed hem his cas / and by the manere of his speche / it semed þ*at* in herte / he baar a cruel Ire / redy to doon vengeance vp on his foos / and sodeynly desired / þ*at* the werre sholde bigynne / but nathelees / yet axed he hir conseil vp on this matere / A Sirurgien / by licence and assent of swiche as were wise / vp roos / *and* vn to Melibeus / seyde as ye may heere ¶Sire quod he / as to vs Sirurgiens ap*er*teneth that we do to euery wight the beste þ*at* we kan / where as we be withholden / and to oure pacientz / þ*at* we do no damage / wher fore / it happeth many tyme *and* ofte / þ*at* whan twey men han euerich wounded oother / o same Sirurgien heeleth hem bothe / wher fore vn to oure Art it is nat p*er*tinent to norice werre / ne p*ar*ties to supporte / but c*er*tes / as to the warisshynge of youre doghter al be it so / þ*at* she p*er*ilously be wounded / we shullen do so ententif bisynesse fro day to nyght þ*at* w*ith* the grace of god / she shal be hool *and* sound / as soone as is possible ¶Almoost right in the same wise / the Phisiciens answerden / saue þ*at* they seyden / a fewe wordes moore / that right as maladyes ben cured by hir cont*ra*ries / right so shal man warisshe werre by vengeance ¶hise neghebores ful of enuye / hise feyned freendes / þ*at* semeden reconsiled / hise flat*er*ers maden semblant of wepyng . and empeyred / *and* agregged muchel of this matere / in preisynge gretly Melibe / of myght of power / of richesse / *and* of freendes / despisynge / the power of hise Adu*er*saries / and seyden outrely / þ*at* he anon / sholde wreke hym on hise foos / and bigynne werre ¶vp roos thanne an Aduocat þ*at* was wys / by leue *and* by conseil / of othere þ*at* weren wise / and seyde / Lordynges / the nede . for the which we ben assembled in this place / is ful heuy thyng and an

Chaucer of Melibeus

ben wise telleth youre cas & herkneth what they seye in conseyl
lynge & yow gouerne after hir sentence Salomon seith werk
alle thy thynges by conseil & thow shalt neuere repente Than
no by the conseil of his wyf Prudence this Melibeus leet
callen a greet congregacion of folk as Surgiens Phisiciens
olde folk and yonge & somme of hise olde enemys reconsiled as
by hir semblant to his loue & in to his grace And ther with al ther
women somme of hise neghebores pt diden hym reuerence moore
for drede than for loue as it happeth ofte / Ther comen also
ful manye subtile flatereres and wise Aduocatz lerned in the
lawe And whan this folk togydre assembled weren this meli
beus in sorweful wise shewed hem his cas And by the manere
of his speche it semed pt in herte he baar a cruel Ire redy to
doon vengeance vp on his foos and sodeynly desired pt the
werre sholde bigynne but natheles yet axed he hir conseil
vp on this matere / A Surgien by licence and assent of swi
che as weren wise vp roos & vn to Melibeus seyde as ye may
heere Sire quod he as to vs Surgiens aperteneth that we
do to euery wight the beste pt we kan where as we be with hol
den and to oure patientz pt we do no damage wher fore it
happeth many tyme & ofte pt whan tweye men han euerich
wounded oother o same Surgien heeleth hem bothe wher
fore vn to oure art it is nat pertinent to norice werre ne parties
to supporte but certes as to the warisshynge of youre doghter
al be it so pt she perilously be wounded we shullen do so en
tentif bisynesse fro day to nyght pt with the grace of god she
shal be hool & sound as soone as is possible Almoost right
in the same wise the Phisiciens answerden saue pt they
seyden a fewe wordes moore that right as maladyes
ben cured by hir contraries right so shal man warisshe
werre by vengeance Hise neghebores ful of enuye hise
feyned freendes pt semeden reconsiled hise flatereres maden
semblant of wepyng and empeireden & agreggeden muchel
of this matere in preisynge greetly Melibe of myght of
power of richesse & of freendes despisynge the power
of hise Aduersaries and seyden outrely pt he anon sholde
wreke hym on hise foos and bigynne werre Vp roos thanne
an Aduocat pt was wys by leue & by conseil of othere
pt weren wise and seyde / Lordynges the nede for the which
we ben assembled in this place is ful heuy thyng and an

heigh matere by cause of the wrong & of the wikkednesse that
hath be doon, and eek by reson of the grete damages þt in tyme
comynge been possible to fallen, for this same cause, and ek
by reson of the grete richesse & power of the parties bothe, for
the whiche resons, it were a ful greet peril to erren in this ma
tere. Wherfore Melibeus this is oure sentence, we conseile
yow aboven alle thyng, þt right anon thow do diligence in
kepynge of thy propre persone, in swich a wise þt thow ne wan
te noon espye ne watche, thy body for to saue. And after þt
we conseille, þt in thyn hous thow sette suffisant garny
son, so þt they may as wel thy body as thyn hous defen
de. But certes for to moeue werre, ne sodeynly for to doon
vengeance we may nat deme in so litel tyme, þt it were
profitable, wherfore we axen leyser & espace to haue deli
beracion in this cas to deme, for the commune prouerbe seith
this, he þt soone demeth, soone shal repente. And eek men
seyn þt thilke Juge is wys, þt soone vnderstondeth a ma
tere & iuggeth by leyser, for al be it so þt al tariyng be
anoyful, algates it is nat to repreue in yeuyng of iugge
ment, ne in vengeance takyng. Whan it is suffisant and
resonable, and that shewed oure lord Jhu crist by ensam
ple, for whan þt the womman þt was taken in auoutrye
was broght in his presence to knowen what sholde be doon
with hir persone, al be it þt he wiste wel hym self what
þt he wolde answere, yet ne wolde he nat answere sodeyn
ly, but he wolde haue deliberacion, and in the ground he
wroot twies, and by thise causes, we axen deliberacion
and we shul thanne by the grace of god conseille thee thyng
that shal be profitable. Vp stirten thanne the yonge folk
atones, and the mooste partie of that compaignye han scor
ned this olde wise man, and bigonnen to make noyse &
seyden, that right so as whil þt iren is hoot men shol
de smyte, right so sholde men wreken hir wronges
whil þt they been fresshe & newe, and with loud voys
they cryden. werre. werre. Vp roos tho oon of thise olde
wise, & with his hand made contenance þt men sholde
holden hem stille, and yeuen hym audience. Lordyn
ges quod he, ther is ful many a man þt crieth werre
werre. þt woot ful litel what werre amounteth. Wer
re at his bigynnyng hath so greet an entree & so large

heigh matere / by cause of the wrongꝭ *and* of the wikkednesse / that hath be doon / and eek by reson of the grete damages / þ*at* in tyme comynge been possible to fallen / for the same cause / And ek by reson / of the grete richesse *and* power of the p*ar*ties bothe / for the whiche resons / it were a ful greet p*er*il to erren in this ma-tere ¶wherfore Melibeus / this is oure sentence ⸵ we conseile yow abouen alle·thyngꝭ. þ*at* right anon thow do diligence in kepynge of thy p*ro*pre p*er*sone / in swich a wise / þ*at* thow ne wan-te noon espye / ne wacche / thy body for to saue ⸵ And after þ*at* we conseille / þ*at* in thyn hous / thow sette suffisant garny-son / so þ*at* they may as wel / thy body / as thyn hous defen-de ¶But c*er*tes / for to moeue werre / ne sodeynly for to doon vengeance / we may nat deme in so litel tyme / þ*at* it were p*ro*fitable / wher fore / we axen leyser *and* espace / to haue deli-beraciou*n* in this cas to deme / for the co*m*mune p*ro*u*er*be seyth this / he þ*at* soone demeth / soone shal repente ¶And eek men seyn / þ*at* thilke Iuge is wys / þ*at* soone vnderstondeth a ma-tere / *and* Iuggeth by leyser / for al be it so þ*at* al taryyngꝭ be anoyful / algates it is nat to repreue / in yeuyng of Iugge-mentꝭ / ne in vengeance takyngꝭ . whan it is suffisant and resonable / and that shewed oure lord Ie*s*u cristꝭ by ensam-ple / for whan þ*at* the womman þ*at* was taken in auoutrye / was broght in his p*re*sence / to knowen / what sholde be doon with hir p*er*sone / al be itꝭ þ*at* he wiste wel hym self / what þ*at* he wolde answere / yet ne wolde he / nat answere sodeyn-ly / but he wolde haue deliberaciou*n* / and in the ground / he wroot twies / and by . thise causes / we axen deliberacion / and we shul thanne / by the g*ra*ce of god conseille thee / thyngꝭ that shal be p*ro*fitable ¶Vp stirten thanne / the yonge folk atones / and the mooste p*ar*tie of that compaignye / han scor-ned / this olde wise man / and bigonnen to make noyse / *and* seyden / that right so / as whil þ*at* Iren is hootꝭ men shol-de smyte ʃ right so sholde men / wreken hir wronges / whil þ*at* they been / fresshe *and* newe / and w*ith* loud voys / they criden · werre · werre ⸵ vp roos tho · oon of thise olde wise / *and* w*ith* his hand made contenance / þ*at* men sholde holden hem stille / and yeuen hym audience ¶Lordyn-ges quod he / ther is ful many a man þ*at* crieth werre ʃ werre ʃ þ*at* woot ful litel / what werre amounteth ⸵ Wer-re at his bigynnyngꝭ hath so greet an entree *and* so large

þ*at* eue*r*y wight may entre whan hym liketh / *and* lightly fynde werre // But certes what ende / þ*at* ther of shal falle ./ it is noght light to knowe // for soothly / whan þ*at* werre is ones bigonne ./ / ther is ful many a child / vnborn of his moder / þ*at* shal sterue yong by cause of thilke werre / or ellis lyue in sorwe / *and* dye in wrecchednesse / and ther fore / er þ*at* any werre be bigonne / men moste haue gret conseil / *and* gret deliberacioun
¶And whan this olde man / wende to enforcen his tale by resons wel neigh all atones / bigonne they to rise / for to breken his tale / and beden hym ful ofte / hise wordes for to abregge / for soothly / he þ*at* p*re*cheth to hem / þ*at* listen nat heren hise wordes / hys sarmon / hem anoyeth // For I*esus* Syrak seith / . That Musyk in wepynge / is a noyous thyng This is to seyn / As muche auaileth / to speken biforn folk to whiche his speche anoyeth / as it is / to synge biforn hym þ*at* wepeth // And whan this wise man say þ*at* hym wanted audience / al shamefast he sette hym doun agayn // For Salomon seith / ther as thow / ne mayst haue non audience / enforce thee nat to speke ¶I se wel quod this wise man / þ*at* the co*mun*e p*ro*u*er*be is sooth // that good conseil wanteth / whan it is moost nede / / yet hadde this Melibeus / in his conseil many folk / þ*at* p*ri*uely in his ere / conseiled hym certeyn thyng. and conseiled hym the cont*ra*rie / in general audience
¶Whan Melibeus hadde herd / þ*at* the gretteste p*ar*ty of his conseil / were acorded / þ*at* he sholde make werre / anon he consented / to hir conseilyng *and* fully affermed hir sentence
¶Thanne dame Prudence / whan þ*at* she say / how þ*at* hyr housbonde / shoop*e* hym / for to wreke hym on his foos / *and* to bigynne werre / she in ful humble wise / whan she say hir tyme / seyde hym thise wordes ¶My lord quod she / I you biseche / as hertely as I dar *and* kan / ne haste yow nat to faste / and for alle gerdons / as yif me audience // For Piers Alfonce seith / . who so þ*at* dooth to thee / outher good / or harm / haste thee nat to quiten it / for in this wise / thy freend wol abyde / and thyn enemy / shal the lenger lyue in drede // The p*ro*u*er*be seith / he hasteth wel / þ*at* wysly kan abide / and in wikked haste / is no p*ro*fit ¶This Melibe / answerde vn to his wyf Prudence // I p*ur*pose nat quod he / to werken by thy conseil / for many causes and resons / For certes euery wight wolde holde me thanne a fool / this is to seyn / If I for thy conseilyng wolde chaunge

þt euery wight may entre whan hym liketh / & lightly fynde werre / But certes what ende þt ther of shal falle it is noght light to knowe / for soothly whan þt werre is ones bigonne / ther is ful many a child unborn of his moder / þt shal sterue yong by cause of thilke werre / or ellis lyue in sorwe & dye in wrecchednesse / And therfore er þt any werre be bigonne / men moste haue gret conseil / & gret deliberation

¶ And whan this olde man wende to enforcen his tale by resons wel neigh alle atones bigonne they to rise for to breken his tale / and beden hym ful ofte hise wordes for to abregge / for soothly he þt precheth to hem þt listen nat heren hise wordes his sermon hem anoyeth / ffor Jhesus Syrak seith / That musik in wepynge is a noyous thyng / This is to seyn / As muche auaileth to speken biforn folk to whiche his speche anoyeth / as it is to synge biforn hym þt wepeth / And whan this wise man say þt hym wanted audience / al shamefast he sette hym doun agayn / ffor Salomon seith / ther as thow ne mayst haue non audience enforce thee nat to speke ¶ I se wel quod this wise man þt the comune prouerbe is sooth / that good conseil wanteth whan it is moost nede // yet hadde this Melibeus in his conseil many folk þt priuely in his ere conseiled hym certeyn thyng / And conseiled hym the contrarie in general audience

¶ Whan Melibeus hadde herd þt the gretteste party of his conseil were accorded þt he sholde maken werre / anon he consented to hir conseilyng & fully affermed hir sentence

¶ Thanne dame Prudence whan þt she say how þt hir housbonde shoop hym for to wreke hym on his foos & to bigynne werre she in ful humble wise whan she say hir tyme seyde hym thise wordes ¶ My lord quod she I yow biseche as hertely as I dar & kan ne haste yow nat to faste and for alle gerdons as yif me audience / ffor Piers Alfonce seith / who so þt dooth to thee outher good or harm haste thee nat to quyten it / for in this wise thy freend wol abyde / and thyn enemy shal the lenger lyue in drede / The prouerbe seith he hasteth wel þt wysly kan abide / and in wikked haste is no profit ¶ This Melibe answerde vn to his wyf Prudence / I purpose nat quod he to werken by thy conseil / for many causes and resons / ffor certes euery wight wolde holde me thanne a fool / this is to seyn / If I for thy conseilyng wolde change

thynges þt ben ordeyned & affermed by so manye wise ¶ Secound
ly I seye þt alle wommen ben wikke and noon good of hem alle
for of a thousand men seith Salomon I foond o good man but
certes of alle wommen good womman foond I neuere ¶ And also certes
if I gouerned me by thy conseil it sholde seme þt I hadde yeue
to thee ouer me the maistrie and goddes forbode þt it so were
ffor Jhesus Syrak seith that if the wyf haue maistrie she is
contrarious to hir housbonde ¶ And Salomon seith neuere
in thy lyf to thy wyf ne to thy child ne to thy freend ne yif
no power ouer thy self ffor bettre it were þt thy children
aske of thy persone thynges þt hem needeth than thow see
thy self in the handes of thy children ¶ And also if I wolde
werke by thy conseilyng certes my conseil moste som tyme be
secree til it were tyme þt it moste be knowe and this ne
may nat be ¶ Whan dame Prudence ful debonairly & with
gret pacience hadde herd al that hir housbonde liked for to
seye thanne axed she of hym licence for to speke and
seyde in this wise ¶ My lord quod she as to youre firste
reson certes it may lightly been answered for I seye þt it is
no folie to chaunge conseil whan the thyng is chaunged
or ellis whan the thyng semeth oother weyes than it was
biforn ¶ And moore ouer I seye þt though þt ye han sworn
& bihight to perfourne youre emprise & natheles ye weyue
to perfourne thilke same emprise by iuste cause men shol
de nat seyn therfore þt ye were a liere ne forsworn for
the book seith þt the wise man maketh no lesyng whan
he turneth his corage to the bettre And al be it so þt youre
emprise be establissed & ordeyned by gret multitude of folk
yet thar ye nat accomplice thilke same ordinaunce but yow
like for the trouthe of thynges & the profit ben rather founde
in fewe folk þt ben wise & ful of reson than by gret multi
tude of folk ther euery man crieth & clatereth what þt hym
liketh Soothly swich multitude is nat honeste ¶ And to the
secounde reson where as ye seyn þt alle wommen ben wikke
saue youre grace certes ye despise alle wommen in this wyse
and he þt al despiseth al displeseth as seith the book And
Senec seith that who so wole haue sapience shal no man
dispreise but he shal gladly teche the science þt he kan with
oute presumpcion or pride and swiche thynges as he noght
ne kan he shal nat been ashamed to lerne hem & enquere

thynges *pa*t ben ordeyned / *and* affermed / by so manye wise ¶Secoundly I seye / *pa*t alle wo*m*men ben wikke / and noon good of hem alle / for of a thousand men / seith Salomon / I foond o good man / but c*er*tes of alle wo*m*men / good wo*m*man foond I neu*ere* [2247] ¶And also c*er*tes / if I gou*er*ned me by thy conseil / it sholde seme / *pa*t I hadde yeue to thee ouer me the maistrie / and goddes forbode / *pa*t it so were / For I*esus* Syrak seith / that if the wyf haue maistrie / she is contrarious / to hir housbonde ¶And Salomon seith / Neu*er*e in thy lyf / to thy wyf / ne to thy child / ne to thy freend / ne yif no power ouer thy self / For bettre it were / *pa*t thy children axen of thy p*er*sone thynges *pa*t hem nedeth / than thow see thy selfꝭ in the handes of thy children ¶And also / if I wolde werke by thy conseilyngꝭ c*er*tes my conseil / moste som tyme be secree / til it were tyme / *pa*t it moste be knowe / and this ne may nat be ¶Whan Dame Prudence ful debonairly *and* w*ith* gret pacience hadde herd / al that hir housbonde liked for to seye // thanne axed she of hym / licence for to speke / and seyde in this wise ¶My lord quod she / as to youre firste reson / c*er*tes it may lightly been answered / for I seye *pa*t it is no folie to chaunge conseil / whan the thyng is chaunged / or ellis / whan the thyng semeth oother weys / than it was biforn ¶And moore ouer I seye / *pa*t thogh *pa*t ye han sworn *and* bihightꝭ to p*ar*fourne youre emprise / *and* nathelees ye weyue to p*ar*fourne thilke same emprise by iuste cause // / men sholde nat seyn therfore *pa*t ye were a lyer*e* / ne forsworn / for the book seith / *pa*t the wise man / maketh no lesyngꝭ whan he turneth his corage to the bettre / [2257] And al be it so / *pa*t youre emp*ri*se be establissed *and* ordeyned / by gret multitude of folkꝭ yet thar ye nat accomplice thilke same ordinance / but yow like / for the trouthe of thynges *and* the p*ro*fitꝭ ben rather founde in fewe folk / *pa*t ben wise *and* ful of reson / than by gret multitude of folk ⁄ ther eu*er*y man crieth *and* clatereth what *pa*t hym liketh / soothly swich multitude / is nat honeste ¶And to the seconde resou*n* / where as ye seyn / *pa*t alle wo*m*men ben wikke / saue youre g*ra*ce / c*er*tes ye despise alle wo*m*men in this wyse / and he *pa*t al despiseth / al displeseth / as seith the bookꝭ . and Senecꝭ seith / that who so wole haue Sapience / shal no man dispreise / but he shal gladly teche / the science *pa*t he kan / w*ith*oute p*re*sumpcion or p*ri*de / and swiche thynges / as he noght ne kan / he shal nat ben ashamed to lerne hem *and* enquere of lasse folk than hym self [2262] ¶And sire / þ*at* ther hath be ful many a good wo*m*man / may lightly be preued / for c*er*tes sire / oure lord Ie*s*u crist wolde neuere han descended / to be born of a wo*m*man / if alle wo*m*men hadde be wikke / And after that for the grete bou*n*tee þ*at* is in wo*m*men / oure lord Ie*s*u c*ri*st whan he was risen fro deth to lyf / appered rather to a womman / than to his apostles / And though þ*at* Salomon seith / þ*at* he ne foond neuere womman good / it folweth nat therfore / þ*at* alle wommen ben wikke / for thogh þ*at* he ne foond no good wo*m*man / c*er*tes many another man / hath founde many a wo*m*man ful good and trewe [2267] ⁋ Or ellis p*ar* auenture / the entente of Salomon / was this / þ*at* as in sou*er*eyn bou*n*tee / he foond no womman / this is to seyn / þ*at* ther is no wight þ*at* hath sou*er*eyn bou*n*tee / saue god allone / as he hym self recordeth / in his Eu*a*ngelie / for ther nys no creature so good / þ*at* hym ne wanteth som what of the p*er*feccioun of god / þ*at* is his makere ¶Youre thridde reson is this / ye seyn / þ*at* if ye gou*er*ne yow by my conseil / it sholde seme / þ*at* ye hadde yeue me the maistrie and the lordshipe / ouer youre p*er*sone ¶Sire sauf youre g*ra*ce / it is nat so / for if so were / þ*at* no man sholde be conseiled / but oonly of hem / þ*at* hadde lordshipe *and* maistrie of his p*er*sone / men wolde nat ben conseiled so ofte / [2272] for soothly thilke man þ*at* axeþ conseil of a purpos / yet hath he free choys / wheither he wole werke by that conseil / or noon ¶And as to youre ferþe reson / ther ye seyn / þ*at* the Ianglerye of wo*m*men / kan hide thynges that they woot nat / as who seith / þ*at* a womman kan nat hide that þ*at* she woot. Sire thise wordes been vnderstonde of wo*m*men þ*at* ben Iangleresses *and* wikked / of whiche wo*m*men men seyn / þ*at* thre thynges / dryuen a man out of his hous / that is to seyn / Smoke / droppyng of reyn / *and* wikked wyues / and of swiche wo*m*men seith Salomon / þ*at* it were bettre dwellen in desert than w*ith* a wo*m*man þ*at* is riotous / [2277] and sire by youre leue / þ*at* am nat I. / for ye han ful ofte assayed my grete silence *and* my grete pacience / and eek how wel þ*at* I kan hiden *and* hele thynges / þ*at* men oghte*n* secrely to hyde ¶And soothly / as to youre fifthe reson / wheras ye seyn / þ*at* in wikked conseil / wommen venquysse men / god woot thilke reson / stant heere in no stede ⁋ For understond now /. ye axen conseil / to do wikkednesse / and if ye wol werke wikkednesse / and youre wyf restreyneþ þilke

of lasse folk than hym self ¶ And oure þt they hath be ful many
a good woman may lightly be preued / for certes oure / oure lord
Jhu crist wolde neuere han descended / to be born of a woman /
if alle women hadde be wikke / and after that / for the grete
bountee þt is in women / oure lord Jhu crist whan he was risen
fro deth to lyf / appered rather to a womman / than to his a
postles / and though þt Salomon seith / þt he ne foond neuere
womman good / it folweth nat therfore / þt alle wommen
ben wikke / for thogh þt he ne foond no good woman / certes
many another man / hath founde many a woman ful good
and trewe / Or ellis per auenture / the entente of Salomon / was
this / þt as in souereyn bountee / he foond no womman / this is
to seyn / þt ther is no wight / þt hath souereyn bountee / saue
god allone / as he hym self recordeth in his Euangelie / forther nys no creature so good / þt hym ne wanteth som what
of the perfection of god / þt is his makere ¶ youre thridde re
son is this / ye seyn / þt if ye gouerne yow by my conseil / it
sholde seme / þt ye hadde yeue me the maistrie and the lord
shipe / ouer youre persone ¶ Sire sauf youre grace / it is nat so /
for if so were / þt no man sholde be conseiled / but oonly of
hem / þt hadde lordshipe & maistrie of his persone / men wol
de nat ben conseiled so ofte / for soothly thilke man þt axeþ
conseil of a purpos / yet hath he free choys / wheither he
wole werke by that conseil / or noon ¶ And as to youre ferþe
reson / ther ye seyn / þt the janglerye of women / kan hide
thinges that they woot nat / as who seith / þt a womman
kan nat hide that þt she woot · Sire thise wordes been
vnderstonde of women þt ben jangleresses & wikked / of
whiche women men seyn / þt thre thinges / dryuen a man
out of his hous / that is to seyn / smoke / droppyng of
reyn / & wikked wyues / and of swiche women seith Salo
mon / þt it were bettre dwellen in desert / than wt a woman
þt is riotous / and sire by youre leue / þt am nat I · for ye han
ful ofte assayed my grete silence & my grete patience / and
eek how wel þt I kan hiden & hele thinges / þt men oghte
secrely to hyde ¶ And soothly / as to youre fifthe reson / wher
as ye seyn / þt in wikked conseil / wommen venquysse men /
god woot / thilke reson / stant heere in no stede / ffor vnder
stond now / · ye axen conseil / to do wikkednesse / and if yo
wol werke wikkednesse / and youre wyf restreyneþ þilke

sikkes ypos / & ouercometh yow by reson & by good conseil / certes youre
wyf oghte rather be preysed / than yblamed / Thus sholde ye vn
derstonde the Philosophre þt seith / In wikked conseil wommen ven
quyssen hir housbondes ¶ And ther as ye blamen alle wommen
& hir resons / I shal shewe by manye ensamples / þt many a
womman hath be ful good / and yet ben / & hir conseils holsom
& pfitable ¶ Eke som men han seyd / þt the conseilyng of wo
men / is outher to deere / or ellis to litel of prys / but al be it
so / þt ful many a womman is badde / & hir conseil vile & noght
worth / yet han men founde / ful many a good womman & ful
discrete & wys in conseilynge ¶ Lo Iacob / by conseil of his
moder Rebekka wan the benesoun of ysaak his fader / and
the lordshipe ouer alle his brethren ¶ Iudith by hir good conseil
deliuered the Citee of Bethulye in which she dwelled / out of the
handes of Olofernus þt hadde it biseged & wolde it al destroye
¶ Abigail / deliuered Nabal hir housbonde fro Dauid the kyng þt
wolde han slayn hym / & apaised the Ire of the kyng by hir
wit / & by hir good conseilyng / ¶ Hester by hir good conseil en
haunced gretly the peple of god in the regne of Assuerus the
kyng / . And the same bountee in good conseilyng / of many a good
womman may men telle ¶ And moore ouer / whan þt oure lord
hadde creat Adam oure forme fader / he seyde in this wise /
It is nat good to be a man allone / make we to hym an help
semblable to hym self ¶ Heere may ye se / þt if þt wommen
were nat goode & hir conseil good & pfitable / oure lord god
of heuene wolde neither han wroght hem / ne called hem
help of man / but rather confusion of man / And ther seyde
ones a clerk in two vers ¶ What is bettre than gold / Iaspre /
¶ What is bettre than Iaspre / wisdom / and what is bettre than
wisdom / womman / and what is bettre than good womman /
no thyng ¶ And sire / by manye of othere resons may ye seen /
þt manye wommen ben goode / & hir conseil good & pfitable .
And ther fore sire / if ye wol truste to my conseil / I shal resto
re yow youre doghter / hool & sound / and eek I wol don
to yow so muche / þt ye shul haue honour in this cause .
¶ Whan Melibe hadde herd the wordes / of his wyf Pruden
ce / he seyde thus ¶ I se wel / þt the word of Salomon is
sooth / he seith þt wordes þt ben spoken discreetly by ordi
naunce / beth honycombes / for they yeue swetnesse to the soule /
& holsomnesse to the body / And wyf / by cause of the swete

Auro quid melius · iaspis · quid iaspide · sensus ·
Sensu quid · mulier · quid muliere · nichil ·

wikked p*ur*pos / *and* ou*er*cometh yow by reson *and* by good conseil / [2282] *cer*tes youre wyf oghte rather be preysed / than yblamed // Thus sholde ye vnderstonde the Philosophre / þ*at* seith / In wikked conseil / wo*m*men venquyssen hir housbondes ¶And ther as ye blamen alle wo*m*men / *and* hir resons / I shal shewe by manye ensamples / þ*at* many a womman hath be ful good / and yet ben / *and* hir conseils holsom *and* p*ro*fitable ¶Eke som men han seyd / þ*at* the conseilyng of wo*m*men / is outher to deere / or ellis to litel of prys // but al be it so / þ*at* ful many a wo*m*man is badde / *and* hir conseil vile *and* noght worth ∫ yet han men founde / ful many a good wo*m*man *and* ful discrete *and* wys in conseilynge [2287] ¶Lo Iacob / by conseil of his moder Rebekka / wan the beneyson of ysaak his fader / and the lordshipe ou*er* alle his bretheren ¶Iudith by ⟨hir⟩ good conseil deliu*er*ed the Citee of Bethulye in which she dwelled / out of þe handes of Olofernus þ*at* hadde it biseged / *and* wolde it al destroye ¶Abigail / deliu*er*ed Nabal hir housbonde / fro Dauid the kyng þ*at* wolde han slayn hym / *and* apaised the Ire of the kyngꝭ by hir witꝭ *and* by hir good conseilyngꝭ ¶Hester by hir good conseil / enhaunced gretly the peple of god in the regne of Assuerus the kyngꝭ . and the same bou*n*tee in good conseilyngꝭ of many a good wo*m*man / may men telle [2292] ¶And moore ouerꝭ / whan þ*at* oure lord / hadde creat Adam oure forme fader / he seyde in this wise / It is nat good to be / a man allone / make we to hym an help / semblable to hym self / ¶Heere may ye se / þ*at* if þ*at* wommen were nat goode / *and* hir conseil / good *and* p*ro*fitable / oure lord god of heuene / wolde neither han wroght hem / ne called hem help of man / but rather / confusion of man // And ther seyde ones a clerkꝭ in two vers ¶What is bettre than gold / Iaspre / ¶What is bettre than Iaspre / wisdom [2297] // And what is bettre than wisdom / wo*m*man // and what is bettre than good womman / no thyng ¶And sire / by manye of othere resons may ye seen / þ*at* manye wo*m*men ben goode / *and* hir conseil good *and* p*ro*fitable And ther fore sire / if ye wol truste to my conseil / I shal restore yow youre doghter / hool *and* sound / and eek / I wol doon to yow so muche / þ*at* ye shul haue honour in this cause ¶Whan Melibe hadde herd the wordes / of his wyf Prudence / he seyde thus [2302] ¶I se wel / þ*at* the word of Salomon / is sooth //· he seith / þ*at* wordes þ*at* ben spoken discretly by ordinance / beth honycombes / for they yeue swetnesse to the soule / *and* holsomnesse to the body // And wyf / by cause of the swete

⟨Auro quid melius ./ iaspis ∫ quid iaspide ./ sensus ∫
Sensu quid ./ amber ∫ quid muliere ./ nichil ∫⟩

wordes / and eek⁊ for I haue assayed *and* preued / thy grete sapience *and* thy grete trouthe / I wol gouerne me by thy conseil / in alle thyng⁊ ¶Now sire / quod dame Prudence / and syn ye vouche sauf⁊ to been gou*er*ned by my conseil / I wol enforme yow / how ye shal gou*er*ne yow self⁊ in chesynge of youre conseil*ours* ¶Ye shal first in alle youre werkes / mekely biseken to the heighe god / þ*at* he wol be youre conseillour⁊ *and* shapeth yow to swich entente / þ*at* he yeue yow conseil / *and* confort⁊ as taughte Thobie his sone [2307] ⁄ At alle tymes / thow shalt blesse god *and* praye hym to dresse thy weyes / and looke þ*at* alle thy conseils ben in hym for euere moore ¶Seint Iame eek seith ⁄ If any of yow / haue nede of Sapience / axe it of god / and afterward thanne shal ye take conseil in your self / *and* examyne wel youre thoghtes / of swiche thynges as yow thynketh / þ*at* is best for youre p*ro*fit⁊ and thanne shal ye dryue fro youre herte / thre thynges / that been cont*ra*riouse to good conseil / that is to seyn / Ire / Coueitise / *and* hastynesse [2312] ¶First⁊ he þ*at* axeth conseil of hym self / c*er*tes he moste be with outen Ire / for many causes ¶The firste is this ⁄ he þ*at* hath greet Ire *and* wrathe in hym self / he weneth alwey þ*at* he may do thyng⁊ þ*at* he may nat do ⁄ And secoundly / he þ*at* is Irous *and* wroþ / he ne may nat wel deme / and he þ*at* may nat wel deme / may nat wel conseille ⁄ The thridde is this / that he þ*at* is Irous *and* wroþ as seith Senek⁊ ne may nat speke / but blameful thynges / [2317] and w*ith* hise viciouse wordes / he stireth oother folk to angre / *and* to Ire // And eek sire / ye moste dryue coueitise / out of youre herte / For the Apostle seith / þ*at* Coueitise / is the roote of alle harmes / and trust wel / þ*at* a coueitous man ne kan nat deme / ne thenke / but oonly to fulfille the ende of his coueitise / *and* c*er*tes / that ne may neu*er*e been acompliced / for eu*er*e / the moore habundance þ*at* he hath of richesse / the moore he desireth [2322] ¶And sire / ye moste also / dryue out of youre herte / hastifnesse / for c*er*tes ye may nat deme for þe beste / a sodeyn thoght⁊ þ*at* falleth in youre herte / but ye moste auyse yow on it⁊ ful ofte / for as ye herde her biforn / the co*mun*e p*ro*u*er*be is this / that he / þ*at* soone demeth / soone repenteth / Sire ye ne ben nat alwey / in lyke disposiciou*n* / for c*er*tes / som thyng⁊ þ*at* som tyme semeth to yow / þ*at* it is good for to do / another tyme / it semeth to yow the cont*ra*rie / [2327] whan ye han taken conseil in your self / and han demed by good deliberaciou*n* / swich thyng / as yow semeth best⁊ ¶Thanne rede I yow / þ*at* ye kepe it secree biwrey nat youre conseil / to no p*er*sone / but if so be þ*at* ye wenen

wordes / and eek for I haue assayed & preued thy grete sapience
& thy grete trouthe / I wol gouerne me by thy conseil / in alle
thyng / ¶ Now sire quod dame Prudence / and syn ye vou
che sauf to been gouerned by my conseil / I wol enforme yow
how ye shal gouerne yow self in chesynge of youre conseilours
¶ Ye shal first in alle youre werkes mekely biseken to the heighe
god / þt he wol be youre conseillour / & shapeth yow to swich
entente / þt he yeue yow conseil & confort / as taughte Thobie
his sone / At alle tymes thou shalt blesse god & praye hym
to dresse thy weyes / and looke þt alle thy conseils ben in hym
for euere moore ¶ Seint Jame eek seith / If any of yow haue
nede of sapience axe it of god / and afterward thanne shal ye
take conseil in youre self / & examyne wel youre thoghtes / of
swiche thynges as yow thynketh þt is best for youre profit / and
thanne shal ye dryue fro youre herte thre thynges / that been
contrariouse to good conseil / that is to seyn / ire / coueitise & hasty
nesse ¶ First he þt axeth conseil of hym self / certes he moste be
with outen ire / for many causes ¶ The firste is this / he þt hath
greet ire & wrathe in hym self / he weneth alwey þt he may do
thyng þt he may nat do / and secoundly / he þt is irous & wroth
he ne may nat wel deme / and he þt may nat wel deme / may
nat wel conseille / The thridde is this / that he þt is irous & wroth
as seith Senek / ne may nat speke / but blameful thynges / and wt
hise viciouse wordes he stireth other folk to angre & to ire / and
eek sire / ye moste dryue coueitise out of youre herte ffor the
apostle seith / þt coueitise is the roote of alle harmes / and trust
wel / þt a coueitous man ne kan nat deme ne thenke but oonly
to fulfille the ende of his coueitise & certes that ne may neuere
been acompliced / for euere the moore habundance þt he hath of
richesse / the moore he desireth ¶ And sire ye moste also dryue
out of youre herte hastifnesse / for certes ye may nat deme for the
beste a sodeyn thoght / þt falleth in youre herte / but ye moste
auyse yow on it ful ofte / for as ye herde her biforn the comune prouerbe
is this / that he þt soone demeth / soone repenteth ¶ Sire ye ne
ben nat alwey in lyke disposicion / for certes som thyng þt som
tyme semeth to yow þt it is good for to do / another tyme it se
meth to yow the contrarie / Whan ye han taken conseil in youre
self / and han demed by good deliberacion swich thyng as
yow semeth best ¶ Thanne rede I yow þt ye kepe it secree /
Biwrey nat youre conseil to no persone / but if so be þt ye wenen

sikerly þt thurgh youre bywreyyng youre condicion shal ben to
yow moore ꝓfitable / ffor Jhesus Syrak seith / Neither to thy foo
ne to thy freend discoure nat thy secree ne thy folie / for they
wol yeue yow audience & lokyng & supportacion in thy ꝑ
sence / & scorne thee in thyn absence ¶ Another clerk seith þt
scarsly shaltow fynden any ꝑsone þt may kepe conseil secrely
¶ The book seith whil þt thow kepest thy conseil in thyn herte /
thow kepest it in thy ꝑson / And whan thow biwreyest thy
conseil to any wight he holdeth thee in his snare / And ther
fore yow is bettre to hide youre conseil in youre herte / than
preyen hym to whom ye haue biwreyed youre conseil þt he
wol kepen it cloos & stille ¶ ffor Seneca seith / If so be þt thou
ne mayst nat thyn owene conseil hyde / how darstow preyen
any oother wight thy conseil secrely to kepe / But nathelees
if thow wene sikerly þt thy biwreyyng of thy conseil to a
ꝑsone wol maken thy condicion to stonden in the bettre plyt
thanne shaltow tellen hym thy conseil in this wise ¶ ffirst
thow shalt make no semblant wheither thee were leuere pees
or werre or this or that ne shewe hym nat thy wyl & thyn
entente / for trust wel þt comenly thise conseillours ben flatereres /
namely the conseillours of grete lordes / for they enforcen hem
alwey rather to speke plesante wordes enclynynge to the
lordes lust than wordes þt ben trewe or ꝓfitable / And therfore
men seyn þt the riche man hath selde good conseil / but if he
haue it of hym self / And after that thow shalt conside̱re
thy freendes & thyne enemys And as touchynge thy freen
des thow shalt considere / whiche of hem þt been moost
feithfull & moost wise & eldest & moost approued in con
seillyng / And of hem shaltow aske thy conseil as the cas re
quyreth ¶ I seye þt first ye shul clepe to youre conseil
youre freendes þt ben trewe / ffor Salomon seith þt right
as the herte of a man deliteth in sauour þt is soote / right
so the conseil of trewe freendes yeueth swetnesse to the soule
¶ He seith also ther may no thyng be likned to the trewe freend
for certes gold ne siluer ben noght so muche worth as the
goode wyl of a trewe freend / And eek he seith þt a trewe
freend is a strong defense / who so þt it fyndeth certes he
fyndeth a gret tresor ¶ Thanne shul ye eek considere / if þt youre
trewe freendes been discrete & wise / for the book seith / Axe
alwey thy conseil of hem þt been wise And by this same

sikerly / þat thurgh yowr*e* bywreyyng’ youre condiciou*n* shal ben to yow moore p*ro*fitable // For I*esus* Syrak seith // Neither to thy foo ne to thy freend / discou*er*e nat thy secree / ne thy folie / for they wol yeue yow audience / *and* lokyng’ *and* supportaciou*n* in thy p*re*sence / *and* scorne thee in thyn absence [2332] ¶Another clerk seith / þat scarsly shaltow fynden any p*er*sone / þat may kepe conseil secrely ¶The book seith / whil þat thow kepest thy conseil in thyn herte / thow kepest it in thy p*ri*son / And whan thow biwreyest thy conseil to any wight’ he holdeth thee in his snare / And ther fore yow is bettre to hide youre conseil in youre herte / than preyen hym / to whom ye haue biwreyed youre conseil / þat he wol kepen it’ cloos *and* stille ¶For Seneca seith / If so be / þat thou ne mayst nat’ thyn owene conseil hyde / ⸗ how dorstow preyen any oother wight’. thy conseil secrely to kepe [2337] // But nathelees / if thow wene sikerly / þat thy biwreyyng’ of thy conseil to a p*er*sone / wol maken thy condicion / to stonden in the bettre plyt’ thanne shaltow telle hym thy conseil / in this wise ¶First thow shalt make no semblant / wheither thee were leu*er*e / pees or werre / or this / or that / ne shewe hym nat thy wyl *and* thyn entente / for trust wel þat co*mun*ely / thise conseillours ben flat*er*ers / namely / the conseillours of grete lordes / for they enforcen hem alwey / rather to speke plesante wordes / enclynynge to the lordes lust’ than wordes þat ben trewe / or p*ro*fitable / [2342] And therfore men seyn / þat the riche man hath selde good conseil / but if he haue it of hym self / And after that’ thow shalt considere thy freendes / *and* thyne enemys / And as touchynge thy freendes / thow shalt considere / whiche of hem þat been moost feithfull / *and* moost wise / *and* eldest’ and moost approued in conseillyng’ and of hem / shaltow axe thy conseil / as the cas requyreth ¶I seye / þat first ye shul clepe to youre conseyl / youre freendes / þat ben trewe [2347] // For Salomon seith / þat right’ as the herte of a man / deliteth in sauour þat is soote ⸗ right so the conseil of trewe freendes / yeueth swetnesse to the soule / ¶He seith also / ther may no thyng be likned to the trewe freend / for c*er*tes / gold ne siluer’ ben noght so muche worth / as the goode wyl / of a trewe freend // And eek he seith / þat a trewe freend is a strong defense / who so þat it fyndeth / certes he fyndeth a gret tresor ¶Thanne shul ⟨ye⟩ eek considere / if þat youre trewe freendes been discrete *and* wise / for the book seith // Axe alwey thy conseil / of hem þat been wise / [2352] And by this same reson / shul ye clepen to youre conseil / of yowre freendes / þ*at* ben of age / swiche as han seighen / *and* ben expert of manye thynges / *and* ben approued in conseilynges / for the book seiþ/ þ*at* in olde men is the sapience / and in longe tyme the Prudence ¶And Tullius seith / þ*at* grete thynges / ne ben nat ay acompliced by strengthe / ne by delyuernesse of body / but by good conseil / by Auctoritee of p*er*sones / *and* by Science / the whiche thre thynges / ne been nat fieble by age / but c*er*tes they enforcen / and encressen day by day / And thanne shal ye kepe this / for a general rule ⁄ First shal ye clepe to youre conseil / a fewe of youre freendes / þ*at* ben especiale ⁄ For Salomon seith / manye freendes / haue thow / but among a thousand / chees thee oon / to be thy conseillour for al be it so / þ*at* thow first ne telle thy conseil / but to a fewe / thow mayst afterward telle it to mo folk if it be nede / but looke alwey þ*at* thy conseillours haue thilke thre condicions / þ*at* I haue seyd bifore / that is to seye / þ*at* they be trewe / wise / *and* of old exp*er*ience / And werk nat alwey in euery nede / by o conseillour allone / for som tyme bihoueth it to be conseiled by manye / for Salomon seith / Saluacion of thynges / is wher as ther ben manye conseilours ¶Now sith þ*at* I haue told yow / of which folk ye sholde be conseilled / ./ now wol I teche yow / which conseil ye oghte eschue ¶First / ye shul eschue / the conseillyng of fooles / for Salomon seith / take no conseil of a fool / for he ne kan nat conseille / but after his owene lust and his affecciou*n* / ¶The book seith / that the p*ro*pretee of a fool is this ⁄ he troweþ lightly / harm of euery wight *and* lightly troweth alle bou*n*tee in hym self // Tow shalt eek eschue / the conseillyng of alle flaterers / swiche as enforcen hem rather to preise youre p*er*sone by flaterye / than for to telle yow the soothfastnesse of thynges ¶Wherfore Tullius seith / Among alle the pestilences þ*at* been in frendshipe / the gretteste is flaterye / And therfore is it moore nede / þ*at* thow eschue *and* drede flaterers / than any oother peple ⁄ The book seith / thow shalt rather drede *and* flee fro the swete wordes / of flaterynge preiseres / than fro the egre wordes of thy freend / that seith thee thy sothes ¶Salomon seith / that the wordes of a flaterer*e* / is a Snare to cacchen Innocentz ⁄ He seith also / þ*at* he þ*at* speketh to his freend / wordes of swetnesse / and of

Thenn shul ye clepen to youre conseil of youre freendes þt
ben of age swiche as han seyghen & ben expert of manye
thynges & ben approued in conseilynges / for the book seiþ þt
in olde men is the sapience / and in longe tyme the pruden
ce / And Tullius seith / þt grete thynges ne ben nat ay a
compliced by strengthe / ne by delyuernesse of body / but
by good conseil / by auctoritee of persones & by science / the
whiche thre thynges / ne been nat fieble by age / but certes
they enforcen / and encressen day by day And thanne shal
ye kepe this / for a general rule / ffirst shal ye clepe to you
re conseil / a fewe of youre freendes / þt ben especiale / ffor
Salomon seith / manye freendes / haue thow / but among a
thousand chees thee oon to be thy conseillour / for al be it
so / þt thow first ne telle thy conseil / but to a fewe / thow
mayst afterward telle it to mo folk / if it be nede / but
looke alwey þt thy conseillours haue thilke thre condici
ouns / þt I haue seyd bifore / that is to seye / þt they be tre
we / wise / & of old experience / And werk nat alwey in
euery nede by o conseillour allone / for som tyme biho
ueth it to be conseiled by manye / for Salomon seith / Sal
uacion of thynges is wher as ther ben manye conseilours
Now sith þt I haue told yow / of which folk ye sholde be
conseilled / now wol I teche yow / which conseil ye oghte
eschue ffirst / ye shul eschue / the conseillyng of fooles /
for Salomon seith / take no conseil of a fool / for he ne kan
nat conseille / but after his owene lust and his affection /
The book seith that the proprete of a fool is this / he troweþ
lightly harm of euery wight / & lightly troweth alle bountee
in hym self // Thow shalt eek eschue / the conseillyng of alle
flatererys / swiche as enforcen hem rather to preise youre per
sone by flaterye / than for to telle yow the soothfastnesse
of thynges Wherfore Tullius seith among alle the
pestilences þt been in freendshipe / the grettest is flaterye
And therfore is it moore nede þt thow eschue & drede fla
tereres than any oother peple / The book seith thow shalt
rather drede & flee fro the swete wordes of flateryng
preiseres than fro the egre wordes of thy freend / that seith
thee thy sothes Salomon seith / that the wordes of a fla
terer is a snare to cacchen innocentz / He seith also þt
he þt speketh to his freend wordes of swetnesse and of

who so trusteth
in the reconsiled
is for the most
part alweis
begilled.

plesance setteth a net biforn his feet to cacchen hym / And ther
fore seith Tullius / Enclyne nat thyne erys to flatereres / ne
tak no conseil of wordes of flaterye ¶ And Caton seith / Avyse
thee wel / & eschue wordes of swetnesse & of plesance ¶ And
eek thow shalt eschue the conseillyng of thynne olde enemys
þt ben reconsiled / The book seith / that no wight retourneth
saufly in to the grace of his olde enemy / And ysope seith / ne
trust nat to hem / to whiche thow hast had som tyme werre or
enemytee ne telle hem nat thy conseil / And Seneca telleth
the cause why / It may nat be seith he / that wher as greet
fyr hath longe tyme endured þt ther ne dwelleth som va
pour of warmnesse / And therfore seith Salomon / In thyn
olde foo trust neuere / for sikerly / though thyn enemy be reconsiled
& maketh thee cheere of humylitee / & louteth to thee wt his
heed / ne trust hym neuere / for certes he maketh thilke feyned
humylitee moore for his p[ro]fit than for any loue of thy p[er]so
ne by cause þt he deemeth to haue victorie ou[er] thy p[er]sone by
swich feyned contenance / the which victorie he myghte nat
haue by stryf or werre ¶ And Peter Alfonce seith / make
no felawesshipe / wt thyne olde enemys / for if thow do hem
bontee they wol puten it in to wikkednesse ¶ And eek thou
most eschue the conseillyng of hem þt ben thy seruantz
& beren thee greet reuerence / for p[er]auenture they seyn it
moore for drede than for loue / & therfore seith a Philo
sophre in this wise / Ther is no wight p[er]fitly trewe to
hym þt he to soore dredeth / And Tullius seith / Ther nys
no myght so greet of any Emperour / þt longe may endure
but if he haue moore loue of the peple than drede ¶ Thou
shalt also eschue the conseillyng of folk þt ben dronke
lewe / for they ne kan no conseil hyde / ffor Salomon seith /
Ther is no p[ri]uetee ther as regneth dronkenesse ¶ Ye shal
also han in suspect / the conseillyng of swich folk / as conseil
le yow a thyng p[ri]uely & conseille yow the contrarie open
ly / ffor Cassidorie seith / That it is a maner sleighte to
hyndre whan he sheweth to doon a thyng openly / and wer
keth pryuely the contrarie ¶ Thow shalt also haue in sus
pect the conseillyng of wikked folk / ffor the book seith /
The conseillyng of wikked folk is alwey ful of fraude
And Dauid seith / Blisful is that man / þt hath nat fol
wed the conseillyng of shrewes ¶ Thow shalt also eschue

plesance / setteth a Net biforn his feet' to cacchen hym // And therfore / seith Tullius // Enclyne / nat thyne erys to flatereres / ne tak no conseil / of wordes of flaterye ¶And Caton seith // Auyse thee wel / *and* eschue wordes of swetnesse *and* of plesance ¶And eek thow shalt eschue / the conseillyng of thynne olde enemys þat ben reconsiled [2372] // The book seith / that no wight retourneth saufly in to the gr*a*ce of his olde enemy // And Ysope seith / Ne trust nat to hem / to whiche / thow hast had som tyme werre / or enemytee / ne telle hem nat thy conseil // And Seneca / telleth the cause why // It may nat be seith he / that wher*e* as greet fyr / hath longe tyme endured / þat ther ne dwelleth som vapour of warmnesse // And ther fore seith Salomon // In thyn olde foo / trust neu*ere* / for sikerly / thogh thyn enemy be reconsiled / *and* maketh thee / cheere of humylitee / *and* louteth to thee w*ith* his heed / ne trust hym neu*ere* / [2377] for c*er*tes / he maketh thilke feyned humylitee / moore for his p*ro*fit' than for any loue of thy p*er*sone / by cause þat he demeth / to haue victorie ou*er* thy p*er*sone / by swich feyned continance / the which victorie / he myghte nat haue / by strif' or werre ¶And Peter Alfonce seith // Make no felaweshipe / w*ith* thyne olde enemys / for if thow do hem bou*n*tee / they wol p*er*uerten it in to wikkednesse ¶And eek' thou most eschue / the conseillyng' of hem þat ben thy seruantz *and* beren thee gret reu*er*ence / for p*ar* auenture / they seyn it moore / for drede than for loue / *and* therfore / seith a Philosophre / in this wise // Ther is no wight p*ar*fitly trewe / to hym / þat he to soore dredeth // And Tullius seith / Ther nys no myght so gret' of any Emp*er*our / þat longe may endure / but if he haue moore loue of the peple than drede [2382] ¶Thou shalt also eschue the conseillyng' of folk þat ben dronkelewe // for they ne kan no conseil hyde // For Salomon seith / Ther is no p*ri*uetee / ther as regneth dronkenesse ¶Ye shal also han in suspect' the conseilyng of swich folk' as conseile yow a thyng p*ri*uely / *and* conseille yow / the cont*ra*rie openly // For Cassiodorie seith / That it is a maner*e* sleighte to hyndre / whan he sheweth to doon a thyng openly / and werketh pryuely the cont*ra*rie ¶Thow shalt also haue in suspect' the conseilyng' of wikked folk // For the book seith / The conseilyng of wikked folk' is alwey ful of fraude [2387] // And Dauid seith // Blisful is that man / þat hath nat folwed the conseilyng of sherewes ¶Thow shalt also eschue

440-41 in another hand: who so trusteth a foe reconsiled, is for the most part alweis begilled Hg (2376)

the conseilyngꝭ of yong folk / for hir conseil is nat rype ¶Now sire / sith I haue shewed yow / of which folkꝭ ye shul take youre conseil / and of which folkꝭ ye shul folwe the conseil ⫽. now wol I teche yow / how ye shul examyne youre conseil / after the doct*ri*ne of Tullius ¶In the examynynge thanne of youre conseillour / ye shul considere many thynges // [2392] Alderfirst thou shalt considere / þat in thilke thyngꝭ þat thow p*ur*posestꝭ / *and* vp on what thyngꝭ thow wolt haue conseil / þat ve*r*ray trouthe / be seyd *and* conserued / this is to seyn / telle trewely thy tale / for he þat seith fals / may nat wel be conseiled / in that cas / of which he lyeth ¶And after this / thow shalt considere / the thynges þat acorden / to that thow p*ur*posest for to do / by thy conseillours / if reson acorde ther to / and eekꝭ if thy myghtꝭ may atteyne ther to / and if the moore partꝭ *and* the bettre p*ar*tꝭ of thy conseillours / acorde ther to / or no ¶Thanne shaltow considere / what thyng shal folwe of that conseilyngꝭ as hate / pees / werre / gr*ace* / p*rofi*tꝭ or damage / *and* many othere thynges / [2397] And in alle thise thynges / thow shalt chese the beste / and weyue alle othere thynges ¶Thanne shaltow considere / of what roote is engendred the matere of thy conseil / and what fruyt it may conceyue *and* engendre ¶Thow shalt eek considere alle thise causes / from whennes they ben sprongen ⫽ And whan ye haue examyned youre conseil / as I haue seyd / *and* which p*ar*tie is the bettre *and* moore p*ro*fitable / *and* han approued it / by manye wise folk / *and* olde ./ thanne shaltow considere / if thou mayst p*ar*forme it / *and* maken of itꝭ a good ende [2402] ¶For reson wol natꝭ þat any man sholde bigynne ⟨a⟩ thyngꝭ. but if he myghte p*ar*forme it / as hym oghte ⫽ Ne no wight sholde ⟨take⟩ vp on hym so heuy charge / þat he myghte nat beren it ⫽ For the p*ro*uerbe seith /. he þat to muche embraceth / destreyneth litel ⫽ And Caton seith / Assay to do swich thyngꝭ as thow hast power to doon / lest þat the charge / opp*re*sse thee so soore / þat thee bihoueth / to weyue thyngꝭ þat thow hast bigonne ⫽ And if so be / þat thow be in doute / wheither thow mayst p*ar*fo*ur*ne a thyngꝭ or noon ./ chees rather to suffre / than bigynne / [2407] ⫽ And Peter Alfonce seith ¶If thow hast myght to doon a thyngꝭ of which thow most repente / it is bettre / nay / than ye / this is to seyn / þat thee is bettre / to holde thy tonge stille / than for to speke ¶Thanne may ye vnderstonde by strenger resons / þat if thow hast powerꝭ to

the conseilyng of yong folk for hir conseil is nat rype ¶ Now
sire sith I haue shewed yow of which folk ye shul take you
re conseil and of which folk ye shul folwe the conseil now
wol I teche yow how ye shul examyne youre conseil after
the doctrine of Tullius ¶ In the examynynge thanne of youre
conseillours ye shul considere many thynges Alderfirst
thou shalt considere þt in thilke thyng þt thou purposest &
vp on what thyng thou wolt haue conseil þt verray trouthe
be seyd & conserued this is to seyn telle trewely thy tale
for he þt seith fals may nat wel be conseiled in that cas
of which he lyeth ¶ And after this thou shalt considere
the thynges þt acorden to that thou purposest for to do by thy
conseillours if resoun acorde ther to and eek if thy myght
may atteyne ther to and if the moore part & the bettre part
of thy conseillours acorde ther to or no ¶ Thanne shaltow
considere what thyng shal folwe of that conseilyng as ha
te pees werre grace ꝓfit or damage & many othere thynges
And in alle thise thynges thou shalt chese the beste and wey
ue alle othere thynges ¶ Thanne shaltow considere of what
roote is engendred the matere of thy conseil and what fruyt
it may conceyue & engendre ¶ Thou shalt eek considere alle
thise causes from whennes they ben sprongen And whan
ye haue examyned youre conseil as I haue seyd & which
ꝑtie is the bettre & moore ꝓfitable & han approued it by
manye wise folk & olde thanne shaltow considere if thou
mayst ꝑforme it & maken of it a good ende ¶ ffor reson wol
nat þt any man sholde bigynne a thyng but if he myghte
ꝑforme it as hym oghte ne no wight sholde take vp on hym
so heuy charge þt he myghte nat beren it ffor the prouerbe
seith he þt to muche embraceth destreyneth litel And
Caton seith assay to do swich thyng as thou hast power
to doon lest þt the charge oppresse thee so sore þt thee biho
ueth to weyue thyng þt thou hast bigonne And if so
be þt thou be in doute whether thou mayst ꝑforme
a thyng or noon chees rather to suffre than bigynne
And Peter Alfonce seith ¶ If thou hast myght to doon a
thyng of which thou most repente it is bettre nay
than ye this is to seyn þt thee is bettre to holde thy
tonge stille than for to speke ¶ Thanne may ye vnder
stonde by strenger resons þt if thou hast power to

pforme a werk of which thow shalt repente / thanne is it bettre
þt thow suffre than bigynne / Wel seyn they þt defenden euery
wight to assaye a thyng of which he is in doute whether he
may pforme it or no ¶ And after whan ye haue examyned
youre conseil as I haue seyd biforn & knowen wel þt ye
may pforme youre emprise conferme it thanne sadly til it
be at an ende ¶ Now is it reson & tyme þt I shewe yow
whanne & wherfore þt ye may chaunge youre conseillours
wt oute youre repreue / Soothly man may chaungen his
purpos and his conseil if the cause cesseth or whan a newe
cas bitideth / for the lawe seith þt vp on thynges þt newely
bitideth / bihoueth newe conseil ¶ And Seneca seith / If thy
conseil is come to the eyris of thyn enemy / chaunge thy conseil
¶ Thow mayst also chaunge thy conseil / if so be þt thou fynde
þt by errour or by oother cause harm or damage may bity
de ¶ Also if thy conseil be deshoneste or ellis cometh of des
honeste cause / chaunge thy conseil / for the lawes seyn that
alle biheestes þt ben deshoneste / ben of no value / And eek if
it so be þt it be impossible or may nat goodly be pformed or
kept / And take this for a general rule / that euery conseil þt
is affermed so strongly þt it may nat be chaunged for no co
dicion þt may bityde / I seye that thilke conseil is wikked
¶ This Melibeus whan he hadde herd the doctrine of his wyf
dame Prudence answerde in this wise ¶ Dame quod he as
yet in to this tyme ye han wel & couenably taught me as
in general how I shal gouerne me in chesynge & in the wt hol
dyng of my conseillours / But now wolde I fayn þt ye wol
Melibeus de condescenden in especial & telle me how liketh yow / or
what semeth yow by oure conseillours þt we han chosen in
oure psent nede ¶ My lord quod she I biseke yow in al humi
blesse þt ye wol nat wilfully replie ayein my resons / ne
distempre youre herte / though I speke thyng þt yow displese /
for god woot þt as in myn entente / I speke it for youre beste
for youre honour & for youre pfit eke / And soothly I hope þt
youre benyngnytee wol taken it in pacience ¶ Trusteth me
wel quod she þt youre conseil as in this cas ne sholde nat
as to speke pprely be called a conseilyng / but a mocion or
a moeuyng of folie in which conseil ye han erred in many
a sondry wise ¶ First & forward ye han erred in the assem
blyng of youre conseillours / for ye sholde first han cleped a

p*ar*forme a werk of which thow shalt repente / thanne is it bettre / þ*at* thow suffre / than bigynne / wel seyn they / þ*at* defenden euery wight to assaye / a thyng of which he is in doute / wheither he may p*ar*forme it or no ¶And after / whan ye haue examyned youre conseil / as I haue seyd biforn / *and* knowen wel þ*at* ye may p*ar*forme youre emp*ri*se / conferme it thanne sadly / til it be at an ende ¶Now is it resou*n* *and* tyme / þ*at* I shewe yow / whanne *and* wherfore / þ*at* ye may chaunge youre conseillours / w*ith* oute youre reproue / Soothly / man may chaungen his purpos / and his conseil / if the cause cesseth / or whan a newe cas bitideth / for the lawe seith / þ*at* vp on thynges / þ*at* newely bitideth / bihoueth newe conseil ¶And Seneca seith / If thy conseil is come / to the erys of thyn enemy / chaunge thy co*n*seil ¶Thow mayst also chaunge thy conseil / if so be þ*at* thou fynde þ*at* by errour / or by oother cause / harm / or damage / may bityde ¶Also / if thy conseil be deshoneste / or ellis cometh of deshoneste cause / chaunge thy conseil / for the lawes seyn / that alle bihestes / þ*at* ben deshoneste / ben of no value / And eek if it so be / þ*at* it be inpossible / or may nat goodly be p*ar*formed / or kept / And take this / for a gen*er*al rule / That eu*er*y conseil / þ*at* is affermed so strongly / þ*at* it may nat be chaunged / for no co*n*diciou*n* / þ*at* may bityde /. I seye / that thilke conseil is wikked This Melibeus / whan he hadde herd / the doct*ri*ne of his wyf / Dame Prudence /. answerde in this wise ¶Dame quod he / as yet in to this tyme / ye han wel *and* couenably taught me / as in gen*er*al / how I shal gou*er*ne me / in chesynge / *and* in the w*ith*holdyng of my conseillours / But now wolde I fayn / þ*at* ye wolde condescenden in especial / *and* telle me how liketh yow / or what semeth yow / by oure conseillours / þ*at* we han chosen in oure p*re*sent nede ¶My lord quod she / I biseke yow / in al humblesse / þ*at* ye wol nat wilfully / replye ayein my resons / ne distempre youre herte / thogh I speke thyng þ*at* yow displese / for god woot þ*at* as in myn entente / I speke it for youre beste / for youre hono*ur* / *and* for youre p*ro*fit eke / And soothly I hope / þ*at* youre benygnytee / wol taken it in pacience ¶Trusteth me wel quod she / þ*at* youre conseil / as in this cas / ne sholde nat as to speke p*ro*prely / be called a conseilyng but a mociou*n* or a moeuyng of folie / in which conseil / ye han erred / in many a sondry wise ¶First *and* forward / ye han erred / in the assemblyng of youre conseillours / for ye sholde first han clepid a

536 ⟨Melibeus⟩ Hg (2424)

fewe folkꝭ to youre conseil / and after / ye myghte han shewed itꝭ to mo folkꝭ if it hadde be nede ¶But c*er*tes / ye han sodeynly clepid to youre conseil / a gret multitude of peple / ful chargeant / *and* ful anoyous for to heere ¶Also ye han erred / for ther as ye sholde oonly / han clepid to youre conseil / youre trewe freendes / olde / *and* wise ·ʃ/ ye han yclepid straunge folkꝭ. yong folkꝭ / false flatereres / *and* enemys reconsiled / *and* folk / þ*at* doon yow reu*er*ence withouten loue ¶And eek also / ye han erred / for ye han broght w*ith* yow / to youre conseil . / Ire / Coueitise / *and* hastifnesse /. the whiche thre thynges / ben contrariouse / to eu*er*y conseil honeste / *and* p*ro*fitable /. the whiche thre thynges / ye han nat anientissed / or destroyed hem / neither in your*e* selfꝭ ne in youre conseillours / as ye oghte // ¶Ye han erred also / for ye han shewed to youre conseillours / youre talentꝭ *and* youre affecciou*n* / to make werre anon / *and* for to do vengeance / they han espied by youre wordes / to what thyngꝭ ye ben enclyned ⁊ And ther fore / han they conseilled yow / rather / to youre talentꝭ than to youre p*ro*fitꝭ ¶Ye han erred also / for it semeth / þ*at* yow suffiseth / to han ben conseilled / by thise conseil*our*s oonly / *and* w*ith* litel auys / wher as in so gretꝭ *and* so heigh a nede / it hadde ben necessarie / mo conseilours / *and* moore deliberaciou*n* / to p*ar*forme youre emp*ri*se ¶Ye han erred also / for ye ne han nat examyned youre conseil in the forseyde manere / ne in due manere / as the cas requyreth ¶Ye han erred also / for ye han maked no diuisiou*n* bitwixe youre conseilours / this is to seyn / bytwixe youre trewe freendes / *and* youre feyned conseilours / ne ye ne haue nat knowe the wyl / of youre trewe freendes / olde / and wise / but ye han cast alle hir wordes / in an hochepotꝭ *and* enclyned youre herte / to the moore partꝭ *and* to the gretter nombre / *and* ther be ye condescended ⁊ And sith ye woot wel / þ*at* men shal alwey fynde / a gretter nombre of foolis / than of wise men / and therfore / the conseils þ*at* ben at congregacions / and multitudes of folk / ther as men take moore reward / to the no*m*bre / than to the sapience of p*er*sones / ye se wel / þ*at* in swyche conseillynges / foolis han the maistrie ¶Melibeus answerde agayn / and seyde / I graunte wel þ*at* I haue erred / but ther as thow hast toold me her biforn / þ*at* he ne is nat to blame / þ*at* chaungeth his conseillours / in c*er*teyn cas / *and* for certeyne Iuste causes ·ʃ/ I am al redy / to chaunge my conseilours / right as thow wolt deuyse ⁊ The p*ro*u*er*be seith / that for to do synne / is ⟨humanum⟩ mannyssh / but c*er*tes / for to p*er*seu*er*e longe in synne

fewe folk to youre conseil and after ye myghte han shewed it to
mo folk if it hadde be nede ¶ But certes ye han sodeynly cleped
to youre conseil a greet multitude of peple ful chargeant & ful
anoyous for to heere ¶ Also ye han erred for ther as ye sholde
oonly han cleped to youre conseil youre trewe freendes olde
& wise ye han ycleped straunge folk, yong folk, false flate
reres & enemys reconsiled & folk þt doon yow reuerence with
outen loue ¶ And eek also ye han erred, for ye han broght wt
yow to youre conseil ire coueitise & hastifnesse, the whiche
thre thynges ben contrariouse to euery conseil honeste & pfita
ble, the whiche thre thynges ye han nat anientissed or destroyed
hem, neither in youre self ne in youre conseillours as ye oghte
¶ Ye han erred also for ye han shewed to youre conseillours you
re talent & youre affection to make werre anon & for to do
vengeance, they han espied by youre wordes to what thyng
ye ben enclyned, and ther fore han they conseilled yow rather
to youre talent than to youre pfit ¶ Ye han erred also for it se
meth þt yow suffiseth to han ben conseilled by thise conseilours
oonly & wt litel avys wher as in so greet & so heigh a nede
it hadde ben necessarie mo conseillours & moore deliberacion
to pforme youre emprise ¶ Ye han erred also, for ye ne han nat
examyned youre conseil in the forseyde manere, ne in due ma
nere as the cas requireth ¶ Ye han erred also for ye han ma
ked no diuision bitwixe youre conseillours, this is to seyn bi
twixe youre trewe freendes & youre feyned conseillours ne
ye ne haue nat knowe the wyl of youre trewe freendes olde
and wise but ye han cast alle hir wordes in an hochepot
& enclyned youre herte to the moore part & to the gretter nom
bre & ther be ye condescended, and sith ye woot wel þt men
shal alwey fynde a gretter nombre of foolis than of wise
men, and ther fore the conseils þt ben at congregacions and
multitudes of folk ther as men take moore reward to the no
bre than to the sapience of psones ye se wel þt in swiche
conseillynges foolis han the maistrie ¶ Melibeus answerde
agayn and seyde I graunte wel þt I haue erred but ther
as thow hast toold me her biforn þt he ne is nat to bla
me þt chaungeth his conseillours in certeyn cas & for cer
teyne iuste causes I am al redy to chaunge my conseillours
right as thow wolt deuyse The puerbe seith that for to do
synne is [humanum] mannyssh but certes for to perseuere longe in synne

is werk of the deuel ¶ To this sentence answerde anon dame
Prudence & seyde / Examyneth quod she youre conseil &
lat vs se the whiche of hem han spoken moost resonably &
taught yow best conseil / And for as muche as þt the examinaci
on is necessarie / lat vs bigynne at the Surgiens and at the
Phisiciens þt first speeken in this matere / I sey yow þt the
Surgiens & Phisiciens han seyd yow in youre conseil discretly
as hem oghte / and in hir speche seyden ful wysly / that to the
office of hem aperteneth to doon to euery wight honour & pfit / &
no wight to anoye / and after hir craft to doon gret diligence
vn to the cure of hem / whiche þt they han in hir gouernance
¶ And sire / right as they han answered wysly & discretly / right
so rede I / þt they be heighly & souereynly gerdoned for hir no
ble speche / and eek for they shullen do the moore ententif bisy
nesse / in the curacion of thy doghter deere / ffor al be it so / that
they ben youre freendes / ther fore shal ye nat suffren þt they
serue ^you^ for noght / but ye oghte the rather gerdone hem & shewen
hem youre largesse / And as touchynge the proposicion / which þt
the Phisiciens encresceden in this cas / this is to seyn / that in
maladies / that a contrarie / is warissed / by another contrarie
I wolde fayn knowe / how ye vnderstande thilke text / & what
is youre sentence ¶ Certes quod Melibeus / I vnderstonde it / in
this wise / that right / as they han doon me a contrarie / right so shol
de I / doon hem another / for right as they han venged hem on
me & doon me wrong / right so shal I venge me vp on hem /
& doon hem wrong / & thanne haue I cured / a contrarie by another
¶ Lo lo / quod dame Prudence / how lightly is euery man encly
ned to his owene desir / & to his owene plesance / Certes quod
she the wordes of the Phisiciens / ne sholde nat han ben vnder
stonden in that wise / for certes wikkednesse / is nat contrarie
to wikkednesse / ne vengeance / to vengeance / ne wrong / to
wrong / but they ben semblable / And ther fore o vengeance
is nat warissed by another vengeance / ne o wrong by a
nother wrong / but euerich of hem encresceth & aggreggeth
oother ¶ But certes the wordes of thise Phisiciens / sholde ben
vnderstonde in this wise / ffor good & wikkednesse / ben two
contraries / and pees & werre / vengeance & suffrance / discord &
acord / and many othere thynges / But certes / wikked shal be
warissed by goodnesse / discord by acord / werre by pees /
and so forth of othere thynges / And her to acordeth Seynt /

is werk of the deuel ¶To this sentence / answerde anon dame Prudence / *and* seyde ⹎ Examyneth quod she youre conseil / *and* lat vs se / the whiche of hem / han spoken moost resonably / *and* taught yow best conseil / And for as muche / as þ*at* the examinacion is necessarie / lat vs bigynne / at the Sirurgiens / and at the Phisiciens / þ*at* first speeken in this matere ⹎ I sey yow / þ*at* the Sirurgiens *and* Phisiciens / han seyd yow in youre conseil / discretly / as hem oghte / And in hir speche / seyden ful wysly / that to the office of hem ap*er*teneth / to doon to euery wight honour *and* profit. *and* no wight to anoye / and after hir craft to doon gret diligence vn to the cure of hem / whiche þ*at* they han in hir gou*er*nance

¶And sire / right as they han answered wysly *and* discretly / right so rede .I. / þ*at* they be heighly *and* soue*er*eynly gerdoned / for hir noble speche / and eek for they shullen / do the moore ententif bisynesse / in the curaciou*n* of thy doghter deere ⹎ For al be it so / that they ben youre freendes / therfore / shal ye nat suffren / þ*at* they serue ⟨you⟩ for noght. but ye oghte / the rather gerdone hem / *and* shewen hem youre largesse ⹎ And as touchynge the p*ro*posiciou*n* / which þ*at* the Phisiciens / encresceden in this cas / this is to seyn / that in maladies / that a cont*ra*rie / is warisshed / by another contrarie I wolde fayn knowe / how ye vnderstande thilke text *and* what is youre sentence ¶Certes quod Melibeus / I vnderstonde it in this wise ⹎ that right as they han doon me a cont*ra*rie / right so / sholde I / doon hem another / for right as they han venged hem on me / *and* doon me wrong right so / shal I venge me vp on hem / *and* doon hem wrong *and* thanne haue I cured / a cont*ra*rie by another

¶Lo / lo / quod dame Prudence / how lightly is euery man enclyned / to his owene desir / *and* to his owene plesance ⹎ Certes quod she / the wordes of the Phisiciens / ne sholde nat han ben vnderstonden / in that wise ⹎ for c*er*tes / wikkednesse / is nat contrarie to wikkednesse / ne vengeance / to vengeance / ne wrong to wrong but they ben semblable ⹎ And therfore / .o. vengeance is nat warisshed / by another vengeance / ne .o. wrong by another wrong but euerich of hem encresceth / *and* aggreggeth oother ¶But c*er*tes / the wordes of thise Phisiciens / sholde ben vnderstonde / in this wise ⹎ For good *and* wikkednesse / ben two cont*ra*ries / and pees *and* werre / vengeance *and* suffrance / discord *and* acord / and many othere thynges ⹎ But c*er*tes / wikked / shal be warisshed by goodnesse / discord . by acord / werre . by pees / and so forth of othere thynges ⹎ And her to / acordeth Seynt

Poul the Apostle / in many places / he seith / Ne yeldeth noght harm for harm / ne wikked speche / for wikked speche / [2482] but do wel / to hym þ*at* dooth ⟨to⟩ thee harm / *and* blesse hym / þ*at* seith to thee harm / And in manye othere places / he amonesteth pees *and* acord ¶But now wol I speke to yow / of the conseil / which þ*at* was yeuen to yow / by the men of lawe / *and* the wise folk þ*at* seyden alle by oon acord / as ye han herd bifore // That ou*er* alle thynges / ye shal do youre diligence to kepe youre p*er*sone / *and* to warnestore youre hous / [2487] *and* seyden also / þ*at* in this cas / ye oghten for to werke / ful auysely / *and* w*ith* greet deliberaciou*n* ¶And sire / as to the firste point that toucheth / to the kepyng of youre p*er*sone / ye shul vnderstonde / that he þ*at* hath werre / shal euere moore deuoutly *and* mekely / preyen / byforn alle thynges / þ*at* I*esus* crist of his mercy / wol han hym in his p*ro*teccioun / *and* ben his souereyn helpyng at his nede ¶For c*er*tes in this world / ther is no wight þ*at* may be conseilled ne kept suffisantly / w*ith* oute the kepyng of oure lord I*es*u Crist [2492] ¶To this sentence / acordeth the p*ro*phete Dauid / that seith / If god ne kepe Citee / in ydel / waketh he þ*at* it kepeth ¶Now syre / thanne shul ye / co*m*mitte the kepyng of youre p*er*sone / to youre trewe freendes / þ*at* been approued and yknowe / *and* of hem / shul ye axen help / youre p*er*sone for to kepe // For Catou*n* seith / If thou hast nede of help*e* / axe it of thy freendes / for ther nys noon so good a Phisicien / as thy trewe freend [2497] ¶And after this / thanne shul ye kepe yow / fro alle straunge folk *and* fro lyeres / *and* haue alwey / in suspect hir compaignye ¶For Piers Alfonce seith / Ne taak no compaignye / by the wey / of a straunge man / but if so be / þ*at* thow haue knowe hym / of a lenger tyme / And if so be / þ*at* he falle in to thy compaignye / p*ar*auenture / w*ith* outen thyn assent. enquere thanne / as subtilly as thow mayst / of his conu*er*sacioun / *and* of his lyf bifore / and feyne thy wey / Sey / þ*at* thow wolt go thider / as thow wolt nat go / And if he bereth a spere / hoold thee on the right syde / And if he bere a swerd / hoold thee on the left syde [2502] ¶And after this / thanne shal ye kepe yow wysly / from al swich maner*e* peple / as I haue seyd bifore / *and* hem *and* hir conseil eschewe ¶And after this / thanne shal ye kepe yow in swich manere / that for any p*re*sumpcion of youre strengthe / þ*at* ye ne despise nat ne attempte nat the myght of youre Aduersarie / so lite / þ*at* ye lete / the kepyng of youre p*er*sone / for youre p*re*sumpciou*n* / for eu*er*y wys man / dredeth his enemy / And Salomon seyth

Poul the Apostle in many places / he seith / ne yeldeth noght harm
for harm / ne wikked speche / for wikked speche / but do wel to hym
þt dooth thee harm / & blesse hym / þt seith to thee harm / And in ma
nye othere places he amonesteth pees & acord ¶ But now wol
I speke to yow / of the counseil / which þt was yeuen to yow / by the
men of lawe / & the wise folk / þt seyden alle by oon acord / as ye
han herd bifore / that ouer alle thynges / ye shal do youre diligence
to kepe youre persone / & to warnestore youre hous / & seyden also
þt in this cas / ye oghten for to werke / ful auysely / & wt greet
deliberacion ¶ And sire / as to the firste point / that toucheth to
the kepyng of youre persone / ye shul vnderstonde / that he þt
hath werre / shal euere moore deuoutly & mekely / preyen by
forn alle thynges / þt Ihesu crist of his mercy / wol han hym
in his proteccion / & been his souereyn helpyng at his nede ¶ For
certes in this world / ther is no wight / þt may be conseilled ne
kept sufficiantly / wt oute the kepyng / of oure lord Ihesu crist /
¶ To this sentence / acordeth the prophete Dauid / that seith / If god
ne kepe citee / in ydel / waketh he þt it kepeth ¶ Now sire /
thanne shul ye / committe the kepyng of youre persone / to youre
trewe freendes / þt been approued and yknowe / & of hem shul
ye axen help / youre persone for to kepe / ffor Caton seith / If thou
hast nede of help / axe it of thy freendes / for ther nys noon so
good a phisicien / as thy trewe freend ¶ And after this / thanne
shul ye kepe yow fro alle straunge folk / & fro lyeres / & haue
alwey in suspect hir compaignye ¶ ffor Piers Alfonce seith /
Ne taak no compaignye / by the wey / of a straunge man / but
if so be / þt thow haue knowe hym of a lenger tyme / and
if so be / þt he falle in to thy compaignye / parauenture / wt outen
thyn assent / enquere thanne / as subtilly as thow mayst /
of his conuersacion / & of his lyf bifore / and feyne thy wey /
sey þt thow wolt go thider / as thow wolt nat go / And if he
bereth a spere / hoold thee on the right syde / And if he bere a
swerd / hoold thee on the left syde ¶ And after this / thanne
shal ye kepe yow wisely / from al swich manere peple / as I
haue seyd bifore / & hem & hir conseil eschewe ¶ And after
this / thanne shal ye kepe yow in swich manere / that for
any presumpcion of youre strengthe / þt ye ne despise nat /
ne accompte nat / the myght of youre aduersarie / so lite / þt
ye lete the kepyng of youre persone / for youre presumpcion / for
euery wys man / dredeth his enemy / And Salomon seith

Dredeful is he þt of al hath drede / ffor certes he þt thurgh the
hardynesse of his herte & thurgh the hardynesse of hym self
hath to gret presumpcioun / hym shal yvel bityde ¶ Thanne
shal ye evere mo countrewayte enbuyssementz & al espiaille
¶ ffor Senek seith þt the wise man þt dredeth harmes / escheweth harmes ne he ne falleth in to perils / þt perils eschueth
and al be so þt it seme þt thow art in siker place / yet
shaltow alwey do thy diligence in kepyng of thy persone /
this is to seyn / ne be nat necligent to kepe thy persone / nat
oonly fro thy grettest enemys / but fro thy leeste enemy
¶ Senek seith / a man þt is wel avysed / he dredeth his leste
enemy / Ovyde seith / that the litel wesele / wol slee the
grete bole / & the wilde hert ¶ And the book seith / a litel thorn
may prikke a kyng / ful soore / And an hound / wol holde the
wilde boor / But natheles I sey nat / thow shalt be so coward þt thow doute ther / wher as is no drede / The book
seith / that som folk have gret lust to deceyve / but yet they
dreden hem to be deceyved / yet shaltow drede to been
empoysoned / & kepe thee / from the compaignye of scorners
¶ ffor the book seith / with scorners / make no compaignye / but
flee hir wordes / as venym ¶ Now as to the seconde point
where as youre wise conseilours / conseiled yow / to warnestore youre hous with gret diligence / I wolde fayn knowe
how þt ye understonde thilke wordes / & what is youre
sentence ¶ Melibeus answerde & seyde / Certes I understonde it in this wise / that I shal warnestore myn hous
with toures / swiche as han castelles & othere manere edifices & armure & artelries / by whiche thynges I may my
persone & myn hous so kepen & defenden / þt myne enemys
shul been in drede / myn hous for to approche ¶ To thys
sentence / answerde anon Prudence / warnestoryng / quod
she of heighe toures / & of grete edifices / with grete costages /
& with gret travaille / and whan þt they been accompliced / yet
be they nat worth a stree / but if they been defended / by trewe freendes / that been olde / and wise ¶ And understonde
wel / þt the gretteste / and the strengeste garnyson / þt ryche
man may have / as wel / to kepen his persone / as his goodes /
is þt he be biloved with his subgetz and with his neighebores ¶ ffor thus seith Tullius / that ther is a manere
garnyson / þt no man may venquysse ne disconfite / and þt

is a lord to be

¶Weleful is he / þ*at* of aƚƚ hath drede // For c*er*tes / þ*at* thurgh the hardynesse of his herte / *and* thurgh the hardynesse of hym self / hath to gret p*re*sumpciou*n* / hym shal yuel bityde ¶Thanne shal ye eu*er*e mo countrewayte emboyssementz *and* al espiaille ¶For Senek seith / þ*at* the wise man þ*at* dredeth harmes / escheweth harmes / ne he ne falleth in to p*er*ils / þ*at* p*er*ils escheweth / And al be so / þ*at* it seme / þ*at* thow art in siker place // yet shaltow alwey do thy diligence / in kepyng of thy p*er*sone / this is to seyn / ne be nat necligent to kepe thy p*er*sone / nat oonly fro thy grettest enemys / but fro thy leeste enemy ¶Senek seith // A man þ*at* is wel auysed / he dredeth his leste enemy // Ouyde seith // that the litel wesele / wol slee the grete Bole / *and* the wilde hert ¶And the book seith / a litel thorn may prikke a kyng ful soore / And an hound / wol holde the wilde boor // But nathelees / I sey nat / thow shalt be so coward / þ*at* thow doute / ther / wher as is no drede // The book seith / that som folk haue gret lust to deceyue / but yet they dreden hem / to be deceyued / yet shaltow drede / to been empoysoned / *and* kepe thee / from the compaignye of scorn*er*es / ¶For the book seith / with scorn*er*es / make no compaignye / but flee hir*e* wordes / as venym ¶Now as to the seconde point where as youre wise conseilours / conseiled yow / to warnestore youre hous / w*ith* gret diligence // I wolde fayn knowe / how þ*at* ye vnderstonde thilke wordes / *and* what is youre sentence ¶Melibeus answerde *and* seyde // Certes / I vnderstonde it in this wise / that I shal warnestore myn hous / w*ith* toures / swiche as han Castelles / *and* othere manere edifices / *and* armure / *and* Artelries / by whiche thynges / I may my p*er*sone *and* myn hous / so kepen *and* defenden / þ*at* myne enemys shul been in drede / myn hous for to approche ¶To thys sentence / answerde anon Prudence // Warnestoryng quod she of heighe toures / *and* of grete edifices / w*ith* grete costages / *and* with gret t*ra*uaille / and whan þ*at* they been accompliced / yet be they nat worth a stree / but if they been defended / by trewe freendes / that been oolde / and wise ¶And vnderstonde wel / þ*at* the gretteste / and the strengeste garnysou*n* / þ*at* ryche man may haue / as wel / to kepen his p*er*sone / as his goodes // is þ*at* he be biloued with his subgetz and with his neighebores ¶For thus seith Tullius / that ther is a manere garneson / þ*at* no man may venquyse ne discomfite / and þ*at*

is a lord to be

is / a lord / to be bilоued / of his Citezeins / and of his peple ¶Now sire / as to the .iij^e^ poynt' wher as youre olde and wise conseilours / seiden / þ*at* yow ne oghte nat sodeynly / ne hastily / proceden in this nede / but þ*at* yow oghte p*ur*ueien and apparailen yow in this cas / with greet diligence and greet deliberaciou*n* ./ [2532] trewely / I trowe þ*at* they seyden right wisely / and right sooth ¶For Tullius seith / In euery nede / er thow bigynne it' apparayle thee / with greet diligence / thanne seye I / þ*at* in vengeance takynge / in werre / in bataile / and in warnestorynge / er thow bigynne / I rede þ*at* thow apparaile thee ther to / and do it' with greet deliberaciou*n* ¶For Tullius seith / that long apparailynge biforn the bataile / maketh short victorie [2537] / And Cassidorus seith / the garneson is strenger / whan it is long tyme auysed ¶But now lat vs speke of the conseil þ*at* was acorded by youre neighebores swiche as doon yow reu*er*ence / with outen loue / youre olde enemys reconsiled / youre flaterers / þ*at* conseileden yow c*er*teyne thynges pryuely / and openly conseileden yow the cont*ra*rie / The yonge folk' also / þ*at* conseileden yow / to venge yow / and make werre anoon [2542] And c*er*tes sire / as I haue seyd biforn / ye han greetly erred / to han clepid swich maner folk / to youre conseil / whiche conseilours been ynow repreued bi the resons foreseyd / but nathelees / lat vs now descende to the special ¶Ye shuln first p*ro*ceden after the doctryne of Tullius / Certes / the trouthe of this matere / or of this conseil / nedeth nat / diligently enquere / for it is wel wist' whiche they been / that han doon to yow / this trespas and vileynye / [2547] and how manye trespasours / and in what manere / they han to yow doon al this wrong' and al this vileynye ¶And after this / thanne shulle ye examyne the .ij^e^ condiciou*n* / which þ*at* the same Tullius addeth in this matere / for Tullius put a thyng / which þ*at* he clepeth consentynge / this is to seyn / who been they and whiche been they / and how manye þ*at* consenten to thy conseil in thy wilfulnesse / to do hastif vengeance / and lat vs considere also / who been they and how manye been they / and whiche been they / þ*at* consenteden / to youre Aduersaries [2552] ¶And certes / as to the firste poynt' it is wel knowen whiche folk' been they / þ*at* consenteden / to youre hastif wilfulnesse / for trewely alle tho / þ*at* conseileden yow to maken sodeyn werre / ne been nat youre freendes / Lat vs now considere whiche been they þ*at* ye holde so greetly youre freendes / as to youre p*er*sone / for al be it so / þ*at* ye be myghty and ryche ./ c*er*tes / ye ne been / but

is a lord to be biloued of his Citezeins and of his peple ¶ Touch
ynge as to the .iij.e point / wher as youre olde and wise consei
lours seiden / þt yow ne oghte nat sodeynly ne hastily proce
den in this nede / but þt yow oghte purueien and apparaillen yow
in this cas / with greet diligence and greet deliberacion : trewe
ly I trowe þt they seyden right wisely and right sooth ¶ ffor
Tullius seith / In euery nede er thow bigynne it / apparaille
thee with greet diligence / thanne seye I / þt in vengeance takyn
ge / in werre / in bataille and in warnestorynge er thow bigynne
I rede þt thow apparaille thee ther to / and do it / with greet delibe
racion ¶ ffor Tullius seith / that long apparaillynge biforn the
bataille / maketh short victorie / And Cassidorus seith / the gar
nyson is strenger / whan it is long tyme auysed ¶ But now
lat vs speke of the conseil þt was acorded by youre neighebores
swiche as doon yow reuerence with outen loue / youre olde enemys
reconsiled / youre flatereres / þt conseileden yow certeyne thynges
pryuely / and openly conseileden yow the contrarie / The yonge folk
also / þt conseileden yow to venge yow and make werre anoon
And certes sire as I haue seyd biforn / ye han greetly erred to han
cleped swich maner folk to youre conseil / whiche conseillours
been ynow repreued bi the resons forseyd / but natheles lat
vs now descende to the special ¶ ye shuln first procede after
the doctryne of Tullius / Certes the trouthe of this matere or
of this conseil nedeth nat diligently enquere / for it is wel wist
whiche they been that han doon to yow / this trespas and vilei
nye / and how manye trespasours / and in what manere they
han to yow doon al this wrong / and al this vileynye ¶ And
after this thanne shulle ye examyne the .ij.e condicion which
þt the same Tullius addeth in this matere / for Tullius put a
thyng which þt he clepeth consentynge / this is to seyn / who
been they and whiche been they / and how manye þt consenten
to thy conseil in thy wilfulnesse / to do hastif vengeance / and lat
vs considere also / who been they and how manye been they and
whiche been they / þt consenteden / to youre aduersaries ¶ And
certes as to the firste point / it is wel knowen whiche folk
been they / þt consenteden / to youre hastif wilfulnesse / for trewe
ly alle tho þt conseileden yow to maken sodeyn werre ne been
nat youre freendes / lat vs now considere whiche been they
þt ye holde so greetly youre freendes as to youre persone / for
al be it so þt ye be myghty and ryche : certes ye ne been but

allone / for certes / ye ne han no child but a doghter / ne ye ne
han bretheren / ne cosyns germayns / ne noon oother ney kyn
rede / wher fore / þt youre enemys / for drede sholden stynte to ple
de wt yow / or destroye youre persone ¶ Ye knowe also þt youre
richesses / moten be despended in diuerse parties / and whan þt
euery wight hath his part / they ne wollen take but litel re
ward to venge thy deeth / but thyne enemys been .iij. and
they han manye children / bretheren / cosyns and oother ney
kynrede / and though so were / thow haddest slayn of hem .ij.
or .iij. yet dwellen ther ynowe / to wreken hir deeth / and to
sle thy persone / and though so be / þt youre kynrede be moore sy
ker and stedefast / than the kyn of youre aduersarie / yet nathe
lees youre kynrede / nys but a fer kynrede / they been but litel
syb to yow / and the kyn of youre enemys / been ney syb to hem /
and certes as in that / hir condicion is bet than youres ¶ Than
ne lat vs considere also / if the conseilynge of hem þt conseileden
yow to taken sodeyn vengeance / wheither it acorde to reson /
and certes / ye knowe wel nay / for as by right and reson / ther
may no man take vengeance on no wight / but the iuge þt
hath the iurisdiccion of it / whan it is ygraunted hym to
take thilke vengeance hastily / or attemprely / as the lawe
requireth ¶ And yet more ouer / of thilke word / that Tullius
clepith consentynge / thow shalt considere / if thy myght and
thy power / may consente and suffise / to thy wilfulnesse and
to thy conseilours / and certes / thow mayst wel seyn / that nay /
for sikerly as for to speke proprely / we may do no thyng / but oon
ly swich thyng / as we may do rightfully / and certes / rightfully
ne mowe ye take no vengeance / as of youre propre auctoritee /
thanne mowe ye seen / that youre power ne consenteth nat
ne acordeth nat / with youre wilfulnesse ¶ Lat vs now exa
myne the .iij. point / that Tullius clepith consequent / thow
shalt vnderstande / that the vengeance þt thow purposest for
to taken / is the consequent / and ther of folweth another venge
ance / peril / and werre and othere damages with oute nombre
of whiche / we been nat war / as at this tyme ¶ And as tou
chynge the .iiij. point / that Tullius clepith engendrynge /
thow shalt considere / that this wrong / which that is doon to
thee / is engendred / of the hate of thyne enemys / and of the
vengeance takynge vp on that wolde engendre another
vengeance / and muchel sorwe / and wastynge of richesses /

allone / for certes / ye ne han no child / but a doghter ne ye ne han bretheren / ne cosyns germayns / ne noon oother ney kynrede / wherfore / þ*at* youre enemys / for drede sholden stynte / to plede w*ith* yow / or destroye youre p*er*sone ¶Ye knowe also / þ*at* youre richesses / moten be despended in diu*er*se parties / and whan þ*at* euery wight hath his part they ne wollen take but litel reward / to venge thy deeth // but thyne enemys / been .iij.^e and they han manye children / bretheren / cosyns / and oother ney kynrede / and thogh so were / thow haddest slayn of hem .ij.^o or .iij.^e yet dwellen ther ynowe / to wreken hir deeth / and to sle thy p*er*sone // and thogh so be / þ*at* youre kynrede be moore syker and stedefast than the kyn of youre adu*er*sarie ·/ / yet nathelees / youre kynrede / nys but a fer kynrede / they been / but litel syb to yow / and the kyn of youre enemys / been ney syb to he*m* / and certes as in that hir condicion / is bet than youres ¶Thanne / lat vs considere also / if the conseilynge / of hem þ*at* conseileden yow to taken sodeyn vengeance / wheither it acorde to reson And c*er*tes / ye knowe wel nay ·/ for as by right and reson / ther may no man take vengeance on no wight but the Iuge þ*at* hath the Iurisdicciou*n* of it whan it is ygraunted hym to take thilke vengeance hastily / or attemprely / as the lawe requereth ¶And yet more ouer of thilke word / that Tullius clepith / consentynge ·/ thow shalt considere / if thy myght and thy power may consente and suffise / to thy wilfulnesse and to thy conseilours / And certes / thow mayst wel seyn / that nay / for sikerly as for to speke p*ro*prely / we may do no thyng but oonly swich thyng as we may do rightfully / and c*er*tes / rightfully ne mowe ye take no vengeance / as of youre p*ro*pre auctoritee / thanne mowe ye seen / that youre power ne consenteth nat / ne acordeth nat with youre wilfulnesse ¶Lat vs now examyne the .iij.^e poynt that Tullius clepith Consequent // Thow shalt vnderstande / that the vengeance þ*at* thow purposest for to taken / is the consequent and ther of / folweth another vengeance / peril / and werre / and othere damages with oute nombre /. of whiche / we been nat waar / as at this tyme ¶And as touchynge the .iiij.^e poynt that Tullius clepith engendrynge / thow shalt considere / that this wrong which that is doon to thee / is engendred / of the hate of thyne enemys / and of the vengeance takynge vp on that wolde engendre another vengeance / and muchil sorwe / and wastynge of richesses /

as I seyde [2582] ¶Now sire / as touchynge to the poynt that Tullius clepith causes / which þ*at* is the laste poynt ./ thow shalt vnderstonde / þ*at* the wrong þ*at* thow hast receyued hath c*er*teyne causes / whiche þ*at* clerkes clepen Oriens and Efficiens / and Causa longinqua / and causa p*ro*pinqua / this is to seyn the fer cause / and the ny cause / the fer cause / is almyghty god that is cause of alle thynges // the neer cause / is thy thre enemys / [2587] the cause accidental / was hate / the cause material / been the .v. wou*n*des of thy doghter / the cause formal / is the manere of hir werkynge / that broghten laddres and clomben / In at thy wyndowes / the cause final / was for to sle thy doghter / it lettyd nat / in as muche as in hem was // but for to speke of the fer cause ./ as to what ende they shul come / ./ or what shal finally bityde of hem in this cas ./ ne kan I nat deme / but by coniectynge and by supposynge / [2592] for we shuln suppose / that they shul come to a wikked ende / by cause / þ*at* the book of decrees seith ¶Selden / or w*ith* greet peyne been causes ybroght to good ende / whan they been baddely bigonne ¶Now sire / if men wolden axe me / why þ*at* god suffrede men to do yow this vileynye ./ certes I kan nat wel answere / as for no soothfastnesse // for the Apostle seith / that the sciences and the Iugementz of oure lord god almyghty / been ful depe / ther may no man co*m*p*re*hende ne serchen hem suffisantly [2597] ¶Natheless / by c*er*teyne p*re*sumpcions and coniectynges / I holde *and* bileue / that god / which þ*at* is ful of Iustice and of rightwisnesse / hath suffred this bityde / by Iuste cause resonable ¶Thy name is Melibe / this is to seyn / a man that drynketh hony / thow hast ydronke so muchil hony / of swete temporel richesses and delices and honours of this world / that thow art dronken / and hast forgeten Ie*s*u *crist* thy creatour / [2602] thow ne hast nat doon to hym / swich honour and reuerence as thee oghte ./ ne thow ne hast nat wel taken kepe / to the wordes of Ouyde // that seith / vnder the hony of the goodes of the body ./ is hyd the venym / that sleth the soule ¶And Salomon seith // If thow hast founden hony / ete of it that suffiseth / for if thow ete of it out of mesure ./ thow shalt spewe / and be nedy and poore / [2607] and p*ar*auenture / Crist hath thee in despit and hath torned awey fro thee his face / and his erys of misericorde / and also he hath suffred / þ*at* thow as I seyde. ¶ Now sire as touchynge to the poynt that Tullius clepith causes which þt is the laste poynt. thow shalt vnderstonde þt the wrong þt thow hast receyued hath certeyne causes whiche þt clerkes clepen Oriens and Efficiens and Causa longinqua and causa propinqua this is to seyn. the fer cause and the ny cause the fer cause is almyghty god that is cause of alle thynges / the neer cause is thy thre enemys / the cause accidental was hate / the cause material been the .v. woundes of thy doghter / the cause formal is the manere of hir werkynge that broghten laddres and clomben In at thy wyndowes / the cause final was for to sle thy doghter / it letted nat in as muche as in hem was / but for to speke of the fer cause. as to what ende they shul come / or what shal finally bityde of hem in this cas. ne kan I nat deme / but by coniectynge and by supposynge / for we shuln suppose / that they shul come to a wikked ende / by cause þt the book of decrees seith ¶ Selden or with greet peyne been causes ybroght to good ende whan they been baddely bigonne ¶ Now sire if men wolden axe me why þt god suffrede men to do yow this vileynye: certes I kan nat wel answere / as for no soothfastnesse / for the Apostle seith / that the sciences and the Iugementz of oure lord god almyghty / been ful depe / ther may no man comprehende ne serchen hem suffisantly ¶ Nathelees by certeyne presumpcions and coniectynges I holde and bileue / that god which þt is ful of Iustice and of rightwisnesse hath suffred this bityde / by Iuste cause resonable ¶ Thy name is Melibe / this is to seyn / a man that drynketh hony / thow hast ydronke so muchil hony / of swete temporel richesses and delices and honours of this world that thow art dronken / and hast forgeten Ihu crist thy creatour / thow ne hast nat doon to hym swich honour and reuerence as thee oghte. ne thow ne hast nat wel taken kepe / to the wordes of Ouyde / that seith / vnder the hony of the goodes of the body. is hyd the venym / that sleeth the soule ¶ And Salomon seith / If thow hast founden hony / ete of it that suffiseth for if thow ete of it out of mesure. thow shalt spewe and be nedy and poore / and parauenture / Crist hath thee in despit and hath torned awey fro thee his face and his eyes of misericorde / and also he hath suffred / þt thow

hast been punysshed in the manere þt thow hast ytrespased
Thow hast doon synne agayn oure lord Crist / for certes the
iij. enemys of mankynde that is to seyn the flessh the
feend and the world thow hast suffred hem entre in to thyn
herte wilfully by the wyndowes of thy body and hast nat
defendid thy self suffisantly agayns hir assautes & hir
temptaciouns so þt they han woundid thy soule in .v.
places / this is to seyn the dedly synnes þt been entred
in to thyn herte by thy .v. wittes / and in the same manere
oure lord Crist hath wold & suffred þt thy .iij. enemys
been entred in to thyn hous by the wyndowes and han
ywoundid thy doghter in the forseyde manere ¶ Certes
quod Melibe / I se wel þt ye enforce yow muchil by wor
des to ouercome me in swich a manere þt I shal nat venge
me of myne enemys shewynge me the perils & the yueles
þt myghten falle of this vengeance / But who so wolde
considere in alle vengeances the perils and yueles þt myght
ten sewe of vengeance takynge: a man wolde neuere ta
ke vengeance and that were harm / for by the vengeance
takynge been the wikked men disseuered fro the goode men
and they þt han wil to do wikkednesse restreyne hir wik
ked purpos whan they seen the punysshynge & chastisyn
ge of trespassours / And yet seye I moore that right as
a singuler persone synneth in takynge vengeance of a
nother man: right so synneth the juge if he do no ven
geance of hem that it han disserued / ffor Senek seith thus
That maister he seith is good þt preueth shrewes / and
as Cassidore seith / a man dredeth to do outrages whan
he woot & knoweth þt it displeseth to the juges and the
souereyns / and another seith / The juge þt dredeth to do
right maketh men shrewes / and Seint Poul thapostle
seith in his epistle whan he writeth vn to the Romayns /
That the juges beren nat the spere wt outen cause but they
beren it to punysshe the shrewes & mysdoers & for to defen
de the goode men ¶ If ye wol thanne take vengeance of
youre enemys: ye shul retourne or haue youre recours
to the juge þt hath the jurisdiccion vp on hem & he shal
punysshe hem as the lawe axeth & requereth ¶ A quod
Melibe this vengeance liketh me no thyng / I bithenke
me now & take hede how fortune hath norisshed me fro

hast been punysshed in the manere þ*at* thow hast ytrespased ¶Thow hast doon synne agayn oure lord Crist // for certes / the .iij.e enemys of mankynde / that is to seyn / the flessh / the feend / and the world / thow hast suffred hem / entre in to thyn herte wilfully / by the wyndowes of thy body / and hast nat defendid thy self suffisantly agayns hir assautes *and* hir temptacions / so þ*at* they han woundid thy soule . in .v. places // this is to seyn / the dedly synnes / þ*at* been entred in to thyn herte by thy .v. wittes // And in the same manere / oure lord Crist hath wold *and* suffred / þ*at* thy .iij.e enemys been entred in to thyn hous by the wyndowes / and han ywoundid thy doghter in the forseyde manere ¶Certes quod Melibe / I se wel / þ*at* ye enforce yow muchil by wordes / to ou*er*come me in swich a manere / þ*at* I shal nat venge me of myne enemys / shewynge me the p*er*ils *and* the yueles / þ*at* myghten falle of this vengeance // But who so wolde considere in alle vengeances / the p*er*ils and yueles þ*at* myghten sewe of vengeance takynge ./ a man wolde neuere take vengeance / and that were harm / for by the vengeance takynge / been the wikked men disseuered / fro the goode men / and they þ*at* han wil to do wikkednesse ./ restreyne hir wikked purpos / whan they seen the punysshynge *and* chastisynge of trespassours // And yet seye I moore / that right as a singuler p*er*sone / synneth / in takynge vengeance of another man ./ right so synneth the Iuge / if he do no vengeance of hem that it han disserued // For Senek seith thus // That maister he seith is good / þ*at* preueth shrewes // And as Cassidore seith // A man dredeth to do outrages / whan he woot *and* knoweth / þ*at* it displeseth / to the Iuges and the souereyns // And another seith // The Iuge þ*at* dredeth to do right⁊ maketh men shrewes // And Seint Poul thapostle seith in his epistle whan he writeth vn to the Romayns / That the Iuges / beren nat the spere / wi*th* outen cause / but they beren it⁊ to punysshe the shrewes *and* mysdoers / *and* for to defende the goode men ¶If ye wol thanne take vengeance of youre enemys ./ ye shul retourne / or haue youre recours to the Iuge / þ*at* hath the Iurisdiccioun vp on hem / *and* he shal punysshe hem / as the lawe axeth *and* requereth ¶A quod Melibe / this vengeance liketh me no thyng⁊ I bithenke me now *and* take hede / how fortune hath norisshed me / fro my childhode / *and* hath holpen me / to passe many a strong pass Now wol I assayen hir*e* / trowynge w*ith* goddes help*e* / þ*a*t she shal helpe me / my shame for to venge / ¶Certes quod Prudence / if ye wol werke by my conseil // ye shul nat assayen fortune / by no wey / ne ye shul nat lene / or bowe vn to hire / after the word of Senek ⸗ for thynges þ*a*t been folily doon / *and* þ*a*t been in hope of fortune // shullen neue*r*e / come to good ende / And as the same Senek seith ⸗ The moore cleer / *and* the moore shynynge þ*a*t fortune is / // the moore brotil *and* the sonner broke she is / trusteth nat in hir*e* / for she nys nat stedefast ne stable / for whan thow trowest to be moost seur or syker of hir help*e* / she wol faile thee *and* deceyue thee ¶And wher*e* as ye seyn / that fortune hath norisshed yow fro youre childhode // I seye / þ*a*t in so muchil / shul ye the lasse truste in hire *and* ⟨in⟩ hir wit ⸗ For Senek seith ⸗ What man þ*a*t is norisshed by fortune // she maketh hym to greet a fool ¶Now thanne / syn ye desire / *and* axe vengeance / *and* the vengeance / þ*a*t is doon after the lawe / *and* bifore the Iuge / ne liketh yow nat / *and* the vengeance / þ*a*t is doon in hope of fortune / is pe*r*ilous *and* vncerteyn // thanne haue ye noon oother remedie / but for to haue youre recours / vn to the soue*r*eyn Iuge / þ*a*t vengeth / alle vileynyes *and* wronges / and he shal venge yow / after that hym self witnesseth / wher*e* as he seith ⸗ leueth the vengeance to me / and I shal do it ¶Melibe answerde ⸗ If I ne venge me nat of the vileynye / þ*a*t men han doon to me // I . somne / or warne hem / þ*a*t han doon to me that vileynye / *and* alle othere / to do me another vileynye / for it is writen / If thow take no vengeance of an old vileynye // thow somnest thyne Adue*r*saries / to do thee a newe vileynye ⸗ And also / for my suffrance / men wolden do me so muchil vileynye / þ*a*t I myghte neither bere it ne sustene / and so sholde I been put *and* holden oue*r* lowe ⸗ For men seyn / I muchil suffrynge / shul manye thynges falle vn to thee / whiche yow shalt nat mowe suffre ¶Certes quod Prudence / I g*ra*unte yow / þ*a*t ouer muchil suffrance / is nat good / but yet ne folweth it nat ther of / þ*a*t euery pe*r*sone / to whom men don vileynye / take of it vengeance / for that ape*r*teneth *and* longeth al oonly to the Iuges / for they shul venge the vileynyes *and* iniuries / and therfore / tho two auctoritees / þ*a*t ye han seyd aboue / been oonly [oonly] / vnderstonden in the Iuges

my childhode & hath holpen me to passe many a strong paas Now wol I assayen hire trustynge wt goddes help þt she shal helpe me my shame for to venge Certes quod Prudence if ye wol werke by my conseil ye shul nat assayen fortune by no wey ne ye shul nat lene or bowe vn to hire after the word of Senek for thynges þt been folily doon & þt been in hope of fortune shullen neuere come to good ende And as the same Senek seith The moore cleer & the moore shynynge þt fortune is the moore brotil & the sonner broke she is Trusteth nat in hire for she nys nat stedefast ne stable for whan thow trowest to be moost seur or siker of hir help she wol faille thee & deceyue thee And wher as ye seyn that fortune hath norisshed yow fro youre childhode I seye þt in so muchil shul ye the lasse truste in hire & in hir wit ffor Senek seith What man þt is norisshed by fortune she maketh hym to greet a fool Now thanne syn ye desire & axe vengeance & the vengeance þt is doon after the lawe & bifore the Juge ne liketh yow nat & the vengeance þt is doon in hope of fortune is perilous & vncerteyn thanne haue ye noon oother remedie but for to hanne youre recours vn to the souereyn Juge þt vengeth alle vileynyes & wronges and he shal venge yow after that hym self witnesseth wher as he seith Leueth the vengeance to me and I shal do it Melibe answerde If I ne venge me nat of the vileynye þt men han doon to me I somne or warne hem þt han doon to me that vileynye & alle othere to do me another vileynye for it is writen If thow take no vengeance of an old vileynye thow somnest thyne aduersaries to do thee a newe vileynye And also for my suffrance men wolden do me so muchil vileynye þt I myghte neither bere it ne sustene and so sholde I been put & holden ouer lowe ffor men seyn In muchil suffrynge shul manye thynges falle vn to thee whiche yow shalt nat mowe suffre Certes quod Prudence I graunte yow þt ouer muchil suffrance is nat good but yet ne folweth it nat ther of þt euery persone to whom men don vileynye take of it vengeance for that aperteneth & longeth al oonly to the Juges for they shul venge the vileynyes & iniuries And therfore tho two auctoritees þt ye han seyd aboue been oonly oonly vnderstonden in the Juges

for whan they suffren ouer muchil the wronges & vileynyes to be doon
wt outen punysshynge / they somne nat a man al oonly for to
do newe wronges but they comanden it ¶ Also a wys man seith
That the iuge þt correcteth nat the synnere / comandeth & biddeth
hym do synne / And the iuges & souereyns myghten in hir land
so muchil suffre of the shrewes & mysdoerys þt they sholden
by swich suffrance by proces of tyme wexen of swich power
& myght þt they sholden putte out the iuges & the soueryns from
hir places & at the laste maken hem lese hir lordshipes ¶ But
lat vs now putte þt ye haue leue to venge yow / I seye ye be
nat of myght & power as now to venge yow / for if ye wol
maken comparison vn to the myght of youre aduersaries : ye
shul fynde in manye thynges þt I haue shewid yow er this
þt hir condicion is bettre than youres / And therfore seye I
þt it is good as now þt ye suffre & be pacient / ¶ fforther
moore ye knowen wel that after the co[m]e sawe / it is a wood
nesse a man to stryue wt a strenger or a moore myghty man
than he is hym self / & for to stryue wt a man of euene streng
the that is to seyn / with as strong a man as he is / it is pil
and for to stryue wt a wayker man / it is folye / and therfore
sholde a man flee stryuynge as muchil as he myghte / ffor Salo
mon seith / It is a greet worship to a man / to kepen hym fro
noyse & stryf / and if it so bifalle or happe þt a man of gretter
myght & strengthe than thow art / do thee greuance : studie &
bisie thee rather to stille the same greuance / than for to ven
ge thee / ffor Senek seith / That he putteth hym in greet pil þt
stryueth wt a gretter man than he is hym self / and Caton
seith / If a man of hyer estaat or degree or moore myghty
than thow do thee anoy or greuance : suffre hym / for he þt ones
hath greued thee may another tyme releue thee & helpe /
¶ yet sette I cas / ye haue bothe myght & licence for to venge yow :
I seye þt ther be ful manye thynges þt shul restreyne yow
of vengeance takynge & make yow for to enclyne to suffre
& for to han pacience in the wronges þt han been doon to
yow ¶ ffirst & foreward / If ye wol considere the defautes þt
been in youre owene persone / for whiche defautes god hath
suffred yow haue this tribulacion as I haue seyd yow
her biforn / ffor the poete seith / That we oghten paciently
taken the tribulacions þt comen to vs / whan þt we thyn
ken & consideren þt we han disserued to haue hem / and

it is madnes to
strive wth a
mightier then
thy selfe .....
wth the equall
dangerous and wth
the inferiour
follie .

for whan they suffren ou*er* muchil / the wronges *and* vileynyes to be doon w*ith* outen punysshynge ./ they somne nat a man al oonly / for to do newe wronges / but they comanden it [2662] ¶Also / a wys man seith / That the Iuge / þat correcteth nat the synnere ./ comandeth *and* biddeth hym do synne // And the Iuges *and* souereyns / myghten in hir land so muchil suffre of the shrewes *and* mysdoerys / þat they sholden by swich suffrance by p*ro*ces of tyme / wexen of swich power *and* myght þat they sholden putte out the Iuges *and* the sou*er*eyns / from hir places / *and* at the laste / maken hem lese hir lordshipes ¶But lat vs now putte / þat ye haue leue to venge yow / [2667] I seye / ye be nat of myght *and* power / as now to venge yow / for if ye wol maken comparison / vn to the myght of youre Adu*er*saries ./ ye shul fynde in manye thynges þat I haue shewid yow er this þat hir condiciou*n* / is bettre than youres / and therfore seye I / þat it is good as now / þat ye suffre *and* be pacient ¶Forther moore / ye knowen wel / that after the co*mun*e sawe ./ it is a woodnesse / a man to stryue w*ith* a strenger / or a moore myghty man / than he is hym self / *and* for to stryue / w*ith* a man / of euene strengthe / that is to seyn / with as strong a man as he is ./ it is p*er*il / [2672] and for to stryue w*ith* a wayker man / it is folye // and therfore / sholde a man fle stryuynge / as muchil as he myghte // For Salomon seith // It is a greet worship*e* to a man / to kepen hym fro noyse *and* stryf // And if it so bifalle / or happe / þat a man of gretter myght *and* strengthe / than thow art do thee greuance ./ Studie *and* bisie thee rather / to stille the same greuance / than for to venge thee [2677] // For Senek seith / That he putteth hym in greet p*er*il / þat stryueth w*ith* a gretter man / than he is hym self // And Catou*n* seith // If a man / of hyer estaat or degree / or moore myghty than thow / do thee anoy / or greuance ./ suffre hym / for he þat ones hath greued thee / may another tyme / releue thee *and* helpe

¶Yet sette I cas / ye haue bothe myght / *and* licence for to venge yow ./ I seye / þat ther be ful manye thynges / þat shul restreyne yow / of vengeance takynge / [2682] *and* make yow / for to enclyne to suffre *and* for to han pacience / in the wronges / þat han been doon to yow ¶First *and* foreward / If ye wol considere the defautes / þat been in youre owene p*er*sone ./ for whiche defautes / god hath suffred yow haue this tribulaciou*n* / as I haue seyd yow her biforn // For the Poete seith / That we oghten paciently taken / the tribulacions þat comen to vs / whan þat we thynken *and* consideren / þat we han disserued to haue hem // And

924-28 in another hand: it is madness to strive with a mightier than they selffe, with they equall perilous, and with they inferior follie. Hg (2671-72)

./ Chaucer of Melibeus ./

Seint Gregorie seith / That whan a man / considereth wel / the nombre of his defautes and of his synnes ./ [2687] the peynes *and* the tribulaciou*n*s þ*at* he suffreth / semen the lesse vn to hym / And in as muche as hym thynketh / his synnes / moore heuy *and* greuous ./ in so muche / semeth his peyne the lighter and the esier vn to hym ¶Also / ye owen / to enclyne *and* bowe youre herte / to take the pacience / of our lord Ie*s*u crist⁊. as seith Seint Peter / in hise Epistles ⁊ Ie*s*u crist he seith / hath suffred for vs / *and* yeuen ensample to eu*er*y man / to folwe *and* sewe hym / [2692] for he dide neu*er*e synne / ne neu*er*e cam ther a vileynous word / out of his mouth / Whan men cursed hym / he cursed hem noght⁊ And whan men betten hym / he manaced hem noght⁊ ¶Also / the grete pacience / which Seintes / þ*at* been in Paradys / han had / in tribulacions þ*at* they han ysuffred / w*ith* outen hir desert⁊ or gilt⁊ oghte muchil stire yow to pacience ¶Forther moore / ye sholde enforce yow to haue pacience / [2697] considerynge / þ*at* the tribulacions of this world / but litel while endure / *and* soone passed been *and* goon / And the ioye þ*at* a man seketh to haue by pacience in tribulaciou*n*s ./ is p*er*durable / after that⁊ the Apostle seith / in his Epistle / The ioye of god he seith / is p*er*durable / that is to seyn / eu*er*e lastynge ¶Also / troweth *and* bileueth stedefastly / þ*at* he nys noght wel ynorisshed ne wel ytaught⁊ þ*at* kan nat haue pacience / or wol nat receyue pacience ⁊ For Salomon seith ⁊ That the doctrine *and* the wit of a man / is knowen by pacience [2702] ⁊ And in another place he seith / That he þ*at* is pacient⁊ gou*er*neth hym by greet prudence ⁊ And the same Salomon seith ⁊ The angry *and* wrathful man / maketh noyses / And the pacient man / attempreth hem *and* stilleth ⁊ he seith also ⁊ It is moore worth to be pacient⁊ than for to be right strong⁊ And he þ*at* may haue the lordshipe of his owene herte ./ is moore to preyse / than he þ*at* by his force / or strengthe / taketh grete Citees ⁊ And ther fore / seith Seint Iame in his Epistle / That pacience / is a greet v*er*tu of p*er*feccioun [2707] ¶Certes quod Melibe / I graunte yow / dame Prudence / þ*at* Pacience / is a greet v*er*tu of p*er*feccioun / but euery man / may nat haue the p*er*feccioun / þ*at* ye seken / ne I nam nat of the no*m*bre / of right p*ar*fite men / for myn herte / may neuere be in pees / vn to the tyme / it be vengid ⁊ And al be it so / þ*at* it was greet p*er*il to myne enemys / to do me a vileynye / in takynge vengeance vp on me ./ [2712]

Seint Gregorie seith / That whan a man considereth wel the
noumbre of his defautes and of his synnes: the peynes &
the tribulacions þt he suffreth / semen the lesse vn to hym /
And in as muche as hym thynketh his synnes / moore heuy & greuous / in so muche / semeth his peyne the lighter
and the esier vn to hym ¶ Also / ye owen to enclyne & bowe
youre herte / to take the pacience / of oure lord Ihu crist / as
seith Seint Peter in hise Epistles / Ihu crist he seith / hath
suffred for vs / & yeuen ensample to euery man / to folwe &
sewe hym / for he dide neuere synne / ne neuere cam ther a vi
leynous word / out of his mouth / whan men cursed hym /
he cursed hem noght / and whan men betten hym / he mana
ced hem noght / ¶ Also / the grete pacience which Seintes þt
been in Paradys / han had / in tribulacions þt they han y
suffred / wt outen hir desert / or gilt / oghte muchel stire yow
to pacience ¶ fferther moore / ye sholde enforce yow to haue
pacience / considerynge þt the tribulacions of this world but
litel while endure / & soone passed been & goon / and the ioye
þt a man seketh to haue by pacience in tribulacions / is p̃du
rable / after that the Apostle seith / in his Epistle / The ioye of
god he seith / is p̃durable / that is to seyn / eue lastynge ¶ Al
so troweth & bileueth stedefastly / þt he nys noght wel ynou
rissed ne wel ytaught / þt kan nat haue pacience / or wol
nat receyue pacience / ffor Salomon seith / That the doctrine
& the wit of a man is knowen by pacience / And in another
place he seith / That he þt is pacient / gouerneth hym by greet
prudence / And the same Salomon seith / The angry &
wrathful man / maketh noyses / and the pacient man / at
tempreth hem & stilleth / he seith also / It is moore worth
to be pacient / than for to be right strong / And he þt may ha
ue the lordshipe of his owene herte / is moore to preyse /
than he þt by his force / or strengthe / taketh grete Citees / And
ther fore / seith Seint Iame in his Epistle / That pacience is
a greet vertu of p̃feccion ¶ Certes quod Melibe / I graunte
yow / dame Prudence / þt Pacience / is a greet vertu of p̃fec
cion / but euery man / may nat haue the p̃feccion / þt ye se
ken / ne I nam nat of the nombre / of right p̃fite men / for
myn herte / may neuere be in pees / vn to the tyme / it be
venged / And al be it so / þt it was greet pil to myne ene
mys / to do me a vileynye / in takynge vengeance vp on me:

mj

yet token they noon hede of the peril / but fulfilden hir wikked
wyl & hir corage / And therfore me thynketh men oghten nat
repreve me though I putte me in a litel peril for to venge me / &
though I do a greet excesse that is to seyn þt I venge oon outra
ge by another // A quod dame Prudence ye seyn youre wil
& as yow liketh / But in no caas of the world a man shol
de nat do outrage ne excesse for to vengen hym / ffor Cassi
dore seith / That as yvele doth he þt vengeth hym by outra
ge as he þt doth the outrage / And therfore ye shul venge
yow after the ordre of right that is to seyn by the lawe
and nat by excesse ne by outrage / And also if ye wol ven
ge yow of the outrage of youre adversaries in oother manere
than right comandeth ye synnen / And therfore seith Se
nek / That a man shal nevere venge shrewednesse by shre
wednesse / And if ye seye þt right axeth a man to defen
de violence by violence and fightynge by fightynge
Certes ye seye sooth whan the defense is doon anon wt
outen intervalle or wt outen taryynge or delay for to defen
den hym & nat for to vengen hym / And it bihoveth þt
a man putte swich attemperance in his defense þt men
have no cause ne matere to repreven hym þt defendeth
hym of excesse & outrage / Pardee ye knowe wel þt ye
maken no defense as now for to defende yow but for to
venge yow / and so seweth it þt ye han no wyl to do
youre dede attemprely and therfore me thynketh that
pacience is good / ffor Salomon seith / That he þt is nat
pacient shal have greet harm ¶ Certes quod Melibe I
graunte yow þt whan a man is inpacient & wrooth of
that þt toucheth hym nat and þt apperteneth nat un to hym
though it harme hym it is no wonder / ffor the lawe seith
That he is coupable þt entremetteth hym or medleth wt
swich thyng as apertenet nat un to hym ¶ And Salomon
seith That he þt entremeteth of the noyse or stryf of
another man is lyk to hym þt taketh an hound by
the erys for right as he that taketh a straunge hound by
the erys is outher while biten wt the hound right in
the same wise is it reson þt he have harm þt by hys
inpacience medleth hym of the noyse of another man
wher as it aperteneth nat un to hym / But ye knowe
wel þt this dede that is to seyn my grief & my disese

yet token they noon hede of the p*er*il / but fulfilden / hir wikked wyl *and* hir corage ⸍ And therfore me thynketh / men oghten nat repreue me / thogh I putte me in a litel p*er*il / for to venge me / *and* thogh I do a greet excesse / that is to seyn / þat I venge / oon out*ra*ge by another // A. quod dame Prudence / ye seyn youre wil *and* as yow liketh ⸍ But in no caas of the world / a man sholde nat do out*ra*ge ne excesse / for to vengen hym [2717] ⸍ For Cassidore seith ⸍ That as yuele / dooth he þat vengeth hym by out*ra*ge / as he / þat dooth the out*ra*ge ⸍ And ther fore / ye shul venge yow / after the ordre of right ⸍ that is to seyn / by the lawe / and nat by excesse / ne by out*ra*ge ⸍ And also / if ye wol venge yow / of the out*ra*ge of youre Adu*er*saries in oother man*er*e than right' comandeth ∫ ye synnen ⸍ And therfore seith Senek ⸍ That a man shal neu*er*e venge / shrewednesse / by shrewednesse / And if ye seye / þat right axeth a man / to defende violence by violence / and fightynge by fightynge ∫ [2722] Certes / ye seye sooth / whan the defense / is doon anon / w*ith* outen int*er*ualle / or w*ith* outen taryynge / or delay / for to defenden hym / *and* nat for to vengen hym ⸍ And it bihoueth / þat a man putte swich attemp*er*ance in his defense / þat men / haue no cause / ne matere / to repreuen hym þat defendeth hym / of excesse *and* outrage ⸍ Pardee ye knowe wel / þat ye maken no defense as now / for to defende yow / but for to venge yow / [2727] and so seweth it' þat ye han no wyl / to do youre dede attemprely / and therfore / me thynketh / that pacience is good ⸍ For Salomon seith ⸍ That he / þat is nat pacient' shal haue greet harm ¶Certes quod Melibe / .I. graunte yow / þat whan a man / is inpacient' *and* wrooth / of that' þat toucheth hym nat' and þat ap*er*teneth nat vn to hym / thogh it harme hym / it is no wonder ⸍ For the lawe seith / That he is coupable / þat entremetteth hym / or medleth / w*ith* swich thyng' as ap*er*tenet nat vn to hym ¶And Salamo*n* seith / That he þat entremeteth of the noyse / or stryf / of another man ∫ is lyk to hym / þat taketh an hound by the erys / [2732] for right as he / that taketh a straunge hound by the erys / is outherwhile / biten w*ith* the hound ∫ right in the same wise is it resou*n* / þat he haue harm / þat by hys inpacience medleth hym / of the noyse / of another man / wher*e* / as it ap*er*teneth nat vn to hym ⸍ But ye knowe wel þat this dede / that is to seyn / my grief *and* my desese toucheth me right ny / And therfore / thogh I be wrooth / and inpacient it is no m*er*uaille / and sauynge youre *gra*ce / I kan nat se / þat it myghte greetly harme me / thogh I tooke vengeance / [2737] for I am richer*e and* moore myghty / than myne enemys been / and wel knowen ye / þat by moneye *and* by hauynge grete possessions / been alle the thynges of this world gouerned // And Salomon seith // That alle thynges / obeyen to moneye ¶Whanne Prudence / hadde herd hir housbonde auanten hym / of his richesse *and* of his moneye dispreisynge / the power of his Adu*er*saries ./ she spak *and* seyde in this wise // Certes deere sire / I graunte yow / þat ye been / riche *and* myghty / [2742] *and* þat the richesses been goode / to hem / þat han wel ygeten hem / *and* þat wel konne vsen hem // For right as the body of a man / may nat lyue w*ith* oute the soule ./ namoore may it lyue / with oute the temporel goodes / and by richesses / may a man gete hym grete // ¶And therfore / seith Pamphilles // If Anetherdes doghter / he seith / be riche ./ she may chese / of a thousand men / which she wol take to hir housbonde // for of a thousand men ./ oon wol nat forsaken hir*e* / ne refusen hir*e* [2747] // And this Pamphilles seith also // If thow be right happy / that is to seyn / If thow be right riche ./ thow shalt fynde / a greet nombre of felawes *and* freendes / and if thy fortune chaunge / that thow wexe poore ./ farwel freendshipe *and* felaweshipe / for thow shalt been / al allone / with outen any compaignye / but if it be / the compaignye of poore folk ¶And yet seith this Pamphilles moore ouer // That they þat been / thralle *and* bonde of lynage / shuln be maad / worthy and noble by the richesses / and right so as by richesses / ther comen manye goodes ./ right so by pou*er*te / come ther manye harmes *and* yueles [2752] // for greet pouerte / constreyneth a man / to do manye yueles // And therfore clepeth Cassidore / pou*er*te / the moder of Ruyne / that is to seyn / the moder of ou*er*throwynge / or fallynge down ¶And therfore / seiþ Piers Alfonce // Oon of the gretteste Adu*er*sitees of this world / is / whan a free man by kynde / or of burthe / is constreyned by pou*er*te / to eten / the almesse of his enemy [2757] // And the same seith Innocent in oon of his bookes // he seith / That sorweful *and* myshappy / is the condiciou*n* of a poore beggere / for if he axe nat his mete ./ he dyeth for hungir /

toucheth me right ny / and ther fore thogh I be wrooth and
inpacient / it is no merueille / And sauynge youre grace I kan
nat se / þt it myghte greetly harme me / though I took ven
geance / for I am richer & moore myghty / than myne ene
mys been / and wel knowen ye / þt by moneye & by hauyn
ge grete possessiouns / been alle the thynges of this world
gouerned / And Salomon seith / That alle thynges obey
en to moneye ¶ Whanne Prudence hadde herd hir hous
bonde auanten hym / of his richesse & of his moneye
dispreisynge the power of his aduersaries / she spak &
seyde in this wise / Certes deere sire / I graunte yow
þt ye been riche & myghty / & þt the richesses been goode
to hem þt han wel ygeten hem / & þt wel konne usen
hem / ffor right as the body of a man / may nat lyue wt
oute the soule / namoore may it lyue with oute the tem
poreel goodes / and by richesses / may a man gete hym grete /
¶ And ther fore seith Pamphilles / If a netherdes doghter
he seith be riche / she may chese of a thousand men which
she wol take to hir housbonde / for of a thousand men oon
wol nat forsaken hire ne refusen hire / And this Pam
philles seith also / If thow be right happy / that is to seyn
If thow be right riche / thow shalt fynde a greet nombre
of felawes & freendes / and if thy fortune change / that
thow wexe poure / farwel freendshipe & felaweshipe /
for thow shalt been / al allone with outen any compaig
nye but if it be / the compaignye of poure folk ¶ And yet
seith this Pamphilles moore ouer / That they þt been
thralle & bonde of lynage / shuln be maad worthy and
noble by the richesses / and right so as by richesses ther
comen manye goodes / right so by pouerte come ther ma
nye harmes & yueles / for greet pouerte constreyneth a
man to do manye yueles / and ther fore clepeth Cassidore
pouerte / the mooder of ruyne / that is to seyn / the mooder of
outhrowynge / or fallynge doun ¶ And ther fore seith Piers
Alfonce / Oon of the grettest aduersitees of this world is
whan a free man by kynde / or of birthe / is constreyned
by pouerte to eten the almesse of his enemy / And the
same seith Innocent / in oon of his bookes / he seith that
sorweful & myshappy / is the condicioun of a poure beg
gere / for if he axe nat his mete / he dyeth for hunger /

And if he axe he dyeth for shame / And algates necessitee constreyneth
hym to axe / And ther fore seith Salomon / That bettre is to dye
than for to haue swich pouerte / And as the same Salomon seith
Bettre it is to dye of bitter deeth / than for to lyuen in swich
wise ¶ By thise resons þt I haue seyd vn to yow / and by ma
nye othere resons þt I koude seye / I graunte yow þt riches
ses been goode to hem þt geten hem wel / and to hem þt wel
vsen tho richesses / And ther fore wol I shewe yow / how ye
shul haue yow and how ye shul bere yow in gaderynge of
richesses / and in what manere ye shul vsen hem ¶ ffirst / ye
shul geten hem wt outen greet desir by good leyser sekyngly
and nat ouer hastily : ffor a man þt is to desirynge to geten
richesses / abandoneth hym first to thefte & to alle othere yue
les / And ther fore seith Salomon / he þt hasteth hym to bisi
ly to wexe riche / shal be noon Innocent / he seith also / that
the richesse þt hastily cometh to a man / soone & lightly gooth
and passeth from a man / But that richesse þt cometh litel &
litel / wexeth alwey & multiplieth / And sire / ye shullen gete
richesses by youre wit & by youre trauaille vn to youre ꝓfit /
and that with outen wrong or harm doynge to any other
ꝑsone / ffor the lawe seith / that ther maketh no man hym
self riche / if he do harm to another wight / this is to seyn
that nature defendeth & forbedeth by right / þt no man make
hym self riche vn to the harm of another ꝑsone ¶ And Tul
lius seith / that no sorwe ne no drede of deeth / ne no thyng
þt may falle vn to a man is so muchel agayns nature / as a
man to encresse his owene ꝓfit / to the harm of another man /
And though the grete men and the myghty men geten richesses
moore lightly than thow / yet shaltow nat be ydel ne slow /
to do thy ꝓfit / for thow shalt in alle wise fle ydelnesse / ffor
Salomon seith / that ydelnesse techeth a man to do manye yue
les / And the same Salomon seith / that he þt trauailleth & bisieth
hym to tilien his lond / shal ete breed / but þt is ydel and
casteth hym to no bisynesse ne ocupacion / shal falle in to po
uerte and dye for hunger / And he þt is ydel & slow / kan ne
uere fynde couenable tyme for to do his ꝓfit / ffor ther is a
versifiour seith / that the ydel man excuseth hym in wynter /
by cause of the grete coold / and in somer / by enchesoun of
the hete / ffor thise causes seith Caton / waketh and encli
neth yow nat ouer muchel for to slepe / for ouer muchel

And if he axe / he dyeth for shame / and algates / necessitee constreyneþ hym to axe // And therfore seith Salomon // That bettre is to dye / than for to haue swich pou*er*te // And as the same Salomon seith / Bettre it is / to dye of bitter deeth / than for to lyuen in swich wise ¶By thise resons / þ*a*t I haue seyd vn to yow / and by manye othere resons / þ*a*t I koude seye / I graunte yow / þ*a*t richesses been goode / to hem þ*a*t geten hem wel / and to hem / þ*a*t wel vsen tho richesses // And ther fore wol I shewe yow / how ye shul haue yow / and how ye shul bere yow in gaderynge of richesses / and in what manere ye shul vsen hem ¶First ye shul geten hem / *with* outen greet desir by good leiser sekyngly and nat ouer hastily ./ For a man þ*a*t is to desirynge to geten richesses / abandoneth hym first to thefte / *and* to alle othere yueles // And therfore seith Salomon // he þ*a*t hasteth hym to bisily to wexe riche / shal be noon Innocent // he seith also / that the richesse / þ*a*t hastily cometh to a man ./ soone *and* lightly / gooth and passeth from a man // But that richesse / þ*a*t cometh litel *and* litel / wexeth alwey *and* multiplieth // And sire / ye shullen gete richesses / by youre wit *and* by youre t*ra*uaille vn to youre p*ro*fit / and that with outen wrong or harm doynge / to any oother p*er*sone // For the lawe seith // that ther maketh no man hym self riche ./ if he do harm / to another wight // this is to seyn / that nature defendeth *and* forbedeth by right þ*a*t no man make hym self riche / vn to the harm of another p*er*sone ¶And Tullius seith / that no sorwe / ne no drede of deeth / ne no thyng þ*a*t may falle vn to a man / is so muchel ageyns nature / as a man / to encresse his owene p*ro*fit to the harm of another man ./ / And thogh the grete men and the myghty men geten richesses moore lightly than thow ./ yet shaltow nat be ydel ne slow / to do thy p*ro*fit for thow shalt in alle wise / fle ydelnesse // For Salomon seith // that ydelnesse techeth a man to do manye yueles // And the same Salomon seith // that he þ*a*t t*ra*uaileth *and* bisieþ hym / to tilien his lond ./ shal ete breed / but þ*a*t is ydel and casteth hym to no bisynesse ne ocupaciou*n* / shal falle in to pouerte and dye for hunger / And he þ*a*t is ydel *and* slow ./ kan neuere fynde couenable tyme / for to do his p*ro*fit // For ther is a v*er*sifiour seith // that the ydel man excuseth hym in wynter / by cause of the grete coold / and in somer / by encheson of the hete // For thise causes seith Caton // waketh / and enclineth yow nat ouer mychel / for to slepe // for ouer mychel reste / norissheth and causeth manye vices // And therfore / seith Seint Ierome ¶Dooth so*mm*e goode dedes / þat the deuel / which is oure enemy / ne fynde yow nat vnocupied / for the deuel / ne takeþ nat lightly / vn to his werkynge / swiche as he fyndeth ocupied in goode werkes ¶Thanne thus / In getynge richesses / ye mosten fle ydelnesse / [2787] and afterward ye shul vse the richesses whiche ye haue geten / by your*e* wit and by youre t*ra*uaille / in swich / a manere / þat men holde yow nat to scars / ne to sparynge / ne to fool large / that is to seyn / ouer large a Spender*e* // For right as men blamen an Auarous man / by cause of his scarsitee *and* chyncherie ʃ in the same wise is he to blame / þat spendeth ouer largely / and therfore seith Catou*n* // Vse he seith thy richesses / þat thow hast ygeten / [2792] in swich a manere / þat men haue no matere ne cause / to calle thee / neither wrecche ne chynche / for it is greet shame to a man / to haue a poore herte and a riche purs // he seith also / the goodes þat thow hast ygeten / vse hem by mesure / that is to seyn / Spende mensurably / for they / þat folily wasten and despenden / the goodes þat they han ʃ whan they han namoore p*ro*pre of hir owene ʃ they shapen hem / to take the goodes of another man [2797] // I seye thanne / that ye shal fle Auarice / vsynge youre richesses in swich manere / þat men seye nat þat youre richesses been ybiryed / but þat ye haue hem in youre myght and in youre weldynge // For a wys man / repreueth the Auaricious man *and* seith thus / in two vers // Wherto and why / biryeth a man his goodes by his grete Auarice / and knoweth wel / þat nedes moste he dye [2802] for deeth / is the ende of euery man / as in this p*re*sent lyf / And for what cause / or encheson / ioyneth he hym / or knytteth he hym / so faste vn to his goodes / þat alle hise wittes / mowen nat disseueren hym / or departen hym fro hise goodes / and knoweth wel / or oghte knowe / þat whan he is deed / he shal no thyng bere w*ith* hym out of this world // And therfore / seith Seint Austyn // That the Auaricious man / is likned vn to helle / [2807] þat the moore it swolweth / the moore desir it hath to swolwe *and* deuoure / And as wel / as ye wolde eschewe to be called an Auaricious man or chynche ʃ as wel sholde ye kepe yow *and* gou*er*ne yow in swich a wise / þat men calle yow nat fool large // Ther fore seith Tullius // The goodes he seith of thyn hous / sholde nat been hidde ne kept so cloos ʃ but þat they myghte been opned by pitee *and* debonairetee / that is to seyn ʃ

reste, norissheth and causeth manye vices / And ther-fore seith
Seint Jerome ¶ Dooth somme goode dedes, þt the deuel, which is ou
re enemy, ne fynde yow nat vnocupied / for the deuel, ne takeþ
nat lightly vn to his werkynge, swiche as he fyndeth ocupied
in goode werkes ¶ Thanne thus, In getynge richesses / ye mos
ten flee ydelnesse / and afterward ye shul vse the richesses whiche
ye haue geten by youre wit and by youre trauaille, in swich a
manere, þt men holde yow nat to scars, no to sparynge, ne
to fool large, that is to seyn, ouer-large a spender / ffor
right as men blamen an Auarous man by cause of his scar
sitee & chyncherye, in the same wise is he to blame þt spen
deth ouer largely / And therfore seith Caton / vse he seith thy
richesses þt thow hast ygeten, in swich a manere, þt men haue
no matere ne cause, to calle thee neither wrecche ne chynche /
for it is greet shame to a man, to haue a poore herte and a
riche purs / he seith also, the goodes þt thow hast ygeten vse
hem by mesure, that is to seyn, spende mesurably / for they
þt folily wasten and despenden the goodes þt they han, whan
they han namoore propre of hir owene, they shapen hem, to
take the goodes of another man / I seye thanne, that ye shul
flee Auarice / vsynge youre richesses in swich manere, þt men
seye nat, þt youre richesses been yburyed, but þt ye haue
hem in youre myght, and in youre weldynge / ffor a wys
man repreueth the Auaricious man & seith thus, in two
vers / wher-to and why, burieth a man his goodes by his
grete Auarice, and knoweth wel, þt nedes moste he dye-
for deeth is the ende of every man, as in this present lyf / And
for what cause, or encheson, ioyneth he hym, or knytteth he
hym, so faste vn to his goodes, þt alle hise wittes mowen-
nat disseueren hym, or departen hym fro hise goodes / and-
knoweth wel, or oghte knowe, þt whan he is deed he shal no
thing bere wt hym out of this world / And therfore seith
Seint Austyn / that the Auaricious man, is likned vn to-
helle, þt the moore it swolweth the moore desir it hath to
swolwe & deuoure / And as wel, as ye wolde eschewe to be
called an Auaricious man or chynche, as wel sholde ye kepe
yow & gouerne yow in swich a wise, þt men calle yow nat
fool large / Ther fore seith Tullius / The goodes he seith of
thyn hous, sholde nat been hidde ne kept so cloos, but þt they
myghte been opned by pitee & debonairetee, that is to seyn-

to yeue hem part / þt han greet nede / ne thy goodes sholden nat
be so open / to be euery mannes goodes ¶ Afterward in getyng
of youre richesses and in vsynge hem / ye shul alwey / haue
thre thynges in youre herte / that is to seyn / oure lord god /
Conscience / and good name ¶ ffirst / ye shul haue god in
youre herte / and for no richesse / ye shullen do no thyng which
may in any manere displese god / that is youre Creatour
& makere / ffor after the word of Salomon / it is bettre to haue
a litel good with the loue of god / than to haue mychel good &
tresor / and lese the loue of his lord god / And the prophete seith
that bettre it is to been a good man / & haue a litel good and
tresor / than to be holden a shrewe / & haue grete richesses / and
yet seye I ferther moore / that ye sholden alwey doon youre
bisynesse / to gete yow richesses / so þt ye gete hem / with good
conscience / And thapostle seith / that ther nys thyng in this
world / of which we sholden haue so greet ioye / as whan
oure conscience / bereth vs good witnesse / And the wise man
seith / The substance of a man / is ful good / whan synne is
nat in mannes conscience ¶ Afterward / in getynge of youre
richesses / & in vsynge of hem / yow moste haue greet bisy
nesse & greet diligence / þt youre goode name / be alwey kept
& conserued / ffor Salomon seith / that bettre it is & moore
it auaileth a man / to haue good name / than for to haue grete
richesses / And therfore he seith in another place / Do greet
diligence seith Salomon in kepynge of thy freend / and of
thy goode name / for it shal lenger abyde with thee than
any tresor / be it neuere so precious / And certes / he sholde nat be
called a gentil man / that after god & good conscience / alle
thynges left / ne dooth his diligence & bisynesse / to kepen
his goode name / And Cassidore seith / that it is signe of a
gentil herte / whan a man loueth & desireth / to haue a good
name / And therfore seith Seint Austyn / that ther been
two thynges þt arn necessarie & nedefulle / and that is good
conscience & good loos / that is to seyn / good conscience / to
thyn owene persone inward / and good loos for thy neighebore
outward / And he þt trusteth hym so muchel in his goode
conscience / þt he displeseth / and setteth at noght / his goode
name or loos / and rekketh noght though he kepe nat his
goode name / nys but a cruwel cherl ¶ Sire now haue
I shewed yow / how ye shul do / in getynge richesses / & how

to yeue hem part þ*at* han greet nede / ne thy goodes sholden nat be so open / to be euery mannes goodes ¶Afterward / in getyng of youre richesses / and in vsynge hem // ye shul alwey / haue thre thynges in youre herte ∥ that is to seyn / oure lord god / Conscience / and good name ¶First ye shul haue god in youre herte / and for no richesse / ye shullen do no thyng which may in any manere displese god / that is youre Creatour *and* makere ∥ For after the word of Salomon / It is bettre to haue alitel good / w*ith* the loue of god // than to haue mychel good *and* tresor / and lese the loue of his lord god ∥ And the p*ro*phete seith // That bettre it is to been a good man / *and* haue alitel good / and tresor // than to be holden a shrewe / *and* haue grete richesses ∥ And yet seye I ferther moore / that ye sholden alwey doon youre bisynesse / to gete yow richesses / so þ*at* ye gete hem / with good conscience ∥ And thapostle seith / that ther nys thyng in this world / of which / we sholden haue so greet ioye / as whan oure conscience / bereth vs good witnesse ∥ And the wise man seith ∥ The substance of a man / is ful good / whan synne is nat in mannes conscience ¶Afterward / in getynge of youre richesses / *and* in vsynge of hem // yow moste haue greet bisy-nesse *and* greet diligence / þ*at* youre good name / be alwey kept *and* conserued ∥ For Salomon seith ∥ that bettre it is *and* moore it auaileth a man / to haue good name / than for to haue grete richesses / And therfore / he seith in another place ∥ do greet diligence seith Salomon in kepynge of thy freend / and of thy goode name / for it shal lenger abyde with thee / than any tresor / be it neu*er* so p*re*cious ∥ And c*er*tes / he sholde nat be called a gentil man / that after god *and* good conscience / alle thynges left ne dooth his diligence *and* bisynesse / to kepen his goode name ∥ And Cassidore seith / that it is signe of a gentil herte / whan a man / loueth *and* desireth / to haue a good name ∥ And therfore / seith seint Austyn ∥ that ther been two thynges / þ*at* arn necessarie *and* nedefulle / and that is good conscience / *and* good loos ∥ that is to seyn / good conscience / to thyn owene p*er*sone inward / and good loos for thy neighebore outward ∥ And he / þ*at* trusteth hym so muchil in his goode conscience / þ*at* he displeseth / and setteth at noght his goode name or loos / and rekketh noght thogh he kepe nat hys goode name // nys but a cruwel cherl ¶Sire / now haue I shewed yow / how ye shul do / in getynge richesses / *and* how ye shullen vsen hem / And I se wel / þ*at* for the trust⁊ þ*at* ye han in youre richesses / ye wol moeue werre *and* bataille /. I consei-le yow / þ*at* ye bigynne no werre / in trust of youre richesses / for they ne suffisen noght⁊ werres to mayntene / And ther-fore seith a Philosophre / That man þ*at* desireth / and wole algates han werre ʃ shal neu*ere* haue suffisance / for the richer þ*at* he is ʃ the gretter despenses moste he make / if he wol haue worship*e* *and* victorie ⁋ And Salomon seith / That the gretter richesses þ*at* a man hath / the mo despendours he hath ⁋ And deere sire / al be it so / þ*at* for youre richesses / ye mowe haue muchel folk ʃ yet bihoueth it nat⁊ ne it is nat good / to bigynne werre / wher*e* as ye mowe / in oother man*ere* haue pees vn to youre worship*e* *and* p*ro*fit ⁋ for the victorie of bataill*es* þ*at* been in this world / lyth nat⁊ in greet nombre / huc or multitude of peple / ne in the vertu of man / but it lyth in the wyl / *and* in the hand / of oure lord god almyghty / and ther fore Iudas Machabeus / which was goddes knyght⁊ whan he sholde fighte ageyn his Aduersarie / þ*at* hadde a gretter nombre *and* a gretter multitude of folk⁊ and strenger than was the peple / of this Machabe ʃ yet he reconforted his litel compaignye / and seyde / right in this wise ⁋ Als lightly quod he / may oure lord god almyghty / yeue victorie to fewe folk⁊ as to manye folk⁊ for the victorie of a batai-le / cometh nat⁊ by the grete nombre of peple / but it come / fro oure lord god of heuene ⁋ And deere sire / for as muchel as ther is no man certeyn / if it be worthy / þ*at* god yeue hym victorie / or naght⁊ after that Salomon seith ʃ ther fore eu*er*y man / sholde greetly drede / werres to bigynne ⁋ And by cause þ*at* in batailles / fallen manye p*er*ils / *and* happeth outher while / þ*at* as soone is the grete man slayn / as the litel man / And as it is ywriten / in the seconde book of kynges ⁋ The dedes of batailles / been Auenturouse *and* no thyng c*er*teyne / for as lightly / is oon hurt w*ith* a spere / as another ¶And for ther is greet p*er*il in werre ʃ therfore shol-de a man / fle *and* eschewe werre / in as muchel / as a man may goodly ⁋ For Salomon seith / he þ*at* loueth p*er*il / shal falle in peril ¶After þ*at* Dame Prudence / hadde spoken in this manere / Melibe / answerde *and* seyde ¶I se wel Da-me Prudence / that by youre faire wordes *and* by youre re-sons / þ*at* ye han shewed me ʃ þ*at* the werre / liketh yow no

ye shullen vsen hem / And I se wel þt for the trust þt ye han
in youre richesses / ye wol moeve werre & bataille / I consei
le yow þt ye bigynne no werre in trust of youre richesses
for they ne suffisen noght / werres to mayntene / And ther
fore seith a philosophre That man þt desireth and wole
algates han werre / shal neuere haue suffisance / for the
richer þt he is / the gretter despenses moste he make / if he
wol haue worship & victorie / And Salomon seith / that
the gretter richesses þt a man hath / the mo despendours he
hath / And deere sire / al be it so þt for youre richesses / ye
mowe haue muchel folk : yet bihoueth it nat / ne it is nat
good to bigynne werre / wher as ye mowe in oother manere
haue pees vn to youre worship & profit / for the victorie of hic
batailles þt been in this world / lyth nat in greet nombre
or multitude of peple / ne in the vertu of man / but it lyth
in the wyl & in the hand of oure lord god almyghty / And
ther fore Iudas Machabeus / which was goddes knyght -
whan he sholde fighte agayn his aduersarye / þt hadde a
gretter nombre & a gretter multitude of folk and strenger
than was the peple of this Machabe - yet he reconforted
his litel compaignye / and seyde right in this wise / Als
lightly quod he may oure lord god almyghty yeue victorie
to fewe folk as to manye folk / for the victorie of a batai
le / cometh nat by the grete nombre of peple / but it come
fro oure lord god of heuene / And deere sire / for as muchel
as ther is no man certeyn / if it be worthy þt god yeue
hym victorie or naught / after that Salomon seith / ther
fore euery man sholde greetly drede werres to bigynne ~
And by cause þt in batailles fallen manye perils / & happeth
outher while / þt as soone is the grete man slayn / as the
litel man / And as it is ywriten in the seconde book of
kynges ~ the dedes of batailles been auentirouse & no
thyng certeyne / for as lightly is oon hurt with a spere as
another / And for ther is greet peril in werre / therfore shol
de a man flee & eschewe werre / in as muchel as a man
may goodly / ffor Salomon seith / he þt loueth peril shal
falle in peril ¶ After þt dame Prudence hadde spoken
in this manere / Melibe answerde & seyde / I se wel da
me Prudence that by youre faire wordes & by youre re
sons þt ye han shewed me / þt the werre liketh yow no

thyng / but I haue nat yet herd youre conseil / how I shal do in
this nede ¶ Certes quod she I conseile yow / þt ye accorde wt
youre aduersaries / & þt ye haue pees wt hem / ffor Seint
Iame seith / in hise epistles / That by concord & pees / the smal-
le richesses wexen grete / & by debaat & discord / the grete riches
ses fallen doun / And ye knowen wel / þt oon of the grettest
& moost souereyn thyng / þt is in this world / is vnitee & pees
And ther-fore seyde oure lord Ihu crist to hise Apostles / in this
wise / wel happy & blessed been they / þt louen & purchacen
pees / for they been called children of god ¶ A quod Melibe
now se I wel / þt ye louen nat myn honour / ne my worshipe
ye knowen wel / þt myne aduersaries han bigonnen this de
baat & brige by hir outrage / & ye se wel / þt they ne requeren
ne preyen me nat of pees / ne they asken nat to be reconsi
led / wol ye thanne / þt I go meke me & obeye me to hem &
crye hem mercy / for sothe that were nat my worship / ffor
right as men seyn / þt ouer greet homlynesse engendreth
despisynge / so fareth it / by to greet humylitee or mekenesse
¶ Thanne bigan dame Prudence to maken semblant of wra
the & seyde / Certes sire sauf youre grace I loue youre honour
& youre profit as I do myn owene / & euere haue doon / ne ye ne
noon other / seyen neuere the contrarie / And yet if I hadde seyd
þt ye sholde han purchaced the pees & the reconsiliacion / I ne
hadde nat muchel mystake me / ne seyd amys / ffor the wise
man seith / The dissension bigynneth by another man / &
the reconsilyng bigynneth by thy self / And the prophete seith
ffle shrewednesse / & do goodnesse / seke pees & folwe it / as
muchel as in thee is / yet seye I nat / þt ye shul rather pursue
to youre aduersaries for pees / than they shuln to yow / for I
knowe wel / þt ye been so hard herted / þt ye wol do no thyng
for me / And Salomon seith / That he þt hath ouer hard an herte /
atte laste he shal myshappe & mystyde ¶ Whanne Melibe
hadde herd dame Prudence make semblant of wrathe he sey
de in this wise / Dame I prey yow / þt ye be nat displesed / of
thynges þt I seye / for ye knowe wel / þt I am angry & wrooth
& that is no wonder / and they þt been wrothe witen nat wel
what they doon / ne what they seyn / Ther-fore the prophete seith
That troubled eyen han no cleer sighte / but seyeth & consei
leth me as yow liketh / for I am redy to do right as ye wol
desire / & if ye repreue me of my folie / I am the moore holden

thyng but I haue nat yet herd youre conseil / how I shal do in this nede ¶Certes quod she / I conseile yow / þ*at* ye acorde w*ith* youre Adu*er*saries / *and* þ*at* ye / haue pees w*ith* hem // For Seint Iame seith / in hise epistles / That by concord *and* pees / the smale richesses / wexen grete / *and* by debaat *and* discord / the grete richesses fallen doun / [2867] And ye knowen wel / þ*at* oon of the gretteste *and* moost souereyn thyng þ*at* is in this world / is vnitee *and* pees / And therfore seyde oure lord Ie*s*u crist to hise Apostles / in this wise // Wel happy *and* blessed been they / þ*at* louen / *and* pur chacen pees / for they been called children of god ¶A quod Melibe now se I wel / þ*at* ye louen nat myn honur ne my worshipe // Ye knowen wel / þ*at* myne Adu*er*saries han bigonnen / this debaat *and* brige by hir*e* out*rage* / [2872] *and* ye se wel / þ*at* they ne requeren ne preyen me nat of pees / ne they asken nat to be reconsiled ./ wol ye thanne / þ*at* I go meke me *and* obeye me to hem *and* crye hem m*er*cy ./ for sothe / that were nat my worship*e* // For right as men seyn / þ*at* ouer greet homlynesse / engendreth despisynge ./ so fareth it by to greet humylitee / or mekenesse / ¶Thanne bigan Dame Prudence / to maken semblant of wrathe *and* seyde [2877] // Certes sire / sauf youre g*ra*ce / I loue youre honur *and* youre p*ro*fit / as I do myn owene / *and* euer*e* haue doon / ne ye / ne noon oother / syen neuere the cont*rar*ie // And yet if I hadde seyd / þ*at* ye sholde han p*ur*chaced the pees *and* the reconsiliaciou*n* ./ I ne hadde nat muchel mystake me / ne seyd amys // For the wise man seith // The dissensiou*n* / bigynneth by another man / *and* the reconsilyng bigynneth by thy self // And the p*ro*phete seiþ / Fle shrewednesse / *and* do goodnesse / [2882] seke pees *and* folwe it as muchel as in thee is // yet seye I nat þ*at* ye shul rather p*ur*sue to youre Adu*er*saries for pees / than they shuln to yow ./ for .I. knowe wel / þ*at* ye been so hard herted / þ*at* ye wol do / no thyng for me // And Salomon seith / That he þ*at* hath ou*er* hard an herte / atte laste / he shal myshappe *and* mystyde ¶Whanne Melibe hadde herd dame Prudence / make semblant of wrathe / he seyde in this wise [2887] // Dame / I pray yow / þ*at* ye be nat displesed / of thynges þ*at* I seye / for ye knowe wel / þ*at* I am angry *and* wrooth / *and* that is no wonder / and they þ*at* been wrothe / witen nat wel what they doon / ne what they seyn // Therfore / the p*ro*phete seith / That troubled eyen / han no cleer sighte / but seieth *and* conseileth me / as yow liketh / for I am redy / to do / right as ye wol desire / [2892] *and* if ye repreue me of my folie ./ I am the moore holden to loue yow / *and* to preise yow Ꝟ For Salomon seith Ꝟ That he þ*at* repreueth hym þ*at* dooth folie ʃ he shal fynde gretter gr*a*ce / than he / þ*at* deceyueth hym by swete wordes ¶Thanne seyde dame Prudence / I make no semblant’ of wrathe ne of angir’ but for youre grete p*ro*fit Ꝟ For Salomon seith Ꝟ he is moore worth / þ*at* repreueth / or chideth a fool / for his folie / shewynge hym semblant of wrathe ʃ [2897] than he þ*at* supporteth hym *and* preiseth hym / in his mysdoynge / *and* laugheth at his folie Ꝟ And this same Salomon seith afterward Ꝟ That’ by the sorweful visage of a man / that is to seyn / by the sory *and* heuy contenance of a man ʃ the fool correcteþ *and* amendeth hym self ¶Thanne seyde Melibe / I shal nat konne answere vn to so manye resons / as ye putten to me *and* shewen / seieth shortly / youre wil *and* youre conseil / *and* I am al redy / to fulfille *and* par*for*ne it [2902] ¶Thanne / Dame Prudence / discou*er*ed al hir wyl vn to hym / *and* seyde Ꝟ I conseile yow quod she / abouen alle thynges / þ*at* ye make pees bitwene god *and* yow / *and* beth reconsiled vn to hym *and* to his gr*a*ce / for as I haue seyd yow here biforn ʃ god hath suffred yow / to haue this tribulaciou*n* *and* disese / for youre synnes / and if ye do / as I seye yow / god wol sende youre Adu*er*saries vn to yow / [2907] *and* maken hem falle at youre feet’ redy to do youre wyl *and* youre comandementz Ꝟ For Salomon seith / whan the condicion of man / is plesant’ *and* likynge to god ʃ he changeth the hertes of the mannes Adu*er*saries / *and* constreyneth hem / to biseken hym of pees *and* of gr*a*ce / and I pray yow / lat me speken w*ith* youre Adu*er*saries / in pryuee place / for they shal nat knowe / þ*at* it be of youre wyl / or youre assent’. [2912] and thanne / whan I knowe hir wyl *and* hir entente ʃ I may conseille yow / the moore seurly ¶Dame quod Melibe / dooth youre wyl / *and* youre likynge / for I putte me hoolly / in youre disposicion *and* ordinance ¶Thanne Dame Prudence / whan she say the goode wyl of hir housbonde ʃ she delyueride / *and* took auys in hir self / thynkynge / how she myghte brynge this nede / vn to a good conclusiou*n* *and* to a good ende ʃ [2917] And whan she saugh hir tyme / she sente for thise Adu*er*saries / to come vn to hire / in to a p*ri*uee place / *and* shewed wysly vn to hem / the grete goodes / þ*at* comen of pees / *and* the grete harmes *and* p*er*ils / þ*at* been in werre / *and* seyde to hem / in a goodly manere ʃ/ how þ*at* hem oghten haue greet repentance / of the Iniurie *and* wrong’ þ*at* they hadden doon / to Melibe hir lord / *and* vn to hire / *and* to hir doghter // [2922] And whan they herden / the goodliche wordes / of Dame Prudence ʃ they weren so supprised *and* rauysshed / *and* hadden so

to loue yow & to preise yow / ffor Salomon seith / that he þt re
preueth hym þt dooth folie / he shal fynde gretter grace than he þt
deceyueth hym by swete wordes ¶ Thanne seyde dame Pruden
ce / I make no semblant of wrathe ne of angre / but for youre gre
te profit / ffor Salomon seith / he is moore worth / þt repreueth or
chideth a fool for his folie shewynge hym semblant of wra
the / than he þt supporteth hym & preiseth hym in his mysdo
ynge & laugheth at his folie / and this same Salomon seith
afterward / that by the sorweful visage of a man / that is to
seyn / by the sory & heuy contenance of a man / the fool correcteth
& amendeth hym self ¶ Thanne seyde Melibe / I shal nat kon
ne answere vn to so manye resons as ye putten to me & shewen
seith shortly youre wil & youre conseil / & I am al redy to fulfille
& parfourne it ¶ Thanne dame Prudence / discoued al hir wyl
vn to hym & seyde / I conseille yow quod she aboven alle thyn
ges þt ye make pees bitwene god & yow / & beth reconsiled vn
to hym & to his grace / for as I haue seyd yow heer biforn / god
hath suffred yow to haue this tribulacion & disese for youre
synnes / and if ye do as I seye yow / god wol sende youre adu
ersaries vn to yow & maken hem falle at youre feet / redy to do
youre wyl & youre comandementz / ffor Salomon seith / whan
the condicion of man is plesant & likynge to god / he chaungeth
the hertes of the mannes aduersaries & constreyneth hem to bise
ken hym of pees & of grace / and I praye yow / lat me speken wt
youre aduersaries in pryuee place / for they shal nat knowe þt it
be of youre wyl or youre assent / and thanne whan I knowe hir
wyl & hir entente / I may conseille yow the moore seurly ¶ Da
me quod Melibe / dooth youre wyl & youre likynge / for I putte
me hoolly in youre disposicion & ordinaunce ¶ Thanne dame
Prudence whan she saugh the goode wyl of hir housbonde / she
delibered & took auys in hir self / thynkynge how she myght
te brynge this nede / vn to a good conclusion & to a good ende
and whan she saugh hir tyme / she sente for thise aduersaries
to come vn to hir in to a pryuee place / & shewed wysly vn to hem
the grete goodes þt comen of pees / & the grete harmes & perils
þt been in werre / & seyde to hem in a goodly manere / how þt
hem oghten haue greet repentance / of the iniurie & wrong þt
they hadden doon / to Melibe hir lord & vn to hir / & to hir dogh
ter // and whan they herden the goodliche wordes of dame
Prudence / they weren so surprised & rauysshed & hadden so

greet ioye of hem þt wonder was to telle / A lady quod they ye
han shewed vn to vs the blessynge of swetnesse after the sawe
of Dauid the prophete / ffor the reconsilynge which we ne been nat
worthy to haue in no manere, but we oghten requeren it wt greet
contricioun & humylitee ye of youre grete goodnesse haue presen
ted vn to vs / Now se we wel þt the science & the konnynge
of Salomon is ful trewe for he seith That swete wordes mul
tiplien & encressen freendes & maken shrewes to be debonaire &
meke / Certes quod they we putten oure dede & al oure matere &
cause al hoolly in youre goode wyl & been redy to obeye vn to the
speche & comandement of my lord Melibe / And therfore deere
& benigne lady we preien yow & biseken yow as mekely as we
konne & mowen þt it like vn to youre grete goodnesse to fulfille
in dede youre goodliche wordes for we consideren & knowelichen
þt we han offendid & greued my lord Melibe out of mesure so
ferforth þt we been nat of power to maken his amendes / &
therfore we oblige & bynde vs & oure freendes for to do al his
wyl & his comandementz / but perauenture he hath swich he
uynesse & swich wrathe to vsward by cause of oure offense þt
he wole enioyne vs swich peyne as we mowe nat bere ne
sustene / And therfore noble lady we biseken to youre womman
ly pitee to taken swich auisement in this nede þt we ne oure
freendes be nat desherited & destroyed thurgh oure folie ¶ Cer
tes quod Prudence it is an hard thyng & right perilous þt a
man putte hym al outrely in the arbitracion & juggement and
in the myght & power of hise enemys / ffor Salomon seith
leeueth me & yeueth credence to that þt I shal seyn ¶ I seye
quod he ye peple & gouernours & gouernours of holy chirche
to thy sone to thy wyf to thy freend ne to thy brother ne
yeue thow neuere myght ne maistrie of thy body whil thow
lyuest / Now sithen he defendeth þt man sholde nat yeue
to his brother ne to his freend the myght of his body: by a
strenger reson he defendeth & forbedeth a man to yeue hym
self to his enemy And natheles I conseille yow þt ye mys
truste nat my lord for I woot wel & knowe verraily þt he is
debonaire & meke large curteys & no thyng desirous ne co
ueitous of good ne richesse for ther nys no thyng in this world
þt he desireth saue oonly worshipe & honour ¶ fforther mo
re I knowe wel & am right seur þt he shal no thyng do in
this nede wtouten my conseil And I shal so werken in this

greet ioye of hir*e* / þ*at* wonder was to telle / A lady quod they / ye han shewid vn to vs / the blessynge of swetnesse / after the sawe of Dauid the p*ro*phete / For the reconsilynge / which we ne been nat worthy to haue in no manere / but we oghten requeren it w*ith* greet contriciou*n* *and* humylitee ʃ ye of youre grete goodnesse / haue p*re*sented vn to vs / Now se we wel / þ*at* the science / *and* the konnynge of Salomon / is ful trewe / for he seith / That swete wordes / multiplien *and* encressen freendes / *and* maken shrewes / to be debonaire *and* meke / Certes quod they / we putten oure dede *and* al oure matere / *and* cause / al hoolly / in youre goode wyl / *and* been redy to obeye vn to the speche *and* comandement of my lord Melibe / And therfore deere *and* benygne lady / we preyen yow / *and* biseken yow / as mekely / as we konne *and* mowen / þ*at* it like / vn to youre grete goodnesse / to fulfille in dede / youre goodliche wordes / for we consideren *and* knowelichen / þ*at* we han offendid *and* greued / my lord Melibe / out of mesure / so ferforth / þ*at* we been nat of power to maken his amendes / *and* ther fore / we oblige *and* bynde vs *and* oure freendes / for to do al his wil *and* his comandementz / but p*ar*auenture / he hath swich heuynesse *and* swich wrathe to vsward / by cause of oure offense / þ*at* he wole enioyne vs / swich peyne / as we mowe nat bere / ne sustene / And therfore noble lady / we biseken to youre wo*m*manly pitee / to taken swich auisement in this nede / þ*at* we ne oure freendes / be nat desherited *and* destroyed / thurgh oure folie ¶Certes quod Prudence / it is an hard thyng *and* right pe*r*ilous / þ*at* a man putte hym al outrely in the arbitraciou*n* *and* Iuggement and in the myght *and* power of hise enemys / For Salomon seith ʃ Leeueth me / *and* yeueth credence / to that þ*at* I shal seyn ¶I seye quod he / ye peple / *and* gouernours / *and* gouer*n*ours of holy chirche / to thy sone / to thy wyf / to thy freend / ne to thy brother / ne yeue thow neuere myght ne maistrie of thy body / whil þow lyuest / Now / sithen he defendeth / þ*at* man sholde nat yeue to his brother ne to his freend / the myght of his body .ʃ by a strenger reson / he defendeth *and* forbedeth a man / to yeue hym self to his enemy / And nathelees I conseille yow / þ*at* ye mystruste nat my lord / for I woot wel *and* knowe ve*r*raily / þ*at* he is debonaire *and* meke / large / curteys / *and* no thyng desirous / ne coueitous / of good / ne richesse / for ther nys no thyng in this world þ*at* he desireth / saue oonly / worship*e* *and* honour ¶Forther moore I knowe wel *and* am right seur / þ*at* he shal no thyng do in this nede / w*ith* outen my conseil / and I shal so werken in this cause / þ*at* by the g*ra*ce / of oure lord god / ye shul be reconsiled vn to vs ¶Thanne seyden they with o voys // Worshipful lady / we putten vs *and* oure goodes al fully / in youre wyl *and* disposicioun / *and* been redy to come / what day þ*at* it like vn to youre noblesse / to lymyte us / or assigne us / for to maken / oure obligacion *and* boond / as strong' as it liketh un to youre goodnesse / [2957] þ*at* we mowe fulfille / the wyl of yow / *and* of my lord Melibe ¶Whanne Dame Prudence / hadde herd the answeres of thise men ./ she bad he*m* go agayn p*ri*uely / *and* she retourned / to hir lord Melibe / *and* tolde hym / how she fand hise Adu*er*saries ful repentant' knowelichynge ful lowely / hir synnes *and* trespas / *and* how they weren redy / to suffren al peyne / requerynge / *and* prayynge hym / of m*er*cy *and* pitee [2962] ¶Thanne seyde Melibe // he is wel worthy / to haue p*ar*doun *and* foryifnesse of his synne / þ*at* excuseth nat his synne / but knowelicheth *and* repenteth hym / axinge Indulgence // For Senek seith // Ther*e* is the remissiou*n* *and* foryifnesse / where as the confessiou*n* is / for confessiou*n* / is neighebore to Innocence // And he seith / in another place

that hath shame of his synne *and* knowelicheth it // And therfore / I assente *and* conferme me to haue pees ./ [2967] but it is good / þ*at* we do it nat w*ith* outen thassent' *and* wil of oure freendes ¶Thanne was Prudence / right glad *and* ioyeful / *and* seyde // Certes sire quod she / ye han wel *and* goodly answerd / for right as by the conseil / assent' *and* help / of youre frendes / ye han ben stired / to venge yow / *and* make werre ./ right so / w*ith* outen hire conseil / shul ye nat acorde yow / ne haue pees with youre Adu*er*saries [2972] // For the lawe seith // Ther nys no thyng so good / by wey of kynde / as a thyng' to been vnbounde / by hym þ*at* it was ybounde // And thanne Dame Prudence / w*ith* outen delay / or taryynge / sente anon messages / for hir kyn / *and* for hire olde freendes / whiche þ*at* were trewe *and* wise / and tolde hem by ordre / in the p*re*sence of Melibe / al this matere / as it is aboue exp*re*ssed *and* declared / *and* preyde hem / þ*at* they wolde yeuen hir*e* auys *and* conseil / what best were to do / in this nede // And whan Melibees freendes / hadde taken hir*e* auys *and* deliberaciou*n* of the forseyde matere / [2977] *and* hadden examyned it' by greet bisynesse *and* greet diligence ./ they yaue ful conseil / for to haue pees *and* reste / *and* þ*at* Melibe / sholde receyue w*ith* good herte / hise Adu*er*saries / to foryifnesse *and* m*er*cy // And whanne Dame Prudence / hadde herd the assent' of hir

1366 in a modern hand: Cellui est presque innocent Hg (2967)

cause, þt by the gce of oure lord god, ye shul be reconsiled un to us
¶ Thanne seyden they with o voys / worshipful lady, we putten
us & oure goodes al fully in youre wyl & disposition, & been
redy to come what day þt it like un to youre noblesse to lymy
te us or assigne us, for to maken oure obligation & bond
as strong, as it liketh un to youre goodnesse, þt we mowe ful
fille the wyl of yow & of my lord Melibe ¶ Whanne dame
Prudence hadde herd the answeres of thise men, she bad he
go agayn prively & she retourned to hir lord Melibe & tolde
hym how she fand hise adversaries ful repentant, knowel
ichynge ful lowely hir synnes & trespas, & how they weren
redy to suffren al peyne, requerynge & prayynge hym of
mercy & pitee ¶ Thanne seyde Melibe, he is wel worthy to
have pardon & foryifnesse of his synne, þt excuseth nat his
synne, but knowelicheth & repenteth hym, axinge indulgen
ce / ffor Senek seith, Ther is the remission & foryifnesse, whe
re as the confession is, for confession is neighebore to inno
cence / And he seith in another place — Cellui est presque innocens
that hath shame of his synne & kno
welicheth it / And therfore I assente & conferme me to have
pees, but it is good þt we do it nat wt outen thassent & wil
of oure freendes ¶ Thanne was Prudence right glad & joye
ful & seyde, Certes sire quod she, ye han wel & goodly an
swerd, for right as by the conseil assent & help of youre fren
des ye han ben stired to venge yow & make werre, right so
wt outen hir conseil shul ye nat accorde yow ne have pees
with youre adversaries / ffor the lawe seith / Ther nys no
thyng so good by wey of kynde, as a thyng to been unbown
de by hym þt it was ybounde / And thanne dame Prudence
wt outen delay or tariynge sente anon messagers for hir
kyn & for hir olde freendes, whiche þt were trewe & wise,
and tolde hem by ordre in the presence of Melibe al this ma
tere as it is above expressed & declared, & preyde hem þt they
wolde yeven hir avi[…] & conseil what best were to do in
this nede / And whan Melibees freendes hadde taken hir
avys & deliberacion of the forseyde matere, & hadden exa
myned it by greet bisynesse & greet diligence: they yave
ful conseil for to have pees & reste, & þt Melibe sholde re
ceyve wt good herte hise adversaries to foryifnesse & mercy
And whanne dame Prudence hadde herd the assent of hir

lord melibe / & the counseil of his freendes / acorde wt hire wil and
hire entencion / she was wonderly glad in herte & seyde / Ther
is an old pverbe quod she seith / that the goodnesse þt thow maist
do this day do it / & abide nat ne delaye it nat til tomorwe
And therfore I conseille þt ye sende youre messages / swiche
as been discrete & wise vn to youre aduersaries / tellynge hem
on youre bihalue / þt if they wol trete of pees & of acord / þt
they shape hem / wt outen delay or tariynge / to come vn to
vs / Which thyng pfered was in dede / and whanne thise
trespassours & repentynge folk of hire folies / that is to seyn
the aduersaries of melibe hadden herd / what thise messageres
seyden vn to hem / they weren right glad & ioyeful / & answer
den ful mekely & benygnely / yeldynge graces & thankynges
to hire lord melibe & to al his compaignye / & shopen hem wt
oute delay to go wt the messageres / & obeye to the comandement
of hire lord melibe / and right anon they tooken hire wey / to
the court of melibe / & tooke wt hem somme of hire trewe freen
des / to make feith for hem / & for to been hire borwes / And
whan they were come to the pfence of melibe / he seyde hem
thise wordes / It standeth thus quod melibe & sooth it is / þt
ye causelees & wt outen skile & reson / han doon grete iniuries
& wronges to me / & to my wyf Prudence / & to my doghter
also / for ye han entred in to myn hous by violence / & haue
doon swich outrage / þt alle men knowen wel / þt ye han descr
ued the deeth / And therfore wol I knowe & wite of yow / whe
ther ye wol putte the punysshynge & chastisynge & the venge
ance of this outrage / in the wil of me & of my wyf / or ye wol
nat ¶ Thanne the wiseste of hem thre answerde for hem alle
& seyde / Sire quod he / we knowen wel / þt we been vnworthy
to comen vn to the court / of so greet a lord & so worthy as ye
been / for we han so gretly mystaken vs / & han offended & gilt
in swich a wise / agayn youre heigh lordshipe / þt trewely we han
deserued the deeth / but yet for the grete goodnesse & debonairetee
þt al the world / witnesseth of youre psone / we submitten vs / to
the excellence & benygnytee of youre gracious lordshipe / & been
redy to obeye / to alle youre comandementz / bisekynge yow / þt
of youre merciable pitee / ye wol considere oure grete repen
tance & lowe submission / & graunten vs foryeuenesse / of ou
re outrageous trespas & offense / for wel we knowen / þt youre
liberal grace & mercy / strecchen ferther / in to goodnesse / than

lord Melibe / *and* the conseil of his freendes / acorde w*ith* hir*e* wyl / and hir*e* entenciou*n* ./ she was wonderly glad in herte / *and* seyde // Ther is an old p*r*o*uer*be quod she / seith // that the goodnesse þat thow maist do this day / do it *and* abide nat ne delaye it nat til tomorwe / And therfore I conseille / þat ye sende youre messages / swiche as been discrete *and* wise vn to youre Adu*er*saries / tellynge he*m* on your*e* bihalue / þat if they wol trete of pees *and* of acord / þat they shape hem / w*ith* outen delay or taryynge / to come vn to vs / which thyng p*ar*fo*ur*ned was in dede / and whanne thise trespassours *and* repentynge folk of hir folies / that is to seyn / the Adu*er*saries of Melibe / hadden herd / what thise messagers seyden vn to hem ./ they weren right glad *and* ioyeful / *and* answereden ful mekely *and* benygnely / yeldynge *gra*ces *and* thankynges / to hir*e* lord Melibe *and* to al his compaignye / *and* shopen hem w*ith* oute delay to go w*ith* the messagers / *and* obeye to the comandement of hir*e* lord Melibe / And right anon they tooken hir*e* wey / to the court of Melibe / *and* tooke w*ith* hem so*m*me of hir trewe freendes / to make feith for hem / *and* for to been hir*e* borwes // And whan they were come / to the presence of Melibe ./ he seyde hem thise wordes ¶It standeth thus quod Melibe *and* sooth it is / þat ye causelees *and* w*ith* outen skile *and* resou*n* / han doon grete Iniuries *and* wronges to me / *and* to my wyf Prudence / *and* to my doghter also / for ye han entred in to myn hous by violence / *and* haue doon swich out*ra*ge / þat alle men knowen wel / þat ye han deserued the deeth // And therfore wol I knowe *and* wite of yow / wheither ye wol putte the punysshynge *and* chastisynge / *and* the vengeance of this out*ra*ge / in the wil of me / *and* of my wyf or ye wol nat ¶Thanne the wiseste of hem thre / answerde for hem alle / *and* seyde // Sire quod he / we knowen wel / þat we been vnworthy to comen vn to the court of so greet a lord *and* so worthy / as ye been / for we han so gretly mystaken vs / *and* han offendid *and* gilt in swich a wise / ageyn youre hey lordshipe / þat trewely / we han deserued the deeth / but yet for the grete goodnesse *and* debonairetee / þat al the world / witnesseth of youre p*er*sone / ./ we submitten vs / to the excellence *and* benygnytee of youre *gra*cious lordshipe / *and* ben redy tobeye / to alle youre comandementz / bisekynge yow / þat of youre m*er*ciable pitee / ye wol considere oure grete repentance *and* lowe submissiou*n* / *and* *gra*unten vs foryeuenesse / of oure out*ra*geous trespas *and* offense / for wel we knowen / þat youre liberal *gr*ace *and* mercy / strecchen ferther in to goodnesse / than doon oure out*ra*geouse giltes *and* trespas in to wikkednesse / al be it þ*at* cursedly *and* dampnablely / we han agilt ageyn youre hey lordshipe ¶Thanne Melibe / took hem vp fro the ground ful benygnely / [3017] *and* receyued hir obligaciou*n*s *and* hir bondes by hir othes / vp on hir plegges *and* borwes / *and* assigned hem a c*er*teyn day / to retourne vn to his court for to accepte *and* receyue the sentence *and* Iugement þ*at* Melibe wolde comande / to be doon on hem / by the causes aforeseyd // whiche thynges ordeyned .∫ eu*er*y man reto*ur*ned to his hous // And whanne þ*at* dame Prudence saugh hir tyme / she feyned / *and* axed hir lord Melibe / [3022] what vengeance he thoghte to taken of hise Aduersaries ¶To which / Melibe answerde *and* seyde // Certes quod he .I. thynke *and* purpose me fully / to disherite hem / of al þ*at* eu*er*e they han / and for to putte hem in exil / for eu*er*e ¶Certes quod Dame Prudence / this were a cruel sentence / *and* muchel ageyn reson / for ye been ric... ynow *and* han no nede of oother mennes good / [3027] *and* ye myghten lightly in this wise / geten you a coueitous name / which is a vicious thyng *and* oghte been eschewid / of euery man / for after the sawe of the word of thapostle // Coueitise / is roote of alle harmes / And therfore / it were bettre for yow / to lese so mychel good of youre owene / than for to take of hir*e* good / in this man*er*e / for bettre it is / to lese good w*ith* worshipe / than it is / to wynne good w*ith* vileynye *and* shame / [3032] And eu*er*y man / oghte do his diligence *and* his bisynesse / to geten hym a good name / and yet shal he nat oonly bisien hym in kepynge his goode name .∫ but he shal also / enforcen hym alwey / to do som thyng by which he may renouelle his goode name // For it is writen / That the olde goode loos / or good name of a man / is soone goon *and* passed / whanne it is nat newed / ne renoueled // *and* as touchynge þ*at* ye seyn / ye wol exile youre Adu*er*saries .∫ [3037] that thynketh me / muchel agayn resou*n* / *and* out of mesure / considered the power / þ*at* they han yeuen yow vp on hem self // And it is writen / that he is worthy to lesen his p*ri*uilege / þ*at* mysvseth / the mygh *and* the power þ*at* is yeuen hi*m* / And I sette cas / ye myghte enioyne hem that peyne / by right *and* by lawe / which I trowe ye mowe nat do / [3042] I seye / ye myghte nat putte it to execuciou*n* p*ar* auenture / *and* thanne were it likly / to retorne to the werre / as it was biforn / And ther fore / if ye wole / þ*at* men do yow obeisance .∫ yow

1448 in another hand: Radix omnium malorum est Cupiditas Hg (3030)

doon oure outrageouse giltes & trespas in to wikkednesse al be
it þt cursedly & dampnablely we han agilt ageyn youre hey
lordshipe ¶ Thanne Melibe took hem vp fro the grounde ful
benygnely & receyued hir obligaciouns & hir bondes by hir
othes vp on hir pledges & borwes & assigned hem a certeyn
day to retourne vn to his court for to accepte & receyue the
sentence & Jugement þt Melibe wolde comande to be doon on
hem by the causes aforeseyd / Whiche thynges ordeyned /
euery man retorned to his hous / And whanne þt dame Pru
dence saugh hir tyme / she freyned & axed hir lord Melibe /
what vengeance he thoghte to taken of hise Aduersaries .
¶ To which Melibe answerde & seyde / Certes quod he . I
thynke & purpose me fully to disherite hem of al þt euere
they han and for to putte hem in exil for euere ¶ Certes quod
dame Prudence this were a cruel sentence & muchel ageyn
resoun for ye been riche ynowh & han no nede of other men
nes good & ye myghten lightly in this wise geten yow a
coueitous name / which is a vicious thyng & oghte been
eschewed of euery man / for after the sawe of the word of
thapostle / Coueitise is roote of alle harmes / And ther fore / Radix omnium malorum est cupiditas
it were bettre for yow to lese so muchel good of youre owe
ne / than for to take of hir good in this manere / for bettre it
is to lese good wt worshipe / than it is to wynne good wt
vileynye & shame / And euery man oghte do his diligence
& his bisynesse to geten hym a good name / And yet shal
he nat oonly bisien hym in kepynge his goode name / but
he shal also enforcen hym alwey to do som thyng by
which he may renouelle his goode name / ffor it is writen /
That the olde goode loos or good name of a man is soone
goon & passed / whanne it is nat newed ne renouelled / &
as touchynge þt ye seyn ye wol exile youre Aduersaries /
that thynketh me muchel ageyn resoun & out of mesure /
considered the power þt they han yeuen yow vp on hem
self And it is writen that he is worthy to lesen his priui
lege þt mysuseth the myght & the power þt is yeuen hi(m) /
And I sette cas ye myghte enioyne hem that peyne by
right & by lawe which I trowe ye mowe nat do / I seye
ye myghte nat putte it to execucion par auenture / & thanne
were it likly to retorne to the werre as it was biforn /
And ther fore if ye wol þt men do yow obeisance yow

moste deme moore curteisly / this is to seyn / ye moste yeue moore
esy sentences & Jugementz / ffor it is writen / that he yt moost
curteisly comaundeth / to hym / men moste obeyen / & therfore I
pray yow yt in this necessitee & in this nede / ye caste yow to ouer
come youre herte / ffor Senek seith / that he yt ouercomeþ his herte
ouercomeþ twies / And Tullius seith / ther is no thyng so comendable
in a greet lord / as whan he is debonaire & meke & apeseth hym
lightly / And I pray yow yt ye wol forbere now to do vengean
ce in swich a manere yt youre good name may be kept & conser
ued / & yt men mowe haue cause & matere to preise yow of
pitee & of mercy / & yt ye haue no cause to repente yow of thyng
yt ye doon / ffor Senek seith / he ouercometh in an yuel manere
yt repenteth hym / of his victorie / wherfore I prey yow lat mercy
be in youre herte / to theffect & entente / yt god almyghty haue mercy
on yow in his laste Jugement / ffor Seint Jame seith in his epistle
Jugement withoute mercy shal be doon to hym / yt hath no mercy of
another wight / ¶ Whanne Melibe hadde herd the grete skiles
& resons of dame Prudence & hir wise informacions & te
thynges / his herte gan enclyne to the wil of his wyf / consi
derynge hir trewe entente / conformed hym anon & assented
fully / to werken after hir conseil & thonked god of whom proce
deth al vertu & al goodnesse / yt hym sente a wyf of so greet discrecion /
And whanne the day cam / yt hise aduersaries sholde apperen
in his presence / he spak to hem ful goodly & seyde in this wise /
Al be it so yt of youre pride & hy presumpcion & folie & of youre
necligence & vnkonnynge ye haue mysborn yow & trespased
vnto me / yet for as muchel as I se & biholde youre grete hu
militee & yt ye been sory & repentant of youre giltes / it con
streyneth me to do yow grace & mercy / wherfore I receyue yow
to my grace & foryeue yow outrely alle the offenses / Iniuri
es & wronges / yt ye haue doon agayns me & myne / to this
effect & to this ende / yt god of his endelees mercy / wole atte
tyme of oure dyynge foryeuen vs oure giltes yt we han
trespassed to hym in this wrecched world / for doutelees if
we be sory & repentant of the synnes & giltes / whiche we
han trespased in the sighte of oure lord god / he is so free
& so merciable / yt he wole foryeuen vs oure giltes & bryn
gen vs to the blisse that neuere hath ende . . . .

Here is ended Chaucers tale of Melibe

moste deme moore curteisly / this is to seyn / ye moste yeue / moore esy sentences *and* Iugementz // For it is writen / that he / þ*at* moost curteisly co*m*mandeth / to hym / men moste obeyen / [3047] *and* therfore I. pray yow / þ*at* in this necessitee / *and* in this nede / ye caste yow to oue*r*-come your*e* herte // For Senek seith // that he þ*at* oue*r*comeþ his herte oue*r*comeþ twies // And Tulli*us* seith // ther is no thyng so com*men*dable in a greet lord / as whan he is debonaire *and* meke / *and* apeiseth hym lightly // And I pray yow / þ*at* ye wol forbere now to do vengean-ce / [3052] in swich a manere / þ*at* youre good name / may be kept *and* conse*r*-ued / *and* þ*at* men mowe / haue cause *and* matere / to preise yow / of pitee *and* of me*r*cy / *and* þ*at* ye haue no cause / to repente yow of thyng þ*at* ye doon // For Senek seith // he oue*r*cometh / in an yuel manere þ*at* repenteth hym / of his victorie // Wherfore / I prey yow / lat me*r*cy be in youre herte / [3057] to theffect *and* entente / þ*at* god almyghty haue me*r*ci on yow in his laste Iugement // For Seint Iame seith / in his epistle // Iugement w*ith* oute me*r*cy / shal be doon to hym / þ*at* hath no me*r*cy / of another wight ¶Whanne Melibe hadde herd / the grete skiles *and* resons of dame Prudence / *and* hir wise Informaciou*n*s *and* te-chynges / his herte gan enclyne / to the wyl of his wyf / consi-derynge hir trewe entente / conformed hym anon *and* assented fully / to werken after hir conseil / [3062] *and* thonked god / of whom p*ro*ce-deth al v*er*tu / *and* al goodnesse / þ*at* hym sente a wyf of so greet discrec*iou*n // And whanne the day cam / þ*at* hise Adue*r*saries / sholde appieren / in his p*re*sence / he spak to hem ful goodly / *and* seyde in this wise //

¶Al be it so / þ*at* of youre pride / *and* by p*re*sumpciou*n* *and* folie / *and* of youre necligence *and* vnkonnynge / ye haue mysborn yow / *and* trespased vn to me / [3067] yet for as muchel / as I se *and* biholde youre grete hu-mylitee / *and* þ*at* ye been sory *and* repentant of youre giltes / it con-streyneth me / to do yow g*ra*ce *and* me*r*cy / Wherfore / I receyue yow to my g*ra*ce / *and* foryeue yow outrely alle the offenses / Iniuri-es *and* wronges / þ*at* ye haue doon / ageyns me *and* myne / [3072] to this effect *and* to this ende / þ*at* god / of his endelees me*r*cy / wole atte tyme of oure dyynge / foryeuen vs oure giltes þ*at* we han trespassed to hym / in this wrecched world / for doutelees / if we be sory *and* repentant of the synnes *and* giltes / whiche we han trespased / in the sighte of oure lord god / he is so free *and* so me*r*ciable / þ*at* he wole foryeuen vs oure giltes / *and* bryn-gen vs to the blisse / that neuere hath ende

¶Here is endid / Chaucers tale / of Melibe

¶The Prologe / of the Persons tale	1 ¶Heere folweth the Prologe / of the Persou*n*s tale
By that the Mau*n*ciple hadde his tale al ended	Mau*n*ciple / ended'
The Sonne // fro the south lyne is descended	sonne / was descended'
So lowe / that he nas nat to my sighte	sigħte
Degrees .29. as of highte	Degrees / nyne and twenty / as in higħte
Ten of the Clokke / it was / so as I gesse	was tho / as
For .xj. foot' and litel moore / or lesse	elleuene foot' or litel
My shadwe was / at thilke tyme as there	
Of swiche feet / as my lengthe parted weere	feet' were
In .6. feet equal / of p*ro*porciou*n*	sixe feet'
Ther with / the Mones exaltaciou*n*	Moones
I mene Libra / alwey gan ascende	meene
As we were entryng' at a Thropes ende	we /
For which oure hoost' as he was wont to gye	¶For
As in this cas / oure Ioly compaignye	caas /
Seyde in this wise / lordynges euerichon	euerichoon
Now lakketh vs / no tales / mo than oon	vs
Fulfild is my Sentence / and my decree	Fulfilled sentence /
I trowe / þat we han herd of ech degree	that
Almoost' fulfild is al myn ordinaunce	
I pray to god / so yeue hym right good chaunce	rigħt
That telleth this tale / to vs lustily	
Sire preest quod he / artow a Vicary	¶Sire
Or arte a p*er*son / sey sooth by thy fey	
Be what thow be / ne breke thow nat oure pley	thou thou
For euery man saue thow / hath toold his tale	thou /
Vnbokele / and shewe vs / what is in thy Male	vs
For trewely / me thynketh by thy cheere	
Thow sholdest / knette vp wel a greet matere	Thou sholdest' knytte mateere
Telle vs a fable anon / for Cokkes bones	
¶This p*er*son / answerde al atones	P*er*sou*n* answerde /
Thow getest fable noon / ytoold for me	Thou ytoold'
For Poul / that writeth vn to Thymothe	Paul / Thymothee
Repreueth hem / þat weyuen Soothfastnesse	that weyueth soothfastnesse
And tellen fables / and swich wrecchednesse	
Why sholde I sowen draf' out of my fest'	sowen /
Whan I may sowen whete / if þat me lest'	

32 Paulus ad Thimotheum El

1 *206r*

The prologe of the Persons tale

By that the Maunciple hadde his tale al ended
The sonne fro the south lyne is descended
So lowe that he nas nat to my sighte
Degrees .29. as of highte
Ten of the clokke it was so as I gesse
ffor .xi. foot and litel moore or lesse
My shadwe was at thilke tyme as there
Of swiche feet as my lengthe parted were
In .6. feet equal of pporcion
Ther with the mones exaltacion
I mene Libra alwey gan ascende
As we were entryng at a thropes ende
ffor which oure hoost as he was wont to gye
As in this cas oure ioly compaignye
Seyde in this wise lordynges euerichon
Now lakketh vs no tales mo than oon
ffulfild is my sentence and my decree
I trowe þt we han herd of ech degree
Almoost fulfild is al myn ordinaunce
I pray to god so yeue hym right good chaunce
That telleth this tale to vs lustily
Sire preest quod he artow a vicary
Or arte a pson sey sooth by thy fey
Be what thow be ne breke thow nat oure pley
ffor euery man saue thow hath toold his tale
Vnbokele and shewe vs what is in thy male
ffor trewely me thynketh by thy cheere
Thow sholdest knytte vp wel a greet matere
Telle vs a fable anon for cokkes bones
This pson answerde al atones
Thow getest fable noon ytoold for me
ffor Paul that writeth vn to Thymothe
Repreueth hem þt weyuen soothfastnesse
And tellen fables and swich wrecchednesse
Why sholde I sowen draf out of my fest
Whan I may sowen whete if þt me lest

ffor which I seye / þt if yow list to heere
Moralitee and vertuous matere
And thanne / þt ye wol yeue me audience
I wole ful fayn / at Cristes reuerence
Do yow plesance leueful / as I kan
But trusteth wel / I am a Southren man
I kan nat geste / rom / ram / ruf by lettre
Ne god woot / rym holde I but litel bettre
And ther fore if yow lest / I wol nat glose
I wol yow telle / a myrie tale in prose
To knytte vp al this feste / and make an ende
And Ihu for his grace / wit me sende
To shewe yow the wey / in this viage
Of thilke pfit / glorious pilgrymage
That highte Jerusalem celestial
And if ye vouche sauf / anon I shal
Bigynne vp on my tale / for which I preye
Telle youre auys / I kan no bettre seye
But nathelees / this meditacion
I putte it ay / vnder correction
Of clerkes / for I am nat textuel
I take but the sentence / trusteth wel
Ther fore I make protestacion
That I wol stonde to correction
Vp on this word / we han assented soone
ffor as it semed / it was for to doone
To enden / in som vertuous sentence
And for to yeue hym space and audience
And bede oure hoost / he sholde to hym seye
That alle we / to telle his tale hym preye
Oure hoost / hadde the wordes for vs alle
Sire preest quod he / now faire yow bifalle
Sey what yow list / and we wol gladly heere
And with that word / he seyde in this manere
Telleth quod he / youre meditacion
But hasteth yow / the sonne wole adoun
Beth fructuous / and that in litel space
And to do wel / god sende yow his grace

Explicit prohemium

For which I seye / þ*at* if yow list to heere
Moralitee / and vertuous matere
And thanne / þ*at* ye wol yeue me Audience
I wole ful fayn / at Cristes reuerence
Do yow plesance / leueful / as I kan
But trusteth wel / I am a Southren man
I kan nat geste / rom / ram / ruf / by lettre
Ne god woot / rym holde I but litel bettre
And ther fore if yow lest / I wol nat glose
I wol yow telle / a myrie tale in prose
To knytte vp al this feste / and make an ende
And Ie*s*u for his g*ra*ce / wit me sende
To shewe yow the wey / in this viage
Of thilke p*ar*fit glorious pilgrymage
That highte Ierusalem celestial
And if ye vouche sauf anon I shal
Bigynne vp on my tale / for which I preye
Telle youre auys / I kan no bettre seye
But nathelees / this meditaciou*n*
I putte it ay / vnder correcciou*n*
Of clerkes / for I am nat textuel
I take but the sentence / trusteth wel
Ther fore / I make protestaciou*n*
That I wol stonde / to correcciou*n*
¶Vp on this word / we han assented soone
For as it semed / it was for to doone
To enden / in som v*er*tuous sentence
And for to yeue hym / space and audience
And bede oure hoost he sholde to hym seye
That alle we / to telle his tale hym preye
¶Oure hoost hadde the wordes for vs alle
Sire preest quod he / now faire yow bifalle
Sey what yow list and we wol gladly heere
And with that word / he seyde in this manere
Telleth quod he / youre meditaciou*n*
But hasteth yow / the sonne wole adoun
Beth fructuous / and that in litel space
And to do wel / god sende yow his grace

¶Explicit prohemium

ELLESMERE

if that
a*n*d mateere
wol fayn /
plesaunce / leefful
geeste / Rum / Ram / Ruf /
woot
therfore / list
al*le* feeste /
grace /
[2] To shewe
p*ar*fit /
highte /
¶But
Clerkes / textueel
but sentence / weel
Therfore / make a protestaciou*n*
stonde
as vs semed /
hym

¶Explicit / prohemium

[2] ¶P*er*sou*n* *206v*

¶Here bigynneth / the Persons tale*

Ier*emie* .6°. State sup*er* vias / *et* videte *et* inter*r*ogate de semitis antiquis / que sit via bona / *et* ambulate in ea / *et* inuenietis refrigeriu*m* an*im*ab*us* ves*tr*is *et cetera*

Ovre swete lord / god of heuene / that no man wole p*er*isse / but wole þ*at* we comen alle to the knoweliche of hym / and to the blisful lyf / þ*at* is p*er*durable / [75] amonesteth vs / by the p*ro*phete Ieromie / that seith in this wise Stondeth vp on the weyes / and seeth / and axeth of olde pathes / that is to seyn / of olde sentences / which is the goode wey / and walketh in that wey / and ye shal fynde refresshynge for youre soules *et cetera* ¶Manye been / the weyes espirituels / that leden folk / to oure lord I*es*u crist and to the regne of glorie / of whiche weyes / ther is a ful noble wey and a ful couenable / which may nat faile / to man ne to womman / þ*at* thurgh synne hath mysgoon / fro the righte wey of Ierusalem celestial / [80] and this wey / is clepid Penitence / of which / men sholde gladly herknen and enquere w*ith* al his herte / to wite / what is penitence / and whennes / it is clepid penitence / and in how manye maneres / been the accions / or werkynges of penitence / and how manye spices / ther ben of penitences / and whiche thynges / ap*er*tenen *and* bihouen to penitence / whiche thynges / destourben penitence / ¶Seint Ambrose seith that penitence / is the pleynynge of man / for the gilt þ*at* he hath doon / and namoore to doon any thyng for which hym oghte to pleyne ¶And som dectour seith Penitence / is ⟨þe⟩ waymentynge of man / þ*at* sorweth for his synne / and pyneth hym self / for he hath mysdoon [85] Penitence / w*ith* c*er*teyne circumstances / is verray repentance of a man / þ*at* halt hym self in sorwe / *and* oother peyne for hise giltes / and for he shal be verray penitent he shal first biwailen / the synnes / þ*at* he hath doon / and stedefastly / p*ur*posen in his herte / to haue shrift of mouthe / and to doon satisfacciou*n* / and neu*er*e to doon thyng for which hym oghte moore to biwaile / or to compleyne / and to continue in goode werkes / or ellis / his repentance may nat auayle

*Ellesmere variants for ParsT on pages 1013–1024.

Here bigynneth the Persons tale

Jer. 6° State super vias et videte et interrogate de semitis
antiquis que sit via bona et ambulate in ea et inuenie
tis refrigerium animabus vestris &c

Oure sweete lord god of heuene, that no man wol
perisse but wole þt we comen alle to the knoweliche
of hym and to the blisful lyf þt is perdurable a
monesteth vs by the prophete Ieremie that seith in this wise
Stondeth vp on the weyes and seeth and axeth of olde pa
thes that is to seyn of olde sentences which is the goode
wey and walketh in that wey and ye shal fynde refressh
ynge for youre soules &c Manye been the weyes espiri
tuels that leden folk to oure lord Ihu crist and to the regne
of glorie of whiche weyes ther is a ful noble wey and
a ful couenable which may nat faile to man ne to wom
man þt thurgh synne hath mysgoon fro the righte wey
of Ierusalem celestial and this wey is cleped Penitence
of which men sholde gladly herknen and enquere wt al
his herte to wite what is penitence and whennes it is
cleped penitence and in how manye maneres been the accions
or werkynges of penitence and how manye speces ther
been of penitences and whiche thynges apertenen & biho
uen to penitence whiche thynges destourben penitence
Seint Ambrose seith that penitence is the pleynynge of
man for the gilt þt he hath doon and namoore to doon
any thyng for which hym oghte to pleyne And som doc
tour seith penitence is waymentynge of man þt sor
weth for his synne and pyneth hym self for he hath
mysdoon Penitence wt certeyne circumstances is verray
repentance of a man þt halt hym self in sorwe & oother
peyne for hise giltes and for he shal be verray penitent
he shal first biwailen the synnes þt he hath doon and
stedefastly purposen in his herte to haue shrift of mouthe
and to doon satisfaction and neuere to doon thyng for which
hym oghte moore to biwaille or to compleyne and to conti
nue in goode werkes or ellis his repentance may nat auaille

ffor as seith Seint Isidre / he is a Iapere and a gabbere and
no verray repentant / þt eft soone dooth thyng / for which hym
oghte repente / wepynge and nat for to stynte to do synne
may nat auaile / But natheles men shal hope / þt at euery
tyme þt man falleth be it neuer so ofte / þt he may arise thurgh
penitence if he haue grace / but certeinly it is greet doute / for
as seith Seint Gregorie / vnnethe ariseth he out of his synne
that is charged wt the charge of yuel usage / and ther fore
repentant folk / þt stynte for to synne & forlete synne er þt
synne forlete hem holy chirche halt hem siker of hir salua
cion / and he þt synneth & verraily repenteth hym in his laste /
holy chirche yet hopeth his saluacion by the grete mercy of oure
lord Jhu crist for his repentance / but taak the siker wey / and
now sith þt I haue declared yow what thyng is penitence /
now shul ye vnderstonde þt ther been .iij. accions of penitence /
[A]ccions of penitence. The firste is þt if a man be baptised after þt he hath synned / Seint
Augustyn seith / but he be penitent for his olde synful lyf / he may
nat bigynne the newe clene lyf / for certes / if he be baptised with
oute penitence of his olde gilt / he receyueth the mark of baptes
me / but nat the grace / ne the remission of hise synnes / til he ha
ue repentance verray / Another defaute is this / that men doon
deedly synne after þt they han receyued baptesme / The
thridde defaute is / that men fallen in venyal synnes after
hir baptesme fro day to day / ther of seith Seint Augustyn /
That penitence of goode and of humble folk / is the penitence
[Sp]eces of penance. of euery day / The speces of penance been .iij. / that oon of
hem is solempne / Another is commune / and the thridde is pri
uee / Thilke penance þt is solempne is in two maneres / as
to be put out of holy chirche in lente / for slaughtre of children
and swich maner thyng / Another is whan man hath synned
openly / of which synne the fame is openly spoken in the contree
and thanne holy chirche by Iugement destreyneth hym for to
doon open penance // Commune penance is that preestes enioynen
men comunly in certeyn cas / as for to goon parauenture naked in
pilgrymage or barefoot / Pryuee penance is thilke þt men
doon al day for priuee synnes / of whiche we shryue vs priuely
Bihoueth to penitence. and receyue pryuee penance / Now shaltow vnderstande
what bihoueth and is necessarie to verray pfit penitence and
this stant on .iij. thynges / Contricion of herte / Confession of
mouth and Satisfaction / for which seith Seint John Crisostom

For as seith Seint Isydre ⁊ He is a Iapere / and a gabber*e* / and no verray repentant þ*at* eft soone dooth thyng / for which hym oghte repente ⁊ Wepynge / and nat for to stynte to do synne / may nat auaile [90] ⁊ But nathelees men shal hope / þ*at* at euery tyme þ*at* man falleth / be it neuer so ofte / þ*at* he may arise þurgh penitence / if he haue g*ra*ce / but c*er*teynly / it is greet dowte / for as seith Seint Gregorie ⁊ Vnnethe [vix] ariseth he out of his synne / that is charged / w*ith* the charge of yuel vsage / and ther fore / repentant folk / þ*at* stynte for to synne / *and* forlete synne / er þ*at* synne forlete hem / holy chirche / halt hem siker of hir*e* sauacion / and he þ*at* synneth / *and* verraily repenteth hym in his laste / holy chirche / yet hopeth his sauaciou*n* by the grete m*er*cy of oure lord I*es*u crist for his repentance / but taak the siker [tene certu*m*] wey / And now / sith þ*at* I haue declared yow / what thyng is penitence / now shul ye vnderstonde / þ*at* ther been .iij. accions of penitence / [95] ¶The firste is / þ*at* if a man be baptised / after þ*at* he hath synned ⁊ Seint Augustyn seith / but he be penitent / for his olde synful lyf / he may nat bigynne / the newe clene lyf / for c*er*tes / if he be baptised with oute penitence of his olde gilt / he receyueth the mark of baptesme / but nat the g*ra*ce / ne the remissiou*n* of hise synnes / til he haue repentance verray ¶Another defaute is this / that men doon deedly synne / after þ*at* they han receyued baptesme / ¶The thridde defaute is ⁊ that men fallen in venyal synnes after hir*e* baptesme / fro day to day [100] ⁊ ther of seith Seint Augustyn ⁊ That penitence / of goode and of humble folk. is the penitence of euery day / ¶The speces [species] of penau*n*ce / been .iij. ⁊ that oon of hem / is solempne ⁊ Another is co*m*mune ⁊ and the thridde is priuee ¶Thilke penau*n*ce þ*at* is solempne / is in two maneres /. as to be put out of holy chirche in lente / for slaughtre of children / and swich manere thyng ¶Another is / whan man hath synned openly / of which synne / the fame / is openly spoken in the contree / and thanne holy chirche / by Iugement destreyneth hym / for to doon open penance / / Co*m*mune penau*n*ce is / that preestes enioynen men co*m*munly / in c*er*teyn cas / as for to goon p*ar*auenture naked in pilgrymage / or barefoot [105] ¶Pryuee penau*n*ce / is thilke þ*at* men doon al day for p*ri*uee synnes / of whiche / we shryue vs pryuely and receyue pryuee penance ¶Now shaltow vnderstande / what bihoueth and is necessarie to verray p*ar*fit penitence / and this stant / on .iij. thynges ⁊ Contriciou*n* of herte ⁊ Confessiou*n* of Mouth / and Satisfacciou*n* ⁊ for which / seith Seint Iohn Grisostom*us*

48 [iij. A]ccions of penitence Hg (96)

58 [iij. Sp]eces of penaunce Hg (102)

69 [What] bihoueth to penitence Hg (107)

¶Penitence destreyneth man / to accepte benygnely eu*er*y peyne / þ*at* hym is enioyned / with contriciou*n* of herte / *and* shrift of Mowthe / w*ith* satisfacciou*n* / and in wirkynge of alle manere humylitee / and this is fruytful penitence agayn .iij. thynges / in whiche we wrathe oure lord I*es*u crist 110 / this is to seyn / by delit in thynkynge / by reccheleslesnesse in spekynge / by wikked synful wirkynge / and agayns thise / wikkede giltes is penitence / that may be likned vn to a tree / ¶The roote of this tree / is contriciou*n* / þ*at* hideth hym in the herte of hym / þ*at* is verray repentant right as the roote of a tree hideth hym in the erthe / Of the roote of Contriciou*n* spryngeth a stalke þ*at* bereth branches / and leues of confessiou*n* / and fruyt of satisfacciou*n* / for which / crist seith in his gospel / Dooth digne fruyt of penitence / for by this fruyt may men knowe this tree / and nat by the roote / that is hyd / in the herte ⟨of⟩ man / ne by the branches / ne the leues of Confessiou*n* 115 / And therfore / oure lord I*es*u crist seith thus / by the fruyt of hem / shul ye knowe hem / Of this roote eek spryngeth a Seed of gr*a*ce / the which Seed / is moder of Sikernesse / and this Seed / is egre and hoot / the gr*a*ce of thys Seed / spryngeth of god thurgh remembrance on the day of dome / *and* on the peynes of helle / Of this matere / seith Salomon / that in the drede of god / man forleteth his synne / the hete of thys seed / is the loue of god / *and* the desirynge of the Ioye p*er*durable / 120 this hete / draweth the herte of man to god *and* dooth hym hate his synne / for soothly / ther is no thyng þ*at* sauoureth so wel to a child / as the mylk of his norice / ne no thyng is to hym moore abhomynable / than thilke mylk / whan it is medled w*ith* oother mete / right so the synful man / þ*at* loueth his synne / hym semeth / it is to hym moost swete of any thyng / but fro þ*at* tyme / þ*at* he loueth sadly oure lord I*es*u crist / *and* desireth the lyf p*er*durable / ther nys to hym / no thyng moore abhomynable / // for soothly / the lawe of god / is the loue of god / for which / Dauid the p*ro*phete seith ¶I haue loued thy lawe *and* hated wikkednesse *and* hate / he þ*at* loueth god / kepeth his lawe *and* his word // 125 this tree saugh the p*ro*phete Daniel in spirit vp on the auysion of Nabugodonosor / whanne he conseiled hym / to do penitence // Penance / is the tree of lyf / to hem þ*at* it receyuen / *and* he þ*at* holdeth hym in verray penitence / is blessed / after the sentence of Salomon ¶In this penitence or Contriciou*n* / man shal vnderstonde iiij. thynges / that is to seyn / what is Contriciou*n* / and whiche ben the causes / þ*at* moeuen a man to Contriciou*n* / and how he

The Person.

Penitence destreyneth man to accepte benyngnely euery peyne þt hym
is enioyned / with contricion of herte & shrift of mouth / wt satis
faction / and in werkynge of alle manere humylitee / and this is
fruytful penitence agayn .iij. thynges in whiche we wratthe oure
lord Ihu crist / this is to seyn / by delit in thynkynge / by recche
lesnesse in spekynge / by wikked synful werkynge / and agayns
thise wikkede giltes is penitence / that may be likned vn to a tree
The roote of this tree is contricion / þt hideth hym in the herte of
hym þt is verray repentant / right as the roote of a tree hideth
hym in the erthe / Of the roote of Contricion spryngeth a stalke
þt bereth braunches and leues of confession / and fruyt of satis
faction / for which / crist seith in his gospel / dooth digne fruyt
of penitence / for by this fruyt may men knowe this tree / and
nat by the roote / that is hyd / in the herte of man / ne by the bran
ches / ne the leues of Confession / And therfore oure lord Ihu crist
seith thus / by the fruyt of hem / shul ye knowe hem / Of this
roote eek / spryngeth a seed of grace / the which seed / is moder
of sikernesse / and this seed / is egre and hoot / the grace of this
seed spryngeth of god thurgh remembrance on the day of doome
& on the peynes of helle / Of this matere seith Salomon / that
in the drede of god / man forleteth his synne / the hete of this
seed / is the loue of god / & the desirynge of the ioye perdurable
this hete / draweth the herte of man to god & dooth hym hate
his synne / for soothly ther is no thyng þt sauoureth so wel
to a child / as the mylk of his norice / ne no thyng is to hym
moore abhomynable / than thilke mylk / whan it is medled wt
oother mete / right so the synful man / þt loueth his synne
hym semeth it is to hym moost swete of any thyng / but fro þt
tyme þt he loueth sadly oure lord Ihu crist / & desireth the lyf
perdurable / ther nys to hym / no thyng moore abhomynable
for soothly / the lawe of god / is the loue of god / for which
Dauid the prophete seith / I haue loued thy lawe & hated wikked
nesse & hate / he þt loueth god / kepeth his lawe & his word
this tree saugh the prophete Daniel in spirit vp on the auysion of
Nabugodonosor / whan he conseiled hym / to do penitence
Penitence is the tree of lyf / to hem þt it receyuen / & he þt holdeth
hym in verray penitence is blessed / after the sentence of Salo
mon / In this penitence or Contricion / man shal vnderstonde
iiij. thynges / that is to seyn / what is Contricion / and whiche
ben the causes / þt moeuen a man to Contricion / and how he

sholde be contrit / and what contricion auailleth to the soule / thanne
is it thus / that contricion is the verray sorwe þt a man receyueth
in his herte for hise synnes wt sad purpos to shryue hym & to
do penance & neuere moore to do synne / And this sorwe shal ben
in this manere / as seith Seint Bernard / It shal ben heuy and
greuous & ful sharp & poynant in herte / ffirst / for man hath
agilt his lord & his Creatour / and moore sharp & poynaunt
for he hath agilt / his fader celestial / and yet moore sharp &
poynaunt / for he hath wrathed & agilt / hym þt boughte hym /
þt wt his precious blood / hath delyuered vs fro the bondes of syn
ne / & fro the crweltee of the deuel / & fro the peynes of helle
¶ The causes þt oghten moeuen a man to Contricion been . vj .
[C]auses to meue a [ma]n to contricion .1. ffirst / a man shal remembren hym of hise synnes / but looke
þt thilke remembrance / ne be to hym no delit / by no wey / but greet
shame & sorwe for his gilt / for Iob seith / synful men / doon
werkes worthy of Confession / And therfore seith Ezechie / I
wol remembre me alle the yeres of my lyf in bitternesse of myn
herte / And god seith in the Apocalips / Remembre yow / fro when
nes þt ye ben falle / for biforn that tyme þt ye synned / ye
were the children of god / and lymes of the regne of god / but
for youre synne / ye ben woxe thral & foul and membres of
the feend / hate of Aungeles / sclaundre of holy chirche / &
foode of the false serpent / perpetuel matere of the fyr of helle /
And yet moore foul and abhomynable / for ye trespasen so ofte
tyme / as dooth the hound þt retorneth to ete his spewyng & Bonum
yet be ye fouler / for youre longe continuynge in synne and
youre synful vsage / for which ye been roten in youre synne
as a beest in his donge / swiche manere of thoghtes maken
a man haue shame of his synne & no delit / as god seyth
by the prophete Ezechiel / ye shal remembre yow of youre
weyes / and they shullen displese yow / sothly / synnes been
the weyes þt leden folk to helle ¶ The seconde cause þt oghte .2.
make a man to han desdeyn of synne / is this / that as seith
Seint Peter / who so þt dooth synne / is thral of synne / &
synne put a man in greet thraldom / And therfore seith the
prophete Ezechiel / I wente sorweful in desdayn of my self
¶ Certes wel oghte a man haue desdayn of synne & with
drawe hym fro that thraldom & vileynye / And lo what
seith Seneca in this matere / he seith thus / though I wiste
þt god / neither god ne man / ne sholde neuere knowe it / yet

sholde be contrit / and what Contriciou*n* auaileth to the soule // thanne is it thus /. that Contriciou*n* is the verray sorwe / þ*a*t a man receyueth in his herte for hise synnes / w*ith* sad purpos to shryue hym *and* to do penance *and* neuere moore to do synne / and this sorwe / shal ben in this manere / as seith Seint Bernard // It shal ben heuy and greuous *and* full sharp*e* / *and* poynau*n*t in herte [130] // first for man hath agilt his lord *and* his Creatour / and moore sharp *and* poynau*n*t for he hath agilt his fader celestial / and yet moore sharp*e* *and* poynau*n*t / for he hath wrathed *and* agilt hym þ*a*t boughte hym / þ*a*t w*ith* his p*re*cious blood / hath delyu*er*ed vs fro the bondes of synne / *and* fro the creweltee of the deuel / *and* fro the peynes of helle

¶The causes / þ*a*t oghten moeuen a man to Contriciou*n* / been .vj. / First / a man shal remembren hym of hise synnes / but looke þ*a*t thilke remembrance / ne be to hym no delit by no wey / but gret shame *and* sorwe for his gilt // for Iob seith / Synful men / doon werkes worthy of Confessiou*n* / And therfore / seith Ezechie // .I. wol remembre me alle the yeris of my lyf / in bitternesse of myn herte [135] // And god seith in the Apocalips*e* / Remembre yow / fro whennes þ*a*t ye ben falle / for biforn that tyme þ*a*t ye synned / ye were the children of god / and lymes of the regne of god / but for youre synne / ye ben woxe / thral *and* foul and membres of the feend / hate of Aungeles / Sclaundre of holy chirche / *and* foode of the false serpent p*er*petuel matere / of the fyr of helle / And yet moore foul and abhomynable for ye trespasen so ofte tyme / as dooth the hound / þ*a*t retorneth to ete his spewyng *and* yet be ye fouler / for youre longe contynuynge in synne and youre synful vsage / for which / ye been roten in youre synne as a beest in his donge / Swiche manere of thoughtes / maken a man haue shame of his synne *and* no delit as god seyth by the p*ro*phete Ezechiel / [140] ye shal remembre yow of youre weyes / and they shullen displese yow soothly / Synnes been the weyes þ*a*t leden folk to helle ¶The seconde cause / þ*a*t oghte make a man to han desdeyn of synne / is this / that as seith Seint Peter // who so þ*a*t dooth synne / is thral of synne / *and* synne put a man in greet thraldam / And therfore // seith the p*ro*phete Ezechiel / I wente sorweful / in desdayn of my self //

¶Certes wel oghte a man / haue desdayn of synne *and* with drawe hym fro that thraldom *and* vileynye // And lo / what seith Seneca in this matere / he seith thus / though I wiste þ*a*t god / neither god ne man / ne sholde neu*er*e knowe it / yet

124 [vj. C]auses to meue a [ma]n to contricioun .1. Hg (133)

137 Vomite (in another hand) Hg (139)

144 .2. Hg (142)

wolde .I. haue desdayn / for to do synne ¶And the same Seneca also seith ⹎ .I. am born to gretter thynges / than to be thral to my body / or than for to maken / of my body a thral / [145] ne a fouler thral may no man ne wo*m*man make of his body / than for to yeue his body to synne / al were ⟨it⟩ the fouleste cherl / or the fouleste wo*m*man þ*at* lyueth and leest of value / yet is he thanne moore foul *and* moore in seruitute / euere fro the hyer degree þ*at* man falleth / the moore is he thral and moore to god *and* to the world vil *and* abhomynable ¶O goode god / wel oghte man haue greet desdayn of synne / sith þ*at* thurgh synne / ther he was fre / now is he maked bonde / And ther fore / seith Seint Augustyn ¶If thow hast desdayn of thy seruant if he agilte or synne ⸗ haue thow thanne desdayn / þ*at* thow thy self sholdest do synne / [150] take reward of thy value / þ*at* thow ne be to foul to thy self ⹎ Allas / wel oghten they thanne haue desdayn / to ben seruantz *and* thralles to synne / *and* soore ben ashamed of hem self þ*at* god of his endelees goodnesse / hath set hem in heigh estat or yeuen hem wit strengthe of body / heele / beautee / p*ro*sp*er*itee / and boghte hem fro the deeth w*ith* his herte blood ⸗ þ*at* they so vnkyndely agayns his gentilesse / quyten hym so vileynsly to slawghtre of hir owene soules ¶O goode god / ye wo*m*men // þ*at* been so greet beautee / remembreth yow / of the p*ro*u*er*be of Salomon ⹎ he seith / [155] likneth a fair womman þ*at* is a fool of hir*e* body / lyk to a ryng of gold / þ*at* were in the groyn of a Sowe / for right as a Sowe wroteth in euerich ordure ⸗ so wroteth she hir*e* beaute in stynkynge ordure of synne ¶The thridde cause / þ*at* oughte moeue a man to Contricion / is drede of the day of dome / and of the horrible peynes of helle / For as Seint Ierome seith / At euery tyme / þ*at* me remembreth of the day of dome / I quake / for whan I ete and drynke / or what so þ*at* I do / euere semeth me / þ*at* the trompe sowneth in myn ere / [160] Riseth ye vp þ*at* ben dede *and* cometh to the Iugement ¶O goode god / muchel oghte a man to drede swich a Iugement / ther as we shullen ben alle / as seith Seint Poul / biforn the Sete / of oure lord I*es*u crist where as he shal maken / a gen*er*al congregacioun / wher*e* / as no man may ben absent for certes / there ne auaileth noon essoyne / ne excusaciou*n* / and nat oonly / þ*at* oure defautes shullen be Iuged / but eek þ*at* alle oure werkes / shullen openly be knowe / [165] and as þ*at* seith Seint

173 nota de pulcritudine Mulierum malarum [*later*] Hg (155)

179 .3. Hg (158)

wolde I haue desdayn for to do synne. And the same Seneca also
seith / I am born to gretter thynges / than to be thral to my bo
dy / or than for to maken of my body a thral / ne a fouler thral
may no man ne womman make of his body / than for to yeue his
body to synne / al were it the fouleste cherl / or the fouleste womman
þt lyueth and leest of value / yet is he thanne moore foul &
moore in seruitute / euere fro the hyer degree þt man falleth / the
moore is he thral and moore to god & to the world vil & abho
mynable. O goode god / wel oghte man haue greet desdayn
of synne / sith þt thurgh synne / ther he was free / now is he
maked bonde / And therfore seith Seint Augustyn. If thow
hast desdayn of thy seruant if he agilte or synne / haue thow
thanne desdayn / þt thow thy self sholdest do synne / take
reward of thy value / þt thow ne be to foul to thy self / Al
las / wel oghten they thanne haue desdayn to ben seruantz
& thralles to synne / & soore ben ashamed of hem self þt god
of his endelees goodnesse hath set hem in heigh estat / or ye
uen hem wit / strengthe of body / heele / beautee / prosperitee /
and boghte hem fro the deeth with his herte blood / þt they so
vnkyndely agayns his gentilesse quyten hym so vileynsly
to slaughtre of hir owene soules. O goode god ye wo
men þt been of so greet beautee / remembreth yow of the
proverbe of Salomon / he seith / likneth a fair womman þt is
a fool of hir body / lyk to a ryng of gold þt were in the
groyn of a sowe / for right as a sowe wroteth in euerich
ordure / so wroteth she hir beautee in stynkynge ordure of
synne. The thridde cause / þt oughte moeue a man to 3
contricion / is drede of the day of doome / and of the horri
ble peynes of helle / ffor as Seint Jerome seith / at euery
tyme þt me remembreth of the day of doome I quake / for
whan I ete and drynke / or what so þt I do / euere semeth
me þt the trompe sowneth in myn ere / riseth ye vp þt ben
dede & cometh to the Juggement. O goode god / muchel
oghte a man to drede swich a Juggement / ther as we shul
len ben alle / as seith Seint Poul / biforn the sete of oure
lord Jhesu crist / wher as he shal maken a general congrega
cion / wher as no man may ben absent / for certes there
ne auailleth noon essoyne ne excusacion / and nat oonly
þt oure defautes shullen be Juged / but eek þt alle oure
werkes shullen openly be knowe / and as þt seith Seint

no[ta] de p[er]fectione mulierum

Bernard / ther ne shal no pletynge availe / ne no sleighte ¶ We
shullen yeue rekenynge of euerich ydel word / there shul we han
a iuge / þt may nat ben deceyued ne corrupt. And why / for
certes / alle oure thoghtes ben descouered as to hym / ne for prey
ere / ne for mede / he wol nat ben corrupt / and therfore seith Salo
mon / the wrathe of god ne wol nat spare no wight / for prey
ere ne for yifte / and therfore at the day of doome / ther nys noon
hope to escape / Wherfore as seith Seint Anselme / fful gret
anguisse shullen the synful folk haue / at that tyme / ther
shal the sterne & wrothe iuge / sitte aboue / and vnder hym
the horrible pit of helle open to destroye hym þt moot biknowen
hise synnes / whiche synnes openly ben shewed biforn god /
and biforn euery creature / and on the left syde / mo deueles
than herte may bithynke / for to harye and drawe the syn
ful soules / to the pyne of helle / and wt inne the hertes of
folk / shal be the bitynge conscience / & with oute forth / shal
be the world al brennynge / whider shal thanne the wrech
ched synful man fle to hyde hym / certes he may nat hy
de hym / he moste come forth and shewe hym / for certes / as
seith Seint Jerome / the erthe shal caste hym out of hym /
and the see also / & the eyr also / þt shal ben ful of thon
der clappes & lightnynges / Now soothly / who so wel
remembreth hym of thise thynges / I gesse that his synne
shal nat torne hym in delit / but to gret sorwe / for drede
of the peyne of helle / and therfore seith Job to god / Suf
fre lord / þt I may a while biwayle & wepe er I go / wt
oute returnynge to the dirke lond / couered with the derknes
se of deeth / to the lond of mysese & of derknesse / where as
is the shadwe of deeth / where as ther is / noon ordre / or
ordinaunce / but grisly drede þt euere shal laste ¶ Lo here
may ye seen / þt Job preyde respit a while / to biwepe and
wayle his trespas / for soothly o day of respit / is bettre
than al the tresor of this world / and for as muche / as a
man may acquyte hym self biforn god by penitence in
this world / and nat by tresor / therfore sholde he preye to
god / to yeue hym respit a while / to biwepe & biwaylen
his trespas / for certes / al the sorwe þt a man myghte
make fro the bigynnyng of the world / nys but a litel
thyng at regard of the sorwe of helle ¶ The cause why
þt Job clepeth helle / the lond of derknesse / vnderstondeth

Bernard / ther ne shal no pletynge auaile / ne no sleighte ¶We shullen yeue rekenynge of euerich ydel word / there shul we han a Iuge / þ*a*t may nat ben deceyued / ne corrupt. and why / for c*er*tes / alle oure thoghtes / ben descou*er*ed as to hym / ne for prayere / ne for mede / he wol nat ben corrupt and therfore seith Salomon / the wrathe of god ne wol nat spare no wight for prayere / ne for yifte / And therfore / at the day of dome / ther nys noon hope to escape / Wherfore / as seith Seint Anselme / Ful gret anguisse / shullen the synful folk haue / at that tyme / ther shal the stierne *and* wrothe Iuge / sitte aboue / and vnder hym / the horrible pit of helle open to destroye hym þ*a*t moot biknowen hise synnes / whiche synnes / openly ben shewed biforn god / and biforn euery creature / [170] and on the left syde / mo deueles than herte may bithynke / for to harye and drawe the synful soules / to the pyne of helle / and w*ith* Inne the hertes of folk / shal be the bityng conscience / *and* with oute forth / shal be the world al brennynge / Whider shal thanne / the wrechched synful man fle to hyde hym / certes / he may nat hyde hym / he moste come forth and shewe hym / for c*er*tes / as seith Seint Ierome / the erthe shal caste hym / out of hym / and the See also / *and* the Eyr also / þ*a*t shal ben / ful of thonder clappes *and* lightnynges / Now soothly / who so wel remembreth hym of thise thynges / I gesse that his synne shal nat torne hym in delit / but to gret sorwe / for drede of the peyne of helle / [175] And therfore / seith Iob to god / Sufre lord / þ*a*t I may awhile biwayle / *and* wepe er I go / w*ith* oute returnynge to the dirke lond / cou*er*ed / with the derknesse of deeth / to the lond of mysese *and* of derknesse / where as is the shadwe of deeth / where as ther is / noon ordre / or ordinau*n*ce / but grisly drede þ*a*t eu*er*e shal laste ¶Lo here may ye seen / þ*a*t Iob preyde respit awhile / to biwepe and wayle his trespas / for soothly / o day of respit / is bettre than al the tresor of this world / And for as muche / as a man may acquyte hym self biforn god by penitence in this world / and nat by tresor / / therfore sholde he preye to god / to yeue hym respit awhile / to biwepe *and* biwaylen his trespas / for certes / al the sorwe þ*a*t a man myghte make fro the bigynnyng of the world / nys but a litel thyng at regard of the sorwe of helle [180] ¶The cause / why þ*a*t Iob clepeth helle / the lond of derknesse / / vnderstondeth that he clepeth it lond / or erthe / for it is stable *and* neu*er*e shal faile / dirkꝰ. for he þ*at* is in helle / hath defaute of light material / for certes the derke lightꝰ þ*at* shal come out of the fyr þ*at* eu*er*e shal brenne / shal turne hym al to peyne / þ*at* is in helle / for it sheweth hym / to the horrible deueles / þ*at* hym tormenten / couered w*ith* the derknesse of deeth // that is to seyn / þ*at* he þ*at* is in helle shal haue defaute of the sighte of god / for c*er*tes the sighte of god / is the lyf p*er*durable // The derknesse of deeth / ben the synnes þ*at* the wrecched man hath doon / whiche þ*at* destourben hym / to se the face of god / right as a dirk clowde bitwixe vs and the sonne ¶Lond of myseise / by cause þ*at* ther ben .iij. manere of defautes agayns .iij. thynges / þ*at* folk of this world / han in this p*re*sent lyf // that is to seyn /. honours /. delices /. and rychesses // Agayns hono*ur* / han they in helle / shame *and* confusiou*n* for wel ye wootꝰ þ*at* men clepen honour / the reu*er*ence / þ*at* man dooth to man / but in helle / is noon hono*ur* ne reu*er*ence / for c*er*tes / namoore reu*er*ence / shal be doon to a kyngꝰ than to a knaue // for which / god seith / by the p*ro*phete Ieremye // thilke folkꝰ þ*at* me despisen / shulle ben in despitꝰ ¶Hono*ur* is eek clepid greet lordshipe / ther shal no wight seruen oother / but of harm and tormentꝰ // Honour is eek clepid / greet dignytee *and* heighnesse / but in helle shul they ben al fortroden of deueles // As god seith // the horrible deueles / shullen goon *and* comen vp on the heuedes of dampned folk // And this is / for as muche as the heyer*e* þ*at* they were in this p*re*sent lyf / the moore shulle they ben abated and defouled in helle ¶Agayns the richesse of this world / shul they han myseyse of pouerte / and this pou*er*te / shal be in .iiij. thynges / In defaute of tresor / of which þ*at* dauid seith // the riche folkꝰ þ*at* embraceden *and* oneden al hir herte to tresor of this world / shulle slepen / in the slepynge of deeth / and no thyngꝰ ne shal they fynden in hir*e* handes / of al hir*e* tresor // And moore ouer / the Misayse of helle / shal ben in defaute of mete / *and* drynke / for god seith thus by Moyses // they shul ben wasted with honger / and the bryddes of helle / shul deuouren hem / w*ith* bitter deeth / and the galle of the dragon / shal ben hire drynke / and the venym of the dragon / hire morsels // And forther ouer / hire Miseyse / shal ben / in defaute of clothyngꝰ for they shullen ben naked in body / as of clothyngꝰ saue the fyr / in which they brenne *and* othere filthes / and naked shul they ben of soule / of alle man*er*e v*er*tues / which þ*at* is / the clothyng of soule / where

that he clepeth it lond or erthe for it is stable & neuer shal faile
dirk . for he þt is in helle hath defaute of light material / for
certes the derke light þt shal come out of the fyr þt euere shal
brenne shal turne hym al to peyne þt is in helle / for it she
weth hym to the horrible deueles þt hym tormenten / couered
wt the derknesse of deeth / that is to seyn þt he þt is in helle
shal haue defaute of the sighte of god / for certes the sighte of
god is the lyf perdurable / The derknesse of deeth ben the syn
nes þt the wrecched man hath doon / whiche þt destourben hym
to se the face of god / right as a dirk clowde bitwixe vs and
the sonne ¶ Lond of mysese / by cause þt ther ben . iij . manere
of defautes agayns . iij . thynges þt folk of this world han
in this present lyf / that is to seyn . honours . delices . and ri
chesses / Agayns honour han they in helle / shame & confusion
for wel ye woot þt men clepen honour the reuerence þt man
doth to man / but in helle is noon honour ne reuerence / for certes
namoore reuerence shal be doon to a kyng than to a knaue / for
which god seith by the prophete Jeremye / thilke folk þt me despi
sen / shulle ben in despit ¶ Honour is eek cleped greet lordshipe
ther shal no wight seruen oother / but of harm and torment /
Honour is eek cleped greet dignytee & heighnesse / but in helle
shul they ben al fortroden of deueles / As god seith / the horri
ble deueles shullen goon & comen vp on the heuedes of dam
ned folk / And this is for as muche as the hyer þt they were
in this present lyf / the moore shulle they ben abated and defouled
in helle ¶ Agayns the richesse of this world / shul they han
mysese of pouerte / and this pouerte shal be in . iiij . thynges
In defaute of tresor / of which þt Dauid seith / the riche folk þt
embraceden & oneden al hir herte to tresor of this world shul
le slepen in the slepynge of deeth / and no thyng ne shal they
fynden in hir handes / of al hir tresor / And moore ouer the
misayse of helle / shal ben in defaute of mete & drynke / for
god seith thus by moyses / they shul ben wasted with hunger
and the briddes of helle / shul deuouren hem wt bitter deeth
and the galle of the dragon / shal ben hir drynke / and the
venym of the dragon hir morsels / And forther ouer / hir
misese / shal ben in defaute of clothyng / for they shullen ben
naked in body as of clothyng / saue the fyr in which they
brenne & othere filthes / and naked shul they ben of soule / of
alle manere vertues / which þt is the clothyng of soule / Where

ben thanne the gaye robes & the softe shetes & the smale shertes
¶ lo what seith god of hem by the prophete ysaye / that vnder hem
shul ben strawed motthes & hir couertures shullen ben of
wormes of helle ¶ And forther ouer / hir myseyse shal ben
in defaute of freendes / for he is nat pouere that hath goode freen
des / but there is no freend / for neither god ne no creature shal
ben freend to hem / and euerich of hem shal haten oother with
dedly hate / the sones & the doghtren / shullen rebellen agayns
fader & moder / and kynrede agayns kynrede / and chiden &
despisen euerich of hem oother / bothe day & nyght / as god
seith by the prophete Michias ¶ And the louynge children that whi
lom loueden so flesshly euerich oother / wolden euerich of hem
eten oother / if they myghte / for how sholde they louen hem to
gidre / in the peyne of helle / whan they hateden euerich of
hem oother / in the prosperitee of this lyf / for truste wel hir
flesshly loue / was dedly hate / as seith the prophete Dauid
who so that loueth wikkednesse / he hateth his soule / and who
so hateth his owene soule / certes he may loue noon oother
wight in no manere / and therfore / in helle is no solas / ne
no freendshipe / but euere / the moore flesshly kynredes that ben
in helle / the moore cursynges / the moore chidynges / and the
moore dedly hate ther is among hem ¶ And forther ouer
they shul haue defaute of alle manere delices / for certes
delices ben after the appetites of the .v. wittes / as sighte .
herynge . smellynge / . sauorynge . and touchynge / but
in helle / hir sighte shal be ful of derknesse & of smoke
and therfore ful of teeres / and hir herynge / ful of waymen
tynge and of gryntynge of teeth / as seith Ihesu crist / hir
nosethirles / shul ben ful of stynkynge stynk / and as
seith ysaye the prophete / hir sauorynge / shal be ful of bit
ter galle / & touchynge of al hir body / ycouered with fyr
that neuere shal quenche / & with wormes that neuere shul dy
en / as god seith / by the mouth of ysaye / and for as mu
che as they shul nat wene that they may dyen for peyne /
and by hir deeth flee fro peyne / that may they vnderstonde
in the word of Iob / that seith / there as is the shadwe of deeth /
¶ Certes / a shadwe / hath the liknesse of the thyng / of which
it is shadwe / but shadwe / is nat the same thyng of which
it is shadwe / right so fareth the peyne of helle / it is lyk
deeth / for the horrible angwissh / and why / for it peyneth

ben thanne the gaye robes / *and* the softe shetes / *and* the smale shertes ¶Lo / what seith god of hem / by the p*ro*phete Ysaye // that vnder hem / shul ben strawed Moththes / *and* hir*e* coue*r*tures / shullen ben of wormes of helle ¶And forther ouer / hir*e* myseyse / shal ben in defaute of frendes / for he is nat pouere / þ*a*t hath goode frendes / but there is no freend / for neither god / ne no creature shal ben freend to hem / and euerich of hem / shal haten oother / w*ith* deedly hate [200] // the sones *and* the doghtren / shullen rebellen agayns fader *and* moder / and kynrede agayns kynrede / and chiden *and* despisen / euerich of hem oother' bothe day *and* nyght // as god seith / by the p*ro*phete Michias ¶And the louynge children þ*a*t whilom loueden so flesshly euerich oother / wolden euerich of he*m* eten oother / if they myghte // for how sholde they louen hem togidre / in the peyne of helle / ʃ whan they hateden euerich of hem oother / in the p*ro*spe*r*itee of this lyf / for truste wel / hire flessħly loue / was dedly hate / as seith the p*ro*phete Dauid ʃ who so þ*a*t loueth wikkednesse / he hateth his soule / and who so hateth his owene soule / ce*r*tes / he may loue noon oother wight in no manere / [205] and therfore / in helle is no solas / ne no frendshipe / but eu*er*e / the moore flesshly kynredes þ*a*t ben in helle / the moore cursynges / the moore chidynges / and the moore dedly hate / ther is among hem ¶And forther ouer / they shul haue defaute / of alle manere delices / for certes / delices ben after the appetites of the .v. wittes / as Sighte /. Herynge /. Smellynge /. Sauorynge /. and touchynge / but in helle / hir*e* sighte / shal be ful of dirknesse *and* of smoke and therfore ful of teerys / and hir*e* herynge / ful of waymentynge and of gryntynge of teeth / as seith Ie*s*u c*r*ist' hire nosethirles / shul ben ful of stynkynge stynk' // And as seith Ysaye the p*ro*phet // hir*e* sauorynge / shal be ful of bitter galle / *and* touchynge of al hir body / ycouered w*ith* fyr þ*a*t neuere shal quenche / *and* w*ith* wormes / þ*a*t neu*er*e shul dyen / as god seith / by the mowth of Ysaye [210] // And for as muche / as they shul nat wene / þ*a*t they may dyen for peyne / and by hir*e* deeth fle fro peyne / that may they vnderstonde in the word of Iob // that seith / there as is the shadwe of deþ / ¶Certes / a shadwe / hath the liknesse of the thyng' / of which it is shadwe / but shadwe / is nat the same thyng' of which it is shadwe // right so / fareth the peyne of helle / it is lyk deeth / for the horrible angwissħ / and why / for it peyneth

309 nota bene Hg (211)

hem eu*er*e / as thogh men sholde dye anon / but c*er*tes they shal nat dye / for as seith Seint Gregorie / to wrecche kaityues / shal be deeth w*ith* oute deeth / *and* ende w*ith* outen ende / *and* defaute w*ith* oute failynge / for hir*e* deeth / shal alwey lyuen / *and* hire ende shal eu*er*e mo bigynne / *and* hir*e* defaute / shal nat' faile / [215] And therfore / seith Seint Ioħn the Eu*a*ngelist ⁏ they shullen folwe deeth / *and* they shal nat fynde hym / *and* they shul desiren to dye / and deeth shal fle fro hem ⁏ And eek Iob seith / þ*at* in helle / is noon ordre of rewle / and al be it so / þ*at* god hath creat alle thynges in right ordre / *and* no thyng w*ith* outen ordre / but alle thynges / be*n* ordeyned *and* nombred / yet nathelees they þ*at* ben dampned / ben no thyng' in ordre / ne holden noon ordre / for the erthe ne shal bere hem no fruyt ⁏ for as the p*ro*phete dauid seith / god shal destroye / the fruyt of the erthe / as fro hem / ne water / ne shal yeue hem no moysture / ne the Eyr no refresshyng' ne fyr no light [220] ⁏ for as seith Seint Basile ⁏ the brennynge of the fyr of this world / shal god yeuen in helle / to hem þ*at* ben dampned / but the light' *and* the cleernesse / shal he yeuen in heuene to hise children / right as the goode man / yeueth flessħ to hise children / *and* bones to hise houndes / and for they shullen haue noon hope to escape / seith Seint Iob / atte laste / þ*at* ther shal horrour *and* grisly drede dwelle with outen ende // Horrour is alwey drede of harm þ*at* is to come / *and* this drede shal euere dwelle in the hertes / of hem þ*at* ben dampned / and therfore han they lorn al hire hope / for .vij. causes ⁏ First' for god þ*at* is hir Iuge / shal be w*ith* oute m*er*cy to hem / ne they may nat plese hym / ne noon of hise halwes / ne they ne may yeue no thyng' for hir*e* raunsou*n* / [225] ne they haue no Voys / to speke to hym / ne they may nat fle fro peyne / ne they haue no goodnesse in hem that they may shewe / to delyuer[e h]em fro peyne / And therfore seith Salomon ⁏ the wikked man dieþ *and* whan he is deed / he shal haue noon hope / to escape fro peyne ¶Who so thanne wolde wel vnderstonde thise peynes *and* bithynke hym wel / þ*at* he hath disserued thilke peynes for hise synnes / c*er*tes he sholde haue moore talent' to siken *and* to wepe / than for to syngen *and* to pleye ⁏ for as þ*at* seith Salomon / who so þ*at* hadde the science to knowe the peynes þ*at* ben establised *and* ordeyned for synne / he wolde make sorwe / thilke science / as seith Seint Augustyn / maketh a man / to waymente in his herte / [230] ¶The .iiij.ᵉ poynt that

352 The .iiij.ᵉ mevere to contricioun Hg (231)

hem ende as thogh men sholde dye anon but certes they shal nat dye / for as seith Seint Gregorie / to wrecche kaytyues shal be deeth withoute deeth / & ende withouten ende / & defaute withoute failynge / for hir deeth shal alwey lyuen / & hire ende shal eueremo bigynne / & hir defaute / shal nat faille / And therfore seith Seint John the Euangelist / they shullen folwe deeth / & they shal nat fynde hym / & they shul desiren to dye / And deeth shal fle fro hem / And eek Job seith / that in helle / is noon ordre of rewle / And al be it so that god hath creat alle thynges in right ordre / & no thyng withouten ordre but alle thynges been ordeyned & nombred / yet natheless they that been dampned been no thyng in ordre / ne holden noon ordre / for the erthe ne shal bere hem no fruyt / for as the prophete Dauid seith / god shal destroye the fruyt of the erthe / as fro hem / ne water ne shal yeue hem no moysture / ne the eyr no refresshyng / ne fyr no light / for as seith Seint Basile / the brennynge of the fyr of this world shal god yeuen in helle / to hem that been dampned / but the light & the cleernesse shal be yeuen in heuene to hise children / right as the goode man yeueth flessh to hise children & bones to hise houndes / And for they shullen haue noon hope to escape / seith Seint Job atte laste that ther shal horrour & grisly drede dwelle with outen ende // Horrour is alwey drede of harm that is to come / & this drede shal euere dwelle in the hertes / of hem that been dampned / And therfore han they lorn al hire hope for .vij. causes / ffirst for god that is hir Juge shal be withoute mercy to hem / ne they may nat plese hym / ne noon of hise halwes / ne they ne may yeue no thyng for hir raunson / ne they haue no voys to speke to hym / ne they may nat fle fro peyne / ne they haue no goodnesse in hem that they may shewe / to delyuere hem fro peyne / And therfore seith Salomon / the wikked man dieth & whan he is deed / he shal haue noon hope / to escape fro peyne ¶ Who so thanne wolde wel understonde thise peynes & bithynke hym wel / that he hath disserued thilke peynes for hise synnes / certes he sholde haue moore talent to siken & to wepe / than for to syngen & to pleye / for as that seith Salomon / Who so that hadde the science to knowe the peynes that been establised & ordeyned for synne / he wolde make sorwe / thilke science as seith Seint Augustyn maketh a man to waymente in his herte / ¶ The .iiij. point that

The .iiij. meuere to contricion

oghte make a man haue contricion is the sorwefull remembrance
of the good þt he hath left to doon here in erthe / & eek the good
þt he hath lorn / Soothly the goode werkes þt he hath left / either
they ben the goode werkes þt he wroghte er he fil in to deedly
synne / or ellis the goode werkes þt he wroghte whil he lay in
synne / Soothly the goode werkes þt he dide biforn þt he fil in
synne / ben al mortefied & astoned & dulled by the ofte syn
nynge / That othere goode werkes þt he wroghte / whil he lay
in dedly synne / they ben outrely dede / as to the lyf perdurable
in heuene / Thanne thilke goode werkes þt ben mortefied by
ofte synnyng / whiche goode werkes he dide while he was in
charitee / ne mowe neuere quyken agayn / wt oute verray peni
tence / and ther of seith god / by the mowth of Ezechiel / that
if the rightful man returne agayn from his rightwisnesse
& werke wikkednesse / shal he lyue / nay / for alle the goode
werkes þt he hath wroght / ne shulle neuere ben in remem
brance / for he shal dye in his synne / and vp on thilke cha
pitre / seith seint Gregorie thus / that we shul vnderstonde
this principally / that whan we doon dedly synne / it is for
naught thanne to reherse or drawen in to memorie the goode
werkes þt we han wroght / biforn / for certes in the werkynge
of the dedly synne / ther is no trust to no good werk þt we
han doon biforn / that is to seyn as for to haue ther by the
lyf perdurable in heuene / but natheles the goode werkes
quyken agayn and comen agayn & helpen & auaylen to ha
ue the lyf perdurable in heuene / whan we han contricion
but soothly the goode werkes þt men doon / whil þt they been
in dedly synne / for as muche as they weren doon in dedly
synne / they may neuere quyken agayn / for certes thyng þt ne
uere [illegible] lyf / may neuere quyken / and natheles al be it
þt they ne auayle noght to han the lyf perdurable / yet auay
len they to abregen of the peyne of helle / or ellis to gete
temporal richesses / or ellis þt god wole the rather enlumyne
& lighte the herte of the synful man to haue repentance
and eek they auailen for to vsen a man to doon goode werkes
þt the feend haue the lasse power of his soule / and thus
the curteys lord Ihu crist / ne wole þt no good werk be lost
for in som what it shal auayle / but for as muche as the
goode werkes / þt men doon whil they ben in good lyf / ben al
amortised by synne folwynge / and eek sith þt alle the

oghte make a man haue cont*ri*ciou*n* / is the sorweful remembrance of the good / *pa*t he hath left to doon here in erthe / *and* eek / the good *pa*t he hath lorn / Soothly / the goode werkes *pa*t he hath left either they ben the goode werkes *pa*t he wroghte er he fil in to deedly synne / or ellis / the goode werkes *pa*t he wroghte / whil he lay in synne / Soothly / the goode werkes *pa*t he dide biforn *pa*t he fil in synne / ben al mortefied / *and* astoned / *and* dulled / by the ofte synnynge / That othere goode werkes *pa*t he wroghte / whil he lay in dedly synne / they ben outrely dede / as to the lyf p*er*durable in heuene // thanne thilke goode werkes *pa*t ben mortefied by ofte synnyng which goode werkes he dide while he was in charitee / ne mowe neu*er*e quyken agayn / w*ith* oute verray penitence / [235] and ther of seith god / by the mowth of Ezechiel / that if the rightful man returne agayn from his rightwisnesse / *and* werke wikkednesse / shal he lyue ʃ / nay / for alle the goode werkes *pa*t he hath wroght ne shulle neuere ben in remembrance / for he shal dye / in his synne / and vp on thilke chapitre / seith Seint Gregorie thus // that we shul vnderstonde this / p*ri*ncipally / that whan we doon dedly synne / it is for nawght thanne to reherse / or drawen in to memorie / the goode werkes *pa*t we han wroght biforn ¶for c*er*tes / in the werkynge of the dedly synne / ther is no trust to no good werk. *pa*t we han doon biforn / that is to seyn / as for to haue ther by / the lyf p*er*durable in heuene / [240] but nathelees / the goode werkes quyken agayn and comen agayn *and* helpen *and* auaylen / to haue the lyf p*er*durable in heuene / whan we han Contricion / but soothly the goode werkes *pa*t men doon / whil *pa*t they been in dedly synne / for as muche / as they weren doon in dedly synne / they may neuere quyken agayn / for c*er*tes / thyng *pa*t neuere [ha]dde lyf / may neuere quyken / and natheles / al be it / *pa*t they ne auayle noght to han the lyf p*er*durable / yet auaylen they / to abreggen of the peyne of helle / or ellis / to gete temporal richesses / or ellis / *pa*t god wole the rather enlumyne *and* lighte / the herte of the synful man to han repentance ʃ And eek they auailen / for to vsen a man to doon goode werkes / *pa*t the feend / haue the lasse power of his soule / [245] and thus the curteys lord I*es*u crist ne wole *pa*t no good werk be lost for in som what it shal auayle / but for as muche as the goode werkes / *pa*t men doon whil they ben in good lyf ben al amortised by synne folwynge ʃ / and eek sith *pa*t alle the goode werkes þ*at* men doon / whil they ben in dedly synne / ben outrely dede / as for to han / the lyf p*er*durable / wel may þ*at* man / þ*at* no good werk ne dooth / synge thilke newe frenshe song **Iay tout p*er*du / mon temps *et* mon labour** // For certes synne bireueth a man / bothe goodnesse of nature / *and* eek the goodnesse of grace / for soothly / the grace of the holy goost fareth lyk fyr / þ*at* may nat ben ydel / for fyr faileth / anon / as it forleteth his werkynge / and right so g*ra*ce faileth / anon as it forleteth his werkynge / thanne leseth the synful man / the goodnesse of glorie / that oonly / is bihight to goode men þ*at* labouren and werken / Wel may he be sory thanne þ*at* oweth al his lyf to god / as longe as he hath lyued / and eek as longe as he shal lyue / þ*at* no goodnesse ne hath / to paye with his dette to god / to whom he oweth al his lyf / for truste wel / he shal yeue acountes as seith Seint Bernard / of alle the goodes þ*at* han ben yeuen hym in this p*re*sent lyf / and how he hath hem despended / nat so muche / þ*at* ther shal nat p*er*isse an heer of his heed / ne a moment of an houre ne shal nat p*er*isse of his tyme / þ*at* he ne shal yeue of it a rekenynge ¶The .v.the thyng / þ*at* oghte moeue a man to Contriciou*n* / is remembrance of the passion þ*at* oure lord I*es*u crist suffred for oure synnes / for as seith Seint Bernard / Whil þ*at* I lyue / I shal haue remembrance of the trauailes þ*at* oure lord I*es*u crist suffred in p*re*chynge / his werynesse in t*ra*uailynge / hise temptacions whan he fasted / hise longe wakynges whan he preyed / hise teerys whan þ*at* he weep for pitee of good peple / the wo / and the shame / *and* the filthe þ*at* men seyden to hym / of the foule spittyng þ*at* men spitte on his face / of the buffettes / þ*at* men yaue hym / of the fowle Mowwes *and* of the repreues þ*at* men to hym seyden / of the nayles / wi*th* whiche he was nayled to the croys / and of al the remenant of his passiou*n* / þ*at* he suffred for my synnes / and no thyng for his gilt // And ye shal vnderstonde / þ*at* in mannes synne / is euery manere ordre of ordinance / turned vp so down / for it is sooþ þ*at* god /. and reson /. and sensualitee. *and* the body of man / ben so ordeyned / þ*at* euerich of thise .iiij. thynges / sholde haue lordshipe ouer that oother / as thus /. god sholde haue lordshipe ouer resou*n* / *and* resou*n* ouer Sensualitee / *and* Sensualitee ou*er* the body of man / but soothly / whan man synneth / al this ordre / or ordinance / is turned vp so down / and therfore

411 The .v.the mevere t[o] contricioun Hg (255)

goode werkes þt men doon whil they ben in dedly synne ben
outrely dede as for to han the lyf perdurable / wel may þt man
þt no good werk ne dooth synge thilke newe frenshe song /
Jay tout perdu mon temps & mon labour / ffor certes syn
ne bireueth a man bothe goodnesse of nature & eek the good
nesse of grace / for soothly the grace of the holy goost fareth
lyk fyr þt may nat ben ydel / for fyr faileth anon as it
forleteth his werkynge and right so grace faileth anon as it
forleteth his werkynge / thanne leseth the synful man the
goodnesse of glorie that oonly is bihight to goode men þt la
bouren and werken / wel may he be sory thanne þt oweth al
his lyf to god as longe as he hath lyued / and eek as longe
as he shal lyue þt no goodnesse ne hath to paye with his
dette to god to whom he oweth al his lyf / for truste wel he
shal yeue acountes as seith Seint Bernard / of alle the goo
des þt han ben yeuen hym in this present lyf / and how he hath
hem despended nat so muche þt ther shal nat perisse an heer
of his heed ne a moment of an houre ne shal nat perisse of
his tyme þt he ne shal yeue of it a rekenyng / The .v.the — The .v.the meuere [...] contricion
thyng þt oghte moeue a man to contricion is remembrance
of the passion þt oure lord Jhesu crist suffred for oure synnes
for as seith Seint Bernard / whil þt I lyue I shal haue re
membrance of the trauailes þt oure lord Jhesu crist suffred in
prechynge / his werynesse in trauaillynge / hise temptacions whan
he fasted / hise longe wakynges whan he preyed / hise teeris
whan þt he weep for pitee of good peple / the wo and the
shame & the filthe þt men seyden to hym / of the foule spit
tyng þt men spitte on his face / of the buffettes þt men
yaue hym / of the foule mowes & of the repreues þt men
to hym seyden / of the nayles with whiche he was nayled
to the croys and of al the remenant of his passion þt he
suffred for my synnes and no thyng for his gilt / and ye
shal vnderstonde þt in mannes synne is euery manere
ordre of ordinance turned vp so doun / for it is sooth þt
god . and reson . and sensualitee . & the body of man ben so
ordeyned þt euerich of thise . iiij . thynges sholde haue lord
shipe ouer that oother / as thus . god sholde haue lordshi
pe ouer reson & reson ouer sensualitee & sensualitee ou
the body of man / but soothly whan man synneth al this
ordre or ordinance is turned vp so doun / and therfore

thanne for as muche as the reson of man ne wol nat be subget
ne obeisaunt to god þt is his lord by right / therfore leseth it the
lordshipe þt it sholde haue in sensualitee & eek ouer the body of
man / and why for sensualitee rebelleth thanne agayns reson
and by that wey leseth reson the lordshipe ouer sensualitee &
ouer the body for right as reson is rebel to god right so is bothe
sensualitee rebel to reson & the body also / and certes this desordinaun
ce & this rebellion oure lord Ihu crist aboghte vp on his precious body
ful deere / and herkneth in which wise / for as muche thanne as re
son is rebel to god therfore is man worthy to haue sorwe and
to be deed / this suffred oure lord Ihu crist for man after þt he
hadde be bitraysed of his disciple and distreyned & bounde so þt
the blood brast out at euery nayl of hise handes / as seith Seint
Augustyn / and forther ouer for as muchel as reson of man ne
wol nat daunte sensualitee whan it may / therfore is man wor
thy to han shame / and this suffrede oure lord Ihu crist / for man
whan they spette in his visage / and forther ouer for as muche
thanne as the caytif body of man is rebel bothe to reson & to
sensualitee therfore is it worthy the deeth / and this suffred oure
lord Ihu crist for man vp on the crois wher as ther nas no part
of his body free withoute greet peyne & bitter passion / and al this
suffred Ihu crist þt neuere forfeted / to muchel am I peyned for the
thynges þt I neuere deserued and to muche defouled for shendshi
pe þt man is worthy to haue / and therfore may the synful
man wel seye as seith Seint Bernard / acursed be the bitternesse
of my synne for which ther moste be suffred so muche bitternesse
for certes after the diuerse disordinaunces of oure wikkednesses / was
the passion of Ihu crist ordeyned in diuerse thynges / as thus
Certes synful mannes soule is bitraysed of the deuel by coue
tise of temporel prosperitee & scorned by deceyte whan he cheseth
flesshly delites / and yet is it tormented by inpacience of aduersi
tee and bispet by seruage & subiection of synne / and atte laste
it is slayn fynally / for this desordinaunce of synful man was
Ihu crist first bitraysed and after that was he bounde / þt cam
for to vnbynde vs of synne & of peyne / thanne was he biscor
ned þt oonly sholde ben honoured in alle thynges of alle thyn
ges / thanne was his visage þt oghte be desired to be seyn of al
mankynde in which visage angels desiren to looke vileynsly
bispet / thanne was he scourged þt no thyng hadde agilt / and
fynally thanne was he crucified & slayn / thanne was acompli

thanne / for as muche as the reson of man / ne wol nat be subget ne obeisau*n*t to god / þ*at* is his lord by right / // therfore leseth it the lordshipe / þ*at* it sholde haue in sensualitee / *and* eek ouer the body of man / and why / for sensualitee rebelleth thanne agayns resou*n* / and by that wey / leseth reson the lordshipe ouer sensualitee *and* ouer the body / for right as reson is rebel to god / right so is bothe sensualitee rebel to reson *and* the body also // and c*er*tes this desordinau*n*ce *and* this rebelliou*n* / oure lord I*es*u crist aboghte / vp on his p*re*cious body ful deere / and herkneth in which wise // for as muche thanne / as reson is rebel to god / therfore is man worthy to haue sorwe / and to be deed / this suffred oure lord I*es*u crist for man / after þ*at* he hadde be bitraysed of his disciple and destreyned *and* bounde so / þ*at* the blood brast out at euery nayl of hise handes / as seith Seint Augustyn // And forther ouer for as muchel as reson of man ne wol nat daunte sensualitee whan it may // / therfore / is man worthy to han shame / and this suffrede oure lord I*es*u crist for man whan they spette in his visage // and forther ouer for as muche thanne / as the kaytif body of man / is rebel / bothe to resou*n* *and* to sensualitee / therfore / is it worthy the deeth / and this suffred oure lord I*es*u c*ri*st for man vp on the croys / wher*e* as ther nas no part of his body free w*ith* oute gret peyne *and* bitter passiou*n* / and al this suffred I*es*u crist þ*at* neu*er*e forfeted //[3] to muchel am I peyned for the thynges þ*at* I neuere deserued and to muche defouled for shendshipe / þ*at* man is worthy to haue // And therfore / may the synful man wel seye / as seith Seint Bernard / Acursed be the bitternesse of my synne / for which / ther moste be suffred so muche bitternesse / for c*er*tes after the diu*er*se discordau*n*ces of oure wikkednesses / was the passiou*n* of I*es*u crist ordeyned in diu*er*se thynges // As thus // Certes synful mannes soule / is bitraysed of the deuel by coueitise of temporel p*ro*sp*er*itee / *and* scorned by deceyte / whan he cheseth flesshly delites / and yet is it tormented by inpacience of Adu*er*sitee / and byspet by seruage *and* subieccio*u*n of synne / and atte laste / it is slayn fynally // for this desordenau*n*ce of synful man / was I*es*u crist first bitraysed / and after that was he bownde / þ*at* cam for to vnbynde vs / of Synne *and* of peyne // thanne was he biscorned / þ*at* oonly sholde ben honoured in alle thynges of alle thynges / thanne was his visage þ*at* oghte be desired to be seyn of all mankynde in which visage Angels desiren to looke / vileynsly bispet / thanne was he skourged / þ*at* no thyng hadde agilt and fynally / thanne was he crucefied *and* slayn // thanne was acompli-

[3] *Out* Hg El. Other MSS read:

forfeted //] And therfore reasonabely may be seyd of Iesu in this manere [to muchel Gg f.] And thus he seide [t.m. Cn-En[3] f.] and saide [t.m. Ra[2] f.] And þerfor may he say [t.m. Ll[2] f.] Wele myght he say [t.m. Py.

ced the word of Ysaie / He was wounded for oure mysdedes / *and* defouled by oure felonyes ¶Now sith þ*a*t Ie*s*u crist' took vp on hym self the peyne of alle oure wikkednesses ʃ / muchel oghte synful man wepe *and* biwayle / þ*a*t for hise synnes / goddes sone of heuene / sholde al this peyne endure ¶The .vj.[the] thyng' þ*a*t oghte moeue a man to Contriciou*n* is the hope of .iij. thynges / ʃ that is to seyn / foryeuenesse of synne / and the yifte of grace wel for to do / and the glorie of heuene / w*ith* which god shal gerdone man for hise goode dedes / And for as muche / as Ie*s*u crist' yeueth vs thise yiftes of his largesse *and* of his soue*r*eyn bou*n*tee / therfore is he clepid **Ie*s*us Nazarenus rex Iudeor*um*** ¶Ie*s*u is for to seyn / Saueour / or Sauaciou*n* / on whom men shal hope / to haue foryifnesse of synnes / which þ*a*t is p*ro*prely / Sauacion of synnes / [285] and therfore / seyde the Au*n*gel to Ioseph / thow shalt clepe his name Ie*s*us / þ*a*t shal saue his peple of hir*e* synnes / And heer of / seith Seint Peter / ther is noon oother name vnder heuene þ*a*t is yeue to any man / by which a man may be saued / but oonly Ie*s*us ¶Nazarenus / is as muche for to seye / as florissynge / In which a man shal hope / þ*a*t he / þ*a*t yeueth hym remissiou*n* of synnes / shal yeue hym eek' *gra*ce wel to do / for in the flour / is hope of fruyt' in tyme comynge / and in foryifnesse of synnes / hope of g*ra*ce wel to do ¶I was at the dore of thyn herte seith Ie*s*us / *and* clepede for to entre / he þ*a*t opneth to me / shal haue foryifnesse of synne / I wol entre in to hym by my g*ra*ce / and sowpe w*ith* hym / by the goode werkes þ*a*t he shal doon / whiche werkes / ben the foode of god / and he shal sowpe w*ith* me / by the grete ioye þ*a*t I shal yeue hym [290] / thus shal man hope / þ*a*t for hise werkes of penau*n*ce / god shal yeue hym his regne / as he byheteth hym in the gospel. ¶Now shal man vnderstonde / in which manere shal ben his contriciou*n* / I seye / that it shal ben vniu*er*sal and total / this is to seyn / a man shal be verray repentau*n*t / for alle hise synnes þ*a*t he hath doon / in delit of his thoght'. for delit is ful p*er*ilous / for ther ben two manere of consentynges / that oon of hem / is clepid / consentynge of affeccion / whan a man / is moeued to ⟨do⟩ synne / and thanne deliteth hym longe / for to thynke on that synne / and his reson / ap*er*ceyueth wel þ*a*t it is synne / agayns the lawe of god / and yet his resou*n* / refreyneth nat his fool delit / or talent' though he seeth wel apertly / þ*a*t it is agayns the reuerence of god / al though his resou*n* / ne consente nat / to doon the

477 The .vj.[the] m[evere to] con[tricioun] Hg (283)

501 In what manere o[ghte] ben thy contricioun Hg (292)

as the word of ysaie / he was wounded for oure mysdedes &
defouled by oure felonyes ¶ Now sith þt Jhu crist / took up on
hym self the peyne of alle oure wikkednesses / muchel oghte
synful man wepe & biwayle þt for hise synnes goddes sone
of heuene sholde al this peyne endure ¶ The vj.the thyng þt
oghte moeue a man to contricion is the hope of .iij. thynges /
that is to seyn foryeuenesse of synne and the yifte of grace
wel for to do and the glorie of heuene wt which god shal ger
done man for hise goode dedes / And for as muche as Jhu crist
yeueth us thise yiftes of his largesse & of his souereyn bountee
ther fore is he cleped Jhus Nazarenus rex iudeorum ¶ Jhu is for
to seyn Saueour or Saluacion on whom men shal hope to ha
ue foryifnesse of synnes which þt is propely saluacion of syn
nes And therfore seyde the angel to Joseph / thow shalt clepe
his name Jhus þt shal saue his peple of hir synnes And heer
of seith seint Peter / ther is noon oother name under heue
ne þt is yeue to any man by which a man may be saued but
oonly Jhus ¶ Nazarenus is as muche for to seye as florisshynge
In which a man shal hope þt he þt yeueth hym remission of
synnes shal yeue hym eek grace wel to do for in the flour is
hope of fruyt in tyme comynge and in foryifnesse of synnes
hope of grace wel to do ¶ I was at the dore of thyn herte seith
Jhus & clepede for to entre he þt openeth to me shal haue foryif
nesse of synne I wol entre in to hym by my grace and soupe
wt hym by the goode werkes þt he shal doon whiche werkes
ben the foode of god and he shal soupe wt me by the grete
ioye þt I shal yeue hym thus shal man hope þt for hise
werkes of penance god shal yeue hym his regne as he by
heteth hym in the gospel. ¶ Now shal man understonde
in which manere shal ben his contricion I seye that it shal
ben universal and total this is to seyn a man shal be ver
ray repentant for alle hise synnes þt he hath doon in de
lit of his thoght. for delit is ful perilous / for ther ben two ma
nere of consentynges that oon of hem is cleped consentyn
ge of affection whan a man is moeued to synne and than
ne deliteth hym longe for to thynke on that synne and his
reson aperceyueth wel þt it is synne agayns the lawe of god
And yet his reson refreyneth nat his foul delit or talent
though he seeth wel apertly þt it is agayns the reuerence
of god / Al though his reson ne consente nat to doon tho

The .vj. the thing / iij con.

In what manere s[hulde] ben thy contricion

synne in dede / yet seyn somme doctours y^t swich delit y^t dwelleth
longe it is ful perilous al be never so lite / and also a man shol
de sorwe namely for al that evere he hath desired agayn the
lawe of god with parfit consentynge of his reson for ther of is
no doute y^t it is dedly synne in the consentynge for certes ther
is no dedly synne y^t it nas first in mannes thoght & after
that in his delit & so forth in to consentynge & in to dede wher
fore I seye y^t many men ne repenten hem never of swiche
thoghtes & delites ne nevere shryven hem of it but oonly of the
dede of grete synnes outward ¶ Wher fore I seye y^t swiche wik
ked delites & wikked thoghtes ben subtil bigylers of hem y^t
shullen ben dampned ¶ Moore over man oghte to sorwen for
hise wikked wordes as wel as hise wikked dedes / for certes the
repentaunce of a singuler synne & nat repente of alle hise othe
re synnes / or ellis repente hym of alle hise othere synnes and
nat of a synguler synne may nat availe / for certes god al
myghty is al good and ther fore outher he foryeveth al or
ellis right noght and her of seith Seint Augustyn ¶ I woot
certeynly y^t god is enemy to everich synnere and how thanne
he y^t observeth o synne shal he have foryevenesse of the re
menant of hise othere synnes ? nay ¶ And forther over con
tricion sholde be wonder sorweful and anguissous and ther
fore yeveth hym god pleynly his mercy and ther fore whan my
soule was anguissous w^t inne me I hadde remembrance of
god y^t my preyere myghte come to hym ¶ fforther over contri
tion moste be continuel and y^t man have stedefast purpos to shry
ve hym & for to amende hym of his lyf for soothly whil con
tricion lasteth man may evere have hope of foryevenesse and
of this cometh hate of synne y^t destroyeth synne bothe in hym
self & eek in othere folk at his power / for which seith david
ye y^t loven god hateth wikkednesse / for trusteth wel to love
god is for to love that he loveth & hate that he hateth ¶ The
laste thyng y^t men shal understonde in contricion is this wher
of availeth contricion ¶ I seye y^t somtyme contricion delyue
reth man fro synne of which y^t david seith I seye quod da
uid that is to seyn I purposed fermely to shryve me & thow
lord relessedest my synne and right so as contricion availeth
nat w^t outen sad purpos of shrifte if man have oportuny
tee / right so litel worth is shrifte or satisfaction with oute
contricion / And moore / contricion destroyeth the prison of helle

& and maketh wayk

synne in dede / yet seyn so*m*me doctours / þ*at* swich delit þ*at* dwelleþ longe / it is ful p*er*ilous / al be neuer so lite / [295] and also / a man sholde sorwe / namely / for al that euere he hath desired agayn the lawe of god / with p*ar*fit consentynge of his resou*n* / for ther of is no doute / þ*at* it is dedly synne / in the consentynge / for c*er*tes ther is no dedly synne / þ*at* it nas first' in mannes thoght' *and* after that' in his delit' *and* so forth / in to consentynge *and* in to dede / Wherfore I seye / þ*at* many men ne repenten hem neuere of swyche thoghtes *and* delites / ne neu*er*e shryuen hem of it / but oonly / of the dede of grete synnes outward ¶wher fore I seye / þ*at* swiche wikked delites *and* wikked thoghtes / ben subtil bigyleris of hem þ*at* shullen ben dampned ¶Moore ouer / man oghte to sorwen for hise wikked wordes / as wel / as hise wikked dedes / for c*er*tes / the repentance of a singuler synne *and* nat repente of alle hise othere synnes / or ellis repente hym of alle hise othere synnes / and nat of a synguler synne / may nat auayle / [300] for c*er*tes / god almyghty / is al good / and therfore / outher he foryeueth al / or ellis right noght / And her of seith Seint Augustyn ¶I woot c*er*teynly / þ*at* god is enemy to euerich synnere / And how thanne / he þ*at* obserueth o synne / shal he haue foryeuenesse of the remenant' of hise othere synnes ./ nay ./ ¶And forther ouer Contriciou*n* / sholde be wonder sorweful and anguissous / and ther fore / yeueth hym god / pleynly his m*er*cy / and therfore / whan my soule was anguissous w*ith* Inne me / I hadde remembrau*n*ce of god / þ*at* my prayere myghte come to hym ¶Forther ouer / Cont*ri*ciou*n* moste be continuel / and þ*at* man haue stedefast p*ur*pos to shryue hym / *and* for to amende hym of his lyf / [305] for soothly / whil Contricion lasteth / man may euere haue hope of foryeuenesse / And of this / cometh hate of synne / þ*at* destroyeth synne / bothe in hym self' *and* eek in othere folk' at his power / for which seith Dauid / ye þ*at* louen god / hateth wikkednesse / for trusteth wel / to loue god / is for to loue that he loueth / *and* hate that he hateth ¶The laste thyng' þ*at* men shal vnderstonde in Contriciou*n* / is this / wher of auaileth Contriciou*n* ¶I seye / þ*at* som tyme / Contriciou*n* delyuereth man fro synne / of which þ*at* Dauid seith / I seye quod Dauid / that is to seyn / I. purposed fermely to shryue me / *and* thow lord / relessedest my synne / and right so as Contriciou*n* auaileth nat / w*ith* outen sad purpos of shrifte / if man haue oportunytee ./ right' so / litel worth is shrifte / or satisfacciou*n* / with oute Contriciou*n* / [310] And moore / Contricion destroyeth the prisou*n* of helle

And maketh wayk'

544 nota Hg (307)

and maketh wayk⁊ *and* feble / the strengthes of the deueles / *and* restoreth the yiftes of the holy goost⁊ *and* of alle goode v*er*tues / and it clenseth the soule of synne *and* delyuereth the soule fro the peyne of helle / *and* fro the compaignye of the deuel / and fro the seruage of synne / *and* restoreth it⁊ to alle goodes espirituels *and* to the compaignye co*m*munyou*n* of holy chirche / and forther ouer⁊ it maketh hym / þ*at* whilom was sone of Ire / to be sone of grace / and alle thise thynges / be preued by holy writ / and therfore / he þ*at* wolde sette his entente / to thise thynges / he were ful wys / for soothly / he ne sholde nat thanne in al his lyf / haue corage to synne / but yeue his body *and* al his herte / to the seruyce of Ie*s*u crist⁊ *and* ther of doon hym ho*m*mage / for certes / oure swete lord Ie*s*u crist hath sparid vs so debonairly in oure folies / þ*at* if he ne hadde pitee of mannes soule / a sory song / we myghten alle synge

¶Explicit p*ri*ma pars penitencie./ ¶Et incipit se*cun*da pars eiusdem

The seconde partie of Penitence / is Confessiou*n* / that is signe of Contriciou*n* ¶Now shul ye vnderstonde / what is / Confessiou*n* / *and* wheither it oghte nedes be doon / or noon / *and* whiche thynges ben couenable to v*er*ray Confessiou*n* ¶First⁊ shaltow vnderstonde / þ*at* Confession is verray shewynge of synnes to the preest⁊ this is to seyn v*er*ray / for he moot confesse hym of alle the condiciou*n*s þ*at* bilongen to his synne / as ferforþ as he kan / al moot be seyd / *and* no thyng excused / ne hid / ne forwrapped / *and* nat auau*n*ce hym of hise goode werkes ⁊ And forther ouer / it is necessarie to vnderstonde / whennes þ*at* synnes spryngen / *and* how they encressen / *and* whiche they ben ¶Of the sprynge of Synnes / as seith Seint Paul in this wise ⁊ that right as by a man / synne entred first⁊ in to this world / and thurgh that synne deth / ./ right so thilke deth / entred in to alle men þ*at* synneden / and this man was Adam / by whom synne entred in to this world / whan he brak⁊ the comandementz of god / and therfore / he þ*at* first was so myghty / þ*at* he sholde nat haue deyed / bicam swich oon / þ*at* he moste nedes dye wheither he wolde or noon / *and* al his p*ro*genye þ*at* is in this world / þ*at* in thilke man synneden ¶Looke / þ*at* in thestat of Innocence / whan Adam *and* Eue / naked weren in Paradys

And maketh wayk & feble the strengthes of the deueles & resto
reth the yiftes of the holy goost & of alle goode vertues And it
clenseth the soule of synne & delyuereth the soule fro the peyne
of helle & fro the compaignye of the deuel And fro the serua
ge of synne & restoreth it to alle goodes espirituels & to the
compaignye communyon of holy chirche And forther ouer it
maketh hym þt whilom was sone of ire to be sone of grace
And alle thise thynges he preued by holy writ And therfore
he þt wolde sette his entente to thise thynges he were ful wys
for soothly he ne sholde nat thanne in al his lyf haue corage
to synne but yeue his body & al his herte to the seruyce of
Ihu crist & ther of doon hym homage for certes oure swete
lord Ihu crist hath spared vs so debonairly in oure folies þt
if he ne hadde pitee of mannes soule a sory song we mygh
ten alle synge

Explicit prima pars penitentie Et incipit secunda
pars eiusdem

The seconde partie of Penitence is Confessioun that is
signe of Contricioun Now shul ye vnderstonde what
is Confessioun & wheither it oghte nedes be doon or noon &
whiche thynges ben couenable to verray Confessioun First
shaltow vnderstonde þt Confessioun is verray shewynge of
synnes to the preest this is to seyn verray for he moot confesse
hym of alle the condiciouns þt bilongen to his synne as ferforth
as he kan Al moot be seyd & no thyng excused ne hid ne for
wrapped & nat auante hym of hise goode werkes And forther
ouer it is necessarie to vnderstonde whennes þt synnes sprin
gen & how they encreessen & whiche they ben Of the sprin
gynge of synnes as seith Seint Paul in this wise that
right as by a man synne entred first in to this world And
thurgh that synne deth right so thilke deth entred in to alle
men þt synneden And this man was Adam by whom syn
ne entred in to this world whan he brak the comaundementz
of god And therfore he þt first was so myghty þt he shol
de nat haue deyed bicam swich oon þt he moste nedes dye
wheither he wolde or noon & al his progenye þt is in this
world þt in thilke man synneden Looke þt in thestat of
Innocence whan Adam & Eue naked weren in Paradys

and no thyng ne hadden shame of hir nakednesse / How þt the serpent
þt was moost wily of alle othere bestes þt god hadde maked / seyde to
the woman / Why comanded god to yow / ye sholde nat eten of every
tree in Paradys / the woman answerde / Of the fruyt quod she of
the trees in Paradys we feden us / but soothly / of the fruyt of
the tree þt is in the myddel of Paradys god forbad us for to ete
ne nat touche it / lest per aventure we sholde dyen / the serpent
seyde to the woman / nay nay / ye shul nat dyen of deth / for sothe
god woot / þt what day þt ye eten ther of / youre eyen shulle
opne & ye shul ben as goddes / knowynge good & harm / the
womman saugh / þt the tree was good to fedynge / and fair to
the eyen & delitable to sighte / she took of the fruyt / of the tree
& eet it / & yaf it to hire housbonde / & he eet / & anon the eyen of
hem bothe opnede / and whan þt they knewe þt they were naked
they sowed of ffyge leves in manere of breches to hiden hire
membres / here may ye seen þt dedly synne hath first sugges
tion of the feend as sheweth here by the naddre / and afterward
the delit of the flessh as sheweth here by Eua / and after that
the consentynge of reson as sheweth here by Adam / for truste
wel / though so were þt the feend tempted Eue that is to seyn
the flessh / and the flessh hadde delit in the beautee of the fruyt
deffended / yet certes til þt reson / that is to seyn Adam / consen
ted to the etyng of the fruyt / yet stood he in the estat of Inno
cence ¶ Of thilke Adam toke we thilke synne original / for of
hym flesshly descended be we alle & engendred of vile & corrupt
matere / and whan the soule is put in oure body / right anoon
is contract original synne / and that þt was erst / but oonly pey
ne of concupiscence is afterward bothe peyne & synne / and
ther fore be we alle yborn sones of wrathe & of dampnacion
perdurable if it nere baptesme þt we receyven / which bynymeth
us the culpe / but for sothe the peyne dwelleth with us as to
temptacion / which peyne highte concupiscence / and this concu
piscence whan it is wrongfully disposed or ordeyned in man
it maketh hym coveite by coveitise of flessh flesshly synne
by sighte of his eyen as to erthely thynges / and eek coveiti
se of heynesse by pryde of herte ¶ Now as to speke of the
firste coveitise / that is concupiscence after the lawe of oure
membres þt weren lawefulliche ymaked & by rightful Juge
ment of god / I seye for as muche as man is nat obeisant
to god that is his lord ther fore is the flessh to hym desobeisant

and no thyng ne hadden shame of hir nakednesse / [325] how þat the serpent þat was moost wily of alle othere bestes þat god hadde maked / seyde to the wo*m*man // why comanded god to yow / ye sholde nat eten of euery tree in Paradys ⁄ // the wo*m*man answerde / Of the fruyt quod she of the trees in Paradys / we feden vs / but soothly / of the fruyt of the tree þat is in the myddel of Paradys / god forbad vs for to ete / ne nat touche it / list p*ar* auenture we sholde dyen // the serpent seyde to the wo*m*man / nay / nay / ye shul nat dyen of deth / for sothe god woot þat what day þat ye eten ther of / youre eyen shulle opne / *and* ye shul ben as goddes / konnynge good *and* harm // the womman saugh / þat the tree was good to fedynge / and fair to the eyen / *and* delitable to sighte / ⁄ she took of the fruyt of the tree *and* eet it / *and* yaf it to hir*e* housbonde / *and* he eet *and* anon the eyen of hem bothe opnede / and whan þat they knewe þat they were naked / they sowed of Fyge leues in manere of breches / to hiden hire membres [330] // Here may ye seen / þat dedly synne / hath first sugges-tiou*n* of the feend / as sheweth heere by the Naddre / and afterward the delit of the flessh̄ / as sheweth heere by Eua / and after that the consentynge of resou*n* / as sheweth heere by Adam / for truste wel / thogh so were / þat the feend tempted oon / that is to seyn the flessh̄ / and the flessh hadde delit in the beautee of the fruyt deffended / ⁄ yet c*er*tes til þat reson / that is to seyn Adam / consen-ted to the etyng of the fruyt yet stood he / in the estat of Inno-cence ¶Of thilke Adam / toke we thilke synne original / for of hym / flesshly descended be we alle *and* engendred / and vile *and* corrupt matere / and whan the soule / is put in oure body / right anoon is contract original synne / and that / þat was erst but oonly pey-ne of concupiscence / is afterward / bothe peyne *and* synne / And ther fore be we alle yborn sones of wraththe *and* of dampnaciou*n* p*er*durable / if it nere baptesme / þat we receyuen / which bynymeþ vs the culpe / but for sothe / the peyne dwelleth with vs as to temptaciou*n* / which peyne / highte concupiscence / [335] and this concu-piscence / whan it is wrongfully disposed / or ordeyned in man / it maketh hym coueite by coueitise of flessh̄ / flesshly synne / by sighte of hise eyen / as to erthely thynges / And eek coueiti-se of heynesse by pryde of herte ¶Now / as to speke of the firste coueitise / that is concupiscence / after the lawe of oure membres þat weren lawefulliche ymaked *and* by rightful Iuge-ment of god / I seye / for as muche / as man is nat obeisau*n*t to god / that is his lord / therfore / is the flessh̄ to hym desobeisau*n*t thurgh concupiscence / which þ*at* yet is clepid norissynne of synne *and* occasiou*n* of synne / therfore / al the while þ*at* a man hath in hym the peyne of concupiscence / it is impossible / but he be tempted som tyme *and* moeued in his flessh to synne / and this thyng may nat faile as longe as he lyueth / it may wel wexe feble and faile by v*er*tu of baptesme *and* by the *gra*ce of god / thurgh penitence / [340] but fully ne shal it neuere quenche / þ*at* he ne shal somtyme / be moeued in hym self but if he were al refreided by siknesse / or by malefice of sorcerye / or colde drynkes / for lo / what seith Seint Paul / the flessh coueiteth agayn the spirit / *and* the spirit agayn the flessh / they ben so contrarie *and* so stryuen / þ*at* a man may nat alwey do as he wolde ¶The same Seynt Paul / after his grete penau*n*ce in water *and* in londe / in water by nyght *and* by day in gret p*er*il *and* in gret peyne in londe / in famyn *and* thurst in cold and clothlees *and* ones stooned almoost to the deth / yet seyde he / Allas .I. kaytif man / who shal delyuere me fro the prison of my kaytif body / And Seint Ierom / whanne he longe tyme hadde woned in desert where as he ne hadde no compaignye / but of wilde bestes / wher*e* as he hadde no mete / but herbes / *and* water to his drynke / ne no bed / but the naked erthe / for which his flessh / was blak as an Ethiopen for hete *and* ney destroyed for cold /. [345] yet seyde he / þ*at* the brennynge of lecherye / boylede in al his body ¶Wherfore I woot wel sikerly / þ*at* they ben deceyued / þ*at* seyn / þ*at* they ne be nat tempted in hire body / Witnesse on Seint Iame the Apostel / that seith / that euery wight is tempted in his owene concupiscence / that is to seyn / that euerich of vs / hath matere *and* occasiou*n* / to be tempted / of the norissynge of synne. þ*at* is in his body / And therfore / seith Seint Iohn the Eu*a*ngelist / If þ*at* we seyn / þ*at* we be w*ith* oute synne / we deceyuen vs selue and trouthe is nat in vs / ¶Now shul ye vnderstonde in what manere / þ*at* synne wexeth *and* encresceth in man ¶the firste thyng is thilke norissynge of synne / of which I spak biforn / thilke flesshly concupiscence / [350] and after that comth the subieccio*un* of the deuel / this is to seyn / the deueles bely / w*ith* which he bloweth in man / the fyr of flesshly concupiscence / and after that a man bythynketh hym / wheither he wol doon or no / thilke thyng to which he is tempted / and thanne / if þ*at* a man w*ith* stonde

244

thurgh concupiscence / which þt yet is clepid norisshinge of synne & occasion of synne / therfore al the while þt a man hath in hym the peyne of concupiscence it is impossible / but he be tempted som tyme & moeued in his flessh to synne / And this thyng may nat faile as longe as he lyueth / it may wel wexe feble and faile by vertu of baptesme & by the grace of god thurgh penitence / but fully ne shal it neuere quenche / þt he ne shal som tyme be moeued in hym self / but if he were al refreyded by siknesse / or by malefice of sorcerye / or colde drynkes / for lo what seith seint Paul / the flessh coueiteth agayn the spirit & the spirit agayn the flessh / they ben so contrarie & so stryuen / þt a man may nat alwey do as he wolde / The same seynt Paul after his grete penance in water & in londe / in water by nyght & by day in gret peril & in gret peyne / in londe in famyn & thurst / in cold and clothlees & ones stooned almoost to the deth / yet seyde he allas / I kaytif man / who shal delyuere me fro the prisoun of my kaytif body / And seint Jerom / whanne he longe tyme hadde woned in desert / where as he ne hadde no compaignye but of wilde bestes / wher as he hadde no mete but herbes & water to his drynke / ne no bed but the naked erthe / for which his flessh was blak as an Ethiopen for hete & ney destroyed for cold / yet seyde he þt the brennynge of lecherye boylede in al his body / wherfore I woot wel sikerly þt they ben deceyued þt seyn þt they ne be nat tempted in hire body / witnesse on seint Jame the Apostel that seith / that euery wight is tempted in his owene concupiscence / that is to seyn / that euerich of vs hath matere & occasion to be tempted of the norisshinge of synne þt is in his body / And therfore seith seint John the Euangelist / If þt we seyn þt we be wt oute synne / we deceyuen vs selue and trouthe is nat in vs / Now shul ye vnderstonde in what manere þt synne wexeth & encresseth in man / The firste thyng is thilke norisshinge of synne of which I spak biforn / thilke flesshly concupiscence / And after that comth the subieccion of the deuel / this is to seyn the deueles bely / wt which he bloweth in man the fyr of flesshly concupiscence / And after that a man bythynketh hym / wheither he wol doon or no / thilke thyng to which he is tempted / And thanne if þt a man wt stonde

and weyue the firste entisynges of his flessh / & of the feend thanne
is it no synne / and if so be þt he do nat so / thanne feeleth he
anon a flawmbe of delit / and thanne is it good to be war / and
kepe hym wel / or ellis he wol falle anon in to consentynge of
synne / & thanne wol he do it if he may haue tyme & place / and
of this matere seith moyses / by the deuel in this manere ¶ The
feend seith / I wol chace & pursue the man by wikked suggestion /
and I wol hente hym by mouynge or styrynge of synne & I
wol departe my prise or my preye by deliberacion / & my lust
shal ben acompliced in delit / I wol drawe my swerd in consen
tynge / for certes right as a swerd departeth a thyng in two peces /
right so consentynge departeth god fro man / and thanne wol I
sle hym wt myn hand in dede of synne / thus seyth the feend /
for certes thanne is a man al deed in soule / and thus is synne
acompliced by temptacion / by delit / & by consentynge / & thanne
is the synne cleped actuel ¶ For sothe synne is in two maneres
outher it venyal / or dedly synne / Sothly whan man loueth a
ny creature moore than Ihu crist oure creatour / thanne is it ded
ly synne / and venial synne is it / if man loue Ihu crist lasse
than hym oghte / for sothe the dede of this venial synne is ful
perilous / for it amenuseth the loue þt men sholde han to god moo
re & moore / and therfore if a man charge hym self wt manye
swiche venial synnes / certes but if so be þt he som tyme deschar
ge hym of hem by shrifte / they mowe ful lightly amenuse in
hym al the loue þt he hath to Ihu crist / and in this wise skip
peth venial in to dedly synne / for certes the moore þt a man char
geth his soule wt venial synnes / the moore is he enclyned to
falle in dedly synne / and therfore lat vs nat be necligent to
deschargen vs of venial synnes / for the prouerbe seith / that manye
smale maketh a greet / and herkne this ensample / A greet wa
we of the see comth som tyme wt so greet a violence / that it
drencheth the ship / and the same harm doon som tyme the sma
le dropes of water / þt entreth thurgh a litel creuesse in to the
thurrok & in the botme of the ship / if men be so necligent þt men
ne descharge hem nat by tyme / and therfore al thogh ther be
a difference bitwixe thise two causes of drenchynge / algates the
ship is dreynt ¶ Right so fareth it som tyme of dedly synne /
& of anoyouse venials synnes / whan they multiplie in a man
so gretly þt thilke worldly thynges þt he loueth / thurgh which
he synneth venially / is as greet in his herte as the loue of

and wayue the firste entisynges of his flessħ / *and* of the feend / thanne is it no synne / and if so be / þ*at* he do nat so / thanne feeleth he anon a flawmbe of delit / and thanne is it good / to be war and kepe hym wel / or ellis he wol falle anon in to consentynge of synne / *and* thanne wol he do it / if he may haue tyme *and* place / And of this matere seith Moyses / by the deuel / in this manere ¶The feend seith / I wol chace *and* p*ur*sue the man / by wikked suggestiou*n* / and I wol hente hym / by moeuyng or stiryng of synne / *and* .I. wol departe my prise / or my preye by deliberaciou*n* / *and* my lust shal ben acompliced in delit / I wol drawe my swerd in consentynge / [355] for c*er*tes / right as a swerd departeth a thyng in two peces / right so consentynge / departeth god fro man / and thanne wol I sle hym w*ith* myn hand in dede of synne / thus seyth the feend / for certes / thanne is a man al deed in soule / and thus is synne acompliced / by temptaciou*n* / by delit *and* by consentynge / *and* thanne is the synne clepid actuel ¶For sothe / synne is in two man*er*es / outher it venyal / or dedly synne / Soothly / whan man loueth any creature / moore than Ie*s*u crist oure creatour / thanne is it dedly synne / and venial synne is it if man loue Ie*s*u crist lasse than hym oghte / for sothe / the dede of this venial synne is ful p*er*ilous / for it amenuseth the loue þ*at* men sholde han to god moore *and* moore / and therfore / if a man charge hym self w*ith* manye swiche venial synnes / certes / but if so be / þ*at* he som tyme descharge hym of hem by shrifte / they mowe ful lightly amenuse in hym / al the loue / þ*at* he hath to Ie*s*u crist / [360] and in this wise skippeth Venial / in to dedly synne / for c*er*tes / the moore þ*at* a man chargeth his soule / w*ith* venial synnes / the moore is he enclyned to falle in dedly synne / And therfore / lat vs nat be necligent / to deschargen vs of venial synnes / for the p*ro*u*er*be seith / that manye smale / maketh a greet / And herkne this ensample / A greet wawe of the See / comth som tyme / w*ith* so greet a violence / that it drencheth the Ship*e* / and the same harm / doon som tyme / the smale dropes of water / þ*at* entreth thurgh a litel creuesse in to the Thurrok / *and* in the botme of the ship*e* / if men be so necligent þ*at* men ne descharge hem nat by tyme / and therfore / al thogh ther be a difference / bitwixe thise two causes of drenchynge / algates the Ship*e* is dreynt ¶right so fareth it som tyme of dedly synne / *and* of anoyouse venials synnes / whan they multiplie in a man so gretly / þ*at* thilke worldly thynges þ*at* he loueth / thurgh which he synneth venially / is as gret in his herte / as the loue of god / or moore / [365] and therfore / the loue of euery thing7 þ*at* is nat byset in god / ne doon p*ri*ncipally for goddes sake / al þ*at* a man loue it lasse than god / yet is it venial synne / *and* dedly synne / whan the loue of any thyng7 weyeth in the herte of man / as muche / as the loue of god / or moore ¶Dedly synne. / as seith Seynt7 Augustyn is / whan man turneth his herte fro god / which that is verray sou*er*eyn bowntee / þ*at* may nat chaunge / *and* yeueth his herte / to a thyng / þ*at* may chaunge *and* flitte / and certes / that is euery thyng7 saue god of heuene / for sooth is / þ*at* if a man yeue his loue / the which þ*at* he oweth al to god w*ith* al his herte / vn to a creature / *cer*tes as muche of his loue as he yeueth to thilke creature / so muche he bireueth fro god / and therfore / dooth he synne / for he þ*at* is dettour to god / ne yeldeth nat to god al his dette / that is to seyn / al the loue of his herte / [370] ¶Now sith man vnderstondeth generally / which is venial synne / thanne is it couenable / to tellen specially of synnes / whiche þ*at* many a man p*ar* auenture ne demeth hem nat synnes / *and* ne shryueth hym nat7 of the same thynges / *and* yet nathelees they been synnes / and soothly / as thise clerkes writen / this is to seyn / þ*at* euery tyme þ*at* man eteth or drynketh / moore than suffiseth to the sustenau*n*ce of his body / in *cer*teyn he dooth synne // and eek / whan he speketh moore than it nedeth / it is synne // eek7 whan he herkneth nat benygnely þe co*m*pleynte of the pouere // eek7 whan he is in heele of body / and wol nat faste / whan oother folk7 fasten / with outen cause resonable // eek / whan he slepeth moore than nedeth / or whan he comth by thilke encheson / to late to chirche / or to othere werkes of charitee // eek / whan he vseth his wyf / with oute souereyn desir of engendrure / to honour of god / or for the entente / to yelde to his wyf the dette of his body [375] // eek7 whan he wol nat visite the syke / *and* the prisoner / if he may // eek / if he loue wyf or child / or oother worldly thyng7 moore than reson requereth // eek7 if he flatre / or blau*n*dise moore than hym oghte / for any necessitee // eek7 if he amenuse / or withdrawe the almesse of the pouere / // eek7 if he apparaileth his mete / moore deliciously / than nede is / or ete it to hastily / by likerousnesse // eek / if7 he tale vanytes / at chirche / or at goddes seruyce / or þ*at* he be a talker*e* of ydel wordes / of folye / or of vileynye / for he shal yelde acounte of it7 at the day of dome // eek / whan he biheteth / or assureth to do thynges / þ*at* he ne may nat p*ar*fourne // eek / whan þ*at* he / by lightnesse / or folye / mysseyth / or scorneth his neighebore

god or moore / and ther-fore / the love of every thyng / þt is nat byset in god / ne doon principally for goddes sake / al þt a man love
it lasse than god / yet is it venial synne / & dedly synne whan
the love of any thyng weyeth in the herte of man / as muche
as the love of god or moore ¶ Dedly synne / as seith Seint
Augustyn is / whan man turneth his herte fro god / which that is
verray sovereyn bountee / þt may nat chaunge / & yeveth his herte / to a thyng þt may chaunge & flitte / and certes / that is every
thyng / save god of hevene / for sooth is / þt if a man yeve his love the which þt he oweth al to god with al his herte / un to a creature / certes as muche of his love as he yeveth to thilke creature /
so muche he bireveth fro god / and ther-fore dooth he synne / for
he þt is dettour to god / ne yeldeth nat to god al his dette / that
is to seyn / al the love of his herte / ¶ Now sith man underston-
deth generally / which is venial synne / thanne is it covenable to
tellen specially of synnes / whiche þt many a man peraventure
ne demeth hem nat synnes / & ne shryveth hym nat / of the same thynges / & yet natheles they been synnes / and soothly / as
thise clerkes writen / this is to seyn þt every tyme þt man eteth
or drynketh moore than suffiseth to the sustenance of his body
in certeyn he dooth synne / and eek whan he speketh moore than
it nedeth / it is synne / eek whan he herkneth nat benygnely þe
compleynte of the povere / eek whan he is in heele of body and
wol nat faste / whan oother folk fasten / with outen cause resonable / eek whan he slepeth moore than nedeth / or whan he
comth by thilke encheson / to late to chirche / or to othere werkes of
charitee / eek whan he useth his wyf / with oute sovereyn desir
of engendrure / to honour of god / or for the entente / to yelde to
his wyf the dette of his body / eek whan he wol nat visite the
syke & the prisoner / if he may / eek / if he love wyf or child
or oother worldly thyng / moore than reson requereth / eek
if he flatre / or blandise moore than hym oghte / for any necessitee / eek if he amenuse / or withdrawe the almesse of the povere
/ eek if he apparaileth his mete / moore deliciously than nede
is / or ete it to hastily by likerousnesse / eek / if he talo vanytes
at chirche / or at goddes servyce / or þt he be a talker of ydel
wordes / of folye / or of vileynye / for he shal yelde acounte
of it at the day of dome / eek whan he biheteth / or assureth
to do thynges / þt he ne may nat parfourne / eek whan þt he
by lightnesse or folye / mysseyeth / or scorneth his neighebore

ech / whan he hath any wikked suspecion of thyng ther he ne woot
of it no soothfastnesse / thise thynges & mo withoute nombre
ben synnes as seith Seint Augustyn ¶ Now shal men understonde þt al be it so þt noon erthely man may eschewe alle veniale synnes / yet may he refreyne hem by the brennynge love
þt he hath to oure lord Jhu crist / and by preyeres & confession
& othere goode werkes / so þt it shal but litel greve / for as seith
Seint Augustyn / If a man love god in swich manere þt al that
evere he dooth is in the love of god / or for the love of god verraily for he brenneth in the love of god / looke how muche þt a drope of water þt falleth in a fourneys ful of fyr anoyeth or
greveth / so muche anoyeth a venial synne un to a man þt is
pfit in the love of Jhu crist / Men may also refreyne venial
synne by receyuynge worthily of the pcious body of Jhu crist
by receyuynge eek of holy water / by almesdede / by general
confession of Confiteor at masse & at complyn / & by blessynge of bisshopes & of preestes / & by othere goode werkes .. ..

De Septem pccis mortalibz

Now is it bihovely thyng to telle whiche ben dedly synnes / that is to seyn chieftaynes of synnes / alle they
renne in o lees / but in dyuerse manere / now ben they cleped chieftaynes / for as muche as they ben chief and sprynge of alle
Superbia othere synnes ¶ Of the roote of thise .vij. synnes thanne is
pryde the general roote of alle harmes / for of this roote spryngen certeyn braunches / as Ire . Envye . Accidie or Slewthe .
Avarice or Coveitise / . to commune understondynge . Glotonye .
and lecherye / and everich of thise chief synnes hath hise
braunches and hise twigges / as shal be declared in hire chapitres folwynge / and though so be þt no man kan outrely
tellen the nombre of twigges & of the harmes þt comen of
braunches pryde pryde / yet wol I shewe a partie of hem / as ye shul under-
stande ¶ Ther is Inobedience / Avauntynge / ypocrisye /
Despit / Arrogance / Inpudence / Swellynge of herte / Insolence /
Elacion / Inpacience / Stryf / Contumacie / Presumpcion / Ir-
reverence / Pertinacie / veyne glorie / and many another
[Inob]edience twig þt I kan nat declare ¶ Inobedient is he þt desobeieth for despit to the comaundementz of god & to hise sovereins
[Avaun]ting & to his goostly fader ¶ Avauntour is he þt bosteth of the

eek whan he hath any wikked suspeciou*n* of thyng ther he ne woot of it no soothfastnesse [380] /. thise thynges / *and* mo with oute nombre ben synnes / as seith Seint Augustyn / ¶Now shal men vnderstonde / þ*at* al be it so / þ*at* noon erthely man may eschewe alle veniale synnes / yet may he refreyne hem by the brennynge loue þ*at* he hath to oure lord I*es*u crist and by preyeres *and* confession / *and* othere goode werkes / so / þ*at* it shal but litel greue /. for as seiþ Seint Augustyn /. If a man loue god in swich manere / þ*at* al that euere he dooth / is in the loue of god / or for the loue of god verraily / for he brenneth in the loue of god / looke / how muche þ*at* a drope of water þ*at* falleth in a furneys ful of fyr anoyeth / or greueth / so muche / anoyeth a venial synne vn to a man / þ*at* is p*ar*fit in the loue of I*es*u crist /. Men may also / refreyne venial synne / by receyuynge worthily / of the p*re*cious body of I*es*u crist [385] by receyuynge eek / of holy water / by almes dede / by general confession / of Confiteor / at masse *and* at Complyn / *and* by blessynge of Bisshopes / *and* of preestes / *and* by othere goode werkes

¶De Septem p*e*cc*at*is mortalib*us*

NOw is it bihouely thing to telle / whiche ben dedly synnes / that is to seyn / chieftaynes of synnes / alle they renne in o lees / but in dyu*er*se manere / now ben they clepid chieftaynes / for as muche as they ben chief / and sprynge of alle othere synnes ¶Of the roote of thise .vij. synnes / thanne is pryde / the general roote of alle harmes / for of this roote / spryngen certeyn brau*n*ches / as / Ire /. Enuye /. Accidie / or Sleuthe /. Auarice / or Coueitise /. to co*m*mune vnderstondynge /. Glotonye /. and Lecherye /. and euerich of thise chief synnes / hath hise brau*n*ches and hise twigges / as shal be declared / in hire chapitres folwynge / and though so be / þ*at* no man kan outrely tellen the nombre of twigges *and* of the harmes þ*at* comen of Pryde / yet wol I shewe a partie of hem / as ye shul vnderstande [390] ¶Ther is / Inobedience / Auantynge / Ypocrisye / Despit Arrogau*n*ce / Inpudence / Swellynge of herte / Insolence / Elaciou*n* / Inpacience / Stryf / Contumacie / Presumpciou*n* / Inreuerence / Pertinacie / Veyne glorie / and many another twig þ*at* I kan nat declare ¶Inobedient is he / þ*at* desobeieth for despit / to the comandementz of god / *and* to hise sou*er*eins / *and* to his goostly fader ¶Auantour / is he þ*at* bosteth / of the

770 [De] Superbia Hg (388)
778 [The] braunches [of] Pryde Hg (390)
783 [Ino]bedience Hg (392)
785 [Auan]tyng Hg (393)

harm / or of the bowntee þ*at* he hath doon ¶Ypocrite is he / that hideth / to shewe hym / swich as he is / and sheweth hym / swich as he nawght is ¶Despitous is he / that hath desdeyn of his neighebore / that is to seyn / of his euenecristen / or hath despit / to doon / that hym oghte to do [395] ¶Arrogau*n*t is he þ*at* thynketh / þ*at* he hath thilke bountees in hym / þ*at* he hath nat / or weneth þ*at* he sholde haue hem / by hise desertes / or ellis he demeth / þ*at* he be that he nys nat ¶Impudent is he þ*at* for his pryde / hath no shame of his synne ¶Swellynge of herte is / whan man reioyseth hym of harm þ*at* he hath doon / ¶Insolent is he / that despiseth in his Iugement alƚ oother folk / as to regard of his value / *and* of his konnynge / *and* of his spekynge / *and* of his berynge ¶Elaciou*n* is / whan he ne may neither suffre to haue maister ne felawe [400] ¶Inpacient is he / þ*at* wol nat ben ytaught ne vndernome of his vice / *and* by stryf werreieth trouthe wityngly *and* deffendeth his folye ¶Contumax is he / þ*at* thurgh his Indignaciou*n* / is agayns euerich auctoritee / or power / of hem þ*at* ben hise souereyns ¶Presumpciou*n* is / whan a man vndertaketh an Emprise / þ*at* hym oghte nat do / or ellis þ*at* he may nat do / and that is called Surquydie ¶Inreuerence is / whan men do nat honour ther as hem oghte to doon / and waiteth / to be reue*r*enced ¶Pertinacie / is whan a man deffendeth his folye / *and* trusteth to muche to his owene wit / ¶Veyne glorie is / for to haue pompe *and* delit in thise temporel heynesses *and* glorifie hem / in worldly estatz [405] ¶Ianglynge is / whan a man speketh to muche biforn folk *and* clappeth as a Melle / *and* taketh no kepe / what he seith ¶And yet is ther a pryuee spice of pryde / that waiteth / first to be salewed / er he wole salewe / al be he lasse worthy / than that oother is p*ar* auenture / and eek he wayteth / or desireth / to sitte / or ellis / to goon aboue hym in the weye / or kisse pax / or ben ensensed / or goon to offrynge / biforn his neighebore / and swiche semblable thynges / agayns his duetee p*ar* auenture / but þ*at* he hath / his herte and his entente in swich a proud desir / to be magnyfied *and* honoured / biforn the peple ¶Now ben ther / two maneres of pryde / that oon of hem / is with Inne the herte of man / and that oother is w*ith* oute / of whiche soothly / thise forseyde thynges / *and* mo than I haue seyd ape*r*te-

788 [Despitous ?] Hg (395)
790 Arroga[nt] Hg (396)
793 Impudent Hg (397)
794 Swelling of [herte] Hg (398)
796 Insolent Hg (399)
798 Elacioun Hg (400)
799 Inpacient Hg (401)
802 Contumax Hg (402)
804 Presumpcioun Hg (403)
806 Inreuerence Hg (403)
808 Pertynacie Hg (404)
810 Veyn glorye Hg (405)
811 Ianglynge Hg (406)
813 Desir of worshi[p] Hg (407)
822 .ij. maners of pri[de] Hg (409)

harm or of the bountee þt he hath don ¶ Ypocrite is he that
hideth to shewe hym swich as he is / and sheweth hym
swich as he nawght is ¶ Despitous is he that hath desdeyn Desp[itous]
of his neighebore / that is to seyn of his euenecristen / or
hath despit to doon that hym oghte to do ¶ Arrogant is he Arrogan[t]
þt thynketh þt he hath thilke bountees in hym þt he hath
nat or weneth þt he sholde haue hem by hise desertes / or
ellis he demeth þt he be that he nys nat ¶ Impudent is he Impudent
þt for his pryde hath no shame of his synne ¶ Swellynge Swelling of
of herte is whan man reioyseth hym of harm þt he hath don
¶ Insolent is he that despiseth in his iugement alle other Insolent
folk as to regard of his value & of his konnynge & of
his spekynge & of his berynge ¶ Elation is whan he Elation
ne may neither suffre to haue maister ne felawe ¶ Im Impacient
pacient is he þt wol nat ben ytaught / ne vndernome of
his vice & by stryf werreieth trouthe wityngly & deffen
deth his folye ¶ Contumax is he þt thurgh his indignaci Contumax
on is agayns euerich auctoritee / or power of hem þt ben
hise souereyns ¶ Presumption is whan a man vnder Presumpcion
taketh an emprise þt hym oghte nat do / or ellis þt he
may nat do and that is called Surquydie ¶ Irreuerence Irreuerence
is whan men do nat honour ther as hem oghte to doon
and waiteth to be reuerenced ¶ Pertinacie is whan a man Pertynacie
deffendeth his folye & trusteth to muche to his owene wit
¶ Veyne glorie is for to haue pompe & delit in thise tempo Veyn glorye
rel heynesses & glorifie hem in worldly estatz ¶ Janglynge Janglynge
is whan a man speketh to muche biforn folk & clappeth
as a melle & taketh no kepe what he seith ¶ And yet is Desir of worsh[ip]
ther a pryuee spice of pryde / that waiteth first to be sa
lewed er he wole salewe / al be he lasse worthy than that
oother is parauenture / and eek he wayteth / or desireth
to sitte / or ellis to goon aboue hym in the weye or
kisse pax / or ben ensensed / or goon to offrynge biforn
his neighebore and swiche semblable thynges agayns
his duetee parauenture / but þt he hath his herte and
his entente in swich a proud desir to be magnyfied
& honoured biforn the peple ¶ Now ben ther two ij maners of p[ride]
maneres of pryde / that oon of hem is withinne the her
te of man / and that oother is withoute / of whiche sooth
ly thise forseyde thynges & mo than I haue seyd apte

nen to pryde þt is in the herte of man / And that othere speces of pride
ben with oute / but natheles that oon of thise speces of pryde is
signe of that oother / right as the gaye levesel atte taverne is sig
ne of the wyn þt is in the celer / And this is in manye thynges
clothing as in speche & contenaunce & in outrageous array of clothyng / for
certes if ther ne hadde be no synne in clothyng / Crist wolde nat
so soone haue noted & spoke of the clothyng of thilke riche man
in the gospel / And as seith seint Gregorie that precious clothyng
is coupable for the derthe of it & for his softnesse & for his stran
genesse & degisynesse and for the superfluitee or for the inordinat
scantnesse of it / Allas may man nat seen as in oure dayes
the synful costlewe array of clothynge & namely in to muche
superfluitee or ellis in to desordinat scantnesse / As to the firste
synne that is in superfluitee of clothynge which þt maketh it
so deere to harm of the peple / nat oonly the cost of enbrawdynge
the degyse endentynge or barrynge / owndynge / palynge or ben
dynge & semblable wast of clooth in vanytee / but ther is also
the costlewe furrynge in hir gownes / so muche pownsonynge
of chisel to maken holes / so muche daggynge of sheris / forth with
the superfluitee in lengthe of the forseyde gownes / trailynge in
the dong & in the myre on horse & eek on foote / as wel of man
as of womman þt al thilke trailynge is verraily as in effect /
wasted / consumed / thredbare & roten with donge / rather than it
is yeuen to the pouere / to greet damage of the forseyde pouere
folk / And that in sondry wise / this is to seyn þt the moore þt
clooth is wasted / the moore moot it coste to the peple for the scars
nesse / And forther ouer if so be þt they wolde yeue swich pown
sonyd & dagged clothynge to the pouere folk / it is nat couenient
to were for hir estat / ne suffisant to beete hire necessitee / to kepe
hem fro the destempraunce of the firmament / Vp on that oother
syde to speke of the horrible desordynat scantnesse of clothyng /
as ben thise kutted sloppes or hanselyns þt thurgh hir shortnesse
ne keuere nat the shameful membres of a man to wikke entente
Allas somme of hem shewen the shap & the boce of hir horrible
swollen membres þt semeth lik the maladie of hyrnia in the
wrappynge of hir hoses / and eek the buttokes of hem þt faren
as it were the hyndre part of a she ape in the fulle of the moone
And moore ouer the wrecched swollen membres þt they shewe
thurgh degisynge in departynge of hire hoses in whit and reed
semeth þt half hir shameful pryuee membres weren flayn

nen to pryde / þ*at* is in the herte ⟨of⟩ man / And that othere speces of pride ben with oute / but natheles / that oon of thise speces of pride / is signe of that oother / right as the gaye leuesel atte Tau*er*ne / is signe / of the wyn / þ*at* is in the Celer ⁋ And this is in manye thynges / as in speche *and* contenau*n*ce / *and* in out*ra*geous array of clothyngꝭ for c*er*tes / if ther ne hadde be no synne in clothyngꝭ crist wolde nat so soone haue noted *and* spoke of the clothyngꝭ of thilke riche man in the gospel ⁋ And as seith Seint Gregorie / that p*re*cious clothyngꝭ is cowpable / for the derthe of itꝭ *and* for his softnesse / *and* for his strau*n*genesse *and* degisynesse / and for the sup*er*fluitee / or for the inordinat scantnesse of it ⁋ Allas / may man nat seen as in oure dayes / the synful costlewe array of clothynge / *and* namely in to muche sup*er*fluitee / or ellis in to desordinat scantnesse ¶As to the firste synne / that is in sup*er*fluitee of clothynge / which þ*at* maketh it so deere to harm of the peple / nat oonly / the cost of enbrawdynge / the degyse / endentynge / or barrynge / owndynge / palynge / or bendynge / *and* semblable wastꝭ of clooth in vanytee ⁋ but ther is also the costlewe furrynge in hire gownes / so muche pownsonynge of chisel / to maken holes / so muche daggynge of sheris / forth / w*ith* the sup*er*fluitee / in lengthe of the forseyde gownes trailynge in the dongꝭ *and* in the Myre on horse / *and* eek on foote / as wel / of man / as of wo*m*man / þ*at* al thilke trailynge / is verraily as in effectꝭ wasted / consumed / thredbare / *and* roten w*ith* dongꝭ rather / than it is yeuen to the pouere / to gret damage / of the forseide pouere folk / and that in sondry wise / this is to seyn / þ*at* the moore þ*at* clooth is wasted / the moore moot it coste to the peple for the scarsnesse / and forther ouer / if so be / þ*at* they wolde yeue swich pownsonyd *and* dagged clothynge to the pouere folk / it is nat co*n*uenientꝭ to were / for hir*e* estatꝭ ne suffisant to beete hire necessitee / to kepe hem / fro the destemp*er*ance of the firmamentꝭ ¶Vp on that oother syde / to speke of the horrible desordynat scantnesse of clothyngꝭ as ben thise kutted sloppes / or hanselyns / þ*at* thurgh hir*e* shortnesse / ne keuere natꝭ the shameful membres of a man to wikke entente / ⁋ Allas / so*m*me of hem shewen the shap*e* *and* the boce of hir*e* horrible swollen membres / þ*at* semeth lik the maladie of hirnia / in the wrappynge of hir*e* hoses / and eek the buttokes of hem / þ*at* faren as it were the hyndre part of a she Ape / in the fulle of the Moone / ⁋ And moore ouerꝭ the wrecched swollen membres / þ*at* they shewe thurgh degisynge / in departynge of hire hoses in whit and reed / semeth / þ*at* half hir*e* shameful pryuee membres weren flayn /

830 [c]lothing Hg (412)

¶And if so be / þ*at* they departen hire hoses in othere colours / as [is] whit *and* blew / or whit *and* blak / or blak *and* reed / *and* so forth / thanne semeth it as by variau*n*ce of colour / þ*at* half the partie of hire pryuee membres / ben corrupt by the fyr of Seint Antony / or by cancre / or othere swiche meschau*n*ces // Yet of the hyndre part of hire buttokes / it is ful horrible for to se / for c*er*tes in that partie of hir*e* body / ther as they purgen hir*e* stynkynge ordure / that foule partie / shewe they to the peple proudly in despit of honestetee / which honestetee þ*at* Ie*s*u crist *and* hise frendes obseruede / to shewe*n* in his lyue ¶Now / as of the outrageous array of wo*m*men / god woot þ*at* thogh the visages of so*m*me of hem / seme ful chaste *and* debonaire // yet notifie they in hire array of atyr / likerousnesse *and* pride [430] ¶I seye nat þ*at* honestetee in clothynge / of man or wo*m*man / is vncouenable / but c*er*tes the sup*er*fluitee / or the desordinat skantitee of clothynge / is reprouable /

¶Also / the synne of Aornement / or of apparaille / as in thynges þ*at* ap*er*tenen to ridynge / as in to manye delicat horses þ*at* ben holden for delit þ*at* they ben so faire / fatte / *and* costlewe / and also many a vicious knaue mayntened by cause of hem / and in to curious harneys / as in Sadeles / in croupers / peytrels / and brydles coue*r*ed w*ith* p*re*cious clothyng *and* riche barres *and* plates of gold *and* of siluer / for which / god seith / by Zakarie the p*ro*phete / ¶I wol confounde / the ryderes of swiche horses // thise folk taken litel reward / of the ridynge of goddes sone of heuene / *and* of his harneys / whan he rood vp on an Asse / *and* ne hadde noon oother harneys / but the pouere clothes of hise disciples / ne we ne rede nat þ*at* euere he rood on oother beest [435] I speke this for the synne of sup*er*fluitee / *and* nat for resonable honestetee / whan resou*n* it requereth ¶And forther ouer / c*er*tes pride is gretly notified in holdynge of gret Meynee / whan they ben of litel profit / or of right no profit and namely / whan that Meynee / is felonous *and* damageous to the peple / by hardynesse of hey lordshipe / or by wey of offices / for c*er*tes swiche lordes / sellen thanne hir lordship / to the deuel of helle / whan they sustenen / the wikkednesse of hir*e* meynee / or ellis / whan thise folk of lowe degree / as thilke þ*at* holden hostelries / sustenen the thefte of hir*e* hostelers / *and* that is / in many manere of deceites / [440] thilke manere of folk ben the flyes / þ*at* folwen the hony / or ellis the houndes / þ*at* folwen the careyne / Swich forseide folk / stranglen spiritually hir*e* lordshipes / for which thus

880 pride in thinges t[hat] longeth to ridy[nge] Hg (432)

894 pride of Meyne Hg (437)

And if so be þt they departen hire hoses in othere colours as is
whit & blak or whit & blak or blak & reed & so forth than
ne semeth it as by variance of colour þt half the partie of
hire privee membres ben corrupt by the fyr of seint Anto
ny or by cancre or othere swiche meschaunces / yet of the hyn
dre part of hire buttokes it is ful horrible for to se for certes
in that partie of hir body ther as they purgen hir stynkyn
ge ordure that foule partie shewe they to the peple proudly
in despit of honestetee which honestetee þt Ihu crist & hise frein
des observede to shewe in his lyue ¶ Now as of the outrage
ous array of women god woot þt though the visages of some
of hem seme ful chaste & debonaire yet notifie they in hire array
of atyr likerousnesse & pride ¶ I seye nat þt honestetee in clo
thynge of man or woman is unconvenable but certes the sup
fluitee or the desordinat scantitee of clothynge is reprouable
¶ Also the synne of aornement or of apparaille as in thynges
þt apertenen to rydynge as in to manye delicat horses þt ben hol
den for delit þt they ben so faire fatte & costlewe and also ma
ny a vicious knaue mayntened by cause of hem and in to
curious harneys as in sadeles in crouperes peytrels and
brydles couered wt precious clothyng & riche barres & plates of
gold & of siluer for which god seith by Zakarie tho prophete
¶ I wol confounde the ryderes of swiche horses / thise folk ta
ken litel reward of the rydynge of goddes sone of heuene &
of his harneys whan he rood vp on an asse & ne hadde noon
oother harneys but the poure clothes of hise disciples ne
we ne rede nat þt euere he rood on oother beest / I speke this
for the synne of superfluitee & nat for resonable honestetee
whan reson it requereth ¶ And forther ouer certes pride is gret
ly notified in holdynge of gret meynee whan they ben of litel
profit or of right no profit and namely whan that meynee
is felonous & damageous to the peple by hardynesse of hey
lordshipe or by wey of offices for certes swiche lordes sellen
thanne hir lordship to the deuel of helle whan they sustenen
the wikkednesse of hir meynee or ellis whan thise folk
of lowe degree as thilke þt holden hostelries sustenen tho
thefte of hir hostelers & that is in many manere of decei
tes thilke manere of folk ben the flyes þt folwen the hony
or ellis the houndes þt folwen the careyne swich forseide
folk stranglen spiritually hir lordshipes for which thus

pride in thinges that longeth to rydyng

pride of meyne

seith Dauid the prophete [W]ikked deth mote come vp on thilke lord
shipes And god yeue þt they mote descende in to helle adoun
adoun for in hire houses been iniquitees & shrewednesses
And nat god of heuene And certes but if they doon amende
ment right so as god yaf his benysoun to Pharao by the ser
uyce of Jacob & to laban by the seruyce of Joseph right
so god wol yeue his malisoun to swiche lordshipes as suffre
nen the wikkednesse of hir seruantz but they come to amende
ment/ pryde of the table appereth eek ful ofte for certes riche men
ben cleped to festes and pouere folk ben put awey & rebuked
[A]lso in excesse of diuerse metes & drynkes And namely swiche
manere bake metes & disshmetes brennynge of wilde fyr
& peynted & castelled with papir & semblable wast so þt it
is abusion for to thynke/ And eek in to gret preciousnesse of
vessel & curiositee of mynstralcie by whiche a man is stired
the moore to delices of luxurie [I]f so be þt he sette his her
te the lasse vp on oure lord Jhu crist certeyn it is a synne &
certeynly the delices myghte ben so grete in this cas þt man mygh
te lightly fallen by hem in to deedly synne [T]he especes that
sourden of pryde soothly whan they sourden of malice ymagi
gyned & auysed & forncast or ellis of usage ben deedly syn
nes it is no doute And whan they sourde by freletee vnauy
sed sodeynly & sodeynly withdrawe agayn al be they greuou
se synnes I gesse that they ne be nat deedly [N]ow myghte
men axe wher of þt pryde sourdeth & sprynketh And I seye
som tyme it spryngeth of the goodes of nature And som tyme
of the goodes of fortune & som tyme of the goodes of grace
[C]ertes the goodes of nature stonden outher in goodes of body
or goodes of soule Certes goodes of body been heele of body
strengthe delyuernesse beautee gentrie franchise [G]oodes
of nature of the soule ben good wit sharp vnderstondynge sub
til engyn vertu naturel good memorie [G]oodes of fortune
ben richesses hye degrees of lordshipes preisynges of the pe
ple [G]oodes of grace ben science power to suffre spirituel
trauaille benygnitee vertuous contemplacion withstondynge
of temptacion And semblable thynges of whiche forseyde
goodes certes it is a ful gret folie a man to pryden hym in
any of hem alle [N]ow as for to speke of goodes of natu
re god woot þt som tyme we han hem in nature as muche to
oure damage as to oure profit [A]s for to speke of heele of

of the table
[...]e of mete
[...] of cometh pryde
[...]odes of body
[...]s of the soule
[...]s of fortune

seith dauid the p*ro*phete ¶Wikked deth mote come vp on thilke lordshipes / and god yeue / þ*at* they mote descende in to helle adown / adown / for in hire houses / been Iniquitees *and* shrewednesses / and nat god of heuene / and certes / but if they doon amendement / right so as god yaf his benysou*n* to Pharao by the seruyce of Iacob / *and* to Laban by the seruyce of Ioseph / right so / god wol yeue his malisou*n* to swiche lordshipes / as sustenen the wikkednesse of hir*e* seruantz / but they come to amendement pride of the table apeereþ eek ful ofte / for c*er*tes riche men ben clepid to festes / and pouere folk ben put awey *and* rebuked / ¶Also in exces / of diu*er*se metes *and* drynkes / and namely swiche manere bake metes *and* disshmetes brennynge of wilde fyr *and* peynted *and* castelled with papir / *and* semblable wast / so þ*at* it is abusiou*n* for to thynke / And eek in to gret p*re*ciousnesse of vessel / *and* curiositee of Mynstralcie / by whiche / a man is stired the moore / to delices of luxure ¶If so be þ*at* he sette his herte the lasse / vp on oure lord Ie*s*u crist c*er*teyn it is a synne / *and* c*er*teynly the delices / myghte ben so grete in the cas / þ*at* man myghte lightly fallen by hem in ⟨to⟩ dedly synne ¶The especes that sourden of pride / soothly whan they sourden of malice ymagyned *and* auysed / *and* forncast or ellis of vsage / ben dedly synnes / it is no doute / and whan they sourde by freletee / vnauysed sodeynly / *and* sodeynly / withdrawe agayn / al be they greuouse synnes / I gesse / that they ne be nat dedly ¶Now myghte men axe / wher of þ*at* pryde sourdeth *and* spryngeth / and I seye Som tyme it sprynge*th* of the goodes of nature / and somtyme of the goodes of fortune / *and* som tyme / of the goodes of grace / ¶Certes the goodes of nature / stonden outher in goodes of body / or goodes of soule / Certes / goodes of body / been heele of body / strengthe / delyuernesse / beautee / genterie / franchise ¶goodes of nature of the soule ben good wit sharp*e* vnderstondynge / subtil engyn / v*er*tu naturel / good memorie ¶goodes of fortune / ben richesses / hey degrees of lordshipes / preisynges of the peple ¶goodes of g*ra*ce / ben Science / power to suffre spiritual t*ra*uaille / benygnytee / v*er*tuous contemplaciou*n* / withstondynge of temptacion ¶and semblable thynges / of whiche forseyde goodes / certes it is a ful gret folie a man to pryden hym in any of hem alle / ¶Now as for to speke of goodes of nature / god woot þ*at* som tyme we han hem in nature / as muche to oure damage / as to oure profit ¶As for to speke of heele of

906 Gloss unintelligible. Hg (442)
914 [Pride] of the table Hg (444)
916 [Exces]se of mete Hg (445)
923 And yf thou wyest what thyng yt were Coneng to lerne [*in another hand*] Hg (447)
929 [Whe]r of cometh pryde Hg (450)
934 [g]oodes of body Hg (452)
936 [goode]s of the soule Hg (453)
937 [good]es of fortune Hg (454)

body / *cer*tes it passeth ful lightly / *and* eek it is ful ofte enchesou*n* / o[f] the siknesse of the soule / for god woot the flessh is a ful greet enemy to the soule / and therfore / the moore þ*at* the body is hool / the moore be we in p*er*il to falle ¶ Eke / for to pryde hym in hys strengthe of body / it is an heigh folye / for certes / the flessh coueiteth agayn the spirit / *and* ay the moore strong þ*at* the flessh is / the sorier may the soule be / and ouer al this / Strengthe of body *and* worldly hardynesse / causeth ful ofte many man / to p*er*il *and* meschau*n*ce [460] ¶ Eke / for to pryde hym of his genterye / is ful gret folie / for ofte tyme / the genterie of the body / bynymeth the genterie of the soule / *and* eek / we ben alle / of .o. fader *and* of o moder / *and* alle we ben of o nature roten / and corrupt bothe riche *and* pouere / for sothe / o manere gentilrye / is for to preise / that apparayleth mannes corage w*ith* v*er*tues / *and* moralitees / *and* maketh hym cristes child / for truste wel / þ*at* ou*er* what man þ*at* synne hath maistrye / he is verray cherl to synne ¶Now / ben ther general signes of gentilesse / as eschewynge of vice / or rybaudye *and* s*er*uage of synne / in word / in werk / and contenau*n*ce / *and* vsynge v*er*tu / curteisye / *and* clennesse / *and* to be liberal / that is to seyn / large by mesure / for thilke that passeth mesure / is folye *and* synne [465] ¶ Another is / to remembre hym of bounte / þ*at* he of oother folk hath receyued ¶ Another is / to ben benygne / to hise goode subgetz / wher fore as seith Senek ther is no thyng moore couenable to a man of heigh estat / than debonairetee *and* pitee / and therfore thise flyes / þ*at* men clepe bees / whan they maken hire kyng they chesen oon þ*at* hath no prikke / wher with he may stynge ¶ Another is / a man to haue a noble herte *and* a diligent to attayne to hye v*er*tuouse thynges[4] [469] ¶Certes also / who þ*at* prydeth hym in the goodes of fortune / he is a ful gret fool / for som tyme / is a man a gret lord by the morwe / þ*at* is a kaytif *and* a wrecche / er it be nyght [471] and som tyme / the richesse of a man / is cause of his deeth / somtyme the delices of a man / ben cause of the greuous maladie / thurgh which he dyeth ¶ Certes / the co*m*mendaciou*n* of the peple / is somtyme ful fals / *and* ful brotil for to triste / this day they preise / to morwe they blame / god woot desir to haue the co*m*mendaciou*n* eek of peple / hath caused deth / to many a bisy man ¶Now certes / a man to p*ri*de hym in the goodes of grace / is eek an outrageous folye / for thilke yiftes of g*r*ace / that sholde haue turned hym to goodnesse

970 nota Hg (468)

[4] 470 follows 474 in Hg.

body / Also it passeth ful lightly / & eek it is ful ofte enchesoun of
the siknesse of oure soule / for god woot the flessh is a ful greet
enemy to the soule / and therfore the moore þt the body is hool
the moore be we in peril to falle // Eke for to pryde hym in his
strengthe of body / it is an heigh folye / for certes the flessh co
ueiteth agayn the spirit / & ay the moore strong þt the flessh is
the sorier may the soule be / and ouer al this / strengthe of
body & worldly hardynesse causeth ful ofte many man to
peril & meschance // Eke for to pryde hym of his gentrye
is ful greet folie / for ofte tyme / the gentrye of the body by
nymeth the gentrye of the soule / & eek we ben alle of o
fader & of o moder / & alle we ben of o nature roten and
corrupt bothe riche & pouere / for sothe o manere gentrye
is for to preise / that apparayleth mannes corage wt vertues
& moralitees / & maketh hym cristes child / for truste wel þt ou
what man þt synne hath maistrye / he is verray cherl to syn
ne / Now ben ther general signes of gentillesse / as eschewyn
ge of vice / or rybaudye & seruage of synne / in word / in werk
and contenance / & vsynge vertu / curteisye & clennesse / & to
be liberal / that is to seyn / large by mesure / for thilke that
passeth mesure is folye & synne // Another is to remembre
hym of bounte þt he of oother folk hath receyued // Another
is to ben benygne to hise goode subgetz / wherfore as seith
Senek / ther is no thing moore couenable to a man of heigh
estat than debonairetee & pitee / and therfore thise flyes þt
men clepe bees / whan they maken hir kyng / they chesen oon
þt hath no prikke wher with he may stynge // Another is
a man to haue a noble herte & a diligent to attayne to hye
vertuouse thynges / Certes also who þt prydeth hym in the
goodes of fortune / he is a ful greet fool / for som tyme is a
man a greet lord by the morwe þt is a kaytif & a wrecche er
it be nyght / and som tyme the richesse of a man is cause of
his deeth / som tyme the delices of a man ben cause of the
greuous maladie thurgh which he dyeth / Certes the comen
dacion of the peple is som tyme ful fals & ful brotil for
to truste / this day they preyse to morwe they blame / god
woot desir to haue the comendacion eek of peple hath cau
sed deth to many a bisy man / Now certes a man to pryde
hym in the goodes of grace is eek an outrageous folye / for
thilke yiftes of grace that sholde haue turned hym to goodnesse

and to medicine turneth hym to venym & to confusion as seith
seint Gregorie ¶ Now sith þt so is þt ye han understonde what
is pryde & whiche ben the speces of it & whennes pryde
sourdeth & spryngeth / now shul ye understonde which is
the remedie agayns pryde and that is humylitee or meke
nesse that is a vertu thurgh which a man hath verray knowe
leche of hym self & holdeth of hym self no prys ne deyntee
as in regard of hise desertes considerynge euer his freletee

maners of humilite ¶ Now ben ther .iij. maneres of humylitee as humylitee in
herte ¶ another humylitee is in mouth ¶ the thridde in hise
werkes ¶ The humylitee in herte is in .iiij. maneres ¶ that oon
is whan a man holdeth hym self as naught worth biforn
god of heuene / another is whan he ne despiseth noon other
man ¶ the thridde is whan he ne rekketh nat though men holde
hym noght worth / the ferthe is whan he nys nat sory of
his humyliacion ¶ Also the humylitee of mouth is in .iiij.
thynges ¶ in atempree speche ¶ and in humblesse of speche
and whan he biknoweth wt his owene mouth þt he is
swich as hym thynketh þt he is in his herte ¶ another is
whan he preiseth the bountee of another man and no
thyng ther of amenuseth ¶ humylitee eek in werk is in .iiij.
maneres / the firste is whan he putteth othere men biforn
hym ¶ the seconde is to chese the loweste place ouer al
the thridde is gladly to assente to good conseil / the ferthe is
gladly to stonde to the award of his souereyn or of hym þt
is hyer in degree certeyn this is a gret werk of humylitee

Inuidia

After pryde wol I speke of the foule synne of En
uye which þt is as by the word of the philosophre
sorwe of oother mannes prosperitee and after the word of
Seint Augustyn it is sorwe of oother mennes wele and
ioye of oother mennes harm ¶ This foule synne is plat
ly agayns the holy goost al be it so þt euery synne is a
gayn the holy goost yet natheles for as muche as boun
tee aperteneth proprely to holy goost & enuye cometh proprely of
malice ther fore is proprely agayns the bountee of the holy goost
¶ Now hath malice .ij. speces that is to seyn hardnesse of
herte in wikkednesse or ellis the flessh of a man is so blynd

and to medicine / turneth hym to venym *and* to confusiou*n* / as seyth Seint Gregorie ¶Now sith *þat* so is / *þat* ye han vnderstonde / what is pryde / *and* whiche ben the speces of it / *and* whennes pryde sourdeth *and* spryngeth // Now shul ye vnderstonde / which is the remedie agayns pride / and that is humylitee / or mekenesse / that is a v*er*tu / thurgh which / a man hath v*er*ray knoweleche of hym self / *and* holdeth of hym self' no pris ne deyntee / as in regard of hise desertes / considerynge eu*er*e his freletee ./ ¶Now ben ther .iij. maneres of humylitee / As humylitee in herte ¶Another humylitee / is in Mouth ¶the thridde in hise werkes ¶The humylitee in herte / is in .iiij. man*er*es ¶that oon is / whan a man holdeth hym self as naught' worth / biforn god of heuene // Another is / whan he ne despiseth noon other man ¶the thridde is / whan he ne rekketh nat' thogh men holde hym noght worth // the ferthe is / whan he nys nat sory of his humyliaciou*n* ¶Also the humylitee of Mouth / is in .iiij. thynges ¶In·Atempree speche ¶and in humblesse of speche // // And whan he biknoweth w*ith* his owene Mouth / *þat* he is swich / as hym thynketh *þat* he is in his herte ¶Another is whan he preiseth the bountee of another man / and no thyng ther of amenuseth ¶Humylitee eek in werk' is in .iiij. maneres // the firste / is whan he putteth othere men biforn hym ¶the seconde is / to chese the loweste place ouer al ./ // The thridde is / gladly to assente to good conseil // the ferthe is / gladly to stonde to the award of his souereyn / or of hym / *þat* is hyer in degree / certeyn / this is a gret werk of humylitee ./

¶Inuidia

After pryde / wol I speke / of the foule synne of Enuye / which *þat* is / as by the word of the philosophre Sorwe of oother mannes p*ro*sp*er*itee / and after the word of Seint Augustyn / it is sorwe of oother mennes wele / and ioye of oother mennes harm ¶This foule synne / is platly agayns the holy goost' al be it so *þat* euery synne / is agayn the holy goost' yet nathelees for as muche as bountee ap*er*teneth p*ro*prely to holy goost' *and* enuye cometh p*ro*prely of malice / ther fore is p*ro*prely agayns the bountee of the holy goost' ¶Now hath malice .ij. speces / that is to seyn / hardnesse of herte in wikkednesse / or ellis the flessh of a man is so blynd

994 [.iij.] maners of humilite Hg (478)

þ*a*t he considereth nat þ*a*t he is in synne / or rekketh nat þ*a*t he is in synne / which is / the hardnesse of the deuel [¶]That other spece of Enuye / is whan þ*a*t a man werreyeth tro[u]the / whan he woot þ*a*t it is trouthe / *and* eek whan he werreyeth / the gr*a*ce þ*a*t god hath yeue to his neighebore / *and* al this / is by enuye / Certes / thanne is enuye / the worste synne þ*a*t is / for soothly / alle othere synnes / ben som tyme / agayns o special v*er*tu but c*er*tes / enuye is agayns alle v*er*tues / *and* agayns alle goodnesses / for it is sory of alle the bountees of his neighebore / *and* in this manere / it is dyuers from alle othere synnes / for wel vnnethe / is ther any synne / þ*a*t it ne hath / som delit in hym self / saue oonly enuye / þ*a*t euer*e* hath in hym self angwissħ *and* sorwe [490] ¶The speces of Enuye ben thise / ¶Ther is first sorwe of oother mennes goodnesse and of hir*e* p*ro*sp*er*itee / and p*ro*sp*er*itee / is kyndely matere of Ioye / thanne is Enuye / a synne agayns kynde ¶The seconde spece of Enuye / is Ioye of oother mannes harm / and that is p*ro*prely lyk to the deuel that euere reioyseth hym of mannes harm ¶Of thise .ij. speces comth bakbitynge / and this synne of bakbitynge / or detraccion / hath certeyn speces / as thus / Som man preiseth his neighebore / by a wikked entente / for he maketh alwey a wikked knotte atte laste ende / alwey he maketh a .but. at the laste ende / þ*a*t is digne of moore blame / than worth is al the preisynge ¶The Seconde spece is / þ*a*t if a man be good / *and* dooth / or seith a thyng to good entente / the bakbiter*e* wol turne al thilke goodnesse vp so down / to his shrewede entente [495] ¶The thridde / is to amenuse / the bountee of his neighebore ¶The ferthe spece of bakbitynge / is this / that if men speke goodnesse of a man / thanne wol the bakbitere seyn / p*ar* fey / swich a man / is yet bet than he in despreisynge / of hym þ*a*t men preise ¶The fifthe spece is / for to consente gladly / and herkne gladly / the harm þ*a*t men speke of oother folk / this synne is ful greet *and* ay encreseth / after the wikked entente of the bakbitere ¶After bakbitynge comth grucchynge or Murmuraciou*n* / and som tyme / it spryngeth of Inpacience agayns god / *and* som tyme agayns man ¶Agayns god is it whan a man gruccheth agayn the pyne of helle / or agayns pouerte / or los of catel / or agayn reyn / or tempest or ellis gruccheth / þ*a*t shrewes han p*ro*sp*er*itee / or ellis / for þ*a*t goode men han aduersitee / [500] and alle thise thynges / sholde men suffre paciently / for they comen by the rightful Iugement *and* ord⟨i⟩nau*n*ce

1035 The speces of E[nuye] Hg (491)

1040 Bakbityng Hg (493)

1055 Gr[u]cchyng Hg (499)

þt he considereth nat þt he is in synne or rekketh nat þt he is in synne / which is the hardnesse of the devel / That other spece of Envye is whan þt a man werreyeth trouthe whan he woot þt it is trouthe / & eek whan he werreyeth the grace þt god hath yeue to his neighebore / & al this is by envye / Certes thanne is envye the worste synne þt is / for soothly alle othere synnes ben som tyme agayns o special vertu but certes envye is agayns alle vertues / & agayns alle goodnesses for it is sory of alle the bountees of his neighebore / & in this manere it is dyuers from alle othere synnes / for wel vnnethe is ther any synne þt it ne hath som delit in hym self / saue oonly envye þt euere hath in hym self angwissh & sorwe ¶ The speces of Envye ben thise ¶ Ther is first sorwe of oother mennes goodnesse and of hir prosperitee / and prosperitee is kyndely matere of Ioye / thanne is Envye a synne agayns kynde ¶ The seconde spece of Envye is Ioye of oother mannes harm / and that is proprely lyk to the devel that euere reioyseth hym of mannes harm ¶ Of thise .ij. speces cometh bakbitynge / and this synne of bakbitynge or detraction hath certeyn speces / as thus / Som man preiseth his neighebore by a wikked entente / for he maketh alwey a wikked knotte atte laste ende / alwey he maketh a · but · at the laste ende þt is digne of moore blame / than worth is al the preisynge ¶ The seconde spece is þt if a man be good & dooth or seith a thyng to good entente / the bakbitere wol turne al thilke goodnesse vp so doun to his shrewede entente ¶ The thridde is to amenuse the bountee of his neighebore ¶ The ferthe spece of bakbitynge is this / that if men speke goodnesse of a man / thanne wol the bakbitere seyn parfey swich a man is yet bet than he in despreisynge of hym þt men preise ¶ The fifthe spece is for to consente gladly and herkne gladly the harm þt men speke of oother folk / this synne is ful greet / & ay encreseth after the wikked entente of the bakbitere ¶ After bakbitynge cometh grucchynge or murmuracion and som tyme it spryngeth of inpacience agayns god / & som tyme agayns man ¶ Agayns god is it / whan a man gruccheth agayn the peyne of helle / or agayns pouerte or los of catel / or agayn reyn or tempest / or ellis gruccheth þt shrewes han prosperitee / or ellis for þt goode men han aduersitee / and alle thise thynges sholde men suffre paciently for they comen by the rightful Iugement & ordinance

The speces of E

Bakbityng

Grucchyng

of god ¶ Som tyme cometh grucchynge of Auarice / as Iudas grucched
agayns the Magdeleyne whan she enoynte the heued of oure lord
Ihu crist wt hire precious oynement / this manere of murmure is
swich as whan men grucchen of goodnesses þt hem selue doon
or þt othere folk doon of hir owene catel ¶ Som tyme comth
murmure of pryde as whan Symon the Pharisee grucched agayn
the Magdeleyne whan she approched to Ihu crist & weep at his
feet for hir synnes / And som tyme it sourdeth of Envye
whan men discouen a mannes harm þt was pryuee or bereth
hym on hand thyng þt is fals ¶ Murmure eek is ofte amonges
seruantz þt grucchen whan hir souereyns bidden hem to don
leueful thynges And for as muche as they dar nat openly wt
seye the comaundementz of hir souereyns yet wol they seyn
harm & grucche & murmure pryuely for verray despit whiche
wordes men clepe the deueles pater noster though so be þt
the deuel ne hadde neuere pater noster but þt lewed folk ye
uen it swich a name ¶ Som tyme it comth of Ire or pryuee
hate þt norisseth rancour in herte as afterward I shal declare

…ernesse ¶ Thanne comth eek bitternesse of herte thurgh which bitternesse
euery good dede of his neighebore semeth to hym bitter and
…cord unsauoury ¶ Thanne comth discord þt unbyndeth alle manere
…rnynge of frendshipe ¶ Thanne comth scornynge of his neighebore
…cusinge al do he neuer so wel ¶ Thanne comth accusynge as whan
man seketh occasion to anoyen his neighebore which þt is lyk
the craft of the deuel þt waytieth bothe nyght & day to accu
…alignite sen us alle ¶ Thanne comth malignitee thurgh which a man
anoyeth his neighebore pryuely if he may And if he nat ne
may algate his wikked wil ne shal nat wante as for to
brennen his hous pryuely or empoysone or sleen hise bestes
remedies for envie & semblable thynges ¶ Now wol I speken of the reme
die agayns this foule synne of Envye ¶ First is the loue
of god principal and louynge of hym self & of his neigh
bore for soothly that oon ne may nat ben wt outhen that
oother And truste wel þt in the name of thy neighebore thow
shalt understonde the name of thy brother for certes alle we
haue o fader flesshly & o moder that is to seyn Adam and
Eue & eek o fader Spirituel that is god of heuene thy
neighebore artow holden for to loue & wilne hym alle good
nesse And ther fore seith god loue thy neighebore as thy self
that is to seyn to saluacion bothe of lyf and soule & moore

of god ¶Som tyme / cometh grucchynge of Auarice / as Iudas grucched agayns the Magdeleyne / whan she enoynte the heued of oure lord I*es*u crist w*ith* hire p*re*cious oynement // this manere of m*ur*mure is swich as whan men grucchen of goodnesses þ*at* hem selue doon or þ*at* othere folk doon / of hir*e* owene catel ¶Som tyme comth Murmur*e* of pryde / as whan Symon the pharisee / grucched agayn the Magdeleyne / whan she approched to I*es*u crist *and* weep*e* at his feet for hir*e* synnes // And som tyme / it sourdeth of Enuye / whan men discou*er*en a mannes harm þ*at* was pryuee / or bereth hym on hand thyng þ*at* is fals [505] ¶Murm*ur* eek is ofte amonges seruantz / þ*at* grucchen / whan hir*e* sou*er*eyns bidden hem to doon leueful thynges / and for as muche as they dar nat openly w*ith* seye the comandementz of hir*e* sou*er*eyns / yet wol they seyn harm *and* grucche *and* m*ur*mure pryuely for v*er*ray despit / whyche wordes / men clepe the deueles pater noster / though so be / þ*at* the deuel / ne hadde neu*er*e pater noster but þ*at* lewed folk / yeuen it swich a name ¶Som tyme it comth of Ire / or pryuee hate þ*at* norisseth rancour in herte / as afterward I shal declare ¶Thanne comth eek bitternesse of herte / thurgh which bitternesse / euery good dede of his neighebore semeth to hym bitter and vnsauoury [510] ¶Thanne comth discord / þ*at* vnbyndeth alle manere of frendshipe ¶Thanne comth scornynge[5] of his neighebore al do he neuer so wel ¶Thanne comth accusynge / as whan man seketh occasiou*n* to anoyen his neighebore / which þ*at* is lyk the craft of the deuel / þ*at* wayteth bothe nyght *and* day to accusen vs alle ¶Thanne comth Malignitee / thurgh which a man anoyeth his neighebore pryuely if he may / and if he nat ne may / algate / his wikked wil ne shal nat wante / as for to brennen his hous pryuely / or enpoysone / or sleen hise bestes *and* semblable thynges / ¶Now wol I speken of the remedye agayns this foule synne of Enuye ¶first is the loue of god principal / and louynge of hym self / *and* of his neighebore / for soothly / that oon ne may nat ben w*ith* outhen that oother / [515] and truste wel / þ*at* in the name of thy neighebore / thow shalt vnderstonde / the name of thy brother / for certes / alle we haue o fader flesshly *and* o moder / that is to seyn Adam and Eue / *and* eek o fader Spirituel / that is god of heuene / thy neighebore artow holden for to loue *and* wilne hym alle goodnesse / and ther fore seith god / loue thy neighebore as thy self / that is to seyn / to sauacion / bothe of lyf and soule / *and* moore

1081 [Bitt]ernesse Hg (510)
1083 [Dis]cord Hg (511)
1084 [Sco]rnynge Hg (1084)
1085 [Ac]cusinge Hg (512)
1088 [M]alignite Hg (513)
1092 remedies for enuie Hg (515)

[5] *Out* Hg El part of 511. Gg reads:
s. as whanne a man sekyth occasioun to anoyen h. n.

ouer / thow shalt loue hym in word / *and* benygne amonestynge / *and* chastisynge / *and* conforte hym / in hise anoyes *and* preye for hym w*ith* al thyn herte // And in dede / thow shalt loue hym in swich wise / þ*at* thow shalt doon to hym in charitee / as thow woldest þ*at* were doon to thyn owene p*er*sone / and therfore / thow ne shalt doon hym no damage in wikked word / ne harm in his body / ne in his catel / ne in his soule by entisynge of wikked ensample [520] ¶Thow shalt nat eek desiren his wyf ne none of hyse thynges ¶Vnderstoond eek þ*at* in the name of neighebore / is co*m*prehended his enemy / *cer*tes man shal loue his enemy for the comandement of god / and soothly / thy freend shaltow loue in god // I seye / thyn enemy shaltow loue for goddes sake / by his comandement / for if it were resou*n* / þ*at* man sholde hate his enemy / for sothe / god nolde nat receyuen vs to his loue þ*at* ben hise enemys / ¶Agayns .iij. manere of wronges þ*at* his enemy dooth to hym / he shal doon .iij. thynges / as thus / // Agayns hate *and* rancour of herte / he shal loue hym in herte / // Agayns chidynge *and* wikked wordes / he shal preye for his enemy // Agayns the wikked dede of his enemy / he shal doon hym bountee / [525] for crist seith / loueth youre enemys / *and* preieth for hem / þ*at* speke yow harm / *and* eek for hem / þ*at* yow chacen and pursuen / and dooth bountee / to hem þ*at* yow haten ¶Lo thus comandeth vs oure lord I*es*u crist to do to oure enemys / for soothly / nature dryueth vs to louen oure frendes / *and par*fey oure enemys / han moore nede to loue / than oure frendes / and they þ*at* moore nede haue / *cer*tes to hem shal men doon goodnesse / and certes in thilke dede haue we remembrau*n*ce of the loue of I*es*u crist þ*at* deyde for hise enemys / and in as muche as thilke loue is the moore greuous to p*ar*fourne / so muche is the moore gret the merite / and therfore the louynge of of oure enemy / hath confounded the venym of the deuel / for right / as the deuel is desconfited by humylitee / right so is he wownded to the deth / by the loue of oure enemy / [530] certes thanne is loue the medicyne þ*at* chaceth out the venym of enuye fro mannes herte ¶the speces of this pas shullen ben moore largely declared / in hir*e* chapitres folwynge

¶Ira

After Enuye / wol I discryuen the synne of Ire / for soothly / who so þ*at* hath enuye vp on his neighebore

euer thow shalt loue hym in word & benygne amonestynge
& chastisynge & conforte hym in hise anoyes & preye for hym
wt al thyn herte / And in dede thow shalt loue hym in swich
wise / þt thow shalt doon to hym in charitee as thow woldest
þt were doon to thyn owene persone / And therfore thow ne shalt
doon hym no damage in wikked word ne harm in his body
ne in his catel ne in his soule by entisynge of wikked ensam
ple ¶ Thow shalt nat eek desiren his wyf ne none of hyse
thynges ¶ Understoond eek / þt in the name of neighebore is
comprehended his enemy / certes man shal loue his enemy for the
comandement of god / and soothly thy freend shaltow loue
in god / I seye thyn enemy shaltow loue for goddes sake by
his comandement / for if it were reson / þt man sholde hate
his enemy / for sothe god nolde nat receyuen vs to his loue
þt ben hise enemys ¶ Agayns . iij. manere of wronges þt
his enemy dooth to hym / he shal doon . iij. thynges / as thus
Agayns hate & rancour of herte / he shal loue hym in herte
Agayns chidynge & wikked wordes / he shal preye for his ene
my / Agayns the wikked dede of his enemy he shal doon
hym bountee / for crist seith / loueth youre enemys & preyeth
for hem / þt speke yow harm & eek for hem þt yow chacen
and pursuen / and dooth bountee to hem þt yow haten ¶ lo
thus comandeth vs oure lord Jhu crist to do to oure enemys
for soothly / nature dryueth vs to louen oure freendes & parfey
oure enemys han moore nede to loue than oure freendes / and
they þt moore nede haue / certes to hem shal men doon goodnes
se / and certes in thilke dede haue we remembraunce of the loue
of Jhu crist þt deyde for hise enemys / and in as muche as
thilke loue is the moore greuous to parfourne / so muche is the
moore gret the merite / and therfore the louynge of of oure
enemy hath confounded the venym of the deuel / for right
as the deuel is desconfited by humylitee / right so is he woun
ded to the deth by the loue of oure enemy / certes thanne is
loue the medicyne þt chaceth out the venym of enuye fro
mannes herte ¶ The speces of this paas shullen ben moore lar
gely declared in hir chapitres folwynge

¶ Ira

After Enuye wol I discryuen the synne of Ire / for
soothly who so þt hath enuye vp on his neighebore

anon he wole comunely fynde hym matere of wratthe in word or in
dede agayns hym to whom he hath envye / and as wel cometh ire of pride
as of envye / for soothly he þt is proud or envious is lightly wroth
¶ This synne of ire after the discryvyng of Seint Augustyn is
wikked wil to ben avenged by word / or by dede ¶ Ire after the
philosophre is the fervent blood of man yquyked in his herte /
thurgh which he wole harm to hym þt he hateth / for certes the
herte of man by eschawfynge & moevynge of his blood wexeth
so trouble þt he is out of alle jugement of reson // But ye shal
understonde þt ire is in two maneres / that oon of hem is good &
that oother is wikke / the good ire is by jalousie of goodnesse
thurgh which a man is wroth wt wikkednesse & agayns wikked
nesse / and therfore seith a wys that ire is bet than pley / this ire
is wt debonairetee & it is wroth wt oute bitternesse nat wroth
agayns the man but wroth wt the mysdede of the man as seith
the prophete David ¶ Irascimini & nolite peccare ¶ Now underston
deth þt wikked ire is in .ij. maneres / that is to seyn sodeyn ire
or hastif ire with oute avysement / & consentynge of his reson /
the menyng & the sens of this is þt the reson of a man ne
consente nat / to thilke sodeyn ire and thanne is it venyal / A
nother ire is ful wikked þt cometh of felonye of herte avysed
& cast bifore wt wikked wil to do vengeance & ther to his reson
consenteth and soothly this is dedly synne ¶ This ire is so dis
plesant to god þt it troubleth his hous & chaceth the holy goost
out of mannes soule and wasteth & destroyeth the liknesse of
god that is to seyn the vertu þt is in mannes soule / & put in
hym the liknesse of the devel & bynymeth the man fro god þt
is his rightful lord / this ire is a ful gret plesaunce to the
devel / for it is the develes fourneys þt is eschawfed wt the
fyr of helle for certes right so as fyr is moore myghty to
destroye erthely thynges than another element right so ire
is myghty to destroye alle spirituel thynges / looke how þt
fyr of smale gleedes þt ben almoost dede under the asshen
wolen quyke agayn whan they ben touched wt brymston
right so ire wole evere mo quyke agayn whan it is touched
by the pryde þt is covered in mannes herte / for certes fyr ne may
nat come out of no thyng / but if it were first in the same
thyng naturelly / as fyr is drawen out of flyntes with
steel / and right so as pryde is ofte tyme matere of ire right
so is rancour norice & kepere of ire ¶ Ther is a maner tree

as seith Seint ysidre

Ira

[a]non he wole co*mm*unely fynde hym matere of wraththe / in word or in dede / agayns hym / to whom he hath enuye / and as wel / comth Ire of p*ri*de / as of enuye / for soothly / he *þa*t is proud or enuyous / is lightly wroth ¶This synne of Ire / after the discryuyng of Seint Augustyn / is wikked wil to ben auenged / by word / or by dede ¶Ire after the philosophre / is the feruent blood of man / yquyked in his herte / thurgh which / he wole harm / to hym *þa*t he hateth / for c*er*tes the herte of man / by eschawfynge *and* moeuynge of his blood / wexeth so trouble / *þa*t he is out of alle Iugement of resou*n* // But ye shal vnderstonde / *þa*t Ire is in two maneres / that oon of hem is good *and* that oother is wikke / the goode Ire is / by Ialowsie of goodnesse / thurgh which / a man is wrooth w*ith* wikkednesse *and* agayns wikkednesse / and therfore seith a wys / that Ire is bet than pley / this Ire is w*ith* debonairetee / *and* it is wroth w*ith* oute bitternesse / nat wroth agayns the man / but wroth / w*ith* the mysdede of the man / as seith the p*ro*phete Dauid ¶Irascimini *et* nolite peccare ¶Now vnderstondeth / *þa*t wikked Ire / is in .ij. maneres / that is to seyn / sodeyn Ire or hastif Ire with oute auysement *and* consentynge of his reson / the Menyng *and* the sens of this is / *þa*t the reson of a man ne consente nat to thilke sodeyn Ire / and thanne is it venyal / Another Ire / is ful wikked / *þa*t comth of felonye of herte auysed / *and* cast bifore w*ith* wikked wil to do vengeau*n*ce / *and* ther to his resou*n* consenteth / and soothly / this is dedly synne ¶this Ire / is so displesant to god / *þa*t it troubleth his hous / *and* chaceth the holy goost out of mannes soule / and wasteth *and* destroyeth the liknesse of god / that is to seyn / the v*er*tu / *þa*t is in mannes soule / *and* put in hym / the liknesse of the deuel / *and* bynymeth the man fro god / *þa*t is his rightful lord / this Ire / is a ful gret plesau*n*ce to the deuel / for it is the deueles forneys / *þa*t is eschawfed w*ith* the fyr of helle / for c*er*tes / right so as fyr is moore myghty to destroye erthely thynges / than another Element / right so Ire is myghty / to destroye alle spirituel thynges / Looke / how *þa*t fyr of smale gleedes / *þa*t ben almoost dede vnder the Asshen wolen quyke agayn / whan they ben touched w*ith* brymston / right so / Ire wole euere mo quyke agayn / whan it is touched by the pryde *þa*t is cou*er*ed in mannes herte / for c*er*tes / fyr ne may nat come out of no thyng but if it were first in the same thyng naturelly / as fyr is drawen out of flyntes with Steel / and right so / as pryde is ofte tyme matere of Ire right so is rancour norice *and* kepere of Ire ¶Ther is a manere tree

as seith Seint ysidre[6]

[6] The remainder of the Hg MS has been lost.

¶Heere bigynneth Chaucers tale of Melibee

yong man called
bigat wyf that
doghter that Sophie / . bifel
he / desport / feeldes
wyf / and left
dores / yshette ¶thre hise
foes / espyed
and
been and wyf / and
doghter with
places ¶this
feet . hire handes / . erys / .
nose / . hir
mouth deed / and Melibeus /
and saugh meschief //
lyk man wepe crie
¶Prud*ence* bisoghte
crie and
eu*ere* wyf Prudence /
hir*e* / vpon Ouide / book / that
is loue / where
mooder wepen deeth
hir*e* child /
wept a certein tyme ¶And thanne /
with
preyen hir*e* wepyng stynte ¶For
resou*n* housbonde
and crie / certein space / . And saugh
hym / ¶Allas /
your*e* lyk
your*e*
[2]doghter / with god

warisshe escape /
that right deed // oughte
deeth ¶Senek man /
[¶Seneca]
deeth
he /
deeth / [¶Melibeus]
and ¶What stente /
greet wepe //
self wepte deeth / Lazarus hys freend
¶Prudence [¶Prudence]
answerde / . Certes woot / Attempree wepyng
deffended is sorwe /
rather Paul
reioyse with that make*n*
with wepen ¶But though
ygraunted / / outrageous deffended /

Senek ¶Whan that frend eyen
[¶Seneca]
been teeris / Al though
teeris
lat
for goon freend / diligence
gete freend /
freend
that Inne
youre herte /
seith ¶A that [¶*Iesus* Syrak]
herte / florissynge But
hise drye ¶He eek /
thus / That man ¶Salomon [¶Salomon]
That Motthes shepes
anoyeth
clothes / *and* tree / right
wherfore / deeth
of op*ere* goodes temporels
pacience ¶Remembre yow
children temporeel
and tribulaciou*n* / yet seyde
thus ¶Oure biraft right as
wold right blessed be
lord ¶To forseide [¶Melibeus]
wyf Prudence ¶Alle and
therwith with
sorwe that noot doone ¶Lat
Prudence and that
[¶Prudence]
been your*e* and conseil-
lyng
and gou*er*ne hir*e* [¶Salomon]
and thou neu*er* repente ¶Thanne /
Melibeus / leet
folk / . surgiens / Phisiciens
and so*m*me reconsiled
semblau*nt* and in ther
neighebores / that
ofte / ¶Ther
subtille flatereres and
folk / togidre weren /

---

17 Ouidius de remedio amoris Hg El (2166)

36 qualiter Iesus Christus fleuit propter mortem lazari Hg El (2177)

39 Apostolus paulus ad Romanos El

59 Memorandum de Iob El (2189)

---

[1] ¶Chaucer on *153v*

[2] ¶Melibee *154r*

[3]speche / semed wel / that crueel
vengeaunce hise foes / that
but hire
matiere ¶A Surgien
weren and to seyde /
Surgiens aperteneth /
wight that been withholde /
that wherfore
and that men /
oon surgien wherfore /
werre
supporte /. But certes / warisshynge
youre doghter /
that
nyght that with
and ¶Almoost / right
that
woordes moore / That right maladies /
been contraries / right so / shul men warisshe
vengeaunce ¶Hise neighebores
freendes that reconsiled / and hise flatereres /
semblant wepyng empeireden and
agreggeden
matiere greetly Melibee / myght /
and freendes
seiden outrely that anon
wreken foes
Aduocat that and conseil
that were seide /. nede for which
been assembled is a ful
heigh matiere / and wikkednesse
resoun damages that
comynge / fallen for this same
and eek
resoun and
resouns / matiere
¶wherfore / Melibeus sentence /
conseille
that right anon / thou do thy diligence
wise thou wante
espie / thy persone for saue ¶And
that
conseille thou sufficeant garnisoun
þat / may / wel body
certes / werre / or sodeynly
vengeaunce / demen / that
profitable /. Wherfore and
For prouerbe seith
thus ¶He that deemeth. eek
that wys that matiere
and leyser ¶for that alle tariyng
anoyful / algates / repreue yeuynge
Iuggement
takyng sufficeant
resonable ¶And crist
that womman / that Auowtrie
broght
hire it so that
that ⟨yet⟩ he
ground [4]he
wroot by deliberacioun /
shal thanne grace god /
thee thyng /
profitable / ¶Vp
partie / compaignye scorned
the olde men and
right that Iren sholden
smyte / / right so / men sholde
been fresshe and with

criden werre / werre ¶Vp tho /
and with contenaunce / that
stille Audience ¶Lordynges
man / that
werre / that litel amounteth ¶werre
entryng and large /
that euery wight and
werre / but certes / ende that shal ther of bifalle /
nat For
bigonne / child mooder /
that of that ilke werre / elles
and wrecchednesse /. And
bigynne / greet conseil and greet
wende / resons /
ny alle rise
soothly /
that that heeren his
sermon
anoieth ¶For Iesus Syrak seith / that Musik
[¶Iesus Syrak]
wepynge anoyous thyng /. this seyn /
auailleth
bifore folk /
is synge / that wepeth /. And this
man /
saugh that and al
agayn ¶For seith / thou
noon [¶Salomon]
Audience / see
commune That
moost ¶Yet Melibeus conseil /
folk that eere conseilled certeyn
conseilled contrarie Audience
Whan that partie
[¶Melibeus]
weren accorded maken anoon /
consented
conseillyng and hire sentence /
Thanne saugh / that hir
[¶Prudence]
housbonde wreken hise foes / and
werre / saugh
seide to hym yow
biseche and
yeueth Audience ¶For [¶Petrus]
seith ¶who that to that oother good
it. wise
wole enemy
drede ¶The prouerbe seith / wel that wisely
abyde / And This Melibee [¶Melibee]
Prudence ¶I purpose he
werke resouns
¶For certes / euery wight fool
¶this I. conseillyng
chaungen
that been ordeyned and affermed wyse ¶Secoundely
that been *and* alle
¶For men a good man [5]but
wommen / certes /
If seme that
ouer god forbede / that weere
¶Iesus Syrak] ¶For Iesus
¶Salomon] contrarious seith ¶Neuere
child / yeue
self /. that
aske persone / that thou be
children / ¶And if
conseillyng / Certes / conseillyng
tyme knowe this /
¶Prudence] noght be Whanne
Prudence / and with

123 Nota de Iudicibus et eorum Iudicijs El (2221)

191 Nota secundum Salomonem El (2247)

[3] ¶Chaucer *154v*
[4] ¶Melibee *155r*
[5] ¶Chaucer *155v*

greet pacience /
seye ⸗/ hym
youre
resoun / ligħtly answered ¶For
seye / that
folie / conseil ⸗. chaunged ¶or
elles / semeth / ootherweyes /
mooreouer that thouġh ye
and bihiġht parfourne
emprise ¶And nathelees /
parfourne / emprise luste cause ⸗
therfore / that liere forsworn ¶For
man
bettre ¶And that youre
and greet folk ⸗
nat thilke ordinaunce /
like ¶For thynges / and been
founden
folk that been wise / and resoun /
greet
folk man / and clatereth /
that
liketh ¶Soothly / multitude ¶As to
resoun /. where been wikke ⸗
Saue grace / certes despisen
wommen /
| and |
¶Seneca] sapience /
| despise but gladly / techen that
kan withouten
presumpcioun pride / And
thynges //
nat been and
folk / self /. And sire / that been many
ligħtly ¶For sire / oure
crist neuere haue descended
wommen / hadden ben
bountee that crist
deeth lyue / appeered womman /
hise Apostles
¶And thouġh that salomon that
neuere
womman that wommen
wikke For though that womman /.
| ful many founden /
trewe ¶Or elles salomon
that bounte womman /
that wiġht
recordeth hys For
that what /
that makere ¶Youre [6]thridde
this ¶ye seyn / if it
seme that maistrie /
youre persone ⸗. sire saue youre grace / so ⸗
For if it were so that conseilled /
hem that hadden and wolden
ben conseilled ⸗ For soothly /
that asketh

oonseil youre fourthe
resoun ¶ther seyn Ianglerie
wommen hath hyd
wiste noġht. As that womman
hyde that she woot ¶sire
been and
wommen / seyn that
hous ¶that seyn droppyng
Reyn /. and and swiche [¶Salomon]
dwelle with
that riotous ¶And sire youre
that .I. / haan

silence / and pacience . ⸗ And
eek wel / that hyde and that
oġhte
secreely youre resoun / where
that wommen venquisshe men
¶god resoun stede ¶For vnderstoond
now / asken conseil
wole werken youre wif restreyneth thilke
and resoun and
wyf / oġhte rather to be preised /
yblamed ¶Thus
that venquisshen
wommen
and resouns ⸗ ⸗ shewe yow by
that
womman / ben been /
conseils ful hoolsome
and ¶Eek / that conseillynge
elles pris ¶But
and conseil and
worth / and
and wise conseillynge ¶Loo
by good conseil
mooder benysoun Ysaak /
ouer hise hire conseil /
[¶de Iudith]
deliuered Bethulie the
Olofernus / that biseged and
wolde haue al destroyed it
¶Abygail housbonde kyng that
[¶de Abygail]
haue and apaysed
and conseillyng ¶Hester / enhaunced |
[¶de Hestere]
| greetly by hir good conseil the god /
kyng ¶and conseillyng
womman whan oure lord

self good / to been alloone /
helpe
that that wommen
goode and conseils goode
wolde neuere han wroġht called hem /
rather confusioun man ¶and
oones [7]two vers ⸗ what
bettre / gold ⸗ Iaspre
Iaspre ⸗ wisedoom ¶And
wisedom / ⸗ womman ⸗. And
than a good womman ⸗
sire / othre resons / seen
that been and
conseils goode and profitable ⸗
therfore sire / triste restoore
yow / and sound / And .I.
do
that cause /
¶Melibee] Whan Melibee herd
wordes
¶Salomon] wel that Salomon
seith that been discreetly
ordinaunce /
been honycombes / yeuen
and hoolsomnesse body ¶And
thy sweete
and preued sapience /
and gouerne
¶Prudence] thyng / Now sire
sauf /
shul youre self / youre conseillours
shul first / mekely / heiġhe
youre conseillour /. And yow /

---

257 Of .iij. thynges þat dryuen a man out of his hous El (2276)

279 Nota de Rebekka El (2288)

---

[6] ¶Melibee *156r*

[7] ¶Chaucer *156v*

¶Thobias] that conseil and
sone ¶At thou and hym /
looke / conseils / been
¶*Sanct*us Iacobus] eu*er*emoore ¶Seint
eek seith ⁊. yow
sapience / god ¶And afterward / shul
taken conseil of youre ⟨self⟩ and your*e*
swich thyng thynketh
youre p*ro*fit / And
shul your*e* herte. thynges
co*n*seil / That
coueitise / and hastifnesse
c*er*tes / been
manye causes / the this ¶he
and wratthe wene*þ* that
that do ¶And secoundely / that
and wrooth /

conseille ¶The and wrooth
¶Seneca] Senec but he blame
folk / Angre and Ire ¶And
sire / coueitise
¶Ap*ost*olus] seith ¶That coueitise is roote
harmes ⁊ And trust
that noght deme thynke /
oonly /
and
accompliced / habundaunce
sire /
c*er*tes / deeme the
beste by a thought / that
For herde biforn / The co*m*mune
this ¶That he deemeth /
repenteth ¶Sir*e* /
be alwey disposiciou*n* ¶for
somtyme
that it Another tyme
contrarie / conseil of your*e*
deemed deliberacion
you list best / that it [8]secree /
conseil that
that thurgh your*e* biwreyyng your*e* condiciou*n* /
be
Yow the moore p*ro*fitable ¶For I*es*us seith /
[¶I*es*us Syrak]
frend secree
Audience and lookynge / to supportaciou*n*
and Absence clerk That
shaltou that conseil sikerly |
thou
thou p*ri*sou*n* / and thou biwreyest
wight / snare ¶And therfore
hyde youre youre
praye hem / han that
wole it seith ¶If [¶Seneca]
nat hyde ⁄ darstou prayen
wight sikerly kepe ¶But
If thou *þ*at the biwreiyng
make condiciou*n* plyt /.
shaltou tellen conseil ¶First
thou semblant
that. wille and
For wel / co*m*en*li*
been flatereres /
namely conseill*our*s
rather speken
lust. been trewe
p*ro*fitable ¶And therfore /
seeld conseil if
self ¶And thou co*n*sidere

freendes and enemys ⁊. freendes ⁄
thou wiche hem /
feithful and moost and conseillyng.
And hem shalt thou aske caas
requireth
first / conseil
youre freendes that been trewe ¶For
seith ¶That right [¶Salomon]
man soote /
so / soule.
also ¶ther freend ⁊
c*er*tes siluer / beth nat worth
wyl freend ¶And that
freend / deffense /
*þ*at hym fyndeth / certes /
greet tresour ¶Thanne ye that your*e*
freendes / and ¶For
book seith /

resou*n* / conseil youre freendes that
been seyn and been expert in manye
and been conseillynges ¶For
book seith / that
in the olde Sapience /
that been accompliced
deliu*er*nesse
p*er*sones and science /
c*er*tes /
enforcen encreescen thanne / shul
gen*er*al reule ¶First shul clepen your*e*
youre freendes that been especiale / for
seith ¶Manye freendes thou /
thousand chese For
that thou [9]telle thou
afterward
alwey / that conseillours / condiciou*ns*
seyn / that
oold exp*er*ience ¶And werke
oon counseill*our* allone ¶For somtyme bihooueth
¶Salomon] been conseilled manye ⁊ For
seith ¶Saluaciou*n*
is / where been conseill*ours*
Now / sith I toold folk /
been
counseilled / ⁄ conseil / oghte
| to eschewe ¶First eschue fooles ⁊
¶Salomon] For taak
noght affecciou*n*
that p*ro*pretee this ¶he troweth
lightly eu*er*y wight / and lightly /
self ¶Thou conseillyng of |
flatereres / hem / your*e*
flaterye yow /
¶Tullius] Tulli*us* seith ¶Amonges
that freendshipe / flat*er*ie /
nede thou and flatereres /
peple ¶The thou
and flee / sweete
freend /
sothes ⁊ Salomo*n*
snare chacche with Innocentz ¶He that
of swetnesse
plesaunce / net
cacche hym ¶And therfore
Tullius / Enclyne eres
¶Cato] taaketh conseil of the
flaterye ⁊. And seith ¶Auyse
and eschue the wordes / and
plesaunce ¶And
eek thou conseillyng thyne
enemys /

---

323 Of .iij. thynges *þ*at been contrariouse to good conseil El (2311)

365 How a man shal tellen his conseil El (2338)

400 Nota secundum Salomonem El (2357)

413 Of conseillours *þ*at a man oghte to eschue El (2363)

---

[8] ¶Melibee *157r*

[9] ¶Chaucer *157v*

that been reconsiled ¶The book seith /. wight
saufly / grace enemy ¶And Isope
whiche thou werre
¶Seneca] conseil ¶And Seneca
why ¶It where greet
that
¶Salomon] warmnesse ¶And therfore
Salomon ¶In
foo neu*er*e ¶For though
enemy / reconsiled
and thee chiere and lowteth
with
heed neu*er*e ¶For
humilitee /
that deemeth /
feyned contenance / nat |
¶Petrus Alfonce] | wynne / by seith /.
felawshipe / with enemys / For thou
it /
hem / that been
and greet they doon it
loue ¶And
¶Ph*ilosoph*us] wise /. wight
¶Tullius] dredeth ¶And seith / Ther
myght greet that
haue / lo[10]ue peple / than for drede
eschue / conseiling that been
they kan hyde ¶For seith /
[¶Salomon]
shul
also / conseillyng folk.
conseille
thyng and contrarie openly
¶For Cassidorie seith / .that man*er*e sleighte
[¶Cassidorus]
thyng
p*ri*uely ¶Thou shalt also / suspect.
conseillyng folk /. book
conseillyng folk.
/.And seith ¶blisful folwed /
[¶Dauid]
conseilyng ¶Thou eschue /
conseillyng yong folk. NOw
youre
conseil /
shal youre
youre
manye thynges ¶Alderfirst
that thou purposest / and
thou wolt
and tale
¶For that conseilled / cas
lieth ¶And thou
acorden thou purposest /
conseillours resou*n* accorde therto / .And eek /
myght
atteine And and part
conseillours or noon shaltou
folwe / after hir conseillyng.
grace / and manye thynges
| ¶Thanne / of alle thou
considere
engendred matiere fruyt
may conserue *and* ¶Thou
fro been sprongen ¶And
han seyd / and
and and hast it
folk and olde ¶tha*n*ne shaltou considere / it thou
p*ar*fourne it and it
¶For c*er*tes / resou*n*

nat that man / a myghte /
p*ar*fourne it oghte ¶Ne wight /
take
heuy a charge that myghte
bere it ¶For [¶p*ro*u*er*be]
seith /. that distreyneth litel ¶And
Catou*n* seith ¶Assay thyng. thou
[¶Cato]
lest that charge thee / that
that thou bigonne /
thou thou mayst p*ar*fourne
noon / chese rather / suffre bigynne
¶And Piers Alfonce thou myght
[¶Petrus Alfonce]
thou repente thee / it nay
ye ¶this that bettre / holde
vnderstonde /
that thou po[11]wer /
p*ar*fou*r*ne which thou
that thou suffre bigynne ¶wel they
wight assaye any thyng
p*ar*fou*r*ne it noon / and han
you*r*e wel / that
p*ar*fourne sadly
NOw and tyme
wha*n*ne and that you*r*e
with outen repreue ¶Soothly / a man
pu*r*pos co*n*seil
caas bitydeth ¶For seith that thynges
¶Seneca] bityden / senec / seith /.
comen / eeris enemy change
conseil
¶Thou If be / that
thou mayst fynde /
that harm damage
dishonest. ellis / dishoneste
conseil /. For seyn ¶that
bihestes that been dishoneste / been
value ¶And eek / If
| so be p*ar*fourned
kept ¶And general reule / that euery conseil
that chaunged condiciou*n*
that bityde ¶I þat wikked /
¶Melibeus] This whanne herd
wyf
Prudence / wyse he
yet and couenablely taught me
general / gouerne me
in the chesynge / and withholdynge
/ but that
condescende and me /
yow that
¶Prudence] nede My yow
that wilfully replie agayn resou*ns* /
thogh that displese /
For that it
and youre p*ro*fite eke / that
benyngnytee /
that youre conseil caas nat
p*ro*p*er*ly / conseillyng
moeuyng folye / erred
¶First / and erred thassemblynge
conseillours / For haue cleped
folk / you*r*e after myghte
folk / been cleped
youre conseil greet peple
chargeant and
¶Also / there sholden
oonly haue cleped conseil frendes olde
and wise / ycleped
folk / and yong folk.

---

473 how a man shal examine his conseillours after the doctrine of Tullius El (2392)

517 how a man may chaungen hise conseillours with outen repreue El (2414)

---

[10] ¶Melibee *158r*

[11] ¶Chaucer *158v*

and and haue yow conseil / coueitise / and hastifnesse / thing*es* been cont*ra*riouse conseil / honeste and p*ro*fitable / thre / ye anientissed youre conseillours yow ogħte ¶Ye shewed’ [12]to youre and werr*e* and youre wordes been therfore / they rather conseilled yow your*e* your*e* þat it suffiseth / been conseilled conseillours and wiþ Auys / where greetꝛ and heigħ been necessarie conseillours / and p*ar*fourne youre emprise youre conseil / man*ere* man*ere* caas requireth ¶Ye han nat maked youre conseillours ¶this bitwixen your*e* and your*e* conseillours ⸝ han wil olde wise castꝛ hire wordes and herte p*ar*tie / and and ther*e* been condescended ¶And wel alwey / fynde fooles / co*n*seils that been congregaciou*n*s folkꝛ. there reward’ nombre / that swiche fooles Melibe*us* [¶Melibeus] that erred ⁊ there thou heerbiforn / nys blame hise conseillours c*er*tein caas / and c*er*teine causes ¶I redy conseillours / rigħt deuyse ⸝ ¶The seith /. [¶p*ro*u*er*be] synne mannyssħ / certes / synne / sentence answereth Prudence and seyde ¶Examineth your*e* and [¶Prudence] see / most resonablely / and taugħt conseil ⁊. muche examynaciou*n* bigynne surgiens phisiciens / that firstꝛ matiere ¶I that surgiens and phisiciens conseil discreetly / oughte ¶And speche seyd wisely / ap*er*teneth eu*er*y wigħt honou*r* and p*ro*fit / and wigħt for to and in hir craft / greet gou*er*naunce / And sire / rigħt wisely and discreetly / I that been and gerdoned eekꝛ sholde do / bisynesse of youre doghter þat been your*e* therfore that yow nogħt / ogħte hem and shewe your*e* largesse ¶And p*ro*posiciou*n* ⸝ that Phisiciens encreesceden caas / that oon cont*ra*rie warisshed contrarie / ⸝ hou vnderstonde this text / and what I. it [¶Melibeus] wise ¶that rigħtꝛ rigħt I another ⁊ For rigħtꝛ [13]venged and wrongꝛ ⸝ Rigħt vpon and wrongꝛ. and cured oon contrarie ¶Prudence] Lo.lo enclined and plesau*n*ce ¶Certes she been vnderstonden in thys wise ⁊. For cont*ra*rie vengeance vengeau*n*ce / wrongꝛ. been semblable ¶And o vengeau*n*ce / warisshed vengeau*n*ce / o wroongꝛ wroongꝛ encreesceth and agreggeth of the been vnderstonden wise ¶For and been contraries and vengeau*n*ce and suffrau*n*ce / discord’ and accord’ *and* manye wikkednesse / warisshed discord’ accord’ / werre thyng*es* heer to accordeth seint [¶Paulus Ap*osto*lus] Paul manye places ¶He seith nat But dooth thee and hym harm ¶And places and accord’ ¶Butꝛ and that accord’ / bifore ¶That ye sholde doone kepen your*e* and warnestoore your*e* hous ¶And also that caas / yow ogħten werken auysely and sire / pointꝛ. toucheth werre eu*er*emoore / mekely and deuoutly / preyen biforn that his grete mercy wol and been nede ⁊. For c*er*tes / In world wigħt that sufficeantly withouten cristꝛ [¶Dauid p*ro*phet*a*] sentence accordeth dauid / seith ⁊ kepe the Citee / ydel that sire / ye co*m*mitte / p*er*sone that knowe / and [¶Cato] help*e* / kepe ¶For seith ¶If help / freendes ⁊ For freend’ ¶And yow folk / and and [¶Petrus Alfonce] alwey hir*e* seith ⁊ taak / compaignye weye of straunge men / be thou hym tyme ¶And that he be falle compaignye p*ar*auenture w*ith*outen assentꝛ. / thou maystꝛ and wey ⁊. seye that thou goostꝛ thider thou natꝛ and rigħt and on his liftꝛ syde / ¶And thanne / shul wisely alħ manere peple And and eschewe / ¶And shul p*re*sumpciou*n* that dispise ne acounte [14]nat myghtꝛ Adu*er*sarie / litel / that your*e* p*re*sumpciou*n* / euery enemy ¶And seith [¶Salomon]

[12] ¶Melibee *159r*

[13] ¶Chaucer *159v*

[14] ¶Melibee *160r*

¶weleful that alle
drede / for certes / that thurgħ
and thurgħ
greet ¶Thanne /
shul euere moore
embusshementz and alle
senec seith ¶That man / he dredeth |
| ne [¶Seneca]
that eschueth ⁊
be it so / seme that thou art place /
dilligence kepynge persone
¶this seyn Ne
oonly / for gretteste for thy
[¶Senek—enemy ⁊ *Out* El]
¶Ouyde [¶Ouidius]
bole / and hert ¶And book / seith ⁊ A
thorn /
a greet kyng soore ⁊.
boor ¶But nat thou be coward /
that thou drede ¶The book
somme folk .han greet lust yet
deceyued ¶Yet shaltou
empoisoned And yow / Scorneres
seith ⁄ scorneres
wordes
Where conseillours conseilled yow
warnestoore
with gret diligence ¶I.
that vnderstonde / and
Melibeus and seyde ¶Certes
vnderstande [¶Melibeus]
it wise ¶That warnestoore
with and
and Armure / and
and hous deffenden that
enemys /
Approche TO this
Prudence ⁊ .Warnestooryng [¶Prudence]
toures and with costages
and greet trauaille / whan that yet
be defended
freendes been / olde vnderstoond
that gretteste strongeste
that a riche
wel persone hise goodes ⁄
is / that biloued / amonges hys hise
Tullius ¶That [¶Tullius]
garnysoun / that venquysse disconfite /
that
lord biloued hise Citezeins /
NOw
thridde point .where olde / conseillours
seyden ¶That oghte sodeynly
hastily proceden
that purueyen apparaillen
caas greet deliberacioun ¶trewely /
that right wisely right
seith / thou it / Apparaille
[¶Tullius]
thee with diligence ¶Thanne that
takyng
In bataille / warnestooryng
I. rede / thou apparaille
greet deliberacioun
¶Tullius] [15]¶For
seith ¶The longe apparaillyng
¶Cassidorus] bataille / victorie ⁊.
seith ¶The garnysoun
stronger / longe But
speken / that accorded
youre neighebores /
reuerence withouten Love /
flatereres / that conseilled
priuely / openly / conseilleden
contrarie ¶The folk
that conseilleden yow anon
¶And certes biforn /
cleped / manere folk conseillours
ynogh by resouns aforeseyd /
procede /
doctrine Tullius ¶Certes / matiere /
nat
yow
trespassours
doon / vileynye ¶And
this thanne / shul seconde condicioun /
that Tullius / matiere ¶For
thyng. that seyn ⁊.
been they and how manye / that
conseil / doon vengeance ¶And
also
that consenteden youre Aduersaries ¶And
It knowen /
that trewely /
tho that conseilleden yow /
freendes ¶Lat considere / they /
that freendes ⁄ persone ⁊ For
that riche / certes / been nat but
certes / child
bretheren germayns / ooþer neigh
wherfore that enemys sholde stinte /
with knowen also that
mooten been dispended / parties /
wight part. taken reward
vnge deeth ⁊. But thre /
manie ny
And though were that thou
ynowe
persone ⁊ .And though be that siker
stedefast. of aduersarie ⁊
nathelees

youre enemys ny hem /
And certes / condicioun / bet
conseillyng conseilleden
yow / vengeaunce / accorde
resoun ⁄
nay ⁊ right resoun /
taken wight / that
graunted hym /
hastily attemprely
requireth moore ouer / that
clepeth consentynge / .thou myght
[16]thy power / consenten wilfulnesse /
conseillours ⁄ certes / thou nay
¶For sikerly / proprely ⁄ thyng.
doon rightfully ⁄ And rightfully
Auctoritee
¶thanne nat
accordeth nat youre
thridde point clepeth Consequent ¶Thou
vnderstonde that thou
take / consequent ⁊ .And vengeaunce /
peril / nombre /
be war /
fourthe point. clepeth engendrynge ⁄
thou
engendred
takynge / vpon
muchel sorwe richesses
as to point that
clepeth that point .thou
that thou receyued /
certeine
Causa propinqua /. seyn /

703 Nota / of the strongeste garnysoun that may be El (2526)

[15] ¶Chaucer *160v*

[16] ¶Melibee *161r*

cause cause ¶The god /
thynges ¶The enemys
¶The Accidental / hate ¶The
fyue woundes doghter ¶The manere
werkynge cloumben in

wyndowes ⁄ The doghter / It
letted nat was ¶But speken
cause / come /
caas / .I. deeme ⁄.
supposynge ¶for shul
ende /. that book of
seith ⁄ .seelden or with peyne /
ybroght /
whanne sire /
If wolde that suffred
Certes /
soothfastnesse ¶For thapostle [¶Apostolus]
Iuggementz almyghty /
suffisantly /
presumpciouns and
bileeue which that rightwisnesse
bityde resonable ⁄.
Thy Melibee
hony ¶Thou muchel hony
sweete temporeel richesses / honours
thou forgeten / crist
thou hym
oughte / thou nat
ytaken Ouide ¶That seith ⁄ [¶Ouidius]
body /
sleeth salomon seith ¶If [¶Salomon]
thou
thou it mesure / thou
poure / And par auenture / Crist
despit / turned face hise
eeris Misericorde ¶And also /
[17]suffred / that thou
punysshed manere that hast trespassed
¶Thou synne / oure
crist. For certes.
.iij. flessh /
feend world / ⁄ thou
wilfully
defended hire assautes / and hire
temptaciouns / so / that wounded
soule / in
places / deedly synnes that
herte / wittes ⁄.
crist woold and that .iij.
entred /
ywounded doghter Certes
¶Melibee] Melibee / wel that
muchel
me / swich manere that nat /
enemys and
that myghten
myghte
takynge / neuere

disseuered men
¶And that wyl
wikkednesse /
purpos / punyssynge and
of the trespassours ¶And ⟨I⟩ moore / .that right

man ⁄/ right so /
¶Seneca] hem / Senec thus
That that proueth shrewes ¶And
¶Cassidorus] seith ¶A outrages /
soot and that it displeseth Iuges / and
souereyns ¶Another seith ¶The [¶Nota]
right. shrewes ⁄.

Paule the Apostle /
epistle / Romayns ⁄
Iuges with
beren punysse and mysdoeres / and to

enemys / youre
Iuge that Iurisdiccion and
punysse and requireth A
¶Melibee] Melibee / vengeance /
thyng ¶I
and heede / Fortune /
norissed me
childhede / and a stroong
¶Now with that
¶Prudence] venge Certes Prudence
¶If conseil / nat assaye
Fortune nat lene bowe / vnto hire
¶Seneca] Senec ¶For thynges / that and
that Fortune / neuere
ende ⁄.
Senec seith ¶The cleer and
shynyng that Fortune is / brotil / and
broken
is ⁄ stidefast
stable thou seur and siker
hire helpe ⁄ faille thee / and where
seyn Fortune norissed
youre childhede /.
that [18]in muchel /
ye / hire
and in wit ⁄. senec
that norissed [¶Seneca]
Fortune / hym a greet fool
and vengeance / and vengeance / that
lawe and nat And
vengeance that Fortune and vncertein
Thanne
vnto Iuge that
and wronges / .And
where seith ⁄.
Melibee answerde ⁄. [¶Melibee]
nat. vileynye that me .I.
sompne that vileynye
vileynye ¶For writen
¶If thou oold vileynye ⁄ / thou sompnest
Aduersaries vileynye ¶And
do to me muchel
that myghte it susteene /
and lowe ¶For seyn / In muchel
thee ⁄ whiche / thou
Certes Prudence .I. graunte
[¶Prudence]
yow that ouer muchel suffraunce nys yet
that doon
vileynye and

and iniuries ⁄ .And ther fore / Auctoritees / that
oonly vnderstonden Iuges /
muchel and the vileynyes
with punysshynge / sompne
it ¶Also
that Iuge that synnere and
synne ¶And and souereyns
muchel and mysdoeres / that

and myght / that out and
and atte laste lesen hire
that been
nat myght and wole
comparisoun / myght Aduersaries /
thynges / that shewed this /
that hire youres ¶And I
that that and
sawe /
man / with

805 In libro decretalium El (2594)
859 Paulus Apostolus ad Romanos El (2630)

17 ¶Chaucer *161v*

18 ¶Melibee *162r*

self / .And stryue with man
strong he / it peril / .
And with weyker folie ¶And
flee muchel myghte ¶For
[¶Salomon]
and stryf ¶And bifalle that
myght and thou art .
greuaunce / studie / and
bisye rather stille /
[19]same greuaunce /
¶Seneca] Senec seith / That greet
that
¶Cato] with self ¶And
seith / man myghty
thou / anoy greuaunce /
that oones
thee / another tyme / may releeue and helpe /
caas / myght and licence / yow /
.I. seye that that
of and suffre /
and the thynges / that
¶First and foreward / if wole that
persone /
yow
¶Poeta] heer biforn ¶For seith
oghte
taken that vs whan we
and that hem ¶And
¶Gregorius] seith / That man
wel
hise defautes / synnes / . and
that suffreth / semen / hym
muche / hise synnes
and greuous / lighter
an owen for to and
pacience crist / As
seint Peter Epistles ¶Iesu
vs folwe and
word moup / whan
noght .
noght . ¶Also which the seintes that
had tribulaciouns that ysuffred
with gilt . oghte muchel stiren
¶Forthermoore / yow /
that tribulaciouns but
and and goone ¶And
that man / tribulaciouns / is
that seith epistle ¶The
god / seith seyn euerelastynge ¶Also
trowep and that nat
ynorissed
ytaught that
¶Salomon] pacience / seith ¶That
and pacience ¶And
seith ¶that that pacient .
prudence ¶And seith and
man atempreth
and stilleth ¶He also / worth
pacient . right strong . that
herte /
that force strengthe
Citees ¶And
therfore / Epistle ¶That
¶Melibee] Melibee / .
yow that pacience /
euery man perfeccioun

956 Petrus in epistolis El (2691)
968 Apostolus in epistola El (2700)
981 Iacobus in epistola El (2707)

[19] ¶Chaucer *162v*

nombre / right
[20]herte / neuere been tyme
venged / so that
vp me / .
tooken heede fulfilleden /
and corage ¶And therfore /
though peril And
though I. that venge
another A youre wyl / [¶Prudence]
and liketh / but
doon hym ¶For [¶Cassidorus]
yuele that vengeth
he that outrage / . therfore /
right / seyn
noght excesse outrage ¶And
If
yow outrage manere
right comandeth / synnen / Senec / .
vengen by shrewednesse
¶And that right axeth / man
defenden
fightyng fightyng /
sooth defense anon with
Interualle with tariyng
delay deffenden
and vengen hym / ¶And that
deffense / that men
cause matiere / that deffendeth
hym
and outrage / for ellis were it agayn resoun ¶Pardee /
knowen that
deffense deffende yow
sheweth that wyl
youre attemprely / . And thynketh
seith ¶That he that [¶Salomon]
Certes Melibee / I [¶Melibee]
that man and
that pat noght that
though for seith /
coupable that entremetteth or with
seych aperteneth Salomon
[¶Salomon]
seith / that entremetteth hym of noyse
strif /
man / . lyk that
eris / For right he hound
eris / with hound Right
that that his
inpacience noyse
where as hym ¶But knowen
wel / that grief and disese /
right ny / . though wrooth
inpacient . merueille / And grace /
seen / that myghte though
vengeaunce /
richer / and myghty
And that and
gouerned ¶And seith ¶That [¶Salomon]
moneye Whan [¶Prudence]
hym and moneye /
dispreisynge hise spak / and
wise ¶Certes / sire yow
that been and myghty / and that
hem han hem and wel
hem / . [21]right nat lyuen with
soule / outen temporeel
And for richesses / grete freendes |
¶Pamphilles] therfore Pamphilles ¶If
A netherdes doghter
seith he / riche / chesen

[20] ¶Melibee *163r*
[21] ¶Chaucer *163v*

thousand men / |
| for thousand men /
hire / hire ¶And
also ¶If right happy / .
thou right riche / thou fynde
and freendes ⁊. And Fortune change /
thou poure / farewel / and
thou be alloone *with*
poure yet
seith / moreouer ¶That that been
and lynage shullen been maad
richesses ¶And right so /
goodes / . right
and yueles / . pouer*te*
¶Cassidorus] yueles / . therfore /
mooder mooder
¶Petrus Alfonce] ou*er*throwynge
doun ¶And therfore seith
Alfonce ⁊. world
man / kynde or by burthe
co*n*streyned
pouer*te* eten Almesse
enemy ¶*And*
¶Innocencius] hise bookes ⁊. He that
and poure beggere /
mete / hunger / .
And algates constreyneth
¶Salomon] axe ¶And bet it is
pouerte ⁊ ¶And seith
¶Bettre is deeth lyuen /
that seid
resons that seye ⁊ / grau*n*te
that
goode hem / that to hem that
richesses ¶And therfore hou

manere /
hem with desir / leyser sekyngly /
nat hastily / that gete
abaundoneth and yueles ¶And
¶Salomon] Salomon ¶He that bisily /
riche Innocent ¶he also / .
richesse that man / and lightly /
fro man ¶but that that and
litel and multiplieth ¶And shul geten
and trauaille profit.

p*er*sone ¶For seith / him-
seluen riche / harm wight ⁊ This
that deffendeth and right that
¶Tullius]
seith ⁊ þat deeth /
that agayns
man encressen man ⁊
though [22]and
lightly thou / .yet shaltou been
slow
profit. thou wise flee ydelnesse ¶For
seith / . ydelnesse / [¶Salomon]
yueles
¶And ⁊ That he that trauailleth and bisieth
hym land / eten breed
but he that ydel /
occupacio*un* / pouer*te* /
hunger ¶And that slow /
neu*er*e
tyme doon profit ⁊.
seith / [¶Vnde v*er*sificator]
coold / som*er* / enchesou*n*
heete ⁊. ⟨seiþ⟩ Catou*n* ⁊. waketh
enclyneth [¶Cato]
nat yow ou*er* muchel / slepe /
ou*er* muchel
reste norisseth vices ⁊.

Ierome ⁊. Dooth goodes / that
[¶*Sanct*us Ieronim*us*]
vnocupied ⁊. For deuel taketh
lightly werkynge occupied

flee ydelnesse ⁊. And afterward richesses /
geten youre wit youre trauaille /
that nat yow / scars
sparynge
spendere / for
right Auaricious cause /
scarsetee
and chyngerie / In blame that
largely ⁊. And Caton ¶Vse seith /
[¶Cato]
richesses that thou geten that
haue /
matiere neiþer
is a greet pou*er*e
purs ¶he that thou
spende hem mesurably / they
that folily / that
owene / hem
man ¶I shul
fleen richesses / that
nat yburyed /
myght weeldynge ¶For
rep*re*ueth man / and
[¶Vnde v*er*sificator]
vers ¶Wherto *and* burieth hise goodes
wel that dye /
deeth eu*er*y p*re*sent lyf ¶And
enchesou*n*
hise that wittes
from
that
with hym / world ¶And ther fore
Augustyn ⁊ man [¶Augustin*us*]
that swelweth /
swelwe and eschewe /
man / chynche /
and yow / that nat
large ¶Therfore Tullius ⁊. [¶Tullius]
hous / ne sholde nat hyd / cloos
[23]but that
myghte opened and debonairetee ¶that
seyn /
yeuen part to hem that greet nede / .
goodes / shullen
been opene / been
¶Afterward / getynge
your*e* hem /
herte / . Oure
¶First /
your*e* thyng.
creatour
¶Salomon] and maker*e* ¶For
Salomon ¶It
a litel good with god / haue / muchel
and
¶*prophet*a] tresour / god ¶And
seith ⁊
is / man and litel good
tresour / been and
richesses ¶And
sholde your*e*
bisynesse that hem *with*
¶Ap*osto*lus] conscience ¶And seith ⁊.
world / of
¶Sapiens] Conscience bereth
witnesse ¶And
seith ⁊ man
nat ¶Afterward
and hem /

[22] ¶Melibee *164r*

[23] ¶Chaucer *164v*

and that youre
¶Salomon] and conserued ⁊.
salomon seith /. is / and
auailleth man haue a good
richesses ⁊ place ¶do greet
salomon / kepyng freend /
abide
tresour / precious ¶And certes nat
and
left. and
¶Cassidorus] good name ¶And
seith ¶That of |
herte ⁊ man and desireth
han
¶Augustinus] name ¶And therfore
Seint Augustyn ¶That
that and that
Conscience and loos / þat Conscience /
inward /
outward /. he that muchel
that noght
noght though his
name / · crueel cherl / Sire /
do and how /
and that that
wole and bataille ¶I conseille
that trust youre
noght mayntene ¶And therfore /
¶Philosophus] Philosophre ¶That man / that
werre / suffisaunce /
that is /
¶Salomon] wole and victorie ¶And
seith ⁊.
that
hath ¶And that youre
folk nat.
good where mowe manere /
and [24]profit ¶For victories
that world / lyen nombre
of the peple / vertu lith
and hand almyghty ¶And
therfore / knyght.
fighte agayn aduersarie that
greet nombre / and folk /
was this peple of Machabee /.
seyde right wise ¶Als
lightly almyghty
to a fewe many folk.
comth
from heuene ¶And muchel /
certein / if he be that
victorie naught / . After
seith / therfore / [¶Salomon]
euery man drede bigynne
¶And cause / that perils / and
that slayn
man /. writen /
kynges batailles auenturouse / and
lightly hurt with spere
another ⁊. And gret werre / therfore /
man flee and eschue muchel
goodly ⁊. seith /. He that peril
[¶Salomon]
peril After that dame
Melibee and see [¶Melibee]
Prudence wordes / and resouns
that me / that werre
thyng. yet
Certes she conseille that
accorde with [¶Prudence]
and that ye with hem ¶For Seint
epistles ¶That and
richesses and debaat and discord /
doun ¶And wel that
and souereyn thyng. that
vnytee and pees
¶And therfore / crist Apostles
wise ¶wel and
that louen and purchacen
god A Melibee /. [¶Melibee]
that honour / worshipe
¶Ye wel that Aduersaries /
bigonnen debaat
and bryge / outrage / and wel that
reconsiled
¶wol that go and meke and
and
crie mercy ⁊/. For worshipe
right that hoomlynesse /
despreisynge /. humylitee mekenesse
Thanne semblant wratthe /
and seyde ¶Certes grace / youre honour
[¶Prudence]
and youre profit as and ye
neuere contrarie ¶And yit
that purchaced pees / and
reconsiliacioun / ⁊
mystaken amys /.
seiþ ¶The and [¶Sapiens]
¶propheta] by-[25]gynneth self ¶And
seith ⁊.
Flee shrewednesse and and
is ¶Yet that
pees yow ⁊. I
that that do thyng
¶Salomon] me ¶And
salomon seith ⁊. he that
and mystyde ⁊ Whanne Melibee
Prudence maken semblant wratthe /
¶Melibee] wise ¶Dame prey yow that
that wel that and wrooth /
and that been wel /
¶propheta] don seyn ¶Therfore /
seith
¶That sighte ¶but seyeth and
me redy do right
desire / and folye / holden /
¶Salomon] yow and preyse yow ¶For
seith ⁊ .That
that folye / grace that
sweete wordes Thanne seide
¶I wratthe ne Anger / but
¶Salomon] profit ¶For seith ⁊.
that
fool folye semblant
wratthe /
that and peyseth hym mysdoynge
and laugheth folye ¶And Salomon /
afterward ⁊. That
and contenaunce man /
correcteth
1 Melibee] and self Thanne
Melibee ¶I nat
answere to manye faire resouns / and
seyeth shortly wyl and and
redy
¶Prudence] and parfourne it Thanne
| to and seyde ¶I conseille she
that pees / and and
and grace ⁊ For biforn /.
yow and disese

1219 In .ij.do libro Regum El (2858)

1232 Sanctus Iacobus in epistolis El (2866)
1236 Dominus Apostolis suis El (2869)

[24] ¶Melibee *165r*

[25] ¶Melibee *165v*

And do sey Adversaries
yow fallen youre
¶Salomon] youre and
comandementz ¶For seith ⁊.
condicioun man plesaunt and
god / . chaungeth
Aduersaries and
hym / and grace / prey
speke with
Aduersaries priuee shul that
or of youre And thanne knowe /
¶Melibee] wil and hire entente / . yow
seurely Dame
Melibee / wil and youre likynge / .
¶Prudence] disposicioun and ordinaunce Thanne
saugh housbonde / |
delibered and self .thinkinge / myghte
conclusioun / and ende / .
saugh
hire pryuee and wisely
goodes that and har[26]mes and
that and manere / .hou that
oughten / repentaunce / that
Melibee and to And
hire doghter
And herden wordes
Prudence / and rauysshed / and
that telle ¶A
shewed
prophete / for we been
but oghte with
and humylitee /
vnto vs ¶Now that science and
Salomon trewe ¶For seith ⁊
sweete
and encreescen and and
meeke ¶Certes they ./ and
matere and
youre and obeye to
and Melibee ¶And
and preien yow and biseke yow as mekely
and that lyke fulfillen
and
that offended and greued lord Melibee
mesure / .
that be hise amendes / and
therfore / and bynden vs and
freendes / for to doon
and hise comandementz ⁊ ¶but heuynesse /
and wratthe vs ward / that
swich a peyne / bere
susteene / . and biseke /
auysement that we /
desherited ne destroyed thurgh
folye Certes
and right that [¶Prudence]
outrely / and Iuggement.
myght and enemys ¶For seith ⁊
[¶Salomon]
and to that I
quod he ¶ye peple / folk and gouernours of hooly chirche
¶to freend / broother /
thou myght thou
lyuest ¶Now deffendeth / that shal
yeuen
broother / myght body ⁄ by |
resoun deffendeth / and yeuen
self enemy ¶And you / that ye /
nat lord / wel / and
that is /
and meeke / and thyng desirous
coueitous
good richesse ¶for thyng
world
that and honour ¶Forther moore /

wel / and right that
thyng doon
with And
that / by grace been
Thanne they o.
[27]voys ⁊ worshipful lady
and fully wil and and
redy / comen / youre noblesse
vs vs maken
obligacioun and boond
youre that fulfille
wille and Melibee Whan
¶Prudence] men / hem /
goon and retourned
Melibee / and
foond knowelechynge
lowely and and were
redy al requirynge
preiynge hym
¶Melibee] and pitee ⁄ Thanne
Melibee ¶he worthy
and
knowelecheth it Indulgence
¶Seneca] ¶For Senec / seith ⁊. ther
and foryifnesse /
as confessioun is ¶For Confessioun Confessioun
Innocence
[And he seith—knowelicheth it *Out* El]

and corforme
pees / good nat with
the assent wyl
¶Prudence] freendes Thanne
Prudence right and
and seyde ¶Certes sire she answered
For right and helpe youre freendes /
been yow maken werre ⁄ right
with accorden
youre Aduersaries ¶For seith ⁊ ther
thyng good vnbounde
ybounde ¶And Dame Prudence
withouten delay tariynge /
anon hire messages hire
kyn and wyse /
Melibee mateere /
abouen and preyden þat
doon
nede ¶And freendes
forseide mateere /
it diligence / And
conseil and and þat Melibee /
aduersaries / and mercy And
whan dame Prudence
Melibee / and hise freendes accorde
wille
¶Prudence] entencioun /
in hire herte / and seyde ¶Ther
she seith ⁊ .That thou mayst
and to morwe
¶And therfore / conseille
youre messages
and wise / hem
þat wole accord / that
with tariyng comen
dede ¶And
and hire
Melibee / Messagers
hem / right and answereden
benignely / graces thankynges
hir Melibee
outen Messagers
hir Melibee ¶And right anon / wey
Court Melibee / and tooken hem /
maken hem borwes / and

[26] ¶Melibee *166r*

[27] ¶Chaucer *166v*

co[28]men / *pre*sence Melibee /
wordes It Melibee / and it
that [¶Melibee]
and resou*n*
wronges / me and Prudence ⁄ and
doghter
violence and
outrage wel haue disserued
deeth / and therfore / and
punyssement *and* the chastisynge /
wyl and wyf Prudence / or
nat Thanne / thre he*m* alle
and seyde ¶Sire vnworthy /
Court lord and worthy
been ⁄ For greetly and
offended and agilt
swich agayn heigh that
disserued and debonairetee
witnesseth in your*e* p*er*sone / submytten
benignitee your*e* gracious and been
to obeie your*e* that
your*e* repentau*n*ce
lough submyssiou*n* graunten vs foryeuenesse
knowe your*e*
lib*er*al m*er*cy / strecchen he*m* ferther
goodnesse
and
agayn your*e* heigh
lordshipe Thanne Melibee / ground
benignely receyved hir*e* boondes
hir*e*
othes hir*e* and assigned
Court.
receyue
Iuggement Melibee comande
hem aforeseyd / ordeyned /.
whan
saugh freyned lord
Melibee /
vengeance / thoughte / Adu*er*saries
To which Melibee seyde ¶Certes he / I
[¶Melibee]
desherite
hem / exil eu*er*e Certes
[¶Prudence]
dame crueel sentence and agayn
resou*n* / ynough and
and myghte lightly wise gete

eschued euery good man ¶For
the Apostle / .Coueitise therfore
[¶Ap*osto*lus]
muchel
taken hir good manere /
is lesen with is wynne *with*
vileynye shame /.
eueri man oghte to doon
name /. And yet
bisie hym / kepynge of his good name.
also
good name / for
þ*at* good loos *and*
and whan newed

renouelled ¶And
touchynge / wole your*e* Adu*er*aries /
resou*n* and [29]mesure /
power yeue
self ⁄. it writen þ*at*
worthy /
mysuseth / myght hym
¶And myghte þ*at* peyne
right trowe / do /. seye
mighte putten and
likly retourne were
therfore / wole obeisance / ye
deemen yeuen
Iuggementz ¶For þ*at* he
comandeth / hym moost
And I
prey yow
¶Seneca] herte ¶For Senec seith /. That
ou*er*cometh herte /
¶Tullius] twies ¶And Tullius seith ¶Ther
comendable
in greet meeke / and appeseth I
lightly / I. prey yow wole
vengeance
man*er*e / goode name kept
conserued /
and mowe and mateere /
preyse yow
mercy / and cause thyng
¶Seneca] doon ¶For Senec seith ¶He ouercometh
hym victorie / wherfore pray
been in your*e* mynde *and* in your*e* entente
almyghty m*er*cy
Iuggement ⁄ ¶For seint seith Epistle
¶Iuggement outen m*er*cy m*er*cy
¶Melibee] wight Whanne Melibee
herd
and resou*n*s Dame and hir*e*
informaciou*n*s
enclyne wil wif
entente and conformed and
fully and p*ro*cedeþ
v*er*tu and alle wyf / discreciou*n*
whan cam Adu*er*saries
appieren
p*re*sence / spak vn to and
wyse
your*e* and p*re*sumpciou*n* and of
yow and trespassed
me. yet muche / see and
your*e*
and and giltes /
doon grace and mercy ¶Therfore /
grace and
and wronges doon agayn and
and that god m*er*cy
at the
diynge that
hym wrecched world / For
and and giltes
trespassed sighte god /
and merciable / that giltes and
to his blisse / neu*er*e ende.Amen

¶Heere is ended / Chaucers tale / of Melibee / and of Dame Prudence

1483 Iacobus in epistola El (3059)

[28] ¶Melibee *167r*

[29] ¶Melibee *167v*

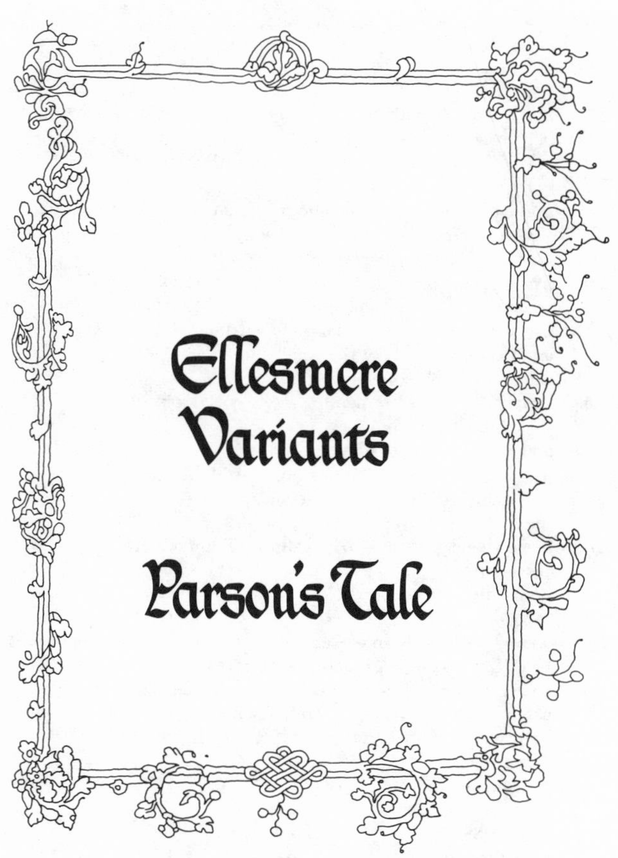

[1] ¶Heere bigynneth / the P*er*soun*s* tale

¶Ier*emie* .6°. State sup*er* vias *et* videte *et* interrogate de viis antiquis / que sit via bona / *et* ambulate in ea *et* inuenietis refrigerium animab*us* vestris *et cetera*[2]

Oure sweete lord heuene
that knoweleche
and the lif / that p*er*durable / .
vs Ieremie / and seith / thys wyse /
¶Stondeth

et cetera / been espirituels
that Crist
Of whiche noble wey /
a couenable / fayle [3]to no man /
that thurgh mysgoon righte
cleped
which man with
wyten Penitence / whennes
cleped Penitence / maneres accioun*s*
Penitence / speces /
been of Penitence / thynges
and bihouen
Penitence / and whiche Penitence /
seith / Penitence /
for gilt to do
oghte pleyne / doctour
seith / Penitence the that
self
mysdoon ¶Penitence / with v*er*ray
man that and
And v*er*ray penitent
first biwaylen synnes that doon
stidefastly /
thyng.
oghte moore biwayle / and continue
elles auaille / .
Ysidre ¶he Iaper*e*
v*er*ray repentant. that eftsoone thyng.
oghte repente / . to synne / ⌈¶No*ta*⌉
auayle ¶But nathelees / hope / . that eu*ery*
neu*er* thurgh
Penitence / *grace* / . but certeinly /
doute / For
Gregorie / vnnethe ariseth of synne /
charged with And therfore /
and
hooly chirche / holdeth sauaciou*n* / .
And that and v*er*raily laste / .
hooly sauaciou*n* / m*er*cy /
Crist repentau*n*ce
taak ⟨tene⟩ the siker ⟨certu*m*⟩ wey / ¶And
sith I penitence /
that acciou*ns* Penitence /
firste accioun of Penitence / is that a man be baptized after that
synned / .
seith / penytent lyf.
lif / . baptized /
outen gilt
remission his
verray / this
baptesme
is / . venial
hir day ¶Ther Augustyn
⌈¶Augustin*us*⌉
¶That and humble folk / .
Penitence / .iij. ¶That
hem / solempne ¶Another /
co*m*mune ¶And pr*i*uee /
penance that solempne As
hooly lente
maner ¶Another thyng is / whan a man
fame
hooly chirche Iuggement
do penaunce / ¶Co*m*mune penaunce
men in certeyn caas / p*ar*auen[4]ture /

13 Nota de Penitence El (81)
19 What Penitence is El (84)

39 Nota secundum sanctum Gregorium El (92)
48 The firste accioun of penitence El (96)
49 Nota secundum sanctum Augustinum El (97)
53 The .ij.de accioun of penitence El (99)
55 The .iij.de accioun of penitence El (100)
58 Of .iij. speces of penaunce El (102)
60 Of penaunce solempne El (103)
65 Of commune penaunce El (105)

[1] ¶P*er*sou*n* *206v*

[2] Miniature of the Parson in left margin.

[3] *207r*

[4] ¶prima pars| *207v*

pilg*ri*mages / or bare foot penau*n*ce
thilke / that
alday priuee
whiche they shryue hem p*ri*uely
p*ri*uee penau*n*ce
what is bihouely and necessarie / to v*er*ray
penitence /. And
stant thynges ⁊. herte ⁊.
¶Ioh*ann*es Crisostom*us*]
Mouth / [¶]and Satisfacciou*n* /. Crisostom
destreyneth a man euery peyne that
Contriciou*n* h*er*te and shrift
mouth / with
werkynge man*er*e
thynges wratthe
Crist ⁊. This thynkynge [¶]by reccheleesnesse
spekynge ⁊. and by werkynge ⁊ And
thise Penitence
The Contriciou*n* / that herte /
hym v*er*ray repentau*n*t. right hydeth
erthe ¶Of
that braunches Confessiou*n* /
satisfacciou*n*
¶For which Crist gospel /. dooth
Penitence /.
of braunches /
ne by the Confessiou*n* Crist /
thus /. ye shul knowe*n* hem ¶Of
seed a grace / seed / is mooder
sikernesse / seed /
hoot the grace of this
seed /
god / thurgh remembrance of the day of doome /
¶Salomou*n*] and helle ¶Of
matere Salomon That
synne ¶The heete this
and desiryng / ioye
This heete / of a man god / and
haten
that
child / Milk Norice / thyng |
| moore abhomynable Milk with
¶Not*a* exemplum] mete ¶Right
man that
semeth / that it is to hi*m* moost sweete of any thyng. but fro that
that crist. and lif
him abhomynable /
god / for
¶david p*ro*pheta] I. lawe /
and that loued and his word
¶This saugh Daniel / in the Auysiou*n* of
| the kyng / Nabugodonosor / whan hym
¶Penaunce / hem that and
v*er*ray
contriciou*n* /
.iiij. thynges Contriciou*n* /.
been contriciou*n* /.
contrit. *and* what contriciou*n* / auailleth
soule ¶Thanne
thus / þat contriciou*n* / v*er*ray sorwe / that

his with purpos / hym / and
penau*n*ce / and neu*er*emoore been
¶*Sanct*us Bernardus] seint Bernard ¶It
been
greuous / and[5] ful sharp*e* and poynau*n*t
herte ¶First
lord / sharp*e* and poynau*n*t
hys celestial /. sharp*e* and
poynaunt. and agilt that boghte hym /.
| which with blood haþ deliuered vs /
and fro the crueltee of the deuel and
causes that oghte moeue
¶First remembre looke he /
that thilke remembrau*n*ce. delit greet
and gilt ¶For [¶Iob]
werkes / Confessiou*n* ¶And therfore
Ezechie / [¶Ezechias]
me / yeres lyf
herte ¶And Apocalips*e* ¶Remembreth
whe*nn*es
been falle /.

youre been woxen and foul / and me*m*bres
feend / Aungels / sclaundre of hooly and
serpent. p*er*petueel matere of the fir of helle /.
abhomynable / trespassen
hound / retourneth / eten
spewyng. and
continuyng *and*
be synne /
dong ¶Swiche thoghtes /
man / to haue synne / and delit.
seith /
Ezechiel ⁊. reme*m*bre
shuln yow /. soothly synnes
weyes / that cause that oghte
man / haue synne this /. That
Peter /. that / of synne /. And
[¶*sanct*us Petrus]
synne / thraldom ⁊. therfore
p*ro*phete / Ezechiel / .I. self /.
[¶Ezechiel p*ro*phet*a*]
| And c*er*tes / synne / and withdrawe
hym / from and vileynye /. and
matere ⁊. He seith thus /. though wiste /
[¶Seneca]
that it. yet
I [¶Idem Seneca]
seith / .I.
fouler thral /
maken to / yeuen
synne /. it womman
that lyueth / foul /
seruitute /. eu*er*e / that falleth /.
thral / and moore / and to
world abhomynable /
man / haue desdayn
that thurgh free /
bonde ¶And therfore / seyth Augustyn /. If thou
[¶*Sanct*us Augustinus]
seruant. agilte / synne /. thou
that thou self / synne /.
reward that thou be /
self ¶Allas
desdayn been seruauntz

---

67 Of priuee penaunce El (106)

69 What is bihouely to parfit penitence El (107)

76 Of .iij. thynges in whiche we wratthe oure lord Iesu crist El (110)

79 How penaunce may be likned to a tree El (112)

84 dominus in Euaungelio El (115)

89 Of a seed þat spryngeþ of Contricioun El (117)

94 Of the heete of this seed El (120)

110 Of .iiij. thynges longynge to contricioun El (128)

114 What contricioun is El (129)

124 Of .vj. causes þat oghten moeue a man to contricioun El (133)

125 The firste cause of contricioun El (134)

130 dominus in Apocalipse El (136)

140 dominus per Ezechielem prophetam El (140)

144 The .ij.de cause of contricioun El (142)

---

5 ¶Penitencie *208r*

and soore been self that god /
estaat /.
wit / prosp*er*itee /
[6]the deeth / with blood / that
vnkyndely / quiten vileynsly /
slaughtre wo*m*men /
that
¶Salomon] prou*er*be
Salomon ¶He seith /. wo*m*man / that
ryng gold / that
a Soughe For right a Soughe / euerich
ordure / wroteth hire beautee in the stynkynge
that oghte
Contriciou*n* / doome /
¶*Sanct*us Ieronimus] helle ¶For seint
seith /. At eu*er*y
doome / .I. quake /.
ete or drynke / that eu*er*e
ere Riseth vp ye that been
dede / and Iuggement
oghte man / swich Iuggement.
¶*Sanct*us Paulus] been
as seint Poul seith / Seete
Crist. make /
wher*e* been absent /. *cer*tes / there
I auailleth noon Essoyne / excusaciou*n* And
that Iugged /. eek that
knowe ¶And as seith
¶*Sanct*us Bernardus] Bernard ./ shal /
pledynge auaille ne sleighte /. We
yeuen euerich word / ther
that been deceyued And why./
certes been descouered hym /.
preyere /
¶Salomon] meede / he shal nat been corrupt ¶And
Salomon
¶The wratthe god / wight /.
preyere
yifte /. and therfore doom /
¶*Sanct*us Anselmus] escape ¶Wherfore /
Seint Anselm. / greet
angwyssh / shul folk haue that tyme /.
shal / and wrothe Iuge aboue /.
horrible put of destroyen
that noot biknowen
been god
creature ¶And in the deueles /
her*t*e bithynke /. drawe /
soules peyne helle ¶And with
folk bitynge Conscience / and
brennynge /. wrecched
flee / hiden hym ¶*cer*tes nat hyden
shewen hym ¶For certes /
¶*Sanct*us Ieronim*us*] seint Ierome /.
Erthe casten
and the Eyr that be ful /
and lightnynges / ¶Now
gesse / þat synne /
nat turne delit greet
helle /. therfore god ¶Suffre
that .I. may a while biwaille / and wepe / go with
returnyng. derke lond / cou*er*ed
and
deeth /.
that euere ¶Loo / heere
respit a while /
waille a respit.
of the world ¶And muche
man / acquiten self /

173 Notate vos mulieres et cauete El (155)

179 The .iij.[de] cause of contricioun El (158)

217 Iob ad deum El (176)

[6] ¶prima pars *208v*

Penitence
[7]this tresor • /
respit a while / to biwepe / and biwaillen
trespas /. sorwe / that
make / bigynnyng
regard helle /
that derknesse /. vnderstondeth /
lond of Erthe / stable / and neuere faille
that light mat*er*ial
certes / light that fyr / that
peyne
hi*m* that cou*er*ed
with deeth /. that that he helle /
sighte of god /. certes / the sighte
p*er*durable ¶The been synnes /
that hath / whiche that
to see right as doop a derk clowde /
Misese / that been man*er*es
defautes / agayn that folk /
lyf /. seyn honours / delices / richesses
¶Agayns honour / haue co*n*fusiou*n*
For that men that honour
doþ man /. honour reu*er*ence /.
reu*er*ence doon there to knave ¶For
Thilke folk /
shul been ¶Honour /
cleped greet lordshipe / and heighnesse / but in helle /

been deueles /. And god seith //. the
[¶*dominus* dicit]
deueles shulle and comen / of the dampned
folk /. is muche / hyer that
present lyf /. been
helle / richesses world /
mysese of pou*er*te / been foure thynges /.
that Dauid seith ¶The folk / that
and hir*e* shul
slepe / in deeth /.
hir hir tresor ¶And
myseyse been / mete and drinke /.
Moyses /. They been hunger
briddes hem with the bitter
been hire
dragou*n* / morsels ¶And hir*e*
mysese / been clothyng.
they shulle be
clothyng.
brenne / and *and* naked been
soule / as of
is of the soule /. Where
been
Robes / and the smale shetes / and the softe shertes
¶Loo / of ysaye /. That
been strawed Motthes / and shulle been

230 Why Iob clepeth helle the lond of derknesse El (181)

240 Of the derknesse of deeth El (185)

242 Of the lond of Misese El (186)

246 Of honours delices and richesses El (187)

249 dominus per Ieremiam prophetam El (189)

257 Agayns the richesses of this world El (192)

259 Of defaute of tresor vnde dauid El (193)

262 Of defaute of mete and drynke El (194)

265 dominus per Moysem El (195)

268 Of defaute of clothyng El (196)

275 dominus per Ysayam prophetam El (198)

275 Of defaute of freendes El (199)

[7] ¶Penitencie *209r*

hir myseyse been /
freendes / for he nys nat poure that freendes /
frend god creature /
been eu*er*ich oother with
hate / The and[8] the dogħtren / rebellen /
and mooder / chiden and
oother and nyght.
children / that
flesshly hem /
myghte /. sholden loue togidre
helle / hated ech of
oother lyf ¶For hir
flesshly deedly Dauid
¶who so that soule /.

wight manere /. therfore / is
freendshipe / but flesshly
kynredes / that been
helle /.
deedly
defaute man*er*e delices /. c*er*tes
delices / been wittes /. As sighte /.
herynge. smellynge /. Sauorynge. / touchynge /.
hir sighte derknesse and smoke.
therfore / teeres /. hir
waymentynge /
crist. hir
nosethirles shullen be stynk.
¶Ysayas p*ro*ph*et*a] p*ro*phete /. hir sauoryng
galle /. and ycou*er*ed with fir
that neu*er*e and with wormes that neuere
Mouth Ysaye /. muche
that
hir deep flee vnderstonden
¶Iob] by the word of Iob /. that seith / ther
deeth
¶Certes thyng.
shadwe /. but shadwe
¶Exemplum] shadwe ¶Right so
deeth angwissh /. why
though they sholde c*er*tes /
¶*sanct*us Gregorius] dye ¶For /
Gregorie ¶To caytyues /
with oute and ende with outen ende / and
with hir and
hir ende / eu*er*emo and hir defaute
nat
faille ¶And Euangelist /. They
and they shul hym /. and
¶Iob] flee he*m* ¶And that
helle rule /. so that
creat right and
thyng / withouten
but been and nombred /.
nathelees / that
been dampned / been in the ordre /
ordre /.
¶Dauid p*ro*ph*et*a] fruyt ¶For Dauid
seith ¶god destroie
moisture /. refresshyng.
¶*Sanct*us Basilius] light ¶For
seint Basilie ¶The

been dampned /. light / and shal be yeuen

children /. right
children and houndes /. And
¶*Sanct*us Iob] escape seint Iob
laste ¶that
horrour / and drede / dwellen
ende /. Horrour /
drede / that and eu*er*e
that been And therfore /
hir*e* causes ¶First. [9]that
be / with outen hem /. and they nat
halwes /. ne they /
hir raunsou*n* /. voys /
hym /. peyne /.
hem / they mowe shewe deliuere hem
peyne ¶And Salomon ¶The dyeth /
[¶Salomon]
and deed.
thanne / vnderstande the peynes /
and weel / that deserued his
certes /
and to wepe /. and to pleye / For that
Salomon /. that [¶Idem Salomon]
that been establissed and
Thilke seint [¶*Sanct*us Augustin*us*]
man / waymenten
herte ¶The fourthe point
maken man to haue contricion /
remembrau*n*ce
that left doon / heere
erthe /. And eek
that lorn ¶soothly / left /. outher
been / that he hath wroght. fel /
synne /. elles / that
wroghte / while
synne ¶soothly / that he dide / biforn that
been mortefied and astoned and
ofte synnyng
The othere that he wroghte /
deedly þei been lyf
heuene ¶Thanne werkes / that been
synnyng. dide / whil
charitee /. with outen v*er*ray penitence /.
mouth Ezechiel ¶That
rightful man /
and lyue nay /.
that shul neu*er*e been remembrau*n*ce /
dyen synne ¶And Chapitre /
seint thus. That shulle
[¶*Sanct*us Gregorius]
this p*ri*ncipally /. deedly
noght rehercen memorie
werkes / that biforn ¶For
deedly trust that
biforn /. is for to seyn /. by
p*er*durable / heuene /. nathelees /.
comen agayn / and helpen and auaillen /
contriciou*n* /.
soothly / that men whil they
deedly were deedly
synne. quyke agayn /. For þ*at* neu*er*e
lyf. neu*er*e quykene / nathelees /.
it
that auaille noght /. p*er*durable ./
auaillen
abregge helle /. elles / geten

---

282 dominus per Michaiam prophetam El (210)

288 Dauid propheta Qui diligit iniquitatem odit animan suam El (204)

294 How the dampned shul haue defaute of alle manere delices El (207)

304 dominus per Ysayam El (210)

318 Sanctus Iohannes Euaungelista El (216)

335 How the dampned han lorn al hir hope for .vij. causes El (225)

352 Of the .iiij[e] point þat oghte maken a man to haue contricioun El (231)

364 dominus per Ezechielem El (236)

---

[8] ¶prima pars *209v*

[9] ¶Penitencie *210r*

richesse ./ elles / that wole /
enlumyne /
and lightne man / haue repentaunce / .
and auaillen /
that soule / . And
curteis crist / . wole that werk
lost .
somwhat auaille / . muche /
werkes that doon / been
lyf / . been
| mortefied / by folwynge. eek /
that
werkes / that been in deedly synne / been
dede / for haue perdurable / .
[10]may that man
that werk song
¶Iay tout/ labour ¶For certes /
and eek
grace / ¶For soothly / hooly
that been ydel / . for fyr / fayleth / anoon
wirkynge / rigħt so. grace fayleth anoon
the*n* man
oonly bihigħt that
werken ⁄. wel thanne / that
lif eek
that
dette / lyf ⁄. For trust
[¶*Sanct*us Bernardus] yeuen acountes /
seint Bernard / goodes /
that han be lyf . and how /
nogħt muche / . that
heed / . moment houre /
that rekenyng fifthe
thyng that contriciou*n* /
passiou*n* / that *crist*
[¶*Sanct*us Bernardus] seint Bernard ¶Whil that .I.
*tra*uailles / that lord crist suffred
*pre*chyng / . trauaillyng . temptaciou*ns*
fasted / . wakynges / preyde / .
teeres /
that weep*e* / peple / .
and filthe / that hym / .
spittyng /
that spitte in his face / . of. buffettes that
yauen hym / .
foule mowes / and of / the repreues / that
seyden / .
croys / . remenant passiou*n* that
thyng gilt ¶And
shul that man*ere* of
ordre or ordinau*n*ce / doun ¶For
sooth / that
god and resou*n*. *and* sensualitee / and been |
that euerich / foure lordshipe /
ou*er* oother / .
ou*er* resou*n* / . and resou*n* ou*er* sensualitee / . and sensualitee ouer
man / .
ordre ordinau*n*ce / doun / ¶And
resou*n* subget
obeisant god that rigħt / . therfore /
that haue / ouer sensualitee / and ou*er*
man / . why ⁄ For resou*n* / .
that resou*n* sensualitee / and
body / . rigħt resou*n*
god ⁄ / rigħt so /
sensualitee / resou*n* / and the body also ¶And
disordinau*n*ce

and abogħte
herkneꝑ wise / ¶For thanne
resou*n* /
god ⁄ therfore /
deed / . that
disciple / distreyned and bounde / so that
[¶*Sanct*us Augustinus] | his blood / brast out
seint
Augustyn ¶And ouer / resou*n*
man /
[11]sensualitee may / therfore
haue shame suffred man /
spetten visage / ¶And muchel
caytyf and
therfore deeth ¶And
crist where ther was no part
free / with outen greet and bitter passiou*n* ¶And
forfeted / .[12]
that neu*ere* deserued defouled /
shendshipe
that haue And [¶*Sanct*us Bernardus]
seint Bernard
synne / . muchel bitternesse / .
For certes / disconcordau*n*ces
crist . thynges / as thus
¶Certes / deuel /
temporeel prosp*er*itee / and deceite
flesħly delices / Inpacience Adu*er*sitee
and dispeir by seruage and *and*
fynally. ¶For disordinaunce man
crist bitraysed / bounde that
vnbynden synne and peyne / byscorned
that oonly / sholde han been
thynges and of alle thynges
¶Thanne visage / that of al
man kynde / Aungels
bispet / . scourged / that And
finally / crucified and slayn ¶Thanne
ysaye / that seith / that he wounded /
and [¶Ysayas]
defouled for oure felonies / that
self / wikkednesses / . ogħte
wepen and that synnes
sixte
ogħte contriciou*n* / thynges / .
foryifnesse synne / . grace /
do heuene / . with which /
gerdone a man dedes / ¶And muche
crist
largesse / and bou*n*tee / .
cleped / **Iudeor*um*** ¶ **Ies*us*** / is |
saluaciou*n* whom / shul
that *pro*prely / saluaciou*n*
Aungel Iosepħ Thou clepen
that sauen hir synnes / .
of seint Peter / . Ther heuene /
that man by which / saued
[¶*Sanct*us Petrus]
Ies*us* ⁄ / . **Nazarenus** / ⟨for⟩
florissħynge /
in hope / . that he
eek grace / . wel for to flour

---

411 Of the .v[e] thyng þat oghte moeue a man to contricion El (255)

424 How in mannes synne is euery manere of ordre or ordinaunce turned vp so doun El (260)

---

[10]¶prima pars *210v*

---

477 Of the .vj.[e] thyng that oghte moeue a man to contricioun thurgh hope of .iij. thynges El (283)

486 How the Aungel spak to Ioseph El (286)

---

[11]¶Penitencie *211r*

[12]*Out* Hg El. Other MSS read:

forfeted ⁄] And therfore reasonabely may be seyd of Iesu in this manere [to muchel Gg f.] And thus he seide [t.m. Cn-En[3] f.] and saide [t.m. Ra[2] f.] And þerfor may he say [t.m. Ll[2] f.] Wele myght he say [t.m. Py.

comynge / .   synnes
grace / wel for to   atte dore
Iesus and cleped   entre / .   that openeth
synne / .   grace /   soupe
with hym[13] by   that
been   soupe with
that   yeuen hym ¶Thus   hope / . for
penaunce / that god   yeuen   bihooteth
gospel   shal a man
manere /   been   contricioun / .
been   total / /   seyn A   verray
repentaunt   that   doon   delit
perilous. / For ther been /   manere
of consentynges / .   cleped
affecioun whan a man   to do synne / and |
synne / .
reson aperceyueth it wel that
resoun /   foul delit   talent .
though   se   apertly / that   is /
reuerence
god / .   though   resoun
consente noght   doon that |
that   delit that dwelleth
be it neuere   ¶And
sorwe   euere
god   parfit   resoun / .
that   deedly synne in consentynge ⁊. For certes /
deedly   that   first /   thought . and
delit / . and   and   dede / .
that   neuere   swiche
and   it .
outward . wherfore   that
delites / and   been subtile bigileres /   that
be   ouer   sorwe /
wikkede   as for hise wikkede dedes / .
certes /
repentaunce   synguler   and
synnes / .   elles repenten hym /
auaille / .   certes /   almyghty
ther fore / he foryeueth
elles   noght . and heer of seith seint Augustyn / . |
¶Sanctus Augustinus] | that god
synnere / . and
that   synne / .   foryifnesse
remenaunt
synnes ⁄ / nay /   ouer / contricioun
sorweful /   angwissous / .
god
angwissous with   me / .   remembrance
god that   preyere myghte   hym /
contricioun
continueel / .   that   purpos
shriuen
and   amenden   lyf / . For
contricioun
foryifnesse / and
comth   synne / . that
¶Dauid]   self / . and   oother folk .
power ⁊. For   Dauid
that
and   hateth /
that man   contricioun /
of / auayleth contricioun
that som tyme / contricioun / delivereth
¶Dauid] | a man fro synne / .
that Dauid seith / ⁊ .I.   Dauid
[14]that is to seyn ¶I purposed   and
Lord / relessedest / my synne ¶And right so as contricioun
auailleth
noght with outen   oportunitee ⁄ /
right so /   with outen
contricioun / ¶And moore ouer contricioun /
prisoun   helle /
wayk and fieble / alle the   and restoreth /
hooly goost and
and deliuereth the soule /
helle / and
and restoreth   espirituels / And
compaignye and communyoun
hooly chirche ¶And forther ouer / .
hym that   grace / .
thynges been   hooly writ .
that   entente   wys / .

yeuen   body / and   herte /
seruice
crist / . and   hommage / . for soothly / oure sweete
crist .   spared   that
soule

¶Explicit prima pars penitencie ⁊.
Et sequitur secunda pars eiusdem

partie
contricioun /
is confessioun / . and   nedes /   doon
noon / . and
been   ¶First
that confessioun /   verray
preest .   verray / .   moste confessen
hym /   condiciouns / that   ferforth
and   thyng excused   hyd
and noght auaunte thee of thy goode werkes / ¶And
that
and   encreessen and   been
synnes seith Seint   wise / .
right   world .
thurgh   deeth / . Right   deeth
that   whom /
brak   comaundementz
god. / And   he that   myghty / that
dyed /   oon that
and   progenye in this
world that   that in thestaat
Innocence /   and Eue   weren
Paradys /
nakednesse / .   that
that   beestes / that   maked ⁄
womman / .   comaunded   nat eten /
Paradys ⁄ The   answerde / .   fruyt
she /
soothly[15] of the

---

501 How a man shal be contrit El (292)
506 Of two manere of consentynges El (293)
523 How a man oghte to repenten hym for hise wikkede wordes as wel as for hise wikkede dedes El (300)
532 How contricion sholde be wonder sorweful El (304)
537 How contricioun moste be continueel El (305)
545 Wher of Contricioun auailleth El (308)
551 How contricion destroyeth the prisoun of helle El (311)
558 how contricioun maketh him that whilom was sone of Ire to be sone of grace El (313)
572 What confession is El (318)
578 Of spryngynge of synnes secundum Paulum El (322)
587 Of the temptacioun of Adam in Paradys El (325)

---

[13] ¶prima pars *211v*

[14] ¶Penitencie *212r*

[15] ¶Secunda pars *212v*

tree / that
| and nat touchen it /. lest dyen ¶The
wo*m*man /. nay /. nay /. deeth /
woot that day / that of /.
shul
opene / and shul been
goddes knowynge good and harm ⁄ ¶The
wo*m*man thanne saugh / that feedyng. *and*
and to the sighte / tree /
and eet it / and yaf to and he eet and anoon
openeden /. that that
fige leues a maner*e* hir*e*
me*m*bres / ¶There may that deedly
feend. naddre /. And afterward.
Eue /. And
resou*n* /. Adam /. For trust
though that tempted Eue / that
flessh hadde delit fruyt /
defended /. yet certes / til that resou*n* /
etynge fruyt. he in thestaat
Innoce*n*ce
tooke original /.
hym flesshly / and engendred /
and corrupt
mateere / body. right anon /
synne /. and that *þat*
and synne /. and
therfore / born / wratthe and
baptesme that bynymeth
culpe /. but vs ⁄
temptaciou*n*. highte concupiscence / whan it is
man /.
flesshly
sighte thynges /. and coueitise
hynesse / ¶Now as for to speken
Concupiscence
membres / that and rightful Iuggement
god ¶I seye obeisaunt
god lord disobeisaunt
thurgh Concupisce*n*ce which yet is cleped norissynge
synne /
and synne /. that hym /
Concupiscence /.
somtime and flessh synne ./
thyng
nat faille lyueth /. fieble
faille baptesme / and grace
thurgh
fully / neu*ere* quenche /. that
self. refreyded
sorcerie / drynkes /. For
¶S*anct*us Paulus] seint Paul ¶the
and the spirit flessh /. been
stryuen /. that doon wolde /
seint Paul penau*n*ce / [16]and
lond /. nyght and greet p*er*il /
greet
peyne /. In lond / famyne / in thurst
coold cloothlees and
stoned deeth // allas I
caytyf man /. deliu*ere* prisou*n*
caytyf body ¶And seint Ierome / whan
[¶S*anct*us Ieronim*us*]
desert / he hadde
beestes / where he ne hadde mete
and
flessh Ethiopeen heete /
and ny coold /. that
lecherie boyled body / wherfore /
sykerly / that they been that seyn / that

624 Of coueitise of Concupiscence El (337)

[16] ¶Penitencie *213r*

hir witnesse Apostel /.
that wight concupiscence /.
seyn
and occasiou*n* tempted synne / that
body /. And therfore Seint Eu*au*ngelist ⁊.
If that that we beth with
synne /. we deceyue
selue / vs shal vnderstonde /
man*ere* / that wexeth / or encreesseth
¶The thyng. synne
biforn /. flesshly concupiscence /.
that /
with
fir flesshly concupiscence /. bithynketh
no thing
tempted /. And thanne /. that withstonde
weyue entisynge and
if it so that
anoon / flambe delit /. good
war /
kepen wel elles /
synne ./ and it. and place ⁊.
Moyses deuel
seith / wole and pursue
suggestiou*n*. /
wole hente hym by moeuynge / or stirynge of synne. / I
prise praye and lust
been elit. consentynge /.
For certes / right thyng peces ⁄ /
right
sleen hym / with synne /. seith
feend /.
soule /.
acompliced temptaciou*n* delit. and
consentynge /. and
synne / cleped Actueel maneres /.
outher / it is venial / deedly synne ¶Soothly /
creature crist tha*n*ne deedly
synne ⁊. And it. crist
hym /. For synne /
perilous loue / that
and moore And self with
synnes /. be that
shrifte /. lightly
hym all loue that crist. wise /
venial deedly synne[17] For certes / that
man /
soule with synne enclyned /
fallen in to deedly synne /. and lat
necligent
¶*prouerbium*] synnes ¶For seith that
¶exemplum] maken a greet ¶And
ensample ⁊. A greet
see tyme with greet
shipe ¶And harm dooth
that entren / thurgh creuace
thurrok. and that they / |
tyme /. And though
difference drenchynge /. algates /
ship*e* dreynt ¶Right somtyme
deedly
and veniale
greetly / that that he louep thurgh whiche

654 Sanctus Iacobus Apostolus El (348)
658 Sanctus Iohannes Euaungelista El (349)
659 how synne wexeth or encreesseth in man El (350)
674 Moyses per demonem El (355)
683 Of synne in two maneres venial and deedly El (358)

[17] ¶Secunda pars *213v*

venyally / . greet herte
therfore thyngꝭ. that biset
god sake / . al though that
synne / . and deedly
thyngꝭ. wexeth muchel
¶*Sanct*us Augustin*us*] moore / ¶Deedly synne /
Seint
Augustyn / is. whan a man /
ver*r*ay soue*r*eyn bou*n*tee / that and
to thyngꝭ that and flitte / .
heuene / . For that
with herte / . creature / .
certes / as muche as he yeueth of his loue
ther fore synne / .
that god / .
seyn herte NOw
gene*r*ally / synne / . itꝭ
that auenture /
and hem
and nathelees / synnes ¶Soothly /
seyn / . that at eue*r*y that a man

certein synne ¶And eekꝭ than nedeth /
synne ¶Eke / benignely the
compleintꝭ poure ¶Eke / body
faste whan hym oghte faste / with outen cause resonable
¶Eke nedeth / .
enchesou*n*
charite ¶Eke / wyfꝭ. outen
engendrure to the hono*ur* god / .
wyfꝭ body ¶Eke / natꝭ
sike and prisoner may ¶Eke /
loue / or childꝭ / .
thyngꝭ. resou*n* requireth ¶Eke /
flatere blandise / oghte /
necessitee
¶Eke / amenuse Almesse
poure
¶Eke / apparailleth mete
ete to hastily likerousnesse ¶Eke / if
vanytees
seruice / that
vileynye / . yelde*n*[18] acountes
doome ꝑ. Eke /
that natꝭ p*ar*fourne ¶Eke / whan that
lightꝭ nesse folie / mysseyeth /
¶Eke /
Thise thynges and nombre /
been seintꝭ Augustyn NOw
that that man / eschue
venial
synnes / . he restreyne hym / loue /
that cristꝭ. and confessiou*n*
and werkes / . so that greue ꝑ.
seith [¶*Sanct*us Augustin*us*]
seint Augustyn ¶If that
eu*er*e god / and for ver*r*aily /
Looke that
water / that fourneys fyr anoyeth
greueth / muche that
p*ar*fit / crist / ¶Men
crist ꝑ.
receyuyng eekꝭ hooly water / .
Almesdede / .
confessiou*n* Confiteor and at
and
Bisshopes and of preestes and oothere goode werkes

¶Explicitꝭ secunda pars Penitencie

726 Of manye diuerse synnes El (372)

[18] ¶Penitencie *214r*

¶Sequit*ur* de septem p*ecca*tis mortalib*us* / et/ eor*um* dependencijs circumstancijs *et* specieb*us*

¶De Sup*er*bia

itꝭ thyngꝭ. been the deedly
this is Chieftaynes synnes / .
butꝭ diu*er*se maneres ¶Now been
cleped Chieftaynes /
been chiefꝭ. sprygen
synnes / roote /
pride gen*er*al harmes / . For
certein braunches / . As Ire. Enuye. or Slewthe.
Coueitise Glotonye.
Lecheryen And synnes
braunches *and* hise twigges hir*e* Chapitres
folwynge / . And thogh be that
telle / and that cometh
pride / . p*ar*tie vnderstonde
Inobedience. Auauntynge. Ypoc*r*isie.
Despit. Arrogance. Inpudence. herte. Insolence
Elaciou*n*. Inpacience. Strif. Contumacie. Presumpciou*n*.
Irreuerence.
P*er*tinacie.
that that disobeyeth [¶Of Inobedience]
despitꝭ god / . and soue*r*eyns / .
and fader / ¶Auauntour
he / that bosteth [¶Of Auauntynge]
bou*n*tee / that [¶Of Ypocrisie]
hideth hym is / .
¶Of despitꝭ] noghtꝭ is[19] ¶Despitous
seyn of euene c*r*istene /
¶Of Arrogance] despitꝭ doon
oghte ¶Arrogant he /
that thynketh / bou*n*tees hym thatꝭ
noghtꝭ that desertes / .
¶Of Inpudence] elles / demeth that
nat / ¶Inpudent is he / .
that pride / hise synnes
is / . whan a man hym / that
¶Of Insolence] ¶Insolent he / .
Iuggementꝭ alle othere
value / . and konnyngꝭ. and
¶Of Elaciou*n*] spekyngꝭ. and beryngꝭ
suffre /
¶Of Inpacience] he / . that been ytaught
and strif wityngly / and
¶Of Contumacie] folye /
he / . that thurgh Indignaciou*n*
auctoritee that been
¶Of p*re*sumpciou*n*] soue*r*eyns
emprise that oghte elles thatꝭ
¶Of Irreu*er*ence] and this is
surquidie / ¶Irreu*er*ence
natꝭ hono*ur* / there
¶Of P*er*tinacie] waiten
reu*er*encedꝭ ¶P*er*tinacie is. whan man
hise folies. and muchel in his witꝭ.
glorie / is pomp*e* and in his temporeel
hynesse / and
hym in this worldly estaatꝭ ¶Ianglynge /
¶Of Ianglynge] whan men speken
folkꝭ. and clappen
Mille / and taken kepe what they seye /
yetꝭ
p*ri*uee spece of pride / waiteth firstꝭ for to
salewed

794 Of swellynge of herte El (398)

809 Of veyne glorie El (405)

813 Of othere priuee speces of pride El (407)

[19] ¶Superbia *214v*

worth /
auenture /. waiteth
elles wey /
pax /. been encensed / offryng'
neigħebore /
that hath
desir magnified'
and honoured been ther
maneres pride /.
with oute /. soothly
thynges and seyd /
pride that of man / and pride /
been oute /. natheles
oother. / right' leefsel signe
wyn that Celer /. and
As and and in outrageous
clothyng'.
Crist wolde nat'
| haue noted and spoken
¶*Sanctus* Gregorius] gospel /.
Seint' Gregorie ¶That
it'. and softenesse / And strangenesse
and degisynesse / superfluitee / and for
inordinat'
it' ¶Allas / men
clothynge /. and namely /
elles / desordinat' As
synne / in that
peple /. cost' of embrowdynge /
degise / endentynge / barrynge /
palynge / wyndynge / or
and clooth / vanitee / [20]also
| costlewe hir gownes /. powsonynge
chisel sheres / forth with
superfluitee forseide gownes / trailynge /
and Mire horse and eek' men
wommen /. that trailyng' verraily
with donge /
poure / greet damage forseyde poure
folk /. wise /. that' the moore that
moore it costeth peple scantnesse |
¶And that yeuen swich powsoned
and clothyng / poure folk /.
nat' conuenient'
were estaat' suffisant' hire
distemperance Up þat
side / speken disordinat
clothyng'.
been haynselyns / that thurgħ
couere of man wikked entente
¶Allas /
shewen the boce of hir shape and the horrible
that semeth / Hirnia
hir eek' hem faren /
part' Ape Moone
¶And membres that shewe /
thurgħ the degisynge departynge hire
semeth that hir priuee flayne
be that departen colours /. is
whit' and blak'. or whit' and blew / or blak / and reed and so
forth /.
colour that partie
hire priuee membres were fir seint
Cancre / or by oother swich meschaunce ¶Of
part' hir buttokes. see /. For certes /
partie hir hir
partie prowdly
despit' honestitee / the which honestitee that
and freendes
shewen in hir lyue NOw / of
that though
chaast' and debonaire / hire
Atyr and pride sey nat' that honestitee
clothynge
or disordinat' scantitee repreuable
aornement' apparaille / is in thynges
that ridynge /. as / that been hoolden
delit'. that been
fatte and costlewe /. and also / to many
knaue / that is sustened by hem / In
harneys /. Crouperes / peytrels
bridles with and riche / barres and plates
and siluer /. which
I confounde rideres
horses ¶This
reward
harneys on the Asse / and
poure ne /
[21]ne nat'. that euere beest'
this /
and honestitee /
reson it' requireth And forther / certes greetly
greet meynee / be
profit' or right no profit'. meynee /
and peple heigh
Offices /. For
lordshipe whanne
hir meynee ¶Or elles / this folk
that sustenynge
hostilers / and
¶Thilke folk / been flyes that
elles / that careyne /. forseyde
folk' hir lordshipes /. which /
¶Dauid *propheta*] Dauid
prophete / ¶Wikked deeth moote
vp thilke lordshipes /.
that moote descenden helle al doun /
| al doun /. hire iniquitees and
heuene /. amendement'.
right / as Pharao / seruice
and Laban / seruice
Iosepħ. / right
hir seruauntz / but' if they
Pride table / appeereth ofte./
been cleped poure been put'
and rebuked
Also excesse and drynkes /.
namely /
dissħ metes fir /
and peynted and and that'
thynke And greet'
and
moore luxurie / if that herte /
the lasse crist /. certeyn
certeinly / been in this caas / that
myghte

---

821 Of two maneres of pride El (409)
837 Of superfluitee and outrageous array of clothinge El (416)
854 Of disordinat scantnesse of clothynge El (422)

---

875 Of outrageous array of wommen El (430)
880 Of outrageous apparaille of thynges that apertenen to ridynge El (432)
886 dominus per zakariam prophetam El (434)
894 Of pride in holdynge of greet meynee El (437)
914 Of pride of the table El (444)
915 Of excesse of diuerse metes and drynkes El (445)
918 Of to greet preciousnesse of vessel and curiositee of Mynstralcye El (446)

---

[20] ¶Superbia *215r*

[21] ¶Superbia *215v*

lighṫly / falle to deedly The
soothly / ymagined /
| auised and forncast /. elles been deedly
doute /. And sourden freletee vnauysed /
| and sodeynly withdrawen ayeyn / been
synnes /. been deedly Now
that pr*i*de sourdeth / and spryngeth seye /
| somtyme it spryngeth / som tyme /
Fortune /. and grace
¶Certes / stonden /
or in goodes soule ¶Certes /
been heele of body.
| as strengthe / deliuernesse /
gentries / franchise / ¶Goodes
soule / been vnderstondynge.
enygn. vertu natureel. memorie / ¶Goodes
Fortune /
been richesse / hyghe lordshipes.
¶Goodes grace / been science. power /
spiritueel
trauaille. benignitee . contemplaciou*n*.
temptaciou*n* / and thynges /.
goodes. greet folye / priden hym /
alle NOw speken nature /.
that hem /
[22]damage / pr*o*fit speken
body /. certes / passeth lightly / and eek
is / enchesou*n* of
of oure soule /. flessh /
soule /. that
falle ¶Eke / pride his
folye /. For flessh
spirit /. and ay / strong that flessh
be /. strengthe
and many a man /
and meschaunce ¶Eek / pride gentrie /
greet gentrie binymeth
gentrie soule /. and eek o
fader / and mooder /. and been
roten.
corrupt and poure ⁊. For
man*ere* gentrie /
apparailleth with v*er*tues
and and child. that ouer
maistrie / is / a v*er*ray
NOw been generale gentillesse /.
vice and ribaudye / and synne /. werk /.
contenau*n*ce /. and curteisye. and clennesse /. and
liberal /. mesure /.
folie and synne ¶Another
bou*n*tee / that folk receyued ¶Another
be benigne subgetis ⁊. wherfore seith
senek ¶ther thing heigh
⌈¶Seneca⌉
estaat. and pitee And therfore / that
⌈¶No*ta*⌉
clepeth bees /. hir*e* kyng.
that wherwith stynge ¶Another

herte / and heighe
Certes[23] who so prideth hym /
Fortune /. is / greet fool /.
tyme
greet morwe /. that caytyf and
wrecche
nyght. somtyme /
deꝑ / somtyme / man / is cause
maladye / thurgh dyeth Certes /
somtyme / fals and brotel
triste /. preyse / blame
desir / haue co*m*mendaciou*n* eek of the peple /
deeth / man NOw certes /
eek / folie /.
yifte
and seith
seint NOw that that
han vnderstonde
pride / and been it. and
pride
sourdeth / and spryngeth[24] NOw
agayns the synne of pride /. mekenesse /.
vertu thurgh which. man / verray
self and deyntee /.
euere
NOw been man*er*es of humylitee /. as
herte /. and another humylitee in his[25] mouth ¶The
humilitee maneres
man / self noght worth
heuene ⁊. Another is /. oother
¶The he rekketh nat. though
noght worth ¶The
humiliaciou*n* / humilitee mouth /.
atte*m*pree speche ¶And speche
¶and biknoweth with mouth /. that
that is /.
bou*n*tee man /.
thyng amenuseth / ¶Humilitee eek
werkes
maneres ¶The firste is /
hym ¶The seconde al
¶The thridde to conseil ¶The
to stonde gladly / award hise souereyns /.
that
is in hyer degree /. c*er*tein greet

¶Sequit*ur* de Inuidia

Pride speken / Enuye
which is / Philosophre /
sorwe / p*ro*speritee /. After
seint Augustyn /. mannes

---

924 Of the especes that sourden of pride El (448)
929 Wher of pride sourdeth and spryngeth El (450)
933 Of goodes of nature El (451)
934 Of goodes of body El (452)
936 Of goodes of nature of the soule El (453)
937 Of goodes of Fortune El (454)
938 Of goodes of grace El (455)
948 Of pride of strengthe of body El (459)
954 Of pride of gentrye El (461)
961 Of generale signes of gentillesse El (464)
974 Of pride in the yiftes of grace El (at 983 in Hg) (470)
983 Of pride in the goodes of Fortune El (471)
979 Of commendacioun of the peple El (473)
990 Of humilite or mekenesse El (476)
993 Of .iij. maneres of humilitee El (478)
995 Of .iiij. maneres of humilitee in herte El (479)
1001 Of .iiij. thynges of humilitee of mouth El (481)
1005 Of .iiij. maneres of humilitee in werkes El (482)
1013 What Enuye is secundum Philosophum et secundum Augustinum El (484)

---

[22] ¶Sup*er*bia *216r*

[23] 470 follows 474 in Hg

[24] El breaks the line after *spryngeth* and begins a new section, with the heading:
¶Remediu*m* cont*ra* pe*c*catu*m* Sup*er*bie

[25] **¶Remediu*m* cont*ra* Sup*er*biam** *216v*

othere harm / ¶This synne
hooly /. al be it so / that synne agayns
the hooly goost /. muche / bountee /
to the hooly. and Enuye comth
malice /. therfore is it proprely / agayn bountee
hooly
two speces /. seyn
wikkednesse /. elles / flessħ of man
blynd /
that he considereþ natꝰ that synne /.
natꝰ that
synne /. is deuel / ¶That oother
⌈ speche of malice / is whan a man trouthe /
that trouthe /. And eek / werreyeth
grace /
that and Enuye /
¶Certes / Enuye that is /. For
synnes been tyme oonly / agayns vertu /.
certes / Enuye and
goodnesses /. sory / bountees
and diuers
¶For thatꝰ
delitꝰ in it selfꝰ. Enuye / that euere in it
and Enuye / been thise /
Ther firstꝰ.
mannes goodnesse / and of his prosperitee.
Ioye /. Enuye
ioye
harm /. deuel /.
two speces /
bakbitynge/. synne / bakbityngꝰ
detraccion /
certeine thus ¶Som neighebore
wikke entente /.
[26]atte ende /. alwey / but / atte laste
that
blame /.
seconde that and thingꝰ
entente /. goodnesse /
doun / shrewed thridde is /
amenuse
bountee fourthe bakbityngꝰ
this /. thatꝰ a man /.
bakbitere seyn /. pardee / swich yetꝰ bet than he /
dispreisynge / that fifte spece is this /. for
gladly gladly to the that
of / folk ꝰ. and encreesseth /
bakbitere After bakbityngꝰ cometh
grucħchyngꝰ Murmuracioun /. somtyme
god /. and somtyme
it is / peynes helle /.
pouerte /. catel. agayn tempestꝰ
elles that prosperitee /.
elles / that
Aduersitee / thynges
paciently /. rightful Iuggementꝰ and ordinaunce

comth grucchingꝰ
Magdaleyne /. enoynte /
cristꝰ. with hire oynementꝰ ¶This manere murmure
swich. man gruccheth / goodnesse /
hym self dooth /.
that oother doon hir ¶Somtyme /
murmure pride /. Simon
Pharisee / gruchched
Magdaleyne / cristꝰ. and
synnes ¶And somtyme grucchyngꝰ sourdeth
discouereth that
hond / thyngꝰ that ¶Murmure eek /
seruauntz / that hir souereyns hem doon
thynges /. muche / withseye
comaundementz hir
harm / and and priuely /
verray despitꝰ / whiche
clepen Pater be that
neuere Pater noster /. that folkꝰ
tyme / grucchyngꝰ comth priue
hate / that herte /.
cometh thurgħ
neighebor / hym / bitter
vnsauory cometh that
⌈¶Of discordꝰ⌉
freendshipe comth /[27] neighebor /
⌈¶Of scornyngꝰ⌉
weel comth / Accusynge /.
⌈¶Of Accusyngꝰ⌉
occasioun / neighebor / that
lyk /
| to the craftꝰ that waiteth / nyght and
malignitee / thurgħ which ⌈¶Of Malignitee⌉
neighebor priuely / may. he noght |
wil / wante /.
pryuely /. empoysone / beestes /
and [28]NOw remedie /
agayns the foule Enuye / ¶Firstꝰ is the louynge
louyng / of his neighebor as hym self /. |
| for been / with oute
oother /. And that neighebore /. thou
vnderstonde brother For
flesshly / and o mooder /
Eue /. and eekꝰ espiritueel / and that
heuene ¶Thy
neighebore / and goodnesse /.
therfore selue /
saluacioun / of lyf and of soule ¶And
thou and in benigne
and and conforten anoyes / and
with herte / ¶And thou
wise /. that thou thou woldest /
that it were persone /. And thou
shalt /
soule / entissyngꝰ

1021 Of .ij.° speces of malice and the firste is hardnesse of herte El (486)

1024 Of another spece of malice El (487)

1035 Of the firste spece of Enuye El (491)

1038 Of the .ij.de spece of Enuye El (492)

1043 The firste spece of bakbitynge El (493)

1045 The .ij.de spece of bakbityng El (495)

1048 The .iij.de spece El (496)

1049 The .iiij. spece El (497)

1052 The v.e spece El (498)

1055 Of grucchyng or Murmuracioun El (499)

1062 Of grucchyng þat comth of Auarice El (502)

1066 Of murmure þat comth of pride El (504)

1069 Of murmure þat sourdeth of Enuye El (505)

1071 Of murmure amonges seruauntz El (506)

1078 O grucchyng that cometh of Ire El (509)

1081 Of bitternesse of herte El (510)

1083 Of discord El (511)

1084 Of scornyng El (1084)

1085 Of accusyng El (512)

1088 Of Malignitee El (513)

1099 How a man shal loue his neighebore El (517)

---

[26] ¶Inuidia *217r*

[27] *Out* Hg El part of 511. Gg reads:
s. as whanne a man sekyth occasioun to anoyen h. n.

[28] **¶Remedium contra peccatum Inuidie** *217v*

¶Thou nat desiren hise Vnderstoond eek / that neighebor / comp*re*hended enemy ¶*cer*tes louen enemy / by the comandement god /. freend / god ¶I enemy / commandement ¶For reson / þat a man haten enemy /. loue / that been enemys of thynges that hym /. thynges thus ¶Agayns and herte ¶Agayns chidyng and wikkede ¶And agayn wikked enemy /. bou*n*tee ¶For and preyeth hem that harm /. and that pursewen bou*n*tee / that ¶Loo / comaundeth crist. to do / enemys /. For vs / freendes /. and p*ar*fey / loue freendes /. that certes / dede / remembrau*n*ce / that enemys /. loue / p*ar*fourne / in so muche / gretter ther fore / louynge of oure confounded / deuel /. right deuel / disconfited humylitee /. right / so / wounded deeth / by loue enemy ¶Certes. / tha*n*ne medicine / that casteth out Enuye / ma*n*nes ¶The paas / be | *in* hir folwynge declared |

¶Sequitur de Ira

Ire /. For so hath vpon neighebor /. comu*n*ly hym a matere wratthe / word [29]in enuye. And wel enuye /. that wrooth discryuyng seint [¶*sanct*us Augustin*us*] wil / been dede /. Ire Philosophre /. [¶Philosophus]

thurgh which that hateth ¶For man and that is / Iuggement resou*n* But that Ire maneres / good / wikked / ¶The Ire / is Ialousie thurgh with wikkednesse / and wikkednesse /. wys man /. that pley This Ire / [¶Sapiens] with debonairetee /. and wrooth with outen wrooth wrooth / with of / man /. **Dauid Irascimini *et* nolite peccare NOw** [¶Dauid p*ro*phe*ta*] that two man*er*es / that Ire / withouten auisement and co*n*sentynge of resou*n* /. menyng and this / that resou*n* of man it is venial ¶Another Ire that felonie auysed and biforn / with wil / vengeance / and therto / co*n*senteth deedly ¶This Ire / displesant god that and hooly out and destroyeth v*er*tu that and deuel and that is / lord /. this Ire / is greet deuel /. fourneys / that eschawfed / with fir helle. For right so / fir mighty / destroyen than any oother Element. right myghty destroyen spiritueel thynges ¶Looke /. that fir gleedes that been vnder asshen / wollen quike agayn been with brymstoon / right so wol eu*er*emo quyken touched / pride that couered For certes / fir nat comen thyng /. thyng natureelly / fir / steel And right pride Ire /. right rancour / and keper*e* Ire Ther is a maner

1110 How in the name of neighebor is comprehended a mannes enemy El (521)

1116 How a man shal do .iij. thynges agayns .iij. manere of thynges that his enemy dooth to hym El (524)

1149 Of Ire in two maneres El (538)

1151 Of good Ire El (539)

1156 Of wikked Ire in ij.° maneres and the firste is sodeyn Ire El (541)

1159 Of Ire þat comth of felonie of herte auised and cast biforn El (543)

1180 Nota secundum Ysodorum El (551)

---

[29] ¶Ira *218r*

The unique typography of *The Canterbury Tales* is the result of combining hand-drawn special characters and letters with contemporary phototypesetting techniques. Each text page in the entire book was prepared by a process of assembling many pieces, some exceedingly small, into single-page units in order to approximate the style of the original Hengwrt manuscript.

The paper on which this book is printed has an effective life of at least three hundred years.